THE
STUDY
OF
POPULATION

An Inventory and Appraisal

THE
STUDY
OF
POPULATION

An Inventory and Appraisal

Edited by

PHILIP M. HAUSER *and* **OTIS DUDLEY DUNCAN**

 THE UNIVERSITY OF CHICAGO PRESS

CHICAGO AND LONDON

Library of Congress Catalog Card Number: 58-11949

THE UNIVERSITY OF CHICAGO PRESS, CHICAGO 60637
The University of Chicago Press, Ltd., London W.C. 1

Preface

In its *Second Annual Report* (1952) the National Science Foundation stated that "the necessary first step in policy development is the assembly of an adequate body of fact about the current status of science in the United States, including an inventory of our present resources of trained men and facilities." This investigation of the status of demography as a science, initiated in the fall of 1954, was undertaken with the financial support of the National Science Foundation to provide such "an adequate body of fact" for its formulation of policy and program in the field of population research.

The formidable character of the undertaking necessarily made this a team enterprise, both in its direction and in its execution. The direction of the study was in a fundamental sense a collective undertaking of the staff of the Population Research and Training Center, and major credit for the preparation of this volume must go to the contributors to the symposium constituting Parts II, III, and IV. It was the co-operation of center colleagues and the basic work of the writers of the individual chapters in the symposium that made the preparation of Part I, "Demography as a Science," a feasible assignment for the editors.

Remarkable co-operation was obtained from the scholars who were invited to participate in this venture. Only thirty-five persons were approached to obtain the participation of the twenty-seven who wrote the individual chapters. Of the thirty who were able to accept the invitation, one died before he could complete the assignment, and two were forced to relinquish the task because of other commitments. The time schedule drawn up for the conduct of the study was remarkably well maintained on the whole, considering the heavy involvements and commitments of the authors. Although the ease with which it was possible to administer this project was undoubtedly in some measure attributable to the fact that modest honorariums were made available for the preparation of the material, the major factors were the interest and enthusiasm of the individuals working in the field and their dedication to the pursuit of demography as a science and as a profession.

On the whole the contributors to this study have observed its terms of reference with care. Some of the writers, however, departed from the proposed outlines rather more drastically than was desired, and some did not completely adhere to the injunction to avoid preoccupation with social engineering problems—that is, policy matters. All of the chapters, however, provide a good basis for the evaluative work required of the editors, and in none does the consideration of social engineering problems detract seriously from the major mission of the study.

The reader should bear in mind that the contributed chapters were finished at various dates over a period of nearly three years. Consequently, they are not all completely "up to date." The difficulty of co-ordinating a complex enterprise, rather than any lapse of scholarship, should be blamed for any failures to include the latest information or thought on specific questions.

Acknowledgment is due to Harry Alpert of the National Science Foundation, who played a major role in initiating the project and recruiting the editors for this assignment. As has been indicated, we are heavily indebted to our colleagues, Donald J. Bogue, Evelyn M. Kitagawa, and Beverly Duncan, who gave generously of their time and counsel at many strategic points in the design and conduct of the investigation. Grateful acknowledgement is also made of the contribution of Hana Okamoto, who supervised the many exacting general administrative and clerical operations that the work entailed.

PHILIP M. HAUSER
OTIS DUDLEY DUNCAN

Table of Contents

List of Illustrations

List of Tables

xvi   *List of Tables*

1. *Overview and Conclusions*

PHILIP M. HAUSER AND OTIS DUDLEY DUNCAN

Concern about the numbers of people has a long history. But as the subject is understood today, demography, or the study of population, is scarcely three centuries old. Like other fields of scientific inquiry, it has had its ups and downs, its periods of flourishing and eras of stagnation. Despite the lack of temporal perspective, one may state confidently that the present is a period of extraordinary activity in the study of population. The amount, coverage, quality, and detail of the information now being assembled about population are greater than ever before; and the number of scholars engaged in the analysis, interpretation, and dissemination of this information is large by any historical standard. The growth of the field in these respects has been accompanied by a clearer differentiation between students of population and other investigators of human problems, although, as we shall see, demography remains closely related to and dependent on a wide variety of scientific and practical specialties.

Significantly, demographers do not have to expend much energy in justifying the pragmatic importance of their research. There is, on the one hand, a profusion of lay publicists of the "population problem" who keep the field in the public eye and, on the other, a steady demand for the demographer's technical skills on the part of those who need information about population to carry out their various functions in society. Although there will be occasion to comment on the implications of the practical and problematic aspects of population for the development of objective studies in the field, we are here concerned primarily with "demography as a science," i.e., as a body of systematic empirical knowledge, and the means by which such knowledge is accumulated.

This chapter summarizes *The Study of Population* and introduces both the editors' views on "demography as a science" as presented in Part I and the symposium of contributed chapters which make up Parts II, III, and IV. Additional introductory statements appear at the beginning of each of these parts, and an outline of their content will be found at the end of this chapter.

THE FIELD OF DEMOGRAPHY

There is no single standard conception of the scope or framework of demography. Notions of what demography is vary from place to place and from time to time in accordance with varying perspectives and predilections. The number of scientists concerned with population research is considerably greater than the number identifying themselves as "demographers." Moreover, the training of those who are interested in the study of human population phenomena covers a broad spectrum of both the natural and the social sciences. Yet a review of the literature dealing with human population matters and a survey of the disciplines and scholars producing this literature indicate that demography can be described in a systematic and comprehensible manner and that there is considerably more order in the research being done

1

and in the organization of the scholars than may appear at first glance.

For working purposes the following definition is suggested: *Demography is the study of the size, territorial distribution, and composition of population, changes therein, and the components of such changes, which may be identified as natality, mortality, territorial movement (migration), and social mobility (change of status).* Three features of this definition merit brief explication. First, the omission of reference to population "quality" is deliberate, to avoid bringing normative considerations into play. "Population composition" encompasses consideration of variation in the characteristics of a population, including not only age, sex, marital status, and the like, but also such "qualities" as health, mental capacity, and attained skills or qualifications. Second, interest in "social mobility" is made explicit because population composition changes through movements by individuals from one status to another, e.g., from "single" to "married," as well as through natality, mortality, and migration. Third, the term "territorial movement" is preferred to "migration" because the latter ordinarily applies to movements from or to arbitrarily defined areal units rather than to the totality of movements.

It is immediately apparent that many types of scholars at one time or another concern themselves with the data of demography. For example, geneticists, ecologists, geographers, anthropologists, manpower specialists, public health experts, psychologists, sociologists, historians, economists, and students of other disciplines with varying frequency employ demographic analysis in the conduct of their research activities. On the other hand, the scientist identified as a demographer on occasion utilizes the frameworks of other disciplines in relation to demographic problems.

To draw a boundary line around specified demographic phenomena is logically indefensible; likewise, it is not defensible to hold that the demographer is concerned only with such variables or to exclude the scholars of other disciplines from legitimate concern with population data. Certainly this would be inconsistent with the history and facts of population research. It would seem that the critical element in the definition of demography is not the scope of the population or other variables studied but rather the concept of "population" itself, on the one hand, and, on the other, the focus of research attention on population in relation to other systems of variables.

"Population," as a concept, here refers to an actual aggregation of organisms, and explicitly to human organisms. In an abstract and comprehensive sense the study of human populations may be regarded (as has been proposed by some biologists) as a part of a single field of population study at all organic levels, or on an even more abstract level as a subdivision of a concern with "population" in an extended sense, including all forms of collections—even inorganic and hypothetical ones—e.g., as the term "population" is used in statistics.

The apparent confusion arising from the fact that both demographers and non-demographers study human populations in relation to other systems of variables is dissipated if one distinguishes between "demographic analysis" and "population studies." Demographic analysis is confined to the study of components of population variation and change. Population studies are concerned not only with population variables but also with relationships between population changes and other variables—social, economic, political, biological, genetic, geographical, and the like. The field of population studies is at least as broad as interest in the "determinants and consequences of population trends."

Thus, "demography" may be conceived in a narrow sense as synonymous with "demographic analysis" or in a broad sense as encompassing both "demographic analysis" and "population studies." When the demographer is carrying out the "population studies," he is almost certain to regard them as "demography." But it must be recognized that scholars of various disciplines are likely to engage in studies which utilize demographic analysis in relation to other frameworks of analysis and which may appropriately be described as "population studies."

Evidently, "population studies" is not a single "theoretical discipline" with a coherent frame of reference of its own. Instead, it is best characterized as an area of substantive inquiry in which any number of frames of reference may be employed. Each of these is likely to include some categories under which certain types of demographic analysis play a significant role. None of them can exhaust all the potentialities of demographic analysis. It is, therefore, a little hard to think of "population studies" as a subject matter for which an integrated but comprehensive theory could be expounded. Such a body of theory would have to embrace such diverse preoccupations as those of economics, social psychology, and genetics (for example). What is called "population theory," then, must be one of two things: an elaboration of the relationships involved in and techniques employed by demographic analysis or that segment of some particular theoretical scheme which involves population phenomena or makes use of demographic analysis. Such, in brief, is the scope of the field whose appraisal is undertaken in this volume.

We now attempt a summary of the major considerations involved in the evaluation of demography as a science.

In the absence of any standardized procedure or criteria for characterizing and evaluating a science, our summary here is presented from two points of view. First, demography is subdivided in terms of its parts, parts discernible in any science: its frame of reference, its data, its methods of study, and its corpus of knowledge, including theory. Second, demography is examined as a whole in relation to other sciences—both the more advanced and the less advanced disciplines.

EVALUATION BY PARTS

Frame of Reference

From the very definition of the field it follows that demographic research is conducted within an explicit and coherent frame of reference. The most important observation to make about this frame of reference is that demographic analysis is primarily a process of working out the *components* of spatiotemporal variation in population phenomena. Consider the simplest possible case: sheer growth of numbers in a territory closed to migration. The demographer begins by "decomposing" this growth into the positive contribution of natality and the negative contribution of mortality. If the rate of growth in one period differs from that in another, the demographer immediately wishes to ascertain whether the variation in growth rates is produced by variation in natality, in mortality, or in both. To essay a more detailed "explanation" of such a change, he resorts to further decomposition of each of the gross components of growth. Natality is analyzed in terms of the fertility of different age groups of women or in terms of the contributions of different cohorts of married couples and so on. Perchance, if the necessary information is available, such analysis employs further subcomponents, such as the fertility of socioeconomic classes or urban and rural populations. Similarly, mortality is analyzed by age, sex, and various bio-social categories of the population. In principle, there is virtually no limit to the number of combinations of subcomponents that may be studied, although in practice the demographer seldom is able to carry the decomposition of population changes as far as he would like. Having accomplished what he regards as a suitable decomposition of population changes (or variations in rates of change from one period or place to another), the demographer may, of course, put the components back together again, e.g., in the form of a "balance sheet," a mathematical model, a statement of the relative importance of the several components, or the backward or forward projection of population changes, which may involve assumptions about the several components and the ways in which they are likely to change.

The focus on components of population variation is characteristic not only of "demographic analysis" in the strict sense but also of virtually all types of "population studies" wherein an effort is made to explain population change or to ascertain the effects of such changes in terms of social, biological, economic, or other factors. While some highly general conceptual schemes attempt to treat population growth as a single independent or dependent variable, ordinarily the various components of growth are acknowledged to interact differently with environing or conditioning factors. For example, areal variations in levels of living may have complex effects on population growth by way of positive correlation with net migration rates and negative correlation with fertility rates.

Consequently, two major problems confront the investigator studying population from the standpoint of a particular body of substantive theory, such as economics or social psychology. He must not only identify the significant economic or psychological factors for his problem, but he must also devise a suitable subclassification of population variation into components. The failure of many a theory of population can be diagnosed as due to a faulty analysis of components, to the lack of data on the relevant components, or to the obscurity of the connection between supposed causal factors and the components of population change. Malthus, for example, got bogged down at the outset of his famous analysis of the causes and consequences of population growth when he proposed that "the checks which repress the superior power of population, and keep its effects on a level with the means of subsistence, are all resolvable into moral restraint, vice, and misery." Whatever may be said of "moral restraint," it is clear that "vice and misery" may affect the several components of population growth differently; hence the direction of their effects is not constant from one situation to another, as Malthus appeared to assume.

In sum, research within the restricted framework of demographic analysis may be regarded as forming the "core" of demography as a science—we refer here to investigations concerned only with the study of size, territorial distribution, and composition of population, changes therein, and the components of such changes. Research in the form of "population studies" involves not only demographic analysis but also the discovery and explanation of relationships between demographic variation and change and the variables of interest to other disciplines—social, economic, political, geographic, historical, ecological, or biological, as the case may be. Such studies employ a variety of frames of reference—that of demography in relation to those of the other disciplines involved.

Data

Demography is one of the observational, as distinguished from the experimental, sciences. That is, demography is dependent for its data on observation and recording of events occurring in the external world rather than on experiments under more or less controlled conditions in the laboratory. Demography in this respect, therefore, is more like astronomy, geography, or ethnology than like chemistry, physics, or experimental psychology. The data of demography, like those of the other observational sciences, are "spread out" in time and space, and only a minute or negligible portion of demographic events can be observed by any one investigator. Moreover, since the systematic observation and recording of demographic events are of relatively recent origin, most of the demographic facts about prehistoric and even historic men are unknown. Even in the decade 1945–54 only 80 per cent of the world's population was enumerated in some kind of census, and this is undoubtedly a record high in the availability of even limited demographic statistics. One can guess that certainly no more than 10 per cent of all the persons born in the world during the Christian era were ever enumerated in a census, and a considerably smaller proportion than that in previous periods. Furthermore, the lack of demographic data increases rapidly as one moves from mere counts of total population to such other items as distribution, composition, change, and components of change. Finally, the temporal variations in the availability of data have their counterpart in space as well. Even at the present time little or no demographic data are available for large sections of the globe.

It must also be noted that the nature of the data of demography poses a fundamental issue which, to be sure, confronts all social science. This is the problem of "historicism"—that is, the question of the extent to which generalizations drawn from data localized in time and space can lead to generic propositions as opposed to descriptions of unique situations.

On the operational level it may be observed that demographic data, because of their comprehensive and costly character, are necessarily provided in large part by governments. Census and vital registration systems, and in a few countries a population register, are the major sources of data for the demographer. These sources, however, will be supplemented increasingly by sampling surveys and by various administrative record materials. The completeness and quality of demographic data depend largely on techniques of collection which typically involve communication between a collection agent and a respondent. Demographic data, therefore, even though they are often relatively simple and concrete, like other social science data are subject to the errors incident to the process of communication.

Research which contributes to better understanding and control of communicative processes will contribute to improved demographic as well as other social science data. Various techniques have been developed and are still in process of development to improve the coverage and quality of data obtained through canvass of a population or through the filling-out of administrative records. Perhaps the most important of these are the development of pretest and postenumerative surveys designed to improve techniques and procedures of collecting data. Demographers have played an important role in the development of these methods, which will have impact on the improvement of not only demographic but also other types of data.

Data are, of course, a function of a discipline's frame of reference. That is, what constitutes data is determined in part by what is sought for as such, as well as by what is actually in the phenomenal world. The demographer, like other scientists, plays an important role in the "creation" of data by the selection of the variables with which he works and his methods of observing, describing, and classifying them. Many of the vexatious problems which confront demography arise from problems of classifying data, which in turn are compounded by problems of instability or inadequacy of response in the collection process. Taxonomy has been, and will remain, an important area of work for the demographer; and the relationship between taxonomic and data-collection activities may be expected to assume increasing importance, especially as the demographer attempts increasingly to relate demographic to other variables. For, in his attempt to improve predictability and explanation, he will increasingly be faced with the need for a broader range of data and for better data—better metrics, reliability, validity, and precision of the stuff with which he works.

For at least a century demographers have been energetically engaged in bringing to the attention of the responsible officials their needs for more complete, detailed, and reliable data. There has been a series of notable efforts to identify the gaps in demographic data and to specify the steps required to fill those gaps—efforts on the part of international conferences of statisticians, national professional organizations of demographers, international statistical agencies, and private scholars and research organizations, not to overlook the important work of census and vital statistics offices themselves in evaluating the coverage and quality of the data they produce. Significantly, new "gaps" have been recognized as old ones were filled; there are whole bodies of subject matter which are now considered indispensable for demographic analysis that were scarcely covered at all in the population statistics of a few decades ago. Moreover, statements of "gaps" in recent times frequently have emphasized the need for information pertinent to a wide variety of population studies as well as to demographic analysis strictly interpreted, in recognition of the incomplete knowledge of, among other things, the relevance of social and economic changes for population growth and movements.

Methods

The methods of demography include the general methodology of science, the relevant aspects of mathematical statistics, and the techniques of the related sciences to which it contributes and on which it draws. In addition, the demographer has developed a number of specific techniques of demographic analysis. The more distinctive methods of demography, for convenience, are considered from the standpoint of data collection, data evaluation, adjustment or estimation, and analysis of data, including prediction and projection.

Probably the weakest link in the demographic methodological chain has been that relating to the collection of data. As has been indicated, demography shares with other sciences its dependence on the process of communication to obtain much of its data. Moreover, the mass data with which the demographer necessarily deals require also dependence on relatively large-scale administrative procedures, both in "field work" and in "data processing," and dependence on the art of collecting data, which at a number of points is still in a relatively crude state. Evidence of this is given by the rough and ready methods by which schedules are often designed, interviews are conducted, classification systems are devised, and in general, metrics of social and economic data are contrived.

Yet, despite the apposite character of these observations, it must not be overlooked that progress is being made in the art of data collection. A number of books have appeared within the past decade which record this progress and which demonstrate that, with all its weaknesses, data collected by means of an interview can be quite adequate for many purposes. Furthermore, continued technological advance in data-processing has greatly decreased the dependence of the demographer on human beings for data processing. The use of electronic devices by the census offices of the United States and other countries has favorably affected not only the tabulation of data but also a number of other aspects of data processing, including the editing, coding, and publication of information.

It is to be emphasized that the "pretest" and "postenumerative" surveys have provided the demographer with devices which, in the case of the former, permit both experimentation and practice to improve data collection and, in the case of the latter, permit the assessment of the reliability, validity, and precision of data as a preliminary to their use for demographic research.

Finally, it should be noted that data collection techniques have in at least one respect experienced a remarkable development in the last two decades or so, a development that has greatly enriched the scope and quality of demographic data, i.e., the great improvements in the sampling of human populations, which have made the sample survey a major source of substantive information as well as an instrumentality for the improvement of data collection techniques.

Techniques for "evaluating," "adjusting," "correcting," or "estimating" data are an important part of the methodological armamentarium of the demographer. Such techniques have necessarily developed because of the recognized roughness and incompleteness of some of the data with which the demographer works. The competent demographer is one who can reach valid conclusions even when the data are not what they might be. This may be accomplished either by keeping generalization within the limits of error imposed by the data or by adjusting or correcting the data to permit valid generalization of the breadth or scope desired.

A number of specific techniques have been devised for the evaluation of data. In general, they consist of methods of evaluating the coverage, comparability, and quality of the information obtained as evidenced by its reliability, validity, and precision. The specific devices in use have been greatly improved in recent years, partly as a result of increased resources made available for the purpose and partly as a result of improved techniques, including sampling, measurement of response error, and the like. Yet despite the progress made, it is clear that complete coverage, higher reliability, validity, precision, and comparability of data are still hard to come by. With the high costs and relatively limited resources available for the collection of mass population data, it is not possible for any census operation to achieve perfection in coverage, quality, or comparability. Rather, it is increasingly being recognized that it is more realistic to allocate available resources in a manner that permits evaluation of the data so that they may be adjusted or corrected as necessary.

With improved techniques for evaluating census and sampling data, adjustments are increasingly possible. It is standard practice, for example, to adjust birth or death registration statistics for underregistration. It is less common to adjust total population returns for underenumeration, although this is done for some purposes. Practice varies, with purpose, in adjusting erroneous age returns and other types of data.

It should be observed that, ironically enough, although the demographer generally knows better, some of the "corrections" effected on data lead to more rather than less error. For example, it is possible that birth rates based on births adjusted for underregistration and population figures unadjusted for underenumeration may be more erroneous than those in which neither the numerator nor the denominator is adjusted. For it is an elementary principle that a ratio in which numerator and denominator are in error in the same direction and in the same proportion is correct despite error in its components.

For other types of data collected in population censuses or sample surveys, definitive evaluations of error are not available or standard practices for adjustment have not evolved, and it is almost certain that many of these data —such as migration, fertility, labor-force status, occupation and industry statistics—are subject to greater error in response than an item like age. It may be anticipated that, as evaluations of census and survey data improve, it may become common practice to expand the range and types of adjustments made in data or to report errors attributable to "non-sampling" sources along with sampling error to discourage and restrict unwarranted generalizations. Until the reporting of non-sampling error in data becomes an accepted practice, it is likely that many of the conclusions drawn from census and survey statistics, even when sampling error is taken into account, will be subject to the illusory exactitude that comes with ignoring the problem rather than with its resolution. Non-sampling error may often be much greater, as recent analyses have shown, than sampling error. Moreover, the former is by no means as amenable as the latter to control.

Because of the gaps in the availability of many types of demographic information, especially "current" information, the demographer has devised various methods of "estimating" desired data. The most common type of estimation is that of total population on a current basis. Such statistics are necessary for many uses, for practical as well as for research purposes, and the demographer is generally under pressure to calculate them. Total population estimates for a country are relatively easy to prepare, with relatively little error, through a bookkeeping procedure, if current fertility, mortality, and international migration information is available. Population estimates for subareas of a nation are, in general, much more difficult and subject to greater error because of the widespread unavailability of information on internal migration. The mathematical methods of interpolation and extrapolation, the "symptomatic" techniques, "component" methods, and various combinations of methods all fall far short of the desideratum of providing current population figures of known and high accuracy.

Somewhat more complex methods are employed to estimate internal migration, the component of population change in respect of which the data are usually not available or most defective. Through the "aging" of an enumerated population to obtain an "expected" population with which a subsequent census can be compared, estimates of "net migration" are obtained as residuals and are subject to the usual sources of error of residual figures, as well as to special sources of error arising from the relative unreliability and non-comparability of successive census or survey operations.

It is in his analytical techiques, however, that the demographer displays his greatest methodological virtuosity. He has at his disposal, of course, the methods of statistics, to which he has added specific techniques of analyzing demographic materials. For dealing with population composition, metrics such as the sex ratio, dependency ratio, and population pyramid are employed to supplement the more common descriptive statistical measurements; and for dealing with population dynamics, a rather elaborate family of rates has been developed for fertility and mortality especially and to a lesser extent for migration. The more elaborate of these rates or extensions of them are quite elegant in their ability to summarize a mass of information—for example, the death rate of the stationary population or the "intrinsic" birth rate. In general, the rates used by the demographer, whether relatively simple or complex, have in common the objective of obtaining or approximating an a posteriori probability statement.

The more complex analytical devices used in demographic analysis derive largely from comparative studies. The need to "control" differences in population composition so as to isolate fertility or mortality differentials, as the case may be, led to the use of "standardization" procedures and to study of the implications of observed schedules of fertility or mortality as made explicit in the stationary or the stable population or the rates based upon them. Moreover, the demographer has been quite ingenious in devising indirect ways of obtaining desired rates, including the more complex ones, or substitutes for them.

Especially elegant in the eyes of most demographers is the stable population theory and method associated mainly with Alfred J. Lotka. This analytical model for a while was thought to accomplish more than it really could— that is, it was supposed actually to reveal the implications of an observed mortality and fertility schedule divorced from the effects of past demographic behavior. Recent studies have demonstrated the limitations of the stable population, in this and other respects, but it still remains a highly useful and relatively sophisticated analytical tool for many purposes.

The demographer, more than most social scientists, has made explicit ef-

forts to "predict" population, at least in the preparation of "projections" of future population. Although "projections" are regarded by the sophisticated as "conditional" predictions and are used more for analytical than for forecasting purposes, the great pressure placed upon the demographer for such figures and his inability to resist such pressures have placed him in a unique and, up to the point of disillusionment, an enviable position in the eyes of fellow social scientists. Postwar demographic reality which has been brought to bear on prewar population projections has demonstrated unequivocally that while the demographer can "project," he cannot yet "predict." Predictions, in contrast with projections, are dependent on "population studies" rather than solely on "demographic analysis." That is, demographic analysis enables the construction of projections based on assumptions in respect of the course of the components of population change, births, deaths, and migration. But the course of these components of change is tied to non-demographic variables, such as the business cycle or war. Only after economists, political scientists, and others are able to predict the phenomena with which they work with reasonable precision, will the demographer, as a result of population studies which will relate the demographic to the non-demographic variables, be in a position possibly to "predict" as well as to "project." Yet the fact that projections are not predictions and may not serve as reliable forecasts does not detract from their analytical usefulness. The implications of variations in the components of change can be made explicit in such projections and therefore be "analyzed" in an effective manner. The demographer is on sound ground in terms of the methodology of science in calculating population projections for analytical purposes. Unfortunately, this is not always his purpose, for many projections result not from analytical need but rather from the practical pressures of administrators, planners, and technicians both in government and business, who must have some inkling of the possible future course of demographic events on which to base their work. The demographer in meeting such needs may be useful, but his usefulness is achieved in this area often at the expense, rather than as a derivative, of his contribution to science.

The more recent methodological developments of an analytical character are taking two general major directions: one is the increased utilization of longitudinal analyses—as in cohort fertility analysis or generation life tables—the other is the use of various forms of mathematical models, deterministic and stochastic.

The longitudinal analyses, especially of fertility, have yielded new insights into the problem of breaking down current changes into cyclical and secular components. Some such decomposition is required if the ability of the demographer to predict as well as to construct projections of future population is to be improved. The interrelations of fertility behavior and other phenomena may be more amenable to detection and analysis as cohort fertility data can be related to other types of social and economic data.

The use of mathematical models for analytical purposes in demography is still in its early developmental state. Despite the fact that demographers as a group are, in comparison with most social scientists, heavily quantitative and relatively well qualified as statisticians, only a handful of demographers are highly trained mathematical statisticians. Without doubt, the increased utilization of mathematical models in demography, beyond those already incorporated in conventional techniques, must await the appearance of a new generation of scholars with better mathematical training than most contemporary demographers possess. Yet the few who are following the increasing tendency to employ direct mathematical approaches to demographic problems have already gone far enough to indicate that they are well worth further study.

On the whole, it must be acknowledged that there is a certain unevenness about the development of methods in demography. On the one hand, a great deal of technical virtuosity has been lavished on problems that would not even exist were the supply of high-quality data greater than it is. This holds, in particular, with respect to methods of correcting data, estimating population numbers and components of change, and calculating rates by indirect procedures. One possible consequence of the considerable preoccupation with estimation, correction, recovery, and reconciliation of data is that technical pyrotechnics may displace penetrating analysis or that workers with high technical standards may become reluctant to work on scientifically important problems where precision is difficult or impossible to attain. Such at any rate is the impression that outsiders may form of demographic research. However, it has been well said that the maturity of a science is not indicated by its ability to produce results without error (the spurious sense of "exactness") but by its ability to recognize and estimate the range of error in its results. By this criterion, the scientific status of demography, if not high, is doubtless improving.

On the other hand, many techniques of demographic analysis have been elaborated to deal with data which are conventionally available rather than with data which might, under improved circumstances, become available. If the methodologist were to reflect on the matter, he would probably be horrified at the prospect of having "complete" data. There are already means of producing data for which adequate analytical methods are not now available. Published census tabulations of population characteristics sometimes give cross-tabulations involving as many as four or five variables. But it is entirely possible, particularly with electronic tabulation equipment, to produce tabulations with several times this many variables cross-classified. It is probably safe to say that demographers are not prepared to suggest means of exhausting the analytical possibilities of such data as are already potentially available, let alone those that may eventuate from future developments in data collection and processing methods.

To a considerable extent, the development of analytical methods, including those of projecting future populations, has been confined to the invention of certain convenient descriptive statistics and certain more or less elementary breakdowns of population changes into components. The number of hypotheses for whose testing such methods are appropriate is actually rather limited. With the development of more elaborate theories, say, of the interrelations of changes in social structure and of trends of economic growth with population changes, it is almost certain that new methods of demographic analysis will have to be devised, or alternative types of socioeconomic models of population change will have to be explored. As the study of population acquires greater scientific maturity, it may be expected that the methods of study will come to be more intimately related with the theoretical preoccupations of the demographer, less dependent on the accidents of data availability, and less closely tied to merely conventional ways of breaking down population change into components.

Knowledge

What demographers know about population is drawn primarily from Western civilization and almost entirely from the modern period. Information about non-Western areas and about any area before the seventeenth century is fragmentary, and such reconstructions and constructions of total population figures as are available are clothed with ingenuity and imagination and in this regard resemble—even if they sometimes lack as good a factual basis—archeological reconstructions or the constructs of the student of organic evolution. Moreover, even less is known in time and space about the components of population change, fertility, mortality, migration, and the details of population composition and distribution.

The time- and space-bound character of demographic data, as has been mentioned above, poses the fundamental problem that confronts all social science—the problem of historicism. Such knowledge as exists may have little if any generic value, and it may permit no generalization beyond the areas and times from which it was drawn. It may well be that what we "know" is highly biased and that the bias lies in our knowing a few things about rapidly growing populations under the impact of industrialization. The prominent place in world demography of the theory of the "demographic transition" indicates preoccupation with the nature of the population changes we have been able to observe, even in the description and categorization of non-Western and pre-industrial population types. Knowledge about population composition and distribution similarly is drawn from a limited spatiotemporal universe that restricts the generality of the conclusions which have been drawn. Yet, even granting the limitation of historicism, it must be recognized that the corpus of knowledge of the demographer has provided some

measure of predictability and/or explanation of population phenomena over
at least several human generations and
that the evidence points in the direction of increasing rather than decreasing ability to generalize as larger and
larger portions of the globe and longer
time spans are subjected to observation.

Furthermore, implicit in these observations is the notion that knowledge is
more than a collection of census statistics. What makes statistics "knowledge"
is their ordering by a frame of reference, their relevance to hypotheses
which are subjected to testing, and
their incorporation into theory attempting prediction and explanation. It is not
statistics *in vacuo* but data ordered and
shown to be in antecedent or consequent relationships that constitute demographic knowledge. Indeed, the
"body of knowledge" produced by and
at the command of demography includes
facts, propositions, and formulations at
several levels of specificity. To begin
with, there are the "raw" data in census
reports and like sources; these can
hardly be termed "knowledge" or even
"facts" unless and until they are subjected to critical scrutiny and interpretation, for many of these items of supposed information are factually incorrect. Then there is a vast mass of what
might be called "ordered description
and interpretation" of population phenomena. We have in mind the kind of
monographic study which records the
population changes of a particular region over a particular period, perhaps
with some analysis of components of
change in size, composition, or distribution. Often such monographs include
"interpretations" or "implications" of
changes, but usually from a particularistic standpoint rather than in an effort
to test hypotheses systematically.

Out of such studies as well as those
oriented to specific hypotheses, however, there has developed a considerable body of statements of "empirical

regularities" concerning demographic
phenomena. Included herein are such
generalizations as the following: within
broad regions and at any given period
of time the fertility of rural populations
tends to be higher than that of urban
populations; the volume and rate of internal migration tend to fall off with increasing distance; mortality varies with
age in a pattern describable by an
asymmetrical U-shaped curve; and so
on. Each such proposition is supported
by a more or less extensive collection of
studies supporting its approximate validity under the particular conditions of
the study. Many of them, of course, are
subject to the qualification that they do
not hold under all circumstances or
even in all cases in which they have
been checked. It is seldom the case that
an explicit statement can be made as to
precisely what conditions are necessary
for these propositions to hold true. The
evidence supporting certain tentatively
accepted empirical generalizations is
much stronger and more comprehensive
for some of them than for others. It is
generally acknowledged that virtually
all putative empirical regularities are to
some degree at least space- and time-
bound in their validity or applicability.
Alongside this collection of "laws"—if
they may be so termed—one finds analyses concerning patterns of historical
trends of population change which
have been to some degree abstracted
from particular temporal observations
and which represent a certain generalization thereof. Trend analyses often
are set forth comparatively: periods
and regions are characterized as ones
of rapid or slow growth, static or declining fertility, violently fluctuating or
nearly constant mortality, and the like.
The description of typical or characteristic changes involves an element of inference, quite apart from the frequent
incorporation of conjectures made to
bridge gaps in the historical record. But
for the best-documented periods and

places trend analyses may be said to provide a "map" of the pattern of historical change—a map which, like any map, suppresses certain details in the interest of highlighting what are regarded as the more significant contours of the phenomena observed. Such are some of the principal "raw materials" with which any effort at explanation, prediction, or high-order generalization must work—or the "brew" from which scientific theories of population, if there are such, have to be distilled.

What may be properly called a "theory" of population consists of a body of interrelated principles which has at least some degree of empirical support, which affords an explanation or prediction of observed and observable relationships and which has heuristic implications in suggesting hypotheses for investigation. We intend by such a stipulation to exclude from consideration both the purely speculative exposition of "laws" of population growth and the construction of miniscule models of relationships, whether hypothetical or empirical, without systematic relevance to other sets of hypotheses. A review of some of the major attempts to construct theories in the foregoing sense reveals progress but also uncovers certain critical questions as to their adequacy. It should be noted immediately, however, that there is little evidence that the defects of the more important bodies of theory currently in use stem from an ignorance or lack of appreciation of the nature and functions of theory on the part of population students. Despite frequent allegations to the contrary, they appear to be as well informed on the role of theory in science as any group of scientists.

What has been called "analytical theory" consists primarily in working out logicomathematical relationships among components of population change and devising and elaborating schemes for component analysis. As with any body

of "pure" or "formal" theory, of course, the major questions about analytical theory in demography concern its empirical relevance and heuristic value. There is ample evidence in the history of demography of the misuse of analytical theory, e.g., in the interpretation of population projections as literal forecasts or in the treatment of hypothetical reproduction rates as actual underlying growth tendencies of populations. Recent developments in analytical theory have emphasized the possibility that simplified models of population growth may conceal logically or empirically unacceptable assumptions about certain subcomponents of growth. But, apart from refinement and further elaboration of the type of analytical theory developed thus far, the crucial issue is how best to construct models incorporating both the relationships employed in demographic analysis and the relationships between components of population change and factors thought to be related thereto, as deduced from sociological, economic, and biological theories, and the like.

Among the most highly developed conceptual schemes—if not "theories" in the meaning used here—are probably those deriving from Malthusian and optimum-population formulations. Perhaps the major contribution of such formulations has been to provide a highly general framework for the discussion of problems of the adjustment of population to resources and policy questions related thereto. They have not been notably helpful in identifying the immediate factors governing population changes, predicting rates of growth or patterns of movement in the short run, or explaining the various empirical regularities discovered in population research. There is evidence of increasing sophistication on the part of those who construct economic-demographic models with respect to the functions and limitations of such models; there is less evidence of any impending break-through with respect to means of bringing such models into operational contact with available data on the course of population change.

The widely accepted collection of propositions and inferences concerning the pattern of modern population growth known as "transition theory" represents an effort to discern a principle of order in the congeries of observed historical trends. As a form of generalized description, transition theory can make a pretty good case for itself, though the "goodness of fit" is by no means perfect. As concerns explanation and especially prediction, however, transition theory has succeeded only in suggesting certain major complexes of poorly defined influences on components of population change. Transition theory provides a valuable framework for appraising the population predicament of countries that appear to be on the verge of modernization. However, the influences on population growth that it postulates are closely bound up with the particular historical circumstances of population growth in Western counries. Hence, there is a big question as to whether it can provide more than vague, general suggestions about the factors likely to govern growth in the future. Because the theory is an attempt to generalize from a particular body of historical facts, it raises in perhaps the clearest form the issue of "historicism," i.e., that of whether such generalizations can successfully be applied to new situations.

Partly because of their feeling that available theories failed to isolate the specific factors governing population change, one school of demographers recently has turned to the intensive investigation of psychosocial attributes of married couples and to the systematization of hypotheses concerning relationships between such attributes and behavior bearing on fertility. Implicit in this attempt is the assumption that through the psychological study in depth of the units making up a population it is possible to understand some of the forces producing population variation and change. Whether or not defects in research design and inadequacies of observational techniques are to blame, it must be said that this viewpoint has thus far brought forth comparatively little hard evidence in its favor. What is significant, however, is that it exemplifies the growing feeling among students of population that to develop general explanatory theories which will withstand close contact with the data it will be necessary to delve rather deeply into the resources of theory provided by the various natural and social sciences which bear on the study of population. There is increasing dissatisfaction with the type of study that merely employs a routine of demographic analysis for descriptive purposes without seeking to test hypotheses grounded in the generic propositions of a science related to demography. The numerous and ingenious recent attempts to develop models to account for patterns of migratory flow represent another instance in point. Underlying such models are sociologically plausible assumptions concerning mass behavior or postulates derived from human ecology concerning community structure and the balance of population and opportunities. The fact that few of these nascent theories have come to maturity may mean that such efforts are misdirected, or it may merely signify that the concerted attempt to exploit the possibilities of self-conscious model-building is new and still in the tentative stage.

It is worth stressing that the import of these observations is the need to recognize the increasing importance of "population studies" as a supplement to "demographic analysis" for advancing demographic knowledge in general, that is, for increasing the ability of the demographer to predict and explain population phenomena.

Although demographers give evidence of increasing awareness of the nature and role of theory in the building of natural science, there may well be room for even more deliberate effort than is now evidenced in the construction and testing of theories. Moreover, there is reason to believe that much might be gained from greater emphasis on the major function of theory, namely, prediction and explanation. Such a focus might do much to eliminate from efforts to develop theory in demography and related disciplines what still remains in the way of *misconceptions* of theory. Included with such misconceptions would be "speculation" (undisciplined generalization with a minimum of data and global explanatory intent), "philosophizing" (more or less disciplined deductive elaboration of propositions without an adequate empirical basis and often, also, with global explanatory intent), mere taxonomy (the construction of classifications out of context of empirical research, often out of touch with the phenomenological world, and therefore of limited value for prediction and explanation), and mere concept creation (the creation of imagery, often couched in neologisms, deriving from speculation or philosophizing rather than from research contacts with data).

Perhaps the most common deficiency of "contributions" to theory in social science in general as well as in demography, manifest often in the types of "misconceptions" to which reference is made above, lies in preoccupation with a part rather than with the whole of the structure of science. This deficiency takes two common forms: "specialization" in theory construction with little or no contact with empirical research and, usually evident in the same investigator, concentration on one or a few

of the functions of theory rather than with the function of theory in a holistic sense.

It may be argued that division of labor is useful in science as in other realms or that division of labor of the type indicated also occurs in the natural sciences. This argument, however, is a specious one in failing to detect the significant difference between the context in which the division of labor between "theory construction" and "empirical research" occurs, say, in physics for the natural sciences and in sociology for the social sciences. In physics the theoretician works with an impressive cumulative fund of knowledge based on empirical research—usually knowledge produced in a laboratory under the conditions of an experimental as distinguished from an observational science. In sociology, by reason of the common misconceptions of theory described above and the relative paucity of the fund of knowledge at this early stage in the development of the discipline, the theoretician is as likely as not to work with propositions based on common sense (his) or, in any case, without the benefit of a relatively large cumulative fund of verified knowledge. The absence of such a fund of knowledge may in part account for the fact that theoreticians in the social sciences often turn to "system" building. Systems have been and can be constructed without benefit of a fund of empirical research results, as has been so amply demonstrated in sociology during the nineteenth and early twentieth centuries. Fortunately, even though systems are still being constructed in sociology, the activity is a limited one and no longer occupies the attention of the predominant proportion of sociologists.

Even in demography, which in many respects occupies an intermediate position between physics and general sociology, much of what is known as theory, at least that which has come down from the nineteenth and early twentieth centuries, is more like sociological theory than theory in physics. However, there is increasing evidence that demography is turning away from activities of the type designated above as "misconceptions" of theory and is attempting to construct theory in accord with the imagery of science as it obtains in the natural sciences.

The construction of theory in this sense may be said to consist of an awareness of and adherence to the following essential principles: first, the recognition of the objective of any science as prediction and explanation; second, the deliberate effort to make explicit essential aspects of the frame of reference, concepts, methodology, and the fund of knowledge which serve as a point of departure for research; third, the utilization of conceptual frameworks, methodology, and the existing fund of knowledge to good effect in exercising the "art of science" which is research; fourth, the designing of research in a manner which clarifies the conditions under which the knowledge gained may be accepted as valid and permits replication of these conditions by others; and, fifth, the construction of theory as the tentative product of empirical research in the form of heuristic implications, that is, in a form conducive to further research. Unless the division of labor in the building of science is co-ordinated and integrated in terms of such a model and unless theory construction, if pursued independently of empirical research, is tied to the existing fund of knowledge, including previous theory, efforts to "theorize" are likely to do little to advance the state of science.

It would be gratifying if, in considering the prospect for demography as a body of knowledge, it were possible to deal more specifically and conclusively with some of the issues raised in respect of certain major foci of theory in the field. But to resolve these issues, other than by fiat, would be to anticipate accurately the future course of the discipline. Of one thing we can be sure—nothing in demography, any more than in any other science, is ever "finished." Data, concepts, methods, and collections of factual information are always in a state of becoming, and theoretical schemes for ordering and structuring these elements of science are themselves subject to evolutionary change. As of now, with the perspective open to us by virtue of achievements to date, it seems likely, for example, that to achieve any high order of explanation and prediction of population changes, demography will have to cast its theories at least partly in historical terms. Such theories, it need hardly be pointed out, are subject to the same general canons of adequacy as other types of theories. They may, however, prove to be of more limited applicability and of lesser abstractness than might be desired. We are not prepared to foreclose possible theoretical developments of other types, but we strongly suspect that the issue of "historicism" will be involved, explicitly or implicitly, in efforts to build population theories for some time to come. Similarly, we cannot here resolve the issue as to whether students of population must fashion their theories in terms of social-psychological variables in order to achieve explanation and prediction. But, again, we suspect that the fruitfulness of this path of development will be a question with which the discipline must continue to grapple.

We cannot even state with complete confidence that the current preoccupation of some demographers, along with other social scientists, with formal model-building augurs well for the discipline. As has been made clear, however, if such efforts are to be undertaken, it is important that they be informed by adequate conceptions of the role of theory in science. We can be sure that, if they are not, the irrelevancy of "models" or "theories" will sooner or later become apparent. One of the major advantages enjoyed by demography, in comparison with many sister disciplines, is a clear perception of the limits of its empirical knowledge. Claims as to the extension of these limits are relatively rapidly and decisively put to test. The prospect is that the life expectancy of "theories" that overreach themselves will be continually reduced in the future.

EVALUATION OF DEMOGRAPHY
AS A WHOLE

The status of demography as a science, insofar as it may be explicated through consideration of its parts, has been set forth above, from a point of view which embodies the biases and predilections of the editors. Certainly the observations above, together with the documentation contained in the remainder of this volume, indicate that demography has a not unimpressive answer to the questions which have been raised in respect of its frame of reference, its data, its methods, and its corpus of knowledge. This is not to say that demography is devoid of problems in any, let alone all, of these various ingredients of any science. But it would seem that all of the essential components of science are to be found in the work of demographers. There is evidence of growth and development in each of the parts of the science which have been surveyed. The corpus of knowledge of demography includes substantial, albeit time- and space-bound, facts about population and population change; and the discipline commands improving conceptual frameworks, hypotheses, and theory which order the facts and point to their interrelationships in an effort to achieve predictability and explanation.

Yet consideration of the parts of a science does not necessarily provide a general picture of its status, for a science, like any organic and developing entity, is more than the sum of its parts. Consequently, an evaluation of demography as a whole is essayed in the paragraphs which follow, with full awareness that it also is subject to the biases of the writers; but, it may be emphasized, the evaluation is essayed only after exposure to the symposium as a kind of integration and synthesis of previous experience in the field.

As an introductory to our holistic evaluation of demography it is in order to provide a brief historical perspective. Some of the earliest interests in population numbers and composition, as old as human history, are those relating to the curiosity of the state and its functionaries in respect of matters of taxation and defense and of the church in respect of moral law and the sacraments, particularly as they related to marriage, birth, and death. These interests, while essentially "non-scientific," were significant for the development of demography as a scientific discipline, for they led to record-keeping activities which provided the first batches of population data for analysis and from which census-taking and vital registration systems emerged as primary sources of population data.

Population study became identified with science as "political arithmetic" in the works of John Graunt, *The Bills of Mortality*, and Sir William Petty, *Politicall Arithmetick*, published in 1662 and 1690, respectively. It is not without significance that Petty and Graunt were both on the original list of fellows of the Royal Society. Moreover, the relation of demography to natural science in its origins is further manifested in the work of a third original fellow of the Royal Society, Halley, of comet fame, who published the first life table. The interest of these pioneers in population data was a concrete manifestation of the application of the "Baconian" method—the method of empirical research—to human phenomena. In fact, in this respect the study of population was one of the milestones in the development of social science.

Although population as a field of study may be said to have originated in empirical observation and quantitative description and analysis, it was popularized and undoubtedly stimulated to more rapid development than it would have otherwise experienced by a political tract written in an atmosphere of political and philosophical dissension rather than empirical research. Malthus in his famous rejoinder to Godwin, among other things, demonstrated that broad generalization without too much regard for facts, especially if it has current political relevance, can attract more attention than sound scholarship. But whether one agrees with Reuter that Malthus "attempted the familiar pseudoscientific task of seeking facts to provide a scientific formulation for the pre-conceived theory" or with Bogardus that Malthus "offered to the world the first carefully collected and elaborated body of data dealing with what he called *the* social problem . . . which may be counted in a sense, the beginning of modern sociological study," it is incontrovertible that the *Essay on the Principle of Population* exerted a tremendous influence on the popular mind, on political action, and also on subsequent scholarly developments in both social and natural science.

The widespread attention given to Malthus undoubtedly contributed to the development of demography. Such consideration as was given to the relation of population to resources and to *the* population problem was supplemented, however, during the nineteenth century by various other interests which found expression in the study of population growth and charac-

teristics. The interest of the biologist in the variability of the characteristics of human populations, in the role of heredity and race in explaining human behavior, in evolution, and in ecology led to a number of studies which embraced and developed both the substantive problems and techniques of demography. These interests arising from natural science sources manifest in the subsequent development of human genetics, biometrics, and aspects of human ecology and human geography were supplemented by the emergence of an interest in vital phenomena on the part of the rapidly expanding field of public health and on the part of the medical profession.

The development of demography from its social science lineage is traceable primarily through economics and through continuing government interest in population phenomena. Economists picked up Malthus' famous principle of population and elaborated it into the "law of diminishing return." Ricardo and Mill placed Malthus' ideas in the center of economic thinking and literature. In consequence, the consideration of population as a social study for most of the nineteenth century and the early part of the twentieth was confined largely to the writings and deductions of economists.

The impetus given to demography by continuing government interest in population was linked to economic policy considerations, on the one hand, and population record-keeping, on the other. The thought given to population matters by the Mercantilists in England, the Physiocrats in France, and the Cameralists in Germany represents the first of these influences; the development of modern census-taking and vital registration systems, the second.

During much of the twentieth century economists paid relatively little attention to population phenomena. More recently, economists have renewed their interest in population as a factor in economic development, both in advanced and less advanced cultures. During most of this century, however, economists' interest in population as an element in deductive theorization dwindled, and population as a field of empirical research was a flame that was never quite kindled.

This did not mean, however, that demography as a field of study languished. On the contrary, with the increasing availability of population data, empirical research greatly increased. Research activity was carried on by a diversity of scholars—persons of quite different academic origins. They included, in keeping with the heritage of demography, both natural and social scientists. The natural scientists were primarily biometricians and public health and medical personnel, with an occasional geneticist, ecologist, geographer, and even physicist. The social scientists tended primarily to be sociologists and statisticians with social science training, many of whom were engaged in government service on various tasks related to the compilation of population and vital statistics. Research contributions were also made by actuaries and mathematical statisticians. The first half of this century produced a sizable population literature containing many quantitative data and embodying relatively sophisticated demographic techniques in addition to the rapidly developing techniques of statistics.

In view of this historical background it is in order, first of all, to note that demography has in the contemporary scene become a science rather than a polemical field for the resolution of policy problems. This is not to say that demographers, as citizens, do not still, from time to time, make known their views on contemporary problems or participate in activities directed at their solution. But it is almost universally recognized among population students that a sharp division of labor must be effected between research with its related scientific activities and "social engineering" behavior directed toward the formation or implementation of policy. To be sure, there are still fringe groups, whose objective is primarily problem solution, who attempt identification with demography. The preponderant proportion of demographers, however, although aware of the implications and utility of their findings for many practical purposes—including such uses as national policy formation, marketing, city-planning, economic development programs, and the like—recognize that their function is that of pursuing and finding knowledge rather than that of preoccupation with policy formation, program administration, and problem solution. These latter, it is recognized, are the tasks of the social engineer and not of the social scientist.

As a science, demography, as has been noted, is not a unitary field. On the contrary, demography not only combines the interests of a number of separate scientific disciplines, but it also straddles the natural and social sciences. This is true of its personnel as well as of its problems for research, its data, its methods, and its corpus of knowledge. The distinction which has been elaborated above between "demographic analysis" and "population studies" tends to point to a hard core of interest, centrally located in demography, with a peripheral area merging into all the disciplines which are involved in population studies.

In lacking unitary character demography is not unique among the sciences. Other recognized sciences tend also to lack a readily identifiable unitary character. Anthropology, for example, includes subfields which cut across other disciplines, such as physical anthropology and archeology, as well as linguistics, ethnology, and social anthropology. A science, in practice, exists either as an abstract area of interest as fixed by a given orientation and frame of reference, such as chemistry or economics, or as a common area of research focused on a given field or fields of phenomena, such as geography, anthropology, or demography. In actuality, a science is always some combination of the two, but the mixtures may differ.

In respect of any of the sciences which deal with man there is almost always the latent question of whether they can actually be "sciences." And there are, of course, schools of thought which hold that the "social sciences" are not sciences and that they should more appropriately be termed "social studies." To avoid polemics on this issue, and with the confidence based on the documentation provided by the symposium, it may be flatly stated that demography is a science because it embodies all the essential elements of scientific outlook and method. Demographers, like other scientists, are dedicated to persistent search for truth. Similarly, demographers are committed to the use of scientific method—that is, certain principles of procedure, including the acceptance of generalization only on the basis of evidence, the use of objective and communicable techniques which are subject to replication, the recognition of the tentative character of knowledge in the sense that it is always assumed that better knowledge can be obtained, and the relentless determination to continue testing available generalizations and to add to the fund of knowledge. Furthermore, it is not irrelevant that demography also possesses a cadre of professional personnel who are dedicated to research and training in demography.

In general, demography with all its limitations seems to measure up reasonably well as an observational science concerned with human populations and therefore, necessarily to some

extent, also with the cultural, economic, and political contexts in which they appear. In the narrow area of "demographic analysis," demography, in comparison with the social sciences, is relatively well advanced in the quantification of its data, in the rigor of its analytical methods, and in the extent to which it can predict and explain phenomena. In the broader area of "population studies" it is subject to the same limitations of data, methods, and predictability and explanation in respect of cultural, social-psychological, economic, political, biological, ecological, or geographic variables as are the various sciences concerned with these phenomena. These limitations become apparent in efforts to predict or explain population phenomena by means of non-demographic concepts and principles or in efforts to treat population as an independent variable to predict or explain the other systems of variables.

Compared with the more advanced natural sciences, demography makes a less favorable showing, even as regards its achievements in demographic analysis. The main documentation for this observation is to be found in the relatively small proportion of the variability in population phenomena which present demographic knowledge can explain. To be sure, total population changes can be "explained" completely by the components of change—fertility, mortality, and spatial movement. In this narrow and restricted sense demographic analysis can fully account for population change. But the demographer has pitifully inadequate ability to predict or explain the components of population change and especially changes in fertility and migration. In respect of this type of problem, the demographer, like other social scientists, has barely begun the climb up the ladder of scientific achievement.

It may be that demography, to the extent that it is a social science, will always have a lower order of predictability and explanation than the observational natural sciences because of the greater variability of "social" than of "natural" phenomena and because of the problem posed by historicism. That is, it is certainly the case today, and it may remain so indefinitely, that the demographer accounts for much smaller proportions of the variability in population phenomena than does the astronomer in the behavior of the heavenly bodies and that the demographer, even though his generalizations are based on empirical findings, knows relatively little about the descriptive validity of his data or the limits of the universe to which his generalizations apply.

Yet, despite these limitations, it is indisputable that the demographer in producing demographic research does contribute to a fund of knowledge of a character vastly superior to "common sense" or other non-scientific forms of professed knowledge about population phenomena. Moreover, despite the historicism of demographic knowledge, such predictive and explanatory findings as are available have considerable relevance for units of time and space that are meaningful to human beings. That is, findings which are limited in the natural-science sense, in that they have applicability for only a few decades and for a given culture or civilization rather than for all of mankind, are nevertheless an important addition to knowledge both for the purpose of science, which is understanding, and for various practical purposes in problem solution in the fields of social engineering.

At least a brief reference to demography as a profession is desirable to complete this summary description and evaluation of the discipline. As a profession, demography is a relatively small field, attracting at the most a few hundred persons in the United States and probably not more than one or two thousand in the entire world. These numbers do not include, of course, scholars engaged in population studies who do not identify themselves as "demographers."

As a field of training demography is far from being a uniform or standardized field. It is not a separate department of instruction in any university in the United States. It has no common curriculum with a prescribed minimum standard of training. Courses in demography, while primarily concentrated in departments of sociology in the United States, actually appear in a wide spectrum of departments in the social and natural sciences or in applied fields such as public health and medicine. In consequence, the present generation of demographers is to a considerable extent "self-trained," in the sense that they have acquired specialization in the field by concentrating in it, largely on their own, while acquiring professional competence in one of the recognized social or natural sciences. The modal disciplinary training of contemporary demographers is sociology, which has produced about three-fifths of the members of the Population Association of America and about half of those in the International Union for the Scientific Study of Population. In fact the modal demographer in the United States is a Ph.D. in sociology teaching at a college or university (26 per cent of the members of the Population Association of America).

On the other hand, it must be recognized that although a large proportion of demographers are sociologists, only a small proportion of sociologists are demographers. In view of the fact that training in sociology is still, by and large, non-quantitative, demographer-sociologists represent an important fraction of the "hard" or quantitatively trained sociologists. The relatively small proportion of sociologists who become demographers are disproportionately trained in a handful of centers at a few universities. Of fifty-eight Ph.D.'s earned by sociologists specializing in demography, during 1946–54, thirty-seven were conferred by four universities.

Consideration of training and research facilities discloses inadequacies in both and, perhaps, an undesirable concentration of both in relation to sociology. It would appear desirable to encourage the development of demographic training and research facilities in relation to other disciplines in addition to those connected with sociology —especially in relation to such areas as actuarial mathematics, mathematical statistics, economics, geography, and biology. Perhaps of even greater potential for the development of demography would be the organization of training and research facilities to provide greater cross-disciplinary participation than is to be found anywhere today.

In any consideration of research and training facilities the important role of the federal government cannot be overlooked. Especially in such agencies as the Bureau of the Census and the National Office of Vital Statistics, the government has made a significant contribution by providing training facilities for its employees, as well as by conducting demographic research. The government is, of course, the major source of demographic statistics. In consequence, there is a tendency for government demographers to be specialized in the collection of the data and for analytical functions to be relatively ignored. Much could be gained, undoubtedly, from a better-balanced combination of collection and analytical functions in government agencies.

It is doubtful that resources for training and research in demography have kept pace, in recent years, with the growth of the profession. The recent tendency for the major foundations, from which social science research

funds have been available, increasingly to grant funds for research tied to social engineering programs, in preference to "pure" research, undoubtedly tends to make the distinction between science and engineering more difficult to maintain, for the demographer as well as for other scientists. The advent of the National Science Foundation may prove to be an important factor in the further development of demography, for there is increasing evidence that it is prepared to allocate funds both for basic demographic research and for the training of demographers. Activities of the National Science Foundation in this direction, however, have only recently begun and, appropriately, on a quite modest scale.

On the whole, demographers have little difficulty in finding publication outlets. Because of high publication costs, they are hampered, as are all scientists, of course, in the publication of monographic studies. But for the publication of articles the demographer has relatively little difficulty in getting into print. A serious problem exists, however, in the wide scatter of demographic articles. Only one widely known journal in English is available exclusively for demography and one in French. Most of the demographic periodical literature is spread over a large number of non-demographic journals. Fortunately, the *Population Index* (Population Association of America and Office of Population Research, Princeton University), which has as its major function the annotation of current literature, has been available to demographers for nearly a quarter of a century. Despite these resources the documentation problem in demography threatens to become unmanageable, and it is likely that this area will require financial support in the coming years.

Any comprehensive attempt at a sociology-of-knowledge study of demography would result in an elaboration of at least the following striking features of the profession: first, the wide range of disciplines from which demographers are drawn and the fact that it is not recognized as a separate discipline academically in the United States; second, the tendency for differentiation of function among demographers, with specialization in collection of data among government demographers and specialization in analytical and substantive research functions among the academic fraternity; third, the great pressure on demographers for the fulfilment of essentially non-scientific functions such as providing information, estimates, projections, and "practical" interpretations of population data. These features contribute to some of the problems of the profession, including the "marginal" role of the demographer in his discipline of origin; his relatively great specialization and, therefore, often narrow interests; and his too frequent preoccupation with publicizing the information he already possesses instead of concentrating on research which would enrich his corpus of knowledge.

ORGANIZATION AND CONTENT
OF THIS VOLUME

The preceding pages contain a highly distilled summary and statement of implications of the material contained in the four main parts of this volume. One of these parts is a more extended presentation of the editors' conclusions on the matters just summarized. The remaining three comprise a symposium assembled according to procedures to be described presently. This symposium represents the end product of a project whose objectives were to provide a description and evaluation of the data, the fund of knowledge, the theory, and the methods of demography and its various subfields; to examine its relationship to other scientific disciplines; and to indicate important circumstances bearing on the development of demography in various parts of the world. The successful achievement of these specific tasks would, it was hoped, provide a comprehensive picture of demography as a science and a profession as of mid-twentieth century. In the consideration of the status of demography as a science, national boundaries were, of course, necessarily ignored. In the consideration of demography as a profession, attention was focused primarily, although not entirely, on the situation in the United States.

Preparation of the Symposium

In the conduct of the investigation some twenty-seven individual scholars, eight from abroad, were called upon to deal with their special areas of competence or to describe the development and status of demography in their own nations. Each of these scientists was asked to prepare a paper which would serve as a chapter in a published report. To assure coverage of the items desired and some uniformity of treatment, each of the authors was provided with a general statement of the purposes of the investigation and a tentative outline of the chapter to be written. The outline was, in general, one of three varieties. One dealt with the materials to be included in the section on the historical development and current status of demography. The second indicated the items to be considered in treating of the elements of demography—that is, the data, methods, and substantive fields of research. The third described the manner in which the relations between demography and other disciplines were to be discussed.

In orienting each author to the general objectives and purposes of the investigation, emphasis was placed on the fact that the focus of the project was on the field of demography as a science concerned with basic research, rather than on the applications of the findings of research to the treatment or solution of social, economic, political, public health, or medical problems. Since the findings of demography generally have wide applicability to the solution of such "social engineering" problems, major effort could have been devoted to an evaluation of demography as a contributor to various applied fields, including such areas as medicine, public health, marketing, housing, education, social work, and economic development. Although such explorations would undoubtedly have great interest and value, they were outside the scope and purpose of this investigation; and they are, of course, of no concern to the demographer as a scientist, even though they are undoubtedly of personal concern to him—as they are to all persons, as members of families and communities and as citizens.

Although it was necessarily an important specific objective of this study to examine and evaluate the status of demography as a science and as a profession in the United States, demography, like other sciences, has been developed through the co-operation of students in many lands. In consequence, in addition to treating of the data and of the substantive, theoretical, and methodological areas of demography without regard to national boundaries, it was deemed desirable to obtain a description of the development and status of demography in a number of countries other than the United States. Such materials, it was felt, would provide a backdrop against which to see the developments in the United States in broad perspective. It was obviously impractical to include a separate discussion for each country in which population studies have been carried on. For example, it would have required over fifty chapters to represent each nation having one or more members in the International Union for the Scientific Study of Population Problems. However, the several chapters in Part II provide representation both of areas where demographic research has a relatively long and distinguished history and of those in which promising beginnings in the development of demography and rapid initial progress have been made in recent years.

Each of the authors asked to prepare a chapter on the development and status of demography in a particular area was provided with the following outline to guide him in his work.

A. Brief History of the Development of Demography in this Country
   1. When and under what circumstances did demography emerge as a science?
   2. What have been the major circumstances favoring and hindering its development (emphasis on the period since 1930)?
   3. What have been the most significant trends in demographic research with respect to (1) types of problems dealt with, (2) approaches to these problems?
B. Present Status of Demography in this Country
   1. In what fields of demography have the greatest achievements been made?
   2. Which aspects of demography are relatively less developed?
   3. What are the major difficulties in the way of a more rapid development of demography?
   4. How adequate are the facilities presently available for training, research, and publication in demography?
C. Prospects for Demography in this Country
   1. What are the most important facts that appear likely to influence the future development of demography in this country?
   2. What modifications need to be made in present programs of training and research to facilitate this development?
   3. What aspects of demography should be emphasized or developed further in future research?

4. What are the most pressing subjects on which research should be done in the near future?

D. Selected Bibliography

List the more important items which are representative of recent and current work in demography in this country and which illustrate the points made in the preceding sections of the outline.

Although the authors by no means rigidly adhered to this outline, they did, by and large, cover the types of materials indicated.

Several alternatives were available for the organization of demography into "elements" for treatment in this study. The classification finally decided upon reflects, it is felt, the actual divisions of the field as the demographer works in it—that is, it reflects the major subjects of concern in research and in training. A dozen such "elements" were identified for operational purposes and to serve as chapter headings in this part of the report.

Each of the authors dealing with an element of demography, although given wide latitude to develop his chapter in his own way, was provided with the "tentative outline" which follows:

A. Major Interest of Field
  1. Brief introduction—historical development of interest in field.
  2. What do we want to know about it?
B. Data
  1. Nature of the data and sources of data.
  2. Deficiencies of data.
  3. Adjustment of data.
C. Methods
  1. General description of methods.
  2. Function: What purposes do the various methods serve? What kinds of questions will they answer?
  3. How are the methods utilized in research?
  4. Deficiencies of methods—what are their shortcomings?
D. Fund of Knowledge and Evaluation
  1. Frame of reference and basic concepts.

2. Highlights of what we do know, in historical perspective—theory and generalizations.
  a. Facts: historical trends, differentials (regional, socioeconomic), prospects.
  b. Explanatory principles: theory, ordering of facts.
  3. Evaluation of fund of knowledge—strong points and gaps.
E. Next Steps in Research (and obstacles which hinder advance in research)
  1. Data.
  2. Methods.
  3. Substantive.
F. Selected Bibliography (include major and representative works)

The individual authors varied considerably in the extent to which they adhered to this outline, and some departed from it substantially.

The consideration of the relationship of demography to other sciences was restricted to the few disciplines with which it is most closely interrelated. These included ecology, human ecology, geography, physical anthropology, genetics, economics, and sociology. Other disciplines, of course, could also have been included, as is indicated by references thereto at various places in the volume.

To guide the authors of the chapters on the relationship of demography to other sciences, general instructions were also issued in the interest of obtaining some uniformity in coverage and treatment. These instructions indicated that the discussion should cover such topics as the relationship between demography and the specified discipline, the theoretical contribution of each to the other, the status of research, and the accumulation of knowledge concerning the main problems jointly investigated by the two disciplines.

Except for relatively minor matters of format and style the individual chapters are presented substantially as written by their authors. It was the policy of the editors to let the individual scholar say his piece as he wished even though at a number of points the editors would have preferred a different type of treatment, a different allocation of space, or the inclusion or omission of some types of items. The editors decided that they would have their say in Part I of the volume, "Demography as a Science," in which it would be their prerogative among other things to differ with various aspects of the presentation of the individual authors.

The twenty-eight chapters obtained from contributors in the manner outlined above provided the main basis for the summary and evaluation of the status of demography as a science undertaken by the editors. These materials do not, of course, provide the sole basis for the appraisal, which necessarily drew upon the experience of the editors and other sources, particularly with respect to the discussion of professional activities. In view of the fact that the editors are sociologists, it should be mentioned that an effort was made to review the field of demography as a broad interdisciplinary activity rather than as merely a subfield of sociology. Even though it is true that most college and university courses in demography in the United States are at the present time taught in departments of sociology, the fact is that demographers are drawn from a number of disciplines other than sociology, and much of demographic research necessarily involves interdisciplinary frames of reference and methodology. Significantly, fewer than half the contributors to the symposium are sociologists primarily, in terms of their training or current professional activity.

Arrangement of the Volume

The plan of the volume is tantamount to an examination of demography from four standpoints. In Part I, "Demography as a Science" the editors have looked at the discipline in terms of the general or abstract components of any science: its general nature, including scope and frame of reference, its data and methods, and its accumulated knowledge, including theory. The evaluation is completed by an examination of those aspects of demography as a profession that bear on its progress as a science. In Part II, "Development and Current Status of Demography," contributors to the symposium employ a historical and geographic framework for discussing the status of demography, whereas in Part III, "Elements of Demography," following a comparative appraisal of data resources for population research, each chapter takes up a particular substantive field or problem in demography. Here each chapter individually is concerned with the topics of demographic data, research methods, verified hypotheses, and explanatory theories that are treated in a broad way in Part I. Finally, in Part IV, "Population Studies in Various Disciplines," the perspective shifts to an examination of demography in terms of its area of overlap with each of several scientific disciplines with which it is closely related.

It is true, therefore, that each of the four main headings in the report entails a broad treatment of the field of demography. Necessarily, there is some repetition of information and duplication of evaluations from one chapter to another. However, given the rather distinctive perspectives of their four ways of presenting the discipline, the actual amount of substantive overlap is comparatively small.

PART I

Demography as a Science

The principles by which progress in a science proceeds can only be reached by observing that progress. They cannot be deduced a priori or prescribed in advance.

R. F. HARROD

2. The Nature of Demography

PHILIP M. HAUSER AND OTIS DUDLEY DUNCAN

Most of the discussions one reads about the scientific status of a discipline seem to reflect some insecurity or doubt as to whether it is a science. When scientists are confident about what they want to do and are sure they know how to do it, they seldom wonder if their discipline is scientific. The kinds of questions one might raise about the status of a mature and confident science, therefore, differ from those appropriate for appraising an aspiring but hesitant science. We need not begin by raising the question of whether demography is a science. Instead, we indicate in this chapter what kind of science it is, and in subsequent chapters we describe some of its special problems as a science and assess the character of its scientific accomplishments.

There is no standardized procedure or uniform set of accepted criteria for the evaluation of a science. For the purposes of this discussion, however, it is possible to set forth a frame for the evaluation of demography both in a holistic manner and in terms of its component parts as a science. The major constituents of demography as a science, or of any science, are designated by categories like those used here as chapter titles and section headings. That is, demography as a science—like any science—may be analyzed into a field of interest delimited by a frame of reference, data, methods of study, and a corpus of knowledge embracing existential propositions and explanatory principles.

Each of these aspects of science may be subdivided. The "area of interest,"

as delimited by a frame of reference, can be regarded as consisting of a central core and various peripheral subjects which merge with the interests of other disciplines or fall within the scope of other frames of reference. The "data" may be grouped in alternative ways, according to type of source, categories in the frame of reference to which they pertain, methods by which they are obtained, or ways in which they are utilized. The "methods" may be classified in various fashions; here, however, the general logic of scientific method results in the use of fairly standard rubrics in the several disciplines, as indicated by such terms as "observation," "description," "classification," "analysis," "experiment," "control," "verification," and "prediction." Finally, the "knowledge" of the discipline is similarly divisible into such commonly recognized elements as "hypotheses," "facts," "theory," "generalizations," "probability statements," or "laws." The distinctions among the several elements of the corpus of knowledge of a discipline usually involve relatively imprecise judgments as to the degree of generality and credibility characterizing the propositions involved.

These various ingredients of a science conceivably may be examined separately and evaluated in such terms as their presence or absence; their comprehensiveness, relative to the potential of the discipline being surveyed, on the one hand, and to the achievements of an advanced science, on the other; their adequacy, as indicated by their contributions to the ultimate objective of any science—the development of a capacity to "explain" and "predict" phenomena falling within the area of interest.

In evaluating the discipline as a whole, the extent to which predictability and explanation are achieved must be regarded as the ultimate criterion. A high order of achievement would indicate, of course, not only that the discipline as a whole enjoys a relatively high status as a science but also that each of the several phases of scientific work similarly has a high order of merit in the sense of contributing to the objectives of the discipline. A low order of predictability and explanation in a discipline, although indicating the inadequacy of at least some of the discipline's component parts, would not necessarily suggest the specific inadequacies responsible for the deficiencies of the discipline as a whole.

Needless to say, no scales, let alone precise ones, exist for measuring the status of demography as a whole or of any of its constituents listed above. The most that can be hoped for, beyond a statement characterizing these aspects of demography, is a series of qualitative assessments based on the experience and judgment of the writers exercised in terms of their conception and imagery of science. The problem is conceived as one of evaluating the several aspects or components of the discipline in summary terms, not of taking inventory of its methods or theories, for example. To compile such an inventory would be tantamount to writing a treatise on the subject of demography, and neither the editors nor the symposium contributors have taken this as their task.

An obvious difficulty encountered in organizing the discussion is that no "part" of a science can be discussed intelligibly without presuming some acquaintance with the other "parts." To evaluate the data of a science, for example, requires some conception of the methods available for analyzing the data, the kinds of problems for which the data are supposed to be pertinent, and the hypotheses to be tested by the data. Our discussion, therefore, must move along in a somewhat serpentine fashion, with unavoidable backward and forward references to topics other than the one nominally under discussion.

An orientation to the frame of reference of demography is presented in the next section. As this statement makes clear, there is some obscurity in respect to the scope of the field which arises from the very nature of the area of interest and the approaches to it that population students have taken. A consideration of the demographer's frame of reference in relation to that of allied disciplines completes this chapter. Succeeding chapters are concerned with the data and methods of demography, its substantive knowledge including population theory, and aspects of demography as a profession. The "Overview and Conclusions" (chap. i) summarizes our general evaluation of the present status of demography as a science.

SCOPE AND FRAMEWORK

Conceptions of the content and frame of reference of demography vary from time to time, from place to place, and according to the perspective from which they are developed. The number of scientists working on some phase of human population studies is considerably larger than the number who would identify "demography" as their major preoccupation. The specialist in public health, for example, is likely to think of demography primarily in terms of its contributions to the measurement of morbidity, mortality, and conditions related thereto. The economist, however (save, perhaps, the few economists specializing in population), is more likely to discuss population under the heading, say, of the supply of labor as a factor in economic development or as a component of consumer demand. Each such specialist, if he were to give the matter any thought, might regard demography as a convenient source of data or analytical techniques particularly relevant to his own problems and as a specialty otherwise concerned with population in ways unnecessary to understand. For example, public health workers, economic analysts, and practitioners of many other specialties maintain a rather steady demand for information about future populations and appear to expect demographers to satisfy that demand.

Even where close relationships between demography and other disciplines are recognized, the approach to demography taken by the related discipline is likely to be strongly colored by that discipline's theoretical preoccupations. Moreover, inasmuch as most demographers *soi-disant* also are trained and active in some discipline other than demography, they are unlikely to share an identical conception of the latter.

Any effort to define demography in terms broad enough to encompass the variant views of the discipline that arise for the foregoing reasons is bound to produce a formulation that seems arbitrary from one perspective or another. Inevitably such a definition must reflect somewhat the predilections of one who formulates it. Fortunately, for the purposes of this volume, the following formal definition of demography will serve to frame the subsequent discussion without operating as a constraint on any function for which the definition is inappropriate: *Demography is the study of the size, territorial distribution, and composition of population, changes therein, and the components of such changes, which may be identified as natality, mortality, territorial movement, and social mobility (change of status).*

Certain somewhat unusual features

of this definition call for a little explanation.

No reference is made to population "quality." In its usual meaning, this term subsumes such characteristics as physical health, mental capacity, and attained skills or qualifications. The frequency distribution of such characteristics, along with many others, is included in the meaning of "population composition." The latter term, indeed, is understood to have quite a broad denotation, including not only such conventional items as age, sex, marital status, race, and nativity but also classifications of labor-force status and economic characteristics associated therewith; family and household status; school attendance and educational attainment; religious affiliation; various group memberships, social roles, and identifications; anthropometric, biometric, and psychometric traits; genetic makeup; and other measurable or enumerable characteristics of individuals capable of statistical summary in a frequency distribution. From the standpoint of this definition, it is accidental rather than essential that certain such characteristics typically are ascertained in censuses while others are not.

Second, the inclusiveness of "population composition" accounts for the stipulation that demography concerns itself with "social mobility" or changes of status, inasmuch as a population changes in composition not only through natality, mortality, and territorial movement of individuals but also through individuals' movements from one status to another, e.g., from "employed" to "unemployed" with respect to employment status or from "single" to "married" with respect to marital status. The concept of "social mobility," which is appropriate to designate such changes, was given a generic meaning by Sorokin (1927, pp. 3, 6):

Social mobility [is] the phenomenon of the shifting of individuals within social space. . . . (1) Social space is the universe of human population; (2) man's social position is the totality of his relations toward all groups of a population and, within each of them, toward its members; (3) location of a man's position in this social universe is obtained by ascertaining these relations; (4) the totality of such groups and the totality of the positions within each of them compose a system of social coordinates which permits us to define the social position of any man.

More recently, Bogue (1952, p. 566) has emphasized the importance of "extending and generalizing the concept of mobility to all its possible applications" and has indicated the value of "mobility statistics" in studying changes in the composition and distribution of population. It is, of course, advisable in some contexts to distinguish characteristics of "fixed definition," such as age (date of birth), sex, race, genetic makeup, or educational attainment (in respect to adults who are assumed to have completed their formal schooling), from characteristics of "variable definition," which are subject to change through social mobility. Demography must deal with both types of characteristics, however.

Finally, in the formal definition of demography the term "territorial movement" is substituted for the usual term "migration," inasmuch as the latter ordinarily is limited to movement between areal units with more or less arbitrary boundaries.

It must be recognized at once that many types of demographic analysis suggested by the foregoing definition frequently are carried out by investigators not explicitly identified as "demographers"; yet "demographers" may on occasion execute such studies. For example, studies of differential mortality according to type of physical impairment are usually conducted by actuaries. But this circumstance follows primarily from the fact that the req-

uisite data are of interest to, and are gathered by, insurance companies. Studies of population genetics ordinarily are made by geneticists; yet demographers have been known to investigate the genetic implications of socioeconomic differences in natality. Work on the distribution of the population by intellectual capacity and attained skills is more likely to be done by someone called a "manpower" specialist than by a demographer, but "manpower" research often involves participation of professional demographers. Public health research workers are more likely than demographers to study the bearing of birth weight on neonatal mortality, but demographers as well are concerned with the incidence of causes of infant deaths. One thinks of mental illness as the province of the psychiatrist and clinical psychologist, but demographers on occasion have become interested in the incidence, prevalence, and expectancy of mental disease and its differential incidence according to the migration histories of individuals. Whereas in the United States a fairly sharp distinction is made between the specialties of demography, on the one hand, and biometry and anthropometry, on the other, in other countries (such as Italy) this distinction is blurred, if not wholly absent. In short, it seems logically impossible to draw a boundary line around some of the phenomena referred to in the definition of demography and to assert that demography's scope is confined to these and none of the others. Any attempt to do this would be belied by the actual history of demographic research as well as by the recognized opportunities for extending the scope of such research.

From these considerations it appears that the critical element in the definition of demography is not the scope of the population characteristics studied, but rather the concept of "population" itself (see Vance's discussion of the population concept, chap. xiv) and the stipulation that population changes are studied in terms of "components of change." It is, of course, implicit in the definition that "population" refers to an actual aggregate of organisms, not to collections of material entities such as telephone poles or airplane engines or to hypothetical collections such as the set of future outcomes of tossing a coin. The extension of the notion of "population" to aggregates of these and other kinds is, of course, significant, and demography makes use of and contributes to the "renewal theory" and "sampling theory" developed on such an extension. But despite its formal affinity with other kinds of population analysis, demography is substantively concerned with populations of human individuals. It is possible that the discipline will ultimately come to be recognized as a specialty within "general demography" or "biodemography," if the proposal of some biologists to regard population studies at all organic levels as parts of a single field of study are accepted. (Frank's discussion, chap. xxvii, is relevant to this proposal.) But even if it becomes necessary to adopt an etymologically tautological neologism, "human demography" will doubtless continue to be recognizable by its substantive preoccupation with populations of people.

The significance of the proviso that demography deals with "components of population change" needs to be emphasized. Demographers are not unique in their interest in population changes, of course. A political scientist, for example, might discover that wars typically alter temporarily the rate of population growth. The demographer, though interested in this observation, would immediately wish to investigate the components of such a change. Is it due to a change in the death rate? If the latter occurs, are military deaths alone suffi-

cient to account for the change? Does the change in rate of growth also reflect a change in the birth rate? If so, is the latter accounted for by hastening or postponement of marriage, or does marital fertility as well undergo a change? What bearing do the movements of refugees and the like have on rates of population growth? Such questions are susceptible of much further elaboration and refinement as more and more detailed components of the overall change in population growth rate are investigated. This illustration furnishes the occasion for another significant observation: while other kinds of study may take account of population changes and may make reference to population data, it is the use to which such data are put that is somewhat distinctive of demography. The whole apparatus of rates, replacement quotients, standardized indexes, and the like, which constitute the tools of demographic analysis, has been devised with a view to making more precise, detailed, and systematic statements of the components of population change.

Perhaps the major issue raised by the present attempt to define "demography" concerns the relationship between "demographic analysis"—the study of components of population variation and change—and "population studies," conceived as embracing in addition the investigation of relationships between such spatiotemporal variations in population and other bodies of subject matter. (See the distinction between "formal demography" and "population studies" set forth by Lorimer, chap. vi.) It should be stated right away that this issue is not that of how "departments" of knowledge are or should be organized for purposes of academic administration. Instead, it is a matter of the structuring of scientific investigation and the ordering of the results of such. investigation. At the heart of the issue is the premise that to "explain" population changes, one must have recourse to conceptual schemes and bodies of theory developed around such notions as adaptation to environment, economic development, social organization, culture patterns, motivation, and the like—to list only a few examples of "independent variables" which have been suggested. Moreover, one must take account of the contention that interest in population phenomena extends beyond their demographic analysis, and even beyond their explanation, to include what may be designated crudely as their concomitants and effects. In the phrase made famous by a United Nations publication, the field of population studies is at least as broad as that of the "determinants and consequences of population trends."

Thus, "demography" may be conceived in a narrow sense as synonymous with "demographic analysis," or in a broad sense as encompassing both "demographic analysis" and "population studies." When the demographer is carrying out the "population studies," he is almost certain to regard them as "demography." But it must be recognized that scholars of various disciplines are likely to engage in studies which utilize demographic analysis in relation to other frameworks of analysis and which may appropriately be described as "population studies."

Consider an example: the phenomenon of "urbanization." Within the terms in which demography was defined, urbanization can be characterized as a change in the pattern of population distribution. It involves an increase in the relative size of the urban population, a growth in number and size of urban settlements or places, and an increasing concentration of the population in such places. Given the requisite data, a strictly demographic "explanation" of urbanization can be worked out. It may involve internal migration from rural areas to urban places, the settlement of

disproportionate numbers of immigrants from foreign countries in cities, and/or differential natality and mortality of the urban and rural sectors of the population. Some of these components of change may work in opposite directions from others; for example, urban populations may have lower natality and higher mortality than rural, while the prevailing direction of migration is cityward. The "net" change, then, which represents urbanization, is analyzed into its components of gross change. The several components of change may operate differently in different segments of the total time period over which urbanization is being studied. Each of the components mentioned may be further analyzed into components; for example, rural-urban differences in natality may be broken down into components of nuptiality and marital fertility, or rural-urban migration may be analyzed for selectivity by age, sex, and other characteristics. In principle, the demographic analysis of urbanization is never finished, for further analysis into components is always possible. Nevertheless, at any given stage of such an analysis one can say that the *demographic explanation* of urbanization is "complete": either the change in population distribution has been analyzed in terms of an exhaustive set of components, or a "residual" component is included. Moreover, at no stage of the investigation have concepts or techniques other than those of demographic analysis been introduced.

Although, in principle, demographic analysis affords a "complete" explanation of urbanization, no one supposes that it affords a unique or causally sufficient explanation. The phenomenon of urbanization actually requires or entails a whole series of corollary changes (not all of which, by any means, are as yet understood). Urban populations depend on rural ones for food; urbanization, therefore, requires an increase in agricultural productivity per agricultural worker or the development of sources from which food may be imported. In either case, urban industries must be developed whose products may be exchanged for food. Such industries need raw materials; extractive industries, foreign or domestic, must accordingly come into being and grow. The increase of urban populations calls for housing and utilities. Local governments and administrative agencies are created, modified, or elaborated. Transportation routes and communications networks, intra-urban and interurban, are formed. Centralized markets and distribution systems are organized. Some of these things are necessary conditions of urbanization; others are perhaps consequences thereof. Viewed in either light, they require functional analysis, and their interrelationships are complicated. What is more, the process of urbanization itself may have demographic consequences. As cities grow in size, their problems of public health may become exacerbated. Conditions under which urban families live may be conducive to the limitation of their size. If the pattern of urban growth is modified, say in the direction of decentralization, the effects of urbanization on the natality and mortality components of population change may actually become the reverse of those just suggested.

It is evident that to identify conditions under which such a demographic process as urbanization occurs requires reference to a great variety of data, concepts, and hypotheses not comprehended by demographic analysis as such. The same can be said in respect to the attempt to specify non-demographic consequences of the demographic process. Finally, the interplay between demographic analysis and other types of substantive considerations is so complicated by the interaction of different types of change that neither can be said to be a simple "cause" or "effect" of the other. In recognizing the complexity of the problem of describing and explaining such a phenomenon as urbanization, one may be tempted to conclude that demographic analysis as such makes but a limited, even scarcely significant, contribution to the entire problem. However, it is of the utmost importance to notice that in tracing out interactive relationships, one often comes back to some system of components of population change as a frame of reference. If increasing urban density is prejudicial to health, one discovers this by analyzing data on mortality and morbidity. If, as a consequence of living in crowded quarters, urban couples are disposed to limit births, this must be expressed in the facts of natality and differential natality. The organization of urban activities is reflected in patterns of population distribution and movement. The development of new industries and the modifications of occupational structure associated with urbanization are recorded in shifts in population composition. In short, the various components of population change continually figure in the investigation of urbanization as intervening variables linking interrelated structural changes or, at least, as indexes of associated organizational or behavorial changes.

Another important point is that no treatment of urbanization can include "everything." To study it at all one must have a frame of reference, and a frame of reference by its very nature makes empirical investigation selective. There are, of course, many frames of reference with which one can approach the investigation of a phenomenon like urbanization. The economist, for example, might study the relationships among urbanization, trends in per capita income, patterns of investment, modifications of productivity, changes in labor-force participation, and sequences of industrial growth. The social psychologist, by contrast, might concern himself with such things as the adjustment of individuals to urban living, changes in patterns of primary contacts, participation in voluntary associations, and implications of modified patterns of social relationship for socialization of individuals and control of social deviation. Whatever the frame of reference, it is probable, as was indicated, that a thorough study at some point would involve the results of demographic analysis. The particular aspects of population composition and the particular components of population change that would be relevant to one frame of reference might not be of equal utility for another. The direction which demographic studies would take, therefore, would be influenced by the way in which the research problem was formulated. Although, in principle, there is virtually no limit to the degree to which demographic analyses might be elaborated, in the actual context of research only a fraction of the possible analyses would be contemplated.

On the strength of this illustration and on the basis of considering analogous problems, one concludes that "population studies" is not a single "theoretical discipline" with a coherent frame of reference of its own. Instead, it is an area of substantive inquiry in which any number of frames of reference may be employed. Each of these is likely to include some categories under which certain special types of demographic analysis play a significant role. None of them can exhaust all the potentialities of demographic analysis. It is, therefore, a little hard to think of "population studies" as a subject matter for which an integrated but comprehensive theory could be expounded. Such a body of theory would have to embrace such diverse preoccupations as those of economics, social psychology, and genetics (for example). What is called "population theory," then,

must be one of two things: an elaboration of the relationships involved in and techniques employed by demographic analysis, or that segment of some particular theoretical scheme which involves population phenomena or makes use of demographic analysis.

It cannot be claimed that the point of view just expressed is indorsed by all students of population, or even by all contributors to the symposium. It is, in fact, rather common for writers to suggest the desirability of "integrating" population theory and theories emerging from other disciplines. For example, Vance indorses Spengler's stipulation that population theory "requires a multi-science approach." He goes on to state that "the dynamics of population need to be integrated with some basic theory of social change" (Vance, 1956, pp. 91, 93). "Integration with sociological theory" is indicated by Moore (chap. xxxiii) to be a desirable outcome of an adequate theory of population change.

It is fairly clear from the context of such statements that the goal of "integrating" population theory with material from other disciplines is not set forth merely because of some yearning for the unity of science. Rather, it is felt that adequate explanation of demographic phenomena requires systematic reference to variables defined and schemes developed in the several social and natural sciences. This is made clear by Ryder (chap. xviii), who states: "Demography, and fertility analysis as an integral component of it, is a multi-science discipline. The reason for this is clear: the focus of fertility research is a concrete event rather than an analytical abstraction from that event in terms of a special frame of reference" (see also Lorimer's discussion of "interdisciplinary population studies," chap. vi). There does seem to be general agreement, therefore, that the study of population is, of necessity, carried on from the perspectives of several alternative frames of reference (Lorimer, 1957). What is less clear, however, is whether these diverse kinds of study can somehow be brought together in a single "discipline" with a coherent frame of reference and an integrated body of explanatory principles. One might well raise the question of what form such an "integrated" and "multiscience" theory or frame of reference might take. Would not the range of the theory or the scope of the frame of reference have to be nearly as great as that of the collective totality of the social and life sciences or virtually coextensive with what one contributor (Duncan, chap. xxviii) refers to as the "natural history of man"? Is there any genuine prospect that such a synthesis or integration can be accomplished within any time span that can now be foreseen? Are demographers actually well advised to begin contemplating such a task with the accumulation of knowledge presently at their disposal? Would it not be salutary to remember that even physics—surely one of the most advanced sciences—has not yet achieved a complete integration of the various bodies of theory which have arisen in connection with the diverse phenomena included in its area of interest?

The position taken here is that "population studies" designates a field or a body of subject matter which is of common interest to a number of diverse theoretical disciplines and to which are applied the techniques of demographic analysis. There is, no doubt, value in recognizing the field as one in which scholars specialize owing to the diversity and complexity of the technical problems associated with the use of population data. That all such scholars work with a common body of theory, however, is simply not the case, nor does it seem likely that it will soon come to be the case. Each of the various theoretical disciplines employing

population data may come to elaborate its own version of "population theory," which will amount to a specification of the role of demographic analysis and the relevance of population phenomena to the other elements in its frame of reference. Specialists in population studies or "demographers" are well advised to become acquainted with a variety of such frames of reference; this maximizes their usefulness as analysts of demographic data. But the "integration" of all these diverse bodies of theory will come about only when the entire spectrum of social and life sciences —or at least major segments thereof— are "integrated."

It should be pointed out that the majority of the contributions in Part III of the symposium concern "demography," in the strict sense in which that term was defined above; by contrast, in Part IV attention shifts to several perspectives on "population studies"; i.e., population phenomena and demographic analysis are examined within the frames of reference of several disciplines. We have entitled the symposium *The Study of Population,* but we use the term "demography" in various contexts to embrace both types of interest. Our task is actually a dual one—first, to examine the resources and accomplishments of "demographic analysis" as such and, second, to deal with issues arising from the interrelationships of demography and the various sciences whose frames of reference require systematic attention to population.

DISCIPLINES INVOLVED IN POPULATION STUDIES

A careful investigation of the history of science would probably reveal two facts which are inadequately appreciated by writers on population: the concept of "population," as it is used in the several sciences today, is an essentially modern concept, and the concept is one with wide ramifications throughout many branches of science. A recent text in general biology, for example, brings out the impact of recent thinking in terms of populations on evolutionary theory, genetics, and ecology; and the authors have occasion to point out that "systematics clearly based on populations and explicitly nontypological is mainly an achievement of the second quarter of the twentieth century. . . . You belong to the first generation of students of biology to whom the biology of populations can be made familiar from the start" (Simpson *et al.*, 1957, pp. 463–64). An economist, presenting a "reconstruction" of his discipline, finds it expedient to begin his task by observing that "reality, in its quantitative aspect, must be considered as a system of populations" (Boulding, 1950, chap. i).

It is clear, therefore, that the generalization of the population concept has led to developments in fields substantively more or less remote from demography. Such developments, however, can hardly fail to react on demography. In addition, the roster of sciences that in one way or another find it necessary to include systematic consideration of demographic matters seemingly lengthens continually. Although geographers, for example, have long included some study of population in their investigations, it was only quite recently that "population geography" was recognized as a distinctive and important specialty within the field (Ackerman, chap. xxix; Trewartha, 1953; James, 1954). It may be appropriate, therefore, to essay a quick summary of the varied kinds of scientific interests that impinge on the study of population. Certain of the connections between demography and other disciplines are reviewed in detail in Part IV of the symposium. Unfortunately, space limitations precluded the representation there of all the subjects having an important bearing on the study of human populations.

The concept of population is used in perhaps its most abstract sense in the mathematical-statistical developments known as "renewal theory" and "sampling theory." The former, it may be noted, is a direct outgrowth and generalization of mathematical demography. Workers in this field have produced models of the "generalized birth and death process" applicable to any kind of similar items subject to accretion and depletion. Such models may be deterministic or stochastic, with the latter being in the forefront today, in the wake of modern developments of probability theory. In the generalizations which it has involved, much of this work seems to be at some remove from direct applicability in demographic analysis. Nonetheless, the development of a wide array of mathematical models must be viewed as a potential resource for the demographer—one which, it may be supposed, will be exploited more fully as demographers begin to acquire the requisite skills in mathematics. Sampling theory, as is noted subsequently, developed in good part to meet the need for a rationalization of the "representative method" whereby inferences about the composition and dynamics of population are based on examination of a small fraction of the members of the population. In its abstract form, sampling theory involves the generalization of the population concept to make it synonymous with a "universe" of any kind of item susceptible of sufficiently uniform definition. But a significant proportion of the practical applications of sampling theory require the construction of sample designs especially adapted to demographic studies of human populations. Of considerable theoretical interest are the specific theorems concerning samples of "finite populations," which had to be worked out to apply probability theory rigorously to the sampling of human populations, as opposed to the theorems on "infinite populations" typically appropriate for studies, say, of games of chance. There is, then, a close reciprocal relationship between sampling theory and demography, and developments in each owe much to the other.

Within the framework, then, of the generic concept of "population" as a highly abstract view of a "universe" of phenomena comprising recognizable individual elements and concerned with highly general aspects of the phenomena, such as number, composition, distribution, and change, demography is concerned with human population. This concern has indeed contributed, as has been noted, to the development of the concept of population as an abstraction relevant to other fields of interest and in turn has been furthered by interest in non-human populations.

The disciplines with which demography is most closely related are those which also have concern with aspects of human populations directly or as elements of a more broadly defined population. They include in the natural sciences biology, zoölogy, geography, and physical anthropology and in the social sciences sociology, economics, political science, and history. They include also aspects of mathematics and statistics. In Part IV of the symposium not all phases of the interests in human population manifest in these disciplines have been treated. Significant interrelationships are brought out, however, in the separate chapters devoted to ecology, human ecology, geography, physical anthropology, genetics, economics, and sociology.

In the consideration of the relationships of ecology—from the natural-science standpoint—and demography, Frank, in chapter xxvii, has pointed to several aspects of ecology of interest to demography, especially "population ecology." This subfield of ecology so closely parallels demography in outlook and method as to have been termed "biodemography" (Hutchinson and Deevey, 1949). Frank's discussion of the differences between the problems of demography and of population ecology shows that each has certain advantages and deficiencies in comparison with the other in the conduct of research, but it is clear that the basic focus of studying population growth and composition in terms of "demographic analysis" is a common one. It is worthy of note that Frank's treatment of the problem of demographic analysis in the broad framework of ecology is characteristically "hard," that is, quantitative, and that the literature he draws upon is in some measure a literature produced by demographers. His conclusion that "up to the present time, ecology has profited from demography much more than the reverse" may in some sense be true; but it overlooks the basic indebtedness of human ecologists, who often combine this interest with an interest in demography per se, to ecology for both conceptual framework and methods. Frank points to a significant area in ecology which may have much to contribute to demography—theory. Ecological theory may have important implications for demographic theory construction, and Frank's discussion of ecological theory suggests that it would be desirable for demographers to get better acquainted with it.

Duncan's treatment of "Human Ecology and Population Studies" (chap. xxviii) reveals the extent to which both the human ecologist and the demographer have, in fact, drawn upon ecology for general orientation and specific approaches to similar problems. Perhaps the most significant contribution of Duncan's analysis lies in his explicit relating of population to human ecology and his explication of the manner in which demography may be considered a subarea of human ecology. This is a specific example of an area of "population studies" as distinguished from "demographic analysis," and it illustrates the sense in which demography is a "multiscience" discipline, whether population is considered as a dependent or an independent variable in relation to other systems of variables. In his analysis of the major components of human ecological interest, in which population appears as one of the four key elements, Duncan states in a significant way that demography can ill afford to operate without awareness of the place of population in the "ecological complex." Furthermore, in his discussion of "the treatment of demographic problems in human ecology," Duncan has afforded specific instances of the way in which "demographic analysis" may be greatly enriched by ecological population studies. Finally, it may be noted that among the specific "problems and issues" singled out for consideration, the discussion of the relevance of "environment" illuminates not only the interrelationship of population and human ecology but also of both with geography and with the emergent interest in "regional science" (Isard, 1956).

Ackerman elaborates the relationships of geography and demography and indicates the outlook for research in those aspects of geography which have special relevance to population. In his explication of the nature of geography as a discipline he explains how the geographer's interest in population developed and became crystallized in the subarea of "human geography." Significant interrelations with demography are depicted in the description of the geographer's interest in such common problems as collection of demographic data, areal differentiation of population, distributional aspects of population attributes, settlement patterns, and population sustenance. The latter interest he treats in a separate chapter, "Population and Natural Resources" (chap. xxvi). As in Frank's treatment

of ecology and Duncan's of human ecology, it is noteworthy that Ackerman's annotations include references which are drawn from demography, ecology, and human ecology, as well as geography. Geography's claim to a "place in illuminating the scene in which population growth and decline runs its course" is set forth in summary of the trends in geographic research of greatest relevance to demography.

In both the chapters on "Physical Anthropology and Demography" (chap. xxx) and "Genetics and Demography" (chap. xxxi) the interrelations of genetics and demography are considered, with some inevitable duplication albeit variation in emphasis.

Spuhler in his treatment of physical anthropology and demography, in keeping with the major interest of physical anthropology in demography, focuses primarily on the genetics of human populations. He depicts the problems involved in tracing differences in gene frequencies among populations and the implications of random mating and departures from random mating, as in inbreeding and assortative mating, both positive and negative. He also discusses mutation, gene flow, selection, and random drift in gene frequencies. In outlining the geneticist's approach to research, he reveals, on the one hand, the highly mathematical character of developments in human genetics which provide a frame for investigation and, on the other, the inadequate character of the data, including demographic data, available for the geneticist for the study of human populations.

Drs. Kallmann and Rainer, in dealing with the same problems, describe the historical background out of which the modern approach to human genetics emerged and treat more fully specific problems of quality in human populations in at least indicating some of the areas which have been of major concern to eugenicists. In their depiction of specific problems they also show the way in which ecological and sociological considerations, *inter alia*, complement genetic approaches in dealing with variability in populations.

As medical men, Drs. Kallmann and Rainer understandably, although contrary to instructions, also deal with the "engineering" aspects of the implications of the findings of genetics as made manifest in "eugenics." But their treatment of these problems is a far cry from that often evident in the popular and hortatory literature of the subject.

The materials presented both by Spuhler and by Kallmann and Rainer on human genetics show that research in human genetics has undergone considerable development in recent years. But much remains to be done—and the road seems long and difficult—before the geneticist can contribute specifically and significantly toward the explanation of variability in many characteristics of human populations, particularly those with large components of "cultural" mix.

Spuhler's treatment of morphological anthropology points to the ways in which the anthropologist, working with skeletal remains, can contribute to the demographer's knowledge about populations prior to the modern period or in non-Western areas. His brief reference to "duration of periods in the primate life cycle" provides an interesting and generally little-appreciated perspective on the size of human population in relation to other primate populations. Furthermore, his brief reference to "somatic adaptation to the acquisition of culture" points to the major area of interest of the social anthropologist, who unfortunately is not represented in this symposium.

In describing "culture" as a "nongenetic mode of inheritance depending on symbolic contact rather than fusion of gametes" which has greatly "supple-

mented somatic evolution," Spuhler indicates the vast area in which the main explanation for the variability of many highly significant attributes of contemporary human populations is to be found—the area of the cultural and social-psychological, as distinct from the biological, evolutionary, and genetic. The absence of a chapter in the symposium by a social anthropologist is partly the result of the pressure of limited space and partly in recognition of the overlap in the interests of social anthropology and sociology (see chap. xxxiii).

In his discussion of "Economics and Demography" (chap. xxxii) Spengler presents, in effect, a paradigm for "population studies" in which economic and demographic phenomena are interrelated. In doing so, he makes quite explicit the systems of interacting variables, demographic and economic, which may be utilized as dependent and independent variables, respectively. In pointing to the "convergence" of demographic and economic interests, which he incorporates in his own person, he exhaustively illustrates the way in which adequate prediction and explanation in both economics and demography may depend on joint and cooperative investigation. In this frame he outlines the historical developments which made demography, at least in part, an offshoot of the growing interest in political economy and economics during the eighteenth and nineteenth centuries.

Spengler's discussion of demographic data reveals not only common ground for the economist and demographer but also the way in which conceptual frameworks are interrelated. In his explication of economic methods of analysis he shows how they are designed more to reveal the impact of population changes on economic changes than the reverse, and he points to the necessity of multiscience methodological, as well as theoretical, approaches to common problems. Spengler's specific treatment of the interrelations of economic and demographic change constitutes an excellent example of a framework for "population studies" in relation to economic factors. Finally, in pointing to "next steps in research," Spengler outlines the improvements needed in methods and approaches and in substantive areas of investigation.

In calling for improved methods, he again touches a common ground for economist and demographer in outlining the need for longitudinal studies and more effective model construction. Interestingly enough, he concludes that among the needs for further research is the broadening of the area of "population studies" to include investigation of social-psychological as well as economic and demographic variables. In considering substantive areas of research, he emphasizes, among other things, the following areas as requiring increased collaboration between economist and demographer: land and natural-resources use, population and levels of living, age-structural change in relation to economic behavior, economic effects of differential fertility, the relation of population and economic development in the underdeveloped areas of the world, population growth and recreation and health, population growth and "goods that were once free," and population and location of industry. In a number of these areas of research, it may be seen that human ecological considerations of the type discussed by Duncan would also be involved.

Finally, in the consideration of "Sociology and Demography" (chap. xxxiii) Moore treats of the interrelations of demography with the discipline which, more than any other, has captured demography as a subarea in contemporary times, especially in the United States. He finds as features of demography distinguishing it from other subareas of sociology its emphasis on quantification, its interest in the "distributive" rather than unifying aspects of society, and its focus on time and change. These characteristics tend, on the one hand, to give the demographer a certain prestige among sociologists arising from the reflected superior status of the natural sciences and, on the other hand, to make him often a marginal member of the profession, especially if he is completely or nearly identified with demographic research and training.

In elaborating the interrelations of sociology and demography, Moore stresses "functional theory" in the former as most relevant to the latter. He sees this as a major tie in that, in the functional approach in sociology, population may be considered an endogenous variable in the analysis of social systems. In analyzing patterns in society, population phenomena, like other human relations, may be treated from the standpoint of "structural suitability," either in general or in terms of specific societies. Population phenomena may also be studied in relation to various functions, such as the "maintenance of a system of stratification" or "passage rituals." Generalizations are presented in respect of fertility, natural selection, mortality, and migration to illustrate the results of such an approach. Thus, Moore takes the position that the functional approach in sociology "explicitly brings demographic variables into the scheme of sociological theory." He leaves room, however, for other approaches in sociology to encompass demography, including "the 'relativistic' position that emphasizes 'cultural' differences and attempts to establish detailed connections between structural elements in particular social systems and the demographic characteristics of these systems." Furthermore, he also allows for "some independent variability" of demographic phenomena, despite their presence in a social system, and he qualifies his consideration of the structural-functional approach by bringing in the principle of "structural substitutability" and an emphasis on dynamic as well as static analysis.

Moore provides specific examples of the interrelations of demographic and sociological variables, pointing to the alternation of these systems as independent or dependent variables. Ecological considerations, as may be expected, since human ecology is also regarded as a subfield of sociology, enter into some of these considerations. Furthermore, in facing the extent to which variability in population phenomena can be explained by sociological variables, he suggests the desirability of extending the range of investigation to include "psychological" variables. Here again is a good illustration of the way in which the consideration of population phenomena leads to a multiscience approach in "population studies."

Turning from consideration of the relation of sociology to demography, Moore then reverses his focus. In discussing the relation of demographic theory to sociology, he voices a common, although not necessarily well-founded, complaint that demography may have "too little" theory. In the context in which this observation is presented, however, one in which sociology has "too much" theory, it seems that "theory" as Moore uses it in this context embodies much of what are elsewhere in this volume (chap. i) considered as "misconceptions" of theory. For example, Riesman's discussion of the possible relationship of the theory of the demographic transition and personality types, to which Moore makes a passing reference, may be considered an example of "speculation" rather than "theory" in the sense in which the editors treat it. The relative absence of "theory" in this sense in demography as compared with general sociology may be a positive rather than a negative virtue. In elaborating the relation of demographic theory to sociology, Moore also provides specific examples which illustrate other aspects of the nature of "population studies" as well as specific ways in which demography is related to general sociological research.

Thus, in the chapters comprising Part IV of this volume some of the more important interrelations of demography with other fields are explored. In considering these interrelations, the authors contribute to an elaboration and clarification of the distinction between "demographic analysis" and "population studies," and demonstrate how population phenomena, while not subject to monopoly by any unitary scientific discipline, provide a basis for a multiscience approach which may be expected to complement "demographic analysis" and, in the long run, greatly to improve the ability of the demographer to predict and explain. It will undoubtedly follow that "population studies" will, in turn, also help to improve predictability and explanation in the related disciplines.

REFERENCES

BOGUE, DONALD J. 1952. "The Quantitative Study of Social Dynamics and Social Change," *American Journal of Sociology*, LVII, 565–68.

BOULDING, KENNETH E. 1950. *A Reconstruction of Economics*. New York: John Wiley & Sons.

HUTCHINSON, G. E., and DEEVEY, E. S., JR. 1949. "Ecological Studies on Populations." *Surveys of Biological Progress*, I, 325–59.

ISARD, WALTER. 1956. "Regional Science,

the Concept of Region, and Regional Structure," *Papers and Proceedings of the Regional Science Association,* II, 13–26.

JAMES, PRESTON E. 1954. "The Geographic Study of Population," in *American Geography: Inventory and Prospect,* ed. P. E. JAMES and C. F. JONES. Syracuse, N.Y.: Syracuse University Press.

LORIMER, FRANK. 1957. "The Nature of Demography: Implications for Programmes of Instruction," in *The University Teaching of Social Sciences: Demography,* ed. D. V. GLASS. Paris: UNESCO.

SIMPSON, GEORGE GAYLORD, *et al.* 1957. *Life: An Introduction to Biology.* New York: Harcourt, Brace & Co.

SOROKIN, PITIRIM. 1927. *Social Mobility.* New York: Harper & Bros.

TREWARTHA, G. T. 1953. "The Case for Population Geography," *Annals of the Association of American Geographers,* XLIII, 71–97.

VANCE, RUPERT B. 1956. "Is Theory for Demographers?" in *Population Theory and Policy,* ed. J. J. SPENGLER and O. D. DUNCAN. Glencoe, Ill.: Free Press.

3. The Data and Methods

PHILIP M. HAUSER AND OTIS DUDLEY DUNCAN

In this chapter and the succeeding one we have resorted to a breakdown of the science of demography into "data," "methods," and the "body of knowledge," subdividing the last into "factual information" and "theory." Any such scheme, of course, is artificial, and we have been unable to avoid the recurrence of certain themes under several of these headings. Moreover, we have had to emphasize at various points that scientific progress with respect to any of these ingredients is more or less closely bound up with improvements in the others. In particular, as it will appear shortly, it is hardly possible to assess the data of demography apart from the methods used to collect the data and to analyze them.

THE DATA OF DEMOGRAPHY

Demography belongs to that group of empirical sciences whose data are produced by the observation and recording of events occurring naturally in the external world, as contrasted to those whose data are generated by experiments conducted in the laboratory under conditions controlled to a greater or lesser degree by the experimenter. In this respect, demography is analogous to astronomy, geology, ecology, paleontology, meteorology, ethnology, and economics, rather than to such sciences as physics, chemistry, anatomy, physiology, and experimental psychology. Without exaggerating the contrasts between these two types of discipline, one should note certain differences between them which are pertinent to the present discussion.

The data studied by the observational sciences are "spread out"; i.e., any single observer can hope personally to collect only a minute, or even negligible, proportion of the data required to test an empirical proposition which will be of any importance to his discipline. The "spread" is both spatial and temporal. The collection of adequate meteorological data requires that numerous observers (human or mechanical) be stationed at scattered points over a region or even over the whole world; a major barrier to the progress of the discipline is the insufficient number of such observation stations. Similarly, demographic data are collected by cadres of enumerators covering a territory or by corps of registration officials collecting records of vital events or movements in space. Astronomical data are collected in time series to permit determinations of magnitudes and paths of movement on the basis of spatial displacements. Similarly, to develop reliable information on processes of demographic change requires repetition of population enumerations from time to time and the continuous collection of registration data over a period of time. Both astronomy and demography, no doubt, can make indirect and approximate inferences about modes of temporal change from data pertaining to a single instant in time, but, ultimately, the validation of such inferences rests on the ability to accumulate observations in time sequence. By contrast, in the experimental sciences, at least in principle, it is within the capacity of the single investigator (or labora-

45

tory) to make a "crucial experiment" resting on his own observations.

In all kinds of empirical science the investigator's access to the phenomena he wishes to observe is limited, not merely in practice but in principle. The physiologist cannot observe a living organism completely dissected, because dissection brings about death. Microscopic phenomena are beyond the range of the unaided human senses. Such limits to accessibility may be overcome by various devices, each of which has the effect of introducing an additional element, e.g., an instrument, into the observational equation. While limited accessibility, therefore, is not peculiar to the observational sciences, it may take on the special form of "historical inaccessibility" in their case. The geologist is never able to witness directly the transitions between eras, epochs, or periods or to see at work more than a tiny segment of the earth-forming processes. He must, rather, learn to read the fragmentary record of these transitions and processes in the small proportion of the earth's mass that is directly accessible to him. In like fashion, knowledge of the demographic past is limited by the survival of such few records as ever were made of population phenomena, precariously supplemented as they may be with inferences and extrapolation from partial records of related events.

When it is suggested, then, that a measure of demography's status as a science is the adequacy of its basic data, one wants to be sure that an appropriate norm of comparison has been selected, if, indeed, such a comparison is warranted at all. It would be hard to make sense out of the statement that demography's data are less adequate than those of chemistry or experimental psychology: the term "less adequate than" suggests a commensurability that does not exist. Whether one could compare, say, meteorology and demography more meaningfully in this respect is uncer-

tain; but at least it is easy for specialists in demography to appreciate some of the difficulties meteorology faces in trying to get adequate data, because these difficulties are analogous to their own (especially if one includes historical climatology within the scope of meteorology).

Availability of Data

In discussing the adequacy of data for an observational science like demography, one must consider the availability of data over time and space and the nature of the observations recorded at different times and places. Linder's paper (chap. xv) indicates that the aggregate population of the world enumerated in censuses some time during the decade 1945–54 amounted to approximately 80 per cent of the world's estimated total population as of 1953. This is almost surely a record high proportion for any decade in history (or prehistory, for that matter), although it is likely that this number may be surpassed in and around 1960 in response to the United Nations' World Census Program. As compared with sixty-five sovereign countries taking censuses during 1945–54, the number fluctuated between forty-two and forty-nine over the decades between 1895 and 1944, whereas a century ago—the decade 1855–64—only twenty-four censuses were taken. It is questionable whether any census, in the modern sense of the word, was ever taken before the nineteenth century, and only sporadic counts and assessments of population numbers of any kind occurred. One can guess, therefore, that no more than 10 per cent of all the persons born in the world during the Christian era were ever enumerated in a census. (The impossibility of ever knowing the actual figure itself testifies eloquently to kind and degree of inaccessibility of demographic data.)

The availability of census counts also varies considerably over space. Linder's figures indicate that under two-thirds of Africa's population was counted during the decade centered on 1950, while enumeration of almost 100 per cent of the population in Europe was carried out during this period. Whereas there are a few countries with records of a century or a century and a half of periodic censuses, there are other countries where no census has ever been taken.

A total count of population is, of course, only a beginning for demographic study; analytical research requires information on the characteristics of the population and on the vital events occurring in the population. It is pertinent, therefore, that such a rudimentary classification of population as urban and rural residence by sex is available for no more than 56 per cent of the world's population, whereas availability is only 21 per cent for classification by level of education, age, and sex. For only 53 per cent of the world's population are current vital statistics published, and the proportion with reasonably complete statistics of this kind is much less. Statistics of international population movements, covering merely the major categories of arrivals and/or departures, are available for countries containing in the aggregate only 32 per cent of the world's population.

As is true of total population counts, the registration of vital events and movements of population and the classification of population by various characteristics are carried out in varying degrees from region to region, as well as from time to time. It is important to realize that this variation is not of a random character—demographic ignorance is not equally distributed with respect to time periods, places, or subject matter. A number of contributors to the symposium comment on the circumstances that influence the availability of demographic data. For example:

Political and social policy sometimes determine what is to be included in official statistics on population. In the United States the rigorous separation of church and state has prevented a question on religious affiliation from appearing in the population census [Hawley, chap. xvi].

We have very few reliable data concerning the detailed facets of procreative behavior for any population or subpopulation characterized by high fertility. . . . The systematic collection of official data of scientific utility almost seems to require that institutional structure which is most likely to lead to low fertility [Ryder, chap. xviii].

As national governments became stronger and as commerce and industry expanded, the need for statistical data concerning population, vital events, trade, commerce, crime, poverty, and other aspects of social life became widely appreciated [Dorn, chap. xix].

The evolution of records of international migration may be loosely divided into four phases corresponding to the changing preoccupations and policies of sovereign states [Thomas, chap. xxii].

. . . writers are sometimes found to point out the association of demography with representative government. In the United States . . . this relation is fairly direct [Vance, chap. xiv].

Taeuber's paper (chap. xiii) contains much information related to this theme, and her peroration is worth repeating:

Analysis of the present and the past must be made on the basis of whatever data exist, or they cannot be made at all. This is an obvious statement, and its implications for research are far-reaching. Comparable estimates of demographic status and trends may be made by conjecture and analogy, but they will be limited to simple variables, and their validation lies in accepting as axiomatic hypotheses of comparability that should be major subjects of research. Incisive or intricate research must have its hypotheses defined and its methodology developed area by area and culture by culture. If information is qualitative or if quantitative data are not amenable to the usual techniques of demography, the approach and methods of other disciplines must be integrated with those of demography.

Perhaps one more analogy between demography and another science may be cited. Compare the predicament of the student of organic evolution with that of the demographer, as just described. An eminent biologist has speculated that of five hundred million species produced in the entire course of evolution, only some two million are now extant. The remainder of the history of organic variation and development must be inferred from fossils. Fossils constitute a highly selective, as well as an intrinsically incomplete, record of past life. Whole phylogenetic categories may be grossly underrepresented in the fossil record because their tissues were not well suited to preservation or because the areas where they lived have undergone erosion. Moreover, the recovery of fossils is a somewhat fortuitous occurrence.

Data Collection Systems

The data of demography, as has been indicated above, include counts of the population, the classification of population into various categories of composition and distribution, and the measurement of components of change in population—births, deaths, territorial movement or migration, and social mobility. Efforts to create "minimum" lists and to standardize the population characteristics for which information is obtained have been made by the United Nations, the specialized agencies, and other bodies. The extent to which these types of data are available on a global basis is indicated by Linder (chap. xv).

Most of the data of demography are obtained through a process of communication from individual members of the population providing information for themselves or, under certain circumstances, for others in addition to themselves. Some of the data of demog-

raphy, however, are obtained through indirect and analytical methods which utilize the data directly obtained from respondents, as indicated subsequently.

The specific collection systems used in the collection of demographic data include the field canvass of the population through a complete census or sample survey and the establishment and maintenance of a record system, three forms of which may be distinguished as "sources" of population data (see Linder, chap. xv). First, and perhaps most important of these, is the vital registration system—a continuous register of information on births and deaths and related vital events. Second is the population register, a permanent and continuous record of the population maintained on a reasonably current basis. Third is the heterogeneous and increasingly vast system of records maintained in connection with a host of administrative tasks which provide data for demography as by-products of their administrative functions.

In a broad sense, then, the two general direct sources of population data are the field canvass and the record system. The specific techniques involved in the collection of data by means of these systems are considered later in this chapter. Each of these sources presupposes a well-organized and rather highly centralized authority —usually the state, but in earlier times occasionally the ecclesiastic structure. The collection of population statistics also requires a considerable allocation of economic resources, for statistics are a costly commodity. The completeness and accuracy of statistics are, in considerable degree, functions of the attitudes and intellectual level of the population under observation. In sum, a very fortunate conjuncture of political, economic, and social circumstances is required to produce a continual flow of the high-quality data called for by modern demographic analysis. It is under somewhat similar circumstances that demographers are likely to appear. There is no reason to be surprised that demography has made the greatest strides in providing reliable descriptions of the populations of which most demographers are members.

Demographic Data and Other Disciplines

In various places throughout this volume the proposition is advanced that explanatory principles in demography, except for the "necessary relations" discussed by Lorimer (chap. vi), are to be found in other biological and social sciences. Assuming for the sake of the present discussion that this is an accurate diagnosis of the case, the question arises as to what light may be shed on the adequacy of demographic data by a consideration of the uses to which they are put by other disciplines.

In chapter xxvii Frank observes that "demography furnishes what constitutes the most extensive set of populational data" available to the ecologist. It would appear, however, that these data have been useful to the ecologist primarily as a convenient body of material to use in developing methods of analysis and to suggest procedures that might be useful in studies of animal populations. There has been little interest in the last three decades—i.e., since Pearl's studies on the logistic model of population growth in the mid-1920's—in the use of human population data for testing comprehensive theories of population regulation. It may be assumed that human data have two fundamental weaknesses for such purposes: First, the number of generations represented in any series of demographic statistics is far too small to allow all the factors pertinent to a biological theory of population regulation to come into play. No doubt if full statistics existed for all population groups inhabiting the earth since the coming of man, there would be a variety of cases available for comparative analysis of what happens under Malthusian conditions, or when gross environmental changes occur, to mention but two kinds of situations which the biologist would like to study in detail. As Frank indicates, "There seems to be little doubt that the present is an unusual era for man in that there are no constant limits to population increase." It may well be that the validity of what some demographers call "naturalistic" theories of population control could be established only if observations were available for time spans on the order of geologic eras. Second, human populations cannot, like some animal populations, be observed under laboratory conditions. While the contributions of laboratory studies to population ecology are limited, they are recognized by the ecologist as being of critical importance (see chap. xxvii).

Both these qualifications on the use of demographic data might be summed up as a difficulty of perspective: the data available on human populations (or likely ever to be available) do not fit well into the perspective of the population ecologist. This doubtless accounts for the fact that imposing treatises on "The Distribution and Abundance of Animals" are written with scarcely passing reference to human animals.

The historical inaccessibility of demographic data is likewise a formidable obstacle to their use by such sciences as physical anthropology and genetics. For example, there is good reason to suppose that the formation of human varieties and "races" is subject to the principles governing this phenomenon in other organisms, not to overlook the relevance of practices, like monogamy and social endogamy, somewhat distinctive of the human species (chap. xxx). Yet demography is in no position to put at the geneticist's disposal data, say, on the volume, direction, and timing of migrations of a kind that would be useful in studying conditions under which differentiated types emerge. If anything, the exchange of knowledge operates in the reverse manner: inferences about migration may be developed by observations on hybrid populations and the like.

There is much evidence to indicate that archeologists and ethnologists are becoming sensitized to the importance of population factors and population changes for the kinds of problems which they investigate. Again, however, demography is in no position to put at the disposal of these disciplines any *data* not otherwise available to them. The interdisciplinary relationship as far as data is concerned seems to come down to the fact that students of comparative demography and population history would like very much to have statistics for the peoples and communities investigated by archeologists and ethnologists. Demographers may be in a position to suggest techniques of population estimation to these specialists or, in the case of studies on living peoples, to indicate suitable methods of sampling and enumeration for ethnographic surveys. Sampling in some cases provides a means for procuring reliable information where censuses are out of the question. There are, however, considerable difficulties in carrying over standard survey techniques developed on Western populations to the situation faced by ethnographers. Consequently, it has been found that the development of appropriate methods of collecting population data requires close co-operation between the anthropologist and the population statistician.

Earlier remarks on the availability of demographic data are again pertinent to the question of the use of these data by historians and geographers. (The fact that the symposium contains no paper on "History and Demography" is due more to limitations of space than to a failure of the editors to recognize the important ties between these disciplines. Fortunately, there are good statements in the literature which may be consulted. See, for example, Russell, 1948). Both history and geography, of course, make use of population statistics where they are available. To the demographer it may often seem that the historian's use of censuses and like sources is somewhat casual, which is perhaps because the historian's problems so often pertain to periods for which data coming up to standards of modern demography are wholly or partly lacking. There is a specialized subdiscipline of "historical demography" or "demographic history" whose practitioners work in periods antedating modern censuses and registration systems. Here they attempt to derive population estimates from whatever symptomatic data may be available. This is an exacting field of historiography which requires the combined skills of the expert in documentary criticism and the statistician. Significantly, it has been cultivated to a much greater extent by Europeans than by Americans. No doubt a good many American demographers share the following opinion of studies in historical demography: "the possibilities of determining the size and characteristics of past populations with a sufficient degree of accuracy so as to make the data demographically very useful are small. . . . The exact relationship of such summaries to population problems in the modern world would not appear very close" (Jaffe, 1949). On the other hand, a small number of demographers have taken the trouble to train themselves in historiographic techniques and have added their efforts to those of the few historians who are trying to push back the veil of historical inaccessibility to a modest degree. As Taeuber suggests in chapter xiii, the standards appropriate for evaluating this work are quite different from those applied to the elaborate statistical analysis of modern census and registration data.

Given the geographer's primary interest in population distribution, the most distinctive aspect of his concern with demographic data is his need for small-area statistics. This means that a considerable number of censuses are of relatively little use to him, because the practice of tabulating even numbers of inhabitants by small civil divisions is by no means universal. When it comes to population characteristics by small areas, the supply of data is even less. The geographer is perhaps more sensitive than other scientists to the fact that census statistics necessarily are compiled for political areal units for the most part; often these do not combine neatly into the natural "regions" which the geographer often makes the object of his study. In general, the problems of securing adequate population data faced by the geographer are much like those confronting other specialists in the study of population distribution, as discussed in chapters xvii and xxviii.

Special problems of data availability confront the economist undertaking demographic studies, for, as Spengler indicates in chapter xxxii, many of the hypotheses emerging from economic theory suggest rather complicated structural and temporal relationships between population and economic factors. For example, very seldom is the elaborate machinery of time-series analysis developed for economic studies useful for demographic-economic research, because population data are not ordinarily available with the frequency required by such methods. But while the statistics may often fall short of meeting the economist's needs in respect to coverage and frequency, it is probably true that population data are at least as likely to be available on a country-by-country or period-by-period basis as are comprehensive bodies of economic

information. Indeed, the economist is likely to rely heavily on population censuses for his information on employment, occupations, industries, and levels of living.

Turning finally to the use of population data by human ecologists and sociologists, one is tempted to conclude that the problems of obtaining adequate population data for their studies pale into insignificance beside the problem of getting the practitioners of those disciplines to recognize the scientific potentialities of the great quantities of data which do exist. One does not have to search far to find symptomatic indications of a subtle bias against the use of ordinary demographic data on the part of sociologists not explicitly identified as demographers. For example, a recent examination of "the nature of the data and the kinds of statistical analysis that do and do not occur in sociological research," classified articles as "statistical" and "non-statistical." A substantial proportion "of the 'statistical' articles were strictly in the area of demography, population and census analysis. The remaining 'statistical' articles . . . run the gamut of sociological research. For the purposes of this investigation, these latter reports were subjected to intensive examination" (Gold, 1957). Although the author does not clarify in what respects the "purposes of this investigation" render population studies unsuitable for "intensive examination," one may infer that they were somehow uninteresting to him or perhaps had other, more positive disqualifications. Despite the considerable effort devoted to informing sociological investigators of uses to which population data may be put (see Hauser, 1941; Shryock, 1950), sociologist-demographers frequently find their colleagues in sociology to be poorly informed about the availability of many kinds of sociologically relevant data. Shryock (1950, p. 417) comments, "As to the record of sociologists in using 1940 census materials . . . the war may explain a somewhat disappointing performance."

In terms of coverage, the most evident inadequacy of population data for sociological studies is that such data primarily provide distributive descriptions of aggregates rather than structural information about groups or institutions. In any event, such is the usual impression about population data held by sociologists. This assessment may overlook several considerations. First, as Glick's report (chap. xxiv) amply illustrates, the census and sample-survey mechanisms can be adapted to provide "structural" kinds of data. The fact that American family statistics were for so long relatively impoverished probably reflects merely the fact that sociological considerations had not been introduced into the design of the census. Second, many kinds of social process are appropriately studied in terms of data on aggregates rather than on psychosocial "groups." Third, in many instances, data on aggregates may be made to serve as useful indicators of "structural" characteristics.

Another way to put the problem is that data of the kind the sociologist would like to use in investigating "determinants" of demographic variation and change are not available in the form or quantity appropriate for matching them with data from standard demographic sources. This is especially the case in respect to social-psychological variables, observations on which are difficult to make in the framework of a census or vital registration system.

To an extent, the human ecologist shares the plight of the sociologist, in that he would like to relate the conventional sorts of demographic data to characteristics of the units into which populations are organized, and he finds that data collected on a unit basis are not easy to come by, except for such

economic units as stores and industrial establishments. Nevertheless, as is described in chapter xxviii, the human ecologist has directed his ingenuity to the problem of finding indicators of community structure in the store of available population statistics.

Disciplines like sociology and economics, which have recognized a need for developing complex study designs to tease out some of the more complicated interrelations of demographic and socioeconomic variables, have turned increasingly from a reliance on official sources of data to the execution of *ad hoc,* specially designed surveys (see the discussion of this point by Spengler, chap. xxxii). As this tendency continues, there will perhaps be increasing use of the neologism "microdemography" to denote comparatively small-scale studies in which census-type information is collected along with other characteristics thought to be relevant to demographic variation. Granting the obvious utility of this essentially new source of demographic data, one must raise the question of whether such studies contribute new information on problems already dealt with by demography or whether, in fact, they are simply raising new kinds of problems. But this question is appropriately discussed at a later stage.

In summary, the several disciplines closely related to demography make somewhat different demands on population data or require somewhat different types of population data. This circumstance may be a cause, or simply a reflection, of the difficulty in co-ordinating these disciplines for an integrated attack on the problem of explaining population variations from place to place and from time to time. The evidence suggests that some disciplines—for example, human ecology—have gone quite far in shaping their theoretical preoccupations to problems amenable to research with the available data, whereas others—like economics—have preferred to theorize at a given level of abstraction, irrespective of the possibilities of subjecting theories to empirical test with the kinds of population data likely to be available. Perhaps one could conclude that the wide range of demographic inquiry—from sheer empiricism to sheer speculation—results from the wide variety of reactions to the ever difficult problem of securing data adequate for scientific purposes.

Needed Population Data

To discuss meaningfully what data demography needs requires some framework of assumptions about the kind of work demographers will want to do, for as a perfectly abstract proposition, there is virtually no limit to the desirable expansion and improvement of existing data. As is made clear in the papers in Part III, the analytical concepts of demography tend to develop well beyond the analytical possibilities afforded by existing bodies of data. For example, specialists in natality analysis now demand data compiled on a cohort basis and classifications of couples by duration of marriage—information not often available because its uses were unknown in the past. It is likely that for as long as demography grows as a science, it will find need for data of greater coverage and higher quality than any feasible collection system is likely to supply.

On the other hand, the history of data collection systems clearly reveals the influence of developments in demographic analysis on collection procedures. It has been recognized for a long time that comprehensive demographic research can be conducted only for populations covered both by periodic censuses and by standing vital registration systems. Walter F. Willcox—the dean of American demography in his day—spoke of the census and the registration system as the two pillars that support the "arch" of demography. (In theory, a continuous population register can be made to serve both functions. But in practice, countries maintaining such a register have found it necessary to supplement and check it with periodic enumerations.)

The question, therefore, translates itself into: What priorities are indicated in securing data to remedy the most egregious gaps in demographic knowledge? There are then two possibilities: First, the very statement of the "gap" in effect designates the data needed to fill it. For example, demographers might agree that we need to know the birth and death rate in mainland China. The need, therefore, is for an accurate census count co-ordinated with a complete registration of vital events in that country. Second, the kind of "gap" may be such that the problem is precisely to find out what kind of data are needed. For example, demographers would like to understand better the "causes" of the postwar increase in the birth rate in Western countries. The problem here is to know what data, even if they were available, would afford an adequate explanation of that phenomenon.

One might say, therefore, that a most formidable inventory of the "missing" data could rather easily be compiled, understanding "data" here to refer to the kinds available under the best census, vital registration, and administrative statistics systems. The demographer would like to have for every country and other territory of the world complete, periodic censuses of high quality and wide subject-matter coverage, and complete continuing vital registrations and registers of migration, in each case with full information on the characteristics of the individuals involved in the registered event. Such information should be made available not only for each country but for small areal subdivisions thereof. The demographer would like to see such collections of data extended more or less indefinitely backward (by some appropriate magic) as well as forward in time. To the extent that such a program is not merely visionary, many competent specialists have been hard at work in delineating its outlines. Reference has been made to the work of international agencies in this field. It might be added that there is a long history of work by professional statisticians in formulating recommendations for the collection of population data. The efforts of the International Statistical Institute merit special mention; a current example is the report of the committee on the 1960 census of the Population Association of America (Duncan, 1957).

Even supposing that currently proposed international standards of population data collection were met in every particular in every country, one could not assume that the demographer would be satisfied. There are many characteristics of the population that could be informatively analyzed under the heading of "population composition" which are not now carried on census schedules. Even if census data were available in complete detail for an inconceivably fine areal breakdown, there would remain scientifically legitimate purposes for which greater detail would be required. Good uses could be found for data collected far more frequently than any census or survey agency would dare to imagine could be done. Manifestly, on what we may call the "descriptive" side the task of demography is never done and the needs are never met.

Turning to the needs which demographers may have for data which will "explain" demographic phenomena, the possibility of foreseeing and meeting needs is even more remote. One school of population students may hold that natality is most effectively investigated in terms of its complex relationships with consumer expenditures, and an-

other that what are needed are fuller data on the incidence of Oedipus complexes and feelings of emotional insecurity among potential parents. Fortunately for this discussion, for the future which it is useful to envision, such data will necessarily be collected *ad hoc* as supplements to rather than components of standard population data collection systems.

There have been at least two systematic efforts to point to deficiencies and gaps in data which document some of the observations made above. The first, conducted under the auspices of the Population Association of America, was prepared by P. K. Whelpton (1938). The second, based on the deliberations of a United Nations committee of experts, was prepared by Frank W. Notestein (1955).

The first of these reports pointed to gaps and deficiencies in data arising from its consideration of "needed population research" in 1938. The second, reflecting significant post–World War II developments, pointed to gaps and deficiencies in "data" as well as "knowledge" from the focus of the "relationships between population trends and economic and social conditions." Both reports were in large measure oriented to data and knowledge needed for "policy" purposes. This orientation reflects a condition demography tends to share with other social sciences—the fact that funds and other research resources are apt to be available primarily as by-products of "social engineering" interests—interest in social, economic, or political problems and policy.

The Whelpton report was concerned more with data needed for "demographic analysis" than for "population studies." In the Notestein report the emphasis was reversed. This shift in focus undoubtedly reflects the increasing interest of demographers in the relationships between demographic variables and other systems of variables to improve both the prediction and explanation of demographic phenomena. In both reports the point was made that the "basic data" of the type derived from census and vital registration systems need improvement in coverage and quality, and also geographically and historically as far as possible. Also, in both reports, although with the difference in emphasis indicated above, the need to obtain supplementary and complementary data from sources other than census and vital registration systems is indicated.

The quest for more data and better data is a perennial one in demography, as in all science. The improvement in demographic and related data will undoubtedly, however, continue to be limited by the changing conceptual framework and research interests of the demographer; the techniques available for obtaining the information with desired reliability, validity, and precision; the resources available for obtaining data, which tend to be restricted within governmental budgetary frameworks and fluctuating foundation interests in "applied" as contrasted with "basic" research; and the values of differing cultures which dictate what information may be politic or impolitic to obtain (for example, "religion" in the United States or "race" in Mexico).

Of these limiting factors, changing frameworks and techniques are more subject to the control of demographers than the other factors. Moreover, they are more likely to be the factors which determine what the needs for new data are, through which pressures are exerted on the other limiting factors so that the needed data become available. Needless to say, as demographic conceptual frameworks and techniques change and improve, "old" data may become regarded as increasingly defective, and "new" data previously impossible or not feasible to obtain may become available for research.

THE METHODS OF DEMOGRAPHY

The methods employed by the demographer include, of course, the general methodology of science, the techniques of mathematical statistics, and those of the specific natural science and social science disciplines with which demography is interrelated and on which it draws. In addition, demographic methods include a number of specific techniques which, if not entirely restricted to demographic use, have been in large measure developed in efforts to obtain and summarize information about population and to analyze and predict population phenomena.

These techniques of demographic research are classifiable into three not necessarily mutually exclusive categories for convenience in treatment: the techniques through which data are collected; the techniques by means of which data are evaluated, adjusted, corrected, or estimated; and the techniques by means of which demographic data are analyzed, including the techniques utilized for purposes of "prediction" or "projection." Because of the crucial nature of data collection methods and the fact that they are not discussed at length in the symposium, a somewhat fuller treatment of them than of the other methods of demography will be essayed in this chapter.

Methods of Data Collection

Demographic data are collected either by means of a canvass of the population on a complete or a sample basis or by means of a record system, such as a vital records system, a population register, or other public and private records.

The population canvass.—Field canvass methods have evolved over the years both in connection with census operations undertaken by many governments and more recently also in connection with sample survey operations (United Nations, 1949, 1957*b*). The key steps involved in the field canvass method may be listed as: field procedures to assure unduplicated and complete coverage of the population canvassed; the design of a schedule or questionnaire containing the inquiries to which responses are sought; the interview with the respondent by an enumerator; and the processing of information collected to achieve consistent, uniform, additive, and manageable data. Each of these steps is further divisible into a series of specific techniques which individually and aggregately affect the validity, reliability, and precision of the data which are collected. Some indication of the state of the art in respect to each of these steps is essayed in the paragraphs which follow.

The wide variety and dispersed locations of forms of human habitation, the mobility of populations, and problems of accessibility conspire to defeat efforts at complete census coverage. Principles have been evolved in the course of the years, however, by census offices throughout the world (United Nations, 1949, 1957*b*). Yet, despite strenuous efforts and considerable financial outlay, censuses still fail to achieve complete enumeration. The best techniques or combinations of techniques to obtain complete coverage are yet to be discovered. A number of the more advanced census and statistical organizations recognize this goal as an important one for continued research and experimentation.

Although complete coverage is probably not achieved by any national census, the data obtained, bearing in mind the Aristotelian injunction in respect of accuracy, are complete enough for many research purposes. But it is necessary for some research uses, as well as for some administrative uses, to "correct" or "adjust" the data. Moreover, it is particularly hazardous to use census data for minority and other relatively small groupings of the population for whom net underenumeration may greatly exceed the average underenumeration.

The design of a schedule and the preparation of instructions for its completion constitute an important aspect of the method of collecting data. These instruments are in large measure products of the experience and judgment of the persons who construct them rather than applications of routines based on objective and well-defined procedures. Yet, although this observation is a commonplace to persons in the census and survey field, it should not be permitted to obscure the progress that has been achieved in recent years in increasing the effectiveness of schedules as means for obtaining desired demographic and other data.

In the course of about a century and a half of systematic and periodic census-taking, the form and content of the census schedule have materially changed. From blank sheets of unruled paper which served the marshals who took the first census of the United States in 1790 (Wright and Hunt, 1900), the census schedule has become a large printed and ruled document which, by 1960, in response to the requirements of the equipment which is to be used, will be an exceedingly complex-appearing document maximizing the use of "precodes" and containing numerous "boxes" for special markings to be subject to microphotographic and electronic equipment.

The availability of advanced equipment, however, has had more effect on standardizing and making objective the form than the content of census schedules. Determination of the content, not in terms of subjects to be investigated —which reflect, of course, the needs of governments and of the society as interpreted by the properly constituted bodies—but the substantive way questions are put to obtain the desired information, is still in a relatively primitive state.

In this realm progress has been achieved largely through informal accumulation of experience but also, and especially in recent years, through systematic applications of social science, especially work in social psychology, psychology, and sociology on the interview. Developments in the use of "open" and "closed" or "structured" and "unstructured" questions, "sorter" and "multiple" (Kahn and Cannell, 1957) questions, the "funnel sequence" of questions, "self-enumeration," indirect approaches, "projective" tests, and scale analysis are indicative of the increasing efforts to achieve more systematic and objective ways of designing schedules in respect of content.

These efforts are relatively recent, and the state of knowledge and the research devoted to increasing knowledge in this area are, on the whole, still quite meager. The design of a schedule involves both problems of communication—concept, symbolic meaning, and response—and problems of measurement—validity, reliability, and precision. Fortunately, many of the data with which the demographer works in conventional demographic analyses are subject to relatively little response error or to response errors which can be reasonably well controlled (Durand, 1950).

The data which are used in broader types of studies, however, especially those which overlap the interests of such disciplines as social psychology, may be subject to much greater error of this kind (Eckler and Pritzker, 1951). These deficiencies arise in part from the deficiencies of the techniques available for the design of schedules and instructions and in part from problems of conducting the interview.

Undoubtedly the weakest link in the chain of techniques utilized in obtaining information by means of the census method is the interview—the situation in which the enumerator obtains answers to the inquiries on the schedule from a respondent. It is in the interview that the complex sequence of techniques to obtain census data meets its most severe test—for it is here that the validity and reliability of the information obtained, and much of its precision, are determined. Yet it is in the interview that the most difficult problems, those about which ignorance is the greatest, are encountered. Among these problems are the various "obstructions" to communication (Kahn and Cannell, 1957), such as problems of motivation, psychological barriers, language difficulties, and the uncertainties and, as yet, unpredictable sequences of behavior which may arise in the process of enumerator-respondent interaction. One important source of response error in the interview arises from the usual census practice of obtaining the information for all members of a household from only one respondent—usually the adult household member easiest to find at home. Various devices are being tested to reduce this source of error, all of which have in common the use of "self-enumeration" forms.

The techniques of processing the mass information collected by a census have obvious implications for the timeliness of demographic data. But processing techniques may also vitally affect the accuracy and quality of the information collected, and it is this latter effect which is, perhaps, of greater concern to the demographer.

More than in any of the other aspects of the census method, the techniques of processing data have been subject to technological advance. Desk adding and calculating machines, punched card equipment, and, more recently, electronic equipment have revolutionized the processing of mass data and have contributed materially to their increased timeliness, accuracy, and quality. The advantage of machine technology for timeliness and accuracy is obvious; that in regard to quality is not as easy to visualize. The major contribution of machines to the quality of census data is to be found in their use for "editing" of census schedules—that is, in the use of punched card tabulating equipment and, more recently, electronic digital computers for checking the internal consistency of responses over a wide range of items with great speed and accuracy.

The processing of mass census data may be subclassified into "editing," "coding," "punching," "tabulating," and "result-work" procedures which precede the publication of a census report. In these processes machine technology has contributed least to coding. Machines with prodigious capacity can perform in hours, with greater accuracy, editing, punching, tabulating, and result-work tasks which formerly required days, weeks, or months for batteries of clerks. It is possible to eliminate entirely the work of "punching," transferring information onto a punch card or tape, by means of "mark-sense" or "Fosdic"—Film Optical Sensing Device for Input to Computers (see Taeuber, 1958)—equipment, and thus greatly to reduce error arising from this transcription of data as well as to achieve great gains in time and cost.

A final item to be treated under data processing is that relating to verification of the several steps mentioned. In this realm mathematical statistics and technology have combined to provide highly effective and inexpensive methods of verification by means of acceptance sampling, specifically, quality control methods, applicable to mass clerical operations. When the processing has been mechanized, verification, of course, is achieved by machine methods. In the use of electronic digital computers all processes are automatically machine verified.

One aspect of the processing of data, deserving treatment by itself rather than as an aspect of "processing" and little affected by technology, is that relating to the classification of data—the design of classification systems to make vast bodies of data manageable without greatly impairing their usefulness for research and other purposes. The "classification" of data is, of course, a procedure common to all science and one which may vitally affect the analysis of data and the inferences which may be drawn. An item such as sex involves a relatively simple and completely objective classification system corresponding to phenomenological reality. An item such as age, while also posing relatively simple problems of classification, does pose some difficulties arising from variability and bias in response. By reason of errors in the reporting of age, with responses tending to heap at zero, five, and even numbers, classifications of age not only perform the usual function of making data manageable but also serve to "smooth" the age distribution. Such categories as "color or race" and "marital status" pose greater problems in respect to designing classifications; not only are there questions about their theoretical meaning, but one must also bear in mind the probable errors in the data to which they are applied.

Classification systems involve the adoption of more or less arbitrary subcategories and definitions and must take into account the possible disparities between appearance and reality. The adoption of such categories imposes an order on the phenomenological world that may facilitate the manipulation of the data and of research; but it may also lead to errors of reification, the attribution to the phenomena of characteristics more a function of the investigator than of the actual world. The arbitrary character of classification systems and their influence on the analysis and inferences which can be drawn becomes more serious in respect of many of the social, psychological, and economic characteristics with which some types of population studies are concerned. Among the more difficult and vexing of the classification problems involved are those in relation to "social-economic" status or indexes thereof, occupation, industry, personality types and traits, and attitudes.

Virtually all of the foregoing discussion of the field canvass method applies with equal force to the sample survey. The specific techniques of field procedure, design of schedules, the interview, and processing of data are also utilized in the sample survey. The difference lies merely in the use of part of the population to represent the whole.

The selection of "part" to represent the "whole" with which to do research and make inferences about the whole is a problem common to all science. The specific techniques with which to draw a suitable part vary, of course, with the nature of the universe or the phenomena which are to be investigated. In a universe that is made up of units which are completely homogeneous for purposes of the research to be undertaken, the selection of any unit will serve the purpose. In a universe that is made up of heterogeneous units, however, the selection of a portion of them to represent the whole is not so simple. On the basis of developments in mathematics and mathematical statistics, however, theory and methods have been evolved which make such a selection completely objective. Moreover, statistical theory and method enable the investigator to calculate the sampling error of his data, that is, to know, within specified limits of uncertainty, the difference between the results obtained from the sample and those which would have been obtained from a complete census.

Although probability theory on which sampling methods are based dates back to the seventeenth century and although Laplace's classic work on probability was written a century and a half ago (Laplace, 1812), the developments in theory and practice which have made the sample survey an exceedingly powerful tool for population study are largely the product of the last two or three decades. It is in the development of "restrictive random designs" as against simple random sampling, and particularly in the emergence of "area probability sampling," that the sample survey has emerged as a major instrumentality for producing population as well as other types of data (Yates, 1949; Hansen, Hurwitz, and Madow, 1953).

Sampling has been extended to many aspects of data collection and data-processing with great gains in timeliness, economy, and quality. From a substantive standpoint one of the more important uses of sampling in data collection is that in conjunction with the census. In this usage the number of inquiries in a complete census undertaking is limited, and sampling methods are employed within the framework of the census for a number of the inquiries. The use of sampling in conjunction with the census was employed in the United States in 1940 to extend the range of the subjects on which information was obtained for relatively large geographic areas. In 1950, sampling was used in conjunction with the census to provide information for "small areas" as well as large areas. In 1960 it is likely that the use of sampling in conjunction with the census will be greatly extended and that only a few basic items will be included in the complete canvass.

The justification for the use of sampling methods lies, of course, in its contribution to increased timeliness, decreased costs, and improved quality of the data. The gains in timeliness and costs obviously arise from the great decrease in the number of persons to be enumerated and items to be processed. The gain in quality of data is not so readily apparent. It derives from the feasibility of increasing the expenditure per person enumerated, over that practiced in a complete census enumeration. For example, in a relatively small sample survey it may be feasible to include two questions for ascertaining age, such as "age last birthday?" and "date of birth?" when it is too costly to do this in a complete canvass. Moreover, the reduction in the number of units to be interviewed or handled permits the selection of better and more highly paid enumerators, more intensive and prolonged training, more thorough field procedures, and the like. It is out of considerations of this kind that the disparity between the complete census report in 1950 and the small sample survey, the Monthly Report on the Labor Force, a difference of some four million workers, was resolved in favor of the sample (the census was based on a canvass of forty-three million, the sample survey, twenty-five thousand, households). Analyses of the nature of the discrepancy reveal that it was the census and not the sample that was in error. The sample was also subject to error, of course, but in this instance the census "undercount" of workers was greatly in excess of the sampling and response errors of the sample.

The sample survey then, by reason of its low time and money costs, has advantages over the census method in producing data for demographic and other uses. It cannot, of course, replace the census as a medium through which statistics are obtained for small areas, e.g., the some fifty thousand minor civil divisions of the United States, the census tracts within large cities, and the small places—towns and villages; but it can become the more important source of data on composition and characteristics of the population, including the more complex forms of social, psychological, and economic data in which the demographer may be interested. The increasing importance of the Current Population Survey of the United States Bureau of the Census (see the Bureau's *Catalog of United States Census Publications,* quarterly) as a source of demographic data, the recently initiated Morbidity Survey (United States Department of Health, Education, and Welfare, 1957), and the increasing number of sample surveys throughout the world (United Nations, *Statistical Papers,* Ser. C) attest to the rapidity with which the sample survey is becoming a major source of demographic data, and especially of data beyond the items usually used in demographic analysis.

The pretest and postenumerative surveys to which reference is made below are, of course, both sample survey enterprises. They represent an exceedingly useful form of sampling in that the "parts" which they work with may be used as a basis for designing or evaluating the "whole."

The conduct of a field canvass, like the use of any technique of science, is an art. It is an art which includes a number of highly objective and routinized procedures, but it also includes techniques dependent on the experience and judgment of the personnel engaged in taking the census.

To maximize the efficiency of census procedures and to achieve some control over the various sources of error in response or in measurement, it has increasingly become the practice of modern census organizations to "pretest" their schedules, instructions, and procedures. Moreover, since in the taking of a census as in any art "practice makes perfect," the pretest serves as a rehearsal as well as an experiment. In the United States census it has become a working rule to include in the census undertaking only inquiries and procedures which have been subjected to rigorous pretesting.

The pretest can be employed to experiment over a wide range of substantive and procedural matters. It can be used to evaluate alternative procedures varying from the testing, recruiting, and training of personnel to alternative ways of editing or tabulating data. Furthermore, the pretest can be employed to test alternative inquiries to obtain the desired information and, in some measure, to anticipate and control errors of response and of measurement.

The "pretest" is a device, then, which permits both experimentation and practice to improve the census results with which the demographer works. It has greatly improved (United Nations, 1957a) census data, but it still has many limitations in usage. A complete analysis of pretest results is often impossible because of census time and cost budgets, and the pretest often cannot give completely adequate answers to questions relating to the reliability, precision, and, especially, the validity of data. In consequence, many types of questions in regard to the limitations of the data remain unanswered even when pretests have been employed. To provide the desired answers, at least in part, the "postenumerative" survey is employed.

It is the primary function of the postenumerative survey to evaluate the completeness and quality of census results. Obviously, the findings of a postenumerative survey cannot be used to help to improve the census which it follows; its contribution to the improvement of the census lies in its addition to the fund of knowledge with which to plan the next and subsequent censuses. The results obtained from a postenumerative survey, however, do provide a great deal of information on the limitations of the census and a basis for adjusting or correcting the data, where

that is possible and desirable in light of the uses to which they are to be put. A particularly useful product of the postenumerative survey is the measurement it can provide of differential underenumeration or differences in quality of data for the various population subcategories or groupings. Such information is indispensable for many comparative studies. The postenumerative sampling survey is the best device yet developed with which to measure the errors of a complete census, errors in coverage as well as in the quality of the data (Hansen, Hurwitz, and Pritzker, 1953). Moreover, such a use of sampling makes it possible to separate errors in census and sample collections of data into their components—sampling error, response error, sampling bias, and response bias (Eckler and Hurwitz, 1957).

In pretest and postenumerative surveys the sampling survey becomes, in addition to a method of collecting data, a technique for measuring coverage and quality, providing factors for adjusting and correcting data and pointing to ways of improving the data with which the demographer works. Since the developments described are of relatively recent origin, these devices have just begun to make their significant contribution to the improvement of the data of demography.

Record systems.—There are three major types of record systems which provide data for the demographer. These are the vital registration system, the population register, and the administrative records of various government offices which provide demographic statistics as a by-product. In addition there are also record systems from non-governmental sources—particularly those of insurance companies, which often have great value.

The registration of births, deaths, marriages, divorces, and related vital events is essential for various administrative purposes both public and private. Information based on vital records used in conjunction with data obtained from a population census provides basic data on population dynamics—that is, information on fertility and mortality as components of population change and on marriage and divorce as components of net family formation.

The development of a vital registration system and procedures for deriving adequate statistics therefrom is not an easy task. In the more highly developed countries vital registration systems have taken many decades to achieve reasonably complete coverage and to provide usable statistics. In the United States, characterized by a federal system involving voluntary co-operation between the federal and state governments, all states were not in the registration system until as recently as 1933.

To provide adequate data for demography, a vital registration system must include procedures to assure the filing of a uniform record for every vital event—for example, live birth, death, stillbirth, and marriage; to provide for complete and usable answers to the inquiries on the record form; and to enable the information in the record form to be processed for statistical purposes —that is, edited, coded, tabulated, and presented, preferably through some central office which provides vital statistics for the nation and its subdivisions on a comparable basis. Principles and procedures for achieving these objectives have been evolved over the years (United Nations, 1953).

The filing of a uniform record for every vital event requires the organization of a comprehensive system of local registration offices and detailed procedures to assure co-operation of the general population, medical and other functionaries concerned with vital events, and government officials. The complex and comprehensive character

of such an organization and set of procedures makes difficult the achievement of 100 per cent registration of vital events and accounts for varying degrees of underregistration in the more advanced as well as the less developed countries. The major motivation for achieving complete registration of vital events is usually to be found in connection with the administrative and legal uses of the data. Demographic and statistical uses, however, also exert pressures for achieving complete registration. In the more developed countries death registration is usually virtually complete and birth registration nearly so.

Needless to say, it is essential for statistical purposes that a uniform record be available for each vital event so as to permit the compilation of statistics. In centralized national systems this is relatively simple to achieve; in a federal system like the United States the achievement of uniform record forms is a more complex matter which may require legislative and administrative action by each of the forty-eight states, the District of Columbia, and the several independent city or county registration systems. Although each separate registration system in the United States is free to design its own record forms, a standard core for each form has been accepted on a voluntary basis which does enable the United States to compile uniform vital statistics.

In the United States, although vital events relating to fertility and mortality have achieved a reasonably satisfactory state of completeness of registration, data relating to marriage and divorce, especially divorce, are still in a relatively primitive state. The United States national committee on vital and health statistics in a recent report (1957) has recommended the establishment of a "marriage registration area" comparable to that established for vital statistics in 1915. Even such a recommendation is not yet possible in respect to divorce statistics, which required "thorough study" before recommendation could be made.

Certain basic items relating to vital events have been incorporated in the standard form used for the recording of births, deaths, marriages, divorces, and the like. The information desired about each event, however, is still a matter for discussion on both the international and national scenes (United Nations, 1953). Moreover, the same types of problems which were discussed above relative to the obtaining of information through censuses apply to vital record forms. The collection of the information is dependent on the process of communication in a setting which is frequently more complex than that involved in the field canvass operation and often under conditions which are more difficult because of the emotion and sentiment associated with vital events. The recording of vital information, however, may in some respects pose fewer problems than the population canvass because of the special training of the functionaries who record the information—the physician, the undertaker, and the registrar. All in all, not too much reliable information is at hand as a basis for evaluating the validity, reliability, and precision of the information entered on vital record forms. Particularly perplexing is the extent to which information entered on vital records is comparable with that obtained through the population canvass, a matter of special importance in the construction of vital statistics rates in which the population-canvass information is the denominator. In consequence, vital rates, especially those of an "item-specific" character dependent on such relatively complex characteristics as occupation, are subject to relatively great and as yet largely unmeasured error.

Principles and procedures conducive to the compilation of adequate vital statistics have been the subject of national and international consideration over the years (United Nations, 1953). An especially difficult aspect of the procedures involved in the production of accurate vital statistics has been that relating to the reporting and classification of causes of death. This particular problem has been the subject of a large number of national and international conferences which among other things have resulted in the preparation of international lists of causes of death, the sixth decennial revision of which, including "lists of diseases" for the first time as well as "causes of death," is now in international usage.

Although it is generally recognized that the vital statistics of the United States, especially those relating to fertility and mortality, are quite adequate for many of the research uses to which they are put by demographers, they are far from being completely satisfactory. Specific needs for improvements—administrative, methodological, and substantive—have been spelled out in the report "National Vital Statistics Needs" prepared by the United States national committee on vital and health statistics (1957), to which reference has already been made.

The population register.—In a number of European countries a continuous population register is maintained to serve a number of legal and administrative functions. Such registers are important sources of demographic information and may provide the equivalent of a cross-section population census or a continuous flow of data on vital events. The population register, furthermore, may be used as a direct source of information on territorial movements or internal migration. Sweden affords an excellent example of the use of the population register, among other things, as a device for obtaining demographic data (Thomas, 1941). In Sweden the register is kept on a current basis by annual re-registration of households through the obligatory participation of the landlord; since the register serves for various purposes, including taxation, voting, and housing, comprehensive coverage is assured. Internal movements require registration at the place of destination as well as notification at the place of origin of the movement. The excellent population register in Sweden accounts for the fact that demographic statistics for Sweden span a period of some two hundred years.

The United States does not maintain a population register. In fact, such efforts as have been made from time to time toward the establishment of such a register, as, for example, during World War II to help meet the national emergency, have been frowned upon by many members of Congress as contributory to the establishment of a police state. Short of acute national emergency or catastrophe, it does not appear that a comprehensive national population register will be established in this country. But the expanding coverage of various social security programs is creating a file which, in time, may include all persons in the United States and which may incorporate many of the elements of a population register. However, because a population register does not contribute demographic data for the United States and is not likely to in the foreseeable future, discussion of this means of obtaining population information will be restricted to the observations made above.

Other administrative record systems. —Various record systems of both public and private agencies also serve as sources of demographic data, even though usually for restricted or special populations or for relatively short periods of time. One of the most important and also the most comprehensive of such record systems in various countries, including the Unied States, is that relating to various social security pro-

grams. In the United States, for example, files maintained for old-age and survivors insurance, unemployment compensation, and employment services are increasingly contributing to the flow of data useful for demographic purposes (e.g., Bogue, 1950). During World War II other federal record systems contributed to the pool of demographic knowledge, especially records of the Selective Service System and of the Office of Price Administration, which maintained rationing records. Records of such agencies as the Department of Defense, Veterans Administration, Federal Emergency Relief Administration, Department of Agriculture, Department of Justice (especially Immigration and Naturalization Service), Bureau of Indian Affairs, and Treasury Department (Bureau of Internal Revenue) from time to time provide demographic information about the particular populations with which they deal. Such data have various demographic uses, providing information not only about the populations concerned but also external checks against data obtained through census or sample surveys.

At the state level various record systems are also important sources of population statistics, especially those relating to marriage and divorce, which under our federal system are maintained only locally. At the present time marriage and divorce statistics in the United States are among the most deficient in the Western world, and efforts are under way to improve the methods of obtaining these data and to produce comprehensive and adequate marriage and divorce statistics.

Finally, private records may also contribute to the pool of population data. Especially important in this respect, because of their relatively large coverage, are the records of the great insurance companies. The Metropolitan Life Insurance Company has, in fact, for many years been the source of valuable demographic statistics and analysis, and it regularly publishes a statistical bulletin.

Methods of Evaluating, Adjusting, and Estimating Data

The degree of accuracy required in data is a relative thing and a function of the use to which the data are put. As has been indicated, there are many sources of error in demographic data. For some purposes, such as observation of broad trends and macroscopic changes, errors in population data may be insignificant. For other purposes, such as an analysis of differential fertility or mortality in specific areas, defective data may greatly distort the conclusions which may be drawn.

One of the most important tasks of the demographer in the conduct of his research is the assessment of the validity, reliability, and precision of the data with which he is working. The competent demographer can use deficient data when no other information is available and still reach valid conclusions. In general, this may be accomplished in either of two ways: by restricting generalizations to propositions which may be regarded as valid because of demonstrably limited error in the data or by adjusting or correcting the data so as to reduce their error and make them usable for the purposes intended. Specific techniques are available for implementing either of these alternatives, some in the general techniques of statistics and some specifically devised by the demographer for dealing with his special problems.

The major criteria for evaluating a data collection system include the coverage, the comparability, and the quality of the data it produces. The term "coverage" may be taken to include both the completeness with which the target population or class of events is enumerated or registered and the range of information obtained about the unit of observation.

In regard to completeness, the recent experience of the United States census and registration system gives some indication of the magnitude of the problem under relatively favorable conditions. Careful, though not necessarily accurate, estimates indicate that the 1950 census enumeration represented a net undercount of 1.5 to 3.5 per cent, comprising a somewhat larger gross undercount compensated by a small amount of duplication and overcounting of the *de jure* population. There is no reason to suppose that substantially greater or lesser coverage was achieved in the earlier censuses of the twentieth century. A notorious example of underenumeration is the census of 1870, taken under the disturbed conditions following the Civil War. It has been estimated that the official population total for that year should be increased by 3.3 per cent, with the bulk of the error occurring in the South.

Birth registration tests, which involved matching of census schedules and registration certificates on an individual basis, were carried out in conjunction with the 1940 and 1950 censuses. These tests indicated that approximately 92.5 and 98 per cent of the births occurring in the United States were being registered in the respective years. Prior to 1933 the effective underregistration was much greater, because not all states were included in the registration area. With the approach to completeness represented by the 1950 figure, it has become doubtful whether such tests will be conducted in connection with future censuses.

Higher standards of completeness are doubtless maintained by certain European countries whose populations are smaller, more homogeneous, less mobile, and more accustomed to contacts with bureaucracy than that of the United States. By contrast, extreme de-

ficiencies in enumeration, and especially
in vital registration, are common in
many of the less-developed areas where
experience in data collection is limited
and the population is apathetic if not
resistant to procedures of enumeration
and registration (see the pertinent discussions by Mortara, Chandrasekaran,
and Taeuber, chaps. xi–xiii).

Considerable variability in subject-
matter coverage is indicated in Linder's
tabulation (chap. xv) of the items included in various national censuses. In
part, this results from the fact that inquiries appropriate in one social setting
may be unsuitable or even downright
meaningless in another. As Jaffe (chap.
xxv) points out, for example, refined
inquiries on labor-force status are appropriate only in an economy in which
a sharp distinction is made between the
non-working and the working population, with the bulk of the latter being
employed persons receiving monetary
compensation for their services. Expansion of the subject-matter coverage of
a census increases the expense of taking
it and may also involve a cost in lowered quality of data if the enumeration
form becomes unduly complex. Both
consequences may be averted, to a degree, by substituting samples for complete enumerations within the census
framework.

Problems of subject-matter coverage
in vital statistics are perhaps even more
difficult than in censuses. The vital record is usually completed by a person
who, though perhaps medically educated, lacks training in procedures of
collecting social data. The birth or
death certificate is basically a legal document, secondarily a device for collecting statistics. There are difficulties in
securing adequate coverage that result
from its doing double duty. A remarkable anachronism was the fact that a
century after its registration system was
established, England's birth certificate
did not call for the age of the mother

at the birth of the child; appropriate
legislation requiring this information
was passed only in 1938.

Problems of comparability arise when
demographers make comparisons involving data from different periods,
places, or data collection systems. Because science in its most fundamental
aspect is a systematic procedure for
making comparisons, it is readily seen
that comparability is close to the heart
of demography's status as a science, as
far as adequacy of data is concerned.
Lack of comparability arises, in the first
instance, from dissimilarities in coverage. It has been rare, if not unknown,
in the history of population enumerations for two censuses to have exactly
the same subject-matter coverage. Even
if similar basic lists of items are covered in two censuses, there are likely to
be detailed but significant differences
in definition of categories or enumeration rules. A perennial problem in comparability is the one encountered in
matching census and vital statistics,
which must be done, of course, to calculate vital rates. For example, it is
questionable whether a meaningful occupational death rate can be computed
from United States data, because the
population covered in the census labor-
force question on occupation is not the
same as that covered by the occupation
item on the death certificate—quite
aside from the problem of how accurately occupations are ascertained in
either inquiry. Problems of temporal
comparability, and the enormous labor
that has been expended to deal with
them, are described in Dorn's discussion
of cause-of-death statistics (chap. xix).

Another basic form of non-comparability is differential accuracy. If, for example, vital registration has been improving in completeness, birth and
death rates will show apparent increases
in the absence of any true change in
natality or mortality. There are numerous instances in the demographic lit-

erature of hasty generalizations about changes in vital rates that involve precisely this mistake. It is an elementary principle of statistics that a ratio in which the numerator and the denominator are both in error in the same direction and in the same proportion is correct despite the inaccuracy of its components. In recent years it has been standard practice for American demographers to correct birth statistics for underregistration, making use of the factors discovered in the birth registration test. It is much more unusual for the base populations to be corrected for underenumeration, owing, presumably, to the lack of firm estimates of degree of underenumeration. It is a somewhat ironical possibility that, as a result, many of the "corrected" birth rates that have been published are further from the truth than uncorrected rates derived directly from official statistics.

Much more obscure kinds of noncomparability are those incident to the transfer of analytical methods and concepts developed on the basis of Western demographic experience to the kinds of materials available on, say, Oriental and native African populations (see Taeuber's discussion, chap. xiii).

The third criterion of data adequacy —quality—is perhaps best considered under the heading of errors that may be present in data. The discussion of data collection methods above and most of the papers in Part III indicate the formidable problems in obtaining reasonably accurate statistics in each of the subject-matter fields of demography. When one considers the complexity of the routines of data collection, recording, and processing and reflects that errors may occur at each of these stages and their several substages, the possibilities of inaccuracy seem impressive. One expert on enumerative surveys has taken the trouble to set down a list of more than a dozen distinct types of error that need to be recognized in designing surveys (Deming, 1944). In discussions of census data most attention has been given, perhaps, to two sorts of error: coverage errors (already discussed under completeness) and response errors. The latter include the well-nigh universal tendencies to misstate age, failure of the respondent to report characteristics carrying social stigma (e.g., an unmarried woman with children may report herself as widowed), refusal to respond to questions, and simple ignorance with respect to questions calling for somewhat complex information. Demographers have developed considerable skill in the detection and correction of some of these kinds of error. For example, there are several ingenious tests of the degree of age misstatement based on the estimation of digit preferences. Where such tests have been applied comparatively, the results often have been in the direction expected: the proportion of erroneous statements declines as a population becomes better educated and as more care is exercised in enumeration.

A special word needs to be said about migration data, for much of the foregoing refers implicitly only to population numbers and characteristics and to births and deaths. It is clear from Thomas' discussion (chap. xxii) that the collection of information on international movements is usually, if not always, a by-product of administrative activities intended to control such movements and rarely is designed with primarily scientific needs in mind. The resulting grievous inadequacies of international migration statistics are well known, if not always fully appreciated.

The situation is somewhat different with respect to internal migration. Only in countries maintaining continuous population registers are internal movements recorded as they occur. Whereas one might expect such a system to be optimal from the standpoint of generating demographic data, the inherent complexities of the task of keeping track of all changes of residence has militated strongly against the realization of its theoretical potentialities. Nonetheless, some of the most illuminating materials on migration have come from countries with this type of records. In other countries two main types of methods of securing migration data are employed. Censuses may collect retrospective migration histories of individuals—actually, segments of such histories. As explained by Bogue (chap. xvii), careful analysis of information on place of birth or place of previous residence can disclose much about basic patterns of internal migration. Nonetheless, the method has inherent defects: only the moves of persons now living are reported; moves occurring within the migration interval are not reported; and so on. The indirect, or residual, methods of calculating migration described in chapter xvii are used a good deal in the absence of pertinent direct information. The accuracy of these methods depends heavily on the comparability of vital statistics and census data. All things considered, it is unquestionably true that migration is the least satisfactorily measured of the three components of population change: mortality, natality, and movement.

To overcome grave deficiencies in availability of data, demographers have built up a whole technology of population estimation (treated subsequently and in Grauman's discussion, chap. xxiii). In terms of the numbers of people to which it refers, a much higher proportion of demographic "knowledge" consists of estimates and guesses than of actual results of observation. It is true that much of the effort devoted to current estimates of population is motivated by practical needs rather than scientific interests. However, much of the support for hypotheses about fundamental patterns of demographic change derives essentially from suppositions about population conditions in times and places for which no precise observations can be had. The ingenuity of demographers in filling such gaps— for better or worse—may perhaps match that of the paleontologist in reconstructing the course of evolution from scattered fossil fragments.

To compensate for deficiencies in quality of data, much effort is devoted to the estimation of errors and to the devising of appropriate correction factors. Similarly, to resolve problems of comparability, intensive study is given over to methods of reconciling discrepant information and of making comparisons where, strictly, comparisons cannot be made. It might be remarked that the marginal return to such efforts is highly variable. In some cases, minor adjustments of data result in making available for analysis considerable bodies of information that otherwise would be scientifically suspect. In other instances, quite heroic efforts to produce plausible estimates yield results that cannot be accepted as worth much more than quite casual judgments.

The study of errors, like the need for estimates, stimulates the development of appropriate technologies. For example, the practice of taking enumerative check surveys in connection with censuses is spreading rapidly and is becoming accepted as an indispensable part of census-taking.

Techniques for "adjusting," "correcting," or "estimating" data are an important part of the methodological armamentarium of the demographer. Such techniques have necessarily developed because of the recognized roughness of some of the data with which the demographer works.

The most common adjustments or corrections of demographic data have centered largely on problems of "completeness" in census enumerative procedures or vital records registration procedures. Vital statistics, particularly birth and death statistics, are often "corrected" for "underregistration," and census statistics, less often, are adjusted for "underenumeration." Adjustment of census data is often undertaken, also, for misreporting of age—for the tendency for age reporting to "heap" at five, zero, and to a lesser extent at even numbers.

Various methods, as has been indicated above, have been used over the years to obtain estimates of "underregistration" or "underenumeration" (see discussions by Linder, chap. xv; Ryder, chap. xviii; and Dorn, chap. xix). In general they have compared actual registration or enumeration with external and independently obtained comparable bodies of data (Eckler, 1953) or with registration or census data, or both, extended from earlier to more recent dates to obtain "expected" populations for purposes of comparison (Coale, 1955). In using "internal" comparisons the estimate of underenumeration or underregistration is derived, in effect, from inconsistencies in the data from time to time.

In 1940 and 1950 in the United States, rather elaborate tests of completeness of registration and enumeration were undertaken in conjunction with the decennial census operations (U.S. Bureau of the Census, 1953). The results have provided demographers with important information, on the basis of which such corrections of the data can be made as may be necessary. Moreover, the government publishes natality and mortality data on both a "registered" and "adjusted for underregistration" basis (U.S. Bureau of the Census, 1957).

Adjustment procedures for misreporting of age vary from the simple device of grouping ages to complex actuarial methods of smoothing age distributions. For many demographic purposes the grouping of ages into suitable class intervals provides adequate correction of age-heaping. For some analytical purposes, however, especially in connection with the construction of life tables or the stationary or stable populations, the more complex techniques are necessary and are available (see Hawley, chap. xvi).

Of a quite different character are the techniques of "estimating" demographic data when they are not available from census, survey, or record sources. The most common type of "estimate" is that of a population for an "intercensal" or "postcensal" date. In general, three types of estimating procedures have been evolved: mathematical techniques of interpolation or extrapolation; "symptomatic" techniques involving the use of data believed to be highly correlated with population change; and combinations of these methods, which may include the use of births and deaths both as symptomatic indicators and as components of natural increase (Bogue and Duncan, 1958). In addition, current "estimates" for a nation as a whole, as in the United States, may be calculated by the equivalent of a "bookkeeping" method, by algebraically adding births, deaths, and migration to the most recent census results.

The methods available for current population estimation for areas smaller than a nation as a whole are at best a poor substitute for the unavailable data, more specifically, data on internal migration, which together with birth and death data would permit the use of the "bookkeeping" method. However, they do provide, at least for larger areas, a useful set of current statistics (Shryock, 1957). Experimental work now under way indicates that composite methods may be developed to improve the accuracy of current population estimates and to make them available for smaller areas. It is probably true that, on the whole, pressure for current population estimates comes more from "social engineering" sources—public health, marketing, city-planning, economic development, and the like—than from research needs, although the latter are also served by the availability of current estimates.

Another frequently utilized set of estimation techniques are those for obtaining estimates of internal migration (see Bogue, chap. xxi; Grauman, chap. xxiii). Such data are usually not available, and the demographer, to obtain some notions of the magnitude and character of internal migration, has been forced to devise indirect methods to obtain them. In general, these methods involve the calculation of an "expected" population obtained by "aging" an earlier enumerated population with which the current enumerated population is compared. The difference is taken to be a measurement of net migration. Rough as the results may be, it is clear that they provide exceedingly useful information about internal migratory movements.

Finally, other types of data may be adjusted and estimated for special study purposes (e.g., Edwards, 1943). The above noted methods, however, are by far the most common ones employed in demography.

Methods of Analyzing Data

Without question the greatest virtuosity in method displayed by the demographer is that in the analytical techniques he employs. In addition to the general techniques of descriptive statistics and statistical inference, he has devised or adapted methods especially to deal with problems of demographic analysis.

For dealing with population "statics" the demographer depends largely on general statistical descriptive techniques with some special rates and graphic devices which have become widely used. In this latter category are such things as the sex ratio, the dependency ratio, the index of displacement, and the population pyramid (see Hawley,

chap. xvi). To deal with population dynamics, demography has developed a rather comprehensive and elaborate set of "rates" designed to measure vital events or components of population change, such as natality, mortality, morbidity, marriage, divorce, and migration. This is not the place to describe or even to catalogue the various population rates (see Ryder, chap. xviii; Dorn, chap. xix). On the whole, demographic rates are designed to measure change and are calculated as approximations to a posteriori probability statements. In at least one instance, the "mortality rate" of the life table, a reasonably intensive effort is made to approximate a true a posteriori probability statement.

The more complex techniques of demographic analysis have resulted from comparative demography—from efforts to compare demographic phenomena in space or in time. In attempting such comparisons—for example, in comparing the mortality of two or more populations in space or the same population(s) over time—it became clear that if the age and sex composition of the respective populations were not "controlled," the differences would reflect differences in population composition as well as differences in mortality. To deal with this problem, techniques of standardization were developed or adapted, including techniques of indirect standardization (Linder and Grove, 1943; Kitagawa, 1955).

As an extension of mortality analysis and also as a way of effecting standardization for comparative mortality studies, the development of the life table provided the demographer and the actuary with relatively powerful analytical tools (see Dorn, chap. xix). Moreover, by using the life table as a "stationary" population, the demographer is able, within a framework of explicit assumptions, to set forth the implications of observed age-specific mortality rates in terms of the type of population structure they would generate (Dublin, Lotka, and Spiegelman, 1949).

Perhaps the most ingenious of demographic analytical methods arose in response to a basic question which troubled demographers for some time: What were the implications of observed natality and mortality for population reproduction, that is, for the ability of the population to replace itself in the longer run? (see Lorimer, chap. vi; Hyrenius, chap. xx). The analytical framework developed around the "stable population" concept enabled the demographer to set forth the implications of the observed age-specific fertility rates, as well as mortality rates, in terms of the type of population structure they would generate. By this means the demographer was able, in some measure, if not completely (Dublin and Lotka, 1925), to analyze away the effects of current population age structure, the product of past demographic history, while assessing the replacement implications of observed current fertility and mortality. The general birth, death, and natural increase rates of the "stable population" (the so-called true or intrinsic rates) were in contrast with observed general birth, death, and natural increase rates. The measure of generation reproduction, the "net reproduction" rate, was recognized as a function of the stable population, and the "gross reproduction" rate indicated the implications of observed fertility if there was no mortality. The demographer has also been ingenious in devising indirect ways of obtaining these rates or of obtaining substitute rates for them when the data do not permit their direct calculation.

One aspect of the techniques designed to make explicit the implications of observed mortality and natality rates deserves special mention. That is, in form, the rates constructed to achieve this objective—either the gross and net reproduction rates on a generation basis or the "true" or "intrinsic" rates on an annual basis—appear to refer to the future in a way which gives them the aura of predictions. Actually, the one thing the demographer is usually certain of is that the age-specific death and birth rates used in constructing the stable population will not prevail indefinitely. Yet, the fact that the rates, in form, describe a phenomenon that would occur at a future date led lay persons, and sometimes persons who should have known better, to interpret them as having predictive value. It is rather interesting that the effort to analyze cross-sectional data led to rates which took the form of predicting the future in a way that is not warranted; and contrariwise, as is indicated below, efforts to predict the future in the form of population projections often have little value as predictions but may serve as important analytical models. It may be observed that these apparently perverse results flow, in each instance, from the failure to recognize the function and limitations of concepts as tools in science.

More recent methodological developments have focused on still another vexing problem, that of distinguishing cyclical and other variations in time from secular trend in fertility. The nature and limitations of the data forced the demographer to make time analyses of fertility from measures of current fertility (see Ryder, chap. xviii). But current fertility is not necessarily a good indicator of the fertility of a woman over her entire reproductive period. With the increasing ability of populations to control their fertility—to defer fertility or to make up for deferrals—trends in current fertility may well prove to be poor indicators of trends in generation fertility. This problem became an acute and embarrassing one when demographers were unable to tell whether the postwar boom in fertility represented merely a cyclical upturn or a reversal in secular trend.

This time-analysis problem led to greater attention to longitudinal, as opposed to cross-section, study and to the emergence of "cohort fertility" analysis. Such analysis focuses on the fertility of birth or marriage cohorts of women and arranges the data in such a way as to make possible the time analysis of "completed fertilities" of women or their cumulative fertility at specific stages in their childbearing careers, for comparison with other cohorts at comparable stages. This longitudinal approach, bolstered by controlling other variables, such as age at marriage, duration of marriage, and parity, has already contributed greatly to the unscrambling of secular trend from other time variations; and it may be expected to contribute even more as longer series of cohort data become available (Hajnal, 1947; Whelpton, 1954). The results of cohort fertility studies have tended to emphasize the value of longitudinal analysis in general; and cohort mortality analysis, generation life tables, work histories, and other cohort analytical approaches will undoubtedly receive more attention in the future. Such a conclusion is suggested by the recent appearance of a number of studies concerned with occupational and industrial mobility which involve variations on the cohort approach and technical innovations in the handling of "mobility statistics" (Bogue, 1950; Rogoff, 1953; Glass, 1954; Blumen *et al.*, 1955). These studies, incidentally, provide evidence that methodological developments are likely to follow upon the expansion of demographers' substantive and theoretical interests into new fields.

In addition to the foregoing analytical methods, it should be noted that the current tendency to construct formal mathematical-statistical models, deterministic or stochastic, is evidenced in respect of demographic as well as other phenomena (Karmel, 1947, 1948*a, b;* Kendall, 1949; Yntema, 1952; Goodman, 1953; Henry, 1953). To date, however, with the exception of stable population theory, such model-building in demography has been relatively limited. Of a somewhat different character are the efforts of demographers to calculate empirical population "projections" which are further considered below.

Largely as a result of practical interests in population forecasts, the demographer has devoted considerable energy to population prediction and projection (see Grauman, chap. xxiii). The quantitative nature of demographic data and method lends itself readily to the calculation of future populations. But projections of future population often have diverged rather widely from the actual course of population change.

The errors in the estimates of future population for contemporary Western countries have generally been attributed primarily to the difficulty of anticipating the course of the birth rate and the magnitude of migration flows. Projections of future population based on the aging of the population already born, that is, projections based solely on mortality, under recent conditions have provided more accurate forecasts than projections of future population including the components of fertility and migration. The prediction of the course of the birth rate or of internal migration is much more hazardous than the prediction of mortality because of the much greater sensitivity (under modern conditions) of the former to variations in social, economic, and political variables. In consequence, the demographer can hardly predict the course of the birth rate or migration with great accuracy until students of other disciplines are able to achieve good predictability of such phenomena as the course of the business cycle, hot or cold wars, or technological developments. Moreover, it may be that demographic predictions will always have limitations imposed by "historicism." However, even if predictions were restricted to a relatively short period, such as a few decades or even a few years, they would still have considerable utility as devices for exploring the implications of current population trends or as bases for planning and administration.

As a result of the great changes in population phenomena produced by World War II, which belied many of the prewar expectations of demographers, it has been increasingly recognized that demographers have definite limitations in their ability to predict future populations (Davis, 1949). Demographers have become increasingly aware of the fact that they are able to make only conditional predictions, that is, predictions which are tied to specific assumptions. Thus, the demographer increasingly speaks of his predictions as "projections"—that is, indications of the course of population change within the framework of explicitly stated assumptions. The prudent demographer is now likely to be quite modest about the extent to which his "assumptions" may be expected to hold.

In the light of these developments population projections may be regarded as a form of model-building rather than as predictions or forecasts of events. They may often be used as if they were predictions or forecasts because they are the best that can be done in efforts to foresee population changes. But the demographer must admit that he is in no position to indicate whether his assumptions, usually based implicitly on the continuation of past trends in social, economic, political, and other events, will hold.

Population projections as models may, of course, have important analytical uses and, in consequence, may be thought of as analytical as well as predictive techniques. Variations in the assumptions on which projections are made may illuminate the interaction of demographic and non-demographic variables and thus help to "explain" as well as to predict. It is well to realize, however, that demographers have not ordinarily used the comparison of projected or predicted changes with actual changes as a means of testing the adequacy of explanatory theories.

This is not the place to review in detail the techniques of calculating future populations. Suffice it to say that the methods are, like the methods of current population estimation, classifiable into three types: forms of mathematical extrapolation, empirical forms of component projections, and combinations of the above methods. As in respect of other demographic techniques, the demographer has, on the whole, displayed technical competence in utilizing and adapting mathematical techniques of extrapolation and in devising empirical methods for calculating future populations, including the widely used techniques of component projection and ratio estimation.

REFERENCES

BLUMEN, ISADORE, *et al.* 1955. *The Industrial Mobility of Labor as a Probability Process.* Ithaca: Cornell University Press.

BOGUE, D. J. 1950. *An Exploratory Study of Migration and Labor Mobility Using Social Security Data.* Oxford, Ohio: Scripps Foundation.

———. 1952. "The Quantitative Study of Social Dynamics and Social Change," *American Journal of Sociology*, LVII, 565–68.

———, and DUNCAN, BEVERLY. 1958. "A Composite Method for Estimating Postcensal Population of Small Areas by Age, Sex, and Color," MS accepted for publication in *Vital Statistics—Special Reports*. Washington, D.C.: National Office of Vital Statistics.

COALE, ANSLEY J. 1955. "The Population

of the United States in 1950 Classified by Age, Sex, and Color: A Revision of Census Figures," *Journal of the American Statistical Association*, L, 16–54.

DAVIS, J. S. 1949. *The Population Upsurge in the United States.* Stanford, Calif.: Food Research Institute.

DEMING, W. E. 1944. "On Errors in Surveys," *American Sociological Review*, IX, 359–69.

DUBLIN, L. I., and LOTKA, A. J. 1925. "On the True Rate of Natural Increase," *Journal of the American Statistical Association*, XX, 305–39.

DUBLIN, L. I., LOTKA, A. J., and SPIEGELMAN, M. 1949. *Length of Life.* New York: Ronald Press.

DUNCAN, O. D. 1957. "Report of the Committee on the 1960 Census, Population Association of America," *Population Index*, XXIII, 293–305.

DURAND, JOHN D. 1950. "Adequacy of Existing Census Statistics for Basic Demographic Research," *Population Studies*, IV, 179–99.

ECKLER, A. Ross. 1953. "Extent and Character of Errors in the 1950 Census," *American Statistician*, VII, 15–19.

———, and HURWITZ, W. N. 1957. "Response Variance and Biases in Censuses and Surveys." Presented at meetings of International Statistical Institute, Stockholm; to be published.

———, and PRITZKER, LEON. 1951. "Measuring the Accuracy of Enumerative Surveys," *Bulletin of the International Statistical Institute*, Vol. XXXIII, Part 4.

EDWARDS, ALBA M. 1943. *Comparative Occupation Statistics for the United States, 1870 to 1940.* Washington, D.C.: Government Printing Office.

GLASS, D. V. (ed.). 1954. *Social Mobility in Britain.* Glencoe, Ill.: Free Press.

GOLD, DAVID. 1957. "A Note on Statistical Analysis in the *American Sociological Review*," *American Sociological Review*, XXII, 332–33.

GOODMAN, LEO A. 1953. "Population Growth of the Sexes," *Biometrics*, IX, 212–25.

HAJNAL, J. 1947. "The Analysis of Birth Statistics in the Light of the Recent International Recovery of the Birth-rate," *Population Studies*, I, 137–64.

HANSEN, M. H., HURWITZ, W. N., and MADOW, W. G. 1953. *Sample Survey Methods and Theory.* Vol. I: *Methods and Applications.* New York: John Wiley & Sons.

HANSEN, M. H., HURWITZ, W. N., and PRITZKER, L. 1953. "The Accuracy of Census Results," *American Sociological Review*, XVIII, 416–23.

HAUSER, P. M. 1941. "Research Possibilities in the 1940 Census," *American Sociological Review*, VI, 463–70.

HENRY, LOUIS. 1953. *Fécondité des mariages: Nouvelle méthode de mesure.* ("Travaux et documents de l'Institut National d'Études Démographiques," Cahier No. 16.) Paris: Presses Universitaires de France.

JAFFE, A. J. 1949. Book review, *American Sociological Review*, XIV, 442–43.

KAHN, R. L., and CANNELL, C. F. 1957. *The Dynamics of Interviewing.* New York: John Wiley & Sons.

KARMEL, P. H. 1947. "The Relations between Male and Female Reproduction Rates," *Population Studies*, I, 249–74.

———. 1948a. "The Relations between Male and Female Nuptiality in a Stable Population," *ibid.*, pp. 353–87.

———. 1948b. "An Analysis of the Sources and Magnitudes of Inconsistencies between Male and Female Net Reproduction Rates in Actual Populations," *ibid.*, II, 240–73.

KENDALL, D. G. 1949. "Stochastic Processes and Population Growth," *Journal of the Royal Statistical Society*, Ser. B, II, 230–64.

KITAGAWA, EVELYN M. 1955. "Components of a Difference between Two Rates," *Journal of the American Statistical Association*, L, 1168–94.

LAPLACE, P. S. 1812. *Théorie analytique des probabilités.* Paris.

LINDER, F. E., and GROVE, R. D. 1943. *Vital Statistics Rates in the United States, 1900–1940.* Washington, D.C.: Government Printing Office.

NOTESTEIN, F. W. 1955. "Gaps in Existing Knowledge of the Relationships between Population Trends and Economic and Social Conditions," in *Proceedings of the World Population Conference, 1954*, Vol. VI. New York: United Nations.

Rogoff, Natalie. 1953. *Recent Trends in Occupational Mobility*. Glencoe, Ill.: Free Press.

Russell, J. C. 1948. "Demographic Pattern in History," *Population Studies*, I, 388–404.

Shryock, H. S., Jr. 1950. "Opportunities for Social Research in the 1950 U.S. Census of Population," *American Sociological Review*, XV, 417–23.

——. 1957. "Development of Postcensal Estimates for Local Areas," in National Bureau of Economic Research, *Regional Income*. ("Studies in Income and Wealth," Vol. XXI.) Princeton: Princeton University Press.

Taeuber, Conrad. 1958. "Progress on 1960 Censuses of Population and Housing," *American Statistician*, XII, 8–9.

Thomas, Dorothy S. 1941. *Social and Economic Aspects of Swedish Population Movements*. New York: Macmillan Co.

United Nations. 1949. *Population Census Handbook*. New York: United Nations.

——. 1953. *Principles for a Vital Statistics System*. New York: United Nations.

——. 1957a. "Notes for a Methodology of Census Tests." (ST/STAT/P/L.24.) New York: United Nations (mimeographed for limited distribution).

——. 1957b. "Enumeration in Population Censuses." (ST/STAT/P/L.25.) New York: United Nations (mimeographed for limited distribution).

——. Various dates. "Sample Surveys of Current Interest," *Statistical Papers*, Ser. C. New York: United Nations.

United States Bureau of the Census. 1953. *Infant Enumeration Study, 1950*. Washington, D.C.: Government Printing Office.

——. 1957. *Statistical Abstract of the United States*. Washington, D.C.: Government Printing Office.

——. *Catalog of United States Census Publications*. Washington: Government Printing Office, published quarterly.

United States Department of Health, Education, and Welfare. 1957. "The National Health Survey Act," *Public Health Reports*, LXXII, 1–8.

United States National Committee on Vital and Health Statistics. 1957. "National Vital Statistics Needs," *Vital Statistics—Special Reports*, XLV, 219–69.

Whelpton, P. K. 1938. *Needed Population Research*. Lancaster, Pa.: Science Press.

——. 1954. *Cohort Fertility*. Princeton: Princeton University Press.

Wright, C. D., and Hunt, W. C. 1900. *History and Growth of the United States Census, 1790–1900*. Washington, D.C.: Government Printing Office.

Yates, Frank. 1949. *Sampling Methods for Censuses and Surveys*. New York: Hafner Publishing Co.

Yntema, L. 1952. *Mathematical Models of Demographic Analysis*. Leiden: J. J. Groen & N. V. Zoon.

4. Demography as a Body of Knowledge

PHILIP M. HAUSER AND OTIS DUDLEY DUNCAN

In a sense, science is like exploration: beginning in a small region whose contours have been charted, it expands over the world, bringing new continents to light, establishing their coastlines with ever greater precision, and adding more and more detail to the maps of their interiors. At any time the scientist's map of the universe, then, would show much information for some regions, sketchy data and conjectures for others, and expanses of unexplored territory for still others. Scientific progress would result in the shrinkage of the second two categories and would necessitate the preparation of more maps on larger scales to accommodate the accumulation of knowledge about the areas under exploration. Were this imagery accurate, one might take inventory at some point in time, indicating which areas are relatively well known, which are now being penetrated, and which remain virtually terra incognita.

There are, of course, grave difficulties with such a metaphor. The very development of science not only brings into view continents whose existence was hitherto unsuspected but itself creates an expansion of the universe to be investigated. In a very real sense, the more we know, the less we know, for new knowledge continually forces a reassessment of the relative importance of areas of ignorance.

FACTUAL INFORMATION

For the sake of a quick perspective, let us for the moment maintain a naïve view of the task of demographic science. What do we actually know of the most elemental facts of human population?

For temporal perspective, population history might be divided into (1) the half-million or million years of prehistory which witnessed the evolution of man to his modern form and the evolution of his culture (in certain areas) to the stage of settled communities of some size; (2) the pre-Christian period of history; (3) the Christian era, down to (4) the modern era, which as far as population history is concerned may be said to encompass the last three centuries.[1]

Little enough is known of biological and cultural evolution during prehistory, as the anthropologist would be quick to agree. Still less is known about the population phenomena of this period. Archeological data—skeletal remains and fragments of material culture—provide a basis only for rough inferences or guesses, supplemented as they may be with analogies from contemporary primitive peoples. (Very few of the latter, in fact, have been subject to more than the most cursory demographic study.) This whole period, then, is almost entirely demographic "terra incognita." One may expect the quantity and value of the conjectures about it to increase as archeologists and physical anthropologists come to appre-

[1] This paragraph and the ones to follow do not purport to state results of careful scholarship. Neither the symposium nor the background of the editors includes any substantial coverage of historical demography. The purpose of the discussion, as was indicated, is to provide a "quick perspective."

ciate the insights that may be gained from conceptualizing the life of prehistoric man in demographic as well as morphological and cultural terms.

From the dawn of history to the beginning of the Christian era (approximately) only the very haziest outlines of population developments have been discerned. Historians know, very roughly, the limits of the areas inhabited by "civilized" peoples and under their military control from time to time. The expansion of the ecumene can be depicted in broad terms, but what the population changes accompanying this expansion were is uncertain. That the several millenniums witnessed a slow growth of world population but at rates varying considerably from time to time seems highly probable; little effort has been made to estimate details of these changes except in a few very restricted areas and periods.

The justification for recognizing a third period, approximately coinciding with the beginning of the Christian era, is that some scholars have been willing to hazard fairly comprehensive guesses as to what the magnitude of world population and its general pattern of distribution were at that time. Bennett (1954, chap. i) cites estimates by Beloch and Wright of the numbers inhabiting the continent of Europe at the beginning of the era and four hundred years earlier. Various scholars have put together series purporting to show the growth of population in China since 400 B.C. (Taylor, 1956; Usher, 1956), although there is a good deal of variation in their interpretations of the source materials. Usher (1956) attempted a map of "stages of settlement" in Eurasia in A.D. 14; significantly, the next dates for which he gives comparable estimates are 1340 and 1600. Historians seem fairly confident about major cycles of population increase and decrease in the Mediterranean-European world during the Christian era

(Russell, 1956), and Bennett has ventured estimates of world population subdivided by continents at fifty-year intervals from A.D. 1000 on. None of the figures for this entire period, of course, is more than a carefully reasoned estimate, although greater confidence may be placed in the estimates for certain countries at certain times than for the figures for entire continents at any time during the entire period. None of the figures is derived from a "census" in the modern sense of the term; the available materials include partial counts and lists of various kinds to which highly approximate adjustment factors must be applied, and these are generously supplemented with conjectures based on fragmentary information about settlement patterns, subsistence techniques, trade activity, and the like. The analytical value of the estimates, say, for studies correlating population movements and economic changes is compromised by the fact that the population estimates depend in part on what is known or suspected about economic conditions—the two are not wholly independent items of information.

The "modern" period is dated from 1650, primarily because the estimates of world population by continents made by Willcox and Carr-Saunders for that date have been widely accepted by demographers as a basis for describing population trends since that time (Bennett, 1954; United Nations, 1956). These estimates, like those for earlier dates, are highly conjectural. However, the "modern" period does witness the beginning of considerable interest in the facts of population, manifested in the appearance of numerous contemporary population estimates. The beginnings of essentially modern forms of population enumeration and registration also fall within this period. In general, the more recent the date within this period, the greater the coverage of world population by censuses. Even the most recent figures for world population, however, incorporate estimates for fairly sizable populations. It is doubtless no accident that the "modern" period in terms of our knowledge of the facts of population growth coincides with the "modern" period in terms of patterns of growth. The period since 1650 has witnessed a growth of world population at continually increasing rates—rates considerably above those believed to prevail over any other extended interval during the last couple of millenniums. One might add that the concept of "world population" as anything more than an arbitrary summation of regional populations only begins to take on meaning within the modern period. During this period the major subdivisions of the world have become economically and socially interrelated to such a degree that population growth in one region responds more or less directly to conditions in other regions; prior to this time population trends in the various world regions probably moved in virtual independence of one another. This is not to say that in the modern period growth takes place at a uniform rate in all regions—far from it. But forces of commerce, settlement, immigration, cultural diffusion, and military conflict come to be global influences on population in this period.

It is clear that most of what demographers "know" about population pertains to the modern period, and to the more recent part of it, at that. Moreover, it seems certain that this will always be the case, with the exception that more may be learned about the future as it becomes the present. There is a great deal that can be done with the methods of historical and archeological investigation to establish a plausible generalized account of the character of population changes in the more or less remote past. But however prodigious the efforts of such investigators, they

will not be able to provide the counterpart of the relatively precise quantitative material available for populations subject to census and registration systems. This should be a sobering observation for anyone who cares to reflect on the status of demography as a science. If the basic data needed for what is now understood as demographic analysis are forever unavailable—except for the tiniest fraction of the period in which human populations have inhabited the earth—the generalizations reached by applications of demographic analysis must be appropriately limited in scope. In attempting broad propositions about the course of population change, demographers of course resort to largely deductive methods of historical reconstruction or typology (as in descriptions of "pre-industrial" or "high growth potential" populations). Whether these compare favorably with the kinds of retrospective extrapolations appearing in other sciences has seldom been discussed.

The situation is actually even more serious than has been indicated. What is "known" about population in the modern period pertains largely to populations which have themselves undergone "modernization," i.e., principally the populations of European countries and regions settled by Europeans. In identifying the "terra incognita" of demography, therefore, one needs not only the historical perspective of the preceding paragraphs but some assessment of the availability of information on a regional basis for the "modern" period. Some indication of the nature of the problem is given in Linder's paper (see Table 1, chap. xv). Whereas an estimated 99.7 per cent of the population of Europe was enumerated in a census sometime within the period 1945–54, the corresponding figure for Asia was 85.4 per cent, and for Africa only 63.7 per cent. The situation for the mid-twentieth century was no doubt more favorable than that at any preceding time.

What these facts mean is that knowledge of population change tends to be highly selective of populations and time periods in which rapid changes occur. The modern period as a whole, as was indicated, is one of rapid growth—world population is now five times as large as it was a scant three centuries ago. The countries for which the most data are available and about which most is known, on the whole, are those experiencing outstandingly high rates of growth during this period. It is not too much to say that this circumstance has given a strong bias to contemporary population theory. What is often regarded as the major theoretical accomplishment in the field is the theory of "demographic transition," i.e., a generalized account of the components of population change and the socioeconomic circumstances attending the rapid population growth of (primarily) European peoples in the modern period. One finds in the literature some discussion and documentation of populations not undergoing rapid secular growth—but primarily from the standpoint of their prospects for doing so ("high growth potential") or the consequences of their completion of a rapid growth cycle (countries of "incipient decline"). No doubt this bias reflects a preoccupation with problems thought to be relevant for contemporary population policy, as well as the differential availability of factual information. Whatever the explanation, it is almost certain that the contours of the relatively unexplored portion of the universe of demographic phenomena are strikingly different from those of the relatively well-explored portion.

Before dropping the analogy of scientific "exploration," still a third perspective should be suggested. Knowledge of total population size and rate of growth is, of course, only the starting point of the knowledge the demographer would like to accumulate. He is interested almost as much in the facts of population distribution and composition as in those of size and growth, and he aspires to measure the components of change in size, distribution, and composition. It may be taken as axiomatic that the knowledge of these matters is less complete than that of total numbers. Censuses, for example, vary greatly in subject-matter coverage and detail of tabulation, and in general they provide more meager information on composition and distribution the more remote the period in which they were taken. Similar comments apply to vital statistics and other sources of demographic data. Comments made earlier about the selectivity of knowledge on population change apply with even greater emphasis to knowledge of the components of population change. Although it is by no means true that demographers have analyzed all the data at their disposal, by and large the factual knowledge they have accumulated reflects the volume and adequacy of the available data. Hence the discussion of demographic data in chapter iii and the information in chapter xv of the symposium give a pretty good indication of what demographers know on the strictly factual level or what they can be expected to know as a result of ongoing research.

The "naïve" view of scientific exploration is, of course, inadequate for the assessment of a discipline as a body of scientific knowledge. The discussion has already acknowledged, implicitly, that a collection of census tables by itself does not constitute "knowledge." In the scientific sense, knowledge comprises not discrete "facts" but, at a minimum, critically analyzed information ordered in terms of a conceptual scheme. Moreover, the kind of knowledge to which a science aspires is of a general and abstract character, taking the form of an integrated set of propositions having both empirical validity and predictive, explanatory, and heuristic value. In short, scientific knowledge is "theoretical" knowledge, however rudimentary may be the "theory" within which facts find their place. Having indicated roughly the limitations on demographic knowledge arising from the selective availability of factual information on population, it is appropriate to review the character of the theoretical knowledge established by population research. It will be well to consider at some length the character of the theory with which students of population operate. As may be anticipated from earlier remarks, to take up "population theory" is to project the discussion out of the realm of "demography" in the strict sense of our earlier definition and into a consideration of alternative frames of reference in the study of population. Some issues that arise from the juxtaposition of such alternatives will emerge rather clearly in the treatment of theory.

POPULATION THEORY

Social scientists, including demographers, frequently voice one of two complaints about their respective disciplines: either the discipline is too much preoccupied with theory and theories, or it does not give enough attention to theory. A superficial review of intellectual history suggests that there is a cyclical alternation in the relative popularity of the two views. Whether or not this is a fair generalization, it seems to be true that students of population have become more conscious of supposed theoretical shortcomings in recent years than they were a couple of decades ago, and there seems to be less apprehension now than formerly that demography will succumb to the temptation to substitute "armchair" cogitation for empirical research.

The view that demography is short on theory is most succinctly stated in the symposium by Moore (chap. xxxiii): "If a standard complaint about sociology is that it has 'too much' theory, a standard complaint about demography is that it has 'too little.' What is generally meant in the case of sociology is that competing conceptual systems and theories have not been adjudicated and that empirical generalizations are often not related in any systematic way. What is generally meant in the case of demography is that a pervasive preoccupation with refinement of measurement and with *ad hoc* explanations for observations leads to an avoidance of the fundamental question, What do we want to know?" In similar vein Vance (1956, p. 88) states, "It seems some time since we have made any investment of our own in basic theory." These are not isolated judgments. For example, a sociologist refers to "the demographer's indifference to theory" (Jones, 1956, p. 42), and one of the editors of this volume has made casual reference to the "tendency . . . to produce discrete, descriptive studies with little or no attention to theoretical framework" (Hauser, 1956, p. 78).

Such assessments are not to be taken lightly, for if they have substance, they indicate basic inadequacies in at least one "part" of population study which must be impeding the advance of the field as a whole. Before accepting these judgments at face value, however, it is well to make a fairly careful survey of the field to determine wherein and to what degree they may be justified. We will consider first whether demographers and students of population appear to have an adequate conception of the nature and functions of theory in science. To anticipate the conclusion, it seems that they are reasonably sophisticated on this score. Consequently, any theoretical shortcomings cannot be charged wholly to a lack of appreciation of theory. Second, we shall examine selected bodies of theory and attempt, without summarizing them in detail, to bring out various issues that have arisen in connection with efforts to formulate theories of population.

Demographers' Conceptions of Theory

Students of population spend relatively little time in debating subtle points in the philosophy of science or in self-criticism at a very general methodological level. Consequently, one finds in the literature comparatively few discussions by demographers of the nature of scientific theory and related topics. It does not follow that demographers as a class are unusually naïve about such matters, for they doubtless are as fully exposed as anyone else to the methodological discussions that go on in other disciplines. The evidence of the present symposium is that demographers understand pretty well what science is all about and what theory has to do with it.

This symposium furnishes a sample of demographers' views on the role of theory, but it will be expeditious to supplement its materials by reference to a collection of papers reprinted under the title *Population Theory and Policy* (Spengler and Duncan, 1956), and to other essays. From these materials one can assemble a fairly representative selection of demographers' views on what constitutes scientific theory and what the functions of theory are. Following a somewhat informal digest of these views, attention will be given to some of the issues that may be involved in the evaluation of demography as a science from the standpoint of its theory.

What are the elements or "ingredients" of theory, as demographers have identified them? The term "theory" sometimes is used in a general and nontechnical way to refer to "men's views concerning the causes and the consequences of population movement and change" (Spengler and Duncan, 1956, p. 3); in this broad sense theory is inclusive of doctrine, speculation, discussion, investigation, and virtually any other treatment of population. The same authors note, however, that in the development of population theory, "conjectures" appeared early, to be superseded only fairly recently by "explanatory principles," which in turn tended to find their place in "an organized body of scientific knowledge centered about population" in the late eighteenth century.

Another somewhat casual use of the term "theory" identifies it with the semi-speculative elaboration of highly general "laws" of population growth. Among the "theories" of population of this kind that demographers still sometimes discuss are those of Marx, Sadler, Doubleday, Spencer, Gini, Dumont, and Carr-Saunders, many of which are polemically oriented to the views of Malthus (Spengler and Duncan, 1956, pp. 5–54). It is probably true that a majority of contemporary demographers with strong empirical orientations regard such broad "theories" or speculative generalizations as discredited and question their value even as patterns for the kind of theoretical development that students of population should attempt. Insofar as one finds among some demographers a lingering antagonism to the very idea of "theory," such antagonism is doubtless directed in large part to this kind of theorizing.

Coming to the more limited and specific usages of the term "theory" and the more careful considerations of what theory comprises, several "kinds" of theory may be identified. Lorimer, in chapter vi, presents a statement on "analytical theory" described as the "mathematical development of . . . necessary relations" among population phenomena (see also A. J. Lotka, 1956*a*, *b*); this type of theory is contrasted with the "purely hypothetical construction" of a contingent relationship, such as is found in the logistic growth formula (Lorimer, chap. vi). Another contributor describes theory as a "group of related empirical generalizations" (Moore, chap. xxxiii). Elsewhere, "theory" seems to be used synonymously with "models into which enter functional relations, the general character and direction of which, but not their specific and concrete content, are known" (Spengler, chap. xxxii). The notions of "frame of reference" and "referential concepts" are employed in one contribution (Duncan, chap. xxviii), and the importance of developing "concepts" useful for population theory is stressed in another (Vance, chap. xiv). The use of "theoretical estimating models" employing "stable relationships" derived from empirical studies is described by Grauman (chap. xxiii). At least one paper in the symposium discusses purported "laws" of population, but in the sense of fairly specific empirical uniformities (Dorn, chap. xix).

One formal attempt to indicate a "specific sense" for the term "theory" suggests that it embraces "both the construction and use of hypotheses and the transformation of hypotheses, together with what already is known, into models designed to represent reality in relatively simple and comprehensible terms." It is further suggested that the function of theory is "to make data meaningful, to reveal what relationships obtain, to disclose what data are important, and to permit economical use of data" (Spengler and Duncan, 1956, p. 86). A slightly different emphasis is found in a volume with "theory" in its title which refers to "the complex of related definitions, classifications, and hypotheses which give potential facts their meaning." It also indicates that one of the primary objects of "theory construction" or "model-building" is "the careful formulation of a set of interrelated ideas from which it is possible to deduce meaningful theorems, by which we mean simply a body of conceivably refutable propositions" (Leibenstein, 1954, p. 5). An unusually (for demography) explicit discussion of the elements of theory indicates that there are at least four: a "frame of reference," a "set of deductive propositions" which concern interrelationships among variables which the frame of reference defines, a "set of empirical propositions" which have been verified by systematic observation, and "crude empirical propositions" which have been thus far validated only by common-sense observation (Davis, 1955, p. 542).

Some of the functions of theory are implied in the statements already cited; nonetheless, it is well to inquire explicitly what demographers think theory does.

"Analytical theory," according to its exponents, provides a "frame for empirical investigations" (Lorimer, chap. vi), or as Lotka put it, "formal relations will serve us as guides in the examination and interpretation of the empirical data" (1956, p. 135). Moreover, such theory may be used to "discover relations not otherwise apparent among actual processes" (Lorimer, chap. vi). Whereas "the study of necessary relations . . . can never reveal to us any fact of which the truth is not already contained in the premises," such truths and the interrelations of facts are not necessarily self-evident and have to be brought out "in the investigation of general demography by the deductive method" (Lotka, 1956*a*, p. 96). (What is here called "analytical theory" is sometimes referred to by other writers as "pure theory" or "formal theory.")

The theoretical role of the "frame of reference," as described by Davis (1955), is to "define variables," and the frame of reference is "mainly a matter of purposive definition." It "provides a systematic criterion of relevance" and "a set of interrelated categories in terms of which an empirical system is to be described." It may be used to discover instances in which phenomena have failed to be "fully described within the system" and thus as an aid in locating "important gaps in available knowledge." A somewhat different function is suggested by Frank (chap. xxvii): "at least some general population theory may provide a frame of reference: it should be able to define limits within which all organic populations must exist." Analogously, Moore indicates that "one major function of sociological theory at the highest level of generalization is the identification of universals in social systems," a contention relevant to the present inquiry, inasmuch as "a view of human societies in terms of requisite functions explicitly brings demographic variables into the scheme of sociological theory" (chap. xxxiii).

Thomas (chap. xxii) maintains that the "formulation of questions to be addressed to the empirical data necessarily entails model-building," and he indicates that "theorists have applied a variety of methods" at "different levels of abstraction" to this end; reasons are given for supposing that "construction of models" will be of aid in filling "important gap[s] in our fundamental concepts." Vance (1956, p. 92) states that "the function of theory is not to give answers to all questions which may arise; rather it is to see that in the unfolding of science the 'right' questions get asked in the 'right' context."

Moore implies that "generalizations can be derived" from an appropriate "theoretical approach" and that a suitable theory "provides avenues for . . . wider empirical generalizations" (chap. xxxiii). Spengler suggests that through the "use of theory and models" certain "effects of demographic change" can be

ascertained, and "their magnitude is roughly determinable, even in the absence of much information" (chap. xxxii). More specifically, Lotka (1956*a*, p. 96) points out that "the study of Population Analysis along deductive lines . . . enables us, on occasion, to obtain indirectly information for which the direct observational data have not been, or for one reason or another can not be, obtained," and Grauman (chap. xxiii) states that "theoretical estimating models" can be constructed "from which quantities can be inferred that are consistent with some given quantities *under average conditions.*" These claims may be compared with the caution voiced by Leibenstein (1954, p. 6) regarding the example of "theory construction or model-building" with which he is concerned. It cannot, he states, "in any way add to the stock of factual knowledge in the sense of additional empirical or historical information," although it "may lead to one or more non-trivial theorems or propositions that can be put in such form as to be conceivably falsifiable by empirical research." He notes, however, that "a theory need not be correct to be useful," inasmuch as the questions it raises (a function already mentioned) may lead to a correct theory.

The function of theory in organizing knowledge is stressed by some writers. Thus Vance suggests that theory could provide for demography "a binder for its diverse findings" (1956, p. 88). Moore believes that the "theory of demographic transition" can provide "integration with sociological theory" and "incorporation of other areas of demographic research into a 'main body' of principles of social, including demographic, change" (chap. xxxiii).

It may be an accident of sampling, but it is curious that in the discussions under review not much emphasis is placed on "explanation" as a function of theory. However, Westoff (1956, p.

401) refers to "theories which were advanced to explain . . . relationships discovered" and were "largely of the so-called 'ex post facto' variety and at best . . . can be considered as only more or less plausible inferences." He appears to suggest that explanations are better generated as "analytical hypotheses" formulated in advance of studies. Two closely related functions are identified by Peacock (1956, p. 202). In his view a suitable population theory has "general interpretative value," insofar as it clarifies issues in discussions, although it is incapable of resolving questions of fact. Secondly, it may have "use for prediction purposes."

In a tentative synthesis of the materials so far presented, one may conclude that, according to demographers, the "ingredients" of theory include: (*a*) concepts defined within a frame of reference; (*b*) empirical propositions, generalizations, or laws (which may vary in generality and credibility); (*c*) propositions, hypotheses, or theorems deduced or constructed from other elements of theory, with these taking the form of (*d*) "necessary relations," "models" incorporating necessary and/or empirical relations, or "purely hypothetical constructions." One might, therefore, be said to be "theorizing" if he were engaged in such diverse activities as defining new concepts, elaborating a frame of reference, stating assumptions, making deductions, or constructing explanatory or predictive models.

If the last statement is accepted, it can be interpolated here that a good deal of "theorizing" in demography takes the form of making what are called "population projections" (discussed in chap. xxiii). A projection is the deduction, from a set of assumed quantities and relationships, of a "model" of future population change. Although projections often are made with the intent of supplying or suggesting a forecast of future events, it has been emphasized, by Hajnal (1955, p. 309) among others, that "a projection can be useful as a piece of analysis even if its accuracy is low."

In summary of the functions of theory alluded to by demographers, it appears that theory may be used to organize knowledge; guide or frame empirical research, furnish criteria of relevance, or raise questions for investigation; define variables; identify "universals" and limits of empirical variation; disclose gaps in knowledge; infer unknown quantities; generate propositions; explain relationships; interpret facts; and predict. The emphasis placed on one or another of these functions may vary, of course, from one demographer to another, as may the amount of attention given to each of the several listed "ingredients" of theory.

The foregoing somewhat atomistic summary of the views of various population students on the nature of theory and the functions of theory probably does scant justice to any one of them. Nonetheless, certain critical observations appear to be in order, without implying that the criticisms pertain to any one writer in particular.

To begin with, in comparison with the conception of the nature and objectives of science stated in chapter ii, there is relatively little emphasis in the statements of demographers on the explanatory and predictive functions of theory. At least in the opinion of many writers on scientific method, what distinguishes propositions of a "theoretical" character from mere empirical generalizations is that the former state considerations as a consequence of which certain empirical regularities are expected to obtain and indicate conditions under which such regularities will hold; i.e., theories are supposed to "explain" and "predict" the facts at the command of a discipline. Moreover, the greater the number and variety of such facts that are brought under the scope of a theory, the more powerful the theory is supposed to be. If this crucial feature of scientific theory is neglected, it becomes possible to accept as "theories" various bodies of discourse which incorporate several of the ingredients of theory (such as concepts, definitions, and deductions) but which fail to perform the principal function of theory. It may well be, for example, that one of the typical shortcomings of population theories is that they are stated so generally or abstractly that they fail to "make contact" with the facts or with regularities which have thus far been established empirically or, what comes down to the same thing, that their predictions are of such a general character that they are not readily refuted or confirmed by evidence now available or likely soon to become available.

Second, the preceding criticism may be closely related to the fact that demographers appear to emphasize insufficiently that "theory" is but one element or aspect of a corpus of scientific knowledge which does not develop in isolation from other aspects of science. Thus, in failing to emphasize sufficiently the distinctive function of theory, demographers may also have neglected to bring out the close interrelationship between theoretical development, the accumulation of substantive knowledge, and the verification of hypotheses.

Third, it is not evident in the cited writings of demographers that "theories" may be stated at widely varying levels of generality and with greater or lesser scope of applicability. It is possible that some of the concern over lack of theory in population studies reflects a failure to recognize that the functions of theory can be performed at different levels of specificity and that each level is potentially significant for some purposes. For example, a "theory" at the least specific level may merely indicate what variables are related to popula-

tion variation and change. The content of the "theory" would then be in the form, "Y, a dimension of population variation or change, is explained by variables $X_1, X_2 \ldots X_n$." More specifically, the "theory" may be able to specify in qualitative terms how these several variables are interrelated; or it may go further and suggest the direction of the effect of one variable on another, perhaps specifying the mathematical form of a model of population change, without being able to supply the actual values of the parameters in the model. At the most specific levels a "theory" may actually permit the derivation of numerical estimates of such parameters or, finally (as in the case of a population projection, for example), predict the value of some particular variable to be observed at a specified place and time. It would appear that the level of generality and the scope of applicability of theories are related in such a way that it is difficult to achieve the level of specificity desired while maintaining as broad a scope as would be desired. To achieve broad scope, it may be necessary to go to the level of least specificity, at which the most a theory can say is that "such and such factors are probably involved." Of course, the "explanations" and "predictions" yielded by a theory at this level are likely to be so vague as to be trivial and uninteresting. On the other hand, where a theory specifies a mathematical form for certain interrelationships (the logistic theory of population growth is a good example for the point at issue here, apart from other considerations which call into question its acceptability as a theory), it is likely to be found that it applies only under certain special circumstances; moreover, it may prove impossible to specify exactly what these circumstances are. In sum, a richer conception of the levels of generality of population theories would enable demographers to develop more useful notions of the functions they may expect population theories to perform.

A final observation on demographers' conceptions of theory is that most of the writers appear to assume that population theory should emanate from a single frame of reference, whether it be that of some single discipline (such as sociology) or that of a hypothetical "multiscience" but "integrated" discipline of population study. They appear, in general, to have overlooked the implications of the fact that studies of population are conducted from a wide variety of frames of reference and that the explanations and predictions stemming from one may be quite different in character from those produced by another. In particular, insufficient attention seems to have been given to specifying the relationship between the mode of explanation in terms of "components of change" (which we identified earlier as the characteristic type of explanation afforded by demographic analysis per se) and "causal," "functional," "motivational," or other kinds of explanation afforded by the theories prevailing in the several disciplines giving systematic attention to population. Some further consideration of this problem appears a little later in connection with our discussion of "psychosocial theories of fertility."

Some Issues in Evaluating Population Theory

The preceding materials are sufficient to demonstrate the generally sophisticated, though not wholly adequate, conceptions of the nature and function of scientific theory held by demographers and students of population. To venture any evaluation of the status of population theory, however, requires some account of the kinds of theoretical developments that have occurred in the field and the issues to which these give rise. It is, of course, impossible to review here the entire corpus of popula-

tion theories, but it is feasible to pick out some of the major kinds of theoretical work that have attracted considerable attention and to sketch certain of the issues that arise in connection with this work.

Analytical theory.—In chapter vi Lorimer presents some of the problems that have arisen in connection with recent developments in what he calls "analytical theory." His review brings out certain "difficulties" that arise in "practical applications of stable population theory" and that raise "fundamental questions of a theoretical nature." Whereas "analytical theory" was conceived by Lotka as a development of "necessary relations," it appears that his "stable population theory is . . . an abstraction, which is very convenient and efficient in many respects, but which is logically incomplete and, under some conditions, may be erroneous." This passage is significant in suggesting the criterion of "completeness" for a body of analytical theory. It seems appropriate to consider some implications of this criterion.

The way in which the "incompleteness" of Lotka's "analytical theory" of the stable population came to be recognized is adequately described by Lorimer. In brief, it seems to come down to the point that when the "frame of reference" (in the terminology of Davis and others) was broadened to take explicit account of certain variables (sex composition of the population, nuptiality, order of birth) that Lotka had ignored, some of the "necessary relations" involving relationships among the original variables and the additional ones turned out to involve logical inconsistencies or to require assumptions unacceptable on empirical grounds.

One can use a quite simple and homely example to show how this can happen. Demographers make frequent use of the "inflow-outflow" relationship, $P_t = P_0 + B - D + I - O$, where P_t is the size of a population at the end of a t-year period, P_0 is its initial size, and the remaining symbols represent, respectively, the births, deaths, in-migration, and out-migration occurring over the interval. Among other things, this relationship is used to estimate net migration, i.e., the quantity $(I - O)$, given two censuses and the vital statistics of the intercensal period (see Bogue, chap. xxi). The demographer is, of course, here employing the "necessary relation," $I - O = P_t - P_0 - B + D$, which has been deduced on the assumptions involved in this little piece of "analytical theory." Now, apart from errors in the population enumerations and the vital statistics, it is "necessary" for this method to yield an exact value for the net migration quantity. But suppose that P_0 and P_t refer to the initial and terminal populations of a city which annexes some populated territory during the interval. The net migration to the city, in respect to its boundaries at the terminal date, will be estimated with an error approximating in size that of the annexed population. (In applications of the residual method of estimating net migration, demographers try to make appropriate corrections for sizable annexations.) Clearly the "analytical theory" represented by the inflow-outflow relationship encounters "difficulties" in "practical applications," which, if they do not raise "fundamental questions of a theoretical nature," at least force one to recognize that the theory is "incomplete and, under some conditions, may be erroneous." When the "frame of reference" is broadened to take account of an additional variable, modification of territorial boundaries, some of the supposed "necessary relations" are recognized to be factually unacceptable.

If, in this example, P_t and P_0 were used to represent the terminal and initial size of the urban population of a country, the formula would produce an erroneous estimate of net migration to urban territory, not only because some cities annex territory but because some rural places increase in size and become reclassified as urban (or some urban places decline and are reclassified as rural). Again, to avoid misleading implications of the original "necessary relations," the demographer is forced to broaden his "frame of reference."

It appears, therefore, that there is something of a contingent character even in "necessary relations" which have been carefully deduced, particularly if they appear in a somewhat complex body of "analytical theory." It is hard to be sure that all the consequences of such a theory have been worked out, and there is always the possibility that a broadening of the frame of reference will force recognition of certain implications that are unacceptable.

Viewed in this light, there is perhaps not quite so marked a difference between "analytical theory of necessary relations" and "a purely hypothetical construction that may, in some situations, have useful applications," as Lorimer suggests in referring to the "radical distinction" between the two (chap. vi). Both, it appears, "under some conditions may be erroneous." The real distinction between the two is, perhaps, that a "purely hypothetical construction," or what some of the writers previously cited might prefer to call a "model," usually makes it explicit that its frame of reference is quite limited and that certain variables of acknowledged empirical relevance have been ignored in the interest of convenience or simplicity. It is somewhat curious, as a matter of fact, that Lorimer chose to contrast the "logistic formula . . . as a purely hypothetical construction" with Lotka's stable population theory as an example of "necessary relations." In fact, Lotka (1956b and other publications) developed quite a body of "analytical theory" pertaining to logistic growth. Moreover, if the descriptive adequacy of the two constructs were in question, it would doubtless prove possible to exhibit many more empirical examples of growth conforming approximately to the logistic curve than of growth exhibiting the properties of a stable population.

In short, recognition of the criterion of "completeness" leads to the observation that deductive elaboration of assumptions can produce "models" or bodies of "theory" which are only more or less "complete" and consequently more or less serviceable in respect to several of the functions that theory is said to perform: inference, interpretation, explanation, prediction, hypothesis formation, and so on. Indeed, any such construction is by necessity *empirically* incomplete, for it is practically impossible to include in it all variables that may be empirically relevant.

Some further insight on the nature of "analytical theory" is gained by referring to a problem that has been tackled by means of such theory in recent years —in the phraseology of one of the contributions, "the cause of the ageing of populations: declining mortality or declining fertility?" (United Nations, 1954). Students of this problem have been at some pains to point out that "it is a common misconception that the ageing of populations is, or has been, chiefly, if not entirely, the result of declines in mortality" (*ibid.*, p. 30). This conclusion, which appears contrary to "common sense" and to the common knowledge that larger proportions of cohorts now survive to old age than was the case formerly, has been supported by a variety of analytical studies and models. The immediate issues that arise in connection with this work, accordingly, have to do with the appropriateness of the models or analytical methods. It is impossible to enter into the details of these matters, but certain general problems or issues can be pointed out.

In the first place, none of the investigations attempts to "explain" fully any particular observed age distribution or set of observed changes in age distribution. To accomplish the most elementary resolution of such a distribution or set of changes into its components would require reference to the actual movements—both transitory and secular—of natality, mortality, and migration over a period of at least a century. In particular, the investigators have abstracted from the effects of migration by assuming closed populations. Moreover, in one way or another, they have concerned themselves primarily with what may be termed "long-run" changes in age distribution. This requires some formulation of what the pertinent "long-run" changes are, as distinct from observed changes. In the method of analysis proposed by Stolnitz, it turns out that "the age-distribution effects of a given mortality movement are much more readily analyzed in relation to the distribution that would be found at successive periods without such movement, than in relation to the initial distribution" (Stolnitz, 1956b, p. 209). Or, as Coale observes, "We cannot provide a usefully clear analysis of the general case of an arbitrary initial age distribution, arbitrary initial vital rates, and arbitrary vital rate changes. One reason that this case is too complicated is that the age distribution would typically change from its initial form even if the birth and death rates were to remain unaltered" (Coale, 1956, p. 79). Thus, whereas both writers attempt to make their conclusions as "general" as possible, they are forced to make comparisons between alternative hypothetical courses of events as a means of demonstrating their conclusions rather than to rely wholly on the study of variation among empirical instances.

A second point about these studies is that their results depend in part on certain empirical hypotheses or generalizations which are incorporated into the models or analytical framework—in particular, propositions setting forth "typical" patterns of mortality change, based on historical experience. Consequently, the conclusion that "mortality changes tend to have rather limited effect on age structure" (Stolnitz, 1956*b*, p. 178) is not wholly a consequence of the mathematically necessary interrelations of natality, mortality, and age distributions; moreover, inasmuch as the "typical" patterns of mortality change which have been studied derive from past observations, one may "contemplate that the earlier conclusion [that Western mortality trends have fostered the aging of their populations], though based on incorrect reasoning, may yet be borne out by events" (Stolnitz, 1956*b*, p. 215).

A final observation on the age-distribution studies is that they are subject to somewhat the same difficulties as stable population models (which have, in fact, been used in several of these studies); i.e., certain of the assumptions made in the analysis of effects of vital-rates changes on age distributions may turn out to imply empirically questionable hypotheses. In most of the investigations, the procedure has been to "hold constant" fertility to examine effects of mortality changes and to compare the results thus obtained with those produced by fertility changes with mortality "held constant." This procedure, of course, presumes that it is meaningful to postulate the independence of mortality and natality changes. It seems doubtful that such a condition could hold over any very extended period. One of the investigations of age distributions observes:

There is only one sense in which it can be said that the decline in mortality has caused populations to age substantially. At least in the very long run, the level of fertility cannot be entirely dissociated from that of mortality. High fertility, combined with low mortality, results in a rate of population growth which cannot be sustained indefinitely. . . . Hence, unless mortality were to rise again, fertility must eventually also decrease—though possibly at a very much later time [United Nations, 1954, p. 83].

But apart from this relationship, even a short-run change in mortality seems likely to have some impact on natality. If infant mortality declines, couples would have to reduce their fertility by an amount equivalent to the number of infant lives saved if "effective fertility" were not to undergo change. An increase in the probability of surviving through the childbearing period would require changes in nuptial birth rates if total birth rates were to remain constant. Conversely, a change in fertility has the effect of modifying exposure to risk of death from causes associated with childbirth and is, therefore, likely to have an impact on mortality. Whatever the net effects of these and other plausible interrelations of fertility and mortality, they serve to indicate that, like stable population theory, the mode of analysis used in studying determinants of age distribution is "an abstraction, which is very convenient and efficient in many respects, but which is logically incomplete and, under some conditions, may be erroneous."

Malthusian theory.—It would serve no purpose here to review the history of Malthusian controversy, but it should be pointed out that the volume and vigor of this controversy have conspired to keep Malthus' views before the eyes of population students for over a century and a half. It is probably true that most, if not all, of the criticisms of Malthus vouchsafed by modern writers are to be found in the writings of his contemporaries and immediate successors (Smith, 1951). However, the better discussions of the present day have signifi-

cant advantages over those of the past:
access to the accumulation of verified
knowledge about the complex course of
population changes since the time of
Malthus and, presumably, a more sophisticated conception of the nature
and functions of scientific theory, including a distinction between theory
and pronouncements on questions of
policy. Discussions of Malthus which
do not capitalize on at least one of these
advantages, though numerous, may be
ignored for present purposes.

It hardly needs to be mentioned that
no competent and responsible student
of population today indorses Malthus'
work without qualification. The major
issues about Malthusian theory, instead,
seem to be of two kinds: whether to
emphasize the qualifications that must
be placed on Malthus' presentation or
the values remaining in an appropriately reformulated version of Malthusian
theory, and whether such a reformula-
tion, even if free of logical and empirical difficulties, is adequate and sufficiently specific to serve as a basis for
further research and analysis. These
issues are well illustrated in the following summaries of some recent commentaries on Malthus.

A noteworthy statement of the deficiencies of Malthus' writing on the theory of population is that of Davis
(1955), which has already been referred
to in connection with its unusually clear
explication of the nature and functions
of scientific theory. Davis examines successively Malthus' frame of reference,
his theory as a deductive system, and
the empirical generalizations which
Malthus advanced. He finds serious
conceptual inadequacies in the frame
of reference, partly attributable to Malthus' failure to distinguish scientific
from moral ideas; faults in the logical
structure of Malthus' arguments; and
defects in the empirical evidence on
which Malthus relied. Moreover, Malthus' lack of appreciation of the sepa-

rate, if complementary, roles of these
elements of theory is held responsible
for a lack of clarity and consistency in
his presentation and for various weaknesses in his conclusions. On the whole,
Davis' paper is an elegant critique of
the *Essay on Population* which either
reiterates or subsumes most of the significant contributions of earlier critics;
it is a valuable statement of the need
for correcting "those who praise Malthus because they believe his theories
are valid, and those who dispraise him
because they believe his views are unimportant."

Of the writers who have chosen to
emphasize enduring values in Malthus'
work, some have pointed to important
aspects of his work that are sometimes
neglected, while others have brought
out the potentialities of a modernized
statement of the general Malthusian
framework. Representative of the former category is Spengler's (1945) recapitulation of the "*whole* of Malthus's
population theory," laying stress on
views stated in Malthus' *Principles of
Political Economy* which commonly are
overlooked by commentators. It is pointed out, for example, that while Malthus
regarded the available means of subsistence as setting the upper limit to
population growth, the course of
growth prior to reaching such a maximum depended on the effective demand
for labor; moreover, he gave considerable attention to industrialization both
as a means of dissolving obstacles to
the expansion of the demand for labor,
and consequently to the growth of population, and as a factor instituting conditions favorable for controlling population growth.

Two noteworthy restatements of
Malthusian theory, using the tools of
modern economic analysis and stressing
its value as a general system, are those
by Peacock (1956) and Boulding
(1955). Peacock suggests that the "theory is a more general one than is some-

times supposed"; that it is not merely a static "equilibrium theory," but encompasses both short-run oscillations and secular changes; that the "Malthusian analytical framework" can be used to advantage even if one questions the "general validity of the Malthusian assumptions"; and that Malthusian theory must be conceded at least to have "general interpretative value" as a "theory of economic development" as well as specific "applicability . . . at least in the short run, to certain areas." At one point Peacock appears to concede that the "level of abstraction" of the reformulated Malthusian analysis may appear excessive: "the attempt to proceed by successive approximations towards reality seems to take us away from reality altogether. We are prepared to accept the broad strokes of the Malthusian brush to rivet our attention on a fundamental problem, but once we modify the picture with the details required by actual conditions, we seem to lose sight of the significant problem." Boulding contends that the Malthusian model "in its generalized form is applicable to almost any situation of population equilibrium or even dynamics." Like Peacock (and many other writers), he feels that "the Malthusian system, especially as an *equilibrium* system, throws light on many historical situations." Moreover, the system is readily elaborated in terms of dynamic models. In fact, the "very richness of the dynamic-model universe is an embarrassment. The real world is more complex than any of them, and on a priori considerations one model is not much better than another." Nevertheless, study of the simpler dynamic models is claimed to be valuable as a guide to parameters that may be found in the real world.

Optimum theory.—Like Malthusian theory, optimum theory from time to time is pronounced dead by its critics; nonetheless, there continues to be a fairly steady stream of writing on the subject, even if it no longer appears to be at the center of interest. It is, of course, no guarantee of the validity or even the significance of an idea that it inspires discussion, and a great many demographers with primarily empirical interests doubtless agree that the optimum is an example of a "concept forever stillborn" (Vance, 1956, p. 90).

One problem that plagues population theory and research is especially salient in regard to optimum theory: the difficulty of separating normative considerations oriented to problems of policy from factual considerations oriented to research problems. The very term "optimum," of course, signals the intrusion of normative elements into the discussion of population. In fact, a good share of the literature on optimum population is concerned with deciding what criterion is the appropriate one on which to determine an optimum. Clearly, this is an issue which cannot be resolved solely on empirical grounds or by scientific theorizing alone.

There are, however, two kinds of question whose answers are not, in principle, beyond the reach of scientific methods. First, given a supposed relation, $y = y(P)$, in which the variable y is asserted to vary with population, it is, in principle, possible to investigate the existence and form of the relation and to determine whether there is a unique value of P (or range of values) that maximizes y. In making such a determination, it is, of course, necessary in one way or another to take account of other variables which may also be related to y. Whether these operations can be satisfactorily executed with available data is another question. Significantly, the problem is usually treated in purely deductive fashion on *ceteris paribus* assumptions about the other variables. Second, it is possible, again in principle, to determine the relationship of y to some other variable, say x, which likewise may be related to population by a function $x = x(P)$. If the behavior of such functions has been established by scientific methods, the implications of substituting x for y as a criterion of optimum population become much clearer. It may be that y and x are so highly correlated that it makes little or no difference which is the criterion, or they may be so loosely related that optimum population on the one basis is quite different from that on the other. In this measure, then, scientific investigation can make a contribution to the problem of choosing a criterion, without ever being able to resolve the problem of choice per se. It should be mentioned, finally, that (in principle) the scientific side of studies on optimum population can be carried out in terms of some index number, defined, say, as $I \equiv I(x, y)$, investigating the form of its relationship to population, $I = f(P)$, existence of maximum values of I, and circumstances affecting the influence of P on I. Again, however, the acceptance of the index function, $I(x, y)$, as a criterion of optimum population is governed by extra-scientific considerations.

The gist of optimum theory—as an empirical theory, as distinguished from a normative theory—is very simple. Given a criterion, y, the theory asserts that for a specified set of relevant conditions the function $y(P)$ increases over a range of "low" values of P, reaches a maximum, and then decreases as P increases; i.e., $y = y(P)$ is a curve concave to the X-axis with a single hump. This theory—or perhaps more accurately, hypothesis—is deduced on the following kinds of assumptions: a criterion of optimum population, y, usually per capita real income or some closely related variable, is given; conditions with respect to such variables affecting y as resources, technology, and patterns of social organization are assumed to be fixed; and some components (notably

those responding to economies of scale or the division of labor) of the aggregate y are assumed to be subject to increasing returns with increasing P, and others (notably those dependent on extraction of fixed resources) to diminishing returns. On these assumptions, $y(P)$ will have a maximum value at some point, P_o, of intermediate value with respect to the range of P. This value will depend, among other things, on the relative importance of the two kinds of components of y.

To indicate the various refinements that can be made of this formulation is unnecessary for the present purpose, which is to bring out the major issues raised by optimum theory. Some of these issues may be listed in summary fashion: First, the *choice of criterion*, as has been indicated, involves extra-scientific considerations but is subject to clarification by scientific methods, notably in respect to the character of the index-number problem involved in using any aggregative or multivariable criterion of the optimum (Peacock, 1957). Second, the theory is *static*; influences on y, other than P, are held constant. This means, fundamentally, that the nature of the function $y = y(P)$ cannot be established by direct empirical observation, because when P varies in the real world there is also concomitant variation in technology and organization, among other things. Third, the static character of the theory is in contrast to the *volatility of the optimum*, which must be subject to greater or lesser variation with changes in relevant circumstances, including opportunities for trade with other populations. Fourth, optimum theory may entail assumptions about the covariation of population size and population composition that are unacceptable; a population of optimum size may be one with an age composition relatively unfavorable to per capita productivity. In this instance, as in others, the *ceteris paribus* assumption may actually involve logical inconsistencies or unacceptable empirical hypotheses. Finally, these several difficulties call into question both the possibility of *ascertaining the optimum* and of *achieving an optimum population* through the exercise of available population policies (Leibenstein, 1954, chap. ix). Whether or not optimum theory is acceptable as a guide for policy, like the choice of a criterion, involves extra-scientific considerations; but it is, in principle, open to scientific methods to determine whether a given set of policies empirically can produce a population of optimum size. The likelihood that any readily available policies could do so is considered low by critics of optimum theory.

Various answers to these objections to optimum theory have been offered. Possibilities for casting the theory in dynamic, rather than static, terms have been indicated (Leibenstein, 1954, chap. ix). Proponents of optimum theory, conceding that the optimum is subject to change, have given reasons for supposing that it is not highly volatile and, in particular, that it has not increased rapidly in recent decades in industrial countries. Admitting that optimum theory is not a sufficient basis for policy, the proponent may insist that good evidence of an actual population well below or well in excess of the optimum is a highly relevant consideration for framing policy. Finally, despite the difficulties in ascertaining a unique value of the optimum at any given time, the theory is asserted to have value in directing attention to the phenomenon of depressing effects of population growth on per capita income and the desirability of investigating the status of various industries in respect to increasing or decreasing returns (Gottlieb, 1956).

One is led to the conclusion that the potential contributions of optimum theory, whatever they may be, have been prejudiced by the combination of normative and empirical considerations in the framework of a single doctrine and that, partly as a result of this, there has not been a vigorous prosecution of the kind of empirical research suggested by optimum theory (the last point is readily admitted by proponents of optimum theory; see Gottlieb, 1956).

Transition theory.—Certain of the writers (notably Moore and Vance) whose views on the nature of population theory were indicated earlier have cited the "theory of demographic transition" as an example of the kind of theory needed in population studies. No doubt this opinion would be indorsed by a goodly number of demographers, as may be judged from the frequency with which favorable allusions are made to transition theory.

One major aspect of the theory is the "generalization of the historical demographic experience of Western countries which have achieved very low levels of mortality and fertility" (van Nort and Karon, 1955, p. 523). The growth of European peoples in the modern era involved declining mortality, which was produced by "the whole process of modernization" including "rising levels of living, new controls over disease, and reduced mortality" (Notestein, 1945, p. 39). Fertility responded more slowly to modernization but ultimately began a decline through the widespread use of contraception, under the impact of such forces as "the growing individualism and rising levels of popular aspiration developed in urban industrial living" (*ibid.*, p. 40).

The use of transition theory as an "analytic tool" (van Nort and Karon, 1955, p. 523) involves some further generalizations. "The more rapid response of mortality than of fertility to the forces of modernization is probably inevitable" (Notestein, 1945, p. 41). Accordingly, populations may be grouped into three classes according to "demographic type" or "stage of demographic evolution": first, "incipient decline" or transition completed; second, "transitional growth," with mortality declining ahead of fertility; and, third, "high growth potential," or transitional growth not yet begun (Notestein, 1945, 1956). As these categories imply, and as is suggested by a study of the beginnings of economic development and demographic transition in certain non-European countries, "the principles drawn from the European demographic transition are widely applicable throughout the world" (Notestein, 1953, p. 21).

A significant issue that arises in connection with transition theory has to do with its level of generality. On one hand, Vance (1956, pp. 91–93) refers to the "great need for the development of integrated theory of a high order" and suggests that "the framework for one such theory is now emerging" in the work of Notestein and others on the "theory of demographic transition." On the other hand, Notestein himself states: "In demography our theory of the broad processes of population change seems to have been sufficiently tested to prove its general validity. It is adequate to delineate the nature of the problem at hand. But it does not answer the concrete questions on which information is needed either for purposes of prediction or for the formulation of policy. . . . In demography it seems to me that there is less need for work on the over-arching theory of change than for knowledge at lower levels of generality" (Notestein, 1953, p. 27).

Issues as to the validity of this theory (only an incomplete sketch of which has been given here) arise on several levels. First, is the description of population changes among Western peoples accurate? Even apart from short-run fluctuations, certain cases, such as the early decline in birth rates in France and America, require *ad hoc*

explanations. Second, what are the relevant components of the "whole process of modernization"? In presentations of the theory thus far, various lists of such components have been presented, but it is conceded that "at present we cannot either list all of the factors involved or attach precise weights to the factors we can list" (Notestein, 1953, p. 18). Significantly, the factors listed range over several levels of abstraction, from "urbanization," the "development of modern technology," and "economic development," through "ideals and beliefs" and "popular education," to "motivation for the reduction of births." The observation that demographic transition appears to have commenced in some cases where one or another of such factors was absent or not to have begun despite the presence of one or more of them suggests that the theory is as yet incomplete on the explanatory side.

Finally, what of the predictive value of the theory? In the light of the "baby boom," it seems that "incipient decline" is not an accurate short-run forecast for all populations under a regime of controlled vital processes. Instead, the "important fact is that populations of this type can check their growth any time it becomes desirable to do so" (Notestein, 1956, p. 38). The controls on future population growth, therefore, are of a type not taken into account in transition theory as such. With respect to countries undergoing transitional growth, it is clear that the tempo of change currently differs from that observed in countries completing the transition earlier. For example, "the mortality experience of Western nations provides little precedent for the changes taking place in a growing number of the areas usually classified as 'underdeveloped.' . . . The recent trends approach or exceed the most rapid ever encountered among the nations with lowest mortality today" (Stolnitz,

1956*a*, pp. 1–2). Evidence to date, however, tends to favor the gross prediction from transition theory that mortality decline leads natality decline. Regarding the third category of populations: "To say that the principles drawn from the European analysis apply to the world's present areas of high fertility is, of course, a far cry from saying that we may expect events to take a similar course" (Notestein, 1953, p. 21). Reasonable forecasts for such countries require assessment of their initial levels of population density, existing natural resources, and prospects for economic development, among other things; and it is often pointed out that the "values" carried by these populations may not be susceptible to changes from the same sources that purportedly modified Western "values" pertaining to family size. In fact, discussion of transition theory in respect to countries of "high growth potential" less often runs in the direction of making predictions than to a consideration of the nature of their "population problem" and of the desirability of the alternative courses of population policy open to them, whereupon, of course, it wanders outside the realm of strictly scientific discourse.

In terms of its substantive application, therefore, transition theory raises issues in respect to its adequacy as descriptive generalization, as ex post facto explanation, and as prediction. But apart from its validity in any of these respects, transition theory raises an issue of quite general significance which it is well to emphasize in the context of the present discussion. The theory purports to be relevant only, or at least primarily, to what was earlier called the "modern period" of population history, roughly the last three centuries. Cowgill (1956), among others, has pointed out that the sequence of changes comprising a "modern" growth cycle—declining mortality followed by declining natality—is but one of several such possible sequences; that periods of growth in the past probably involved a different sequence; and that the "future cycle," for countries having gone through the "modern cycle," will likewise be distinctive. The circumstances likely to attend the occurrence of one or another type of cycle are outlined, but necessarily in rather hypothetical terms for want of many relevant data. On the basis of such analysis one might inquire whether "transition theory" should be considered a special case of a more general "growth theory" which has yet to be outlined in any detail or whether it should be accepted as a "historical theory" capable only of characterizing a historically unique era. In the latter event, does it become necessary to develop different "historical theories" for all distinguishable historical eras? If one pursues this line of reasoning, must he conclude that to retain its empirical character, the study of population must be cast in the form of "population history" rather than "population theory" in the sense in which "theory" is commonly understood in science as a body of general explanatory propositions? Is it only by confining himself to a particular brief historical period that the population student becomes convinced of the possibility of developing "theory" in a generic sense? Some demographers who stress the present shortcomings of population theory and the desirability of "high-level" or "integrated" theory have nonetheless conceded the improbability of discovering general "laws" of population growth. Can the requirements of "high-level" or "integrated" theory be met by a type of theorizing which accepts, not even a "law," but a somewhat flexible pattern of analysis and explanation, different for each distinguishable era of population history?

Analogous questions can be raised in respect to most theories in the social sciences, and social scientists are arrayed on quite a wide spectrum of positions in regard to "historicism." The issue is one that, in the nature of the case, is probably not resolvable once and for all by abstract reasoning. The purpose in restating it here is to point out that orientations to virtually all kinds of "theories" are conditioned in one way or another by the position taken in regard to "historicism."

Psychosocial theories of fertility.— For about the last twenty years a small group of American demographers have been making investigations of "social and psychological factors affecting fertility." Their efforts have become widely known through the successive reports and summaries (probably exceeding forty in number) of the "Indianapolis Study" and through publicity given the plans for additional studies along somewhat similar lines. It seems highly pertinent to include here some discussion of issues in population theory raised by this work, but in view of space limitations this must be accomplished without presenting a full summary of the Indianapolis results or of theoretical writing bearing on these results. (The reader not already acquainted with this work may consult, among other sources cited later, Kiser and Whelpton, 1956, and Mishler and Westoff, 1955.) At the risk of giving a somewhat distorted conception of the psychosocial studies, attention will be confined here to what seem to be three paramount issues: the role of theory in these studies, the conception of psychosocial factors as intervening variables, and the use of psychosocial hypotheses in explaining fertility trends and variations.

It appears that in organizing the Indianapolis Study, the investigators (an interdisciplinary committee, including social psychologists and other social scientists along with demographers) did not endeavor to formulate a general theory of fertility but addressed themselves to the construction of twenty-three hypotheses concerning "social and psychological factors affecting resort to contraception and the size of the planned family" (Kiser and Whelpton, 1956, p. 257). Subsequently, they were constrained to note that "a recurrent criticism of this Study has been that it lacked sufficient theoretical and conceptual organization" (Mishler and Westoff, 1955, p. 121). Interestingly enough, the presumably unfortunate consequences of this omission are not made wholly clear. In a summary of "methodological lessons" of the Indianapolis Study (Kiser, 1956) the criticism is reiterated that "the twenty-three hypotheses of the Indianapolis Study were not bound together by an integrating theory or organizing principle," but the defects associated with this fault seem merely to be that "too many . . . factors were included," that the "variables were not always precisely defined," and that "the variables . . . were not always measured." These surely are technical or procedural deficiencies rather than matters of "integrating theory" in any generic sense. The investigators appear to assume that working on the basis of "a systematic sociological or psychological theory" (Mishler and Westoff, 1955, p. 121) would improve future studies, as compared with the "'dragnet' approach" (Kiser, 1956, p. 153) of the Indianapolis Study, but the grounds for this belief are not made wholly explicit.

Significantly, in developing plans for further research, the investigators have rejected the scheme of selecting a "particular approach" and "developing a particular theory of fertility" to be "tested through research," because there are "insufficient grounds for selecting any particular 'theory' which would automatically restrict the types and ranges of data gathered." In elaborating this statement, they say:

The theoretical approaches which have been discussed are concerned with different "levels" of data and with different "levels" of interpretation and do not really meet each other head-on as alternative explanations of the same event, that is, some of them are psychological theories and others are sociological theories. By definition each of these separate theories is a restricted formulation which deals with a particular abstraction from the world of behavior. For this reason, each in itself would be inadequate for the prediction of fertility which is a concrete event taking place at a particular point in social-historical time. It would be possible, for example, to develop a relatively adequate interpretation of some psychological aspect of fertility . . . in terms of a psychological theory, but this would not provide an adequate interpretation of fertility performance [Mishler and Westoff, 1955, p. 128].

Among other significant premises of this statement are the assumptions that working with a "particular theory" is antithetical to the "prediction of . . . a concrete event" and that the latter is the appropriate aim for the research. It is by no means clear wherein "the choice is not simply a bow in the direction of eclecticism" (*idem*) and in what respects it represents an advance over laying out twenty-three hypotheses lacking in "sufficient theoretical and conceptual organization." What the investigators do propose to use is a "conceptual framework or 'model' which [permits] the description of the major elements of the concrete situation within which the fertility event takes place" (*ibid.*, pp. 128–29). As expounded, this "conceptual framework" appears to amount to an a priori classification of "dependent variables" and "independent variables," whose use "entails a certain risk that the hypotheses which are formulated will form together less of a unified whole than would be the case if the study were developed in terms of a single body of theory" (*ibid.*, p. 131).

It seems clear that the investigators

of psychosocial factors are greatly concerned about the role of theory in research; this role is considered important, but they are unable to specify clearly, for their purposes, what it is. It may be, too, that they have hit on an issue of signal importance for population studies in general in stating an antithesis between testing a particular theory and the prediction of a concrete event. If, like most demographers, they prefer to attempt the prediction or explanation of concrete events, they seem prepared to sacrifice some of the elegance of an integrated theory.

Turning to the second kind of issue raised by the psychosocial studies of fertility, it may be noted that the investigators have consistently maintained that "to account for the variations in fertility in which we are interested" (Mishler and Westoff, 1955, p. 121) it was necessary to "investigate the social and psychological factors affecting resort to contraception and the size of the planned family" (Kiser and Whelpton, 1956, p. 257). Or as one commentator put it, "The ultimate aim, as he saw it, was to predict intimate individual or paired behavior within a given social context. Thus the study should be focused on motivation" (views attributed to W. E. Moore, in Kiser, 1953, p. 476). It was, however, only in retrospect that any lengthy justification of this position, which apparently was taken to be almost axiomatic, was attempted. In describing plans for new studies, the investigators make reference to a conceptualization by R. M. MacIver involving "three classes of factors (1) the cultural background; (2) the motivations; and (3) means of family limitation. . . . Cultural background factors including such matters as industrialization, emancipation of women, urbanization and extension of public education, could only indirectly contribute to the decline of the birth rate. There had to be a mediation of these factors through motivations or personal desires regarding family limitation. The concept 'means of family limitation' includes contraception, abortion, etc." (Kiser *et al.*, 1956, p. 47). Finally, at least one of the investigators has had the temerity to refer to "causes" of differential fertility and has characterized the Indianapolis Study as a "land mark in this research field . . . the first major study to test empirically substantive hypotheses which raise the question 'why'" (Westoff, 1956, p. 401).

It is also interesting to note the investigators' assumption that "information about the motivations and interests of married couples regarding the planning and having of children and the factors responsible for differences in fertility . . . would be helpful in the event that the development of a national population policy should be undertaken in the United States" (Westoff, 1957, p. 74). Apparently it was believed not only that "motivations and interests" are the critical determinants of fertility but also that these factors are susceptible to manipulation with the means at the disposal of a national population policy. This hypothesis, of course, would require separate investigation, and the students of psychosocial factors have not yet turned their attention to it, perhaps because the probability that such a policy would be implemented now seems smaller than it did in the late 1930's.

One cannot study the summaries of the Indianapolis Study and related literature without noting a certain confusion about the analytical or theoretical role of psychosocial factors. They are variously referred to as "factors affecting fertility," as "mediating" other factors, as "causes," and as both "independent variables" and "dependent variables." This confusion is manifested most clearly in the uncertainty about what the psychosocial factors are supposed to explain. For example, Westoff

(1956, pp. 401–2) refers to the Indianapolis Study as illustrating "the most recent development" in respect to the "interest in the differential fertility of socio-economic groups—research into its causes." He then notes:

One of the major results of the Indianapolis Study has been to highlight the analytical importance of socio-economic status. This importance is manifested, with only few exceptions, in the fact that given relationships between specific variables, for example, general planning, feeling of economic security, feeling of personal adequacy, religious interest, and others, and fertility planning and planned fertility are either considerably weakened or disappear completely when socio-economic status is held constant.

Such a statement comes dangerously close to the circular assertion that the cause of fertility differentials among socioeconomic groups is socioeconomic status. The situation can perhaps be clarified by thinking in terms of partial correlation. Let X_1 be a measure of fertility (say size of completed family), X_2 a measure of socioeconomic status (say income), and X_3 a psychological factor (say "feeling of personal adequacy"). Then the differential fertility of socioeconomic groups, which had been well documented prior to the Indianapolis Study, would be represented by a significant (negative) value of the correlation r_{12}. The investigator of psychosocial factors, conceiving them as "causes," "mediating factors," or the like, discovers that the correlation r_{13} also is significant but that the partial relation $r_{13.2}$ is low or non-significant; i.e., "relationships . . . are either considerably weakened or disappear completely when socio-economic status is held constant." But this is the *wrong correlation* to compute, assuming the investigator is attempting to explain the original socioeconomic differential. To test the hypothesis that the psychological factor explains the socioeconomic differential, one would compute the partial correlation $r_{12.3}$. A necessary condition for accepting the psychological variable as a "mediating factor" or as a "cause" of the socioeconomic differential is that the absolute value of $r_{12.3}$ be less than r_{12}; to afford a complete explanation of the socioeconomic differential, introduction of the psychological factor into the analysis must reduce $r_{12.3}$ to zero, or to a non-significant value.

The foregoing discussion is not intended to reflect unfavorably on the actual analyses of data in the Indianapolis Study, which was carried out with great technical competence and ingenuity. It is meant, however, to show that there appears to have been some lack of clarity in the specification of what the twenty-three hypotheses were designed to explain. That this confusion was not present throughout the work is indicated by the analysis which showed that "the high negative relationships" between socioeconomic status and fertility were "due mainly to their joint relationship to the *planning* of fertility. . . . When differences in contraceptive practice were held constant statistically, the inverse relationship between socioeconomic status and fertility virtually disappeared" (Westoff, 1957, p. 85). This of course satisfies the criterion just stated for explanation of the socioeconomic differential, in this case with "contraceptive practice" as X_3 in the partial correlation model. But it was in the "attempt to unravel the social-psychological variables that underlie these relationships" (*idem*) that there was a failure to adhere to an appropriate model of explanation.

Before leaving the matter of psychosocial factors as intervening variables, it should be pointed out that the findings of the Indianapolis Study do not provide, nor are they claimed by the authors to provide, any very strong support for the hypothesis that psychosocial factors explain differential fertility. In fact, the investigators make repeated reference to the "failure to secure closer relations between psychological factors and fertility" (Kiser, 1956, p. 154). They consider a number of aspects of the study design and analysis that may have accounted for this "failure." Interestingly enough, however, they do not appear to entertain seriously the supposition that psychosocial variables actually are not very important or useful as explanatory factors. In fact, their comments on their results provide a remarkable example of maintaining a hypothesis tenaciously in the face of rather consistently negative evidence. *148178*

This observation leads to a consideration of the third major issue raised by the psychosocial studies, the utility of psychosocial theories in explaining movements and variations in natality. It is made clear in the reports of the Indianapolis Study that in the "background" of the study were such well-documented findings as the secular decline of natality to the low levels observed in the 1930's and the existence of sizable and persistent differentials in natality among regions, rural-urban residence categories, ethnic categories, and socioeconomic levels. Although it is more often implied than stated directly (cf. Westoff, 1956), it appears to have been the hope that the Indianapolis Study would throw light on these trends and differentials. Moreover, as was indicated, there was an expectation that the study would provide knowledge of an instrumental character which could be used in formulating a population policy. It would not be unfair, perhaps, to say that the study aspired to make a contribution in respect to the explanation, prediction, and control of fertility variations and changes. Without suggesting any criticism of the study per se, it is appropriate to raise some questions about the general premise that the study of psychosocial factors can be relied on to make such a contribution.

Let us suppose that such a study demonstrated a high cross-sectional (i.e., at a given period of time) correlation between size of completed family and, say, "feeling of personal adequacy" of parents. (For the present purpose it does not matter whether "feeling of personal adequacy" was measured at the beginning, end, or other point of the childbearing period.) How might such knowledge be used to explain secular trends in the birth rate? Supposing the hypothesized correlation to be positive, it would be necessary to show that a decline in the birth rate was accompanied or preceded by a decrease, on the average, in the "feeling of personal adequacy" of parents. But such a demonstration is beyond the resources of the social sciences, which have not yet learned to resurrect the dead. It would, perhaps, be possible to develop the inference that people were feeling less adequate as the decades went by, say by examining contemporary fiction, impressions of journalists, and the like; but such material hardly meets the standards of population research in regard to representativeness, reliability, and validity. The non-availability of psychological data for past populations renders psychological explanations of past fertility trends untestable. By the same token, it makes untestable any explanation in psychological terms of differences in fertility among categories of the population, or changes therein, insofar as these pertain to populations no longer accessible to psychological observation.

It is, of course, not impossible in principle to accomplish mass observation of psychosocial traits in a contemporary population, given the resources of modern sampling techniques. At present, however, we take no censuses or current population surveys of people's "feelings of personal adequacy." Hence, there is much point to the following observations of a writer considering the "functions that may be served by alternative types of research":

American demographers have devoted major resources . . . to examining the social and psychological determinants of American fertility patterns. It is generally believed that the associations so far established between fertility and socio-economic factors have been more revealing than those involving psychological factors. As a result, much attention has been directed to seeing how the latter aspect of fertility behavior might be clarified. That the psychological concomitants of fertility are central to any adequate system of explanation is obvious. Nevertheless, we may be confronted with a problem of practical emphasis. A little-observed advantage of focusing on social and economic categories is that their distribution in the population is often known. Accordingly, given the fertility behavior within these categories, it is generally possible to deal with fertility in the aggregate. No comparable possibility is now in sight on the psychological side. In this sense attempts to analyze fertility in psychological depth, even if successful, may have only limited bearing on our ability to forecast its course in the large [Stolnitz, 1956c, p. 743].

Indeed, one can go further. The use of psychological variables in demographic prediction or forecasting presumes that the composition of the population by such complex psychological characteristics as "feelings of personal adequacy" itself can be forecast; there is room for skepticism about this. It is possible that Stolnitz was making a gratuitous concession in stating that "the psychological concomitants of fertility are central to *any* adequate system of explanation" (italics added). As noted above, Mishler and Westoff recognized the possibility of explanatory theories at different "levels," the sociological and the psychological.

Moreover, there is a sense in which the use of psychological variables to explain fertility differentials yields little more than an unilluminating truism. To see this clearly, consider a difference of the magnitude represented by the fertility rates of India and France. The French have fewer babies because they "want" fewer and because they "know" how to limit conceptions or, one might say, because of "motivational and cognitive factors affecting fertility."

The study of psychosocial factors need not, of course, be limited to fertility; indeed, one does not have to look far ahead to foresee the emergence of a subdiscipline of "psychological demography," concerned with "why" people migrate, "why" they marry when they do, "why" they enter or leave the labor force, and so on, based on the premise that the only ultimately meaningful explanation of migration, nuptiality, labor-force dynamics, and the like, is one couched in psychological terms (see Vance's discussion of "microdemography," chap. xiv). Psychological reductionism, of course, is no new intellectual position in the social sciences, though it has only lately been seriously entertained as a perspective for population studies. Without in the least suggesting that psychological studies are without value, it seems in order to recognize that explanations can, indeed, be formulated at various "levels" and that different bodies of theory offer alternative perspectives on demographic variation and change—perspectives not all of which are readily reduced to psychological paraphrases. The following statement puts the matter as well as any:

A proper understanding of migration requires a knowledge of its causes. Too often, however, the search for causes becomes a matter of ascertaining the motives of migrants, though the announced motives may or may not have any connection with the factors of change attending migration. . . .

Some have suggested that migration is psychological in origin, beginning with an idea which spreads and gathers impetus through contagion. Interpretations such as these locate the cause of migration in the individual migrants and only secondarily, if at all, in the environmental and communal context. No doubt migration involves psychological elements, but it is also a manifestation of external changes. For an understanding of the general phenomenon it is important to know not why the migrant thinks he has moved but the conditions or characteristics common to all instances of migration and lacking in situations from which there is no migration [Hawley, 1950, p. 328].

Much the same statement can be made concerning the trends in fertility and the fertility differences among regions, categories, and population groups in which the demographer is interested. In this connection, it is interesting to compare statements made by one of the Indianapolis Study investigators, at about the time the study was initiated, on fertility studies and migration studies, respectively:

What may be the most important problems relating to fertility [pertain to] the weight of the various factors determining for individuals and couples the proportion marrying, the age at marriage, the extent to which family limitation is tried, the number of children wanted by couples able to govern family size, and the extent to which these factors may be subject to social control. Few attempts have been made to obtain information on the number of children which people would like to have, and of the various conditions leading them to have more or fewer. . . . Studies of the number of children wanted by couples who practice contraception effectively are also rare. . . . The importance of the subject justifies more intensive research, based on an analysis of reasons made, not by the individuals concerned nor by their friends, but by persons trained to study motives and conditions governing conduct.

. . . .

It is of great importance to understand the reasons which lead some people to move and others to stay where they are. Theoretically and fundamentally, the cause of much of the migration which occurs should be a higher ratio between the number of persons and the capacity to support population in one area than in another. The relation of population to resources will not be considered here, however . . . attention being limited to the more immediate or superficial reasons for or against migrating rather than this deep-seated cause. Motives for migrating may be classified into several groups. . . . In general, it is said that people move because they believe their future situation will be better . . . because they are forced out . . . because they dislike to remain long in any surrounding, or because of some combination of such conditions [Whelpton, 1938, pp. 88–89, 144].

Note that while the "motives" and "reasons" both for wanting children and for migrating are considered "important," it is conceded that, as they concern migration, these amount to "immediate or superficial reasons" rather than a "deep-seated cause." Perhaps it is not irrelevant to suggest that any item of behavior has both "immediate or superficial reasons" and "deep-seated causes," in the sense in which the author used those terms. Analysis of the former is properly carried out by psychological concepts and techniques, but the latter require the investigator to employ some other theoretical framework. It is perhaps a matter of personal predilection on what level or from what perspective a population student chooses to work. However, in view of the widespread popularity of social-psychological approaches and methods, it is perhaps well to call attention to the view that psychological explanations, like any theoretical explanations of phenomena, are empirically incomplete; or as Ogburn and Nimkoff state:

If the proximate cause of a change over time is psychological, that is, expressed in motives, it is often desirable to search further in causes more removed until a cause not psychological is reached. As an illustration, the cause of an increase in adultery may be found in an increase in sexual desire for someone other than one's legal mate. Such covetousness . . . may not be a constant. It may be more common at one time than in another. . . . There is some curiosity therefore as to what has brought about this increase in effective covetousness. The mere statement of increased motivation is not enough. . . . So we look beyond the motive to the conditions that brought it about. . . . Motives are not an adequate explanation of a change in social behavior over a period of time. It is desirable to explain the change in motives in terms of some change in conditions such as a change in science or in technology. . . . Hence in a chain of causes we seldom stop at a psychological cause [Ogburn and Nimkoff, 1955, pp. 23–24].

Finally, if population students are to give serious consideration to Vance's proposal (chap. xiv) that present "macrodemography" should be complemented by a psychosocial "microdemography," they should be aware of the "aggregation problem" (Theil, 1954) that inevitably arises in attempts to co-ordinate "micro" and "macro" approaches.

CONCLUDING OBSERVATIONS

Continued research efforts, in both "demographic analysis" and "population studies," indicate that the corpus of demographic knowledge, including theory, may be expected to increase and to improve in terms of the ultimate criterion of the quality or status of any science—its potential for prediction and explanation. The basis for this conclusion may be found in the following interrelated considerations: the extension of census-taking, vital registration, sampling survey, and other data collection procedures to increasingly greater proportions of the world's population; the increasing scope and quality of information about the population being collected by these means; the continued development of conceptual frameworks and analytical methods in demography and in related sciences reflected in the increasing effectiveness of research design both in demographic analysis and population studies; and the increasing sophistication in demography in respect of the objectives and methodology of science as indicated in more deliberate efforts to build theory in relation to, and in interaction with, empirical research.

The improvements in geographic coverage, scope, and quality of data have been discussed in chapter iii, are presented in some detail in Part III, and require no further elaboration here. Suffice it to repeat that better data are in no small measure a consequence of developments in conceptual frameworks, methods, and in the general state of demography and related disciplines as sciences, as well as a prerequisite and stimulant to further development of demographic knowledge. Some explanation of the third and fourth considerations, however, is called for.

The discussion earlier in this chapter and the materials in Part III, "Elements of Demography," document the way in which improved conceptual frameworks and more effective analytical methods have contributed to the augmentation of demographic knowledge. Hawley (chap. xvi) in his discussion of population composition indicates the way in which the "stable population" as a conceptual framework and analytical tool has added to our knowledge of composition and its possible course of change. Bogue (chap. xvii) in his consideration of population distribution has shown how multivariate analysis can illuminate problems relating to regionalism, urbanization, and industrialization; and in his summary of the field of internal migration (chap. xxi) he has provided a number of examples of the way in which conceptual frameworks can affect the knowledge

which can be gleaned about both migratory streams and behavior of migrants. Ryder (chap. xviii) has documented reasonably fully the way in which improvements in conceptual framework and analytical method have added to our knowledge of changes in fertility over time; and Dorn (chap. xix) has done the same in respect of mortality. Hyrenius (chap. xx) in his succinct discussion has demonstrated the vital role of formal models in the analysis of population growth and replacement. Grauman (chap. xxiii) has similarly demonstrated the role of research techniques and empirical models, embodying both concept and methodology, in population estimation and projection and in the explanation of population change. Glick (chap. xxiv) in his discussion of the family and Jaffe (chap. xxv) in his treatment of the labor force have also shown in their special areas the ways in which improved conceptual frameworks and analytical methods have opened up new areas of interest and research for demography. Finally, Thomas (chap. xxii) in treating of international migration and Ackerman (chap. xxvi) in considering population and natural resources have shown how conceptual frameworks in economics and geography, respectively, have stimulated and helped to create and organize knowledge in demography and in related disciplines.

In the summary and evaluation of the "elements" of demography, then, the authors of the symposium, as well as the observations of the editors, have pointed to the way in which conceptual framework and analytical method have contributed to the improvement of demography as a science and may be expected to continue to do so. Such improvement is effected, of course, by means of the improved data and the more effective research which the more refined conceptual frameworks and methods permit.

The materials in the symposium, including those in Parts II and IV as well as in Part III, together with the discussion of theory in this chapter, tend to bolster the fourth consideration above. That is, these materials serve to document the increasing sophistication of demographers in their research in respect to the objectives and general methodology of science. More specifically, both demographic analyses and population studies give indications of increasing awareness of the role of theory in research and of a conception of theory and an imagery of science that is increasingly advanced as measured by the standards of the natural sciences.

The analyses above of the "elements" and "functions" of theory in demography as contained in the investigations and discussions of demographers may be taken in support of this conclusion. This does not mean, however, that there is no room for further improvement. On the contrary, demographers in general may have much to gain from additional allocation of energy to deliberate efforts directed toward theory-construction in conjunction with the conduct of empirical research. In this connection much might be gained, also, if in such efforts more emphasis were placed on prediction and explanation as the primary function of theory.

REFERENCES

BENNETT, M. K. 1954. *The World's Food.* New York: Harper.

BOULDING, K. E. 1955. "The Malthusian Model as a General System," *Social and Economic Studies,* IV, 195–205.

COALE, A. J. 1956. "The Effects of Changes in Mortality and Fertility on Age Composition," *Milbank Memorial Fund Quarterly,* XXXIV, 79–114.

COWGILL, D. O. 1956. "The Theory of Population Growth Cycles," in *Population Theory and Policy,* ed. J. J. SPENGLER and O. D. DUNCAN. Glencoe, Ill.: Free Press.

DAVIS, KINGSLEY. 1955. "Malthus and the Theory of Population," in *Language of Social Research,* ed. P. F. LAZARSFELD and MORRIS ROSENBERG. Glencoe, Ill.: Free Press.

GOTTLIEB, MANUEL. 1956. "The Theory of Optimum Population for a Closed Economy," in *Population Theory and Policy,* ed. J. J. SPENGLER and O. D. DUNCAN. Glencoe, Ill.: Free Press.

HAJNAL, JOHN. 1955. "The Prospects for Population Forecasts," *Journal of the American Statistical Association,* L, 309–22.

HAUSER, P. M. 1956. "Present Status and Prospects of Research in Population," in *Population Theory and Policy,* ed. J. J. SPENGLER and O. D. DUNCAN. Glencoe, Ill.: Free Press.

HAWLEY, A. H. 1950. *Human Ecology: A Theory of Community Structure.* New York: Ronald Press.

JONES, F. E. 1956. "A Sociological Perspective on Immigrant Adjustment," *Social Forces,* XXXV, 39–47.

KISER, C. V. 1953. "Exploration of Possibilities for New Studies of Factors Affecting Size of Family," *Milbank Memorial Fund Quarterly,* XXXI, 436–80.

———. 1956. "Methodological Lessons of the Indianapolis Fertility Study," *Eugenics Quarterly,* III, 152–56.

———, and WHELPTON, P. K. 1956. "Résumé of the Indianapolis Study of Social and Psychological Factors Affecting Fertility," in *Demographic Analysis,* ed. J. J. SPENGLER and O. D. DUNCAN. Glencoe, Ill.: Free Press.

———, *et al.* 1956. "Development of Plans for a Social Psychological Study of the Future Fertility of Two-Child Families," *Population Studies,* X, 43–52.

LEIBENSTEIN, HARVEY. 1954. *A Theory of Economic-demographic Development.* Princeton: Princeton University Press.

LOTKA, A. J. 1956a. "Population Analysis," in *Population Theory and Policy,* ed. J. J. SPENGLER and O. D. DUNCAN. Glencoe, Ill.: Free Press.

———. 1956b. "Some Recent Results in Population Analysis," in *Population Theory and Policy,* ed. J. J. SPENGLER and O. D. DUNCAN. Glencoe, Ill.: Free Press.

MISHLER, E. G., and WESTOFF, C. F. 1955.

"A Proposal for Research on Social Psychological Factors Affecting Fertility: Concepts and Hypotheses," in *Current Research in Human Fertility*. New York: Milbank Memorial Fund.

NOTESTEIN, F. W. 1945. "Population: The Long View," in *Food for the World*, ed. T. W. SCHULTZ. Chicago: University of Chicago Press.

———. 1953. "Economic Problems of Population Change," in *Proceedings of the Eighth International Conference of Agricultural Economists*. London: Oxford University Press.

———. 1956. "The Population of the World in the Year 2000," in *Demographic Analysis*, ed. J. J. SPENGLER and O. D. DUNCAN. Glencoe, Ill.: Free Press.

OGBURN, W. F., and NIMKOFF, M. F. 1955. *Technology and the Changing Family*. Boston: Houghton Mifflin Co.

PEACOCK, A. T. 1956. "Theory of Population and Modern Economic Analysis," in *Population Theory and Policy*, ed. J. J. SPENGLER and O. D. DUNCAN. Glencoe, Ill.: Free Press.

———. 1957. "Production Functions and Population Theory," *Population Studies*, X, 298–305.

RUSSELL, J. C. 1956. "Demographic Pattern in History," in *Demographic Analysis*, ed. J. J. SPENGLER and O. D. DUNCAN. Glencoe, Ill.: Free Press.

SMITH, KENNETH. 1951. *The Malthusian Controversy*. London: Routledge & Kegan Paul.

SPENGLER, J. J. 1945. "Malthus's Total Population Theory: A Restatement and Reappraisal," *Canadian Journal of Economics and Political Science*, XI, 83–110, 234–64.

———, and DUNCAN, O. D. (eds.). 1956. *Population Theory and Policy*. Glencoe, Ill.: Free Press.

STOLNITZ, G. J. 1956a. "Comparison between Some Recent Mortality Trends in Underdeveloped Areas and Historical Trends in the West," in *Trends and Differentials in Mortality*. New York: Milbank Memorial Fund.

———. 1956b. "Mortality Declines and Age Distribution," *Milbank Memorial Fund Quarterly*, XXXIV, 178–215.

———. 1956c. "Population Composition and Fertility Trends," *American Sociological Review*, XXI, 738–43.

TAYLOR, K. W. 1956. "Some Aspects of Population History," in *Demographic Analysis*, ed. J. J. SPENGLER and O. D. DUNCAN. Glencoe, Ill.: Free Press.

THEIL, H. 1954. *Linear Aggregation of Economic Relations*. Amsterdam: North-Holland Publishing Co.

UNITED NATIONS, POPULATION DIVISION. 1954. "The Cause of the Ageing of Populations: Declining Mortality or Declining Fertility?" *Population Bulletin of the United Nations*, No. 4, pp. 30–38.

———. 1956. "The Past and Future Population of the World and Its Continents," in *Demographic Analysis*, ed. J. J. SPENGLER and O. D. DUNCAN. Glencoe, Ill.: Free Press.

USHER, A. P. 1956. "The History of Population and Settlement in Eurasia," in *Demographic Analysis*, ed. J. J. SPENGLER and O. D. DUNCAN. Glencoe, Ill.: Free Press.

VAN NORT, LEIGHTON, and KARON, B. P. 1955. "Demographic Transition Re-examined," *American Sociological Review*, XX, 523–27.

VANCE, R. B. 1956. "Is Theory for Demographers?" in *Population Theory and Policy*, ed. J. J. SPENGLER and O. D. DUNCAN. Glencoe, Ill.: Free Press.

WESTOFF, C. F. 1956. "The Changing Focus of Differential Fertility Research: The Social Mobility Hypothesis," in *Population Theory and Policy*, ed. J. J. SPENGLER and O. D. DUNCAN. Glencoe, Ill.: Free Press.

———. 1957. "Social Psychological Factors Affecting Fertility: The Indianapolis Study," in *Modern Marriage and Family Living*, ed. MORRIS FISHBEIN and RUBY JO REEVES KENNEDY. New York: Oxford University Press.

WHELPTON, P. K. 1938. *Needed Population Research*. Lancaster, Pa.: Science Press.

5. Demography as a Profession

PHILIP M. HAUSER AND OTIS DUDLEY DUNCAN

If the sociology of knowledge were a well-developed area of research, we should doubtless turn to it for information on how the characteristics of the demographic profession affect the progress of demography as a science. It seems probable that the field of population study would be a promising topic for research in the sociology of knowledge. Historically, it has been divided between scientific research and disciplined speculation, on the one hand, and controversy over social issues, on the other. Clearly, the latter has left its mark on the former. Moreover, it is possible to discern a connection between the emergence of scientific interests in population and what may be called the "professionalization" of demography (see, for example, chap. vi).

This chapter falls considerably short of a treatment of demography as a case study in the sociology of knowledge, and we shall have to content ourselves with some rather miscellaneous observations on contemporary aspects of the professionalization of the field, most of which will pertain to the United States (see, however, chaps. vii–xiii, which contain pertinent information for selected other countries). The discussion focuses on personnel, training, and facilities for training and research.

PERSONNEL

It must be observed at the outset that there is no way to make any precise estimate of the number of "demographers" in the world or even in the United States. This follows from the fact that many people making use of and contributions to population studies do not identify themselves professionally as demographers. On the other hand, some who recognize population as a major field of interest may be concerned only with certain narrowly technical aspects of the subject and may lack interest in "demography as a science." Finally, one would be hard put in some cases to draw a line between professional demographers and persons whose concern with population is oriented primarily to the extra-scientific aspects of its study.

It is, however, quite clear that demography is not a large discipline, as compared with many of the major fields of social and natural science. The current membership of the Population Association of America is around five hundred. No doubt there are a number of persons interested professionally in population in one way or another who are not members, but there are doubtless some members whose interest in or other connection with the field is rather nominal.

The International Union for the Scientific Study of Population lists 395 members from 54 different countries as of November, 1957. Of these 89, or not quite one-fourth, are residents of the United States. The union has somewhat more exacting criteria of professional interest in demography than does the association. If one were to suppose that in countries other than the United States the number who might appropriately be classified as demographers bore the same ratio to membership in the union as does the association membership to union membership in the United States, the world population of demographers would be estimated as of the order of two thousand, or rather less than one demographer per one million population. This estimate seems to be well on the generous side. The per capita number of demographers in the United States must be at least three or four times the world average, and if uniform criteria were applied, this ratio would probably be considerably higher.

Little precise or reliable information on the characteristics of demographers is available. Of the 465 members of the Population Association of America listed in its April, 1956, directory as residing within the continental United States, 224 indicated connections with colleges and universities (including a few graduate students and other non-teaching personnel); 127 were government employees (local, state, national, and international); and the affiliations of the remaining 114 were other than academic or government, or were not stated. Thus, nearly half the members were connected with academic institutions, slightly more than one-fourth were with government agencies, and about one-fourth were otherwise occupied. Although it is a quite imperfect index of "professionalization," the proportion of members holding the doctor's degree is of some interest. This proportion amounted to about 56 per cent for the total membership (excluding those overseas), and to around 75 per cent for the academic, 45 per cent for the government, and 33 per cent for the other members.

An important aspect of the professionalization of demography is that few, if any, demographers were trained as demographers exclusively, since, as will be elaborated later, virtually all academic training in the field is given in one or another department of the natural or social sciences. It is pertinent

to inquire, therefore, from what fields demographers are drawn. Our best information here applies only to holders of doctor's degrees. Approximately three-fifths (62 per cent) of the population association members holding doctor's degrees obtained them in sociology. The proportion was even higher among the academic members, 72 per cent, as compared with 45 per cent among the remaining members. In fact the "typical" or modal member of the Population Association of America can be described as a Ph.D. in sociology teaching at a college or university: 120, or 26 per cent, of the members residing in the United States answer to this description.

There is, however, quite an array of other fields of preparation represented. The 262 members holding doctor's degrees may be classified as follows: 163 sociology; 26 biological and medical sciences (including M.D.'s); 24 economics; 12 statistics and biostatistics; 10 geography; 8 psychology; 7 mathematics; 7 history and political science; and 1 each, anthropology, city-planning, law, philosophy, and physics. Not all of these persons, of course, currently maintain a close identification with the fields in which they were trained. A large number of demographers in government employment would be classified as one or another kind of "statistician" in terms of their job titles or civil service ranks.

Of the 89 United States members of the international union, 46, or almost exactly half, are sociologists by training (irrespective of type of degree held). The remainder are drawn from economics (18), biological and medical sciences (7), mathematics (5), and statistics (5), with 9 from miscellaneous and unknown fields. The fact that the proportion of sociologists is somewhat lower in the international union than in the general membership of the population association may indicate a time trend, since the latter probably includes a larger proportion of young members.

One other bit of information on backgrounds is possibly indicative. Of the eleven persons who served as president of the population association between its founding in 1931 and 1948, only four or five would be classified as sociologists; but of the eleven presidents between 1948 and 1959, eight were sociologists by training, and a ninth, though holding the Ph.D. in economics, is identified with equal accuracy as a sociologist.

One has the strong impression, though no firm verification is available, that the recruitment of demographers from sociology is much more common in the United States than in most other countries, and much more common in the United States at present than at earlier periods. Both inferences accord with the fact of sociology's rapid growth in the United States.

It is only possible to speculate on the implications of the professional connection between demography and sociology. But one significant fact must be kept in mind. Although perhaps a majority of demographers are sociologists, they constitute only a small minority of all sociologists. Between 1946 and 1954 only 4 per cent of students taking master's degrees in sociology had written theses on demographic problems, and only 6 per cent of doctoral dissertations accepted in this period were in demography (Duncan, 1957, Table 7). In the sociological periodical with the highest current circulation, about 11 per cent of all articles report demographic research, although 24 per cent of all articles reporting results of quantitative studies are demographic in character (based on figures given by Gold, 1957). The fact that the number of institutions offering advanced work in demography or granting degrees to candidates specializing in this field is much less than the total number offering graduate work in sociology means that the great majority of sociologists have no close acquaintance with demography or truly professional competence therein. Although the research output of sociologists is probably concentrated on population disproportionately as compared with the distribution of fields of interests among sociologists, demography continues to be considered somewhat tangential to the field by many sociologists. The position of sociology vis-à-vis the study of population is, therefore, somewhat anomalous. On the other hand, it must be conceded that the popularity of sociology as a teaching discipline and the treatment of population—however perfunctory—in most courses in general sociology have probably played an important part in the growth of academic interest in population and in the recruitment of professional demographers.

Information on the growth in numbers of demographers is even more scanty than that on current numbers and backgrounds. However, it seems likely that no more than a handful of persons in the United States would have identified themselves as demographers a couple of generations ago. We are told that only thirty-eight persons attended the first meeting of the Population Association of America in 1931 and that attendance at annual meetings remained low for several years thereafter (Kiser, 1953). At the present time it is around two hundred each year. There are other indications that the professionalization of the field made rapid strides only recently. For example, no longer ago than 1938 the number of professional demographers on the staff of the Population Division of the United States Bureau of the Census was about four, as compared with about eighteen today. The impression of participants is that the organization of demographers in a national association "has had some part in pumping vitality into the government agencies" (Kiser, 1953, p. 110; see also Vance's discussion of the history of the association in chap. xiv).

TRAINING

If one were to study carefully the backgrounds of persons regarded as eminent demographers today, he would probably find that many of them were "self-trained" or that their formal study of the field was for the most part quite limited. At the same time, these people, by their contributions to knowledge and method, have made demography a field in which it is increasingly difficult to gain professional competence without formal training. As this fact becomes more widely realized, there is an increasing amount of discussion of problems of training demographers. For example, the 1957 meetings of the International Statistical Institute and the International Union for the Scientific Study of Population featured a session on training. The topic was also discussed at the 1954 World Population Conference, and UNESCO recently sponsored a survey on the teaching of demography in a number of countries. The general availability of the last report, in particular, allows us to treat this subject rather summarily.

It is widely assumed that the need for trained demographers in many countries with low levels of living and actual or potential severe population pressure is much greater than such countries are likely to meet, without aid, in the foreseeable future (Hauser, 1955). Several important programs have been fashioned to meet this need. The United States Bureau of the Census for some ten years has had a program of in-service training for foreign demographers and has furnished leadership in the Western Hemisphere in efforts to raise standards of census-taking and analysis of population data. Various United Nations technical assistance programs have included formal or informal training of personnel in statistical agencies as one of their objectives. The United Nations has also joined in the sponsorship of two centers of training in demography, in Bombay and Santiago. The fellowship program of the Population Council, Inc., now about five years old, has provided opportunities for advanced study in population for graduate students drawn from all over the world. Many of these have come to the United States for their training, but some have gone to various western European countries.

Turning more specifically to the training of demographers in the United States, including those coming to this country for training from abroad, we are led back to the close institutional relationship between demography and sociology. About nine-tenths of all courses in population offered in colleges and universities of the United States are administered by departments of sociology. Although sociology by no means has a monopoly on the production of graduate students specializing in population, the data given earlier strongly indicate its dominance in this respect. How well sociology may qualify for this responsibility is another question. As was pointed out in another connection:

The evidence . . . warrants the conclusion that a large fraction—perhaps a majority—of persons teaching population courses have only a secondary interest in demography. Most of them are sociologists by departmental affiliation, and presumably by field of training as well. Many took their training in departments where only elementary courses (at most) in population were available. It is quite unlikely that as many as half of them did research in demography for their master's or doctor's dissertations. Finally, the overwhelming majority must teach courses other than population, usually devoting a larger share of their teaching time to non-demographic than to demographic courses. A number of respondents . . . indicated that one of the major problems in teaching population was their own lack of interest or competence in the field [Duncan, 1957, p. 177].

Among the major problems arising in the training of demographers, which, in part, flow from the concentration of training in sociology departments, the following may be listed in summary fashion: (1) Because the majority of undergraduate and graduate students of sociology are only incidentally interested, at best, in population, the demand for courses and research supervision in demography frequently is insufficient to support a specialization of teaching staff in this field. This holds true a fortiori with respect to advanced seminars and courses in demographic research methods which are found only in a few of the larger universities. (2) Because the need for background in mathematics and statistics is much less for some fields of sociology than for training in demography, a large proportion of students are ill equipped to study population, and courses tend to be fashioned to their level of competence rather than to that desirable for specialists in demography. (3) A special problem concerning students from foreign countries is that their undergraduate work in sociology often is insufficient to prepare them for graduate work in that discipline. Consequently, to meet requirements for advanced degrees, they must devote a disproportionate amount of their time to making good their deficiencies in aspects of sociology which—though of some possible relevance to demography—do not bear directly on their objective of attaining competence in demographic analysis. For them, as for others, it is difficult to prescribe curriculums incorporating courses in such relevant fields as economics, biology, and geography, because of the pressure of degree requirements in subfields of sociology other than demography. In spite of the generally acknowledged interdisciplinary character of population studies and the uses made of demographic analysis in a number of fields, no university has yet been successful in setting up a truly cross-disciplinary program of instruction in population, although there are some instances of partial interdepartment collaboration in training. In view of the foregoing circumstances it seems probable that persons with well-rounded training for the study of population will continue for some time to be in large part "self-trained," although the opportunities for basic elementary training in demography are certainly much greater than they were in the past.

FACILITIES

Training in demography is given in a considerable number of academic institutions, though in many of these it amounts to a fairly incidental aspect of specialization in sociology or another discipline. Similarly, population research is carried on not only in a considerable number of universities but also by business, government, welfare, planning organizations, and the like, though the research carried out by many of these is highly segmental in character. There are, in fact, relatively few institutions and agencies that have facilities for demographic training at the professional level or that pursue what might be called comprehensive programs of basic research on population. The concentration of training is indicated by that fact that of fifty-eight doctor's degrees awarded to sociologists specializing in demography during 1946–54, no fewer than thirty-seven were conferred by only four universities, each granting six or more. There were six universities awarding two such degrees each, and nine universities awarding one each (Duncan, 1957, p. 182). There is no equally convenient measure of concentration of basic research output, but the informed demographer would probably be willing to name a half-dozen or so organizations and institutions that would account for a large fraction of recent research literature describable as basic in character. Such concentration is not surprising or disconcerting in itself, for similar concentrations of activity occur in most spheres of social and economic life. There is, however, some question as to whether the number and diversity of research and/or training facilities are sufficient to advance the scientific study of population as rapidly as one might like.

In the United States there are two independently endowed research organizations specializing in basic population research. The Milbank Memorial Fund (New York), in addition to its programs in the public health field, has, since the late 1920's, conducted a continuing series of studies focused on human fertility. The Scripps Foundation for Research in Population Problems, located at Miami University in Ohio, was established in 1922 and has made major contributions in its studies of population trends in the United States, projections of future population, population distribution, and cohort fertility analysis. Neither of these organizations functions to any great extent as a training center other than in the sense of training persons working on its research projects.

There are four centers or institutes of population study set up at major universities that combine the functions of research and training, working closely, in the latter respect, with the sociology departments (or, in one case, with the department of economics and sociology) of their respective universities. These are the Office of Population Research at Princeton University, the In-

stitute of Population Research at Louisiana State University, the Office of Population Research at the University of Washington, and the Population Research and Training Center at the University of Chicago. In general, staff members of these units hold appointments in the sociology department and carry out their training programs as part of the graduate curriculum of that department. For the most part their research activities must be financed by grants and contracts from extra-university sources. Inasmuch as, in each case, an important aspect of the training program is the opportunity for qualified students to participate in actual research, the training program is in good part supported by the research program. It is an interesting commentary on the viewpoint of universities toward social science training that, whereas the provision of laboratory facilities in the natural sciences is a standard item of the regular budget, such facilities in the social sciences, including demography, are likely to be available only as an adjunct to an independently financed research program.

At a number of universities there are research offices which, though not devoted wholly to population research, nevertheless carry on research in the field and afford more or less extensive opportunities for student participation and apprenticeship training. These include the Bureau of Applied Social Research at Columbia University, the Bureau of Social Science Research at American University, the Bureau of Population and Economic Research at the University of Virginia, the Institute for Research in Social Science at the University of North Carolina, and the Institute for Social Research at the University of Michigan. Unlike the centers mentioned in the preceding paragraph, these units may not have a strong integration between their research programs and the training of students, though several of these universities do have highly qualified sociologists specializing in population on their faculties.

Practically all the university centers with population research programs are closely related to departments of sociology. It can only be regretted that there are not at least two or three such centers organized, say, around geographic aspects of population, or integrated with an institute of human biology. It is also unfortunate, at least for demography, that none of the major university centers for the study of statistics has developed a program emphasizing demographic research and problems, and it is likewise unfortunate that there is no center where training in actuarial mathematics is conducted in co-operation with a demography program.

In the absence of firm data on the demand for professional demographers in relation to the supply, one can only record the conjecture that the demand is likely to exceed the supply—at least of highly qualified personnel—for some time to come. It is likely that the formation of additional university centers of population study will be one response to this situation, though one cannot be so optimistic that the need for more diversified types of facility just alluded to will be met any time soon. However, there is no good evidence that the existing facilities are strained by an oversupply of qualified candidates for training.

The supply of candidates is, in fact, a phenomenon meriting further study. As a hypothesis subject to test, it may be asserted that the social sciences are at a disadvantage in recruitment, as compared with many of the natural sciences, inasmuch as young people become committed to social science careers rather late, often after experiencing disappointment in the early stages of some other career or program

of study. It may also be supposed that specialization in population study comes even later for the prospective social scientist, since the opportunity for becoming acquainted with the professional aspects of the field arises only at a late stage of his undergraduate or graduate study. It is perhaps significant, for example, that comparatively few National Science Foundation fellowships for study in demography are awarded in comparison with such equally specialized fields as mathematical economics or experimental psychology. The fellowship program of the Population Council, Inc., alluded to earlier, has required quite active recruitment of suitable candidates. In total, the prospect is somewhat remote for a situation in which opportunities for population study can be extended quite selectively and where the agencies engaged in training are in a position to insist on strong backgrounds in, say, mathematics and statistics as a prerequisite to advanced study in demography.

While the preceding discussion of facilities has focused on university programs of research and training, one must not overlook the important contributions, particularly in research, made by government agencies, over and above their responsibilities for assembling population data. An important aspect of the professionalization of demography is the increase in the number of well-trained demographers located in the Bureau of the Census, National Office of Vital Statistics, and numerous other agencies concerned with population studies in one way or another. These people are, of course, in a highly strategic position in at least one respect: they are close to the sources of data and have the opportunity to familiarize themselves with the manifold circumstances of data collection affecting the analysis and interpretation of data. In discussing the problem of training, Jaffe (1955) has pointed out that the collection and the analysis of data have too often been divorced, in both training and practice.

An important aspect of facilities for both training and research is access to adequate libraries, sources of data, and laboratory equipment. The matter of library facilities is perhaps of some special importance for demography, inasmuch as its literature is so widely scattered in journals of a large number of fields. A small library, therefore, cannot serve demographers as adequately by subscribing to two or three basic periodicals as it could, say, sociologists. One consequence of the scattered demographic literature is that students do not get as comprehensive a view of current research in the field as they should; this problem is only partially met by the publication of bibliographies and anthologies of population literature.

There is an even greater problem in respect to maintaining an adequate library of sources of population data. Such data are published by literally hundreds of agencies throughout the world, and the reports of a single modern population census more than fill a "five-foot shelf." It is a rare library indeed that can claim any great degree of coverage of existing population data. One has only to peer a little into the future, extrapolating the growth of data collection systems, to foresee a problem of staggering magnitude. If population research is even to begin to keep pace with the accumulation of population data, entirely new techniques of disseminating the data must be devised—microphotographic techniques come to mind as one possibility—and/or the conduct of population research must be decentralized and integrated much more closely with the collection of population data. Demography and the collection of demographic data are rapidly evolving beyond the point where the

progress of the field can be left to the individual scholar poring over the census reports that happen to have been acquired by his university's library. It may not be amiss to suggest that the agencies and foundations who may take the facilitation of demographic investigations as one of their objectives should begin to make penetrating and imaginative studies of the sheer "logistics" of population research.

In respect to laboratory facilities it is again questionable whether resources measure up to need, and, again, with the introduction of electronic devices one may visualize the problem becoming more exacerbated before it is ameliorated. At the present time, it is largely "by hook or by crook" that the research worker or the student gains access to an adding machine, desk calculator, or drafting table. It is a major feat of administration to secure even substandard facilities for an occasional "laboratory course" or "workshop." Too often, such facilities must be literally begged, borrowed, or stolen from equipment budgeted to research projects that are by no means overequipped.

One can think of both worthwhile ameliorative measures and heroic "solutions" of the foregoing problems of adequate facilities for population training and research. The obvious common denominator of all such proposals is the need for greater allocation of resources to the facilitation of demographic study. Universities need to change their scale of thinking in respect to budgets for all the social sciences, demography not the least among them. Census offices and the like should seek much fuller support for analytical work and for processing data well beyond the form of raw tabulations. Either governments or philanthropists must some day be called upon to provide funds in large amounts to permit creative solutions to the massive documentation problem. Singly or in concert, demographers need to work with publishers to find means of disseminating more effectively the results of demographic research. There would be little excuse for setting down such obvious proposals were it not for the fact that the potential growth of demography as a science, together with the vast activities which support the science, can take it rapidly toward a "critical mass" which can no longer be handled by traditional expedients.

There is an evident need for information on the economics of demographic research; this is an important aspect of the sociology of knowledge of this field. At present there are no reliable and comprehensive figures on the amount of funds devoted to population research or supporting activities that more or less directly advance the discipline as a science. If such information becomes available, it will prove most instructive to compute the ratio of funds expended on the collection and dissemination of population data to all other funds allocated by government and society to professional and scientific activities in the field of population study. It would be surprising indeed if that ratio were less than ten to one. What the optimum ratio would be can only be conjectured. But there is every reason to believe that support for the second category could be increased several times without approaching the point where the tail wags the dog.

There is some reason to doubt that the growth in resources available for the support of basic research on population has kept pace in recent years with the growth of demography as a profession. During the postwar period, many of the foundations to whom the research worker might turn for support have developed a policy of making grants only or primarily in connection with their particular programs of social action. The foundation picture, so far as demography is concerned, was greatly altered by the formation of the Population Council, Inc., late in 1952. By mutual agreement, applications to the various foundations supporting social research of one kind or another are channeled to the population council when they involve demographic problems.

A conspectus of the council's activities is afforded by a summary of its grant allocations over the period 1953–56, when grants totaling somewhat more than one million dollars were authorized. This total is broken down by major programs as follows (in thousands of dollars):

$ 540 demography
164 demographic fellowships
258 medical research
45 medical fellowships
8 medical genetics fellowships
28 miscellaneous grants

$1,043 total

It should noted that the medical programs are largely concerned with the physiology of human reproduction, a field closely related to demography and bearing on population studies, but not clearly within the scope of either as we have defined them in this volume. It is not possible to make a clear-cut distinction between those grants, in the demography program, that pertained to basic demographic research, as opposed to other types of projects relating to demography as a profession. However, our scrutiny of project titles suggests that about three-fifths of the funds allocated under this program could be classified under the former heading, with the remainder being in support of conferences, travel, training programs, publications, and the like. Or, if one combined the demography and the demographic fellowship programs, it could be said that perhaps half the total funds were allocated to basic research or to the planning and facilitation of basic research. (It should be clear that this estimate represents our appraisal of the actual activities of the council during the stipulated period and is in no sense a summary of any explicit policy of the foundation.)

As we have suggested, although government agencies—the Bureau of the Census and the National Office of Vital Statistics, in particular—make a substantial contribution to the output of basic demographic research, there is little reason to expect a marked expansion of such work on their part in the foreseeable future, highly desirable though such expansion would be. The federal government enters the picture in another way, however, through the National Science Foundation, which "in March 1953 . . . undertook a systematic and continuing study of the present scientific status of the social sciences and of the role of the Foundation with respect to social science research." As a result, the foundation now has a "limited program of support of the social sciences," most aspects of which are open to demography, including "(1) support of basic research; (2) graduate and postgraduate fellowships; (3) support of conferences and symposia; (4) partial support of travel to international conferences; (5) status of science studies; (6) register of scientific and technical personnel; and (7) scientific manpower studies." The actual activities in the population field carried out by the foundation are summarized in a report by Alpert (1957). It may suffice here to indicate only the conclusion that "thus far the amount of participation by demographers has been extremely limited." Although only a handful of fellowships for graduate study in demography had been awarded by the end of 1957, and less than half a dozen research projects had been undertaken under foundation grants, it may be anticipated that the

National Science Foundation will be an important source of support for both training and research in demography in the future.

A final class of facilities to which reference should be made comprises the various media of publication. Demography is virtually unique among social sciences in having commanded the services of the current bibliographic quarterly, *Population Index,* for nearly a quarter-century. The index, besides annotating current literature and listing official publications of population statistics, carries "current items" of scientific and professional interest and a selection of up-to-date demographic summary statistics on the various countries of the world. Edited and published at the Office of Population Research, *Population Index* is jointly sponsored by the office and the Population Association of America. The latter has consistently reaffirmed, over the years, its judgment that a bibliographic service is of greater long-run value than would be an alternative publication in the form of a conventional journal. There has been recurrent discussion of the possibility of establishing such a journal whenever the growth of the association would warrant it. At present the principal journal of demography in English is *Population Studies,* which has been issued since 1947 by the population investigation committee at the London School of Economics. Recently, *Population Review* was established in India. Of non-English journals, probably the most widely used in the United States is *Population,* which has been published since World War II by the Institut National d'Études Démographiques (Paris). The *Population Bulletin,* published by the Population Reference Bureau, is not primarily an outlet for research articles but a medium for furthering the bureau's objective, which is "to make available in accurate, nontechnical form the essential facts upon which rational population policies must be based" (Cook, 1953). The *Population Bulletin of the United Nations* appears irregularly and is largely, though not wholly, devoted to presentation of material related to the research program of the Population Branch.

A glance at a few of the chapter bibliographies in this volume will disclose the wide variety of journals in the social and natural sciences in which demographic materials appear. Demographers frequently argue that this diffusion of publication has an advantage in terms of "spreading knowledge around." However, it does mean that the demography one reads tends to depend heavily on the discipline from which he hails; the lack of centralization of the demographic literature probably militates against the building-up of a common universe of discourse for the variegated students of population.

GENERAL OBSERVATIONS

If one were to essay a sociology-of-knowledge investigation of the field of population study, at least three striking facts about demography as a profession would have to be taken into account. First, demographers are drawn from a number of disciplines. Their scientific investigations and their professional organizations lead them to cross disciplinary boundaries somewhat freely. Since there is no recognition of demography as a discipline in the administrative framework of universities, demographers are sometimes slightly marginal with respect to their home disciplines, whatever they may be. Second, by virtue of demography's dependence on data collected by governments, and for other reasons, the professional activities of demographers tend to be differentiated and specialized according to type of institutional affiliation. By the same token, demography constitutes a somewhat distinctive arena of interaction among representatives of academic, government, business, and other institutions. Third, a large part of the demand for the services of the demographer as a professional person is of an extra-scientific character. There is, of course, the teaching function, which leads primarily to the transmission rather than to the accumulation of knowledge. In addition, demographers are called on to devote a large proportion of their work to providing information, estimates, projections, and interpretations of data from the standpoint of various social engineering uses. Much of the research and publication generated by this demand can be said to have only incidental value, at best, as contributions to "science." From the standpoint of demography as a science, for example, little is gained by making annual estimates of population for towns and cities or by making periodic revisions of population projections by a standardized technique. Except when such exercises lead to new analytical methods or afford some new insight into interrelations between population and socioeconomic circumstances—both of which contributions are comparatively rare—their contributions to scientific knowledge (as discussed in chap. iv) are slight. Perhaps the most charitable view one could take of these activities is that they are the "bread and butter" of the professional demographer. If he learns to carry out these tasks with dispatch, he may have some time and resources left over for research of a more basic character. Another aspect of the demand picture is that demographers are continually called on to provide publicity on current population changes and to interpret demographic problems to various publics. It is not uncommon for what is essentially the same paper to be written over and over again by an eminent demographer, to be published on one occasion in a journal whose audience is welfare workers; on another, real estate agents; on a third, public health officers; and so on. If only knowledge of population accumulated as rapidly as does literature of this kind, one could be sanguine indeed about the prospects of demography as a science.

The professional environment of the demographer, therefore, is one that has certain unusually stimulating features but at the same time one that provides certain distractions from the pursuit of science. It is hazardous, to be sure, to speculate on the motivational patterns of professional people. But if one were to speculate, he might conclude that on the whole the goal of building science constitutes a subordinate and less than autonomous motive. The demographer too often steps out of his role as scientist to allow us to suppose the contrary. Although the student of *Wissenssoziologie* has yet to determine the optimum conditions for scientific progress in a discipline, it may be imagined that the optimum "mix" of stimuli and motivations would be somewhat different from that characterizing demography. At the same time, the progress of demography as a science, as recorded in this volume, must signify that demographers are fumbling toward an appro-

priate integration and balance of their scientific and professional roles.

REFERENCES

ALPERT, HARRY. 1957. "Demographic Research and the National Science Foundation," *Social Forces*, XXXVI, 17–21.

COOK, ROBERT C. 1953. "The Population Reference Bureau," *Science*, Vol. CXVIII, No. 3074.

DUNCAN, O. D. 1957. "The Teaching of Demography in the United States of America," in *The University Teaching of Social Sciences: Demography*, ed. D. V. GLASS. Paris: UNESCO.

GOLD, DAVID. 1957. "A Note on Statistical Analysis in the *American Sociological Review*," *American Sociological Review*, XXII, 332–33.

HAUSER, PHILIP M. 1955. "Population Statistics and Research in Planning Economic Development," *Proceedings of the World Population Conference, 1954*, V, 927–44. New York: United Nations.

JAFFE, A. J. 1955. "Forms of Training in Techniques of Demographic Analysis," *Proceedings of the World Population Conference, 1954*, III, 815–24. New York: United Nations.

KISER, CLYDE V. 1953. "The Population Association Comes of Age," *Eugenical News*, XXXVIII, 107–11.

POPULATION COUNCIL. 1956. *Report of the Population Council, Inc., November 5, 1952, to December 31, 1955*. New York: Population Council, Inc.

———. 1957. *Annual Report, 1956*. New York: Population Council, Inc.

Development and Current Status
of Demography

Introduction to Part II

The historical materials in this part provide a rather comprehensive account of the circumstances attending the beginnings, early development, and recent progress of demography, as these occurred in widely scattered places and over a considerable span of time. It will doubtless be apparent that each period and region has had a distinctive contribution to make to the growth of demography, despite the recurrence of common problems and methods of study. Each has had, as well, its own special obstacles to overcome. Reasons are given why demography appears to have languished at certain periods and why the preoccupations of demographers have varied considerably from place to place. Whereas the contemporary period, on the whole, appears to be one in which demography is making rapid strides as compared with earlier epochs, its progress is uneven—as is probably true of any science—and there remain countries where demography scarcely is recognized as a legitimate field of free investigation and others where a variety of practical obstacles inhibit its potential development.

In chapter vi Lorimer presents a general picture of the emergence and development of demography as a recognizable scientific discipline. Especially noteworthy in his essay are the isolation of some of the major themes of that development and the indication of how these themes have converged to produce the discipline that we know today. It was, of course, impossible for the author to summarize all contributions of historic importance. However, a perusal of his first bibliography—arranged in chronological order from 1589 through 1937—will give the reader a good conspectus of the preoccupations and accomplishments of demographers in the several phases of their discipline's evolution.

Sauvy's account of demography in France (chapter vii) is significant, among other things, as a study in the relationships between the development of demography and the concern about "population problems" on the part of government and public opinion. France is somewhat distinctive among European countries in the length of time and degree to which population research has been oriented to questions of national population policy. However, Sauvy's sketch of the kinds of contributions being made by French demographers makes it clear that policy orientation need not prejudice the standards of scientific work, provided that there is strong institutional support for impartial and objective population studies.

As indicated by Grebenik in chapter viii, Great Britain was the home of pioneer developments in "political arithmetic" as well as a stage for the great public controversies touched off by the statements of Malthus. This essay also makes it clear that the early development of demography, including many of its most important tools of investigation, was by no means primarily attributable to academic interest in the subject. Indeed, Grebenik points out that in Britain—which is typical in this respect of many other countries—demography has some way to go to become firmly established in academic circles.

Demography in Germany, Schubnell points out in chapter ix, has strong roots in eighteenth- and nineteenth-century intellectual movements and scientific developments. In this country, as in others, emphasis has shifted back and forth from abstract theoretical constructions to meticulous empirical and descriptive studies. Here, as elsewhere, the impetus to and support for the latter stem primarily from the recognition of critical social problems consequent upon population changes. A major problem for the healthy development of the discipline is how to maximize the contribution to basic knowledge of the subject made by the newer tools and mechanisms for population research.

The American reader of Costanzo's summary of Italian contributions, chapter x, will doubtless be struck by the close interrelationship of demographic and biometric or anthropometric interests on the part of that country's scholars. Perhaps the author's own preoccupations have led him to emphasize the affinity of these interests, but his historical materials amply confirm that demography in Italy has long had a strong biological orientation. It is equally clear, however, that the distinction between demography and other studies of social and economic problems by statistical methods is not so greatly emphasized here as in some countries and that the close association between demographers and other statistical specialists has been a salutary influence on the study of population.

The case of Brazil, as described by Mortara in chapter xi, is significant in showing the possibility for rapid strides in demography in a country lacking both a long history of scientific interest in the subject and the kind of resources for research that are likely to be taken for granted in countries with well-developed statistical systems. Especially instructive is the ingenuity of demographers in Brazil in making the most of incomplete and defective data. The expedients they have devised will doubtless prove most useful in pursuing population studies in countries lacking reliable vital registration systems and having only one or two censuses conforming to modern standards of data collection.

Chandrasekaran's survey of demography in India, chapter xii, is significant in view of that country's acknowledged chronic population problem, the exigency of which rather highlights the underutilization—until recently—of its store of basic data in the form of decennial censuses since 1881. As is implied by the author, the significant recent strides in the development of scientific demography are not unrelated to the growing recognition of the political and economic import of population conditions. In a country which achieved independence only a little more than a decade ago, it is not surprising that scholars have sensed the potential importance of their contributions only recently. From the author's account of current activities, it appears that India will be one of the leaders among countries sometimes designated as "less developed" in establishing a firm institutional basis for scientific demography.

Taeuber's panorama of demography in the Pacific countries, chapter xiii, brings out variations in adequacy of resources for research and discontinuities and gaps in research activities. Some of the more significant of her observations concern the extent to which population changes and interest therein are imbedded in a cultural-historical matrix; her presentation raises the question of how far techniques and orientations emanating from Western demography can be applied effectively in radically different contexts. Along with the other chapters in this part,

Taeuber's discussion may lead one to wonder whether demography must always in some measure reflect "national character," despite the diffusion of common standards of scientific work.

American demography, as described in some detail by Vance in chapter xiv, has had its own characteristic emphases and shifting foci. One circumstance of particular relevance was the early development of regular census-taking and subsequent notable progress in that field, in marked contrast to the egregious retardation of the vital registration system. On the academic side, Vance indicates the close relationship between demography and sociology that has developed in recent decades— a liaison that has both positive and negative implications for the advancement of population studies. As far as may be judged from comparison with the other accounts given here, demographers in the United States have been unusually successful in building a strong professional organization which, despite its large complement of non-academic members, has traditionally emphasized the facilitation of basic population research.

6. The Development of Demography

FRANK LORIMER

THE BEGINNINGS OF DEMOGRAPHY: POLITICAL ARITHMETIC

A new field of empirical research was opened by John Graunt, who set forth his findings in a pamphlet published in London in 1662: *Natural and Political Observations . . . Made upon the Bills of Mortality.* The "bills of mortality" were current reports on burials, and incidentally on christenings, in a population of nearly half a million persons in the vicinity of London. Weekly reports on burials had been initiated in 1592, during one of the recurrent plagues that spread terror through the city. Kept for a time and then neglected, these reports were resumed by the company of parish clerks during another plague in 1603 and were continued regularly thereafter. The weekly inventories by parishes were summarized in annual reports, and, from 1629 on, the burials were classified by "disease" or "casualty," as reported by "ancient matrons" appointed to this task in each parish. This material attracted the attention of a young merchant inflamed with the enthusiasm of his age for empirical investigations, and he set about studying them in a spirit akin to that of an explorer or chemist. Homage for the foundations of a new science is due both to the unknown parish clerks who initiated these systematic reports and to Graunt, who first used them as a basis for systematic, objective inferences.

London in the mid-seventeenth century, though an unhealthy city, had a lively commercial and intellectual life —as vividly recorded in the diary of Samuel Pepys. John Graunt, born in 1620, the son of a draper, ran a haberdasher's shop in the city and did so successfully. He was also a citizen of the world of ideas. He had attracted the friendship of William Petty, a man of tremendous energy a few years younger than Graunt. Petty, at the time he met Graunt, had been seaman, salesman, student, and inventor; he later became professor of music at Gresham College, professor of anatomy at Oxford, assessor of estates in Ireland, and a wealthy landed proprietor. While studying in Paris, under the influence of Thomas Hobbes, he had conceived the remarkable idea that arithmetic was applicable to political affairs —an idea that eventually found expression in his *Political Arithmetick.* Petty and later Graunt became members of a circle of friends—which included Robert Hooke and Robert Boyle—who met in taverns or chambers, or at Gresham College, to discuss "natural philosophy," "observations," and "experiments." It was in this milieu that Graunt set himself the task of discovering "regularities" in the maze of events recorded in the bills of mortality.

The terms "natural" and "political" in the title of Graunt's pamphlet suggest, at its inception, the dual nature of demography as a biological and social discipline. This suggestion is elaborated in two dedicatory epistles. One dedication presented the study to the president of the newly founded Royal

Society of Philosophers (of which Graunt was not yet a member), "as it relates to Natural History, and as it depends on the Mathematiques of my Shop-Arithmetique." The other presented it to a member of the Privy Council, "as it relates to Government, and Trade."

Prior to this time, populations and their changes had received little systematic attention. Some ancient philosophers, geographers, and historians had been interested in the numbers of persons in nations and cities and in the broad implications of population for political affairs. But even this speculative interest in population had withered—except in the studies of a few unusual scholars, notably the Arab philosopher ibn-Khaldun in the fourteenth century and the Italian Jesuit Giovanni Botero in the late sixteenth century. The latter anticipated Malthus' treatment of factors limiting the growth of population. Census inquiries of a sort were frequently carried out for administrative reasons, but the data from these inquiries were not related to any theoretical issues. In fact, up to the beginning of the seventeenth century there was no word in any modern European language for "population" as a specific concept (Nitti, 1894, English ed., pp. 3–4). The word "population," it seems, was first used by Francis Bacon; it was translated loosely as *peuple* or *monde* in early French editions of his essays. In 1612, in writing "Of the True Greatness of Kingdoms and Estates," Bacon said: "The greatness of an estate in bulk and territory doth fall under measure . . . the population may appear by musters." In 1625, in discussing "remedies" in his essay, "Of Seditions and Troubles," he warned, "Generally it is to be foreseen that the population of a Kingdom (especially if it be not mown down by wars) do not exceed the stock of the Kingdom which should maintain them."

Riccioli, another Italian Jesuit, gathered information on the numbers of persons in different states and presented a scholarly estimate of the earth's population in 1661. He made a substantial contribution, which was used by later demographers. But unlike Graunt, Riccioli did not investigate the processes of population change. The first field study in demography seems to have been an investigation by a Swiss physician, Felix Platter, of the effects of a plague in Basel, 1609–11 (Bickel, 1947, p. 82), but this remarkable undertaking was a relatively isolated event.

Graunt approached his material in a critical spirit and carried out an ingenious and painstaking investigation of its significance. He aimed at a precise statement of the grounds for each inference and presented his basic data in detail. As he put it, "I have, like a silly Scholeboy, coming to say my lesson to the World . . . brought a bundle of Rods wherewith to be whipt, for every mistake I have committed." Of course, he made many mistakes, but he discovered important relations, and at various points he discreetly avoided speculations unsupported by evidence. He found an excess of males over females at birth and measured sex ratios at birth in London and in a rural community, but he made no attempt to explain this phenomenon—limiting his comment to the recommendation that this relation be examined in other populations. He supplemented his London data with a ninety-year set of parish records for Petty's native village—which he treated as representative of rural England.

Graunt found that burials generally exceeded christenings in London but that the reverse relation prevailed in the rural parish. He recognized that the number of christenings in London had been greatly reduced during the two decades preceding his study by the omission of infants born to dissenters, but on the basis of earlier data he estimated the ratio of deaths to births in London as approximately 14 to 13, as contrasted with a ratio of 52 to 63 "in the country." He examined possible reasons for this disparity—both in mortality (taking into account the relative frequencies of deaths from various causes in London and "in the country") and in fertility (taking account of peculiarities in the composition of London's population and of conditions that might lower fecundity in the city). He estimated the increase of London's population from changes in absolute numbers of deaths over a half-century, and he estimated the volume of migration required to account for this increase, in view of the excess of deaths over births. He undertook measurements of relations between population and frequencies of births and deaths, both for London and for the rural community. And for the latter, where weddings were recorded, he used the ratio of births to marriages as an index of fertility. He studied the relative variability of deaths ascribed to particular causes in successive years and in different areas.

The significance of Graunt's contribution has been well stated by Walter F. Willcox: "Graunt . . . discovered . . . the uniformity and predictability of many important biological phenomena taken in the mass. In so doing, he opened the way both for the later discovery of uniformities in many social or volitional phenomena . . . and for a study of these uniformities, their nature and their limits; thus he, more than any other man, was the founder of statistics" (Graunt, 1662, 1939 American ed., Introduction).

There has been considerable controversy over the respective roles of Graunt and Petty in this undertaking. Most early writers accepted Graunt's responsibility for the study, but this position has been challenged. However, the editor of Petty's economic writings (Hull, 1899) and most modern demographers who have examined the material (Greenwood, 1948; Willcox in his Introduction to Graunt; Glass, 1950b) recognize that Petty lacked the intellectual discipline exhibited in the Observations and adduce specific evidence that Graunt was, indeed, the real author. Petty may have stimulated Graunt's initial interest in this sort of an inquiry; he co-operated in obtaining the rural registration data; he later carried through somewhat similar, but more superficial, observations on the Dublin bills of mortality; and he edited a posthumous edition of Graunt's Observations, published by the Royal Society. Moreover, Graunt had promoted Petty's appointment as a professor of music at Gresham College, and Petty, who took a leading role in the organization of the Royal Society, undoubtedly sponsored Graunt's election to the society prior to the issue of its revised charter in 1662; he may also have prompted Charles II's special commendation of Graunt's work on this occasion. There remains an unresolved question about the extent to which Petty may have participated actively in the preparation of the Observations, edited parts of the original text, or written some passages. The question is especially pertinent for a feature of the text which foreshadowed future progress in demography, a schematic life-table design. The initial step in its construction was empirical: an estimate of the proportion of live-born infants who die within the first six years of life. Graunt had developed this estimate (in an early part of his study)—in the absence of any specific information on ages of persons at death —by assigning all deaths due to certain infantile diseases and half of those due to certain diseases with high incidence in childhood to the first six years of life. The subsequent stages in "Graunt's life table" (which is presented near the end of the last chapter dealing with the London material, where it is followed by some passages which seem inconsistent with the rest of the text) were obtained by an application of arbitrary proportions. Willcox suggests that Petty may have contributed this construction, but Glass gives reasons to the contrary. Whoever its author, this was a brilliant conception, even though at this time it lacked any objective control.

Graunt's contribution was hailed by the members of the Royal Society and, through the society, brought to the attention of the scientific world. It was associated with Petty's ideas, which also attracted wide attention. If Graunt was the founder of a new science, Petty was its godfather—giving it a name, "political arithmetic," and enhancing its social position. Petty dealt with population along with many other topics, but his own works do not contain any important technical contributions to demography.

A demand for more precise knowledge in the field of political arithmetic came from the rising interest in insurance schemes, involving the calculation of risks and the assessment of charges. A great advance was made in London by another member of the Royal Society, about thirty years after the publication of Graunt's *Observations*. Edmund Halley, who achieved immortality by charting a comet, constructed the first empirical life table—on the basis of births and deaths, with the latter classified by the ages of persons at death, from the church records of Breslau, Silesia. These records had been used by a clergyman, Kasper Neumann, to produce evidence contrary to prevalent superstitions that particular ages and astronomical events brought special dangers. His study was sent to Leibnitz and by him to the Royal Society of London. Incidentally, such exchange of ideas and information among scientists across national boundaries was an important factor in the early advance of demography, as of other sciences. Halley communicated directly with Neumann and obtained supplemental information for the period 1687–91. Halley realized that exclusive reliance on vital statistics in his undertaking would be proper only with respect to a relatively closed, stationary population. But he satisfied himself that the Breslau material could be used in this way, with some minor adjustments. The city did not have a large migrant population, and the number of births, at least during the period under observation, was only slightly above the number of deaths. He used his data with great ingenuity—relating deaths, at least within the first year of life, to births. He obtained estimates of expected numbers of persons in a stationary population by single years of age through eighty-four years (Halley, 1693).

New investigations into population questions took place around 1700 in England and in France. These studies were related to special inventories of the population in both countries; but the results of these inventories were not officially collated in either country to give national figures, and the inquiries were not repeated in the following decades.

The British Parliament in 1694 levied taxes on marriages, births, and burials, and on bachelors and childless persons; the scheme included a provision for local enumerations of the population in all parts of England and Wales in 1695, to be followed by successive revisions each year. A plan was also drawn to establish a national system of current reports on parish statistics, with provision for information concerning non-conformists as well as members of the established church. This ambitious plan was not carried through in England, though a similar program was put into operation in Sweden during the next century. However, enumerations were actually made in 1695, though they may have been incomplete in some areas. Figures on houses were already available for administrative areas in England and Wales (as of 1690) from hearth-tax records. Gregory King, who set about preparing an estimate of the population of England and Wales, used the enumeration returns for selected areas in London and elsewhere to obtain ratios of persons per house in several kinds of communities (Glass, 1950a). He then applied these ratios to the figures on houses, with adjustments to give estimated numbers of occupied houses in 1695. King also investigated data on burials, presumably as a means of checking his population estimates, but he did not report these calculations in his published results. His final estimate of the population of England and Wales in 1695 (5.5 million), though perhaps somewhat too high, was the most substantial finding on this subject between the time of the Norman Conquest and the first census of England and Wales in 1801.

The title of King's work suggests Graunt's influence: *Natural and Political Observations and Conclusions upon the State and Conditions of England* (1696). King experimented with estimates of age distribution through life-table constructions, and he also used enumeration data on persons by age in some districts, with critical attention to their credibility. His final estimate of the distribution of the population by sex and by age classes in England and Wales was apparently obtained by smoothing figures for about five thousand people "in several places." But when challenged, he defended his results with considerable sophistication by evidence and inferences from his own, Graunt's, and other investigations. The new science of "political arithmetic" was beginning to achieve cumulative power.

A census of the French kingdom was prescribed in 1693 (the year before the act of the British Parliament which contained a similar provision). This was intended primarily to provide information for use in directing the distribution of food within regions during a time of severe shortage (Vincent, 1947). Only a few fragments of the results of this survey have been preserved. Nevertheless, the data thus collected were used for a remarkable enterprise.

France at this time was divided into administrative districts called *généralités*. The chief royal agent in each of these divisions was known as an *intendant*. These *intendants* were ordered in 1697 to prepare *mémoires*, in accordance with a series of prescribed questions, on the geographic, economic, and social conditions of their respective territories. The *mémoires* of the *intendants*, prepared during periods ranging from a few months to a year or more, yielded a comprehensive body of information on conditions in France at the end of the seventeenth century. These *mémoires* are still extant, though only a few have been published. The instructions on the required information included the following items: ". . . Number of towns; approximate number of men in each; number of villages and hamlets; total number of parishes and of souls in each . . . Factories; number of workmen; their maintenance. Where are they trained? . . . Number of workmen leaving as compared with number remaining . . . Consult the old registers to see if the population was formerly more numerous; causes of decline . . ." (Vincent, 1947, p. 68). Information on hand in the offices of the *intendants* from the 1693 survey of the population was apparently used in meeting some of these requirements.

Prior to this survey, Sebastian Vauban, marshal of France, engineer and liberal statesman, had written a *Description géographique de l'élection de Vézelay* (an *élection* being a subdivision of a *généralité*). This included the results of a detailed census of its parishes. There is good reason to suppose that Vauban took part in preparing the instructions to the *intendants*. In any case, he used material in the *mémoires*, with some adjustments, to prepare a first account of the population of France. This was presented in an anonymous publication, *Projet d'une dîme royale* (1707). The first chapter in this publication deals with enumerations, their usefulness, and methods of organization. Vauban recommended annual enumerations of the population, but no significant progress was made in this direction during the next half-century.

Graunt's *Observations* and related inquiries attracted the attention of scholars in several other countries—notably in the Netherlands, Sweden, and various German states. Johann Süssmilch, a Lutheran clergyman, became the leading exponent of demography in the middle decades of the eighteenth century. The first edition of his essay was published in Berlin in 1741: *Die Göttliche Ordnung in den Veränderungen des menschlichen Geschlechts, aus der Geburt, dem Tode, und der Fortplanzung desselben erwissen.* Graunt had discovered "regularities" in apparently fortuitous events, such as marriages, births, diseases, deaths, and movements from place to place. His studies pointed toward a demographic "order," but his findings were given a theological interpretation in a treatise on "physico-theology" by Derham; Süssmilch's interest was aroused by reading this book. Süssmilch posed the question, "Are not vital events, apparently so fortuitous but really so orderly, the expression of a divine mind?" There was never any doubt in his heart about the answer, and he set forth to demonstrate this proposition through observations and empirical inferences. He devoted his active mind for many years to population studies, gathering data, corresponding with other scholars, and preparing his exposition. The second edition, in two volumes, 1761–62, has twelve hundred pages plus an appendix with sixty-eight tables—far more massive than Graunt's incisive treatment in less than a hundred pages! A third edition was published in 1765. Süssmilch's interest was universal and he made the most painstaking estimate of the world's population ever presented up to this time.

The excess of males over females at birth (a ratio not influenced by human behavior), modified by the excess of male deaths to female deaths, allows an approach toward equality of men and women at marriageable ages—thus affording a rational basis for monogamy. This was a cardinal point in "physico-theology." As Süssmilch investigated this phenomenon, his evidence led him to reject a simple formulation. It is this sort of conscientious attention to detail that distinguishes him from the ordinary protagonist of a fixed idea. Findings based on a large series of records (he is said to have been the first to emphasize "the law of numbers," i.e., the increase in the value of findings with increase in the number of cases) led him to conclude that there is generally an excess of women over men among adults. But as might be expected, he had no difficulty in squaring his new observation with his theology. Observing the frequencies of remarriages by men and by women, he noted that men are more prone to accept a new spouse if a first marriage is dissolved by death than are women. There is, in his phrase, a tendency among men toward "successive polygamy." He concluded that God, in his infinite wisdom, had provided for this propensity. He was impressed by an apparent constancy in the distribution of deaths by age classes under different conditions. He found that in most nations (though not in all parts of a nation) there is "normally" a moderate excess of births over deaths, giving a gradual increase of population. He assumed that it is the duty of governments to preserve this tendency, and he thus became one of the early exponents of pro-natalist policies.

Süssmilch obtained vital statistics from 1,056 parishes in Brandenburg and enumeration returns for various cities and provinces in Prussia. He compared his findings with observations in England, those by Struyck on 22 villages in Holland, studies by Wargentin in Sweden, and others. He computed many series of ratios: population to marriages, to births, and to deaths; births to marriages; deaths at particular ages to deaths at all ages; and deaths by cause to deaths from all causes; etc. He constructed life tables for an urban and a rural area in Germany, and in his third edition (1765) he presented the first life table on the population of all Prussia. He observed that death is most frequent in the first weeks of life and declines to a low level which he placed in the vicinity of fifteen years. He found the ratio of deaths to population in Brandenburg villages, 1743–48 (in years not affected by severe epidemics), as one death per 42 or 43 persons and in 1739–48 as one death per 38 or 39 persons. In large cities, such as London, Rome, and Berlin, he estimated one death per 24 to 30 persons.

Süssmilch also studied conditions influencing fertility, including the effects of disease, age at marriage, disruption of marriages by death, prolonged nursing of infants, and fear of pregnancy. He found evidence of declines in rates of marriage in Prussia and in France during the first half of the eighteenth century. He concluded that in rural districts this must generally be due to complete occupancy of the land. He argued that oppressive taxation of peasants in France had led to actual depopulation in some districts. He attributed declines of marriage rates in cities chiefly to "luxury" and high prices. Through his active correspondence he drew the attention of many scientists to various aspects of population changes.

Buffon, writing in France in the mid-eighteenth century, placed the study of human populations in a broad empirical context. He was especially concerned, in the course of his extensive and acute observations on various species, with conditions controlling the oscillations and the relative stability of all natural populations, including man. He made some specific contributions in vital statistics, but his major contribution to demography was a quickening of interest in the development of significant theory in conjunction with precise observations.

One of Graunt's most energetic, if not most acute, successors in England was Thomas Short. His first work, *New Observations . . . on City, Town, and County Bills of Mortality* (1750), can be said truly to contain many "curious observations." In 1767 Short published *A Comparative History of the Increase and Decrease of Mankind in England and Several Countries Abroad . . . ,* with numerous references to the observations of other scientists, including Benjamin Franklin.

Meanwhile, studies in various countries concerned with conditions affecting mortality, the development of life tables, and the computation of annuities were leading to greater precision in the treatment of vital statistics. Some of the notable contributors to this and other aspects of political arithmetic, with dates of important works, are: Kersseboom (Holland, 1740), Struyck (Holland, 1740), Deparcieux (France, 1746), Elvius (Sweden, 1746), D. Bernouille (Switzerland, 1760), Muret (Switzerland, 1766), Wargentin (Sweden, 1766), Price (England, 1771), Lastri (Italy, 1775), Tetens (Denmark, 1785), and Milne (England, 1815).

Most students of vital statistics at this time were forced to rely on information concerning births and deaths, without information on the characteristics of the populations in which these events occurred. More complete information was sometimes obtained for selected classes, such as insured persons or members of religious orders. Some of the eighteenth-century scientists who wrestled with problems of life-table construction, like Kersseboom and Deparcieux, exercised great ingenuity and made significant contributions to the methods of demographic analysis. According to Westergaard (1932, p. 96), Tetens initiated the method of "expected deaths"—in this case to compare the observed frequency of deaths in an insured population with that expected on the basis of its characteristics at the specific rates of a selected life table. Outside of Sweden, where age-specific death rates could be obtained directly from the statistical system, Milne seems to have been the first to derive life-table values from joint information on births and deaths and on the characteristics of a total community. His data for Carlisle were drawn from investigations by a physician, Heysham, on the incidence by age of deaths from smallpox in this community.

The founders of political arithmetic differed widely in social background, ideology, and motivations. But such differences in social orientation and personal motives seem to have been largely irrelevant to their achievements. The critical characteristics that gave their efforts a cumulative force were their enthusiasm for the discovery of previously unknown relations—especially quantitative relations—in the processes of life and death and their respect for empirical observations.

Interest in political arithmetic as a comprehensive discipline declined prior to the rise of modern demographic research. One reason, though this seems paradoxical, may have been the emphasis on new measures for the systematic provision of basic demographic information. In the absence of such information the political arithmeticians had exercised great ingenuity in attempts to answer simple factual questions. The development of official statistical programs required less theoretical orientation, it absorbed much intellectual energy, and it tended to discredit more speculative inquiries. Some of the leaders in this field, notably Quételet, also had strong theoretical interests, but such persons were exceptional. Then, too, the attention of most students of human affairs in the nineteenth century was attracted either to speculative issues with broad social implications or to more immediate political and social affairs. In any case, the enthusiasm of the early pioneers in this field for significant "observations" on population processes as a branch of "natural philosophy" gradually waned —giving way either to more specific inquiries or to larger, less controlled speculations.

Only in the analysis of mortality was there a fairly consistent movement from the early work in political arithmetic to more precise investigations and significant scientific theory. This movement was propelled by two social forces, the demand of insurance societies for more accurate actuarial values and an increasingly scientific approach to the control of diseases—eventually, the acceptance of government responsibilities in the field of public health. Other aspects of population study during the nineteenth century were often developed in the context of more or less unrelated interests.

Collection of the basic data needed for demographic studies involves great effort and expense, but the provision of such data is facilitated by some of their inherent characteristics. In the first place, the primary phenomena of demography are discrete and relatively free from ambiguity. In the second place, much of the information needed by demographers is also wanted for other more immediate uses. Censuses were taken in the Roman, Chinese, and some other ancient nations and in some medieval European states to serve administrative ends. As the functions of governments became more diversified in the modern world, more detailed and precise information was required. The present status of demography as a science must be attributed in large part to the availability of a vast body of appropriate and relatively accurate data, provided in part to serve other interests.

The original motivation for recording births, marriages, and deaths springs mainly from their utility in defining the status and roles of individuals in a society, the inheritance of property, etc. Births, deaths, and marriages are registered with varying fidelity by families, associations, or communities in many different kinds of societies. The recording of vital events was an important aspect of ecclesiastic organization in early modern Europe. (Interest in recording and collecting information on deaths was also stimulated by concern about the recurrence of epidemics, especially in large towns. Rising public interest in sanitation and health brought a new stimulus toward improving vital and sanitary statistics.)

Church registers were a principal source of demographic data in Europe through the eighteenth century. They also laid a foundation for the subsequent development of civil registration systems. Attitudes, habits, and procedures built up around Roman Catholic, Lutheran, Episcopalian, and other church records in Europe were carried over—as were those relating to the community-family archives (*koseki*) in Japan—into the new civil systems. Under these conditions, a partial development of vital statistics usually preceded, and their systematic development advanced in step with, the development of census inquiries in Europe.

This did not happen in the areas of British settlement in North America for three reasons: the diversity of sects; the predominance of such denominations as Baptists, Congregationalists, and Methodists in which the baptism of infants was repudiated or regarded merely as a ceremony without ecclesiastical legal force; and the retention of authority over civil registers by the several states of the United States. On the other hand, in the United States a periodic census was prescribed in the Constitution for political reasons. A century elapsed in this country between the inauguration of a periodic census program and the inauguration of a national vital statistics reporting system. Similarly, the taking of a fairly reliable census in many underdeveloped countries today is a much simpler task than the organization of current vital statistics.

The medieval parish registers in Europe were gradually improved in early modern times with the progress of communication and literacy. This improvement received a strong impetus from the Reformation because records of church affiliation then acquired increased importance. The subject was accorded serious attention in the Council of Trent (1545–63); rules about the proper recording of baptisms, marriages, and burials were made obligatory in all Catholic parishes. Other measures were gradually introduced by kings and parliaments in attempts to assure the registration of vital events relating to citizens of all denominations. Beginning in 1670, annual reports were issued on numbers of recorded births, marriages, and deaths in Paris.

The transformation of parish registers into national statistical systems was carried out with greatest efficiency in the northern European countries. According to a Swedish law of 1748, quite elaborate reports, to be drawn from current records, were to be filled out each year (later every three years) by the pastor of each parish—giving births in each calendar month by sex and by legitimacy, marriages and dissolutions of marriage, and deaths by sex, by age, and by cause. Additional information was required on numbers of households and numbers of persons by sex and by age, with separate classifications for persons fifteen years or over by marital status and by occupation. Reports were required on all persons within a parish, regardless of their religious affiliations. Each pastor's study became "a small statistical laboratory." The population of Sweden was completely enumerated in 1751. Later a municipal population-registration office was established in Stockholm. Eventually an elaborate nationwide system of cross-checks by correspondence was introduced to control the accuracy of the current data. Similar programs have been developed in Denmark, Norway, and the Netherlands (U.S. National Resources Committee, 1938, Appendix C).

A Tabular Commission (Tabell-Kommissionen) was established in Sweden in 1749 to consolidate and analyze the returns from the parishes. The astronomer Per Wargentin, who succeeded Peter Elvius as secretary of the Academy of Science, then became the guiding spirit of demographic research in Sweden. The commission apparently worked with zeal, exploiting the rich material at its disposal and taking account of the contributions of scientists in other countries, e.g., Struyck and Kersseboom in the Netherlands and Deparcieux in France. It investigated conditions associated with variations in mortality and fertility. Demographic information was treated as a state secret in Sweden at this time, and therefore the earliest investigations of the commission were not published. However, as security regulations in Sweden were relaxed, it became possible for Wargentin to publish, in 1766, the first series of observed sex- and age-specific death rates ever reported for any nation—covering the period 1755–63. Comparable data did not become available for most European countries until about the middle of the nineteenth century or for the United States until the twentieth cenury.

Census enumerations were carried out around 1700 in three European countries: England, France, and Iceland. But in no case were the results at this time officially tabulated or analyzed.[1] There had been enumerations of the population in various European cities and states in the sixteenth and seventeenth centuries—some of them complete enumerations of the population by sex, with division by broad age classes (Wolfenden, 1954, p. 6). There were also enumerations of some French and British colonies in America in the seventeenth and eighteenth centuries. There were twenty-five colonial enumerations (nine in New York, four in Rhode Island) within the territory of the United States (Willcox, 1940, p. 68). The series for French Canada began in 1666.

The first continuous series of reliable reports on the population of any nation was, as already noted, that for

---

[1] The enumerations in England and in France have been mentioned above. The returns for Iceland have now been analyzed, and yield very interesting results (Thorsteinsson, 1947).

Sweden—though in this case house-to-house enumerations were soon replaced by the use of data from the continuous accounting system. Enumerations of the population of Prussia were initiated under Frederick the Great in 1748 and were carried out quite frequently thereafter. Periodic censuses, continuing into the present, began in the United States in 1790 and in both England and France in 1801. Census programs were soon established in other countries. As these programs developed, the inquiries gradually became more comprehensive and specific. Between 1855 and 1865, complete enumerations were carried out in twenty-four sovereign countries. The number rose to forty-nine in the years 1925–34 and, after a recession because of the war, to sixty-five in the years 1945–54 (see Linder, chap. xv).

The Constitution of the United States prescribed that an enumeration of the population should be made within three years after the first meeting of Congress and within every subsequent period of ten years (Wright and Hunt, 1900; Rossiter, 1909). There is no definite evidence that any of the founding fathers promoted this measure as a potential vehicle of statistics. Yet prior to the second census, a memorial was addressed to Congress by the American Philosophical Society, signed by Thomas Jefferson, recommending "a more detailed view of the inhabitants of the United States, under several different aspects." Detailed information was requested on numbers of births and on numbers of persons by ages as a means of estimating "the ordinary duration of life in these States . . . and the ratio of the increase of their population," as well as information on citizenship and occupation (Wright and Hunt, 1900, p. 19). Another memorial with similar intent was presented to Congress at about the same time by the Connecticut Academy of Arts.

In the first census (1790) information was obtained from households, and the names of masters of families were listed by locality. The census distinguished free white males sixteen and over from those under sixteen years. Otherwise, persons were distinguished by sex, color, and status (free or slave) but not by age. Inquiries on broad age classes and other topics were gradually extended and defined in successive inquiries from 1800 through 1840. Sadler (1830) used ratios of children under ten to women sixteen through forty-four years for the white population of the United States in 1820, together with data from the 1821 census of Ireland, as indexes of fertility. Professor George Tucker of the University of Virginia, who had participated in the 1840 census program, presented a series of such ratios for states (1843).

By an act of Congress in 1819, passenger lists were required of all vessels arriving in the United States from foreign ports. Information was compiled from these lists by the Department of State, 1820–74, and by the Treasury Department, 1867–95. After the establishment of an Office of Immigration in 1892 (later the Bureau of Immigration and Naturalization), this agency was assigned responsibility for current statistics in the field. The provision of information on immigrants and their children received strong emphasis in census programs during the later decades of the nineteenth and the early decades of the twentieth century.

A radical innovation was introduced in the program of the seventh census (1850). Defects in previous procedures and a rising demand that the census provide more useful and socially significant information corresponding with statistics in other countries were responsible for the change. James D. B. DeBow, editor of the *Commercial Review of the South and West* (New Orleans), shared in the plans and was later appointed to edit the returns. According to the new plan, the information for each individual was entered on a separate line on the population schedule, thus permitting detailed tabulations and cross-tabulations of two or more items.

Another feature of the seventh census was the attempt to derive current vital and social statistics for the preceding year from the census returns. For example, each person was asked about marriage and about school attendance during this year. An attempt was made to estimate births from information on living children at the time of the census and on deaths during the previous year. A special schedule was used for reports on deaths during the previous year. This method of trying to overcome the lack of registration data on vital events was continued through the rest of the nineteenth century but was finally abandoned as unsatisfactory.

Congress in 1902 established the Bureau of the Census as a permanent organ of the federal government; previously each census had been conducted by a special staff that was disbanded when its report was completed. The Bureau of the Census was given responsibility for the collation and publication of mortality statistics, to be provided by states and cities, as of 1900 and subsequent years.

The national death registration area, established at this time, comprised 10 states, the District of Columbia, and 134 cities in other states, i.e., all areas in which the registration of deaths was required by law and in which the returns were judged to meet certain criteria. The area was gradually extended to include the whole nation for the first time in 1933. Various state reports on vital statistics had, however, been published long before this—beginning with Massachusetts in 1842. A national birth registration area was finally established

in 1915. By 1933 it too had been extended to include the entire nation. The registration of births remained seriously incomplete through the 1930's but has been greatly improved since that time. The National Office of Vital Statistics (now an organ of the Department of Health, Education, and Welfare) is also responsible for the analysis and presentation, at the national level, of information on marriages and divorces; but many states still fail to make reports on this subject, and the information provided varies among the reporting states. There is still no adequate federal program for statistics on marriage and divorce.

In Europe the initiation of periodic census inquiries was generally associated with the development of current vital statistics. In France a national vital statistics reporting system had been established during the last decades of the Old Regime. A yearly account of the numbers of births, marriages, and deaths was established for each *généralité* in 1770 and continued until 1783. These vital statistics were partly published in the *Mémoires de l'Académie des Sciences* (1786–88). An enumeration of the population was undertaken in 1790.

A new program for obtaining demographic data was initiated during the Napoleonic era and continued in force thereafter, with gradual improvements and modifications. The revolutionary governments had established the principle of public responsibility for the registration of vital events. In 1800 Lucien Bonaparte, as Minister of the Interior, ordered a general census of the French population. A census was taken in 1801 and at each successive five years (except for interruptions due to war). These enumerations attained a relatively high degree of accuracy during the 1830's. The office of Statistique Générale was established in 1833, with responsibility for census enumerations and current vital statistics. However, detailed information on the distribution of the population by ages did not become available until 1851.

In England and Wales a national system of civil registers was established in 1837 under supervision of the newly organized office of the Registrar General, but the registration of vital events did not become obligatory until 1874. In 1839 William Farr, M.D., then thirty-two years of age, was appointed "compiler of abstracts." Thereafter, he was for many years the mentor, though never the titular head, of official demographic statistics in England and Wales. The British censuses, which had been taken each ten years since 1801, came under the supervision of the Registrar General. Information on quinquennial age classes was first obtained in the next census (1841). Thus detailed information on age composition became available in England, France, and the United States about the same time, in the mid-nineteenth century. The provision of extensive, statistical information on many other questions also came into vogue at about this time.

Westergaard has characterized the years 1830–49 as "the era of enthusiasm." A series of international statistical congresses, organized largely through the initiative of Adolphe Quételet, began with an assembly in Brussels, 1853. These congresses were concerned mainly with the organization of official statistical services, the formulation of standards, and development of international comparability in official statistics. This function was later assumed by the International Statistical Institute, but with greater emphasis on analytical methods and the substantive aspects of statistical inquiries. Major responsibility for the world-wide development and co-ordination of statistical activities relating to demography now rests with the Social and Economic Council of the United Nations, supplemented in the Western Hemisphere by the Inter American Statistical Institute.

The censuses of British India, from 1871 on, provided the first cumulative body of reliable demographic data for a large non-European country. The remarkable official system of family registers in Japan, though unsatisfactory as a source of national statistics, established behavior patterns and procedures that made possible the inauguration of a highly efficient program of census enumerations and vital statistics in 1920. The census of China in 1953–54, if detailed data which support the preliminary announcements are eventually published, will have closed the greatest gap in basic information on the world's population.

The situation of demographic statistics in Latin-America has varied widely. A noteworthy program for the control and development of census data was developed in Brazil under leadership provided by the Instituto Brasileiro de Geografia e Estatística, but systems of vital statistics have been more effectively developed in several other Latin-American countries. A new era of census enumerations in this hemisphere was inaugurated with the 1950 co-operative Census of the Americas.

The efficiency and scope of modern census programs has benefited greatly from the introduction of systematic sampling designs, as well as from the development of mechanical and electronic processes. Apparently, sampling was first used in national census operations in Norway, 1900, and in Denmark, 1901, but it was some time before this technique came into wide use. Large-scale sampling surveys were developed by special agencies in the United States during the 1930's. A sampling design was first used in a decennial census of the United States in 1940.

Shortly thereafter, responsibility for the Monthly Survey of the Labor Force, developed under the Works Progress Administration, was transferred to the Bureau of the Census; this was later developed into the more comprehensive Current Population Survey. The Indian Statistical Institute, under the direction of P. C. Mahalanobis, has been one of the leading agencies in the development of comprehensive sampling programs for economic, social, and demographic data. The sampling census of the African population of Southern Rhodesia, described by J. R. H. Shaul and C. A. L. Myburgh (1948), marks a further advance. The development of efficient sampling designs has revolutionized the intensive investigation of special aspects of demography. Another major line of progress has come through the application of sampling techniques in investigating the accuracy of basic demographic data obtained in different ways.

Demographers are acutely aware of deficiencies and errors in the data at their disposal. They sometimes take for granted the magnitude of these resources, which are indeed the foundation of scientific work in this field. If we think about the work of local registrars in Kansas, Mexico, and Japan; census enumerators in Costa Rica, Iceland, and India; statisticians and clerks in Helsingfors, Rangoon, and Leopoldville, we realize that a host of workers supplies the data required for measuring demographic trends and processes in different parts of the world—to a degree far beyond that which the early demographers would have deemed possible. The cumulative record of the last decade must have involved the entry and processing of billions of items. At the same time, great effort is now being directed to filling gaps and improving the quality of these basic data.

CONTROVERSIES AND INVESTIGATIONS

The study of population questions during the late eighteenth century and all through the nineteenth century was greatly influenced by shifting interests in economic, social, and political problems. One must, therefore, consider the relation of population studies to various social and ideological issues in a study of the development of demography.

Lively controversies about national population trends broke out during the late eighteenth century both in France and in England. There was at this time much uncertainty about general population trends in Europe, and scholars entertained widely different opinions. Montesquieu, taking one extreme position, asserted that the world's population was then only about one-tenth of its magnitude in ancient times (Spengler, 1938, p. 105). Controversy on this subject in France reached a high point with a publication in 1756 by Victor Marquis de Mirabeau, *L'ami des hommes ou traité de la population*. Mirabeau set out to prove that the strength of the nation, dependent on the well-being of its peasants and workers, was being sapped away, as evidenced by the decline of its population. His bold thesis stirred a considerable furor.

This controversy focused attention on a factual question on which it was possible to obtain objective information. Some relevant data may already have been in the hands of the Abbé Jean d'Expilly, who was gathering material for his *Dictionnaire*. Either shortly before or shortly after the publication of Mirabeau's book, D'Expilly engaged in intensive correspondence with the *intendants* to obtain material on the trend of the French population. He was able to obtain vital statistics from about two-thirds of the parishes in France for two periods: 1690–1701 and 1752–63. His figures on vital statistics for provinces, published in early volumes of the *Dictionnaire*, showed in most cases an excess of births over deaths and apparent increases in ratios of births to deaths in the more recent period—contrary to Mirabeau's assumption. His findings were disputed. In 1764, an official order went to all *intendants* to collect comprehensive information on vital statistics. Even prior to this order, La Michodière, *intendant* of Auvergne, had undertaken an intensive investigation of births, marriages, and deaths in this *généralité* and later in Lyons and Rouen. His secretary, Messance, was encouraged to publish the results of these inquiries in 1766. Vincent comments on the unique value of this publication: ". . . for the first time in France, basic data are kept quite distinct from the results to which an analysis of those data might lead" (1947, p. 55). La Michodière became Councilor of State in 1768. He played an active part in initiating a national vital registration system by order of the Controller-General and was later assigned responsibility for the first national reports on this subject. Before the detailed reports on vital statistics were published, Baron de Montyon used this material to publish under the nominal authorship of his secretary, Moheau, his great work: *Recherches et considérations sur la population de la France* (1778). This treatise on demography has been described as "the most general and at the same time the most precise one produced by any statistician in France up to this time" (Levasseur, cited by Vincent, 1947, p. 58).

A decade after De Montyon's treatise, the mathematician Laplace proposed an inquiry into the population of France by observing ratios of populations to births in scattered localities, obtaining an estimated ratio of this sort for the kingdom, and applying this ratio to the total number of births. After the revolution, he obtained authorization to carry out this project—on the Republican New Year's Day, September 22, 1802. A census had been taken the previous year, but it was poorly executed, so Laplace's procedure was not without possible utility; its main defect from this standpoint was the unreliability of his figures on total births. From a theoretical standpoint, his contribution was brilliant. It is true that his sample was uncontrolled, so that it would not now be accepted as representative. Nevertheless, implicitly assuming his sample to be representative, Laplace calculated the mathematical limits of probable error in his estimate. The procedures are described in his *Théorie analytique des probabilités* (1812, pp. 391 ff.), a cornerstone in the development of statistical theory.

Some British writers in the eighteenth century, like Montesquieu in France, had argued that ancient populations were superior in morals, longevity, and size to the people of the modern world (Glass, 1952). Robert Wallace, moderator of the General Assembly of the Church of Scotland, expounded this view (1753). Nevertheless, he held that a tendency toward excessive propagation, if not restrained, would necessarily dissipate any utopian society—thus partially anticipating Malthus. Opposing ideas about the trend of population in England during the eighteenth century were published in the *Philosophical Transactions* of the Royal Society and in popular pamphlets. Richard Price, who became a leading exponent of the thesis that England's population was decreasing, elaborated his views in 1769 in a letter to Benjamin Franklin. Price apparently overestimated the force of mortality and underestimated the population of England and Wales as about five and a half million at this time. His investigations on this subject were included in his essay on reversionary payments

(1771) and expounded with new force and supporting evidence in *An Essay on the Population of England* (1780). His position was attacked, and the contrary thesis was expounded by other writers, notably Arthur Young, William Eden, William Wales, and John Howlett. The weight of economic interests and patriotic sentiments, as well as some objective evidence, favored this position—which was, of course, implicit in the exposition by Malthus (1798). The last notable attempt to estimate the British population from information on houses, ratios of persons per home, persons per birth, and numbers of births was published by Sir Frederick Eden in 1800, on the eve of the first census of England and Wales. His estimate of at least nine million persons was substantiated by the results of the enumeration.

Proposals for obtaining reliable information on the British population had been advanced in academic circles and in Parliament at various times during the eighteenth century. Heysham's heroic work in obtaining trustworthy demographic data for Carlisle (used by Milne for his life table) and Maitland's investigations in London had revealed gross deficiencies in the available current data. The Company of Parish Clerks, responsible for the London bills of mortality, had petitioned in 1735 and again in 1751 for compulsory registration of births and deaths instead of voluntary reports on baptisms and burials. A national registration bill was introduced into Parliament in 1753 but was opposed as conflicting with the sentiments and liberties of the British people. This bill would have provided both a complete registration system and annual enumerations to be carried out in all localities by the overseers of the poor. Another proposal, presented to Parliament in 1758, would have required the compulsory registration of births, deaths, and marriages in all parishes—with registration fees to be used for the support of the Foundling Hospital.

Final enactment by Parliament of a bill providing for a census of England and Wales came in 1800, and the first census was carried out in 1801. Interest in this undertaking had been whetted by the controversy over the trend of population in Great Britain. Price's nephew, William Morgan, criticizing an attempt by John Rickman to estimate population changes during the previous century on the basis of the 1801 returns, alleged that the census "appears to have been instituted for the mere purpose of determining a controversy; and even in this it has totally failed of its object" (Glass, 1956, p. 5). Rickman's own comprehension of the scientific possibilities and limitations of his material was rather meager, but he continued to exercise control over census operations in England and Wales through 1831. These controversies about the actual trend of population in France and in England were, of course, conditioned by the absence of basic information; therefore, they stimulated fruitful scientific inquiries. The nature of the controversy initiated by Malthus at the end of the eighteenth century was more problematic in this respect.

Several eighteenth-century scholars had observed that the potentiality of men, or other organisms, for natural increase might exceed the resources for their support. Benjamin Franklin had published observations on this subject in 1755. Also in 1755 an essay on this theme was published in Paris by an English economist, Richard Cantillon. He drew attention to cultural aspects of the problem, pointing out that the limits of tolerable density of population varied with standards of living and that marriage patterns might be adopted to check the growth of population in excess of these limits. Giammaria Ortes, in a work published in

Venice in 1790, wrote that the actual growth of population, usually well below its potential rate, was checked by limitations of "capital" but tended to prevent any sustained rise in the general welfare. These expositions, however, did not stir any great popular response.

In 1798, Thomas R. Malthus, a young clergyman (1766–1834), published his famous brochure: *An Essay on the Principle of Population as It Affects the Future Improvement of Society, with Remarks on the Speculations of Mr. Godwin, M. Condorcet, and Other Writers*. At this time he had not carried out any empirical investigations and had little familiarity with studies in this field. Thereafter, convinced of the validity of his thesis and finding himself in the midst of a lively controversy, he eagerly explored all aspects of population changes. His later writings on population, presented as successive editions of the essay, covered a wide range of information. Like Süssmilch, he had sincere respect for objective evidence. He never distorted his accounts to serve his theoretical interests. He used basic data critically in his computations, and his attention was frequently arrested by technical problems. Kuczynski (1935*a*, 1936 ed., pp. 42–43) notes that in relating births to marriages Malthus took account of the time lag between these events so as to avoid the bias in relating births to marriages of the same year in an increasing population—a point often neglected at this time. Nevertheless, the main impact of his work for many decades was to engender a bitter controversy.

The "principle of population," according to Malthus, is that the increase of population, which constantly tends to exceed increase of the means of subsistence, is checked only by the resultant intensification of misery and vice unless a "preventive check," restraint

from marriage, intervenes. His assumption about the necessary relations between demographic and economic changes was challenged, but precise measurement of these changes and analysis of their interactions was beyond the scientific resources of Malthus and his critics. So his exposition, involving large issues of social policy which were charged with strong emotion, was more conducive to "speculations" than to empirical studies. His own investigations, focused mainly on demographic processes, were presented as illustrations of his principle, but such information by itself could neither establish nor refute his central thesis. The most powerful attack on his doctrine—that by Karl Marx—was developed with only slight and casual references to any actual demographic phenomena.

Malthus did indeed awaken tremendous interest in England and elsewhere in "the population question," but only a few of the scholars who engaged in this discussion during the following century undertook empirical studies. Among the early nineteenth-century writers, Michael Sadler has perhaps the best claim to be cited as a serious student of conditions influencing population trends. He assembled considerable information in support of the position that fertility is checked by the growth of cities and the increase of wealth; he seems to have been the first to use ratios of children to women of childbearing age as an index of fertility, drawing his data from the United States census of 1820 and the census of Ireland, 1821. He then proposed a new "law of population" as a substitute for the Malthusian thesis. According to Sadler, "the fecundity of human beings under similar circumstances varies inversely as their numbers on a given space" (1828, 1829 ed., p. xxviii). Yet few of those who discussed population theories during the middle decades of the nineteenth century made any contribution to knowledge in demography. Much later, i.e., near the beginning of the twentieth century, several scholars who were initially attracted to population studies by an interest in Malthusian theory—notably Alexander M. Carr-Saunders and Warren S. Thompson—did make important empirical contributions to demography. The exposition by Malthus did not induce any immediate burst of enthusiasm for systematic investigations.

On the contrary, there is considerable evidence to the effect that the Malthusian controversy tended to inhibit the progress of demography as a science—especially in England, where the controversy was most intense. For example, William Farr, the leading English vital statistician during the middle decades of the nineteenth century, took little interest in the study of fertility or the theoretical analysis of population changes. Glass (1956) comments on this point: "Perhaps part of the relative lack of interest in the study of fertility reflected the reaction to Malthus. People who, like Farr, were concerned to improve public health, felt that they were fighting against the influence of Malthus, and thus continually needed to draw attention to the wastage of human life."

The article "Population" (by W. Hooper) in the *Encyclopaedia Britannica* (9th ed., 1890), reflects the neglected state of demography in England at this time. This article, though aimed at a scientific exposition of the subject, is very pedestrian. The only British authors mentioned in a list of nine citations (including works by French, German, Italian, and Belgian scientists) are William Farr and W. A. Guy —the latter a physician who carried out extensive but poorly controlled investigations into conditions affecting mortality. Newsholme's *Elements of Vital Statistics* had appeared during the year

preceding publication of this article (though presumably after its preparation), but there too the treatment of fertility, population structure, and related topics was very sketchy. Hooper's article concludes with an apologetic reference to the Malthusian controversy in its later neo-Malthusian phase:

We cannot here deal with what is known as the "population question." Any adequate discussion of that highly important subject would involve considerations outside the limits of this article. The "population question" is a question of conduct, while the present article seeks only to point out certain well-ascertained facts regarding the phenomenon of superorganic evolution called population.

The basic difficulty in the relation of Malthus to the development of demography as a science is that the problem to which he drew attention, i.c., the interrelation of demographic and economic trends, was too complex for effective scientific treatment with the methods available to him and his immediate successors. The polemical character of his writings also provoked unnecessary controversy and confusion.

The greatest progress in demography during the nineteenth century came through investigations of mortality and related topics. Activity was intensified when, during the second half of the century, national and state governments accepted new responsibilities for protecting the health of their citizens. The first comprehensive public health law in Great Britain was passed by Parliament in 1848. This was followed by the "Shaftesbury Acts" for the improvement of housing, conditions of labor, and other social measures. Similar advances took place in other countries. The expansion of life insurance operations also stimulated investigations in this field and provided valuable data; the companies themselves frequently undertook important studies. These investigations increased the store of substantive knowledge on conditions affecting the frequencies of death—including work in particular occupations, types of residential area, social class status, etc.

The treatment of problems in this field stimulated progress in methods of statistical inference. Scientists recognized the necessity, in investigating the relation of a particular factor to variations in mortality, of controlling the influence of associated conditions. This led, among other advances, to emphasis on specific mortality rates by age and sex and to the development of systems of weighting specific rates in comparing frequencies of mortality under different conditions: the methods of "expected deaths," direct and indirect standardization.

Great intellectual energy was also directed toward improving methods of life-table construction and related theory. Advances moved toward definitive results as reasonably accurate age-specific mortality rates became available from current vital statistics in conjunction with census data on population by sex and by age. The theoretical development of the subject was dependent on the treatment of mortality as a continuous function, with "the force of mortality" considered in an infinitesimal time interval—a principle attributed by Westergaard (1932, p. 92) to Daniel Bernouille (1760) in the course of his work on the age incidence and lethality of smallpox. Studies by Gompertz (1825), Makeham (1860), and others were aimed at a general formula of mortality applicable to the broad age range between childhood and senescence. Wilhelm Lexis (1875), Karl Pearson (1897), and others investigated the distribution of deaths at advanced ages.

Scientists concerned with public health problems made intensive investigations of variations in health, nutrition, conditions of labor, income, etc.

Studies of health thus came to be associated with other inquiries into conditions of life and labor, investigations of variations in size of family, patterns of family life, and fertility. This association acquired increased importance in the later development of population studies.

Interest in fertility during most of the nineteenth century was largely incidental to other concerns and was rather sporadic. There were two reasons for this: there was no obvious reason for any widespread concern at this time about variations or trends in fertility in the Western world from an economic, social, or political point of view; theoretical interest in the processes and structure of population—the mainspring of "pure demography"—was eclipsed by more "practical interests" during the decades that intervened between the decline of political arithmetic and the rise of modern demography.

The absence of any strong social motivation for the study of fertility is obvious. Fertility was (within the times for which we have any information) not so high in Europe as in Asia or in the Americas. Moreover, advances in production generally outstripped increases in population, and in any case the open spaces of the New World then appeared limitless. Differentials in fertility were not very conspicuous in the early nineteenth century, either among most European nations or among social classes within nations. Neither was there any apparent trend toward declines in fertility except in France and North America. There was, therefore, a tendency toward axiomatic acceptance of fertility as a constant. In fact, in the eighteenth and early nineteenth centuries, numbers of births and ratios of population to births in particular parishes were often used as a basis for estimates of the size of total populations.

Fertility was extremely high in America at the beginning of the nineteenth century (owing to the absence of economic restraints on family formation at early ages rather than, as in Asia, to the support of the primary family by larger kinship and social groups). This high fertility was accepted as appropriate to a land of opportunity. Fertility rates in the United States then decreased progressively, with a downward movement beginning much earlier than in most European countries, but this attracted little attention because of the high initial level of fertility, a parallel decline in mortality, and rising immigration. Eventually the contrast between the fertility of native and immigrant stocks stirred alarm, but this theme did not come into play until the 1890's.

Fertility had begun to decline in France near the end of the eighteenth century, and this decrease proceeded progressively through the nineteenth century, causing a significant difference in rates of increase between France and other European countries. But France then enjoyed a relatively strong position as a military power, and the interests of most citizens were focused on internal social and political issues. In fact, in the mid-nineteenth century liberal French statesmen viewed the relatively low fertility of the population with positive satisfaction. Thus, A. Legoyt, chief of Statistique Générale, wrote in 1847 that the moderate fertility of French families was evidence of "intellectual progress, order and foresight" (Spengler, 1938, p. 110). Some anxiety was stirred up when the number of deaths actually exceeded the number of births in 1854 and 1855, but this was relieved when the census of 1861 showed continued increase. Real anxiety about the trend of fertility in France dates from the rise of Prussia as a military power, the defeat of Austria in 1866, and the defeat of France in

1870. Henceforth, fertility became an issue of intense concern to patriotic Frenchmen. Within the next few decades over-all decreases in fertility, low fertility, and social class differences in fertility within large European cities became a subject of major interest throughout Europe.

The earlier, rather incidental and sporadic investigations of fertility had registered some advances in theory and methods. Kuczynski (1935a) gives an excellent review of the development of these studies. One aspect of methodology in this field is particularly interesting from the standpoint of general population theory. Fertility is traditionally conceptualized in Europe as "fertility of marriages" and in the United States as "fertility of persons" (by sex and age)—marital status being treated merely as one of the conditions influencing reproductive behavior. This difference is probably due in large part to differences in types of available data. It may also be due in part to the influence of scientists with biological orientation, notably Pearl and Lotka, on American demography in the 1920's. But the difference in approach also reflects differences in real situations. Postponement of marriage as a means of restricting fertility has been much more important in Europe than in the United States, and the proportions of women who never marry have been higher in many parts of Europe than in America. In any case, European demographers have tended to place greater emphasis than their American colleagues on the differentiation between the formation of conjugal unions and nuptial fertility as major components in total fertility.

The population registers of the Scandinavian countries yielded the earliest precise information on fertility. The Swedish Statistical Commission, under Per Wargentin's leadership, began in 1775 to collect information on confinements by women in quinquennial age-classes. H. Nicander computed age-specific confinement rates for the period 1780–95 which were published in the *Transactions of the Swedish Academy* (1800). These were reviewed by Milne in his *Treatise on the Valuation of Annuities* (1815).

There was a remarkable venture in the investigation of fertility in Scotland in the mid-nineteenth century. In the first year of compulsory registration of vital events, 1855, information was required at each birth on the age of the mother, the date of her marriage, and the number of children previously borne. These requirements were then discontinued; information on ages of mothers at maternity was not again obtained in Great Britain until the 1930's, but the information obtained by this "snapshot" was analyzed intensively. James Stark, as the Scottish Registrar General, presented the data in his first detailed annual report (1861). J. Matthews Duncan used the material for an analysis of fertility in relation to age at marriage, duration of marriage, and other variables (1866). The second edition of his work included a mathematical contribution by Tait. Fifty years later, C. J. and J. N. Lewis (1906) used the 1855 Scottish data for further investigations. Referring to a period when there was very little voluntary control of nuptial fertility, these studies still have great scientific value, but neither the Swedish nor the Scottish materials attracted wide attention during the nineteenth century.

A later development in the organization of statistical services led to the establishment of municipal statistical offices, notably in Germany, Italy, Hungary, and Paris. The directors of these municipal offices were able to obtain more diversified data than were generally afforded by national agencies. Imaginative social scientists in these situations undertook more intensive investigations of interrelations among social and demographic phenomena than had hitherto been possible. The work of Richard Böckh in Berlin and Giorgio Mortara in Milan illustrates this trend.

French interest in fertility in the last half of the nineteenth century was largely speculative. Some studies were developed with critical attention to objective evidence, though this evidence was usually obtained by methods that did not permit rigorous control. Some studies of fertility by French scholars at this time (like the contemporary work of Émile Durkheim in general social theory) were imaginative and acute; they gave conceptual depth and diversity to subsequent investigations in this field. This was true, for example, of the early studies of Frédéric Le Play (1855, 1864, 1871). His ideas were based in large part on meticulous, intensive investigations of particular families. They key factor in the decrease of fertility in France seemed to him to be the decrease of "stability" in French families, which he attributed mainly to changes in the rules of inheritance. The thesis that upward social mobility ("social capillarity") was a major factor in the decline of fertility was advanced with great force by Arsène Dumont (1890).

It is, even now, difficult to measure the influence of such social and psychological factors on fertility with any precision. It was still more difficult to do so with the methods of social research available fifty years ago. But it was possible to measure "differential fertility," i.e., variations in fertility among particular areas at particular times in association with various conditions. Governmental agencies and individual scholars, therefore, gave increasing attention to such investigations in the late nineteenth and early twentieth centuries.

Another motivation for studies of differential fertility came from the exposition of the principles of organic evolution by Charles Darwin. Darwin himself was convinced that his idea had important implications for human destiny. His cousin, Francis Galton, devoted his energies to exploring these implications; his major publications on inheritance in man appeared in 1869, 1883, and 1899.[2] Galton drew Karl Pearson into these inquiries. Pearson became director of the Galton Laboratory of National Eugenics at the University of London in 1907; he developed the laboratory as a center of biometric research. David Heron's monograph on differential fertility in London was published in 1906 as the first number in the series, "Studies in National Deterioration."

Another impulse toward studies of fertility came from movements concerned with poverty, illness, and related social issues. Many who were deeply concerned about these problems pointed to the association of high fertility with poverty and with high infant mortality. They espoused the birth control movement, both as a socially constructive measure and as a matter of personal liberty. This point of view, expounded by Sidney Webb in a Fabian Society penny tract (1907), led to the association of studies of fertility with studies of health and with the general field of social theory and social research.

In America real interest in fertility began with concern about differences between immigrant and native families. General Francis A. Walker, who had

directed the 1890 census, wrote articles on this subject in the *Forum* (1891) and in the *Atlantic Monthly* (1896) which were characterized by strong emotion and loose speculation. He asserted that the influx of immigrants had caused a decline of fertility in the native population, thus tending to replace the native population without affecting the total increase of the population. The first systematic treatment of fertility giving special attention to differences between native and immigrant stocks was presented by John Shaw Billings; his findings were also published in the *Forum* (1893). Intensive investigations of fertility which gave special attention to national origins were soon developed by Walter F. Willcox, Joseph A. Hill, Louis I. Dublin, and others.

These convergent lines of interest led to a burst of activity in the study of fertility, which henceforth became a major field of population research. Significant early studies include those by Böckh (Germany, 1884), Dumont (France, 1890), Rubin and Westergaard (Denmark, 1890), Körösi (Hungary, 1896), J. Bertillon (France, 1899b), Coghlan (New South Wales, 1903), Kiaer (Norway, 1903), Heron (England, 1906), Newsholme and Stevenson (England, 1906), Willcox (United States, 1906), Yule (England, 1906), Beneduce (Italy, 1907–8), March (France, 1907), Mortara (Italy, 1908a, 1909), and Hill (United States, 1910). A great inquiry into the fertility of marriages in England and Wales was carried out by T. H. E. Stevenson, Registrar General, on the basis of data obtained in the 1911 census (Great Britain, General Register Office, 1917–23). A question on number of children ever born was asked of all ever-married women in the United States in the 1890, 1900, and 1910 censuses, but owing to the lack of funds for their ex-

[2] Galton also carried out investigations on fingerprints and published a treatise on this subject. In this undertaking he was closely associated with Alphonse Bertillon, a leading French statistician, anthropologist, and demographer, whose son, Jacques Bertillon, an ardent pro-natalist in charge of vital statistics at Paris, became a leading exponent of population studies in France.

ploitation, the data were left to gather dust.[3]

A broad academic interest in demography, in some respects comparable to the early English enthusiasm for "political arithmetic," developed in Italy around the beginning of the twentieth century. The new impulse seems to have stemmed from the work of Rodolfo Benini, author of *Principi di demografia* (1901). He developed his exposition from an investigation of the characteristics and behavior of individuals, then of small groups—notably the family—and finally of the vital processes of society in association with statistical investigations in related fields. One of his pupils, Giorgio Mortara, following a series of investigations in Milan, published a comprehensive study of the demographic and social characteristics of Italian cities (1908*a*). Investigations of fertility by Beneduce and of mortality and fertility by Mortara appeared about the same time. Also in 1908, Corrado Gini published a statistical investigation of sex determination in man. Gini emphasized biological factors in society. In his thesis, expounded in 1911 and developed in later writings, genetic heterosis is a major force in the rise of nations; differential reproduction, involving loss of reproductive capacity by the elite, is a major force in their decline. Many of his colleagues did not accept this thesis, but the investigation of biological phenomena has been emphasized in many Italian studies. Gini himself treated a wide range of social and economic questions, as well as problems in statistical theory and pure demography. Italian demography has, in fact, been generally characterized by great vari-

[3] Sample data from the 1910 census were later used in studies of fertility sponsored by the Milbank Memorial Fund. A more extensive tabulation of these data was made by the Bureau of the Census in connection with its investigation of returns from the 1940 census.

ety in theoretical interests. Two Italian demographers, Mortara and Bachi, became leaders in the development of this field in other countries: Brazil and Israel. The Italian tradition in demography is reflected in the recent treatise by Marcello Boldrini: *Demografia* (1956).

There was, naturally, great popular interest during the nineteenth century in the territorial expansion of populations, the characteristics of regions, and migration. These were topics on which governmental agencies sought statistical information—though information on actual movements was often limited to data collected at frontiers, chiefly at ports of overseas migration. In the United States information was obtained on the state or country of birth of each person in all census returns from 1850 on.

These topics had loomed large in the early descriptive studies of states, known as "statistics," before this word acquired its present technical meaning. In Europe, studies of the growth and distribution of population in relation to physical conditions and culture came to be recognized as a distinct discipline called "human geography." Its first influential exponent was Frederick Ratzel: *Anthropogeographie* (1882–91). His exposition tended toward environmental determinism. His French colleagues, Paul Vidal de la Blache and Jean Brunhes, avoided this dogmatic tendency, giving more adequate recognition to the role of cultural factors. In the United States some of the early exponents of human geography, notably Ellen Semple and Ellsworth Huntington, held extreme positions that aroused strong opposition from anthropologists and sociologists. Similar opposition between geographers and sociologists did not develop, at least to the same degree, in France or England, and it has now been largely overcome in the United States.

Many historians and geographers have been interested in interpretive studies of population changes and migrations. Dieterici (1859) took up again the task initiated by Riccioli and Süssmilch, an attempt to estimate the earth's population. This work was carried forward with successive revisions by other scholars. Julius Beloch (1886, 1900) published laborious studies of population distribution and trends in the ancient Roman world and in medieval Europe. Historians in various European countries, notably in Italy, used medieval and early modern archives for intensive studies of population changes in cities with a long and varied history.

American and Russian historians have naturally been much concerned with the role of population movements in the social and political life. Population changes involving conquests of the indigenous peoples of the Americas have been a theme of continuous controversy and recurrent investigations. Frederick Jackson Turner's essay, "The Significance of the Frontier in American History" was published in 1893. Population movements were always a subject of central interest to Russian historians. A quarter-century ago Alexandre and Eugene Kulischer (1932) published a broad interpretation of the role of migrations in human history.

In spite of the great human interest in international migrations, the difficulties of obtaining reliable and comparable data or of testing general hypotheses in this field have baffled most scientists. There have been few really systematic treatments of the subject, though progress has been made in recent years. Comprehensive statistics on international migrations were brought together, and prior knowledge on this subject was surveyed in the volumes edited by Walter F. Willcox and Imre Ferenczi under the auspices of the National Bureau of Economic Research (1929–31).

Scientific investigation of conditions associated with migration almost inevitably involves treating local and international movements as aspects of a continuous process. The distinction is essentially artificial—except where attention is focused on local movements which may be relatively isolated from larger currents. International movements inevitably involve local changes, both in areas of origin and in areas of destination. A systematic treatment of migration therefore involves, and usually begins with, the investigation of local conditions and movements.

Imaginative and precise investigations of migration were carried out in Sweden by Gustav Sundbörg, who used the remarkable data of the continuous registration system. Emigration and internal migration were treated as related processes and were studied in relation to other demographic and social changes (including variations in harvests); communities were classified and rural communities divided into two types: agricultural and non-agricultural. Sundbörg's principle treatise in this field was published in 1913. In this case, demographic study in Europe was carried forward by an American demographer (Thomas, 1941).

There had been earlier systematic investigations of internal migration in Germany. Georg von Mayr (1876) published a study of population movements in Bavaria, using census data on place of birth by place of residence. Somewhat later, attention was focused on the movement of German peasants from East Prussian farms to cities and the related in-movement of Polish workers. Some students, observing the low natural increase in cities and large-scale farm-to-city movements, became greatly concerned about *Landflucht*—as related to both quantitative and qualitative population changes. A thesis linking *Landflucht* with deterioration of the nation's population (Georg

Hansen, 1889) attracted wide attention and had many repercussions. Max Weber investigated the same phenomena in their social context, drawing attention to unfavorable conditions in rural areas that might be corrected by liberal political policies. German monographs and articles on migration appeared with considerable frequency from 1890 on. Bleicher (1893) used data on current movements from community registers, but many investigators neglected the registration data. These data were later used by Conrad Taeuber (1931), Konrad Steyer (1935), Fritz Meyer (1936), and Heberle and Meyer (1937). Here again we have direct carry-overs in this field from European sources to American demography.

The English geographer Ravenstein (1885–89) developed a conceptual formulation that exercised considerable influence on later investigations of mobility. He made a painstaking investigation of data on changes in residence of English and American people, chiefly from census reports on place of birth by place of residence. Examining these data, he found evidence of certain regularities or "laws." In his second article (1889) he presented a critical comparative treatment of information from various countries.

In Australia George H. Knibbs (1917) treated migration in his investigation of mathematical relations among demographic phenomena. He aimed at a comprehensive statement of quantitative relations in demography, though he recognized that any such general statement could be only "a rough framework," subject to many corrections, about which "more subtle conceptions" might be formed and explored (pp. 455–56). He viewed the formulation of relations among migratory movements, rates of increase, and the age composition of populations as an essential aspect of this task.

In reviewing various movements shortly before, during, and shortly after the nineteenth century which influenced the development of population studies, we need to take account of a general trend which at first had little direct relation to demography as a science. The progress of industrialization brought a host of new adjustments, conflicts, and problems. It involved the growth of great towns in which housing, sanitation, the acquisition of goods and services, and many other conditions gave rise to acute dissatisfactions. New social alignments were formed, and new political movements arose in relation to the conflicting interests of different social classes. Many scholars turned their attention to the investigation of "social problems," with increasing reliance on quantitative, descriptive material from census inquiries and "social surveys." The studies in London by Charles Booth began with his contributions to the *Journal of the Royal Statistical Society*, from 1886 on. Finally presented in the *Life and Labour of the People of London* (1903), they are perhaps the most notable example of this movement. More or less similar investigations were carried out in many countries.

In the United States, the quantitative treatment of social problems came to be recognized in many universities —notably at Columbia, Chicago, and various state institutions—as an academic discipline (sometimes called "statistics," sometimes "sociology"). Columbia College in New York City was an early center of such activity, first under Richmond Mayo-Smith, then under Franklin Giddings. A course entitled "Social Science: Statistics" at the Graduate School of Political Science, Columbia College, 1884, included under the rubric "statistics of population" the following: race and ethnological distinctions, nationality, density of city and country, sex, age, occupation, religion, education, births, deaths, marriages, mortality tables, and emigration. The other major subjects treated in this course were "economic statistics" and "moral statistics" (Fitzpatrick, 1955). The contents of a text by Carroll D. Wright, *The Outline of Practical Sociology* (1898), are quite similar. The major themes treated under "questions of population" are "immigration, urban and rural population, and special problems of city life." Gradually, certain aspects of these social studies came to be oriented toward the analysis of population changes. "Population problems" came to be recognized in the United States as one of the major fields of sociology.

In Europe, the academic affiliations of quantitative studies on social problems were generally more varied and complex. Moreover, on the Continent such investigations were to a great extent carried on by official agencies, including municipal statistical offices. They were, therefore, generally associated with studies of population changes and vital statistics.

The preceding survey shows various emerging lines of interest related in different ways to the study of population changes. The survey has been rather disjointed and diffuse; so was the actual situation with respect to population studies in the nineteenth century. Before we deal with ways in which these diverse interests were modified and integrated in the emergence of demography as a modern discipline, we must give specific attention to a line of theoretical studies which came to play a key role in this development.

ANALYTICAL THEORY

The mathematical analysis of possible relations among demographic phenomena has provided theoretical frames which have been useful in the development of demography as a science. One line of inquiry has been conceived as the analysis of certain "necessary relations" among demographic processes. In a "closed population" the distribution of persons by age is a function of the previous frequencies of births and of the age-specific death rates. The sex structure of such a population is determined by the proportions of males and females at birth and by sex- and age-specific fertility and mortality rates. Frequencies of births and deaths, in turn, are conditioned by the age and sex structure of populations. These relations involve the succession of generations and rates of natural increase. Analysis of the implications of these relations yields a theoretical structure that has had wide application in the investigation and interpretation of population changes. The parameters of any specific formulation, such as a particular life table, are contingent on particular conditions; they denote processes affected by complex biological and social conditions. But these processes involve structural relations inherent in the nature of biological aggregates which can be developed in abstraction.

Other inquiries have been concerned with the mathematical analysis of other observed or hypothetical relations. The demographer aims at the discovery and formulation of relatively persistent trends and relations, as contrasted with more sporadic changes, and with the investigation of conditions associated with these trends and variations. In this undertaking he needs a large battery of systematic hypotheses and related techniques. As the study of population has progressed, this theoretical apparatus has been gradually enlarged and revised. Many of the formulations thus developed have been derived from, or are associated with, the core relations mentioned in the preceding paragraph. Others are quite independent.

The distinction between "necessary relations" and "hypothetical relations," which was emphasized by Lotka, can be interpreted merely as a distinction in degree rather than in kind. Relations recognized as basic physical conditions in demographic processes operate in conjunction with other biological and social factors which can also be treated as structural relations. In particular, interactions between the male and female members of a population, involved in all mammalian reproduction and socially conditioned in human populations, and the timing of births as influenced by the formation and dissolution of marriages and other conditions limit the applicability of any analytical theory which does not take these conditions explicitly into account. On the other hand, analytical theory in which the family is treated as the reproductive unit in human population is also beset with complications. Family structures vary in different societies; family units overlap through the remarriage of members of dissolved unions; the distinction between familial and non-familial reproduction is rarely absolute; and in some societies the distinction cannot be made with sufficient precision to be very useful. Perhaps any general analytical system in demography requires hypotheses that are to some degree unrealistic, at least in some situations. Recognition of this possibility is not inconsistent with recognition of the pragmatic value of precise analysis and the investigation of the mutual implications of different formulations. It does, however, throw emphasis on the value of frankly hypothetical and relatively specific formulations, as contrasted with more elaborate theoretical models.

The mathematical treatment of possible relations in demography also has entailed certain dangers, though these are extraneous to its essential character. Concentration of attention on the formulation of observed or possible relations in abstraction has sometimes been associated with a neglect of the conditions on which these relations may be contingent or with unwarranted assumptions about the nature of these conditions. Purely hypothetical formulations have sometimes been proclaimed as "laws," assumed to have universal validity without specification of their limiting conditions.

The observation that a population has been increasing at a constant rate during a certain period can be stated in terms of the compound interest formula or, more elegantly, the exponential function. It is then possible to state precisely how many persons there will be in this population at some distant date *if* it continues to increase at this constant rate. Similarly, the logistic curve defines changes in the size of a population at successive times on a more complex but equally arbitrary hypothesis. Or again, the mathematical statement of an observed acceleration of the instantaneous rate of mortality with increases in age through some broad range provides information about the death rate at a particular age from knowledge about its height at some other age, under conditions which cause precisely this acceleration of mortality. But none of these calculations in itself gives any assurance that the required conditions will be fulfilled, and the finding that a formula fits several situations gives no basis for confidence that it will fit a different situation. Many errors in demography have resulted from uncritical interpretations of mathematical implications. Such dogmatic applications of mathematics are quite different from the critical use of mathematics in exploring relations among various aspects of population change.

The development of life tables by Halley and others, which gave substance to the conceptual scheme envisioned by Graunt and Petty, was a first major contribution to the development of analytical theory in demography. A life table can be interpreted in either of two ways: (1) It gives the probabilities of time-units (e.g., years) to be lived between any two precise ages by a cohort of persons (as defined at birth or at any specified age) and their mean expectation of future life at any age, relative to any given or hypothetical schedule of age-specific death rates. This is its primary use for actuarial purposes. (2) It also gives the proportional distribution by ages of a hypothetical closed population formed by a constant succession of births and subject to a constant age-specific schedule of mortality. These conditions define a "stationary population" with constant structure.

Leonhard Euler, a Swiss mathematician from whom Süssmilch sought assistance on various problems, took a second major step in developing the basic principles of a "stable" population (though he did not use this word), i.e., a hypothetical, closed population with a constant schedule of age-specific mortality and a constant rate of increase. Euler (1760) showed that such a population must have a fixed age distribution and other characteristics that can be precisely determined, whether the population is constantly increasing, stationary, or constantly decreasing. Its basic characteristics (apart from sex ratios and the relative frequencies of births to mothers and fathers at different ages, which Euler did not treat) are completely determined by two independent functions which he called the "mortality hypothesis" and the "multiplication hypothesis." The latter can, of course, be resolved into its mortality and fertility components, so that the two independent functions are a "mortality hypothesis" and a "fertility hypothesis"; but the "multiplication hypothesis" can, for many purposes, be treated as one of two necessary determinants of the characteristics of a closed population.[4]

Euler used the expression "$(1)(2) \ldots (n)$" for the proportions of infants born alive who survive to the beginning of the successive years of life—corresponding to the $p(a)$ values in Lotka's notation. He used the expression "$n, n^2 \ldots n^n$" for ratios of numbers of births (or persons) at the end of 1, 2, or n years to the number of births (or persons) at any initial point of time—corresponding to the expression "$(1 + r), (1 + r)^2 \ldots (1 + r)^n$" in current terminology. He then defined the ratio of the number of persons in such a population who reach age a at any moment to the number of births at the same moment as $(n)/n^n$—i.e., in current terms, $p(a)/(1 + r)^a$, or $e^{-ra} p(a)$ where e refers to the base of the system of natural logarithms. He developed a set of related theorems as solutions to a series of questions. He was especially interested in the fact that his formulation could be used to estimate the influence of the increase of a population on the relative frequencies of deaths at different ages at any given time (e.g., during a calendar year) in an actual population which approximated a stable population. Such application of his analysis might, he hoped, improve the derivation of life tables in cases where it was necessary to rely solely on current vital statistics.

Euler's law of the relation of the age structure of a closed population with constant vital rates to its mortality schedule and its rate of increase is basic to stable population theory. Euler did not undertake extensive empirical research in demography; however, he did deal with population questions on

[4] Lotka in his later work restricted the term "stable population" to one defined by the schedule of age-specific fertility for either maternity or paternity, but the neglect of this aspect of later stable-population theory did not invalidate the earlier analyses by Euler and Lotka before this specification was introduced.

several occasions. He supplied Süssmilch with a table showing the numbers of years required for the doubling
of a population at various constant rates
of increase. In his major contribution
to demography, cited above, he used
empirical values obtained by Kersseboom as an illustration, and he concluded his exposition with a tribute to
Süssmilch:

I have only treated these questions in
their generality, without dealing with any
particular population; that requires a large
number of observations under various circumstances. . . . We are greatly indebted to
Mr. Süssmilch who, overcoming almost insuperable obstacles, has furnished us with
many such observations, sufficient to resolve
a large share of the questions arising in this
research. As he has already drawn many
important conclusions from his investigations, we must hope that he will carry forward this science toward its highest possible
degree of perfection [Euler, 1760].

Euler's analysis was neglected for
more than a half-century because of a
failure to appreciate its theoretical importance and because of difficulties be-
setting any direct application of its
principles to the available vital statistics. It was then reviewed by Ludwig
Moser of Königsburg in a systematic
treatment of population theory (1839).
After an introductory discussion of statistical theory in general and the theory of probability in particular, Moser
gave a critical exposition of errors arising from the use of observed frequencies of death in an actual population as
representing the frequencies to be expected in a stationary population
(which he referred to as "Halley's
method"). Kersseboom had calculated
frequencies of death by age in relation
to frequencies of persons reaching previous ages among adults in a small insured population, or in relation to numbers of registered births in dealing with
deaths at early ages, but he had also
used another series on deaths by ages

without reference to changes in the
base population. There were similar
mixtures of "cohort observations" and
"period observations" in the work of
other early demographers, without
clear differentiation of the basic principles involved. Moser gave a clear exposition of Euler's analysis and dealt
with various criticisms and limitations
affecting its application. He noted, for
example, that population increase in
the United States in the early nineteenth century fitted Euler's hypothesis of exponential change quite well but
that the movement of births in France
did not do so. Many populations show
the effects of more or less erratic
changes in births and deaths during
previous decades. Moser insisted that
in practice one must make "double observations" on the numbers of persons
of various ages present in a population
at a particular time and the numbers
of deaths of persons at various ages in
this population in order to obtain true
measurement of mortality. He thus
promoted a new emphasis on valid age-
specific rates of mortality in life-table
construction, and he gave a systematic
exposition of the relevant principles.
Moser also dealt with the measurement
of nuptial and extra-nuptial fertility,
sex ratios at birth, and other demographic questions.

Moser's exposition, including his
statement of Euler's principles, directly influenced Adolphe Quételet, the
Belgian scientist who exerted an enormous influence on the development of
statistics in the mid-nineteenth century,
and the German statisticians associated
with Georg Knapp who had strong theoretical interests. Quételet himself published the first Belgian life table based
on the joint use of census data and vital
statistics. He also wrote a summary of
Moser's exposition of Euler's law,
which was quoted by Maurice Block in
a text on statistical theory and methods. Lotka's first contribution to demo-

graphic theory (1907*a*) was essentially a restatement and simple development of these principles, with the notation: "Compare M. Block, *Traité théorique et practique de statistique,* 1886, p. 209." Apparently, at this time Lotka was not acquainted with Euler's original, more complete statement, though in a later publication (1928) he referred to a corollary theorem in Euler's exposition for which he provided a correction. In his first article on the subject Lotka emphasized the degree to which observed crude birth rates, death rates, and age distributions in populations "where the general conditions of the community are constant and immigration is negligible" conform to the expectations of stable population theory—using a comparison of observed values for England and Wales in the 1880's with the corresponding theoretical values. In concluding the article, Lotka observed that these relations were capable of further development. In his subsequent work he carried this analysis through to an architectonic system.

Lotka, in a second article in 1907, showed that the equations developed in his analysis of demographic functions are also applicable to an isothermal monomolecular reaction. He remarked:

We have illustrated a statistical method which is sufficiently general in its application to comprise such widely different cases as that of the growth of a population under certain conditions on the one hand and that of a simple chemical reaction on the other. The fundamental feature of this method is the splitting up of the characteristics governing the rate of growth of a material aggregate into two factors—the one relating to those properties of the system which determine the formation of new individuals, and the other relating to those properties of the system which determine the limitation of the "life period" of the individual constituents [Lotka, 1907*b*].

Four years later, Lotka and Sharpe developed the fundamental equation of a stable population as a limiting type toward which a closed population tends, given a constant schedule of age-specific mortality, a constant schedule of age-specific fertility, and a constant sex ratio at birth. Lotka then carried out further investigations into the interrelations among vital processes in hypothetical stable populations. However, he did not at this time introduce the idea of the reproduction of generations into his analysis or develop the functions implicit in this relation.

We must return at this point to earlier developments in Europe. Investigations leading toward the analysis of the reproduction of generations (the natural unit of balance between fertility and mortality) were carried out in Germany during the second half of the nineteenth century. Lotka's later work on this subject, in co-operation with Dublin, was apparently quite independent. Nevertheless, the earlier European work merits attention.

The allocation of deaths, as reported by ages within chronological intervals, to moving cohorts of persons who pass birthdays at different times during this interval, was a moot problem in life-table theory at this time. Attempts were made to resolve this problem empirically by obtaining direct information on year of birth as well as age at death in reports on deceased persons. A proposal by Wittsein in 1863 to this effect was taken into account in recommendations approved by the International Statistical Conference at the Hague in 1869. The proper determination of the "complete" (as contrasted with a "curtate") expectation of life involved essentially the same problem. A precise development of life-table theory was then possible through differential and integral calculus. These theoretical aspects of life-table construction were treated in depth by Georg

Knapp (1868). Several colleagues, including G. Zeuner, K. Becker, and W. Lexis, elaborated his analysis. Knapp recognized that the treatment of these relations involved three types of association (*gesammtheit, collectivité*) among the elements of a population. One of his colleagues, Zeuner, constructed three-dimensional models in the analysis of these relations. Others worked with "stereograms," i.e., two-dimensional representations of three-dimensional relations. (The technique was developed further by Perozzo and was discussed by L. Bodio at the International Congress of Hygiene and Demography, Geneva, 1882.) This approach has become classic in actuarial theory (see, for example, Glover, 1923). The treatment of the "surface of mortality" has also been used in the analysis of cohort mortality (see Delaporte, 1941).

This approach led to investigations of generational processes, as contrasted with the usual cross-sectional treatment of vital statistics within a brief time period (e.g., a year). There had, in fact, been some experimentation with direct longitudinal methods of life-table construction. F. von Hermann in Bavaria had attempted to obtain survival quotients directly from data on numbers of deaths by ages in a current year and on numbers of births or numbers of persons reaching earlier ages in the previous experience of the cohorts exposed to risk of death during the current year under consideration; but this procedure was subject to serious disturbance by the movements of migrants. Hermann's results were criticized by Wilhelm Lexis, but he was attracted to this approach on theoretical grounds and devoted considerable attention to possible measures for taking migration into account. (For later statements on the significance of the cohort analysis of mortality, see Derrick, 1927; Delaporte, 1941; Frost, 1939; Merrell, 1947.) Lexis was also influenced by Moser's exposition and by Knapp's more intensive analysis.

Lexis published a theoretical treatise on demographic statistics in 1875. He stated that his investigations were aimed at a conceptual treatment of demographic measurements rather than at the elaboration of statistical techniques for handling particular problems, and he concluded with an application of probability theory to demographic and actuarial problems. He began his exposition with a discussion of ways of measuring the survival of individuals, introduced into a population by births, through successive durations of life. Here he followed the approach developed by Knapp. He then discussed the measurement of the formation and dissolution of marriages and nuptial fertility. He comments at this point, "Couples provide the normal framework of the births which in our previous exposition have been considered as primary phenomena. So the movement of population completes a revolution" (Lexis, 1875, p. 88). He referred to the ages of women at maternity as "reproduction points" and noted that paternity could be treated in the same way. He emphasized the need for data on births by age of mother as well as by calendar year, sex of infant, and status with respect to legitimacy. He also called for data on dissolution of marriages by death or divorce by age and on remarriages by duration of previous status. He then proposed summing the relative frequencies of births at successive ages to a cohort of married women—if data could be obtained over a period of years equal to the childbearing span—taking into account the cumulative frequency of first marriages of women prior to the end of the reproductive span. The concept of gross and net reproduction ratios was thus implicit in his exposition.

The first actual net reproduction ratio was computed by one of Lexis' colleagues, Richard Böckh (1884, pp. 30–34). This achievement was fairly incidental to Böckh's interest in many demographic problems, including various aspects of marriage and fertility. As director of the Berlin statistical office he was able both to direct the collection of data and to carry through their analysis. He acquired data for Berlin in 1879 on age-specific death rates (used for life-table construction), specific data on marriages, and data on births classified by marital status, ages of parents, and order of birth. He applied the age-specific, nuptial-specific maternal fertility rates to the life table for Berlin in the same year to show the total number of births to be expected on these conditions to each female infant born alive (2.172). Dividing this number by *one plus* the ratio of males to females at birth (2.053), he found the reproductivity of the population to be 6 per cent above the replacement level. He also computed the comparable proportion of female infants born alive who subsequently marry and the number of births during married life to each ever-married woman (3.90). He then added an estimated 2/9 of all illegitimate infants, to take account of later legitimizations, so as to give an adjusted value (4.04). He also applied the information on births by order to compute a net prolificacy distribution. Kuczynski later referred to Böckh's procedure in first computing a total fertility ratio and then taking the distribution of births by sex into account as a "detour," but this suggests an undue concentration of interest in gross and net reproduction ratios, apart from the other information supplied by Böckh's procedure.

Böckh, Kuczynski, and Hirschberg computed fifteen net reproduction tables for Berlin for the years 1886 through 1900. Other tables of this type were computed in Germany for Sweden (several periods covering nearly a century), Denmark, France, and a group of German states (Kuczynski, 1935a, 1936 ed., p. 207). Kuczynski states, "Outside of Germany, the first fertility table seems to have been computed in 1925 by Dublin and Lotka." The last table in this early German series seems to have been that by Rahts in 1912.

An independent approach to this problem was developed in the United States in the middle 1920's—apparently on the initiative of Louis I. Dublin. As a vital statistician, Dublin recognized that the crude death rate was deflated and that the crude rate of natural increase was inflated by the current age distribution of the national population, and he assumed that this age distribution might be expected to change appreciably in the coming years. He was also concerned that fertility, which had been declining for a long time in this country, had begun again to decline quite rapidly after its early postwar recovery. The current crude rate of natural increase presented a false picture of the actual situation, concealing its underlying trend. He engaged the cooperation of his colleague, Alfred J. Lotka, in carrying out an investigation to discover the "true" situation, and they co-operated in the preparation of an article setting forth the results of this inquiry. Hence appeared their famous contribution: "On the True Rate of Natural Increase, as Exemplified by the Population of the United States, 1920" (1925). A "Bibliographic Note" gives references to Bowley (1924), Brownlee (1924), Carr-Saunders (1922), Savorgnan (1924), and Brunner (1925), but not to any earlier work. It may seem surprising that Lotka had no familiarity with the German work to which we have referred, especially since he had spent a year in graduate study at the University of Leipzig, 1901–2. However, at that time he had been primarily interested in the physiochemical aspects of organic evolution. If the earlier German demographers had influenced his thinking, he was apparently unaware of this, and he specifically acknowledged (in his reply to Kuczynski) that Böckh's contribution had not come to his attention in 1925. Commenting on his derivation of the ratio of female births in two successive generations from the elements of generational reproduction (probabilities of survival from birth to successive ages, and successive age-specific maternal frequencies), he wrote, "It is singular that this fact should have escaped attention" (1925b).

Lotka now developed a complete general theory of the interrelations of the primary biological processes, including the determination of the age and sex structures and other functions of stable populations and the relations of generational to instantaneous changes in closed mammalian populations under constant conditions. These principles are stated (somewhat less completely than in his later monograph) in two technical papers published in 1925: an Appendix to the joint article cited above and an article in the *Journal of the Washington Academy of Sciences* (1925b). The definitive exposition of his mature demographic theory is presented in a monograph: *Théorie analytique des associations biologiques, Deuxième partie: Analyse démographique avec application particulière à l'espèce humaine* (Lotka, 1934–39).

Lotka's contribution to demography can be likened in some respects to that of Newton to physics. Both achieved a synthesis in analytical theory which had far-reaching significance, and both set a frame for new empirical investigations. Further investigations have revealed limitations in the applicability of these theories which were not at first suspected but which could never have been discovered except through experi-

ments made possible by the precision and scope of these original constructions. Their analyses are still being carried forward in exploring relations not otherwise apparent among actual processes. Coale's recent analytical treatment of the relative influence of variations in fertility and in mortality on the age structure of populations (1956) may be cited as one illustration.

Two difficulties have arisen in the calculation of net reproduction ratios and other functions of a stable population. One difficulty concerns the relation between male and female reproduction ratios. It was initially assumed that the instantaneous rates of natural increase implicit in male and female ratios for the same population must be identical. But the relative numbers of males and females in an actual population may be such (as noted by Vincent, 1946; Hajnal, 1947; Karmel, 1947, 1948) that the reproductive behavior of either sex in a monogamous population could be maintained indefinitely only by a considerable change in the reproductive behavior of the other. To the extent that this is so, neither rate can logically be treated as the intrinsic rate of natural increase implicit in the behavior of an actual population, and there seems to be no logical basis for averaging these rates. Another difficulty arises if a female (or male) net reproduction ratio is defined, following Lotka, as the ratio of female (or male) births in two successive generations implicit in the reproductive behavior and mortality rates of women (or men) at successive ages in a particular population during a specified period (such as a particular year). The reproductive behavior of women (or men) at successive ages in any particular year may deviate widely from the behavior of any actual cohort in successive years. It may, in fact, include elements that could not possibly characterize an actual cohort. For example (as has been shown by Whelpton), the sum of age-specific *first* birth rates per woman at successive ages in the United States in some recent years has been above unity! The vulnerability of gross and net reproduction ratios from cross-sectional data is so great that it is now realized that such ratios may be quite meaningless in certain situations and must, in any case, be used with caution. This difficulty, however, does not arise if the fertility values are derived from the experience of actual cohorts, as in computations by Depoid (1941), Whelpton (1954), and others.

The first of the two difficulties mentioned above, though less likely to cause serious distortions in practical applications of stable population theory, raises more fundamental questions of a theoretical nature. Lotka thought of his work as a development of "necessary relations" inherent in the structure of all "biological collectivities." But he achieved his analytical construction only by treating the reproductivity of individuals of one sex in abstraction from their relations with individuals of the other sex. In mammalian populations conception is necessarily a bisexual process. And in human societies mating is, in varying degrees, institutionally controlled through marriage. Moreover, variations in marriage patterns, e.g., in ages at first marriage and in the stability of marriages, may exert strong influence in the determination of reproductive levels. Monosexual stable population theory is therefore an abstraction which is very convenient and efficient in many respects but which is logically incomplete and, under some conditions, may be erroneous. On the other hand, the introduction of terms relating to the formation of marriages and nuptial fertility as parameters of reproductivity—with complementary functions relating to the dissolution of marriages, remarriages and extramarital fertility (or the arbitrary exclusion of these functions)—obviously complicates the analysis. Moreover, these relations as substantive realities are contingent on particular social conditions, so that their precise definition is necessarily hypothetical.

Analytical theory in demography is a subject of continuing inquiry. Among recent studies in this field are Hajnal's contributions to the work of the United Kingdom's Royal Commission on Population and studies by Coale, Henry, Ryder, and others. These theoretical treatments of demographic processes are being developed in close association with specific empirical investigations. Current theoretical and empirical studies in demography are, actually as well as ideally, complementary aspects of scientific advance in this field. In contrast to formulations of total population change in global terms, current theoretical studies are mainly directed to analyzing the interaction of different aspects of population change and to heuristic formulations as frames of reference for investigating specific demographic phenomena. There are also some recent practical applications of analytical theory by the United Nations staff in the development of methods for preparing population estimates on the basis of incomplete information (*Manuals on Methods of Estimating Populations*, I–III, 1955–56).

DEMOGRAPHY AS A DISCIPLINE AND INTERDISCIPLINARY POPULA-TION STUDIES

Political arithmetic gave promise of becoming a discipline in the late seventeenth and early eighteenth centuries, but its inquiries were generally absorbed in other movements or suffered neglect. Major emphasis shifted to the collection, organization, and publication of quantitative information by official agencies. Statistics gradually emerged as a new discipline, with the theory of probability in the lead role.

Earlier methods of estimation were discredited. Enthusiasm over the first observations of "regularities" in vital events lost its force. Real continuity in the development of interests and methods of inquiry from early to modern times seems to have been largely limited to investigations of mortality and the formulation of life expectancies. If there is any "apostolic succession" from John Graunt to modern demographers, it passes through this rather limited field.

The formation of demography as a discipline during the twentieth century can be sketched in outline. The measurement and formal analysis of mortality had assumed the character of a limited but mature discipline during the nineteenth century. The principles of this discipline were applied, with appropriate modifications, to the measurement and formal analysis of fertility as interest in this subject became lively. Thus demography, centered in vital statistics, acquired greater breadth. Its scope and precision were then substantially advanced by analytical theory of the relations between fertility, mortality, and population structure.

Meanwhile, descriptive treatments of populations, based on information from censuses, civil registers, and other sources, became both more comprehensive and more specific and analytical—dealing with the whole complex of interacting elements in population changes and with the measurement of relations among various phenomena. Quantitative descriptions of population trends revealed large variations among nations and within nations and significant changes in population trends under changing conditions. There was rising interest in the relation of population trends to economic and social conditions. Students from other fields were drawn into the investigation of "population problems." Interest in demography, as such, also led to new investiga-

tions of conditions affecting population changes and their influences on other processes. Thus the field of demography was extended through studies of the "determinants and consequences" of population trends. Meanwhile, advances in other biological and social studies made possible increasingly precise and significant, though generally imperfect, analyses of these relations. This more comprehensive discipline is sometimes referred to as "population studies"; this is in contrast to "formal demography," the treatment of population changes in abstraction from their biological and social contexts.

The word "discipline" is used here in the sense of a field of related studies in which there develops a community of scholars with common interests who stimulate one another in their investigations, a set of related techniques, a cumulative body of knowledge, and certain generally accepted principles of procedure. Such a discipline also tends to acquire an apparatus—associations, periodic publications, and research and training centers. The assumption that demography is a "discipline" does not necessarily imply that it is, or should be, treated as a distinct "school" or "department" within the structure of a university. This is a matter of academic convenience. Actually, of course, various fields of investigation overlap in varying degrees so that distinctions between them are more or less arbitrary, but the functional grouping of closely related studies has operational value.[5]

[5] We have frequently used the word "discipline" rather than "science" in this paper in order to avoid begging the question of the degree to which demography is scientific. We have also used the words "scholar" and "student" on the assumption that the broad category of those seeking to acquire knowledge includes scientists. Our aim is to present as objective an account as possible of the development of demography, with special attention to those aspects of its development which have tended to promote its character as a sci-

The word *démographie* was apparently first used by Achille Guillard: *Eléments de statistique humaine, ou démographie comparée* (1855). The word soon gained currency in Europe as a succinct term for investigations of population changes and vital events. Owing to the fact that in the nineteenth century intensive investigations in this field were mainly concerned with mortality and life expectancies, the word "demography" came to be primarily associated with vital statistics—though it was also used in a broad sense to refer to all population studies.

Demography, in the sense which it acquired during the quarter-century after Guillard's treatise, received explicit international recognition in the fourth international conference on hygiene. The organizers of this conference (Geneva, 1882) decided to include a section on "demography," and the conference was called Congrès International d'Hygiène et Démographie. Bodio (Italy), Böckh (Germany), Jacques Bertillon (France), and Körösi (Hungary) were among the participants in the meetings on demography. The conference at Geneva is referred to as the "fourth conference" (sometimes as the "fifth conference") in the series, but the preceding sessions had not included demography as a distinct subject. There were eight later conferences with the same title, with major emphasis on vital and medical statistics.

Demography received further impetus from the organization of the International Statistical Institute in 1885. Émile Levasseur contributed a study on the area and population of the world for publication in the first bulletin of the institute, 1866–67. Luigi Bodio, director of the statistical office in Italy after 1872, became the first secretary-general of the institute. He gave major attention to the compilation of vital and demographic statistics for various countries, since he had previously prepared and published studies in this field. This program was carried forward until responsibility for such compilations was assumed by official international agencies. The institute has continued to place strong emphasis on the development of demographic statistics.

A visionary conception of "social physics" as a science of man, to include studies ranging from anthropometry through demography to psychology and "moral statistics," was advanced by Adolphe Quételet in the mid-nineteenth century, the "era of enthusiasm" for statistical inquiries. With boundless energy he promoted international cooperation in official statistical programs and conducted research on population, the theory of probability, anthropometry, criminology, and other topics. But his vision of "social physics" was not widely shared by his contemporaries and seems to be even less generally acceptable today.

One demographic inquiry initiated by Quételet attracted relatively little interest at the time, but the same formulation introduced again after the lapse of nearly a century stirred great excitement. In an early treatise Quételet advanced the mechanistic hypothesis that "resistance . . . to the unlimited growth of population increases in proportion to the square of the velocity with which the population tends to increase" (1835, pp. 169–72). At Quételet's suggestion, Pierre-François Verhulst undertook investigations of this proposition which led him to develop the symmetrical "logistic" curve, which becomes asymptotic to some upper limit as a population approaches the full utilization of its resources (Verhulst, 1838, 1845, 1847). Applying this formula to the population of Belgium,

---

ence. Each reader can evaluate the evidence and interpret it in his own terms.

he fixed its ultimate maximum at 9.4 million persons.

Essentially the same formula was developed independently by Raymond Pearl and Lowell J. Reed in 1920. Their treatment, however, was conceived in biological rather than mechanical terms. The functions of a population conforming to the logistic curve were then explored in various mathematical studies by Lotka, Yule, Volterra, and others. The radical distinction between this development and that treated above under "analytical theory" is that this postulates a complete determination of vital processes in man, to the exclusion of the variable influence of social relations, culture, and human creativity—or, more precisely, it analyzes trends to be expected if these social factors are negligible or if they conform in net effect to a fixed pattern. The analytical theory previously considered is restricted to the treatment of necessary relations. It is now generally recognized that for human populations the logistic formula is valid only as a hypothetical construction that may, in some situations, have useful applications.

Pearl's empirical investigations of contraceptive behavior were undertaken with the expectation that they would show that variations in social conditions (other than those interpreted as functions of the density of population) had a negligible influence on fertility. Owing to a defect in the original research design (reliance on data concerning the total previous fertility of "contraceptors" and "non-contraceptors," without differentiation between periods of use or non-use of contraceptives) his first studies seemed to support the hypothesis of biological determinism. After he had corrected the research design, the evidence was clearly in the opposite direction. As a true scientist, Pearl accepted this new evidence as conclusive. The present

writer happened to be in attendance at a symposium at the Milbank Memorial Fund at which Pearl presented his findings (1934). Pearl added a dramatic comment in the course of the subsequent discussion. According to the author's memory, it was: "Gentlemen, you realize that this evidence destroys the basis of most of my life's work." This comment, apart from its human interest, marks a critical change during the twentieth century in the approach to research in demography. It signals the shift from excessive emphasis on biological factors in this field to a more mature approach in the investigation of processes determined by the interaction of biological, social, and cultural factors. There was, for a time, some tendency among social scientists to neglect biological factors, but this overemphasis is also giving way to a more freely exploratory approach.

Governments in various countries have long sponsored the preparation of "compendia" or interpretative "summaries" of the results of census inquiries. In the United States a notable summary, using material from all previous enumerations, was prepared in the census office, seventh census, by James D. B. DeBow: *Statistical View of the United States* (1854). A successor to this survey, in the early twentieth century, was prepared in the new Bureau of the Census by William S. Rossiter: *A Century of Population Growth* (1909). With the progress of time these surveys, both by governmental agencies and by individual scholars, became more analytic and precise—as apparent in the census monograph by Walter F. Willcox: *Twelfth Census: Supplementary Analysis and Derivative Tables* (1906). A comprehensive, analytical account, *Population Trends in the United States*, by Warren S. Thompson and P. K. Whelpton, prepared under the auspices of the President's Research Committee on Social Trends, was published in 1933. This was followed by a publication of the United States National Resources Committee: *The Problems of a Changing Population* (1938). Long before this time, Émile Levasseur had published an impressive exposition and interpretation of population trends, referring primarily to his own country but including a comparative treatment of population in other countries: *La population française* (1889–92). A comparable survey of world population by A. M. Carr-Saunders was published in 1936. Such comprehensive studies drew attention to population as a general field of interest and thus tended to give it greater coherence. They also pointed up particular questions on which positive evidence was lacking or inconclusive.

Political movements aimed at the control of population trends, which became intense in many European countries during the 1930's, placed a strain on the scientific character of demography. Such pressures were resisted in varying degrees by scholars in different countries. The most serious eclipse of scientific work by brutal political forces took place in Germany under the National Socialist regime. There was also a partial but much less devastating eclipse of this sort in Italy. Of course, in all countries quasi-political action programs have offered inducements toward deviations from scientific objectives and respect for the limits of science. This problem was precisely and forcibly stated by Liebmann Hersch in his presidential addresses to the International Union for the Scientific Study of Population and to the World Population Conference in Rome, 1954.

On the other hand, political interest in population has afforded a stimulus and support to scientific demography under conditions where science is respected and protected by liberal traditions and proper safeguards. This was notably so in the series of technical studies on population problems carried out under special government commissions in Sweden in the late 1930's and in the United Kingdom during the 1940's. In France the liberal tradition in population studies was upheld during the preceding years and during the crisis of World War II by Adolphe Landry and his associates. Then in the initial postwar period, 1945, the Institut National d'Études Démographiques was established under governmental auspices but assured complete freedom in scientific inquiries. This has become one of the major centers of demographic research in the modern world. A notable feature of this institute has been its interdisciplinary approach to population studies. Its staff includes analytical demographers, economists, a biologist, a social historian, a social psychologist, and representatives of other disciplines.

In the United States a majority of the most competent students of population questions during the first quarter of the century—notably Dublin, Glover, Lotka, Pearl, Reed, Sydenstricker, Wilson, and Woodbury—were primarily concerned with health, actuarial studies, or the biological sciences, or were drawn into demography from these fields. The scope and orientation of population studies, however, was significantly affected by the entrance of scholars with different backgrounds. Several of those mentioned in the preceding paragraph were mainly concerned with the social aspects of health. In fact, public health investigations are largely social rather than biological studies. Under the auspices of the Children's Bureau, Robert M. Woodbury (1918, 1925) studied variations in infant mortality in relation to living conditions, size of family, etc.; this was one of the first large-scale demographic field studies in this country.

One of the "Hagerstown Morbidity Studies" by Edgar Sydenstricker (1929) was "Differential Fertility According to Economic Status." Later, as director of the Milbank Memorial Fund, Sydenstricker initiated the use by Frank W. Notestein of a sample of the long-neglected data on fertility collected in the 1910 census. This was the beginning of a continuing series of contributions to demography under the auspices of the fund, including studies by Pearl, Stix and Notestein, Kiser, and others.

A rather surprising number of the leaders in American demography entered professional work through graduate studies in the department of sociology at Columbia University, under Franklin Giddings. The first among these was Walter F. Willcox, who wrote his dissertation, *The Divorce Problem—A Study in Statistics,* in 1891.[6]

In this early empirical study, which he credits in part to the influence of Bertillon, he observed the relatively low efficacy of legislation in this field and emphasized the importance of social forces and education. He continued various social studies along with his later work in demography. His breadth of interest within the field of demography was later expressed in such undertakings as his investigation of the increase in the population of the earth and of the continents since 1650, published in the volume on international migration (1931). Robert E. Chaddock (1908) presented a historical and demographic dissertation in the same series, *Ohio before 1850.* William F. Ogburn (1912) presented an investigation, *Progress and Uniformity in Child-labor Legislation: A Study in Statistical Measurement.* As a statistical sociologist at Columbia, 1919–27,

and then at Chicago, he carried out and stimulated others to carry out a wide range of inquiries, including many studies in demography.

Warren S. Thompson approached the study of population through an examination of Malthusian theory, which was also presented as a dissertation in the Columbia series (1915). The first non-government institute for population research was established at Miami University in 1922 by E. W. Scripps, a philanthropic publisher, and Thompson became the director. Its initial program was focused on the economic aspects of population and the characteristics of city populations. P. K. Whelpton, who was trained in agricultural economics, joined the institute as associate director.

A line of social studies closely associated with demography but having somewhat the character of a special discipline, i.e., human ecology, was initiated by a group of scholars at the University of Chicago in the early 1920's: Robert E. Park, Ernest W. Burgess, and R. D. McKenzie. In this approach, principles developed in botany and zoölogy were used to give a conceptual frame for empirical investigations of relations among demographic and social processes in human communities. These concepts were always intended merely as leading principles or hypotheses.

The movement of Negroes to industrial centers stimulated a series of studies on Negro migration which were reviewed and interpreted by Louise V. Kennedy (1930). The economic depression gave further stimulus to studies of the distribution of population, regional variations in social conditions, and internal migration. A series of monographs and special reports, based largely on the results of special field inquiries, was published under the auspices of the Works Progress Administration.

[6] A communication by the same writer concerning the apportionment of Representatives in Congress has appeared as this paper is being edited, May, 1957.

New empirical and analytical investigations of the complex interrelations between population changes and economic processes were developed among economists and economic demographers in the United States as in many other countries. In view of the complexity of this important aspect of population studies and its treatment elsewhere in this symposium, we will not attempt to sketch these developments.[7]

Another approach to population studies was initiated by Frederick Osborn in the late 1920's. He was impressed by the work of Darwin and Galton but had grave doubts about the validity of many current expositions of eugenics. He conceived the idea that an objective inquiry in this field could be carried out by relating the measurement of reproductive trends in the components of a population (classified in various ways) to measurements of their characteristics and by investigating the association of these trends and characteristics with other biological, social, and personal factors. In this inquiry he enlisted the co-operation of some other students, including the present writer. Their joint inquiry was published in 1934 (Lorimer and Osborn, 1934).

Up to the middle 1920's, population projections had received relatively little systematic attention. Estimates of future population were usually based on simple assumptions about absolute or relative increases or on algebraic formulas fitted to previous observations and dealt only with trends in total numbers. The logistic method was essentially of this type, though developed with far more elaborate theory. Edwin Cannan (1895) suggested making future population estimates by dealing separately with the different

[7] A comprehensive review of such studies throughout the world is presented in the United Nations monograph *Determinants and Consequences of Population Trends.*

sex and age components of an initial population and carried out a rather simple experiment of this sort. About thirty years later, A. L. Bowley (1924, 1926) developed more specific applications of this principle. Shortly thereafter, P. K. Whelpton independently developed the same principle and worked through its methodological implications in great detail (1928, 1936). Many variations in methods of population projection using components have been developed since this time in the United States and in other countries.

Interest in population projections has exerted a unifying force in demography. In particular, the component method involves a joint application of knowledge concerning all aspects of population changes involving fertility, mortality, and migration. In fact, such projections are sometimes developed in a purely hypothetical way to reveal the effects of a particular variable, the others being held constant. Otherwise, projections afford critical tests of current knowledge. Demographers recognize that the degree to which actual trends may conform to hypothetical projections will be contingent on circumstances that they cannot foresee. Nevertheless, except in purely experimental calculations, they attempt to set up realistic hypotheses and to indicate a range of likely variations. The lack of success of many projections has revealed errors in inferences, especially about fertility. This experience has intensified efforts to increase knowledge about the influence of changing conditions on demographic processes.

Population studies, or demography, as a field of interrelated interests has gained force rapidly throughout the world since the early 1920's. The first World Population Conference was held in Geneva in 1927. Prior to this time there was no national or international organization in this field and no periodical primarily devoted to population studies. The Geneva conference was organized by Margaret Sanger. The participants were mainly statisticians, biologists, and economists. They had complete freedom in the exchange of ideas and information; the liveliest discussion concerned the scientific evaluation of Pearl's logistic theory. Nevertheless, the scholars at this conference deemed it inappropriate to form a continuing organization under the sponsorship of a proponent of action in a controversial field, and they arranged to meet for this purpose privately in Paris the following year. The International Union for the Scientific Investigation of Population Problems[8] was organized there in 1928, with Raymond Pearl as its first president. The members of the union agreed to promote the organization of scientific associations in various countries. The Population Association of America was organized in 1931, with Henry P. Fairchild as its first president. A large, successful International Population Conference was held at Paris in 1937—following a smaller conference in London, under the auspices of the union (1931), a conference in Rome, organized by an Italian committee (1931), and a conference in Berlin (1935). The structure of the International Union was changed after World War II from an organization of national committees to an organization of individuals in order to obviate the possible exercise of political pressures exerted through autonomous national committees.

The experience of demographers in co-operation with official international agencies has been generally felicitous. A first major development was the League of Nations' sponsorship of a series of population studies under the direction of Frank W. Notestein at the Office of Population Research, Princeton University (established in 1936).

[8] Now the International Union for the Scientific Study of Population.

The provision for a Commission on Population in the charter of the United Nations and the formation of a technical group charged with the development and promotion of population studies in its secretariat has enhanced both the scientific character and the prestige of population studies. These associations were reinforced in the World Population Conference under the auspices of the United Nations (Rome, 1954).

Research and training programs, varying in scope and intensity and with varying degrees of specialization in population studies, have been established at various universities. A foundation devoted to the promotion of study and research in this field has been established by John D. Rockefeller III: The Population Council, Inc. (New York). Research and training centers in demography have recently been established, through the co-operation of the United Nations and member governments, in Santiago and in Bombay. There is an active center for research on migration in the Netherlands and a graduate research program in Australia. There is much active work at a high technical level in Japan and in India. A comprehensive statistical survey, the *United Nations Demographic Yearbook,* is published regularly. The United Nations also issues technical studies on population in special memoranda and in the *Population Bulletin.* There are now three major periodicals in this field: *Population* (Paris), *Population Index* (Princeton), and *Population Studies* (London).

It is evident, in view of the record of lapses and rediscoveries in this incomplete account, that after the early days of active exchange of ideas within the small community of European savants, the progress of demography as a science was hampered for a long time by the relative isolation of scholars in different countries. This situation is to some extent now being corrected. The formation of an international community in this field quickens the extension of knowledge and promotes experimentation with significant hypotheses. It brings another more subtle, perhaps even more important, benefit. It promotes the formation of universal canons of scientific procedure in the treatment of population problems.

It appears that the progress of demography as a science has followed a course between what may be called "leftist" and "rightist" deviations—giving these words a special meaning in this context. On the one hand, it has been distracted at times by speculative dogmas, such as those of Malthus, Marx, and Francis A. Walker. On the other, it has been led into errors by treating mathematical formulations as substantive information and by misapplying physical and biological principles to processes contingent on changing social and cultural factors. It has, nevertheless, constantly tended to recover equilibrium in the on-going process of inquiry.

The character of demography as a discipline is somewhat peculiar. It has a rigorous but limited core of analytical theory and well-defined statistical techniques—though these are constantly subject to new experimentation and revision. It is the first responsibility of a demographer to acquire competence in the principles of "formal demography." But a demographer limited to the merely formal treatment of changes in fertility, mortality, and mobility would be in a position like that of a "formal chemist" observing the compression of mercury with no information about associated changes in temperature or the constitution of the liquid.

The demographer is inevitably involved in investigating the biological and social correlates of demographic processes. These biological and social factors are inherently complex in their nature and in their relations with population changes. They are, in many cases, the object of intensive investigations in other disciplines: the physiology of reproduction, genetics and maturation; the psychology of personality, medicine, economics, sociology, anthropology, etc. The concept of "pure demography," except as the skeleton of a science is therefore an illusion. Significant demography is necessarily interdisciplinary.

Demography must progress through alternating and successive inquiries—with different specializations by various individuals at various times. Some of these inquiries will be carried out by demographers in isolation, taking into account information and principles developed in other disciplines. At the same time, significant contributions on matters of critical importance in demography will be made in other disciplines. One function of the demographer is to define problems on which such contributions by other students are needed. Again, in some cases the most effective attack on a problem may require active collaboration among demographers and students in other fields. Three programs now under way in the United States may be cited as illustrations: a joint investigation of the relation of migration to previous economic development in the United States, by Dorothy S. Thomas (demographer) and Simon Kuznets (economist); a joint investigation of impending population growth and economic development in India, by Ansley J. Coale (demographer) and Edgar M. Hoover (economist); and an investigation of social and psychological factors in the subsequent fertility of wives who have two living children and who reside in metropolitan areas in the United States, by Elliott Mischler (psychologist) and Charles F. Westoff (sociologist) in co-operation with a committee comprising demographers, sociologists, and psychologists. It may be expected that as demography advances, such co-operative inquiries will become increasingly important.

Recognition of the interdisciplinary character of population studies is consistent with recognition of the importance of demography as a discipline. Its critical function, beyond the sphere of formal demography, is the organization of present knowledge and new inquiries relevant to the understanding of population changes and associated biological and social processes. We may recall the dual orientation of demography as set forth by John Graunt, its first exponent: "political and natural observations." The objective analysis of population changes in their biological and social context serves both the enlargement of science and the formation of realistic public policies.

SELECTED BIBLIOGRAPHY

A. Chronological List

Citations and Selected Works through 1937

1589. Botero, Giovanni. *Delle cause della grandezza della città*. Venice. 1st English edition. *A Treatise . . . by Sig. Giovanni Botero*. Translated by Robert Patterson. London: Ockould & Tomes, 1606. American edition: *The Reason of State*. Edited by D. P. Waley. New Haven: Yale University Press, 1956.

1661. Riccioli, Giovanni Baptista. "De verisimili hominum numero," *Geographiae et hydrographiae reformatae* (Bologna).

1662. Graunt, John. *Natural and Political Observations . . . Made upon the Bills of Mortality*. Dedications dated "25 January 1661-2." *The Dictionary of National Biography*, XXII, 426, states that an earlier edition was published in 1661, but this is dubious. A posthumous fifth edition, edited by Petty, was published by the Royal Society in 1676. German edition; Leipzig, 1702. American edition, with Introduction by Walter F. Willcox, and edited by Jacob B. Hollander. Baltimore: Johns Hopkins Press, 1939.

1676. Petty, Sir William. *Politicall Arithmetick* (presented in MS to Charles II and published posthumously by Petty's son). London, 1690.

1683. ———. *Observations upon the Dublin Bills of Mortality*.

1691. ———. *The Political Anatomy of Ireland*. Posthumous publication. *See* Hull, 1899.

1693. Halley, Edmund. "An Estimate of the Degrees of the Mortality of Mankind, Drawn from Curious Tables of the Births and Funerals at the City of Breslaw . . . ," *Philosophical Transactions of the Royal Society of London*, XVII, 596–610. "Some Further Considerations on the Breslaw Bills of Mortality," *ibid.*, pp. 654–56. American edition: *Two Papers on the Degrees of Mortality in Mankind*. Edited by Lowell J. Reed. Baltimore: Johns Hopkins Press, 1942.

1696. King, Gregory. "Natural and Political Observations and Conclusions upon the State and Condition of England." MS, British Museum. American edition: *Two Tracts by Gregory King*. Edited by George E. Barnett. Baltimore: Johns Hopkins Press, 1936.

1707. Vauban, Sebastian. *Projet d'une dîme royale* (published anonymously). Paris.

1739. Maitland, William. *History of the City of London*. London.

1740. Kersseboom, Willem. *Eenige aanmerkingen op de gissingen over den staat van het menschelyk geslagt. . . .* The Hague.

1740. Struyck, Nicolaas. *Inleiding tot de algemeene geographie benevens eenige storrekundige en andere verhandelingen*. Amsterdam.

1741. Süssmilch, Johann Peter. *Die göttliche Ordnung in den Veränderungen des menschlichen Geschlechts aus der Geburt, dem Tode, und der Fortpflanzung desselben orwiesen*. 2d ed., 2 vols., Berlin, 1761–62. *See* Crum, 1901.

1746. Deparcieux, Antoine. *Essai sur les probabilités de la durée de la vie humaine. . . .* Paris: Frères Guerin. 2d ed.; 1760.

1748. Kersseboom, Willem. *Proeven van politique redenkunde. . . .* The Hague.

1749. Buffon, Georges-Louis Leclerc, Comte de. *Histoire naturelle*. Vol. II:

Histoire générale des animaux; histoire particulière de l'homme. Paris: Imprimerie Royale.

1750. SHORT, THOMAS. *New Observations . . . on the City, Town, and County Bills of Mortality.* London: Longman.

1752. HUME, DAVID. Discourse X, "Of the Populousness of Ancient Nations," *Political Discourses.* 2d ed.; London.

1753. WALLACE, ROBERT. *A Dissertation on the Numbers of Mankind in Ancient and Modern Times: In Which the Superior Populousness of Antiquity Is Maintained* (published anonymously). Edinburgh. French translation; London, 1754. French edition; Paris, 1760.

1755. CANTILLON, RICHARD. *Essai sur la nature du commerce en général.* Paris. Modern ed.; Paris: Institut National d'Études Démographiques, 1952.

1755. FRANKLIN, BENJAMIN. *Observations Concerning the Increase of Mankind, Peopling of Countries, etc.* Boston. Reprinted in *Magazine of History*, Extra No. 63 (1918), pp. 215–24.

1755. WEBSTER, ALEXANDER. "An Account of the Number of People in Scotland in the Year 1755." *See* "A Note on the Account . . . ," *Journal of the Royal Statistical Society,* Vol. LXXXV (1922).

1756–58. MIRABEAU, VICTOR, MARQUIS DE. *L'ami des hommes ou traité de la population.* Paris.

1757. BROWN, JOHN. *An Estimate of the Manners and Principles of the Times.* London.

1760. BERNOUILLE, DANIEL. "Essai d'une nouvelle analyse de la mortalité causée par la petite vérole," *Histoire de l'Académie Royale des Sciences, année 1760.* Paris, 1766.

1760. EULER, LEONHARD. "Recherches générales sur la mortalité et la multiplication du genre humâin," *Histoire de l'Académie Royale des Sciences et Belles-Lettres, année 1760,* pp. 144–64. Berlin, 1767.

1760. WALLACE, ROBERT. *Various Prospects of Mankind, Nature, and Providence.* London.

1762–69. D'EXPILLY, ABBÉ JEAN. *Dictionnaire géographique, historique, et politique des Gaules et de la France.* Paris.

1766. MESSANCE (secretary to LA MICHODIÈRE). *Recherches sur la population des généralités d'Auvergne, de Lyon, de Rouen. . . .* Paris.

1766. MURET, J. S. *Mémoire sur l'état de la population dans le pays de Vaud.* Yverdon. Also in *Mémoires . . . société économique de Berne.*

1766. WARGENTIN, PER WILHELM. "Mortaliteten i Sverige, i adledning cef Tabell-Verket," *KVA Handingar,* pp. 1–25. *Mémoires abregés de l'Académie Royale des Sciences de Stockholm,* I, Tome 4. Paris, 1772. *Tables of Mortality Based upon the Swedish Population Prepared and Presented in 1766.* Stockholm: Thule Life Insurance Co., 1940.

1767. SHORT, THOMAS. *A Comparative History of the Increase and Decrease of Mankind. . . .* London: Nicole.

1771. PRICE, RICHARD. *Observations on Reversionary Payments.* London: Cadell. 7th ed.; London, 1812.

1771. YOUNG, ARTHUR. *Proposals to the Legislature for Numbering the People.* London.

1774. ———. *Political Arithmetic.* London.

1778. MOHEAU. *Recherches et considérations sur la population de la France.* (Actual author, ANTOINE J.-B. R. AUGET, BARON DE MONTYON.) Paris. Modern ed.; Paris, 1912.

1780. PRICE, RICHARD. *An Essay on the Population of England.* London: Cadell.

1782. CHALMERS, GEORGE. *An Estimate of the Comparative Strength of Britain during the Present and Four Preceding Reigns.* London.

1788. MESSANCE (secretary to LA MICHODIÈRE). *Nouvelles recherches sur la population de la France avec des remarques importantes sur divers objets d'administration.* Lyon.

1790. ORTES, GIAMMARIA. *Riflessioni sulla popolazione delle nazioni per rapporto all'economia nazionale.* Venice. Reprinted in *Scrittori classici italiani di economia politica,* ed. P. CUSTODI. Vols. XXIV, XLIX. Milan, 1803–16.

1798. MALTHUS, THOMAS R. *An Essay on the Principle of Population, as It Affects the Future Improvements of Society, with Remarks on the Speculations of Mr. Godwin, M. Condorcet, and Other Writers.* London. 2d ed.; 1803. For other editions, *see* GLASS, 1953.

1800. EDEN, SIR FREDERICK MORTON. *An*

Estimate of the Number of Inhabitants in Great Britain and Ireland. London.

1812. LAPLACE, PIERRE SIMON, MARQUIS DE. *Théorie analytique des probabilités.* Paris: Courcier.

1815. MILNE, JOSHUA. *Treatise on the Valuation of Annuities. . . .* London: Longman, Hurst, Rees, Orme & Brown.

1819. SISMONDI, JEAN CHARLES LÉONARD S. DE. *Les nouveaux principes d'économie politique ou de la richesse dans ses rapports avec la population.* Paris: Delaunay.

1821. FOURIER, JEAN BAPTISTE JOSEPH. "Recherches sur la population," *Recherches statistiques sur la ville de Paris . . . d'après les ordres . . . le comte Chabrol.* Paris: Imprimerie Royale.

1825. GOMPERTZ, BENJAMIN. "On the Nature of the Function Expressive of the Law of Human Mortality," *Philosophical Transactions of the Royal Society of London.*

1828. SADLER, MICHAEL T. *Ireland: Its Evils and Their Remedies. . . .* London: Murray. 2d ed.; 1829.

1829. BURN, JOHN S. *The History of Parish Registers.* London: J. R. Smith. 2d ed.; 1862.

1830. SADLER, MICHAEL T. *The Law of Population: A Treatise, in Six Books; in Disproof of the Super-Fecundity of Human Beings, and Developing the Real Principle of Their Increase.* 2 vols. London: Murray.

1835. QUÉTELET, ADOLPHE. *Sur l'homme et le développement de ses facultés.* Paris: Bachelier.

1837. McCULLOCH, JOHN R. *Statistical Account of the British Empire.* London: Knight.

1838. DEMONTFERRAND, F. "Essai sur les lois de la population et de la mortalité en France," *Journal de l'Ecole Royale Polytechnique,* XVI (Memo. 26), 249 ff.

1838. VERHULST, PIERRE FRANÇOIS. "Notice sur la loi que la population suit dans son accroissement," *Correspondance mathématique et physique publiée par A. Quételet* (Brussels), X, 113–21.

1839. FARR, WILLIAM (Compiler of Abstracts, 1839 ff.). *First Annual Report of the Registrar-General.* London. *See also* FARR, 1885.

1839. MOSER, LUDWIG F. *Die Gesetze der Lebensdauer.* Berlin: Veit & Co.

1841. BERNOULLI, CHRISTOLPH. *Handbuch der Populationistik oder der Völker- und Menschenkunde nach statistischen Ergebnissen.* Ulm.

1841. DOUBLEDAY, THOMAS. *The True Law of Population Shewn To Be Connected with the Food of the People.* London. 3d and enlarged ed.; London: Smith, Elder & Co., 1853.

1841. SHATTUCK, LEMUEL. *The Vital Statistics of Boston; Containing an Abstract of the Bills of Mortality for the Last Twenty-nine Years, and a General View of the Population and Health of the City at Other Periods of Its History.* Philadelphia: Lea & Blanchard.

1841 ff. *Massachusetts State Registration Reports.* Office of the Secretary, Commonwealth of Massachusetts.

1841–42. McCULLOCH, JOHN R. *Dictionary, Geographical, Statistical, and Historical, of the Various Countries.* London: Longman, Hurst, Rees, Orme & Brown. (Later editions with varied titles.)

1843. JONES, DAVID. *On the Value of Annuities.* London: Baldwin & Cradock.

1843. TUCKER, GEORGE. *Progress of the United States in Population and Wealth in Fifty Years.* Boston: Little & Brown.

1845. SHATTUCK, LEMUEL. *Census of Boston for the Year 1845.*

1845. VERHULST, PIERRE FRANÇOIS. "Recherches mathématiques sur la loi d'accroissement de la population," *Nouveaux mémoires de l'Académie Royale des Sciences et Belles-Lettres de Bruxelles,* XVIII, 1–38.

1846. TELLKAMPF, THEODOR. *Die Verhöltnisse der Bevölkerung und der Lebensdauer im Königreich Hanover.*

1847. VERHULST, PIERRE FRANÇOIS. "Deuxième mémoire sur la loi d'accroissement de la population," *Nouveaux mémoires de l'Academie Royale des Sciences et Belles-Lettres de Bruxelles,* XX, 1–32.

1850. RATCLIFFE, HENRY. *Observations on the Rate of Mortality and Sickness Existing amongst Friendly Societies.* Manchester.

1850. SHATTUCK, LEMUEL. *Plan for a Sanitary Survey of Massachusetts.* Boston: Dutton & Wentworth.

1850 ff. Hübner, Otto L. *Geographisch-statistische Tabellen.* Frankfurt, 1850–1919.

1851. Moreau de Jonnès, Alexandre. *Statistique des peuples de l'antiquité.* . . . Paris: Guillaumin.

1851. Quételet, Adolphe. "Nouvelles tables de la mortalité pour la Belgique," *Bulletin de la Commission Centrale de Statistique,* Vol. IV.

1854. DeBow, James. *Statistical View of the United States* . . . . Washington, D.C.: Census Office, 7th census, 1850.

1855. Guillard, Achille. *Eléments de statistique humaine ou démographie comparée.* Paris: Guillaumin.

1855. Le Play, P. G. Frédéric. *Les ouvriers européens.* 6 vols. Paris.

1856. Watson, Elkanah. *Men and Times of the Revolution.* New York: Dana & Co. (Cites his 1815 estimate of future United States population, p. 455.)

1857. Elliott, E. B. "On the Law of Human Mortality That Appears To Obtain in Massachusetts, with Tables of Practical Value Deduced Therefrom," *Proceedings of the American Association for the Advancement of Science,* 1857, pp. 51–82.

1859. Dieterici, K. F. W. "Die Bevölkerung der Erde," *Petermanns Geographische Mittheilungen,* 1859, pp. 1–19.

1860. Makeham, W. M. "On the Law of Mortality and Construction of Annuity Tables," *Journal of the Institute of Actuaries,* Vol. VIII.

1861. Legoyt, Alfred. *L'émigration européenne.* Paris: Guillaumin.

1861. Stark, James (Registrar General, Scotland). *First Detailed Annual Report.*

1864. Le Play, P. G. Frédéric. *La réforme sociale en France,* 2 vols. Paris. 7th ed., 3 vols.; 1887.

1866. Duncan, J. Matthews. *Fecundity, Fertility, and Allied Topics.* Edinburgh: Adam & Charles Black. 2d ed., with mathematical exposition by Tait; 1871.

1868. Knapp, Georg F. *Uber der Ermittlung der Sterblichkeit aus den Auszeichnungen der Bevölkerungs-Statistik.* Leipzig.

1869. Quételet, Adolphe. *Physique sociale.* 2 vols. Brussels: Muquardt.

1869. Zeuner, Gustav. *Abhandlungen aus der mathematischen Statistik.* Leipzig.

1871. Le Play, P. G. Frédéric. *L'organisation de la famille.* Paris. 3d ed.; 1884.

1874. Becker, Karl. *Zur Berechnung von Sterbetafeln an die Bevölkerungs-Statistik zu stellende Anderungen.* Berlin.

1874. Knapp, Georg F. *Theorie des Bevölkerungs-Wechsels.* Brunswick.

1875. Great Britain. *Memorandum on the Census of British India of 1871–72.* ("Sessional Papers," cmd. 1349.) London: H. M. Stationery Office.

1875. Lexis, Wilhelm. *Einleitung in die Theorie der Bevölkerungs-Statistik.* Strasbourg: Trübner.

1876. Bodio, Luigi. *Del movimento della popolazione in Italia e in altri stati d'Europa.* Rome. (Similar expositions in *Bulletin de l'Institut International de Statistique,* 1894, 1896.)

1876. Mayr, Georg von. *Die bayerische Bevölkerung nach der Gebürtigkeit.* Munich.

1877. Bertillon, Jacques. "Migration française," *Annales de démographie internationale* (Paris).

1881. Perozzo, L. "Stereogrammi demografici," *Annali di statistica* (Rome), Ser. 2, Vol. XXII.

1882. Curtis, Josiah. "The Registration of Vital Statistics," *National Board of Health, Annual Report,* pp. 335–461.

1882–91. Ratzel, Friedrich. *Anthropogeographie.* Stuttgart: J. Engelhorn.

1882 ff. Congrès International d'Hygiène et de Démographie. *Proceedings,* Vol. IV. Geneva, 1883. (This is the first volume to include "demography" as such.) 14th session, Washington, 1912.

1883. Billings, John Shaw. "The Registration of Vital Statistics," *American Journal of Medical Science,* N.S. LXXXV, 33–59.

1883. Galton, Francis. *Natural Inheritance.* London and New York: Macmillan.

1884. Böckh, Richard. *Statistisches Jahrbuch der Stadt Berlin.* Berlin. (First net reproduction ratio, pp. 30–34.)

1885. Farr, William. *Vital Statistics: A Memorial Volume of Selections from the Reports and Writings of William Farr,* ed. Noel A. Humphreys. London: Sanitary Institute.

1885–89. Ravenstein, E. G. "The Laws of Migration," *Journal of the Royal Statis-*

tical Society, XLVIII, 167–235; LII, 241–305.

1886. BELOCH, (KARL) JULIUS. Die Bevölkerung der griechisch-romanischen Welt. Leipzig: Duncker & Humblot.

1886. BLOCK, MAURICE. Traité théorique et practique de statistique. Paris: Guillaumin. 1st ed., 1875.

1886. Bulletin de l'Institut International de Statistique, Vol. I.

1886–87. LEVASSEUR, ÉMILE. "Statistique de la superficie et de la population des contrées de la terre," Bulletin de l'Institut International de Statistique, Vols. I–II.

1889. HANSEN, GEORG. Die drei Bevölkerungsstufen: Ein Versuch, die Ursachen für das Blühen und Altern der Völker nachzuweisen. Munich: J. Lindauer.

1889. NEWSHOLME, ARTHUR. The Elements of Vital Statistics. London: Sounenschein. 3d ed., rev.; 1899.

1889. WRIGHT, CARROLL D. A Report on Marriage and Divorce in the United States, 1867 to 1886. Washington, D.C.

1889–92. LEVASSEUR, ÉMILE. La Population française. 3 vols. Paris: A. Rousseau.

1890. BÖCKH, RICHARD. "Die statistisches Messung der ehelichen Fruchtbarkeit . . . ," Bulletin de l'Institut International de Statistique, V, No. 1, 159–87.

1890. DUMONT, ARSÈNE. Dépopulation et civilisation. Paris: Vigot.

1890. HOOPER, WYNNARD. "Population," Encyclopaedia Britannica, 9th ed.

1890. RUBIN, MARCUS, and WESTERGAARD, HARALD L. Statistik der Ehen auf Grund der socialen Gliederung der Bevölkerung. Jena: G. Fischer. (Also in Danish, Copenhagen, 1890.)

1891. PRITCHETT, H. S. "A Formula for Predicting the Population of the United States," Journal of the American Statistical Association, N.S. II, 278–86.

1891. WALKER, FRANCIS A. "Immigration and Degradation," Forum, XI, 634–44.

1891. WILLCOX, WALTER F. The Divorce Problem—a Study in Statistics. ("Columbia University Studies in History, Economics, and Public Law," Vol. I, No. 1.) New York.

1893. BILLINGS, JOHN S. "The Diminishing Birth-Rate in the United States," Forum, XV, 467–77.

1893. BLEICHER, H. Die Bewegung der Bevölkerung (in Frankfurt am Main) in Jahre 1891. Frankfurt.

1893. TURNER, FREDERICK JACKSON. "The Significance of the Frontier in American History" (read at World's Columbian Exposition, 1893) in The Frontier in American History. New York, 1920.

1894. NITTI, FRANCOSCO S. La popolazione e il sistema sociale. Rome. English ed.: Population and the Social System. London.

1894. WEBER, MAX. "Entwickelungstendenzen in der Lage der östelbischen Landarbeiter," Archiv für soziale Gesetzgebung und Statistik, Vol. VII.

1895. BERTILLON, JACQUES. De l'influence de l'aisance sur la natalité à Paris (1889–1893). Paris: A.F.A.S.C.

1895. CANNAN, EDWIN. "The Probability of a Cessation of the Growth of Population in England and Wales during the Next Century," Economic Journal, V, 505–15.

1895. MAYO-SMITH, RICHMOND. Statistics and Sociology. New York.

1896. BENINI, RODOLFO. "Di alcuni punti oscuri della demografia," Giornale degli economisti, XII, 97–128, 297–327, 509–34.

1896. KÖRÖSI, JOSEPH. "An Estimate of the Degrees of Legitimate Natality . . . at Budapest," Philosophical Transactions of the Royal Society of London, 186B, pp. 781–875.

1896. WALKER, FRANCIS A. "Restriction of Immigration," Atlantic Monthly, LXXVII, 822–29.

1897. DUMONT, ARSÈNE. "Profession et natalité," Bulletin de la Société d'Anthropologie de Paris.

1897. PEARSON, KARL. The Chances of Death and Other Studies in Evolution. London and New York: E. Arnold.

1897. WILLCOX, WALTER F. "Area and Population of the United States at the Eleventh Census," "Density and Distribution of the Population of the United States at the Eleventh Census," Economic Studies (American Economic Association), II, 200–257, 385–455.

1898. GIDDINGS, FRANKLIN H. The Elements of Sociology. New York: Macmillan.

1898. WRIGHT, CARROLL D. *The Outline of Practical Sociology.* New York.

1899a. BERTILLON, JACQUES. *Statistique internationale résultant des recensements de la population . . . pendant le XIXe siècle.* Paris: G. Masson.

1899b. ——. "La natalité selon le degré d'aisance: Étude à ce point de vue de Paris, Londres, Berlin, et Vienne," *Bulletin de l'Institut International de Statistique,* XI, No. 2, 163–76.

1899. HULL, CHARLES H. *The Economic Writings of Sir William Petty.* Cambridge.

1899. WEBER, ADNA F. *The Growth of Cities in the Nineteenth Century.* ("Columbia University Studies in History, Economics, and Public Law," Vol. XI.) New York.

1900. BELOCH, (KARL) JULIUS. "Die Bevölkerungs Europas in Mittelalter," *Zeitschrift für Socialwissenschaft,* III, 405–23.

1900. SUNDBÄRG, GUSTAV. "Sur la répartition de la population par âge et sur les taux de mortalité," *Bulletin de l'Institut International de Statistique,* XII, No. 1, 89–94, 99.

1900. WRIGHT, CARROLL D., and HUNT, WILLIAM C. *The History and Growth of the United States Census, 1790–1890.* Washington, D.C.: Government Printing Office.

1901. BENINI, RODOLFO. *Principi di demografia.* Florence: G. Barbèra.

1901. CRUM, FREDERICK S. "The Statistical Work of Süssmilch," *Publications of the American Statistical Association,* VII, 335–80.

1902. VERRIJN-STUART, C. A. "Natalité, mortinatalité, et mortalité infantile selon le degré d'aisance dans quelques villes et un nombre de communes rurales dans les Pays-Bas," *Bulletin de l'Institut International de Statistique,* XIII, No. 2, 357–68.

1903. BOOTH, CHARLES. *Life and Labour of the People in London.* 17 vols. London: Macmillan.

1903. COGHLAN, TIMOTHY A. *The Decline of the Birth-Rate of New South Wales, and Other Phenomena of Child-Birth, an Essay in Statistics.* Sydney: W. A. Gullick.

1903. DUMONT, ARSÈNE. *Rapport sur l'âge au mariage et son influence sur la natalité.* (Commission de la Dépopulation, Sous-Commission de la Natalité) Melun: Imprimerie Administrative.

1903. KIAER, A. N. *Statistische Beiträge zur Beleuchtung der ehelichen Fruchtbarkeit.* Christiana.

1903. LEXIS, WILHELM. *Abhandlungen zur Theorie der Bevölkerungs- und Moralstatistik.* Jena.

1905. HARDY, GEORGE F. *Memorandum on the Age Tables and Rates of Mortality of the Indian Census of 1901.* Calcutta: Superintendent of Government Printing.

1905. NEYMARCK, A. *Rapport sans les causes économiques de la dépopulation.* (Commission de la Dépopulation, Sous-Commission de la Natalité.) Melun.

1906. GONNARD, R. *L'émigration européenne au XIXe siècle.* Paris: A. Colin.

1906. HERON, DAVID. *On the Relation of Fertility in Man to Social Status and on the Changes in This Relation That Have Taken Place during the Last Fifty Years.* ("Drapers' Company Research Memoirs: Studies in National Deterioration," Vol. I.) London: Dulan & Co.

1906. LEWIS, C. J., and LEWIS, J. NORMAN. *Natality and Fecundity—A Contribution to National Demography.* Edinburgh.

1906. NEWSHOLME, A., and STEVENSON, T. H. C. "The Decline of Human Fertility in the United Kingdom and Other Countries As Shown by Corrected Birth Rates," *Journal of the Royal Statistical Society,* LXIX, 34–87.

1906. PRINZING, F. *Handbuch der medizinischen Statistik.* Jena: G. Fischer.

1906. WILLCOX, WALTER F. *Twelfth Census: Supplementary Analysis and Derivative Tables.* Washington, D.C.: Government Printing Office.

1906. YULE, G. U. "On the Changes in the Marriage and Birth Rates in England and Wales during the Past Half Century with an Inquiry as to Their Probable Causes," *Journal of the Royal Statistical Society,* LXIX (Pt. II), 88–132.

1907a. LOTKA, ALFRED J. "Relation between Birth Rates and Death Rates," *Science,* N.S. XXVI, 21–22.

1907b. ——. "Studies on the Mode of Growth of Material Aggregates" *American Journal of Science,* XXIV, No. 141, 199–216.

1907. MARCH, LUCIEN. "Les statistiques de familles," *Bulletin de l'Institut International de Statistique*, XVII, 218.

1907. MOMBERT, PAUL. *Studien zur Bevölkerungsbewegung in Deutschland.* Karlsruhe: G. Braunsche.

1907. SUNDBÄRG, GUSTAV. *Bevölkerungsstatistik Schwedens 1750–1900.* Stockholm.

1907. WEBB, SIDNEY. *The Decline in the Birth-Rate.* (Tract 131.) London: The Fabian Society.

1907–8. BENEDUCE, ALBERTO. "Della natalità e della fecondità," *Giornale degli economisti*, XXXV, 673–721, 776–809, 866–91; XXXVI, 149–90.

1908. CHADDOCK, ROBERT E. *Ohio before 1850.* ("Columbia University Studies in History, Economics, and Public Law.") New York.

1908. GINI, CORRADO. *Il sesso dal punto di vista statistico; le leggi della produzione dei sessi.* Milan: R. Sandron.

1908a. MORTARA, GIORGIO. *Le popolazioni della grandi città italiane.* Turin: U.T.E.T.

1908b. ———. *La mortalità secondo l'età et la durata della vita economicamante produttiva.* Rome: Bocca.

1909. ———. *Tavola de sopravvivenza e delle variazioni di stato civile e tavola di natalità per il comune di Milano.* Naples: R. Inst. di Incor. *See also* MORTARA, 1933–37.

1909. ROSSITER, WILLIAM. *A Century of Population Growth, 1790–1900.* Washington, D.C.: Government Printing Office.

1910. HILL, JOSEPH A. "Fecundity of Immigrant Women," *United States Immigration Commission Reports*, XXVIII, 731–823.

1911. BORTKIEWICZ, L. VON. "Die Sterbeziffer und der Frauenüberschuss in der Stationären und in der progressiven Bevölkerung . . . ," *Bulletin de l'Institut International de Statistique*, XIX (Part 2), 63–138.

1911. FAIRCHILD, HENRY P. *Greek Immigration to the United States.* New Haven.

1911. GINI, CORRADO. "Sui fattori demografici dell'evoluzione delle nazioni," *Rivista italiana di sociologia.*

1911. SHARPE, F. L., and LOTKA, A. J. "A Problem in Age-Distribution," *Philosophical Magazine*, Ser. 6, XXI, 435–38.

1911. WELTON, THOMAS A. *England's Recent Progress: An Investigation of the Statistics of Migrations, Mortality, etc. . . . Particular Communities.* London: Chapman & Hall.

1912. FRANCE, BUREAU DE LA STATISTIQUE GÉNÉRALE. *Statistique des familles en 1906.* Paris.

1912. GROTJOHN, ALFRED, and KAUP, J. *Handwörterbuch der sozialen Hygiene.* 2 vols. Leipzig: Vogel.

1912. HUBER, M. "Mortalité suivant la profession, d'après les décès enregistrés en France en 1907 et 1908," *Bulletin de la Statistique Générale de la France*, I, No. 4, 402–39.

1912. OGBURN, WILLIAM F. *Progress and Uniformity in Child-Labor Legislation: A Study in Statistical Measurement.* ("Columbia University Studies in History, Economics, and Public Law.") New York.

1913. ELDERTON, ETHEL M., *et al. On the Correlation of Fertility with Social Value: A Cooperative Study.* ("Eugenics Laboratory Memoirs," No. 18.) London.

1913. GONNER, EDWARD C. K. "The Population of England in the Eighteenth Century," *Journal of the Royal Statistical Society*, LXXVI, 261–96.

1913. SUNDBÄRG, GUSTAV. *Emigrationsutredningen Betänkande.* Stockholm. *See also* THOMAS, 1941.

1914. DUNCAN, JAMES C. "The Fertility of Marriage in Scotland: A Census Study," *Journal of the Royal Statistical Society*, LXXVII, 259–99.

1914. GROTJOHN, ALFRED, and KAUP, J. *Geburtenrückgang und Geburtenregelung im Lichte der individuellen und der sozialen Hygiene.* Berlin: L. Marcus.

1915. LIVI, LIVIO. *La composizione della famiglia.* Rome.

1915. THOMPSON, WARREN S. *Population: A Study in Malthusianism.* ("Columbia University Studies in History, Economics, and Public Law.") New York.

1916. GROSSMAN, H. *Die Anfänge und geschichtliche Entwicklung der amtlichen Statistik in Österreich.* Brno.

1916. WATTAL, P. K. *The Population Problem in India.* Bombay: Bennett, Coleman & Co. 2d ed.; 1934.

1917. EDWARDS, ALBA M. "Social-economic Groups in the United States," *Journal of the American Statistical Association,* XXVIII, 377–87.

1917. KNIBBS, GEORGE H. "The Mathematical Theory of Population, of Its Character and Fluctuations, and of the Factors which Influence Them . . . ," *Census of the Commonwealth of Australia, April, 1911,* I, Appendix A, 1–466.

1917–23. GREAT BRITAIN, GENERAL REGISTER OFFICE. *Census of England and Wales, 1911.* Vol. XIII: *Fertility of Marriage,* Parts I–II. London.

1918. WOODBURY, ROBERT M. "Infant Mortality Studies of the Children's Bureau," *Quarterly Publication of the American Statistical Association,* XVI, 30–53.

1920. PEARL, RAYMOND, and REED, LOWELL J. "On the Rate of Growth of the Population of the United States since 1790 and Its Mathematical Representation," *Proceedings of the National Academy of Sciences,* VI, No. 6, 275–88.

1921. PARK, ROBERT, and BURGESS, ERNEST. *An Introduction to the Science of Sociology.* Chicago: University of Chicago Press.

1922. CARR-SAUNDERS, A. M. *The Population Problem: A Study in Evolution.* London: Oxford University Press.

1922. OGBURN, WILLIAM F., and THOMAS, DOROTHY S. "The Influence of the Business Cycle on Certain Social Conditions," *Journal of the American Statistical Association,* LXVIII, 324–40.

1922. VIDAL DE LA BLACHE, P. M. J. *Principes de géographie humaine.* Paris: Colin.

1923. CHEN TA. *Chinese Migrations, with Special Reference to Labor Conditions.* (United States Bureau of Labor Statistics, Bulletin No. 340.) Washington, D.C.

1923. GLOVER, JAMES W. *United States Life Tables . . . 1901–10.* Washington, D.C.: Bureau of the Census.

1923. SAVORGNAN, FRANCO. "Nuzialità e fecondità delle case sovrane d'Europa," *Metron,* III, 198–225.

1924. BOWLEY, A. L. "Births and Population in Great Britain," *Economic Journal,* XXXIV, 188–92.

1924. GINI, CORRADO. "Premières recherches sur la fécondabilité de la femme,"

Proceedings of the International Mathematical Congress, Toronto, pp. 889–92.

1924. HUNTINGTON, ELLSWORTH. *Civilization and Climate.* New Haven: Yale University Press.

1924. SAVORGNAN, F. "La fecondità della aristocrazia," *Metron,* III, 468 ff.

1925. BRUNNER, C. T. "Local Variations in the Birth-Rate," *Economic Journal,* XXXV, 60–65.

1925. DUBLIN, LOUIS I., and LOTKA, ALFRED J. "On the True Rate of Natural Increase, As Exemplified by the Population of the United States, 1920," *Journal of the American Statistical Association,* XX, 305–39.

1925. INTERNATIONAL LABOR OFFICE. *Les mouvements migratoires de 1920 à 1923.* Geneva.

1925. KNIBBS, GEORGE H. "The Growth of Human Populations and the Laws of Their Increase," *Metron,* V, 147–62.

1925a. LOTKA, ALFRED J. *Elements of Physical Biology.* Baltimore: Williams & Wilkins Co.

1925b. ———. "The Measure of Net Fertility," *Journal of the Washington Academy of Sciences,* XV, 469–72. (There is a collection of ninety-four manuscript papers in three volumes, "Scientific Papers of Alfred J. Lotka," in the Library of Congress.) *See also* LOTKA, 1907, 1934.

1925. NARAIN, BRIJ. *The Population of India.* Lahore: Rama Krishna & Sons.

1925. PEARL, RAYMOND. *The Biology of Population Growth.* New York: Knopf.

1925. THOMAS, DOROTHY S. *Social Aspects of the Business Cycle.* London: G. Routledge & Sons; New York: E. P. Dutton & Co.

1925. WILSON, EDWIN B., and LYTTEN, WILLEM. "The Population of New York City and Its Environs" (critique of logistic forecast), *Proceedings of the National Academy of Sciences,* XI, 137–43. *See also* WILSON and PUFFER, 1933.

1925. WOODBURY, ROBERT M. *Causal Factors in Infant Mortality: A Statistical Study Based on Investigations in Eight Cities.* ("United States Children's Bureau Publications," No. 142.) Washington, D.C. (A preliminary review of the research program was presented in the

Journal of the American Statistical Association, 1918.)

1925. YULE, G. UDNY. "The Growth of Population and the Factors which Control It," *Journal of the Royal Statistical Society,* LXXXVIII (Part 1), 1–58.

1926. BOWLEY, A. L. "Estimates of the Working Population of Certain Countries in 1931 and 1941," *International Economic Conference.* Geneva: League of Nations.

1926. BUER, MABEL C. *Health, Wealth, and Population in the Early Days of the Industrial Revolution (1760–1815).* London: Routledge.

1926. DUBLIN, LOUIS I. (ed.). *Population Problems in the United States and Canada.* (Pollock Foundation for Economic Research, Publication No. 5.) Boston: Houghton Mifflin.

1926. JEROME, HARRY. *Migration and Business Cycles.* New York: National Bureau of Economic Research.

1926. TRUESDELL, LEON E. *Farm Population of the United States, 1920.* Washington, D.C.: Government Printing Office.

1927. COLLINS, SELWYN D. *Economic Status and Health.* (United States Public Health Bulletin No. 165.) Washington, D.C.

1927. DERRICK, V. P. A. "Observations on (1) Errors of Age in the Population Statistics . . . and (2) the Changes in Mortality Indicated by the National Records," *Journal of the Institute of Actuaries* (London), LVIII, 117–59.

1927. SANGER, MARGARET (ed.). *Proceedings of the World Population Conference, Geneva, 1927.* London: Arnold, 1928.

1928. LOTKA, ALFRED J. "The Progeny of a Population Element," *American Journal of Hygiene,* VIII, 875–901.

1928. WHELPTON, P. K. "Population of the United States, 1925 to 1975," *American Journal of Sociology,* XXXIV, 253–71.

1928–31. KUCZYNSKI, R. R. *The Balance of Births and Deaths.* Vol. I. New York: Macmillan. Vol. II. Washington, D.C.: The Brookings Institution.

1929. SHRYOCK, RICHARD H. "The Origin and Significance of the Public Health Movement in the United States," *Annals of Medical History,* N.S. I, 647–65.

1929. SYDENSTRICKER, EDGAR. *Differential Fertility According to Economic Status.*

. . . ("United States Public Health Reports," XLIV, 2101–6. *Hagerstown Morbidity Study No. 11.*) Washington, D.C.

1929–31. WILLCOX, WALTER F. (ed.). *International Migrations.* 2 vols. New York: National Bureau of Economic Research. Vol. I: *Statistics,* compiled by IRME FERENCZI. Vol. II: *Interpretations* (including "Increase in the Population of the Earth and of the Continents since 1650," pp. 33–82).

1930. JAPAN. *Jinko-bu toshin setsumei.* ("Reports of the Population Section.") Tokyo: Jinko shokuryo mondai chosa-kai ("Commission on Food and Population").

1930. KENNEDY, LOUISE V. *The Negro Peasant Turns Cityward: Effects of Recent Migrations to Northern Centers.* ("Columbia University Studies in History, Economics, and Public Law," No. 329.) New York.

1930. SPENGLER, JOSEPH J. *The Fecundity of Native and Foreign-born Women in New England.* ("Brookings Institution Pamphlet Series," Vol. II, No. 1.) Washington, D.C.

1930. SYDENSTRICKER, EDGAR, and NOTESTEIN, F. W. "Differential Fertility According to Social Class . . . Based upon the United States Census Returns of 1910," *Milbank Memorial Fund Quarterly,* XII, 126–33.

1930. THOMPSON, WARREN S. *Population Problems.* New York: Macmillan. 4th ed.; 1953.

1930. USHER, A. P. "The History of Population and Settlement in Eurasia," *Geographical Review,* XX, No. 1, 110–32.

1930. VOLKOV, E. Z. *Dinamika naseleniya SSSR za vosemdesyat let.* Moscow.

1931. BOLDRINI, MARCELLO. *La fertilità dei biotipi.* Milan: Vita e pensiero.

1931. GINI, CORRADO (ed.). *Proceedings of the International Congress for Studies on Population, Rome, 1931.* 10 vols. Rome: Comitato Italiano per lo Studio dei Problemi della Popolazione, 1933–34.

1931. HONJŌ, EIJINŌ. "The Population and Its Problems in the Tokugawa Era," *Bulletin de l'Institut International de Statistique,* XXV, 60–82.

1931. PITT-RIVERS, G. H. L. F. (ed.). *Problems of Population.* International Union for the Scientific Investigation of Population Problems (Conference, London, 1931). London: Allen & Unwin, 1932.

1931. PTOUKHA, A. M. V. "La population de l'Ukraine jusqu'en 1960," *Bulletin de l'Institut International de Statistique,* XXV, No. 3, 59–88.

1931. TAEUBER, CONRAD. "Migration to and from Selected German Cities: An Analysis of Data of the Official Registration System (*Meldewesen*), 1902–1929." Unpublished dissertation, University of Minnesota.

1931. THOMPSON, WARREN S. *Ratio of Children to Women, 1920.* Washington, D.C.: Government Printing Office.

1931. VOLTERRA, VITO. *Leçons sur la théorie mathématique de la lutte pour la vie.* Paris: Gauthier-Villars.

1931. WICKSELL, S. D. "Nuptiality, Fertility, and Reproductivity," *Skandinavist aktuarietidskrift,* XVIII, 125–27.

1931–43. *Archiv für Bevölkerungswissenschaft und Bevölkerungspolitik.* Berlin.

1932. BURGDÖRFER, FRIEDRICH. *Volk ohne Jugend.* Berlin: K. Vowinckel.

1932. ELSTON, JAMES S. *Sources and Characteristics of the Principal Mortality Tables.* Rev. ed. New York: Actuarial Society of America.

1932. KISER, CLYDE V. *Sea Island to City: A Study of St. Helena Islanders in Harlem and Other Urban Centers.* ("Columbia University Studies in History, Economics, and Public Law," No. 368.) New York.

1932. KULISCHER, ALEXANDER, and KULISCHER, EUGENE M. *Kriegs- und Wanderzüge: Weltgeschichte als Völkerbewegung.* Berlin: Gruyter.

1932. MAUCO, GEORGES. *Les étrangers en France.* Paris: A. Colin.

1932. VANCE, RUPERT B. *Human Geography of the South.* Chapel Hill, N.C.: University of North Carolina Press.

1932. WESTERGAARD, HARALD. *Contributions to the History of Statistics.* London: P. S. King & Son.

1932. WOLFE, A. B. "Population Censuses before 1790," *Journal of the American Statistical Association,* XXVII, No. 180, 357–70.

1933. BACHI, ROBERTO. *La mobilità della popolazione all'interno delle grandi città europee.* Rome: Federazione della Proprietà Edililizia.

1933. KISER, CLYDE V. "Trends in the Fertility of Social Classes from 1900 to 1910," *Human Biology,* V, No. 2, 256–73.

1933. McKENZIE, R. D. *The Metropolitan Community.* New York: McGraw-Hill.

1933. MINER, J. R. "Pierre François Verhulst, the Discoverer of the Logistic Curve," *Human Biology,* V, No. 4, 673–89.

1933. MOMBERT, PAUL. "Neuere Erscheinungen zur Bevölkerungslehre und Bevölkerungsstatistik," *Archiv für Sozialwissenschaft,* LXVIII, 594–615.

1933. ROUN, HAROLD F., and STOUFFER, SAMUEL A. "Criteria of Differential Mortality," *Journal of the American Statistical Association,* XXVIII, No. 184, 402–13.

1933. SYDENSTRICKER, EDGAR. *Health and Environment.* New York: McGraw-Hill.

1933. TAEUBER, CONRAD. "Migration to and from German Cities, 1902–29," *Proceedings of the International Congress for Studies on Population, Rome, 1931,* ed. C. GINI, IX, 469–83.

1933. THOMPSON, WARREN S., and WHELPTON, P. K. *Population Trends in the United States.* New York: McGraw-Hill.

1933. UYEDA (UEDA), TEIJIRO. *Future of the Japanese Population.* (Japanese Council, Institute of Pacific Relations.) Tokyo: Nippon Press.

1933. WILLCOX, WALTER F. *Introduction to the Vital Statistics of the United States 1900 to 1930.* Washington, D.C.: Government Printing Office.

1933. WILSON, EDWIN B., and PUFFER, RUTH. "Least Squares and Population Growth," *Proceedings of the American Academy of Arts and Sciences,* LXVIII, No. 9, 287–382.

1933. WINKLER, WILHELM. *Grundriss der Statistik.* Vol. II: *Gesellschaftsstatistik.* Berlin: Spenger.

1933. WOOFTER, T. J. *Races and Ethnic Groups in American Life.* New York: McGraw-Hill.

1933–37. MORTARA, GIORGIO. "Studi sulla natalita in Italia" (a series), *Giornale degli economisti.*

1933–37. UYEDA (UEDA), TEIJIRO (ed.). *Nihon jinko mondai kenkyu* ("Studies in Japanese Population Problems"). 3 vols. Tokyo: Kyocho-kai.

1934. CHARLES, ENID. *Twilight of Parenthood*. New York: W. W. Norton & Co.

1934. HERSCH, LIEBMANN. "Taux globaux et taux composite en démographie," *Revue de l'Institut International de Statistique*, II, 5–25.

1934. KRZYWICKI, L. *Primitive Society and Its Vital Statistics*. Warsaw: Mianowski; London: Macmillan.

1934. KUCZYNSKI, R. R. "Population," *Encyclopaedia of the Social Sciences*, XII, 240–48.

1934. LANDRY, ADOLPHE. *La révolution démographique: Études et essais sur les problèmes de la population*. Paris: Librairie du Recueil Sirey.

1934. LORIMER, FRANK, and OSBORN, FREDERICK. *Dynamics of Population*. New York: Macmillan.

1934. MYRDAL, ALVA, and MYRDAL, GUNNAR. *Kris i befolkningsfrägän*. Stockholm.

1934. PEARL, RAYMOND. "Second Progress Report on a Study of Family Limitation," *Milbank Memorial Fund Quarterly*, XII, 248–69.

1934. ROSS, FRANK A., and KENNEDY, LOUISE V. *A Bibliography of Negro Migration*. New York: Columbia University Press.

1934. ZAHN, FREDERICK. *50 années de l'Institut International de Statistique*. The Hague.

1934–39. LOTKA, ALFRED J. *Théorie analytique des associations biologiques*. Part I: *Principes*. Part II: *Analyse démographique avec application particulière à l'espèce humaine*. Paris: Hermann & Co.

1935. EDIN, KARL A., and HUTCHINSON, EDWARD P. *Studies of Differential Fertility in Sweden*. London: P. S. King.

1935a. KUCZYNSKI, ROBERT R. *The Measurement of Population Growth: Methods and Results*. London: Sidgwick & Jackson; New York: Oxford University Press, 1936.

1935b. ———. "British Demographers' Opinions of Fertility 1660–1760," *Annals of Eugenics*, VI, 139–71.

1935. METHORST, H. W. *Differential Fertility in the Netherlands*. (*Population* [London], Vol. I, special memoir.)

1935. STEYER, KONRAD. *Die Wanderungsbewegung in Ostpreussen: Eine Bevölkerungsstudie*. ("Beiträge zur Statistik der Provinz Ostpreussen," No. 1.) Kaliningrad: Gräfe & Unzer.

1935. SZULC, S. "Die Lebensbilanz der Bevölkerung Polens 1895–1934," *Bevölkerungsfragen, Bericht des Internationalen Kongresses für Bevölkerungswissenschaft, Berlin, 26 August–1 September, 1935*, ed. HARMSEN and LOHSE, pp. 128–36. Munich, 1936.

1935. VOLTERRA, VITO, and D'ANCONA, UMBERTO. *Les associations biologiques au point de vue mathématique*. Paris: Hermann & Co.

1935–40. UNITED STATES WORKS PROGRESS ADMINISTRATION. "Research Monographs" and "Special Report," including: BECK, P. G., and FORSTER, M. C., *Six Rural Problem Areas*. Monograph I. 1935; WOOFTER, T. J., JR. *Landlord and Tenant on the Cotton Plantation*. Monograph V. 1936; WEBB, JOHN M., and BROWN, MALCOLM. *Migrant Families*. Monograph XVIII. 1939; LIVELY, C. E., and TAEUBER, CONRAD. *Rural Migration in the United States*. Monograph XIX. 1939; MANGUS, A. R. *Rural Regions of the United States*. 1940.

1935 ff. *Population Literature*, Vols. I–II (Population Association of America). Continued, 1937 ff., as *Population Index* (School of Public Affairs, Princeton University, and Population Association of America).

1936. CARR-SAUNDERS, A. M. *World Population: Past Growth and Present Trends*. London: Oxford University Press.

1936. DUBLIN, LOUIS I., and LOTKA, ALFRED J. *Length of Life: A Study of the Life Table*. New York: Ronald. Rev. ed., with MORTIMER SPIEGELMAN; 1949.

1936. EL-SHANAWANY, R. "The First National Life Tables for Egypt," *L'Égypte contemporaine*, XXVII, 209–66.

1936. GOODRICH, CARTER, et al. *Migration and Economic Opportunity*. Philadelphia: University of Pennsylvania Press.

1936. GREENWOOD, MAJOR. "English Death-Rates, Past, Present, and Future, a Valedictory Address," *Journal of the Royal Statistical Society*, XCIX, No. 4, 674–707.

1936. HALBWACHS, MAURICE, and SAUVY, ALFRED. "L'espèce humaine," *Encyclopédie française*, VII. Paris: Librairie Larousse.

1936. HARMSEN, H., and LOHSE, F. (eds.). *Bevölkerungsfragen, Bericht des Internationalen Kongresses für Bevölkerungswissenschaft, Berlin, 26 August–1 September, 1935.* Munich: J. F. Lehmann.

1936. QUENSEL, C. E. "Barnantalet i de svenska aktenskapen'" ("Number of Children in Swedish Marriages") *Statsvetensk tidskrift*, XXXIX, 203–26.

1936. SAVORGNAN, F. *Corso di demografia.* Pisa: Nistri Lischi.

1936. UYEDA (UEDA) TEIJIRO. *The Growth of Population and Occupational Changes in Japan.* ("Japanese Council Papers," Institute of Pacific Relations, Conference, Yosemite, California, August 15–29, 1936.)

1936a. VALAORAS, VASILOS G. "A Comparative Study of the Mortality of the Population of Greece," *Human Biology*, VIII, 553–64.

1936b. ——"The Expectation of Life in Ancient Greece," *Practika de l'Académie d'Athènes*, XIII, 401–10.

1936. WHELPTON, P. K. "An Empirical Method of Calculating Future Population," *Journal of the American Statistical Association*, XXXI, 457–73.

1936. WOLFBEIN, SEYMOUR, and JAFFE, A. J. "Demographic Factors in Labor Force Growth," *American Sociological Review*, XI, No. 4, 392–96.

1937. BURGDÖRFER, F. "Familienstatistik und Fruchtbarkeitsmessung," *Revue de l'Institut International de Statistique*, V, 212–26.

1937. CHARLES, ENID. "The Changing Structure of the Family in Australia," *Economica*, N.S. IV, 245–73.

1937. *Les comptes-rendus du Congrès International de la Population.* 8 vols. Paris: Hermann & Co., 1938. *See also:* SANGER (ed.), 1927; PITT-RIVERS (ed.), 1931; GINI (ed.), 1931; HARMSEN and LOHSE (eds.), 1936.

1937. DEPOID, PIERRE. "Influence de la nuptialité sur les taux de reproduction française," *Journal de la Société de Statistique de Paris*, LXXVIII, 342–46.

1937. EDGE, P. GRANVILLE. "The Demography of British Colonial Possessions," *Journal of the Royal Statistical Society*, C, 181–220.

1937. GREEN, HOWARD W., and TRUESDELL, LEON E. *Census Tracts in American Cities.* Washington: Bureau of the Census.

1937. HEBERLE, RUDOLPH, and MEYER, FRITZ. *Die Grossstädte im Strome der Binnenwanderung.* Leipzig.

1937. HUBER, MICHEL, BUNLE, HENRI, and BOVERAT, FERNAND. *La population de la France.* Paris: Librairie Hachette.

1937. ISHII, RYOICHI. *Population Problems and Economic Life in Japan.* Chicago: University of Chicago Press.

1937. KUCZYNSKI, ROBERT A. *Colonial Population.* London: Oxford University Press.

1937. LIVI, LIVIO. *I fattori biologici dell'ordinamento sociale.* Padua.

1937. SOMOGYI, S. "Tavole di nuzialità e di vedovanza per popolazione italiana," *Annali di statistica*, Ser. 7, Vol. I.

1937. THOMAS, BRINLEY. "The Influx of Labour into London and the Southeast," *Economica*, N.S. IV, 323–36.

1937. UYEDA (UEDA), TEIJIRO. "Bevölkerungsfrage und Wirtschaft im heutigen Japan," *Weltwirtschaftliches Archiv*, XLVI, 93–115.

1937. VACLAV, SEKERA. "Les migrations dans les grandes villes pendant la crise économique mondiale," *Statisticky Obzor* (Prague), XVIII, 145–68.

1937–39. BELOCH, (KARL) JULIUS. *Bevölkerungsgeschichte italiens.* 2 vols. Berlin and Leipzig: De Gruyter (posthumous).

B. References

1938–57

BICKEL, WILHELM. 1947. *Bevölkerungs-Geschichte und Bevölkerungs-Politik der Schweiz.* Zurich: Büchergilde Gutenberg.

BOLDRINI, MARCELLO. 1956. *Demografia.* Rev. ed. Milan: Giuffrè.

CHIAO, C. M., THOMPSON, W. S., and CHEN, D. T. 1938. *An Experiment in the Registration of Vital Statistics in China.* Oxford, Ohio: Scripps Foundation for Research in Population Problems.

COALE, ANSLEY J. 1956. "The Effects of Changes in Mortality and Fertility on Age Composition," *Milbank Memorial Fund Quarterly*, XXXIV, 79–114.

DAVIS, KINGSLEY (ed.). 1945. *World Population in Transition.* ("Annals of the American Academy of Political and Social Science," Vol. CCXXXVII.) Philadelphia.

DELAPORTE, PIERRE J. 1941. *Evolution de la mortalité en Europe depuis l'origine des statistiques de l'état civil; tables de mortalité et de survie des générations.* Paris: Statistique Générale de la France.

DEPOID, PIERRE. 1941. *Reproduction nette en Europe depuis l'origine des statistiques de l'état civil.* Paris: Statistique Générale de la France.

DUBLIN, LOUIS I. (ed.). 1939. *The American People; Studies in Population.* ("Annals of the American Academy of Political and Social Science," Vol. CLXXXVIII.) Philadelphia.

FITZPATRICK, PAUL J. 1955. "The Early Teaching of Statistics in American Colleges and Universities," *American Statistician,* IX, 12–18.

FRAZER, W. M. 1950. *A History of English Public Health, 1834–1939.* London.

FROST, WADE H. 1939. "The Age Selection of Mortality from Tuberculosis in Successive Decades," *American Journal of Hygiene,* XXX, 91–96.

GLASS, DAVID. 1950a. "Gregory King's Estimate of the Population of England and Wales, 1695," *Population Studies,* III, No. 4, 338–74. (Cites reference to previous article on this subject by same author, *Eugenics Review,* Vol. XXXVII [1946].)

———. 1950b. "Graunt's Life Table," *Journal of the Institute of Actuaries,* LXXVI, 60–64.

———. 1952. "The Population Controversy in Eighteenth-century England," *Population Studies,* VI, 69–91. (Part I of a projected series of papers, "The Development of British Demography in the Eighteenth and Nineteenth Centuries.")

———. (ed.). 1953. *Introduction to Malthus.* New York: Wiley; London: Watts. (Contains "A List of Books, Pamphlets, and Articles on the Population Question . . . Britain . . . 1793 to 1880," by J. A. BANKS and DAVID GLASS, pp. 81–112.)

———. 1956. "Some Aspects of the Development of Demography," *Journal of the Royal Society of Arts,* CIV, 854–68.

GREENWOOD, MAJOR. 1948. *Medical Statistics from Graunt to Farr.* Cambridge.

GUTMAN, ROBERT. 1956. "The Birth Statistics of Massachusetts during the Nineteenth Century," *Population Studies,* X, 69–94.

HAJNAL, J. 1947. "Aspects of Recent Trends in Marriage in England and Wales," *Population Studies,* I, 72–92.

HENRY, LOUIS. 1953a. "Fondements théoriques des mesures de la fécondité naturelle," *Revue de l'Institut International de Statistique,* XXI, 135–51.

———. 1953b. *Fécondité des mariages: Nouvelle méthode de mesure.* Paris: Institut National d'Études Démographiques.

HERSCH, LIEBMANN. 1954. Address to the World Population Conference. See UNITED NATIONS, 1955–57.

HOGBEN, LANCELOT (ed.). 1938. *Political Arithmetic.* New York: Macmillan.

HONJO, EIJINO. 1941. *Nihon jinko shi* ("History of Japanese Population"). Tokyo: Nihon Nyōron-sha.

KARMEL, P. T. 1947. "The Relations between Male and Female Reproduction Rates," *Population Studies,* I, 249–74.

———. 1948. "The Relations between Male and Female Nuptiality in a Stable Population," *Population Studies,* I, 353–87.

KULISCHER, EUGENE M. 1948. *Europe on the Move.* New York: Columbia University Press.

LANDRY, ADOLPHE. 1945. *Traité de démographie.* Paris: Payot.

LIVI, LIVIO. 1940. *Trattato di demografia.* 2 vols. Padua: A. Milani.

MERRELL, MARGARET. 1947. "Time-specific Life Tables Contrasted with Observed Survivorship," *Biometrics Bulletin,* III, 129–36.

MYRDAL, ALVA. 1941. *Nation and Family: The Swedish Experiment in Democratic Family and Population Policy.* New York and London: Harper & Bros.

NOTESTEIN, F. W., TAEUBER, I. B., KIRK, D., COALE, A. J., and KISER, L. K. 1944. *The Future Population of Europe and the Soviet Union.* Geneva: League of Nations.

PEARL, RAYMOND. 1939. *Natural History of Population.* London: Oxford University Press.

PELLER, SIGISMUND. 1948. "Mortality, Past and Future," *Population Studies,* I, 405–56.

Population (France). 1954. "Histoire et chronologie des réunions et congrès internationaux sur la population," special no.

Population Index. Vol. XVI. 1950. "Alfred

J. Lotka, 1880–1949," pp. 22–29. (Bibliography.)

REED, LOWELL J. (ed.). 1942. *Two Papers on the Degrees of Mortality in Mankind by Edmund Halley.* Baltimore: Johns Hopkins Press.

RUSSELL, JOSIAH COX. 1948. *British Mediaeval Population.* Albuquerque: University of New Mexico Press.

SAUVY, ALFRED. 1956. "Adolphe Landry," *Population,* XI, 609–20.

SAVORGNAN, FRANCO. 1942. *La fecondità dell'aristocrazia e prolusioni e saggi.* Pisa: Nistri-Lischi.

SHAPIRO, SAMUEL. 1950. "Development of Birth Registration and Birth Statistics in the United States," *Population Studies,* IV, 86–111.

SHAUL, J. R. H., and MYBURGH, C. A. L. 1948. "A Sample Survey of the African Population of Southern Rhodesia," *Population Studies,* II, 339–53.

SPENGLER, JOSEPH J. 1938. *France Faces Depopulation.* Durham, N.C.: Duke University Press.

———. 1952. *French Predecessors of Malthus: A Study in Eighteenth Century Wage and Population Theory.* Durham, N.C.: Duke University Press. French edition: *Économie et population; les doctrines françaises avant 1800.* (Institut National d'Études Démographiques, Cahier No. 21.) Paris.

———, and DUNCAN, OTIS DUDLEY (eds.). 1957. *Demographic Analysis: Selected Readings.* Glencoe, Ill.: Free Press.

SPIEGELMAN, MORTIMER. 1955. *Introduction to Demography.* Chicago: Society of Actuaries.

STEPHAN, FREDERICK F. 1947. "History of the Uses of Modern Sampling Procedures," *Proceedings of the International Statistical Conferences,* IIIB, 81–104. Washington, D.C.: International Statistical Institute.

STOLNITZ, GEORGE J., 1955–56. "A Century of International Mortality Trends: I, II," *Population Studies,* IX, 24–55; X, 17–42.

———, and RYDER, NORMAN B. 1949. "Recent Discussion of the Net Reproduction Rate," *Population Index,* XV, 115–28.

TAEUBER, IRENE B. (Supervisor). 1943. *General Censuses and Vital Statistics in the Americas.* Washington, D.C.: United States Bureau of the Census; Library of Congress.

THOMAS, DOROTHY S. 1938. *Research Memorandum on Migration Differentials.* New York: Social Science Research Council.

———. 1941. *Social and Economic Aspects of Swedish Population Movements, 1750–1933.* New York: Macmillan. *See also* UNITED STATES NATIONAL RESOURCES COMMITTEE. 1938.

THORSTEINSON, THORSTEINN. 1947. "The First Census Taken in Iceland in 1703," *Proceedings of the International Statistical Conferences,* IIIB, 614–23. Washington, D.C.: International Statistical Institute.

UNITED KINGDOM, ROYAL COMMISSION ON POPULATION. 1949–50. *Reports; Papers.* Vol. II: *Reports and Selected Papers of the Statistics Committee* (including "The measurement of reproductivity," etc., by JOHN HAJNAL, pp. 338–403).

UNITED NATIONS. 1953. *Determinants and Consequences of Population Trends.* New York.

———. 1955–57. *Proceedings of the World Population Conference, 1954.* 6 vols. New York.

UNITED STATES NATIONAL RESOURCES COMMITTEE. 1938. *The Problems of a Changing Population.* Appendix C, by DOROTHY S. THOMAS, "Continuous Register System of Population Accounting." Washington, D.C.: Government Printing Office.

VINCENT, PAUL. 1946. "De la mesure du taux intrinsèque d'accroissement naturel dans les populations monogèmes," *Population,* I, 699–712.

———. 1947. "French Demography in the Eighteenth Century," *Population Studies,* I, No. 1, 44–71.

WHELPTON, PASCAL K. 1938. *Needed Population Research.* (Auspices of the Population Association of America.) Lancaster, Pa.: Science Press.

———. 1954. *Cohort Fertility.* Princeton: Princeton University Press.

WILLCOX, WALTER F. 1940. *Studies in American Demography.* Ithaca: Cornell University Press.

WOLFENDEN, HUGH H. 1954. *Population Statistics and Their Compilation.* Chicago: University of Chicago Press. 1st ed.; Actuarial Society of America, 1925.

7. Development and Perspectives of Demographic Research in France

ALFRED SAUVY

Although works or texts on population, marriage, and related topics had been numerous since the sixteenth century, demography—the science of population—did not really come into being until the end of the seventeenth century, with the work of Fénelon, Boisguillebert, Vauban, Belesbat, and others. Their inquiries had been stimulated by the poverty and the decrease of the population in that period. Moreover, their work very nearly coincided with the first census.

In the eighteenth century, authors who discussed population were numerous. The general problem with which they were concerned was the cause of depopulation and the means of remedying it. The term "population" came into general use around 1750. The demographic statisticians—Messance, Expilly, Moheau, etc.—wrote especially between 1760 and 1780. In the same period, the physiocrats appeared, for example, Quesnay, whose theory treated economics and population simultaneously.

With the growth of population and liberal ideas the national anxiety was less acute, and research became less voluminous after 1780. Economic demography also underwent an eclipse in the nineteenth century. Despite Guillard's coining of the term "démographie" in 1855, the subdivision of science toward the middle of the century was disastrous for demographic study. Being much too general, demographic studies were disregarded by the specialized faculties of the universities. Demography was at that time an uncoordinated science, with neither teachers nor students; however, elements of demography could be found in human geography and history (faculty of letters), political economy (faculty of law), anthropology (faculty of sciences), and medical biology and hygiene (faculty of medicine).

Toward the end of the nineteenth century demographic inquiries were for the most part of a statistical nature; nevertheless, anxieties, provoked by the drop in natality, prompted a number of works (Bertillon, A. Dumont).

At the beginning of the twentieth century these anxieties were elaborated with no notable effect on demography, and this situation continued until after World War I. Between the two wars, aside from the purely statistical studies in which there was clear improvement, the principal demographic works were executed by miscellaneous individuals who were not responsible professionally for demographic studies (Landry).

After World War II a profound change occurred, basically caused by the collapse of 1940. During four years of occupation and humiliation, France had felt, somewhat vaguely, that this collapse had resulted from a decrease in vitality which had accompanied the excessive sterility of families and the aging which had continued for the past century and a half. In the optimistic atmosphere of the liberation a new national consciousness developed, and with it came the desire for a deliberate population policy.

These considerations prompted the formation of the Institut National d'Études Démographiques, a scientific organization charged with studying all the phenomena of population, in the broadest sense of the word. Thus, its concern was not only with quantitative analysis but with the investigation of causes and consequences of demographic phenomena. About the same time, the central statistical service, the Institut National de la Statistique et des Études Économiques, was expanded considerably, and this permitted an improvement in basic statistical material.

For the most part, however, research was focused on the areas which preoccupied the public. Just as a man is engrossed with the diseased or painful parts of his body, so demographic research was centered primarily around the points where some social malady was indicated. Thus, we see that demography was influenced directly by the very history of population or, more precisely, by anxieties which developed about it.

Progress in statistical matters certainly contributed to giving demographic investigations a more scientific character, but this progress was not the only factor producing improvement. In fact, despite the quality of statistical material (particularly of vital statistics), it was utilized only imperfectly. The defect in methodology remains because of insufficient training in the universities and, until 1945, because of the lack of appropriate organizations responsible for analyzing statistics, drawing conclusions from analyses, and disseminating them. Statistics has not profited from the kind of criticism which would orient it more usefully and has, for this reason, somewhat neglected the social factors, which are always difficult to perceive.

THE PRESENT STATUS OF DEMOGRAPHIC STUDIES[1]

The value of statistical material has been extended considerably further in recent years. Here, we will omit the progress in the field of statistics—which involves census techniques or mathematical methods of analysis—and limit ourselves specifically to purely demographic research.

Owing to the improvement of basic data and its criticism (Depoid), pure or quantitative demography has made considerable progress, particularly in the interpretation of raw statistics. We can cite several topics in which notable advances have been made.

In the measurement of fertility and demographic vitality the notion of "fertility behavior" and the use of birth order permit a sounder judgment of the significance of rates of natality or fertility (Bourgeois-Pichat, Henry). At the same time, physiological sterility has been defined and measured (P. Vincent).

The phenomenon of mortality—particularly of infant mortality—has been analyzed more and more thoroughly (Bourgeois-Pichat), and the mortality of the aged (P. Vincent), with the fundamental distinction between endogenous mortality of a biological nature and exogenous mortality, has been examined (Bourgeois-Pichat, Sutter). Mortality tables have been improved and analyzed (Delaporte).

The demography of underdeveloped countries and particularly of territories dependent upon French authority, about which little was known until re-

[1] In this summary sketch we can mention only a few of the investigations and investigators. We have not attempted to provide bibliographic references for all the authors referred to.

cently, has been studied more adequately (Henry, Chevalier). For Algeria in particular, the basic characteristics and especially the pattern of growth are known today. A special study of Madagascar also has been carried out. Progress in the technique of demographic projections has gone hand in hand with improvements in the measurement of fertility and mortality (Henry, Pressat).

The economically active population has been studied in several ways. Population projections, occupational distribution, and occupational migrations in relation to full employment and technological development have been constructed by Fourastié and Sauvy; Henry has considered the rate of activity according to age and occupation; and projections of expenses resulting from the economically inactivate population and social security (in the broadest sense) have been made by Bourgeois-Pichat.

On the statistical side, the aging of the population has been studied as completely as possible; furthermore, its economic and social consequences have been examined—especially the question of the duration of the economically active life (age of retirement) and, more generally, the fate of aged persons (Daric).

In the field of international migration, research has been carried out on the needs for immigration in relation to economic development and on the assimilation or adaptation of migrants into their new environment (Girard). General European studies have concerned projections for several countries of western Europe (Bourgeois-Pichat) and the results that can be expected from a more or less forced economic integration, especially in terms of employment (Sauvy).

Theoretical investigations of relationships between demographic phenomena and economic and social phenomena have been carried out mainly on the optimum population, considered in its most general aspect: the relationship between welfare and number of people and, above all, change in that number (Sauvy, Buquet). These relationships have not been studied merely from a physical, mechanical point of view—as they most often are. The influence of population size and variation on men's behavior has merited equal attention and has led to the study of manifestations of economic Malthusianism (Sauvy), which brings about a reduction in the desire to produce and progress. Research also has been done on the need for increasing employment in anticipation of an increase in the younger groups of working age (Fourastié, Sauvy).

Among the social problems, three have been given major attention: alcoholism, housing, and education. Because alcoholism has significant demographic consequences, a systematic analysis has been made of the causes of the phenomenon—economic (production) and psychosocial causes, particularly the general attitude toward the opinions and mentality of the drinker (Debré, Girard)—and the national loss on the economic and demographic level has been estimated, notably by a very rigorous mathematical analysis of mortality statistics (Ledermann) and by investigations based on social observation (Malignac).

Research has been carried out on two basic aspects of housing from a demographic point of view: a projection of objective needs according to probable growth (Henry) and an inventory of expressed needs through direct questioning of families (Girard). In the field of education, the projection of school population and school construction needs has been accompanied by penetrating qualitative research on the intellectual level of children (according to age, sex, occupation of parents, region of residence, size of family, etc.) and on academic and occupational orientation (Gilles, Heuyer, Girard, Stoetzel).

Conditions of family life have shown, as in many other cases, that traditional moral considerations must be set aside in favor of a systematic observation and analysis of the facts. Inquiries into family budgets, almost nonexistent until 1945, have been increased. The influence of number of children on the level of living of the family, taking account of family legislation, has been measured systematically (Malignac); at the same time, investigations have been undertaken on the work of the married woman (Daric, Stoetzel, Girard) and the life of the couple (Fougerollas, Duplessis). The evolution of conceptions of the family has been studied systematically (Prigent) in relation to economic development and internal migration.

The new science of population genetics, which straddles genetics and demography, has benefited from careful research on the demographic consequences of consanguinity, particularly on isolates and their dispersal (Sutter, L. Tabah).

Investigations of the history of population have been carried out especially on the prestatistical period. Vital statistics have been reconstructed as far back as 1776, as has the distribution of population by age and sex (Bourgeois-Pichat). Furthermore, a number of investigations in progress are aimed at exploiting parish registers of civil status from the seventeenth and eighteenth centuries (Henry); others comprise work on the origins of contraceptive practices of the family in modern times (Sauvy, Mirochnitchenko).

Numerous investigations of the history of population theories with different focuses (Bourdon, Gemaehling) have been undertaken; they have no systematic character. A translation of J. J. Spengler's book, *French Predecessors of Malthus,* has been followed by the compilation of a bibliography of around three thousand volumes appearing since 1800 and discussing population in its various aspects. Cantillon's *L'essai sur la nature du commerce en général* has been re-edited (Anita Hirsch) and a new edition of the works of Quesnay is in preparation (Jacqueline Hecht).

Generally, the areas which have received the least scientific study are those which have least preoccupied the public interest or those which are not readily amenable to a statistical approach, particularly those which ramify into all the aspects of social life. This is especially the case with the social factors in mortality, and still more in nuptiality. There are few important investigations of social factors in mortality aside from the statistical study of infant mortality (Croze, Febvay). This phenomenon has not been understood in all its relationships with the social setting, so that local surveys have not provided the expected results. Statistics on social factors in fertility are clearly inadequate, and investigations are few or insufficiently thorough. In particular, voluntary sterility has not been examined sufficiently.

The inadequacy of studies of nuptiality is even more extreme. Not only has there been an insufficient study of the living conditions and behavior of men with respect to marriage, but the available statistics themselves have been analyzed only partially (e.g., age differences between husband and wife). This relative disinterest is explained by the fact that nuptiality has not posed any sociopolitical problems in France thus far. While fertility dropped, giving reason for alarm, nuptiality always remained satisfactory despite wars and crises.

We have approached the topic of morbidity from a demographic instead of a medical point of view. Morbidity statistics of a sufficiently general scope are rather rare. The phenomenon of physical or mental morbidity is poorly understood on the demographic level.

Texts and works bearing on internal migration, and especially the rural exodus, are numerous, but the phenomenon too often has been discussed from a local and descriptive angle (regional monographs) or from an administrative standpoint (decentralization of industry). This material is more relevant to geography or administration than to demography. It is true, however, that important studies are in progress. Despite the progress made in the area of social mobility (Girard, Brésard), there has been inadequate research. A number of problems remain to be solved.

There remain several major obstacles to the development of demography. There is a lack of statistical data or factual information on social factors in mortality and fertility. However, the lack of statistics is only an intermediate cause, not a fundamental one. Let us look further. Numerous investigations must be given up as too costly; research of a regional character or that which requires a decentralization of resources suffers from the lack of financial means. Even more serious than this deficiency, the lack of qualified research personnel must be regarded as the basic obstacle. Because the remuneration of qualified individuals is less than that of personnel in private industry or international organizations, recruitment is difficult, and, furthermore, the best-qualified persons who do enter the field often leave it for higher paid positions elsewhere. The questions of financing and personnel ought to be considered together. It is useless to seek financial resources if they cannot be used to good advantage, and it is impossible to train qualified persons without assuring them of satisfactory positions. One can say that the "market" is much too restricted.

The skepticism or indifference of the public is sometimes an important obstacle. The principal gaps occur, we have seen, with respect to questions which require an understanding of the social setting. Not only is the public rather reticent about answering census questions, but it does not always react in a favorable manner to social research.

There is also a lack of liaison between demographers and administrative agencies and private associations. A number of administrative agencies possess useful documents which they not only fail to publish but do not even admit owning. Statistics often are only a by-product of basically judicial and administrative activities. The lack of liaison is even more marked in the case of private associations—for example, the large professional organizations. This lack affects, in particular, questions concerning the economically active population, housing, education, and public health.

There is another lack of liaison between demographers and scientists of other disciplines. Great progress has been made in this direction, for the expressed goal of the Institut National d'Études Démographiques is to bring together various experts (jurists, statisticians, economists, biologists, sociologists, etc.). At the same time, the need for liaison has become more important. Progressive specialization is leading to a partitioning harmful to all sciences, and particularly so to demography, which touches a great number of other sciences without having close relationships with any of them. The liaison is most inadequate in the case of physicians and economists. Physicians have felt, for quite some time, an indifference or even aversion to statistics. Economists, on the other hand, have not given sufficient attention to the importance of demographic and human factors. The reaction of public opinion must be reckoned with, too. Demographic works often are poorly understood by public authorities and the public at large. The misunderstandings which this creates produce additional obstacles to demographic work.

If one takes the word demography in the narrow sense, training for demography requires mathematical instruction as a foundation. Once out of the faculty of science or of preparatory classes in a specialized school, the student can take courses in mathematical statistics, especially at the Institut de Statistique of the University of Paris and at the school of the Institut National de la Statistique. But the needs of private industry have increased faster than the number of students, so the scarcity of personnel is serious. This scarcity persists because of the defective orientation of secondary schools and colleges. The number of students in the liberal arts and law has risen and exceeded the number of professional positions, while the number of students in the sciences is clearly inadequate.

Demographers, in the broader sense of the word, are trained by other means: political economy (in the faculty of law), geography and sociology (in the faculty of letters), etc. Interfaculty institutes function in several universities —for example, Bordeaux, Caen, Lille, Strasbourg, Nancy, Lyon, and Toulouse. As for demographic investigations, they are executed most frequently at the Institut National d'Études Démographiques, which undertakes population studies in the broadest sense. Not only are purely demographic problems —the bookkeeping of population—investigated, but also problems of applied demography—a synthesis of human problems designed to enlighten public opinion and public authorities

while advancing the cause of pure science—are studied.

The Institut National d'Études Démographiques works in liaison with: (a) the Institut National de la Statistique des Études Économiques, which has responsibility for compiling statistics (censuses, vital statistics, etc.) and proceeding to a preliminary analysis (in demography, it functions as a supplier of the Institut National d'Études Démographiques); (b) scientific institutions and organizations, responsible for questions concerning sociology, economics, genetics, family law, history and geography, education, labor, and health; (c) the universities, particularly those mentioned above, where institutes or centers for demographic studies are located; (d) administrative agencies and private organizations which find themselves facing practical problems involving population (especially education, labor, and housing); and (e) the press and organs of mass communication.

Nor is there adequate publication about demography. The major newspapers devote a little more space to demographic questions than formerly; nevertheless, their reports are very inadequate in both quantity and quality, and the public is not well informed. The only periodical devoted to demography is *Population*, published by the Institut National d'Études Démographiques. The publications of the Institut National de la Statistique et des Études Économiques, the *Bulletin de liaison* of the demographic institutes of the universities, and miscellaneous reviews of a social character (such as *Économie et humanisme*), of geography, and of sociology also furnish some information. Some books on demography are published by the Institut National d'Études Démographiques, some by the Institut National de la Statistique et des Études Économiques, and others by private publishers. These are not widely distributed.

One cannot pretend, then, that demographic thought is being expressed successfully. Classical education has almost no room for demography, and the number of people likely to use demographic works is very small. The absence of any kind of popular literature on the subject is usually cited as the cause for this lack of interest.

PROSPECTS FOR DEMOGRAPHY

Because in the past basic progress has partly been made under the sway of sociopolitical necessity and partly dictated by historical events, we can expect that the future development of studies will depend more or less on the acuteness of the problems which arise. For example, comparisons of the growth of population in France and foreign countries can lead to a more attentive study of the problem of contraception and its spread. It would be vain to try to reverse the order; the development of pure demography is desirable in itself, but alone it is not enough. Applications will be impossible if a gap exists between theory and social reality. On the other hand, it would be a mistake to count on only the stimulation of necessity, for this stimulant always arrives too late.

The points where action is possible include (a) an increase in financial means, (b) training of qualified personnel, and (c) dissemination of methods and results. Finances come mostly from the government and co-operation could be obtained if diffusion of knowledge, the essential factor, were increased; if the usefulness of demographic studies were apparent to the public, research would be undertaken on a larger scale by interested organizations (especially professional groups), either by granting financial subsidies

for specific objectives or by deciding themselves to undertake demographic work which appeared useful. This is naturally more a matter of applied demography (economically active population, employment, etc.) than of pure demography.

Modifications of the present programs are needed especially in the framework of instruction. The principal modifications should be the teaching of an abridged course in demography in the secondary schools; a separation from law and political economy and, if possible, the formation of faculties of social science; the teaching of statistics and demography in each university by specialized professors; and the training of personnel from underdeveloped countries, especially the overseas territories. As for research, it must avoid abstraction and isolation and push on in the area of applications. Pure demography will inevitably benefit from this.

The focus of necessary future investigations follows from what has just been said; it is a matter of relating scientific theory and action by showing how the first can aid the second. Therefore, it is necessary to develop research which penetrates the social complex, so as to bring questions which vary empirically or which have not even been formulated into the scientific domain. The three large subjects, fertility, mortality, and nuptiality, must be studied more and more by relating them to social factors. As these social factors cannot always be comprehended by the too rigid and costly classical statistics (census and vital statistics), local inquiries must be multiplied. Such inquiries, although more difficult to utilize, are much more fruitful if conducted in a rigorous, scientific manner.

Demographic projections must be studied in their implications for economic life and, in particular, for the economically active population—aging and the problem of retirement, youth and occupational orientation. Projections for the population of underdeveloped countries need to be made also. The evolution of population ought to be followed more closely on a regional basis. Moreover, demographic research ought to be extended into other areas, notably population genetics, history of population, population theory, comparative legislation, and international migration.

It is possible to select from the preceding statement several questions in which interest is already present and which most urgently require study: (*a*) populations of overseas territories need investigation in terms of their development and the cultural and economic level at which education in contraceptive practices can have some impact, taking care that such studies do not provoke an unfavorable psychological reaction; (*b*) problems of the growth of the economically active population of France require study in order to foresee coming changes and to plan ways of avoiding dislocations after 1960 (the year in which the largest groups reach working age); (*c*) regional demographic projections, a problem related to the foregoing, should be made; and (*d*) social factors in mortality and fertility should be studied by means of special inquiries and improved statistical materials.

In this outline, the danger of separating demography from the social complex which it should take into account is apparent. The progress which has been made always has resulted from the pressure of necessity, and demography's failure to gain esteem has derived from its excessive abstraction. Though conceivable for a physical science, isolation is not desirable for a social science.

SELECTED BIBLIOGRAPHY

Ariès, P. 1948. *Histoire des populations françaises.* Paris: Éditions Self.

Balandier, G. 1956. *Le "tiers monde": Sous-Développement et développement.* ("Institut National d'Études Démographiques, Travaux et documents," Cahier No. 27.) Paris: Presses Universitaires de France.

Bourgeois-Pichat, J. 1950. *Mesure de la fécondité des populations.* ("Institut National d'Études Démographiques, Travaux et documents," Cahier No. 12.) Paris: Presses Universitaires de France.

Boverat, F. 1946. *La vieillissement de la population.* Paris: Éditions Sociales Françaises.

Bunle, H. 1954. *Le mouvement naturel de la population dans le monde de 1906 à 1936.* Paris: Institut National d'Études Démographiques.

Buquet, L. 1956. *L'optimum de population.* ("Pragma Publications de l'Institut Économique Appliquée," No. 6.) Paris: Presses Universitaires de France.

Chevalier, L. 1947. *Le problème démographique Nord-Africain.* ("Institut National d'Études Démographiques, Travaux et documents," Cahier No. 6.) Paris: Presses Universitaires de France.

———. 1951. *Démographie générale.* Paris: Dalloz.

Daric, J. 1948. *Vieillissement de la population et prolongation de la vie active.* ("Institut National d'Études Démographiques, Travaux et documents," Cahier No. 7.) Paris: Presses Universitaires de France.

Fleury, M., and Henry, L. 1956. *Des registres paroissiaux à l'histoire de la population: Manuel de dépouillement et d'exploitation de l'état civil ancien.* (Institut National d'Études Démographiques, Occasional Publication.) Paris.

Fourastié, J. 1957. *Migrations professionnelles: Données statistiques sur leur évolution en divers pays, de 1900 à 1955.* ("Institut National d'Études Démographiques, Travaux et documents," Cahier No. 31.) Paris: Presses Universitaires de France.

FROMONT, P. 1947. *Démographie économique*. Paris: Payot.

GEORGE, P. 1951. *Introduction à l'étude géographique de la population du monde*. ("Institut National d'Études Démographiques, Travaux et documents," Cahier No. 14.) Paris: Presses Universitaires de France.

GIRARD, A., and STOETZEL, J. 1953. *Français et immigrés: L'attitude française et l'adaptation des Italiens et des Polonais*. ("Institut National d'Études Démographiques, Travaux et documents," Cahier No. 19.) Paris: Presses Universitaires de France.

———. 1954. *Français et immigrés: Nouveaux documents sur l'adaptation: Algériens, Italiens, Polonais; le service social d'aide aux immigrants*. ("Institut National d'Études Démographiques, Travaux et documents," Cahier No. 20.) Paris: Presses Universitaires de France.

GRAVIER, J. F. 1954. *Décentralisation et progrès technique*. Paris: Flammarion.

HENRIPIN, J. 1954. *La population canadienne au début du XVIIIème siècle: Nuptialité, fécondité, mortalité infantile*. ("Institut National d'Études Démographiques, Travaux et documents," Cahier No. 22.) Paris: Presses Universitaires de France.

HENRY, L. 1953. *Fécondité des mariages, nouvelle méthode de mesure*. ("Institut National d'Études Démographiques Travaux et documents," Cahier No. 16.) Paris: Presses Universitaires de France.

———. 1956. *Anciennes familles genevoises: Etude démographique: XVIe–XXe siècles*. ("Institut National d'Études Démographiques, Travaux et documents," Cahier No. 26.) Paris: Presses Universitaires de France.

HUBER, M. 1939. *Cours de démographie et de statistique sanitaire*. 6 vols. Paris: Hermann.

———, BUNLE, H., and BOVERAT, F. 1950. *La population de la France: Son évolution et ses perspectives*. 3d ed. Paris: Librairie Hachette.

INSTITUT NATIONAL D'ÉTUDES DÉMOGRAPHIQUES. 1950. *Le niveau intellectuel des enfants d'âge scolaire: Une enquête nationale dans l'enseignement primaire*. ("Travaux et documents," Cahier No. 13.) Paris: Presses Universitaires de France.

———. 1954a. *Économie et population: Les doctrines françaises avant 1800: De Budé à Condorcet. By J. J. SPENGLER*. ("Travaux et documents," Cahier No. 21.) Paris: Presses Universitaires de France.

———. 1954b. *Le niveau intellectuel des enfants d'âge scolaire: La détermination des aptitudes: L'influence des facteurs constitutionnels, familiaux, et sociaux*. ("Travaux et documents," Cahier No. 23.) Paris: Presses Universitaires de France.

———. 1954c. *Études européennes de population—Main-d'œuvre, emploi, migrations. Situation et perspectives*. Paris: Éditions de l'Institut.

———. 1955. *Les Algériens en France: Étude démographique et sociale*. ("Travaux et documents," Cahier No. 24.) Paris: Presses Universitaires de France.

———. 1956. *Économie et population: Les doctrines françaises avant 1800: Bibliographie générale commentée*. ("Travaux et documents," Cahier No. 28.) Paris: Presses Universitaires de France.

———. 1957. *Région Languedoc-Roussillon: Économie et population*. ("Travaux et documents," Cahier No. 30.) Paris: Presses Universitaires de France.

INSTITUT NATIONAL DE LA STATISTIQUE ET DES ÉTUDES ÉCONOMIQUES. 1946. *Les transferts internationaux de population*. Paris.

LAMBERT, J., and COSTA PINTO, L. A. 1944. *Problèmes démographiques contemporains*. Rio de Janeiro: Atlantica Editora.

LANDRY, A., et al. 1945. *Traité de démographie*. Paris: Payot.

LANNES, X. 1953. *L'immigration au France depuis 1945*. ("Research Group for European Migration Problems Publications," Vol. VIII.) The Hague: M. Nijhoff.

LEBRET, L.-J. 1951–55. *Guide pratique de l'enquête sociale*. 3 vols. Paris: Presses Universitaires de France.

LEDERMANN, S. 1956. *Alcool, alcoolisme, alcoolisation: Données scientifiques de caractère physiologique, économique, et social.* ("Institut National d'Études Démographiques, Travaux et documents," Cahier No. 29.) Paris: Presses Universitaires de France.

POUTHAS, C. H. 1956. *La population française pendant la première moitié du XIXème siècle.* ("Institut National d'Études Démographiques, Travaux et documents," Cahier No. 25.) Paris: Presses Universitaires de France.

PRIGENT, R. 1954. *Renouveau des idées sur la famille.* ("Institut National d'Études Démographiques, Travaux et documents," Cahier No. 18.) Paris: Presses Universitaires de France.

REINHARD, M. 1949. *Histoire de la population mondiale de 1700 à 1948.* Paris: Éditions Domat-Montchrestien.

SAUVY, A. 1944. *La population, ses lois, ses équilibres.* Paris: Presses Universitaires de France.

———. 1952. *Théorie générale de la population.* Vol. I: *Économie et population.* Paris: Presses Universitaires de France.

———. 1954. *Théorie générale de la population.* Vol. II: *Biologie sociale.* Paris: Presses Universitaires de France.

———. 1953. *L'Europe et sa population.* Paris: Éditions Internationales.

SORRE, M. 1943–53. *Les fondements de la géographie humaine.* 3 vols. Paris: Librairie Armand Colin.

SUTTER, J. 1950. *L'Eugenique.* ("Institut National d'Études Démographiques, Travaux et documents," Cahier No. 11.) Paris: Presses Universitaires de France.

8. The Development of Demography in Great Britain

E. GREBENIK

The scientific study of population in Great Britain began in the second half of the seventeenth century with the publication of John Graunt's *Natural and Political Observations on the Bills of Mortality*. Graunt, who in Westergaard's words (Westergaard, 1932) opened up "quite a new field for scientific investigations," investigated the registers of baptisms and burials which had been kept in London since the beginning of the seventeenth century and was struck by the regularities exhibited by these figures. His perspicacity was great: he recognized, for instance, the excess mortality of males over females which, coupled with the excess number of boys born, nearly equalized the numbers of the sexes at marriageable age—a fact which Süssmilch later found inspiring; he commented on the underreporting of deaths from syphilis and was the first to construct a rudimentary life table, which was, however, based on a priori reasoning (Glass, 1950). He made a number of population estimates, using different assumptions: he stated that the number of women of childbearing age was equal to twice the number of annual births, that there were twice as many families as women of childbearing age, and that the average number of persons per family was eight. An alternative estimate was based on observations which determined the ratio of deaths to the number of families in a local population. This ratio was then applied in reverse to the deaths in the bills of mortality in order to estimate the population as a whole.

Graunt's contemporary and friend, Sir William Petty, was another contributor to the subject. Greenwood described him as a "perennial boy" forever bubbling over with ideas of varying degrees of quality. Some parts of his work were highly speculative—for instance, he tried to estimate the population at the time of the great flood—but others, such as the estimation of war losses in Ireland and his computation of the money value of a man, were highly practical. He suggested the establishment of a statistical department which would deal with marriages and burials, the number of houses and hearths, the number of persons in different age groups and their marital status, etc. Petty also produced estimates of the population of London, obtained by multiplying the number of houses by a figure purporting to be the average number of persons per house, and another one based upon the ratio of deaths from the plague to those who were supposed to have escaped the disease. He was interested in the rate of population growth and applied the data and methods of Graunt to a variety of different topics and purposes.

The third name which must be mentioned in this connection is that of Edmund Halley, better known as the discoverer of Halley's comet. Halley published a life table of the city of Breslau in the *Transactions of the Royal Society* for 1693. Though his table was constructed from burial figures only, he recognized the principles upon which a correct life table had to be built and was aware of the fact that a life table based on deaths alone assumed that there was a stationary population.

The works of Graunt, Halley, and Petty provided the theoretical foundation for the study of population statistics during the eighteenth century. There was no radical improvement in technique, but the methods employed by the political arithmeticians were used more widely. Interest in the study of mortality was maintained by the growth of life assurance and the increasing practice of granting life annuities. A number of life tables were constructed; the Northampton table computed by Richard Price was commonly used, even though its construction was faulty and it greatly overestimated mortality. A later table was Milne's Carlisle table, which was based on a local census carried out in that city by Dr. John Heysham. And in the early part of the seventeenth century De Moivre, a Huguenot mathematician living in London, attempted to fit Halley's life table by means of a mathematical law.

A certain amount of interest in statistics was also taken by medical practitioners who were concerned with the statistical study of disease and with epidemiology. There were disputes about the relative salubrity of the town and the countryside, and the fatality rates of particular diseases were studied. Some new data were provided, but again no advance was made in methodology, and the first British book devoted entirely to medical statistics (Hawkins, 1829) was largely descriptive in character.

In the meantime, interest in population problems was stimulated from another direction. The population controversy of the eighteenth century was begun by moral philosophers and economists interested in finding a general law governing the growth of human populations. In particular, the question whether the population of Great Britain had increased or declined since 1688 was debated with some acrimony. Such a debate was, of course, possible only because there were no population and vital statistics, but the absence of facts and the a priori nature of the arguments advanced did not make the quarrels any less fierce. An attempt was made to remedy the deficiency in 1753, when a census bill passed through the House of Commons, only to be thrown out by the House of Lords. The controversy was resolved only after regular censuses began in 1801, but the first census was preceded in 1798 by the publication of T. R. Malthus' *First Essay on Population* (Glass, 1952).

Malthus' doctrine and its effect on economic thought has been discussed by many writers, and there is no need to recapitulate it here (see Glass, 1953, for a bibliography).

Malthus' analysis of population growth and its relation to means of subsistence was generally accepted by economists and by public opinion during the first half of the nineteenth century. But acceptance of the diagnosis did not imply acceptance of the remedies he proposed in the second and subsequent editions of his essay, and throughout the nineteenth century many books and pamphlets were published advocating the restriction of births within marriage and instructing the population in methods of birth control (Glass, 1940). Attempts were also made to refute Malthus' general law of population growth and to replace it by some alternatives.

Discussion of population growth was placed on a much firmer basis by the institution of regular censuses in 1801.

The Census Act of 1800 authorized the first census, and since that time a census has been taken every ten years with the exception of 1941. The General Register Office was founded in 1837, when registration of births and deaths became compulsory in England and Wales (it did not begin in Scotland until 1855), and the Registrar General was given responsibility for taking population censuses, as well as for vital registration (Grebenik, 1955). The institution of these measures was part of a more general development of statistics evidenced by the creation of the Statistical Society of London (later the Royal Statistical Society) in 1834, and the Manchester Statistical Society in 1833.

A great many of the advances made in demographic techniques during the nineteenth century were due to the official statisticians in the General Register Office, and in particular to William Farr, who was appointed to the office in 1839 as compiler of abstracts and who remained there until 1880, reaching the rank of superintendent of statistics. Farr created the British system of census-taking and vital statistics, and under his guidance both census enumerations and vital registration became more and more complete. But Farr was more than an administrator; he made notable contributions to the methodology of demography, particularly in the field of life table construction and in the study of occupational mortality. Indeed, in the latter study he and his colleagues at the General Register Office did pioneering work. Registration of deaths was probably reasonably complete fairly early, but registration of births did not become so until 1874, when failure to register a birth was made punishable by a fine.

The interest of the statisticians of the period lay primarily in the field of mortality, as the efforts of the sanitary reformers of the period made a study of these subjects peculiarly appropriate. Very little work was done on fertility, J. M. Duncan's book on the subject (Duncan, 1866) being practically the only work devoted to the topic. Farr also commented on fertility and showed himself aware of the need for including questions relating to maternal age at birth registration, a need which was not met until 1938.

In the general field of population theory, attempts were still made by various writers to obtain general laws of population growth. Malthus' doctrine was no longer accepted as axiomatic, but by and large the economists of the second half of the nineteenth century did not evince any great interest in population; they tended to regard population growth simply as one of their data. It was only at the very end of the nineteenth century that Edwin Cannan, with brilliant acumen, suggested the possibility of population decline (Cannan, 1895) and prepared a population projection.

At the beginning of the twentieth century, therefore, there were two main groups of persons interested in the study of population. The staff of the General Register Office had built up an excellent system of vital registration and census data which were published and commented upon annually. The staff devoted their main attention to the analysis of mortality statistics, and the analysis of fertility data had made little headway. On the other side, there were the economists whose discussions were, with the exception of Cannan, on a more abstract and generalized plane.

DEMOGRAPHY IN THE TWENTIETH CENTURY

In the twentieth century, however, interest began to shift from the study of mortality to the study of fertility. There were a number of reasons for this. The birth rate in the last quarter of the nineteenth century had been falling and the gap between the birth and the death rate had narrowed. Moreover, new discoveries had been made in biology, and Sir Francis Galton had applied the study of heredity to man and had founded the subject of eugenics. In the Galton Laboratory at University College, London, Karl Pearson and his co-workers investigated certain problems of demographic interest, particularly those connected with differential fertility. Ansell in his work on insurance data had already studied the fertility of the middle and upper classes in 1874, and in 1906 D. Heron published his work, "Relation of Fertility in Man to Social Status," in the appropriately named *Drapers' Company Research Memoirs on National Deterioration.* By constructing an index of social class for particular areas and relating this to an index of fertility he was able to show an association between high birth rates and poor social conditions. A few years later Ethel Elderton published her monumental report on the English birth rate in which she dealt with the prevalence of birth control by means of abortion among the working classes of the north of England (Elderton, 1914). The eugenists were preoccupied with the possibility of biological deterioration which, they believed, might result from differential fertility between different sections of the population (see, for instance, Whetham and Whetham, 1909).

It is significant that the first major official investigation into fertility dates from that period. In the census of 1911 a question relating to the fertility of marriage was asked for the first time. Married women were asked to state the duration of their marriage and the total number of children born to them, distinguishing among those born alive, those who had died, and those who were still living. Owing to the inter-

vention of the First World War, the publication of the final report of this inquiry did not take place until 1923, though the fertility tables were published in 1917. The analysis was confined to married women enumerated on the same census schedule as their husbands, and a summary of the results dealing with the fertility of different social groups was given by Stevenson in a paper to the Royal Statistical Society (Stevenson, 1920).

The interest in the declining birth rate at the time is evidenced by the National Birth Rate Commission, set up by the National Council of Public Morals. This commission consisted of a number of public figures, and their terms of reference were to investigate the declining birth rate. Their report added little to the knowledge of the problem, but they spent a good deal of their time discussing the prevalence of contraception and the morality of birth control (National Birth Rate Commission, 1916), without, however, arriving at any very definite conclusion.

The period immediately after the war did not produce major advances in techniques or methods. The economists were primarily concerned with problems associated with the optimum population, and their discussion continued to be highly abstract. Empirical work was still largely confined to the official statisticians, and a scrutiny of the pages of the *Journal of the Royal Statistical Society* of the period shows that only a small section of its space was devoted to vital statistics. Mortality studies continued, among the medical statisticians and epidemiologists, and some interest in the history of population began (Buer, 1926; Griffiths, 1926).

There was no post in any British university devoted exclusively to demography or to population studies, and there were few scholars whose primary interest lay in this field. One of the few exceptions was A. M. Carr-Saunders, who was Charles Booth Professor of Social Science at Liverpool University from 1923 to 1937. Trained as a biologist, he became interested in eugenics and the problem of human population before the war, and his first major work, *The Population Problem,* was published in 1922. It surveyed the general field of population and traced the interactions and relationships of the different aspects from a historical and evolutionary point of view. A number of scholars from different fields took an interest in these problems; some were anthropologists, some geographers, some medical men, some geneticists. However, it was the economists and economic historians who did most of the writing on population. They were still mainly interested in the relationship between population and output—a good deal was written on the optimum theory at the time—and regarded population as one of the variables which was given in their system, rather than as a variable to be explained. Empirical work was left to the vital statisticians, mainly to those in government employment.

The position changed when Professor Lancelot Hogben was appointed to the chair of social biology at the London School of Economics in 1930. Professor Hogben created a research department and gathered around himself a number of assistants who gave considerable attention to population problems and their social and biological aspects. He was joined in the department by R. R. Kuczynski, and among his coworkers was Enid Charles; his assistants included D. V. Glass, who joined the department in 1935. The continued decline in the birth rate resulted in public attention becoming focused on population problems, and Enid Charles's population projections which appeared in 1935 created a good deal of concern. Dr. Charles intended to point out the implications of a continuation of past

fertility trends upon the future population, and she computed three projections on different assumptions, all of which led to the conclusion that the population of England and Wales would begin to decline in the foreseeable future. The public tended to disregard the qualifications with which Dr. Charles's argument was hedged and to treat her projections as actual forecasts. Her work attracted a great deal of attention and led to an increased interest in population problems. Hogben and his colleagues were also instrumental in sponsoring studies dealing with differential fertility, with geographical variation of fertility, and with certain aspects of social selection (Hogben, 1938). The implication of differential fertility on national intelligence also received attention, and Cattell (1937), who forecast a continuous decline in national intelligence, was widely quoted.

Professor Hogben left the London School of Economics in 1937. No successor was appointed, and the Department of Social Biology was dissolved. However, in 1938 R. R. Kuczynski was appointed to a university readership in demography at the London School of Economics. This was the first time that an academic post in Britain had been devoted to demography, though there had been a chair of epidemiology and vital statistics in existence at the London School of Hygiene for some time. This readership is still, at the time of writing, the only post in the subject, though at one time Enid Charles held a readership in demography and vital statistics at the University of Birmingham.

Another important development in the field of demographic research was the foundation of the Population Investigation Committee in 1936. This committee, which has been under the chairmanship of Sir Alexander Carr-Saunders throughout its existence, was founded to pursue research into population problems and to help in forming an enlightened public opinion on the subject. It was originally financed by the Eugenics Society and contained representatives of that society, the British Medical Association, the Royal College of Obstetricians and Gynaecologists, and similar bodies, as well as individual members. It maintained a small staff of research workers, and D. V. Glass acted as its research secretary from its foundation until he was appointed to the chair of sociology at the London School of Economics in 1949. A number of major research projects were sponsored by the committee, in particular a survey of European population policies (Glass, 1940), and many minor papers were published in the learned journals by members of its staff.

The preoccupation with the falling birth rate led to the first major reform in the system of British vital registration since 1837 when the Population (Statistics) Act was passed in 1938. This act was specifically designed to make it possible to collect statistics which would be useful in the analysis of fertility. The act provided that at the registration of a birth questions should be included relating to the age of the mother, the duration of her marriage, and the parity order of the child. It therefore became possible, for the first time, to study age-specific fertility without having to make estimates, to compute reproduction rates, and to study the fertility of marriage by duration. The outbreak of war in 1939 interrupted the regular publication of the figures, but they were made available to students of the subject.

During the war demographic research was naturally in abeyance, but as the war proceeded, increased interest was taken in problems of reconstruction; and as the number of births had fallen considerably in the early years of the war, the government agreed in 1943 to set up a Royal Commission "to examine the facts relating to the present population trends in Great Britain; to investigate the causes of these trends, and to consider their probable consequences; to consider what measures, if any, should be taken in the national interest to influence the future trend of population and to make recommendations." Lord Simon, then Lord Chancellor, was appointed chairman of the commission. The commission was assisted by three expert committees to deal with economic, statistical, and biological and medical problems. The chairmen of these committees, who were also members of the Royal Commission, were Sir Hubert Henderson (who later became chairman of the Royal Commission itself), Sir Alexander Carr-Saunders, and Professor A. W. M. Ellis, respectively. The committees were to advise the Royal Commission on scientific and technical points: the members of the commission itself, with the exception of the three chairmen of the scientific committees, were in no way experts in demography.

The Royal Commission worked for five years and produced its report in 1949. When the report appeared, it was acclaimed and widely featured in the press, but its general impact on public opinion was small, and it was never debated by Parliament. There were a number of reasons for this: enthusiasm for social reconstruction was distinctly smaller in 1949 than in 1944, and the recovery of the birth rate which had taken place from 1943 onward seemed to many to have made the population problem a considerably less urgent one.

But though public opinion did not take much notice of the Royal Commission's recommendations, the work was of considerable importance from the point of view of the development of demography. The commission rejected the net reproduction rate approach to population replacement. This rate, which assumed implicitly that the age of a woman was the most significant factor in determining her fertility, had been criticized by many writers in the late thirties and early forties, but the Royal Commission's report was the first official document in Britain to adopt an alternative approach in terms of the fertility of marriage by duration and to use the cohort method of analysis. Moreover, members of the commission's secretariat, especially J. Hajnal (Hajnal, 1947, 1950), made significant contributions to the development of this new type of analysis and to the problems of measuring population replacement.

The Royal Commission also sponsored two major pieces of demographic field work, the Family Census of 1946 (Glass and Grebenik, 1954) and an inquiry into family limitation (Lewis-Faning, 1949).

The Family Census of 1946 was a special sample survey, covering 10 per cent of ever-married women in Great Britain. The Royal Commission needed statistics on the development of marital fertility for its report. As no fertility questions had been asked in any national census since 1911 and no data on fertility by duration of marriage were available before 1938, an *ad hoc* investigation became necessary. In the family census, the respondent women were asked for the dates of their birth and marriage, the number of their live-born children, and the dates of birth of these children. A question about their husbands' social status was also included. The question relating to the children's date of birth had not been asked in any previous British census, and an analysis of the replies made it possible to compare the fertility of different marriage cohorts at equivalent durations and thus to extend the analysis of mari-

tal fertility to comparatively recent marriage cohorts. Preliminary results obtained from the family census were used in the statistical section of the Royal Commission's report.

The second major inquiry sponsored by the Royal Commission dealt with family limitation and was carried out for them under the auspices of the Royal College of Obstetricians and Gynaecologists by Dr. E. Lewis-Faning. This was the first large-scale inquiry into the subject carried out in Britain; previous information on the subject had to come almost entirely from the records of birth-control clinics (Charles, 1932; Secor Florence, 1930). The field work of Lewis-Faning's inquiry was carried out entirely by medical practitioners; the subjects were largely hospital patients in wards other than gynecological or obstetric. The results of the inquiry are too detailed to summarize here, but they confirmed the wide prevalence of birth-control practices among the married population and the increasing use of appliance methods.

The Royal Commission also considered the organization of the British system of official and vital statistics. They recognized the excellence of the work undertaken by the staff of the General Register Office, but the Statistics Committee of the Royal Commission felt that the practice of appointing to the headship of that office an administrative civil servant without professional experience of demography was unfortunate. They felt that the technical work performed by the office was much more important than its record-keeping functions and therefore that it would be desirable for the head of the office to be a qualified statistician or actuary.

The report of the Royal Commission made it clear that there was no *immediate* danger of an actual population decline in Great Britain and that it was unlikely that there would be an appreciable change in numbers in the near future. This, no doubt, was one of the major reasons for the small impact that the report made on public opinion, and there has not been much officially sponsored research into population problems since. The General Register Office has begun, however, to publish a series of "Occasional Studies on Medical and Population Subjects," which consists of monographs by members of its staff. Of particular interest among these is a compilation of statistics relating to external migration (Carrier and Jeffery, 1953). The office has also taken considerably more interest in morbidity and now issues regular publications on this topic.

On the unofficial side, the Population Investigation Committee has continued to sponsor demographic research. After the end of the war the committee was enabled to extend its activities through generous grants by the Nuffield Foundation and other benefactors. In particular it began the publication of *Population Studies* in 1947. This is the only periodical in the English language (with the exception of *Population Index*, which fulfils slightly different functions) to be devoted entirely to demography.

The Population Investigation Committee has sponsored three major research projects. The first was undertaken in co-operation with the Royal College of Obstetricians and Gynaecologists and the Society of Medical Officers of Health. Undertaken just before the introduction of the National Health Service, it consisted of a study of the extent to which mothers made use of the maternity and similar services provided by public authorities and of the costs incurred in having children. The sample consisted of all births taking place in a particular week in March, 1946, and it has proved possible to follow up the children enrolled in the sample and to obtain data relat-ing to social class differences in development. The survey is still proceeding at the time of writing.

The second major survey was conducted in co-operation with the Scottish Council for Research in Education and was designed to test the hypothesis of a decline in national intelligence. A complete age group of eleven-year-olds was tested in 1947 (a previous survey of a similar nature having been carried out in 1932). Although the inverse relationship between fertility and intelligence was shown to hold, no decline in average intelligence was found. Again it has proved possible to follow up the children tested, and the survey is still proceeding.

The third piece of research dealt with the relationship between fertility and social mobility (Berent, 1952) and was part of a much wider study of social mobility (Glass, 1954), a study in which a number of demographic techniques were used.

A great deal of research on subjects of demographic interest has also been carried out in Professor Hogben's Department of Medical Statistics at the University of Birmingham, principally on the medical and biological aspects of demography (published largely in the *British Journal of Preventive and Social Medicine*); in Professor Baird's Department of Midwifery at the University of Aberdeen, largely on the social aspects of obstetrics; and by the Social Medicine Research Unit of the Medical Research Council on Infant Mortality (see Grebenik, 1954, for an annotated bibliography).

Another aspect of the development of demography is the growth of interest in population development among primitive peoples. Before the war the vital statistics of most British colonial possessions were of a rudimentary character, but in the late thirties and early forties the Colonial Office made efforts to improve the quality of the data collected. When Dr. R. R. Kuczynski retired from the readership in demography at London University in 1941, he accepted the part-time appointment of demographic adviser to the Colonial Office and held this appointment up to the time of his death in 1947. In the course of his duties he advised on censuses taken in a number of colonial areas, and he prepared his monumental *Demographic Survey of the British Colonial Empire* (Kuczynski, 1948–53), in which he brought together the information that was available about British colonial territories. During the postwar period, a good deal of progress was made in improving the quality of colonial census and vital statistics and in applying new methods to those problems (Searle, 1950).

PROFESSIONAL ASPECTS

From the preceding, it is clear that most of the credit for the progress in demography, particularly in its early stages, must go to the civil servants of the General Register Office. They built up a system of census and vital statistics of high quality, and for a very long time they were the only persons whose exclusive duty it was to study population developments and to comment on them. Demography was not taught in the universities, and private scholars interested in population problems regarded the subject as a side line. The principal interest of the few professional demographers in the late nineteenth century lay in the study of mortality. The necessary technical apparatus was practically complete in the 1880's, considerable contributions to the methodology having been made by the well-organized actuarial profession. Moreover, there was unanimity about the desirability of reducing mortality, and infant mortality in particular, so that the study of the subject was one in which civil servants, who were debarred from expressing controversial

views in public, could without impropriety take part. The methods developed in the General Register Office, particularly in the study of occupational mortality, were followed in many other countries.

The problem of the falling birth rate did not become acute until the beginning of the present century, and interest shifted from the study of mortality to that of fertility. Again, the pioneering work was done by the official statisticians, the first major study of fertility being the analysis of the fertility data in the census of 1911. Stevenson, one of the statisticians at the General Register Office, devised the fivefold social status scale which is still used in many studies of differential fertility today. But regular information necessary for the detailed study of fertility did not become available until 1938, and on the whole the contributions of the official statisticians to the development of the methodology, though by no means negligible, were less important than in the case of mortality. This was partly due to the fact that with the increasing complexity of public administration, pressure of routine work on the officials concerned became very much heavier—up to the end of the Second World War, the number of professionally qualified persons at the General Register Office was ridiculously small—but another factor which may have played a part is connected with the relationship between the study of fertility on one hand and problems of family limitation and social policy on the other. Opinions in this field are much less unanimous than in the case of mortality, and civil servants may instinctively shy away from fields in which controversy may arise. Moreover, it seemed to be the policy of the General Register Office to confine activities to the collection and publication of the basic data and to giving advice to other government departments, leaving interpretation and research to unofficial agencies.

In the period immediately after the First World War, however, little interest was taken in the study of demography. The study of population was regarded as a task for the economist. Economics was the best developed of the social sciences in Britain; there were chairs in the subject at Oxford and Cambridge—always a hallmark of a subject's academic respectability—as well as in many other universities. Economists were not disinterested in population, but they tended to be preoccupied with the consequences rather than the causes of population development. Population was taken as one of their data, and few attempts were made to relate population phenomena to social and economic events.

Today, population studies would probably be considered to fall within the province of sociology rather than economics, but the study of sociology was slow to develop in Britain, and the application of empirical methods to the study of society, except in the field of social surveys and the study of living conditions, came relatively late. Empirical work at first tended to be concentrated in the field of social anthropology, and the study of primitive society, and Carr-Saunders' first book drew heavily on anthropological evidence. It was only in the thirties that empirical social research, including demographic research, was started on any significant scale; considerable impetus was given to its development after the Second World War, when, following the report of the Clapham Committee (U.K., 1946), increased financial aid was given to the social sciences in the universities, aid from which demographic research also benefited. At present, departments of sociology and allied subjects exist in most British universities, and a good deal of empirical social research is proceeding.

There is still, however, only one full-time post in the country which is devoted to demography: the readership in demography at the London School of Economics in the University of London. There are several posts on the periphery of the subject, especially on the biological and medical side; thus there are chairs of biometry and eugenics at University College, London; a chair of epidemiology and vital statistics at the London School of Hygiene and Tropical Medicine; a chair of medical statistics at Birmingham; and a Department of Human Ecology at Cambridge. In Oxford there is an Institute of Social Medicine where research on certain aspects of mortality and morbidity is carried on. The Medical Research Council, an official body, maintains a Social Medicine Research Unit which has been responsible among other projects for a large-scale study of infant mortality. But apart from the London readership there are no posts in demography in any of the social science faculties of British universities.

In academic undergraduate courses, it is relatively rare to find demography as a subject. In London it may be taken as an option in the B.Sc. (economics) degree by students specializing in sociology, social anthropology, or statistics. It is taken in Part II of the final examination, where it forms one paper out of five. The training of students specializing in statistics is biased toward the more formal side of the subject, and students are at liberty to offer actuarial statistics as another option. Demography is also an option (as an alternative to criminology) in the B.A. or B.Sc. degree in sociology of London University, where it constitutes one out of nine papers. In the University of Leeds, demography is an option in the B.A. degree in social studies, and in the degree in economics with statistics. The budding actuary is also required to take demography as part of his professional training. The treatment, judging from a perusal of the Institute of Actuaries' textbook (Cox, 1950), is, however, largely formal. The actuarial student will, of course, also have to acquire a detailed and extensive knowledge of life-table construction and of the theory of life contingencies in general. Vital statistics generally figures as a subject in examinations for the diploma in public health, which must be taken by intending medical officers of health, but the knowledge required is fairly elementary. Where degrees or diplomas in statistics are given, some instruction in vital statistics is not infrequently included in the curriculum. At the graduate level opportunities for research exist in those universities which have members of the staff interested in demography, and in London it is possible to take a master's degree in demography by examination.

Thus, demographers tend to be recruited either from statisticians, who will be interested in the more formal side of the subject, or from sociologists, whose primary interests lie in the social aspects of demography. At present the only undergraduate degree which combines the two approaches is the London B.Sc. (economics) with statistics as a special subject, but more commonly the two aspects are brought together only at the graduate level.

The scope for qualified demographers in Britain today is fairly limited. For those who stay in the universities, the absence of posts in demography as such is a bar to academic preferment unless they show interest in a wider field, although there are some scholars whose primary interest is in demography holding appointments in sociology, statistics, medical statistics or public health. Prospects of expansion in the near future depend partly upon the prospects of growth in the social sciences in general, which in turn depend

upon government policy toward the universities, and partly upon developments in the demographic situation. If the birth rate were to fall appreciably below replacement level in the near future, it is possible that interest in demographic research might be stimulated.

Outside academic work, employment opportunities are also limited. The civil service is the only alternative career which offers prospects to demographers, but here again the number is severely limited: the General Register Office and the General Registry Office in Scotland employ about ten qualified professional staff members between them. Moreover, the normal method of entry to these posts is through the statistician grade, and a knowledge of statistics outside the demographic field is required of candidates. They would generally be expected to acquire their specialized knowledge after being posted to the General Register Office. It is possible that there might be openings in the overseas civil service for a small number of demographers, but the number is unlikely to be substantial. In general, anyone wishing to pursue demographic research is likely to acquire the requisite special knowledge on the job, and the incentive to specialize in demography is small.

The lack of career outlets for demographers and the consequent shortage of qualified personnel is one of the major obstacles to the development of demographic research in Great Britain. In spite of the comparative excellence of her statistics, there are still a number of gaps to be filled. Of these, one of the most important relates to the study of marriage. Although the General Register Office is responsible for the tabulation and publication of data relating to marriage, the original information comes from the marriage registers which are in the majority of cases completed by clergymen whose interest in and knowledge of statistics is limited. Hence, the only information that is officially made available about marriage consists of the number of first and subsequent marriages, tabulated by age of the bride and the groom. There is very little work on social class differences in marriage habits, on attitudes to marriage, on intermarriage between different groups, etc. More research on these subjects is urgently needed.

In the study of differential mortality and fertility, attention has been concentrated on occupational and geographical differences. Differentials between social and cultural groups could be investigated with advantage, and sociologists and demographers might well co-operate in an attempt to find the most useful lines of division for that purpose. Attention needs also to be devoted to the study of fertility motivation and sexual behavior. This is a subject which has been left almost entirely untouched and on which information would be desirable.

Most of the research needed lies on the borders of demography proper and sociology, social psychology, and allied disciplines. If the recent expansion in social research continues, there is hope that some of these problems may be tackled in the not too distant future.

SELECTED BIBLIOGRAPHY

ANSELL, C. 1874. *On the Rate of Mortality at Early Periods of Life, the Age at Marriage, the Number of Children to a Marriage, the Length of a Generation and Other Statistics of Families in the Upper and Professional Classes.* London.

BERENT, J. 1952. "Fertility and Social Mobility," *Population Studies*, III, 244–60.

———. 1954. "Social Mobility and Marriage," in *Social Mobility in Britain*, ed. D. V. GLASS. London.

BUER, M. 1926. *Health, Wealth, and Population in the Early Days of the Industrial Revolution.* London: George Routledge & Sons.

CANNAN, E. 1895. "The Probability of a Cessation of Growth of Population in England and Wales during the Next Century," *Economic Journal*, 505–15.

CARR-SAUNDERS, A. M. 1922. *The Population Problem: A Study in Human Evolution.* Oxford: Clarendon Press.

CARRIER, N. H., and JEFFERY, J. R. 1953. *External Migration: A Study of the Available Statistics.* London: H. M. Stationery Office.

CATTELL, R. B. 1937. *The Fight for Our National Intelligence.* London.

CHARLES, ENID. 1932. *The Practice of Birth Control.* London: Williams & Norgate.

———. 1935. "The Effect of Present Trends in Fertility and Mortality upon the Future Population of England and Wales and upon Its Age Composition," *London and Cambridge Economic Service Special Memorandum*, No. 40.

COX, P. R. 1950. *Demography.* Cambridge: Cambridge University Press.

DUNCAN, J. MATTHEW. 1866. *Fertility, Sterility, and Allied Topics.* Edinburgh: A. & C. Black.

ELDERTON, ETHEL. 1914. *Report on the English Birth Rate.* Part I: *England North of the Humber.* London: Dulau & Co.

FARR, W. 1885. *Vital Statistics.* London: Edward Stanford.

FLORENCE, LEILA SECOR. 1930. *Birth Control on Trial.* London: Allen & Unwin.

GLASS, D. V. 1940. *Population Policies and Movements in Europe.* Oxford: Clarendon Press.

———. 1950. "Graunt's Life Table," *Journal of the Institute of Actuaries*, LXXVI, No. 342, 60–64.

———. 1952. "The Population Controversy in Eighteenth Century England," *Population Studies*, VI, No. 1, 69–91.

——— (ed.). 1953. *Introduction to Malthus.* London: Watts & Co.

——— (ed.). 1954. *Social Mobility in Britain.* London: Routledge & Kegan Paul.

GLASS, D. V., and GREBENIK, E. 1954. *The Trend and Pattern of Fertility in Great Britain.* 2 vols. London: H.M. Stationery Office.

GRAUNT, J. 1662. *Natural and Political Observations Mentioned in a Follow-*

ing Index and Made upon the Bills of Mortality, with Reference to the Government, Religion, Trade, Growth, Air, Diseases, and the Several Changes of the Said City. London: John Martyn.

GREBENIK, E. 1954. "Demographic Fieldwork in Great Britain." Paper submitted to the World Population Conference, Rome.

———. 1955. "The Sources and Nature of Statistical Information in Special Fields of Statistics: Population and Vital Statistics," *Journal of the Royal Statistical Society*, Series A, CXVIII, Part IV, 452–62.

GREENWOOD, M. 1948a. *Medical Statistics from Graunt to Farr*. Cambridge: Cambridge University Press.

———. 1948b. *Some British Pioneers of Social Medicine*. London: Oxford University Press.

GRIFFITHS, G. T. 1926. *Population Problems of the Age of Malthus*. Cambridge: Cambridge University Press.

HAJNAL, J. 1947. "The Analysis of Birth Statistics in the Light of the Recent International Recovery of the Birth Rate," *Population Studies*, I, No. 2, 137–64.

———. 1950. "Births, Marriages, and Reproductivity: England and Wales, 1938–47," *Papers of the Royal Commission on Population*, II, 303–422.

HALLEY, E. 1693. "An Estimate of the Degrees of the Mortality of Mankind, Drawn from Curious Tables of the Births and Funerals at the City of Breslaw . . . ," *Philosophical Transactions of the Royal Society of London*.

HAWKINS, F. BISSET. 1829. *Elements of Medical Statistics*. London.

HERON, D. 1906. *On the Relation of Fertility in Man to Social Status, and on the Changes in This Relation Which Have Taken Place during the Last Fifty Years*. London: Dulau & Co.

HOGBEN, L. (ed.). 1938. *Political Arithmetic*. London: Allen & Unwin.

INNES, J. W. 1938. *Class Fertility Trends in England and Wales: 1876–1934*. Princeton: Princeton University Press.

KUCZYNSKI, R. R. 1935. *The Measurement of Population Growth*. London: Sidgwick & Jackson.

———. 1948–53. *A Demographic Survey of the British Colonial Empire*. 3 vols. London: Oxford University Press.

LEWIS-FANING, E. 1949. *Family Limitation and Its Influence on Human Fertility during the Past Fifty Years*. London: H.M. Stationery Office.

NATONAL BIRTH RATE COMMISSION. 1916. *The Declining Birth Rate: Its Causes and Effects*. London: Chapman & Hall.

PETTY, SIR WILLIAM. 1690. *Political Arithmetic*. London: Robert Clavel.

ROYAL COMMISSION ON POPULATION. 1949. *Report*. London: H.M. Stationery Office.

———. 1949–50. *Papers of the Royal Commission on Population*. 5 vols. Vol. 1: cf. Lewis-Faning, 1949. Vol. II: *Reports and Selected Papers of the Statistics Committee*. Vol. III: *Report of the Economics Committee*. Vol. IV: *Reports of the Biological and Medical Committee*. Vol. V: *Memoranda Presented to the Royal Commission*.

SEARLE, W. F., et al. 1950. "Colonial Statistics," *Journal of the Royal Statistical Society*, CXIII, Part III, 271–98.

STEVENSON, T. H. C. 1920. "The Fertility of the Various Social Classes in England and Wales from the Middle of the 19th Century to 1911," *Journal of the Royal Statistical Society*, LXXXIII, Part III, 1–44.

UNITED KINGDOM PRIVY COUNCIL OFFICE AND TREASURY. 1946. *Report of the Committee on the Provision of Social and Economic Research*. London: H.M. Stationery Office.

WESTERGAARD, H. 1932. *Contributions to the History of Statistics*. London: P. S. King & Sons.

WHETHAM, W. C. D., and WHETHAM, C. D. 1909. *The Family and the Nation: A Study in Natural Inheritance and Social Responsibility*. London: Longmans, Green & Co.

9. Demography in Germany

HERMANN SCHUBNELL

HISTORICAL DEVELOPMENT OF POPULA-
TION STUDIES IN GERMANY

In Germany, as in other European countries, the study of population problems initially was based on assumptions stemming from a concern with the history of arts, politics, and economic affairs. With the spread of the natural science approach in recent times, the identification of empirically demonstrable and quantitatively measurable relationships and the causal connections among variables became the goal of scientific investigation. The attempt to observe nature with mathematical precision and to reveal its regularities was extended to the observation of social mass phenomena. Not only population theory (*Bevölkerungslehre*) but also scientific statistics owes its genesis to this procedure. From the beginning the development of both disciplines progressed in a close and reciprocal relationship.

Even though the population phenomena of the Middle Ages in Germany were of great significance, little attention was directed to demographic problems at that time. Until the beginning of the modern era, the events of being born and dying were regarded as "ordained by God." According to the dominant view, they were beyond the realm of human influence. As a consequence of territorial fragmentation, there was no stimulus in the tiny areas for a systematic and comprehensive observation of society in the mass. Only as the modern state developed its structure with centralized administration, fi-

nancial requirements, instruments of military power, and a far-reaching state-directed economic policy did demographic questions gain political significance. To begin with, the population losses and displacements that accompanied the Thirty Years' War increased the need for population policy measures. In the financial and economic policies of the cameralists and mercantilists of the seventeenth and eighteenth centuries, population played a decisive role. The discussion of population problems gained momentum as in no previous century. From the controversy over the advantages and disadvantages of population growth, a sort of theoretical treatment of population questions gradually developed; the exclusive concern, however, was to reach the most advantageous decision regarding population policy. In this prescientific stage of the study of demographic questions, considerations of state politics and economics were dominant. The differences in interpretation stemmed, in large part, from unsystematic and inaccurate circumstances. Until the middle of the eighteenth century, the collection of statistics for administrative purposes was extremely rare. Results of the estimates of population size and growth show how confused and often naïve the conceptions of demographic processes then were.

The universal scholar Gottfried Wilhelm Leibnitz (1646–1716) exerted a great influence on the development of scientific population theory in Germany. He was familiar with the work of the early English political arithme-

203

ticians; he advanced this work through his own ideas and through the spread of knowledge about this new area of scientific investigation. The book written by the pastor Caspar Neumann in 1696, *Reflexionen über Leben und Tod bei denen in Breslau Geborenen und Gestorbenen*, became known through Leibnitz to the English mathematician Halley, who used statistical data contained in it as a basis for his opinions regarding human mortality levels. One may regard Neumann as the first German representative of political arithmetic, even though his scientific accomplishments are not comparable with those of the earlier English arithmeticians.

The most important German representative of this new science, at that time considered something entirely new and original, was the clergyman Johann Peter Süssmilch (1707–67). The title of his work published in 1741, *Die göttliche Ordnung in den Veränderungen des menschlichen Geschlechts,* is indicative of the fundamental theological attitude of Süssmilch and his contemporaries. In places their books sound like exegeses of the Mosaic word: "Be fruitful and multiply, and replenish the earth, and subdue it." But the book is an exposition with scientific properties and the power of proof that resides in exact figures. That this kind of evidence for divine order already entailed a departure from the firm metaphysical foundation of the Christian faith did not enter into the consciousness of the naïvely enthusiastic theological demographers.

Subsequently, in enlarged editions of his published work Süssmilch dealt with population problems from the standpoint of statistics, theory, and population policy in a comprehensive, scientific way for the first time. He brought together into a composite picture the predominantly monographic works of his predecessors and contemporaries; these he sought not only to collect and summarize but also to explain, i.e., to perceive them as part of a universal law. Thereby he also created the basis for the development of a scientific theory of population as well as of scientific statistics in Germany.

Süssmilch had no pupils or direct successors to elaborate this outline of a complete treatise on population, the first to appear in Germany or elsewhere. That was a consequence of events of the late eighteenth and early nineteenth centuries. The French Revolution, the Wars of Liberation, the end of absolutism and mercantilism, ongoing secularization and incipient industrialization, to name only the most important events, produced completely new assumptions for the scientific treatment of demographic questions. Second, the *Essay on the Principle of Population* by T. R. Malthus, which appeared in the same year as the last edition of Süssmilch's work (1798) put population theory, including that in Germany, on a new basis. The historian Heinrich Luden in his *Handbuch der Staatsweisheit oder der Politik,* published in 1811, was the first man in Germany to discuss and thereby spread the Malthusian theory. It found its first German critic only a few years later in J. G. Hoffmann, director of the newly founded Prussian Statistical Bureau, which rendered great services in the improvement of official statistics.

A number of scientific movements played a part in the development of population theory in Germany in the nineteenth century. In large part, the groups concerned with demographic questions worked independently of one another. They include:

1. The jurists, who in the tradition of absolutism and cameralistic administration still regarded population as an object of cameralistic or police or administrative science. Legalistic and politico-economic considerations still were

mingled; the statistically discovered laws of population movement became the basis of administrative police activity, which was at the service of an explicit population policy.

2. The political economists who joined in the Malthusian controversy. The most important representatives of German political economy took sides in the controversy and fought one another vehemently. This contributed, among other things, to a tendency to consider population problems more and more exclusively in their economic aspect and to regard population theory as a subdivision of political economy. In Germany, controversy about the Malthusian doctrine occurred at the time when the economic structure was in transition from a predominantly agrarian to an industrial form. The economic, social, and demographic situation, which was frequently and rapidly changing during this transition, determined at any given time the conclusion as to whether Malthus was right or not. Consequently, population theory became, in a sense, dependent on the circumstances. Among the German political economists, the adherents of Malthusianism were in the majority during the entire nineteenth century. With the beginning of the twentieth century, the proportions of adherents and of critics became more nearly equal, while in terms of scientific influence the critics began to predominate.

3. Finally, the statisticians and mathematicians who conducted further inquiries in the field of political arithmetic. In comparison with the study of the economic side of population problems, which, occasioned by the Malthusian "population law," had been furthered by the demographic and economic conditions of the nineteenth century, the comprehensive treatment of population theory, as Süssmilch had developed it in his first endeavor, received little attention. People again undertook monographic studies dealing with specific problems resulting from improvements in mathematical and actuarial methods and, especially, with the analysis of statistical data which became available in greater abundance from decade to decade. In the first half of the nineteenth century official statistical offices were established in nearly all German states; the major function of the offices at that time was to compile basic population statistics. The investigations of Casper, Hoffmann, and Moser (1839) on life expectancy, which appeared in the first half of the century, were famous. Professor Christian Bernoulli of Basel carried out the first scientific analysis of official statistical data of the early decades of the nineteenth century in his *Populationistik oder Bevölkerungswissenschaft* (published in 1840–41). His method of presenting demographic results was taken over by nearly all later textbooks and in its essentials still is usable today. Until the turn of the century, the most important textbook was the *Allgemeine Bevölkerungsstatistik* of Professor J. E. Wappäus of Göttingen, published 1859–61, which stressed textual interpretation and critical testing of the statistical data.

Similarly, the handbooks and textbooks on population which appeared in the second half of the nineteenth century were almost exclusively statistical demographic presentations. By comparison, the treatment of population theory and population policy receded into the background. Of lasting influence on the development of population statistics and population theory in Germany was the work of G. von Mayr, whose *Bevölkerungsstatistik* appeared in 1897 as the second volume of his *Statistik und Gesellschaftslehre*. Mayr terms population statistics "exact population theory." Though he offers statistical data which were then unique in their completeness, he foregoes the discussion of questions and relationships in population theory. The predominance of the statistical aspect of population studies in the entire nineteenth century and particularly in Mayr's work, which influenced scientific and applied statistics in Germany until quite recently, caused population studies to be identified more and more with population statistics.

Thus, in the nineteenth century demography in Germany was almost exclusively viewed and pursued only in its economic or only in its statistical aspect. Two exceptions should be mentioned: the geographer Ratzel, who in his *Anthropogeographie* created a prominent place for population questions in geography, as well as the cultural scientist W. H. Riehl, whose great work *Die Naturgeschichte des Volkes als Grundlage einer deutschen Sozialpolitik* treats a whole series of demographic problems for the first time in a politico-economic and sociological perspective.

DEMOGRAPHY IN GERMANY DURING THE TWENTIETH CENTURY

The development of demography in Germany in the twentieth century was determined above all by events in the area of population and economic policy. For example, Burgdörfer in 1917, under the impact of the growing decreases in births in western European countries, worked out his method studying the population problem in terms of family statistics. From the side of social hygiene, before the First World War, Grotjahn had taken up the question of the falling birth rate and its effects. In the middle of the 1920's, as a result of the economic difficulties, numerous investigations of the question of overpopulation were carried out, especially by Mombert.

A decade later population policy concepts and objectives prompted a number of investigations on the measurement and the causes and effects of the falling birth rate and its control. The formulation of the problem at any given time in the course of history determines the kind and scope of assignments given to demography by the government and, thereby, in large part the focus of scientific study. Of course, in spite of this preoccupation with specific problems, in certain periods scientific study progressed in those areas that did not happen to be of central interest. For example, in those years in which overpopulation was regarded as the most pressing among the demographic problems of Germany, Harmsen (1927), using France as an example, analyzed the socioeconomic significance of a population decrease in order to make clear the development that was threatening Germany also. The outline of a practical population policy by the same author, appearing in 1931, showed the consequences of differential fertility by social stratum and presented the problems, goals, and means of a biologically, socially, and economically meaningful population policy on the basis of scientific knowledge. The population policy put into practice during the 1930's under the influence of excessive nationalism was not scientifically based and has been rejected by the majority of German demographers.

Until World War II, population studies in Germany were regarded as a subdivision of political economy, to be treated predominantly with statistical methods and, in any case, with the methods of population and economic history. Paul Mombert, who developed a comprehensive but exclusively economic theory of population (1929), was of the opinion that the population problem could be fitted easily into a system of politico-economic theory. To be sure, he saw the relationship between population and society, but his population theory dealt primarily with the relations between population and economy.

It is characteristic, incidentally, that the political economists of the nineteenth and twentieth centuries, who claimed population theory as a subdivision of political economy, held fast to the concept of *Bevölkerungslehre.* The designation *Demographie,* coined by the Frenchman Guillard in 1855 as a synonym for the concept *statistique humaine,* gained acceptance in Germany only in recent years, although the German statistician Ernst Engel took over this term in the year of its origin (1855) and was the first to advocate the recognition of the scientific content of demography as an independent science.

One can characterize the status of demography in Germany at the beginning of World War II as follows: Population studies were regarded as a subdivision of political economy. The emphasis lay on comprehensive population statistics, which, based on objective and regionally differentiated official statistical inquiries, included a wealth of material.

Central in demographic research was the observation of fertility and mortality trends by means of a series of refined methodological procedures. In comparison, the investigation of spatial movements of population was relatively undeveloped. Essentially, until World War II only migratory movements in larger cities, in the metropolises, and in a few provinces could be followed. Only after the introduction of a new registration law in 1938 was it possible to carry out current comprehensive investigations on the basis of arrival and departure registration certificates in all parts of the Reich. But the data were only partially exploited demographically, since these administratively very complicated statistics had to be dropped again at the beginning of the war. After 1945 a number of *Länder*

(provinces), employing varying methods, resumed these observations of internal movement which are so important for an adequate assessment of refugees. Since 1950 these statistics have been gathered by a unified method in all *Länder* of the Republic of West Germany. The results give one an insight into the process of migration according to social and economic characteristics, never before possible in such scope and in such far-reaching detail.

The treatment of the relationships between population and economy had very much receded into the background during the 1930's. Until 1945 a major part of scientific work was dominated by population policy considerations. From the side of an ever more strongly developing sociology, the overemphasis of the arithmetical way of proceeding and the one-sidedness of the numerical investigation of social life were criticized, and a more inductive approach carried on from the sociological perspective was called for. From the discussion with theoretical sociology on the one side and applied statistics on the other, arose the designation of "sociography" or "empirical sociology" (Tönnies, Heberle) for this trend in research which was regarded as a subdivision of sociology. Among the studies in which the sociographic method of research was applied to individual groups in the investigation of social phenomena, the works of T. Geiger (1932) and Heberle-Mayer (1937) should be mentioned as examples of a new kind of method and inquiry in Germany.

After the end of World War II German demographers found themselves facing a new and very difficult situation. Demography was seriously discredited by the misuse which the totalitarian regime had made of the results of demographic research. Therefore, confidence in the objectivity of scientific investigation and treatment of population problems first had to be regained. At the same time, an abundance of population problems had to be solved, among which the more important include: (1) the refugee problem; (2) the reconstruction of official statistics—population statisticians had to ascertain the quantitatively comprehensible facts of the changed demographic situation and make them known to the public; (3) the social changes, caused by the war, and their results; (4) the exceptionally high mobility of certain population groups and its effects; (5) the labor shortage arising in the course of economic reconstruction; (6) the differentiation of the living conditions of modern society on the one hand and their leveling on the other, with their consequences for the structure and development of the population.

From these comprehensive practical problems and through the further elaboration of its scientific procedures, demography in Germany has taken on a new form. It has cut loose from its one-sided dependence on political economy and also from statistics. It is far more sociologically based than before and is on the point of developing into an independent discipline, as in Anglo-Saxon countries. Of course, here no more than in the case of other disciplines does independence signify shutting one's self off or desiring to lay exclusive claim to an object or method of investigation. On the contrary, a significant characteristic of demography and one of its most important tasks in Germany, as elsewhere, is the establishment of relationships with the border disciplines that are important for the study of population problems, whether medicine, anthropology, or the science of history, geography, political economy, or sociology. This is the trend in recent decades in scientific inquiry in general, which is characterized, on the one hand, by going into ever greater detail in problem formulation and research results, and, on the other hand, by attempting to assimilate the detailed findings in a more comprehensive overview and to emphasize the border areas. In this task, demography in Germany, which has been the guest of one science after another during the last century and a half, has gained its independence. Or to put it more exactly, regained it, for in its first representative, Süssmilch, it was—even though on an entirely different level of scientific knowledge—completely independent.

In the postwar development of demography in Germany, Mackenroth (1953) in particular played an important part. The fundamental conception of his population theory is based on an insight which, in its beginnings, is to be found in Karl Marx: there is no universally valid law of population in the sense of a law of natural science; there are only historical, i.e., sociological, population laws of limited historical validity. Population problems stand in a close structural relationship with political, societal, and social conditions. Mackenroth renounced conclusively and with a decisiveness probably still not reached in other countries those demographic theories which, no matter of what origin, tried to give a universally valid natural scientfic explanation in all circumstances. It is the special merit of Mackenroth that he gathered the widely scattered, existing insights for such a population theory into a new and convincing system in accordance with his basic theoretical position.

CURRENT STATUS OF DEMOGRAPHY AS REFLECTED IN RESEARCH ACTIVITIES

As one glances over the scientific works dealing with demographic problems or with areas bordering on demography which have appeared in Germany since the end of World War II, an extraordinary diversity is revealed. The efforts to put social science research on new foundations and to apply its findings to the difficult socio-political and economic problems have worked themselves out in the more specialized area of demography. To show the diverse trends and the breadth of scientific activity, we shall mention only those works that are most important and that characterize the present position of demography most clearly.

In a *Grundriss der Bevölkerungs-wissenschaft*, Von Ungern-Sternberg and Schubnell (1950) have undertaken to present an introduction to the problems as well as a survey of the major results of demographic research. In addition to the text by Mackenroth which has already been mentioned, a comprehensive presentation of population theory has been published by Charlotte Lorenz (1955) in the *Handbuch der Soziologie*. A new approach to ascertaining relationships between population movement and economic structure as well as between population movement and cultural development was undertaken by Wagemann (1948) in his theory of the optimal dimensions of social structures. With his "demodynamics" he tries to construct a population theory which, in contrast to the classical theories, emphasizes the processes of population *movement* and, above all, the accompanying changes in the structure of society.

In the field of mathematical population theory, which had been eminently represented in Germany by Knapp (1874), Becker, Lexis (1877), Von Bortkiewicz (1919), in the postwar period the Austrian Wilhelm Winkler (1948, 1952) carried on the theory of the pure types of the population developed by Sundbärg, Knapp, Bortkiewicz and Lotka and enriched the system of demographic types by a number of additional types. Although we cannot enter into the development of demography in Austria, Winkler is to be mentioned in the presentation of German

demography, since his works have had considerable influence on demograpic research and theory in Germany.

Research on the history of population, for which German demography is indebted to Beloch, Abel, Keyser (1943)—in Switzerland, W. Bickel wrote a comprehensive history of population and population policy (1947) —also was taken up again after the war. In a two-volume work by Kirsten, Buchholz, and Köllmann (1956), relationships between space and population in world history were examined and presented according to areas and countries.

From the anthropological perspective, demographic research has been enriched substantially by the work of Von Eickstedt and Ilse Schwidetzki (1950). Furthermore, mention should be made of the Institut für angewandte natur- und geisteswissenschaftliche Anthropologie in Berlin-Dahlem (Professor H. Muckermann, director), which has carried out demographically significant work.

In the Akademie für Gemeinwirtschaft (Professor Schelsky, director) aspects of the sociology of the family, especially the variation in social level of families with many children, have been investigated.

The problem of the refugee and migrant in wartime and the postwar period has been the object of numerous research studies at various institutions.

At the Institut für Weltwirtschaft at Kiel, which has long carried on demographic research on an international scale, questions concerning the migrant and the labor force potential have been studied (by Edding and Hilde Wander, among others).

The Institut für empirische Soziologie, Hanover/Nuremberg (Professor K. V. Mueller, director), has studied the absorption of the refugees into the indigenous population as well as the relation between talents and social level.

In the Sozialforschungsstelle an der Universität Münster in Dortmund (Professor Brepohl, director) there is a special division for demographic research (under the direction of Professor Ipsen), which has, among other things, turned toward studying the population of Germany and eastern European countries as well as problems of metropolitan population. In this connection one also should mention the many-sided works of Elisabeth Pfeil on the occupational and social assimilation of the displaced persons, on sociological and sociopolitical problems of population in industrial areas, and on metropolitan research.

The Akademie für Staatsmedizin in Hamburg (Professor Harmsen, director) has conducted research on numerous social-hygienic problems of municipal populations, as well as on the health conditions and the demographic status of the population in the Soviet-occupied zone of Germany and in the Soviet Union.

The Herder-Institut in Marburg (Professor Keyser, director), among other things, made the sociobiological effects of the displacement of persons of German ancestry and population conditions in east European countries the objects of its studies.

In close co-operation with the Statistical Office of the Federal Republic, the Institut für Raumforschung, Bad Godesberg (Dr. Dittrich, director), worked on problems relating to migration statistics; and the Bundesanstalt für Landeskunde in Remagen (Professor Meynen, director) completed numerous works in regional anthropogeography and made cartographic use of the results of statistical censuses, including the national census of 1950. The Akademie für Raumforschung und Landesplanung at Hanover (Professor Brüning, director) has instigated and completed a series of demographic research studies. In the series published by this institute, the work by

Scharlau (1953) on population growth and livelihood also appeared.

The Soziographische Institut at the University of Frankfurt am Main (Professor Neundörfer, director) carried out studies on social structure, the results of which are important for many difficult problems of social reform, and also made studies in internal migration, rural-urban migrations, and commuting. Agrarian sociological studies, which dealt largely with demographic problems, were initiated and completed by the Forschungsstelle der Internationalen Konferenz für Agrarwissenschaft (Professor von Dietze, Freiburg im Breisgau, director).

New statistical data—highly detailed on both an areal and a subject matter basis—were required to carry out nearly all the foregoing research projects. The results of population statistics from the prewar and wartime period, insofar as they were still available, were obsolete. Working in close co-operation during the period 1945–50, the provincial statistical offices, the statistical offices of the large cities, and the federal statistical offices reconstructed the systems of official statistics from both an administrative and a methodological standpoint. This work was made very difficult by the differences in legislation and administration among the four zones of occupation. Until the census of 1950 co-operation with the statistical headquarters of the Soviet zone of occupation was still possible, but then it ceased. The compilation of population statistics by uniform methods and the co-ordination of the *Länder* statistics in this area are the responsibility of a part of the Federal Statistical Office, the Abteilung Bevölkerungs- und Kulturstatistik (under the supervision of the director, Dr. Horstmann), which operates in close connection with the scientific institutes and administrative centers requiring population statistics. Scientific projects in the area of population statistics are co-ordinated, and experiences are exchanged.

Even though in the framework of this presentation the listing of scientists, institutes, and similar centers in Germany which are presently engaged in demographic study must necessarily remain incomplete, it nevertheless shows the breadth of demography being carried on in Germany today and the diversity of questions being investigated.

ORGANIZATION OF DEMOGRAPHIC RESEARCH AND TRAINING FACILITIES

In surprising contrast to the present status of demography and to the need for basic demographic research on the part of the state and science are, however, the scientific, organizational, and institutional facilities available to German demography and the financial means at its disposal. The situation would be still more hopeless were it not that new ways are being sought on the basis of private, personal initiative to create acceptance and work possibilities for demography in Germany. Thus, at the end of 1952 German scientists and government officials founded a society for the scientific study of population. Its goals are to further demographic research, to issue a periodical and other publications, and to develop co-operation with foreign and international societies for the purpose of exchanging experiences. Professor Harmsen is president, and Dr. Horstmann is vice-president.

The Deutsche Akademie für Bevölkerungswissenschaft, called into being at the beginning of 1953 (whose president is also Professor Harmsen, vice-presidents Professor Neundörfer and Dr. Horstmann), represents the establishment of an association of the demographers active at German universities, higher schools, and scientific institutes. It is to co-ordinate demographic studies, to plan and support scientific research and publications, and to advocate scientific population studies to the authorities. The means at the disposal of both institutions are very meager and aside from membership contributions consist of insignificant grants by the state and interested individual centers; they do not even suffice to publish a periodical of demographic studies. The *Archiv für Bevölkerungswissenschaft und Bevölkerungspolitik,* founded in 1930 by Professor Harmsen, had to cease publication in 1943. The need of such a periodical is felt not only in Germany but also by demographers in those smaller countries of Europe who have a close relationship with German science but who themselves are unable to maintain independent research facilities and to support a scientific periodical. The Deutsche Statistische Gesellschaft (President Wagner, Vice-President Fürst) also treats demographic problems which are publicized in its periodical, *Allgemeines Statistisches Archiv.* For example, the theme of its annual conference in 1955 was the contribution of statistics to the study of relationships between population and economics. In addition, questions regarding the concept of family and household as well as occupational and regional statistics were discussed. But it would be the task of a special periodical devoted to demographic studies to make research projects and research results known in the national and international sphere, to establish connections with other disciplines, and to give the public current information on the problems and significance of demographic research.

The lack of sufficient scientific, organizational, and financial means of which German demographers have complained results, in large part, from the position of demography in the German research setup and university operation.

At the universities and higher schools

in Germany there are no special chairs of instruction for demography. Demographic problems are dealt with more or less incidentally, in the sphere of various other disciplines, most often as a part of political economy or statistics, or in the framework of anthropological, geographical, social, medical, or sociological lectures. There is no special chair of instruction in population history. Demography is not an examination subject in Germany; demographic research institutes do not exist. Special lectures on general population theory were held after the war only at the universities of Kiel and Freiburg, and in both cases only because of the personal interest of the respective professors. Consequently, it is very difficult for the German student to study demographic problems and to treat them in the framework of a doctoral work or *Habilitationsschrift*. Even in population statistics, which usually are studied along with economic statistics rather than alone, the institutes and seminars in large part lack the means to acquire the necessary literature.

Without going into an extended discussion of the position of demography in the Soviet occupation zone of Germany, it may be said that there also demography as an independent discipline does not exist. The circumstances are similar, by the way, in Austria and in Switzerland. There demographic questions also are dealt with for the most part in connection with lectures on population statistics. Recently, demography was admitted as an examination subject at the University of Zürich; at Neuenburg special lectures are held on demography in its sociological aspect.

As a result of this neglect of demographic research and instruction at the German universities and higher schools there are very few demographers in Germany and practically no possibilities for training students in this specialized area. The demographically trained personnel that are needed therefore must be trained at the previously named institutes, in the statistical offices themselves, or through taking part in scientific research work. Here one is dealing mostly with scientists with a self-contained discipline such as political economy or sociology, history or geography, more rarely medicine or jurisprudence.

PROSPECTS OF DEMOGRAPHY IN GERMANY

Demography in Germany finds itself at the beginning of a new development both in the kind of problems it must solve and in its theoretical-methodological bases and possibilities. The highly differentiated social structure of modern industrial society will have to be studied even more carefully than before by all scientific means in order to have the necessary knowledge for the solution of practical problems in the socioscientific and sociopolitical area. To mention a few examples, such problems lie in the areas of social reform, the social equalization of family burdens, tax legislation, the sociopolitical and labor market effects of rearmament, and the relationships between social policy, economic policy, and the course of the trade cycle. With the further change in the age structure of the population, the special problems of the process of aging will have to be examined more closely, and perhaps also the relationship between biological age and calendar age in connection with employability and the labor supply, the development and maintenance of individual working ability and the possibility of employment in advanced age, the changes in the composition of families and the household accompanying the process of aging, the change in occupations, the care of the aged, etc. To all these questions demography has substantial contributions to make. The mechanization of human labor which is marching on in step with technological progress and, above all, automation will put a new kind of question to be solved in the area of demography. German demographers will have to give special attention to family planning, its sociological reasons and economic effects, which has been studied very little in Germany. The further development of the use of atomic energy will, if it leads to radiation injuries, raise genetic and eugenic problems, and demography must give substantial co-operation in mastering them.

German demography has greatly neglected the treatment of economic problems in the last two decades. The relationships between population and economics—in view of the development of demography as well as of economic theory—may no longer be treated exclusively or predominantly in a static way; they must rather be seen in their dynamics. But here science—political economy, as well as demography—is faced with a broad and as yet little explored area. German demography is indebted to the investigations of August Lösch (1932, 1936) for the first approaches to a theoretical formulation of the relationships between population and economics that brought in the dynamic aspects. The way in which phrasing of the question has changed in the course of time and the contributions of population statistics to the examination of economic-demographic relationships were discussed by Schubnell (1955). The discussion points up a scientific development which was carried on in Germany by political economists and demographers, statisticians and sociologists, and which was connected with names like Mombert, Lösch, Röpke, Zwiedineck-Südenhorst, Winkler, Heberle, Fritz Meyer, Burgdörfer, Isenberg, and Mackenroth, to mention only the most important. The theoretical conception of sociologically based demographic theory also will

produce new possibilities of insight in the examination of relationships between population and economics.

Among the most pressing problems which German demography must investigate in the immediate future are the examination of the structure of families and households and their development; further investigation of population mobility and its connection with sifting and selection processes; the change in the social stratification of the population, its causes and effects; the preparation of scientifically objective and exact material on the question of the sociopolitically requisite equalization of family burdens; examination of the sociopolitical stratification of the population in connection with the questions of social mobility, of income stratification and standard of living; and examination of questions concerning the need for replacement and provision for the population in the various areas of the economy. In the methodological sphere German demography will have to co-operate in the preparation of the 1960 census and in the execution and evaluation of the sample survey (*Mikrozensus*). The theoretical propositions of a sociologically based population theory must be developed further, but at the same time tested again and again by application to concrete problems, and, if necessary, they must be modified. Recently Bickel made a contribution in this direction (1956).

The very mention of these most important research tasks to be carried out in the future indicates the characteristic task of demography to relate the scientific knowledge of various disciplines to one another, to stimulate new studies from its particular point of view, to make the results useful for the practical formulation of questions, and thereby to put into action the results of scientific work. Carrying out these tasks requires the collection of basic quantitative data. To obtain them, methods must be adapted to ascertain ways in which complicated and interdependent events actually develop. This can be achieved only in part by the customary complete population enumeration, since the detailed and dependable ascertainment of complicated characteristics is not possible by self-enumeration of the respondents. The limitations of the complete enumeration are especially evident when qualitative characteristics are requested in addition to the previous quantitative ones, when behavior is to be explained, or when social relationships, social changes, life situations, social mobility, etc. are to be explored.

The Federal Statistical Office has developed in its sample survey of population and employment an instrument which is able to comprehend exactly socioscientific and sociopolitical factual situations of the greatest variety. We are dealing here with a sample survey executed every three months, which includes 1 per cent of the population once a year and 0.1 per cent the other three times. It is carried out with a trained staff of interviewers. Besides the previously customary cross-sectional observation through one-time samples, the sample survey offers the possibility of longitudinal observations. The households included in the sample are questioned repeatedly in a series of quarterly censuses. Thus it is possible to ascertain the individual changes relating to persons, the development of families and households, and thereby the changes in the living circumstances and the social mobility of individuals and population groups in the course of their lives.

The sample survey will become, especially for empirical social research, an indispensable instrument for the rapid, exact, and informative observation of socially and scientifically important facts and changes as well as their causes and effects. Through these censuses carried out under official auspices,

current material will be placed at the disposal of German demography and will be especially valuable for research.

To carry out these tasks so important for the political, social, and economic life of the German population, demography must be supported by the state on an equal basis with the other sciences in Germany. (In Germany there are no universities and great research institutes erected and operated by private, non-governmental means as there are, for instance, in the United States.) Demography also will have to be recognized as an area of research and instruction at German universities and higher schools, as has long been the case in many other countries. Furthermore, sufficient funds must be made available for the establishment and maintenance of demographic institutes and seminars, the publication of a periodical of demographic studies, and the execution of demographic investigations. Even in general education, attention should be given to demographic questions in the framework of education for citizenship. Finally, press, radio, and film must be kept up to date on demographic problems and the results of demographic research; greater publicity must be obtained for this branch of science, which is so important to the life of the nation and to international relations—to be sure, not to shape political opinion with regard to population, but to give a scientifically objective clarification and presentation of the facts in the case.

SELECTED BIBLIOGRAPHY

BERNOULLI, C. 1840–41. *Populationistik oder Bevölkerungswissenschaft.* 2 vols.
BICKEL, W. 1947. *Bevölkerungsgeschichte und Bevölkerungspolitik der Schweiz seit dem Ausgang des Mittelalters.*
———. 1956. "Bevölkerungsdynamik und Gesellschaftsstruktur," *Schweizerische Zeitschrift für Volkswirtschaft und Statistik,* Vol. XCII, No. 3.

BORTKIEWICZ, L. VON. 1919. *Bevölkerungswesen.*

BURGDÖRFER, F. 1917. *Das Bevölkerungsproblem, seine Erfassung durch Familienstatistik und Familienpolitik.*

——. 1932. *Volk ohne Jugend.*

——. 1940. "Bevölkerungsstatistik und Bevölkerungspolitik," in *Die Statistik in Deutschland nach ihrem heutigen Stand*, ed. F. BURGDÖRFER, Vol. I.

——. 1954. *Welt-Bevölkerungs-Atlas*, Part I.

ELSTER, L., WINKLER, W., et al. 1924. "Bevölkerungswesen," *Handwörterbuch der Staatswissenschaften*, Vol. II.

GEIGER, T. 1932. *Die soziale Schichtung des deutschen Volkes.* (*Soziologische Gegenwartsfragen*, Part I.)

GROTJAHN, A. 1914. *Geburtenrückgang und Geburtenregelung.*

——. 1926. *Die Hygiene der menschlichen Fortpflanzung.*

HARMSEN, H. 1927. *Bevölkerungsprobleme Frankreichs unter besonderer Berücksichtigung des Geburtenrückgangs.*

——. 1931. *Praktische Bevölkerungspolitik: Ein Abriss ihrer Grundlagen, Ziele, und Aufgaben.*

HEBERLE, R. 1931. "Soziographie," in *Handwörterbuch der Soziologie*, ed. A. Vierkandt.

——, and MEYER, F. 1937. *Die Grossstädte im Strom der Binnenwanderung.*

IPSEN, G. 1933. "Bevölkerungslehre," in *Handwörterbuch des Grenz- und Auslandsdeutschtums.*

KEYSER, E. 1943. *Bevölkerungsgeschichte Deutschlands.*

KIRSTEN, E., BUCHHOLZ, E. W., and KÖLLMANN, W. 1956. *Bevölkerung und Raum in neuerer und neuester Zeit. 2 vols.* Part I: *Raum und Bevölkerung in der Weltgeschichte* (*Bevölkerungs-Ploetz*). Part II: *Von der Vorzeit bis zum Mittelalter.* Part III: *Vom Mittelalter zur Neuzeit.*

KNAPP, G. F. 1874. *Theorie des Bevölkerungswechsels.*

LEXIS, W. 1877. *Zur Theorie der Massenerscheinungen in der menschlichen Gesellschaft.*

LÖSCH, A. 1932. *Was ist vom Geburtenrückgang zu halten?*

——. 1936. "Bevölkerungswellen und Wechsellagen," *Beiträge zur Erforschung der wirtschaftlichen Wechsellagen*, No. 13.

LORENZ, C. 1955. "Bevölkerungslehre," *Handbuch der Soziologie.*

MACKENROTH, G. 1953. *Bevölkerungslehre: Theorie, Soziologie, und Statistik der Bevölkerung.*

MAYR, G. VON. 1897. *Bevölkerungsstatistik.* (*Statistik und Gesellschaftslehre*, Vol. II.)

MOHL, R. VON. 1858. *Geschichte und Literatur der Staatswissenschaften.* Vol. III: *Geschichte und Literatur der Bevölkerungslehre.*

MOMBERT, P. 1929. *Bevölkerungslehre.*

MOSER, L. 1839. *Die Gesetze der Lebensdauer nebst Untersuchungen über Dauer, Fruchtbarkeit der Ehen, und Tödlichkeit der Krankheiten.*

RATZEL, F. 1882–91. *Anthropogeographie.* Part I: *Grundzüge der Anwendung der Erdkunde auf die Geschichte.* Part II: *Die geographische Verbreitung des Menschen.*

RIEHL, W. H. 1853. *Die Naturgeschichte des Volkes als Grundlage einer deutschen Sozialpolitik.*

ROSCHER, W. 1854. *Grundlagen der Nationalökonomie.* Vol. I: *Theorie der Bevölkerung.*

RÜMELIN, G. VON. 1882. "Die Bevölkerungslehre," in *Handbuch der politischen Ökonomie*, ed. SCHÖNBERG.

SCHARLAU, K. 1953. *Bevölkerungswachstum und Nahrungsspielraum, Geschichte, Methoden, und Probleme der Tragfähigkeitsuntersuchungen.*

SCHUBNELL, H. 1955. "Der Beitrag der Bevölkerungsstatistik zur Untersuchung der Zusammenhänge zwischen Bevölkerung und Wirtschaft," *Allgemeines statistisches Archiv*, Vol. XXXIX, No. 4.

SCHWIDETZKI, I. 1950. *Grundzüge der Völkerbiologie.*

STEIN, L. VON. 1866. "Das Bevölkerungswesen und sein Verwaltungsrecht," *Die Verwaltungslehre*, Part II.

SÜSSMILCH, J. P. 1741. *Die göttliche Ordnung in den Veränderungen des mensch-*

lichen Geschlechts, aus der Geburt, dem Tode, und der Fortpflanzung desselben erwiesen.

UNGERN-STERNBERG, R. VON. 1932. *Die Ursachen des Geburtenrückganges im europaischen Kulturkreis.*

——, and SCHUBNELL, H. 1950. *Grundriss der Bevölkerungswissenschaft (Demographie).*

WAGEMANN, E. 1948. *Menschenzahl und Völkerschicksal: Eine Lehre von den optimalen Dimensionen gesellschaftlicher Gebilde.*

WAGNER, A. 1892. "Bevölkerung und Volkswirtschaft," *Grundlegung der politischen Ökonomie,* Book IV.

WAPPÄUS, J. E. 1859–61. *Allgemeine Bevölkerungsstatistik.* 2 vols.

WINKLER, W. 1948. "Gesellschaftsstatistik," *Grundriss der Statistik,* Part II.

——. 1952. *Typenlehre der Demographie (Reine Bevölkerungstypen).*

10. *Contributions of Italy to Demography*[1]

ALESSANDRO COSTANZO

This paper attempts to indicate the salient aspects of the study of demography in Italy and its development in that country. We will deal only with descriptive and empirical demography, excluding the history of methods of collecting data and omitting consideration of population policies. We make a sharp distinction between population theory, which will be considered only briefly, and the quantitative study of demographic phenomena, which is the main topic of the paper.

POPULATION THEORY

A lively interest in population problems has been expressed by Italian students of political and economic matters, as well as specialists in demography, since the fifteen century. In the period before Malthus important political writers were Machiavelli, Botero, Paruta, Zuccolo, Chiaramonti, Denina, and Brustolini. Economists writing on population included Algarotti, Bandini, Beccaria, Belloni, Briganti, Carli, Cornaro, D'Arco, Filangieri, Genovesi, Ortes, Palmieri, Ricci, Vasco, and Verri. (See Costanzo, 1957.) None of these students denied that population would grow more rapidly than it actually does if it did not encounter obstacles, primarily limits on the means of subsistence. However, they varied greatly in their optimism concerning the possibility and consequences of a disequilibrium between population and subsist-

[1] EDITORS' NOTE.—This is a greatly abridged translation of Professor Costanzo's paper, which, it is hoped, will be published in full in its original form.

ence. Ortes was perhaps the closest to Malthus in his ideas as well as one of the closest chronologically.

There has been much discussion about whether Malthus had any precursors in Italy. Certainly the central idea of Malthusian theory had been expressed long before his time, in Italy as well as in Malthus' own country. Ortes had pointed out the difference in the potential rates of increase of population and the means of subsistence and had stated the law of geometrical growth of population. Geometric growth was also recognized by Cornaro and Zuccolo. The greater success of Malthus' version was doubtless due to the trenchant manner in which he posed the problem and to the pertinence of his discussion to social controversies occurring in the period in which he wrote.

For many decades after Malthus writings on population theory were largely polemical treatments of his actual or supposed ideas. Nineteenth-century writers involved in controversy over Malthusian ideas included such economists and statisticians as Benini, Cagnazzi, Ferrara, Gioia, Loria, G. Majorana, S. Majorana, Martello, Messedaglia, Nitti, Paresi, Pareto, Romagnosi, Rossi, Zorli, Virgili, and others whose views cannot be described individually for lack of space.

It was only toward the middle of the last century that the work of Verhulst, taken up and developed in the 1920's by Pearl and Reed, indicated an empirical method of identifying the law of population growth in terms of the biological, economic, and other forces that determine it. Several Italian investigators also made contributions to this line of theoretical development.

Amoroso (1929) indicated that Malthus was wrong in supposing a direct causal relationship between means of subsistence and population rather than a relationship of interdependence between the two. Amoroso observed that the movement of population results from the action of two forces: the limits and conditions placed on population increase by the means of subsistence (Ortesian action) and the stimulus to productive activity and consequent increase in means of subsistence occasioned by population growth (Smithian action). Defining "demographic elasticity" as the logarithmic derivative of population divided by the logarithmic derivative of the means of subsistence, Amoroso gives an analytical expression of the principles of Ortesian action and Smithian action, arriving at a differential equation which is that of the logistic law of Pearl and Reed. The logistic law is thereby given a new rational interpretation.

This theoretical construction, leading to the simple logistic, was generalized by Vinci (1929, 1930, 1937), whose general dynamic scheme was further analyzed by Vianelli. Vianelli (1935) recognized the difficulty in attempting to express by simple logistic curves the complex circumstances influencing the development of population; he indicated the advantages of generalized logistic formulas and subjected them to some empirical tests. Volterra (1926, 1931) considered the development of populations from the somewhat different point of view of several species living in biological association and produced a well-known mathematical theory on this subject.

In this intellectual climate, which had carried the search for a law of population development into the area of empirical investigation, Gini (1911, 1912, 1930a, b, 1931) presented his cyclical theory of population which both contradicted the biological assumptions of the Malthusian theory and predicated a cycle of development different from that described by the simple logistic curve. Gini denies that the reproductive potential of a population remains constant throughout successive generations; he maintains that it follows a cycle analogous to that of the reproductive capacity of individuals. This vital cycle does not occur synchronously for the various family strains and the several social classes which make up a population. It is in the different rates of increase of these groups that the "key to the evolution of nations" is to be found.

L. Livi (1941) presents a naturalistic conception of the bases of social organization represented by organic characteristics and by the natural variability of somatopsychic characteristics. His central point is the slow maturation of the human individual, requiring care of the mother for an extended period and the defense and sustenance of the family by the father. This circumstance results in the monogamous structure of the family and its vulnerability, which gives rise to the union of families in society for common defense and development.

PRECURSORS OF QUANTITATIVE DEMOGRAPHIC STUDIES

As far back as 1300 the rector of St. John's in Florence used beans to count the number of baptisms, placing a black bean in a receptacle for each boy baptized and a white bean for each girl. This information made possible not only the computation of the total number baptized but at least an approximation of the sex ratio among them— between 110 and 119 boys for every 100 girls baptized. Much later a doctor in Padua, Santorio di Capodistria

(1561–1636) tried to measure, by means of a specially constructed steelyard, the loss of weight due to perspiration. He thus introduced the quantitative method in the study of biological phenomena and initiated the influential biometric orientation. These incidents represent the first steps toward the slow replacement of qualitative evaluation by quantitative examination of the phenomena which concern us here.

But, according to Boldrini, it was only in the second half of the eighteenth century that the empirical spirit of the English political arithmeticians spread through Italy and gave the initial impetus to interests that were to flourish in the nineteenth century. In 1771 P. Verri pointed out the oscillations to which populations were subject from year to year and advised caution in inferring causes of population change from the unreliable data which were then available. G. R. Carli, pointing out that the population of Milan was unknown, indicated that variations in population could be deduced from the reliable marriage and birth statistics appearing in parish records, employing the commonly accepted ratios of "one marriage a year for each hundred of the population and births in the ratio of three to four per hundred." This was not yet on a level of exact quantitative research, but it is evident that for these economists the interest in population went beyond that of establishing its connections with economic phenomena to encompass the study of population as an end in itself.

A forward step had been taken a couple of years earlier by Beccaria, who used data published for the parish of San Sulpizio in Paris on the baptized and the dead, 1715–44, in an attempt to explain the varying sex ratio by age among the dead; he presented a little essay on empirical demography.

Among the first in Italy to apply the new method of demographic investigation was M. Lastri (1775), whose research on the population of Florence is an example of empirical historical demography. He calculated sex ratios of births and demonstrated that not all months of the year are equally fertile, and he noted that the more fertile months were not the same in different countries. He also identified a series of problems with which he could not cope for lack of data, including the ratio of births to marriages, the differential fertility of social classes, and the differential fertility of rural and urban areas.

In 1774 a Veronese doctor, G. V. Zeviani, presented an essay, "On the Numerous Deaths of Babies," which contained the first Italian mortality table (see Boldrini, 1937), probably constructed by Halley's method. As Boldrini observed, the table probably did not represent the true mortality, but it is important in the history of demography as an expression of the author's empirical spirit.

In 1787 G. Toaldo—whose reference to the "astonishing order of Providence" echoed Süssmilch—published seven mortality tables, presumably constructed by the same method as Zeviani's. He investigated the causes of high infant mortality and demonstrated mortality differences between mountain parishes and those of the plains, between men and women, and between the country and the city. In 1828 Cagnazzi constructed mortality tables for the Kingdom of Naples on the basis of death statistics—for males and females and for the city of Naples and the provinces. He speculated about the difference in infant mortality between the provinces and the capital and about the seasonal pattern of deaths. In 1844 De Renzi published tables for the city of Naples, constructed on the basis of more than 180,000 deaths. These were prepared separately for the various sections of the city and were accompanied by observations on the causes of mortality differences among various regions. All these tables were constructed on the basis of numbers of deaths alone; therefore, they did not represent accurately the existing mortality levels. However, this work was evidence of a growing interest in the quantitative study of population.

DEMOGRAPHIC STUDIES IN THE FIRST HALF OF THE NINETEENTH CENTURY

At the beginning of the last century, as the demographic interests of scholars became stronger, they spread into related fields, particularly what would be called today the field of biometry. We must give some attention to these interests, not only because they have been an important part of the Italian contribution to demography, but also because, as Boldrini observes, there is little difference between biometric phenomena in the strict sense and demographic phenomena.

M. Gioja studied seasonal variations in the sex ratio at birth and concluded that heat was favorable to the production of males; Calindri arrived at the same conclusion some years later. Gioja also advanced the hypothesis that stature is influenced by climate, asserting that greater height is common to countries where cold is pungent but not excessive. These studies are worth noting as the first contributions to subjects which were to be taken up later in much greater detail. Even in this early period there were investigations of medical statistics purporting to demonstrate the influence of atmospheric conditions on such characteristics as age at puberty, age at marriage, and life expectancy. There were also studies by Gioja on the impact of famine on demographic phenomena and by Bianchi on differential fertility by occupations.

A statistician and physician, De Renzi (1838) was the first to examine the selective effect of constitution on mortality, in addition to examining the influence of variations of atmospheric pressure and temperature on morbidity. He can therefore be considered a predecessor of the school of constitutional physicians who some decades later were to take up the broader problem of the relationships between body development and morbidity and mortality, and he gave impetus to the recent investigations of constitutional demographers who have meticulously examined the problem posed by these physicians.

DEMOGRAPHIC STUDIES IN THE SECOND HALF OF THE NINETEENTH CENTURY

The Italian contribution to biometric-anthropometric-demographic studies increased rapidly after the middle of the century, producing a voluminous body of investigations that cannot be mentioned individually (see Bodio, 1885). We shall atempt only to give a broad view of these studies.

The application of the statistical method to the study of such social phenomena as criminality, suicide, and prostitution revealed the influence of factors which are independent, or nearly so, of individual volition—age, sex, marital status, social class, educational level, and environmental conditions. These results were supplemented by the contributions of the anthropological school (especially Mantegazza and Lombroso) which related these manifestations of moral life—delinquency in particular—to constitutional characteristics, especially craniometric characteristics. Most of these studies deserve notice, not for the importance of their results nor for their rather elementary methods of research, but because of the vigorous and controversial scientific movement which they initiated. The positive school of criminology—in particular, Lombroso, Ferri, and Garofalo—shifted attention to the criminal himself, starting from the observation that his volition is nullified or modified by his constitution and environment.

In the final decades of the century many demographic phenomena were subjected to quantitative inquiry with more and more advanced methods derived from mathematics and and probability theory. Morselli (1880) represented a notable example of this tendency in his recognition of the need to supplement the study of averages with the analysis of variability.

Among the numerous subjects studied are the classification of the Italian population by age in studies by Rameri, Armenante, Fabris, Novellis, and by Perozzo (1885), who used interpolation to subdivide quinquennial age classes by single years of age; the mortality tables of Rey, Armenante, Fano, and Rameri; and various mortality studies by Sormani, Rameri, Perozzo, Mauro, and Favero. Other investigations were conducted on an explicitly empirical basis, for example: Messadaglia's study on the expectation of life; Morpurgo's investigations anticipating Benini's conclusions on seasonal patterns of conceptions and deaths, the work of Boccardo on the sex ratio, the research of G. S. del Vecchio on the effects of marriages among blood relations, that of Sormani on climatic and seasonal effects on natality and mortality, and the work of Perozzo (1883) which applied elaborate probability schemes to the distribution of marriages according to the age of the spouses.

During this period investigations of historical demography were pursued vigorously, following the valuable earlier studies of Lastri, Rosario, Cagnazzi, Calindri, Scuderi, Serristori, Ferrario, and Zuccagni-Orlandini. Fundamental accomplishments in this field were made by Castiglioni (1862) and especially by Beloch (1886, 1908, and other works), who made noteworthy studies of ancient Italian populations. The interest in historical demography has persisted; it is represented by the work of the Comitato Italiano per lo Studio dei Problemi della Popolazione (1933–40), which led to the publication of a mass of information about the existing demographic data for a number of Italian communities.

An almost contemporaneous interest in biometric and anthropometric studies developed and reached its zenith only in recent years. Lombroso's investigations of group differences in stature were methodologically defective. Perozzo concluded that there was an Italian type with respect to stature, and Raseri erroneously discerned a tendency for Italian stature to diminish over time. R. Livi (1896 and other works) made the first and only great anthropometric study on Italian soldiers; he pointed out Bertillon's error in attributing the bimodal distribution of the stature of draftees to the presence in their district of origin of two racial groups. Pagliani thought he recognized the effect of racial mixture in the distribution of draftees by stature, but the effect that he noticed was merely an artifact of arithmetical rounding.

De Rossi was one of the first to study temporal variations in average stature, a subject studied subsequently by many other scholars. Increases in average stature were noted by Boldrini, L. Livi, and Gini. Fucci thought he recognized a countertendency toward diminution of stature in conscripts called in World War I, but this phenomenon was due to the progressive lowering of age at induction. The present writer (Costanzo, 1948, 1952), in the most recent studies of this problem, used long series of military data to demonstrate an increasing trend in stature for Piedmontese men over a period of nearly a century and a half and for the total group of Italian men twenty years old over a period of about two-thirds of a century.

Systematic Treatment of Demographic Problems

In the latter part of the nineteenth century, demography came to be distinguished from statistics. Investigators no longer found it necessary to contrast "demography"—the empirical, statistical study of population phenomena—with "demology," or population studies undertaken from the standpoint of other natural and social sciences. The former term (coined by Guillard in France) was accepted as embracing the entire field. Thus the way was prepared for the first systematic treatise on the subject. In his *Principles of Demography* Benini (1901) organized his exposition around the two fundamental theories of population quality and population quantity. The former emphasizes individual biosocial differences as a basis of social selection and social cohesion; the latter studies the conditions of continuity and growth of population, with special reference to limitations on the resources necessary to support growth. Benini considered that cohesion and continuity are the salient facts of human society. His work was important in itself, and it became a basis for subsequent extensive empirical investigations using statistical data not available to Benini.

A few years later Colajanni (1904) published a treatise on demography; he arranged his material in terms of the traditional distinction between the state and the movement of population.

Several systematic works have appeared in recent years. Both Zingali (1930) and Savorgnan (1936) follow the traditional plan of organization; the latter introduces considerable sociological material and emphasizes the importance of population as a factor in social evolution. Luzzatto-Fegiz (1951) treats natality, mortality, and migration as a framework for studying population movements, but he also organizes part of his material around the processes of family formation, development, and dissolution. Livi (1940) orders his treatment of demographic phenomena in terms of his naturalistic conception of the bases of social organization. Lasorsa (1952), after an introduction on techniques of data collection and analysis, frames his exposition in terms of morphological and biosocial considerations and emphasizes the regularities observed to exist in such phenomena.

Boldrini (1956), who is to be credited with the most recent systematic work, presents a functional classification based on the distinction between demographic statistics and scientific demography; he stresses the distinction between the tools of scientific research and research itself. It is to the latter that the author devotes most of his attention, and he presents a number of original contributions. He has also accomplished a much-needed systematization of the bio-anthropometric work which is closely related to demography (Boldrini, 1927, 1934, 1950, and other works).

The many contributions of Gini, spread over diverse subjects, are partly integrated by his central conception of the cyclical movement of population and by his views on population policy.

The review of particular demographic problems will necessarily be superficial and selective because of the large number of contributions by recent and contemporary Italian statisticians and demographers.

The Sex Ratio of Births and Conceptions

This problem, which has long attracted Italian scholars, acquired particular interest when developments in genetics seemed to cast doubt on previous demographic findings on the sex ratios of live births, stillbirths, and miscarriages. After Gini's studies early in the century, Boldrini took up the problem in an effort to reconcile the real and supposed facts with genetic theory. He concluded, with the support of studies by Alberti and De Lisi, that the unknown primary sex ratio would not have to differ significantly from the secondary sex ratio ascertained by demographers. The predominance of male fetuses in miscarriages after a certain stage of intra-uterine life is probably compensated—at least in part—by a predominance of females in the very early stages, when the determination of sex is very difficult and subject to considerable error with present clinical techniques. The departure of the ratio from unity even at conception can be explained on hypotheses formulated by geneticists—particularly that of Morgan, which states that the theoretical ratio exceeds unity somewhat because of the greater motility of the spermatozoa carrying the Y chromosome (Boldrini, 1928*a*).

There is no room to mention the numerous studies and discussions of this question, but there is a recent investigation by Colombo (1955) which supports Boldrini's thesis and a contribution by Savorgnan (1955), who agrees with Boldrini and maintains that intra-uterine mortality takes almost equal numbers of males and females. The problems of the relative frequency and sex ratios of plural births have also been investigated by a number of workers, including Benini, Gini, Boldrini, L. Livi, Amato, and Vajani.

Natality

The phenomenon of natality has undergone extensive investigation by scholars using both official compilations of statistics and data secured in special investigations. In his investiga-

tion of illegitimacy Boldrini (1933) stated that the low rate of illegitimacy is partly explained by the high frequency with which illegitimate pregnancies are interrupted and by the high rate of neonatal mortality of illegitimate births. Colombo (1951) has contributed a broad study of the rise of the birth rate which occurred in many countries during World War II. He indicates that a probable cause of this fluctuation is the temporary weakening of rational restraints on the procreative instinct—an interpretation supported by the fact that in many countries the rise in the birth rate has been followed by a decline. Returning to a subject investigated earlier by Mortara, De Castro (1934) studied antenuptial conceptions and pointed out their low frequency in Italy, their prevalence in both large and small cities and in rural areas, their inverse relationship with age of parents, and their relationship with religious sentiments and social conditions of the parents. Vianelli (1939) showed that in depressions the number of illegitimate births increases while legitimate births from antenuptial conceptions decrease—phenomena which he explains in terms of the postponement of marriage. D'Elia (1943) presents a critique of conventional formulas for measuring effective fertility, proposes certain improvements, and indicates the differences between two alternative methods—differences which are rather slight if one disregards periods of rising infant mortality.

The problems which dominate the empirical work on natality, however, are those of the fecundability, prolificacy, and fertility of women. Using data on the wives of soldiers who had received brief leaves during World War I, Boldrini (1919*a*) made the first calculation for a defined population of the fecundability of women, defined as the probability that a woman will conceive when exposed to the risk of fertilization. A simple and ingenious method, employing statistics on first births by number of months elapsed since marriage, was proposed by Gini (1924, 1925). He concluded that the fecundability of women married for the first time is constant from one population to another and constant over time in the same population, despite the great diminution in natality. Further investigations of this problem were made by De Meo and Naddeo. It is impossible to summarize the extensive literature on fertility; important contributions were made by Boldrini, Del Chiaro, D'Elia, De Vergottini (1936, 1937*a, b,* 1939), Federici, Gini, Lasorsa (1954), Lenti (1935, 1937, 1939, 1940), Livi (1940), Maroi, Mortara, Parenti (1939), Paglino, and Vampa.

The problem of differential reproductivity has been illuminated by the studies of Golzio and Battara (1934), who found especially low marital fertility in marriages celebrated in civil ceremonies. (See also Gini, 1936; Federici, 1939.) Savorgnan (1942 and earlier publications) thoroughly studied the fertility of the aristocracy. Boldrini (1932) has given a plausible explanation of the differential fertility of the social classes in terms of the differing constitutional characteristics of the social classes and the variation in fertility by constitutional type.

The causes of the decline in natality have been debated at length. An important study (Molinari, 1933) which attempted to ascertain these causes was sponsored in 1928 by the Istituto Centrale di Statistica; it concerned certain Italian municipalities in which the decline in natality between 1911 and 1921 was particularly pronounced. The results, which were based on questions addressed to municipal officials and must be accepted with caution, indicated that voluntary limitation far outweighed biological factors. Reasons for the use of contraceptive measures were

studied by De Castro (1938). Somogyi's (1933) investigation suggested that both differential fertility and the decline in natality are due to a complex of social and economic factors. Boldrini (1956) studied the trend of marital fertility in terms of duration of marriage; he concluded that declining natality cannot be produced by biological causes, which operate very slowly, but only by the desire to reduce the number of births. Gini (1940), taking up the subject again, reasserted the principles underlying his cyclical theory of population. Declining natality, he stated, is due either to the strengthening of the force of reason or to a diminution in the force of the reproductive instinct. Gini did not exclude reason, but he thought that all the instincts related to reproduction had lost part of their strength. Instinct being a biological phenomenon, the weakening of the reproductive instinct would be an indirect manifestation of a decline in physiological fecundity, and it would have a biological basis.

Mortality

Mortality has been studied at several stages of the life cycle. Alberti's (1934) work on the population of Milan is important methodologically for its contribution to the measurement of abortion. Studies on trends in stillbirths have been made by Lenzi, on the relation of stillbirths to the interval between births by De Vergottini, and on the relation of stillbirths to duration of marriage, order of birth, and occupation by D'Elia. Significant studies of infant mortality, from a variety of viewpoints, have been published by Barberi, Caranti, Del Chiaro, D'Elia, Galvani, and Savorgnan.

But it is perhaps mortality by cause which has attracted the greatest attention. The studies of Uggé (1928) deal with the comparability of cause-specific mortality rates. He shows that international comparisons lead to conclusions on the basis of corrected rates quite different from those on the basis of uncorrected rates. He also indicates that declining death rates from infant diseases, infectious diseases, and acute respiratory diseases contributed heavily to declining mortality in Italy between 1911 and 1921, while mortality from pulmonary tuberculosis, typhoid fever, tumors, apoplexy, and heart disease hardly decreased at all. Boldrini (1928*b*) has classified causes of death in terms of the constitutional or physiological types most susceptible to them. Eliminating the influence of changes in age composition, he shows that the decline in general mortality for the period 1911–21 was mainly due to the decline in death rates from respiratory diseases which affect principally individuals having a long-shaped body structure. Such a finding helps to explain the gradual increase in stature over time (mentioned earlier) in terms of the greater chance of survival of this type as compared with the opposite type possessing a short-shaped body structure. Others contributing studies on cause of death include Niceforo, L. Livi, Ferrari, Tizzano, L'Eltore, and Barberi (1954); Barberi presented a unique investigation of joint causes of death and demonstrated associations among various causes.

The measurement of probabilities of death as a function of age was, as indicated above, one of the topics that first claimed the attention of Italian demographers. This interest has continued. The mortality tables of Perozzo, Bagni, and Beneduce, prepared in connection with the censuses of 1881, 1901, and 1911, respectively, carry forward the earlier series of life tables, but with greatly improved techniques. Later technical contributions to life-table construction were made by F. Vinci, by Mortara (1914)—who prepared the only life tables by single causes of

death—and by Gini and Galvani (1931), who presented life tables for 1921–22 in a work of fundamental importance to this field. Galvani also prepared tables on the basis of the 1931 census. Life tables for 1935–36 were prepared by Mirri, but they had to be limited to females because great numbers of males were out of the country in this period.

Boldrini prepared life tables for several countries describing the rate at which the initial cohort of men about to be drafted underwent attrition. The mortality data were shown in combination with factors representing fitness for military service by age. Boldrini's use of life tables to study this problem of military importance was a unique Italian contribution in this field.

Constitutional Demography

A half-century has now elapsed since Achille de Giovanni founded the Italian school of constitutional demography. He criticized prevailing etiological theories and asserted that the course of disease varies according to morphological type. According to the constitutionalists, harmoniously developed individuals resist mortality longer than those with a long-shaped or a short-shaped body structure. The long-shaped individuals have a strong tendency to contract diseases of the respiratory system and especially pulmonary tuberculosis, while short-shaped individuals are prone to diseases of the circulatory and digestive systems. But the development of the constitutional doctrine, to which Pende and Viola contributed greatly, rested on defective data—data secured in medical clinics and not representative of the general population in which selective mortality occurs. Boldrini (1925 and earlier works) is credited with attacking the problem from the demographic standpoint and with making fundamental contributions to it. According to his results, while the selectivity of pathogenic causes occurs substantially as Giovanni indicated, it is not the harmoniously developed type that proves the strongest but a type characterized by a slight dominance of transverse over longitudinal development, i.e., a moderately short-shaped type.

Boldrini's results were substantially confirmed by a number of investigators and in particular by the research of Costanzo (1936) on the male inhabitants of the town of Casale Monferrato (Piedmont, Italy), who were followed from age twenty until death, the cause of which was ascertained.

Although it is well to suspend judgment pending further studies, data collected by Costanzo (1939) strongly indicate a connection between pigmentation and robustness, as shown by the proportion of males temporarily or permanently unfit for military service; the subjects with light pigmentation were at a disadvantage. The body constitution therefore appears to be a selective factor not only in its morphological aspect but also in certain qualitative characteristics. Owing to this research in constitutional demography, it has become possible to include a new selective factor in the list of known elements producing mortality differentials—such as age, sex, marital status, social condition, and race.

The achievements of constitutional demography are not limited to findings on morbidity and mortality. Boldrini (1931) verified empirically a fertility differential in biotypes in favor of the short-shaped type. Pende and Benedetti likewise found high fertility to be associated with a short-shaped body structure. Despite some uncertainties and inconsistencies, studies in various parts of Italy (for the Comitato Italiano per lo Studio dei Problemi della Popolazione) to ascertain anthropometric and constitutional characteristics of the parents of large families substantially confirmed Boldrini's results.

The recent research in this field, while it was able to reach conclusions which formerly could not be demonstrated, only represents the latest development of ideas already expressed by Renzi. After Quételet's theoretical elaboration, these ideas found applications in the work of the anthropological school, which connected moral and physical characteristics with anthropometric characteristics in a cause and effect relationship.

Nuptiality and Assortative Mating

The aspect of nuptiality which seems to have interested Italian demographers the most is the phenomenon of similarity of spouses. The first studies of marital selection are by Benini (1901), who regarded marriage as a phenomenon of the forces of cohesion and repulsion which play a fundamental role in his qualitative theory of population. Numerous subsequent studies improved the methods of studying the problem and accumulated more knowledge about assortative mating. Contributions by Bachi, Bandettini, Brambilla, Castrilli, D. de Castro, De Meo, De Vergottini (1955), Genna, Mortara, Pompilj, Savorgnan, and Uggé established the importance of age, previous marital status, religion, nationality, economic and social factors, and even some qualitative and quantitative physical characteristics as factors in mate selection.

Although it was carried out later than in some other countries, there has also been some research using existing statistical data to compute nuptial probabilities and changes in marital status as a function of age. The Italian pioneer in these studies was Mortara (1908, 1909), who prepared mortality and nuptiality tables using data of the 1901 census and vital statistics for 1899–1902. Owing to a lack of requisite data, few investigators followed up Mortara's work. Much later, Somogyi (1937) used 1931 census data and 1930–32 vital statistics to prepare nuptiality tables for single persons of both sexes, widows, and widowers; he also prepared tables of widowhood separately for each sex. On the basis of these and life tables he worked out tables for both sexes showing the attrition of the single population by marriage and death. Medani and Parenti (1938) also made contributions to this problem.

A recent study by Colombo (1954) discusses various hypotheses on the basis of which forecasts of trends in marriage rates might be made; this is a subject of considerable interest inasmuch as future movements of natality depend in part on the number of marriages which will occur.

Seasonal Patterns of Demographic Phenomena

Cycles in demographic phenomena—births and deaths in particular—have been studied in terms of seasons and shorter intervals, such as the week. The results are interesting from a sociological standpoint. The findings on births suggest that some biological factor is responsible for the observed patterns. Bresciani-Turroni (1912) pointed out that the seasonal pattern of births varies from one country to another and changes in amplitude over time. Lasorsa (1934) studied seasonal variation in mortality by cause of death, relating its pattern to meteorological conditions and showing that they influence causes differentially.

L. Livi (1938) noted an increase in the number of births registered toward the end of the week and suggested that the phenomenon might reflect the fatigue of the pregnant women. Maroi (1954) found the number of births reported to be largest on Sundays and Mondays and smallest on Fridays and

the seventeenth of the month. This is apparently the consequence of the superstition which considers these days unlucky and induces parents to misreport the birth date. The weekly cycle of deaths coincides with that of births, and this variation, too, does not seem accidental.

Vajani (1955) arrived at another conclusion from data specially collected at the Maternity Hospital in Milan and analyzed in terms of an appropriate probability model. He noted that the observed data vary from the theoretical frequencies only to a degree attributable to chance, and he therefore concluded that the variation is void of any biological significance and is a product of psychological and social factors.

The seasonal variation in births has been recognized for more than a century, and various writers have put forth a number of hypotheses to explain it. Are the causes biological or simply environmental and social? Benini concluded that the same set of physical and psychological factors acts on both mortality and conceptions to produce their seasonal patterns. Gini expressed doubt of a biological explanation and attributed great importance to such social factors as occupation, civil and religious customs, migration, and variations in the number of marriages. These factors are thought to exert such an influence on births that it is impossible to decide whether seasonal variations in reproductive capacity have an independent effect.

In a profound analysis of seasonal variation Luzzatto-Fegiz (1925*a*) noted that the usual explanation of the seasonal pattern of conceptions relates it to presumed variations in the frequency of sexual intercourse. However, this author believed that there is seasonal variation in the procreative power of the male and in the ability of the female to become pregnant. He claimed that the initial maximum of births at the beginning of the year reflects the high fecundity of intercourse in the spring and that the autumn secondary maximum is a consequence of the first. This hypothesis seems to be supported by the similarity in seasonal pattern of legitimate and illegitimate births—which suggests a cause independent of marriage.

Meanwhile, Boldrini (1919*b*) focused attention on the family, asking whether there was seasonal variation in the procreative capacity of individual men and women. He concluded that variation in fecundity over the year cannot be excluded but that it would be a characteristic of the individual instead of the species.

Population Projections

Knowledge of the components of population change was first used in making population projections by Gini and De Finetti (1931); their projections covered the period 1921–61. The results are no longer of practical value, owing to the demographic influence of the war, but the methodological value of the work remains. Recently De Meo (1952, 1954) calculated the probable Italian population up to 2001; because of the plausibility of his hypotheses and the careful methods used, his projections are among the best available. Different hypotheses were employed in the calculations made by Somogyi (1954) and by the Istituto Centrale di Statistica. The latter (so far not published) are based on two series showing the most probable trend of natality and mortality instead of on the so-called optimistic and pessimistic hypothesis.

The projections of Gini and De Finetti were used by Uggé to evaluate the possible social effects of future population changes, particularly the size of military cohorts, the economically active population, and the pattern of consumption and earnings.

Miscellaneous Demographic Problems

A variety of other subjects have been studied by numerous Italian scholars. D'Addario (1934) introduced the concept of "agglomeration" and measured differential population agglomeration in the Italian departments. Gini and others (1933) conducted an extensive inquiry into the center of gravity and the median center of the Italian population, and they calculated the mean centers of numerous demographic, economic, and social phenomena. Uggé and others (1934) calculated the geographical co-ordinates of the Italian population.

Considerable attention was given to the problem of war and population in the years immediately following World War I. Writers such as Gini, Savorgnan, Maroi (1919, 1921), L. Livi, Boldrini, D'Addario, and L'Eltore discussed both the role of demographic factors in the etiology of conflicts and the demographic, eugenic, and dysgenic effects of wars.

An interesting aspect of the evolution of demographic aggregates was discussed by Luzzatto-Fegiz (1925*b*); he examined the processes of expansion, involution, and substitution in the various family lines of a group of immigrants and their descendants where the immigrants were biologically superior to the natives. He indicated that the gradual assimilation of such a group allows customs, institutions, and languages to remain relatively unchanged over long periods.

In the field of vital statistics delayed reports of births have interested Italian demographers ever since Benini called attention to the problem toward the end of the last century. Further contributions were made by Corridore and L. Livi (1929); the latter carried out a research project for the Istituto Centrale di Statistica to determine geographic variations in the frequency of delayed reports. Gini and others (1954) have recently presented new materials which confirm previous conclusions on the subject. Other writers dealing with the problem include D'Addario (1934), Barberi, Battara, and Maroi.

Fortunati (1934) studied variations in natality, mortality, and nuptiality as a function of size of community; his results were recently confirmed by Scardovi (1955).

The differential growth of the social classes as a consequence of differential natality and mortality has been investigated by Gini (1936), L. Livi, and Battara. Uggé (1933) investigated religious differentials in birth rates. An important recent study by Somogyi (1956) contains detailed information on length of pregnancy, birth weight according to length of pregnancy, sex, vitality, legitimacy of births, and multiple births.

Migratory movements, of particular importance in Italy's case, have attracted attention since the beginning of the century. Studies on the economic value of emigrants, assimilation, and eugenic effects of emigration have been contributed by Savorgnan, L. Livi, De Vergottini (1940), Gini, Mortara, Lasorsa, and Parenti and Pierfrancesco (1954).

Calculations of the money value of a man go back to Engel, who had some precursors—at least as far as the concept is concerned—in Italy. At the beginning of the nineteenth century Gioja considered the variation in economic value of individuals according to age and social status; he proposed that the state regulate its treatment of individuals according to their utility and that the punishment of a murderer be varied according to the economic value of the murdered individual. Following Engel's work, the problem was reconsidered at the end of the century by

Raseri and Pareto. The latter calculated the presumed economic loss to Italy resulting from emigration, a problem also investigated by Beneduce and Coletti.

Apart from the special question of emigration, investigations of the money value of a man were made by Mortara (1934 and other works), Pietra and Ferrari, Fua, and De Meo (1947, 1951). De Meo introduced the concept in the field of insurance. Finally, Boldrini's (1956) full discussion bears on the controversial question of whether to take interest into account in computing the money value of a man. He shows that the correct solution of this problem depends on the purposes for which the calculation is made.

CONCLUSION

This has been a brief overview of the evolution and accomplishments of demography in Italy, and only a small number of the significant contributions have been cited. However, the progress made in this field is evident. Later contributions often represent improvements on earlier and more elementary studies. The development of demography in Italy has become more rapid in recent decades as a result of the contributions of the statisticians, including those devoting themselves mainly to methodological problems and subjects other than population.

This great scientific development contrasts strongly with the slight importance given to the teaching of demography in Italy (see Boldrini, 1957). With few exceptions, demographic studies are not included in the student's curriculum or are incidental to his work in related fields.

Fortunati (1939) is correct in his contention that the flourishing of demographic studies in Italy was partly a consequence of the achievement of national unity and the organization of data collection at the national level.

The possibility of further progress in demography seems to be dependent on the availability of more detailed statistical data.

SELECTED BIBLIOGRAPHY

ADDARIO, R. D'. 1934. "L'agglomeramento della popolazione nei compartimenti italiani," *Atti del Congresso Internazionale per gli Studi sulla Popolazione* (Rome, 1931), VI, 647–70.

ALBERTI, S. 1934. *La mortalità antenatale.* Milan: Vita & Pensiero.

AMOROSO, L. 1929. "L'equazione differenziale del movimento della popolazione," *Rivista italiana di statistica,* I, 151–57.

BARBERI, B. 1954. "Some Preliminary Figures on the Joint Causes of Death in Italy," *Bulletin of the International Statistical Institute,* XXXIV, 65–77.

BELOCH, J. 1886. *Die Bevölkerung der griechisch-römischen Welt.* Leipzig: Duncker & Humbolt.

——. 1908. "La popolazione dell'Europa nell'antichità, nel medioevo, e nel rinascimento," *Biblioteca dell'economista,* Ser. V, XIX, 437–503.

BENINI, R. 1901. *Principi di demografia.* Florence: Barbèra.

BODIO, L. 1885. "Saggio di bibliografia statistica italiana," *Annali di statistica.* Rome: Tipografia Bencini.

BOLDRINI, M. 1919a. "I figli di guerra: Ricerche statistiche sulla fecondità dei soldati," *Giornale degli economisti,* LVIII, 293–302.

——. 1919b. "L'epoca di generazione: Contributi statistici alle conoscenze sulla fecondità umana," *Rivista di antropologia,* XXIII, 3–56.

——. 1925. *Sviluppo corporeo e predisposizioni morbose.* Milan: Vita & Pensiero.

——. 1927. *Biometrica: Problemi della vita, delle specie, e degli individui.* Padua: Cedam, Dottor Antonio Milani.

——. 1928a. "Sulla proporzione dei sessi nei concepimenti e nelle nascite," *Contributi del laboratorio di statistica dell'Università Cattolica del Sacro Cuore,* Ser. 1, Vol. III. Milan: Vita & Pensiero.

——. 1928b. "La diminuzione della mortalità e la selezione dei rischi assicura-tivi," *Giornale degli economisti e rivista di statistica.*

——. 1930. "Antropometri," *Trattato italiano d'igiene.* Turin: U.T.E.T.

——. 1931. *La fertilità dei biotipi: Saggio di demografia costituzionalistica.* Milan: Vita & Pensiero.

——. 1932. "Biotipi e classi sociali," *Rivista internazionale di scienze sociali,* Year XL, Ser. 3, III, fasc. 1, 3–28.

——. 1933. "Sulle nascite illegittime in Italia," *Politica sociale,* V, 910–22.

——. 1934. *Biometria e antropometria.* Milan: A. Giuffré.

——. 1936. "La proportion des sexes dans les conceptions humaines," *Revue de l'Institut International de Statistique.*

——. 1937. "La prima tavola italiana di mortalità," *Assicurazioni,* IV, Part 1, 631–46.

——. 1950. *O homen e a sociedade: Introdução ao estudo biometrico do homen.* Rio de Janeiro: Instituto Brasileiro de Geografia e Estatística.

——. 1956. *Demografia.* Rev. ed. Milan: A. Giuffré.

——. 1957. "The Teaching of Demography in Italy," in *The University Teaching of Social Sciences: Demography,* ed. D. V. Glass. Paris: UNESCO.

BRESCIANI-TURRONI, C. 1912. "Studi sulle variazioni stagionali di alcuni fenomeni demografici," *Annali del Seminario Giuridico dell'Università di Palermo,* Vol. II.

CASTIGLIONI, G. 1862. *Introduzione storica sopra i censimenti delle popolazioni italiane dei tempi antichi fino all'anno 1860.* Turin: Stamperia Reale.

CASTRO, D. DE. 1934. "I concepimenti antenuziali," *Atti del Congresso Internazionale per gli Studi sulla Popolazione* (Rome, 1931), VII, 687–736.

——. 1938. "Risultati di un'indagine preliminare sull'estensione dell'uso dei mezzi contraccettivi," *Atti della II Riunione del Comitato di Consulenza per gli Studi sulla Popolazione.* Florence: Casa Editrice Poligraphica Universitaria.

COLAJANNI, N. 1904. *Manuale di demografia.* Naples: L. Pierro.

COLOMBO, B. 1951. *La recente inversione*

nella tendenza della natalità. Padua: Casa Editrice Dottor Antonio Milani.

———. 1954. "Intorno all'estrapolazione della dinamica della nuzialità," *Statistica* (Bologna), XIV, 747–75.

———. 1955. *Sul rapporto dei sessi nelle nascite e nei concepimenti.* Padua: Casa Editrice Dottor Antonio Milani.

COMITATO ITALIANO PER LO STUDIO DEI PROBLEMI DELLA POPOLAZIONE. 1933–40. *Fonti archivistiche per lo studio dei problemi della popolazione fino al 1848.* 9 vols. Rome.

COSTANZO, A. 1936. *Costituzione e mortalità.* Milan: Vita & Pensiero.

———. 1939. "Pigmentazione degli occhi e dei capelli e selezione naturale," *Metron*, XIII, No. 4, 109–33.

———. 1948. "La statura degli italiani ventenni nati dal 1854 al 1920," *Annali di statistica*, Ser. 8, II, 63–123.

———. 1952. "Evoluzione dei caratteri fisici dei maschi casalesi ventenni nati dal 1791 al 1929," *Atti della IX Riunione Scientifica della Società Italiana di Statistica, Roma, 1950*, pp. 241–58.

———. 1957. "Il contributo degli italiani alla teoria della popolazione." Inaugural address, XVII Riunione Scientifica della Società Italiana di Statistica, Rome, 1957.

ELIA, E. D'. 1943. "Sulla misura della natalità residuale," *Rivista italiana di scienze economiche*, Vol. XV, 18 pp.

FEDERICI, N. 1939. *La riproduttività differenziale: Intensità, cause, conseguenze.* Rome: Istituto di Statistica, Facoltà di Scienze Statistiche, Demografiche, e Attuariali.

FORTUNATI, P. 1934. *Natalità, mortalità, e nuzioalità nei comuni del Regno in ordine di intensità di popolazione.* Padua: La Garangola.

———. 1939. "Teoria della popolazione e demografia," in *Contributi italiani al progresso della statistica.* Rome: Società Italiana per il Progresso delle Scienze, pp. 71–115.

GALVANI, L. 1933. "Sulla determinazione del centro di gravità e del centro mediano di una popolazione, con applicazioni alla popolazione italiana censita il 1 dicembre 1921," *Metron*, XI, No. 1, 17–48.

GINI, C. 1911. "Sui fattori demografici dell'evoluzione delle nazioni," *Rivista italiana di sociologia*, XV, 530–35.

———. 1912. *I fattori demografici dell'evoluzione delle nazione.* Turin: Bocca.

———. 1924. "Prime ricerche sulla fecondabilità della donna," *Atti del R. Istituto Veneto di Scienze Lettere e Arti*, LXXXIII, Part 2, 315–44.

———. 1925. "Nuove ricerche sulla fecondabilità della donna," *Atti del R. Istituto Veneto di Scienze Lettere e Arti*, LXXXIV, Part 2, 269–308.

———. 1930a. "The Cyclical Rise and Fall of Population," in *Population.* By C. GINI *et al.* (Harris Foundation Lectures, 1929). Chicago: University of Chicago Press.

———. 1930b. *Nascita, evoluzione, e morte delle nazioni.* Rome: Libreria del Littorio.

———. 1931. *Le basi scientifiche della politica della popolazione.* Catania: Studio Editoriale Moderno.

———. 1936. "Real and Apparent Exceptions to the Uniformity of a Lower Natural Increase of the Upper Classes," *Rural Sociology*, I, 257–80.

———. 1940. "Les facteurs de la décroissance de la natalité à l'époque contemporaine," in *Actas, memórias communicações do congresso nacional de ciencias da população.* Lisbon: Commissão Executiva dos Centenarios Congresso do Mundo Português.

———, and FINETTI, B. DE. 1931. "Calcoli sullo sviluppo futuro della popolazione italiana," *Annali di statistica*, Ser. 6, Vol. X.

———, and GALVANI, L. 1931. "Tavole di mortalità della popolazione italiana," *Annali di statistica*, Ser. 6, Vol. VIII.

———, *et al.* 1933. "Sui centri della popolazione e sulle loro applicazioni," *Metron*, XI, No. 2, 3–102.

———, *et al.* 1954. "Sulla diffusione del ritardo nella registrazione delle nascite avvenute negli ultimi giorni dell'anno," *Bulletin of the International Statistical Institute*, XXXIV, 85–121.

GOLZIO, S., and BATTARA, P. 1934. "Indagini sulla fecondità dei matrimoni contratti con rito civile," *Economia*, XII, 301–23.

LASORSA, G. 1934. "Variazioni stagionali della mortalità secondo gruppi di cause di morte," *Atti del Congresso Internazionale per gli Studi sulla Popolazione* (Rome, 1931), VII, 549–84.

———. 1952. *Demografia.* Rev. ed. Bari: Cacucci.

———. 1954. "Considerazioni sulla fecondità e sui saggi di riproduzione," *Proceedings of the World Population Conference, 1954,* IV, 367–82.

LASTRI, M. 1775. *Ricerche sull'antica e moderna popolazione della città di Firenze per mezzo dei Registri del Battistero di San Giovanni, dal 1451 al 1774.* Florence: Gaetano Cambiagi, Stampatore Granducale.

LENTI, L. 1935. "La fecondità legittima della donna italiana secondo l'età e l'ordine di generazione," *Giornale degli economisti,* LXXV, 809–46.

———. 1937. "La fecondità legittima milanese secondo l'età di entrambi i genitori," *Giornale degli economisti,* LXXVII, 165–72.

———. 1939. "Osservazioni sulle tavole di fecondità," *Giornale degli economisti e annali di economia,* N.S. I, 28–50.

———. 1940. "Calcolo di tavole di fecondità matrimoniale in funzione della durata del matrimonio, per l'Italia, in base all'esperienze 1931 e 1937," *Atti della IV Riunione della Società Italiana di Demografia e Statistica* (Rome, May, 1939), pp. 54–62.

LIVI, L. 1929. "Sulle false dichiarazioni delle date di nascita per i nati alla fine dell'anno e rettifica della distribuzione mensile delle nascite nel triennio 1923–25," *Annali di statistica,* Ser. 6, III, 41–109.

———. 1938. "La fluttuazione settimanale delle nascite," *Economia,* XXI, 371–78.

———. 1940. *Trattato di demografia: Le leggi naturali della popolazione.* Padua: Casa Editrice Dottor Antonio Milani.

———. 1941. *Trattato di demografia: I fattori biodemografici nell'ordinamento sociale.* Padua: Casa Editrice Dottor Antonio Milani.

LIVI, R. 1896, 1905. *Anthropométria militaire.* Rome: Presso il Giornale Medico del R. Esercito.

LUZZATTO-FEGIZ, P. 1925a. "Le variazioni stagionali della natalità," *Metron,* V, No. 4, 53–129.

———. 1925b. "I cognomi di S. Gimignano," *ibid.,* No. 2, pp. 115–53.

———. 1951. *Statistica demografica ed economica.* 2d ed. Milan: Edizioni di Comunità.

MAROI, L. 1919. *I fattori demografici del conflitto europeo.* Rome: Athenaeum.

———. 1921. "La guerra e la popolazione (rassegna di demografia)," *Metron,* I, No. 2, 156–211.

———. 1940. "Nuovi elementi sulla fecondità della città di Roma," *Atti della IV Riunione della Società Italiana di Demografia e Statistica* (Rome, 1939), pp. 63–73.

———. 1954. "La periodicità giornaliera dei nati e dei morti in Italia," *Statistica,* XIV, 412–23.

MEO, G. DE. 1940. "Sulle nascite dei primogeniti in Italia," *Metron,* XIV, No. 1, 79–157.

———. 1947. "Capacità di assorbimento del mercato per le assicurazioni sulla vita in Italia," *Annali dell'Istituto Univ. Navale* (Naples), Vol. XIV.

———. 1951. *Su una forma di assicurazione vita adatta alle caratteristiche del mercato italiano.* Naples: Stabilimento Tipografico G. Genovese.

———. 1952. *Popolazione e forze di lavoro: Prospettive demografiche fino al 2000 per l'Italia Meridionale, Sicilia, Sardegna, Mezzogiorno, e Italia.* Rome: Svimez.

———. 1954. *De quelques critères pour les prévisions du développement futur des populations.* Rome: Svimez.

MOLINARI, A. 1933. "Un'indagine sulle motivazioni della diminuzione delle nascite," *Atti del Congresso Internazionale per gli Studi sulla Popolazione* (Rome, 1931), viii, 473–516.

MORSELLI, E. 1880. *Critica e riforma del metodo in antropologia, fondate sulle leggi statistiche e biologiche dei valori seriali e sull'esperimento.* Rome: Eredi Botta.

MORTARA, G. 1908. "Le popolazioni delle grandi città italiane al principio del secolo ventesimo," *Biblioteca dell'economista,* Ser. 5, XIX, 507–915.

———. 1909. "Tavole di sopravvivenza e

delle variazioni di stato civile e tavola di natalità legittima per la popolazione femminile del comune di Milano (1899–1902)," *Atti del R. Istituto d'Incoraggiamento di Napoli,* Ser. 6, Vol. V.

———. 1914. "Tavole di mortalità, secondo le cause di morte, per la popolazione italiana (1901–1910)," *Annali di statistica,* Ser. 5, VII, 7–82.

———. 1934. "Costo e rendimento economico dell'uomo," *Atti dell'Istituto Nazionale delle Assicurazioni,* VI, 130–69.

PARENTI, G. 1938. "Ancora su due recenti tavole di nuzialità della popolazione italiana," *Giornale degli economisti e rivista di statistica,* LXXVIII, 570–78.

———. 1939. "Su un calcolo approssimato del saggio netto di riproduttività di una popolazione," *Atti della III Riunione della Società Italiana di Demografia e Statistica* (Bologna, 1938), pp. 145–54.

———, and PIERFRANCESCO, B. 1954. "Effetti dell'emigrazione sull'accrescimento e sulla struttura della popolazione totale e in età produttiva (con riferimento ai paesi europei di emigrazione)," *Proceedings of the World Population Conference, 1954,* II, 167–78.

PEROZZO, LUIGI. 1883. "Nuove applicazioni del calcolo delle probabilità allo studio dei fenomeni statistici e distribuzione dei matrimoni secondo l'età degli sposi," *Annali di statistica,* Ser. 3, V, 175–203.

———. 1885. "Sulla classificazione per età della popolazione del Regno secondo il censimento 31 dicembre 1881," *ibid.,* XIV, 85–184.

POMPILJ, GIUSEPPE. 1954. *Sull'omogamia uniforme," Atti della XI e XII Riunione Scientifica della Società Italiana di Statistica* (Roma, 1951), pp. 137–60.

RENZI, S. DE. 1838. *Topografia e statistica medica per la città di Napoli e del Regno.* Naples: dalla Tipografia del Filiatre Sebezio.

SAVORGNAN, FRANCO. 1936. *Corso di demografia.* Pisa: Nistri-Lischi.

———. 1942. *La fecondità dell'aristocrazia.* Pisa: Nistri-Lischi.

———. 1955. "La mascolinità dei concepimenti," *Rivista italiana di economia, demografia, e statistica,* IX, 1–6.

SCARDOVI, ITALO. 1955. "Ricerche speri-

mentali intorno alle relazioni tra popolosità e movimento naturale della popolazione," *Statistica* (Bologna), XV, 187–235.

SOMOGYI, S. 1933. "Sui fattori biologici della natalità," *Economia,* XI, No. 4, 259–81.

———. 1937. "Tavole di nuzialità e di vedovanza per la popolazione italiana, 1930–32," *Annali di statistica,* Ser. 7, I, 199–289.

———. 1954. "Perspectives démographiques pour l'Italie jusqu'en 1971," in *Études européennes de population.* Paris: Institut International d'Études Démographiques.

———. 1956. "Nuovi contributi alla conoscenza dei fenomeni demografici italiani," *Statistica* (Bologna), XVI, 481–548.

UGGÉ, A. 1928. "Confronti internazionali fra la mortalità per singole cause secondo il metodo dei coefficienti tipo," *Contributi del laboratorio di statistica dell'Università Cattolica del Sacro Cuore,* Ser. 1, Vol. III. Milan: Vita & Pensiero.

———. 1933. "Natalità differenziale secondo la religione, e fattori demografici dello sviluppo numerico dei gruppi confessionali," *Atti del Congresso Internazionale per gli Studi sulla Popolazione* (Rome, 1931), VIII, 299–336.

———. 1934. "Di alcuni riflessi economici e sociali del futuro sviluppo della popolazione italiana," *ibid.,* VII, 89–102.

———, GIGLIO, F., and MARTINOTTI, P. 1934. "Le coordinate geografiche della popolazione italiana," *Contributi del laboratorio di statistica dell'Università Cattolica del Sacro Cuore,* Ser. 8, Vol. VII. Milan: Vita & Pensiero.

VAJANI, L. 1955. "Indagine sulla distribuzione dei nati nei diversi giorni della settimana," *Giornale degli economisti,* XIV, 326–48.

VERGOTTINI, M. DE. 1936. "Produttività e prolificità lorda e netta della donna italiana (1931)," *Economia,* N. S. XVIII, No. 3, 144–68.

———. 1937a. "Sulla fecondità della donna italiana," *Annali di statistica,* Ser. 7, I, 321–55.

———. 1937b. "Tavola di fecondità della

donna italiana, secondo l'età e il numero dei figli avuti," *Giornale degli economisti e rivista di statistica,* LXXVII, 89–107.

VERGOTTINI, M. DE. 1939. "Su alcune misure della fecondità matrimoniale," *Atti della III Riunione della Società Italiana di Demografia e Statistica* (Bologna, November, 1938). Florence.

———. 1940. "Saggio di demografia italiana all'estero," *Annali di statistica,* Ser. 7, VI, 49–296.

———. 1955. "Sugli indici di attrazione matrimoniale," *Studi in onore di G. Pietra,* pp. 305–9. Cappelli: Rocca S. Casciano.

VIANELLI, S. 1935. "Evoluzione economica e demografica negli schemi delle curve logistiche," *Rivista italiana di scienze economiche,* VII, 383–444.

———. 1939. "Sulla fecondità legittima e illegittima nel Comune di Bologna," *Atti della III Riunione della Società Italiana di Demografia e Statistica* (Florence, 1938).

———. 1940. "La distribuzione dei morti nelle diverse ore del giorno alla luce di un nuovo schema dinamico," *Atti della IV Riunione della Società Italiana di Demografia e Statistica* (Rome, 1939), pp. 82–96.

VINCI, F. 1929. "La logica della curva logistica," *Rivista italiana di statistica,* I, 386–92.

———. 1930. "Ancora sulla curva logistica," *ibid.,* II, 105–6.

———. 1937. *Manuale di statistica,* Vol. II. Bologna: Zanichelli.

VOLTERRA, V. 1926. "Variazioni e fluttuazioni del numero d'individui in specie animali conviventi," in *Memorie della R. Accademia Nazionale dei Lincei, classe di scienze fisiche, matematiche, e naturali,* Ser. 6, II, fasc. 3, 31–113.

———. 1931. *Leçons sur le théorie mathématique de la lutte pour la vie.* Paris: Gauthier-Villars.

ZINGALI, G. 1930. "Demografia," in *Trattato italiano d'igiene.* Turin: U.T.E.T.

11. Demographic Studies in Brazil

GIORGIO MORTARA

GIORGIO MORTARA

EMERGENCE OF SCIENTIFIC STUDIES OF POPULATION

The development of scientific research in the field of demography has been very slow in Brazil. This lag, on the whole common to Latin-American countries, has had various causes. On the one hand, the great territorial expanse of these countries and the dispersion of their inhabitants, which are reflected in the dimensions of religious and administrative units (parishes, municipalities) posed serious difficulties to the enumeration of the population and the registration of births, deaths, and migration. Either there were no demographic statistics or they were so incomplete that they could not provide usable data for the study of populations, except for a few large cities.

On the other hand, during the initial phase of independent political and social organization and the free economic evolution of these countries, the minds most inclined to scientific research were attracted to medical and technical studies, which offered them numerous possibilities for application and the prospects of immediate advantages for themselves and the societies in the midst of which they were to work. And in the fields of science dealing with population, investigations of the anthropological and psychological characteristics of these peoples, of diverse and mingled origins, and of the contributions of different ethnic or national groups to the development of local civilizations appeared much more interesting than specifically demographic investigations.

Also, one must remember that the unjust contempt for demography in the organization of university programs in Brazil hindered the training of scientists specializing in population research. The needs of government contributed much more than the aspirations of science in bringing about the first attempts at understanding and interpreting facts about the population.

EARLY DEVELOPMENT OF DEMOGRAPHIC RESEARCH

Until 1870 there existed rather vague ideas about the number of inhabitants of Brazil, as is shown by the fine report of J. N. De Souza e Silva (1870), *Investigações sobre os recenseamentos da população geral do Imperio,* compiled at that time. This work brings together and compares the estimates of the population of each province and of the whole country made by administrative agencies and scientists during the near century-long period, 1779–1870. There are almost unbelievable differences between the estimates for dates very near to one another; for example, the province of Pará. was estimated to have 380,000 inhabitants in 1868 and 140,-000 in 1870, while the census of 1872 enumerated 275,000.

In contrast to some previous estimates which—without sufficient justification—had been called "censuses," the inquiry of 1872 was a true census, conducted in a systematic and uniform manner, by parishes and municipalities, over the entire territory of the empire. The census count for the nation as a whole, according to which Brazil had about ten million inhabitants, did not differ much from the last previous estimates, but in the data by provinces the differences were at times very large. The province of Rio de Janeiro, which was estimated to have 1,100,000 inhabitants in 1868, had only 783,000 in 1872; on the other hand, Minas Gerais, the population of which had been estimated at 1,500,000, had 2,040,000. In the municipality of the capital barely 275,000 inhabitants were enumerated in 1872, though its population had been estimated at 510,000 in 1869.

The census of 1872 gave, for the first time, reliable information on the number and the territorial distribution of the population and also on some aspects of its composition, such as sex, the division into free and slave, and nationality. Other information, for example that on age, was very inaccurate: there appeared to be only 150,000 infants under one, against an average of 233,000 in each year of age from five to ten years; there appeared to be over 13,000 centenarians, etc. But the data of this census, which, through a prompt critical analysis, an adequate elaboration, and a wise interpretation, could have furnished valuable components for the scientific study of the demography of Brazil, were used only sporadically for this purpose.

In the second year of the republic, in 1890, a new census was carried out, and another was executed in the final year of the nineteenth century. Neither the execution of these inquiries nor the processing of their data was satisfactory; despite their gaps and errors, however, the data obtained have been used profitably for the study of the demography of the country in the retrospective investigations carried out during the last five years.

Information on the organization and the results of the censuses of 1890 and 1900 was given in the first volume (*Introduction*) of the publication devoted to the presentation of information obtained by the succeeding census, which took place in 1920. It was organized in a remarkably modern way by J. L. S. Bulhões Carvalho, who also directed the publication of the results with an ample commentary; this publication represents the first attempt at a systematic presentation of the different aspects of the population structure of Brazil. Some elements of population dynamics also are considered there: notably, the life tables calculated for the aggregate of the federal capital and thirteen state capitals, and for the federal capital separately, which were the first analyses of this type concerning the Brazilian population.

The data resulting from the 1920 census count were, in several cases, more or less arbitrarily corrected before publication, with the intent of making up supposed omissions. Unfortunately, these corrections often were excessive, and this, along with the frequent failure of the critical sense in the commentaries, diminished the value of a part of the information available in the numerous volumes in which the results of the census have been set forth (Diretoria Geral de Estatística, 1922–30).

Again it was Bulhões Carvalho who gave Brazil the first summary of demographic statistics and demography in his work *Estatística, método e aplicação* (1933), in which he tried to establish the position of his country in the international demographic framework. Despite some deficiencies in method and a few oversimplified interpretations, one can agree that this work marked the beginning of scientific research in the field of demography in Brazil.

Other scientists, younger and better prepared, went on to continue and develop the work of this pioneer. One can recall the studies of J. Kingston on the growth of the population of Brazil after 1920 (these studies led to a substantial reduction in current estimates, which had been vitiated by the overstatements of the census of 1920); the works of L. Galvani and his followers on some aspects of the demography of the state of São Paulo; the methodological studies of A. Pagano; J. P. Fontenelle's abstract on biometry (1934) and his report on public health in the Federal District (1937); and some investigations of public health statistics by E. Rangel, L. N. Briggs (1933), A. Scorzelli, Jr., and L. de Freitas Filho.

Among the scientific works of the period before 1940 in the fields of social science most closely related to demography, it is fitting to recall the investigations of F. J. Oliveira Vianna on the formation and development of the Brazilian people, rich in facts and observations, although sometimes dominated by racial prejudices; the fundamental works of G. Freyre on the social evolution of Brazil, revised and completed later by other investigations; the anthropological studies of Roquette Pinto, and those pursued and developed later by A. Ramos; and R. Simonsen's contributions to the analysis of economic factors in internal migration.

The persevering and enlightened action of M. A. Teixeira de Freitas resulted, in 1936, in the formation of the Instituto Brasileiro de Geografia e Estatística (IBGE), in which the federal government acts in co-operation with the governments of the states and local administrations for the organization of geographical and statistical services and inquiries. Its creation aroused some hope for progress in the collection and publication of demographic statistics.

With regard to the dynamics of population, these hopes have been completely disillusioned. The civil registration statistics on marriages, births, and deaths for the greatest part of the country are unusable even today because of their enormous gaps, which can only be filled to a minor degree by recourse to ecclesiastical statistics, also incomplete and relating only to a part (in general, preponderant) of the population. There are no national statistics of internal migrations; there are no municipal registers of population. In this field, the institute has not been able to operate directly because the registration services depend upon local authorities. But with respect to the condition of the population, the institute, acting directly through one of its agencies, the Serviço Nacional de Recenseamento, has succeeded in collecting a substantial volume of information, which has clarified many aspects of Brazilian demography.

RESEARCH IN CONNECTION WITH THE 1940 CENSUS

The preparation and execution of the census of 1940, begun in 1938, gave a decisive impetus to demographic studies in Brazil. Under the direction of Professor J. Carneiro Felippe, the distinguished chemist and mathematician who sacrificed his life for the success of the great enterprise, this inquiry was organized according to the best criteria suggested by demographic science and technique, with an inflexible rigor, seeking to avoid all manipulation of original information and numerical results.

The period of preparation and collection in the census operation was used profitably to submit the data as a whole and some series of particular data from previous censuses to a critical examination, with the following goals: to determine, within the limits of possibility, the changes in the population of Brazil resulting from natural increase and migration, from 1840 on; to establish the population composition by sex and age; to reconstruct the numbers of births and deaths; and to measure the frequency of these phenomena. By patient work and the application of partly original methods, not only approximate values of birth and death rates for this century-long period, but also life tables for the periods 1870–90 and 1890–1920 and a fertility table for females for a period immediately before the census of 1920 could be calculated. These tables, in turn, furnished the data for the calculation of the rates of Boeckh and Lotka (Mortara, 1940–42, 1944). In the correction of the age composition and calculation of death rates, use was made of the life tables for large cities, which Bulhões Carvalho calculated after subjecting them to some corrections and adjustments (Mortara, 1940–42, No. 4).

The number of births was calculated from the number of infants reported by each census plus the number of deaths occurring before the census to children of the same cohort (estimated by cautious assumptions about infant mortality). After the birth rate for the last years before the census was calculated, the values of the rates over the century-long period could be estimated by interpolation or extrapolation.

The number of deaths in the native population of Brazil was calculated by comparing two successive censuses for the adult ages and by comparing the observed number of survivors at the date of each census with the estimated number of live births occurring after the date of the preceding census for the ages of infancy and adolescence (Mortara, 1940–42, No. 7).

The age distributions of the population and of deaths were corrected by adjustments designed to eliminate the effects of numerous and serious errors of age-clustering and overstating or understating age which had been discovered in the declarations of age of the living and the deceased (Mortara, 1940–42, Nos. 3, 5). The calculation of death rates by age, carried out after these adjustments, also permitted the estimation of the number of deaths of

non-natives of Brazil, which completed the calculation of deaths. The general death rates determined for the periods included between two successive censuses served as bases for the approximate reconstruction of the trend in the death rate over the century-long period (Mortara, 1940–42, No. 6).

The variation of fertility by age of mother was estimated by analogy from the calculated number of births, the age distribution of females, and the trend in fertility in other populations with high natality (Mortara, 1940–42, No. 8).

The provisional results of the census of 1940, known since 1941, by giving the number of inhabitants with an accuracy that was judged satisfactory, confirmed the existence—the possibility of which already had been foreseen in previous studies—of an overestimation on the order of 10 per cent for the total population of Brazil in the published data of the census of 1920 (Laboratório do Conselho Nacional de Estatística, 1948–57a, No. 13, sec. 3). In many cases, corrections already had been calculated in previous studies to arrive at various demographic estimates consistent with similar corrections of the census of 1920; in other cases, these estimates were revised according to the corrected base; in still other cases, calculations which could not have been made previously because of anomalies in the published data of the census of 1920 could be made with some assurance.

Without doubt, the relative magnitude of the errors of these data varies a great deal from state to state, and probably, at times, even the direction of the errors varies from municipality to municipality. Attempts have been made to estimate these errors for some states where they evidently are more serious (Laboratório do Conselho Nacional de Estatística, 1948–57a, No. 13, secs. 6, 7), but it has not been possible to extend this laborious research to all the states, as would have been desirable. Nevertheless, so far as method is concerned, the studies cited above indicate the means which must be employed to attain this goal.

Insofar as the tabulation produced definitive results from the census of 1940, these results were submitted to a critical examination by the Technical Section of the Census Service, established in 1942 under the direction of Professor G. Mortara. Many of the analyses that were carried out by municipalities, by units of the Federation (states, federal territories, Federal District), and for the country as a whole have been presented in a special series of studies (Serviço Nacional de Recenseamento de 1940, 1950–52), which were continued later by the Laboratório do Conselho Nacional de Estatística (1950–52). These studies sought to determine the degree of precision of the data examined, to discover and possibly correct errors of enumeration and of classification, and to make evident—with the aid of international and retrospective comparisons—the real characteristics (occasionally rather different from apparent characteristics) of the structure and trends of the populations of Brazil. An attempt also was made to determine the characteristics of the population distribution, either with reference to area (density), or according to the type of residence (urban agglomerations, rural and scattered habitations).

Among the individual characteristics of populations of Brazil studied in the "Análises," besides sex and age, there can be mentioned color (in the coding of the census, the categories of white, brown, black, and yellow were distinguished), marital status, nationality, place of birth (unit of the Federation or foreign country), the time of settling in Brazil (for the immigrants), place of birth of parents (for native

Brazilians), economic activity (principal and supplementary occupation or non-occupational status), education, knowledge of the Portuguese language, language spoken at home, religion, and ownership of real estate. All these characteristics were studied not only for the population as a whole but also for each sex and age group; economic activity also was studied in relation to color and nationality, and other characteristics were studied in detailed cross-classifications (for example, color, sex, age, literacy). Critical analysis of the census data, which preceded all attempts at interpretation and commentary, often revealed inaccuracies which had to be corrected whenever possible. The data on age, color, and some infirmities (the blind, deaf-mutes), especially, had to be subjected to a minute and rigorous critical examination so that they would provide a sufficiently realistic picture rather than reflect the numerous errors and ambiguities of the original declarations (Mortara, 1954c; Laboratório do Conselho Nacional de Estatística, 1948–57a, Nos. 2, 3, 11).

One part of the works published in a mimeographed edition, either in the series of "Análises" or in the two other series which will be mentioned below, appeared later in a definitive printed edition, revised and co-ordinated, in the series "Estudos de estatística teórica e aplicada," sections "Série demográfica" and "Série cultural" (Laboratório do Conselho Nacional de Estatística, 1948–57a, 1948–57b).

Insofar as the results of the census of 1940 were known, the Technical Section did its part not only to establish the composition and distribution of the population but also to continue and extend research on its dynamics. The greater part of the work on this subject has been issued in two series, the first of which (Serviço Nacional de Recenseamento de 1940, 1942–48b) had as its objective the applications of the census to the reconstruction of the population dynamics, and the second (Serviço Nacional de Recenseamento de 1940, 1944–46) sought to study mortality by the combined use of data on deaths, taken from the vital statistics for some areas of almost complete registration, and data on the living, obtained from the census.

In the series "Aplicações," the estimates of the number of births and the natality rate based on the census (Laboratório do Conselho Nacional de Estatística, 1948–57a, No. 4) were extended to the years around 1940; these calculations were useful in the correction of the infant mortality rates for some areas where death registration was sufficiently complete, while birth registration was not. With the data from the inquiry on fertility included in the census of 1940 (where two questions were asked of adults on the number of children ever born: born alive and stillborn), cumulative rates of fertility and of female prolificacy by age groups could be calculated. Afterward, by differencing the cumulative curve of fertility constructed with the aid of these rates, the simple curve of fertility by age was obtained. By an analogous procedure, the frequency of first-order births and the proportion of fertile women also could be measured separately (Laboratório do Conselho Nacional de Estatística, 1948–57a, No. 5).

By combining the components of the fertility table with those of the life table described previously, the rates of Boeckh and Lotka were calculated again (Laboratório do Conselho Nacional de Estatística, 1948–57a, No. 5, sec. 1). The results of this calculation were of the same order of magnitude as those that had been obtained by a calculation, in part conjectural, for the period around 1920.

The data of the inquiry on fertility also were used fully in the series "Análises" cited above, in which the cumulative rates of fertility and female prolificacy were calculated for the four major color groups, for the native population of Brazil, for the principal foreign-born groups, for the various classes of marital status, and for the different groups according to age at first birth, in which the distribution of births according to birth order also was studied (Laboratório do Conselho Nacional de Estatística, 1948–57a, Nos. 5, 6, 9, 10).

It is appropriate to mention also the study on nuptiality, measured according to the variation by age of the proportion of unmarried females indicated by the census, and the subsequent construction of a table of female nuptiality, which appeared in the series "Aplicações" (see Mortara, 1949). Studies based on the census on the frequency, by age, of new cases of blindness from illnesses or accidents permitted the calculation of the incidence of that infirmity in a cohort (Laboratório do Conselho Nacional de Estatística, 1948–57a, No. 2, secs. 4, 5).

The possibilities and limitations of the procedure of differencing cumulative frequency curves, employed in the work on fertility, nuptiality, and blindness, have been discussed in a special monograph (Mortara, 1948) with the aim of encouraging its use and avoiding its misuse.

Again in the series "Aplicações," the results of the census of 1940 are compared systematically with those of previous censuses, with the aim of correcting and completing the calculations which had been made before on the development of the population of Brazil (Laboratório do Conselho Nacional de Estatística, 1948–57a, No. 13, secs. 4, 5). After the rates of population growth of various units between 1890 and 1940 were determined, these rates were used for a projection of the development of these populations between 1940 and 1950 (Laboratório do

Conselho Nacional de Estatística, 1948–57a, No. 7).

Another group of studies in the series "Aplicações" was devoted to the reconstruction of the patterns of internal migration, according to census data of place of birth in combination with place of residence for the native population of Brazil. With these data, the distribution of natives of each unit of the Federation residing in Brazil could be determined according to the unit in which they were residing, as well as the distribution of natives of Brazil residing in each unit, according to the unit in which they were born. For each unit, the absolute and relative number of natives presently residing in another unit, and that of non-natives presently residing in it were known; thus the balance of migratory movements could be established between each unit and each of the others and could give an idea of the importance of different currents of internal migration (Laboratório do Conselho Nacional de Estatística, 1948–57a, No. 1). Later, a theoretical study, with some examples of application (Mortara, 1955a), was designed to show that these currents could be reconstructed approximately with the aid of census data if the age-specific mortality rates of in-migrants and out-migrants were known.

In the "Estudos sôbre a mortalidade," general death rates, cause-specific mortality rates, infant mortality rates, and age-sex-specific mortality rates all were calculated, and life tables by sex (1939–41) also were constructed for several large cities and for one entire state, that of São Paulo, after some estimates were made and some errors corrected in the original statistics (Serviço Nacional de Recenseamento de 1940, 1945, 1947; Laboratório do Conselho Nacional de Estatística, 1948–57a, No. 18, secs. 4, 6). For the two principal cities, Rio de Janeiro and

São Paulo, the mortality rates by sex, age, and cause of death, combined, were calculated, thus making it possible to construct life tables in which deaths were classified according to their causes (Serviço Nacional de Recenseamento de 1940, 1945, secs. 9–12).

Several life tables were adjusted, either according to an original formula or following the Gompertz-Makeham formula (Serviço Nacional de Recenseamento de 1940, 1945, secs. 2, 3, 6, 7, 8; Laboratório do Conselho Nacional de Estatística, 1948–57a, No. 18, secs. 3, 5, 8, 9).

The methods and results of research on the demography of Brazil undertaken by the Technical Section of the 1940 Census Service during the period 1939–48 have been presented in several reports at international conferences (Mortara, 1950, 1954a), and an English translation of a few selected studies has been published under the auspices of the Population Division of the United Nations (Mortara, 1949).

RESEARCH IN CONNECTION WITH
THE 1950 CENSUS

When the 1940 Census Service was dissolved at the end of 1948, its Technical Section was reconstructed as the Laboratório do Conselho Nacional de Estatística, which continued studies on the demography of Brazil without interruption. Some new aspects of the demography of the country were examined; the frequency of births according to economic and social level was studied with the aid of cumulative rates of fertility calculated from the 1940 census data, for males classified by age, working status, and occupation (Laboratório do Conselho Nacional de Estatística, 1948–57a, No. 10, sec. 5, No. 15, sec. 1).

Besides the series of complementary studies of the "Análises" and the "Aplicações," designed for the continuation of research based on the census of 1940, the laboratory has put out a new series of "Estudos demográficos" in a mimeographed edition (Laboratório do Conselho Nacional de Estatística, 1951–57), one part of which was published in a definitive edition in the "Série demográfica" and "Série cultural" already cited (Laboratório do Conselho Nacional de Estatística, 1948–57a, 1948–57b). This new series was devoted principally to analyses and applications of the results of the census of 1950, which was executed with competence and accuracy under the direction of M. Tulo Hostílio Montenegro, who, since 1945, had examined and analyzed comparatively the census methods employed in the different countries of the Americas.

The studies on the last census have been conducted, in general, according to the same criteria and procedures that were used in previous studies cited above. It is necessary, however, to note that in the tabulation of the census of 1950 urban and rural populations were distinguished in the classifications according to some individual characteristics (sex, age, education, fertility). Thus it was possible to carry out some investigations that the preceding census (which had given only the classification of urban and rural populations by sex) had not permitted. It was now possible to follow the progress of urbanization (Laboratório do Conselho Nacional de Estatística, 1948–57a, No. 17, secs. 2–4); to study fertility by the relation between number of children and number of females of reproductive age in urban, suburban, and rural populations of each unit (Laboratório do Conselho Nacional de Estatística, 1948–57a, No. 16, sec. 2); to analyze comparatively the composition by sex and age of these categories of the population (Laboratório do Conselho Nacional de Estatística, 1948–57a, No. 17, sec. 1); to determine, for each of the

three categories, the degree of literacy according to sex and age, by units, as a whole, by municipalities, and even by districts, subdivisions of municipalities (Laboratório do Conselho Nacional de Estatística, 1948–57b, Nos. 3–8; 1948–57a, No. 17, sec. 5).

Research on the currents of internal migration, worked out with the aid of data from the census of 1950, has permitted an estimate of the importance of the migratory movements which occurred in the interval between the last two censuses and the calculation of the natural increase and the actual increase of urban, suburban, and rural populations. These studies have made evident the amplitude of the currents of migration directed from rural areas toward the cities (Laboratório do Conselho Nacional de Estatística, 1948–57a, No. 17, secs. 3, 4).

By making use of data from two reliable censuses, executed at a ten-year interval, the Laboratório also has been able to calculate—by a comparison of the data of these censuses and with the aid of estimates of natality and of infant mortality—the rates of general and age-sex-specific mortality for the native population of Brazil and for the native populations of the states of greatest demographic importance. Life tables for these populations also have been constructed (Laboratório do Conselho Nacional de Estatística, 1948–57a, No. 19, secs. 4–6).

By combining the vital statistics data of the population with those of the census of 1950, the Laboratório has calculated new life tables by sex (1949–51) for the two large cities of Rio de Janeiro and São Paulo, and the Department of Statistics of the State of São Paulo has made the calculation for the whole of the state (Laboratório do Conselho Nacional de Estatística, 1948–57a, No. 18, secs. 2, 3, No. 19, secs. 1, 2, No. 20). The elaboration of a fertility table, carried out by the Laboratório, also permitted the determination of the coefficients of Boeckh and Lotka for the same state (Mortara, 1955*b*).

The calculations of birth rates have been redone with the results of the census of 1950, which made possible estimates for all the units and for all the municipalities of some states (Laboratório do Conselho Nacional de Estatística, 1951–57, No. 118 and 1948–57*a*, No. 16, secs. 3, 5).

In taking account of the results of the 1950 census, the previous estimates of the development of the population of Brazil and of various units were reviewed, and projections also were prepared on the future trend of that development without, however, overlooking the contingent nature of such projections. Attempts have been made to project the development of the population of Brazil in the course of the second half of the twentieth century and that of the populations of the units until 1960 (Laboratório do Conselho Nacional de Estatística, 1951–57, Nos. 95, 129, 131).

The greater part of the work of the Technical Section and of the Laboratório is made up of critical essays, correction, exposition, and interpretation of demographic statistics. They have sought especially to offer the most precise possible measurement of population phenomena, in order to prepare the indispensable basic information for the scientific study of these phenomena, directed toward research on their causes and consequences. This research has been barely sketched in the works cited; nevertheless, it has not been neglected.

The results of particular investigations have been brought together and co-ordinated in order to obtain a picture of the population of Brazil in its entirety, its distribution, its structure, and its evolution (see, for example, Mortara, 1954*b*; Laboratório do Con-

selho Nacional de Estatística, 1951–57, No. 120). All of one series of reports presented at the World Congress of Population at Rome in 1954, drawn up for the most part by the staff of the Instituto Brasileiro de Geografia e Estatística, had as its objective the description and co-ordinated analysis of the demographic characteristics of Brazil (see Alves, 1954; Da Rocha, 1954; De Andrade, 1954; De Carvalho, 1954; Kingston, 1954; Lyra Madeira, 1954; and Thimóteo de Barros, 1954).

On some special aspects of population phenomena, there is research that goes beyond a simple interpretative description. Examples that can be mentioned are the studies on population composition by sex, age, and marital status; on fertility by marital status (Laboratório do Conselho Nacional de Estatística, 1948–57*a*, No. 9); on the social and economic factors in natality (Mortara, 1954*d*); on voluntary abortions (Laboratório do Conselho Nacional de Estatística, 1954*a*); on the factors underlying different causes of death (Serviço Nacional de Recenseamento de 1940, 1945, secs. 9 and 11; Laboratório do Conselho Nacional de Estatística, 1948–57*a*, No. 13, sec. 2, and No. 20); on the determinants of internal migration (Laboratório do Conselho Nacional de Estatística, 1948–57*a*, No. 17); and on the linguistic assimilation of immigrants (Laboratório do Conselho Nacional de Estatística, 1948–57*b*, No. 2).

RECENT RESEARCH AND PUBLICATIONS

The work of the Instituto Brasileiro de Geografia e Estatística stimulated the activity of demographers, and, at the same time, it offered them indispensable data for carrying out their work and possibilities for disseminating the results of their studies. It is precisely to the independent scholars that we owe the first systematic attempts at a scientific investigation of the causes and consequences of population phenomena.

In the first place, there is the remarkable work of J. Lambert and L. A. Costa Pinto, *Problèmes démographiques contemporains* (1944), devoted primarily to the exposition of facts and of methods which assure the correct description of facts but which also gives a sketch of the interrelations between demographic phenomena and other social phenomena. This book can be considered the first modern manual of demography and population policy published in Brazil.

The *Revista Brasileira de Estatística*, edited since 1940 by the Instituto Brasileiro de Geografia e Estatística, has published numerous demographic studies, produced in part by agencies of the institute itself, but in part the work of independent scholars. Besides the already experienced demographers like J. Lyra Madeira, J. Kingston, O. Pôrto Carreiro, and M. Rodrigues da Silva, some young contributors made their debut, sharpening their critical sense by the analysis of national statistics and developing their capacity for interpretation of demographic phenomena and the influence they exert. Among these young demographers must be mentioned A. V. de Carvalho, E. Thimóteo de Barros, O. L. de Arruda Gomes, M. V. da Rocha, and E. Alves. Among the other contributors were G. Jardim, O. de Andrade, Jr., and A. P. de Toledo Piza.

Another periodical edited by the Instituto Brasileiro de Geografia e Estatística, the *Boletim Estatístico,* although intended principally for the publication of numerical information, accepted several studies in demography. Some other studies have appeared in the *Revista Brasileira dos Municípios,* also edited by the institute.

The periodical publications of the Instituto de Resseguros do Brasil, the Instituto de Aposentadoria e Pensões dos Industriários, and of some other public institutes also have encouraged scientific research not only on matters of direct interest to these institutes but on other demographic subjects. Among the articles published in these reviews, those of J. Lyra Madeira must be mentioned, as well as those of his collaborator, O. Iório, and those of J. D. Soares.

The review, *Conjuntura Econômica,* of the Fundação Getúlio Vargas also has included some studies in demography. Among its contributors, T. P. Accioly Borges and T. R. Raposo De Almeida can be cited. Some other investigations worthy of mention have appeared in the review of the Department of Statistics of the state of São Paulo, through the work of J. C. de Almeida, C. de Freitas Guimarães, M. Dutra Rodrigues Perdigão, R. de Freitas, and other collaborators.

A summary of demography, *Noções de Bioestatística,* for the use of doctors specializing in sanitary statistics, was published by L. de Freitas Filho in 1945; a second edition, revised and enlarged, appeared in 1952. The studies of the Instituto Brasileiro de Geografia e Estatística helped furnish the documentation of that work, which fulfils its purpose well.

Among other recent works concerning Brazilian demography, there is the work of Castro Barretto, which is concerned primarily with the determination of the directives of population policy and employs a historical and social analysis, and the rigorous scientific studies of E. Willems and M. Diégues on the cultural and social assimilation of immigrants. Brazilian literature is sufficiently abundant on this subject, but it has been inspired in part by nationalistic or racial prejudices, which dictate a priori the conclusions of apparently objective research. Nevertheless, dispassionate and factual studies can be cited, such as that of A. Hehl Neiva on Jewish immigration and a few others.

Special mention is merited by the amply documented work of J. F. de Camargo, *Crescimento da população no Estado de São Paulo e seus aspectos econômicos* (1952), which highlights the relations between the demographic development and the economic evolution of the most populous and advanced of the states of Brazil.

The geographic aspects of the demography of this country have been the object of numerous studies published in the *Revista Brasileira de Geografia,* edited since 1939 by the Conselho Nacional de Geografia, which is the other large agency of the Instituto Brasileiro de Geografia e Estatística. Among the contributors who treated these subjects are P. Deffontaines, M. M. F. Silva, L. Câmara, N. Bernardes, R. Bouchaud Lopes da Cruz, L. M. Cavalcanti Bernardes, M. L. da Silva Lessa, E. de Carvalho, E. Coelho de Sousa Keller, E. Gonçalves Egler, and N. Strauch.

The data of the censuses of 1940 and 1950 also have been used by foreigners for studies on the demography of Brazil. One of the most notable of these is contained in the fine book by T. Lynn Smith (*Brazil: People and Institutions,* 1954), which would have been improved if the author had profited from some investigations of the Technical Section and the Laboratório. The commentaries and analyses concerning Brazil in the recent publication of the United Nations, *The Population of South America, 1950–1980,* should be mentioned also.

During the last few years, Brazilian demographers have made some contributions to comparative international research in the field of demography. Notably, we can cite a series of inter-American demographic studies by the Technical Section (Serviço Nacional de Recenseamento de 1940, 1942–43), a

study on the development of Latin-American populations by natural increase and migration (Mortara, 1946–47, No. 3, sec. 1), and the Laboratório's research on changes in the duration of the economically active life and in the population's age composition through the effect of mortality (Laboratório do Conselho Nacional de Estatística, 1954*b*, *c*). Economic aspects of some demographic phenomena have been studied by J. Lyra Madeira. The influence of alimentation on sexual activity and its reflections in fertility have been highlighted, with remarkably original views, by J. de Castro.

PROSPECTS FOR THE DEVELOPMENT OF DEMOGRAPHY

The efficient organization of censuses has eliminated one of the obstacles which hindered the development of demographic studies in Brazil. A second obstacle will be overcome when an efficient organization for the registration of births, deaths, and marriages, at present very incomplete, is established successfully.

The work of scholars could be facilitated and encouraged by the establishment of municipal registers of population, which provide an indispensable basis for statistics on internal migration and a very useful aid for statistics on international migration. Such registers would also be very valuable for purposes of public administration.

It appears improbable, however, that scientific research in the field of demography can attain the desirable breadth and depth without a modification in higher education which would grant this discipline the place it merits among the course materials of economic, social, and administrative sciences. In the faculty of statistical sciences, recently created, there is one course in demographic statistics; in the faculties of philosophy and economics, a half-course. It is necessary to introduce, besides this instruction, courses in demography in which demographic statistics are one of the tools: the principal one, without doubt, but certainly not the only one.

SELECTED BIBLIOGRAPHY

ALVES, E. 1954. "Composition par âge de la population du Brésil," *Revista brasileira de estatística*, Vol. LIX; also in *Proceedings of the World Population Conference, 1954*, Vol. III. New York: United Nations, 1955.

ANDRADE, O. DE. 1954. "Répartition de la population brésilienne selon l'état matrimonial," *Revista brasileira de estatística*, Vol. LIX; also in *Proceedings of the World Population Conference, 1954*, Vol. IV. New York: United Nations, 1955.

BARRETTO, CASTRO. 1944. *Estudos brasileiros de população*. 2d ed.; 1947. Rio de Janeiro: Artes Gráficas Indústrias Reunidas S.A.

———. 1951. *Povoamento e população*. Rio de Janeiro: Olympio.

BRIGGS, L. N. 1933. *Marcha da mortalidade infantil no Rio de Janeiro*. Rio de Janeiro: Inspetoria de Demografia Sanitária.

BULHÕES CARVALHO, J. L. S. 1933. *Estatística, método e aplicação*. Rio de Janeiro: Leuzinger.

CÂMARA, L. 1948. "Estrangeiros em Santa Catarina," *Revista brasileira de geografia*, Vol. II.

CAMARGO, J. F. DE. 1952. *Crescimento da população no Estado de São Paulo e seus aspectos econômicos*. São Paulo: Universidade de São Paulo.

CARVALHO, A. V. DE. 1954. "La natalité au Brésil," *Revista brasileira de estatística*, Vol. LIX; also in *Proceedings of the World Population Conference, 1954*, Vol. I. New York: United Nations, 1955.

CASTRO, J. DE. 1952. *Geopolítica da fome*. Rio de Janeiro: Livraria da Casa do Estudante.

———. 1955. "A fecundidade masculina em São Paulo, segundo a idade e o ramo de atividade," *Revista brasileira de estatística*, Vol. LXIII.

DEFFONTAINES, P. 1939. "Geografia humana do Brasil," *Revista brasileira de geografia*, Vols. I–III.

DIRETORIA GERAL DE ESTATÍSTICA. 1922–30. *Recenseamento do Brasil realizado em 1 de Setembro de 1920*, Vols. I–V. Rio de Janeiro.

FONTENELLE, J. P. 1934. *O método estatístico em biologia e em educação*. Rio de Janeiro: Oliveira & Co.

———. 1937. *A saúde pública no Distrito Federal, 1935 e 1936*. Rio de Janeiro.

FREITAS FILHO, L. DE. 1952. *Noções de bioestatística*. 2d ed. Rio de Janeiro: Gráfica Debret.

———. 1956. *Vida e morte nas capitais brasileiras*. Rio de Janeiro: Instituto Brasileiro de Geografia e Estatística.

GREVILLE, T. N. E., and ARAUJO MORALES, N. L. 1955. "Life Table Studies in Brazil," *Estadística*, Vol. XLVII.

HEHL NEIVA, A. 1944. "Estudo sôbre a imigração semita no Brasil," *Revista de imigração e colonização*, Vol. II.

———. 1947. "Aspectos geográficos da imigração e colonização do Brasil," *Revista brasileira de geografia*, Vol. II.

JARDIM, G. 1954. *População urbana e população rural*. Rio de Janeiro: Serviço Nacional de Recenseamento de 1950.

KINGSTON, J. 1954. "Quelques aspects démographiques et économiques des régions rurales au Brésil," *Revista brasileira de estatística*, Vol. LVIII; also in *Proceedings of the World Population Conference, 1954*, Vol. V. New York: United Nations, 1955.

LABORATÓRIO DO CONSELHO NACIONAL DE ESTATÍSTICA, INSTITUTO BRASILEIRO DE GEOGRAFIA E ESTATÍSTICA. "Estudos de estatística teórica e aplicada" (edited in part by the Gabinete Técnico do Serviço Nacional de Recenseamento de 1940):

1948. "Série biométrica," No. 1.

1948–57a. "Série demográfica," Nos. 1–23.

1948–57b. "Série cultural," Nos. 1–10.

———. 1950–52. "Estudos complementares das análises de resultados do censo demográfico de 1940," Nos. 1–16, "Das aplicações dêsse censo," No. 1.

————. 1951–57. "Estudos demográficos," Nos. 1–230.

————. 1954*a*. "Inquérito sôbre os abortos no Distrito Federal," Nos. 1–2.

————. 1954*b*. "La durée moyenne de la vie économiquement active," *Revista brasileira de estatística,* Vol. LVIII; also in *Proceedings of the World Population Conference, 1954,* Vol. III. New York: United Nations, 1955.

————. 1954*c*. "Illustration de l'influence de la mortalité et de la natalité sur la composition par âge de la population," *Revista brasileira de estatística,* Vol. LVIII.

————. 1955. "Quelques renseignements sur les études de statistique regionale au Brésil," *Bulletin de l'Institut International de Statistique,* Vol. XXXV.

————. 1955–57. "Contribuições para o estudo da demografia das regiões Nordeste, Norte, Sul," Nos. 1–3.

LAMBERT, J., and COSTA PINTO, L. A. 1944. *Problèmes démographiques contemporains. I: Les faits.* Rio de Janeiro: Atlântica Editora.

LYRA MADEIRA, J. 1945, 1947. "Ajustamento de tábuas de mortalidade," *Revista do Instituto Brasileiro de Resseguros,* Vols. XXIX, XLI.

————. 1953. "Aspectos econômicos de algumas características demográficas," *Revista brasileira de estatística,* Vol. LVI.

————. 1954. "Perspectives démographiques du Brésil," *Revista brasileira de estatística,* Vol. LIX; also in *Proceedings of the World Population Conference, 1954,* Vol. III. New York: United Nations, 1955.

————. 1956. "Sôbre algumas curvas de saturação empregadas em ajustamentos de dados observados," *Revista brasileira de estatística,* Vol. LXVIII.

MONTENEGRO, T. H. 1952. *Métodos dos censos de população das nações americanas.* Rio de Janeiro: Serviço Nacional de Recenseamento de 1950. Original text in Spanish appeared in *Estadística,* No. 9 (1945).

MORTARA, G. 1940–42. "Estudos sôbre a utilização do censo demográfico para a reconstrução das estatísticas do movimento da população do Brasil" (Nos. 1–8), *Revista brasileira de estatística,* Vols. I–VII, IX.

————. 1942. *Curso de elementos de estatística demográfica.* Rio de Janeiro: Instituto Brasileiro de Geografia e Estatística. Reprinted 1953.

————. 1944. "As tábuas de sobrevivência e suas aplicações na demografia," *Revista brasileira de estatística,* Vols. XVII, XIX.

————. 1946–47. "Estudos brasileiros de demografia" (Nos. 1–3). Rio de Janeiro: Fundação Getúlio Vargas.

————. 1948. *Análise comparativa de diversos critérios aplicáveis no estudo biométrico do desenvolvimento de caracteres coletivamente típicos em função da idade.* Rio de Janeiro: Instituto Brasileiro de Geografia e Estatística.

————. 1949. *Methods of Using Census Statistics for the Calculation of Life Tables and Other Demographic Measures, with Applications to the Population of Brazil.* ("Population Studies," No. 7.) New York: United Nations.

————. 1950. "Sur les méthodes appliquées pour la reconstitution du mouvement de la population du Brésil à l'aide des recensements démographiques," *Bulletin de l'Institut International de Statistique,* Vol. XXXII.

————. 1951. "Objectivos e métodos da demografia," *Revista brasileira de estatística,* Vol. XLVI.

————. 1953*a*. "Durée de la vie économiquement active suivant la mortalité," *Bulletin of the International Statistical Institute,* Vol. XXXIII.

————. 1953*b*. "Contributions of the Brazilian Institute of Geography and Statistics to Population Studies," *Bulletin of the International Statistical Institute,* Vol. XXXIII.

————. 1954*a*. "Les méthodes de mesure de la fécondité des populations où l'enregistrement des naissances est inexistant ou défectueux," *Revista brasileira de estatística,* Vol. LVIII; also in *Proceedings of the World Population Conference, 1954,* Vol. IV. New York: United Nations, 1955.

————. 1954*b*. "Structure and Development of Brazil's Population," *Population Studies,* Vol. VIII.

————. 1954*c*. "Les erreurs dans les déclarations de l'âge dans les recensements brésiliens de 1940 et de 1950," *Bulletin de l'Institut International de Statistique,* Vol. XXXIV.

MORTARA, G. 1954*d.* "The Brazilian Birth-Rate: Its Economic and Social Factors," in *Culture and Human Fertility.* By F. LORIMER *et al.* Part V. Paris: UNESCO.

———. 1955*a.* "Nota sôbre o cálculo das migrações interiores baseado nos censos," *Revista brasileiro de estatística,* Vol. LXI.

———. 1955*b.* "Essai de calcul du taux de reproduction pour la population de l'état de São Paulo." Paper presented at the twenty-ninth session of l'Institut International de Statistique, Petrópolis.

———. 1955*c.* "Sulla dipendenza della composizione per età di una popolazione dalla mortalità," *Giornale degli economisti,* Vol. XIV, Nos. 1–2.

———. 1956. "Indícios da freqüência das uniões conjugais livres em alguns Estados do Brasil," *Revista brasileira de estatística,* Vol. LXVI.

———. 1957. *A fecundidade da mulher no Brasil.* Rio de Janeiro: Instituto Brasileiro de Geografia e Estatística.

ROCHA, M. V. DA. 1954. "La mortalité au Brésil," *Revista brasileira de estatística,* Vol. LX; also in *Proceedings of the World Population Conference, 1954,* Vol. I. New York: United Nations, 1955.

SCORZELLI, A. 1944. "Aspectos bioestatísticos da mortinatalidade no Distrito Federal," *Boletim de higiene e saúde pública,* Vol. III.

SERVIÇO NACIONAL DE RECENSEAMENTO DE 1940, INSTITUTO BRASILEIRO DE GEOGRAFIA E ESTATÍSTICA. 1942–43. "Estudos de demografia interamericana," Nos. 1–6.

———. 1942–48*a.* "Análises de resultados do censo demográfico," Nos. 1–412.

———. 1942–48*b.* "Applicações do censo demográfico para a reconstrução e a emenda das estatísticas do movimento da população," Nos. 1–42.

———. 1944–46. "Estudos sôbre a mortali-dade nas grandes cidades brasileiras," Nos. 1–46.

———. 1945. "Estudos sôbre a mortalidade no Distrito Federal e no Município de São Paulo," *Revista brasileira de estatística,* Vol. XXIV.

———. 1947. "Estudos sôbre a mortalidade nos Municípios do Recife e de Salvador, Pôrto Alegre, Belo Horizonte, e Belém," *Revista brasileira de estatística,* Vol. XXIX.

———. 1950–52. *Censo demográfico.* (1 vol., national series; 24 vols., regional series.)

SERVIÇO NACIONAL DE RECENSEAMENTO DE 1950, INSTITUTO BRASILEIRO DE GEOGRAFIA E ESTATÍSTICA. 1951–53. *Censo demográfico: Seleção dos principais dados.* (1 brochure for Brazil and 22 for the units of the Federation.)

———. 1951–56. "Documentos censitários." (Ser. A, Nos. 1–5; Ser. B, Nos. 1–8; Ser. C, Nos. 1–16; Ser. D, Nos. 1–7.)

———. 1954–56. *Censo demográfico.* (1 vol., national series; 25 vols., regional series.)

SILVA, M. M. F. 1946. "Tentativa de classificação das cidades brasileiras," *Revista brasileira de geografia,* Vol. III.

SMITH, T. L. 1954. *Brazil: People and Institutions.* Rev. ed. Baton Rouge: Louisiana State University Press.

SOUZA E SILVA, J. N. DE. 1870. *Investigações sôbre os recenseamentos da população geral do Imperio e de cada provincia por si, tentadas desde os tempos coloniaes até hoje.* Rio de Janeiro: Tipografia Nacional. Reprinted, Rio de Janeiro: Serviço Nacional de Recenseamento de 1950, 1951.

THIMÓTEO DE BARROS, E. 1954. "Les migrations intérieures au Brésil," *Revista brasileira de estatística,* Vol. LVIII; also in *Proceedings of the World Population Conference, 1954,* Vol. II. New York: United Nations, 1955.

UNITED NATIONS. 1955. *The Population of South America, 1950–1980.* New York.

12. Survey of the Status of Demography in India

C. CHANDRASEKARAN

Indian history has ample evidence of early attempts at the collection of population data. *The Arthasastra of Kautilya,* a monumental work dating back to 321–269 B.C.—in the Maurya period which reached its peak at the time of the Great Asoka—contains a detailed description of methods for conducting population, economic, and agricultural censuses. During the time of Akbar the Great, another bright period in Indian history, the administration report known as the *Ain-i-Akbari* included comprehensive data pertaining to population, industry, wealth, and many other characteristics. Such attempts at the collection of statistical data were not always kept up in India, perhaps because of its political vicissitudes, and it is only from about the middle of the nineteenth century that continuous data on India's population are available.

Systematic attempts to carry out population censuses were made between 1865 and 1872, when such censuses were taken in different parts of the country, though not at the same time. From 1881, population censuses have been conducted on an all-India basis once every ten years. These censuses have provided a mine of information on demographic subjects, but demographic analyses of the data have been very limited until recently. The position has been aptly put by the Population Data Committee: "There is often much more information available than is realised, and especially in India, we must be ready to dig for it and not wait for it to be handed over ready-made." The census, at least in its earlier stages, was conceived essentially as an administrative undertaking, and the persons appointed as census commissioners or census superintendents of the states were often foreign administrators posted temporarily to these offices. Probably because of the individual inclination of these persons or because of a different concept of the purpose of the census, the reports of the earlier census authorities paid greater attention to discussions of the anthropology of the people and to such subjects as religion, caste, or tribe than to a detailed study of the census data and of their social and economic implications.

The presence of a foreign government also was not conducive to an appreciation of the importance of the census or of its findings, either by the public or by academic men. There was a general tendency to consider the census as a governmental activity intended chiefly to foster the interests of the government. Indicative of this attitude was the staging of the boycott of the 1931 census as part of the Civil Disobedience Movement. The political use which was being made of the census data to establish communal representation in the legislatures was resented in nationalist circles and increased the apathy toward the census.

249

The setting was hardly suitable for the development of a scientific attitude toward the census, for the population problem had then become a political question. The British administrators were prone to point out that the large size of the population of India was the cause of India's poverty, while Indians imbued with the spirit of nationalism were eager to maintain the contrary and to show that the British rule was the cause of poverty in India. According to them, the relatively slow growth of the population was in itself a reflection on the British administration. Thus the inhibiting effect of the political situation was a fundamental handicap in the development of demography until at least the third decade of the present century.

The increasing attention paid to demography and the growing recognition of its importance are part of the political, economic, and intellectual changes which have swept the country in the last two or three decades. The period between 1931 and 1945, when the Second World War ended, was also accompanied by an increase in activity in population studies by individual scholars and by various groups. While the emphasis prior to 1931 was on the study of death rates and life tables, subsequent to this date interest began to extend to a consideration of problems of differential fertility and of population projection. Factors contributing to such interest were probably the following. The 1931 census had included in the census schedule the following items on fertility: duration of married life with present wife, sex of the first born (whether quick or still-born), number of children born alive, and number of children still living. The inclusion of such questions, particularly after public discussions of the dangers of early motherhood which preceded the passing in 1930 of the Sarda Act (which raised the age at marriage of

girls to fourteen years), stirred up considerable interest in fertility problems among individual scholars. In addition, the publication of such books as *Measurement of Population Growth* by Kuczynski and the *Twilight of Parenthood* by Enid Charles created interest in the use of gross and net reproduction rates as measures for studying the rate of growth of population.

Evidence of the growing interest in demography was the holding of the First Indian Population Conference in February, 1936, under the auspices of the University of Lucknow. At this conference an attempt was made to forecast the population of India in 1941, and there was discussion of the need for family limitation from a number of points of view. The Second All-India Population and First Family Hygiene Conference was held in Bombay in 1938, at which the results of a number of scientific studies were presented. The conference heard the reports of a field study on the differential fertility of some of the population groups of the Cochin State and of another on the fertility of the Amil community in Sind. The conference was also presented with papers on a variety of subjects including economics of employment vis-à-vis demographic reconstruction, the sociological analysis and forecast of population increase, population and employment in India, and logistic law of growth and structure of Indian population.

Dr. Enid Charles's statement in the *Twilight of Parenthood* that "the population of India was slowly increasing" led to an interesting discussion in 1936 between Dr. K. C. K. E. Raja, a public health worker, and Professor Adarkar, essentially an economist. Dr. Raja maintained that the rate of growth was likely to be greater in the decade 1931–41 as compared to the previous decades and surmised that Dr. Enid Charles's reading might prove to be a serious underestimate of the trend of events. Professor Adarkar disagreed with Dr. Raja and held the view that the weight of evidence then was heavily in favor of future stability and decline of the population in India. In fact, Professor Adarkar's contention was that Dr. Raja was rather anxious to support the official expression found in the public health commissioner's report of 1931 that the "Indian population was growing at an alarmingly rapid rate." In any case, the fact that such discussion about the growth of India's population took place in the quinquennium prior to the Second World War is a point illustrating that the population question had begun to receive increasing attention by the intelligentsia of the country.

The forecast of a population of 400 million for India in 1941, made at the First Indian Population Conference, acted as a spur for Dr. Radhakamal Mukerjee to publish in 1938 his book on *Food Planning for Four Hundred Millions*. Although this book, true to its title, emphasized the need for rational agricultural development, it did not fail to point out the diversity of academic skills that are required for the investigation of population problems. In the Preface to his book Dr. Mukerjee stated: "Agriculture and Industrialization, nutrition and food customs, the balance of births and deaths and differential fertility among the various social grades, health, efficiency and standard of living, medicine and public hygiene are all implicated in population investigations, which must require the cooperation of experts in diverse fields." Dr. Mukerjee's book was followed by the publication in 1939 of *India's Teeming Millions* by Professor Gyan Chand, who attempted to highlight the population problem from the economic point of view, essentially with the help of published statistics. In the words of the author ". . . the problem presents enormous difficulties

in the task of national reconstruction, but if we temper our faith with a vivid appreciation of the facts of today, we are bound to realize the gravity of the situation as it exists and is developing and also the necessity of taking action to bring it under control."

While individual research workers were attempting to interpret the available data on population, the rapid growth of population observed in the 1931 and 1941 censuses emphasized their consideration from the standpoint of social and economic planning. The National Planning Committee, set up in 1938 under the chairmanship of Pandit Jawaharlal Nehru, the present Prime Minister, and including representatives of governments, established a subcommittee which considered the problems of population from the point of view of food supply and nutrition, social reform, unemployment, and social welfare. A glimpse of the new consciousness which was coming into being can be seen from a resolution of this committee, which read:

In the interests of social economy, family happiness, and national planning, family planning and a limitation of children are essential; and the State should adopt a policy to encourage these. It is desirable to lay stress on self-control, as well as to spread knowledge of cheap and safe methods of birth control. Birth Control Clinics should be established and other necessary measures taken in this behalf and to prevent the use or advertisement of harmful methods.

The government emphasized the importance of population data when, in 1944, the then Department of Education, Health, and Lands set up the Population Data Committee and stated, "in view of the importance of problems concerning growth of population in relation to reconstruction planning, the Government of India have constituted an expert committee to examine and advise the Government of India on the available data relating to growth of population." This committee consisted of Mr. W. M. Yeatts as chairman and Sir Theodore Gregory, Professor P. C. Mahalanobis, Professor K. B. Madhava, and Dr. K. C. K. E. Raja as members. The committee paid special emphasis to the statistical problems related to the age tabulation of the 1941 census, which could not be completed because of the financial stringency caused by the Second World War, and also made recommendations for the use of sampling methods for the estimation of vital statistics rates. In particular, they pointed out the use which could be made of the household lists prepared at the census as a sampling frame for obtaining demographic data and recommended their safekeeping.

About the same time the Health Survey and Development Committee, set up by the government to help in making plans for postwar development in the health field, made a comprehensive review of the field of population from the quantitative and qualitative points of view and pointed out some of the important gaps in existing knowledge. With a view to improving the quality of population statistics, the committee suggested the appointment of a registrar general of vital and population statistics at the center and of provincial registrars in the various provinces. One of its chief recommendations was that "the population problem should be the subject of continuous study." In the view of the committee, population studies should be organized and conducted on as broad a basis of collaboration as possible, with the registrar general, the provincial registrars and their trained statisticians, the health departments, and the departments of economics, sociology, statistics, and genetics in the universities, wherever such existed, participating in them.

One of the main difficulties in carrying out demographic studies on the Indian population has been the lack of reliable basic data. Even the census data have not been free from obvious inaccuracies. The unreliability of the age data has been pointed out in all censuses. The deficiencies in other types of data have also been evident whenever attempts were made to study these in detail. But more defective than the census data have been those of vital statistics registration. The absence of accurate birth and death data made demographic analyses more difficult and curbed the enthusiasm of many pioneer workers.

It was after the development of modern statistical science in the country, thanks to the initiative of Professor P. C. Mahalanobis and of the Indian Statistical Institute, that statisticians began to take an interest in demographic research. The presence of trained statisticians not only helped in the evaluation of the accuracy of routine population data but also made it possible to obtain fresh data by *ad hoc* surveys. The Indian Statistical Institute began collecting data on fertility by field inquiries as early as 1937. By 1942 such *ad hoc* surveys had covered 9,000 weaving families and 1,000 agricultural families in rural Bengal, 1,000 middle class families in Calcutta, and 3,500 working class families in five industrial centers in Bengal. About the year 1945, the All-India Institute of Hygiene and Public Health, which had already carried out a number of studies on population trends, began a series of intensive researches, under the guidance of Dr. C. Chandrasekaran, in the demographic field. In the newly constituted Singur Health Centre methodological problems related to the obtaining of birth and death rates and to the estimation of the extent of birth and death registration by field surveys were taken up. An important field study instituted at that time was a survey of the reproductive patterns of

8,000 women selected from the city of Calcutta and the rural areas and an investigation of the effects of economic and social factors on these patterns. A study on Parsi demography, from published data, was undertaken by this institute in 1946–47. In this study the relatively high accuracy of the data available for the Parsis in India was used to exemplify modern demographic analysis. Another institute which has been interesting itself in population studies is the Gokhale Institute of Politics and Economics. As early as 1942, Mr. N. V. Sovani of this organization published a study called *The Population Problem in India: A Regional Approach.* Although it is primarily an institute for economic research, since 1951, following a grant from the Rockefeller Foundation, a section in demography and population studies has been established in it. The institute has since carried out a number of surveys in mortality and fertility.

Of late, official reports show a growing keenness to apply demographic principles and analyses. The 1941 census report contained an interesting note by Mr. Satya Swaroop which attempted to assess the cumulative effect of the reduction of infant mortality on the size of India's population in 1951 and 1961. The report of the 1951 census by the census commissioner for India is a complete departure from the pattern of previous census reports. This report has attempted to interpret the past changes in the size and structure of India's population and to point out their implications for the level of living of the population. The report also makes a plea for a reduction in the birth rate of the country. The 1951 census also attempted for the first time in the history of the Indian census to make an assessment of the accuracy of the census count by a recheck in the field. In commending this task to the various census superintendents of the states, the census commissioner was no doubt influenced by the importance given to such checks by the United Nations. The recommendations of the United Nations Population Commission on census methods have also been acknowledged in planning other features of the 1951 Indian census.

The importance of demographic research as an aid to social and economic planning received fresh impetus about the year 1950. In that year, following a recommendation of the Economic and Social Council, an agreement was reached by the government of India and the United Nations to undertake jointly a field study on the interrelationships of economic, social, and population changes. The plan and purpose of the study received wide publicity, particularly at the time when the Planning Commission of the Government of India was beginning to prepare the First Five-Year Plan for economic development. Furthermore, the holding of a session of the International Union for the Scientific Study of Population in New Delhi in December, 1951, brought to the capital a number of foreign demographers. Their presence immediately after the publication of the stimulating book entitled *The Population of India and Pakistan* by Kingsley Davis was very welcome. The Planning Commission held discussions with a number of them and was able to get a clear insight into the ramifications of the population problem and the importance of considering population trends and factors affecting them while planning for economic development. Meanwhile, interest in family planning was growing in the Health Ministry, and at its invitation Dr. Abraham Stone was sent to India by the World Health Organization to start a pilot project in the rhythm method of family planning. The Planning Commission had useful discussions with Dr. Stone which, as can be gauged from the program on family planning included in the First Five-Year Plan, led to the creation of additional interest in demography.

This program emphasized the need to "obtain an accurate picture of the factors contributing to the rapid population increase in India." One of the seven points in the program was the study of the interrelationships between economic, social, and population changes, the information from which was expected to provide "the necessary background for the formulation of a national population policy based on factual information." Another point in the program was the "collection from representative sections of the population of information on reproductive patterns and on attitudes and motivations affecting the size of the family." In recommending this program, the Five-Year Plan suggested that the problems of population and family planning might be divided into those relating to (1) policy and approach and (2) research and programs, and intrusted each of these tasks to a separate committee.

The Programme and Research Committee, with its demographic subcommittee, considered the problems of demographic research and training at a number of sessions, but the concrete lines of action recommended by them have been few. These few have included the provision of financial grants to two or three schemes for studying birth and death rates and fertility patterns. The setting up of four demographic units in places where some demographic work was already being undertaken, such as the Delhi School of Economics, the Gokhale Institute of Politics and Economics, the All-India Institute of Hygiene, and the Indian Statistical Institute, were recommended by this committee.

Meanwhile, studies carried out recently in the population field show a high degree of demographic skill. At the World Population Conference held in Rome in 1954, for instance, two papers—one by Mahalanobis and Ajit Das Gupta and the other by Chandrasekaran—were presented; they dealt with the design of statistical surveys and the examination of the accuracy of the data obtained from such surveys. The studies currently undertaken in India deal with such specific fields of demographic interest as fertility, labor force, and urbanization. Such studies have resulted essentially from the government's plans for social and economic development. Work connected with family planning projects has given an insight into the complexity of factors which affect fertility and the necessity for understanding these properly if the government policy of effecting a check on India's birth rate is to be pursued vigorously. Similarly, the aim of banishing unemployment within a reasonable number of years has made it necessary to estimate accurately the size of the labor force in the future and the number of persons for whom job opportunities will need to be provided. The need for studying the relationship between the secondary and tertiary sectors of the economy has encouraged a study of the growth of industrial towns in India.

PRESENT STATUS OF DEMOG-
RAPHY IN INDIA

From the brief history of demography given in the previous section, one point stands out; i.e., until now this branch of knowledge has developed without any definite plan or direction. Academic interests of individual scholars and national exigencies have been the two dominating forces on the growth of demography in the past. As a result, certain fields of demography have received far greater attention than others. For instance, a number of statistical studies have been carried out on mortality, fertility, and future population size. In contrast, the amount of work done in economic demography has been extremely limited and far from commensurate with the demands made in this field by the problems arising out of the country's economic planning. Little attention has been paid to the social and economic problems related to population movement, although the population censuses have, as a rule, provided valuable basic data which could be used for this purpose. There is also little evidence in the scientific publications of the recognition of demography as a social science and of the importance of social and cultural factors in population dynamics.

A major reason for the lack of an all-round development in demography has been the absence of proper training and research facilities. An inquiry made by Mr. N. V. Sovani[1] a few months ago in connection with the teaching of demography project of the International Union for the Scientific Study of Population showed that in all of the twenty-six universities in India which replied to his questionnaire, demography did not form a separate subject in courses leading to the Bachelor's degree. Whatever teaching is provided is given within the framework of other disciplines, mainly sociology, economics, and statistics. The teaching of the subject at the undergraduate level, in the economics or sociology courses, is rudimentary and is confined to giving elementary ideas on vital statistics and population theories. The courses in statistics emphasize the calculation of statistical measures of fertility and mortality.

There is no chair in demography at any of the universities. In two universities, i.e., Bombay and M. S. University, Baroda, there are two optional

[1] I am indebted to Mr. Sovani for allowing me to make use of his findings.

papers in demography at the postgraduate Master's examination in economics. The two papers form a pair out of six to seven such in advanced economics, and the candidate has to choose two pairs from among these. While Baroda offers teaching related to the two papers in demography, in Bombay there is no such facility, and the candidates have to prepare on their own. In the Lucknow University there is a paper in demography in the examination leading to the M.A. degree in economics. The introduction of a paper on population for the M.A. examination at the Aligarh University has been proposed. The statistician's diploma examination of the Indian Statistical Institute includes an optional paper on population and vital statistics.

The facilities for demographic research (apart from the newly created Demographic Research and Training Institute, which will be referred to later) have also been limited, and there has been no institution in India devoting itself entirely to this work. The All-India Institute of Hygiene and Public Health at Calcutta, the Gokhale Institute of Politics and Economics at Poona, the Indian Statistical Institute at Calcutta, and the J. K. Institute of Sociology and Human Relations at Lucknow—to mention only some of the institutions which have undertaken research studies in the past—have other major preoccupations. Demographic research work undertaken by their staff has often been in addition to their normal duties; of late, however, the Gokhale Institute and the Indian Statistical Institute have established separate demographic sections.

A recent development of considerable importance has been the setting up of the Demographic Teaching and Research Centre under the joint sponsorship of the government of India and the Sir Dorabji Tata Trust. The United

Nations is also supporting this project on the understanding that this center will admit for training a certain number of students from other countries of Asia and will assist these countries in the development of research into their demographic problems. In accepting the proposal for collaboration with the United Nations, the government of India expressed the hope that this center "will prove to be an important contribution towards the study and evaluation of population problems in Asian countries in order to facilitate the planning of sound national programmes of reconstruction." The institution consists of a number of co-operating units: (1) the main unit with its staff of a co-ordinating officer, a statistician, a demographer, and clerical and other subordinate personnel; the staff will be strengthened by the United Nations to enable the center to perform its international functions stated above; (2) the Indian Cancer Research Centre, Bombay, with its two units dealing with human variation and the physiology of human reproduction, respectively; (3) the Tata Institute of Social Sciences, Bombay; (4) the Department of Sociology of the University of Bombay; and (5) the Gokhale Institute of Politics and Economics, Poona.

It is the task of the main unit to promote, in collaboration with the other units mentioned earlier, integrated programs of teaching and research. The institute will admit fellows for training. The period of training will last for two years. The program of teaching during the first year will cover theoretical training in the different subjects dealt with by individual units of the organization as well as practical work and participation in the research undertaken by the center. During the second year each student will be posted, in turn, to these different units to participate in their work. It is expected that, with this background of training, the outgoing student will be able to associate himself effectively with the planning of development programs at the national and state levels and to become a useful member of a center for the teaching of demography. A few outstanding fellows will be provided with opportunities to pursue higher studies in their own subjects, with a view to enable them to secure doctorate degrees in these subjects. After such specialization, these fellows should, it is felt, be able to fulfil to a greater extent the tasks of organizing departments of demography in universities and of making contributions to planning and research in their own fields of study.

In addition to the Demographic Research and Training Centre, the government of India has recently taken steps to establish demographic units which will "form the nuclei from which interest in demographic problems will be promoted and a free flow of trained workers in this field will be encouraged." Two such units are to be set up immediately, one in the Delhi School of Economics and the other at Calcutta. The unit at Calcutta will be run by the Indian Statistical Institute in collaboration with the All-India Institute of Hygiene and Public Health. These units will, it is understood, have considerable latitude in determining their fields of interest.

PROSPECTS FOR DEMOGRAPHY IN INDIA

The prospects are extremely bright for further development of demography in India. The fact that the government of India has shown initiative in the provision of centers for training and research in this field augurs well for the future. In addition to the facilities available in the country, Indian students have also the opportunity for overseas training provided by international agencies such as the Colombo

Plan and the United Nations and by private organizations such as the Population Council of New York. There is, therefore, assurance that in the immediate future India will have a number of persons trained in demography and qualified to undertake important tasks in this field.

The need for demographic work will arise essentially from the requirements of the government programs for social and economic development. Various departments of the government have already taken steps to obtain the assistance of demographers either as consultants or as full-time staff members. A Standing Committee for Population and Vital Statistics has also been set up at the center, with representation from several ministries and the central statistical organization, to consider problems of co-ordination arising in the collection of demographic data. This is an important step, since in the future the handicap to demographic work is not likely to arise so much from the want of demographic skill as from the lack of adequate demographic data.

Demography in India has had its ups and downs, and it will require a keen student of the history of civilizations to explain how in this country, which held the pride of place in the collection and use of demographic data in the third century B.C., the status of this subject became as low as it did in the middle of the last century. Whatever the factors which were responsible for this change, the last hundred years have seen a slow but growing interest in this field of science. Today demography has well-nigh regained its importance, and the chances are that the immediate future will see its status rise still higher.

SELECTED BIBLIOGRAPHY

ADARKAR, B. P. 1938. "The Future Trend of Population Growth in India," *Sankhyā*, III, 41–48.

ANON. 1957. "Growth of Industrial Towns in India," *Eastern Economist,* Vol. XXVIII.

CHAND, GYAN. 1939. *India's Teeming Millions.* London: Allen & Unwin.

CHANDRASEKARAN, C. 1948. "Some Aspects of Parsi Demography," *Human Biology,* XX, 47–89.

——. 1952. "Cultural Patterns in Relationship to Family Planning in India," in *Report of the Proceedings of the Third International Conference on Planned Parenthood.* Bombay: Family Planning Association of India.

——. 1955. "Fertility Survey in Mysore State, India," in *Current Research in Human Fertility.* New York: Milbank Memorial Fund.

——. 1957. "Present Day Demographic Trends," *Journal of the Indian Public Health Association,* Vol. I.

——, and SEN, MUKTA. 1948. "Enquiry into the Reproductive Patterns of Bengalee Women," in *Report of the Indian Research Fund Association.*

CHANDRASEKHAR, S. 1946. *India's Population: Fact and Policy.* New York: John Day.

——. 1955. *Population and Planned Parenthood in India.* London: Allen & Unwin.

COALE, ANSLEY J., and HOOVER, EDGAR M. 1956. "Population Growth and Economic Development in India, 1956–1986" (preliminary draft privately circulated for critical review). Princeton: Office of Population Research, Princeton University.

DANDEKAR, V. M., and DANDEKAR, KUMIDINI. 1953. *Survey of Fertility and Mortality in Poona District.* (Gokhale Institute of Politics and Economics, Publication No. 27.) Poona.

DAS GUPTA, AJIT, and MAJUMDAR, M. 1955. *India: 1951–2001.* (Population projections working paper for United Nations seminar on population in Asia and the Far East held at Bandung.) Calcutta: Indian Statistical Institute.

——, et al. 1955. *Couple Fertility.* ("The National Sample Survey," No. 7.) Reprinted in *Sankyhā,* XVI, 230–434.

DAVIS, K. 1951. *The Population of India*

and Pakistan. Princeton: Princeton University Press.

GHOSH, D. 1946. *Pressure of Population and Economic Efficiency in India.* New Delhi: Indian Council of World Affairs.

——, and VARMA, RAMA. 1939. "A Study in Indian Fertility," *Eugenics Review,* XXXI, 115–19.

GHURYE, G. S. (ed.). 1940. *Indian Population Problems.* (Report and proceedings of the Second All-India Population and First Family Hygiene Conference.) Bombay: Karnatak.

GOPALASWAMI, R. A. 1953. *Census of India, 1951.* Vol. I: *India.* Part 1A: "Report." Delhi: Manager of Publications.

GOVERNMENT OF INDIA AND UNITED NATIONS. "Population Survey in Mysore State, India" (to be published).

HEALTH SURVEY AND DEVELOPMENT COMMITTEE. 1946. *Report.* 4 vols. Delhi: Manager of Publications.

JAIN, S. P. 1939. *Relationship between Fertility and Economic and Social Status in the Punjab.* (Punjab Board of Economic Enquiry, Publication No. 64.) Lahore.

MAHALANOBIS, P. C. 1946. "Problems of Current Demographic Data in India." (Paper presented at a special meeting of the Population Association of America, on "A World View of Population Studies.")

——. 1950. "Why Statistics?" Presidential address in *Proceedings of the Thirty-seventh Indian Science Congress.*

——, and DAS GUPTA, AJIT. 1955. "The Use of Sample Surveys in Demographic Studies in India," in *Proceedings of the World Population Conference, 1954,* Vol. VII, Meeting 21. New York: United Nations.

MATHEN, K. K. 1954. "Public Opinion Survey on Certain Aspects of the Population Problem," *Indian Journal of Medical Research,* XLII, 619–34.

MUKERJEE, RADHAKAMAL. 1938. *Food*

Planning for 400 Millions. London: Macmillan & Co.

NATIONAL PLANNING COMMITTEE. 1947. *Population: Report of the Sub-Committee.* ("National Planning Committee Series," No. 6.) Bombay: Vora.

RAJA, K. C. K. E. 1937. "A Forecast of Population in India at the Census of 1941," *Indian Journal of Medical Research,* XXIV, 1183–91.

——. 1956. "The Demographic Teaching and Research Centre," *Journal of Family Welfare,* II, 209–12.

SARKAR, BENOY KUMAR. 1940. "The Economics of Employment vis-à-vis Demographic Reconstruction," in *Indian Population Problems,* ed. G. S. GHURYE. (Report and proceedings of the Second All-India Population and First Family Hygiene Conference.) Bombay: Karnatak.

SINHA, J. 1954. "Fertility and Age at Marriage," *Bulletin of the International Statistical Institute,* XXXIII, 113–26.

SOVANI, N. V. 1942. *The Population Problem in India: A Regional Approach.* (Gokhale Institute of Politics and Economics, Publication No. 8.) Poona.

——. 1948. *The Social Survey of Kolhapur City.* Part I: *Population and Fertility.* (Gokhale Institute of Politics and Economics, Publication No. 18.) Poona.

——. 1952. "The Problem of Fertility Control in India: Cultural Factors and Development of Policy," in *Approaches to Problems of High Fertility in Agrarian Societies.* New York: Milbank Memorial Fund.

SWAROOP, S., and LAL, R. B. 1938. "Logistic Law of Growth and Structure in Indian Population," *Population,* II, 100–121.

TILAK, V. R. K. 1957. "Population Growth and Labour Force in India" (unpublished).

WATTAL, P. K. 1934. *The Population Problem in India.* Bombay: Bennett, Coleman.

13. Demographic Research in the Pacific Area

IRENE B. TAEUBER

The development of population statistics in Europe, the peopling of the Americas and Oceania by Europeans, and the expansion of European administrative power produced a regional bias in demographic research and theory. The data and the hypotheses were derived from European cultural experience. A more adequate knowledge of the world's population and a more generalized theory alike require research on other peoples, other cultures, and other regions.

The Pacific is the most populous of the world's ocean regions. In 1954 some 1.35 billion people lived in the nations that touched its shores or on the islands that dotted its waters (United Nations, Statistical Office, 1955, Table 1). In the western Pacific, the U.S.S.R. and Communist China dominate the mainland of Asia, but there is a coastal arc that extends from Sakhalin through Japan, the Ryukyus, Taiwan, and the Philippines to the Indonesian Archipelago, Australia, and New Zealand. In the eastern Pacific a single land barrier stretches from Alaska to Tierra del Fuego. Here are the English-speaking continental areas of Canada and the United States and the Spanish-speaking countries from Mexico through Central America, Colombia, Ecuador, Peru, and Chile. Then there are islands scattered throughout the ocean from the coastal fringe of Asia to the western coast of the Americas.[1]

The major concentrations of people are on the Asian mainland. The 884 million population of the Soviet Union, Korea, Communist China, and Pacific Southeast Asia is one-third that of the world. It is two-thirds that of the Pacific region. The population of the coastal fringe numbers 219 million, while all the American nations from Canada to Chile have a population of 248 million. This last number is sizable, but it is only 18 per cent of the total figure for the Pacific region. The islands between the coastal fringe of Asia and the shores of the Americas have an estimated population of 1.5 million, 0.1 per cent of the regional total.

The strategic significance of Pacific demography need not be stressed. Almost 800 million of the 884 million mainland people belong to the Soviet Union or Communist China, and the Communist area has been extended into North Korea, northern Indochina, and Sakhalin Island. The 220 million people of the coastal fringe include the 88 million of a Japan still largely unarmed and the 81 million of a neutralist Indonesia. The combined population of Australia and New Zealand is less than 12 million. The tiny islands are important, but their peoples are few indeed. As contrasted with Asia, the western American nations are sparsely settled. Canada has 15 million people, while Chile has 6.5 million. The population of 248 million for the

[1] The Institute of Pacific Relations included the Pacific nations of the Americas and the Soviet Union in its definition of the area of interest.

259

Americas from the Arctic to the Antarctic is dominated by the 162 million of the United States.

There are great differences in density of settlement in the Pacific area, but ratios of people to land are relevant neither to welfare nor to power unless the character and development of the land use and the non-agricultural economy are considered. Here the Pacific is an area of sharp contrast. There are advanced industrial nations —and there are people who live largely by the ancient agricultural ways (Institute of Pacific Relations, International Secretariat, 1949, 1951; Cressey, 1951; Pelzer, 1941; Stamp, 1936; Wickizer and Bennett, 1941). Neither the modern nor the ancient economies are localized geographically or aligned politically. Mainland Asia includes the Soviet Union; the coastal fringe includes Japan, Australia, and New Zealand; the Americas include Canada and the United States.

Reconnaissance of the demography of half the world's population is difficult to handle simply and in brief space. The work could be documentary, a listing of sources for data and publications of research. It could describe the data and research systems that have swept across the area over the centuries. The economic approach is tempting, with its differentiations of agricultural, mixed, and industrial areas. There are also the questions of the rates of population growth and the prospects for the future as death rates are reduced drastically among peoples whose birth rates presumably remain high.

The orientation here is not the status of data, for that is covered elsewhere (in the contribution to this volume by Forrest Linder). Neither is it the population problems. Great as they may be and massive as the literature is, there has been little scientific analysis of them. The approach, rather, lies in the types of data and the research questions that are particularly significant for the Pacific region. The area emphasis is placed on nations or territories where population data and demographic research are not developed or are developed in unconventional ways. The substantive emphasis is placed on problems that require new hypotheses or the modification of old ones for the new physical and cultural contexts.

THE STATUS OF DATA

Tabulations of demographic data included in the *Demographic Yearbook* of the United Nations indicate a hiatus for major portions of most of the regions of the Pacific. The population figures that were cited earlier were dominated by non-censal estimates. Growth, distribution, structure, and characteristics are all conjectural for these non-enumerated populations. Even where a census was reported, that census was often remote in date, published incompletely if at all, or limited to segments of the population.

Censuses

The inadequacies of data differ from one area of the Pacific to another, from one type of culture and economy to another. The great area of ignorance is the Asian mainland. The Soviet Union had a census in 1939, but few data were published. Communist China had a census-registration in 1953–54, but the data were even more limited than those for the Soviet Union. Korea's last census under the Japanese was the war survey of 1944; South Korea's census of 1949 was quite deficient, and tabulations were ended when North Korea invaded in June of 1950. French enumerations in Indochina were limited to portions of the peninsula. Thailand and Malaya had censuses in 1947. Thus such a basic characteristic as age is known through a postwar census for about 25 million of the 850 million or more people of the Pacific nations of the Asian mainland.

The area of greatest knowledge is the eastern Pacific, i.e., the nations of the Americas (U.S. Bureau of the Census and Library of Congress, 1943). The data from Canada and the United States are those of advanced industrial nations. The statistical systems of the Latin nations are less advanced than those in America north of the Rio Grande, but censuses were taken in or near 1950 in all the Pacific nations of the Americas except Peru, and here there was a census in 1940. The major problems are those of the quality of data and the adequacy of tabulations rather than the absence of enumeration.

In the independent nations of Asia's coastal fringe, the state of demographic statistics is related to the state of economic development. Japan, Australia, and New Zealand have advanced statistical systems and recent census data, fully tabulated. The Republic of Indonesia has had no census; the last census under the Netherlands was that in 1930. The Philippines had a census in 1948, and there were earlier censuses under Spain and the United States. Taiwan took a census in 1956, and there is a functioning registration system. Censuses have been taken recently in most of the territories of the coastal fringe, though in New Guinea only non-indigenous inhabitants were included.

The final region of the Pacific consists of the other islands between the eastern coast of Asia and the western coast of the Americas. Most of the people in these islands have been enumerated recently, the United States Trust Territory of the Pacific, the British Solomon Islands, and the New Hebrides being outstanding exceptions.

The registration of vital statistics and the recording of migration have the same general pattern of development as the enumerative censuses. Availability, completeness, and accuracy are related either to the economic development and educational level of the nation itself or to the policies and plans of the administering power for the territory.

Population Registrations

The great demographic tradition of the Pacific region is that of population registration. The history among the Chinese goes back to ancient days, though it may be that most of the figures thought to be based on counts or registrations are largely *ad hoc* judgments. In recent centuries registration has been an aspect of the organization of population into small groups (the *chia*) and the organization of these into larger groups (the *pao*) (Chao, 1938; Chen Ta, 1948; Jaffe, 1947*b*; Liu, 1935; National Tsing Hua University, 1944; Skinner, 1951; Taeuber, 1948). The major function has been control of the population at the local level, but the administration of that control early involved the use of identifying placards on dwelling places and the keeping of local records. In theory, the inspection of these records and their summation at successively higher levels could yield information on population size and distribution, births and deaths, and movements to and from specified areas. This would be a continuing population inventory. In fact, the reputed compilations seldom involved anything more complex than one figure for all China. Only now are the provincial figures for the Ching Dynasty being published (Yen Chung-pin, 1955). The systematic and prolific compilation and publication so characteristic of the Japanese did not occur among the Chinese.

The origins of the registration system of Japan lie in China. The alien forms were introduced in virtual copy, but the adaptations in use and the altered context created a system of household registers (*koseki*) that was distinctively Japanese. Population registers were to provide the data for the periodic reallocation of land envisioned in the Great Reform of the seventh century A.D. (Taeuber, 1957). The operation of a complex registration and reporting system was impossible in the Yamato domains of the period. The fragments of data that survive suggest that the continuing declines in reported populations over the early centuries mirror an altered structure of administrative power rather than depopulation. However, a great tradition was established.

Nationwide registration was restored under the Tokugawa as a part of the control mechanism of a powerful centralized state. There was regulation of residence, economic activity, manners, morals, and apparel. Civil registers were kept, and there were also religious registers to insure the extirpation of Christianity. When population became recognized as a problem in the early eighteenth century, the *shogun* ordered the *daimyo* to submit periodic reports on numbers of commoners. The first report was in 1721; it was followed by a series of reports at six-year intervals from 1726 to 1852. For many of these years the compilations are available by sex for the *kuni* into which the country was then divided. Annual figures are available for some of the *han* (clans). There were some reports on births, deaths, marital status, and social class.

The coverage of the Tokugawa registers was incomplete, for the people without social class, the *daimyo*, the *samurai*, and the imperial family, together with their retainers, were omitted. The registers were also inaccurate, and the procedures differed in the domains of the different *daimyo*. In 1872 a new survey of the population was undertaken, and new registers were established. Continuing efforts were put into the improvement of the *koseki* records and the reporting system based on them. Initially, there were annual reports giving age and sex structure as well as numbers. Each five years from 1898 through 1918 there were "censuses," detailed compilations of the registration data by age, sex, marital status, and residence. The data remained defective. The first enumerative census was taken in 1920; thereafter there were complete censuses in decennial years, simplified censuses in quinquennial years. Vital statistics remained by-products of the *koseki* system, with procedures that traced back to the registration laws of the seventh century A.D. in Japan and to the T'ang codes in China. A Chinese registration system that never yielded reputable data in China was molded into one of the world's most extraordinary data systems by the Japanese.

The Chinese registration system, or a modification of it, diffused into neighboring areas, but adherence was limited and results inadequate. The great extension occurred as the Japanese extended their empire. In Korea the registration system remained so deficient that major adjustments were required each time an enumerative census was taken (Park, 1955; Taeuber, 1946*b*; U.S. Library of Congress, 1950*b, c, d*). Registration came late in the Ryukyus, and it was incomplete. In Taiwan, on the other hand, the Japanese administration of a basic Chinese institution produced data of notable accuracy (Barclay, 1954*a, b*). In Kwantung and the South Manchuria Railway Zone the registers remained deficient, though there were annual reports on population, births, and deaths. The great extension of the modern Japanese record system to a Chinese population occurred in Manchukuo (Taeuber, 1945*b*; U.S. Library of Congress, 1951). The levels of completeness and accuracy in Kwantung and Manchukuo were below those in Taiwan but above those for other Chinese populations on the mainland.

The other great registration system in the Pacific area was that of the Catholic church. In the Latin-American countries, the Philippines, and the Spanish islands of the southwest Pacific there were records of converts, baptisms, and deaths. These ecclesiastic registers were not safe guides to population developments, however, for the converted peoples were a variable and perhaps unrepresentative portion of the total; vital events had to be deduced from records of religious rites; and neither births nor deaths could be allocated precisely to the populations that produced them.

There have been other registration systems in the Pacific, notably that established by the Netherlands in Indonesia. There are large registration systems operating today, including those of Communist China on the mainland and Nationalist China on Taiwan.

THE STATUS OF RESEARCH

The status of research in the individual countries of the Pacific area is related to the general status of academic development, particularly in the social sciences and statistics. There is an implicit assumption here that should be made explicit. Studies in the humanities, literature, and linguistics contain much that is relevant to demography. The activities of governments and religious groups in the collection and publication of figures provide material for demographic research. Writings on population problems and policies, together with the pronouncements and records of central governments and elites, are also materials for analysis. None of these types of materials are themselves research.

The collection, processing, and tab-

ulation activities that produce data are preludes to research. Over any considerable period of time there should be close relationships between the procurement of data by an indigenous government and the analysis of those data, whether in government agencies or by universities and research institutions. There are lags and discontinuities here, however. Neither in the past nor the present have the statistical activities of colonial governments generated significant research among the governed people.

In the Pacific as a whole, the development of demographic research is related to the development of the industrial and educated population. In Canada, the United States, Australia, and New Zealand, statistical systems, technical training, and academic and other facilities are advanced. These are countries where scientific contributions are anticipated rather than exceptional events.

The other industrial country in the Pacific region is Japan. This is also the other country with an advanced statistical system. Demographic research is less advanced technically than in the English-speaking industrial countries of the region, but it is prolific and its technical levels are advancing rapidly. Since all other countries with substantial developments of demographic research are Western, the technical and scientific contributions are in Western languages. This linguistic factor plus the recency of Japan's modernization and the isolation of the years of war created difficult conditions for scholarship. Counteracting these deterrent factors, though, was the long pre-eminence of the population problem of Japan and the antiquity of the interest in it. The report of the Commission on Food and Population in 1930 did not lead to government programs to reduce the rate of population growth, but it did lead to recognition of demographic research as a function of government. There is an Institute for Research on Population Problems under the administration of the Welfare Ministry, with functions that extend to the government as a whole. There are special research reports, and there is a demographic journal, *Jinko mondai kenkyu*. The quasi-official Foundation Institute for Population Research also has a long history; in the imperial period it issued a journal, *Jinko mondai*. It has served to bring scientific, governmental, university, and business groups together in the formulation and recommendation of policy.

It is not possible to summarize either the research projects or the publications of Japan in brief compass.[2] The evaluation is also difficult, for the research is highly competent in some fields, quite limited in others. It is important to note, however, that demographic research is a part of comprehensive and widely ramified activities in population and related fields. In addition to the statistical development previously mentioned, there are major publicity programs. The Population Problem Council of the Mainichi papers subsidizes research and publication; the Mainichi papers present frequent coverage of the population problem and summarize current research and statistics. There has been national debate on policy, and there is formulation of policy recommendations for the government. The Institute of Public Health of the Welfare Ministry sponsors research and training for planned parenthood. The national permissive legislation and the resort to abortion have provided pressures for more acceptable policy and have led to research on family limitation practices

[2] A rather comprehensive bibliography for Japan and the areas of the former empire is included in Taeuber, 1958. A general bibliography was prepared by Japan's National Commission for UNESCO, 1952.

and the choices among means. Activity and research in the population field in Japan are essentially indigenous, though many of the demographers, statisticians, and doctors received some of their training in the West.

The oldest colonial statistics of the Pacific area are those of the Spanish and the Portuguese, but research was delayed and limited. The conquests of Spain were followed by depopulation among the Indians in many areas (Bennett, 1948; Cook, 1940, 1943, 1949a, b; Cook and Simpson, 1948; Steward, 1946–50). State and church alike were concerned with this reaction to conquest, so systems of records and special surveys were ordered. The concern extended over the domains of Spain, whether North or South America, the Philippines, or the islands of the southwest Pacific. Indigenous people were not participants in the plans for statistics or for policy, and they were trained neither for understanding nor for research.

There were early attempts at enumeration in the independent nations of the Americas, and periodic censuses and vital statistics have been accepted by practically all the Latin countries as essential functions of modern states (Inter American Statistical Institute, Temporary Organizing Committee, 1941). Emphasis has been placed on the collection of data and the training of operational personnel, but the development of evaluation and analysis is retarded (Arias B., 1953, 1956; Almaraz Ugalde and Becherelle, 1954; Barrera, 1954; Bocaz S., 1953; Burnight *et al.*, 1956; Centro interamericano de bioestadistica, 1955a, b, c, d; Costa Rica, 1953, 1957; El Salvador, 1954). Quantitative social science is neither a developed nor a prestige field in the universities. Population analysis has had low priority in comparison with disciplines such as medicine, economics, and finance. Moreover, questions of population research are frequently suspect because of possible relations between research and the definition of population problems.

The populations of the area from the Rio Grande to Tierra del Fuego are better known than they were a few decades ago, but the area remains one of ignorance insofar as incisive comparative analysis is concerned. However, several interrelated developments are all favorable to a major concentration on demographic research in the individual countries and within the region in the near future. The rapidity of population growth creates problems in the present and fears for the future (United Nations, Population Division, 1954; United Nations, Social Affairs Division, Population Branch, 1955). National, regional, and urban planning requires processed, if not analyzed, demographic data. There are pressures for higher education in all areas, and educational systems are being expanded. In the Indian countries the identification with the indigenous heritage is favorable to historical and contemporary studies that have substantial demographic components. And, finally, these countries are part of the larger world. Individually and collectively, they are responsive to its intellectual currents and its scientific developments. The activities of hemispheric and other international organizations may focus attention on population structures, growth, and prospects. If so, the resultant activities occur within a regional context and so stimulate comparable analysis within the areas and co-operative analysis of problems and processes that extend beyond national boundaries.

The story of demographic research in the nations that recently achieved independence is quite different from that of the United States, the British Commonwealth countries, Japan, or the republics in Latin-America. In the past,

demographic research, as data collection, was carried out in the tradition of the colonial power, in most instances by nationals of that power or by persons closely directed by them. There was only limited research by Filipinos and Americans on the population of the Philippines, whether in the colonial or the national periods. In Indonesia there was some analysis of population dynamics, and there was major concern, some research, and some movement toward policy in Java. Today indigenous research is limited by political instabilities and economic difficulties, but there are evidences of serious interest (Boeke, 1942, 1947, 1953; Furnivall, 1944, 1948; Heeren, 1955; Human Relations Area Files, 1955; Keyfitz, 1953; Keyfitz and Widjojo, 1954; Klein, 1953–54; Netherlands Indies, 1938; University of Indonesia, 1956).

The most developed systems of colonial statistics were those under Japan. Here there was an approach to research by ruling and indigenous peoples alike. There was some analysis in many fields, but the great literature was in the fields of mortality and morbidity. There was some comparative analysis of individual colonial populations, but until the years of the Co-Prosperity Sphere there was little concept of the empire as an area or a subject for research. There were village studies in the colonies and affiliated areas, and there were many studies of the movements and the colonizations of the Japanese themselves. Here, however, there is a peculiar situation. There were data of great practical and theoretical significance, and there were some trained personnel among the Japanese and the indigenous people. Population growth was rapid, and population was recognized as a severe problem. Yet there was little research on the population problems of the colonies. The answer probably lies in the timing of developments. The great advance of technically competent demographic research in Japan came in the thirties, but it was also in the thirties that freedom of research was limited by the state. In this perspective, the demographic research that was carried out may attest the indefatigable energy of the Japanese students. Collection and evaluation of the literature of this period would be required for final evaluation of the extent of the scientific developments or of the status of demographic research.

The status of research in French Indochina is difficult to describe or to evaluate in comparative terms. There was no census that covered all the associated states, and vital statistics were limited to local areas. There was major research on human geography, though, and there were medical, social, and anthropological studies of localities and groups (French Indochina, 1929; Gourou, 1936, 1940*a*, *b*; Robequain, 1939, 1946; Zelinsky, 1950).

Political and economic conditions have retarded demographic research in the new nations. Among the areas formerly subject to or affiliated with Japan, Sakhalin, North Korea, Kwantung, and Manchukuo are in the Communist world and subject to its statistical and research limitations. In the early years developments in South Korea permitted some focus on demographic statistics, but the situation altered sharply after the invasion of 1950 (Lautensach, 1950; McCune, George, 1950; McCune, Shannon, 1956; Park, 1955). The records of Taiwan had been products of the Japanese who were repatriated to Japan. Trained and experienced Taiwanese were few, and the Chinese from the mainland were experienced only in the tradition of the *pao-chia* registration and control system. The state of siege precluded untrammeled research. The elements of a population problem, trained personnel, university growth, and external interest and assistance all exist in Taiwan. The future of research rests more on political and military considerations than on the tenet of scientific relevance.

The data and the research of the Federation of Malaya and the Crown Colony of Singapore remain in the British tradition as exemplified in classic form in India and Ceylon (Cooper, 1951; Malaya, 1949; Singapore, 1947; Smith, 1952). The migrant colony of Hong Kong has been so dominated by immediate problems that analysis has been limited severely since the armies of Japan plunged southward. The research in the lesser British territories of the Pacific will be noted later.

The record of the United States in demographic research in its Pacific territories is not a laudable one. The data and the research in Hawaii are similar to those in continental United States (Adams, 1937; Burrows, 1947; Glick, 1942; Lind, 1955; Shapiro, 1939). Rather complex data are collected in Alaska, and there have been some studies. A detailed census was taken in the Ryukyus in 1950, and the registration system is being improved; but there is a notable deficiency in demographic research (Emerson *et al.*, 1949; Taeuber, 1955). The status of data and research in the other territories has been low. Simple censuses have been taken each decade in the Panama Canal Zone and the Pacific territories. There has been research in many fields, but demography remains an exception. No census has been taken in the United States Trust Territory of the Pacific since the Japanese took the last of their enumerative censuses of Nanyo-gunto, the mandated islands, in 1940 (Stanford University, 1949; Taeuber, 1950*b*; Yanaihara, 1940. But for the new developments, see U.S. Government of American Samoa, 1957).

Population figures and descriptions of institutions and behavior related to marriage, birth, and death are abundant for the island peoples (McArthur, 1957). Demographic research is limited since official data tend to be inadequate for technical manipulation (note the quantitative and qualitative limitations to the studies cited in Elkin, 1953, and Keesing, 1953*b*). Anthropologists have studied many of the cultures intensively, though, and demographic structure and trends were often considered. Population decline was the spectacular process, and it was recognized as a symptom of social disorganization (Cilento, 1928; Fiji, 1896; Gini, 1938; Hogbin, 1939; Kooijman, 1955; Lambert, 1934; Lessa, 1955). The transition to growth was regarded initially simply as the cessation of decline. Rapid growth in the current period is responsible for an increasing interest in population research among administrators, native leaders, and international organizations (Belshaw, Horace, 1956; Cato, 1955; Coulter, 1941; Keesing, 1934, 1945; Lambert, 1938). The recent analysis of population trends in Tikopia may presage a type of anthropological-demographic co-operation that will contribute substantially to knowledge of method and process (Borrie *et al.*, 1957; Firth, 1936; Hunt *et al.*, 1954; Lessa, 1955; Murrill, 1950; Powdermaker, 1931).

The advance of research on the populations of the tiny islands is far more rapid than that on the gigantic population of China. Here there have been great controversies on such unanswerable questions as the size of the population (Fitzgerald, 1936; Krotevich, 1955; Rockhill, 1912; Wang, 1932–33, 1935; Willcox, 1926, 1937, 1940). The development of research has been frustrated by the immensity of the tasks and by the political instabilities. The emphasis has always been placed on official figures. By the early twentieth century there were direct influences of Western developments, and so laws, regulations, and schedules were pre-

pared for enumerative censuses (Chao, 1938; Lieu, 1933; Wang, 1932–33, 1935). Whether the intellectual aspects of preparation were well or ill performed, they had little relevance to data. There was neither the general nor the specific administrative organization for adequate performance. There was neither the concept nor the technique for surveys among an illiterate and suspicious people. The reputed censuses of 1910, 1912, and 1928 yielded figures of largely unknown origin and obviously gross inaccuracies. After 1928 there was a restoration of *pao-chia* registration, but the procedures and administration were defective. The purpose was police control, not government statistics or research. Once again there were many figures, but there were no data for definitive analysis of numbers, trends in numbers, sex ratios, age structures, or vital rates.

In the brief period from the late twenties to the late thirties there were strong movements leading toward research. Doctors, social scientists, and demographers trained in the West were returning to China, and the co-operation and funds of Western institutions, mainly American, permitted a growth of statistical data both as by-product of health and other activities and as direct product of field study (Buck, J., 1937; Ch'iao, 1934; Ch'iao *et al.*, 1938; Lee, 1935; Notestein, 1938; Seifert, 1935; Thompson, W., 1938).

The Japanese research personnel of the South Manchuria Railway Company had long studied China's population and economy. With the conquest of Manchuria, scholars from Japan and the staff and students of the developing universities started making population studies (Beardsley *et al.*, 1950; Iwamura, 1948; Koyama, 1940; Miura and Shinozuka, 1952; Sato, 1951; Taeuber, 1945*b*). Experimental censuses and a national census of 1940 produced quantities of data for analysis (bibliographies in Taeuber, 1957, and U.S. Library of Congress, 1951). Again, timing barred the progress of research. The Japanese who survived war and repatriation are laboring somewhere in Japan, few in population research on Manchuria or northeast Asia.

Some research continued in free China during the war (Chen Ta, 1946; National Tsing Hua University, 1944). Developments began again after 1945, and again there were plans, the training of personnel, and initial activities. There is no complete record of events after the Communist domination of the mainland. The Communists, as the regimes before them, introduced their rule with a survey of the population (Krotevich, 1955). This time there was control of the country with an administrative organization that reached the village level, and there were widespread activities. Through combinations of enumeration, registration, compilation, and estimation, figures on the total numbers of the Chinese were produced between mid-1953 and late 1954. Since summation of totals was done at local levels and transmitted upward, it is doubtful whether there are even collections of schedules in provincial and national offices. There are major activities in registration and in vital records, but there are few figures for evaluation. There are publications on research and policy, but the original documents do not seem to be available to scholars in the United States.

All the studies that have been made in China demonstrate the difficulties of demographic research. Few have contributed unequivocal conclusions about the demography of China or the demographic behavior of people of Chinese culture. Field work required the adaptation of Western concepts and techniques to China, but that adaptation was seldom made. People were illiterate, suspicious, and superstitious. The discipline of research organization was not firm, controls were inadequate, and publication consisted more of description than of analysis. It is interesting to speculate on how many of the difficulties were the usual ones of early statistical and research development and how many were inherent in the culture of China. The available information on Communist China indicates a persistence of the non-numerical approach to the handling of numbers, the projection of global answers on limited and faulty evidence, and the acceptance of much of the mythology of Chinese demographic characteristics and population trends. There is now a centrally organized government with economic plans and population policies. Whether its activities will serve to create ever more elaborate demographic propaganda or to stimulate demographic research remains a question.

It would be logical to include the status of demographic research in the Soviet Union in this résumé. That story is omitted on the grounds that it, like the stories of the other industrial nations, is part of the advance of demography in general rather than in the Pacific area. The research that is most relevant to the comparative demography of Far Eastern peoples is that of the Soviet Far East. Here Asian peoples were parts of and subjected to the political organization and forced economic transformation of an industrializing state.

These comments on demographic research have proceeded area by area, with major emphasis on demographic research within national or territorial boundaries. This is the research that is the most developed. There is a paucity of demographic research on the processes and consequences of the interactions among cultures. There are few comparisons of variables among peoples of different cultures and physical conditions. There is little testing of hypotheses about similarities and differences in demographic response to political, economic, and social change. As long as these types of research are not undertaken, ignorance of the demography of the Pacific region will remain. And that ignorance precludes either a knowledge of world population or a demography that can assert and demonstrate that it is not culture bound.

SOME QUESTIONS FOR RESEARCH

The questions for demographic research in the Pacific region are not unique to that region. In this area, however, there are many types of demographic structures and processes, and there are complex interrelations of milieu and culture with human reproduction and survival. Both the preconditions to biological and cultural survival and the ranges of variation that are consistent with survival can be studied in the laboratories of the Pacific. Control of all the factors differentiating development and status would leave a residue of biological, social, and economic factors that are universal. There may be interrelations among these universal factors that are essential to the survival of groups. Those peoples who have disappeared biologically are removed from the possibilities for research, but there have been and are declining peoples. In the Pacific there are also the demographic-cultural adjustments that have produced the most numerous of all peoples, the Chinese.

Consideration of some of the questions for research in the Pacific region is not a design for research. The raising of the questions may serve some purpose, for it is important that limited studies be so formulated that they are relevant to wider problems and hypotheses. It is desirable also that research be cumulative and that new research be more than a reaffirmation of already established relationships. Perhaps the most desirable first step in Pacific demography is the evaluation of the existing fund of knowledge. Only thus will there be knowledge of what is known, and only thus can the hypotheses for further research be developed efficiently.

A major theoretical and practical question is that of the relations between population growth, industrialization, and urbanization. The Pacific region includes major areas for comparative study. Canada, the United States, Australia, and New Zealand are all countries in advanced transition. In global perspective, the economies are highly developed, incomes and educational levels are high, and mortality and fertility are low. Relative to western and northern Europe, fertility is high. The possible numbers of research projects here are great. The data are available or could be procured through censuses, surveys, and registration procedures or special field research; and the professional personnel and facilities exist in the individual countries.

The Soviet Union has undergone rapid economic development in the last four decades. The pattern and control of that development have differed from the earlier experiences of the nations of western and northern Europe. The demographic correlates of the process have been studied for the U.S.S.R. as a whole and its major regions (Lorimer, 1946). A demographic transition occurred, but its timing and its cultural context differed from earlier transitions. At one critical stage the government acted to force declines in fertility through the legalization of abortions. Then the government adopted comprehensive social and population policies to stay the declines in fertility. These refer to the Soviet Union as a whole. The important question from the standpoint of the Pacific is that of Soviet Asia. What were the consequences of the altered political structure, the economic changes, and the population policies on the peoples of Asian Russia, and particularly of the Soviet Far East? This is comparative cultural analysis, but it may have political relevance, for Soviet Asia is the sparsely settled land of Asia.

Japan is a significant nation in which to study the demography of industrialization and urbanization, for it is neither Western in culture nor Christian in religion. The premodern demographic balance involved substantial limitation of family size by abortion and infanticide. The economic development came late, and it was rapid. In Japan, as in the West and in Russia, there was a decline in mortality and a long period of population increase, but there was a decline in fertility whose rate eventually surpassed that in mortality. In the years since 1948, the Japanese have permitted abortions, and fertility has declined rapidly. The problems of analysis in the interrelations of social structure, traditional values, and attitudes are immense and complex, but the results of such research have both practical value and theoretical relevance. The experiences of the Soviet Union and Japan suggest that declines in fertility may be quickened by the nature of the processes of economic change and urbanization and that the provision of facilities for abortion may result in early and substantial reductions in rates of population growth. If this is so, the historic experience of Europe may not permit the derivation of projections that are not time and culture bound. Furthermore, the trends in the U.S.S.R. and Japan may not be a basis for estimating the future for such nations as China and Indonesia.

Still other types of studies of the demographic transition could be made on the basis of Pacific experience. The developments in Chile merit special study. Here there has been substantial and continuing urbanization, and there has been a long decline in mortality (Bocaz S., 1953; Centro interamericano de bioestadistica, 1955a, b, c, d; U.S. Library of Congress, Hispanic Foundation, 1954). The national data suggest a fairly rapid decline in fertility almost two decades ago and then a plateau. The heavy and evidently increasing resort to abortion raises major questions of demographic-economic interrelations and of motivations. Perhaps there is blocked economic development and a blocked demographic transition. Only incisive research in Chile can yield the nexus of interrelations in what appears to be a most significant variation in the pattern of modernization.

Most considerations of the concept of the demographic transition have emphasized the changing rates of growth of national populations, although there have also been studies of differentials in mortality and fertility within groups of the national populations. Is the transition in fact a national process, a correlate of an economic development of an industrial type which characterizes the nation as a whole? Or do economic and social groups in rural and urban areas reveal persistent patterns of fertility, the national transition being primarily a product of the altered social-economic and urban-rural composition of the population? The experience of Japan suggests that both processes occurred during her rapid transition, i.e., that there was declining fertility in all groups but that a substantial portion of the national decline was due to the altered structure and residence of the population. The census data that the Japanese collected in their colonies permit analysis of the fertility of the component groups in many populations.

The preceding discussion of the demographic changes associated with economic modernization has involved the implicit assumption that there was a premodern pattern of levels and relations from which decline occurred. There is evidence in the Pacific area that this is not so, but there has been little systematic research on premodern vital balances or on the initial reactions of fertility and mortality to the forces of development. Rates of natural increase were so high in the American colonies as to suggest that fertility had risen under the favorable conditions of the New World. Decline in fertility was in process by the beginning of the nineteenth century, and the declines in the early nineteenth century characterized rural and urban areas alike. In Japan the initial reactions to Western contact involved increases in mortality and in fertility. Maximum fertility occurred in the period between the greatly reduced incidence of the limitation practices of the indigenous society and the widespread adoption of the limitation practices of the modern period.

The ideal procedure would require analysis of the demography of many peoples and cultures prior to contact with the West. An approach to such retrospective research can be achieved in some instances by anthropologists, but it can never be adequately quantitative. However, there can be analysis of many cultures similar to and different from each other in known ways, and there can be analysis of peoples of the same culture in different resources and developmental situations. A vital balance that involved substantial limitation of fertility seems to have existed among many of the premodern cultures of the western Pacific. In the delicately balanced economies of the islands, a high fertility that permitted rapid population growth was hazardous. Increasing numbers would force death rates upward, but famine and disease might eliminate the entire population. If fertility were below mortality and if the relationship continued, the population would disappear.

The analysis of limitations to reproduction among non-literate peoples could be relevant to the great problems of today if the factors in the limitation were defined in terms of forces and interrelations. The question of motivations is significant, for there is a common assumption that precautionary limitation of fertility in the interests of individual or family development is a unique product of the modern industrializing and urbanizing society.

The altered levels of fertility and mortality that accompanied industrial development and urban growth are but one facet of the demography of the contact and interpenetration of cultures. The movement of Western people into the Pacific region had devastating consequences for some of the people who lived in the region; the indirect contacts with Western culture often led to substantial growth. Something of the complexity of the processes of contact are noted here.

The migrations of Europeans across the Atlantic and the gradual occupation of the Americas were demographic tragedy for most of the native peoples (Cook, 1940, 1943, 1949*a, b;* Cook and Simpson, 1948; Kroeber, 1939; Steward, 1946–50; Wissler, 1938). In North America the course of events led almost to extermination. The results of contact were similar in Chile, though here the intermixture was greater. The general course of events seems to have been displacement, disturbed economic functioning, social disorganization, and decline or disappearance. Conflict accounted for some of the mortality, but the major factor was disease. Eventually the epidemics and the endemic diseases were brought under control, famines were eliminated, and death rates were reduced. Birth rates remained high, and there was the familiar story of rapid population increase among people whose resources, skills, and adaptability were low.

In America north of the Rio Grande, in some areas of Middle America, and in the southern part of South America the Indians were relatively few in numbers, so there was amalgamation or ethnic succession. In the areas of the great Indian civilizations, the story was quite different. Here the immigrants were Spanish men who came as soldiers, priests, or adventurers. The labor for economic exploitation had to be that of the Indians. The family arrangements had to involve Indian women. Thus there was a rigid social structure that was firmly based in economy, state, and church. On the other hand, there was intermixture in a situation in which the children were assimilated into the upper group. There developed a rough parallelism in the ethnic and social structures of the populations. The numerical relations of the groups and the evolutions of the social structures themselves produced gradations from top to bottom in some cases, virtual discontinuities in others. Political revolutions that were both social and agrarian in origin altered these associations in some areas, barely touched them in others. Selective urban migration and selective access to schools and other channels of upward mobility were aspects of the continuities in social-economic and ethnic structures. The evolutions of national populations, the regional and social-economic differentials in vital processes, and the prospects for change are all related to these structures, their persistences, and their plasticities. So also are income distributions, rates of savings, and business entrepreneurship.

The demographic research in the Spanish cultures is intricate if the basic questions extend beyond the measurement of population composition and change into the historic interrelations and the present relationships. Historians are laboring on the depopulations that followed the conquest and the change to growth that occurred later. International and national research is beginning on current demographic situations, particularly the continuation of high fertility under conditions of rapidly declining mortality. The basic research that involves the social structures, the political and cultural instabilities, and the types of economic relations and trends is scarcely touched.

The influence of the Indian or other indigenous group on the population history in the contact situation is a significant aspect of the demography of the Spanish areas. Hispanic America covers a great area. Spain also occupied and united the areas that are now the Republic of the Philippines, and she ruled many of the lesser islands of the Pacific. The demographic influences here may be those involved in Spanish rule, or they may be those involved in Spanish Catholicism as it touched the many peoples from the Andean highlands to the coral atolls.

The Pacific is also a region for the study of the demographic aspects of the Western economic penetration that occurred along with conquest and political rule. All the American nations were once colonies, but revolutions occurred long ago. The classic colonialism is that of the western Pacific. The diversities in areas, economies, peoples, cultures, and governing powers are great enough to permit partially controlled research on the factors and processes that produced the typical colonial pattern of demographic development. Britain controlled Malaya, Singapore, Hong Kong, and many lesser islands, and influenced Thailand. The Indochinese peninsula was French, while Indonesia was Dutch. Japan controlled a great colonial area directly and ruled northeastern China indirectly. Spain, Portugal, and Germany were once major colonial powers in the Pacific. The United States controlled the Philippines in the past. The areas of present responsibility include Alaska, Hawaii, the Ryukyus, the Trust Territory of the Pacific, and several other islands. These diverse situations permit the design of research projects that extend the demography of colonialism beyond the specifically descriptive.

The lesser islands of the Pacific have been mentioned occasionally, but they have been treated casually in the consideration of the key problems for research. The island peoples are by definition marginal insofar as the evolution of the numerous peoples and the great cultures are concerned. Their demographic balances over the centuries have not produced rapidly increasing populations that occupied expanding areas. The reasons for the differences in the historic destinies of populations are worthy of speculation and susceptible to limited study. The slow growth may be a product of the particular physical environment in which the group finds itself. Or the limitations in culture and growth may have been forces in the movement to the marginal physical environment.

The peoples of the individual islands are the responsibilities of the great powers who must be concerned with their welfare. Anthropological research is relevant to the fulfilment of these responsibilities, and so anthropology has been furthered as academic discipline and administrative guide. Declining population was regarded as a symptom of cultural ill-health, and much attention was focused on its prevalence, its causes, and its possible cures. The missions and the doctors alike opposed practices that had reduced fertility in the indigenous cultures; acculturation involved the passing of the old practices. The initial result of Western contact was increased mortality. The

consequent phase for the survivors seems to have involved substantially increased fertility and increasingly reduced mortality. Then the miracles of public health were brought to the islands, and death rates were reduced to very low levels. Population increase is replacing population decline as the welfare problem for administering powers. The balances that preserved the peoples of the islands in the indigenous cultures must indeed have been delicate ones. Or perhaps there were alternating periods of growth and decimation, with disappearance the fate of those whose fertility was inadequate or superabundant for the fragile economic development permitted by the islands.

The major demographic research interest in the island populations lies in the plasticity of the cultural forms and processes that condition marriage, family, childbearing, mortality, and migration. Here it may be possible to sketch the specifications for lethal variations, although not to estimate their frequencies. It may be, on the other hand, that the cultures had compensating mechanisms for modifying vital processes or migration before the continued operation of the original forces had lethal consequences.

There are possibilities for significant research in the islands on the divergent types of institutional and psychological bases that lead to similar levels of fertility, mortality, and population growth. Ultimately, it may be fruitful to explore the hypothesis that there were functional relations between fertility and mortality. This question has a theoretical relevance that extends beyond the southwest Pacific, or indeed beyond the demography of the non-literate peoples. The existence of a growth potential in the reproductive mores of a population may be an essential aspect of survival in competition and of economic and territorial expansion. Such a potential might be a hazard where such competition was not required and where expansion was not possible. A structure of theory that involves cultural adaptability and selective survival is consistent with many of the facts concerning vital balances among mainland and island peoples. The critical empirical question is the persistence or change in the vital balances under altered economic and environmental conditions that do not involve an indigenous culture in contact with an industrial culture. The demographic balances of the island cultures and the demographic changes in the industrial cultures may be manifestations of the fundamental processes of adaptability in cultural dynamics. If so, the high mortality that threatened the disappearance of the island peoples and the sharply reduced mortality that threatens catastrophe to the multitudinous mainland peoples are both manifestations of a cultural contact that shattered functional associations once prevalent in the indigenous cultures.

The greatest of the research fields in the Pacific, and the least cultivated, is that of China and the Chinese. The reconstruction of the growth of the population of China is scarcely susceptible to scientific investigation. There are major possibilities for research in the demography of the Chinese or, more precisely, in the demographic patterns of peoples of Chinese culture. The economic practices, the institutions, and the values of the Chinese have led over the centuries to the production of the world's largest population. The mortality has been high, and the hazards of famine, epidemic, and natural catastrophe have been major. Fertility has been high enough to insure survival in the difficult times and to insure growth over the centuries, but there are known to be institutional deterrents and personal limitations to maximum reproduction. As China undergoes industrialization and urbanization, the se-

lectivities in migration and the demographic responses to urban life become important factors not alone in the structure of urban populations but in the efficiency of industrialization. There is the correlated question of the speed with which change occurs in the villages.

The ideal analysis of the Chinese population would require census data and vital statistics for areas and groups within China. An analysis of differentials in vital rates, migration, and population structure would permit comparisons of the demography of China with that of other nations. The analysis within China and the comparisons with other nations that were similar in economy or in culture might provide an objective basis for evaluating the future prospects for China. The difficulty is that the pre-Communist Chinese within China had not been subjected to forced economic development. Thus China's own history may have limited relevance to the prediction of the reactions of Chinese to the new order that is being formed.

The discussion of the ideal in Chinese research is a guide to the formulation of research problems, but there have not been and there are not now the adequate census and registration data to permit the ideal analysis. That research which is possible within China depends on the data which are available and accessible. For the population of the central area of mainland China there are some official statistics and some special studies that permit analysis of numbers, land-resource relations, economic activities, marital status, family structure, migration patterns, mortality, and fertility. Then there are materials on Chinese outside China, primarily the data of colonial censuses, surveys, and registration procedures. These colonial censuses and the related vital statistics cover Chinese from different areas and subcultures within China who are living in different parts of the Pacific region under varying economic, social, and political conditions. In northeast Asia there are comparable data on Chinese in the Kwantung Leased Territory, the South Manchuria Railway Zone, and Manchukuo. There are comparable data for Koreans in Korea, Manchukuo, and Japan, and for Japanese in Japan, Korea, Manchukuo, and North China.

There are many research-oriented projects that could lead to an appreciable contraction of the perimeters of ignorance surrounding China and the Chinese. A resurvey of the historical records would seem justified, provided only that analytical techniques were used for the evaluation. The cultural patterning of the responses to questions and the practices in registration are legitimate projects since knowledge of bias is essential to the analysis and interpretation of contemporary as well as past statistics. Analysis of the similarities and differences in Japanese and Chinese culture is significant, for the family patterns and the Confucian relations of the generations of the Japanese trace directly to China.

THE PACIFIC AS AREA AND FIELD FOR RESEARCH

This survey of data and questions for research has been limited. Great fields have been noted sketchily if at all. There has been no note on that intermediate analysis which is often included with research, i.e., the estimation of numbers, distribution, characteristics, or change for use in policy decisions or administrative programs. The differential rates of growth of the various peoples remain unnoted, as do the forecasts of future growth. The formal demographic approach has been secondary to the consideration of the interrelations of external factors and specific demographic variables in the generation of growth or decline. The

reasons for these biases are inherent in the consideration of the Pacific region as a demographic laboratory. The emphasis is placed on that which may be distinctive rather than on that which has no specificity in place and time.

There is another major deficiency in the presentation, and that is the lack of connection between the statement on data and the statement of questions for research. The data that were described included major segments of the traditional statistics on the numbers and characteristics of people and on the rates at which births and deaths occurred. The questions for research involved many that were historical and cultural. They concerned the demography of cultural contact and social change; the interrelations of population, economy, social structure, and value systems; the relations of variables in preliterate, transitional, and modern cultures; and the impact of cultural variables on demographic structure and process. The ancient and the modern demographic statistics of many Pacific areas are both defective for the design of research that provides answers for the questions posed. Field research is often barred either because the processes are historical or because the areas are not open to research.

Analysis of the conventional data of censuses and vital statistics is critically important, but such data are selective of areas, time periods, cultural types, and levels of economic development. Modern data are products of the modern period among economically developed peoples or those ruled by others who are thus developed. The data for measurement vanish in periods of crisis, instability, or revolutionary change, and they are unlikely to reappear for some time if the political or cultural changes have been major. But in this situation of major change, the projection of the measured trends of earlier periods is a questionable procedure.

The use of conventional techniques in the analysis of the demography of the Pacific peoples faces the insuperable barriers of an absence of adequate quantitative data for major and highly selected portions of the area. Ramified activities are under way to extend and improve the data collection processes. There are regional concentrations of efforts under the Inter American Statistical Institute and the South Pacific Commission. There is technical assistance under the United Nations and the Colombo Plan, as well as through the International Cooperation Administration of the United States.

If the prospects for demographic data in the statistically underdeveloped areas of the Pacific were assessed on the basis of the past experience of today's developed areas, the outlook for research materials in the immediate future would be dark. Here, as in so many aspects of social change in the Pacific, the past may not permit prediction of the future. Techniques of sample surveys and machine processing of data can be imported rather than invented. Methods and techniques in schedule design, survey methods, and analysis can be adapted rather than developed *de novo*. The fundamental fact, however, is that the conventional data for demographic analysis do not now exist for great populations, and they may not exist for many populations for considerable periods in the future.

Analysis of the present and the past must be made on the basis of whatever data exist, or they cannot be made at all. This is an obvious statement, and its implications for research are far-reaching. Comparable estimates of demographic status and trends may be made by conjecture and analogy; but they will be limited to simple variables, and their validation lies in accepting as axiomatic hypotheses of comparability that should be major subjects of research. Incisive or intricate research must have its hypotheses defined and its methodology developed area by area and culture by culture. If information is qualitative or if quantitative data are not amenable to the usual techniques of demography, the approach and methods of other disciplines must be integrated with those of demography.

There are no definitive conclusions on the possibilities or the prospects for demographic research in major portions of the Pacific area. Surveys of data and exploratory analysis are essential. The alternative to the analysis of the materials that exist is the absence of analysis. Since the populations concerned are a considerable portion of the world's total and since the area includes many natural experiments in demographic structures and interrelations, a negative answer to the possibilities for research cannot be accepted.

SELECTED BIBLIOGRAPHY

ADAMS, ROMANZO. 1937. *Interracial Marriage in Hawaii: A Study of the Mutually Conditioned Processes of Acculturation and Amalgamation.* New York: Macmillan Co.

ALMAREZ UGALDE, A., and BRAVO BECHE-RELLE, M. A. 1954. "Tablas de vida para la República Mexicana en 1950," *Revista del Instituto de Salubridad y Enfermades Tropicales,* XV, 39–50.

ARIAS B., JORGE. 1953. "Tablas de mortalidad para el Municipio de Guatemala 1921–1940–1950," *Revista de Colegio Médico de Guatemala,* IV, 315–34.

———. 1956. "Algunos errores en la declaracion de edad en censos de población de 1950 en Centro America y Mexico," *Estadística,* XIV, 403–25.

BARCLAY, GEORGE W. 1954a. *Colonial Development and Population in Taiwan.* Princeton: Princeton University Press.

———. 1954b. *A Report on Taiwan's Population to the Joint Commission on Rural Reconstruction.* Princeton: Office of

Population Research, Princeton University.

BARRERA, H. E. 1954. "Tablas de vida de la ciudad de Quito," *Revista ecuatoriana de higiene y medicina tropical,* XI, 89–105.

BEARDSLEY, RICHARD K., *et al.* 1950. *Bibliographic Materials in the Japanese Language on Far Eastern Archaeology and Ethnology.* Ann Arbor: University of Michigan Press.

BELSHAW, CYRIL S. 1950. *Island Administration in the South West Pacific: Government and Reconstruction in New Caledonia, the New Hebrides, and the British Solomon Islands.* London: Royal Institute of International Affairs.

BELSHAW, HORACE. 1956. *Population Growth and Levels of Consumption, with Special Reference to Countries in Asia.* New York: Institute of Pacific Relations.

BENNETT, WENDELL C. (ed.). 1948. *A Reappraisal of Peruvian Archaeology.* (Society for American Archaeology Memoir No. 4.) Menasha, Wis.

BOCAZ S., ALBINO. 1953. "Curva de Gompertz aplicada al crecimiento de la población chilena," *Estadística chilena,* No. 7, pp. 239–40. "La curva de la población de Chile," *ibid.,* No. 9, pp. 369–70. "Curva de Gompertz aplicada al crecimiento de la ciudad de Santiago," *ibid.,* Nos. 10–11, p. 453.

BOEKE, JULIUS H. 1942. *The Structure of Netherlands Indian Economy.* New York: International Secretariat, Institute of Pacific Relations.

———. 1947. *Indische Economie.* Book I: *De Theorie der Indische Economie.* 2d rev. ed. Haarlem: H.D. Tjeenk Willink.

———. 1953. *Economics and Economic Policy of Dual Societies as Exemplified by Indonesia.* New York: International Secretariat, Institute of Pacific Relations.

BORRIE, W. D., FIRTH, RAYMOND, and SPILLIUS, JAMES. 1957. "The Population of Tikopia, 1929 and 1952," *Population Studies,* X, 229–52.

BOURGEAU, JAN. 1950. *La France du Pacifique: Nouvelle-Calédonie et dépendances, Wallis et Futuna, Nouvelles-Hébrides, établissements français de l'Océanie.* Paris: Société d'Éditions Géographiques, Maritimes, et Coloniales.

BUCK, J. LOSSING. 1937. *Land Utilization in China.* Vol. I: *Land Utilization in China.* Vol. II: *Atlas.* Vol. III: *Statistics.* Chicago: University of Chicago Press.

BUCK, PETER H. (Te Rangi Hiroa.) 1938. *Vikings of the Sunrise.* New York: Frederick A. Stokes Co.

———. 1945. *An Introduction to Polynesian Anthropology.* (Bulletin No. 187.) Honolulu: Bernice P. Bishop Museum.

BURNIGHT, R. G., *et al.* 1956. "Rural-urban Fertility in Mexico," *American Sociological Review,* XXI, 3–7.

BURROWS, EDWIN G. 1947. *Hawaiian Americans: An Account of the Mingling of Japanese, Chinese, Polynesian, and American Cultures.* New Haven: Yale University Press.

CATO, A. C. 1955. "Fijians and Fiji-Indians: A Culture-contact Problem in the South Pacific," *Oceania,* XXXVI, 14–34.

CATOR, W. J. 1936. *The Economic Position of the Chinese in the Netherlands Indies.* Chicago: University of Chicago Press.

CENTRO INTERAMERICANO DE BIOESTADÍSTICA. 1955a. *Confrontacion de los censos de 1940 y 1952 de Chile mediante las estadísticas de mortalidad.* Santiago de Chile: Escuela de Salubridad.

———. 1955b. *Estudio de la tendencia de la natalidad en diversas edades de la mujer, en Chile, en el periodo de 1931–1952.* Santiago de Chile: Escuela de Salubridad.

———. 1955c. *Integralidad del registro de nacimientos y oportunidad de la inscripcion en Chile, periodo 1917–1953.* Santiago de Chile: Escuela de Salubridad.

———. 1955d. *Tablas de vida para Chile, ambos sexos, hombres, mujeres, 1951–1953.* Santiago de Chile: Escuela de Salubridad.

CHANG CHUN-JO. 1939. *A Study of Military Colonization during the Successive Dynasties* (in Chinese). Shanghai: Commercial Press.

CHAO CH'ENG-HSIN. 1938. "Recent Population Changes in China," *Yenching Journal of Social Studies*, I, 1–48.

CH'EN, C. C. 1937. "Ting Hsien and the Public Health Movement in China," *Milbank Memorial Fund Quarterly*, XV, 380–90.

CHEN HAN-SENG. 1949. *Frontier Land Systems in Southernmost China: A Comparative Study of Agrarian Problems and Social Organization among the Pai Yi People of Yunnan and the Kamba People of Sikang*. New York: Institute of Pacific Relations.

CHEN TA. 1929. *Emigrant Communities in South China: A Study of Overseas Migration and Its Influence on Standards of Living and Cultural Change*. New York: Institute of Pacific Relations.

———. 1946. "Population in Modern China," *American Journal of Sociology*, Vol. LII, Part II.

———. 1947. "Factors of Urban Growth in China," *Proceedings of the International Statistical Conference*. Calcutta: Eka Press.

———. 1948. "The Need of Population Research in China," *Population Studies*, I, 342–52.

CH'IAO CH'I-MING. 1934. *A Study of the Chinese Population*. New York: Milbank Memorial Fund.

———, et al. 1938. *An Experiment in the Registration of Vital Statistics in China*. Oxford, Ohio: Scripps Foundation for Research in Population Problems.

CILENTO, RAPHAEL W. 1928. *The Causes of the Depopulation of the Western Islands of the Territory of New Guinea*. Canberra: Government Printer.

CLYDE, PAUL H. 1948. *The Far East: A History of the Impact of the West on Eastern Asia*. New York: Prentice-Hall.

COLE, FAY-COOPER. 1945. *The Peoples of Malaysia*. New York: Van Nostrand Co.

COOK, SHERBURNE F. 1940. *Population Trends among the California Mission Indians*. ("Ibero Americana," Vol. XVII.) Berkeley: University of California Press.

———. 1943. *The Conflict between the California Indian and White Civilization*. Vol. I: *The Indian versus the Spanish Mission*. Vol. II: *The Physical and Demographic Reaction of the Non-mission Indians in Colonial and Provincial California*. Vols. III–IV: *The Conflict between the California Indian and White Civilization*. ("Ibero Americana," Vols. XXI–XXIV.) Berkeley: University of California Press.

———. 1949a. *The Historical Demography and Ecology of the Teotlalpan*. ("Ibero Americana," Vol. XXXIII.) Berkeley: University of California Press.

———. 1949b. *Soil Erosion and Population in Central Mexico*. ("Ibero Americana," Vol. XXXIV.) Berkeley: University of California Press.

———, and SIMPSON, LESLEY B. 1948. *The Population of Central Mexico in the Sixteenth Century*. ("Ibero Americana," Vol. XXXI.) Berkeley: University of California Press.

COON, CARLETON S., and ANDREWS, JAMES M., IV (eds.). 1943. *Studies in the Anthropology of Oceania and Asia, Presented in Memory of Roland Burrage Dixon*. ("Papers of the Peabody Museum of Archaeology and Ethnology, Harvard University," Vol. XX.)

COOPER, EUNICE. 1951. "Urbanization in Malaya," *Population Studies*, V, 117–31.

COSTA RICA, DIRECCIÓN GENERAL DE ESTADÍSTICA Y CENSOS. 1957. *Tablas de vida de Costa Rica, 1949–1951*. San José.

COSTA RICA, MINISTERIO DE ECONOMÍA Y HACIENDA. 1953. *Atlas estadístico de Costa Rica*. San José.

COULTER, JOHN W. 1941. *Land Utilization in American Samoa*. Honolulu: Bernice P. Bishop Museum.

CRESSEY, GEORGE B. 1951. *Asia's Lands and Peoples: A Geography of One-third the Earth and Two-thirds Its People*. 2d ed. New York: McGraw-Hill.

DE YOUNG, JOHN E. 1955. *Village Life in Modern Thailand*. Berkeley: University of California Press.

DOBBY, E. H. G. 1946. "Some Aspects of the Human Ecology of Southeast Asia," *Geographical Journal*, CVIII, 40–54.

———. 1951. *Southeast Asia*. New York: John Wiley.

DU BOIS, CORA. 1944. *The People of Alor: A Social-psychological Study of an East*

Indian Island. . . . Minneapolis: University of Minnesota Press.

———. 1949. *Social Forces in Southeast Asia.* Minneapolis: University of Minnesota Press.

EL SALVADOR, DIRECCIÓN GENERAL DE ESTADÍSTICA Y CENSOS. 1954. "Tabla de vida abreviada para la Republica de El Salvador, años 1949–1951," *Boletín estadístico,* No. 13, pp. 26–30.

ELKIN, A. P. 1953. *Social Anthropology in Melanesia: A Review of Research.* London: Oxford University Press.

EMBREE, JOHN F., and DOTSON, LILLIAN O. 1950. *Bibliography of the Peoples and Cultures of Mainland Southeast Asia.* ("Southeast Asia Studies.") New Haven: Yale University Press.

EMERSON, RUPERT, et al. 1949. *America's Pacific Dependencies: A Survey of American Colonial Policies and of Administration and Progress toward Self-Rule in Alaska, Hawaii, Guam, Samoa, and the Trust Territory.* New York: American Institute of Pacific Relations.

FAIRBANK, JOHN K., and LIU KWANG-CHING. 1950. *Modern China: A Bibliography Guide to Chinese Works, 1898–1937.* Cambridge: Harvard University Press.

FEI HSIAO-T'UNG and CHANG CHIH-I. 1949. *Earthbound China: A Study of Rural Economy in Yunnan.* Rev. English edition. London: Routledge & Kegan Paul.

FIJI, GOVERNMENT. 1896. *Report of the 1893 Commission on Depopulation.* Suva.

FIRTH, RAYMOND W. 1936. *We, the Tikopia: A Sociological Study of Kinship in Primitive Polynesia.* London: G. Allen & Unwin.

———. 1939. *Primitive Polynesian Economy.* London: George Routledge & Sons.

———. 1946. *Malay Fishermen: Their Peasant Economy.* London: Kegan Paul, Trench, Trubner & Co.

FITZGERALD, CHARLES P. 1936. "Further Historical Evidence for the Growth of the Chinese Population," *Sociological Review,* XXVIII, 267–73.

———. 1947. "The Consequences of the Rebellion of An Lu-shan upon the Population of the T'ang Dynasty," *Philo-biblon: A Quarterly Review of Chinese Publications,* II, 4–11.

FRENCH INDO-CHINA, ÉCOLE FRANÇAISE D'EXTRÊME-ORIENT. 1929. *Bibliographie de l'Indochine française.* Vol. I, 1913–26; Vol. II, 1927–29; Vol. III, 1930. Hanoi: Imprimerie d'Extrême-Orient.

FURNIVALL, J. S. 1944. *Netherlands India: A Study of Plural Economy.* New York: Macmillan Co.

———. 1948. *Colonial Policy and Practice: A Comparative Study of Burma and Netherlands India.* Cambridge: Cambridge University Press.

GINI, CORRADO. (ed.). 1938. *Bibliografia sulla demografia delle popolazioni primitive.* Rome: Commissione per lo Studio della Demografia delle Popolazioni Primitive.

GLICK, CLARENCE. 1942. "The Relation between Position and Status in the Assimilation of Chinese in Hawaii," *American Journal of Sociology,* XLVII, 667–79.

GOUROU, PIERRE. 1936. *Les paysans du delta tonkinois: Étude de géographie humaine.* Paris: Les Éditions d'Art et d'Histoire.

———. 1940a. *La terre et l'homme en Extrême-Orient.* Paris: Armand Colin.

———. 1940b. *L'utilisation du sol en Indochine française.* Paris: P. Hartmann.

HAN, C. T. 1946. *An Estimate of Chinese War Losses in the Sino-Japanese War, 1937–1943* (in Chinese). Nanking: Institute of Social Sciences, Academia Sinica.

HAWLEY, AMOS. 1954. "Fertility of an Urban Population in the Philippines," in *Papers in Demography and Public Administration,* pp. 27–45. Manila: University of the Philippines, Institute of Public Administration.

———. 1955. "Rural Fertility in Central Luzon," *American Sociological Review,* XX, 21–27.

HEEREN, H. J. (ed.). 1955. *The Urbanization of Djakarta.* Djakarta: Institute for Economic and Social Research, Djakarta School of Economics, University of Indonesia. ["Urbanisasi Djakarta," *Ekonomi dan Keuangan Indonesia,* Vol. VIII.]

HOGBIN, H. IAN. 1930. "The Problem of Depopulation in Melanesia, As Applied to Ontong Java (Solomon Islands)," *Journal of Polynesian Society*, XXXIX, 43–66.

——. 1939. *Experiments in Civilization: The Effects of European Culture on a Native Community of the Solomon Islands*. London: G. Routledge & Sons.

HUMAN RELATIONS AREA FILES. 1955 ff. IRIKURA, JAMES K. *Southeast Asia: Selected Annotated Bibliography of Japanese Publications*. KENNEDY, RAYMOND. *Bibliography of Indonesian Peoples and Cultures*. Rev. ed. 2 vols. PELZER, KARL J. *Selected Bibliography of the Geography of Southeast Asia, Part III: Malaya*. UNIVERSITY OF CHICAGO, PHILIPPINE STUDIES PROGRAM. *Selected Bibliography of the Philippines.* . . . YUAN TUNG-LI. *Economic and Social Development of Modern China: A Bibliographical Guide*. New Haven: Yale University Press.

HUNT, EDWARD E., *et al.* 1954. "The Depopulation of Yap," *Human Biology*, XXVI, 21–51.

INSTITUTE OF PACIFIC RELATIONS. 1932. *Problems of the Pacific, 1931*. (Fourth Conference, Hangchow and Shanghai.) Chicago: University of Chicago Press. (Reports were issued for the conferences from 1927 through 1939.)

——, INTERNATIONAL SECRETARIAT. 1949–51. *The Development of Upland Areas in the Far East*. 2 vols. New York.

INTER AMERICAN STATISTICAL INSTITUTE, TEMPORARY ORGANIZING COMMITTEE. 1941. *Statistical Activities of the American Nations, 1940*. Washington, D.C.

IWAMURA, SHINOBU. 1948. "The Structure of Moslem Society in Inner Mongolia," *Far Eastern Quarterly*, VIII, 34–44.

JAFFE, A. J. 1947a. "Notes on the Rate of Growth of the Chinese Population," *Human Biology*, XIX, 1–11.

——. 1947b. "A Review of the Censuses and Demographic Statistics of China," *Population Studies*, I, 308–37.

JAPAN, NATIONAL COMMISSION FOR UNESCO. 1952. *Literature on Population Problems in Japan (1945–1951)*. Tokyo: Chuwa Printing Co.

JARAMILLO, T. J. 1941. "Estimated Population of the Philippines," *Journal of Philippine Statistics*, I, 135–43.

KEESING, FELIX M. 1934. *Modern Samoa: Its Government and Changing Life*. London: Allen & Unwin.

——. 1945. *The South Seas in the Modern World*. Rev. ed. New York: John Day Co.

——. 1953a. *Culture Change: An Analysis and Bibliography of Anthropological Sources to 1952*. Stanford, Calif: Stanford University Press.

——. 1953b. *Social Anthropology in Polynesia: A Review of Research*. London: Oxford University Press.

KERNER, ROBERT J. 1939. *Northeastern Asia: A Selected Bibliography, Contributions to the Bibliography of the Relations of China, Russia, and Japan, with Special Reference to Korea, Manchuria, Mongolia, and Eastern Siberia, in Oriental and European Languages*. 2 vols. Berkeley: University of California Press.

KEYFITZ, N. 1953. "The Population of Indonesia," *Ekonomi dan Keuangan Indonesia*, Vol. VI.

——, and WIDJOJO, NITISASTRO. 1954. *Soal Penduduk dan Pembangunan Indonesia*. ("Population Problems and the Development of Indonesia.") Djakarta.

KLEIN, WILLEM C. (ed.). 1953–54. *Nieuw-Guinea: De Ontwikkeling op economisch, sociaal, en cultureel Gebied, in Nederlands en Australisch Nieuw-Guinea*. The Hague: Staatsdrukkerij-en Uitgeverijbedrijf.

KOOIJMAN, S. 1955. "Population Study of the Marind-Anim," *South Pacific Commission Quarterly Bulletin*, V, 21–23.

KOYAMA, EIZO. 1940. "Shina Manshu ni okeru shorai jinko no suitei" ("An Estimate of the Future Population of China and Manchoukuo"), *Jinko mondai kenkyu*, I, 60–70.

KROEBER, ALFRED L. 1939. *Cultural and Natural Areas of Native North America*. ("University of California Publications in American Archaeology and Ethnology," Vol. XXXVIII.) Berkeley: University of California Press.

KROTEVICH, S. 1955. "Vsekitayskaya perepis' naseleniya 1953 g." ("All China Census of Population, 1953"), *Vestnik Statistiki*, No. 5.

LAMBERT, SYLVESTER M. 1934. *The Depopulation of Pacific Races.* (Special Publication XXIII.) Honolulu: Bernice P. Bishop Museum.

———. 1938. *East Indian and Fijian in Fiji: Their Changing Numerical Relation.* (Special Publication XXXII.) Honolulu: Bernice P. Bishop Museum.

LANG, OLGA. 1946. *Chinese Family and Society.* New Haven: Yale University Press.

LATTIMORE, OWEN. 1940. *Inner Asian Frontiers of China.* New York: American Geographical Society.

LAUTENSACH, HERMANN. 1950. *Korea: Land, Volk, Schicksal.* Stuttgart: K. F. Koehler Verlag.

LEE, F. C. H. 1935. "An Analysis of Chinese Rural Population," *Chinese Social and Political Science Review,* XIX, 22–44.

LESSA, WILLIAM A. 1955. "Depopulation on Ulithi," *Human Biology,* XXVII, 161–83.

LIEU, D. K. 1933. "The 1912 Census of China," *Bulletin de l'Institut International de Statistique,* XXVI, No. 2, 85–109.

LIND, ANDREW W., with ROBERT SCHMITT. 1955. *Hawaii's People.* Honolulu: University of Hawaii Press.

LIU, NANMING. 1935. *Contribution à l'étude de la population chinoise.* Geneva: Imprimerie et Éditions Union.

LOEWENTHAL, RUDOLF. 1949. *Bibliography of Russian Literature on China and Adjacent Countries, 1931–1936.* Cambridge: Russian Research Center, Harvard University.

LOOMIS, CHARLES P. (ed.). 1953. *Turialba: Social Systems and the Introduction of Change.* Glencoe, Ill.: Free Press.

LORIMER, FRANK. 1946. *The Population of the Soviet Union: History and Prospects.* Geneva: League of Nations.

———. 1954. *Culture and Human Fertility: A Study of the Relation of Cultural Conditions to Fertility in Non-industrial and Transitional Societies.* Paris: UNESCO.

McARTHUR, NORMA. 1957. *The Populations of the Pacific Islands.* Part I: "Territories of French Oceania." Part II: "Cook Islands and Niue." Part III: "American Samoa." Part IV: "Western Samoa and the Tokelau Islands." Part V: "Tonga." Part VI: "Fiji." Part VII: "Papua and New Guinea." Part VIII: "Netherlands New Guinea." Canberra: Australian National University, Department of Demography.

McCUNE, GEORGE M., with ARTHUR L. GREY, JR. 1950. *Korea Today.* Cambridge: Harvard University Press.

McCUNE, SHANNON. 1956. *Korea's Heritage: A Regional and Social Geography.* Tokyo: Tuttle.

MALAYA, FEDERATION OF MALAYA AND COLONY OF SINGAPORE. 1949. *A Report on the 1947 Census of Population.* By M. C. DEL TUFO. London: Crown Agents for the Colonies.

MEEL, H. DE. 1951. "Demographic Dilemma in Indonesia," *Pacific Affairs,* XXIV, 266–83.

MENDES CORRÊA, A. A. 1944. *Timor Português: contribuições para o seu estudo antropológico.* Lisbon: Imprensa Nacional.

MILLS, LENNOX A. 1942. *British Rule in Eastern Asia: A Study of Contemporary Government and Economic Development in British Malaya and Hong Kong.* London: Oxford University Press.

MIURA, UNICHI, and SHINOZUKA, FUSAJI. 1952. "Population Ecology of the Mongolians in Manchuria," *Archives of the Population Association of Japan,* No. 1, pp. 37–46.

MUKERJEE, RADHAKAMAL. 1936. *Migrant Asia.* Ser. 3, Vol. I. Rome: Comitato Italiano per lo Studio dei Problemi della Popolazione.

MURRILL, RUPERT I. 1950. "Vital Statistics of Ponape Island, Eastern Carolines," *American Journal of Physical Anthropology,* VIII, 185–94.

NATIONAL TSING HUA UNIVERSITY, CENSUS RESEARCH INSTITUTE. 1944. *Supplement* [to the *Report on the Population Census of 1942 and Civil Registration Work in the Model Civil Registration Districts of Yunnan,* by Yunnan Province, Working Committee on the Model Lakeside Civil Registration Districts] (in Chinese). Kunming.

———. 1946. *Preliminary Report on the Population Census and Vital Registra-*

tion for District Chengkung and District Kunyang, Yunnan Province (in Chinese). Peking.

NETHERLANDS AARDRIJKSKUNDIG GENOOTSCHAP, MET DEN TOPOGRAFISCHEN DIENST IN NEDERLANDSCH-INDIE. 1938. *Atlas van tropisch Nederland.* The Hague: Martinus Nijhoff.

NETHERLANDS INDIES, CENTRAAL KANTOOR VOOR DE STATISTIEK. 1938. *Catalogus der Boekwerken betreffend Nederlandsch-Indie:Aanwezig in de Bibliotheek van het Centraal Kantoor voor de Statistiek. . . .* Batavia: Department van Economisch Zaken.

NEWMAN, MARSHALL T., and ENG, RANSOM L. 1947. "The Ryukyu People: a Biological Appraisal," *American Journal of Physical Anthropology,* V, 113–58.

NOTESTEIN, FRANK W. 1938. "A Demographic Study of 38,256 Rural Families in China," *Milbank Memorial Fund Quarterly,* XVI, 57–79.

OLIVER, DOUGLAS L. 1951. *The Pacific Islands.* Cambridge: Harvard University Press.

PARK, CHAI BIN. 1955. "Statistical Observations on Death Rates and Causes of Death in Korea," *Bulletin of the World Health Organization,* XIII, 69–108.

PELZER, KARL J. 1941. *An Economic Survey of the Pacific Area.* Part I: *Population and Land Utilization.* New York: International Secretariat, Institute of Pacific Relations.

———. 1945. *Pioneer Settlement in the Asiatic Tropics: Studies in Land Utilization and Agricultural Colonization in Southeastern Asia.* New York: American Geographical Society.

———. 1949–50. *Selected Bibliography on the Geography of Southeast Asia.* Part I: *Southeast Asia-General.* Part II: *The Philippines.* ("Southeast Asia Studies.") New Haven: Yale University Press.

PENTONY, B. 1953–54. "Psychological Causes of Depopulation of Primitive Groups," *Oceania,* XXIV, 142–45.

PHILIPPINES, BUREAU OF THE CENSUS AND STATISTICS. 1954. *Statistical Handbook of the Philippines, 1903–1953.* Manila.

POWDERMAKER, HORTENSE. 1931. "Vital Statistics of New Ireland as Revealed in Genealogies," *Human Biology,* III, 351–75.

PURCELL, VICTOR. 1951. *The Chinese in Southeast Asia.* London: Oxford University Press.

RADCLIFFE-BROWN, A. R. 1930. "Former Numbers and Distribution of the Australian Aboriginals," *Official Yearbook of the Commonwealth of Australia,* No. 23, pp. 671–96.

REED, STEPHEN W. 1943. *The Making of Modern New Guinea, with Special Reference to Culture Contact in the Mandated Territory.* Philadelphia: American Philosophical Society.

REID, CHARLES F. (ed.). 1939. *Bibliography of the Island of Guam.* (One in a series on the territories and outlying possessions of the United States.) New York: H. W. Wilson Co.

ROBEQUAIN, CHARLES. 1939. *L'évolution économique de l'Indochine française.* Paris: P. Hartmann.

———. 1946. *Le monde malais: Péninsule malaise, Sumatra, Java, Borneo, Célèbes, Bali et les petites îles de la Sonde, Moluques, Philippines.* Paris: Payot.

ROBERTS, S. H. 1927. *Population Problems of the Pacific.* London: G. Routledge & Sons.

ROBSON, R. W. (comp.). 1945. *The Pacific Islands Handbook, 1944.* North American edition. New York: Macmillan Co.

ROCKHILL, WILLIAM W. 1912. *The 1910 Census of the Population of China.* Leyden: E. J. Brill.

SATO, HIROSHI. 1951. "Study on the Palisade in Manchuria," *Annals of the Hitotsubashi Academy,* Suppl. No. 1, pp. 32–44.

SEIFERT, HARRY E. 1935. "Life Tables for Chinese Farmers," *Milbank Memorial Fund Quarterly,* XIII, 223–36.

SHAPIRO, HARRY L. 1939. *Migration and Environment: A Study of the Physical Characteristics of the Japanese Immigrants to Hawaii and the Effects of Environment on Their Descendants.* New York: Oxford University Press.

SINGAPORE, DEPARTMENT OF SOCIAL WELFARE. 1947. *A Social Survey of Singapore: A Preliminary Study of Some Aspects of Social Conditions in the Mu-*

nicipal Area of Singapore. Singapore: G. H. Kiat.

SKINNER, G. WILLIAM. 1951. "A Study in Miniature of Chinese Population," *Population Studies*, V, 91–103.

———. 1957. "Chinese Assimilation and Thai Politics," *Journal of Asian Studies*, XVI, 237–50.

SMITH, T. E. 1952. *Population Growth in Malaya: An Analysis of Recent Trends*. London: Royal Institute of International Affairs.

STAMP, L. DUDLEY. 1936. *Asia: A Regional and Economic Geography*. 3d ed. London: Methuen.

STANFORD UNIVERSITY. SCHOOL OF NAVAL ADMINISTRATION. 1949. *Handbook on the Trust Territory of the Pacific Islands*. Washington, D.C.: Navy Department, Office of the Chief of Naval Operations.

STEWARD, JULIAN H. (ed.). 1946–50. *Handbook of South American Indians*. . . . (U. S. Bureau of American Ethnology Bulletin 143.) Washington, D.C.: Government Printing Office.

SUN E-TU ZEN and DE FRANCIS, JOHN. 1956. *Chinese Social History; Translations of Selected Studies*. Washington, D.C.: American Council of Learned Societies. (A translation of 25 articles cited in their *Bibliography on Chinese Social History: A Selected and Critical List of Chinese Periodical Sources*.)

TAEUBER, IRENE B. 1940. "The Demography of the Netherlands Indies," *Population Index*, VI, 150–54.

———. 1942. "The Demography of the Philippines," *ibid.*, VIII, 3–9.

———. 1944. "Colonial Demography: Formosa," *ibid.*, X, 147–57.

———. 1945a. "French Indo-China: Demographic Imbalance and Colonial Policy," *ibid.*, XI, 68–81.

———. 1945b. "Manchuria as a Demographic Frontier," *ibid.*, pp. 260–74.

——— (with EDWIN BEAL, JR.). 1946a. *Guide to the Official Demographic Statistics of Japan*. Part I: *Japan Proper, 1868–1945*. *ibid.*, Suppl., October, 1946.

———. 1946b. "The Population Potential of Postwar Korea," *Far Eastern Quarterly*, V, 289–307.

———. 1947. "Hokkaido and Karafuto: Japan's Internal Frontiers," *Population Index*, XII, 6–12.

———. 1948. "Current Estimates of the Size and Distribution of China's Population," *ibid.*, XIV, 3–20.

——— (with GEORGE W. BARCLAY). 1950a. "Korea and the Koreans in the Northeast Asian Region," *ibid.*, XVI, 278–97.

——— (with CHUNGNIM C. HAN). 1950b. "Micronesian Islands under United Nations' Trusteeship: Demographic Paradox," *ibid.*, pp. 93–115.

——— (with CHIA-LIN PAN). 1952. "The Expansion of the Chinese: North and West," *ibid.*, XVIII, 85–108.

———. 1955. "The Population of the Ryukyu Islands," *ibid.*, XXI, 233–63.

———. 1956. "Population Policies in Communist China," *ibid.*, XXII, 261–74.

———. 1958. *The Population of Japan*. Princeton: Princeton University Press.

TAYLOR, CLYDE R. H. 1951. *A Pacific Bibliography: Printed Matter Relating to the Native Peoples of Polynesia, Melanesia, and Micronesia*. ("Memoirs of the Polynesian Society," Vol. XXIV.) Wellington, N. Z.: Polynesian Society.

TÊNG SSŬ-YÜ. 1950. *New Light on the History of the Taiping Rebellion*. Cambridge: Harvard University Press.

THOMPSON, LAURA A. 1940. *Fijian Frontier*. New York: Institute of Pacific Relations.

———. 1941. *Guam and Its People: A Study of Culture Contact and Colonial Education*. New York: Institute of Pacific Relations.

THOMPSON, WARREN S. 1938. "An Experiment in the Registration of Vital Statistics in China," *Les comptes-rendus du Congrès International de la Population*, III, 56–69.

TREWARTHA, GLENN T. 1951. "Chinese Cities: Numbers and Distribution," *Annals of the Association of American Geographers*, XLI, 331–47.

———. 1952. "Chinese Cities: Origins and Functions," *ibid.*, XLII, 69–93.

———, and ZELINSKY, WILBUR. 1955. "Population Distribution and Change in Korea, 1925–1949," *Geographical Review*, XLV, 1–26.

ULMER, HENRI. 1936. "Note sur les dénombrements des pays d'Extrême-Orient," *Revue de l'Institut International de Statistique,* III, 413–26. Also in *Bulletin de l'Institut International de Statistique,* XXIX, No. 3, 4–18.

UNITED KINGDOM, COLONIAL OFFICE. 1950. *Social Science Research in Sarawak.* By E. R. LEACH. London: H.M. Stationery Office.

UNITED NATIONS, ECONOMIC COMMISSION FOR ASIA AND THE FAR EAST. 1948 ff. *Economic Survey of Asia and the Far East, 1948—.*

UNITED NATIONS, POPULATION DIVISION. 1948. *The Population of Western Samoa.* ("Reports on the Population of Trust Territories," No. 1.)

——. 1951. "International Migrations in the Far East during Recent Times: The Countries of Emigration," *Population Bulletin,* No. 1, 13–30.

——. 1952. "International Migrations in the Far East during Recent Times: The Countries of Immigration," *ibid.,* No. 2, 27–58.

——. 1953. "Aspects of Urbanization in ECAFE Countries," *Economic Bulletin for Asia and the Far East,* IV, 1–15. "Addendum," *ibid.,* V, 60–64.

——. 1954. *The Population of Central America (Including Mexico), 1950–1980.* ("Future Population Estimates by Age and Sex," Report I, ST/SOA, Ser. A, "Population Studies," No. 16.) New York: United Nations.

UNITED NATIONS, SOCIAL AFFAIRS DIVISION, POPULATION BRANCH. 1955. *The Population of South America, 1950–1980.* ("Future Population Estimates by Sex and Age," Report II, ST/SOA, Ser. A, "Population Studies," No. 21.)

UNITED NATIONS, STATISTICAL OFFICE. 1955. *Demographic Yearbook, 1955.*

UNITED STATES BUREAU OF THE CENSUS AND LIBRARY OF CONGRESS. 1943. *General Censuses and Vital Statistics in the Americas.* Washington, D.C.: Government Printing Office.

UNITED STATES GOVERNMENT OF AMERICAN SAMOA. 1957. *Census of American Samoa, September 25, 1956.* Pago Pago: Office of the Governor.

UNITED STATES LIBRARY OF CONGRESS. 1950a. *Indochina: A Bibliography of the Land and the People.* By CECIL C. HOBBS et al.

——. 1950b. *Korea: An Annotated Bibliography of Publications in Western Languages.* By HELEN D. JONES and ROBERT L. WINKLER.

——. 1950c. *Korea: An Annotated Bibliography of Publications in Far Eastern Languages.* By EDWIN G. BEAL, JR., with ROBERT L. WINKLER.

——. 1950d. *Korea: An Annotated Bibliography of Publications in the Russian Language.* By ALBERT PARRY et al.

——. 1951. *Manchuria: An Annotated Bibliography.* By PETER A. BERTON et al.

——, HISPANIC FOUNDATION. 1954. *Handbook of Latin American Studies, 1951.* Gainesville: University of Florida Press.

UNIVERSITY OF INDONESIA, INSTITUTE FOR ECONOMIC AND SOCIAL RESEARCH. 1956. *The Population of Indonesia.* Djakarta: Fakultet Ekonomi, Universitet Indonesia.

VALENZIANU, CARLO. 1940. *Renaissance démographique en Oceanie française.* Ser. 3, Vol. III. Rome: Comitato Italiano per lo Studio dei Problemi della Popolazione.

——. 1949. "Enquête démographique en Oceanie française," *Population,* IV, 93–114.

VANDENBOSCH, AMRY. 1941. *The Dutch East Indies: Its Government, Problems, and Policies.* Berkeley: University of California Press.

VIAL, L. G. 1937. "Some Statistical Aspects of Population in the Morobe District, New Guinea," *Oceania,* VIII, 283–307.

WANG SHIH-TA. 1932–33. *The Minchengou Investigation of 1909–1911: A New Study Based on Recently Discovered Documents* (in Chinese). Academia Sinica, Institute of Social Sciences.

——. 1935. *A New Estimate of China's Population* (in Chinese). Academia Sinica, Institute of Social Sciences.

WICKIZER, VERNON D., and BENNETT, MURRAY K. 1941. *The Rice Economy of Monsoon Asia.* Stanford, Calif.: Stanford University, Food Research Institute.

WILLCOX, WALTER F. 1926. "China's Population—400,000,000 or 300,000,000?" *Chinese Students' Monthly*, XXII, 23–29.

——. 1937. "The Population of China and Its Modern Increase," *Revue de l'Institut International de Statistique*, V, 3–14.

——. 1940. *Studies in American Demography*. Ithaca: Cornell University Press.

WISSLER, CLARK. 1938. *The American Indian*. 3d ed. New York: Peter Smith.

WITTFOGEL, KARL A., and FENG CHIA-SHÊNG. 1949. *History of Chinese Society: Liao, 907–1125*. Philadelphia: American Philosophical Society.

WOLFF, WERNER. 1948. *Island of Death: A New Key to Easter Island's Culture through an Ethno-psychological Study*. New York: J. J. Augustin.

YANAIHARA, TADAO. 1940. *Pacific Islands under Japanese Mandate*. London: Oxford University Press.

YUN CHUNG-PIN et al. (eds.). 1955. *A Compilation of Selected Statistical Materials on the Economic History of Modern China* (in Chinese). Appendix, pp. 362–74. Peking.

ZELINSKY, WILBUR. 1950. "The Indochinese Peninsula: A Demographic Anomaly," *Far Eastern Quarterly*, IX, 115–45.

14. The Development and Status of American Demography

RUPERT B. VANCE

The term "demography" was first used in its French form in 1855 by Achille Guillard in his *Eléments de statistique humaine ou démographie comparée* (Paris, 1855) only a few years after the origin of the phrase "vital statistics." The subject matter of demography is a population, and any group studied by statistical methods can be considered a population. Demography, however, applies only to human beings, and since it has a Greek root (*demos*) in common with democracy, writer are sometimes found to point out the association of demography with representative government. In the United States it will be seen that this relation is fairly direct.

THE HISTORICAL EMERGENCE OF DEMOGRAPHY IN THE UNITED STATES

The United States Census, 1790—

There is some debate as to whether Canada, Sweden, or the United States originated the modern census, but there seems no doubt that the American government was the first to write a continuing census of the population into its basic constitution. Both the nature and the function of the United States census were determined by political rather than by scientific considerations. The census office thus differs from purely scientific bureaus of the government in that it is subject to conflict and diverse pressure between popular claims and scientific demands (Willcox, 1940, p. 75). Democracy played its part, and the very federalism which made the census obligatory delayed the registration of vital statistics for almost a century and a half.

To apportion representation and direct taxes, the Constitution (Art. I, sec. 3) provided that an enumeration of the population must be made within three years after the first meeting of Congress and each decade thereafter. The Constitution was ratified in 1789, and the first census was taken in 1790. It is thus the oldest continuing census based on enumeration in the field, and it has possibly had more scientific influence than any other.

A distinguished French statistician wrote, "The United States affords the unique example of a people who established their statistics on the very day when they organized their government and regulated in the same document the census of their inhabitants, their civil and political rights and the future of their country." To this General Francis Walker made the apt reply that his country did this for "political and not for philosophic reasons" (Willcox, 1940, p. 80).

When the first American census was taken in 1790, it was customary for nations to regard their statistical data as state secrets. The census of 1790 was published as a public document—a slight volume of fifty-six pages. It gave a total count of 3,929,214. The returns were presented exactly as received from the United States marshals, and indications are that those officials carried out the census as they individually thought best. It is not known for sure that the provisions of the law were ever transmitted to them. The count fell short of the expectations of leading statesmen, and statisticians today feel it represents a serious undercount (Holt, 1929, p. 4).

It is noteworthy that Thomas Jefferson, as president of the American Philosophical Society, signed a memorial to Congress asking that the scope of the census be broadened to include the characteristics of the population. The census of 1830 was the first to use printed schedules, but the census itself was printed so badly that it had to be republished. Occasionally columns of the published reports did not yield their ostensible totals. The census of 1840 contained so many gross errors that a protest was made by the young American Statistical Association (Holt, 1929, p. 13).

The census was not made a permanent bureau until 1902, first in the Department of the Interior and finally in its permanent home, the Department of Commerce, in 1913. Previous to 1902 the census had an uncertain existence, for all work stopped and the whole organization was disbanded between enumerations. The director of the census was engaged only for a year or two, had no continuity in office, and often saw his position abolished before the census figures were fully tabulated and published (Holt, 1929, p. 1).

Early American Demographers

American demography, however, has been fortunate in its early practitioners. Many were able civil servants who carried the work of census and vital statistics beyond numerical description into analysis and interpretation. Sometimes they held other bureau offices in order to carry on the work between census periods.

Lemuel Shattuck (1793–1859), after setting up the vital registration system of Massachusetts based on that of England (1842), was called to Washington and did much to bring the federal census of 1850 up to standards then prevailing in Europe. James D. B. DeBow (1820–67), remembered as a Southern partisan and editor of *DeBow's Review,* served as the superintendent of the 1850 census, which he compiled and edited. He strongly advocated the maintenance of a permanent staff between censuses. Francis Amsa Walker (1840–97)—an able economist and a notable theorist of immigration—supervised the census of 1880, probably the most elaborate statistical survey of a nation's activities published up to that time, and was the ablest early director. Carrol Davidson Wright (1840–1909), chief of the first state bureau of labor statistics in Massachusetts and first chief of the federal bureau of labor statistics, completed the eleventh census. These men all made themselves demographers to whom the discipline owes a great deal. The descriptive level at which they worked can be indicated by a comment of General Francis A. Walker in 1893: "I do not know," he wrote, "of a single man who has ever held a position in this country as head of a statistical bureau or as a statistician who ever had any elementary training for his work" (Cummings, 1918, p. 574). General Walker was not writing from bias, for in the same connection he wrote that "a strong passion for statistics early developed itself in the life of our people. . . . No government in the world has ever lavished money and labor more generously upon statistical inquiry nor has any people ever performed more cheerfully and patiently in this respect" (Cummings, 1918, p. 573).

The Development of Vital Statistics

In theory and in science a census and a vital statistics system are inseparable. As Walter F. Willcox once wrote, a census system which does not flower in a registration system is about as futile as capital which does not result in income (1940). It required 143 years for the United States to develop a registration system.

The unhappy separation of census and vital statistics dictated by the dual nature of American federalism had not gone unnoticed. Early in the nineteenth century the surgeon general of the War Department began a series of reports on army mortality which were to run for a long time. Manfully the census began a long struggle to cope with the problem. The census of 1850 developed a separate schedule devoted to current mortality with listings of the characteristics, the month, and the cause of death of everyone who had died during the year ending June 1, 1850.

In the meantime states and cities acting independently were setting up good registration systems. Others tried and failed, and some took no part in the early efforts. John Shaw Billings, M.D. (1838–1913), for thirty years surgeon general of the United States, was among the first to see the futility of gathering vital statistics by census returns. He advocated a national office which should "secure by paying for them, uniform and complete registration returns from the several States" (Willcox, 1940, p. 485).

Billings, a many-sided man, made other contributions to demography. As a supervisor of the census he walked through a room where hundreds of clerks were hand-tallying items from schedules and remarked to a young engineer, Herman Hollerith: "There ought to be some mechanical way of doing this job, something on the principle of the Jacquard loom, perhaps, whereby holes on a card regulate the pattern." Hollerith's invention, developed in the machine shop of the Bureau of the Census, secured simultane-

ous tallying by means of electrical contacts through holes punched in cards (Willcox, 1940, p. 89). Without this development neither the modern census nor the record-keeping of business corporations could be carried out.

When the census was reorganized as a permanent office in 1899, a division of vital statistics had been included. Congress, on recommendation of the director, had adopted a resolution requesting state authorities to co-operate with the census in setting up a uniform system of registration of births and deaths. It had been repeatedly demonstrated that vital statistics obtained only once every ten years by census enumeration were worthless. Finally, in 1910 mortality questions were eliminated from the census schedules. Annual mortality statistics have been published for the official registration areas since 1899, when they covered approximately 40 per cent of the total population.

Not until 1909 was the effort made to present statistics on births. It proved unsuccessful, and no report was published. Birth statistics from the official birth registration area were first published in 1915. Ninety per cent estimated coverage was required for the admission of a state to the official area. This development was finally completed in 1933 when, with the qualification of Texas, the last state was admitted to the official registration area. The census of 1940 thus marked a significant turning point for demography. For the first time in our history national vital statistics were available for analysis along with the necessary population base. No states have been dropped since completion of the area, although regression is believed to have occurred in some states. The first nationwide treatment of the completeness of birth registration was made in connection with the census of 1940. It was concluded that the national registration of births was 92.5 per cent complete. Death registration is more highly developed.

Demography and Immigration Statistics

The United States represents the modern world's greatest experiment in international and internal migration. In spite of continued interest in the subject, there is no annual record of internal migration, and the annual statistics of foreign immigration were not adequately developed until the establishment of the United States Bureau of Immigration in 1892.

The registration of immigrants began with an act of 1819 providing that lists of passengers from foreign ports be deposited with local collectors of customs. From this time on "the history of these statistics is a complicated story of changes in source, definitions and classifications" (B. Thomas, 1954, p. 42). Different units of time and different age categories have been used. For the first half of the nineteenth century no records were kept of the distribution of immigrants by sex. The figures usually quoted are those from the census returns of the foreign-born as compiled by the United States Immigration Commission of 1911. It seems certain that up to 1903 the term "immigrant" applied only to steerage passengers, so that aliens traveling first and second class were not counted. No distinction was made between permanent and temporary immigrants until 1906, and no figures were gathered on emigrants until 1907. Until the 1890's "the officials employed to cope with the immigrants were notoriously few and ill paid." Some of the returns on the hundreds of thousands passing through Ellis Island were just guesswork. Old records show names with no population characteristics entered by the harried clerks. In addition, the leakage through Canada furnished an appreciable but undetermined amount of immigration (B. Thomas, 1954).

Some of the confusion in immigration statistics can be traced to contradictions in the laws. One act (1882) was designed to keep out paupers and those likely to become public charges. Other acts (1885, 1887, 1888) aimed to exclude those "under contract or agreement . . . express or implied." If the immigrant got past one set of inspectors who tried to prove he was a pauper, he faced another group intent on showing that he had a job. If the statistics seem inconsistent, it is because the immigrant, in John R. Commons' words, "strives to show first that he can support himself and then he strives to show that he does not know of any job by which he can support himself" (B. Thomas, 1954).

Finally an adequate statistical system was developed when a Bureau of Immigration was set up (1892) with its officials stationed at the ports. Internal migration offers another story.

Adequate statistics by themselves have never created demography. Here a notable development for the science grew out of concern with immigration as an American social problem. For its time, the *Reports of the Immigration Commission* (1911) represented an achievement of some distinction. The commission, made up of congressmen and distinguished citizens, employed an able research staff. Its forty-two volumes were research reports—not routine testimony. Often descriptive, the studies developed basic statistics, analyzed the immigrants' economic adjustments, presented the sociological processes of assimilation and mobility, drew vivid pictures of the traffic in crime and prostitution, and—in the case of Franz Boas' report on bodily changes in the descendants of immigrants—posed new scientific problems. As a notable example of the nation's concern with its peculiar social problems, the report served to give an impetus to demographic studies and to portray an attitude which may have prevented such studies from being thoroughly objective. The findings were made available to the general public in a summary volume which went through several editions (Jenks and Lauck, 1926).

Demography and the Scientific Disciplines

For its final development demography waited for the emergence of university scholarship and related academic disciplines. As mathematics moved into statistics and as sociology and political economy moved from philosophy to empirical studies, demography was given the firmer basis demanded of a mature discipline.

Representative of this early movement when statistics itself was mainly descriptive was the work of Richmond Mayo-Smith (1854–1901) at Columbia University (1880–1900). Mayo-Smith taught the first course in statistics offered in any American university and made important contributions to the quantitative approach to social science. He held that sociologists had exaggerated the complexity of social phenomena by adopting a complex terminology drawn from biological analogies and that they had increased the difficulties of their science by the individual collection of data (Lundberg, 1933, p. 237). In his courses taught over a period of twenty years and in his two influential texts, *Statistics and Sociology* (1895) and *Statistics and Economics* (1899), Mayo-Smith made substantive contributions to the content of demography as a growing discipline. *Statistics and Sociology* was soundly based on the "great censuses of 1890–91 in half a dozen major countries" and represented in Mayo-Smith's own words "a systematic effort . . . to present the statistics of population in such a way as to show their real signifi-

cance." His mode of analysis made systematic use of practically all the categories to which demographers are now accustomed. In *Statistics and Economics* he had a chapter dealing with population as labor force which developed an analysis of workers and dependents in terms of the sex and age distribution of persons gainfully employed.

The development of an integrated and self-consistent body of materials variously called population problems, population studies, or simply population was a function that had to be performed in the universities. It came slowly and piecemeal, largely within the context of economic and social problems as defined by Thomas R. Malthus (1766–1834), and influenced by the American outlook on "social Darwinism" and the country's concern with immigration. Demography's late development of a sophisticated outlook can be attributed in part to the fact that it grew up in the context of concern with "American social problems"—considered not as scientific problems but as "controversial" problems in the popular sense. At Harvard, Thomas Nixon Carver called attention to population in his courses and in a text in social problems written in 1915; A. B. Wolfe at Ohio State, H. P. Fairchild at Yale, and Edward A. Ross at Wisconsin were among those who gave population courses a standing in the university curriculum. James A. Field went from Carver's classes to develop one of the best of the early population courses in the department of economics at the University of Chicago. That his untimely death deprived the discipline of an able scholar was shown in his posthumous *Essays on Population* (1931). In 1923 Edward B. Reuter at the University of Iowa published the first American text in population, *Population Problems*—a title used by practically all his successors. It was followed in 1926 by *Population Problems*, a collection of papers edited by Louis I. Dublin. In 1930 appeared Warren S. Thompson's more comprehensive *Population Problems*—a text which with its various revisions apparently has dominated the academic field (1953). These volumes did more than attest to the importance of demography; they set the body of doctrine and by their existence served to create new courses in the growing discipline.

Demography Comes of Age

As demography came of age in the United States in the early decades of the twentieth century, scientific observation, description, and analysis tended to coalesce at higher levels.

Government agencies improved their data by issuing compilations which brought time series under review and revision. This phase can be dated from 1879 when the Bureau of the Census became responsible for the annual issue of the *Statistical Abstract*. Co-operation with the Social Science Research Council resulted in 1949 in the publication of *Historical Statistics of the United States, 1789–1945*, a scholarly attempt to extend many demographic series as far back into history as possible.

The census and appropriate agencies reviewed vital statistics data and in 1943 published an authoritative compilation, *Vital Statistics Rates in the United States, 1900–1940* (Linder and Grove, 1943). This offered a bench mark from which all registration statistics before 1940, official and unofficial, could be compared. The bureau gradually developed intercensal estimates to give historical continuity to vital rates and demographic series. The establishment in 1940 of the Monthly Current Population Survey on a sample basis was a logical extension of these developments.

A new level of interpretation and analysis had long been needed from the bureaus involved in the processing of data. This was met in the 1920's by a brilliant innovation—the development of the census monograph. Instead of presenting statistics with barely enough comment to keep its figures from being misunderstood, the bureau hired outside experts, made them temporary employees, and encouraged them to follow new leads in the use of unpublished census tabulations. Distinctive volumes based upon the 1920 census were published on population increase (Rossiter, 1922), farm population (Truesdell, 1926), farm tenancy (Goldenweiser and Truesdell, 1924), school attendance (Ross, 1924), immigrants and their children (Carpenter, 1927), the ratio of children to women (Thompson, 1931), and women in gainful occupations (Hill, 1929).

The way in which demography developed from the confluence of many streams is shown in the career of the man who may well be called America's first demographer, Walter F. Willcox. His dissertation, *The Divorce Problem: A Study in Statistics* (1891) came out of Columbia University's graduate combination in statistics, economics, and sociology. As a chief statistician in the census office, Willcox wrote interpretive reports on the twelfth and earlier censuses and later wrote an *Introduction to the Vital Statistics of the United States, 1900 to 1930* (1933). As professor of economics and statistics at Cornell, he helped train some of the country's leading demographers. After World War I, Willcox came to know most of the important figures in world demography in the International Statistical Institute. In connection with his work on international migration with the National Bureau of Economic Research and the International Labor Office of the League of Nations, he clarified United States immigration statistics and developed the estimates of the growth of world population by continents from 1650 to 1935 (Willcox, 1931, II, pp. 33–82). Out of this grew the important theory of the demographic transition. In several respects Willcox qualifies as the father of American demography—an impression reinforced in 1940 by the publication of his volume, *Studies in American Demography* (1940). This volume, containing revisions of important papers published in government reports from 1893 to 1940, showed that while Willcox practiced his trade in the market place of demography, the government bureau, he kept abreast of every trend.

STATUS OF DEMOGRAPHY IN THE UNITED STATES

Demography developed out of two different lines of approach: (1) the problem approach of Thomas Robert Malthus (1776–1834) and (2) the statistical analysis of population aggregates represented in the work of John Graunt (1627–74) and Adolphe Quételet (1796–1874). Failure to fuse these two approaches helps to explain present scientific dilemmas in the discipline. Malthus' formulation emphasized the economic aspect of population growth and led, as R. D. McKenzie pointed out (1934), to the conceptualization of demography as a congeries of social problems—poverty, unemployment, standard of living, and even war. This in turn has given rise to a number of subjective concepts—overpopulation, underpopulation, population optimum. So far these concepts have not proved amenable either to statistical treatment or to objective analysis. Stemming from this background, the literature in America has produced such emotional titles as *Mankind at the Crossroads, Standing Room Only, The Shadow of the World's Future, The Menace of Color, The Passing of the Great Race, The Rising Tide of Color, Danger Spots in World Population,* *Population on the Loose, Human Survival,* and *The Geography of Hunger.*

In the study of population aggregates, the true demographic approach, attention is focused on the dynamic movements of populations as biosocial groups. In this approach scientific progress has been made. In the description and analysis of vital processes, concepts have been developed which are objective and useful as tools in scientific analysis. Studies of population trends, population replacement, and population distribution have proved subject to verification and are thus cumulative. The gap persists, however, between the two lines of development—a fact made evident in the analysis of the status of American demography, its theories and techniques.

Population Dynamics and Social Change

Malthusian theory hardly applied to the American situation since the nation's period of greatest poverty coincided with its period of sparse settlement. Malthusianism, however, meant population theory, and it is one of the ironies of American demography that Malthusian theory continued to be a part of the American doctrine whether it fitted conditions or not. In the United States population growth and social change were intensified, and it is fitting that we consider American contributions to demographic theory and techniques from this point of view.

Economic and political expansion proved to be of prime importance in the history of United States demography. The young nation developed one of the highest rates of population increase known and became the world's most extensive experiment in international migration—facts duly noted by Robert Griffin in his presidential address before the London Statistical Society when he spoke of the unparalleled increase of the population of the

United States as "the greatest political and economic fact of the age, altering the whole idea of the balance of power in Europe."

The nation early became preoccupied with the "foreign immigrant" as a social problem, and since the settlement and exploitation of the country also involved Negro slavery, racial and ethnic analysis became staples of American demography. The stream of foreign immigration and the mode of settlement from the eastern seaboard also made it inevitable that the nation should become a great experiment in internal migration.

The appropriation of "open resources" dictated economic trends which included rapid industrialization and urbanization. Superimposed on the westward movement, these trends gave renewed impetus to internal migration and to a rapid shift in occupations which affected birth rates and the pattern of population replacement. As natural increase declined among the various social strata, differential fertility became important in relating questions of quantity and quality to national policy. Finally, some portion of the economic surplus from this development was assigned by a generous philanthrophy to scientific research, and American foundations joined the United States government as fiscal underwriters of demographic science.

For a time it appeared that the great depression of the 1930's would halt both economic expansion and population growth. Strangely enough, the impetus demography needed to attain maturity in the United States came from the impact of the depression. Population as human resources took its place at the forefront of analysis, and policy-making gave impetus to the work of scholars, government agencies, and foundation programs. Demography in this period reached a new level of creative scholarship, and the pattern which emerged made distinctive contributions to analysis and theory.

Warren S. Thompson and P. K. Whelpton furnished the definitive account of United States population status and history (1933); Frank Lorimer and Frederick Osborn provided a significant analysis of the trend and dynamic impact of differential fertility (1934); Carter Goodrich and others developed an economic analysis of the course and function of population redistribution in the depression (1936). The definitive statement on metropolitan growth and organization was written by R. D. McKenzie (1933). The regional approach to population status and cultural adequacy was developed for the South by Howard W. Odum (1936). In one of the most enlightened of government reports, *The Problems of a Changing Population,* the National Resources Committee raised the need and promises of population adjustment to a new analytical level (1938). Memorandums on migration by Warren S. Thompson (1937), Rupert B. Vance (1938), and Dorothy S. Thomas (1938) and one on needed population research by P. K. Whelpton (1938) pushed forward the frontiers of research. The record of demography's most productive decade was brought to a close by a definitive work on life expectancy by Louis I. Dublin and Alfred J. Lotka, *Length of Life* (1936; 2d ed. by Dublin, Lotka, and Spiegelman, 1949), and Raymond Pearl's most important book, *The Natural History of Population* (1939), a firsthand study of the role of contraception in differential fertility.

The substantive achievement of the thirties has not been repeated in the analysis of the American scene. The Second World War diverted the attention of scholars from domestic problems so that the data of the 1940 census remained comparatively unexploited during the decade succeeding. One exception was found in the approach to cultural demography developed for the South as the seedbed of the nation by Rupert B. Vance and Nadia Danilevsky in *All These People* (1945).

The First World War had little effect on United States demography, but in the postwar period American demographers deserted provincialism to turn their attention to world-wide analysis. Before the 1940's, several American demographers had ranged abroad to find suitable topics. This was to be expected in view of the increased developments in American scholarship and resources. E. F. Penrose's analysis of the bearing of population theories on the economics of Japan (1934), Joseph J. Spengler's treatment of declining fertility in France (1938), John W. Innes' study of the emergence of class differentials in fertility in England and Wales (1938), and Dorothy S. Thomas' use of exceptional official statistics in tracing Swedish population movements from 1750 to 1933 (1941) all antedated America's involvement in the postwar world.

With the rise of the United Nations, at the end of hostilities, Americans devoted a sustained attention to world demography that transcended the problem of undeveloped areas. In this research the newly founded office of Population Research at Princeton University (1936) took commanding lead on the basis of its previous work for the League of Nations. Frank Notestein and associates had used the new techniques of population projection to determine future population numbers and components of major European regions by 1970 (1944). Wilbert E. Moore had applied new techniques of measuring population pressure to the less-developed areas of southern and eastern Europe (1945), while Dudley Kirk had analyzed the trend of Europe's population increase and migra-

tion in the period between the two world wars (1946). Using life-table analysis and projection techniques, Frank Lorimer had built up estimates of population composition to replace the destroyed Soviet census of 1939 and thus was able to analyze the history and prospects of Soviet population increase (1946).

Work on the demography of underdeveloped areas also opened new vistas for American scholarship. Kingsley Davis made use of the sustained series of the Indian censuses in the first thoroughgoing study to merge oriental demography with sociological analysis (1951). George W. Barclay studied the population problem of Taiwan (Formosa) in relation to its culture (1954). This creative series was completed with Irene Taeuber's richly documented demography of Japan (1958). Warren S. Thompson, in an analysis of the troubled Pacific area, related population growth to the international scene (1946). T. Lynn Smith has written the cultural demography of Brazil (1946). In all Latin-America, the demography of Puerto Rico has been most thoroughly studied (Hatt, 1952; Hill *et al.*, 1955a; Stycos, 1956). Finally, Josiah C. Russell, a medieval historian, used demographic techniques on documents in the British archives to write the period's most impressive contribution to historical demography (1948). The period's most notable contribution to American studies was found in a new series of census monographs from the 1950 enumeration (U.S. Census Monographs 1955——). American demography thus rounded out the two decades at the middle of the century with a richly documented contribution to science.

The Task of Demography and the American Contribution

Undoubtedly there are two vantage points from which we might view the present status of demography in America. From a substantive point of view we might well list the achievements and the gaps that exist in the contemporary analysis and description of the United States population. From the vantage point of theory we might attempt an exposition of the task of demography and evaluate America's contribution thereto. In spite of its hazards we chose the second problem for our attack.

A population, to begin with, must be regarded as a large-scale human group in the course of change. Population, as James A. Field pointed out, thus "comes to involve all the activities—economic, cultural and social—to which men attach value" (1931). The development of a scientific concept of population is the first task of demography. Field pointed out that the concept "population" has the dynamic implication of its verb—the process of peopling. Crucial here is the work which focuses on the mathematics of self-renewing processes. Demography owes to A. J. Lotka the operational definition of the concept of population and virtually all of demography's entire core of analytical development. He introduced into the discipline a powerful tool, the analysis of a closed population changing at given rates of death and procreation. Lotka and Louis I. Dublin wrote the first paper which showed that a "population increasing at a prescribed rate and subject to a prescribed life table will assume a definite age distribution with a constant birth and death rate" (Lotka and Dublin, 1925). With F. R. Sharpe, Lotka worked out the answer to the following problem: Given the age distribution in an isolated population at any instant of time, the life table, the birth and death rate at every age of life, and the ratio of male to female births, find the age distribution at any subsequent instant (1911). This

analysis was the first to derive the "true rate" of natural increase.

While not so rigorous, the best substantive work was Robert R. Kuczynski's analysis of the balance of births and deaths in Europe—done in the United States under the aegis of an American research institution (1928–31). Kuczynski developed the gross and net reproduction rates using only arithmetic methods. Lotka's work went further and developed a theory of self-renewing aggregates which also applies to atomic fission. His theoretical writings on evolution and biological associations were published in French, and although they remain untranslated to this day, they have greatly affected the development of demography (1934, 1939).

Lotka's mathematical formulation thus merges with Field's social science definition to round out the population concept. Field wrote: "The term may be taken to mean the provision and stock of men, and hence the material and stuff out of which human affairs come and by reason of which the problems of the numbers and quality of the human stuff exists. . . . Such a dynamic interpretation is necessary to express the sense of process, going on, growth, significant action, together with the control of the process" (1931).

Lotka's work serves to show that important scientific concepts are not created by definition; they develop out of discoveries in a given science and grow by virtue of two processes: the operations necessary to realize the concept and the function it performs in the explanatory process. Thus fertility, mortality, and migration are not to be regarded as concepts; they are simply the categories which demographers investigate. The concept of *a population*, however, ranks among the most valuable yet developed in the field of demography. When a science discovers or creates a complex idea of proved explanatory value and capable of logical manipulation, it has developed a true concept. Thus the term "population," already freighted with meaning from ecology and sociology, became such a concept when it was invested with the operations performed by A. J. Lotka and others. As such, it serves an explanatory function when applied to any phenomena demonstrated to be identical or similar.

It seems safe to say that no other concept of equal explanatory value has yet been developed in demography. Optimum population would be such a term were it capable of statistical manipulation. It is a tribute to American demography to say that population redistribution is at the stage where it could be qualified as such a concept. Given adequate data and sufficient theoretical import, ideas of regions and rural-urban distribution can be fitted into differential rates of birth, death, and migration to determine the degree to which the population will redistribute itself over the succeeding generation (Goodrich, 1936; Vance, 1938). In the same way, the term "population replacement" could be applied to the different rates at which each social class will be replaced in the succeeding generation—provided that such strata can be identified in the population and that rates of social mobility can be calculated. At present, difficulties of data and statistical operations loom so large that these concepts have not made their appearance among the achievements of American demography.

American demography accordingly has arrived at the position in social science where it must be judged by its peers (Vance, 1952a). Any criticism of the historical development of demography in the United States must report that it lingered too long in the descriptive state—sometimes without benefit of accurate observation. The discipline, in

Philip M. Hauser's words, has developed an extremely high ratio of techniques and data to ideas (1948). It rightly emphasizes precision; it wrongly neglects the importance of ideas. In reviewing more than a thousand recent migration studies, Dorothy S. Thomas rendered the crisp judgment that the majority were "planlessly empirical and trivial in content" (Malzberg and Lee, 1956, p. 3). The discipline is most vigorous in those analytic techniques which discover process and lead to the accurate measurements necessary for description. This in turn has led back —and rightly so—to the search for more valid observation. The theoretical orientation of demography still appears its weakest spot, largely because the goal of analysis often appears to be solely description.

Population deals with normal, nonpathological processes. As the discipline has followed the usual course of science, it developed along several levels of exposition and interpretation: science (1) as valid observation, (2) as substantive description, (3) as technical and logical analysis, and (4) as scientific theory. It is proposed to view American research in fertility, mortality, migration, population growth, etc., from this point of vantage. American demography has attempted the development of several ambitious theories, and it is their near failure which has made the American science fearful of theory today.

Growth Cycles, the Demographic Transition, and Population Projections

Empirical tests of the supposedly universal principles of Malthus have been one of the preoccupations of American demography. Such tests of necessity waited upon the accumulation of observations of population over time (Willcox, 1931). The theory of population growth represents a point at which doctrines of population pressure converged with high-level mathematical analysis. Once a center of study, this approach represents both the achievements and failures of American demography. The approach was pioneered by Raymond Pearl, and it can be discussed in terms of his contribution (1925).

The basic idea in Pearl's work proved simple enough. Population, instead of increasing at a constant rate, tends to follow the growth curve of biological organisms, increasing rapidly during embryonic development, slowing down and stabilizing as it reaches an upper limit. This analysis of changing rates of growth, free of the irrational features of straight-line increment, was first suggested by P. F. Verhulst in 1845, in a logistic curve with the following equation: $P = K/(1 + e^{a+bx})$. Represented graphically, this equation was used by Pearl and Lowell J. Reed to represent the sequential change of rates of increase in a rising trend line whose inflections proceed from an assumed "zero" to an upper limit K in the fashion of a stretched-out **S** curve. Pearl's experiments on fruit flies (*Drosophila melanogaster*) in the limited environment of a milk bottle agreed with the somewhat restricted number of observations available on the growth of world population. His work, *The Biology of Population Growth* (1925), approached the status of a full-blown theory of growth cycles, and can be summed up as follows:

The long-run tendency of population growth can be represented by a curve which starting from a previously established stationary level, representing the supporting capacity of its region at the prevailing level of culture, productive technique, and standard of living—rises at first slowly, then at an increasing rate, finally leveling out as the curve approaches an upper asymptote which represents the supporting capacity of the environment at the last stage of culture development.

Never repudiated or refuted in an all-out critical attack, the theory of logistic growth cycles nevertheless has been quietly superseded. There are several reasons for this. Like other projections, logistic growth did not carry forward into the accurate prediction of future populations. Fitted alike in Pearl's scheme to the increase of the population of Algiers, the United States, and the world, the theory was forced to face the fact that in the populations studied growth had not begun at a stationary level, nor had it reached the stabilized level represented by K. More important, Pearl worked without tracing the trend lines of fertility and mortality and without knowing of the concept of the demographic revolution. As analysis of the demographic transition came into its full development, the concept seemed better to explain the pattern of growth represented by the logistic curve. In the opening "demographic gap" caused by the downswing of deaths and in the new equilibrium attained when fertility decline closes the gap at the new low level of births and deaths, the demographic transition offers a concise statement of the transition from high-level births and deaths. Such a statement now appears to represent the hypothesis needed in demographic dynamics.

This achievement, cumulative in the true empirical sense, has largely been the work of American scientists Walter F. Willcox (1931, II, 33–82), Frank Notestein—the classic statement— (1945), Warren S. Thompson (1948), and others who incorporated the work of the British demographer A. M. Carr-Saunders (1936). Controversy has arisen over the validity of the transition theory (Hatt *et al.*, 1955; van Nort and Karon, 1955), but the theory fills several requirements of high-level analysis: it is dynamic rather than static, and it takes account of demographic interrelations among countries and among groups within countries in terms of culture contacts and social interaction (Spengler, 1952).

Finally, as carried through in the transition from high-level to low-level vital rates, the emergence and "clo-

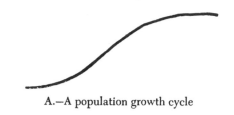

A.—A population growth cycle

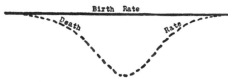

B.—The mechanics of Cycle I (the primitive cycle).

C.—The mechanics of Cycle II (the modern cycle).

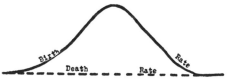

D.—The mechanics of Cycle III (the future cycle).

E.—The mechanics of Cycle IV

Fig. 1.—Theoretical types of population growth cycles. (From Donald O. Cowgill, "The Theory of Population Growth Cycles," *American Journal of Sociology*, LV [1949], 163–70.)

sure" of the "demographic gap" appears to follow a logistic curve of growth. In a significant analysis, Donald O. Cowgill (1949) has developed this portion of the theory. He showed that this historic trend is one of four growth cycles which yield an **S** curve of population growth. Such growth "could be inaugurated by either an increased birth rate or a decreased death rate and terminated by either a decreased birth rate or an increased death rate." In this analysis these variables yield four simple theoretical patterns of growth. Cycle I is the primitive cycle assumed in Malthusian theory where the birth rate remains stationary while the death rate falls, then rises. Cycle II is represented by the historic transition in the West. Cycle III, typified by the "baby boom," is initiated by a rising birth rate and terminated by its recession. Cycle IV, which represents the reverse of Cycle II, would be initiated by a rising birth rate and terminated by a subsequent rise in the death rate. Cycle IV, which has not been encountered in demographic history, represents something of a logical improbability.

By reducing cycles of population growth to their component trends, this analysis serves to remove the last trace of "cosmic necessity" and "mathematical mysticism" from logistic growth; thus it demonstrates that "closure" and stabilization, instead of being accepted as inevitable, can be treated simply as a hypothesis for historic change. Such change is logical just as the Industrial Revolution is logical; it may happen and it may not. If it does happen it will occur in a certain fashion. This loss in theory may prove to be a gain in population analysis.

It is apparent also that when such natural increase of a population is distributed over time, each of the four cycles will yield a normal curve of distribution of this increase. When such increase is made cumulative, the result is a true **S** curve. This is evident in the inspection of Cycles I and II. The logistic curve of population growth is equivalent to a normal curve of population increase made cumulative over a given time span.

The logic of population growth also carries over into population projections —a field assiduously cultivated by American demographers. Figures of future population, it has been suggested, offer better tests of logistic growth than can be found in the conflicting estimates of populations of the past. Before 1910 practically all population forecasts were based on some method of extrapolating historic trends—either the trend of the total population or of its rate of growth. Other methods were developed, based on the principle of the logistic curve.

The empirical method developed by P. K. Whelpton and Warren S. Thompson introduced further components of growth by specifying the age-specific rates of fertility and mortality (Thompson and Whelpton, 1943). Furthermore, it yields age and sex projections because the projections begin with actual age and sex cohorts to which are applied the appropriate age-specific rates to yield the succeeding age and sex groupings (Whelpton, 1947). For cohorts already born this method has given excellent results; substantial errors have entered, however, because of the rapid changes in births—errors which become cumulative as the new cohorts themselves enter the reproductive age. Population projections thus have not proved to be successful undertaking on the part of American demographers. By 1950 the most valid of all these future estimates was Whelpton's old logistic calculation of 1928— a projection which the demographer himself had ceased to use (1928).

Widespread fluctuation in births has undermined population projections and has led demographers to study historical changes in the fertility of cohorts of women over each reproductive generation. Whelpton's work, *Cohort Fertility* (1954), introduced variables heretofore unaccounted for since he analyzed fertility adjusted to age, parity, fecundity, and marriage. Finally, by studying changes in completed cumulative fertility, Whelpton sought to determine whether actual declines or increases in family size have taken place. Fluctuation in births, it is felt, can best be understood by the historical treatment of actual changes in cohort fertility. In the analysis of hypothetical cohorts, annual rates are projected after the manner of the gross reproduction rate. Thus in population growth over time Whelpton is able to show that births are postponed, made up, and anticipated in line with economic trends and that conflicting trends exist by parity; i.e., fifth order births and over will continue to decline while first to fourth order births are increasing. In short, Whelpton has applied the technique of the generation life table, with complications, to the fertility of the cohorts of women born at successive periods.

We may conclude that the dynamic aspects of American demography have helped determine the nature of the concept of population and have developed some highly useful mathematical models to represent the process of population growth as that of a self-renewing aggregate. In sociology a great deal of care and ingenuity has been devoted to developing a theory of social change. Some suggestion of possible integration of the processes of population growth and of culture change now appears in the offing.

Macro-micro Analysis in Demography

Scientists have studied dynamics in the changes in the total social system; they realize that parallel changes occur in systems of human motivation and attitudes. In the trend lines of population growth and changing rates of cohort fertility the demographer is confronted with interaction between two parallel sets of phenomena: Economics now handles this problem by parallel systems of *macro-* and *micro-* analysis. Kenneth E. Boulding, who has done much to develop economic analysis along this line, writes (1955, p. 237):

There are two main branches in modern economic analysis, to which the names "microeconomics" and "macroeconomics" may conveniently be given. Microeconomics is the study of particular firms, particular households, individual prices, wages, incomes; individual industries, particular commodities. . . . Many economic problems and policies, however, are concerned not so much with individual prices, commodities, and firms, but with *aggregates;* not with the price of cheese, but with the price of everything, or the "general level" of prices. . . . Macroeconomics, then, is that part of the subject which deals with the great aggregates and averages of the system rather than with particular items in it, and attempts to define these aggregates in a useful manner and to examine how they are related and determined.

Bringing this type of analysis closer to the phenomena treated in sociology, Neil W. Chamberlain has pointed out (1955, p. 4):

Economic relations, as one category of social relations, are subject to our conclusions concerning the mutually conditioning relationship between individuals and culture. In economic analysis the micro-model is built solely on the individual and deals with interpersonal relations only. The macro-model, on the other hand, deals with *aggregate* relations, being similar in this respect to the concept of culture (another aggregate); indeed macro-economic relations can be viewed as an aspect of culture dealing with organized repetitive influences on individual economic behavior. The micro and macro relations of eco-

nomic analysis thus correspond to the individual and culture in sociological theory. The conclusion that individual and culture are interrelated so that one can be explained only in terms of the other can be transformed to micro and macro economic analysis. Neither can explain economic behavior adequately without the other.

Fertility as the crux of the population problem shows the necessity of the new analysis. No projections, no extrapolations, no models of inevitable growth of themselves now appear capable of projecting trend lines for future fertility. To account for these shifts, demography turned to environing conditions, major changes in the social system over the generations, such as industrialization, urbanization, secularization, rising levels of living, and the increased development of technology. But since these large-scale explanations by themselves provided inadequate explanations of changes in forms of behavior they must be related to changes in individual motivation and attitudes. Here the family appears to occupy the niche occupied by the firm in micro-economics. One simple illustration should suffice. It is not simply the discovery of contraception in the society but the decision on the part of families to use contraceptives which operates to limit the size of families. The first application of this conceptual apparatus to demographic theory represented an ambitious approach to the Malthusian dilemma of undeveloped countries. Leibenstein (1954) used economic and demographic factors in interaction in an attempt to determine the dynamic impetus required to move off "dead center" a society stalled in the Malthusian "trap." This impetus would be determined when the annual rate of capital investment came to exceed the annual rate of population increase.

With the aid of bio-statisticians and

public health people, mortality now appears as one of the best explored topics in American demography. To a large extent this is due to the explanatory function of macro-analysis in advanced civilizations.

Thus in the study of declining mortality, demography has demonstrated statistically the mass effect of the introduction of serums, vaccines, the chlorination of water, sanitary organization, drainage, sewage, etc., by type of disease. This operates in the macrosystem. No micro-analysis seems involved in this situation, for legal measures make chlorinated water and pasteurized milk the only types available. Vaccination, enforced for certain diseases, is compulsory, and if no problems of individual decision are involved, the macro-analysis gives the complete picture of mortality decline. These controls are the kind envisaged by sanitarians, since public health measures are so calculated that they cannot be defeated by individual choices of the human factor.

In this same area, however, the progress of medicine may leave the discipline with problems of individual choice. Why does not mortality decline at a rate commensurate with the advance of medical science? Here macroanalysis must be supplemented by micro-analysis. Decisions to seek medical aid and hospital care are modes of behavior, individual actions subject to micro-analysis. Access to hospital areas and economic ability to pay for medical care may be subject to macro-analysis, but the individual decision to make use of medical facilities must be sought at the level where these social forces impinge on the individual and the family unit.

Mortality studies are weakest where they come closest to the influences of socioeconomic categories. Mortality, by size of community, can be studied from mass data, but the important problem of mortality by occupation has not been explored since the 1930 census and then for only ten states (Whitney, 1934). In United States demography, this problem has to do with the correct ordering of observations. Death certificates can be matched against base occupations only in census years; individuals may change occupations several times over their life careers; the occupation usually given at age sixty-five will have to be replaced by the major occupation on the death certificates if these studies are to be continued. The last occupation may have less bearing on mortality than the major life calling. Finally, unless the category "retired," given in labor force statistics for those age sixty-five and over, is supplemented by major occupation, large numbers of deaths cannot be allocated.

Parallel macro-micro relationships are now shown to exist in the newer studies of fertility. Here the family can be treated as analogous to the firm in micro-economics. Once contraception becomes a matter for family decision, childbearing becomes a voluntary action, and the macro-analysis of social trends will be recognized as insufficient. Thus fertility by marriage, fecundity, parity, etc., can be calculated alongside the trend line of social change, but the meanings will not be obvious unless attitude surveys can make clear the interaction between these two sets of phenomena as movements in the social system go over into changes in individual motivation.

In a study of the Hutterites, the total social system was seen to converge in a complex giving high valuation to fertility, and no special study was made of individual attitudes (Eaton and Mayer, 1954). In a cross-cultural survey, *Culture and Human Fertility*, Lorimer (1954) undertook to relate primitive macro-systems (social structure, kinship, etc.) to fertility without determining underlying attitudes in the micro-systems. In the Indianapolis study, such conditions of the total social system as urbanization, education, Protestant religion, and occupation were made the basis of selection of those low-fertility families whose attitudes were to be studied (Whelpton and Kiser, 1946–56). Moreover, hypotheses set up to account for decisions in family size were drawn from the total system analysis. In Puerto Rico studies, the relation of these two systems was made more explicit in the work of Hill, Back, and Stycos (1955a, b, c), for the analysis moved from the conditions in the total social system to the attitudes and motivations of the families operating within that system. A dilemma was found in this study: decisions about family size were found to fit neither with the macro-system nor with reported attitudes.

Cultural conditions—shifting from time to time and from group to group—are not likely to show uniform correspondence of macro- and micro-conditions. Differential fertility has been viewed as the varying incidence of system changes on families in different social strata (Notestein and Sydenstricker, 1930; Kiser, 1942). Reversals of fertility trends, baby booms, and the convergence of differentials will offer a test of factors sustaining as well as depressing the birth rate (Woofter, 1949).

Internal Migration

Such a scheme indicates a direction demography will take in future migration analysis. Macro-analysis, using available statistics in the manner developed by O. E. Baker (1933), C. H. Hamilton (1934), and others will seek to show the net flow of migration among such locations as states, rural-urban areas, etc. This, along with the resulting analysis of changing economic opportunity, furnishes the macro-picture. Micro-analysis should then focus on the decision to migrate. Thus the

fundamental choice may be the decision whether to migrate or not, with place as a matter of secondary choice. This phenomenon does not come out in the analysis of the over-all statistics. Heretofore, these things have been discussed in terms of distance, barriers to communication, means of travel, etc., but we have not really come to grips with the micro-analysis of migration until we have studied human action systems. The joining of these two trends could mean new major achievements in American demography. Once this is accomplished, we will be able to return to the study of growth cycles, population fluctuations, and trends in fertility with improved techniques and more enlightened theory.

Certainly a major gap in American demography is found in our failure to cope with the problem of internal migration. No annual registration of migration exists. Only in the migration questions of 1940 did the census begin to deal with the problem of adequate observation and enumeration. As a consequence, most migration analyses in the United States end at the point where they should begin. The derivation of net figures on migrations between given areas too often satisfies this type of research. Since these figures represent net balance of inflow and outflow, their characteristics cannot be regarded as the characteristics of a real population. The best conceptualization of the migration stream—that of Samuel Stouffer—dates from 1940: "The number of persons going a given distance is directly proportional to the number of opportunities at that distance and inversely proportional to the intervening opportunities" (1940). Daniel O. Price gave statistical formulation to the vectors of internal migration, showing, for example, the relation between direction and distance (1948). As an identifiable element in the population stream, Negro migration has been best studied in its cultural and social context (Woofter, 1920; Kiser, 1932).

Until the work of Lee, Price, and associates (1953), the United States had only one general analysis of internal migration. We could truthfully say that the major work in internal migration had been done twenty years ago by C. W. Thornthwaite (1934) and had not been repeated. In Sweden and other countries these figures would serve as data for the analysis of the migration process, not as the conclusion of an arduous investigation. Thus we have the ironic situation in which many American demographers have regarded the work of a man such as E. G. Ravenstein as speculative theory while the estimates of net migration are hailed as sound empirical research.

Finally, the opportunity for experimental analysis remains comparatively unexploited in demography. Gilbert W. Beebe organized a project which enabled him to demonstrate the extent to which a contraceptive program would lower the fertility of a rural West Virginia county (1942). Rupert B. Vance (1956) and Francis C. Madigan, S.J. (1957), used the mortality records of Catholic religious orders to determine whether men and women would have similar life expectancy if they followed similar styles of life, and arrived at the conclusion that the longevity of United States women has its basis in biology.

We may close this section of the survey by glancing at (1) a closed chapter, (2) an achievement, and (3) a bright promise in recent American demography.

A closed chapter in American demography is the disappearing treatment of minority groups. First to go was immigration. Harry Jerome's important demonstration of the impact of business cycles on international migrations (1926) may belong in the field;

M. L. Hansen's account of the Atlantic migration (1940) and Oscar Handlin's *The Uprooted* (1951) definitely do not. Two texts, however, indicate its continuing importance (Davie, 1936; Taft and Robbins, 1955). The place of the Negro in American life has definitely become a sociological specialty, living apart from demography.

An achievement is to be found in the development of the labor force concept—pioneered by the United States census—and it is an achievement ranging all the way from theory to more valid observation back to improved analysis. A major controversy over the unemployment figure of the 1930 census led demographers to examine the older concept of the "gainfully employed"; this led to a complete reappraisal of basic questions in the census, and these new observations led to better analysis and better theory (Ducoff and Hagood, 1947; Jaffe and Stewart, 1951). An analysis making use of the labor force concept was able to show that the loss of a hundred jobs in the United States from 1930 to 1937 meant not 100 but 176 unemployed (Vance, 1945, pp. 324–25, 333).

The most promising development imminent in the United States appears to be the fusion of the new urban studies with demography. Great progress has been made in studies of world urbanization, human ecology, regionalism, and the growth of the metropolitan community, with especially notable work by Kingsley Davis (1956), Vance and Demerath (1954), Philip M. Hauser (1944), O. D. Duncan (1951), and Donald J. Bogue (1950, 1953). Unlike demography proper, this area has not remained innocent of theory. Accordingly, the fusion of these studies with the substantive content and analytical techniques of demography marks a distinct stage of achievement. Duncan and Duncan (1957) in *The Negro Population of Chicago* have best shown the impact of a racial migration on the ecology of a great city. Since social change definitely affects population growth and urbanization and since the development of metropolitan communities constitutes one of the greatest changes in the United States, this development will give new direction to major lines of investigation in American demography. Undoubtedly the next few decades will show great advance in population studies in the United States. There remains one question: How well are the forces of science organized for the tasks ahead?

CIRCUMSTANCES AFFECTING THE FUTURE
DEVELOPMENT OF DEMOGRAPHY

So far we have discussed demography in terms applicable to many nations of Western culture. We come now to an assessment of the future development of demography in the United States. How have American scholars faced up to the particular problems of their scientific discipline? In the past what circumstances have favored or hindered the development of the discipline? If we can identify the trends, can we determine their movements in the future? Will they persist? Will they be deflected? If so, in what way?

*The Population Association
of America, 1931——*

The professional organization of population specialists in the United States was accomplished in 1931 when the Population Association of America was founded, with Henry Pratt Fairchild as its first president. While several reasons have been assigned for the late date of this development, there are really two: the demographers already had an important part in the conduct of several learned societies, and lay interest in the controversial aspects of

population may have delayed the demographers' decision to organize.

Population sections were regularly scheduled by various social science societies; there was a tendency for census personnel to participate in the programs of the American Statistical Association and for university demographers to concentrate in the American Sociological Society. Membership was overlapping and programs sometimes interchangeable—phenomena which have continued since the demographers organized. Final impetus to organization was given when the association called a conference on population studies in relation to social planning at Washington, D.C., May 2–4, 1936. The membership list, issued soon after, showed 195 members. The success of the association was assured when anonymous contributors underwrote the cost of financing the secretary's office.

The core of the new organization came out of the American National Committee of the International Population Union, which was reconstructed to serve as the research committee of the association. Abroad, there was a tendency to view those savants who attended conferences of the union as spokesmen for their respective governments. In the popular mind the scientific study of population was still confused with the spread of propaganda for birth control. The organization of the association was delayed in the hope of avoiding entanglement in demographic controversy with the various natalists, pro-natalists, and depopulationists. Propagandists were not made welcome, and the original organization was carefully set up with only scientists on the executive board.

Accordingly, very little popular interest in population problems finds reflection in the association, for it is definitely not a layman's organization. While this choice may have retarded popular education in demographic matters, it definitely has improved the scientific status of demography in the United States. Most of the "crackpot" books on population are now written by non-members. For a period, the "freeze-out" left the direction of the work of the association to the board of directors. After the association's professional characteristics became fixed, a new constitution was written, and the association assumed its present democratic complexion. Demography in the United States has greatly benefited from the absence of the sensationalism and factional conflict which accompanies controversy in demography.

The association began the publication of a bibliographic quarterly, *Population Literature*, in 1934. This was taken over by Princeton University in 1936. *Population Bulletin*, a popular monthly issue of some twelve to sixteen pages, has been published since 1945 by the Population Reference Bureau. In France, England, and several other countries with a smaller public, well-known demographic journals are published. In the United States the demographer who wishes to keep abreast of the literature must subscribe to journals in statistics, economics, geography, public health, biology, eugenics, and sociology. While bibliographical needs have been met by *Population Index*, an able quarterly of world-wide coverage, it is often questioned as to whether sufficient resources can be demonstrated to justify the establishment of a journal centering in demography. The struggle for survival of such periodicals as *Human Biology* and *Human Fertility* indicates the risks involved. Obviously, the need is partly met by the publication program of the United Nations and the many releases of the Bureau of the Census. Attempts have been made to fill the gap, and they may well succeed.

The Universities

Population will remain a teaching discipline, and all other areas of demographic interest—government, research interests, and the foundations—will draw their strength from demography in the colleges. Irene Taeuber points out, "The fact that demography cuts across the boundaries of so many of the defined fields of knowledge and of academic concentration has had a deep influence on the patterns of its organization as a research field and as academic discipline" (1946).

Historically, demography has been nurtured and supported within the tent of one particular discipline, sociology. Since sociology is more highly promoted as an academic subject in the United States than elsewhere, this association has had its advantages. The interests of sociologists have been wide-ranging, usually broad enough to require work in family sociology, statistics, social economics, cultural history, and other topics suitable for work in demography.

There are drawbacks, however, and the teaching of demography has certain "soft spots." A recent survey by the Population Association of America disclosed a certain lack of professionalism in the field. Many who teach courses in population lack affiliation with their professional association; some lack professional training in the discipline and do no research in the field; some, in fact, teach a textbook course by request of the college administration simply as a side line. There are teachers in the field who have no knowledge of statistics beyond arithmetic and little knowledge of the literature beyond that of the text they teach. This group constitutes a small minority; while not peculiar to small colleges, the group can be held responsible for the failure of demography to attract and recruit an indeterminate number of able students.

With present resources and the diverse specialties found within sociology, it is not to be expected that more than six or eight universities will be equipped to carry on the research and teaching program required for distinguished graduate work. Outstanding demographers can be found in many institutions, but the requirements of good research programs, well-equipped statistical facilities, and sufficient graduate stipends for training strictly limit the number of centers. Harvard, once a center, has de-emphasized demography in its training. Pennsylvania, under the leadership of Dorothy Swaine Thomas, has re-entered the field. Columbia, Chicago, North Carolina, Princeton, and Washington (at Seattle) continue to feature demography as a specialization in conjunction with statistics, human ecology, and rural and urban sociology.

In one respect the all-encompassing nature of sociology has in itself offered handicaps, for there is the danger of attempting to duplicate in one department the function of specialists distributed in many. While this type of "empire-building" is not peculiar to sociology, it is generally felt that attempts to circumscribe demography within a conventional department have not been too successful. Few institutions have yet achieved the co-operation or the organizational form required to engage the interests of their economists, statisticians, and health and biological specialists in a unified attack on the problems of demography. Thus, in well-equipped universities rich in personnel, demography has not used these resources to full potential, and demographic theory has not attained the high level required in graduate teaching and research.

It is not held that demography is in worse plight here than in other coun-

tries, but apart from a few research institutes demography has not found the means of achieving its full potential. Outside of these few well-known universities the academic leadership needed for this achievement is not yet in sight. New forms of co-operation will be needed to bring such fields as economics, public health, and genetics nearer to the center of demographic training.

Demography would be much less advanced were it not for the liberal support and the well-considered policies of American foundations. Even here there has been criticism—criticism not altogether based on the problem of whether foundation largess, like rain, falls upon both the just and the unjust. Two diverse procedures in use may be pointed out here. Foundation support may be granted for a definite project with an organization specifically set up for the purpose and dismantled when the task is completed. A valuable achievement of this type was the study of population redistribution which produced *Migration and Economic Opportunity* (Goodrich, 1936). Such operations have proved very successful for special programs. They also have the virtue that, if they fail, they are not long remembered and their sponsors do not long invite criticism for the failure.

Better known are the permanent institutes doing research in population and supported by foundation grants in conjunction with a university. Here foundations will support specific projects, but continuity will have to be furnished by the institute or "bureau." Among the most productive has been the Scripps Foundation at Miami University in Oxford, Ohio. Of all American foundations it appears to have received the greatest returns from a comparatively small endowment. Scripps, however, has suffered from lack of a teaching connection. Since its research was not tied in with a university graduate school, its contribution to teaching has been limited to work with a few interns. The Milbank Memorial Fund has sponsored health and population studies, has developed a publishing program (including a journal), and annually brings the country's leading demographers together in scientific round tables (Milbank Memorial Fund, 1946–57). Permanent institutes located at universities carry certain built-in hazards even while they distribute the benefits of scholarship. They absorb more funds than even the most resourceful universities can provide; they are subject to continual hazards of refinancing; only directors full of ideas can expect to secure continued support; the search for renewed support is likely to turn even men who like to live dangerously from scholars into promoters and "budgetary experts." Government contracts then come along to fill out and complicate the picture.

The critics, no doubt, are correct when they say that "endowment for research has led to research for endowment" and that the modern scholar has shed the quiet garb of academic security to assume that of the scientific promoter of a corporate organization which must be continually supplied with funds. This, however, is not the question at issue. We are not concerned with the problem of "what makes Sammy run?" We have to ask whether this process has been productive for demography and whether it will continue. To both questions the answer must be "yes." The organization of the Population Council in 1953, with a large fellowship program, is an indication that demography will secure more adequate support in the future and that competition for these resources will produce more able demographers and eventually insure a better product.

Among the more successful of these permanent research organizations are the Office of Population Research at Princeton University; the Population Center at the University of Washington, Seattle; and the newly founded Population Research and Training Center at the University of Chicago. Other institutes such as those at North Carolina and Columbia support demographic studies. One important American corporation has performed some of the functions of both the foundation and the research institute. The Metropolitan Life Insurance Company has supported a distinguished research division with scientists whose work has gone far beyond the demands of actuarial science and has published the research of its statistical division in a bulletin made available to all interested demographers.

Government

Government in its various arms has greatly improved those scientific services which obviously mean so much to the development of demography. The modern census has reached a state of technical and scientific proficiency; it has been responsive to the needs and to the advice of the scientific fraternity; it has made use of panels of scientific specialists in planning its own operation. Free of the "boom and bust" policy which once prevailed, the census bureau is no longer dismantled and put into storage in intercensal periods. Similar traditions persist, however, in regulations which provide that unexpended budgets revert to the general fund and in the pressure on the Bureau of the Census which sometimes leaves it unable to finish the work it is commissioned to do. In the 1950 census certain basic tabulations would have gone unpublished had it not been for foundation assistance. Budgetary considerations are responsible for the fact that valuable tabulated materials go unpublished in each census period. Some demographers seem never to learn of these resources; others are unable to pay for them out of their own limited budgets.

Much work is done on farm and rural population by the United States Department of Agriculture—notably the basic estimates in the series on rural-urban migration begun in 1920. Agriculture experiment stations regularly publish rural population studies, most of which have been simple but adequate descriptive accounts. The few to break new ground have developed technical measures of calculating migration—interstate, rural-urban, etc. On the fringes of demography this work has been of value in extension services and has aided in the formulation of agricultural policy.

Demographers and the learned world in general have a certain responsibility here. They are the basic consumers of government statistics, and they convey their analyses to both the scientific and the general public. When demographers and university research specialists consistently fail to make use of certain tabulations, that series stands in danger of being abandoned. Commercial interests know what data they require of the census and exert influence to see that they are secured. Academic people are also organized and make requests through their learned societies. When these requests are granted, there is often no assurance that demographers are committed to do important research in the series requested. The function of the census is subject to controlled review, and as the task of the census becomes more expensive, "lean decades" and "lean topics" may operate to break the continuity of needed series. Demographers, by the very nature of their task, must wage unceasing warfare against the threatened loss of valuable information. Their best weapon is the demonstration that scientific results and public use follow from census enumerations.

Great changes are to be expected in American demography of the future. Many demographers of the past lacked advanced statistical training. Others to whom theory meant only Malthus or the population optimum came to profess a certain lack of interest in ideas. It is safe to predict that in the future few demographers who are not versed in mathematical statistics will gain distinction. High level techniques, however, will still be sought for the substantive contributions they can make. Here it is safe to say that the ablest demographers must also be subtle masters of theory in society, economy, social psychology, and culture. It is fundamentally the lack of ideas, not a lack of data and techniques, that has retarded demography. The demographer of the future will probably be more of a specialist; thus he will be more difficult for the layman to understand. Kingsley Davis, for example, has expressed the view that in the future demographers will become specialists in fertility, with training also in family sociology; in mortality, with training in public health; or in migration, with training in economics. All will be statisticians, and specialists in underdeveloped areas will also be economists. Some, however, may be generalists who will interrelate the divergent specialties of this already complex field.

SELECTED BIBLIOGRAPHY

Baker, O. E. 1933. "Rural-urban Migration and the National Welfare," *Annals of the Association of American Geographers,* June, 1933.

Barclay, G. W. 1954. *Colonial Development and Population in Taiwan.* Princeton: Princeton University Press.

Beebe, G. W. 1942. *Contraception and Fertility in the Southern Appalachians.* Baltimore: Williams & Wilkins Co.

BOGUE, D. J. 1950. *The Structure of the Metropolitan Community: A Study of Dominance and Subdominance.* Ann Arbor: University of Michigan Press.

———. 1953. *Population Growth in Standard Metropolitan Areas 1900–1950, with an Explanatory Analysis of Urbanized Areas.* Washington, D.C.: Government Printing Office.

BOULDING, K. E. 1955. *Economic Analysis.* 3d ed. New York: Harper & Bros.

CARPENTER, N. 1927. *Immigrants and Their Children, 1920: A Study Based on Census Statistics Relative to the Foreign Born and the Native White of Foreign or Mixed Parentage.* Washington, D.C.: Government Printing Office.

CARR-SAUNDERS, A. M. 1936. *World Population.* Oxford: Clarendon Press.

CHAMBERLAIN, N. W. 1955. *A General Theory of Economic Process.* New York: Harper & Bros.

COWGILL, D. O. 1949. "The Theory of Population Growth Cycles," *American Journal of Sociology,* LV, 163–70.

CUMMINGS, J. E., *et al.* 1918. "Statistical Work of the Federal Government of the United States," in *The History of Statistics,* ed. J. KOREN. New York: American Statistical Association.

DAVIE, M. R. 1936. *World Immigration, with Special Reference to the United States.* New York: Macmillan Co.

DAVIS, K. (ed.). 1945. "World Population in Transition," *Annals of the American Academy of Political and Social Science,* No. 237 (January, 1945).

———. 1951. *The Population of India and Pakistan.* Princeton: Princeton University Press.

———, and HERTZ, H. *Patterns of World Urbanization.* New York: Macmillan Co. (to be published).

DUBLIN, L. I. (ed.). 1936. "The American People: Studies in Population," *Annals of the American Academy of Political and Social Science,* No. 188 (November, 1936).

———. (ed.). 1926. *Population Problems in the United States and Canada: An Outgrowth of Papers Presented at the Eighty-sixth Annual Meeting of the American Statistical Association.* Boston: Houghton Mifflin Co.

———, LOTKA, A. J., and SPIEGELMAN, M. 1936. *Length of Life: A Study of the Life Table.* New York: Ronald Press Co. Rev. ed.; 1949.

DUCOFF, L. J., and HAGOOD, M. J. 1947. *Labor Force Definition and Measurement: Recent Experiences in the United States.* New York: Social Science Research Council.

DUNCAN, O. D. 1951. "Optimum Size of Cities," in *Reader in Urban Sociology,* ed. P. K. HATT and A. J. REISS, JR. Glencoe, Ill.: Free Press.

———, and DUNCAN, BEVERLY. 1957. *The Negro Population of Chicago.* Chicago: University of Chicago Press.

EATON, J. W., and MAYER, A. J. 1954. *Man's Capacity to Reproduce: The Demography of a Unique Population.* Glencoe, Ill.: Free Press.

EVANS, G. H., JR. 1950. *Basic Economics: A Macro- and Micro-Analysis.* New York: Alfred A. Knopf.

FIELD, J. A. 1931. *Essays on Population and Other Papers.* Chicago: University of Chicago Press.

GOLDENWEISER, E. A., and TRUESDELL, L. E. 1924. *Farm Tenancy in the United States: An Analysis of the Results of the 1920 Census Relative to Farms Classified by Tenure, Supplemented by Pertinent Data from Other Sources.* Washington, D.C.: Government Printing Office.

GOODRICH, C., *et al.* 1936. *Migration and Economic Opportunity: The Report of the Study of Population Redistribution.* Philadelphia: University of Pennsylvania Press.

HAMILTON, C. H. 1934. *Rural-Urban Migration in North Carolina 1920–1930.* Raleigh, N.C.: North Carolina State College.

HANDLIN, O. 1951. *The Uprooted: The Epic Story of the Great Migrations That Made the American People.* Boston: Little, Brown & Co.

HANSEN, M. L. 1940. *The Atlantic Migration, 1607–1860: A History of the Continuing Settlement of the United States.* Cambridge: Harvard University Press.

HATT, P. K. 1952. *Backgrounds of Human Fertility in Puerto Rico: A Sociological Survey.* Princeton: Princeton University Press.

HATT, P. K., FARR, N. L., and WEINSTEIN, E. 1955. "Types of Population Balance," *American Sociological Review*, XX, 14–21.

HAUSER, P. M. 1948. "Present Status and Prospects of Research in Population," *American Sociological Review*, XIII, 371–82.

———, and TEPPING, B. J. 1944. "Evaluation of Wartime Population Estimates and of Predictions of Postwar Population Prospects of Metropolitan Areas," *American Sociological Review*, IX, 473–80.

HILL, J. A. 1929. *Women in Gainful Occupations, 1870 to 1920: A Study of the Trend of Recent Changes in the Numbers, Occupational Distribution, and Family Relationship of Women Reported in the Census as Following a Gainful Occupation.* Washington, D.C.: Government Printing Office.

———. 1936. "Composition of the American Population by Race and Country of Origin," *Annals of the American Academy of Political and Social Science*, No. 188, pp. 177–84.

HILL, R., BACK, K. W., and STYCOS, J. M. 1955a. "Family Action Potentials and Fertility Planning in Puerto Rico," in *Current Research in Human Fertility.* New York: Milbank Memorial Fund.

———. 1955b. "Family Structure and Fertility in Puerto Rico," *Social Problems*, III, 73–93.

———. 1955c. "Intra-family Communication and Fertility Planning in Puerto Rico," *Rural Sociology*, XX, 258–71.

HIMES, N. E. 1936. *Medical History of Contraception.* Baltimore: Williams & Wilkins Co.

HOBBS, A. H. 1942. *Differentials in Internal Migration.* Philadelphia: University of Pennsylvania Press.

HOLT, W. S. 1929. *The Bureau of the Census: Its History, Activities, and Organization.* Washington, D.C.: Brookings Institution.

INNES, J. W. 1938. *Class Fertility Trends in England and Wales: 1876–1934.* Princeton: Princeton University Press.

JAFFE, A. J. 1951. *Handbook of Statistical Methods for Demographers: Selected Problems in the Analysis of Census Data.* Washington, D.C.: Government Printing Office.

———, and STEWART, C. D. 1951. *Manpower Resources and Utilization: Principles of Working Force Analysis.* New York: John Wiley & Sons.

JENKS, J. W., and LAUCK, W. J. 1926. *The Immigration Problem: A Study of American Immigration Conditions and Needs.* 6th ed.; revised and enlarged by R. D. SMITH. New York and London: Funk & Wagnalls Co.

JEROME, H. 1926. *Migration and Business Cycles.* New York: National Bureau of Economic Research.

KIRK, D. 1946. *Europe's Population in the Interwar Years.* Geneva: League of Nations.

KISER, C. V. 1942. *Group Differences in Urban Fertility.* Baltimore: Williams & Wilkins Co.

———. 1932. *Sea Island to City: A Study of St. Helena Islanders in Harlem and Other Urban Centers.* New York: Columbia University Press.

KUCZYNSKI, R. R. 1928–31. *The Balance of Births and Deaths.* 2 vols. New York: Macmillan Co.

LANDIS, P. H., and HATT, P. K. 1954. *Population Problems: A Cultural Interpretation.* 2d ed. New York: American Book Co.

LEE, E. S., *et al.* 1953. *Net Intercensal Migration 1870–1940.* 3 vols. Philadelphia: University of Pennsylvania. (Dittograph.)

LEIBENSTEIN, H. 1954. *A Theory of Economic-Demographic Development.* Princeton: Princeton University Press.

LINDER, F. E., and GROVE, R. D. 1943. *Vital Statistics Rates in the United States, 1900–1940.* Washington, D.C.: Government Printing Office.

LIVELY, C. E., and TAEUBER, C. 1939. *Rural Migration in the United States.* Washington, D.C.: Government Printing Office.

LORIMER, F. 1946. *The Population of the Soviet Union: History and Prospects.* Geneva: League of Nations.

———. 1954. *Culture and Human Fertility.* Paris: UNESCO.

———, and OSBORN, F. 1934. *Dynamics of Population: Social and Biological Sig-*

nificance of Changing Birth Rates in the United States. New York: Macmillan Co.

LOTKA, A. J. 1934–39. *Théorie analytique des associations biologiques.* Part I: *Principes.* Part II: *Analyse démographique avec application particulière à l'espèce humaine.* Paris: Hermann & Co.

———, and DUBLIN, L. I. 1925. "On the True Rate of Natural Increase of a Population," *Journal of the American Statistical Association,* XX, 305.

———, and SHARPE, F. R. 1911. "A Problem in Age Distribution," *Philosophical Magazine,* XXI, 435.

LUNDBERG, G. A. 1933. "Richmond Mayo-Smith," *Encyclopedia of the Social Sciences,* X, 237.

McKENZIE, R. D. 1933. *The Metropolitan Community.* New York and London: McGraw-Hill.

———. 1934. "The Field and Problems of Demography, Human Geography, and Human Ecology," in *The Fields and Methods of Sociology.* ed. L. L. BERNARD. New York: Ray Long & Richard R. Smith.

MADIGAN, F. C., S. J. 1957. "Are Sex Mortality Differentials Biologically Caused?" *Milbank Memorial Fund Quarterly,* XXV, 202–23.

———, and VANCE, R. B. 1957. "Sex Differential Mortality: A Research Design," *Social Forces,* XXXV, 193–99.

MALZBERG, B., and LEE, E. S. 1956. *Migration and Mental Disease.* New York: Social Science Research Council.

MAYO-SMITH, R. 1895. *Statistics and Sociology.* New York: Macmillan Co.

———, 1899. *Statistics and Economics.* New York: Macmillan Co.

MILBANK MEMORIAL FUND (New York):
1946. *Post War Problems of Migration.*
1947. *Problems in the Collection and Comparability of International Statistics.*
1948. *International Approaches to Problems of Underdeveloped Areas.*
1949. *Modernization Programs in Relation to Human Resources and Population Problems.*
1952. *Approaches to Problems of High Fertility in Agrarian Society.*
1954. *Interrelations of Demographic, Economic, and Social Problems in Selected Undeveloped Areas.*
1955. *Current Research in High Fertility.*
1956. *Trends and Differentials in Mortality.*
1957. *The Nature and Transmission of the Genetic and Cultural Characteristics of Human Populations.*

MOORE, W. E. 1945. *Economic Demography of Eastern and Southern Europe.* Geneva: League of Nations.

NATIONAL RESOURCES COMMITTEE. 1938. *The Problems of a Changing Population.* Washington, D.C.: Government Printing Office.

NOTESTEIN, F. W. 1945. "Population: The Long View," in *Food for the World.* T. W. SCHULTZ (ed.). Chicago: University of Chicago Press, pp. 36–57.

———, and SYDENSTRICKER, E. 1930. "Differential Fertility According to Social Class: A Study of 69,620 Native White Married Women under 45 Years of Age Based upon United States Census Returns of 1910," *American Statistical Association Publications,* XXV, 9–32.

———, et al. 1944. *The Future Population of Europe and the Soviet Union: Population Projections, 1940–1970.* Geneva: League of Nations.

ODUM, H. W. 1936. *Southern Regions of the United States.* Chapel Hill: University of North Carolina Press.

PEARL, R. 1925. *The Biology of Population Growth.* New York: Alfred Knopf.

———. 1939. *The Natural History of Population.* New York: Oxford University Press.

PENROSE, E. F. 1934. *Population Theories and Their Application, with Special Reference to Japan.* Stanford, Calif.: Stanford University, Food Research Institute.

PRICE, D. O. 1948. "Distance and Direction as Vectors of Internal Migration, 1935 to 1940," *Social Forces,* XXVII, 48–53.

REUTER, E. B. 1923. *Population Problems.* Philadelphia: J. B. Lippincott Co.

ROSS, F. A. 1924. *School Attendance in 1920: An Analysis of School Attendance in the United States and in the Several States, with a Discussion of the Factors Involved.* Washington, D.C.: Government Printing Office.

ROSSITER, W. S. 1922. *Increase of Population in the United States 1910–1920: A Study of Changes in the Population of Divisions, States, Counties, and Rural and Urban Areas, and in Sex, Color, and Nativity at the Fourteenth Census.* Washington, D.C.: Government Printing Office.

RUSSELL, J. C. 1948. *British Medieval Population.* Albuquerque: University of New Mexico Press.

RYAN, B. 1953. "Fertility Values Among the Buddhists of Ceylon," in *Proceedings of the Annual Conference.* New York: Milbank Memorial Fund.

SIEVERS, A. M. 1952. *General Economics: An Introduction.* Philadelphia: J. B. Lippincott Co.

SMITH, T. L. 1946. *Brazil: People and Institutions.* Baton Rouge: Louisiana State University Press.

———. 1948. *Population Analysis.* New York: McGraw-Hill.

SPENGLER, J. J. 1938. *France Faces Depopulation.* Durham, N.C.: Duke University Press.

———. 1952. "Population Theory," in *A Survey of Contemporary Economics,* Vol. II, ed. B. F. HALEY. Homewood, Ill.: Richard D. Irwin, Inc.

STIX, R. K. and NOTESTEIN, F. W. 1940. *Controlled Fertility.* Baltimore: Williams & Wilkins Co.

STOUFFER, S. 1940. "Intervening Opportunities: A Theory Relating Mobility and Distance," *American Sociological Review,* V, 845–67.

STYCOS, J. M. 1956. *Family and Fertility in Puerto Rico: A Study of the Lower Income Group.* New York: Columbia University Press.

TAEUBER, I. B. 1946. "Population Studies in the United States," *Population Index,* XII, 254–69.

———. 1958. *The Population of Japan.* Princeton: Princeton University Press.

TAFT, D. R., and ROBBINS, R. 1955. *International Migrations: The Immigrant in the Modern World.* New York: Ronald Press Co.

THOMAS, B. 1954. *Migration and Economic Growth.* Cambridge: Cambridge University Press.

THOMAS, D. S. 1938. *Research Memorandum on Migration Differentials.* New York: Social Science Research Council.

———. 1941. *Social and Economic Aspects of Swedish Population Movements, 1750–1933.* New York: Macmillan Co.

THOMPSON, W. S. 1931. *Ratio of Children to Women 1920: A Study in the Differential Rate of Natural Increase in the United States.* (United States Bureau of the Census Monograph No. 11.) Washington, D.C.: Government Printing Office.

———. 1937. *Research Memorandum on Internal Migration in the Depression.* New York: Social Science Research Council.

———. 1946. *Population and Peace in the Pacific.* Chicago: University of Chicago Press.

———. 1948. *Plenty of People: The World's Population Pressures, Problems, and Policies and How They Concern Us.* New York: Ronald Press Co.

———, and WHELPTON, P. K. 1933. *Population Trends in the United States.* New York: McGraw-Hill.

———. 1943. *Estimates of Future Population of the United States, 1940–2000.* Washington, D.C.: National Resources Planning Board.

THORNTHWAITE, C. W. 1934. *Internal Migration in the United States.* Philadelphia: University of Pennsylvania Press.

TRUESDELL, L. E. 1926. *Farm Population of the United States: An Analysis of the 1920 Farm Population Figures, Especially in Comparison with Urban Data, Together with a Study of the Main Economic Factors Affecting the Farm Population.* Washington, D.C.: Government Printing Office.

UNITED STATES BUREAU OF THE CENSUS. 1949. *Historical Statistics of the United States 1789–1945: A Supplement to the Statistical Abstract of the United States.* Washington, D.C.: Government Printing Office.

———. 1950. *Catalog of United States Census 1790–1945.* By H. J. DUBESTER.

Washington, D.C.: Government Printing Office.

———. 1946 ff. *Catalog of the United States Census Publications.* Washington, D.C.: Government Printing Office.

UNITED STATES CENSUS MONOGRAPHS. New York: John Wiley & Sons.

BANCROFT, G. (1958). *The American Labor Force.*

BERNERT, ELEANOR. 1958. *America's Children.*

DUNCAN, O. D., and REISS, A. J., JR. 1956. *Social Characteristics of Urban and Rural Communities, 1950.*

GLICK, P. C. 1957. *American Families.*

GRABILL, W. H., KISER, C. V., and WHELPTON, P. K. 1958. *The Fertility of American Women.*

HUTCHINSON, E. P. 1956. *Immigrants and Their Children, 1850–1950.*

MILLER, H. P. 1955. *Income of the American People.*

SHELDON, H. 1958. *The Older Population of the United States at Mid-Century.*

TAEUBER, C., and TAEUBER, I. B. 1958. *The Changing Population of the United States.*

UNITED STATES IMMIGRATION COMMISSION. 1911. *Reports of the Immigration Commission.* 42 vols. Washington, D.C.: Government Printing Office.

VAN NORT, L., and KARON, B. P. 1955. "Demographic Transition Re-examined," *American Sociological Review*, XX, 523–27.

VANCE, R. B. 1938. *Research Memorandum on Population Redistribution within the United States.* New York: Social Science Research Council.

———. 1952a. "Is Theory for Demographers?" *Social Forces*, XXXI, 9–13.

———. 1952b. "The Demographic Gap: Dilemma of Modernization Programs," in *Approaches to Problems of High Fertility in Agrarian Societies.* New York: Milbank Memorial Fund.

———, and DANILEVSKY, N. 1945. *All These People: The Nation's Human Resources in the South.* Chapel Hill: University of North Carolina Press.

———, and DEMERATH, N. J. (eds.). 1954. *The Urban South.* Chapel Hill: University of North Carolina Press.

———, and MADIGAN, F. J., S.J. 1956. "Differential Mortality and the Style of Life of Men and Women: A Research Design," in *Trends and Differentials in Mortality.* New York: Milbank Memorial Fund.

WALKER, F. A. 1891. "Immigration and Degradation," *Forum*, XI, 638–42.

———. 1896. "Restriction of Immigration, *Atlantic Monthly*, LXXVII, 824.

WHELPTON, P. K. 1928. "Population in the United States, 1925–1975," *American Journal of Sociology*, XXXIV, 253–70.

———. 1938. *Needed Population Research.* Lancaster, Pa.: Science Press.

———. 1947. *Forecasts of the Population of the United States 1945–1975.* Washington, D.C.: Government Printing Office.

———. 1954. *Cohort Fertility: Native White Women in the United States.* Princeton: Princeton University Press.

———, and KISER, C. V. 1946–56. *Social and Psychological Factors Affecting Fertility.* 4 vols. New York: Milbank Memorial Fund.

WHITNEY, J. S. 1934. *Death Rates by Occupation: Based on Data of the U.S. Bureau of the Census.* New York: National Tuberculosis Association.

WILLCOX, W. F. 1891. *The Divorce Problem: A Study in Statistics.* New York: Columbia University Press.

———. (ed.). 1931. *International Migrations.* 2 vols. New York: National Bureau of Economic Research.

———. 1933. *Introduction to the Vital Statistics of the United States, 1900 to 1930.* Washington, D.C.: Government Printing Office.

———. 1940. *Studies in American Demography.* Ithaca: Cornell University Press.

WOOFTER, T. J. 1920. *Negro Migration: Changes in Rural Organization and Population of the Cotton Belt.* New York: W. D. Gray Co.

———. 1949. "Factors Sustaining the Birth Rate," *American Sociological Review*, XIV, 357–66.

Elements of Demography

Introduction to Part III

This series of a dozen chapters makes up what is virtually an encyclopedia of modern demography. The description is apt because, like any encyclopedic presentation, these chapters necessarily are selective rather than exhaustive in the treatments of their topics. If the reader is primarily interested in learning what demographers have to say about the principal subjects they investigate, he may well concentrate his reading on this part. Naturally, the chapters present few of the data supporting either the summarized conclusions of population research or the authors' judgments of how such research ought to be prosecuted. The materials are to be regarded as "authoritative" in the only sense in which that term may be used in science; i.e., they represent carefully considered statements by highly qualified persons, but not necessarily statements for which conclusive proof is available or evaluations which would be unanimously indorsed by the profession. There was no intention that this part should constitute a detailed presentation of the content of the discipline, after the fashion of a textbook. Despite their considerable average length, these papers are concisely written and presuppose a mature reader. In some passages the authors manifestly are addressing their remarks to fellow demographers rather than to the beginner or the educated layman, but technicalities are not overemphasized.

The presentation begins with a subject—the availability of demographic data on a world basis—which is germane to all the rest of the volume. In chapter xv Linder describes the major types of data sources, indicates the various defects to which they are subject, and reviews the world coverage of a number of specific items of data as of recent times. His paper also summarizes the history of co-operative international efforts to improve, broaden, and standardize the collection of basic population statistics. The evidence indicates a large measure of progress by comparison, say, with the situation of a century ago but a much larger measure of shortcoming with respect to even a minimum uniform program of data collection. The spatiotemporal differentials in coverage and quality of population data described by Linder go far to explain the uneven character of demographic knowledge as revealed in the succeeding chapters.

In chapter xvi Hawley enumerates the major items that have traditionally been of concern to the demographer under the heading of population composition. He also indicates the excellent reasons why a particular range of population characteristics has made up the core of interest in the subject, and he suggests important aspects of composition that are commonly neglected. That its analysis affords a natural starting point for many kinds of population studies is implied by Hawley's observation that population composition constitutes a framework on which rests the institutional structure of the whole society. Whereas compositional components of fertility, mortality, and migration have been subjected to much study by demographers, there has been a relative neglect of the kind of problem that Hawley identifies as the analysis of the specific demographic requirements of each social institution.

Bogue's presentation of the field of population distribution (chapter xvii) goes somewhat beyond an interest in numbers and density of inhabitants by territorial subdivisions of a national territory or their classification by urban-rural residence and the like. It suggests, in effect, that each topic in demography is subject to study from the "distributive approach," which emphasizes areal components of demographic variation and complements the more conventional "aggregative approach." The major contribution of the chapter is to spell out both the broader and the more specific implications of the former approach, indicating reasons why it may be expected to produce contributions to knowledge which are beyond the reach of traditional techniques. Additional materials on population distribution, as the problem is more conventionally treated, will be found in chapters xxvi, xxviii, and xxix.

Any misconception that demography deals with problems which are intrinsically simple will be dispelled by a reading of chapter xviii. Here Ryder indicates that shortcomings of our basic knowledge of human fertility are due to inadequate specification of the variables to be explained and non-operational conceptualization of explanatory factors, as well as to deficiencies in the supply of fundamental data. It is also made plain that no single discipline can at present supply a complete explanation of the trends and differentials in fertility that demographers have identified. Social influences are translated into biological consequences through a variety of specific linkages; moreover, there is good reason to believe that the determinants of fertility behavior are subject to variation over time and from one culture area to another. Of special interest in the chapter is the formulation of considerations involved in choosing a rationale for computing fertility rates.

Demographic studies of mortality, as Dorn indicates in chapter xix, have objectives different from, though complementary to, those of medical and public-health studies. Analysis of trends and differentials in mortality enables the demographer to discover socio-environmental influences on mortality rates, although his interpretation of such findings often has been handicapped by inadequate knowledge of etiology and by a variety of deficiencies in the data available for mortality studies. Of perennial concern and exasperating difficulty is the problem of analyzing trends in longevity as affected by changes in the prevalence of various causes of death. This difficulty may be regarded as a paramount illustration of indeterminacy of results when they are based on materials of varying reliability and precision classified in terms of shifting principles. Despite the handicaps to its study, the field of mortality analysis has accumulated an impressive collection of fairly dependable empirical regularities, a number of which are summarized by Dorn.

The combination of natality and mortality rates into an over-all measure of population reproduction or replacement is the problem discussed by Hyrenius in chapter xx. He presents the elegant mathematical relationships that have been developed in attacks on this problem and indicates various moot points still surrounding the use and interpretation of such mathematical models. As the author indicates, the motivation for proposals on methods of measuring replacement has been the need for an understanding of what lies behind crude indexes of natality and mortality together with the hope of finding ways to infer underlying population trends. It is now apparent, however, that the quest for a single index of reproductivity was misguided and that each of a variety of indexes plays a role in analyzing population growth by answering a specific question.

In chapter xxi Bogue identifies the main problems confronting the student of internal migration. To a greater extent than even the investigator of natality or mortality, the migration specialist is dependent on indirect and partial evidence; hence there has arisen a body of techniques for estimating migration, most of which are subject to considerable error. The need for rational principles for constructing migration rates—a problem hitherto somewhat neglected—is also brought out by Bogue. Finally, the author indicates that progress in developing effective explanatory models of the migration process depends on making observation much more specific with respect to the situations instigating migration and the conditions associated with differential migration rates among various segments of a population.

International migration as a problem for demographic-economic analysis is covered by Thomas in chapter xxii. The student of this subject continually has forced upon him a circumstance that all demographers must grapple with at least occasionally—the lack of comparability of different sources of information, particularly information for different countries. Another problem emphasized elsewhere in the volume, "historicism," likewise is brought to the fore here, inasmuch as a large part of the migration that can be described statistically consists of the transatlantic movement of the nineteenth and twentieth centuries, which occurred under conditions without exact historical parallel and with small likelihood of being repeated. Nonetheless, significant progress has been made in identifying causes of fluctuations in the migratory flow and in isolating, partly through the use of formal models, the effects of migration on sending and receiving countries.

The practical and scientific needs met by population estimates and projections are indicated by Grauman in chapter xxiii, which also provides a survey of the principal techniques used by demographers to produce such figures. The author rightly emphasizes that calculations of unknown populations as well as uses of such calculations inevitably must involve the exercise of "expert judgment" in greater or lesser degree, although it is possible to specify conditions under which such calculations are likely to be relatively reliable as opposed to those in which they are primarily conjectures. Contrary to the position taken by some demographers, the presentation here does not make a sharp distinction between *estimates*, based on at least a minimum of direct or symptomatic evidence, and *projections*, which rest on sheer extrapolation from the known to the unknown.

The treatment of family statistics by Glick in chapter xxiv demonstrates that a wide range of demographic problems is placed in a somewhat different light if viewed from the standpoint of the natural groups in which people actually live rather than from the standpoint of the individual. Nuptiality and marital status are of obvious importance for fertility analysis, and they also have a bearing on mortality. In migration studies it is important to take account of differential movement according to household composition and stage of the family cycle and to distinguish streams of migration in which families moving as units form an important part of the total as opposed to those made up largely of unattached individuals. This chapter gives a valuable account of conceptual and operational problems involved in compiling and interpreting family statistics.

The intimate relationship between working-force analysis and other demographic problems is stressed by Jaffe in chapter xxv. The field of working-force analysis makes a direct bridge between demography strictly conceived and studies of economic structure, fluctuations in economic activity, and economic development. Indeed, the very concept of the working force as a clearly distinguishable component of the population is shown to be relative to the stage of economic development, inasmuch as the differentiation of the working from the non-working population is indefinite in predominantly agricultural, subsistence economies. A notable contribution of working-force investigations to demography in general is the stimulus they have given to the collection of sample survey data at frequent intervals. Thus, much of our knowledge of recent short-run population changes in the United States has been gained as a by-product of the monthly survey of the labor force conducted by the Bureau of the Census since 1940.

A special aspect of the study of population distribution is taken up in chapter xxvi, wherein Ackerman deals with the distribution of population in relation to the distribution of resources. It is made plain that no simple interpretation of population-resource ratios is warranted, inasmuch as their effects depend upon absolute size of population and territory, technological development, and the organization of trade relationships, as well as other factors. Possible correlations between population distribution and patterns of resource use and management are described, and the author provides a framework for investigations of the problem of resource adequacy. The discussion here makes it plain that neither the "alarmist" nor the "optimistic" popular appraisal of trends in resource adequacy is supported by present knowledge and theory. Here, as is so often the case in respect to "population problems," the actual situation turns out to be a good deal more complex than the lay publicist of the problem is likely to realize.

15. World Demographic Data

FORREST E. LINDER

TYPES OF DATA REQUIRED FOR A SCIENCE OF DEMOGRAPHY

The status of demography as a science depends upon the type, range, and quality of data available for the objective study of population, as well as upon the theoretical structure with which these facts can be classified, interrelated, and interpreted. Demography is largely a quantitative science, at times restricted to little more than the exposition or description of demographic statistics. At this level of development, the data considered necessary for demography also have been limited, and limited largely to direct data on population, vital statistics, and migration.

But even in this context, "population data" must cover more than information on the total number and geographic distribution of people. Consideration of the major features of population composition is essential even in the simplest demographic studies. Essential types of population data include geographic distribution; urban-rural or community size group data; relation of present and former residence; personal characteristics such as age, sex, and marital status; economic characteristics of occupation, industry, and related factors; educational and cultural characteristics; data on nuptiality and fertility; household composition; and various other topics which may be investigated by means of population censuses.

In the same way, vital statistics data required for a demographic science are more than the total count or the crude rate of births, deaths, and marriages. Obviously, the full detail of vital statistics includes many items of information which may be peripheral to demographic interests and which pertain more to medical science. Such topics are items like weight at birth, period of gestation, hospitalization, and type of birth, i.e., single or plural issue. Mortality items such as type of certification, hospitalization, and specific categories of cause of death also may be peripheral to purely demographic needs. On the other hand, the major characteristics of the event or child and of the parents are essential natality data for demography. Such mortality items as the geographic distribution of deaths, the age and sex distribution of deaths, and the economic and cultural factors characterizing variation in mortality cannot be ignored by a developing science.

Fetal mortality is of lesser demographic interest except as an element of what might be considered as negative fertility or as a major component of pregnancy wastage. For marriage and divorce most of the characteristics of the event and of the participants are pertinent demographic data except, perhaps, for such purely legal types of statistical information as the legal causes for divorce.

The importance of the geographic distribution of population needs no special emphasis here, and in this connection both international and internal migration data must be included among the desirable basic demographic statistics. The theoretical requirements exceed a mere count of arrivals and departures, since limited use can be made of the data unless some of the personal, economic, and social characteristics of the migrants are known.

Population data, vital statistics, and migration statistics constitute the principal types of statistics required for demography in its traditional and limited sense. However, as already stated, a limitation to these types of information would, for the most part, restrict demography to an expository form of science. Without doubt there is much progress yet to be made in the observation of demographic phenomena, in their precise definition, classification, and description. And even though these first stages of development have not been fully achieved, demography is rapidly becoming an explanatory science—a process of evolution which will require increased consideration of data not strictly demographic. This broadened scope can be seen by the emphasis given by the United Nations Population Commission to the study of the interrelations of demographic factors with economic and social factors.

If demography is defined in broader terms, then the data required for a science of demography must be extended to include many other social and economic statistics. However, the range of essential social and economic data can be determined only as success is achieved in finding and interpreting consistent and rational interrelations among these different elements.

The term "social statistics" is generally vague and ambiguous. It has been defined (United Nations Statistical Office, 1954a) in a broad sense as the statistics that are

. . . concerned with the status, and the changes in status, of various population groups, in regard to such factors as occupation, earnings, nutrition, housing, education, recreation, family life, community activities, cultural activities and interests; special interest is usually attached to the conditions of "vulnerable" groups, such as children, aged people, physically handicapped, labourers in lower-paid occupations, and, on certain conditions, wage earners and other broad groups generally. Social statistics also include numerical information on the administration and results of measures taken by governments, local authorities, employers, trade unions and welfare organizations to improve living and working conditions.

It is clear that social statistics defined in this comprehensive way include topics which are also considered within the sphere of other disciplines. It is this obvious overlapping which emphasizes that a developing science of demography will be necessarily concerned with an increasing variety of social data.

The relation between demography and economic statistics is not dissimilar. The scope of "economic statistics" is perhaps more generally and clearly understood than that of "social statistics," and this scope includes such topics as agricultural and industrial production and consumption, internal and external trade, transport, construction, and various types of financial statistics. A few of these topics may be remotely and indirectly related to demographic questions; whereas others, such as agricultural production, have a direct and predominant bearing on questions of population distribution and growth.

It is obvious that a comprehensive study of the availability and quality of data essential for a scientific demography would involve a detailed inventory and appraisal of almost the complete scope of statistical knowledge. No such encyclopedic coverage can be attempted here. In fact, more progress must be achieved in demographic analysis before the pertinent social and economic factors are isolated and their influence on population measured. The major part of the following discussion will be limited to a discussion of strictly demographic data, but demographic research is increasingly concerned with other social and economic variables.

THE PROBLEM OF EVALUATING DATA

The evaluation of world demographic data is a task the scope and complexity of which is difficult to exaggerate. Even with a limitation of the task to the consideration of demographic data in the narrower sense, there are literally hundreds of topics and subtopics which should be considered, and any general statement regarding availability or quality would differ with each. The statistical information available on each of these topics would have to be considered separately for each of the more than two hundred sovereign countries, trust territories, dependencies, colonies, condominia, international administrations, etc., which may be considered the separate statistical units composing the inhabited world. To complete the picture, each topic for each area would need to be studied not only in terms of the present status but also in terms of historical development.

The numerous elements to be considered in a complete presentation become almost identical with the factors affecting interarea and intertemporal comparability of demographic statistics and include the problems of measuring historical development, present coverage, and quality.

The evaluation of demographic data in terms of quality is a major problem in itself. A limited number of objective quantitative tests are possible. Examples of these are the examination of age distributions for undue heaping at certain digits or the comparison for consistency of age distributions in successive censuses. But the number and power of such tests is almost trivial in view of the numerous aspects of quality appraisal for which there are no direct or even approximate tests.

By far the greatest factor influencing quality of data is the validity and consistency of respondents' replies to the census enumerator or to the vital records registrar. Such data as sex and age may be relatively precise, but the validity of information received for, let us say, cause of death varies enormously. Variation in the quality of original data is so great that a statement that so-and-so many countries publish statistics on cause of death may have no real meaning as an evaluation of the availability of this particular item of demographic data.

Closely related to this point is the variation in tabulated data due to differences of definition, classification, and processing procedures. The problem is not just one of establishing uniform definitions and methods. It also involves the question of whether such standards, even if followed, result in data with the same meaning. In a different context, this problem has been described (Linder, 1955) as follows:

In reality, the goal of complete formal international comparability in census statistics, to be achieved through standard international recommendations, is probably a false goal, or at least an oversimplification of what can be accomplished. If there were universal agreement on a definite set of census items, together with uniform definitions, uniform enumeration and editing instructions, standard classifications and tabulations, and if every country adhered literally to these standards, the resulting statistical tabulations would still be far from having uniform meaning for every country.

For a few simple biological items there are no important conceptual difficulties. The number of people and their distribution by age and sex are items which theoretically could be made comparable for all areas by establishing uniformity of definition and equal quality of results. But items, such as marital condition, relation to head of household, ethnic nationality, educational or economic status are characteristics intrinsically related to the social and economic organization of each country. A standard international definition for such characteristics can achieve comparable statistics only to the extent that the social and economic features of the country are similar. In two dissimilar countries, it may be that greater comparability of meaning for a census item can be obtained if the census question is asked in distinctly different ways.

The measurement of the coverage of available statistics is theoretically simpler than the measurement of quality, but in practical terms the problems are equally difficult. Questions of coverage are of three types—omitted areas, omitted groups, and general incompleteness.

Both population censuses and vital statistics tabulations are defective for some countries because of omitted areas. For general population censuses an effort is made in almost all cases to cover the total national area, and any parts of the country omitted may be only vaguely known or described. Even so, it is obvious that some of the more inaccessible areas in any country having a large and difficult terrain are, for all practical purposes, inadequately covered in the censuses.

For vital statistics this situation is often more serious. The gradual development of the registration system in a country may mean that data are presently available only for a designated group of cities, for districts covered by organized health units, or for defined registration areas. Fortunately, in most cases the area omissions in vital statistics are clearly defined if the omissions are important or if the tabulated data cover a limited registration area.

Census data or vital statistics may also be defective because of omitted population groups. Usually such omissions are intentional. For example, a census count may include only nationals of a country—omitting large groups of foreign residents. Or, as has been the case in some parts of Africa, detailed census information may be collected for the so-called European population and only more summary data for the "native" inhabitants. In other instances, certain ethnic or cultural groups may be unintentionally completely or partially omitted if the areas of their residence coincide with areas not adequately covered by the census or by vital registration.

A detailed examination of the statistics and the methods of their collection usually makes possible some qualitative, if not quantitative, appraisal of the effect of omitted areas or groups. These qualifications make up a large proportion of the numerous footnotes required in any extensive compilation of international statistics. The problem of the general incompleteness of a census enumeration or of vital registration is more difficult to appraise. Objective tests of incompleteness are possible, but only a limited number of countries have ever made such studies of their own data.

These questions of comparability and completeness can be considered again in reference to specific types of data. Where registration, from all evidence, is more than 99.9 per cent complete, one can say confidently that basic vital statistics data exist for that country. But what can be said in a case where vital statistics data are published regularly and currently but where the basic rates are only a fraction of the magnitude that should be expected and where all other evidence indicates a serious underregistration? Do vital statistics exist for such a country, or do they not? Factors of quality and comparability determine the measure of extent. A careful case-by-case description can, of course, state the facts as they are known, but a *summary* evaluation of demographic statistics for all the world must do great violence to such scientific preciseness.

All of the above factors, and others, would need to be considered for past periods in a complete historical review of the development of demographic statistics. The additional factor of changes in national boundaries, caused by consolidation or division of areas, must then also be considered. As is the case with a description of the present situation, the historical development is difficult to see clearly because of a general lack of sufficient technical notes in national publications appraising the effect of the factors affecting comparability.

An enumeration of the above factors is sufficient to show that the analysis of the availability of demographic data can be only approximate. The following sections of this chapter are based, therefore, on an examination of *official* population and vital statistics, and for the most part only on those official statistics which are available in national publications or are supplied to the United Nations in reply to questionnaires. This approach ignores a vast number of fragments of official data that may be available for a country, as well as a diversified fund of more obscure unofficial demographic information. Such data can be found and used in the course of intensive demographic research concerned with a limited area and time, but they are not easily available for general demographic purposes or for studies of broader scope.

Furthermore, the following analyses must, for sheer lack of space and time, be concerned primarily with the major and more universal statistical variables, and the consideration of only these major variables gives a somewhat exaggerated or optimistic view. Data for minor and less common variables are naturally less available than data for the major variables; and, in addition, for the former there may be greater heterogeneity in definition, classification, and general quality.

MAJOR SOURCES OF DATA

A summary review of completeness and adequacy of demographic data could be made in several different ways. One method, and probably a fruitful method, would be to classify demographic problems or interests into a limited number of categories and then to examine the availability of data for each category.

For example, one category of problems might be the estimation of future population size. For this category an analysis could be made of the essential character of the problem, the factors bearing upon its solution, and the data required for an ideal solution. The available data could then be measured against these requirements, and some concept of the adequacy of existing demographic statistics for this purpose could be obtained. Similar topic-by-topic analyses could be made for other fields of demographic research—internal migration, family size and composition, economic characteristics of the population, and other general problems—so as to cover the whole scope of demographic interests. A study of existing data from this axis of observation might reveal some areas for which data are now largely satisfactory and others where the required data are completely inadequate.

In spite of its promise, the above approach must await further work by the analytical demographer, since it depends upon a formulation and definition of problem areas and upon a clear statement of the kinds of data that are desirable or essential for the study of these various types of demographic problems. In addition, the method is somewhat cumbersome, since a single item or type of data may be essential for the study of a large number of different problems. The more conventional method of examining the adequacy of demographic data, either in a general way or for a specific problem, is an operational approach examining in turn the type of data produced by each source or method of collection. This approach is simpler, since in this way each class of data need, for the most part, be studied only once. In addition, the examination of data according to the method of its collection brings to light changes in methodology which may be necessary for the improvement of coverage or quality.

In general, the various methods of collecting demographic data yield two broad types of information. One of these types, "cross-section" or "instantaneous" data, results from a census or survey. The other type, "continuous" data, results from a procedure by which data are collected on a continuing basis as the events under observation occur. Continuous data are produced by a registration system for births and deaths, by a record of the flow of migrants across an international control point, or by any continuous administrative operation for which related statistics are a by-product (e.g., many forms of social security statistics). This dichotomous classification gives an important characteristic of the data. It is not, however, precise enough to form the basis of an operational study of data. To do this, it is necessary to describe more exactly the operations which could be a source of important demographic data. The principal sources are (1) the population census, (2) the civil registration system, (3) the international migration control system, (4) the continuous population register, (5) the *ad hoc* or periodic survey, and (6) various continuous administrative operations. Because of their varied character and their relatively minor importance at the present time, it is not necessary to discuss the last two of these sources in detail.

The Population Census

Most students of demography understand, at least in general terms, the procedure that is implied by the phrase "a population census." It is understood to mean an enumeration of the population in which specified information is collected and compiled for each individual. However, there is no established international definition of a "census," and, in practice, this term has been used to cover a rather wide variety of procedures. These differ in many ways—for example, in purpose, in method, and in results. A population census taken for the primary purpose of collecting statistical data is likely to be quite different in method and result from a population registration taken primarily for the purpose of administering a rationing program. Collection procedures may also differ in method, such as in the application of sampling, in the phasing of the enumeration, and so forth.

Lacking an accepted international definition of a census, the United Nations *Demographic Yearbook* in the 1949–50 issue stated some general requirements which were set up to qualify a population count for inclusion in the publication as a "census." These requirements were (1) that it covered the majority of the population, (2) that it was obtained by the method of individual enumeration, and (3) that it was effected within a time period of less than a year. These criteria served to exclude a large number of approximate or partial population figures. However, the criteria are hardly adequate as a statement of the essential features of the population census method.

A more recent attempt to state these essential features is given in the Draft International Recommendations now being considered for use in the 1960 world population census program (United Nations Statistical Office, 1955*a*, p. 3). This document defines and describes a population census in the following terms:

A census of population may be defined as the total process of collecting, compiling and publishing demographic data pertaining, at a particular time, to all persons in a defined territory.

The essential characteristics of a census are:

(1) *Universality*—the census enumeration should include every member of the community, without omission or duplication.

(2) *Simultaneity*—all census facts should refer to one well-defined point of time.

(3) *Individual units*—a census implies that separate data are recorded for each individual. A procedure by which "totalled" or summarized data are collected for groups of individuals is not a census.

(4) *Defined territory*—the coverage of a census operation should relate to a precisely defined territory.

(5) *Compilation*—the compilation and publication of data by geographic areas and by basic demographic variables is an integral part of a census.

The Civil Registration System

Demographic data relating to births, deaths, and other vital events can be collected by different methods, but not all of these are equally satisfactory. Attempts to collect such data by a census procedure have not been considered successful. The census method fails because the instantaneous census method is ill-adapted to portray a continuous process. At best, a census could obtain birth and death data only for a short defined period, perhaps the twelve-month period before the census, and such a restricted period of observation would be inadequate for the study of what may be rather rapid temporal changes in mortality and fertility. In addition to this limitation, it has been shown that the census method gives very incomplete and inaccurate birth and death data, largely because of the inability of the respondent to report, or to report accurately, dates and circumstances of an event which occurred at some time in the past.

The special survey is a more successful method of collecting vital statistics. Basically, of course, a special survey is subject to the same limitations and defects as a census. In fact, some of the limitations may be more severe. On the other hand, a special survey could have the collection of data on vital events as a specific purpose, and extra precautions could be taken to insure completeness and accuracy. Neither method would provide data adequate for the major needs of demographic research. Except for special purposes, the only satisfactory source of vital statistics is records of the civil registration of vital events.

In *Principles for a Vital Statistics System* (United Nations Statistical Office, 1953*a*) such a system is defined (in Principle No. 101) as "including the legal registration, statistical recording and reporting of the occurrence of, and the collection, compilation, analysis, presentation, and distribution of statistics pertaining to 'vital events,' which in turn include live births, deaths, foetal deaths, marriages, divorces, adoptions, legitimations, recognitions, annulments, and legal separations."

By this definition it is apparent that vital statistics are, for the most part, derived from registration. This method is defined (in Principle No. 102) as "the continuous and permanent, compulsory recording of the occurrence and the characteristics of vital events primarily for their value as legal documents as provided by law and secondarily for their usefulness as a source of statistics."

International Migration Control

As in the case of population statistics or vital statistics, migration data can be obtained by a variety of procedures. In some instances, data pertaining to international migration movements are obtained in connection with a regular population census. Generally, such data relate only indirectly to the volume or characteristics of the migration movement of the current period. Migration data can also be obtained from special surveys, such as special censuses or registrations of aliens. However, special inquiries using censuses or survey techniques do not take place frequently, and such sources can usually be ignored except for data which would be useful for special purposes or *ad hoc* analyses.

Migration statistics, internal as well as international, can also be derived from general population registers, but very few countries in the world have systems of continuous population registers of the necessary type. As is the case with special surveys, this procedure can hardly be regarded as a source of regular or current data for most parts of the world.

Most migration data, therefore, are collected at international frontiers, and these data are mostly by-products of the administrative operations of frontier control. International compilations of migration data are almost exclusively limited to data from this source. Because most migration data originate from administrative operations not primarily designed to produce statistical data, it is difficult to give an operational definition of the sources of migration statistics. Different organizational arrangements exist in the different countries of the world. In most cases, different administrative agencies of the government have responsibility for control over different classes of migrants, and the channel of statistical reporting may be quite different for migrants using different modes of travel. These arrangements result in different definitions, and the compiled statistics cannot have a satisfactory degree of international comparability. (A more complete discussion of the organizational and conceptual problems in compiling international migration statistics is found in United Nations Statistical Office, 1953*b*.)

Continuous Population Register

The continuous population register is often referred to as a source, or a possible source, of demographic data. However, as is the case with migration statistics, this source hardly represents a well-defined procedure. Only a small number of countries have continuous population registers, and these vary widely in their purpose, design, and usefulness as a source of statistical information. Most population registration systems are established for administrative purposes, and different national purposes result in different designs and functions.

Some population registration systems are designed primarily as a mechanism for establishing personal identity. Within these systems the identification may be limited to invariant items, such as sex, date of birth, place of birth, name, name of parents, or the system may require personal identification in terms of changing characteristics, such as place of residence, marital status, occupation, and names of children.

The geographic basis of the system may also vary. Some systems may be almost free of any geographic classification, since the record files are centralized nationally or for major divisions of the country. Even where the record files are decentralized, the records may be filed not according to place of present residence but according to place of birth or, in one instance, according to the residence of the family head—which may be a place where the individual concerned has never lived.

Registers also vary according to the unit of registration. In some instances the individual is the unit of the record. In other instances the immediate family group or a broader kinship or household group may be the unit. The differences in the register system and its organization are accompanied by differences in type and detail of the items recorded.

Considering all of these factors, the "continuous population register" can hardly be looked upon as a single methodological concept, and in operation the population registers that exist do not produce useful demographic statistics—at least in proportion to the theoretical possibilities that often are claimed for these procedures. In theory, a continuous population register could produce valuable data, since a continuous system could collect up-to-date information and since the register could facilitate the interrelation of different types of data from various sources. However, no country has found a population register a satisfactory substitute for a periodic census, and systems for registering vital statistics and for border control of migrants are essential whether or not the census and vital registration data are also used in maintaining a continuous register.

With negligible exceptions, therefore, the continuous population register is not a source for the international compilation of regular and comparable demographic statistics. The sources remain limited for the most part to the periodic census, the current vital registration, and the various procedures for controlling and recording frontier crossings.

POPULATION CENSUS STATISTICS[1]

Numberings of the people and national "stocktakings" are known to have been conducted from very ancient times, though such counts were not originally called censuses. Based on the Latin word *censere,* which means "to appraise," the term "census" usually refers to the official enumeration of the population of a country. By extension, the term also is used to describe statistical surveys in the fields of housing, agriculture, industry, etc.

The purpose and method of popula-

[1] For a more complete discussion of census history see United Nations (1949*a,* chap. i).

tion enumerations can be significantly different whether or not they were considered as censuses and regardless of the epoch in which they took place. Little is known about the methods and purposes of the ancient enumerations. There are references to population enumerations made between 3000 and 2000 B.C. in Babylon, Egypt, and China, but it seems that these were only partial registrations and probably were taken for the assessment of fiscal, military, and labor liabilities. Other population counts are recorded in the Old and New Testaments. When Solon introduced tax censuses in Athenian administration in 594 B.C., the people were divided into four classes according to income from landed estates. This type of census eventually developed into an electoral record, and it seems that the practice remained in force until the time of Herodotus. Under the Roman census procedures the members and property of every family were enumerated quinquennially for taxation purposes. The Greek and Roman registrations also were limited, since they were confined to certain segments of the territory and population, and both served other than statistical purposes, inasmuch as they provided rolls of citizens for determining their civil status and corresponding liabilities. After the sacking of Rome (A.D. 410) the practice of systematic census-taking appears to have fallen into disuse. However, compilations made in Europe during the Middle Ages—although they can hardly be said to resemble closely either ancient or modern censuses—to some extent took the place of these counts.

It was a long time before census-taking was revived, and when surveys on a national scale were resumed it was with a different objective. The purpose of national censuses is no longer military recruitment or taxation but to supply factual knowledge for the guidance of essential functions of government. There is no record until the seventeenth century of periodic records of population for purposes other than determining obligations to the state. The first modern census was taken in the Canadian province of Quebec (then called La Nouvelle-France) in 1666, and it covered the basic items of sex, age, marital status, and occupation. During the first part of the eighteenth century, seven censuses of Nova Scotia (then Acadia) and six of Newfoundland were also taken. In Europe a registration of local citizenship was commenced in Urttemburg in 1622, and parish registries were made compulsory in Sweden in 1686, but systematic records of population do not appear to have begun generally until the eighteenth century. In 1719, Frederick William I of Prussia began his half-yearly accounts of population, occupation of houses, and finances and taxes. Enumerations of people took place in Hesse-Darmstadt, 1742; Hesse-Cassel, 1747; Sweden, 1748; Gotha, 1754; Saxony and Hanover, 1755; Brunswick, 1756; Denmark, 1769; Bavaria, 1777; Mecklenburg-Strelitz, 1784; German-Austria, 1785; Spain, 1787; the Two Sicilies, 1788; Savoy and Nice, 1789; the United States, 1790; England and France, 1801; New South Wales, 1828; and Belgium, 1831 (Australia, Commonwealth Bureau of Census and Statistics, 1917, p. 5).

The fact that a "census" was taken in a certain year is, however, not of great importance. It expresses the fact that some enumeration of the population was made in that area at that time, but it does not show that useful demographic data were obtained or that a pattern of enumeration was established.

As an illustration of the development of the census method, the case of the United States censuses will be examined in more detail. The first general population enumeration of the United States was made in 1790, but neither the Constitution, which calls for an enumeration every ten years, nor the experts who examined the 1790 census called it a census. On the contrary, in a report submitted to the Senate in 1900 on censuses in the United States, it is stated (Wright, 1900, p. 13) that the American enumeration of 1790 could not be regarded as a census in the current sense of the word.

It was not until at least 1850 that the United States began to take censuses in the modern sense. In the first census, the marshals of the judicial districts were responsible for the enumeration; they recorded the name of the head of the family, some of his personal characteristics, and various particulars relating to his family and slaves. But there were no printed schedules, and information was collected without a systematized manner of recording. A printed schedule was used for the first time in 1830, but the particulars relating to each individual were still not recorded separately. It was not until 1850 that the United States census questionnaire had a line for the characteristics of each person enumerated. One has to pass over two more censuses—until 1880—before enumerators and supervisors were specially selected and trained, and it was also during the census of 1880 that the first attempt was made to reduce the period of enumeration. In the case of censuses prior to 1880 the enumeration lasted from ten to twenty months, but in 1880 an attempt was made to shorten the period to one month. In the census of 1890 perforated cards and mechanical equipment were used for the first time in the United States. This system was invented by Mr. Hollerith, an employee of the census bureau, and it revolutionized census procedure.

What has been said about censuses in the United States is also true of many other countries. Thus in Switzerland, though the first census was taken in 1798, the first modern census was not taken until 1860 (League of Nations Health Organisation, 1928, p. 23); in England and Wales, the first census was in 1801, but the present system was not adopted till 1841 (League of Nations Health Organisation, 1925, pp. 17–19; Statistical Society of London, 1840). In France, the first census was in 1801, but this census was limited to the resident population; the census of 1836 was the first for which detailed instructions were issued, and it was not until 1841 that both the resident and non-resident populations were enumerated (League of Nations Health Organisation, 1927, pp. 31–32). In Ireland, the first enumeration was made in 1813, but the first modern census is regarded as that of 1841 (League of Nations Health Organisation, 1929, pp. 23–24). In Chile, though there were enumerations of the population in 1831–35 and 1843, it was not till 1854 that a modern type of census was taken; in Colombia a series of censuses date from 1825 to 1864, but the first modern census is regarded as that of 1870 (United States Department of Commerce, Bureau of the Census, and Library of Congress, 1943). Similarly, though a count was taken in Egypt in 1882, the first census in the modern sense of the word is regarded as that of 1897 (Worthington, 1946, p. 187).

Little will be gained by going into the moot question of where the modern census originated—whether it was in North America or Europe. The current type of national census started in many countries in the last three-quarters of the nineteenth century, and the institution of the census has rapidly gained a permanent place in the organization of nearly all modern states. Whatever the history of census-taking, the purely statistical purpose of the census is recognized more and more, although in some parts of the world the use of enu-

meration for non-statistical purposes still persists. It is almost standard in Western countries to find in the census legislation very strict provisions protecting the confidentiality of the individual information furnished for the census. In some countries such information cannot even be given by the census office to any other government agencies; thus it cannot be used for taxation, military conscription, police, or other purposes.

However, as now conceived, a census of population implies more than a counting or an enumeration; it includes the total process of collecting, compiling, and publishing demographic data primarily for the value of the statistical information thus obtained. The idea of periodicity is also implicit, since it is evident that census data are of greater value if censuses are taken at regular intervals.

Each country has the major responsibility for the improvement of its own census methods, and such responsibility will continue to be primarily national. However, as in other technical fields, innovations and improvements in population census methodology have been crossing national boundaries for many decades, either formally or informally. There is no fixed point which marks the beginning of the formal exchange of technical knowledge among countries. There is no doubt that census problems were among the first considered at organized international meetings dealing with statistical matters. The First International Statistical Congress, held in Brussels in 1853, adopted a resolution which is perhaps the first formal international recommendation on the subject (Congrès International de Statistique, 1872, p. 35; here translated from the original French). This resolution recommended the following:

I. Population censuses should be nominal and based on the concept of the *de facto* population. However, special information may be collected to establish, according to circumstances, the size of the *de jure* population.

II. Censuses will be taken every ten years; they will take place during the month of December.

III. There will be a schedule for each family or household.

IV. Special enumerators will be in charge of the distribution and collection of the schedules and will see to it that they are accurately filled in or will fill them themselves according to instructions.

V. Censuses will deal with:

 a) Surname and first name, age, place of birth, language spoken, religion, marital status, occupation or condition, fixed or habitual residence, temporary residence, or only in transit in the commune, children receiving public or private education, distribution of houses according to stories and number of rooms used for living by each family, gardens around houses.

 b) Illnesses and apparent infirmities: blind persons, deaf-mutes, insane persons at home or in public or private institutions, idiots.

VI. It will be necessary to process the census data of each country according to uniform methods which will permit international comparisons.

The resolution, although passed more than one hundred years ago, includes many of the basic features that still are stressed in current international recommendations on population censuses. Subsequent international statistical meetings have confirmed, modified, or elaborated certain points of the 1853 resolution.

The Second International Statistical Congress, held in Paris in 1855, recommended detailed census classifications for the statistical programs of large cities. At the fourth congress, held in London in 1860, a long resolution, covering in greater detail essentially the same points as the 1853 resolution, was adopted. It was published together with a proposal by the organizing commission on the topic of occupations. The 1860 resolution also included new items, such as the establishment of population registers, additional types of housing data to be collected, definition of the urban population, and surveys collateral to the census.

The population census resolution adopted by the Fifth International Statistical Congress, held in 1863 in Berlin, emphasized the need for improved methods for distinguishing the *de facto* and the *de jure* population as well as for the active participation of the population in the preparation and taking of a census. The sixth congress, held in Florecnce in 1867, passed a resolution dealing almost entirely with procedures for obtaining the *de facto* and the *de jure* population.

It seems that neither the third congress (held in Vienna in 1857) nor the seventh congress (held in The Hague in 1869) adopted resolutions relating to population censuses. However, at the Eighth International Statistical Congress, held in St. Petersburg in 1872, the following "international minimum" requirements (basically similar to those approved by the 1853 Congress) were agreed to: (*a*) the census should be nominal; (*b*) it should enumerate the *de facto* population; (*c*) it should be decennial; (*d*) it should be completed within twenty-four hours; (*e*) the individual information to be obtained should include name, age, sex, relationship to household, civil status, occupation, religion, language, education, birthplace and nationality, residence, and special mention of such infirmities as blindness, deaf-mutism, cretinism, idiocy, and insanity (Australia, Commonwealth Bureau of Census and Statistics, 1917, p. 13; Institut International de Statistique, 1899). In addition, the eighth congress recommended that population censuses should be taken in the years ending in zero.

This subject received greater impetus at the sixth session of the International Statistical Institute, also in St. Petersburg in 1897, when Joseph de Körösy submitted a proposal recommending that all countries of the world participate in a "century census" in 1900—if possible as of December 31—covering the minimum information already agreed to by the congress of 1872. It was decided at that conference to approve this proposal in principle and to call it to the attention of the governments (Institut International de Statistique, 1899, Part 1, pp. 200–207, 215–18; Part 2, pp. 220–50; Körösy, 1881).

There are indications that the recommendations of 1897 and earlier were considered by various countries planning population censuses during the first part of the twentieth century. Follow-up resolutions were adopted by a number of regional conferences, such as the conferences of Australian statisticians held in Hobart, 1890, and Sydney, 1900; the first and second Pan-American scientific congresses held in Santiago de Chile, 1908, and Washington, D.C., 1915; and the fourth and the fifth international conferences of American states convened in Buenos Aires, 1910, and Santiago de Chile, 1923.

In Europe—through the work of the International Statistical Institute, the International Labor Office, the Committee of Statistical Experts of the League of Nations, the International Institute of Agriculture, and other bodies—there was the hope, around 1930, that population censuses would be established on a firm, regular pattern with a high degree of intercountry comparability. The advent of World War II destroyed that possibility for a time and disrupted the census tradition of most of the European countries.

A strong revival of international cooperation in the field of censuses began

in 1943, this time among the American nations. The Inter American Statistical Institute, which had been created in 1940, sponsored an active and successful regional program known as the 1950 Census of the Americas. In 1947, this regional program became the strongest sector of the 1950 world-wide program of national population censuses developed under United Nations sponsorship. In these world and regional programs, international census standards were developed, technical manuals prepared, training courses organized, and technical assistance to individual countries provided (in the form of experts, tabulation, and printing equipment).

Because population censuses are not a yearly continuing function of governments but one organized anew at periodic intervals, international recommendations have emphasized the initiation of census activity. This is in contrast to the emphasis in resolutions dealing with current types of statistics—such as vital statistics. In the latter case, resolutions deal more with the gradual reorganization or improvement of existing services. However, population census recommendations on the organization, timing, and initiation of co-ordinated census activities should not obscure the continuous international efforts to improve the standardization and comparability of technical procedures, definitions, and classifications.

Recommendations on these technical topics, developed for use in censuses taken around 1950, are given in detail in the *Handbook of Population Census Methods* (United Nations Statistical Office, 1954*b*). Studies of census methods used during the decade 1945–54 and preliminary recommendations for the 1960 World Census of Population are now being prepared by the United Nations Statistical Office (1955–56). In these publications consideration is given to the definition and classification of all major census items—including age, marital status, nationality, language, place of birth, educational characteristics, fertility, and economic characteristics.

Because of their extensive character and importance, special note might be made of the two main classifications of economic characteristics. The international standard industrial classification of all economic activities was approved by the Statistical Commission at its third session (April–May, 1948) and recommended for international use by the Economic and Social Council at its seventh session (July–August, 1948). This classification and previous drafts of similar classifications have been drawn up for use in both economic and population censuses. The international standard classification of occupations has been developed by the International Labor Office. Its present form—a classification of seventy-two minor groups within the framework of the ten major groups—has been adopted as a provisional classification by the Eighth International Conference of Labor Statisticians. The classification is still being studied and revised. Because of the close relationship which must be maintained between population and vital statistics, it is appropriate that these classifications be used also for vital statistics.

Although participation and co-operation in the 1950 international census program was generally good, much remains to be done by national statistical administrations and international organizations to insure that accurate censuses are taken at least every ten years throughout the world and that their results are processed and published more rapidly. It has been rightly pointed out that, apart from methods to reduce the high cost of censuses, there is also the question of adapting census techniques in countries in which the bulk of the population is dispersed in large and not easily accessible areas, partly illiterate, and suspicious of the census. To reduce costs and to achieve more accurate results, the use of scientifically planned sample surveys as a supplement of the complete census inquiry has been suggested. Even when sampling is not used in connection with the census, a simplification of the questionnaire is urged by some as a method of obtaining accurate results in countries facing the difficulties mentioned. These proposals confront the demographer with a dilemma. A simplification of the census schedule will undoubtedly improve the accuracy of the census data and the speed with which they may be tabulated and published, but this implies a curtailment of data available for analysis.

The present coverage of population census statistics can be measured by a study of the censuses which have been taken in the past decade. The statistical task accomplished in connection with the censuses taken in the period 1945–54 can be better appreciated when the census program of that decade is considered against a background of previous census activities.

In the first half of the nineteenth century demographic data from census sources were available for only a relatively small proportion of the world's people, the population census tradition being established primarily in European and North American countries. In the decades around 1860 and 1870, only about 200 million persons were covered by census enumerations—less than 20 per cent of the world's population. After this, there was a rapid rise, and in the decade around 1880 the total had increased to over 500 million, or approximately a third of the world's people. In the period around 1900, when approximately 800 million persons were included in national census enumerations, census activity covered half the world's population.

The increase continued until the number of persons enumerated in the decade around 1930 was 1,200 million, and in the decade around 1940 it was 1,300 million. For each of these periods the proportion of the world's population covered was approximately 57 or 58 per cent. The increase in the total number of persons enumerated did not represent proportional increases in world coverage because census work did not advance as rapidly for some of the large and fertile populations of Asia, Africa, and Latin America as for the European countries.

54, in terms of total numbers of people covered, would be a more modest increase over recent decades, since the proportion of the world covered would have been only 61.5 per cent.

The census activity during 1945–54 was widespread. Practically all of Europe west of the U.S.S.R. had a census in this period. In the Western Hemisphere, all the sovereign countries and the major territories and dependencies have had a census since 1944—with the exception of Peru, which had a census in 1940; Jamaica, which had a census in 1943; the Netherlands Antilles

TABLE 1

AGGREGATE POPULATION ENUMERATED IN CENSUSES DURING 1945–54
AND PER CENT OF TOTAL POPULATION, BY CONTINENTS

(Based on Estimated Populations for Mid-1953)

Continent	Total Population (Thousands)	Population Enumerated, 1945–54 (Thousands)	Per Cent of Total Population Enumerated
Total	2,493,000*	1,995,830	80.1
Africa	208,000	132,494	63.7
North America	229,900	226,627	98.6
South America	118,100	106,343	90.0
Asia	1,307,000	1,116,276	85.4
Europe	403,100	402,014	99.7
Oceania	13,900	12,076	86.9

* Including the U.S.S.R.

The decade 1945–54 was a period of substantial increase in census activity. The world consists of approximately 214 sovereign countries, trust territories, and non-self-governing territories and has a total population of some 2,490 million (1953 estimate). On the basis of available information, 159 areas with an estimated population of almost 2 billion, or slightly over 80 per cent of the world total, were enumerated during the 1945–54 decade.

This large proportion covered is achieved partly because of the census of the Chinese mainland in 1954. This one census contributes approximately one-fourth of the total number of enumerated persons. Without this large single addition to the number enumerated, the census achievement for 1945–

(1930); Surinam (1921); and Uruguay, which has not had a census since 1908. Many of the important areas in Africa and most of the major countries of Asia have taken censuses within the past decade. The U.S.S.R., Indonesia, Burma, Afghanistan, Iran, Ethiopia, and some of the smaller countries of the Middle East are the principal areas which were not enumerated in this period.

The geographic coverage of these recent censuses can be seen in Table 1, which shows for each continent the aggregate population and the per cent of the total population enumerated during 1945–54. Europe and North America lead, with the proportions enumerated over 98 per cent, and in all of the other continents except Africa the proportion of the population enumerated exceeded the world percentage of 80.

The total number of people and the proportion of the world population enumerated in any period are sharply affected by whether or not several countries with very large populations have taken censuses during that period. From the standpoint of available data, this is the important criterion. From a long-range point of view, an equally important factor is whether the census procedure itself is being adopted by an increasing number of countries. This is perhaps a more significant and stable

countries were taken in that period—a figure 33 per cent greater than the highest previous figure for the one-hundred-year span covered by Table 2.

The geographic distribution of the growth in the use of the population census method deserves some note. European countries adopted the census procedure early, and the number of censuses in each decade is fairly high during most of the one-hundred-year period. The low figures for the period around 1940 are, of course, atypical—a consequence of the war. On the other hand, earlier decades show relatively

TABLE 2

NUMBER OF SOVEREIGN COUNTRIES TAKING A POPULATION
CENSUS: EACH TEN-YEAR PERIOD FROM 1855 TO 1954*

Time Periods	Total	Africa	North America	South America	Asia and Oceania	Europe
1855–64	24	0	4	2	1	17
1865–74	29	0	2	5	3	19
1875–84	37	1	5	4	6	21
1885–94	35	0	6	3	6	20
1895–1904	44	2	7	5	7	23
1905–14	42	2	7	4	6	23
1915–24	48	2	9	4	11	22
1925–34	49	2	8	2	10	27
1935–44	44	3	9	6	9	17
1945–54	65	2	12	8	15	28

* This table is based on the history of areas which were sovereign in 1954. The changes shown in the table are not due, therefore, to an increase or decrease in the number of countries existing at any period. For example, India, Burma, and Pakistan are each counted as having taken censuses in decades prior to their separate existence as independent countries, whenever their combined populations were enumerated.

measure of progress than an index based on the total number of persons enumerated.

Table 2 gives the number of sovereign countries in each continent which have taken population censuses in each ten-year period from 1855 to 1954. The number of countries taking censuses increased slowly during the forty-year period 1855–94. For the period 1895–1904 there was a sharp increase from 35 to 44. Then for the fifty-year period 1895–1944 there was no significant increase, the number of censuses for sovereign countries ranging from 42 to 49 for the five decades. By contrast, the decade 1945–54 showed a striking increase; sixty-five censuses of sovereign

little census activity in other parts of the world and rapid increases in more recent periods, especially in the last decade. For this period the number of American censuses increased to twenty from a previous high of fifteen, and the number of censuses in Asia and Oceania increased from a previous high of eleven to fifteen.

The availability of data on total population can be measured simply by the number and distribution of persons enumerated. At least equally important to the demographer are the other items of information collected and compiled by the censuses. Detailed studies by the United Nations of the schedules used by fifty-two sovereign countries in censuses taken during the decade 1945–54 show the consistency or variety of enumerated items (United Nations Statistical Office, 1955*b*).

Table 3 summarizes for each of these fifty-two countries the types of data collected. This table gives only broad types of data and does not indicate the method of obtaining the information or the schedule question. The same general topic can be investigated in a variety of ways, and for this reason the resulting tabulations may not be as uniform or comparable as may be implied by an examination of Table 3. Also, some important items commonly included in census tabulations are not listed in Table 3. These are items such as total population, urban-rural distribution, family composition, and population dependent upon agriculture. Such topics are usually compiled by tabulation from a combination of one or more schedule items and, accordingly, do not appear explicitly as schedule items. Also, it is understood that a census schedule may include a number of administrative or control items which are not listed in the table.

It is obvious that there is a wide variety of data covered by the different national censuses. It also is evident that the magnitude of the census operation, as indicated by the number of schedule items, varies from country to country. Table 3 lists thirty-one types of data, and the frequency distribution of the numbers of these types of data included in the fifty-two censuses is given in Table 4. One country includes only twelve of these items in its census; whereas three countries include as many as twenty-four topics. The largest frequencies were for censuses of eighteen and nineteen types of data.

It is obvious that a count of the number of items in a census has no absolute meaning, since the number is determined partly by how the individual questions or entries are grouped into "type of data." However, it is apparent that there is considerable heterogeneity in the content of census enumerations among countries. To a certain extent this is to be expected, since a census is designed primarily to serve national purposes and since not all census topics have equal value or validity for every country. Nevertheless, on items of international interest a satisfactory degree of general utilization has probably not been achieved.

It might be thought offhand that statistically advanced countries would use the census method for the investigation of a wider range of items than would other countries. Where technical and other resources are inadequate, the failure of many censuses has resulted from an overloading of the schedule. On the other hand, statistically backward countries have fewer other sources of data, and the census offers an opportunity to obtain important information which could not otherwise be known. While no definite conclusion can be made, it is interesting to note that if continents are listed in order from those using the smallest average number of census items to those using the largest average number of census items, the order is: Oceania, Europe, America, Asia, and Africa. Few would dispute that this is also an approximate rank order of statistical development.

The detailed information in Table 3 is summarized, by continents, in Table 5. From this table it can be seen that certain topics are almost universally included. Name, geographic location, sex, age, marital status, and occupation are included in each of the fifty-two censuses. Other items, such as citizenship, place of birth, industry, status, and relation to household head are omitted only in exceptional cases. The economic characteristics of occupation, industry, and status are included in almost every census. Items relating to unemployment are also quite usual, al-

TABLE 3—SUMMARY OF TYPES OF DATA COLLECTED IN THE POPULATION CENSUSES OF SELECTED COUNTRIES, 1945–54*

("X" indicates that the given type of data was collected; "–" that it was not collected)

Type of Data Collected	Africa			America																			
	Egypt (1947)	Libya (1954)	Un. of So. Africa (1951)	Argentina (1947)	Bolivia (1950)	Brazil (1950)	Canada (1951)	Chile (1952)	Colombia (1951)	Costa Rica (1950)	Cuba (1953)	Dominican Rep. (1950)	Ecuador (1950)	El Salvador (1950)	Guatemala (1950)	Haiti (1950)	Honduras (1950)	Mexico (1950)	Nicaragua (1950)	Panama (1950)	Paraguay (1950)	United States (1950)	Venezuela (1950)
Identification and geographic data:																							
Name	X	X	X	X	X	X	X	X	X	X	X	X	X	X	X	X	X	X	X	X	X	X	X
Geographic location	X	X	X	X	X	X	X	X	X	X	X	X	X	X	X	X	X	X	X	X	X	X	X
Data on residence	X	X	X	X	–	X	X	–	–	–	X	X	–	X	X	–	X	–	–	–	–	X	X
Personal characteristics:																							
Sex	X	X	X	X	X	X	X	X	X	X	X	X	X	X	X	X	X	X	X	X	X	X	X
Age	X	X	X	X	X	X	X	X	X	X	X	X	X	X	X	X	X	X	X	X	X	X	X
Marital status	X	X	X	X	X	X	X	X	X	X	X	X	X	X	X	X	X	X	X	X	X	X	X
Citizenship (legal nationality)	X	X	X	X	X	X	X	X	X	X	X	X	X	X	X	X	X	X	X	X	X	X	X
Place of birth	X	X	X	X	X	X	X	X	X	X	X	X	X	X	X	X	X	X	X	X	X	X	X
Economic characteristics:																							
Economically active and inactive population	X	X	X	X	X	X	X	X	X	X	X	X	X	X	X	X	X	X	X	X	X	X	X
Occupation, profession or craft	X	X	X	X	X	X	X	X	X	X	X	X	X	X	X	X	X	X	X	X	X	X	X
Industry or branch of economic activity	X	X	X	X	X	X	X	X	X	X	X	X	X	X	X	X	X	X	X	X	X	X	X
Status (as employer, employee, etc.)	X	X	X	X	X	X	X	X	X	X	X	X	X	X	X	X	X	X	X	X	X	X	X
Unemployment	X	X	X	X	X	X	X	X	X	X	X	X	X	X	X	X	–	X	–	X	X	X	X
Secondary occupation	–	–	–	–	–	X	–	–	–	–	–	X	–	–	–	–	–	X	–	–	–	–	–
Time worked	X	–	–	–	–	–	X	–	–	–	X	–	–	–	–	–	X	X	–	–	–	X	X
Income	–	–	X	–	–	–	X	–	X	–	–	X	–	–	–	–	–	X	–	X	–	X	X
Households:																							
Relationship to head of household	X	X	X	X	X	X	X	X	X	X	X	X	X	X	X	X	X	X	X	X	X	X	X
Data on parents or dependents	X	–	–	–	–	–	–	–	–	–	–	–	–	–	–	–	–	–	–	–	–	–	X
tiality and fertility:																							
N uptiality	X	–	–	X	–	–	–	–	–	–	–	–	–	–	–	–	–	–	–	–	–	X	–
Number of children born	X	–	–	X	–	X	–	–	–	–	X	X	–	–	–	–	–	X	–	X	–	X	X
Number of children living	X	–	–	X	–	X	–	–	–	–	–	–	–	–	–	–	–	–	–	–	–	–	–
Educational characteristics:																							
Level of education	X	X	–	X	X	X	X	X	X	X	X	X	X	X	X	X	X	X	X	X	X	X	X
Literacy	X	X	X	X	X	X	–	X	X	X	X	X	X	X	X	X	X	X	X	X	X	–	X
School attendance	–	X	–	X	X	–	X	X	–	X	X	X	–	X	X	–	–	–	X	X	X	X	X
Cultural characteristics:																							
Language	–	–	X	–	X	X	X	–	–	X	–	X	X	–	X	–	–	X	X	X	X	–	–
Religion	X	X	X	X	–	X	X	X	–	–	–	X	–	–	X	–	–	X	X	–	–	–	–
Ethnic characteristics	X	–	X	–	–	X	X	–	–	X	X	X	–	–	X	–	–	–	–	–	–	X	–
Native customs	–	–	–	–	X	–	–	–	X	–	–	–	X	–	X	–	X	X	–	–	–	–	–
Social data:																							
Physical and mental disabilities	X	X	–	X	–	–	X	X	–	–	–	X	X	–	–	–	–	–	–	–	–	–	X
Migrants and refugees	X	X	X	X	–	–	X	–	–	–	X	–	–	–	–	–	–	–	–	–	–	–	–
Military service	–	–	–	–	X	–	X	X	–	–	–	–	–	–	–	–	–	–	–	–	–	X	–
Social insurance and family expenditures	–	–	–	–	–	–	–	–	–	–	–	–	–	–	–	–	–	X	–	X	–	–	–

Type of Data Collected	Asia								Europe																					Oceania	
	Ceylon (1953)	India (1951)	Iraq (1947)	Japan (1950)	Pakistan (1951)	Philippines (1948)	Thailand (1947)	Turkey (1950)	Austria (1951)	Belgium (1947)	Denmark (1950)	Finland (1950)	France (1954)	Ger. Fed. Rep. (1950)	Greece (1951)	Iceland (1950)	Ireland (1951)	Italy (1951)	Luxembourg (1947)	Netherlands (1947)	Norway (1950)	Portugal (1950)	Spain (1950)	Sweden (1950)	Switzerland (1950)	Un. Kingdom (1951)	Yugoslavia (1953)	Australia (1954)	New Zealand (1951)
Identification and geographic data:																													
Name	X	X	X	X	X	X	X	X	X	X	X	X	X	X	X	X	X	X	X	X	X	X	X	X	X	X	X	X	X
Geographic location	X	X	X	X	X	X	X	X	X	X	X	X	X	X	X	X	X	X	X	X	X	X	X	X	X	X	X	X	X
Data on residence	–	–	X	X	X	X	X	X	X	X	X	X	X	X	X	X	X	X	X	X	X	X	X	X	X	X	X	–	X
Personal characteristics:																													
Sex	X	X	X	X	X	X	X	X	X	X	X	X	X	X	X	X	X	X	X	X	X	X	X	X	X	X	X	X	X
Age	X	X	X	X	X	X	X	X	X	X	X	X	X	X	X	X	X	X	X	X	X	X	X	X	X	X	X	X	X
Marital status	X	X	X	X	X	X	X	X	X	X	X	X	X	X	X	X	X	X	X	X	X	X	X	X	X	X	X	X	X
Citizenship (legal nationality)	X	X	X	X	X	X	X	X	X	X	X	X	X	–	X	X	–	X	X	X	X	X	X	X	X	X	X	X	–
Place of birth	X	X	X	X	X	–	X	X	X	X	X	X	X	–	X	X	–	X	X	X	X	X	X	X	X	X	X	X	X
Economic characteristics:																													
Economically active and inactive population	X	X	X	X	X	X	X	X	X	X	X	X	X	X	X	X	X	X	X	X	X	X	X	X	X	X	X	X	X
Occupation, profession or craft	X	X	X	X	X	X	X	X	X	X	X	X	X	X	X	X	X	X	X	X	X	X	X	X	X	X	X	X	X
Industry or branch of economic activity	X	X	–	X	X	X	X	X	X	X	X	X	X	X	X	X	X	X	X	X	X	X	X	X	X	X	X	X	X
Status (as employer, employee, etc.)	X	X	–	X	X	X	X	X	X	X	X	X	X	X	X	X	X	X	X	X	X	X	X	X	X	X	X	X	X
Unemployment	X	X	–	X	X	X	–	X	X	X	X	X	X	X	X	X	X	X	X	X	X	X	X	X	X	X	–	X	X
Secondary occupation	–	X	–	–	X	X	–	–	X	X	–	X	–	X	–	X	–	–	X	–	X	–	X	X	X	–	X	–	–
Time worked	–	–	–	X	–	X	–	X	–	–	–	X	–	X	X	–	–	–	–	–	–	–	–	–	–	–	–	–	X
Income	X	–	–	–	X	X	–	–	–	–	–	–	–	–	–	–	–	–	–	–	–	–	–	–	–	–	–	–	X
Households:																													
Relationship to head of household	X	X	X	X	X	X	X	–	X	X	X	X	X	X	X	X	X	X	X	X	X	X	X	X	X	X	X	X	X
Data on parents or dependents	X	–	–	–	–	–	–	–	–	–	X	–	–	–	–	–	–	X	–	–	–	X	X	–	X	–	–	–	–
tiality and fertility:																													
N uptiality	X	–	–	X	X	–	–	–	–	X	X	X	X	–	–	X	–	–	X	X	X	X	X	–	X	X	X	X	–
Number of children born	X	X	–	X	X	X	–	–	–	X	–	X	X	X	X	X	–	–	X	X	X	X	X	–	X	X	X	X	–
Number of children living	X	X	–	–	X	–	–	–	–	X	–	–	–	–	–	–	–	–	X	–	–	X	X	–	X	–	X	X	X
Educational characteristics:																													
Level of education	X	X	–	X	X	X	X	X	X	X	–	X	X	–	X	X	–	X	–	X	X	X	X	–	–	–	X	–	–
Literacy	X	X	X	–	X	X	X	X	–	X	–	–	–	–	X	–	–	X	–	–	–	X	X	–	–	–	X	–	–
School attendance	–	–	–	X	X	X	–	X	X	–	–	X	X	–	–	–	X	–	–	–	–	X	X	–	–	X	–	–	–
Cultural characteristics:																													
Language	X	X	–	–	X	X	X	X	X	X	–	X	–	X	X	–	–	–	–	–	–	–	–	–	X	X	X	–	–
Religion	X	X	X	–	X	X	X	X	X	–	–	X	–	X	X	X	–	–	X	X	X	X	–	–	X	X	X	X	X
Ethnic characteristics	X	X	–	–	–	X	–	–	–	–	–	–	–	–	–	–	–	–	–	–	–	–	–	–	–	–	X	X	X
Native customs	–	–	–	–	–	–	–	–	–	–	–	–	–	–	–	–	–	–	–	–	–	–	–	–	–	–	–	–	–
Social data:																													
Physical and mental disabilities	X	–	X	–	–	X	–	–	X	–	–	X	–	X	X	X	–	–	–	–	–	X	X	–	X	–	X	–	–
Migrants and refugees	X	X	–	X	X	–	–	–	–	–	–	–	–	X	–	–	–	X	–	–	–	–	–	–	–	–	–	X	X
Military service	–	–	–	–	–	–	–	–	–	–	–	–	–	–	–	–	–	–	–	X	–	–	–	–	–	–	–	–	X
Social insurance and family expenditures	–	–	–	–	–	–	–	–	–	–	–	–	–	X	–	–	–	–	–	–	–	–	–	–	–	–	–	–	–

* Source: Table 1, United Nations Statistical Office (1955*d*). This table is a summary presentation and shows only whether or not each type of data listed was collected. An indication that data on a given subject were collected does not necessarily mean that a specific question employing similar terminology was used on the census schedule. For an additional explanation of the meaning of the entries and for a list of the studies on individual subjects containing de tails of the methods used in the investigation of each topic, see the text.

though there is wide variety in the kinds of information asked, and in the larger number of cases the information is related to prior occupation. Other items relating to the economic characteristics of the population are not so commonly included. Information on secondary occupation was requested in seventeen censuses, time worked in fourteen, and income in twelve.

Items on nuptiality and fertility also were not generally included. Some information on nuptiality was collected by twenty countries, but the questions were not uniform among the countries. Twenty-nine countries asked for information on the number of children born, and fourteen on number of children living.

For educational characteristics, it is interesting to note that level of education was investigated in forty-one censuses. Each of the twenty American censuses, seven of the eight Asian censuses, and twelve of the nineteen European censuses included information on this topic. Level of education was included more frequently than literacy (thirty-four countries), and although the problems of international comparability are greater, level of education now seems to be recognized as a more useful item.

The information collected on cultural characteristics varied widely. The most common item, religion, was used in thirty-two censuses. Language information, such as mother tongue, language spoken, or ability to speak specified languages was included in half of the fifty-two censuses. Very special items such as those on ethnic characteristics or information on native customs regarding food, clothing, or living habits were included in only a few censuses, and the information requested varied.

The total population covered and the geographic areas included in the population censuses during 1945–54 can be considered satisfactory. Also, the main

topics covered show an increasing consistency. Much more remains to be achieved, but the current stage of development shows that tremendous strides have been taken toward the use of comparable international census concepts.

Unfortunately, the demographer's interests and needs are not met unless technical advances at the collection stage increase the resulting data available for population research. The ultimate test must be the extent to which

TABLE 4

FREQUENCY DISTRIBUTION OF
NUMBER OF TYPES OF DATA
COLLECTED IN POPULATION
CENSUSES OF FIFTY-TWO
COUNTRIES, 1945–54

Number of Types of Data	Frequency
24	3
23	3
22	6
21	5
20	4
19	8
18	8
17	4
16	6
15	1
14	2
13	1
12	1

the needed facts and figures are tabulated and published. A definitive analysis of available census data which will result from the enumerations taken during 1945–54 cannot be made at this time. In many countries the full tabulation and exploitation of census data may extend over a period of years. Practically all of the data which will ultimately become available from censuses taken prior to 1950 are already at hand, and many of the data from censuses taken in 1950 and 1951 are either published or available in preliminary form (except for some of the more complicated or lower priority tabulations). However, for censuses taken during 1952–54 only scattered results may be available except for total counts for a country or for major civil divisions. Re-examined five years after the close of the period, the available data may considerably exceed those at hand in 1955.

of census tabulation, the aggregate population of areas for which recent census data are available and the per cent that these aggregates are of the world population. This table is based on responses to United Nations questionnaires, including responses received

TABLE 5

NUMBER OF COUNTRIES COLLECTING EACH TYPE OF CENSUS DATA:
FIFTY-TWO COUNTRIES, 1945–54*

Type of Data Collected	Total	Africa	America	Asia	Europe	Oceania
Total number of censuses studied.....	52	3	20	8	19	2
Identification and geographic data:						
Name.............................	52	3	20	8	19	2
Geographic location..................	52	3	20	8	19	2
Data on residence....................	39	3	10	6	19	1
Personal characteristics:						
Sex..............................	52	3	20	8	19	2
Age..............................	52	3	20	8	19	2
Marital status......................	52	3	20	8	19	2
Citizenship (legal nationality)..........	49	3	20	8	17	1
Place of birth......................	49	3	20	7	17	2
Economic characteristics:						
Occupation, profession, or craft.........	52	3	20	8	19	2
Industry or branch of economic activity..	51	3	20	7	19	2
Status (employer, employee, etc.).......	51	3	20	7	19	2
Unemployment......................	47	3	18	6	18	2
Secondary occupation.................	17	..	3	3	11	..
Time worked........................	14	1	6	3	3	1
Income............................	12	1	7	3	..	1
Households:						
Relationship to head of household......	51	3	20	7	19	2
Data on parents or dependents.........	8	1	1	1	5	..
Nuptiality and fertility:						
Nuptiality..........................	20	1	2	3	13	1
Number of children born..............	29	1	8	5	14	1
Number of children living.............	14	1	2	3	6	2
Educational characteristics:						
Level of education...................	41	2	20	7	12	..
Literacy...........................	34	3	18	7	6	..
School attendance....................	26	1	14	4	7	..
Cultural characteristics:						
Language...........................	26	1	11	6	8	..
Religion............................	32	3	8	7	12	2
Ethnic characteristics.................	15	2	7	3	1	2
Native customs......................	6	..	6	..	..	..
Social data:						
Physical and mental disabilities.........	20	2	6	3	9	..
Migrants and refugees................	14	3	3	4	2	2
Military service......................	6	..	4	..	1	1
Social insurance and family expenditures.	3	..	2	..	1	..

* These data are derived from Table 1, United Nations Statistical Office (1955d).

Nevertheless, of the censuses of sovereign countries taken in 1945–54, thirty-one were taken before 1950 and thirty-nine in the years 1950 and 1951, and a preliminary investigation of available data is possible.

Table 6 shows, for each major type

during 1955, for which data are published in recent issues of the United Nations *Demographic Yearbook*. Table 6 may be based to some extent on data not yet available in national publications, since countries frequently release data to the United Nations for publication prior to publication in their own official statistical compilations.

Table 6 reveals a number of interesting points about the availability of different types of data. In the first place, population totals for various geographic divisions of a country are the most generally available type of table. National totals are universal, and population totals for major civil divisions are available for 79.6 per cent of the world population.

than half the world's people. Distributions by sex and age in quinquennial age groups cover 55.9 per cent of the population, and population distributions by sex and age in single years of age now seem to be an essential part of most tabulation programs, being available for 46.2 per cent of the world. Tabulated data for some other items are, however, not so generally produced. Tabulations of the population

TABLE 6

AGGREGATE POPULATION OF AREAS FOR WHICH DIFFERENT TYPES OF
CENSUS DATA ARE AVAILABLE AND PER CENT THAT THESE
AGGREGATES ARE OF TOTAL WORLD POPULATION*

Type of Information	Aggregate Population Covered (in Thousands)	Per Cent of World Population Covered
Population by major civil divisions	1,980,745	79.6
Population, urban and rural, by sex	1,394,898	56.1
Population by size of locality and sex	1,268,515	51.0
Population by quinquennial age groups and sex	1,389,714	55.9
Population by single years of age and sex	1,149,368	46.2
Population by marital status, age, and sex	1,145,748	46.1
Population by country of birth and sex	1,150,101	46.2
Population by citizenship and sex	1,150,644	46.3
Population by size of household	621,625	25.0
Population, total and economically active, by sex	1,296,442	52.1
Population, total and economically active, by age and sex	697,645	28.1
Economically active population by industry, status, and sex	1,208,247	48.6
Population by language spoken and sex	820,847	33.0
Population by religion and sex	913,378	36.7
Population by ethnic composition and sex	383,205	15.4
Population by literacy, age, and sex	680,908	27.4
Population by level of education, age, and sex	515,935	20.8
Population by school attendance, age, and sex	498,686	20.1
Female population by age and size of family (number of children born alive)	604,006	24.3
Female population by age and size of living family (number of children living)	64,813	2.6

* The percentages shown in this table are based on an estimated world population of 2,487,000,000 in mid-1953 and on the totals of the estimated mid-year population in 1953, or the nearest year available, of the areas for which relevant information is shown in the United Nations *Demographic Yearbook* for 1955.

ulation. Other compilations of the geographic population distribution are available for lesser percentages. Data by some form of "urban-rural" classification are available for 56.1 per cent and population classified by size of locality for 51.0 per cent.

Data on sex, age, and marital status are available for most censuses that complete a tabulation program involving any degree of cross-tabulation; even so, data for this fundamental cross-tabulation are available for less

by literacy, sex, and age, for example, have been made or released for only 27.4 per cent of the peoples of the world. Data on fertility are even less commonly produced.

To the demographer interested in world-wide analysis, the figures shown in Table 6 mark the limits of what is now feasible. There is considerable knowledge of total population and its distribution, but information on population characteristics diminishes rapidly as the analytical interest goes beyond the most common and traditional census items.

VITAL STATISTICS[2]

Vital registration refers to the legal recording with the authorized officials of certain identifying and descriptive characteristics of a vital event, primarily births, deaths, marriages, or divorces. An important aspect of this concept is the word "legal." Legal recording in the modern world usually means recording in an official or civil register. The use of civil records primarily established for their legal value influences greatly the scope and character of present-day vital statistics.

Civil registers, however, are of relatively recent origin. Except for fragmentary registration during the pre-Christian era, the recording of vital events was originally the unco-ordinated concern of the ecclesiastical authorities. In Europe, systematic maintenance of ecclesiastical registers was established in Spain in the fifteenth century. By 1538 the clergy of England were being required to record baptisms, marriages, and burials. In the following year (1539) France required the curates to keep registers of baptisms and burials. The early years of the seventeenth century saw similar parish registers set up in Sweden, Canada (Quebec), Finland, and Denmark. As early as A.D. 720, there appears to have been a system of registration of births, deaths, and marriages in some parts of Japan. Buddhist temple registers were established there in 1635.

All of these European and Asiatic registers were ecclesiastical, designed for the purpose of recording baptisms, burials, and weddings. It remained for the countries of the Western Hemisphere to introduce civil registers in which government officials replaced the clergy as registrars. Perhaps the first of these were the early civil registers of births and deaths established by the Incas in Peru; the second resulted from the civil registration laws of the colonies of Massachusetts and New Plymouth. The secularization of vital registration continued with the adoption of the Napoleonic Code in 1804, and by 1900 the majority of countries had established a legal basis for a civil registration system.

Civil registers have many advantages over those maintained by the church. In a civil register, records are made of births, deaths, and marriages rather than of baptisms, burials, and weddings. Moreover, the coverage, not being restricted to members of certain religious faiths, theoretically includes the total population. Also, the records can include more relevant data than those usually included in documents prepared as religious records.

Although vital registration—either ecclesiastical or civil—has had a long history, it was not until 1662 that the records were put to any use other than legal. The realization of this new use of vital records must be credited to John Graunt, who saw the possibilities of using "bills of mortality" for purposes of statistics (Graunt, 1665). Statistical use of the registers spread to Germany and France, but it remained for Dr. William Farr, compiler of abstracts in the newly created General Register Office of England and Wales, to systematize vital statistics. His development of a system of national vital statistics in England and Wales was the beginning of vital statistics as they are known today. His penetrating analyses of the deficiencies in vital statistics and the methods of achieving improvement are still models for workers in the field.

Efforts to improve vital statistics must take cognizance of the fact that vital statistics—even of the simplest

[2] For a more complete discussion of the history of vital registration, see United Nations Statistical Office (1955c, chap. i).

type—do not exist for a large number of areas. For an additional group of countries data are fragmentary and defective. Moreover, for the parts of the world where substantial data do exist, there are problems of comparability—some simple, some complex. Efforts to develop vital statistics where none exist, to improve the coverage where data are fragmentary, and to improve the quality and the comparability of definitions, classifications, and tabulations for those statistics which are routinely compiled have been going on for many years. Work in the establishment of vital statistics systems and the improvement of coverage is carried out primarily at the national level. It is therefore not well documented except in scattered national sources. The third aspect, being done at the international level, can more easily be traced. In contrast to the early international census recommendations, much of the early international work in vital statistics was concerned with specific classification problems, and general reviews of the methods and problems of organizing a vital statistics system were undertaken only later.

The first major study of this type was a review of the organizational patterns of vital statistics systems and the procedures used in forty-three areas; it was carried out and published by the International Statistical Institute in 1921, and a revision was issued in 1929. Both presentations sought to summarize the essential elements of the vital statistics systems and to present them in the form of reference tables. No attempt was made to formulate recommendations on the different points presented, although various unrelated recommendations had been made in the first thirteen regular sessions of the institute.

The Health Organisation of the League of Nations attacked the problem of variation in registration and compilation methods by studying in detail, and individually, the systems in twenty-two selected countries. A comprehensive report for each area studied was published between 1924 and 1930 (League of Nations Health Organisation, 1924–30), but no systematic attempt was made to draw recommendations from the studies.

As a part of its general program to promote the development of national statistics, the Statistical Commission of the United Nations at its fourth session, in 1949, requested that a study of the different systems of vital registration be made in order to promote comparability of definitions, adequacy and comparability of classifications and tabulations, and development of effective registration systems. In response to this resolution, the United Nations Statistical Office initiated a series of studies of national vital statistics practices. Over one hundred geographic areas, sovereign and non-sovereign, were surveyed by correspondence, and the responses were analyzed by a cross-section comparative method. Conclusions drawn from this survey form the basis of general United Nations recommendations for improvement of vital statistics, published as *Principles for a Vital Statistics System* (United Nations Statistical Office, 1953*a*). The methodological studies, together with histories of vital registration and compilation of vital statistics, are published in the *Handbook of Vital Statistics Methods* (United Nations Statistical Office, 1955*c*).

The recommendations given in the principles suggest the improvement and standardization of vital statistics. The principles include a basic list of items for live birth, death, fetal death, marriage, and divorce, with priorities indicating immediate and more advanced goals of data collection; standards for registration of vital events; statistical recording, reporting, collecting, and tabulation procedures; needs for co-ordination; place of sampling, surveying, record linkage; and evaluation of the system. These international recommendations provide, therefore, a comprehensive guide for the organization and administration of a vital statistics system.

These general and comprehensive studies and recommendations were preceded by work on specific classification problems. Probably the first recognition of the need for internationally comparable vital statistics was expressed in the desire for a uniform classification of causes of death. This recognition came from the International Statistical Congress in 1853, at which Dr. William Farr and Dr. Marc d'Espine were requested to prepare a uniform nomenclature of causes of death applicable to all countries. Although the original classifications were not universally accepted, some of the principles of classification were carried over into later lists.

The first international list of causes of death was approved at an international conference called to consider this problem in 1900. The list went through three editions under the auspices of the institute. The League of Nations participated in the fourth and fifth revisions, and in 1946 responsibility for the development of the list was delegated to the World Health Organization. In 1948 a major revision of the classification took place, and the classification was extended to cover morbidity as well as mortality. This sixth revision of the list, entitled "International Statistical Classification of Diseases, Injuries, and Causes of Death," is published as Supplement 1 to the bulletin of the World Health Organization (1948). A seventh revision of the classification is now being prepared by the World Health Organization, and this revision will become the international standard after 1955.

The classification of certain other items—birth order, period of gestation, hospitalization, etc.—presents problems of unique interest to the field of vital statistics. Other basic vital statistics classifications—occupation, industry, status, level of education, etc.—should be kept in agreement with the corresponding classifications used for population censuses. A discussion of the classification of these various items can be found in the *Handbook of Vital Statistics Methods.*

Equally important is agreement on standard definitions of the essential vital statistics variables. Again, many of the definitions in vital statistics are the same as those recommended for population censuses, but others apply only to information on vital events. One of the most fundamental international definitions relates to the distinction between live birth and stillbirth.

International standardization of the definition of live birth and stillbirth was first attempted by the International Statistical Institute at its 1915 session, when it had for consideration a definition developed by the Royal Statistical Society's Special Committee on Infantile Mortality. According to the International Statistical Institute, the criterion for determining the presence of life or its absence (stillbirth) should be "any sign of life." The League of Nations Health Committee (1925) subsequently undertook a study of the problem and recommended in 1925 that the criterion should be "breathing" rather than "any sign."

Both of these definitions had adherents, and in various countries the legal implications of the two definitions were quite different. In 1950, the World Health Assembly adopted a new definition at the recommendation of its Expert Committee on Health Statistics. The new definition of live birth had as its object the registration and statistical reporting of every product of conception which shows any sign of life after birth. The reverse of the live-birth definition is that of "fetal death" rather than "stillbirth," and it was designed to eliminate the variation among countries in the criterion chosen for "evidence of life" or its absence.

International definitions for statistical purposes of the other major vital events (death, marriage, and divorce) are set forth in *Principles for a Vital Statistics System.* However, in order to achieve international comparability, other items of information collected for vital statistical purposes should be clearly defined. To assist in standardization, the United Nations has set forth (in Principle 309) a recommended definition of the following items:

age
attendant at birth
birth order
cause of death
certifier
date of birth
date of marriage
date of occurrence
date of registration
duration of marriage
hospitalization
industry
legitimacy
level of formal education
literacy
live-birth order
marital status
marriage birth order
number of children born to this mother
number of dependent children
number of previous marriages
occupation
period of gestation
place of occurrence
place of usual residence
status
total birth order
type of birth
type of certification
weight at birth

A fully developed vital registration system would form the source of rich and useful demographic data. Such a system would provide current and complete data on the number of births, deaths, stillbirths, marriages, and divorces covering every segment of the population and all areas of the country. The system would yield monthly and annual indexes showing trends of totals and detailed annual classifications and cross-classifications by a number of biological, social, and economic characteristics.

Comparing this utopian standard with the systems actually existing, there can be seen a tremendously wide range of development. For many areas of the world there exist not even the most rudimentary statistical data on vital events. Even the gross rate of addition to the population or the gross population loss due to death is not known with any precision. For other countries of the world the vital statistics system is efficient and accurate and yields a wealth of useful data. Even for those systems, however, there is still progress to be made in improving the exactness of the information or in extending the data to new variables.

A complete analysis of the present availability of vital statistics should be based on a master cross-tabulation showing for each area of the world the existence or absence of data for each vital event classified according to each essential variable and with an indication for each item of the degree of completeness, currency, and accuracy. Such a table would be impossible to make and difficult to comprehend. A more convenient summary view can be seen by taking several cross-cuts through this theoretical table.

The *United Nations Population and Vital Statistics Reports* ("Statistical Papers," Ser. A), is published quarterly and presents *inter alia* all recent available official statistics of live births and deaths for each of the approximately 214 geographic units of the world.

These data are not all uniform in definition and vary widely in quality. Nevertheless, they measure in a gross way the availability of total birth and death statistics.

The issue of this report published in April, 1955 (Vol. VII, No. 2), includes provisional total data for some areas for 1954, although for a few areas the most recent figures are for 1947. Disregarding this time range, the report can be used to obtain a fair appraisal of the extent of total birth and death figures for the world and each of its major regions. The April, 1955, issue gives an

hand, totals of births and deaths are available for only 36.7 per cent of the African population and 43.0 per cent of the population of Asia. These extremes show not only the uneven development of registration systems throughout the world but also the serious deficiencies of data which exist in the regions with acute problems of population growth.

The importance of vital statistics in the study of population and the breadth of the possible analysis of these statistics in relation to other biological, economic, and social factors is shown by

TABLE 7

PROPORTION OF THE WORLD POPULATION, BY REGIONS, FOR WHICH DATA
ON TOTAL BIRTHS AND DEATHS ARE AVAILABLE*

| | POPULATION (IN THOUSANDS) | | | PER CENT OF TOTAL POPULATION | | |
	Total	Vital Statistics Available	Vital Statistics Not Available	Total	Vital Statistics Available	Vital Statistics Not Available
World total..	2,493,000	1,318,580	1,174,420	100	52.9	47.1
Africa.........	208,000	76,248	131,752	100	36.7	63.3
Asia...........	1,307,000	562,636	744,364	100	43.0	57.0
Europe........	403,100	380,211	22,889	100	94.3	5.7
North America..	229,900	225,100	4,800	100	97.9	2.1
Oceania	13,900	12,025	1,875	100	86.5	13.5
South America...	118,100	62,360	55,740	100	52.8	47.2
Other†.........	213,000	....	213,000	100	....	100

* This table is based on data in United Nations Statistical Office (1955e). Population data are for mid-1953.
† Primarily U.S.S.R.

estimated world total population of some 2,490 million. Of these peoples of the world, vital statistics are published for 1,319 million, or 52.9 per cent. Thus, it can be concluded at once that the most basic vital statistics are lacking for almost one-half of the world's people.

Similar data are given for the different continental areas in Table 7, which shows that the proportion of the population for which total vital rates are available varies widely. In North America data are given for 225,100 thousand of the continental population of 229,900 thousand. Europe also shows a high proportion of the population covered, 94.3 per cent. On the other

the variety of substantive items included in the vital statistical report forms of various nations.[3] An examination of all the available reporting forms for the major sovereign countries of the world showed that live-birth forms for sixty countries contained fifty-five different items; death forms for sixty-one countries contained fifty-two items; stillbirth, for fifty-seven countries, forty-nine items; marriage, fifty-six countries, fifty-eight items; and divorce, forty countries, forty-two items.

[3] For a detailed discussion, see United Nations Statistical Office, 1955c, chap. ix. This chapter gives tables showing the individual items included in the report forms of each nation studied.

In the aggregate, the number and type of the items included are impressive; if data for each item were collected by each country, the analytical possibilities would be almost unlimited. However, for individual countries the number of live-birth items ranges from 4 to 34 with a median of 19–20 items. The variation is similar for the number of items collected for other vital events.

For all types of vital events a few generalizations are valid. In the first place, there are a few basic and traditional items related to time, place, and the major characteristics of the participant which are collected by the majority of countries for each event. Such items are so fundamental that they should be universal. At the other extreme, there are a large number of

TABLE 8

ITEMS ON LIVE-BIRTH STATISTICAL REPORT FORMS

Items of Substantive Information on the Live-birth Statistical Report Forms
of Sixty Areas, in Rank Order by Frequency of Inclusion*

Item	Frequency	Item	Frequency
Sex of infant	60	Industry of mother	14
Date of birth of infant	54	Status (employer, employee, etc.) of father	13
Place of registration of birth	51	Status (employer, employee, etc.) of mother	12
Legitimacy	50	Race or color of father	8
Date of birth of mother, or age	50	Race or color of mother	8
Date of registration of birth	48	Citizenship of infant	8
Birth registration number of infant	46	Religion of infant	8
Type of birth	46	Period of gestation	7
Occupation of father	45	Origin of mother	6
Place of birth (geographic) of infant	43	Literacy of mother	5
Date of birth of father, or age	41	Duration of marriage of mother	5
Number of children born to mother	41	Race or color of infant	5
Occupation of mother	37	Literacy of father	5
Place of residence of mother	36	Origin of father	5
Name of infant	34	Is infant premature or full term?	4
Hospitalization	30	Weight of infant at birth	4
Citizenship of father	28	Date of baptism of infant	3
Citizenship of mother	28	Health condition of infant	3
Stillborn or liveborn?	27	Language spoken and/or mother tongue of mother	3
Attendant at birth	24	Language spoken and/or mother tongue of father	3
Name of mother	23	Birth registration number of father	2
Name of father	22	Birth registration number of mother	2
Place of residence of father	22	Delivery normal or otherwise?	2
Date of marriage of mother	20	Length of infant at birth	1
Place of birth of mother	20	Duration of hospitalization of mother	1
Place of birth of father	19	Health condition of mother	1
Industry of father	16		
Religion of father	15		
Religion of mother	14		

* Source: United Nations Statistical Office (1955c, chap. ix).

The items shown on the statistical report forms for each of the events—birth, death, stillbirth, marriage, and divorce—are listed in Tables 8, 9, 10, 11, and 12. In these tables the items are listed in rank order by frequency of inclusion. Many variations in the exact form of questions and the amount of detail have been disregarded. Tables 8–12 show the potential value as well as the present deficiencies of vital statistics for demographic analysis

items collected by only a few countries. These items reflect varying economic or social situations, interest in special demographic or medical research problems, or experimental innovations in collecting new types of data. Such items should not remain fixed or be collected on a world-wide basis. Variation and fluidity are desirable here.

Between these groups stands another class of items. These are items of

TABLE 9

ITEMS ON DEATH STATISTICAL REPORT FORMS
Items of Substantive Information on the Death Statistical Report Forms
of Sixty-one Areas, in Rank Order by Frequency of Inclusion*

Item	Frequency	Item	Frequency
Sex of decedent	61	Date of marriage of decedent	9
Date of birth of decedent, or age	60	Stillbirth or death?	7
Cause of death	57	Origin of decedent	6
Marital status	54	Place of birth of mother and/or father	6
Place of death registration	53	Diet of infant (decedent)	6
Date of death	52	Birth registration number of decedent	5
Occupation of decedent	49	Age of mother and/or father	5
Date of death registration	48	Industry of mother and/or father	5
Death registration number	46	Birth order of decedent (if infant)	4
Place of death (geographic)	44	Duration of marriage of decedent	4
Place of residence of decedent	44	Identification number of decedent	4
Name of decedent	39	Literacy of decedent	4
Certifier of cause of death	36	Social security number of decedent	3
Citizenship of decedent	33	Place of birth registration of decedent	3
Hospitalization	31	Age of decedent at marriage	2
Medical attendance during last illness	31	Date of birth of mother	2
Legitimacy of decedent (if under one year)	30	Status (employer, employee, etc.) of mother and/or father	2
Place of birth of decedent	29	Was decedent premature or full term?	2
Industry of decedent	22	Were mother and/or father of decedent alive at death of decedent?	2
Religion of decedent	17	Citizenship of mother and/or father	2
Occupation of mother and/or father	15	Language of decedent	1
Race or color of decedent	14	Place of marriage of decedent	1
Name of mother and/or father	12	Place of marriage registration of decedent	1
Status (employer, employee, etc.) of decedent	12	Weight and length of decedent at birth	1
Number of children born to the decedent	11	Race or color of mother and/or father	1
Date of birth of surviving spouse, or age	11		
Duration of stay in place of death	10		

*Source: United Nations Statistical Office (1955c, chap. ix).

TABLE 10

ITEMS ON STILLBIRTH STATISTICAL REPORT FORMS
Items of Substantive Information on the Stillbirth Statistical Report Forms
of Fifty-seven Areas, in Rank Order by Frequency of Inclusion*

Item	Frequency	Item	Frequency
Sex of fetus	57	Industry of mother	16
Date of delivery	49	Date of marriage of mother	16
Place of registration	48	Time of death (before, during, after labor, etc.)	15
Legitimacy	47	Industry of father	15
Date of birth of mother, or age	45	Place of birth of father	14
Type of birth	43	Race or color of mother	11
Date of registration	42	Religion of mother	11
Registration number	40	Religion of father	11
Place of delivery (geographic)	37	Status (employer, employee, etc.) of mother	10
Occupation of father	37	Status (employer, employee, etc.) of father	10
Place of residence of mother	36	Race or color of father	9
Number of children born to mother	36	Duration of marriage of mother	5
Hospitalization	35	Origin of mother	5
Certifier or attendant	35	Origin of father	5
Occupation of mother	34	Weight of fetus at delivery	3
Date of birth of father, or age	32	Literacy of mother	3
Cause of stillbirth (fetal death)	31	Literacy of father	3
Stillbirth, live birth, or death?	27	Birth registration number of mother	2
Name of mother	26	Birth registration number of father	2
Name of fetus	24	Is fetus premature or full term?	2
Citizenship of mother	24	Length of fetus at delivery	1
Period of gestation	23	Language of mother	1
Name of father	23	Language of father	1
Citizenship of father	20		
Place of residence of father	17		
Place of birth of mother	17		

*Source: United Nations Statistical Office (1955c, chap. ix).

general applicability which have, for the most part, passed the experimental stage and which show the extension of traditional vital statistics to new areas of interest. These items include variables relating vital events to the distributions of the basic economic, social, and cultural characteristics of the populations concerned. The use of these

event, the date of its occurrence and registration, and the main personal characteristics of the individuals involved—such as sex, age, and place of usual residence—are almost universal.

For live births (Table 8) legitimacy, age of mother and father, type of birth (i.e., twin, triplet, etc.), occupation of

TABLE 11

ITEMS ON MARRIAGE STATISTICAL REPORT FORMS
Items of Substantive Information on the Marriage Statistical Report Forms
of Fifty-six Areas, in Rank Order by Frequency of Inclusion*

Item	Frequency	Item	Frequency
Date of birth of bride, or age	54	Industry of bride	9
Date of birth of groom, or age	54	Relationship of bride to groom	9
Marital status of bride	52	Relationship of groom to bride	9
Marital status of groom	52	Race or color of bride	8
Place of marriage registration	49	Race or color of groom	8
Occupation of groom	46	Names of fathers of participants	8
Marriage registration number	44	Occupation of fathers of participants	8
Date of marriage	43	Number of children of previous marriages of bride	7
Date of marriage registration	42	Number of children of previous marriages of groom	7
Occupation of bride	41	Date of dissolution of last marriage of bride	6
Citizenship of bride	37	Date of dissolution of last marriage of groom	6
Citizenship of groom	37	Origin of bride	5
Place of residence of groom	35	Origin of groom	5
Place of residence of bride	33	Names of mothers of participants	4
Name of groom	28	Identification number of bride	3
Name of bride	27	Identification number of groom	3
Place of marriage	27	Language spoken and/or mother tongue of bride	3
Place of birth of bride	24	Language spoken and/or mother tongue of groom	3
Place of birth of groom	24	Occupations of mothers of participants	2
Religion of bride	19	Places of birth of fathers of participants	2
Religion of groom	19	Places of birth of mothers of participants	2
Literacy of groom	19	Legitimacy of bride	1
Number of previous marriages of bride	18	Legitimacy of groom	1
Number of previous marriages of groom	18	Citizenship of fathers of participants	1
Literacy or level of formal education of bride	18	Citizenship of mothers of participants	1
Type of marriage (civil, religious, customary)	14	Places of residence of fathers of participants	1
Number of children (of bride) legitimized by this marriage	13	Places of residence of mothers of participants	1
Status (employer, employee, etc.) of bride	13		
Status (employer, employee, etc.) of groom	13		
Officiant of marriage	12		
Industry of groom	10		

* Source: United Nations Statistical Office (1955c, chap. ix).

ulations concerned. The use of these types of items is not well developed, and it is in this area that the greatest gaps exist in the potentially available vital statistics.

Many of the items most often used in demographic analysis are included in the statistical report forms of a majority of countries. The place of the

father, and number of children born to the mother are included in the forms of at least two-thirds of the sixty countries studied. But most of these topics are so fundamental to natality analysis that any omission of them is surprising. Many other items—national origin of mother, race, mother's language, religion, etc.—occur with less frequency, and some of these indicate special national interests or problems. Important as they may be for adequate analysis of the data for certain countries, it would not be expected that data on these items would be collected by all countries of the world. Other items which occur with lesser frequency show the interest of certain countries in using the vital registration system to collect information of a quasi-medical character. Items of this type are the countries collect such data simultaneously or that any countries do so continuously. The total fund of demographic knowledge may be increased if different countries develop different research studies. At least the demographer should not expect to find universal data for such specialized fields of study.

For mortality the situation (as shown in Table 9) is analogous. The

TABLE 12

ITEMS ON DIVORCE STATISTICAL REPORT FORMS
Items of Substantive Information on the Divorce Statistical Report Forms
of Forty Areas, in Rank Order by Frequency of Inclusion*

Item	Frequency	Item	Frequency
Number of children of divorcees........	32	Party found guilty...................	6
Date of divorce or final court decision...	31	Status (employer, employee, etc.) of divorcees	6
Date of birth of divorcees, or age.......	31	Type of divorce (mutual consent, other).	6
Grounds for divorce	30	Separation prior to divorce............	6
Occupation of divorcees..............	28	Date of marriage registration..........	5
Place of divorce (geographic and/or court)	28	Industry of divorcees.................	5
Registration number.................	26	Number of previous marriages of divorcees	5
Date of divorce registration...........	24	Place of residence (last common) of divorcees	4
Date of marriage being dissolved.......	23	Party to whom divorce granted........	4
Party who requested divorce (petitioner).	22	Race or color of divorcees............	4
Place of divorce registration...........	20	Type of marriage (civil, religious, customary).......................	4
Place of residence of divorcees (at time of divorce).........................	19	Marriage registration number..........	3
Citizenship of divorcees..............	19	Alimony...........................	3
Religion of divorcees.................	14	Place of marriage registration.........	3
Names of divorcees..................	13	Fees paid..........................	2
Duration of marriage being dissolved....	12	Age of divorcees at time of marriage.....	2
Place of birth of divorcees............	9	Identification numbers of divorcees.....	2
Date of petition....................	9	Legitimacy of divorcees..............	2
Literacy or level of formal education of divorcees.......................	9	Origin of divorcees..................	2
Number of previous divorces of divorcees	8	Language spoken and/or mother tongue of divorcees.......................	1
Place of marriage (geographic) being dissolved............................	8		
Marital status of divorcees prior to the marriage.........................	7		

* Source: United Nations Statistical Office (1955c, chap. ix).

questions on prematurity, weight at birth, nature of delivery, and the health condition of the mother and child. Since these items relate to the medical or biological aspects of natality, they have universal applicability, and in most instances they provide material for special scientific studies which have some validity beyond the geographic area for which the study was made. In such cases it is not necessary that all time and place of the event and the personal characteristics of the deceased generally are covered. In addition, the medical information on the cause and circumstances of the death is collected by practically all of the sixty-one areas for which the reporting forms were examined. Other items collected by smaller numbers of countries show concern with national interests or with special demographic or medical studies. The few comments on live births and deaths illustrate the kind of information which can be obtained from a study of Tables 8–12.

Although the coverage of items included in the report forms of various countries is uneven, information on only the most common items would produce an impressive number of tabulations and cross-tabulations. Unfortunately, there are many items of information included on the statistical report forms which are not converted

the *Demographic Yearbook* are concerned with a limited number of topics which are considered to be available in most countries and which have general international interest. It is possible to examine those topics for which a systematic international collection is made; however, the study of these internationally collected items will give only an approximation of the information available, and since the international items are selected for widespread

TABLE 13

AVAILABILITY OF NATALITY DATA

Aggregate Population of Areas for Which Different Types of Natality Data
Are Available and Per Cent That These Aggregates
Are of the World Population*

Type of Information	Aggregate Population Covered (Thousands)	Per Cent of World Population
Number of live births	1,371,854	55.16
Crude birth rates	1,342,960	54.00
Number of live births by age of mother	819,347	32.95
Birth rates specific for age of mother	640,374	25.75
Number of legitimate live births by age of mother	599,710	24.11
Legitimate birth rates specific for age of mother	430,416	17.31
Number of live births by age of father	480,564	19.32
Birth rates specific for age of father	367,733	14.79
Number of live births by live-birth order	706,869	28.42
Birth rates by live-birth order	570,683	22.95
Live births by age of mother and live-birth order	570,663	22.95
Birth rates by live-birth order specific for age of mother	471,702	18.97
Legitimate live births by duration of marriage: number and percentage distribution	410,880	16.52

* Source: The percentages shown in this table are based on an estimated world population of 2,487,000,000 in mid-1953 and on the totals of the estimated mid-year population in 1953, or the nearest year available, of the areas for which relevant information is shown in the United Nations *Demographic Yearbook, 1954*, Tables 8–20, pp. 242–455.

into tabulated data. One of the great inefficiencies of the vital statistics system is the waste of information collected but never published, or at least never published in readily available sources. This is true even of many of the advanced countries, where important information on such items as the occupation of the father (for live births) or the occupation of the deceased (for deaths) is rarely compiled.

For most of the topics, there is no convenient way to get a measure of the world-wide availability of information. The United Nations questionnaires for

availability, the data available for items of lesser frequency are generally much less complete.

Gross indexes of the availability of natality, mortality, stillbirth, marriage, and divorce data are given in Tables 13 to 16. Each of these tables lists the types of tabulations of major importance and the aggregate population of the areas for which the tabulation is available. The tables also give the percentage of the estimated world population covered by this aggregate population. The percentages are based on an estimated world population of 2,487 million in mid-1953, and the aggregate population is based on the estimated mid-year population of each area in 1953 or the nearest year available. The areas for which relevant information is available are those shown in issues of the United Nations *Demographic Year-*

ble because the time reference is not necessarily the same in various tables published in the *Demographic Year-book*. For example, Table 16 shows that total marriage data are available for approximately 37 per cent of the

TABLE 14

AVAILABILITY OF MORTALITY AND INFANT MORTALITY DATA
Aggregate Population of Areas for Which Different Types of Mortality Data
Are Available and Per Cent That These Aggregates Are
of the World Population*

Type of Information	Aggregate Population Covered (Thousands)	Per Cent of World Population
General mortality data:		
Number of deaths...	1,347,956	54.20
Crude death rates	1,313,257	52.80
Number of deaths by month of occurrence..	1,151,198	46.29
Deaths by age and sex....................	1,058,718	42.57
Death rates specific for age and sex........	661,992	26.61
Deaths and death rates by cause..........	631,948	25.41
Deaths by cause, age, and sex.............	579,165	23.29
Infant mortality data:		
Infant deaths...........................	1,278,846	51.42
Infant mortality rates...................	1,279,076	51.43
Deaths under one year of age by age and sex..	1,010,858	40.65
Infant mortality rates by age and sex.......	1,008,539	40.55

* Source: The percentages shown in this table are based on an estimated world population of 2,487,-000,000 in mid-1953 and on the totals of the estimated mid-year population in 1953, or the nearest year available, of the areas for which relevant information is shown in the following issues of the United Nations *Demographic Yearbook, 1951*, Tables 15, 16, 20, 21, 23, pp. 206–87, 336–95, 420–73; 1952, Tables 15, 21, pp. 256–63, 360–413; 1953, Table 9, pp. 166–75; 1954, Tables 28–31. pp. 516–97.

TABLE 15

AVAILABILITY OF STILLBIRTH DATA
Aggregate Population of Areas for Which Different Types of Stillbirth Data
Are Available and Per Cent That These Aggregates Are
of the World Population*

Type of Information	Aggregate Population Covered (Thousands)	Per Cent of World Population
Number of stillbirths (late fetal deaths).......	1,175,911	47.28
Stillbirth ratios.........................	1,175,911	47.28
Number of stillbirths by age of mother.......	606,035	24.37
Stillbirth ratios specific for age of mother.....	555,636	22.34
Number of stillbirths by age of mother and total-birth order.......................	458,903	18.45
Stillbirth ratios specific for age of mother and total-birth order.......................	438,065	17.61

* Source: The percentages shown in this table are based on an estimated world population of 2,487,000,000 in mid-1953 and on the totals of the estimated mid-year population in 1953, or the nearest year available, of the areas for which relevant information is shown in the United Nations *Demographic Yearbook, 1954*, Tables 22–27, pp. 462–515.

book which gave for each topic the most complete recent coverage.

These tables may not be strictly comparable with each other, and they may be only approximately comparable from item to item within the same ta-

world's population but that crude marriage rates are available for a slightly larger percentage, 39 per cent. These percentages are based primarily on Table 32 of the 1954 issue of the *De-mographic Yearbook,* where the rates included cover a time span of 1920–53, whereas the percentage for the data on number of total marriages relates to the shorter time span of 1946–53. The longer time span permits the inclusion of marriage rates for certain areas for which data were not available during the more recent shorter time interval. However, these minor variations in the bases of compilation for Tables 13–16 do not invalidate the use of these percentage indexes as an over-all measure of the availability of vital statistics.

With reference to live births, the United Nations demographic questionnaires request information only on a very limited number of items—total number, sex, age of mother and father, legitimacy, birth order, duration of marriage, and month of birth. With the exception of duration of marriage, all of this information was collected by more than two-thirds of the countries studied in Table 8. In spite of this, information on the number of live births by age of mother is available for no

TABLE 16

AVAILABILITY OF MARRIAGE AND DIVORCE DATA

Aggregate Population of Areas for Which Different Types of Marriage Data
Are Available and Per Cent That These Aggregates Are
of the World Population*

Type of Information	Aggregate Population Covered (Thousands)	Per Cent of World Population
Marriage data:		
Marriages	914,410	36.77
Crude marriage rates	963,225	38.73
Marriages by age of participants	611,958	24.61
Marriage rates specific for age and sex	476,593	19.16
Marriages by previous marital status of participants	447,994	18.01
Divorce data:		
Divorces	733,036	29.47
Crude divorce rates: (final decrees per thousand population)	729,078	29.32
Divorce rates per thousand married couples	634,638	25.52

* Source: The percentages shown in this table are based on an estimated world population of 2,487,000,000 in mid-1953 and on the totals of the estimated mid-year population in 1953, or the nearest year available, of the areas for which relevant information is shown in the following issues of the United Nations *Demographic Yearbook, 1949–50*, Tables 32, 34, pp. 430–51, 454–58; 1954, Tables 32–35, pp. 598–621.

Table 13 gives percentage indexes of the availability of natality data. Information on the total number of live births is available for approximately 55 per cent of the total world population. (This percentage differs from the figure of 52.9 per cent given in Table 7. The difference arises from the fact that the figures in Table 7 are based entirely on a postwar period, whereas the trend tables in the yearbook in some cases include prewar data from areas for which statistics are no longer available internationally.) The table also gives data for other variables included in the yearbook tables.

more than 33 per cent of the world's population; data on legitimate live births by age of mother are available for only 24 per cent; and information on the important variable of birth order is available for only slightly more than one-quarter of the world's people. As may be seen from Table 13, the picture is even less favorable when the availability of rate information is examined. Most vital statistics variables must be converted to a rate basis before they can readily be interpreted, and this requires that, in addition to the birth information, there be a comparable population base. Although data on live births by age of mother are available for 33 per cent, birth rates specific for this variable are available for only 26 per cent. Similar reductions of the percentages can be noted for the other rate figures.

In summary, elementary data on the crude birth rate are available for slightly more than half of the world's population, but live birth rates specific for age of mother, age of father, birth order and duration of marriage are available for one-quarter or less of the world's population. Gross and net reproduction rates are available for about 28 per cent of the world's population (based on the 1954 *Demographic Yearbook*, Table 21, pp. 456–61).

As would be expected, the situation is essentially the same for mortality data. Since natality and mortality data are derived from the same general system, the efficiency of this system determines approximately to the same extent the availability of data for each of these vital events. For mortality, the United Nations collection is limited to total population, sex, age, month, cause of death, type of certification, and occupation of the deceased. Data available on occupation of deceased and type of certification have not been published in the United Nations *Demographic Yearbook* because of their paucity and obvious lack of comparability. However, the other items—sex, age, month and cause of death—are collected almost universally by the sixty-one countries which were examined in Table 9, and it might be expected that rather complete tabulations of these few variables would be generally available. Such is not the case. Table 14 gives the indexes of availability for these mortality tabulations. The crude death rate is available for essentially the same part of the world as is the crude birth rate. Deaths by sex and age are more generally available (more than 42 per cent of the world's population) than the analo-

gous information on live births by age of mother. However, owing to a lack of appropriate population figures, death rates specific for age are available for little more than one-quarter of the world; this is essentially the same percentage as that for birth rates specific for age. Accurate information on the number of deaths by cause of death is, of course, fundamental to the study of mortality, and Table 14 indicates that these important data are available for only approximately one-quarter of the world.

Table 15, which gives indexes of the availability of stillbirth data, shows a similar picture. However, stillbirth ratios or rates are not computed on a population base; they are usually related to the total number of live births. Whenever stillbirth data are available, there is almost always available a corresponding live-birth figure with which a rate can be computed. Therefore, although for live births and for deaths there was a noticeable difference between the raw data and rate information, in the case of stillbirths this difference is negligible. The same factor holds for infant mortality, and Table 14 indicates that total infant deaths and infant mortality rates are available for the same proportion of the world's people.

Table 16 gives similar information for marriage and divorce data. Data for these events are generally less available than for birth and death statistics. This is true because in some areas of the world marriage and divorce statistics are not registered through the same system as births and deaths, and, having less demographic and public health interest, statistics on these events have not been considered as important as statistics on births and deaths. Total marriage statistics are available for slightly more than one-third of the world's population, whereas total divorce information is available for less than 30 per cent. In both instances the percentages for specific marriage and divorce tabulations are less than for total figures.

INTERNATIONAL MIGRATION STATISTICS

Among the major sources of regular demographic statistics, the population census is unique because it is designed almost entirely for the data which it produces. Vital statistics or data from a vital registration system are to some extent a by-product of a system established to produce vital records for legal and official uses. But the objective of a vital records system is to provide an accurate recording of facts. This administrative objective is not in conflict with the requirements of a statistical system, and the vital records system can usually be modified so as to serve adequately the statistical objectives.

The situation for international migration statistics is quite different. In this case, governments establish administrative machinery for the control of persons crossing their frontiers, and any statistical data arising from these administrative measures are usually incidental. Frontier crossings may be classified as arrivals or departures, and according to the purpose and the intended duration of travel. Each type of border crossing may be subject to regulation, and regulations for different modes of travel—train, bus, plane, or car across land frontiers and ship or plane across water frontiers—may be administered by different governmental organizations. These factors make it difficult to establish within any country a simple, direct system for collecting data on the various types of international population movement. In addition, governments are hesitant to add to the usually complicated procedures involved in foreign travel, and there exists a definite reluctance to require that forms be filled out if they are needed for statistical purposes only.

Accordingly, each government usually collects only the data needed for its own administrative purposes; since these differ from country to country, it becomes extremely difficult, if not impossible, to compile international migration statistics that are satisfactory in coverage and comparability.

In spite of these difficulties, continuous efforts have been made to develop international recommendations for procedures which could be adopted by countries so as to provide more satisfactory migration statistics. A summary of the historical development of international work in this field, as well as the 1953 United Nations recommendations for the improvement of international migration statistics, is given in *International Migration Statistics* (United Nations Statistical Office, 1953*b*).

In this report the major steps preceding these latest international recommendations are described:

... During the nineteenth century and at the beginning of the twentieth, some consideration was given to migration statistics by the International Statistical Institute at its sessions of Vienna in 1891, Budapest in 1901 and Berlin in 1903, and again at the sessions held at Rome in 1926, Warsaw in 1929 and Madrid in 1931. Migration statistics were also considered at the International Conference on Emigration and Immigration at Rome in 1924, and at the Commercial Conference of the Inter-Parliamentary Union held at Rio de Janeiro in 1927. ... In addition, the Committee of Statistical Experts of the League of Nations considered international tourist statistics at their fifth session in 1936, and made on this subject some recommendations that are relevant to the classification of arrivals and departures. ...

The efforts of the International Labour Organisation and of the United Nations in this field have been persistent and systematic, and deserve more detailed attention. Since its creation just after the first World War, the International Labour Organisation has been concerned with the international co-ordination of migration statistics, considered mostly from the man-power angle; various technical bodies of the United Nations Organization have also been active in promoting the improvement of these data from the broader demographic, economic and social points of view. The text of the recommendations and resolutions on migration statistics passed by the International Labour Conference in 1922, the resolutions of the International Conference on Migration Statistics convened in 1932 at Geneva by the International Labour Organisation and the 1949 Draft Recommendations for the Improvement of Migration Statistics, prepared by the United Nations Population Commission and endorsed in the same year by the Statistical Commission, can all be found in "Problems of Migration Statistics"[4] as well as in the original reports of the conferences or commissions.

In the United Nations *Demographic Yearbook* for 1954 an attempt was made to collect and publish all available migration data for certain specified tables. Data were collected by questionnaires sent to governments and supplemented by information extracted from official publications and documents. The heterogeneity of the published data is indicated by the footnotes qualifying the tabular data and is due partly to the variety of governmental sources and procedures from which the statistical information is derived.

The various sources, as indicated by codes in the yearbook tables, are:

I. Port statistics, provided by the shipping authorities and based on ship or aircraft manifests or other administrative documents or on individual forms completed by each traveller.
II. Statistics of frontier control, provided by the police or immigration authorities.
III. Statistics based on coupons detached at points of departure and arrival from

[4] United Nations (1949*b*).

identity documents issued to migrants by their own country.
IV. Passport statistics; being the number of passports issued to certain categories of prospective travellers.
V. Statistics of local population registers, provided by the authorities in charge of the registers, based on entries recording declarations of change of residence.
VI. Other statistics, including those obtained in connection with the enforcement of regulations concerning immigration, work-permits for aliens, transport contracts for emigrants, etc.

Of these various sources of statistics, most migration data are derived from port statistics or statistics of frontier control. However, the use of other sources is substantial; the following listing shows the frequency with which different sources were used for the derivation of data published in the 1954 *Demographic Yearbook*: port and frontier control, fifteen countries; coupons detached from identity documents, two; passports issued, three; population registers, nine; and other sources or not stated, ten. This tabulation is based on sources for thirty-six countries; several countries use more than one source.

The available data on international migration suffer not only because of the variety of administrative procedures from which they are derived but also because of variations in the type of international population movement included in the statistics of various countries. All movements of civilians across national frontiers may be classified under several categories:

A. *Frontier traffic*—defined as the movement of persons residing in frontier areas and moving frequently back and forth across the border (as in going to and from work).
B. *Major categories of arrivals*
　　1. Permanent immigrants, i.e., nonresidents (nationals and aliens) in-

tending to remain for a period exceeding one year.

2. Temporary immigrants, i.e., non-residents intending to exercise for a period of one year or less an occupation remunerated from within the country.
3. Visitors, i.e., non-residents intending to remain for a period of one year or less without exercising an occupation remunerated from within the country.
4. Residents (nationals and aliens) returning after a stay abroad not exceeding one year.
5. Total arrivals (sum of categories 1–4).

C. *Major categories of departures*
1. Permanent emigrants, i.e., residents (nationals and aliens) intending to remain abroad for a period exceeding one year.
2. Temporary immigrants departing.
3. Visitors departing on completion of visit.
4. Residents (nationals and aliens) intending to remain abroad for a period of one year or less.
5. Total departures (sum of categories 1–4).

While all of these categories have demographic and sociological interest, some of them pertain to special problems. For instance, data on frontier traffic are usually of special interest, and such information as may exist is usually excluded from compilations of migration statistics. Similarly, the categories of arriving or departing visitors or national residents departing for or returning from a stay abroad of a year or less are not of major importance from a demographic point of view. Although the United Nations recommendations suggest that a count be made of the totals of the various categories, they do not recommend that detailed statistics be compiled for these groups of travelers. Most of the statistics available for certain classes of visitors or departing and returning residents are found in compilations of "tourist statistics."

There is more substantial demographic interest in temporary immigrants arriving and departing, since this category implies some form of economic activity in the country of immigration. However, in spite of the possible importance of this category—at least to certain countries—the United Nations recommendations only draw attention to the usefulness of detailed statistics for this group, and collection of detailed data is suggested only if required for national purposes. Accordingly, most available statistics on international migration are limited to data on permanent immigrants and permanent emigrants. For the various reasons indicated before, even this limited class of statistics is highly deficient in comparability and in coverage.

The general coverage of the international migration data published in the *Demographic Yearbook* for 1954 is shown in Table 17. This table gives for each published type of migration statistics the aggregate population of the areas for which data are available and the per cent that these aggregates are of the world population. Some data on major categories of arrivals and departures are available for countries having an aggregate population of almost 800 million people, or about 32 per cent of the world population. An inspection of the data actually published will show, however, great variation in geographic coverage. For example, only six countries present data on frontier traffic, whereas twenty-six have data on permanent emigrants or immigrants.

Coverage of the few other items is substantially less than that for the totals of the categories of arrivals and departures. In general, data on migrants by sex and age, country of last residence, or intended residence are available only for countries including approximately a fifth of the world's population. From the standpoint of over-all coverage, migration data are more deficient than most categories of population census or vital statistics.

INTERNATIONAL COMPILATIONS
OF STATISTICS

The problems of missing, fragmentary, and non-comparable data are revealed when data for a number of countries are assembled. One of the first of such international compilations was contained in the five issues of the *Annuaire international de statistique,* published between 1916 and 1921 by the International Statistical Institute. This publication was followed by the

lished for the years 1922 to 1938 by the Epidemiological Intelligence Service of the Health Organisation. The Health Organisation also had issued, between 1924 and 1930, a series of six international health yearbooks covering data for a maximum of thirty-four areas.

The data presented in these publications were summarized and analyzed with special attention to comparability in the *Summary of International Vital Statistics,* issued by the Bureau of the Census, United States Department of Commerce (1940). To bring up to date this compendium of population and

TABLE 17

AVAILABILITY OF INTERNATIONAL MIGRATION DATA

Aggregate Population of Areas for Which Different Types of International Migration Data Are Available and Per Cent That These Aggregates Are of the World Population

Type of Information	Aggregate Population Covered (Thousands)	Per Cent of World Population
Major categories of departures and/or arrivals..	788,954	31.72
Emigrants by country of intended permanent residence................................	461,384	18.55
Immigrants by country of last permanent residence...................................	508,255	20.44
Emigrants by age and sex..................	430,197	17.30
Immigrants by age and sex................	486,064	19.54

* Source: The percentages shown in this table are based on an estimated world population of 2,487,000,000 in mid-1953 and on the totals of the estimated mid-year population in 1953, or the nearest year available, of the areas for which relevant information is shown in the United Nations *Demographic Yearbook, 1954,* Tables 39–43, pp. 634–79.

International Statistical Institute's *Aperçu de la démographie des divers pays du monde,* issued in 1922 for the years 1911–19. Supplemental volumes were issued in 1925, 1927, 1929, and 1931, and the last issue, in 1939, contained data for the years 1929–36. Both of these series were copiously footnoted to emphasize the lack of comparability in the data.

The League of Nations carried on the compilation of international population and vital statistics in its seventeen statistical yearbooks, issued each year from 1927 to 1942–44 by the Economic Intelligence Service, and in the *Annual Epidemiological Reports,* pub-

vital statistics, the same office (under a new name) issued in 1947 a *Summary of International Vital Statistics 1937–1944* (United States Public Health Service, 1947). This summary emphasized the lack of comparability in an extensive descriptive and analytical text, as well as in footnotes.

A series "Statistique internationale du mouvement de la population" has appeared in publications of the Statistique Générale de la France since 1907. These have been summarized in *Le mouvement naturel de la population dans le monde de 1906 à 1936,* published by the Institut National d'Études Démographiques in 1954.

The compilation and publication of international population and vital statistics became the responsibility of the United Nations when the Economic and Social Council at its fourth session (February 28–March 29, 1947) recommended that the United Nations publish "a demographic yearbook, containing regular series of basic demographic statistics, comparable within and among themselves, and relevant calculations of comparable rates . . ." (United Nations, 1947).

The first United Nations *Demographic Yearbook*, which was general in content and related to data for years prior to 1949, was prepared by the Statistical Office of the United Nations, in collaboration with the Department of Social Affairs, and published in 1949. Subsequent issues, for 1949–50, 1951, 1952, 1953, and 1954 have been assembled on a rotation plan which featured special aspects of demographic statistics while continuing to show a core of basic tables each year. The sixth issue (1954) contains special tables on natality, as did the 1949–50 issue; the 1952 volume featured population data; the 1951 issue, mortality. The seventh issue will again pay special attention to population, including data from all censuses taken between 1945 and 1954.

In the field of population and vital statistics, the United Nations *Demographic Yearbook* is supplemented by the World Health Organization *Annual Epidemiological and Vital Statistics*, Part 1, the fifth edition of which—relating to data for 1952—was issued in 1955. The first and second issues of this work were retrospective, covering series for 1939–46 and 1947–49, respectively, and providing continuity with the *Annual Epidemiological Reports* issued previously by the Health Organisation of the League of Nations. The third, fourth, and fifth editions give data primarily for the years 1950, 1951, and 1952.

SELECTED BIBLIOGRAPHY

AUSTRALIA, COMMONWEALTH BUREAU OF CENSUS AND STATISTICS. 1917. *Census of the Commonwealth of Australia, April, 1911. Vol. I.* (Statistician's Report Including Appendixes.) Melbourne.

CONGRÈS INTERNATIONAL DE STATISTIQUE. 1872. *Compte-Rendu général des travaux du Congrès International de Statistique aux sessions de Bruxelles, 1853; Paris, 1855; Vienne, 1857; Londres, 1860; Berlin, 1863; Florence, 1867; et La Haye, 1869.* St. Petersburg: Ministre de l'Intérieur de Russie.

DUDFIELD, R. 1901. "Census Taking," *Journal of the Institute of Actuaries,* Vol. XXXV.

GRAUNT, J. 1665. *Natural and Political Observations Mentioned in a Following Index, and Made upon the Bills of Mortality.* 4th ed. Oxford: William Hall, for John Martyn and James Allestry, Printers to the Royal Society.

INSTITUT INTERNATIONAL DE STATISTIQUE. 1899. "Compte-Rendu de la sixièmes session de l'Institut International de Statistique," *Bulletin of the International Statistical Institute,* Vol. XI, Parts I–II.

————. 1916–21. *Annuaire international de statistique.*

————. 1922–39. *Aperçu de la démographie des divers pays du monde.*

INSTITUT NATIONAL D'ÉTUDES DÉMOGRAPHIQUES. 1954. *Le mouvement naturel de la population dans le monde de 1906 à 1936. Paris.*

KÖRÖSY, J. DE. 1881. *Projet d'un recensement du monde: Étude de statistique internationale.* Paris: Guillaumin & Co.

LEAGUE OF NATIONS, ECONOMIC INTELLIGENCE SERVICE. 1927–42/44. "Statistical Year-Books."

LEAGUE OF NATIONS, HEALTH COMMITTEE. 1925. *Report of the Committee Studying Dead-Birth,* C. M. 1925, C. 224, M. 80.

LEAGUE OF NATIONS, HEALTH ORGANISATION. 1924–30a. "Statistical Handbook Series," Nos. 1–14. Geneva.

————. 1924–30b. "International Health Yearbooks."

————. 1925. *The Official Vital Statistics of England and Wales.* ("Statistical Handbook Series," No. 3.) Geneva.

————. 1927. *The Official Vital Statistics of*

the French Republic. ("Statistical Handbook Series," No. 9.) Geneva.

LEAGUE OF NATIONS, HEALTH ORGANISATION. 1928. *The Official Statistics of Switzerland.* ("Statistical Handbook Series," No. 12.) Geneva.

———. 1929. *The Official Statistics of Ireland: The Irish Free State and Northern Ireland.* ("Statistical Handbook Series," No. 11.) Geneva.

———, EPIDEMIOLOGICAL INTELLIGENCE SERVICE. 1922–38. "Annual Epidemiological Reports."

LINDER, F. E. 1955. "Adherence of National Censuses to International Recommendations," in *Proceedings of the World Population Conference, 1954.* Vol. IV. New York: United Nations.

ROYAL STATISTICAL SOCIETY. 1840. "Report to the Council of the Statistical Society of London, from the Committee Appointed to Consider the Best Mode of Taking the Census of the United Kingdom in 1841." *Journal of the Royal Statistical Society,* III, 72–102.

UNITED NATIONS. 1947. *Resolutions Adopted by the Economic and Social Council.* (E/437.) Lake Success, N.Y.: United Nations.

———. 1949a. *Population Census Handbook.* Provisional edition. Lake Success, N.Y.: United Nations.

———. 1949b. *Problems of Migration Statistics.* ("Population Studies," No. 5.) Lake Success, N.Y.: United Nations.

———, STATISTICAL OFFICE, 1948–57. *Demographic Yearbook.* New York: United Nations.

———. 1953a. *Principles for a Vital Statistics System.* ("Statistical Papers," Ser. M, No. 19.) New York: United Nations.

———. 1953b. *International Migration Statistics.* ("Statistical Papers," Ser. M, No. 20.) New York: United Nations.

———. 1954a. *Survey of Social Statistics.* ("Statistical Papers," Ser. K, No. 1.) New York: United Nations.

———. 1954b. *Handbook of Population Census Methods.* ("Studies in Methods," Ser. F, No. 5.) New York: United Nations.

———. 1955a. *Population Census Programme, Draft International Recommendations.* (ST/STAT/P/L.1.) New York: United Nations.

———. 1955b. *Population Census Programme.* (ST/STAT/P/L.2–16.) New York: United Nations.

———. 1955c. *Handbook of Vital Statistics Methods.* ("Studies in Methods," Ser. F, No. 7.) New York: United Nations.

———. 1955d. *Population Census Programme, 1945–54 Experience—Types of Data Collected.* (ST/STAT/P/L.2.) New York: United Nations.

———. 1955e. *Population and Vital Statistics Reports.* ("Statistical Papers," Ser. A, Vol. VII, No. 2.) New York: United Nations.

———. 1955–56. *Population Census Programme.* (ST/STAT/P/L. 1–21.) New York: United Nations.

UNITED STATES, DEPARTMENT OF COMMERCE, BUREAU OF THE CENSUS. 1940. "Summary of International Vital Statistics," *Vital Statistics, Special Reports,* IX, No. 36, 345–461.

———, and LIBRARY OF CONGRESS. 1943. *General Censuses and Vital Statistics in the Americas.* Washington, D.C.: Government Printing Office.

UNITED STATES, PUBLIC HEALTH SERVICE, NATIONAL OFFICE OF VITAL STATISTICS. 1947. *Summary of International Vital Statistics 1937–1944.* Washington, D.C.: Government Printing Office.

WORLD HEALTH ORGANIZATION. 1939 ff. *Annual Epidemiological and Vital Statistics.*

———. 1948. *Manual of the International Statistical Classification of Diseases, Injuries, and Causes of Death: Sixth Revision of the International Lists of Diseases and Causes of Death Adopted 1948.* Vol. I. (*Bulletin of the World Health Organization,* Suppl. 1.) Geneva.

WORTHINGTON, E. B. 1946. *Middle East Science.* London: H.M. Stationery Office.

WRIGHT, C. D. 1900. *The History and Growth of the United States Census.* (Prepared for the Senate committee on the census.) Washington, D.C.: Government Printing Office.

16. Population Composition

AMOS H. HAWLEY

THE MEANING OF COMPOSITION

When the term "composition" appears in discussions about population, it usually marks a turning point from the gross and general to the refined and specific. It calls attention to the existence of various internal differentials which influence the comparability of populations or of demographic phenomena. Strictly speaking, composition refers to the distribution within a population of one or more individually carried traits or attributes. There seem to be four general and related objectives served by a study of composition: (1) Data on composition make possible an elaboration of the description of a population and therefore permit detailed interpopulation comparisons. They are frequently used in testing the representativeness of strata in a sample drawn from a known universe. (2) Such data also constitute an inventory of the human resources of a society. (3) The data describe the variables essential for analyzing demographic processes, e.g., birth, death, migration, and growth. In the absence of direct information on demographic processes, composition data, particularly age and sex data, provide a means for estimating the incidence of birth and death. (4) Demographic variables, together with population size, are important conditions affecting the formation and change of social structure.

The individual traits or attributes to which the term "composition" refers are usually those believed to have some significance for one or more of the uses of detailed data about population. Thus, while the list of characteristics by which individuals are differentiated can be extended to great length, not all are relevant. Relevance may be more often approximated than fully realized. Its achievement is compromised by the state of existing knowledge, by the adequacy of observational techniques, and by budgetary restrictions. To a very large degree, compositional elements are those characteristics of individuals which are enumerable by non-professional personnel employing census procedures. Accessibility to observations, in other words, is an important determinant of what is subsumed under composition. Accessibility, of course, is itself subject to various interpretations. Nevertheless, in most instances a balance is struck between the relevance and the obtainability of the data.

The individual characteristics to which composition generally refers include sex, age, marital status, place of birth, education, occupation, labor force status, industry, relation to head of household, and other such features. Rarely, however, does customary usage of the term "composition" embrace such characteristics as physical and mental health, extended kinship relations, social class position, or accumulated wealth. Doubtless, exclusions of these kinds are due more to the difficulties encountered in securing reasonably accurate data than to negative decisions about their usefulness.

Information about population composition is obtained primarily from official censuses. Reliance on the complete, periodic enumeration is yielding at many points, however, to a growing use of sample enumerations, especially for data needed in intercensal intervals, but also as adjuncts to the complete enumeration. Composition data are also gathered in connection with the registration of births, deaths, and marriages. But since information from this source describes only the part of the population that has experienced a vital event within a given time interval, it does not provide knowledge of the composition of the total population. An exception is found in countries which maintain continuous population registers, notably Belgium, Sweden, and the Netherlands (National Resources Committee, 1938, pp. 276–97).

Because population data originate almost exclusively with governmental agencies, they are defined and obtained primarily to serve the administrative purposes of political entities. Thus the elements of composition that are represented in official statistics differ from nation to nation. For example, where a characteristic is possessed more or less uniformly by the members of a population, as with language or mother tongue in Japan, information about the characteristic has little or no administrative value. Accordingly, a question about mother tongue is not included on the Japanese census schedule, though such a question appears in the censuses of many other nations. For the same reason, some of the more advanced nations have deleted questions about literacy from their census schedules, e.g., Canada, Czechoslovakia, Switzerland, and the United States. The censuses of Finland and Ireland omit questions about nationality.

Political and social policy sometimes determine what is to be included in official statistics on population. In the United States the rigorous separation of church and state has prevented a question on religious affiliation from appearing in the population census. The new social policy in India brought an end to the regular enumeration of caste membership. Lack of experience with systematic census enumerations, the absence of a tradition of record-keeping in a culture, and other local circumstances affect the availability and the quality of data on composition. In an effort to improve and standardize census practices relating to composition data the Population Commission of the United Nations recommended, in 1948, a list of twelve subjects for inclusion in the censuses to be taken in 1950: total population, sex, age, marital status, place of birth, citizenship (legal nationality), mother tongue, educational characteristics, fertility data, economic characteristics, urban and rural population, and households, including relationship to head of household (United Nations, 1949, p. 3).

INTERPOPULATION COMPARISONS

An appreciation of the nature of composition data and of the range of their variability can best be obtained by interpopulation or international comparisons. The selection of composition elements treated here will be limited to those not discussed elsewhere in this volume and for which usable data are available.

Sex constitutes one of the most readily observable elements of population composition. Its universal recognition reduces the error of reporting to a minimum and its simple dichotomy invites few problems of classification. At the same time, sex is undoubtedly one of the most important of all demographic characteristics. Sex composition affects directly the incidence of birth, death, and marriage; it appears as a differential in migrant status, occupational distribution, and in virtually all other distributions of characteristics; and it is used as a basis of distinction in almost every aspect of social structure.

Sex composition is conventionally expressed as a ratio of males per 100 females, the sex ratio. A series of sex ratios for a number of selected countries is shown in Table 18. The third column of that table shows a variation of sex composition from 87 males per 100 females in Iraq (1947) to over 106 in British Borneo (1951). In most cases, however, the ratios depart from unity by small amounts either positively or negatively. When the sex ratios for all ages are compared with those for age 0–1, certain inconsistencies appear. As a rule, the sex ratio at birth exceeds 100 and varies inversely with the frequency of prenatal losses. Where prenatal losses are low, as in the high level-of-living areas of the West, the sex ratios at birth are usually around 105 to 106. On the other hand, in low level-of-living areas where the frequencies of prenatal losses are relatively high, sex ratios at birth vary around 102. Furthermore, under conditions of stable birth and death rates and no net migration, mortality differentials, which normally favor females, produce a steady decline of the sex ratio with each advance of age; the ratio arrives at unity between ages forty and fifty, depending on the particular schedule of age-specific mortality rates obtaining, and for the total population averages 94 to 97 males per 100 females. The principal exceptions to this pattern of variation occur where maternal mortality is high enough to offset the relatively low mortality of females in the non-reproductive ages. In the light of this knowledge, the ratios for Turkey seem to be much too high—suggesting a large underenumeration of females. A similar inference may be applied to India, the Philippines, Puerto Rico, and Venezuela, though the high ratios for all ages may be due at least partially to high maternal mortality. The ratios shown for British Borneo, India, and the Union of South Africa are curious. When the sex ratio for all ages

exceeds the ratio for the first year of life, one or more of several circumstances may be responsible: (1) there may have been an underreporting of male infants; (2) an underreporting of male infants may have been combined with an underenumeration of females in ages above one year; (3) the ages of infant males may have been over-

TABLE 18

MALES PER HUNDRED FEMALES, BY COUNTRY AND LATEST CENSUS YEAR*

COUNTRY	CENSUS YEAR	MALES PER HUNDRED FEMALES	
		All Ages	Age 0–1
British Borneo....	1951	106.5	100.3
India............	1951	105.6	102.9
Union of South Africa.........	1946	103.5	96.8
Venezuela........	1950	102.8	104.2
Puerto Rico......	1950	101.0	102.5
Turkey..........	1950	101.0	113.8
Philippines.......	1948	100.7	107.5
Dominican Republic.............	1950	100.5	101.2
Costa Rica.......	1950	99.7	104.3
Bechuanaland....	1946	99.1	94.4
Sweden..........	1950	99.2	106.5
United States.....	1950	98.6	103.7
Denmark.........	1950	98.4	103.3
Norway..........	1950	98.3	105.1
Egypt...........	1947	98.1	103.2
Mexico..........	1950	97.0	102.1
Japan...........	1950	96.2	104.2
Nigeria..........	1952	95.8	97.3
Paraguay.........	1950	95.5	103.9
Haiti............	1950	94.5	97.6
Switzerland.......	1950	93.0	105.5
Spain...........	1950	92.8	105.0
Yugoslavia.......	1948	92.6	105.0
United Kingdom..	1951	92.4	105.4
Austria..........	1951	86.6	104.0
Iraq.............	1947	87.2	.....

* Source: Computed from data in United Nations *Demographic Yearbook, 1953* (1954), Table 4; United Nations *Demographic Yearbook, 1954* (1955), Table 3.

stated or the ages of female children understated; (4) there may have been a substantial net immigration of males; or (5) there may have been a substantial net emigration of females. In the absence of net migration as a cause of unexpected sex ratios, a combination of ratios such as that observed in the four countries constitutes presumptive evidence of census errors. Ratios of less than ninety-four for all ages—as in Switzerland, Spain, Yugoslavia, the

United Kingdom, Austria, and Iraq—while abnormal, may be due to excess war mortality among males or to net emigration of males.

Age shares the universal recognition accorded to sex. Its obvious importance for a wide range of demographic and social phenomena has led every people to give attention to age, though with varying degrees of precision. Age restricts participation in reproduction and fixes the outer limits on the number of babies that can be born at any one time. The age distribution of a population also affects the incidence of mortality and influences the number of deaths that can occur in a given time interval. Since physical capability and mental maturity are associated with age, the roles and responsibilities of a society are distributed according to the age attained. This is most conspicuous in the composition of the labor force, but it is visible also in the membership of all social categories recognized by a society. It is manifested, too, in the distinctive age composition of migrants. Needless to say, there are large differences in the treatment of age in different societies.

The age composition of a population is a product of the birth, death, and migration rates that have operated over a period of three to four generations. It is a record of the effects of historical events that have influenced vital rates during the lifetime of the living members of a population. An accurate reading of that record from the age distribution of a given census year, however, is impossible without the aid of supplementary information. Still, given the present state of knowledge, fairly dependable inferences about the nature of recent and current trends can be made from age distribution data.

The distributions in Table 19 embrace virtually the full range of differences among populations about the world in the middle of the twentieth century. At one extreme are populations with two-fifths or more of their members under fifteen years of age, a little over one-half in ages fifteen to sixty-four years, and negligible proportions sixty-five years of age and over. Such a distribution is characteristic of a population in which high birth and death rates prevail. At the other extreme are populations with about one-fifth of their totals in the youngest age group, two-thirds or more between ages fifteen and sixty-four, and 7 per cent or more in the oldest age group. Populations of this type, found mainly in Europe, North America, and Oceania, are distinguished by low birth and death rates. Their peculiar distributions have resulted from comparatively recent declines in fertility, supplemented in North America, and Oceania by substantial net immigrations. To the extent that the large proportions in ages fifteen to sixty-four are the products of former high fertility rates, the population at these ages cannot be fully replaced on the basis of the fertility rates which gave rise to the groups under fifteen years of age. Such populations experience rising average ages. The age compositions of certain other countries are in transitional phases. In Japan and Yugoslavia death-rate decline is well advanced, whereas birth rates have only recently begun to fall. Recent declines in mortality unaccompanied by changes in fertility may account for the large numbers under fifteen years of age in the Dominican Republic, Paraguay, and the Philippines. On the other hand, the age composition of Egypt appears to have been more or less constant through the forty years preceding the census of 1947 (El-Badry, 1955). The dynamics of age composition have been analyzed by Lorimer (1951) with various assumptions regarding changes in vital rates.

A high proportion of the population in the years of childhood means a heavy dependency burden on the economically active members of the population. There are over 90 persons under fifteen and over sixty-five years of age for every 100 persons fifteen to sixty-four years of age in Paraguay, the Philippines, and the Dominican Republic; in Switzerland, the United Kingdom, and Austria there are fewer than 50 de-

composition of India and Spain, shown in Table 19, since neither of these populations has experienced substantial declines of fertility or large net gains through migration. Errors of age reporting are of various kinds. In societies where illiteracy is prevalent and life is primitive, the precise measurement of age serves no useful purpose. Accord-

TABLE 19

PERCENTAGE AGE DISTRIBUTION OF SELECTED POPULATIONS,
BY COUNTRY, FOR LATEST CENSUS YEAR*

Country and Census Year	Under 15	15–64	65 and Over	Ratio of under 15 and 65 and Over to 15–64
Dominican Republic (1950)	44.5	52.5	2.8	90.1
Philippines (1948)	44.4	52.5	3.1	90.6
Paraguay† (1950)	43.7	52.2	3.8	91.0
Puerto Rico (1950)	43.2	52.8	3.9	89.2
Costa Rica (1950)	42.9	54.1	2.9	84.6
Mexico (1950)	41.7	54.7	3.1	81.9
Venezuela‡ (1950)	41.6	55.4	2.8	80.1
British Borneo (1951)	39.5	59.3‖	1 2#	68.6
Turkey (1950)	38.3	58.3	3.3	71.3
Egypt (1947)	38.1	58.8	3.1	70.1
Haiti (1950)	37.8	58.2	3.9	71.8
Union of South Africa (1946)	37.5	57.9	4.3	72.1
Bechuanaland (1946)	36.3	58.5	4.6	69.9
Japan§ (1950)	35.5	59.5	5.0	68.1
Yugoslavia (1948)	32.0	62.3	5.7	60.5
United States (1950)	26.9	64.9	8.2	54.1
Spain (1950)	26.2	66.5	7.2	50.2
Denmark (1950)	26.2	64.5	9.1	54.7
India (1951)	37.4	59.0	3.6	69.5
Norway (1950)	24.3	66.0	9.7	51.5
Switzerland (1950)	23.5	66.8	9.6	49.5
Sweden (1950)	23.4	66.3	10.2	50.6
United Kingdom (1951)	22.2	66.8	11.0	49.7
Austria (1951)	22.9	66.5	10.6	50.4

* Source: Computed from data in United Nations *Demographic Yearbook, 1953* (1954), Table 3; United Nations *Demographic Yearbook, 1954* (1955), Table 3. Unknown ages are omitted.

† Adjusted for underenumeration.

‡ Excluding jungle populations, estimated at 67,067 in 1950.

§ Estimated on the basis of a sample drawn from census returns.

‖ Includes ages 15–69 years.

Includes ages 70 years and over.

pendents per 100 persons in the productive ages. These data cannot be regarded as better than first approximations, however. In most parts of the world participation in the labor force begins before age fifteen and continues beyond age sixty-five, as is indicated in Table 20.

The erroneous reporting of age is a persistent problem. It is probable that this lies behind the unexpected age

ingly, individuals seldom know their ages. In such instances, as in the British East African census of 1948 (Martin, 1953), the practice is to instruct enumerators to estimate individual ages within broad categories. Errors also result from a preference for certain digits, e.g., zeros, fives, and even numbers. Technically advanced populations as well as less advanced populations exhibit a digit preference, though to a lesser degree. Individuals who fear that accurate recording will expose them to the undesirable effects of economic, military, or other official policies may report erroneous ages. It is for this reason that census agencies often protect the confidential character of individual data.

Marital status is a third element of composition of considerable importance. It has direct bearing on the computation of measures of reproduction

TABLE 20

PERCENTAGE OF ECONOMICALLY ACTIVE MALES AMONG ALL MALES IN SELECTED AGES, BY COUNTRY*

Country and Census Year	10–14 Years	65 Years and Over
Industrial countries:		
United States (1940)	1.2	41.8
Australia (1933)	3.1	43.4
Sweden (1940)	1.9	42.6
France (1936)	14.2	53.7
Semi-industrial countries:		
Japan (1930)	14.1	64.0
Italy (1936)	26.9	61.8
Greece (1928)	21.4	78.8
Portugal (1940)	26.2	87.0
Jamaica (1943)	4.0	62.3
Panama (1940)	19.7	82.9
Agricultural countries:		
Peru (1940)	22.8	82.6
Brazil (1940)	30.4	75.1
Turkey (1945)	48.7	79.0
Egypt (1937)	63.4	85.6
Philippines (1939)	26.5	53.1
U.S.S.R. (1926)	58.0	69.3

* Adapted from John D. Durand, "Population Structure as a Factor in Manpower and Dependency Problems of Underdeveloped Countries," in *Population Bulletin of the United Nations*, No. 3 (New York: United Nations, 1953), Table 1, p. 4.

(subject to the extent that illegitimate births are socially stigmatized). Data on marital status distribution describe the behavior of a population in the formation and dissolution of marital unions. When viewed comparatively, such data are useful indicators of social, economic, and cultural differences among countries. An illustration is provided in Table 21. In India 18 per cent of the males and less than 4 per cent of the females fifteen years of age and over are single, while in Ireland the comparable proportions are 55 per cent

and 45 per cent. It is clear that the frequency of marriage is higher and that the average age of marriage is lower in India than in Ireland. Although the comparison points to a significant difference between the societies of India and Ireland, the basis of the difference is not apparent. It could reflect differences in the length of training and formal schooling, in economic opportunities, or in other aspects of the social structures. Comparisons of marital status distributions provide a basis for important research questions. It may be significant that the largest proportions married are found, with one or two exceptions, in non-Christian countries, while the smallest proportions married occur in Christian countries in which Roman Catholicism predominates. The sex differences in the proportions widowed are noteworthy. They are due to sex differences in mortality and to differences in opportunities for remarriage. In general, where the proportions married are high, the proportions widowed are also high. The disparity between the sexes is widened in areas where recent wars have taken a heavy toll of males.

An accurate classification of population by marital status presents serious difficulties. The principal ambiguity occurs in connection with the definition of the married. Couples living in common law or consensual marriages may or may not report themselves as married, depending not only on the legal status of such unions in their locality but also on their knowledge of that legal status. An increasing number of national census offices are making special efforts to secure an accurate reporting of the consensually married. A second source of uncertainty regarding who is married arises from separations which may be *de facto* or legal. How are the separated members of a marriage union to be classified, and does the answer apply uniformly to both legal and consensual marriages? Although the way such questions are treated may depend on the uses to be made of the information, an official census agency must adapt its statistics to the most general use. The current tendency, therefore, is to report the separated as a distinct class. Perhaps some of these considerations account for the failure of the degree of familiarity with culture and the receptivity to new ideas and information on the part of individuals. In this sense, educational status has direct relevance for a wide array of concerns, ranging from measurements of fertility, morbidity, mortality, and other demographic events to inventories of the human resources of so-

TABLE 21

PERCENTAGE DISTRIBUTION OF PERSONS FIFTEEN YEARS OF AGE AND OVER, BY MARITAL STATUS, BY SEX, AND BY COUNTRY*

COUNTRY AND CENSUS YEAR	MALE						FEMALE					
	Total	Single	Married	Widowed	Divorced	Unknown	Total	Single	Married	Widowed	Divorced	Unknown
India (1931).....	100.0	18.1	73.1	8.8†	.....	.....	100.0	3.6	70.5	25.9†	.....	.....
Bulgaria (1934)..	100.0	24.2	70.7	4.6	.4	.1	100.0	16.9	70.6	12.0	.4	.1
Turkey (1935)...	100.0	25.3	71.6	2.5	.3	.3	100.0	12.2	65.9	20.9	.7	.3
U.S.S.R. (1926).	100.0	29.7	65.4	3.9	.5	.5	100.0	22.9	59.2	16.4	1.1	.4
France (1946)...	100.0	30.5	62.4	5.5	1.2	.3	100.0	25.0	54.9	17.9	1.5	.7
Egypt (1937)....	100.0	31.2	64.7	2.7	1.2	.2	100.0	13.7	65.1	19.1	2.0	.1
Japan (1930)....	100.0	32.3	60.9	5.4	1.4	.....	100.0	21.2	61.6	15.4	1.8	.....
Australia (1947).	100.0	32.8	61.8	3.9	.9	.6	100.0	26.3	61.5	10.8	1.0	.4
U.S. (1940).....	100.0	33.2	61.2	4.3	1.3	.....	100.0	25.8	61.0	11.5	1.7	.....
Denmark (1945).	100.0	32.4	60.9	4.6	1.9‡	.2	100.0	28.8	58.8	9.4	2.8‡	.2
England and Wales (1931)..	100.0	35.6	59.2	5.0	.2	.....	100.0	35.4	53.4	11.1	.1	.....
Sweden (1945)...	100.0	36.2	56.7	4.9	1.1	1.1	100.0	32.1	55.3	9.7	1.6	1.3
Italy (1936).....	100.0	37.4	57.3	5.3	.....	.....	100.0	33.1	53.9	13.0	.....	.....
Canada (1941)§..	100.0	39.7	55.2	4.0	1.0‡	.1	100.0	33.0	56.9	8.7	1.3‡	.1
Spain (1940)....	100.0	41.1	53.3	5.6	.....	.....	100.0	37.7	47.7	14.6	.....	.....
Brazil (1940)....	100.0	44.3	51.9‖	3.7	.....	.1	100.0	37.2	51.9‖	10.7	.....	.2
Finland (1940)...	100.0	44.7	50.5	4.2	.6	.....	100.0	39.9	46.5	12.8	.9	.....
Chile (1940)	100.0	48.7	46.8	4.5	.....	.....	100.0	42.4	46.3	11.3	.....	.....
Ireland (1946)...	100.0	55.1	39.5	5.4	.....	.....	100.0	44.9	42.7	12.4	.....	.....

* Source: *Demographic Yearbook, 1949–50* (New York: United Nations, 1950), Table 5.
† Includes divorced.
‡ Includes separated.
§ Excludes Newfoundland.
‖ Includes 0.3 per cent consensually married.

of the number of married males to equal the number of married females in over 120 populations listed in the *Demographic Yearbook, 1954* (United Nations, 1955, pp. 136–94).

The importance of education in the modern world is so evident that it needs no exposition. As a demographic characteristic, educational status is used as an index of level of sophistication, of socioeconomic position, or, in general,

cieties and the possibilities of systematic social change. It is for such reasons that educational data are collected by the census agencies of most nations.

The simplest measure of the educational level of a population is the frequency of illiteracy. Table 22 presents illiteracy rates, by sex, for a number of selected countries. It will be observed that illiteracy, for both sexes as reported by the various national censuses, varied from 92 per cent in Indonesia to 1 per cent in Finland. The range is somewhat larger for females than for males. In fact, the frequency of illiteracy is substantially higher for females in all areas except those in which very low rates prevail, i.e., Canada, France, and Finland. Although the countries shown in Table 5 were selected only to show the range of differences, many countries in which illiteracy is prevalent have never taken a census. And many countries in which illiteracy rates approximate zero have ceased to ask questions about literacy in their censuses.

The comparability of the rates shown in Table 22 leaves much to be desired. The minimum ages to which the literacy data apply vary from zero to fifteen; hence the base population on which rates are computed differs from country to country. Furthermore, census questions are phrased in various ways; some ask only whether the individual can read and write, and some supplement such a question with others concerning ability to read only and, in a few instances, ability to write. The supplementary questions on ability to read and ability to write make possible identification of the semiliterate. Even so, the level of the ability to read and write is usually undetermined. In some censuses the literacy questions pertain to any language, while in others they apply to specific languages. The Population Commission of the United Nations has urged adoption as a criterion of literacy the ability to read and write a simple message in any language. Given standard procedures in all of the items that have been mentioned, problems of comparability will persist as a result of differences in language universes and in accumulated literatures.

Of course, measures of the frequency of literacy are at best a crude evidence of educational composition, except for countries where relatively little formal

TABLE 22

ILLITERACY BY SEX, FOR SELECTED COUNTRIES, WITH CENSUS YEAR
AND MINIMUM AGE AT WHICH QUESTION WAS ASKED*

COUNTRY	CENSUS YEAR	MINIMUM AGE AT WHICH QUESTION WAS ASKED	PERCENTAGE ILLITERATE		
			Total	Male	Female
Indonesia	1930	15	92	85	97
India	1931	5	91	85	98
Egypt	1937	5	85	77	94
Turkey	1945	0	70	56	83
Nicaragua	1940	7	63	..	..
Malaya	1947	15	62	43	84
Burma	1931	10	60	39	82
Brazil	1940	5	57	52	62
Peru	1940	6	57	45	68
Portugal	1940	7	49	40	56
Colombia	1938	7	44	42	46
Ceylon	1946	5	42	30	56
Greece	1928	10	41	23	58
Philippines	1948	10	40	..	..
Chile	1940	7	28	26	30
Yugoslavia	1948	11	25	15	34
Spain	1940	10	23	17	29
Italy	1931	10	22	18	25
Argentina	1947	14	14	..	..
Canada	1931	10	4	4	3
France	1936	10	4	3	4
Finland	1930	10	1	1	1

* Source: UNESCO, *Facts and Figures* (New York, 1952).

schooling is available. Where feasible, however, educational composition is best described in terms of the number of years of school completed and the numbers enrolled in school, by age and sex. Although twenty-nine of the fifty-three censuses surveyed by the Population Commission of the United Nations (United Nations, 1949, p. 80) included questions on the level of educational attainment, the question was not asked of all members of the populations in all cases. Only twenty-three censuses included questions on school attendance, and irregular application to the populations concerned is also characteristic of the censuses.

To the extent that nationality differences in a population represent differences in mode of life, in political alignments, or in other phases of collective life, they enter into considerations of composition. As elements of composition, nationality characteristics may appear in either one of two forms. Indigenous nationality groups may have been combined into a single political entity by conquest, treaty, or federation, as in Switzerland, Czechoslovakia, and the Balkan countries. Often these groups remain as permanent ethnic enclaves in the larger population. On the other hand, nationality differences may be transitory, changing their complexion from time to time as waves of immigrants succeed one another and subsequently lose their identities in the common culture of a hospitable state. Such has been the experience in the American countries and, most recently, in Israel. In those circumstances nationality differences can be sustained for not more than two or three generations after immigration has ceased. Nationality composition, in other words, does not in all cases lend itself to comparative treatment.

Another problem arises from the lack of a simple, standard classification to which the world's diversity of national-

ity or ethnic types may be reduced. The progeny of mixed marriages add further complications to the classification of types. A partial solution to these difficulties is found in the substitution of the citizenship concept for nationality. Although citizenship carries somewhat different connotations, its greater adaptability to statistical requirements compensates for the loss of meaning. Citizenship composition, moreover, is a matter of obvious administrative interest.

Although this discussion does not exhaust the range of content subsumed under the term "population composition," enough has probably been said to indicate which kinds of data are involved and what their variability may be. Each element of composition possesses unique properties and is subject, therefore, to errors peculiar to itself. The task of achieving census accuracy is actually a multiplicity of tasks, each specific to a particular type of data.

The improvement of composition data presents different problems in different parts of the world. In highly organized modern states with long experience in census-taking, improvement is largely a matter of perfecting census procedures or of securing more adequate financing of census activity. Some sources of error, however, seem to be inherent in the periodic character of the census, especially in the problems of staffing. Mobilizing a large staff of enumerators for short-term employment results in problems of selection, incentive, and careful field supervision. Where enumerators are drawn from the ranks of civil officials, such problems are less serious. Even so, the scope of the task is so great that it admits many opportunities for error. Sampling provides a solution to this as well as to other faults in census-taking; it offers the possibility of maintaining a permanent staff of skilful and experienced enumerators. Until sampling becomes general practice, the problems of controlling enumerator behavior will continue to be a major preoccupation of census agencies.

In countries which have had little experience with census practices, the improvement of population data is bound to be a discouragingly slow process; for it requires more than a census model and a staff of competent technicians. A reasonably reliable census depends ultimately on the population's appreciation of the administrative needs for such data. Sophistication of this kind cannot be expected where communications are undeveloped and illiteracy is prevalent. Under such conditions, it is even unlikely that government officials will supply adequate funds for an efficient statistical agency. Government irresponsibility has its counterpart in the citizens' lack of trust of government, often manifested in suspicion and hostility toward a census. Census data can only be as accurate as the replies to enumerators' inquiries. Durand (1950, p. 188) has observed that by lenient tests gross census errors prevail in African countries and are frequent in Asiatic and Latin-American countries. Most of the countries which have never taken a census are in the same continental areas, and it is in these parts of the world where people are least prepared to render accurate information about themselves. Indeed it is difficult to understand how demographic data for the populations of the so-called underdeveloped countries can be improved more rapidly than the maturation of their societies to higher levels of organization. The quality of demographic data is, among other things, an index of the degree of social, economic, technical, and political development attained by a population.

METHODS AND APPLICATIONS

It has been seen that age and sex are pivotal characteristics in analyses of composition; the distributions of all other characteristics are contingent in one way or another on age and sex distributions. This results not alone from the fundamental social and economic importance of age and sex but also from their independent variability. As biological properties of individuals, age and sex are in no way determined by marital status, education, or other such demographic traits. Furthermore, both age and sex are intrinsically subject to systematic variation which can be known in advance of the actual event. That is, with given numbers of births and deaths, a given age schedule of mortality, and no migration, an expected age and sex composition will emerge.

The systematic variation of age may be illustrated with the stationary population, a key concept in demographic work. This concept denotes a population in which births and deaths are equal and which has the age composition of the life table. The stationary populations shown in Table 23 are those of countries selected to represent different levels of mortality. The percentage distributions show the survival frequencies at each age resulting from the country's age schedule of mortality for a given calendar year (or midyear). India, with the highest level of recorded mortality of all countries employing modern statistical practices, has a stationary population with a fifth or more of the total in the 0–9 year age group and only 7 to 8 per cent 60 years of age and over. New Zealand, with one of the lowest levels of mortality, has but one-seventh of its total stationary population in the 0–9 year age group and over 19 per cent at ages 60 years and over.

A related concept is that of the stable population, one with constant age-sex-specific mortality rates, constant age-specific fertility rates, and a constant sex ratio at birth. Such a population has a fixed rate of natural increase and an unchanging, or stable, age and sex composition, the mathematical relations in which were developed by Lotka (1939). Although the stable population is a mathematical construct, El-Badry (1955) has observed, after adjustment for classification errors, a close approximation to stable conditions in the actual population of Egypt through

trinsic death rate, defined as the total death rate in the stable population, the lower the average age of the population. With natural increase rates uncontrolled, such a relationship does not obtain, as a comparison of the stable age compositions for a given country at different levels of natural increase shows. In other words, it is only in the stationary population, i.e., where natu-

TABLE 23

STATIONARY POPULATIONS FOR SELECTED COUNTRIES*

Sex and Age	India 1949–50†	Belgian Congo‡ 1950–52	El Salvador 1953	Argentina 1947	France 1950–51§	United States 1949–51	New Zealand 1950–52
Male:							
Total........	100.0	100.0	100.0	100.0	100.0	100.0	100.0
0– 9.........	22.2	20.7	16.6	15.6	14.9	14.7	14.2
10–19.........	18.8	18.4	15.6	15.2	14.7	14.5	14.1
20–29.........	16.9	16.8	14.7	14.9	14.4	14.3	13.9
30–39.........	14.6	14.8	13.6	14.6	14.2	14.0	13.7
40–49.........	12.0	12.3	12.4	13.4	13.3	13.4	13.3
50–59.........	8.6	9.2	10.7	11.8	12.0	12.0	12.3
60–69.........	4.9	5.4	8.4	8.7	9.5	9.4	10.1
70–79.........	1.7	2.1	5.3	4.6	5.5	5.6	6.2
80 and over....	.3	.3	2.7	1.2	1.5	2.1	2.2
Female:							
Total........	100.0	100.0	100.0	100.0	100.0	100.0	100.0
0– 9.........	22.3	19.9	16.0	14.7	13.7	13.7	13.5
10–19.........	18.7	17.9	15.1	14.4	13.6	13.6	13.4
20–29.........	17.1	16.3	14.4	14.0	13.5	13.4	13.3
30–39.........	14.5	14.5	13.5	13.7	13.3	13.3	13.2
40–49.........	11.4	12.3	12.4	12.9	12.9	12.9	12.9
50–59.........	8.3	9.5	11.0	11.9	12.1	12.0	12.2
60–69.........	5.1	6.1	8.8	9.9	10.5	10.4	10.6
70–79.........	2.1	2.9	5.7	6.3	7.4	7.3	7.6
80 and over....	.5	.6	3.1	2.2	3.0	3.4	3.3
Life expectancy at age 0:							
Male.........	32.4	37.6	49.9	56.9	63.6	65.5	68.3
Female.......	31.7	40.0	52.4	61.4	69.3	71.0	72.4

* Source: *Demographic Yearbook, 1954* (New York: United Nations, 1955).

† Based on data for an area with 294,749,000 inhabitants in 1951.

‡ Based on a 4 per cent sample of the native population.

§ Exclusive of the Saar.

the forty years from 1907 to 1947. Illustrations of stable populations with differing intrinsic vital rates, as worked out by Lorimer (1951), are shown in Table 24. The effects of differing age schedules of mortality may be determined by comparing the age compositions in corresponding rows for each of the three countries listed in the stub of the table. For example, where natural increase is held constant at —5 per thousand per year, the higher the in-

ral increase is 0, that age composition is entirely a function of the age schedule of mortality.

The stable population is used primarily for examining the relationships between age and sex composition and vital rates. Were it not for the time and the detailed data required for computing the stable population, it undoubtedly would have a much wider application in demographic work. The stationary population is a more available tool.

Detailed life tables are prepared periodically for many areas, and where these are lacking, the construction of abridged life tables is a relatively simple matter. Consequently, the stationary population and the principles it involves find very general use in the adjustment and correction of demographic data.

For example, if age is reported correctly, the ratio of the number in one

Since there has been no sharp change in mortality experience within the periods embraced by adjacent age groups, shown in Table 25, the irregularities in the age ratios may be due, as Coale (1955) points out, either to unusual cohort size brought about by past migrations or to the tendency toward preferential age reporting. Coale's correction for unusual cohort size is to divide each age ratio by an adjusted av-

TABLE 24

STABLE POPULATIONS WITH SELECTED SCHEDULES OF
MORTALITY AND RATES OF CHANGE*

COUNTRY AND DATE OF LIFE TABLE	RATE OF NATURAL INCREASE (PER THOUSAND)	INTRINSIC VITAL RATES (PER THOUSAND)		PERCENTAGE OF TOTAL POPULATION IN SPECIFIED AGES						
		Birth Rate	Death Rate	0–14	15–64	15–19	20–49	50–59	60–64	65 and Over
New Zealand 1931–38	− 5	12.35	17.35	18.4	65.4	6.4	39.8	13.1	6.1	16.2
	0	14.94	14.94	21.4	65.0	7.0	40.5	12.1	5.4	13.6
	5	17.87	12.87	24.7	64.1	7.7	40.7	10.9	4.7	11.2
	10	21.08	11.08	28.1	62.7	8.3	40.5	9.8	4.1	9.2
	20	28.52	8.52	35.3	58.8	3.4	38.9	7.6	2.9	5.9
Japan 1926–30	− 5	18.50	23.50	22.9	66.7	7.5	42.0	12.1	5.1	10.4
	0	21.90	21.90	26.1	65.3	8.2	41.9	10.9	4.4	8.6
	5	25.65	20.65	29.5	63.6	8.8	41.3	9.7	3.8	7.0
	10	29.70	19.70	32.9	61.5	9.3	40.4	8.5	3.2	5.6
	20	38.83	18.83	40.1	56.4	10.2	37.7	6.4	2.2	3.5
India 1921–31	− 5	32.73	37.73	31.6	64.3	9.6	44.1	7.9	2.7	4.1
	0	37.40	37.40	34.8	61.9	10.1	42.7	6.9	2.3	3.3
	5	42.39	37.39	38.1	59.3	10.4	41.0	5.9	1.9	2.6
	10	47.64	37.64	41.4	56.6	10.8	39.2	5.1	1.6	2.0
	20	59.12	39.12	47.9	50.8	11.2	35.1	3.6	1.0	1.2

* Source: Lorimer (1951), p. 32.

age group to the average of the number in two adjacent age groups should approximate unity. This assumes a pattern of variation through the age range such as that found in the stationary population. The close approximation of age ratios to unity in the United States stationary population is observable in Table 25, though substantial departures from unity begin to appear after age 35. By contrast, age ratios for the enumerated population show fairly radical fluctuations from what is expected.

erage of the age ratios for the respective cohort in every census in which it has been enumerated. Deviations from unity after that correction has been made are attributable to the heaping effects of age preferences. Coale's corrected ratios show clearly a tendency toward five-year age heaping. Some gain in accuracy would result, however, from a prior weighting of the age ratios in the enumerated population by the corresponding ratios in the stationary population.

Myers' "index of preference" provides another test, based on a single-year age distribution, of the extent to which age is misclassified owing to reporting errors. If age were correctly reported, a summation of individual year age groups at each digit of age from 0 through 9 should yield approximately 10 per cent of the population for each digit of age. One-half the sum of the deviations from 10 per cent in the actual population constitutes the "index of preference." As stated, the method includes a slight bias, for in any decennial age class, e.g., 10–19, the numbers of people decline at each higher digit. Hence the numbers at digits below 5 exceed 10 per cent, while those at digits above 5 fall below 10 per cent. The blended method, developed by Myers (1940 and 1954), eliminates that bias. This method involves summing the digit populations ten times, using starting ages 13 to 22, successively. The ten series of sums are then added together and the combined figure for each digit

distribution in any large population of ages is random.

An application of the blended method is shown in Table 26. The heaping at digits 0 and 5 is pronounced. Just as

TABLE 25

RATIOS OF POPULATION IN GIVEN AGE GROUPS TO AVERAGE OF POPULATIONS IN TWO ADJACENT AGE GROUPS, UNITED STATES STATIONARY AND ENUMERATED POPULATIONS

AGE	STATIONARY POPULATION 1949–51		ENUMERATED POPULATION 1950	
	Male	Female	Male	Female
5– 9....	.999	.999	.964	.967
10–14....	1.001	1.000	.944	.928
15–19....	1.001	1.001	.947	.936
20–24....	1.001	1.001	.990	1.014
25–29....	1.000	1.001	1.062	1.066
30–34....	1.002	1.001	.981	.984
35–39....	1.004	1.002	1.032	1.037
40–44....	1.006	1.004	1.006	.998
45–49....	1.008	1.005	.986	.983
50–54....	1.012	1.007	1.010	1.014
55–59....	1.014	1.010	1.013	1.007
60–64....	1.016	1.014	1.001	.976
65–69....	1.016	1.022	1.046	1.076
70–74....	1.011	1.028	.948	.958
75–79....	.986	1.018	.942	.955

TABLE 26

POPULATION AT EACH DIGIT OF AGE AS PERCENTAGE OF THE TOTAL POPULATION, CONTINENTAL UNITED STATES, BY CENSUS YEAR, 1880–1950*

DIGIT OF AGE	CENSUS							
	1880	1890	1900	1910	1920	1930	1940	1950†
0............	16.8	15.1	13.2	13.2	12.4	12.3	11.6	11.2
1............	6.7	7.4	8.3	7.7	8.0	8.0	8.5	8.9
2............	9.4	9.7	9.8	10.2	10.2	10.3	10.4	10.2
3............	8.6	9.1	9.3	9.2	9.4	9.4	9.6	9.7
4............	8.8	9.0	9.5	9.4	9.4	9.6	9.7	9.7
5............	13.4	12.3	11.3	11.5	11.3	11.2	10.7	10.6
6............	9.4	9.6	9.4	9.6	9.7	9.6	9.6	9.8
7............	8.5	8.9	9.3	9.1	9.4	9.3	9.6	9.7
8............	10.2	10.4	10.2	10.7	10.6	10.5	10.3	10.2
9............	8.2	8.5	9.7	9.4	9.6	9.8	10.0	10.1
Total.....	100.0	100.0	100.0	100.0	100.0	100.0	100.0	100.0
Index....	10.4	7.8	4.7	5.6	4.5	4.3	3.0	2.2

* Source: Myers (1954), p. 828.
† Based on 20 per cent sample.

reduced to a percentage of the total. The index remains half the sum of the deviations from 10 per cent. The "index of preference" does not draw its assumptions from the stationary population; the assumption is that the digit

noteworthy is the evidence of increasing accuracy of age reporting by the population; the index has declined continuously from 10.4 in 1880 to 2.2 in 1950.

Given grouped age data and either

no single-year distributions or demonstrably erroneous single-year distributions, it is still possible to distribute the grouped data by single years by one of several graduation procedures. The most widely used procedure is the application of the Sprague multipliers (Jaffe, 1951, pp. 94 ff.). This method extrapolates from reasonably accurate five-year group totals single-year numbers which sum to the actual number

Age	Stationary Population 1949–51*	Native White 1950
Total	97.2	97.6
0– 4	104.7	104.4
5– 9	104.5	104.0
10–14	104.4	104.1
15–19	104.2	100.8
20–24	103.8	96.4
25–29	103.3	95.4
30–34	102.9	95.5
35–39	102.5	96.4
40–44	101.8	97.3
45–49	100.5	97.0
50–54	98.4	95.9
55–59	95.0	94.6
60–64	90.4	92.2
65–69	84.6	87.4
70–74	78.2	84.9
75–79	71.4	81.6
80–84	64.6	76.2
85 and over	60.0	65.3

* Sex ratios in the life-table population multiplied by 105.5.

enumerated for the five-year age group. Since the weights used are based on an osculatory fifth difference formula, the method is inadequate for age groups at either end of the life span (0–4 and 95–99) and for those next to the extreme age groups (5–9 and 90–94). Graphic methods of graduation are usually employed in the two age groups at the ends of the age range, though several improved mathematical procedures are available for the purpose.

The stationary population serves also as a basis for testing the accuracy of census enumerations of sex, by age. A population not subject to changes through migration, such as the native white population, including those living abroad, should have age-group sex ratios comparable to the sex ratios of corresponding age groups in the stationary population. Although the sex ratios for the total stationary and the total native white populations of the United States shown in Table 27 are not significantly different, the age-group comparisons reveal imposing discrepancies. In the native-white population sex ratios drop below unity at age 20–24 instead of age 50–54, as in the stationary population. At ages above 60 the ratios among native whites are considerably higher than the expected ratios. The two columns in Table 27 are not completely comparable because the stationary population is derived from the life table for the total United States population rather than from that for native whites only. The native white ratios, moreover, have not been adjusted for military mortality.

Some of the difference between the two columns of Table 27 is due to the calendar-year basis of the stationary population, in contrast to the cohort composition of the native white population, each cohort in which has passed through different mortality experiences. This inconsistency may be resolved by substituting expected sex ratios based on a cohort life table for the stationary population ratios, as Coale has done (1955, pp. 17–19). The expected sex ratio is computed from the products of the survival rates for each decennium in which the cohort has been in the population. For example, the expected sex ratio for the age group 30–34 in 1950 is derived by multiplying the survival ratio of age 20–24 to age 30–34 in 1940–50 by the survival ratio of age 10–14 to age 20–24 in 1930–40 by the survival ratio of age 0–4 to 10–14 in 1920–30 for each sex. The resulting male value is then divided by a corresponding female value and multiplied by 1.055, the sex ratio at birth, to arrive at an expected sex ratio for a given cohort.

Survival ratios may be applied to successive cohorts in order to test the accuracy of census reporting of various other demographic characteristics. In estimating the accuracy of the enumeration of foreign-born populations, for example, when the ten-year survival rates from an appropriate life table are applied to the age distribution of the foreign-born in 1940 and the results ad-

ulations of unmarried persons of each sex. Hajnal's (1950, pp. 407–9) nuptiality table incorporates the principle of the attrition table in simplified form. In Table 28 columns 2 and 3 show first-marriage probabilities. Column 4 is the cumulative product of the probabilities in column 3; column 5 shows the differences between successive figures in column 4; the survival ratios in column 6 are derived from a single-person life table; and column 7 is the product of columns 5 and 6. The figures in col-

TABLE 28

FEMALE FIRST MARRIAGES ACCORDING TO 1938 NUPTIALITY, ENGLAND AND WALES*

Age (1)	Probability of First Marriage (2)	Probability of Remaining Unmarried (3)	Proportion Single at End of Period (4)	Proportion Marrying According to Gross Nuptiality (5)	Survivors in Life Table of Single† (6)	Marriages in Stationary Population† (7)
15–19	.10690	.89310	.89310	.10690	9,235	987
20–24	.52850	.47150	.42110	.47200	9,156	4,322
25–29	.53063	.46937	.19765	.22345	9,042	2,020
30–34	.27989	.72011	.14233	.05532	8,914	493
35–39	.15169	.84831	.12074	.02159	8,766	189
40–44	.07992	.92008	.11109	.00965	8,583	83
45–49	.05185	.94815	.10533	.00576	8,346	48
50–54	.03019	.96981	.10215	.00318	8,027	26
55–59	.01811	.98189	.10030	.00185	7,605	14
60–64	.01077	.98923	.09922	.00108	7,035	8
65–69	.00917	.99083	.09831	.00091	6,248	6
70–74	.00214	.99756	.09807	.00024	5,193	1.2
75–79	.00016	.99939	.09801	.00006	3,757	0.2
All ages	......	......	......	.90199	.....	8,197

* Source: Hajnal (1950), p. 407.
† Per 10,000 female births.

justed for net migration, by age, the expected numbers of foreign-born ten years of age and over in 1950 are derived. The same procedure may be employed for any other age-related characteristic for which life tables and other essential data are available.

Survival ratios are also employed in the computation of expectancy tables which combine the probabilities of occurrence of two or more events. Grabill's (1945) attrition tables for single persons, for example, apply the age-specific marriage rates for single males and for single females to the respective survival ratios to obtain stationary pop-

umn 7 describe the expected first marriages in a stationary population with constant marriage rates. This column expresses a calendar year's experience rather than that of a given cohort aging through its life span. An expectancy table of this type may be constructed for any demographic characteristic (or event) which is acquired after birth, such as school completion or naturalization of the foreign-born. Brown (1951) has adapted the procedure to an analysis of the family-unit composition in a stationary population.

Cohort analysis, i.e., analysis based on the survival experience of a given cohort of births through a period of years, lends itself to many uses beyond the measurement of census accuracy. It has had frequent use in population projections, particularly short-run projections of specific population groups, such as school-age children and entrants into the labor force. Siegel and Hamilton (1952) have explored the applicability of cohort analysis for estimating net migration (see Price, 1955). Whelpton (1954) has developed cohort fertility tables, with birth-order parity, marital status, and fecundity controlled, as a refinement of measures of net reproduction. And Hajnal (1953) has employed cohort analysis to estimate the proportions marrying at various ages from the proportions single at earlier ages. These and other applications of cohort analysis are treated elsewhere in the present volume and therefore need no elaboration here.

Since the incidence of many phenomena varies by age and sex, the distributions of these characteristics can exert a large influence on the magnitudes of various demographic rates and measures. Differences between crude birth, death, or marriage rates—for example, between the populations of two or more areas or of two or more time periods—may be due to differences in age or sex composition as well as to local peculiarities in fertility, mortality, or marriage. Hence, in many comparisons it is desirable to remove the effects of differential age or sex distribution. A widely used device for exercising the desired control is standardization. In direct applications of this technique the age composition of a "standard population" is substituted for the actual age composition, and the age-specific frequencies observed in the actual population are applied to the "standard" age distribution to obtain an adjusted or standardized total rate.

TABLE 29

PROCEDURE FOR THE STANDARDIZATION OF THE TOTAL (CRUDE) DEATH RATES OF
MAINE AND SOUTH CAROLINA, 1930*

AGE (IN YEARS)	STANDARD MILLION FOR THE U.S., 1940	MAINE				SOUTH CAROLINA			
		Population† 1930	Deaths† 1930	Specific Rates (per 100,000)	Expected Deaths in Standard Million	Population† 1930	Deaths† 1930	Specific Rates (per 100,000)	Expected Deaths in Standard Million
0– 4.......	80,100	75,037	1,543	2,056	1,647	205,076	4,905	2,392	1,916
5– 9.......	81,100	79,727	148	186	151	240,750	446	185	150
10–14.......	89,200	74,061	104	140	125	222,808	410	184	164
15–19.......	93,700	68,683	153	223	209	211,345	901	426	399
20–24.......	88,000	60,575	224	370	326	166,354	1,073	645	568
25–34.......	162,100	105,723	413	391	634	219,327	1,910	871	1,412
35–44.......	139,200	101,192	552	545	759	191,349	2,377	1,242	1,729
45–54.......	117,800	90,346	980	1,085	1,278	143,509	2,862	1,994	2,349
55–64.......	80,300	72,478	1,476	2,036	1,635	80,491	2,667	3,313	2,660
65–74.......	48,400	46,614	2,433	5,219	2,526	40,441	2,486	6,147	2,975
75+.......	20,100	22,396	3,056	13,645	2,743	16,723	2,364	14,136	2,841
Total...	1,000,000	796,832	11,082	1,390.8‡	12,033	1,738,173	22,401	1,288.8‡	17,163

* Source: Linder and Grove (1943), pp. 61, 67.
† Deaths and population of unknown age are excluded.
‡ Crude death rate per 100,000 population.

An illustration is provided in Table 29. While the comparison of crude death rates of 13.9 and 13.0 per 1,000 population for Maine and South Carolina favors South Carolina, the difference between the standardized rates, 12.0 and 17.2, respectively, is in the opposite direction.

Alternative methods of holding constant the effects of compositional variables include indirect standardization and the closely related "method of expected cases" proposed by Westergaard (see Woodbury, 1922, and Turner, 1949). The indirect method of standardization is particularly applicable when the age-specific rates of the phenomenon in question are not available for all populations compared. This method simply applies the age-specific rates observed in one population (which then becomes the standard population) to the observed age distributions of the other populations. The sum of the products for each population is the expected frequency, the frequency that would have occurred had the adjusted population had the age-specific rates found in the standard population. The indirectly standardized rate is then obtained by multiplying the total or average occurrence rate in the standard population by the ratio of the observed to the expected numbers in the second population. (See Linder and Grove, 1933, pp. 69–71; Jaffe, 1951, pp. 44 ff.)

The principal problem involved in the standardization procedure is that of selecting an appropriate standard population, for the standardized rate is affected by the choice of standard. In many instances the problem is not a serious one, especially where the question asked is: what would be the difference between rates of a given phenomenon in two populations, if both had had the age composition of one of the populations? Where a large number of populations are to be compared,

the selection of the standard population is a more critical matter. The general practice is to select a population which does not differ radically from those being compared. Until recently the population of England and Wales in 1901 was widely used as the standard for international comparisons. Since World War II, the population of the United States in 1940 has come into general use as an international standard. Some students, however, prefer a stationary population for intranational comparisons. The effects of different

TABLE 30

STANDARD MILLIONS, MEDIAN AGES, AND RATIOS OF STANDARDIZED DEATH RATES OF SOUTH CAROLINA AND MAINE BASED ON EACH STANDARD MILLION*

	Standard Millions	Median Age	Ratio of Standardized Death Rates: South Carolina to Maine
England and Wales, 1901.............		23.96	1.43
Proposed by International Statistical Institute, 1917.......		24.45	1.41
United States, 1930...		26.51	1.44
United States life tables (Whites and Negroes), 1929–31..		31.20	1.36
United States, 1940...		28.03	1.43

* Source: Linder and Grove (1943), p. 80.

standard populations on the ratio of the standardized death rate in South Carolina (1930) to the standardized death rate in Maine (1930) are shown in Table 30. It is apparent that carefully chosen standards produce small differences in such ratios.

Although standardization has been illustrated only in connection with age composition, it may be used to control the influences of sex, nativity, ethnic status, occupation, income, and other variables. Moreover, it is possible to standardize for two or more variables simultaneously by subclassifying variables. However, specific rates of occurrence for all subclasses, which demand more detailed information than is often available, are required. Nor is standardization limited to the adjustment of vital rates. It is used in such problems as controlling the size-of-city distribution of population in observations of regional differences as in the ratio of physicians to population (see Duncan, 1948). Standardization is especially useful as a device for treating demographic characteristics as independent variables.

While defects exist in the techniques available for the analysis and adjustment of composition data, most are of minor importance. In fact, the statistical tools that have been developed are far more advanced than are the observational devices used to obtain data. This disjunction is nowhere better illustrated than in the life table and the various derivations from it. Conceptually, the life table is a powerful statistical tool; yet because its accuracy rests on the completeness of death registration and the completeness of enumeration of the single-year populations used as bases for computing age-specific mortality rates, life-table values more often than not contain substantial errors. The task facing demography is the qualitative improvement of the data with which it deals.

The principal shortcoming of the operating tools of demography lies in their calendar year basis. They are designed to describe relationships at a single point in time, and the results pertain to other time periods only on the unlikely assumption that all relevant conditions remain unchanged. The outstanding exception to the calendar year limitation of most demographic tools is found in cohort analysis. For reconstructions of past changes, as applied to generation fertility by Glass and Grebenik (1954), for example, cohort analysis is a tool of unequivocal utility. Whelpton (1947) and others have adapted cohort analysis to the

projection of trends of population growth and in doing so have painfully disclosed a demographic dilemma: the decisive factors which control population movements of all kinds are nondemographic in character. Critics of the projections made by demographers, who incidentally have spoken with the advantage of hindsight (see Davis, 1949), appear to demand that the demographer assume responsibility for assumptions which rightfully belong to economists, political scientists, and sociologists.

IMPLICATIONS OF COMPOSITION

Each institution of a society, in the degree to which its processes are specialized, presupposes a certain number and type of population. Hence the composition of the total population constitutes a framework on which rests the institutional structure of the whole society. This does not contradict the fact that many elements of composition, e.g., marital status, occupation, education, are themselves functions of the form and the mode of operation of existing institutions. Any particular distribution of characteristics, regardless of origin, establishes limitations on the number and the kinds of institutions that may exist at the moment or, what is in effect the same thing, on the extent of short-run institutional changes. Composition is a limiting and permissive, rather than an efficient, causal factor. While it does not follow that the mere presence of large numbers of single people otherwise eligible for marriage will result in a high marriage rate, the number of marriages that can occur in any interval is fixed by the number of eligible people available. Likewise, whether the tool-and-die workers in a given population find employment for their skills depends on market conditions, availability of capital, international politics, or other factors; but the number of such workers limits, momentarily at least, the rate of expansion of industries that depend on their skills (a situation which was actually encountered in the United States in the early 1940's). Presumably it was such considerations as these that led Whelpton (1938, pp. 170–83) to discuss the notion of an optimum composition of population. Present knowledge, far from having arrived at optimum composition, is sketchy even on the associations of particular demographic traits with particular institutions.

The economic implications of composition, especially of age distribution, have been extensively treated, though for the most part in speculative terms. Demographers have confined their attention largely to the relation of age composition to the labor force—its relative size, rates of entry and departure, and other features which can be investigated on the assumption of given age limits to the labor force population. Although economists generally have been content to deal with the relation of population to the economy on a macroscopic scale, many attempts to probe specific relationships have been made. They have dealt with the effects of changing age composition on the efficiency and adaptability of labor, on the incidence of savings and investment, on the volume of consumption, on the size of industrial plants, and on retirement insurance and annuity costs. Their efforts have been hampered, however, by the absence of pertinent theory, by a lack of appropriate data, and by the problem of applying suitable controls.

The fairly precise age-grading within educational institutions establishes a close relationship between age composition and the number of teachers, classrooms, and other needed facilities. The relationship has been extensively explored with the character or quality of educational service held constant (see Dewhurst, 1947, chap. 13). Attention has also been given to the effect of changing age composition on the creation of new families and the demand for additional housing units (see Whelpton, 1947, pp. 58–59). The great upsurge of the marriage rate in the United States in the 1940's, with the consequent aggravation of an already critical housing shortage, was due in part to the very large number of individuals fifteen to nineteen years of age in 1940 who arrived at marriageable ages during the next few years. Irregularities of composition produce successive institutional disturbances as the different demographic categories pass through the life cycle. The aging of the population—particularly the rapid accumulation of persons over sixty-five years of age, whose numbers may be more than doubled between 1955 and 1975 (U.S. Bureau of the Census, 1955; Notestein, 1954)—has spurred interest in the probable effects on community services of all kinds. This has been left largely to speculation, however. A few preliminary studies pertaining to this problem have been made, such as that by Hawley (1941), which dealt with the association of the complement of retail and commercial service establishments in United States cities with age, as well as with other elements of composition. But that and other studies of its kind employed a simple subdivision of classes, rather than the more revealing multiple regression analysis, as its analytical model.

Much interest in the relation of age to political institutions has been premised on the assumption that conservatism increases with age. Accordingly, so the reasoning has gone, an aging population means more conservatism in politics and government. This argument was greatly weakened by the observation that age is at best an index of other factors, such as accumulated wealth (Miles, 1935) or low level of educational achievement (Stouffer, 1955, pp. 104–8), with which conservatism is more closely associated. On the other hand, where age categories coalesce into vested interest groups, age composition may be expected to reflect itself in voting patterns.

Virtually all the systematic work concerned with sex composition has dealt with its influence on marriage expectancies. Beyond that, the implications of sex composition appear largely in informal observations regarding the effects of sex imbalance—as induced by war or pioneer settlement, for example —on moral precepts and community disorder.

The formation of new families has concerned economists because of the assumed relationship between housing demand and capital formation (Hansen, 1945), but the importance of family composition of a population for other aspects of the economy has received only passing attention. Lansing and Morgan (1955) have observed that successive stages in the family cycle are accompanied by different income and expenditure patterns. There is a suggestion in their study that the distribution of families by family-cycle stages may be more significantly related to consumption than is age or other individually carried traits. Perhaps the family-cycle stage composition of population will also prove to be a more influential factor in determining the volume and diversity of religious, recreational, and other institutionalized services. Glass and Davidson (1951) have made some use of family stages in their estimates of household structure and housing needs in a stationary population.

The implications of ethnic and racial composition have seldom been subjected to quantitative investigation. Janowitz (1952, p. 34) has noted the decline of the foreign language press in the United States as an effect of the attrition of foreign-born residents. There are frequent references to the

implications of the relative numbers of minority group members for the distribution of political power. One author has put forth a hypothesis that the maintenance of minority status is a function of the extent of residential concentration of an alien group (Hawley, 1944).

There is sufficient evidence to indicate an institutional basis in the composition of population, but scarcely any research has been designed to arrive at a relatively precise measure of that relationship. Although demographic characteristics are frequently employed as controls, they are seldom treated as independent variables, and their effects in various combinations, so far as this writer is aware, have never been explored. Yet the class of problems under discussion here represents one of the important contact points of demography with other social sciences.

A desirable point of departure for research in composition, using demographic characteristics as controls or as independent variables, is a comparative analysis of their relevance. For many purposes, there is probably a degree of redundance among age, education, income, occupation, marital status, family status, and other such traits. In the interest of parsimony, the redundance should be located and, if possible, measured. The significances of various demographic characteristics are quite possibly different in different cultures; if this is true, it would argue for repetitions of the analysis of demographic variables in a variety of cultural contexts. Such studies would undoubtedly shed light on the utility of a standard census format for all countries of the world and on the comparability of demographic data.

A related problem concerns the specific demographic requirements of each institution of society. This problem is a special case of the general question concerning the influence of population size. In view, however, of the confusing findings from research on the larger question, it would appear that the proper starting point is with the number and type of populations necessary for the support of particular institutions. The research task is complicated by the "economies" derived from institutions sharing clienteles, as it were. Institutions are not discrete phenomena; they occur in combination, and some do not appear until others are present. A workable institutional theory and a taxonomy are prerequisites to progress in the determination of the demographic requirements of institutions. The research tools to be employed are dependent on the form taken by institutional theory.

Assuming that specific demographic requirements for particular institutions are ascertained, the next question concerns the amount of variation in the number of people of a defined type that may occur without affecting changes in the form or function of the related institution or cluster of institutions. Research on this problem would throw some light on the demographic basis of equilibrium in social structure. On the other hand, the use of demographic changes as indicators of actual or expected social changes is contingent on knowledge about the tolerances of population size variability.

SELECTED BIBLIOGRAPHY

BROWN, S. P. 1951. "Analysis of a Hypothetical Stationary Population by Family Units: A Note on Some Experimental Calculations," *Population Studies,* IV, 380–94.

COALE, ANSLEY. 1955. "The Population of the United States in 1950 Classified by Age, Sex, and Color: A Revision of Census Figures," *Journal of the American Statistical Association,* L, 16–54.

DAVIS, JOSEPH S. 1949. *The Population Upsurge in the United States.* ("War-Peace Pamphlets," No. 12.) Stanford, Calif.: Stanford University, Food Research Institute.

DEWHURST, J. F., *et al.,* 1947. *America's Needs and Resources.* New York: Twentieth Century Fund.

DUNCAN, OTIS DUDLEY. 1948. "Regional Comparisons Standardized for Urbanization," *Social Forces,* XXVI, 430–33.

DURAND, JOHN D. 1950. "Adequacy of Existing Census Statistics for Basic Demographic Work," *Population Studies,* IV, 179–99.

EL-BADRY, M. A. 1955. "Some Demographic Measurements for Egypt Based on the Stability of Census Age Distributions," *Milbank Memorial Fund Quarterly,* XXXIII, 1–38.

GLASS, DAVID V., and GREBENIK, E. 1954. *The Trend and Pattern of Fertility in Great Britain.* London: H. M. Stationery Office.

GLASS, RUTH, and DAVIDSON, F. G. 1951. "Household Structure and Housing Needs," *Population Studies,* IV, 395–420.

GRABILL, WILSON H. 1945. "Attrition Life Tables for the Single Population," *Journal of the American Statistical Association,* XL, 364–74.

HAJNAL, JOHN. 1950. "Births, Marriages, and Reproductivity, England and Wales, 1938–1947," in *Papers of the Royal Commission on Population.* Vol. II: *Reports and Selected Papers of the Statistics Committee.* London: H. M. Stationery Office.

———. 1953. "Age at Marriage and Proportions Marrying," *Population Studies,* VII, 111–36.

HANSEN, ALVIN H. 1945. "Postwar Employment Outlook," in *Economic Reconstruction,* ed. SEYMOUR HARRIS. New York: McGraw-Hill.

HAWLEY, AMOS H. 1941. "An Ecological Study of Urban Service Institutions," *American Sociological Review,* VI, 629–39.

———. 1944. "Dispersion versus Segregation: Apropos of a Solution of Race Problems," *Papers of the Michigan Academy of Science, Arts and Letters,* XXX, 667–74.

JAFFE, A. J. 1951. *Handbook of Statistical Methods for Demographers: Selected Problems in the Analysis of Census Data.*

Bureau of the Census. Washington, D.C.: Government Printing Office.

JANOWITZ, MORRIS. 1952. *The Community Press in an Urban Setting*. Glencoe, Ill.: Free Press.

LANSING, JOHN B., and MORGAN, JAMES N. 1955. "Consumer Finances over the Family Cycle," *Consumer Behavior*. Vol. II: *The Life Cycle and Consumer Behavior*, pp. 36–51. New York: New York University Press.

LINDER, FORREST E., and GROVE, ROBERT D. 1943. *Vital Statistics Rates in the United States, 1900–1940*. Bureau of the Census. Washington, D.C.: Government Printing Office.

LORIMER, FRANK. 1951. "Dynamics of Age Structure in a Population with Initially High Fertility and Mortality," *Population Bulletin*, No. 1, pp. 31–41.

LOTKA, A. J. 1939. *Théorie analytique des associations biologiques*. Part II: *Analyse démographique avec application particulière à l'espèce humaine*. Paris.

MARTIN, C. J. 1953. "Some Estimates of the General Age Distribution, Fertility, and Rate of Natural Increase of the African Populations of British East Africa," *Population Studies*, VII, 181–99.

MILES, WALTER R. 1935. "Age in Human Society," in *A Handbook of Social Psychology*, ed. CARL MURCHISON, pp. 596–682. Worcester, Mass.: Clark University Press.

MYERS, ROBERT J. 1940. "Errors and Biases in the Reporting of Ages in Census Data," *Transactions of the Actuarial Society of America*, XLI, Part 2, 395–415.

———. 1954. "Accuracy of Age Reporting in the 1950 United States Census," *Journal of the American Statistical Association*, XLIX, 826–31.

NATIONAL RESOURCES COMMITTEE. 1938. *The Problems of a Changing Population*. Washington, D.C.: Government Printing Office.

NOTESTEIN, FRANK. 1954. "Some Demographic Aspects of Aging," *Proceedings of the American Philosophical Society*, XCVIII, 38–45.

PRICE, D. O. 1955. "Examination of Two Sources of Error in the Estimation of Net Migration," *Journal of the American Statistical Association*, L, 689–700.

SIEGEL, JACOB S., and HAMILTON, C. HORACE. 1952. "Some Considerations in the Use of the Residual Method of Estimating Net Migration," *Journal of the American Statistical Association*, XLVII, 475–500.

STOUFFER, SAMUEL A. 1955. *Communism, Conformity, and Civil Liberties*. New York: Doubleday & Co.

TURNER, RALPH H. 1949. "The Expected Cases Method Applied to the Non-White Labor Force," *American Journal of Sociology*, LV, 146–56.

UNITED NATIONS. 1949. *Population Census Methods*. ("Population Studies," No. 4.) New York: United Nations.

———. 1955. *Demographic Yearbook, 1954*. New York: United Nations.

UNITED STATES BUREAU OF THE CENSUS. 1955. *Revised Projections of the Population of the United States, by Age and Sex: 1960 to 1975*. (Ser. P–25, No. 123.) Washington, D.C.

WHELPTON, P. K. 1938. *Needed Population Research*. Lancaster, Pa.: Science Press.

———. 1947. *Forecasts of the Population of the United States, 1945–1975*. Bureau of the Census. Washington, D.C.: Government Printing Office.

———. 1954. *Cohort Fertility: Native White Women in the United States*. Princeton: Princeton University Press.

WOODBURY, ROBERT M. 1922. "Westergaard's Method of Expected Deaths As Applied to the Study of Infant Mortality," *Journal of the American Statistical Association*, XVIII, 366–76.

17. *Population Distribution*[1]

DONALD J. BOGUE

THE FIELD OF POPULATION DISTRIBUTION DEFINED

The population of a whole country may be studied in two ways—as the residents of a single areal universe or as the residents of a congeries of sub-universes of which each sub-universe has a particular location in space. The first approach, the "aggregative," emphasizes the whole; the second approach, the "distributive," emphasizes the parts. These two approaches are complementary, since each answers a class of questions that the other cannot. Both may be used to study population composition, population trends, and the dynamics of population change. In fact, any population phenomenon that can be studied by one approach may be studied also by the other, and with profit in most instances.

The distinction between the two approaches may be clarified by an example. In the United States (as in many other nations) mortality rates declined throughout most of the nineteenth century and in the present century. The aggregative approach would trace this decline for the total population over the years. It would stratify the population by sex, age, marital status, occupation, and a variety of other characteristics; compute rates for each stratum or combination of strata; and note the trend over time within each. Age-sex-color specific rates (and other specific rates) of mortality for the entire United States for a series of time periods would be the statistical evidence to be examined and interpreted by this approach. A comparison of the rates for the various strata and an interpretation of the difference found would constitute a major share of this analysis. Such research would be termed a study of differential mortality in the population at large.

At any one time the mortality rates for a nation may vary considerably from place to place. Rates in some regions may be higher than those in other regions; rates in the cities may be higher than those in rural areas; rates for certain neighborhoods within the cities may be higher than those for other neighborhoods. Thus there is internal diversity, or "place variance," in mortality. What appeared at first to be a single rate for the nation now appears to be simply the average of the rates for the subareas—the subarea rates being weighted in proportion to their relative shares of the whole. This place variance may be important for both theoretical and practical reasons. If mortality rates are persistently higher in some areas than in others, there must be particular reasons for the diversity. The distinguishing feature of population distribution research is its concern

[1] This paper expresses a theoretical and research viewpoint that has guided eight years of research in the field of population distribution. The funds for this long-term study were granted by the Rockefeller Foundation. In addition, much of the presentation relies upon the responses of fellow demographers to an inquiry about their recent and current research activities. The author acknowledges with thanks the splendid response which permits him to speak with confidence about the present status of research in this particular area.

for place variance. In the example be-ing considered here, the distribution approach to mortality would specify that rates should be established for each of various subdivisions of the country in addition to those established for the country as a whole. The major research task would be to interpret the interarea variance in rates and the trend in this variance.

To account for the diversity among areas, or place variance, one may pos-tulate two types of explanations—differ-ential composition and differential inci-dence or prevalence of the phenomenon being studied. If wide differences in mortality are noted among a sample of areas, these differences may be due to the fact that the populations of some areas are concentrated in the age groups at which mortality is high, while the populations of other areas contain dis-proportionately large shares of persons in the ages where mortality rates are low. Similarly, differential race, sex, and other composition can lead indi-rectly to differential mortality. Study of how differential population composition leads to differential population behavior is one of two major aspects of distribu-tional analysis.

There is also a possibility that in some areas mortality operates with greater force upon particular age-sex-color (and other) groups than upon others. The extent of this variation, with the compositional aspect held con-stant, is the second important aspect of distributional study. By controlling dif-ferential composition, one is able to study the impact of a variety of social and economic conditions upon a popu-lation phenomenon. In mortality analy-sis, one could standardize the rates for subareas for sex, age, color, occupation, income (and possibly other factors) in order to determine whether the inter-area differences that persist can be ac-counted for in terms of differences in climate, medical and health services,

and the knowledge and health practices of the residents. A major practical con-tribution of this analysis is that it lo-cates unique residence groups in the population that deviate from the aver-age. These may be problem areas in need of special administrative action, or they may be areas of outstandingly good performance, perhaps indicating a type of administrative action that should be adopted in other areas.

A type of distributive population re-search performed frequently is the in-vestigation of single local populations. For example, the trends in the size and composition of the population of a par-ticular city or state are frequently the object of intensive reserach. These stud-ies do not isolate a universe of variance but usually note only the difference be-tween the single population studied and the universe from which it was drawn (such as nation, region, state). Another type of analysis, not strictly of the distributive type, is exploratory re-search. For studies of this type, a par-ticular local population is taken as being roughly representative of the general population, and the interrela-tionships in this population are assumed to be similar to those in the general population or in some major segment of it. The emphasis is not upon varia-tion but upon presumed lack of signif-icant variation.

To summarize, the field of popula-tion distribution research may be de-fined as the study of a nation's or a community's population in terms of areal subdivisions, such as regions, states, socioeconomic areas, urban-rural residence, and census tracts. This in-cludes the study of the composition of population residing in the smaller areal units as well as the study of the total number of inhabitants. It includes mo-bility research (studies of migration and movement within and between these units of area). It also includes studies over time of change in size and composition of the population of areal units.

The number and variety of studies in population distribution are very large and are increasing rapidly. Yet this is an area of study with which many professional demographers have only a slight familiarity, for their research has tended to be of the aggregative type. Much of the distributive population research has been done by persons who would not regard themselves as population specialists. As a result, the field is amorphous. It has few underlying methodological, conceptual, or theoretical principles by which continued research could lead to cumulative increase in predictability and control of population events in local areas.

The objective of this paper is to inventory this field of research, to describe each of its major subtypes, and to summarize briefly a theoretical viewpoint and methodology that could be of use in bringing greater coherence and validity to the findings of future population research.

AN INVENTORY OF RESEARCH IN
POPULATION DISTRIBUTION

In order to ascertain the present status of research in this particular field of population, a comprehensive bibliography was compiled. The following sources were consulted: Joint Reference Library,[2] *Public Affairs Information Service, Population Index*, the annual census of research of the American Sociological Society, and the annual report of degrees granted, in the *American Journal of Sociology*, July issues, 1950–55. Articles dealing with some phase of the distributive aspect of population were included. (Because it was impossible to make a complete international list, the bibliography was con-

fined to the work of analysts in the United States. It would have been highly desirable to include a listing of work being done in other countries, but the resources for performing this task were not available, and the compiler was not qualified.) In addition, letters were addressed to eighty-two persons in the United States who are known to be interested in this type of work or who are chairmen of sociology departments where such research could be performed. In spite of this determined effort to gain a complete coverage of recently completed and current research on population distribution, many items may have been inadvertently missed.

The items in this bibliography have been grouped into the following categories, by type of areal unit:[3] regions, states, and local—general; metropolitan and urban (including suburbs and fringes); rural (total) and rural nonfarm; and rural farm and agricultural. The subjects with which this research deals are listed in the stub of Table 31. The entries of Table 31 are a cross-classification of the nine categories of areal units against most of the possible research topics in the field of population distribution. By noting the combination of areal units and subjects, it is possible to state which are favored topics and which are neglected or bypassed. From the tabulation of Table 31, from familiarity with the titles, and from actually examining as many of the reports as could be obtained, the following conclusions have been reached:

1. There is a primary emphasis in distributional research on the number of inhabitants and growth in total size. The total population, density of popula-

[2] The valuable help of Georgia Keck and Marianne Yates, librarian and assistant librarian of the Joint Reference Library, Chicago, is gratefully acknowledged.

[3] Donald J. Bogue (comp.), *Bibliography of Research in Population Distribution, Published and Underway: 1950–55* (Oxford, Ohio: Scripps Foundation, Miami University). This document is too large to include in this chapter, but a copy may be obtained from the publisher at a nominal cost.

tion, trends in total population growth, and forecasts of total population are items of extraordinary interest. By comparison, the specific demographic processes receive much less research attention.

2. In a high proportion of cases interest centers on single areas; conse-

quently, much of the research consists of case studies in which the history of development and description of present conditions constitute the major part of the work. Workers who are employed by municipal governments or who teach in city universities tend to write about the city of their residence. Workers

TABLE 31

POPULATION DISTRIBUTION RESEARCH STUDIES COMPLETED, 1950–55, AND UNDER WAY, MAY, 1955, BY SUBJECT

SUBJECT OF RESEARCH	COMPLETED RESEARCH					RESEARCH UNDER WAY			
	Total, All Areas	Regions, States, or Combinations of Areas	Urban and Metropolitan	Rural (Total) and Rural Non-farm	Rural Farm and Agricultural	Total, All Areas	Regions, States, or Combinations of Areas	Urban and Metropolitan	Rural, Including Farm and Non-farm
Total, all topics.....	553	264	228	32	29	150	82	50	18
Total population size and growth...............	84	29	48	5	2	10	4	4	2
Population estimates and forecasts.............	71	52	16	0	3	8	6	1	1
General population composition and trends....	131	51	64	10	6	45	26	14	5
Components of population change...............	5	4	1	0	0	3	1	1	1
Patterns of population distribution, density, or land use...............	25	2	22	1	0	10	2	6	2
Migration and mobility..	69	42	20	3	4	23	16	4	3
Race, color, nativity, ethnic origin............	21	9	10	1	1	8	4	4	0
Age....................	15	11	2	1	1	4	2	2	0
Sex....................	2	2	0	0	0	1	0	1	0
Mortality, longevity, life tables	18	14	1	3	0	3	3	0	0
Fertility...............	16	7	6	1	2	10	8	2	0
Family and household....	12	4	5	0	3	3	0	2	1
Marriage, divorce, widowhood................	6	4	2	0	0	3	2	1	0
Health, morbidity, medical services..........	17	10	3	3	1	1	1	0	0
Education..............	4	4	0	0	0	2	2	0	0
Labor force, employment status...............	26	11	10	3	2	4	0	2	2
Income................	2	2	0	0	0	0	0	0	0
Occupation............	3	1	2	0	0	4	3	1	0
Level of living, economic conditions............	9	4	1	1	4	0	0	1	0
Retail trade, manufacturing, government, service industries in relation to population	9	1	8	0	0	1	0	1	0
Commuting............	7	0	7	0	0	1	0	1	0
Other.................	1	0	1	0	0	6	2	3	1

who are employed by state governments or who teach in state universities tend to write about the state of their residence. There appears to be a widespread sense of responsibility for maintaining a current analysis of the local population as a service to the local community or state.

3. There is also a heavy emphasis upon description and history rather than upon statistical inference. The recent trends and present composition of the population are recited, frequently with only a brief statement (or no statement at all) of the specific processes that could give rise to these results. Most of this descriptive work is coupled with exclusive interest in a single area—city or state. This means that the deviation of the local area from the national total is often described but not interpreted. The end product in many cases is a dot map or a shaded map showing where and how intensively the population is concentrated. Although the production of such maps is certainly a worthwhile activity, it is only the beginning of distributional analysis.

4. There is comparatively little intensive analysis of the distributional aspects of particular population events. Instead, the approach has tended to be of a "shotgun" variety, wherein all population events for a particular area are considered (frequently in a very cursory fashion). Where intensive studies of particular aspects of population have been undertaken, all too often the scope of the inquiry has continued to be largely historical and descriptive rather than analytical and explanatory. Studies of the population of states by counties and of cities by census tracts have frequently demonstrated and described intercounty and intertract variation for a given event and have shown how it has changed over time but have not undertaken to explain the variation. In some instances, analysts in neighboring areas have performed essentially the same analysis for their respective areas independently of each other. Because they used slightly different techniques, categories, and combinations of data, their results are not fully comparable. Because the analysis of particular events has proceeded on this area-by-area basis, there is a proliferation of studies on certain popular topics and a deficit of distributional studies on others. Several important topics have been left unstudied for some of the major states, metropolitan areas, and cities. This must mean that much statistical information tabulated for these areas remains unanalyzed. In the inventory of current and recently completed research, the number of studies which are complete distributional analyses for a single topic is very small.

5. Many of the agencies who sponsored population distribution research are not research but administrative agencies. Many research persons in this field work in close alliance with local administrative agencies, and in many instances this orientation causes the research to be biased and selective in its interpretation. However, the frequency with which the studies are published by local administration bodies attests to the fact that local officials consider the studies important. One of the outstanding characteristics of population distribution research is that it has tried to be useful to local administrative groups. Population distribution research is one of the few types of social research for which local agencies have found use and for which they show enthusiasm.

6. There is scarcely a topic that has been studied at the national level that has not been studied at the local level at least once.

7. By and large, the distributional analysis for urban and metropolitan populations is much more developed than that for rural. The rural farm population has received much more atten-

tion than the rural non-farm. In fact, the rural village population is a badly neglected area of study; almost the only attention given it has been as a part of state and regional studies. Even here, attention has been turned almost entirely to total population and size of place rather than to socioeconomic characteristics and demographic processes in village population.

8. Also neglected are the small and medium-size cities. Metropolitan areas have received a large share of the distributional analysis for urban populations. The hinterland city is allowed to remain virtually unstudied; yet it is among such cities that some of the widest variations in population phenomena are to be found.

9. Several compositional aspects of population have received very little distributional analysis. Among them are race, nativity, educational attainment, school enrolment, income, occupation, marital status, family composition, and sex composition. Even the topics of major interest to demographers have been badly neglected on the distributional level. Distributional fertility and mortality studies are not numerous; they averaged less than one per seven states and less than one per twenty metropolitan areas.

10. An outstanding "popular" topic for distributional analysis is migration and spatial mobility. This topic ranks fourth in frequency, falling after studies of total population size, general composition, and population estimates and forecasts.

11. Within recent years there has been a movement to enlarge the scope of inquiry and to allow groups of persons to work together in order to encompass a larger territory and to integrate their findings. As yet, this movement has been much more pronounced in the study of rural population than in the study of urban population. The current work of the Division of Farm Population, Agricultural Marketing Service, in organizing, systematizing, and integrating the distributional research of state colleges is outstanding in this respect.

12. A hasty check of the authors' names shows that a surprisingly high percentage of them are not members of the Population Association of America. Many of their studies show evidence of little rigorous training in demographic methods. This indicates that population analysis, as a profession and field of specialization, has not yet had its full impact upon the field of population distribution.

Table 31 also shows that the volume of research under way at the present time is very large and that the characteristics of this research are similar to those stated for published research. At the present time, more time and more funds are being spent for the study of internal population distribution and redistribution than for any other single phase of demography. Unfortunately, this research is largely piecemeal, unintegrated, and descriptive. Much of it is pure fact-reporting and trend-tracing—aimed at testing no particular hypothesis or arriving at no fundamental explanation. Yet this is one of the most widely supported types of population research. Administrative agencies of many types support this work, read it, and attempt to use it in arriving at solutions to their problems. Studies that do attain scientific validity are widely read and appreciated, and scientific statements that validly apply to particular local areas are needed. In their concern with the cosmic problems, demographers may have failed to appreciate the fact that population problems become, in effect, problems of local areas. In their drive to be scientific and objective they have separated themselves from a group of professional city planners, welfare workers, businessmen, and others who are anxious to make use of their services.

Given this situation, the problem becomes what to do about it. How can the population researcher perform work that would lead to a more scientific study of population distribution, a study that will still retain and even enhance its usefulness to local persons?

A PHILOSOPHY FOR THE STUDY OF POPULATION DISTRIBUTION

Why Study Local Areas at All?

The following questions can be asked: Is not the extent of inter-area variation greatly overemphasized? Would not a detailed and comprehensive analysis for the entire United States, for each population topic listed in the stub of Table 31, provide sufficiently precise information to satisfy the needs of population experts and public administrators alike? The answers to these questions are negative. The extent of interarea variation, or deviation from the national average, is much greater than many demographers seem to realize. Only a very few local areas in a nation can use the national averages and national trends as a reliable guide and an interpretation of what to expect in a local area.

As a fundamental example, take the facts of rate of growth. The population of the United States grew by 14.5 per cent between 1940 and 1950, but the individual counties of the nation varied considerably (see Table 32). Only 364 of the 3,103 counties and independent cities fall in the growth-interval in which the average national rate falls. Instead of following the national trend, almost one-half of the units lost population. This situation is typical. For almost any population event, the statistics for the nation are only an average value; the individual areas of the nation deviate widely from this average. Usually the coefficient of variation (the

standard deviation divided by the arithmetic mean) is at least 50 per cent. This is the point at which many statisticians would claim that an average begins to lose its meaning and usefulness as a measure of central tendency, for it is characteristic of only a small proportion of cases.

However, much of this variation is not of a random, unexplainable variety. It reflects the operation of unique combinations of local conditions. Variations in physical environment, social conditions, and type of economy may be expected to exert a marked influence upon

TABLE 32

DISTRIBUTION OF COUNTIES BY RATE OF POPULATION CHANGE, UNITED STATES: 1940–50

Rate of Change	Number of Counties	Per Cent of Counties
Total..............	3,103	100.0
Increase:		
20 per cent or more...	520	16.8
10.0 to 19.9 per cent...	364	11.7
5.0 to 9.9 per cent...	307	9.9
0.0 to 4.9 per cent...	394	12.7
Decrease:		
0.0 to 4.9 per cent...	414	13.3
5.0 to 9.9 per cent...	396	12.8
10.0 to 19.9 per cent...	520	16.8
20.0 per cent or more..	188	6.1

population events. It is well known that these factors vary greatly among the parts of most nations. The population rates and proportions for a local area do not deviate aimlessly from year to year from corresponding measures of the national population; instead, they tend to show a persistent direction, degree, and rate of change. Their behavior is much more orderly than the wide range of variation about the national total might lead one to presume. But this orderliness results from differential population composition and differential environmental conditions—the force of unique conditions in the local area upon the relative status of these local areas. Only by studying population events in small-area units can these conditions and statuses be incorporated into the analysis as explanatory factors.

How Can the Population Analyst "Break Through" the Descriptive Phase?

Because his area deviates from the national average and because he suspects that this situation is not accidental but due to a unique combination of local conditions, the population analyst interested in a particular area tends to

variation of the events and attributes in a number of different areas and observation of which characteristics that vary among the areas covary with the population event. This requires that a hypothesis be formulated about what specific aspects of the environment are related to the population events. If a given factor varies independently of the population event (does not covary with it), it may be presupposed not

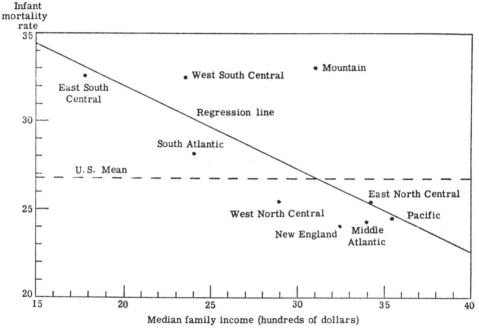

Fig. 2.—Scattergram of infant mortality rate for the white population of the United States plotted against income of families, by geographic divisions: 1950.

resort (as has been stated) to a complete description of a population event. He lets this substitute for an explanation of the event. It is readily apparent that this is not all that is needed. Any local area has numerous unique attributes. By description alone, it is difficult to determine which of these attributes is responsible for deviant population events. The factors that produce given population events can be ascertained only by a broad comparative analysis, such as observation of the

to be an explanatory factor for the deviation of the local area from the national average.

An example will help clarify this. Figure 2 is the scattergram of infant mortality rates for the white population in the United States (infant deaths per 1,000 births) for 1950, by geographic division. The average (national) rate is drawn through these points as a horizontal dotted line. Median family income is the scale of the X-axis. The infant mortality rates of white infants are plotted as a scattergram against median family income in each of the nine geographic divisions. If the factor "family income" were independent of the population event "infant mortality," the data of Figure 2 would be scattered randomly around the horizontal line. However, this is not the case. Infant mortality rates tend to be scattered about a regression line that specifies a progressive decline in infant mortality with the rise in median family income—the solid line of Figure 2. Thus, variations in infant mortality rates tend to be systematically related to variations in family income.

Data for observing this directly are not available, for births and deaths are not tabulated according to the income of the family into which they are born. This relationship can be observed only by subdividing the land area of the total universe in such a way that both infant mortality and family income may be observed to vary from one area to another. The fact that they tend to covary inversely leads to the hypothesis that they are related, either directly or through a common variable.

Multiple and Alternative Hypotheses

Family income is not the only factor with which infant mortality may covary. There is great variation among local areas in such other factors as occupation, education of parents, color, age of mother, health of mother, medical care, and housing facilities. A regression line between infant mortality and each of the above traits may show that all are significantly related to the rate of infant deaths. This does not necessarily mean that all are causally related. Certain of these factors may have common elements. Controlling these elements may remove the apparent effect of certain factors; thus, in order to arrive at a more comprehensive explanation, it is necessary to test all possible hypotheses. This testing re-quires the use of analytical methods capable of handling several factors simultaneously. These methods must be capable of measuring the effect attributable to each variable while holding constant the effect of the other variables. By such a procedure, it may be possible to explain a large share of the initial variance from the national average by the multiple covariance in a set of environmental factors. However, the "environmental factors" considered as variables are not conceived of as exerting a direct effect upon population. They are assumed to be indexes of forces and influences that are greater at a given time in a given type of socioeconomic system.

Uncontrolled Assignment of Treatments and Uncontrolled Replication

This view of population distribution is not one of regional causation; instead, it is a particular type of research design. It is no more than a reasoning by analogy from certain research designs employed by statistical analysts in the biological sciences, wherein varying quantities of various factors are assigned as treatments to individuals, with replication for sets of individuals to permit estimation of uncontrolled variables. The population researcher is powerless to determine the amount of each factor to be administered to each group, and he cannot specify how many times an experiment is to be repeated. If he employs these same statistical methods, he must do so under conditions of uncontrolled assignment of treatments and uncontrolled replication. His classification of the population according to traits, behaviors, or conditions is a substitute for assignment of treatment. His division of the entire area into subareas, each with its unique attributes, is a substitute for replication of the experiment. Both of these acts are accomplished after the events being studied have taken place and do not have the effect of randomizing errors—as in the case of controlled assignment of treatment and controlled replication. The population behavior of each subarea, together with the unique combination of traits observed for each subarea, becomes raw data for a multiple-variable analysis in which the data for each area are a single set of observations.[4]

This line of approach is indirect, and the factors which it finds to be nonrandomly related to population events cannot be interpreted as being causal. Cause must be inferred from theoretical considerations and (if possible) from more direct measurement. In the example considered above, if infant births and deaths were both classified by income of parents, the relationship could have been established directly by cross-tabulation. Unfortunately, the array of "causal factors" with respect to which population data are cross-tabulated is very small. There are only two approaches by which information about these factors may be brought to bear upon population phenomena: the "ecological" approach outlined here and direct field enumeration of the population. Neither of these can be a complete substitute for the other. Rapid progress in demography calls for a greatly accelerated development of both.

Cross-classification versus Areal Distribution

From the foregoing, it is evident that if a given attribute, characteristic, or condition is regarded as being a factor in population behavior, it may be incorporated into the research study in two ways. It may be introduced distributively, as a varying attribute of the areas, or it may be introduced directly, as an attribute of the persons enumerated. In the latter case, it would be statistically manipulated by cross-classifying it with the population events. Hence, in some circumstances, there may be a choice of the way in which a variable is introduced. In this case, a distributive analysis would be made for each cell of the cross-classification or for certain summary measures derived from the cross-classification. Thus, if mortality data for subareas were tabulated by age, color, and sex, a mortality index standardized for these three factors might be computed for each area before launching into an analysis of other factors related to the areas.

Successive reduction of the size of the area for which observations are made would make it possible eventually to identify persons in terms of the space which they occupy. Similarly, progressive multiple cross-classification would make it possible to identify individuals in terms of combinations of characteristics which they alone possess. Thus, at the extreme, one approach excludes the other. Any research study must be a compromise between the degree of cross-classification and the size of the areal unit employed in a distributive analysis. In most instances a distributional approach without cross-classification is undesirable, and vice versa. The extent to which each approach should be emphasized will vary with the problem. Where there are no cross-classifications or where the population being studied is too small to support elaborate cross-classification, the distributional approach may receive emphasis. On the other hand, direct information available from cross-classification should be used as long as it is reliable. The distributional approach presupposes that the population for each local area will be cross-classified by a variety of factors, for there is interarea variation in relationships inferred from cross-classified data, as there is in single distributions. Under very few circumstances could an elaborate multiple-

---

[4] This phase of the philosophy of population distribution has been stated in detail in Bogue and Harris (1954), chap. i.

variable cross-classification of the population for an entire country be more informative than a less elaborate cross-classification with some area detail.

Summary

When carried out as a "shotgun" approach to the description of a particular local area, population distribution studies are less effective than they might otherwise be, either as contributors of scientific knowledge or as the basis for administrative decisions concerning problems in the area. However, when undertaken as a multiple-variable analysis of particular population events for a sample of areas, population distribution studies are capable of contributing a great deal of indirect information about the environmental factors that underlie population events. This manner of approach, which may be called "ecological," is a gross analogy to the field experiments of agronomists and biologists. It should be employed where direct cross-tabulated information for the local areas is not available, and it should make the maximum possible use of cross-tabulated information that is available. Knowledge provided by this approach is especially useful because it keeps the analyst informed about the adequacy of his explanations and because it may be expressed in a form which permits its application to specific local areas.

AREAS FOR USE IN THE ANALYSIS OF POPULATION DISTRIBUTION

To this point, the discussion has proceeded as if the choice of areas to be used in distributional analysis were self-evident or immaterial, but this is not the case. Given a particular territory whose surface is diverse, there is an infinite variety of ways in which it may be carved into subareas. If an average value is to be computed for each subarea, it is evident that the range of variability of the averages may be made arbitrarily small or arbitrarily large and that the "average of the averages" may be raised or lowered simply by gerrymandering the boundaries. There are two major schools of thought among geographers and other distributional analysts in their delimitation of areas.[5] One is the "homogeneous area" school, and the other is the "nodal area" school. The first group maintains that to be of maximum usefulness for scientific analysis areas should be of maximum internal homogeneity. Data collected for homogeneous areas show a greater range of variation for phenomena and for factors selected as explanatory variables. Each set of observations (data for a single area) tend to be confounded with fewer other variables. Thus, both population events and the variables that may be used to explain variations occur in their "purest" form when collected for units of area where internal homogeneity with respect to the factors being considered has been maximized.

The maximization of homogeneity should not be confused with the maximization of relationships. If one were interested in demonstrating a given relationship by appropriate gerrymandering, it would be possible to bias the analysis in the direction desired. This would be accomplished by maximizing the covariation of the variables involved. However, if there are points of disjuncture in the distribution of particular variables, and if the distribution for each of a number of variables is studied so that singly each distribution covers a minimum range of values, independent of the range of values covered by distributions for other variables, the variation of the means for the areas delimited will have been maximized without necessarily biasing the data collected for these units of area. This is espe-

[5] These two approaches are discussed in greater detail in Bogue (1955).

cially true where homogeneous areas are delimited by a "unique set of characteristics" approach (in which the particular characteristics that are of outstanding economic and social significance in a given locale are given greater weight in arriving at the definition) rather than by the "fixed characteristics" approach.

The "nodal area" school maintains that modern economies are highly organized divisions of labor, in which particular territories orient their activities toward nodal centers—in most cases, large metropolitan centers. Thus this school is committed to emphasizing metropolitan regionalism. The obvious units of area to be employed in the statistical analysis are metropolitan regions, with each region perhaps divided into a few major subareas. Boundaries to such areas are determined not by homogeneity of characteristics but by functional interrelationships—lines of flow of goods and services and points at which competing nodes serve the hinterland areas. Internally, nodal regions are marked by diversity of characteristics rather than by homogeneity. One of the characteristics of metropolitan centers is their tendency to lie at or near the boundaries of major discontinuities in homogeneity. Seemingly, one function of such nodes is to articulate and integrate the special needs of adjoining areas that are unlike each other.

Unfortunately, students of distribution have adopted an "either-one-or-the-other" approach to these two ideas. Although they are not mutually exclusive, neither are they compatible. Each has been able to demonstrate, by the most trustworthy statistical tests, that it represents a valid point of view, holding constant variables representing the point of view of the other. In view of these facts, it is naïve to contend that one of these schools is wholly "correct" and that the other is "incorrect." A more tenable view is that a refined distributional analysis is one which takes account of both ideas simultaneously. This view asserts that uniform (homogeneous) areas and nodal areas are two equally valid and equally important ways of viewing an inhabited territory.

Recent research (Bogue, 1949, 1954) has delimited both nodal areas and homogeneous areas for the United States, but no research has been published that employs both units simultaneously. The premises upon which such research would be conducted may be described, however. Since nodal regions are integrated in terms of exchange and flows, their internal structure consists of the routes of movement, the volume of movement, and the types of commodities moved from each part to every other part. Because the node is the organizing center, most of the routes will converge upon it, and the indexes of movement for most types of commodities will diminish with increased distance from the node to the outer boundary. The distance gradient, which is so often reported in studies of functional areas, is thus a major device for studying the internal structure of nodal areas. It would be an erroneous conclusion, however, to presume that distance gradients and other measures of internal structure of nodal areas are uninfluenced by the characteristics of the territory to which they pertain. Gradients for mountainous areas would differ from those for a semiarid prairie, and both could be unlike the gradient for a fertile and well-watered prairie. The boundaries of uniformity tend to be points of discontinuity or change in slope of gradients or points at which other changes in division-of-labor relationships occur.

It is here that the importance of recognizing uniform regions in the study of nodal areas becomes important. The territory that actually is integrated by a given node is not the "uniform fertile plain" postulated by Von Thünen and assumed by most subsequent students. Instead, the hinterland is characterized by a variety of conditions. Some parts may be mountainous regions devoted to mining and cattle-raising, as in the Denver metropolitan hinterland. Still other parts may be less fertile upland where small subsistence farms predominate, as in the Nashville metropolitan hinterland. Instead of working with "ideal types" or trying to visualize metropolitan relations from the data for rare territories where absolute uniformity is approached, nodal relationships should be observed in real-life situations. This can be done by explicitly introducing environmental differences as an additional set of factors. The homogeneous regions and subregions may be used as an economic and geographic base to show what activities the node integrates. They may, therefore, become an integral part of the internal structure of particular nodal regions. Without this all-important economic base, the hinterlands of all nodes appear to be identical. The unique functions which individual metropolitan centers perform are determined, in no small part, by the unique characteristics of their hinterlands; unless these unique features are known, it is difficult to comprehend how or why a particular metropolis performs the combination of functions it does. Thus, a realistic approach to the question, "Should population distribution analysis make use of homogeneous units of area or nodal units of area?" is "Use should be made of both—simultaneously in many cases."

THE REGION AS A SET OF INTERRELATED VARIABLES

The preceding discussion has an important implication: if one simultaneously introduces several environmental characteristics as independent variables into a distributional analysis (where a population event is assumed to be the dependent variable) and if together these variables succeed in "explaining" or "accounting for" the phenomenon, does not this very finding destroy the significance of regions and regionalism? Why use the term "regionalism" or "regional effect" as a sort of mysterious force if the elements that compose this force are known? Do not the units of area used in the analysis suddenly cease to be important in their own right? Are they not merely a not-too-important vehicle for arriving at the measurement of a statistical relationship? For example, a multiple-variable analysis may show that all differences among geographic units in mortality rates disappear when interregional differences in urban-rural, occupational, racial, and income distribution are taken into account simultaneously. If this happens, should we not stop talking about "The South" and other "regions" as if they are distinctive socioeconomic and geographic units and regard regional events as being fully explained by a series of explicit variables? The rules of parsimony require us to discard a concept when it is no longer necessary, and the "region" concept may be merely an intervening variable that we can abandon as soon as we know what variables it represents. Moreover, is it not true that as a nation undergoes industrialization, urbanization, and integration into a nodal (metropolitan) structured economy, the geographic and other differences that give local areas their unique characteristics tend to become ineffective as differentiators of the population? It may well be asked whether the concept of "regional effect" is not simply a worn-out idea left over from the heyday of environmental determinism in geography.

Although this argument may sound plausible, it is not valid. It mistakes basic assumptions employed in our measuring devices for reality. Most statistical systems for handling several variables simultaneously assume that variables can occur in almost every conceivable combination. Actually, the variables which may be used to measure the various aspects of environment cannot and do not occur in this way; they occur in space in more or less distinctive combinations and ranges of value, and the boundaries of the areas within which a particular combination is present are quite distinct. (In some cases such boundaries are sharp lines, while in others they are fairly narrow bands of transition.) Moreover, the particular combination of variables that occurs in a given place tends to be unmistakably related to geography, market position, or other traits rendered significant by the type of technology and economy present. The term "region" is merely a shorthand term for a unique cluster of interrelated conditions, traits, or forces present in an area at a given time. These clusters are so distinctive that not only geographers but economists, administrators, and even the general public take note of them.

Multiple-variable analysis helps to clarify the substantive content of a particular set of regions but does not become a synonym for regions. Instead of rendering the concept superfluous, it gives added and deeper meaning by helping to evaluate the relative weight of the forces at work in each of the distinctive socioeconomic clusters that we call regions.

Moreover, the notion that progressive urbanization and industrialization will cause these distinctive clusters to disappear cannot be supported either by theory or by observation. In fact, the contrary appears to be true. A market economy seems to cause places to seize upon whatever unique site, locational or physical characteristics they have that may provide the basis for profitable specialization. This is simply one form of adjustment to maximize their share of income in the total economy. For example, slight variations in soil quality, climate, and terrain can, under the influence of the modern market, differentiate "tobacco land" from other farmland or cause one section to specialize in "cash grain," another in livestock farming, and still a third in dairying. The economists of location have long argued that a similar situation holds for non-agricultural activities —there is a general region or regions within which a given industry can survive because the cost of assembling the necessary materials and marketing the product is less than it would be in other areas.

Thus, instead of minimizing geographic differences, the modern metropolitan economy may emphasize them. In this process, interregional differences that once were large may disappear, while new differences may appear. Instead of becoming a homogeneous mass, industrialized populations tend to become a patchwork of specialized populations tied together by a geographic as well as intracommunity and intercommunity division of labor. Modern research is helping to underscore the usefulness of regional variables as a readily observable set of major national divisions.

LIMITATIONS OF THE DISTRIBUTIVE APPROACH

The mode of analysis that has been illustrated—relating the behavior of population groups to some factor that characterizes the group or its environment (or to changes in such factors)— has definite limitations. Since the units of observation are areas, the findings cannot be generalized to persons but must be applied to areas, although the relationships established for samples of areas (the so-called ecological correlations) do have significant implications for the expected results among random samples of persons drawn from each area. Procedures for evaluating and refining these implications have not been adequately explored, but it is plausible to expect that the implications would be greatly enhanced if the areas under observation had maximum homogeneity.

Another limitation arises from the fact that areas are not independent of each other but are contiguous to or have explicit location in relation to each other area. This may give rise to a covariation among the variables based solely on contiguity or proximity. The error may be expected to decline as the number of variables considered simultaneously is increased. This is especially true if the factors that express the covariance due to contiguity are explicitly introduced as separate variables.

Because of these limitations, the findings of a distributive analysis must be applied only to problems in which the unit of study is the area. Even here, the findings should be accepted as being tentative and approximate. Only after a given analysis has been replicated should the findings be considered verified generalizations. If this seems a heavy price to pay, it should be remembered that the same price must be paid in many other lines of social research before a comparable level of plausibility is reached.

ILLUSTRATIVE HYPOTHESES FOR DISTRIBUTIONAL ANALYSIS

The preceding review of population distribution research has been critical of much current work in the field. The review has outlined principles for delimiting areal units and has proposed a philosophy for a revised mode of procedure. It is now appropriate to discuss concrete research programs of population distribution that may be undertaken. Two such programs are described. They are illustrations only; a similar approach could be made for virtually all topics of population study.

A Distributional Analysis of Mortality and Morbidity

Although mortality rates have declined to a low level and although area-to-area differences have lessened in the last quarter-century, such differences still exist. It is generally agreed that differences in mortality are due largely to differences in social, economic, and health conditions among the areas; to the quality of medical services per capita; and to attitudes, knowledge, and concern with health among the residents. However, it is not known how much of these differences in mortality and morbidity are due to each of these factors, independent of the others. The following questions could be asked for total mortality, for total morbidity, for each cause of death, and for each type of illness: What factors are associated with varying incidence? What special factors are associated with unusually low and high incidence? How much change is associated with how much variation in each factor? What is the relative importance of each factor? Where are the areas of highest concentration of incidence, and what remediable factors appear to be responsible in each area? Where are the areas of greatest decline in incidence, and what factors are responsible in each area? In all the above examples, comparisons should be controlled for population composition. In order to answer these questions, a multiple-variable analysis should be made for a sample of subareas, such as state economic areas. This would require tabulation by age, color, and sex for each subarea. It is impossible to perform such a study now because of the lack of data; state units are too large and heterogeneous for such an analysis, and county data are not cross-tabulated in sufficient detail. Life tables, with only a few exceptions, cannot now be prepared for any truly homogeneous area. Life expectancy, longevity, and mortality by cause of death need to be studied among local environments—both within metropolitan areas and within regions.

Distributional Fertility Analysis

Variations in fertility among the population are greater than variations in mortality. It has been demonstrated that much interarea variation persists when age and color composition are controlled, and much work has been devoted to showing that fertility differentials exist among various occupational, income, religious, social, and other groups. But as yet there has been no measure of how much variation in fertility each factor explains when all others are controlled or of how much variation remains when all these factors are considered simultaneously. These questions need to be answered not only for a single instant of time but for several instants, so that changes and trends can be noted. This would call for a multiple-variable distribution analysis of fertility measures for the white and non-white population separately, controlled for age and marital status. It would involve a study design similar to that proposed for the study of mortality. Fertility data with the necessary cross-tabulations are not now available for such a study. At present, demographers are devoting a large amount of energy to the question of *how* fluctuations in fertility occur; yet of equal importance is the unanswered question of *why* they occur in a sociological and socioeconomic sense. An intensive distributional analysis of interarea variation in fertility and of interarea change in differences in fertility should throw considerable light on this subject, although a major handicap is the lack of generally accepted measures of fertility for use in an "open" population (a population that can be influenced by migration).

POPULATION DISTRIBUTION, COMPARATIVE INTERNATIONAL DEMOGRAPHY, AND UNDERDEVELOPED COUNTRIES

At the present time the international aspects of demographic events are being stressed, with greatest emphasis being placed upon underdeveloped countries. It is currently fashionable to compare the size, growth trends, and composition of the population of whole countries and to discuss the population problems of whole countries. These procedures assume, implicitly, either that each country is a homogeneous area or else that it is a single nodal unit. In almost all cases this is not true; most of the principal countries of the world are internally diverse. Hence, as the study of international demography progresses, there will be an increasing emphasis upon the comparison of countries in terms of their regions and subregions. The demographers of each country will appreciate that they do not have a single "population problem" but that their population problems are manifold, with each problem having spatial location within some one part of the country. Each problem can be expected to have special complications that are related to the geographic, economic, cultural, and historical traits that are unique to its locus. Administrators in each country will also come to see that their national population problems are the problems of particular areas and that the solutions must be devised in terms of the environmental circumstances.

In addition, the processes of industrialization and commercialization will lead to extensive mobility and migration among the population. Urbanization and metropolitanization may be expected to be a by-product of the industrialization process. Demographers in all nations will undoubtedly become much more concerned about internal migration than they are at present.

In short, although the attention of international demographers is now focused intently upon national aggregates, it may be predicted with a fair degree of assurance that this will be altered in the near future and that international demography will enter a phase of intensive distributional analysis. If this proves to be the case, one can hope that the transition from aggregative to distributional analysis will be made directly, without the discipline's having to go through the wasteful case-study descriptive phase that has characterized much of the work in the field to date.

SUMMARY AND CONCLUSION

The study of population distribution, in terms of volume of effort expended, is the largest single field of population study. Unfortunately, it has developed largely outside the main stream of population thought and has been carried forward by people who have been considered as "fringe" demographers by the professional population analysts. Most of the world's leading demographers have been concerned largely with national aggregates.

This chapter has tried to show that the distributional approach need not be one of descriptive case study. In fact, this approach can be a method which provides information about interrelationships between population events and environmental conditions obtainable in no other way. It is to be hoped that the study of population distribution will be accepted as one of the core areas of population study and that a scientific philosophy and methodology will be worked out in greater detail. Recent trends in research indicate that this will prove to be the case.

This chapter has purposely avoided some of the topics traditionally discussed under the term "population distribution." This includes a discussion of the relation of population to physical resources, the "carrying capacity" of land, optimum population, "population pressure," population trends toward increased agglomeration and urbanization with increasing technological complexity, and the intraregional and interregional interdependence that develops as a population distributes itself to exploit its environment. These are important aspects of the subject, but they all involve specific applications of the principles developed here. The object here has been to spell out some of the basic principles of study design in the field of population distribution so that work on these problems may produce a more rapid cumulation of scientific knowledge in the field of demography.

SELECTED BIBLIOGRAPHY[*]

BOGUE, DONALD J. 1949. *The Structure of the Metropolitan Community.* Ann Arbor: University of Michigan Press.

———. 1954. "An Outline of the Complete System of Economic Areas," *American Journal of Sociology,* LX, 136–39.

———. 1955. "Nodal versus Homogeneous Regions, and Statistical Techniques for Measuring the Influence of Each," preprint, *Proceedings of the Conference of the International Statistical Institute,* Rio de Janeiro.

———, and HARRIS, DOROTHY L. 1954. *Comparative Population and Urban Research via Multiple Regression and Covariance Analysis.* ("Scripps Foundation Studies in Population Distribution," No. 8.) Oxford, Ohio: Scripps Foundation, Miami University.

[*] For additional references see bibliographies for chapters xxviii and xxix.

18. Fertility

N. B. RYDER

There is no event in personal history more significant for the future than becoming a parent, and there is no pattern of behavior more essential for societal survival than adequate fertility. This is the subject of the present chapter: the determinants of birth. The individual and social importance of proper knowledge of this vital activity cannot be overstated. The network of familial relationships, the pattern of familial activities, and the structure of familial rights and responsibilities are transformed by the entrance of a baby. On the aggregate level, although the law of large numbers prohibits such a dramatic parallel, changes in procreative behavior are influential accompaniments of virtually every variation in the fortunes of society. A disturbance of the rate of production of new members portends for the population successive modifications in the numbers of consumers in each higher age group, the demands imposed on the educational structure, the flow of young adults into the labor force, the housing requirements of newlyweds, and so on throughout the life span to the ages beyond retirement when the old seek to derive financial if not psychological security from their savings, their progeny, and their government. It is thus not surprising that the policy-makers in business and in government are avid consumers of those data concerning past, present, and future births which it is the obligation of the fertility analyst to understand.

The practitioners consecrated to this task represent a catholic variety of specialties. The fields of learning which have been most immediately concerned with and instrumental in the understanding of fertility are sociology, biology, and, to a lesser extent, economics, anthropology, and psychology. No science concerned with man has ignored or could properly ignore the "facts of life." Notable among the contributors from fields of applied research are actuaries, doctors, public health workers, and government statisticians. This variegated list documents the proposition that demography, and fertility analysis as an integral component of it, is a multiscience discipline. The reason for this is clear: the focus of fertility research is a concrete event rather than an analytical abstraction from that event in terms of a special frame of reference. The many consequences of this consideration for the characteristics of the subject range from the firmly empiricist orientation of inquiry and the fruitfulness of cross-fertilization to conceptual disorder and lack of theoretical acuity. The form of the following presentation betrays this situation by proceeding from plane to plane ever deeper into the substrata of causation. Demography is now almost exclusively a province of sociology, the deepest and most complex as well as the least developed of the levels of knowledge-seeking.

Prior to the acquisition of reliable data for large population aggregates, fertility analysis perforce consisted of reasonable speculation and deduction applied to the selected kinds of information available to the observant individual. Thus, until perhaps three centuries ago, the history of thought in this area was a catalogue of the opinions of statesmen and philosophers and a documentation of the varieties of behavior. This thought was virtually devoid of the quantitative appraisal which is the essence of systematic science. Many systems of political thought included expressions of values in the sphere of childbearing, in terms of approval or disapproval of practices which might promote or discourage expansion of the numerical dimensions of the state. The incidence of such practices can be inferred only vaguely from the frequency and energy of these exhortations. But gradually the relevance for human affairs of the measurement of simple attributes of the body politic came to be realized, and a trickle of data from scattered places provided a minimal substructure for informed inquiry. At the close of the eighteenth century, demography was vaulted into a position of political prominence by the publication of a highly provocative essay on population by an English clergyman, Thomas Robert Malthus.

The model of demographic dynamics which Malthus introduced, and which still serves as a focus for many discussions of theory and policy, was undoubtedly a stimulant to the increasing scope and quality of population data; but the form was not conducive to fertility research because Malthus regarded fertility more as a parameter than as a variable. The "passion between the sexes" was considered constant, and the relationship between progress and population growth was established through the agency of mortality variation. During the nineteenth century two distinct sets of ideas were developed in opposition to the view of the constancy of fertility. The first was

that the transformation in man's ways of life, associated with the idea of progress, weakened his generative faculties through some unspecified physiological nexus and thus caused fertility to decline. The second was that a critical component of progress was man's decision to control his output of children, to extend the sphere of rationality into the area of reproduction, and to bring into the world only those who could be raised in that standard of life he deemed essential or desirable. Much research of the past half-century can be viewed as attempts to study the relevance and validity of these two hypotheses and, by extension, to determine whether the primary responsibility for research in this area lies with the biological or the social sciences.

As more and better statistical information was produced for a number of countries of Western culture, during the later part of the nineteenth and earlier part of the twentieth centuries, it became clear that fertility was not constant but falling. The possibility of imminent diminution of numbers for many nations, laid bare by these observations, made study of the causal nexus of fertility decline both crucial and urgent. The immediate question may be stated briefly: Had fertility declined because people were unable to bear or because they were unwilling to bear? Pertinent statistical documentation of possible answers has only recently been attempted, and it is still relatively imperfect and incomplete. It may be asserted with confidence that fertility regulation, or the use of effective means to gain reproductive ends, is predominantly responsible for differences of fertility in time, in space, and between classes of the population distinguished by socioeconomic and other criteria.

Such an answer in turn poses an array of questions concerning the sources of differences between populations in the proportion of people who are effectively in control of their procreation and in the character of reproductive ends. Research in these areas has proceeded in terms of both individual behavior and institutional structures. The extension of our frame of reference to intersocietal comparison symbolizes the most critical problem for current fertility research: The underdeveloped areas, where mortality is declining as a component and inevitable accompaniment of progress, portend a progress-negating explosion of numbers unless fertility is limited as effectively as in the West, and much more quickly.

By means of official enumeration and registration systems, many national and subnational governments produce data concerning the populations under their jurisdiction. While these records are intended in part for policy and administration purposes, they are also frequently available in anonymous statistical form as secondary sources of research data; in fact, they have been the mainstay of fertility analysis. The registration system may provide cumulative summaries, for successive time periods, of population movements like birth, death, migration, marriage, and marital dissolution, as well as demographic and other relevant characteristics of the individuals involved in these events. With respect to birth, the most significant items of information concern the parents, e.g., dates of birth, marriage, and previous fertility and pertinent socioeconomic variables. The enumeration system, typified by the decennial census, provides a balance sheet of the distributions of members of the population by numerous attributes. Virtually all this information may be characterized as a summary statement of events which have occurred to the enumerated individuals prior to census date. This form of state-

ment emphasizes that, ideally, registration and enumeration are substitutable, although intercensal departures from the population are unclassifiable by the census. Thus a primary basis is provided for evaluation and correction of inaccuracies in either basic source.

Clearly the registration system, through the tabulation of births by parental characteristics, is a tremendous boon to the fertility analyst; but the enumeration system is also of great importance and is a virtually essential counterpart of birth registrations. The population at census date may be asked for a summary of reproductive history including age, length of marriage and other details of marital history, parity (cumulative fertility) and correlative information such as ages of parents and perhaps of children, and socioeconomic classifications. In addition, the census provides a reference background for the events recorded by registration since the information that a particular group of individuals became parents cannot be fully interpreted without an assessment of the number of individuals in that group who were available for parenthood. The rationale behind this basic occurrence/exposure ratio calculation is discussed at greater length in the following exposition of measurement techniques. Finally, in the absence of registration data, a record of the population by age at a point of time is a record of the survivors (after death and migration) of births during previous periods and accordingly may be used, within the limitations of the related data, to reconstruct a history of fertility.

While it may be taken for granted that the data yielded by enumeration and registration procedures are to some extent erroneous, the analytic consequences of this fact are reduced by the considerations that: (1) the level of accuracy may frequently exceed that necessary for hypothesis verification;

(2) most data are logically related to other pieces of knowledge and can be approximately corrected; (3) even in the absence of a satisfactory correction basis, the extent and direction of inaccuracy may be identified and its bearing on the hypothesis in question may be assessed in a useful if less quantitative manner, since error is a phenomenon of human behavior with its own patterns of regularity and is therefore amenable to scientific analysis. Types of error may be classified as follows: for the events eligible for registration, there may be overregistration, underregistration, and non-registration (the last referring to sectors of the population for which a registration process does not exist) and for the characteristics of the individuals connected with the events, there may be misclassification (such as age misstatement) or non-classification (such as age not stated). An identical list exists for individuals eligible for enumeration and for their characteristics. In the present discussion attention is focused on underregistration, underenumeration, and misclassification.

The essence of all procedures for correction of faulty enumeration and registration data is the comparison of identical or logically related information, for the same individual or aggregate, from two or more independent sources. Three procedures comprise most research in this area: (1) An area sample of the population may be enumerated at approximately the same time as the total census and the samples compared with the census enumeration of the same area, as in the 1950 Post-Enumeration Survey of the United States census. (2) The results of two censuses at times (t_1) and (t_2) may be compared for logically identical aggregates, such as those aged (a) at time (t_1) and those aged $(a + t_2 - t_1)$ at time (t_2). Due allowance must be made for mortality and migration

during the intercensal period, for example, a record of deaths and migrants in the cohort of period $(t_1 - a)$ during the interval between times (t_1) and (t_2). (3) Registered births of time (t_1) may be compared with enumerated individuals aged $(t_2 - t_1)$ in a census at time (t_2), due allowance being made for deaths and migrants of the birth cohort of time (t_1) during the interval between times (t_1) and (t_2).

Any of these three procedures of comparison may be conducted on a name-by-name rather than on an aggregate comparison basis; the former enables the identification of several sources of error not verifiable in the latter. For those individuals represented in both sources, inconsistencies of classification may be informative on misclassification in either source, particularly if one source is superior in quality to the other. Those individuals present in one source but not in the other represent one part of the underenumeration or underregistration in the deficient source. The other component of underenumeration or underregistration consists of individuals present in neither source. Comparisons over a time interval imply the data on population movements during the interval, a third possible source of error. It goes without saying that the process of identifying individuals or aggregates from two sources is also subject to error. In addition to these essentially arithmetical comparison procedures, data from a single source may be compared with expectation derived from the accumulated body of knowledge in the area. This approach to the problem, while implicit in the activity of any perceptive investigator, presents not only the problem of less precise correction bases, but also the dilemma that the corrected data are to that extent jeopardized in their function of testing the same body of knowledge.

Although the attributes which are

known or suspected to be determinants of error are too numerous and too variable to permit simple summary, a few general propositions may be presented. The adequacy of enumeration depends on: (*a*) the efficiency of the enumeration procedure, particularly the selection, training, supervision, and payment of enumerators, the experience of the enumerating organization, and the rapport of its sponsors; (*b*) the characteristics of the population which may pose difficulties, particularly the mobility of the individual (and such related characteristics as the permanence of housing). Underregistration differs from underenumeration in that the individuals directly connected with the event in question create the data; their adequacy may be expected, therefore, to depend on the experience of the population with record-keeping, on the general level of sophistication, and on the level and efficacy of enforcement of sanctions for non-performance. Surrogates of authority, such as doctors, hospital staffs, ministers, and undertakers, will tend to yield better data than individuals unconnected with officialdom. Finally, errors of misclassification may be subdivided into categories of randomness and bias. Random errors are most likely to arise as a function of ignorance—because the informant reports data on other individuals, because the individual reporting for himself has a low level of intelligence or education, and because the question is complex or refined in detail or relates to a remote event. Bias is most likely to arise when the informant perceives information as being to his own advantage or disadvantage, so that answers are pulled toward higher status in his frame of reference. As examples, age misstatement follows a pattern of overrepresentation in the young adults and in the categories bordering on less desirable age groups; the foreign-born tend to claim native birth; and the non-white attempt to pass as white. Of particular significance for fertility research is the tendency for reported marital status to correspond appropriately with parity and with residential arrangements in agreement with reproductive norms.

Turning next to methodology, the discussion will be developed progressively from the simpler to the more complex measures, and will finally be summarized. The most common and most elementary measure of fertility is the crude birth rate. Given a population identified in space and time, then the crude birth rate is the ratio of the number of births occurring to members of the population during a particular time period to the total number of person-years of life of the population during that period, i.e., the exposure to risk of occurrence of birth. The crude birth rate is usually expressed as a rate per thousand person-years. The practice of approximating the denominator, by multiplying the population size at the midpoint of the period in question by the number of years represented in the numerator, is responsible for the customary description of the rate as "births per thousand population." Notwithstanding this practice, the inclusion of time in the denominator is always implicit and appropriate since any event requires not only actors but also the passage of time.

The principles underlying the computation of the crude birth rate—identification of an exposed population and of births to this population in terms of certain attributes, including time—may be extended without modification to the computation of rates for classes and subclasses of the population. For example, the age-specific fertility rate represents a crude birth rate for each age group in the population, the numerator being births to parents of a given age group and the denominator the number of person-years spent in that age group in the time period concerned.

A possible ambiguity arises here, since each birth is represented by two parents, who are not generally of the same age. Properly speaking, therefore, age specification implies either counting each birth twice and dividing the resultant rates by two for uniformity of dimension with the crude birth rate or specifying parental sex as well as age.

Female age-specific fertility rates are by far the most common, primarily for reasons of convenience. If the crude birth rate be symbolized by b, the fertility rate for age group a by $f(a)$ and the proportion of the population in age group a by $c(a)$, then b is identical with the sum of the products $f(a) \cdot c(a)$ over all ages. This illustrates a fundamental analytic approach which has been widely used in fertility research: the computation of rates at various levels of specificity for attributes x_i, in order to distinguish between differences in fertility at lower levels of specificity caused by differences in $f(x_i)$ and by differences in the distribution of the population, $c(x_i)$, by those particular attributes. There are three problems implicit in this basic approach: (1) the specificity problem, or what variables should be considered in terms of their influence on fertility and their distribution in the population (to which the most appropriate general reply would seem simply to be the highest level feasible in terms of available data); (2) the index problem, or how the n-dimensional table of rates resulting from the specification of n variables can be reduced to manageable compass in a single fertility index for convenient comparison between groups; (3) the temporal aggregation problem, or which rates should be considered as the analytical unit for purposes of temporal comparison.

The index problem does not exist if only one component of the population be distinguished as the appropriate exposure denominator for the births of a period, i.e., if specificity results in only one rate. A common fertility measure, for example, is the ratio of births during a time period not to the total person-years of the population but to the person-years for females in the reproductive ages (such as 15–44, inclusive), these being the component of the population more specifically exposed to and responsible for the observed births. An approximate counterpart of this measure, using only enumeration data, has been applied extensively and successfully, particularly in the United States, where the relative length of the census series contrasts markedly with the relative brevity of the birth registration series. This measure is the ratio of the number of children in age group 0–4 (or some other conveniently chosen range) to the number of women 15–44 (likewise an arbitrary representation, in this case of the reproductive span). Using the ages indicated here, the child-woman ratio, as it is customarily termed, is an approximation to the ratio of births in the five years preceding census date to the person-years of exposure in age group 15–44 in that quinquennium; the approximation depends for its accuracy on the relation of infant and child mortality and migration to the differences of size of the cohorts passing through the reproductive ages in the precensal period.

Solutions to the index problem may be exemplified for the set of age-specific fertility rates for females. If a rate be computed for each of, say, n age groups, then the index which summarizes these n rates is the sum of these rates, each assigned an appropriate weight; and the index problem becomes one of selecting weights. One elementary and relatively satisfactory solution is the use of equal weights, and the index resulting from this procedure is customarily termed the "total fertility rate." This measure may be conceptualized as the mean parity, at the end of fertile life, for a cohort of women passing through the reproductive age span without mortality and experiencing in each age the fertility rates being summarized. Derivative from this concept is the gross reproduction rate, a simple modification of the total fertility rate obtained by multiplying it by the proportion of births which are female, or alternatively and more directly by including only female births in the computation of the original age-specific fertility rates. It will readily be seen that the gross reproduction rate is a measure of female replacement under mortality-free conditions and is thus a fertility counterpart to the net reproduction rate discussed in the chapter on reproduction.

A second solution closely allied to the reproduction rates is the stable birth rate, obtained by weighting the age-specific fertility rates by the stable age distribution implicit in these rates and in a set of age-specific mortality rates. The stable birth rate is directly analogous to the crude birth rate in form, with a potentially permanent age distribution substituted for the actual age distribution of the population which supplies implicit weights in the computation of the crude birth rate. A third type of solution to the index problem, related to an empirical rather than to a mathematical model, is the selection of some "standard" age distribution as a source of weights for the component fertility rates. This type of solution is convenient but arbitrary since the resultant index is a function of the standard chosen and since there are no universally acceptable guiding principles for this selection.

The temporal aggregation problem arises because there is a meaningful alternative set of fertility measures, a set deriving from the identification of the fertility of a population in time by specifying the temporal location of the parents (in the denominators of the various measures) rather than the temporal location of the births (in the numerators). For example, a group of females may be identified by the attribute of birth during a particular time period, i.e., as a birth cohort. As this cohort passes through the reproductive span, aging *pari passu*, its exposure to risk of occurrence of birth and its number of births may be registered in each age; accordingly, a set of age-specific fertility rates may be generated in precisely the same way as for a period of observation of births. Indexes which summarize cohort fertility-age functions may be computed in the ways described for periods above, and, since they will in general differ in their temporal variations from the time series for their period counterparts, a choice between these is required on analytic grounds. The most general basis of an answer to this decision problem is in terms of the perceived importance in the concrete situation of the particular circumstances and conditions of a period relative to the persistent interrelationships among the cohort's lifetime experiences. In practice the temporal aggregation problem is often ignored or answered by default in favor of the period approach, in the absence of the time series of data necessary for computing cohort measures.

We have raised three problems which are present in the construction of fertility measures—the specificity problem, the index problem, and the temporal aggregation problem—and illustrated them by reference to one specified variable, age of female. In the following paragraphs we will discuss a few other variables. The specification of these has increased our understanding of fertility. In each case different indexes may be employed to summarize the set of rates generated, as analogues of the indexes suggested for age-specific rates, and in each case the set of rates may be specified temporally by a period **or** by a cohort referent. Many difficulties in comparing fertility studies and generalizing from them ensue from the different solutions to the problems of specificity, of index construction, and of temporal aggregation. Establishing formal relationships among these for simple models of demographic change is an important task which has been accomplished to date only in fragmentary form. Since the cohort approach to temporal aggregation deserves priority on general analytical grounds, it must be noted that such analysis requires patience. Agencies concerned with policy formation cannot afford the lapse of time essential for relatively complete reproductive records; these agencies will therefore have recourse to information assembled by successive time periods. Accordingly, two important areas of research are identified: (1) establishment of the nature of the relationship between temporal variations in various fertility parameters, from a cohort and from a period viewpoint; (2) determination of the optimal means for assessing incomplete reproductive experience for cohorts, in terms of the demands of current fertility analysis. The importance of this kind of research varies directly with the volatility of procreative behavior.

Since we are concerned with a process which is normatively confined to married couples and which is a major focus of married life, an obvious extension of the principle of exposure specification is into the area of marriage. Records for a birth cohort of individuals throughout the fertile ages may be used to distinguish, for each age of experience, the person-years of married and unmarried exposure, the numbers of legitimate and illegitimate births, and fertility rates specific for marital status as well as for age. The same computations may be made for periods. In either case the table of rates may be summarized in index form by interposing a population distribution by age and marital status derived from one of the models suggested above. As before, the index problem may be avoided by computing the ratio of the number of legitimate births to the total number of person-years of married life within the fertile age span, for the cohort or for the period.

Another measure which has analytic utility in this cohort case and which provides an example of still another principle of distinction among fertility measures is the ratio of legitimate births to (first) marriages. Each is cumulated to the end of the age of fertility, and the ratio is equal to the measure of marital fertility divided by the mean duration of marriage within the fertile period. Thus we may distinguish between time-free measures, which are ratios of the numbers of two related events, and measures of the occurrence/exposure form, which are additionally functions of the passage of time. The period analogue of the cohort birth-marriage ratio is not commonly used; the events recorded in the numerator and denominator, respectively, do not generally occur to the same individuals, and the meaning of the measure is thereby obscured. Attempts to rectify this difficulty by computing the ratio of births of year t to marriages of year t-n, where n represents an approximation to the mean interval between marriage and birth, have not been regarded as successful.

The specification of marital status may be extended into consideration of marital duration as well, since the fertility of married couples is known to vary markedly with the length of time elapsed since marriage. And again, fertility rates specific for female age and duration of marriage may be computed for cohorts or for periods and may be summarized in indexes by the various procedures noted. Several special considerations about marital duration may be introduced at this point. In the first place, marital duration may be used as a specified variable without age; and, since it is a variable of the same type as age (denoting the passage of time since occurrence of a significant event in personal history), the models from which indexes were derived for age-specific measures may be readily adapted to duration-specific fertility. Furthermore, this adaptation permits the temporal division of fertility experience for successive marriage cohorts as well as for successive birth cohorts. Consecutive events may be assembled and summarized for people sharing a given period of marriage and thus united by the common circumstances of their socioeconomic environment at like stages of their family cycle. The marriage cohort approach to fertility has the further advantage that the unit of study can be a couple, an eminently appropriate unit for reproductive analysis, rather than, as has been customary in age-specific fertility, an individual.

This is an appropriate point at which to note the technically awkward problem that the husband and/or the wife may have been married more than once, so that the marital duration of a couple may be interpreted in several different ways. Finally, for a variety of plausible reasons the age at marriage of husband and of wife (remarriage again posing the problem of plural possible definitions) may be expected to be related in interesting ways to the fertility of the couple. However, since the variables of age, duration of marriage, and age at marriage are algebraically related, the specification of any two of these in a scheme of measurement automatically implies the concealed operation of the third.

It has been suggested in the preceding paragraphs that marital status, and more particularly marital duration and age at marriage, are important variables in the computation of fertility rates for periods and for cohorts. One facet of this suggestion is the subdivision of reproductive experience into separately considered components by reference to date of marriage. The procreative history may also be broken into components by distinguishing births by order, and women (or couples) by parity. Only women with $n-1$ previous births are exposed to the risk of occurrence of an nth birth, and future fertility is clearly a function of past fertility. Accordingly a most fruitful recent direction of development of measures has been in the area of parity-specific fertility, for periods and for cohorts, and with age or duration as auxiliary specified variables for the purpose of model-building and index-construction. Unlike the other variables suggested for specification, parity has the unique feature of being itself a measure of fertility to date for the individual or couple concerned. This variable is the only one which permits computation of the range and differentiation of individual procreative performance in the population being studied. It shares with marital duration, however, a possible ambiguity of definition. Parity may be defined as number of conceptions, number of live births and stillbirths, or number of live births; and its referent may be the total reproductive record of the wife, of the husband, or of the present marriage.

Fertility rates specific for parity may be computed on the occurrence/exposure basis in the same manner as fertility rates specific for duration. Another measure, the precise analogue of the birth-marriage ratio, uses the birth or marriage cohort as the temporal aggregation basis. This is the parity progression ratio, operationally defined for parity n as the proportion of women who, having achieved nth parity, proceed to achieve at least $(n+1)$th parity. The resultant series of ratios is time-free in the same sense as the birth-marriage ratio, but in the present case the passage of time in question is the interval between the *n*th birth and the (*n*+1)th birth (or the end of the fertile age span if the *n*th birth is the final one). This brings into focus the proposal of measures specific for the time interval since the preceding birth and enlarges upon the consideration of parity as a fertility variable in the same way as marital duration amplified the variable of marital status. Little research has been done on interval-specific fertility because the requisite data are very rare. The reference to birth interval as a useful variable for fertility specification completes a neat set of demographic variables which have been introduced into the literature of fertility measurement. These variables, six in number, may be arranged in three pairs, as follows: (1) number and age; (2) marital status and marital duration; (3) parity and birth interval. Each pair consists of a status, marked by the occurrence of a demographic event, and an interval, or lapse of time since that occurrence. Fertility research on this plan verges on the reconstruction of complete procreative histories and is closely allied with the study of the family life cycle.

The consideration of birth interval as a significant discriminator of exposure to the risk of birth raises a point concerning the meaning of exposure in the operational definition of specific fertility rates, which is important because of its role as a bridge between the measures based on data from secondary sources and the measures used in intensive research into fecundity and fertility control. The basic rates discussed above have as numerator a sum of events and as denominator a product-sum of person-years of exposure, but the criterion of exposure has been merely the achievement of a particular status. To be explicit, after the (*n*−1)th birth a woman is not exposed to the risk of occurrence of an *n*th birth until a period of time sufficient for the termination of pregnancy elapses. Thus, from a physiological viewpoint every conception results in erasing from the exposure record a time interval which is included as exposure in the above measurement schemes. The proportion of the potentially fertile population which is temporarily sterile at any time because of pregnancy may be a meaningful component in explaining fertility differentials, particularly during periods when fertility is fluctuating. Refined treatment of this factor should include the consideration of pregnancies which culminate in no live births or in more than one live birth as well as those yielding one live birth. Finally, it seems clear that married status is neither necessary nor sufficient for exposure in a physiological sense and in particular that the incidence of premarital conception is high enough in most societies to warrant careful allowance for premarital exposure.

SOCIAL VARIATIONS IN FERTILITY

Our first concerns in this section are movements of national fertility with the passage of time and international differences in fertility at a given time. There are severe restrictions on this analysis because of limited data. As a crude generalization, the higher the fertility, the less information we have available. Our broadest generalizations in time and space must rely on the simplest of measures, the crude birth rate, and our interpretation of the role of demographic influences mentioned in the preceding section is for the most part inferential rather than statistically controlled. We know practically nothing about fertility prior to the nineteenth century. With a fair degree of confidence we may assert that fertility in most of the world was very high, with a crude birth rate between 40 and 50 per thousand, but it was markedly lower, perhaps between 30 and 40 per thousand, in western and northern Europe. The probable components of lower fertility in the latter area are a higher age at marriage, a lower proportion married, and a smaller number of births per married couple. The difference in crude birth rates would almost certainly have been greater were it not for a more healthy regime in western and northern Europe than in the rest of the world. One exception is the United States, where a highly favorable age distribution and nearly universal early marriage, based in large part on immigration, combined with relatively healthful conditions and a labor shortage relative to resources to give a crude birth rate above 50 per thousand per annum.

The pioneers in the Western transition toward low fertility were three nations—France, the United States, and Ireland—but the last two deviated from the subsequent general pattern. The source of the American fertility decline lay in the non-continuance of the peculiar conditions giving abnormally inflated fertility in the earlier years; the Irish fertility decline was, on the demographic level, a product of a very late age at marriage, a very low proportion ever married, and a relatively high emigration. Throughout the latter half of the nineteenth century, the other countries of northern and western Europe followed France along the path of fertility reduction, a trend that continued unchecked—and only minimally disturbed by the First World War—until the end of the great depression of the 1930's. As the years passed, more countries on the cultural periphery of the initiating area were pulled into the transition process, in central and to some extent in southern and eastern Europe, as well as in the populations of predominantly northwest European and particularly British origin in other continents. The details differ from country to country but, as an approximate generalization, the later the date of inception of the decline, the more rapid its pace. Japan is the only country outside the orbit of Western civilization which at this writing has participated in this vital revolution, and it is highly relevant for later analysis to note that this is the only non-Western country with a relatively indigenous non-colonial industrial revolution.

The primary demographic source of the fall in fertility was a decline in the mean completed parity of married women from the neighborhood of seven to a level below three. Parity distributions were progressively attenuated at the higher levels, with a tendency toward a pronounced mode at two. From a timing standpoint, the decline was achieved by cessation of childbearing at progressively earlier marital durations rather than by delayed initiation of marital fertility or longer birth intervals. Age-specific fertility for the total population declined at a somewhat slower pace than marital fertility. The proportion of reproductive person-years spent by females in the married state was increased by a declining rate of marital dissolution (an accompaniment of declining mortality), and the decrease by delayed marriage or by sex imbalance consequent upon predominantly male immigration was not as great. In turn, the crude birth rate declined at a slower pace than the total fertility rate because the potentially parental part of the age distribution was relatively inflated by declining net reproductivity.

In the past two decades birth rates have risen markedly in countries which experienced the decline described above, and the new higher fertility level seems more than temporary. The demographic components of explanation of this rise may be summarized as follows (with due recognition that the experience is as yet too short to be analyzed satisfactorily for recent young marriages): (1) the proportion married of total person-years of reproductive life has increased markedly because of a pattern of earlier and more frequent marriage and continuing improvements in survival; (2) within marriage the proportion infertile has declined markedly, although high parities continue to become rarer and the modal family size is still two; (3) the mean age of childbearing has declined; (4) there has been a transitory fluctuation in annual fertility caused by the postponement and subsequent occurrence of births, either directly within marriage or indirectly through postponed marriage, although the timing pattern of marriages and births may subsequently have been accelerated. Such fertility fluctuations are an important feature of areas for which adequate data exist, but the time lag between postponement and recovery had previously been brief. The fluctuation of the past two decades appears to be unique in magnitude in demographic history and therefore poses peculiar problems of proper analytical perspective.

In concluding this brief sketch of the spatiotemporal differentials in fertility, it must be re-emphasized that the data supporting the above generalizations are highly limited in space, in time, and, most importantly, in cultural variability. As far as we know, most of the world continues to have relatively high and stable fertility, founded on universal and early marriage and high completed parity. Important temporal variations have probably been confined to the short run, and cultural similarities have been more evident than cultural differences. These observations have their most solid foundation in the fundamental truism that, for most of the world for most of man's history, environmental difficulties meant high mortality levels, and the cultures which did not match these with abundant fertility

failed to survive. We have very few reliable data concerning the detailed facets of procreative behavior for any population or subpopulation characterized by high fertility.

Just as there are major differences in fertility among nations at a point of time, so within nations various social, economic, and cultural groups have been observed to have markedly dissimilar patterns of childbearing. The primary source of this information, except for special-purpose small-scale studies, is the census, in large part through the medium of cross-classifications of completed parity with other demographic and socioeconomic information for married women but also through use of the child-woman ratio as an approximate fertility measure. Another potentially important source of information is the combination of registered births with census data on exposure for particular socioeconomic and cultural categories, but this type of measure is complicated because its components come from different sources which may not be comparable in definition and accuracy. This difficulty varies in severity with the complexity of the attributes concerned, as is the case, for example, with paternal occupation.

The variables in terms of which fertility variations have most frequently and successfully been described within Western nations are income, education, occupation, race, nativity, religion, and community size (including in the last the fundamental distinction between rural and urban residence). In terms of the nature of their relationships (in the past) to fertility, these variables may be classified under three headings, although obvious interdependencies partially destroy the usefulness of the classification: (1) for occupation, education, and community size, the fertility continuum has run from high to low in terms of the proximity of the group to urbanization, industrialization, and specialization; (2) for income (as well as other status associations like education and occupation) fertility has tended to vary inversely with status; (3) for the religious, ethnic, and racial cultures and subcultures, Roman Catholic fertility has been higher than Protestant, foreign-born fertility higher than native-born, and non-white fertility higher than white (these classifications tending to be associated with status). There are some hints of a pattern discernible in the mass of detailed and conflicting evidence available. This pattern may be presented in the form of a model of internal fertility dynamics accompanying the decline of fertility in the West. As the occupational structure has gradually been transformed from an agricultural to an industrial focus, those participating most closely in this transformation have modified their fertility downward. By socioeconomic class, the higher the status of the persons concerned, the earlier their fertility decline; the new childbearing pattern has gradually filtered down through the social ranks. The new style of fertility has met pockets of resistance in subcultures with boundary-maintaining mechanisms which are, for the time being at least, relatively effective.

At the upper and lower asymptotes of this model, fertility varies directly with socioeconomic status, but because of the temporal sequence of classes in the pattern of decline, inverse differentials (as reported in the preceding paragraph) are most commonly observed. Thus the differentials observed in any particular study require interpretation, insofar as the model is valid, in terms of the particular phase of the fertility transition which is under observation. Some substantiation of this thesis is available. Fertility differentials in general are somewhat smaller now than they have been in the past. Fertility by income is not now a monotonic decreas-

ing function but tends to have a reverse-J shape. However, most data are less than adequate for segregation of the function, status, and subculture components of fertility variation in time-series form. In fact, the existence of each differential, independent of the others, as established by a reliable form of multivariate analysis, is a largely unaccomplished objective. Difficulties in this area are presented not only by the obvious interdependencies among such variables as race, income, and occupation but also by the variety of fertility measures used in different studies. Some of these are of a period and others of a cohort type; some are restricted to marital fertility, while others are concerned with general fertility; some are in the form of indexes or rates, and others utilize ratio-type measures.

Indeed, the problems and potentialities of differential fertility analysis seem to be more impressive than the results to date. The following questions may be cited as both important and relatively unanswered: (1) To what extent are fertility differentials the result of differences in marital fertility as distinguished from differences in nuptiality, and what has been the relative importance of each at various phases in the sequence of fertility decline? A subsection of this area of inquiry is the interdependence of age at marriage (of husband and of wife) with occupation, income, and education. (2) To what extent are national fertility trends the consequence not of the evolution of the fertilities of population components but of trends in the distribution of the population by these components? (3) Granted that fertility variations through time are occurring within subgroups of the society, to what extent are these a function of movement between subgroups as distinct from internal variation? Particular aspects of this problem include the migrants from rural to urban areas, the migrants through social space (who, in the few studies documenting the problem, seem to have fertilities which vary inversely with the rate of ascension), and the converts from one religious persuasion to another. (4) Do those who experience a change in status differ in fertility from those whose status is static, and, if so, do they resemble more in reproductive behavior the subgroup which is their source or that which is their destination? (5) To what extent are the data on differential fertility which have been accumulated for many countries during the last twenty-five years a reflection in part of the economic and political upheavals of this era? There is no overriding reason for believing that differential responses to short-run phenomena by the various social segments will correspond in degree or in direction with their responses to long-run change. For example, the recent rise in fertility in the past two decades has been most pronounced among those groups which previously had the lowest fertility. Indeed, most of our evidence refers to a period characterized by fluctuation, and the results may accordingly be somewhat misleading for long-run analysis.

In summarizing the problem areas of the materials in this section, we note two critical limitations on the suitability of available data for the formation of universal generalizations. In the first place, our knowledge about underdeveloped areas of the world is largely inferential because enumeration and registration systems are absent or rudimentary. The systematic collection of official data of scientific utility almost seems to require that institutional structure which is most likely to lead to low fertility. Even for the nations of greatest statistical strength, the possible control of demographic influences on fertility is inadequate for the scheme of variables outlined in the discussion

of methods, and all refined series are short. In the second place, our knowledge of fertility for the urban-industrial nations is most firmly grounded in evidence relating to a period of transition and fluctuation, in which the obvious and immediate importance of some dynamic variables may be concealing more fundamental influences. Study of the relationships between fertility movements for national and regional aggregates and movements of social and economic indexes for the same aggregates has been neglected. Despite the multitude of references to the hypothesis that fertility movements are a function of the level of income or employment, few studies of this relationship have yet been made.

Two other problems paradoxically plague the development of demography: the success of technical developments in the measurement field and the abundance of data. In much recent research the enthusiasm for technical refinement of models and data of a complex and intellectually satisfying kind has provided an excuse for the failure to grapple with basic analytical questions which are less amenable to quantification and mathematization. On the second count, despite the manifest weaknesses of present secondary source materials in many areas, the scientific advance of demography is hobbled by the wealth of data possessed relative to other social sciences. It does not seem unfair to assert that the existence of vast stores of official data concerning fertility has made the development of the subject excessively dependent on these stores, so that the forms in which data are presented in these sources have become the frames of reference for analysis. To put the point in the form of a question: Have demographers chosen their methods and concepts because they are theoretically relevant or because the data already exist in these forms?

Official data are presented, because of administrative reasons and because of the nature of data collection, in a spatiotemporal framework. Data are provided in year-by-year form for detailed geographic units. One consequence has been an overwhelming reliance on period-type indexes, despite the facts that people bear children over a considerable span of time and that their behavior in successive time periods is highly interdependent. Another consequence has been a proliferation of studies documenting fertility differences between groups which differ in geographical location, at most only a correlate of social facts. Finally, there has been a persistent focus of research on fertility as a function of those independent variables which are most suitable for official collection, i.e., readily quantifiable data in relatively non-sensitive areas of behavior. Variables like education, occupation, and income are relevant, but it is obvious that they represent overlapping penumbras of meaning and that they are susceptible of wide ranges of interpretation. The vast amount of research that can be done with these data has perhaps stood in the way of research for which specific hypotheses are formulated. Both methodology and data collection should be directed by hypotheses and theories, rather than the other way around. This criticism is, of course, not specific to demography but typical of much social science research. Maybe the heart of the problem is that a poverty-stricken field of science must make do with the cheapest data available.

FECUNDITY

With this section we begin the discussion of the physical processes, conditions, and actions which lead to the occurrence of births and which are thus the proximate sources of fertility variation. These may be divided in an elementary fashion, without intent of ig- noring the subtlety of the distinction in particular cases, into the spontaneous and passive physiological context, i.e., the fecundity-sterility continuum and the deliberate and intentional control or manipulation of the variable elements in that context. Necessary but not sufficient conditions for fertility are coitus (except for artificial insemination) and fecundity. Fecundity is a term for a physiological complex which includes ovulation on the part of the female, ejaculation of viable spermatozoa on the part of the male, union of sperm and ovum in the Fallopian tube, implantation of the ovum in the wall of the uterus, and intrauterine nurture and protection of the fetus from embryonic stage through to delivery of a living child. In some cases it may be possible to ascribe infecundity to inadequacies of the male or of the female, but there are also cases in which the fundamental problem is incompatibility, in the sense that both male and female might participate in a fertile union with another mate.

The terms "fecund" and "sterile" may be used on several levels of temporal referent. An individual may be described as sterile if he or she could become a parent in no union at any time. This would be true, for example, of a woman who had undergone a hysterectomy. A distinction may also be made between fecundity as of a point or short period of time, and fecundity as descriptive of a person's or a couple's total reproductive history. In particular, a woman's ovulation is generally synchronized with her menstrual cycle, and she is considered less likely to be able to participate in a fertile union in the period centered on her menstruation than in the period most removed from menstruation. Ovulation ceases upon conception and is not resumed until some time after delivery. There may be an anovulatory period following delivery, probably related to some extent to lactation. Furthermore, morbid conditions may temporarily reduce the likelihood of birth. The problem of fecundity evaluation is concerned not only with the conditions necessary for conception but also with those requisite to successful pregnancy and parturition. The degree of fecundity of a couple may be measured by the ratio of conceptions to exposed ovulations or by the inverse of this, the mean length of time required to conceive. Fecundity in this sense may be expected to vary from couple to couple, independently of the menstrual and pregnancy cycles, and from time to time and as a systematic function of age for the same couple.

Difficulties in defining fecundity are associated with measurement difficulties. In a sense, the ultimate test of fecundity is the occurrence of birth. If a birth occurs, the couple concerned were fecund in the time period concerned. On the other hand, if a couple exercises no interference with the probability of birth, and engages in regular and not too infrequent coitus, but do not have a birth, then their fecundity is doubtful. The degree of this doubt varies directly with the length of time concerned. In terms of the total procreative history a couple's fecundity—assuming absence of attempts to regulate fertility—may be measured by the couple's parity. In a context of coitus without control, fecundity and fertility are synonymous. There is, however, a subtle and critical conceptual difficulty concealed within this trichotomy of fecundity, coitus, and control. Behavior affecting the frequency of births is classifiable under one heading if there is knowledge of the trichotomy but under another heading in the absence of that knowledge. Moreover, the influences on fertility may be classified as cultural or individual, and regulation takes on an entirely different meaning for research with each classification. An important area of inquiry lies in distinguishing between influences on fecundity.

It follows from the preceding paragraph that a simple indirect measure of fecundity would be the parity distribution of married women who have completed their reproductivity, in a sociocultural context in which the level of intervention with the fertility process may be assumed on various grounds to be insignificant. In an approximate way, taking into consideration the obvious difficulties of accurate observation in such a context, mean completed parity may be as high as nine or ten, with the upper limit exceeding twenty and the proportion of zero parity close to 5 per cent. The probability of plural birth has a small influence on mean parity, but demographic or socioeconomic differentials cannot be confidently affirmed.

Yet even if parity is correctly enumerated, a number of reservations limit the inference of aggregate fecundity from aggregate fertility, and these reservations also indicate the many interwoven ways in which social patterns influence the manifestations of fecundity: (1) Fertility data for married women can be used to represent the fecundity of all women only on the implausible assumption that there is no selection for fecundity implicit in marriage. If brides and grooms are selected with some regard to health and physique (and this is true at least to the extent that marriage presupposes survival) and if these characteristics are correlated with fecundity, then married couples will tend to be more fecund than random pairs. Marriage, as legitimation of a fruitful sexual union, is a specific selection mechanism. (2) Customs influence the ages of marriage of husband and wife. Late marriage eliminates fecund exposure, whereas early marriage may prejudice fecundity through morbidity attributable to premature exposure. (3) Marriage, and thus exposure, may be terminated for the wife (at least temporarily) by the death of the husband. Marriages which persist to the end of the female's fertile years are selected for health and thus possibly for fecundity. Marriages terminated by death of the husband represent some elimination of exposure for females. Marriages terminated by death of the wife are not included in the computation of mean completed parity. In the presence of persistent infertility, the society frequently justifies marital dissolution by divorce. Conversely, monogamy decreases aggregate fecundity by supporting the continuation in marriage of a sterile couple. (4) To be exhaustive, this list should include such items as the prevalence of polygamy, premarital coitus, permissive attitudes toward alternative means of sexual gratification, and other aspects of procreative behavior influenced by social norms.

Most important of all is the dubious assumption that any society is free of fertility regulation within marriage, not only because knowledge about birth control is universal but also because fertility-limiting practices such as intercourse taboos are widespread. The incidence of fetal mortality is an additional piece of relevant information available from secondary sources. Fecundity is defined in terms of the occurrence not of conception but of birth, and a fetal death is a conception which has failed to come to fruition. There is a considerable body of data, unfortunately of low quality typically, on variations of spontaneous fetal mortality as a function of demographic (such as maternal age, parity, and birth interval) and socioeconomic variables. Such evidence is more properly considered and evaluated in the mortality chapter of this volume.

Another source, at present limited to small and highly selected samples of individuals, consists of clinical observations, based on experimental findings, of physiological characteristics of males and of females which seem to be related to fecundity. In a small proportion of cases it is possible to identify a male, a female, or a couple as having a temporarily or permanently low or zero probability of birth because of pathological conditions of the reproductive system. Among the causes identified are immaturity, dietary deficiencies, neuroses, specific infections, and malignant and benign neoplasm. In addition, any resort to sterilization is clearly a negative influence on fecundity although it is most properly classified for analytical purposes as a type of birth control.

Conversely, couples may increase the probability of conception by obtaining the help of specialists in removing known and modifiable causes of sterility, by seeking assistance through artificial insemination, by using temperature records to synchronize coitus and ovulation, and so forth. For the majority of the population all that can be determined by medical examination is that there is no known reason why the couple concerned cannot have a child.

Records of the time required for conception by couples experiencing regular sexual congress without known regulatory activity furnish a third source of evidence, intermediate between fertility statistics and clinical data. These records reveal considerable variance among couples, with a mean length of time required for conception of approximately four lunar months or ovulations. The presumption of sterility increases with the length of the interval. Until recently such data were available only for restricted and special subsamples of the general population, but a study to be published soon contains an extensive amount of evidence of this type and a record of known sterility indications of the clinical variety, for a sample of the young white married female population of the United States.

Without evidence, we may still infer that, between groups characterized by endogamy, there are hereditary differences in fecundity. As a minor but substantiated example, populations differ in their distribution by blood groups and thus in the proportion of unions in which the blood groups of male and female are different, and incompatibility of blood groups is a demonstrated source of sterility. In addition, there are a number of environmental conditions which undoubtedly play some part in establishing fecundity differentials between populations. Group differentials in fecundity probably correlate with differences in health, both generally and with specific reference to certain types of morbidity, such as venereal diseases, which influence the reproductive process. A high frequency of infertility has been noted among impoverished populations. Societies probably differ in fecundity because of differences in knowledge about fecundity and because of differences in care of the woman during pregnancy and parturition.

Many hypotheses have been suggested to associate differences in the general pattern of life, excluding family limitation, among areas differing in fertility. Some of these hypotheses stress changes in activity patterns, ranging from the less active roles of men to the more active roles of women, and many suggest that an increase in general nervous tension has taken its reproductive toll through a decrease in coital frequency or more directly (and mysteriously) through a decrease in fecundity. Specific dietary possibilities have been advanced, such as rich or excessive food, white bread and other prepared foods, alcohol, etc. The hypotheses suffer in general from one of two defects: a valid cause for a couple's sterility is applied to the general population without evidence that the incidence of the cause for the general population is changing; a factor whose incidence is changing for the general population is claimed as a cause of sterility without corroborative experimental demonstration.

In the specifically sexual area, it is likely that differences in mean coital frequency exist between social groups since this is to some extent a normatively oriented phenomenon, and it is also likely that this is a meaningful variable for the probability of conception and perhaps also for the probability of fetal mortality. Clearly, a very low coital frequency is prejudicial to the conception rate, and probably a very high frequency is too because the quantity and quality of the ejaculate is lowered. However, evidence is very weak concerning both the physiological nexus and the statistical background. It seems likely that coital position also has implications for the probability of conception, and coital position varies among cultures. Finally, some types of interference with reproduction may prejudice the future fecundity of the male or female. Evidence indicates that modern contraceptives have no such deleterious effects, but the more primitive types of fertility regulation may increase the risk of infection and prejudice subsequent fecundity. In particular, abortion procedures may play an important role in reducing the fecundity of most, if not all, populations.

By weighing the information pooled from these sources and by making inferences about the behavior of statistical aggregates, a model of fecundity may be constructed to indicate variations of fecundity by age of woman. It is probable that, for a birth cohort of women, aggregate fecundity increases at first gradually and then rapidly from the zero level in the early teens to a maximum not far below unity in the

early twenties, then declines gradually
for about twenty years and finally more
precipitately until it levels out, during
the forties, in a downward exponential
which apparently approaches zero in
the neighborhood of age fifty. The
probability traced in functional form
for the group is the compounded complement of complete sterility (temporary or permanent) on the part of some
couples and subnormal or low fecundity on the part of some of the remainder. Assumptions are required
concerning coital frequency—which
probably declines with age—as well as
lactation, types of contraception, and
levels of health. Throughout the reproductive period decline may be expected
as an accompaniment of the cumulation of morbid conditions, particularly
those associated with childbearing itself. A high level of fertility in the early
ages represents an exposure to greater
risk of damaging the reproductive apparatus and thus may prejudice fecundity at later ages. Fecundity may depend on parity, although the process of
successive sorting clearly leads to a
concentration of low fecundity women
in the low parities. Previous experience
with fetal deaths as well as with births
may be prejudicial to subsequent fecundity. This model, which could be of
use in establishing the proportion of
possible fertility actually achieved by a
population (and thus, by subtraction,
its level of regulation), must be evaluated in the light of the various traps of
cultural variability noted previously.
As a simple example of the problems
posed, it is difficult to talk about the
fecundity of a female in the absence of
a sexual union.

To summarize this section on fecundity, we may delineate a fourfold division of the components of fecundity:
(1) the genetic basis; (2) environmental influences, particularly those affecting the female's health and her reproductive equipment; (3) variations in

exposure not manifestly associated with
birth control; (4) a complex interstitial
area of interdependency between perceived fecundity and regulatory practices. It has become relatively routine
research practice to assume that the
fertilities of populations being compared do not differ in genetic fecundity. While this is probably invalid, it
is not likely to be seriously so, and the
rudimentary state of knowledge of the
genetic basis of fecundity makes the
practice a strategically sensible one.
But the larger assumption is also commonly made that differences in fertility between populations are solely the
consequence of differences in fertility
regulation. This may be true on balance, but it is clearly false in detail.
Progress in fertility research will be
considerably enhanced by the development of improved diagnoses of infecundity, and their extension from special to general samples of the population, as well as by the cumulation of
reproductive life histories, perhaps in
diary form, of menstruation, copulation, conception, fetal death, and birth.
This will facilitate a more satisfactory
evaluation of the extent to which differing cultural patterns contribute to
overt fertility differentials independently of fertility regulation. The practical research problem is probably the
interdependency of the measurement
of fecundity and the measurement of
fertility regulation.

FERTILITY REGULATION

Demographers agree that the major
influence on fertility variations is the
set of actions consciously taken by possibly fecund couples to influence the
probability of occurrence of a birth either at a particular time or beyond a
particular time. The reasons for their
unanimity on this point will be discussed later. The first problem is to outline the scope and variety of these actions. Many of the activities described

may be carried out without the intention to regulate fertility, but it seems advisable to restrict our attention to intentional control activity, i.e., activity perceived and defined by the couples concerned as regulation. We can regard all other fertility-influencing activity as falling into the fecundity category. The classification into this dichotomy is not always easy, and the problem is relative to the level of knowledge and clarity of purpose of the couples under observation. These matters are discussed at greater length in the section on reproductive institutions.

The scope of regulation is extensive, as will readily be seen from consideration of the chain of events which lead to birth; intervention at any link of the chain may be interpreted as fertility control. A division may first be made between activities intended to decrease the probability of birth and those intended to increase the probability of birth. The latter are so commonly excluded from general discussions that "family limitation" is regarded as a synonym for family planning or birth control, but this would clearly be an incomplete view of the subject. Nevertheless, because of the almost certainly greater empirical significance of the former category and because of the traditional emphasis on it, we will give prior attention to activities which reduce fertility. They may be classified according to their location in the fertility sequence.

First, although coitus is not absolutely essential to the occurrence of birth, because of artificial insemination, it may be regarded as practically so. Any reduction of the frequency of coitus intended to decrease the probability of birth is a means of fertility reduction, the extreme case being celibacy. A most important class of such activity is the combination of delayed marriage and premarital continence. Within marriage, the category includes

abstinence and reduced coital frequency. It should be noted that these means may be institutionalized—particularly in relation to pregnancy, lactation, and menstruation—but they need not be considered as volitional regulation. A third special subtype consists of periodic abstinence, commonly known as the "rhythm" or "safe period" method, which is the practice of restricting coitus to the period in which it is believed that the probability of fertilization of the ovum is least likely. Clearly, the practice and efficacy of this regulatory procedure are relative to the state of knowledge; for example, misinformation probably has increased the probability of conception in the past because of restriction of the coitus to periods then believed to be, but now known not to be, sterile. There is also a wide variety of means of gratifying sexual desires outside the realm of coitus or as variations of coitus. Even if "the passion between the sexes" were constant, the means of gratifying this passion are not confined to completed coitus. In addition to masturbation, homosexual practices, and a wide variety of so-called perversions, this category includes the very important type of fertility regulation known as coitus interruptus, or withdrawal, and a variant of this, coitus reservatus. Aside from coitus interruptus and coitus reservatus, these activities are not necessarily pursued with fertility regulation in mind, but a couple's acceptance of them may be much more feasible than the practice of abstinence from regular coitus.

The other categories of means of fertility reduction all presume that regular completed coitus is occurring. The second category is the variety of operative (and perhaps soon chemical) techniques by which sterilization may be achieved for the female or the male. Although research is now proceeding on the inducement of temporary sterility, present methods of sterilization are irreversible. There is also a possible relationship between lactation and delay in the resumption of ovulation after a pregnancy. It is apparently a widespread belief that the mother who feeds her baby at the breast cannot become pregnant again until lactation ceases. While this is a false generalization, there is probably a correlation in the indicated direction. Accordingly, the practice of lactation intended to reduce the probability of birth must be cited in a complete list and marked as a technique which probably has low efficacy.

Third, sterilization has the unique characteristic at present of influencing all subsequent reproductive experience of the person concerned. Most fertility regulation is probably action taken at every act of coitus to reduce the likelihood of conception at that time. In other words, this is a type of regulation specifically oriented to time. There are two major categories of contraception: the physical and the chemical. The former, divisible into devices used by the female (like the diaphragm) and devices used by the male (such as the condom), consists of the interposition of a physical barrier between the ejaculate and the ovum. The second consists of the use of some type of spermicide either before, during, or after coitus. An intermediate category consists of the practice of douching, which combines the removal of sperm with spermicidal activity. It is clear that in such activities as douching subsequent to coitus the motivational element is paramount. Several studies have reported the prevalence of douching for hygienic reasons, at least according to stated intention. Clearly, the problem here is to distinguish between the intent and the statement. Activities believed to reduce the likelihood of conception are considered meaningful in terms of purpose even if they are re-

mote from rationality, e.g., voiding after coitus or adoption of alternative coital positions.

The final category of fertility regulation is induced abortion. In this case conception has occurred, and the activity is aimed at the prevention of a (live) birth. In other words, abortion consists of efforts to increase the probability of fetal mortality. In terms of probable incidence this is a highly important category, but, because it is throughout the world defined as illegal in most situations, the data concerning its practice are very weak. The legalization of abortion in many circumstances and the provision of efficient facilities for it (as in Russia briefly during the interwar period, and in Japan very recently), have led to a very high reported frequency of abortions. Even in the absence of official approval, the number of abortions has been estimated to be equal to between 20 per cent and 100 per cent of births in various Western nations. Abortion methods, like contraceptive methods, may be classified as chemical or mechanical; the latter include both operative procedures and rudimentary practices like self-inflicted injury. Abortion is of particular distinction as a fertility control technique because its purpose is the prevention of an event which would otherwise have a high probability of occurrence, whereas contraception is aimed at the prevention of an event with a relatively low probability of occurrence. It is appropriate to add a footnote here: for the world as a whole, infanticide is undoubtedly a statistically important practice, distinguishable from abortion only by a fine line. Finally, any practices deleterious to the pregnant mother's health come close to the category of abortion because they increase the probability of fetal mortality, but the problem of ascertaining motivation in such situations makes classification almost impossible.

As mentioned in the introduction to this section, there is an important class of activities, called proceptive regulation, which are designed to increase the probability of birth. Taking into account the necessity of specifying motivation throughout, we may list, in apposition to the fertility reduction categories: (*a*) early marriage; (*b*) increased coital frequency; (*c*) coitus synchronized with ovulation; (*d*) adoption of the coital position most likely to insure contact of sperm and ovum; (*e*) avoidance of activities such as hygienic douching or lactation, which might reduce the probability of conception; (*f*) avoidance of contraceptive activity; (*g*) actions taken to increase fecundity or to reduce sterility. These would include specific treatment to remove causes of sterility, avoidance of sterilization even though indicated as desirable on other grounds, the use of specialists for prenatal care and for care during parturition, and, finally, the acceptance of artificial insemination. These activities are all, as indeed are the other regulatory activities, highly relative to the extent of knowledge. Obviously, deliberate avoidance of these activities should be classed as a fertility reduction practice.

Among the sources of information about fertility regulation there are many which are qualitative or inferential and not amenable to rigorous analysis. Knowledge of the reproductive process has been reported as adequate for control purposes in virtually all times and places. The level of technology is not an important barrier because such means as abstinence, coitus interruptus, and abortion are relatively efficacious without the use of artifacts. The applied science of contraception has expanded rapidly in the past hundred years with the vulcanization of rubber and the manufacture of condoms and diaphragms, with the production of spermicides, and with improved knowledge of ovulation time. Expansion in this area has been paralleled in the channels of information and opinion formation. A complete account would include the discussion of legislation and adjudication regarding the production, sale, and dissemination of information and propaganda about birth control; the results of public opinion polls concerning the propriety of birth control; data on the production and sales of manufactured contraceptives; and an evaluation of the relative roles of propaganda, technology, and attitudes with regard to behavior of this kind. In a crudely quantitative way it is clear that family size among nations has varied inversely with the dissemination of knowledge and the efficacy of techniques of contraception. Fertility regulation in the broad sense may also be inferred from the tendency for the crude birth rate and the crude marriage rate to fluctuate synchronously with conditions like economic depression which can generally be defined as inimical to fertility. Finally, hearsay leaves no doubt that a major proportion of the reduction in potential fertility achieved by couples in industrial societies is intentional.

The inferences and indications of this pile of information have been made more rigorous and quantitative by specific research inquiries into the practice and results of fertility regulation. The data gathered in these inquiries represent relatively complete procreative histories for couples, including dates of conception and parturition, periods of exposure to the risk of conception, extent of use of contraception during these periods, and types of contraception. As the following discussion will make clear, the evidence is too complex to be summarized conveniently, but it is generally accepted that the major source of variations in aggregate fertility is the effective practice of fertility control rather than fecundity differentials. Two general points need to be made about these studies. In the first place, the collections of individuals observed have not been representative of the population as a whole but have been selected in ways which relate closely to fertility, fecundity, and fertility regulation or in ways which emphasize particular socioeconomic characteristics. The analytic limitations implicit in this selectivity have, however, been recognized and minimized; in fact, there now exist unpublished data which do not share the limitations of selectivity. Despite the evident worth of these studies, the outstanding point is that we have very few adequate data on this very important category of human behavior.

Second, these pieces of research are concerned almost exclusively with contraception. In broad societal perspective, the roles of premarital and marital abstinence, sterilization, and abortion are equally important; no study of fertility regulation can be complete if it excludes them from consideration. Nevertheless, the remainder of this section will follow the conventional focus on contraception. Because these other ways of controlling the frequency of births are ignored, it may be noted parenthetically that a comprehensive study would have to cope with the technically difficult problem of units of occurrence varying with the category of regulatory procedure employed. Abstinence means the elimination from exposure of a series of ovulations (usually prior to fertility); sterilization means elimination from exposure of a series of ovulations subsequent to fertility; periodic abstinence is specific to individual ovulations; all other contraception is specific to individual copulations; abortion is specific to conception. Each of these is in its own way conditional upon fecundity. As a single unit applicable to all types of regulation, ovulation may be proposed as relatively satisfactory,

but for those controls specific to copulations coital frequency will have the status of a hidden variable.

Contraception may be measured and analyzed by means of occurrence/exposure rates, in the same way as fertility. Following the suggestion of the above paragraph, we may interpret the frequency of occurrence as the number of ovulations of the wife for which some method of prevention of conception was employed. The meaning of exposure is by no means as simple. The regulation of fertility is conceptualized as the employment of various means to achieve procreative ends. Accordingly, there are three criteria for evaluating exposure: (1) the couple concerned must regard rationality, or the means-end schema, as an appropriate frame of normative reference to apply to reproduction; (2) they must have the end of non-fertility in the time period concerned; (3) they must employ some means in order that the end be achieved; i.e., they must be fecund and engaging in coitus. It is clear that these conditions are not only functions of time throughout the couple's procreative history but also complex continua rather than affirmative-negative dichotomies. Varying degrees of rationality may be employed; ends may be vague, ambiguous, and held with varying degrees of resolution; perceived fecundity may vary between zero and unity. To further complicate the issue, each condition is interwoven with the others in the circumstances of any concrete situation.

One major determinant of the extent and efficacy of contraceptive use is the degree to which the population defines rationality in the procreative sphere as moral or immoral. A question posed to an informant regarding his or her attitude toward fertility regulation will generally elicit an expression of belief, but inquiry into why that belief is held is highly unlikely to be profitable. Generally, the sources of non-rational conduct are unknown to the individual and must be investigated on the sociocultural level. In the absence of attitude inquiry, the classification of couples as rational and non-rational in this respect may be inferred from their actions, provided they are fecund and do not want an unlimited number of children. Considerations of rationality also intrude into the area of choice of contraceptive method. The Roman Catholic church defines all methods of contraception except periodic abstinence, an intrinsically inefficient procedure, as immoral. Thus the efficacy of contraception is influenced by non-rationality.

Contraception is also influenced by esthetic considerations, meaning in general the extent to which fertility regulation interferes with coital satisfaction. Abstinence, coitus interruptus, the use of physical contraceptives, and the general diminution of psychosexual satisfaction by the intrusion of calculation are cases in point. Esthetic considerations may be viewed as components of rational behavior, i.e., ends which are weighed against the end of non-fertility. Analytically, a large probability of a small gain is weighed against a small probability of a large loss.

Another important determinant of the extent and efficacy of contraceptive use is inadequate rationality. This category is multidimensional. The necessity for fertility regulation is conditional upon the level of fecundity of the couple, and the choice of procedure is conditional upon their knowledge. We may profitably distinguish between the state of scientific knowledge of fecundity and contraception during a period and the knowledge actually possessed by the couple concerned. The extent to which a couple know their fecundity is an important factor in evaluating contraceptive rationality because they may eschew contraception when they believe it unnecessary. The category of

rationality about means includes not only the level of knowledge of the couple relative to the state of science at the time and the extent to which the couple attempt to improve their knowledge but also the efficiency with which the selected procedure is employed and the foresight and prudence implicit in the regularity of its use. It seems likely that carelessness as well as intelligence has significant social and psychological correlates. Rationality is probably also relative to the particular contraceptive method used, but this aspect may be regarded as a component of the intrinsic efficacy of the method concerned.

If the problems discussed above can be solved adequately in research, the extent to which a population exercises reproductive rationality by using contraception may be readily evaluated. The other facet of reproductive rationality, the efficacy of contraception, is much more difficult to estimate. If fecundity were known, the actual birth rate for the period of contraceptive exposure could be compared with the expected birth rate in the absence of contraceptive exposure; this comparison would achieve a direct measure of efficacy (or rather of its complement). It is obviously incorrect to estimate the expected birth rate in a context of non-control from the experience of those not using contraception at all since these latter are highly likely to be selected for sterility. The measurement of the efficacy of fertility control is conditional upon the existence of known fecundity in much the same way as the measurement of fecundity is conditional upon the existence of known fertility control. One critical difference, however, is that both fecundity and failure of control may be definitely established by fertility, but success of control and infecundity are inseparable alternative explanations of infertility. The situation must be relatively common in which a couple with the end of non-fertility refuse to test their fecundity by resort to coitus without contraception. In such cases the best inference about fecundity, in the absence of medical indications, will probably be derived from the couple's experience in other periods.

The efficacy of contraceptive use, like the frequency of use, is dependent on the degree of fecundity, and inadequate knowledge of the latter results in inadequate measurement of the former.

The measurement of contraceptive efficacy (by computing the ratio of the fertility rate for controlled exposure to the estimated fertility rate for uncontrolled exposure) can provide data for analyzing efficacy as a function of socioeconomic variables, demographic variables (like age, parity, or duration), or type of method used. The components of the exposure period should ideally be weighted differentially for fecundity if there are important variations in fecundity among the groups being compared; in particular, sterile periods like pregnancy and the puerperium should be eliminated from the denominator. This raises the interesting point that contraceptive efficacy as a characteristic of a particular coital act or ovulation will, in general, differ markedly from efficacy in terms of parity reduction; contraceptive failure eliminates a period of exposure, but contraceptive success must be repeated with each succeeding ovulation. Furthermore, unwanted conceptions may eventuate in accidental or intentional fetal death, or even in sterility.

A second distinctive aspect of efficacy measurement is that a partial success from the standpoint of the aggregate measure—a delay of conception—may be interpreted by the couple concerned as a complete failure (and indeed a birth after a long interval may be interpreted as less desirable than a birth after a short interval). In the third place, even though contraception is ac-

tion against conception, contraceptive failures should be measured by births rather than by conceptions. It would be inconsistent to register as successful birth control an unfertilized ovulation which may be a consequence of infecundity but to register as unsuccessful a conception which is later frustrated by an accidental fetal death; the latter phenomenon is equally part of infecundity. The same consideration would not apply to abortion.

The kind of information necessary for an accurate appraisal of the extent to which fertility regulation is practiced and of the efficacy with which it is practiced, is intrinsically difficult to obtain. Problems of sensitivity and rapport are inevitable in questions about sexual behavior, although recent experience has revealed less difficulty than expected. The most important questions are those which strike at the core of the value system, and these, by the same token, are either the most sensitive questions to answer or the questions for which the couples have no answer. Not only is the area of procreative behavior defined as private and intimate, but the particular behavior may be defined as immoral or illegal— so that a question is tantamount to asking for a confession. This inspires negative reaction and misstatement and is almost certainly a latent factor in problems of recall.

Even if the material were non-sensitive, the questioning procedure is to some extent concerned with a long series of events on which the problem of recall is considerable. This applies especially to questions concerning frequency or, more explicitly, completeness of control as opposed to incidence. For example, it has been observed that couples tend to ascribe accidents to non-use rather than to misuse. Equally severe issues arise in investigating the complementary areas of fecundity and intention. Although sterility has a residue of shame or guilt attached to it, the sensitivity of the area is probably secondary as a research barrier to the competence of the testimony. And for an infertile couple the false confession of sterility may be regarded as less shameful than the true confession of birth control. The determination of a couple's ends runs afoul of hindsight and rationalization regarding the occurrence of a birth. Although prior to conception a couple may have stated that a birth was undesirable, after the fact they may have reconciled themselves completely to the occurrence or have come into possession of information which would have changed their intention. In either eventuality the classification of the birth as a failure of regulation may have an entirely different meaning for the couple and for the analyst. Indeed, to ask a couple to classify a conception as accidental and unwanted is to force them into a partial rejection of their child and a confession of inefficiency; in sociocultural contexts like ours this is a serious charge. Only a skilled and tactful analyst will succeed in coping with research obstacles like these.

One basic distinction will serve as a convenient termination of this section and introduction to the next. We have asked how, to what extent, and with what success couples attempt to influence the consequences of coitus. This identifies as an important research area the socioeconomic correlates of reproductive rationality—using this as an omnibus term to encompass the acceptability of a rational frame of reference for fertility decisions—and the degree to which rationality is approached through regular and effective use of control procedures when fecundity may exist and fertility is not desired. This rationality is a necessary but not sufficient component of explanation of fertility differentials because, given reproductive rationality, fertility will vary with the evaluations of the desirability of birth.

The second distinct and important research area, accordingly, lies in the socioeconomic correlates of reproductive ends. One crucial research finding may be cited as exemplification of the separate relevance of these two questions. Although early studies of differential fertility revealed an inverse relationship between fertility and income, the curve of fertility by income has more recently been observed to have a reverse-J shape, the former inverse relationship being transformed into a direct relationship in the upper reaches of the income distribution. Division of the population by reference to the degree of reproductive rationality has permitted the explanation that, whereas the extent and efficacy of fertility regulation tend to vary inversely with income, the reproductive ends of fertility regulators tend to vary directly with income, and the overt fertility differentials are the product of these conflicting influences.

A tentative explanation of the recent history of Western fertility may be inferred from this point. The major transition from an inefficient to an efficient level of replacement may be attributed for the most part to an extension of reproductive rationality throughout the populations and subpopulations concerned; the difference in fertility between an unregulated and a regulated situation tends to be much greater than the variance of reproductive ends. But the closer toward the pole of completely controlled fertility a population moves, the more significant this variance becomes. Thus, even if the trend toward greater fertility regulation is irreversible, we cannot infer from this the direction of fertility. There is no compelling reason for believing that the determinants of reproductive ends are identical with the determinants of achievement of those ends, although there would seem to be justification for the hypothesis that the probability of rejection of a non-rational pattern of behavior in this area will vary with the gravity of the consequences of non-rational fertility levels. The implications for research are clear: the greater the proportion of the population efficiently controlling its procreation, the greater the emphasis that must be placed on the causal nexus of childbearing decisions. Possibly the recent rise in fertility in the Western world was unexpected partly because of neglect of the distinction made here.

REPRODUCTIVE INSTITUTIONS

The reproductive ends which couples seek to achieve by fertility regulation may be considered the consequence of a complex utilitarian calculus, involving an assessment and evaluation of the utilities and disutilities expected to flow from procreative decisions made at each copulation among desirable but competing alternatives. As an example of the many dimensions of this process, there is the determination of the desired distribution of children by number, age, and sex. The decision concerning timing is related to the physiologically advantageous interval between successive pregnancies as well as to the desired relative ages of children. The time of occurrence of a birth can be influenced negatively with much more accuracy than it can be influenced positively. The sex of a prospective child cannot be influenced, but a child of the desired sex is more likely if the number of children be increased.

Since children are almost always born one at a time, at intervals which are rarely less than a year, there is inherent flexibility of accommodation to changing conditions or attitudes. This is a fortunate circumstance in the light of the uncertainty of various relevant factors in the decisions, such as the woman's ability to cope with the process of bearing and rearing or the success of the husband in his occupational role. Flexibility permits the gradual sharpening of objectives which are unavoidably based on imperfect and derivative data. Because definitions change with a changing context, a sequential inquiry has important advantages. A retrospective inquiry will almost certainly have serious deficiencies since rationalization and selective recall obscure the facts of the past.

To judge from reports of informants, emphases of analysts, and everyday conversation, economy is the paramount determinant of fertility decisions. A child may be viewed as a good produced by the parents for their consumption. The cost of production in terms of items which are immediately quantifiable in monetary terms includes a prospective stream of payments for childbearing, feeding, clothing, housing, educating, and so forth, in addition to the possible loss of income of an otherwise working wife. In return, the child may represent not only a time stream of intangible utilities (which are manifest in the reasons for liking children) but also of revenues from its use in familial production.

The satisfactions of parenthood, or the demand for children, are non-economic in their definition; but the value of a child as a durable production good may be measured by the increase in parental income from direct contributions of labor to the family economic enterprise, from contributions of income derived from non-familial employment, and from the financial security provided parents in their old age. Within this framework of analysis it is clear that, independent of the demand for children as a consumption good, relative to the demand for other goods, the decision on having a child is an inverse function of its cost (discounted for expected revenues) relative to the cost of alternative purchases, on the one hand, and a direct function of the level of income, on the other. Accordingly, a complex set of calculations is required before we may infer that a decline in fertility means a lesser desire for children. Conversely, and with direct relevance for recent events in the United States and elsewhere, we are not entitled to infer from a rise in fertility that there is a greater desire for children, particularly if income is rising at the same time. The paucity of research into fertility economics represents a serious lacuna in demographic analysis. However, such research cannot provide an understandiing of the reasons for the evaluation of children relative to alternative expenditures or of the network of attitudes and norms determining the legitimacy of expectation of revenues from children. This understanding depends on research at the aggregate sociocultural level of analysis in the same way that the interpretation of income and employment trends is a subject for macro-economics.

There are many facets to fertility economics which make inquiry in this area both worthwhile and difficult. The income of the family and its expenditure follow characteristic time patterns which are related to the occupational and the procreative careers. Since reproductive decisions typically come very early in the life cycle of the family and since the costs of these decisions extend a considerable distance into the future, income expectations tend to be more relevant than current income in the decision-making process, although this will also be a function of the couple's economic horizon. An important alternative to investment in a child is investment in a career, sacrificing present consumption for a higher or more secure level of future consumption. In addition, most families have more than one child, and each new member of the family represents a threat to expenditures on or investment in the existent children. The love of children may find its expression in qualitative as well as in quantitative terms. Finally, the theory of fertility economics requires detailed attention to the influence of short-run variations in income. From the experience of the Western world during the 1930's it seems valid to hypothesize that the timing pattern of fertility is highly responsive to fluctuations of economic fortune but that the parity eventually achieved is much less elastic. Parenthetically, we may note that present thinking on fertility may be unduly conditioned by the massive fertility fluctuation of the past several decades. There may be a need for two theories of fertility variation, both spatiotemporally and by social class, the one focused on long-run analysis and the other concerned with determinants of fertility behavior in the short run.

Because the economic components of child cost are more readily quantifiable, we must avoid ranking them as more important than other costs. We may speak in general of the economy of time and the destruction of this resource which a child represents for the mother and to some extent for the father. The physical costs to the wife may be even more important. Childbearing handicaps a woman before, during, and after delivery; the experience is at best painful and at worst may result in maternal morbidity or mortality. To this list must be added the costs of space and comfort, of emotional and physical energy, and of responsibility. A child may represent an asset or a liability to the delicate psychological structure of the family and its constituent individuals. Research into the relationships between fertility regulation and the psychological dimension of family life has been rather unsuccessful, but these factors may still be significant in explaining parity variations from couple to couple. There is one important extenuating circumstance: the identification, conceptualization, and operational definition of the independent psychological variables have not yet achieved a satisfactory level. Whatever the overt significance of socioeconomic variables in the explanation of fertility differentials, these variables must operate through motivational channels.

It is probably manifest in the above notes, which summarize a mass of completed or planned research, that interest has been overwhelmingly concentrated on the negative influences on decisions regarding childbearing. This emphasis is partly a response to the problem of explaining the decline in fertility, but it is also partly a reflection of the cloudy sources of positive motivation, which fundamentally cannot be identified by the individuals concerned. In general, people do not know why they want children. Interviews can yield valuable data on the components of reproductive decisions—ideally a comprehensive array of ordered preferences and valuations and an explicit statement of the norms governing the situation—but they cannot be expected to provide explanations of these values and norms. In the last analysis, it is just as fruitless to ask couples why they have selected a particular set of fertility goals as it is to ask couples why they consider contraception to be right or wrong. The degree of reproductive rationality in a population and the values manifested in decisions about fertility are social facts. They may be explained on the sociological plane by the study of comparative reproductive institutions.

The norms and values which individuals use to decide among alternative courses of action derive from the needs of their social groups and from the particular modes of fulfilment of these needs which have evolved within their culture. The most pertinent societal requisite for this discussion is obviously the physical replacement of members, a need which Homo sapiens shares with every other biological species. Now procreation admittedly has a powerful ally in the sex urge, but the process of bearing and rearing a child is costly in resources, in time, and in maternal health; and the knowledge of ways to satisfy sexual desires without bearing a child is virtually universal. Every society regulates the achievement of replacement and insures that coitus will, in an adequate proportion of cases, be permitted to culminate in birth or that it will not be eschewed for fear of birth. In the face of the heavy mortality which almost all societies throughout almost all of history have faced, because of inadequate control over their environments, replacement could be achieved only by constant pressure on the population to bear children. This pressure can take such diverse forms as orders from the patriarch of a clan to his kindred, the scorn or pity of neighbors for the sterile wife, a national policy for subsidization of childbearing, or an exhortation, ostensibly from a superempirical source, to "be fruitful, multiply, and replenish the earth."

Notwithstanding the ubiquity of pressures favoring fertility, there is no society which can afford to seek maximum procreation. This may be inferred from the proposition that society, in satisfying its need for replacement, cannot ignore such other requirements as maintenance of an adequate scale of living and preservation of the institutional structure. And whatever the particular cultural solutions of these and other problems, they inevitably impinge upon fertility norms. Among the many components of societal structure, the kinship system is clearly central to our present topic. In the following discussion the family is regarded as a social device for coping with the problems of replacement and resource exploitation.

The ways in which fertility is regulated in a society are almost completely determined by the conjuncture of three somewhat autonomous but necessarily interdependent systems of action: the demographic, the technological, and the familial. At considerable risk of oversimplification, we will direct our attention to three societal types, each of which is characterized by distinctive values of the parameters identified above. The characteristics of Type I are high fertility and mortality, labor-intensive agriculture, consanguineal familism, and fertility regulated by abortion, infanticide, and abstinence; and the type is exemplified by the peasant societies of the Far East. The characteristics of Type II are somewhat lower fertility and mortality, labor-extensive agriculture, conjugal familism, and fertility regulated by nuptiality control (particularly delayed age at marriage); the prototype is pre-industrial Europe. The characteristics of Type III are low fertility and mortality, industry, individualism, and fertility regulated by contraception, as in the contemporary West. In the following paragraphs we will attempt to describe the logic of interdependency among the values of the selected parameters for each type, and some outstanding features of the Western transition from Type II to Type III, and conclude the discussion with an assessment of the prospects for transition of the underdeveloped areas of the world from Type I to Type III.

Societies of Type I are characterized by low levels of science and technology, high and fluctuating mortality risks, settled cultivation emphasizing the contribution of labor in quantitative terms, and an extremely limited economic horizon. The kinship system emphasizes the dominance of the family of orientation over the family of procrea-tion, and of consanguineal over conjugal ties. The decision of marriage and the choice of marital partner is in the hands of the family rather than of the individuals concerned. The purpose of marriage is to fulfil group needs of replacement and labor supply by childbearing, and not to provide individual satisfactions. The fact that additional numbers represent potential political and economic assets—particularly since inefficient technology tends to emphasize quantity—takes precedence over the immediate costs to the wife and husband.

Aligned with this network of elements is a pattern of fertility regulation which hedges against replacement failure by early and universal marriage and disapproval of contraception but which avoids the embarrassment of depleted per capita resources by tolerating abortion and infanticide. These societies maintain a precarious equilibrium between the Scylla of population shortage and the Charybdis of food shortage by maximizing the number of conceptions and depressing the number of children. Where the economic horizon is so short as to prevent a rational assessment of the consequences of an increase in family size at the time of conception, abortion and infanticide represent successful resolutions of known problems. Characteristically, abortion and infanticide symbolize the relative insignificance of individual life in such a society.

The reproductive norms characteristic of Type I societies do not consistently operate in favor of fertility. For example, abstinence is commonly enjoined on married couples during special times of the cultural year or during a woman's lactation. Although these taboos are explained by magical references to cleanliness, they clearly have the consequence of extending the birth interval and lessening the likelihood that the woman will be burdened by more than one infant at a time. As a second case in point, a taboo on the remarriage of widows is frequently encountered, and this can reduce exposure considerably in a high mortality context. The existence of norms like these exemplifies the proposition that there is conflict and compromise among the social arrangements for satisfying different functional and structural requirements. Institutionalized abstinence, like contraception taboos and arranged marriage, manifests the supremacy of consanguineal relations over conjugal relations. The taboo on widow remarriage symbolizes the affiliation of the widow and her children not to her husband but to his family; the frequent alternative to this taboo, the levirate, merely underlines this point. Reproductive norms are consistent not so much with the need for high fertility as with the subjugation of the individual and the married couple to the will of the larger group. Maintenance of the social structure takes precedence over demographic replacement, but the form of the social structure serves to guarantee high fertility.

The pivot of social organization in Type II societies is the nuclear family. The economy is agricultural, but the level of technology yields lower levels of mortality and reduces the economic advantages of the large kinship unit—although technology is still inadequate for provision of efficient means of contraception. The outstanding difference between these societies and those of Type I is in the field of marriage. The principal type of fertility regulation is nuptiality control, specifically delayed marriage. The family of procreation is relatively independent of the family of orientation, and, since the predominant form of resource exploitation is agriculture, marriage tends to be conditional upon obtaining land. The decision to marry is the couple's own, and respon-

sibility for support of the family falls on the husband's shoulders. Thus the adjustment of population to resources is achieved by "prudential restraint," postponement of marriage until the union can be economically viable.

In these societies the responsiveness of the marriage rate to economic fluctuations is well demonstrated. Since the production unit is the nuclear family, children are welcomed as potential additions to the labor force. Although contraception is not institutionalized in this type of society, several circumstances make it more likely than in the societies of Type I. The prevalence of late age at marriage seems propitious for the acquisition of techniques of withdrawal by unmarried couples, and these techniques are still available after marriage. Empirically, the fluctuations of fertility with the alternation of good and bad harvests in pre-industrial Europe can only partially be explained by the fluctuations of nuptiality. Finally, the greater respect for individual life and marriage and the more extended economic horizon make withdrawal a probable preference over abortion or infanticide, when economic difficulties arise.

Type II societies provided the context for a vast process of social change. The decline of fertility in the West was only part of a pervasive transformation of social and economic institutions toward societal Type III. The overt agency for this decline was a change in the predominant mode of fertility regulation from nuptiality control to marital contraception. This change was assisted and promoted—but not initiated—by technological innovations which provided adequate supplies of efficient mechanical and chemical contraceptives and by extensive propaganda and education to disseminate these throughout the population, but the germ of the transition was already present in the tradition of prudential restraint, supplemented to some extent by coitus interruptus. Many authors have suggested that the new fertility pattern was a consequence of a general movement from traditionalism toward rationalism in the wake of scientific successes in the physical and biological realms and a consequence of a decline in the authority of formal religion, an inherently conservative force. Granting the crucial significance of such developments, it still seems probable that the new patterns of procreation are no more rational in the current socioeconomic context than were the old patterns in terms of the former way of life. The logic of the new pattern of low fertility in Type III societies is summarized in the following paragraphs, under three broad and interdependent categories of variation: the decline in mortality, the transition from agriculturalism to industrialism, and the changing evaluation of the individual vis-à-vis the family.

In describing the sociocultural background of fertility decline, mortality plays a prominent role as an independent variable. As noted previously, society's problem is not fertility but replacement. The higher the level of mortality, the greater the social emphasis which must be placed on fertility; but, as mortality declines, such emphasis becomes less and less appropriate. Within the familial setting mortality decline means that each birth represents more person-years of child life. The healthier environment is probably correlated with an increase in the ratio of birth to conception and of conception to copulation. Furthermore, the couple stands less chance of a premature termination of their marriage through mortality. Accordingly, a pattern of non-interference with coitus would lead, *ceteris paribus,* to a marked increase in marital fertility as measured by number of living children. The transition from high fertility to low fertil-

ity in national statistics may be viewed in terms of family histories as a transition from families kept small by mortality, through a transitory phase of large families, to a recovery of the small family pattern. The decline in fertility may be understood as a reaction to the conjuncture of growing family size and declining economic advantage of family size. Within the community, sympathy for the unintentionally small family which suffered a labor shortage or risk of extinction would tend to be replaced by pity for the large family straining at its resources and losing its progeny to the migratory process.

The transition from agriculture to industry as the fundamental source of income implies the devaluation of children. A young person on a farm could become a useful member of the family labor force at an early age, serve as apprentice and then partner to his father before inheriting the family farm, and provide the parents with some form of annuity upon their retirement. But the son in an industrial economy is unlikely to be employable until after an expensive and extensive period of education toward which the father is unlikely to be competent to contribute. The economic component of a child's value undoubtedly changes in a negative direction. Highly relevant as an indispensable component of the Type III society is urbanism. The city is a symbol of secular rationality and a repository of interests and associations competitive with the family. In this anonymous world the individual is measured more for himself than for his family connections. In a fundamental sense the family and the city are incompatible groups. Yet urban industrialism represents not only a competitor of the family but also a source of higher income; therefore, the number of children "purchased for consumption" may increase in this environment despite a decline in their relative evaluation.

The last and perhaps most significant component of social change for present purposes is the shift of emphasis from familial interests toward individual interests in the Type III societies. The scope of familial activities has become progressively attenuated as specialized institutions invade provinces like production, education, and recreation. The bonds between parents and children have been weakened as social and spatial mobility established distance between family of orientation and family of procreation. The potential conflict of roles between the familial and the occupational spheres seems to be a particularly fruitful area of inquiry. Parenthood gets its motivating power from the fact that it is an important way for the individual to locate himself in his social world. Its value is lowered as non-familial roles become important sources of prestige. For both husband and wife, involvement in and identification with extra-familial activities must compete with familial activities.

On the other hand, the family is not a less essential social unit than before, since, for example, it remains the indispensable agency in the socialization of children. It is more correct to speak of change than of decline in the family. Marriage and parenthood persist as norms for men and women, but the sociopsychological rationality of their persistence still seems to be undergoing a process of redefinition. Although the urban-industrial society seems clearly incompatible with the large family, it does not follow that the small family has any less viability. The normal way of life still includes marriage, the family is still an essential social institution, and family adjustment to life still may involve transitory difficulties without concession of defeat.

An important facet of the discussion of patterns of fertility regulation has been the transfer of responsibility from the larger kinship group to the immediate family. In the urban-industrial societies of Type III the responsibilities for demographic replacement and for maintenance of the scale of living tend to be shouldered by the state. These policies are predominantly pronatalist in character, and accordingly they represent a recognition of conflict, particularly in economic terms, between individual welfare and population preservation. The costs of childbearing to the couple may be reduced by tax exemptions, family allowances, and social provision of services like health and education. Parenthood may be rewarded by employment preference and exemptions from military service. Finally, there are policies which attempt to influence types of fertility control by the society: legislation defining narrowly the situations of approved abortion and sterilization and legislation limiting the dissemination of contraceptives and information about them through clinics, publications, and sales outlets. These laws tend to be treated as anachronistic by the populace and by enforcement agencies alike. The extent to which population policies, particularly of the welfare kind, represent significant variables in the reproductive calculus of prospective parents is a relatively uninvestigated research problem.

The outstanding contemporary problem for demographic analysis is the future of fertility in the underdeveloped areas of the world. These areas are Type I societies, characterized by peasant agriculture and consanguineal familism. What are the prospects that they, as well as the Type II societies, may experience an evolution toward the Type III model? Demographically it is clear that mortality is quickly coming under control, and it is equally clear that, so far, fertility is not. This vital imbalance is producing a massive population increase because the areas concerned contain nearly two billion people. Because the scales of living are close to subsistence and the areas are for the most part overpopulated, the prevailing predictions are customarily phrased in catastrophic terms provided fertility does not decline quickly. It is a well-established sociological doctrine that institutions of long standing and deeply internalized bases, like the normative pressures for high fertility, are very slow to change. The European experience is used as a model. It is emphasized, for contrast unfavorable to the East, that the rise in the European scale of life was probably dependent on the absence of a dense population base at the beginning of the vital revolution and on the presence of empty lands to the west and east. More explicitly, it has been noted that the decline in fertility was accompanied and to some extent caused by a complete social and economic revolution. Accordingly, a dilemma is posed for the underdeveloped world: attempts to raise the scale of living will be frustrated by the inertia of high fertility, and attempts to lower fertility will be frustrated by the consequent inertia of socioeconomic development.

Although this argument may be highly useful for dramatizing the demographic facets of the plight of the underdeveloped areas, there are a number of respects in which it lacks plausibility. The Type III societies may not be in as fortuitous a position as were the Type II societies (in terms of the population-resource ratio), but the Type III societies face the problem with a superior contraceptive technology and an approximate knowledge of their demographic situation. Moreover, abortion (and even sterilization) need not be as dogmatically unacceptable to them as it has been in the individualistic West, particularly since

abortion has probably been a frequent fact of life throughout their history. Furthermore, population pressure in Europe built up slowly because mortality fell gradually and emigration siphoned off a large part of the surplus; its impact on the scale of life was not extreme because a margin above subsistence existed, and the successes of industrialization yielded rising income.

In the underdeveloped areas today, however, sharp mortality declines are occurring, appreciable migration is unfeasible, the economies are virtually at the subsistence level, and industrialization cannot be rapid enough to forestall the population explosion. The governments of these areas are to some extent prepared to assist fertility regulation, and probably they see far fewer advantages to an increase in population size than their European counterparts of a century or more ago. Since the types of societies concerned and the contexts in which the population problem must be worked out are utterly dissimilar, the most plausible inference is that the analysis of Western experience is inapplicable to the problems of the underdeveloped areas. The implications for needed research and theory are obvious.

The theoretical framework presented in this section, which, in somewhat similar form, is well represented in demographic literature, is deficient in rigor and verification, partly because of the inadequate operationality of key terms like familism, individualism, rationalism, and industrialism. The scope of the explanatory system extends into most provinces of sociology. The vital revolution represents only one quantifiable component of a major transformation of Western economy and society. Demographers have from time to time shown twinges of conscience concerning the shortage of theory in their discipline. Their uneasiness should be palliated by the consideration that the responsibility for theoretical and analytical development in so broad an area cannot be their burden alone. Many components of a dynamic model of socioeconomic change have been constructed, or are in process of current assembly. Provided the demographer recognizes his responsibilities as social theorist and scientist as well as empiricist and technician, he can participate without feelings of inferiority in this complex joint task. Indeed, he has several inherent advantages over other social scientists. Since the demographer defines his problems with regard to concrete referents, rather than analytic elements, he is less prone to focus on one aspect of the subject to the exclusion of others, and, above all, he has the tradition, essential for scientific theory, of devotion to carefully observed quantitative facts.

RESEARCH FRONTIERS

Throughout the body of this chapter numerous problems and potentialities for research in each area of the fertility field have been mentioned. It may be useful to summarize these in conclusion. The most obvious barrier to scientific progress here is the sheer insufficiency of quantitative materials concerning the parameters of procreation and their statistical relationship with demographic and socioeconomic variables. Official enumeration and registration data have been progressively improving, but at present they cover an extremely limited variety of empirical situations. The dearth of data for the high fertility areas explains in large part the theoretical inadequacies of our approach to the population problems of the underdeveloped world. Even the nations which are most mature statistically are commonly deficient in the demographic questions represented on birth registrations, and these nations show too little appreciation of a parity question on the census schedule. We

should encourage regular and frequent sample inquiries which include the details of reproductive history because this source has many advantages over registration materials in current fertility analysis. Although the statistical status of the United States is generally good, the absence of national marriage statistics is a considerable barrier to fertility research.

At present, techniques for controlling secondary source materials are markedly superior to the character and volume of data available for their application. There is, however, important methodological work to be done, particularly with a view to rendering comparable and integrable the results of studies which perforce use fertility measures differing in level of specificity, in type of index, in form of measure, and in temporal aggregation approach. Attempts are being and should continue to be made to establish the formal relationships among the vast array of possible measures differentiated in the above ways, for simple models of demographic change. Research into the necessary linkage among different measures should also be extended into the realms of data concerning fecundity, contraception, and family life, to establish liaison between primary and secondary source research. Finally, methods of measurement are still inadequate to optimal assessment of the procreative histories of birth and marriage cohorts which have not completed the fertile age span.

Although quantification of basic parameters is inadequate on the level of data which can be collected by governments, it is infinitely superior to the position in the area of the immediate causes of fertility variation: fecundity, copulation, and contraception. Improvements in the diagnosis of sterility would be of considerable assistance, but inquiry into differentials in fecundity and fertility regulation for social aggregates will necessarily depend on the accumulation of detailed procreative histories (preferably sequential rather than retrospective and perhaps in diary form) of menstruation, copulation, contraception, conception, and birth. Among the special problems in this area are the following: (1) the relation of coital frequency and lactation to the probability of conception and to demographic and socioeconomic variables; (2) the frequency of abortion and sterilization for the purpose of fertility regulation; (3) the extent of attempts to increase the probability of birth; (4) the extent to which marriage delay is used for fertility regulation; (5) the extent of coitus interruptus in various social contexts.

In the analysis of socioeconomic differentials in fertility, research needs to be transferred from secondary to primary sources. Data are needed on the separate roles played by function, status, and subculture variables in fertility variation. Because these may change throughout the reproductive lifetimes of couples, a family history approach seems highly advisable. In particular, more attention needs to be devoted to the sources of fertility variation between social groups, distinguishing between nuptiality differences and marital parity-specific fertility differences, between those who are socially mobile and those who are not, and between degree of reproductive rationality and nature of reproductive ends. For the field of fertility analysis generally, research is required on the economics of reproductive decisions (including the possible influence of population policies) and on the competition for time and interest among the various roles of prospective parents. Studies like these should help to bridge the present unfortunate and irrational gap between fertility analysis on the one hand and the sociology and economics of the family on the other.

There are also many fruitful prospects for research at the societal level. Too little work has been done on the relationships among temporal variations in fertility measures and in economic indexes for major social aggregates. Work like this, which may provide a basis for a short-run as well as a long-run theory of fertility variation, is seriously impeded by the shortage of persons who are technically competent both in demography and in economics. Indeed, even within demography, the compartmentalization of experts into national fertility, differential fertility, internal and external migration, and mortality probably represents short-term gains at the expense of long-term analytical necessities. A second interstitial area of potentially fruitful cross-fertilization lies between anthropology and demography. Critical insights for the analysis of fertility prospects in underdeveloped areas may develop from the study of the interrelationships among modes of resource exploitation, types of kinship system, and demographic parameters. Finally, a co-operative effort is required to establish a theory of socioeconomic change to encompass the past several centuries of Western history. Although this central task of social science clearly exceeds the demographer's grasp, it is a necessary condition for the explanation of variations in fertility.

SELECTED BIBLIOGRAPHY

DAVIS, K., and BLAKE, JUDITH. 1956. "Social Structure and Fertility: An Analytical Framework," *Economic Development and Cultural Change*, IV, 211–35.

GLASS, D. V., and GREBENIK, E. 1954. *The Trend and Pattern of Fertility in Great Britain: A Report on the Family Census of 1946*. Part I: "Report." Part II: "Tables." (*Papers of the Royal Commission on Population*, Vol. VI.) London: H. M. Stationery Office.

HENRY, L. 1953. *Fécondité des mariages: Nouvelle méthode de mesure*. ("Travaux et documents de l'Institut National d'Études Démographiques," Cahier No. 16.) Paris: Presses Universitaires de France.

HENRY, L. 1954. "Fertility According to Size of Family: Application to Australia," *Population Bulletin of the United Nations*, No. 4.

LEWIS-FANING, E. 1949. *Report on an Inquiry into Family Limitation and Its Influence on Human Fertility during the Past Fifty Years*. (*Papers of the Royal Commission on Population*, Vol. I.) London: H. M. Stationery Office.

LORIMER, F. 1954. "General Theory," in *Culture and Human Fertility*, by F. LORIMER *et al.*, Part I, pp. 13–251. Paris: UNESCO.

MURDOCK, G. P. 1949. *Social Structure*. New York: Macmillan.

SPENGLER, J. J. 1952. "Population Theory," in *A Survey of Contemporary Economics*, ed. B. F. HALEY; II, 83–131. Homewood, Ill.: Richard D. Irwin.

———, and DUNCAN, O. D. (eds.). 1956. *Demographic Analysis: Selected Readings*. Glencoe, Ill.: Free Press.

STIX, REGINE K., and NOTESTEIN, F. W. 1940. *Controlled Fertility*. Baltimore: Williams & Wilkins.

UNITED NATIONS, DEPARTMENT OF SOCIAL AFFAIRS, POPULATION DIVISION. 1953. "Economic and Social Factors Affecting Fertility," in *The Determinants and Consequences of Population Trends*, pp. 71–97. (ST/SOA/Ser. A/17.) New York: United Nations.

WHELPTON, P. K. 1938. "Fertility and Fecundity," in *Needed Population Research*, pp. 40–94. Lancaster, Pa.: Science Press.

———. 1954. *Cohort Fertility: Native White Women in the United States*. Princeton: Princeton University Press.

———, and KISER, C. V. (eds.). 1946–55. *Social and Psychological Factors Affecting Fertility*. 4 vols. New York: Milbank Memorial Fund.

19. Mortality

HAROLD F. DORN

The origin of the practice of registering burials is unknown. Undoubtedly this practice had existed for centuries before burial records were first used for statistical purposes. The original reasons for the registration of deaths quite possibly were in part religious and in part legal and economic since such records were essential for the orderly transfer of property from one generation to another.

Perhaps the earliest record of a rudimentary life table is one credited to the Roman, Ulpian, which dates from the third century A.D. and which apparently was used to determine the provisions of life annuity contracts. Although this table must have given only an approximation of the rate at which a generation died out, it was used in northern Italy for several centuries (Dublin, Lotka, and Spiegelman, 1949).

Records of births and deaths from the fourteenth century exist for a number of Italian cities (Gille, 1949). The keeping of records of baptisms, burials, and weddings by church officials spread throughout Europe. Thomas Cromwell, in 1538, during the reign of Henry VIII, ordered each parish to maintain registers of baptisms, christenings, weddings, and burials (Edge, 1928). This made official a practice that had existed for many years in some parts of England.

In some cities, possibly as a result of the interest in the number of deaths during the recurring epidemics, lists of deaths were published or posted in public places at weekly or less frequent intervals. The first known compilation of these data in London was in 1532 (Pearl, 1920). However, more than a century elapsed before John Graunt published the first comprehensive analysis of the weekly bills of mortality (Westergaard, 1932). The first edition of his book, *Natural and Political Observation Mentioned in the Following Index and Made upon the Bills of Mortality*, which appeared in 1662, must have represented the results of several years' study. Graunt's investigations are generally regarded as the precursor of modern studies of mortality and longevity.

Graunt's book stimulated other persons, not only in England but also on the continent of Europe, to study and analyze the existing parish registers. Perhaps the greatest value of these early studies was the interest they aroused in statistics of population, births, and deaths. Certainly the numerical results give only a crude idea of existing mortality conditions.

Correct measures of longevity and mortality must be based upon reliable censuses of population as well as upon the complete registration of deaths. The early investigators of mortality had neither. The parish registers included christenings, baptisms, burials, and weddings instead of births, deaths, and marriages. Moreover, many of the registers included only records of members of the official state church. Regular censuses of population as we know them today were practically unknown until the beginning of the nineteenth century, although regular counts of population for Sweden based upon pop-

437

ulation registers date from the middle of the eighteenth century.

As a consequence, the early life tables were based upon deaths only. The best known of these are Halley's table derived from deaths in Breslau during 1687–91 and Price's table based on deaths in Northampton, England. The latter was used by the Equitable Office upon its establishment in 1762. Since this table greatly overestimated the actual mortality rates, it proved very satisfactory for establishing life insurance premiums, but for the same reason it was unsatisfactory for fixing the terms of life annuity contracts. Much to its later regret, the government of England adopted Price's table as the basis for its annuity plans. A considerable sum of money was lost before the error in the table was discovered.

The computation of the first mortality table for an entire nation derived from statistics of death and population classified by age and sex is attributed to Per Wargentin, who used the average number of deaths registered in Sweden from 1755 to 1757 and the population registered in 1757. His calculations were made possible by an act passed in 1748, establishing a nationwide system of population registers from which regular reports of the number of births, deaths, and marriages, and the size of the population were made to a central governmental bureau. Thus, the first compulsory nationwide system of registration of vital statistics, applicable to the entire population, was adopted by Sweden in the middle of the eighteenth century.

The statistics collected during the first few years after the establishment of the national registration system were not published, since they were regarded as state secrets. Eventually the government relaxed its restrictions, and in 1776 Wargentin published his famous mortality tables for the period 1755–63. These were the first data to show that

for the entire population of a nation the death rate of males exceeded that for females.

Nearly a century went by before reliable national vital statistics became available for any country except the four Scandinavian nations. As national governments became stronger and as commerce and industry expanded, the need for statistical data concerning population, vital events, trade, commerce, crime, poverty, and other aspects of social life became widely appreciated. Shortly after 1800 regular population censuses were initiated by one country after another. Central statistical bureaus were created to collect and analyze the ever increasing amount of statistical data required by national governments.

Perhaps the most far-reaching event of the first half of the nineteenth century, insofar as medical statistics are concerned, was the establishment of civil registration of vital events throughout England and Wales. This act of Parliament became effective on July 1, 1837, and in 1839 William Farr was appointed Compiler of Abstracts in the General Register Office. Thus began what undoubtedly has been the most distinguished career in medical statistics.

It would have been easy for Farr to accept the prevailing opinion that the primary purpose of civil registration was to maintain a file of legal documents and to have devoted most of his time and energy to perfecting and operating the registration system. Indeed, the only provision for statistics in the Registration Act was that once a year a general abstract of the number of births, deaths, and marriages registered during the previous year should be presented to Parliament. It was fortunate for the future of medical statistics that this task was assigned to Farr, for he had no interest in the preparation of files of documents and in the compilation of statistical tables as an end in themselves; he was interested in statistics as a means of social reform.

Believing that how the people of England lived and died was one of the most important questions of the day, Farr devoted his entire official career to the task of using the records that flowed to the General Register Office to portray important health and social problems and to measure the effects of sanitary legislation. He related causes of death to seasons of the year, residence, density of population, age, sex, and occupation. He visualized a problem and then used on it all of the statistical data at his disposal. In searching for an index of the factors that determine man's state of health and length of life, Farr decided to use occupation. His first study was based on the deaths and the census of population of 1851. This was the beginning of a series of decennial reports that have been continued to this day except for the period around 1941, when World War II prevented the preparation of the report. Most of our knowledge of differential mortality by occupation and social class has been obtained from this series of studies initiated by William Farr.

Vital statistics in the New World—North and South America—developed much more slowly than in Europe, in spite of a promising beginning. Registration in Quebec dates from 1621. The first census in North America and one of the first modern censuses of the world was taken in Quebec in 1666. The General Court of Massachusetts Bay Colony in 1639 ordered that records be maintained of every birth, marriage, and death (U.S. Public Health Service, 1954). In contrast to the almost universal practice in Europe, registration covered all events instead of only church ceremonies, and responsibility for the maintenance of the rec-

ords was placed on civil rather than on ecclesiastical officials.

Other colonies adopted similar regulations, but the laws were not enforced and registration in colonial America never was very effective. The records were kept primarily as legal documents with no serious attempt being made to use them for statistical studies. For the most part the records remained in the local registration offices; only fourteen of the forty-eight states had central death records prior to 1900. The first state to establish a complete—in the sense of coverage of the entire state—central file was Massachusetts in 1841.

The beginning public health movement in the United States demanded reliable vital statistics, but this demand fell upon deaf ears. State legislatures remained largely indifferent, if not directly opposed, to the pleas for the establishment of central offices for the collection of vital statistics.

In 1850, largely due to the influence of Lemuel Shattuck, information concerning the number of deaths during the twelve-month period prior to the census date was collected during the census of population. Corresponding information was collected at each subsequent decennial census until 1900. These data were so incomplete and inaccurate that they were worthless for statistical analysis. Recognizing this fact, the Bureau of the Census established a death registration area for the census of 1880. Included were the states of Massachusetts and New Jersey, the District of Columbia, and a number of large cities where registration was believed to be reasonably complete. The area had 8.5 million persons, or about 17 per cent of the total population of the country.

This practice was continued at the time of the censuses of 1890 and 1900. Six additional states were included in the registration area of 1890—Connecticut, Delaware, New Hampshire, New

York, Rhode Island, and Vermont; and two more—Maine and Michigan—in the area used for the 1900 census.

In 1902 the Bureau of the Census, which previously had functioned only during the census period, was made a permanent agency. The act of Congress creating a permanent census bureau also authorized the annual collection of copies of death certificates from those states and cities having adequate registration systems. A death registration area consisting of ten states—Massachusetts, New Jersey, Connecticut, New Hampshire, New York, Rhode Island, Vermont, Michigan, Maine, Indiana—the District of Columbia, and a number of separate cities in non-registration states was established. The area was predominantly urban and included about 40 per cent of the total population of the United States. A third of a century elapsed before mortality statistics for the entire nation became available with the admission of Texas to the death registration area in 1933. Thus the United States lagged nearly a century behind most of the countries of Europe in establishing national mortality statistics.

DEMOGRAPHIC INTEREST IN THE
STUDY OF MORTALITY

The urge for survival is one of the fundamental biological drives. It is not surprising that since the dawn of recorded history man has been interested in longevity. Florida was discovered by Ponce de León while searching for the fountain of youth. But, however interested he may be as an individual in all aspects of health, the demographer as a scientist is concerned primarily with a limited aspect of this subject. Populations increase in number by the addition of births and immigrants; they decrease in number by death and emigration. Mortality, then, is one of the fundamental factors determining the size of human populations. Mortality influ-

ences not only the total size of a population but also its composition by age, sex, nativity, and race. The demographer's primary interest in mortality is the study of its effect upon the size, composition, and future growth of populations.

This interest, however, embraces more than a study of how mortality affects population change; it also includes the question of why mortality acts as it does. Each individual begins his separate existence with the fertilization of the ovum by the sperm cell. Immediately thereafter, lethal factors begin to operate. By the time the embryo has developed to the stage when it can exist outside the body of its mother, perhaps as many as one out of every five embryos has died. These are the fetal deaths. Of those who survive birth, some die almost at once, so ill-prepared are they for a separate, independent existence. The duration of life of the remainder varies greatly. Only a few will live to greet the first century after their birth.

The explanation of the order of dying-out of a generation is the concern of demography, medicine, and public health. The latter two approach this problem from the point of view of the etiology or cause of ill-health, the means of preventing ill-health, and methods of therapy to alleviate or control the effects of ill-health. The demographer wants to know how physical characteristics, social organization, and environment relate to mortality and longevity.

The factors affecting longevity may be subsumed under (*a*) heredity, (*b*) constitution, and (*c*) environment. By constitution is meant the physical, physiological, anatomical, and psychological traits of man. The most important of these for the demographer are age, sex, and race or ethnic background. Environment includes not only the natural physical surroundings in which man finds himself but also those factors arising from his manner of living, such as habits of eating and drinking, occupation, income, and type of community in which he lives.

The constitutional and environmental factors are most directly related to the problems of demography. The extent to which the length of life is determined by heredity and the possible genetic effects of differential mortality represent the chief concern of demographers with respect to the relationship of heredity and mortality. Part of the lack of interest of demographers in the relationship of heredity to mortality undoubtedly arises from the remarkable increase in the average length of life that has occurred during the past fifty years; the increase is clearly ascribable to advances in medicine, improved medical care, a rising standard of living, and control of adverse environmental conditions. No known changes in the genetic qualities of the population took place immediately before or during this period.

From 1900 to 1952, the expectation of life at birth of the white population of the United States increased from 47.6 to 69.7 years. There is no indication that this steady gain in longevity is likely to terminate in the near future. It seems certain that the time will come when the biological limits on the span of human life will put a stop to the present increase in average length of life, but, until that time appears imminent, demographers undoubtedly will continue to devote most of their attention to the effects of environmental factors upon mortality.

NATURE AND SOURCES OF
MORTALITY DATA

Historically, the basic documentary source of mortality data has been a record of death prepared for legal rather than for statistical purposes. This is in direct contrast to the collection of data concerning the size and composition of the population by means of a census. Although the latter has a legal basis, the data are collected for statistical purposes, and statistical considerations largely determine the types of data collected. The death certificate is a legal document; its utilization for statistical purposes is secondary. This severely restricts both the amount and kind of purely statistical data than can be obtained.

A second difference between population censuses and mortality records is that censuses are conducted by enumeration, while mortality records are obtained by registration. Moreover, registration must be complete. The registration of a sample of deaths would defeat the legal purposes for which the death record is required. Attempts have been made to obtain mortality data either at the time of a population census or by special household surveys. These have been uniformly unsuccessful. Even if the problem of a complete count of deaths by enumeration methods could be solved, there is no prospect that the necessary medical information could ever be obtained from household informants. Registration seems certain to remain the principal source of mortality data.

Since mortality records are legal documents, death certificates must be prepared only for those persons specified by law. Most countries require that the death of every person born alive be registered, but there is no general agreement upon the definition of a live birth. In Spain, Cuba, Bolivia, Ecuador, and Honduras a newborn infant who does not survive the first twenty-four hours after delivery is classified as an abortion and is not counted either as a live birth or as a death. In addition, several countries count only infants living at the time of registration—which may be several days after the date of birth. Live-born infants who die before registration are classified as stillbirths. The World Health Organization (1950) has proposed the following definition of a live birth for international use, but its adoption by all nations will require many years since existing laws must be changed in most instances.

Live birth is the complete expulsion or extraction from its mother of a product of conception, irrespective of the duration of pregnancy, which, after such separation, breathes or shows any other evidence of life, such as beating of the heart, pulsation of the umbilical cord, or definite movement of voluntary muscles, whether or not the umbilical cord has been cut or the placenta is attached; each product of such a birth is considered live-born.

All live-born infants should be registered and counted as such irrespective of the period of gestation and if they die at any time following birth they should also be registered and counted as deaths.

The greatest lack of uniformity in the legal definition of a person for purposes of death registration is for fetal deaths. Both legally and statistically, deaths refer only to persons who were live-born and hence exclude fetal deaths. Although accurate data are not available, there is some evidence that from 15 to 20 per cent of embryos fail to be delivered alive. A fetus dying prior to delivery has generally been called a stillbirth if expulsion or extraction from the mother occurs during the latter part of the period of gestation. No agreement exists, however, concerning the duration of gestation necessary before a fetal death shall be recorded as a stillbirth; the most common durations are from twenty to twenty-eight weeks.

In order to promote international uniformity in the definition of a death for purposes of registration and to focus attention upon the problem of fetal deaths, the World Health Organization (1950) has recommended that the concept of stillbirth be abandoned and

that all fetal deaths be registered. A fetal death is defined as a "death prior to the complete expulsion or extraction from its mother of a product of conception, irrespective of the duration of pregnancy; the death is indicated by the fact that after such separation the foetus does not breathe or show any other evidence of life, such as beating of the heart, pulsation of the umbilical cord, or definite movement of voluntary muscles." The World Health Organization recognized that many years will elapse before this definition can become effective, since it requires changing the existing legal definition of a person in almost every registration area of the world. Although the registration of all fetal deaths irrespective of the period of gestation is a goal to be attained as soon as possible, the World Health Organization has recommended that as a minimum every country should register fetal deaths occurring after the twenty-eighth completed week of gestation.

In order to make possible comparisons of statistics of fetal deaths for countries with differing definitions, the following classification was recommended: (a) less than twenty completed weeks of gestation, (b) twenty completed weeks of gestation but less than twenty-eight, (c) twenty-eight completed weeks of gestation and over, (d) gestation period not classifiable in above groups. Preferably, the term "stillbirth" should be abandoned since existing definitions are not comparable. Recognizing that "stillbirth" would continue to be used by many countries for some time, the World Health Organization recommended that for statistical purposes stillbirth be synonymous with late fetal deaths, that is, those of twenty-eight completed weeks of gestation and over. The recommendations of the World Health Organization have the great merit of providing a uniform definition of a live birth and a fetal death. Until these become generally adopted, the existing tripartite classification of deaths, stillbirths, and fetal deaths will remain in effect.

While official registration documents are the principal source of mortality data, a considerable amount of information concerning special groups of the population has been obtained from the records of life insurance companies. The most notable source of these data has been the publications of the Metropolitan Life Insurance Company concerning the mortality of its industrial policy holders (Dublin and Lotka, 1937; also the *Statistical Bulletin*, a monthly publication). Most of our knowledge of the relationship of height and weight to mortality and of the effect of various physical impairments upon longevity has been derived from actuarial studies of the experience of insured persons (Society of Actuaries, 1954).

DEFICIENCIES OF MORTALITY DATA

Even though the registration of vital events is one of the oldest forms of official record-keeping, reliable information concerning merely the total number of deaths is available for only one-half of the population of the world (United Nations, Statistical Office, 1954). Furthermore, although many economic statistical series such as statistics of trade, finance, and production generally are available for countries where they are most relevant to national problems, mortality statistics are least reliable and extensive in the countries with the highest mortality rates.

Mortality statistics take on their fullest meaning only when the number of deaths is classified by cause and by such characteristics of the deceased as age, sex, race, and occupation. An appraisal of the mortality statistics of every country of the world with respect to these classifications has never been

done and probably is impracticable. A sufficiently comprehensive view of the existing situation can be obtained from a review of the reports on mortality statistics submitted to the United Nations in response to its *Demographic Yearbook* questionnaire (United Nations, Statistical Office, 1954). The following comments refer to the fifty-eight major statistical areas with the most complete and reliable statistics. These areas include 1,229,000,000 persons, or about one-half of the total population of the world. It can be safely assumed that mortality statistics for the remaining half of the world's population are much more inadequate and unreliable than those of the fifty-eight areas.

The number of deaths classified by cause, age, and sex is available for 46 per cent of the total population of the fifty-eight areas, or about one-fourth of the total population of the world. The most frequently available index of the socioeconomic status of the population is occupation. The number of deaths by age, sex, and occupation is available for only seven of the fifty-eight areas, or for only 5 per cent of the population of the areas. For practical purposes, official statistics relating mortality to the socioeconomic status of the population are almost non-existent even for the nations with the most complete systems of vital statistics.

The infant mortality rate, perhaps the most sensitive single index of health conditions, can be computed for 95 per cent of the population of these areas. The reliability of this rate varies from one area to another because of lack of uniformity in the definition of a live birth and an infant death and because of incompleteness of registration. The number of stillbirths classified by period of gestation (which is essential for comparability, owing to varying legal definitions of a stillbirth) is reported by ten areas having 27 per cent of the population of the fifty-eight areas.

These illustrations are sufficient to show that even the simplest and most basic mortality statistics are available, on a national basis, for less than one-half of the population of the world. The greatest deficiency in mortality statistics today is the lack of even a reliable count of the number of current deaths for a majority of the world's population. The quality of the available statistics is summarized in a United Nations report (United Nations, Population Division, Department of Social Affairs, 1954):

> This estimate, which is the best that can be made today, suggests a loss of life of stupendous dimensions in spite of the spectacular reduction in infant and childhood mortality which has occurred in some countries during the past century. With 20 per-cent or more of all fertilizations lost before birth and 15 to 20 per-cent of the live births dying by the fifth year of age, it appears on a conservative estimate that one-third or more of each generation is wasted in the initial stages of its formation.
> . . . The statistics relating to reproductive wastage, which includes foetal deaths from fertilization till birth at full term and infant and childhood deaths up to the fifth year of age, have been summarized in this volume for all countries of the world where this information is available. Only fragmentary information exists in regard to the first part of this wastage, namely foetal deaths, and any generalizations as to its approximate size or probable causation are still open to serious doubt. At the most conservative estimate, it appears that about 20 per-cent of all fertilizations end as foetal deaths before the normal period of gestation is concluded.

The statistics on infant and early child-hood mortality are more reliable and abundant, covering about one-half of the world's population. When these statistics are compared on the international level, however, many weaknesses and defects emerge. In many cases, the official data grossly understate mortality because of incomplete registration of deaths. In other cases, international comparability suffers from variations in definitions of terms or tabulations of data. The statistics of causes of death in infancy and early childhood as well as those on causes of foetal deaths, are notoriously defective on account of poor diagnosis or inadequate reporting of the correct cause. Consequently, these statistics give only an approximate picture of mortality differentials during the first 5 years of life in the various areas of the world.

It would be impracticable to discuss the deficiencies in mortality statistics for each of the countries of the world with the most complete registration systems. The following comments pertain to the mortality statistics of the United States. The principal deficiencies arise from (1) lack of comparability in definitions and deficiencies in reporting, (2) inaccuracies in the data reported, (3) lack of comparability in definitions and practices of the National Office of Vital Statistics and the Bureau of the Census, (4) changing procedures in processing and tabulating statistics and (5) the inflexibility of the registration system of collecting statistics.

Lack of Comparability in Definitions and Deficiencies in Reporting

No adequate test of the completeness of death registration has ever been conducted in the United States. Indeed, it is difficult to devise a satisfactory, practicable test. One of the requirements for admission to the death registration area was a demonstration that at least 90 per cent of deaths were registered. How this was demonstrated has never been divulged.

It is generally believed that except for fetal deaths, infant deaths, and possibly total deaths in some of the more rural and isolated parts of the country the registration of deaths in the United States is essentially complete. The National Office of Vital Statistics has assumed that the underregistration of infant deaths is approximately the same as that of live births. This assumption is based upon the comparison of the variation of infant mortality rates among different areas and the corresponding variation of the completeness of registration of live births. No adequate field study has been conducted. There can be no doubt about lack of comparability in definition and serious underregistration of fetal deaths (Yerushalmy and Bierman, 1952). The minimum period of gestation for the registration of a fetal death ranges from no minimum in Mississippi, New York City, Oregon, and Vermont to six completed months in Rhode Island. The most frequent minimum is twenty weeks or the fifth month. Fifteen states specify no criteria for the evidence of life.

More serious than differences in definition as a cause of incomparability in fetal death statistics is incomplete registration. No data are available for the entire nation, but a careful check in New York City, where registration probably is more complete than for the rest of the country, revealed that from 1943 through 1945, 14 per cent of the fetal deaths occurring during the third trimester and 34 per cent of those occurring during the second trimester of pregnancy were unregistered. In spite of serious deficiencies in registration, the fetal death rate in New York City during 1953 was 107 per 1,000 live births plus fetal deaths. It is estimated that perhaps one-half of all fetal deaths in New York City are reported. If this is true, the corrected fetal death rate would be about 200 per 1,000. The 80,000 fetal deaths reported annually in the United States may represent only one-sixth of the total number. (See Baumgartner *et al.*, 1949, and Erhardt, 1952.)

Inaccuracies in Reported Data

By means of a long-continued process of query and education of physicians and undertakers, the reliability of the entries on death certificates has been greatly improved. There is some evidence of serious misstatement of age for persons more than fifty years old, especially for the non-white population. This has been particularly evident since 1940 and also appears in the census of population. It is generally agreed that owing to errors in age reporting on death certificates and in the census of population the reported death rates at seventy-five years of age and over are of doubtful validity. Mortality rates for the non-white population, although consistently greater than those for the white population from birth until age seventy-five, fall appreciably below those for the white population after that age. Because of errors in the basic statistics, it is customary to derive the mortality rates for the terminal ages in a life table by extrapolation of some curve fitted to the observed data at ages below eighty-five or ninety years.

The validity of statistics by cause of death is dependent upon the quality of medical diagnoses. No national evaluation of the accuracy of medical certification has ever been made in the United States. Without doubt, there has been a marked improvement in the specificity of medical diagnoses during the past two decades. In 1950 only 1.2 per cent of all reported deaths were assigned to unknown or ill-defined causes. This percentage ranged from 0.1 for two states and the District of Columbia to 13.6 for Mississippi.

Studies for local areas have revealed rather large discrepancies between diagnoses reported on death certificates and those derived from post-mortem examination of the same persons (James *et al.*, 1955). It is difficult to evaluate such studies since autopsies frequently are done because of a special interest in a particular case or because of uncertainty concerning the correct diagnosis. Even though medical certification on death certificates may yield fairly reliable statistics for the major broad groups of causes of death, there still is opportunity for considerable improvement both in specificity and in accuracy.

One of the basic axes of classification of vital statistics is residence. Originally, official vital statistics were compiled according to the place of death. The increasing use of hospital facilities for medical care during the past half-century has resulted in an increasing proportion of births and deaths occurring at a place other than the residence of the mother or the usual place of residence of the deceased. In 1952, 92 per cent of all live births in the United States occurred in hospitals. Current figures are not available for deaths, but in 1949 nearly one-half (49.5 per cent) of all deaths took place in institutions, mostly general hospitals. Consequently, mortality statistics for areas smaller than states, when tabulated by place of death, have become increasingly unreliable as an index of health conditions. The numerator, the number of deaths, is by place of occurrence, but the denominator, the population of the place in question, is by place of usual residence.

National and state offices were very slow to recognize the importance of tabulating birth and death statistics by place of residence. A tabulation showing the total number of deaths by place of residence was initiated in 1914 by the Bureau of the Census; however, detailed tabulations by age, sex, race, and cause of death for areas classified by size of population were continued on a place-of-occurrence basis until 1940. A thorough analysis has never been made of the mortality statistics classified by size of community prior to 1940. There is no comparable population for the computation of rates, and even if such populations existed, the rates would be of very limited usefulness.

Since 1940, detailed mortality statistics have been tabulated by place of residence of the deceased. Data obtained as part of the 1950 birth registration test indicate appreciable errors in coding the residence reported on death certificates. The past decade has witnessed a rapid growth of population outside the political boundaries of cities and towns. Many of these built-up unincorporated areas have mailing addresses that are difficult to distinguish from those of the central city. At the same time, the residents of such areas use the hospital and medical facilities of the central city.

A comparison of the residence coded from census records and live-birth certificates for births during January, February, and March, 1950, revealed that the birth rate for urban areas was 6.8 per cent too high and that for rural areas 9.9 per cent too low, owing to misclassification of residence. The magnitude of these errors varied widely by geographic area and type of community. The largest discrepancy existed for births in the rural parts of metropolitan counties, where the number of births adjusted for misclassification of residence exceeded the tabulated number by 21 per cent.

No data concerning the amount of misclassification of the usual residence of deceased persons are available. Since the proportion of deaths that occur in hospitals is smaller than the corresponding proportion of births, the error due to misclassification of residence may be somewhat smaller. Nevertheless, the error may be great enough to impair seriously the usefulness of official mortality statistics classified by size of city.

Lack of Comparability in Mortality and Population Statistics

The computation of valid mortality rates requires comparable definitions and processing practices in the compilation of both death and population statistics. The most serious lacks of comparability have been in the definition of urban and rural residence and in the failure to allocate deaths to the place of residence. As a result, reliable statistics for the study of rural-urban differentials in mortality on a national scale do not exist prior to 1940. The 1940 census period was the first for which the same definition of urban population was used for both mortality and population statistics. Prior to that time, for mortality tabulations "urban" has been defined as including places of ten thousand or more inhabitants, while urban population statistics referred to the population of places of twenty-five hundred or more inhabitants, with certain minor exceptions.

No sooner had the definition of urban and rural population used in tabulating mortality statistics been brought into conformity with that used for population statistics than the Bureau of the Census revised its definition of urban population. During the 1950 census of population, the former definition of urban population was revised to include the urbanized or built-up area around cities of fifty thousand or more population and also unincorporated places of twenty-five hundred inhabitants or more. Without doubt, this new classification is more in keeping with the present location of population by density. Approximately eight million persons who would have been classed as living in rural areas under the 1940 definition were included with the urban population in 1950.

However desirable the 1950 classification of population by urban and rural residence may be for purely de-mographic analysis of population distribution, it has made practically impossible comparability between mortality and population statistics. The urbanized areas around cities have no recognized political boundaries and are constantly changing in extent. Although it is feasible to define a boundary for the purposes of a one-time enumeration of population, no practicable method of coding the residence reported on birth and death certificates in accordance with the census definition has yet been devised. The registration of vital events and the administration of public health programs are on the basis of areas with defined political boundaries. So long as this situation exists, it will be necessary to produce vital statistics for politically rather than demographically defined densely populated areas.

Changing Procedures in Processing and Tabulating

Statistical offices responsible for preparing periodic series of statistics constantly face the problem of choosing between existing definitions and practices which preserve comparability with the past and altered definitions and practices which conform more closely to changes in phenomena. The compilation of mortality statistics is no exception. The changes in procedure that are most important for users of mortality statistics are revisions in the international list of diseases and causes of death and changes in the rules for selecting the principal cause of death.

The international statistical classification of diseases, injuries, and causes of death published by the World Health Organization is widely accepted as the basis for coding the causes of death. In order to keep abreast of advances in medical knowledge and to take advantage of experience gained in coding causes of death, this classification is revised approximately every ten years. Every revision has introduced some degree of incomparability with the past, but the sixth revision (1948) represented a more sweeping change than any of the previous ones. In order to measure the effect of the change in classification, the National Office of Vital Statistics coded a 10 per cent sample of death certificates for 1949 and 1950 according to both the fifth and sixth revisions.

For many causes of death the difference between the two numbers obtained was negligible, being less than 5 per cent. For some causes the difference was so large that a serious lack of comparability was introduced in the time series of death rates. The number of deaths attributed to diabetes by the sixth revision was only 57 per cent of the number based on the fifth revision. For chronic nephritis the number of deaths was decreased by nearly two-thirds. On the other hand, the number of deaths assigned to rheumatic fever was increased 1.7 times. Not all of these differences were due to revisions in the international list. Associated with the sixth revision was a change in the rules for the selection of the principal cause of death. Over 60 per cent of death certificates have two or more separate diagnoses as defined by the three-digit code categories of the sixth revision. Since most tabulations of death statistics include only one cause of death, it is obvious that the rules for the choice of the principal cause will largely determine the rank order of causes of death.

Prior to the adoption of the sixth revision in 1949, the principal cause of death had been selected in accordance with an arbitrary set of coding rules embodied in the *Manual of Joint Causes of Death*. These rules took precedence over the opinion of the physician as recorded on the death certificate. A few other countries also followed this practice; the remainder accepted the opinion of the certifying physician unless it appeared to be obviously incorrect. Beginning in 1949, the National Office of Vital Statistics abandoned the use of the *Manual of Joint Causes of Death,* and it now accepts the opinion of the certifying physician concerning the principal cause of death except when the entries on the death certificate seem to be inconsistent.

In the long run, this change should improve the quality of cause-of-death statistics. Some incomparability will exist until physicians become familiar with the change in procedure, but this is less serious than that which would be introduced by continuing to use the *Manual of Joint Causes of Death*.

Irrespective of what rules are followed in choosing the principal cause of death, the tabulation of mortality statistics by a single cause loses much of the value and meaning of cause-of-death statistics. This has long been recognized, but most vital statistics offices have taken no steps to remedy the situation because of the increased cost of coding more than one cause of death (Janssen, 1940). Abbreviated tabulations for the United States were prepared for 1917, 1925, and 1940.

More than two-thirds of deaths at the present time are attributed to chronic diseases. Usually more than one chronic disease is present at the time of death, and even the attending physician has difficulty in deciding which shall be chosen as the primary cause of death. Frequently it is medically unrealistic to select a single disease since death results from the combined effect of two or more diseases. The importance of tabulating multiple causes of death was pointed out by the World Health Organization when it issued the sixth revision of the international list in 1948, but so far no tabulations for the United States have been published.

Inflexibility of the Registration System

The full significance of mortality statistics can be portrayed only by relating them to the social and economic characteristics of the population or to the environment in which this population lives. The inflexibility of the legal registration system makes the collection of social and economic data as part of the death certificate practically impossible. Any proposed change in the certificate must be approved by each of the forty-eight states and the District of Columbia. Registrars of vital events, many of whom have little interest in statistics, must be persuaded that the changes are desirable. Any change requires a minimum of two or three years, and even then there is no assurance that it will be adopted by every registration area.

The only indicators of socioeconomic status entered on the death certificate are occupation and industry. Uncertainty concerning the comparability of these data with corresponding data from the census of population has prevented any extensive analysis of mortality in relation to occupation and industry. The National Tuberculosis Association, using data for ten states for 1930, prepared a summary of mortality rates for workers grouped into seven broad socioeconomic classes.

The National Office of Vital Statistics has planned a study of mortality of male workers between twenty-five and sixty-five years of age for 1950, by detailed occupation and industry. In order to evaluate the validity of these data, a comparative study of the entries of occupation and industry on birth and death certificates and on the schedule for the census of population has been initiated by the Scripps Foundation. These two studies should clearly establish the validity and usefulness of the entries of occupation and industry on certificates of death.

Adjustment of Data

Any analysis of the trend in mortality in the United States either from all causes or from specific causes must take account of changes in the number of states included in the death registration area and of changes in the classification of causes of death. Only since 1933 have mortality statistics been available for the entire country. Prior to that date, one has the choice of statistics for a constantly changing area or of statistics for a fixed geographic area, such as the original registration states, that clearly is not a representative sample of the United States. Moreover, the choice of a fixed geographic area does not insure comparability in time since the first states to be admitted to the death registration area were in the northeast and north central parts of the nation, where a large proportion of the immigrants who came to the United States during the first two decades of this century took up residence.

In respect to causes of death, the previously mentioned studies in connection with the sixth revision of the international list have provided useful data for judging the comparability of the time trend of mortality rates for specific causes. But, in general, not much can be done about adjusting mortality statistics for known or suspected deficiencies. There is evidence of misstatement of age by elderly persons—especially in the non-white population—perhaps some underregistration of infant deaths, certainly serious underregistration and lack of comparability in the definition of fetal deaths, and undoubtedly some misclassification of residence, but no reliable quantitative estimate of these deficiencies is available; official statistics must be used as published, seasoned with whatever reservations seem appropriate to the author.

Methods of Analysis of Mortality Statistics

The methods of describing and analyzing mortality statistics have been developed over a period of some two hundred years. Many illustrious names are associated with early mortality studies: Lexis, Bernoulli, D'Alembert, Quételet, and Poisson. In addition to vital statisticians, actuaries have played a significant role in the development of the rather extensive body of theory and techniques now available for the analysis of mortality statistics. This fund of knowledge has been essential for the development of one of the largest forms of business activity in the United States, life insurance.

The methods available for the study of mortality have been developed for three main purposes, (a) classification, (b) quantitative description, and (c) analysis. The international list of causes of death has evolved over a period of more than half a century. It probably was the first statistical nomenclature to be widely adopted internationally. The sixth revision was promulgated as Regulation No. 1 of the World Health Organization and is the official basis for classifying deaths according to cause by all member nations.

The principal methods for the quantitative description of mortality data are rates and ratios. A wide variety of these have been developed—crude rates, specific rates, maternal mortality rate, infant mortality rate, neonatal mortality rate, perinatal mortality rate, fetal death rate, stillbirth ratio. Since every mortality rate may be regarded as a weighted average, its value depends upon the weights used in its computation. Many persons have attempted to devise a unique set of weights that would be independent of time and place. This is a futile quest, since such a set of weights does not exist. Three principal methods have emerged from the mass of literature on this subject: the direct method of adjustment, the indirect method of adjustment, and the method of equivalent average rates.

The techniques for the analytical study of mortality have evolved around the mortality table and its derivative, the life table. These permit the analysis of mortality statistics independent of the age composition of a specific, actual population. A wide variety of questions can be answered by these techniques; the following are illustrative: What is the probability of eventually dying from some specific cause of death? What would be the average number of years of life gained by the elimination of a particular cause of death? What is the probability of widowhood and orphanhood in a specific population? What is the relative importance of the various causes of death independent of the existing age distribution of a specific population?

Many methods have been developed for measuring the relative effect of mortality in two or more populations or of changes in mortality for a specific population over time. Among these are the expectation of life, the probable lifetime, proportion of a cohort surviving to some specified age, per cent of possible years of life lived, death rate in a stationary population, the number of potential years of life lost, and adjusted death rates. Considerable discussion of the relative merits of these methods has taken place in the past, and proponents for each method have advanced reasons why it is superior to the others. In fact, no single method is superior to all others for every purpose. Each method answers a somewhat different question, so that the choice of the method should be governed by the purpose of the study.

The mathematical theory of population change and its relationship to births and deaths was developed during the latter part of the nineteenth century by Knapp, Zeuner, Lexis, and others. The most complete exposition of this subject probably is in Czuber's *Wahrscheinlichkeitsrechnung* (1938). No comparable discussion is available in English, although Glover (1921) and Wolfenden (1954) have published fairly comprehensive summaries.

Forecasts of the future trend in mortality rates have been prepared by various persons in order to estimate the gains in longevity that might result from the widespread application of existing knowledge, to project or forecast a component of future population changes, to estimate annuity premiums and reserves for insurance purposes, and to estimate the adequacy of social security plans (Dorn, 1952a; Jenkins and Lew, 1949; Royal Commission on Population, 1950; Notestein *et al.*, 1944).

Mortality rates may be grouped in three principal ways for analytical or forecasting purposes: (*a*) rates showing variation for a constant age according to the year of death—this method yields a time series; (*b*) rates showing variation according to age for a fixed time period—the usual method of tabulation; and (*c*) rates showing variation according to age and year of death or birth—the method of generations. All these methods have been used in the preparation of forecasts of mortality. Several investigations have been made of generation life tables, since this method seemed to offer a more logical basis for forecasting mortality rates.

The usual life table is prepared by taking the current mortality rates at each age during a period of time and constructing from these a hypothetical cohort assumed to be exposed throughout its lifetime to these age-specific rates. The expectation of life computed from such a life table is a hypothetical figure giving the average number of years of life that would be lived by the members of a cohort starting life together and subject thereafter to the schedule of mortality rates used in the construction of the table. As an actual generation goes through life, health conditions change so that persons who survive the first few years of life in Western societies experience improved health conditions during adult life and old age.

It is impracticable to construct a generation life table for a general population by counting year after year the number of deaths and survivors of a specific cohort of births until the last member has died. A satisfactory approximation can be derived, provided that age-specific mortality rates are available for a period of years at least as great as the life span. For example, the survivors of persons born during 1850 were ten years old in 1860, twenty years old in 1870, thirty years old in 1880, and so on. Hence, a generation mortality table can be constructed by taking the death rate at age zero in 1850, at age ten in 1860, at age twenty in 1870, and so on. Furthermore, the progression of mortality by age and calendar time can be observed for consecutive cohorts at various stages of their generation experience in any particular year. (See Dublin and Spiegelman, 1941.)

The investigation of mortality tables constructed in this manner suggested that each generation tended to have a characteristic mortality throughout its span of life (Derrick, 1927). Kermack, McKendrick, and McKinlay (1934a, 1934b) after a study of generation mortality tables for England and Wales, Scotland, and Sweden, concluded that the death rates for the separate age groups (with the exception of the first few years of life) at any particular calendar time depended more upon the date of birth of the individuals concerned than upon the year in question. From this came the hypotheses that the most important factor in determining the mortality experience of a generation was its death rate during the first ten to fifteen years of life and that improved health conditions after those ages exerted only a slight effect upon subsequent mortality.

If $F(t,\theta)$ represents the specific death rate for age θ at time t, then $F(t,\theta) = \alpha(t-\theta)B(\theta)$, in which $\alpha(t-\theta)$ depends only on the time of birth and $B(\theta)$ depends solely on the attained age, θ. If $^sq_x^r$ represents the death rate at age x during calendar year r of persons born at time s, that is, the calendar period $r-x-1$ to $r-x$, the ratios $^{s+n}q_x^{r+n}/^sq_x^r$ eliminate the effect of age, $B(\theta)$, and the trend of the ratios can be used to forecast mortality rates for future years. Unfortunately, mortality rates for the entire United States have not been available for a sufficient number of years to test this theory adequately. The method has not been used extensively in forecasting mortality. Its use was carefully considered by the Royal Commission of Population of Great Britain (1950), but it was finally rejected in favor of exponential trend curves.

Cohort or generation death rates have been effectively used in the analysis of mortality from tuberculosis and lung cancer (Springett, 1950; Dorn, 1954). In each instance, generation death rates revealed aspects of the age selection of these diseases that were concealed by the age-specific mortality rates computed for a fixed calendar period.

The mortality table and the life table are important tools for the demographer. Without them only a crude idea could be obtained of the potential rate of change of human populations; the crude rate of natural increase reflects not only the inherent growth potential of a population but also its current age distribution. The computation of meas-ures of intrinsic natural increase, such as the net reproduction rate or the true rate of natural increase, involves the use of life-table functions. Another application is in the computation of the size and age composition of the stable population that would result from the indefinite continuation of any fixed set of fertility and mortality rates.

The mortality table has several important applications to problems involving the survival of two or more persons. The duration of marriage and the chances of widowhood can be computed by taking into account the ages of both husband and wife and their joint chances of survival. Such computations are required for the estimation of widows' benefits under insurance plans and social security programs. No data are available on the extent of orphanhood in the United States. Estimates based upon survival functions derived from mortality tables have been made of the number of maternal and paternal orphans and of the number of complete orphans.

The mortality table has found its widest application in business and economics, outside the field of demography. It is the foundation stone of all forms of life insurance. Indeed, the first application was in the computation of annuity benefits and insurance premiums. More recently the principles of life-table construction have been applied to the study of depreciation and replacement needs of physical property.

KNOWLEDGE OF MORTALITY

Why do living beings die when they do? What factors determine the duration of life? Why is it that of two fertilized ova, one will not develop to be separated alive from the mother while the other will live an independent existence for eighty years? These are questions to which man has sought the answer for as long as written history exists. The study of longevity per se is properly the province of biology rather than of demography. The demographer's interest in longevity arises in part from the interrelationship of longevity with the biological, social, and economic characteristics of humans as members of population groups.

Although the absolute duration of human life is important, it is the rate of change in the survivorship curve of a generation, i.e., the death rate, that is the primary focus of interest of demography. By themselves, the number of deaths and the size of the population are discrete phenomena whose interrelationship can be only vaguely appreciated. When related by means of a death rate, they form one of the indispensable tools for the study of population change.

It is important to distinguish the concept of span of life from that of average length of life. The span of life is a biological trait; it is the limit beyond which, even under the most favorable conditions, the members of a given species cannot survive. It varies widely among different species. For human beings its numerical value can be estimated only approximately. Certainly it exceeds 100 years. Almost certainly its maximum value is less than 150 years. So far as we know its value cannot be easily altered.

Of more importance to demography is the average duration of life or the average number of years actually lived by a generation. There is no evidence that the span of life differs among various groups of the human race. In contrast, the average length of life not only has changed radically within recorded history but also varies widely among different population groups existing at the same time. It represents the most succinct summary of mortality conditions that has yet been developed.

The analysis of the interrelationships of mortality with other demographic phenomena has been greatly facilitated by the construction of theoretical models. One of the most important of these is built around the concept of a cohort of persons and a stationary population. A cohort is a group of persons who enter a population at the same time. The number of births during a calendar year may be regarded as a cohort, so also may the females who marry during a specified period.

The concepts of cohort and population have a wide application in the analysis of mortality and morbidity statistics and of demographic data. One may think of a population composed of persons with a particular disease, persons in hospitals, persons in an institution, married persons, persons in the labor force, persons eligible for old age pensions, and so on. Every such population is uniquely determined if its increment and decrement rates are known. Its size and composition at any future date theoretically can be determined. Nor is it necessary for a population to be composed of human beings. It can refer to electric light bulbs in a building, poles for carrying power or telephone lines, automobiles of a particular year or model, or any similarly defined group of physical objects to which additions are made and from which withdrawals occur.

If the increment and decrement rates are equal, the resulting population will be stationary, that is, will assume a fixed size and composition. If the increment and decrement rates are not equal but remain fixed, the resulting population will become stable in the sense that its composition by age will become fixed, but its size will change by a constant relative amount during equal periods of time.

The theory of decrement rates and of a stationary population has been developed primarily by actuaries for use in solving problems in insurance. The most widely familiar example of these concepts is the life table. The theory and techniques are basic to the analysis of a variety of demographic, medical, and epidemiological problems and have wide application in industrial statistics. They undoubtedly represent the best-developed analytical tools available to the demographer.

Nations, Population Division, Department of Social Affairs, 1953).

Three centuries later, in 1950, the United Nations estimated that the population of the world numbered 2.4 billion, a fourfold increase since 1650. As a result of this acceleration in the rate of growth, the number of persons

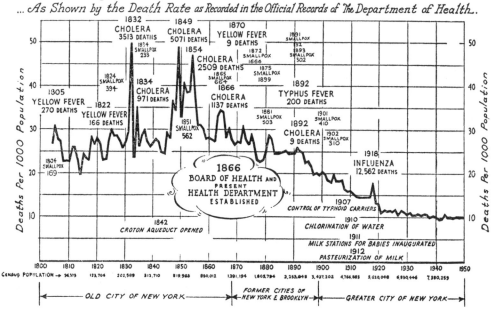

FIG. 3.—Number of deaths per 1,000 population, New York City, 1800–1950. (Reproduced by permission of New York City Department of Health.)

The Decline in Mortality Rates

The most striking demographic event of the past three centuries has been the unprecedented increase in the population of the world. During all the centuries of its existence, the human race has gained only slowly in number prior to 1650, the date of the first acceptable estimate of the world's population. At that time perhaps 545,000,000 persons inhabited the earth. The reliability of this estimate, due to Carr-Saunders, is unknown, but it appears reasonably consistent with subsequent estimates. If anything, it may be too high (United

added to the population of the world during the past century exceeds the total accumulated during the entire previous history of the human race.

There is ample evidence that this increase resulted primarily from a decrease in mortality rates and in spite of a sharp decline in the birth rate in western Europe and North America, a decline that was well under way as early as the first half of the nineteenth century (Dorn, 1952b). Around 1700 the expectation of life at birth of the population of North America and western Europe was between 30 and 35 years and probably had increased very little during the previous three or four centuries (Dublin, Lotka, and Spiegelman, 1949). In 1953 the expectation of life at birth of the white population of the United States was 69.8 years, an increase of approximately 100 per cent (U.S. Public Health Service, National Office of Vital Statistics, 1955).

There are no data indicating that any measurable part of this remarkable increase in average length of life was due to changes in the genetic constitution of the population. Rather, all available

knowledge of preventive medicine, and, more recently, discoveries in pharmacology and chemotherapy—in particular, the antibiotic agents and new insecticides.

These improvements in health have not been shared equally by persons in all parts of the world. In fact, they have been restricted largely to the inhabitants of western and southern Europe, North America, Australia, and New Zealand. Of the countries of Asia, Japan alone has mortality rates that have

TABLE 33

ESTIMATED DEATH RATES FOR REGIONS OF THE WORLD, 1947*

Region	Number of Deaths per Thousand Population	Percentage of Total Population
World	22–25	100.0
Africa	25–30	8.2
America:		
United States and Canada	10	6.7
Latin-America	17	6.6
Asia (except Asiatic U.S.S.R.):		
Near East	30–35	3.1
South Central Asia	25–30	18.3
Japan†	15	3.4
Remaining Far East	30–35	28.3
Europe and Asiatic U.S.S.R.:		
Eastern Europe and Asiatic U.S.S.R.	18	12.1
Rest of Europe	12	12.8
Oceania	12	0.5

* Source: *Demographic Yearbook, 1949–50*, United Nations, 1950.
† In 1953 the death rate in Japan was 8.9.

evidence points to man's increasing control of his environment as the explanation. This increasing control was made possible by four developments: (a) the opening up of new continents, which provided additional sources of food, precious metals, and other commodities, as well as an outlet for surplus population; (b) the expansion of commerce, which made possible the transportation of food and capital goods over long distances; (c) technological changes in agriculture, together with the development of modern industry; and (d) increased control of disease through improved housing, better food and water supplies, adoption of sanitary measures, the growth of the

dropped to a comparable level (Table 33).

As can be seen from Figure 4, some areas of the world during the past decade had mortality rates as high as those existing in England and Wales and Sweden more than a century ago. These comparisons are only approximate since the areas with the highest death rates have either no, or at best incomplete, mortality statistics. If anything, the rates shown in Figure 4 for Mexico and the Moslem population of Algeria are too low owing to underregistration. The death rates for Mexico probably are fairly representative of those for many other Latin-American countries, while those for Algeria may not differ greatly from the mortality rates prevailing in non-European Africa, Asia Minor except Israel, and most of Asia except Japan.

The difference in the level of death rates in contemporary Sweden and the ulation of Algeria, and similar populations, will be patterned after the evolution of mortality in Sweden? Only time can tell, but there are reasons for believing that the changes which required 175 years in Sweden can be

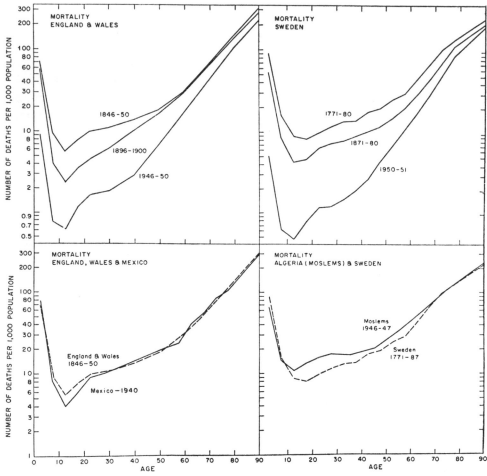

FIG. 4.—Number of deaths per 1,000 population by age: England and Wales, 1846–50, 1896–1900, 1946–50; Sweden, 1771–80, 1871–80, 1950–51; Mexico, 1940; Algeria (Moslems), 1946–47.

Moslem population of Algeria is as great as the difference in level between present-day Sweden and the Sweden of 175 years ago. Not only is the general level comparable but also the shape of the curve by age is similar. Does this suggest that the decrease in the mortality rates of the Moslem population of Algeria is as drastically speeded up in contemporary populations and accomplished in large part in one or two decades.

The present levels of mortality in western Europe and North America were reached only after at least a century and a half of declining death rates and were preceded by sweeping changes in social and economic conditions, in scientic development, and in the diffusion of knowledge. Today the accumulated knowledge of public health and preventive and curative medicine is available for immediate application in countries with high death rates. Personnel, facilities, and financial aid can be provided from outside the country, so that, with only slight cost to the country benefiting, modern health conditions can be superimposed upon a population without being preceded by corresponding changes in its social and economic customs and institutions. A few examples will indicate both the possibilities and the consequences of the application of modern public health methods in countries with high death rates.

In 1940 Ceylon had a population of nearly six million. Its birth rate was around 36 per 1,000 per year. Its death rate had fallen to 21 per 1,000, high by Western standards but about one-third less than that of most Asiatic countries. In 1936, because of an epidemic of malaria, the death rate rose to 37 per 1,000, slightly exceeding the birth rate. As late as 1946 the death rate still exceeded 20 per 1,000. Modern public health measures for the control of malaria and other infectious diseases were instituted. In 1947 the death rate per 1,000 fell to 14.3; in 1948 it was 13.2; and by 1952 it had dropped to 12, a reduction of 60 per cent in six years. The birth rate remained unchanged at a level of nearly 40 per 1,000. Consequently, the crude rate of natural increase doubled, rising from 14.7 per 1,000 in 1945 to 27.5 per 1,000 in 1950. At this rate, the population of Ceylon would double in about twenty-six years.

Even more dramatic is the change in mortality of the Moslem population of Algeria. Since the statistics are incomplete, the following data should be accepted with some reservations, but the general picture undoubtedly is correct. In 1946 the recorded birth and death rates were 42.3 and 31.1 per 1,000, respectively, yielding a crude rate of natural increase per 1,000 of 11.2. In 1952 the birth rate was essentially unchanged, 41.9 per 1,000, but the death rate had fallen to 13.0 per 1,000, resulting in a crude rate of natural increase of 28.9, or 2.6 times that of five years previous.

In contrast to the past, these contemporary changes have been accompanied by only slight changes in the level of living and in the economic and social conditions of the populations con-

TABLE 34

PERCENTAGE OF NEWBORN FEMALE INFANTS EXPECTED TO SURVIVE UNTIL SPECIFIED AGES BASED ON LIFE TABLES FOR INDIA AND THE UNITED STATES*

Age	India 1941–50	United States (White) 1953
1	83	98
5	68	97
20	57	97
50	31	92
60	21	85
80	3	40

* Data for India are from *Demographic Yearbook, 1954*, United Nations. Data for United States are from United States, National Office of Vital Statistics (1955).

cerned. Can these gains be maintained if outside aid is withdrawn? More important, if outside aid is not withdrawn, can they be maintained until fertility rates are lowered to such an extent that the benefits made possible by the application of modern medicine and public health measures are not nullified by a rapid increase in population?

Table 34 shows how a rapid decline in high mortality rates operates to increase the number of births, even with no change in fertility rates, owing to an increase in the proportion of females surviving to the end of the childbearing period. In India slightly over one-half of newborn female infants are alive at age twenty; only three in ten survive to the end of the reproductive period. In the United States, 97 of every 100 newborn white females can expect to reach age twenty, and nine of every ten can expect to survive until the end of the childbearing period.

The reduction in mortality rates of the populations of western Europe and North America has not been the same for each age (Fig. 4). The greatest relative reduction has been from five to fifteen years of age. As a result, the range between the minimum and maximum death rates during the life span has widened. For present-day Sweden, the increase in the death rate from ages ten to fourteen, when the minimum annual rate occurs, until the maximum at ages eighty and over is more than three hundred fold. One hundred seventy-five years ago, the increase from the minimum at ages fifteen to nineteen to the maximum at ages eighty and over was about one-tenth as much or twenty-seven fold.

Differential Mortality

Just as the levels of mortality vary from one nation to another, or vary over time for a given nation, so also do they vary widely among different population groups within a nation. Part of this variation is related to the biological characteristics of a population, namely, age, sex, and ethnic or racial origin; the remainder is related to social and environmental factors like marital status, occupation, social class, size of community, and place of residence. In practice, it is not possible to disentangle the effect of biological from social and environmental factors since the mortality rates at a given moment for a specific population result from the composite effect of these two groups of factors.

The variation of mortality rates by age already has been mentioned. Perhaps the most universal mortality differential with respect to both time and place is that by sex. The first national mortality table computed by Wargentin for Sweden from deaths during the period 1755–63 showed a higher average death rate for men than for women. In England and Wales a corresponding sex differential has existed since the first national mortality rates were computed for the period 1841–45.

In some population groups where the general mortality level is high, the death rates during late adolescence and early adult life have been higher for females than for males owing in large part to excess mortality from tuberculosis and childbearing. As the general level of mortality has decreased, the higher mortality rates for females have dropped more rapidly; today in most countries having relatively low mortality rates those for males are greater than the rates for females throughout the entire span of life.

The sex differential in mortality has slowly widened as death rates have dropped. The life table for the original registration states of the United States for 1900–1902 showed an expectation of life at birth of 48.2 years for white males and 51.1 years for white females. By 1953 the difference had widened to 6.1 years, the figures being 66.8 and 72.9 years, respectively. Undoubtedly, part of the higher mortality among men arises from their greater exposure to occupational and industrial hazards and from differences in manner of living between males and females. The available evidence suggests, though, that much of the sex difference is biological in origin. It has been observed among deaths *in utero* and continues throughout the remainder of the life span with minor exceptions.

The evidence for a biological basis for racial or ethnic differentials is less convincing. In general, the death rate for the white population is the lowest, that for the yellow population is intermediate, and that for the black population is the highest. But this relative standing appears to reflect social, economic, and environmental rather than biological differences. The decline of the mortality rate in Japan to a level comparable to that of western Europe and North America rather clearly demonstrates the absence of any general racial biological traits affecting mortality. It is true that there is some evidence for differences in racial susceptibility to specific diseases, but the extent to which these differences have their origin in biological traits, in contrast to environmental conditions, remains undetermined.

Additional evidence that observed racial differences in mortality reflect social and environmental rather than biological factors is provided by the experience of Negroes in the United States. In 1953, although the expectation of life at birth was definitely lower for non-whites than for whites, it had risen to 59.7 years for non-white males and to 64.4 years for non-white females. Only crude estimates of the level of mortality exist for the Negro population of Africa, but it seems unlikely that the expectation of life at birth is much above that of western Europe during the Middle Ages, or about thirty to thirty-five years. Yet the Negroes of North America and of Africa are of the same racial origin.

Of the social and environmental factors related to mortality, the most is known about geographic and rural-urban differentials. Within all countries marked variations in death rates are found from one region to another. In the United States during 1950, after adjusting for differences in the age composition of the population, a relative difference of about 40 per cent existed between the highest and lowest rates for the forty-eight states. Corresponding geographic variation is found in European countries (United Nations, Population Division, Department of Social Affairs, 1953).

The magnitude of geographic differentials in death rates has decreased as the level of mortality has fallen. The differentials undoubtedly arise from variation in the degree of urbanism, in economic status, in the availability and utilization of medical and health services and facilities, and other social factors. Few studies attempting to account for observed geographic differentials have been made. More than a century ago William Farr proposed that the healthiest districts be identified and used as a measuring rod for improving health conditions in other areas, but this idea has not been extensively followed up.

It is not surprising that the early writers on mortality devoted considerable attention to urban-rural differentials. The filthy and unsanitary condition of most cities makes them fertile breeding grounds for infectious and communicable diseases. Until about 1800, burials were more frequent than christenings during most years; therefore the population of large cities was maintained only by migration from rural areas. At least one-sixth of the population of London is estimated to have perished during the last great epidemic of plague during 1664–65 (Buer, 1926). As late as 1750 the death rate in London is thought to have been between 40 and 50 per 1,000 population.

When discussing urban-rural differentials in mortality, one must differentiate between the contrast among countries and that within a single country. Agricultural populations usually have a shorter average length of life than the populations of highly industrialized nations, but within a given country the rural population historically has experienced lower death rates than the urban population. Advances in medicine, public health, and sanitation combined with the concentration of hospital and medical facilities in cities have resulted in a remarkable improvement in the health of urban populations; today the rural-urban differential in mortality that has been so marked in the past has sharply diminished and in some instances has disappeared.

A thorough analysis of this problem has never been made in the United States. Because of the failure to allocate deaths to place of residence and because of differences in the definition of urban population used in the compilation of population and vital statistics, mortality statistics prior to 1940 are unsatisfactory for the analysis of the variation in death rates by size of community. At the present time, lack of information concerning the amount of misclassification of place of residence in mortality statistics makes uncertain the interpretation of observed differences between urban and rural areas.

A young man's choice of an occupation is perhaps the most important decision affecting his future length of life. The work a man does, the conditions under which this work is done, and the wages received largely determine where he lives, the food he eats, the medical care he receives, and his habits and ways of life. Those who choose a profession or a white-collar job can expect to live longer than those who choose manual labor. Those who become miners or sandstone grinders have a relatively short expectation of future lifetime.

Most of what we know today concerning the relationship of occupation and social class to mortality has come from the decennial studies of occupational mortality in England and Wales, initiated by William Farr in 1851 and continued since then by the General Register Office of England and Wales. Only fragmentary data are available from other countries. Investigations of the special health hazards of specific occupations have been conducted in countries with large industrial populations, but these fall outside the scope of this discussion.

In England and Wales, mortality rates in general are lowest for the professional classes and highest for unskilled laborers. The same general rank order has been found in other countries with comparable statistics. There is some evidence of a narrowing of social class differentials in mortality during recent years (Logan, 1954). Except for occupations with special health hazards, most of the variation in mortality rates by occupational groups probably results from the general living conditions and manner of life of workers in these occupations rather than from the direct effects of the occupations themselves (Stocks, 1938). To test this hypothesis, the Registrar General of England and Wales (1938) compared the social class differentials in mortality of wives with that of their husbands by assigning each married woman the social class of her husband. Not only did wives show the same gradient in mortality by social class as their husbands, but, in addition, the range in death rates was greater for women than for men. Corresponding data are not available for other countries, but there is no reason to doubt the applicability of these findings to the populations of most of the countries of Europe and North America.

Married persons generally have lower age-specific death rates than unmarried. The differentials usually are larger for men than for women. In population groups with a relatively high maternal mortality rate the death rate of young married women sometimes is higher than that of single women. The differentials by marital status undoubtedly arise in part from a selection of healthy persons for marriage and in part from differences in the habits and living conditions of the married and unmarried.

Heredity and Longevity

The observation that some persons live longer than others gave rise to the hypothesis that longevity, in part at least, is determined by heredity. Studies of family history data by Beeton and Pearson, Holmes, Bell, and Wilson and Doering found a small positive correlation between the length of life of parents and their children.

The most extensive attempt to determine the influence of heredity was made by Raymond Pearl. In order to avoid the defects of estimating the effect of heredity upon longevity from genealogical records, Pearl employed field workers to collect the family histories of some one hundred thousand persons living in and around Baltimore (Pearl and Pearl, 1934). The resulting data showed that the sons of fathers who survived until at least age eighty in turn lived longer, on the average, than the sons of fathers who died before reaching age fifty.

Pearl's investigation, like those of his predecessors, because of defects in methodology, cannot be accepted as more than indicating that a portion of the variation in length of life is determined by heredity. To be sure, the span of life is biologically fixed. But within this span there is overwhelming evidence that most of the variation in mortality rates among large population groups, except that between the sexes, has its origin in environmental factors. This statement is not contradicted by the fact that a number of diseases and defects, most of which are relatively rare, have a known genetic mode of transmission from one generation to the next, nor by the fact that the potential length of life of a specific individual may be determined in large part by his inherited constitution (Pearl, 1938). As age-specific death rates become smaller and smaller, genetic influence will assume increasing importance as a determinant of variation in longevity, but for most of the population of the world, environmental factors will long remain the major determinant.

Natural Selection and the Decline in Mortality

Darwin's theory of the role of natural selection in determining the direction of the evolution of living organisms, together with the rediscovery of Mendel's work in genetics, gave a strong impetus to studies of human heredity. The most active and influential group centered around Galton and his followers in Great Britain.

By the end of the nineteenth century, efforts to lower mortality rates by improving the living conditions of large cities had achieved noticeable success. The growing emphasis upon public health programs and, in particular, the continuing campaign to lower mortality rates during infancy and early childhood seemed to some geneticists to be designed, even though unwittingly, to counteract the beneficial effects of natural selection acting through the medium of high death rates. A series of studies by Karl Pearson, Snow, and others attempted to show that a decline in infant and childhood mortality rates would be followed by increased death rates during late adult life. In the United States, Pearl was one of the principal proponents of this theory. The fact that the death rates at the advanced ages were declining very slowly, if at all, and sometimes increasing from one year to the next was interpreted by some as confirmation of the theory. Was it really worthwhile to save the lives of weaklings during infancy and childhood, thus running the risk of their reproducing themselves and bringing about a general deterioration of the biological constitution of the population, only to have them die at increased rates during late adult life?

It is difficult at this time to appreciate fully the intensity of this debate. Needless to say, the advocates of continued efforts to reduce mortality rates won. As Figure 4 clearly shows, a decline in mortality rates, although considerably greater during the early years of life, has taken place at all ages throughout the life span.

The smaller rate of decline at the older ages may be in part the result of the prolongation of life made possible by advances in medicine and surgery. On the other hand, the persons of advanced age are the survivors of generations subjected to the more hazardous health conditions that prevailed during the past century. They may have survived the selective screening of a high mortality from infectious and communicable diseases only to have their future length of life impaired by residual sequelae. The test of this hypothesis will not come until the survivors of children born during the past two or three decades reach late adult life.

The Future Trend of Mortality

More than one-half of the world's population has an estimated death rate in excess of 20 per 1,000 per year. The widespread application of existing knowledge and techniques in preventive medicine, sanitation, and entomology could reduce this death rate to 15 or below in less than a decade. The examples of Ceylon and the Moslem population of Algeria were cited above. Among the nations with a large population, Japan reduced its death rate from 17.6 per 1,000 in 1946 to 8.9 in 1953.

These spectacular declines in mortality rates can be brought about without a marked improvement in the level of living of the population. Whether or not they can be maintained remains to be seen. The implications of a rapid drop in the death rate of one-half of the population of the world from a level of 20 to 25 per 1,000 to 12 to 15 per 1,000 without a comparable decline in fertility are only too obvious. The near balance of the controls on population growth would be upset to an extent probably unequaled in the previous demographic history of the world. Man has been able to modify or control many natural phenomena, but no one has yet discovered how to evade the consequences of biological laws. No species has ever been able to multiply without limit. There are two biological checks upon a rapid increase in the size of a population, a high mortality or a low fertility. The widespread application of existing knowledge can eliminate a high mortality. The unanswered question for the demographer is, can fertility be brought into balance with lower mortality before a rapid increase in population nullifies the gains in average length of life?

The prospect for a continued decline in mortality for the approximately one-quarter of the world's population with a death rate of about 10 per 1,000 is quite different from that of the countries just discussed. For these nations, a decline in the future comparable in magnitude to that of the past fifty years can be achieved only by lowering the mortality rates of late adult life (Table 35).

Whether or not this can be accomplished depends on a set of factors quite different from those responsible for the past decline in mortality rates. The major factors responsible for the increase in longevity in the past were improvements in sanitation, improved personal hygiene, control of infectious and communicable diseases by immunization, elimination of environmental conditions favorable to the spread of disease, better conditions of work, and a general rise in the level of living. Apart from preventive medicine, advances in medicine and surgery have played a relatively minor role. But during the past ten to fifteen years, advances in medicine and surgery have played an increasingly important part in the decline in mortality rates, largely because of developments in chemotherapy, improvements in surgical skill and technique, widespread use of blood and blood derivatives, more reliable methods for the early diagnosis of disease, and a more general use of better-equipped medical facilities. As an illustration of the potential effectiveness of advances in medicine against specific diseases, the case of tuberculosis is instructive. Although the mortality rate from tuberculosis in the United States

mortality during the early years of life already is so low that even a continuation of the existing annual rates of decrease will have only a small effect upon increasing the average length of life of the total population. Large decreases in mortality rates after age forty require a drop in the rates for accidents and the chronic diseases, in particular cancer and the cardiovascular-renal diseases. The possibility of this has been discussed in Jenkins and Lew (1949) and Dorn (1952a).

Laws of Mortality

Interest in the search for natural laws governing the mortality of human pop-

TABLE 35

Proportion of Possible Years of Life That Would Be Lived by Cohorts of 100 Males and 100 Females Subject throughout Life to Mortality Rates of the White Population of the United States, 1953

| | MALES | | FEMALES | |
Age	Number of Person-Years Lived during Each Age Group	Percentage of Possible Years	Number of Person-Years Lived during Each Age Group	Percentage of Possible Years
0–19	1930	96	1946	97
20–39	1874	94	1919	96
40–59	1702	85	1820	91
60–79	1024	51	1339	67
80–99	149	7	272	14

has been falling for more than half a century, the discovery of effective chemotherapy during the past decade opened a new era in the struggle against this disease. In 1945 the death rate was 39.9 per 100,000. Eight years later, in 1953, the death rate had decreased more than 60 per cent to 14.8 per 100,000. Nor is there any indication that this spectacular rate of decline will soon be halted.

Unlike the past, important declines in mortality rates in the future will depend upon advances in medicine and surgery. This does not mean that the factors which brought about the increase in average duration of life in the past will not continue to be effective in the future. Rather, it means that

ulations arose at an early date. In part, this was in keeping with the general belief, widely held at that time, in the existence of natural and divine laws by which human behavior could be guided or explained. In part, however, this interest had a practical basis. The lack of computing aids made very laborious the calculation of monetary values from a mortality table for determining the provisions of insurance and annuity contracts. Moreover, the discovery of a natural law governing mortality would compensate to some extent at least for the unreliability of the available mortality statistics.

The first to propound a law of mortality was De Moivre in 1725. From the only mortality tables available, those by Graunt and Halley, he deduced the hypothesis that the decrements in the curve of survivorship were constant throughout most of the life span. As more complete and reliable mortality data became available, De Moivre's hypothesis was shown to be false.

A century after De Moivre, Gompertz proposed a theory of mortality that, with some modifications, has continued to be accepted until the present. In 1825 he advanced the hypothesis that the force of mortality—the instantaneous death rate—was a compound of two factors, one independent of constitution and age and the other a direct function of age. He restricted his law to the age range of approximately ten to sixty years. Within this age range the force of mortality increased at a geometric rate with age.

Subsequently, about 1860, Makeham proposed a modification of Gompertz' law that made it generally applicable to most mortality tables from about age twenty until the end of the life span. Makeham's formula, representing the force of mortality by $A+BC^x$, where x denotes age and A, B, and C are constants, greatly simplified the calculation of joint life probabilities. Although Makeham's formula is of considerable practical importance today in life insurance, it no longer is regarded as more than a mathematical formula that satisfactorily graduates many mortality tables over the range of ages characterized by an increasing mortality rate.

In the decennial supplement of the Registrar General for the decade 1861–70, William Farr suggested that the relationship between the death rate and density of population could be expressed by the formula $R=CD^m$, where R is the death rate, D is density of population, and C and m are constants. According to Farr's calculations, m was approximately one-eighth. From this he concluded that the death rate increased

with the eighth root of the density of population. Farr used the crude death rate in deriving this relationship even though he was fully aware that variation in this rate for different areas could be due, in part, to variation in the age and sex composition of the populations. More careful studies using death rates adjusted for differences in age composition revealed that the value of m was not constant either from area to area or from one time to another, but so great was Farr's reputation that interest in the formula continued until many years after his death. As the continued fall in the death rate of large cities demonstrated that mortality could be effectively reduced by sanitation and public health programs, it became apparent that no inherent relationship existed between density of population and length of life.

Karl Pearson in a memorable book, *The Chances of Death and Other Studies in Evolution* (1897), dissected the curve of deaths into five periods, each characterized by a distinct pattern of mortality that could be expressed by a definite mathematical law. The five periods were infancy, childhood, youth, middle age or maturity, and old age or senility. He represented Death as a marksman, using the separate causes of death as his arrows. As these were launched, they selected persons in a specific age range for their target. This was a very graphic representation of mortality. Although it is true that the total mortality rate, as well as those for specific causes of death, varies among the broad age periods proposed by Pearson, both the total variation and the rank order of causes of death constantly change as one disease after another is brought under control. Today, Pearson's laws of mortality are regarded merely as a graphic method of representing the pattern of mortality by age.

The most plausible of all the mortality laws suggested to date is that of Kermack, McKendrick, and McKinlay (1934*a*, 1934*b*), mentioned above in the discussion of generation mortality tables. Greenwood (1936), after an extensive analysis of death rates in England and Wales, concluded that their hypothesis described remarkably well the past trend in mortality but expressed reservations concerning its value for forecasting mortality. The concept of generation mortality tables is very useful in demographic analysis, but the general applicability of the hypothesis advanced by Kermack, McKendrick, and McKinlay has yet to be demonstrated.

Evaluation of Existing Knowledge of Mortality

The analytical study of mortality data antedates that for any of the other core subjects of demography—fertility, migration, marriage, divorce, and number and composition of the population. It is now nearly three centuries since Graunt published his pioneer analysis of the bills of mortality of London. How shall the knowledge concerning the demographic aspects of mortality that has been accumulated in this interval be characterized?

a) Most of our knowledge has been derived from only a small part of the world's population. This knowledge is essentially the experience of the population of a single continent, Europe, and it covers the period since the Industrial Revolution and the settlement and development of North America, Australia, and New Zealand. There is reason to believe that some of this knowledge holds true for the remainder of the world's population, but how much cannot be ascertained until more comprehensive and reliable mortality statistics become available.

b) Knowledge of mortality is quantitative. Just as the study of the growth of populations requires a knowledge of mortality, so the analysis of mortality statistics requires reliable population statistics. The history of mortality statistics bears eloquent testimony to the fact that without reasonably complete and reliable statistics of deaths and population almost nothing of permanent value to demography can be learned about mortality. A wide variety of quantitative measures of mortality have been developed.

c) Studies of mortality have been largely descriptive and limited to showing variation in death rates by age, sex, race, geographic locality, rural and urban residence, marital status, and occupation.

d) Compared to fertility, few studies attempting to explain variations in mortality have been made. The early vital statisticians and students of population were more interested in mortality than in fertility. This is not surprising, since population change was more closely related to variations in mortality than in fertility. The first annual report of the Registrar General of England and Wales devoted one page to marriage and birth statistics and about sixty pages to mortality statistics. This distribution of interest between mortality and fertility statistics continued until the 1920's.

By that time the decline in fertility had reached the point where it appeared to presage an eventual decrease in the size of the population of many nations. The focus of interest shifted from mortality to fertility, and a literal flood of studies of the trend in fertility —the reasons for its decline, variation among different groups of the population, and the implication for future population change—appeared during the following two decades. The data for these studies came from a variety of sources: birth-registration records, the census of population, and special surveys of individuals and families. In contrast, most studies of mortality have been based solely on death certificates. Experience has demonstrated that reliable information concerning mortality cannot be obtained by a census of population or by special or household surveys.

The inflexibility and limitations of the registration system of collecting mortality statistics has restricted available information largely to that required for legal purposes. The principal exception is information concerning the usual occupation of the deceased. Doubts about the comparability of these data with those from the census of population have prevented any extensive analysis of occupational mortality except for England and Wales.

e) Studies of mortality have had a practical basis. The development of mortality statistics has gone hand in hand with the development of life insurance and public health programs. The reports of the Registrar General of England and Wales have contributed more to our knowledge of mortality than those of any other country. The character and direction of these reports was set by William Farr, undoubtedly the world's most influential medical statistician. Farr visualized mortality statistics as a means of improving the living conditions of the population. To this end he directed his great energy and fertile imagination. It is not surprising that the strongest support for mortality statistics today comes from persons interested in public health.

f) The development of mortality statistics has lagged behind the development of their principal consumer, public health programs. The chief causes of death today are the chronic diseases. Little is known of their etiology. As a rule, they develop gradually, without the episodic onset of most infectious and communicable diseases. Their course often is affected by modes of living and environmental conditions. As a result, interest has been directed toward predisposing conditions and methods of early detection and diagnosis.

The long duration of many chronic diseases has emphasized the need for morbidity data. Death is only the terminal stage of a disease that may incapacitate for many years. The difficulty and indeed the impracticability of adapting the registration system to provide the data necessary for the guidance of public health programs in countries with low mortality is forcing public health officials to turn to other sources of information.

NEXT STEPS IN RESEARCH

No attempt has been made to separate the following discussion into recommendations applicable to the so-called highly developed and underdeveloped countries. Although many countries do not have even a reliable count of the total annual number of deaths, most of the countries usually classed as highly developed have one or more inadequacies in their mortality statistics, and the nature of these varies from country to country. For example, Sweden, which has the longest consecutive series of national mortality statistics, did not adopt the international list of causes of death until after 1950. The United States did not have mortality statistics for the entire country until 1933 and did not publish a detailed classification of the number of resident deaths by age, sex, race, and cause for urban and rural areas until 1940. Only in England and Wales has any extensive effort been made on a national basis to study the association of mortality with indexes of social and economic conditions.

Data

Knowledge of mortality, just as of any other field of inquiry, is restricted by the type of data available to the research worker. To correct existing inadequacies the following steps are suggested:

a) Complete systems of reliable mortality statistics need to be developed for the major part of the world's population. The analysis of population trends and the measurement of health problems cannot proceed so long as the elementary facts about the size and composition of the population and the trend and variation in the number of births and deaths are lacking. Adequate mortality data still are unavailable for more than one-half of the world's population.

b) Although national statistics should not be cast in the same mold, the international comparison of mortality statistics is severely restricted by lack of comparability in registration practices, definitions, and tabulation practices. The World Health Organization and the United Nations (1953) have initiated important steps to improve comparability, but only a beginning has been made.

c) The present low level of infant mortality achieved in Australia, New Zealand, and some countries of Europe and North America has focused attention upon the problem of fetal mortality. Although only crude estimates are available, probably between 15 and 20 per cent of all pregnancies terminate in a fetal death. As was pointed out in the discussion of deficiencies in mortality statistics, the World Health Organization has proposed a uniform definition and classification for fetal deaths. Not only do existing definitions differ between nations, but within a nation like the United States registration practices differ among the forty-eight states. The statistics of fetal mortality require rebuilding from the very beginning.

d) In the countries with the lowest mortality rates, future increase in longevity comparable to that of the recent past will be possible only by a sharp reduction in the death rates during late adult life. The leading causes of death at these ages are the chronic diseases. The incidence and course of many of these diseases appear to be affected by modes of living and environmental conditions. It is especially important that mortality statistics of these diseases be related to social and economic factors. This will require not only a more complete utilization of existing data but also the collection of new information.

e) Studies are needed of the predisposing and precipitating causes of ill-health due to chronic diseases. Death represents only the final episode in an illness that may have existed for many years. Mortality should be related to morbidity. The collection of morbidity statistics will require the development of new techniques since the registration system is not well adapted to this purpose.

f) Data concerning multiple causes of death should become a regular part of tabulations of mortality statistics. At least 60 per cent of the death certificates in the United States have more than one diagnosis. It is becoming increasingly unrealistic to base the study of causes of death upon only one of these diagnoses.

Methods

Mortality statistics traditionally have been a by-product of vital registration. For legal purposes there is no substitute for complete registration of all deaths. The development of a satisfactory registration system has required many years in countries with the best mortality statistics. But the most acute need for adequate vital statistics today exists in the least-developed countries of the world, where present registration systems are seriously incomplete. Such countries can hardly wait for decades to develop an adequate registration system before obtaining the mortality and other vital statistics needed to measure the health problems of their populations. Moreover, most of them do not have the personnel or resources to establish quickly a workable national registration system. Modern developments in sampling theory and practice have made possible the collection of representative national vital statistics, pending the development of a complete registration system. The possibility of the use of sampling methods, particularly in the less-developed areas of the world, to provide needed mortality statistics should be seriously studied. An excellent discussion of the use of sampling for vital statistics will be found in Hauser (1954).

The rapid development in recent years of built-up, unincorporated suburban areas outside the corporate limits of many of the larger cities in the United States has made obsolete former definitions of urban and rural populations. In recognition of this the Bureau of the Census, at the time of the 1950 census, revised the definition of urban population to include persons living in the urban fringe around cities of 50,000 or more population. Since these fringe areas do not have politically defined boundaries, no practicable method of compiling mortality statistics in accordance with the definition of urban used in the census of population has yet been devised.

A new basis for tabulating mortality statistics by size of community needs to be developed. This method should avoid the errors of misclassification that cast doubt upon the validity of current vital statistics by size of community and at the same time should be based on a definition of urban and rural that is demographically sound. So long as public health activities are organized on the basis of political subdivisions it will be necessary to compile vital statistics in the same manner, but for demographic analysis supplementary tabulations are required on a basis that is more in keeping with the actual distribution of population by size of community.

Analytical Studies

Since the need and possibilities for undertaking analytical studies of mortality vary from one nation to another, the following comments apply specifically to the United States:

a) *Urban-rural differentials in mortality.*—One of the first illustrations of differential mortality in medical literature was the higher death rate among city dwellers in contrast to rural residents. Although this differential generally is assumed to exist at the present time, no comprehensive study on a national basis has ever been made in the United States. Although errors in classifying residence cast doubt upon the interpretation of current mortality statistics by size of community, these errors could be avoided by the use of metropolitan counties. Another study of this kind, conforming to the existing distribution of population, should be designed to test a new basis for classifying mortality statistics by size of community.

b) *Geographic differentials.*—Almost a century ago, William Farr proposed that the healthy districts of England and Wales be used as a yardstick of public health. Except for states as a whole, very little analysis of geographic variation in death rates has been made in the United States. While the range between states with the highest and lowest mortality rates has been decreasing, in 1950, after adjusting for differences in the age composition of the population, the highest rate was 40 per cent higher than the lowest. Much greater variation undoubtedly would be found if smaller, more homogeneous geographic units were used.

The county is the preferable unit for forming such areas since the basic demographic data are available and since the allocation of deaths to county of residence can be made without appreciable error. Two groupings of counties suggest themselves: metropolitan and non-metropolitan counties within each state or the economic subregions defined by the Bureau of the Census in co-operation with other agencies and recognized for the first time in the tabulation of the 1950 census of population.

c) *Mortality by occupation and socioeconomic groups.*—Although information on the usual occupation and industry of the deceased has appeared on death certificates since the establishment of the death registration area in 1900, no analysis has ever been made of these data except that published by the National Tuberculosis Association for seven broad social and occupational groups based upon the deaths of male workers in ten states during 1930.

One of the major deterrents to a study of occupational mortality has been uncertainty concerning the comparability of the entries of occupation and industry on death certificates with those on the census of population schedule. Fortunately, studies have been planned to determine whether the occupational data are sufficiently reliable to warrant their analysis. If they are too unreliable to be used, an effort should be made to substitute some other index of socioeconomic status on both birth and death certificates.

d) *Fetal mortality.*—Present knowledge about fetal mortality is as deficient as that about infant mortality fifty years ago. At the same time, the fetal mortality rate probably is as high as the infant mortality rate was at the beginning of the century. The primary need at present is improvement in registration and adoption of a uniform definition of fetal death. Nevertheless, studies based on existing data should not be neglected, for this is one method of keeping attention focused on the problem and

thus of contributing to the gradual improvement of the basic information. More use could be made of the perinatal mortality rate, since registration of fetal deaths is most complete for deaths occurring during the last three or four months of gestation.

e) *Increasing sex differential in mortality.*—Males experience a higher mortality rate from the early months of intra-uterine life until the end of the natural life span. As death rates have fallen, the excess mortality among males has increased. In 1900 the age-adjusted death rate for white males was 10 per cent higher than that for white females. By 1950 this differential had increased to 48 per cent. There is no evidence that it will not continue to increase.

To what extent is the higher mortality among males due to greater occupational hazards? How much of it may be attributed to biological differences? The sex differential is now large enough to warrant an attempt to discover the answer to these and similar questions.

f) *High mortality rates at the older ages.*—Not only has the decline in mortality rates among males in the United States failed to keep pace with the decline in mortality rates among females, but the decline in mortality rates for males more than forty years of age also has not kept pace with the corresponding decline for males in most of the countries of western Europe, Canada, Australia, and New Zealand (Dublin and Spiegelman, 1952). To a lesser extent the same is true concerning the relative rate of decrease in the death rates among females above fifty years of age. During the first half of the life span, the mortality rates for males and females in the United States are among the lowest in the world. During the latter half of the life span, the rates for females are near the average of those for comparable countries, but the rates for males are among the highest of those for comparable countries. Several hypotheses have been advanced to explain this reversal of the relative rank of mortality in the United States, but none of these has been adequately tested. Additional studies are called for.

SELECTED BIBLIOGRAPHY

BAUMGARTNER, LEONA, WALLACE, HELEN M., LANSBERG, EVA, and PESSIN, VIVIAN. 1949. "The Inadequacy of Routine Reporting of Fetal Deaths," *American Journal of Public Health*, XXXIX, 1549–52.

BUER, M. C. 1926. *Health, Wealth, and Population in the Early Days of the Industrial Revolution.* London.

CZUBER, E. 1938. *Wahrscheinlichkeitsrechnung*, Vol. II. 4th ed. Berlin: Teubner.

DERRICK, V. P. A. 1927. "Observations on (1) Errors of Age in the Population Statistics of England and Wales, and (2) the Changes in Mortality Indicated by the National Records," *Journal of the Institute of Actuaries*, LVIII, 117.

DORN, H. F. 1952a. "Prospects of Further Decline in Mortality Rates," *Human Biology*, XXIV, 235–61.

———. 1952b. "The Effect of Public Health Developments upon Population Growth," *Annals of the New York Academy of Sciences*, LIV, Art. 5, 742–49.

———. 1954. "The Increase in Cancer of the Lung," *Industrial Medicine and Surgery*, XXIII, 253–57.

DUBLIN, L. I., and LOTKA, A. J. 1937. *Twenty-five Years of Health Progress.* New York: Metropolitan Life Insurance Co.

———, and SPIEGELMAN, M. 1949. *Length of Life.* Rev. ed. New York: Ronald Press.

DUBLIN, L. I., and SPIEGELMAN, M. 1941. "Current versus Generation Life Tables," *Human Biology*, XIII, 439–59.

———. 1952. "Factors in the Higher Mortality of Our Older Age Groups," *American Journal of Public Health*, XLII, 422–29.

EDGE, P. G. 1928. "Vital Registration in Europe: The Development of Official Statistics and Some Differences in Practice," *Journal of the Royal Statistical Society*, XCI, 346–79.

ERHARDT, C. L. 1952. "Reporting of Fetal Deaths in New York City," *Public Health Reports*, LXVII, 1161–67.

GILLE, H. 1949. "The Demographic History of the Northern European Countries in the Eighteenth Century," *Population Studies*, III, 3–65.

GLOVER, J. W. 1921. *United States Life Tables, 1890, 1901, 1910, and 1901–1910.* Washington, D.C.: Government Printing Office.

GREENWOOD, M. 1936. "English Death Rates: Past, Present, and Future," *Journal of the Royal Statistical Society*, XCIX, 674–707.

HAUSER, P. M. 1954. "The Use of Sampling for Vital Registration and Vital Statistics," *Bulletin of the World Health Organization*, XI, 5–24.

JAMES, G., PATTON, R. E., and HESLIN, A. SANDRA. 1955. "Accuracy of Cause-of-Death Statements on Death Certificates," *Public Health Reports*, LXX, 39–51.

JANSSEN, T. A. 1940. "Importance of Tabulating Multiple Causes of Death," *American Journal of Public Health*, XXX, 871–79.

JENKINS, W. A., and LEW, E. A. 1949. "A New Mortality Basis for Annuities," *Transactions of the Society of Actuaries*, I, 369–466.

KERMACK, W. O., McKENDRICK, A. G., and McKINLAY, P. L. 1934a. "Death Rates in Great Britain and Sweden: Some General Regularities and Their Significance," *Lancet*, CCXXVI, 698–703.

———. 1934b. "Death Rates in Great Britain and Sweden: Expression of Specific Mortality Rates as Products of Two Factors and Some Consequences Thereof," *Journal of Hygiene*, XXXIV, 433–57.

LOGAN, W. P. D. 1954. "Social Class Variations in Mortality," *British Journal of Preventive and Social Medicine*, VIII, 128–37.

NOTESTEIN, F. W., *et al.* 1944. *The Future Population of Europe and the Soviet Union.* Geneva: League of Nations.

PEARL, R. 1920. "Some Landmarks in the History of Vital Statistics," *Quarterly Publications of the American Statistical Association*, XVII, 221–23.

———. 1938. "The Search for Longevity," *Scientific Monthly*, XLVI, 462–83.

———, and PEARL, RUTH DeWITT. 1934. *The Ancestry of the Long-Lived.* Baltimore: Johns Hopkins Press.

REGISTRAR GENERAL. 1938. "Occupational Mortality," *Decennial Supplement, Eng-*

land and Wales, 1931, Part IIa. London: H. M. Stationery Office.

ROYAL COMMISSION ON POPULATION. 1950. *Papers of the Royal Commission on Population.* Vol. II: *Reports and Selected Papers of the Statistics Committee.* London: H. M. Stationery Office.

SOCIETY OF ACTUARIES. 1954. *Impairment Study, 1951.* Chicago: Society of Actuaries.

SPRINGETT, V. H. 1950. "A Comparative Study of Tuberculosis Mortality Rates," *Journal of Hygiene,* XLVIII, 361–95.

STOCKS, P. 1938. "The Effect of Occupation and of Its Accompanying Environment on Mortality," *Journal of the Royal Statistical Society,* CI, 669–709.

UNITED NATIONS. 1953. *Principles for a Vital Statistics System.* ("Statistical Papers," Ser. M, No. 19.) New York.

–––, POPULATION DIVISION, DEPARTMENT OF SOCIAL AFFAIRS. 1953. *The Determinants and Consequences of Population Trends.* New York.

–––. 1954. *Foetal, Infant, and Early Childhood Mortality.* Vol. I: *The Statistics.* New York.

UNITED NATIONS, STATISTICAL OFFICE. 1954. "Types of Vital Statistics Available in Different Countries," *Bulletin of the World Health Organization,* XI, 177–99.

UNITED STATES PUBLIC HEALTH SERVICE. 1954. "History and Organization of the Vital Statistics System," *Vital Statistics of the United States, 1950,* Vol. I, chap. i. Washington, D.C.: Government Printing Office.

–––, NATIONAL OFFICE OF VITAL STATISTICS. 1955. *Vital Statistics of the United States, 1953,* Vol. I. Washington, D.C.: Government Printing Office.

WESTERGAARD, H. 1932. *Contributions to the History of Statistics.* London: P. S. King & Son.

WOLFENDEN, H. H. 1954. *Population Statistics and Their Compilation.* Rev. ed. Chicago: University of Chicago Press.

WORLD HEALTH ORGANIZATION. 1950. "Technical Report Series," No. 25.

YERUSHALMY, J., and BIERMAN, JESSIE M. 1952. "Major Problems in Fetal Mortality," *Vital Statistics, Special Reports,* Vol. XXXV, No. 13. Washington, D.C.: National Office of Vital Statistics.

20. Population Growth and Replacement

HANNES HYRENIUS

INTRODUCTION

In the development of demography as a science, studies of methods for measuring mortality began relatively early, while it took considerable time before the other population factors were made the subject of methodological research. The studies of fertility began during the latter part of the nineteenth century; methods for analyzing nuptiality, divorces, and migration followed somewhat later. The main reason for the growing interest in methods of measuring fertility was that the birth rate in some populations had undergone such considerable changes that these changes had also caused changes in the age distributions.

Previously, the birth rate—although sometimes fluctuating considerably—together with a somewhat lower mortality rate had given rise to a clear and fairly stable pyramidal form in the age structure of populations. The decrease in mortality during the nineteenth century in a number of European countries did not have any great effect on the general shape of the age distributions. The incipient decrease in the birth rate, which first became clear in some of the bigger cities in Europe, directed interest toward the increasing effect of these changes on the value of the crude birth rate as a measure of fertility.

The first construction of age-specific fertility rates, leading in due course to the idea of reproduction rates, seems to have been made and used by R. Boeckh, chief of the statistical bureau of the city of Berlin. In 1896 he derived such rates for Berlin for the year 1879. From these rates he also constructed age-standardized measures of the natural increase. From these first attempts the general ideas and the methods of constructing specific reproduction rates and age-standardized rates of natural increase for studying "the balance of births and deaths" were derived through the efforts of a number of statisticians, sociologists, and others in a number of countries.

During the 1920's R. R. Kuczynski completed the two-volume work, *The Balance of Births and Deaths* (1928, 1931), which gave data on reproduction for all countries with available statistics. Among these were two countries with data back to the middle of the eighteenth century (Sweden, Finland) and six countries with data from the first half of the nineteenth century.

As the importance of using adequate measures of natality and natural increase became more and more obvious, vital statistics were improved all over the world. The use of reproduction rates as summarizing indicators of population development has subsequently become more widespread. During the course of time, the concept and the methods of application have, however, been subject to discussion and severe criticism. The result has been modifications and new methods of application of the original idea and also more careful interpretations of what various types of reproduction numbers may disclose. A short list of contributions to the theory and methodology from a number of workers is given at the end of this chapter.

472

METHODS FOR MEASURING NATURAL
INCREASE AND REPRODUCTION

Let $l(x)$ be the life-table survivor rate and $f(x)$ the age-specific fertility rate. These notations may be taken as referring entirely to one sex at a time. If desirable, reference to a specific sex may be made by the letters M or $F-l_F(x)$, etc.

The age-standardized birth rate introduced by Boeckh was

$$b = \int_0^\omega l(x) \, f(x) \, dx \Big/ \int_0^\omega l(x) \, dx . \quad (1)$$

As the life-table mortality rate is

$$d = 1 / e_0 = l_0 \Big/ \int_0^\omega l(x) \, dx , \quad (2)$$

the difference becomes an age-standardized measure of natural increase:

$$n = b - d . \quad (3)$$

Instead of this difference between the two standardized crude rates, one may compare the numbers of births which would occur in the life-table population when applying the given set of age-specific fertility rates, the numerator of (1), with the constant number of births underlying the stationary population itself, $l(0)$. This would in fact be equivalent to *comparing the size of two consecutive generations*.

In this original form, the definition of the *net reproduction rate* is given by

$$R = \int_0^\omega l(x) \, f(x) \, dx \Big/ l(0) . \quad (4)$$

In practice, the infinitesimal treatment is, of course, replaced by a finite approach with sums instead of integrals. Furthermore, as the sex proportion is fairly constant, one uses fertility rates, $f(x)$, including both sons and daughters and, possibly, based on confinements. A reduction to live-born daughters is then easily made by applying the sex proportion.

If $q =$ ratio of number of live-born girls to total number of born or live-born children or confinements, we then have

$$R = q \sum_0^\omega L_F(x) \, f_F(x) . \quad (5)$$

Here, $L_F(x)$ is the stationary age distribution, given by

$$L_F(x) = \tfrac{1}{2} [l_F(x) + l_F(x+1)] . \quad (6)$$

If mortality did not reduce the reproductive capacity of a group of girls during their lifetime or before the end of the fertile period, the total result of fertility would be given by

$$R' = \int_0^\omega f(x) \, dx \quad (7)$$

or

$$R' = q \sum_0^\omega f_F(x) . \quad (8)$$

This is the *gross reproduction rate*. By applying the mean-value theorem, we may write

$$R' = R \cdot l_F(\xi) , \quad (9)$$

where ξ is a mean value of x, situated near the average age of mothers at childbirth. This formula offers an easy way of making fairly good approximations of R.

The net reproduction rate as defined above may be considered a generation-long, age-standardized rate of natural increase with the stationary age distribution as standard. In a sense, such a measure is self-contradictory. The logical objections are eliminated by the method introduced by Alfred Lotka (1934–39, Part II). Instead of the stationary age distribution, Lotka used a stable age distribution with a specific annual rate of net increase, $l(x)e^{-rx}$. Here, r is Lotka's *true rate of natural increase*, defined by "Lotka's fundamental equation."

$$1 = \int_0^\omega l(x) \, e^{-rx} f(x) \, dx . \quad (10)$$

For practical computations, Lotka fitted a Gaussian curve to the function $l(x)f(x)$, i.e., the age distribution of new mothers in the life-table population. Through this approach r can be calculated from the first moments of the age distribution of mothers (among them the net reproduction rate, R). A somewhat better method was later given by S. D. Wicksell (1931). It can, however, easily be demonstrated that the true rate of natural increase differs negligibly from the *annual net reproduction rate* derived from the generation-long net reproduction rate by the simple way of the formulas for compound interest:

$$R = e^{rM} , \qquad (11)$$

from which

$$r = \frac{1}{M} \log_e R \quad \text{or} \quad r = R^{1/M} - 1, \quad (12)$$

where M is the mean age of mothers.

CRITICISM AND IMPROVEMENTS OF ORIGINAL METHODS

The general idea of pooling expressions of the various demographic elements into one single figure may, as such, be criticized. During the decades that have followed the pioneer works by Kuczynski and Lotka, a great number of demographers have been trying to improve the original ideas and methods in order to avoid some of the obstacles and drawbacks of the reproduction rates and to make them more sensitive to changes in the separate factors of reproduction.

The general forms of reproduction rates (gross, net, generation-long, and annual) have heretofore been defined for the female sex only. There is, of course, nothing to prevent us from making exactly the same constructions for the male sex. We would then compare the size of two consecutive male generations. The formulas will obviously be the same as given above, with the exception that the sex quotient q in equations (5) and (8) is to be replaced by $(1 - q)$. The empirical results will, however, differ from the corresponding results for females. This is one of the points on which efforts have been concentrated during the last two decades.

The differences between male and female reproduction measures can be explained by the sex disproportion at birth and the sex differences in mortality and migration. Furthermore, the age patterns of new fathers and new mothers differ considerably. The effect of these factors will give rise to differences in the fertility rates derived by relating the same observed births alternatively to the male and female adult populations. These anomalies have been studied during the two last decades by a number of demographers, among them P. H. Karmel (1947), R. J. Myers, A. H. Pollard, L. Törnqvist, and H. Hyrenius (1948).

The first calculations of net reproduction rates were based on fertility rates by age only. It soon became obvious, however, that differences between populations or persistent changes in time within a population with regard to nuptiality may have a great influence on the size and changes of the final reproductivity. Among the first contributions to this development was a study by S. D. Wicksell (1931). Later, further differentiations were introduced with regard to age at childbirth and duration of marriage or age at marriage and duration of marriage (H. Hyrenius, 1948; C. Clark and R. E. Dyne, 1946). The influence upon legitimate fertility by order of births (parity) was introduced by P. K. Whelpton (1946) as a separate variable in measuring reproduction.

Parallel with the efforts to improve the technique of measuring reproductivity—which usually have led to complications in formulas and calculations —have been attempts to simplify the calculations. Among these is W. S. Thompson's (1931) *replacement index*.

If the age distribution within the fertile ages—say 20–44 years—does not vary too much, an acceptable measure of fertility is obtained directly from the age distribution by

$$b = P_{0-4}/P_{20-44}, \qquad (13)$$

where P_{0-4} denotes the actual population in ages 0–4, etc. In the stationary age distribution, the corresponding fertility measure is

$$\beta = L_{0-4}/L_{20-44}. \qquad (14)$$

From these rates, the net reproduction rate can be estimated by the quotient

$$I = \frac{b}{\beta} = \frac{P_{0-4}/P_{20-44}}{L_{0-4}/L_{20-44}}. \qquad (15)$$

Empirical applications parallel with more detailed calculations of net reproduction rates show that the replacement index is a good indicator within fairly wide limits.

The method suggested by Thompson is based on census data plus a suitable life table and can therefore be used for countries and small areas where no fertility data are available or where such data are inconsistent with the necessary data on the population in fertile ages. The method can be further developed, and other measures on reproduction can be constructed mainly by means of census data.

One such method is based on the average number of children per married woman in ages where fertility has ceased to be of any numerical importance (say 45 or 50). Starting with a stationary population with $l_F(0)=1,000$ and $l_M(0)=1,056$, say, we would for full reproduction require 2,056 children born alive by this population during its lifetime, up to forty-five or fifty years of age among the women. By some simple assumptions about nuptiality and illegitimate fertility and about mor-

tality among married couples it is possible to estimate the number of these children who are born outside marriage or who have become orphans. The remainder are proportioned among the married couples still living together when the wife is, say, forty-five. The average number of children thus constructed can be used for judging to what degree the factual average number is sufficient for regeneration.

The method of analyzing reproductivity just mentioned is, of course, not generally applicable. Under certain circumstances, however, the family data of population censuses may give important information concerning the changes of fertility (proportion of childless marriages, changes in number of families with many children, etc.).

THE GENERATION (COHORT) ASPECT

The original idea of a net reproduction rate implies that one follows the reproductive behavior of a group of newborn girls—or boys—during a generation in order to derive the size of the daughter-generation (or son-generation). In practical applications this underlying condition of the net reproduction rate has long been overlooked. In fact, demographers have formally applied the definitions to series of age-specific fertility rates which have not referred to one and the same generation (*generation-fertility rates*) but which have been observed during a year or period for all generations living in fertile ages at the same time (*period-fertility rates*).

In most routine applications of reproduction measures demographers until recently have not considered any alternative to period rates at all. Insofar as period rates have been deliberately chosen rather than generation rates, the reason has mainly been the desire to obtain current summarizing measures of the reproductive level during a specific period. This need for up-to-date information still plays a role in spite of the results revealed in recent studies on the differences between generation rates and period rates.

The calculation of reproduction rates for generations can be carried out for any considerable length of time only in a few countries. Comparative studies of series of both generation and period rates have in some respects revised previous conclusions about the level of reproduction and temporal changes in it. The practical results of this may be characterized as modified interpretations of the data and as attempts to pay more attention to the underlying trend value of fertility and reproductivity. The relative merits of the two types of rates have been discussed during recent years by a number of demographers. Reference may be made to works by J. Hajnal (1947), H. Hyrenius (1951), P. Vincent (1946), and T. J. Woofter (1947).

The generation approach has been improved in various ways in order to allow a more up-to-date analysis of data. Because of the continuing decrease in mortality, one may start with a group of 1,000 girls of age fifteen instead of a group of 1,000 newborn girls. The calculated number of offspring must then be reduced by partly extrapolated mortality rates up to the age of fifteen.

In populations with widespread birth control, the age pattern of fertility has undergone continuous changes, with greater concentration on the age scale. The proportion of births among women in the higher fertile ages has decreased considerably in a number of countries. These circumstances make it possible to base the calculation of generation reproduction rates mainly on an age interval of perhaps fifteen years, e.g., 20–34. The remainder can be estimated by means of extrapolations which will give rise to very limited errors.

Instead of using a generation of births of a specific year or a group of persons who reach a chosen age during a specific year, one might perform the calculations from the number of marriages contracted during a specific year. By this method, which is called the *cohort method,* one is under certain conditions able to reduce the time interval required for obtaining acceptable results. In some countries and population groups with low fertility, about 90 per cent of the births may occur within the first twelve years after marriage.

When starting with a cohort of marriages, one must supplement the calculations of legitimate births by estimates of the illegitimate births, after which the future number of marriages can be calculated by using extrapolated values of mortality and nuptiality rates. This approach may seem complicated and sometimes dangerous, especially with regard to the extrapolations involved. However, the possible errors are fairly limited, and the shorter time dispersion must be considered advantageous. The method just indicated is only one among several ways of constructing generation or cohort measures of reproductivity.

INCLUSION OF MIGRATION FOR A MEASURE OF TOTAL POPULATION GROWTH

The classical concept of a reproduction rate as a summarizing measure of population growth deals solely with the net result of fertility and mortality or, in other words, with closed populations. In reality, however, most populations are also affected by gains and losses through migration. Although this cannot be considered a natural or general component of population growth, it would, under certain circumstances, be desirable to obtain an age-standardized measure not only of the natural increase but also of the total growth.

If one studies the way in which and

the extent to which a generation replaces itself by a new generation while subject to a certain net migration, the final result can be given in a form having a meaning analogous to that of a reproduction rate. Such a rate, incorporating the effect of net migration, has been called a *replacement rate* (Hyrenius, 1954).

The definition of the replacement rate is given by the following formula:

$$S = \int_0^\omega k(x) f(x) dx$$
$$\simeq q \sum_0^\omega K(x) f(x). \quad (16)$$

Here, $k(x)$ is a survivor rate similar to $l(x)$ but including the effect of both the mortality, $\mu(x)$, and the net migration, $\nu(x)$;

$$k(x) = e^{-\int_0^x [\mu(z)+\nu(z)]dz}. \quad (17)$$

From this, $K(x)$ is calculated as an analogue to $L(x)$. An *annual* replacement rate or "annual rate of total increase," s, in Lotka's sense, may be obtained by the relation

$$1 = \int_0^\omega k(x) e^{-sx} f(x) dx. \quad (18)$$

For total populations of countries net migration is usually relatively limited; therefore the replacement rate does not differ very much from the net reproduction rate. During periods of heavy migration, however, such as the emigration from European countries during the last decades of the nineteenth century and up to the First World War, replacement rates have a special and significant meaning. Another case where replacement rates would be of importance is to be found when different population groups are studied, for instance, the development of agricultural and rural populations as compared with industrial and other populations.

Summarizing various qualities of a

replacement rate, the idea would seem to be applicable and useful when based on a generation or when based on periods of some length (a) if there is a more or less permanent although varying net emigration or (b) if there is a more or less permanent net immigration and, at the same time, fertility and net migration are concentrated in a fairly short age interval.

NUMERICAL ILLUSTRATIONS

The following applications of reproduction measurements are taken from data on the population of Sweden. This

TABLE 36
CALCULATION OF GROSS AND NET REPRODUCTION RATE

Age x	Years Lived by 1,000 Live-born Girls (Stationary Age Distribution) $L(x)$	Age-specific Fertility Rates (Confinements) $f(x)$	Calculated Number of Confinements $L(x)f(x)$
15–19....	4868	38.9	189
20–24....	4851	126.0	611
25–29....	4830	128.0	618
30–34....	4804	93.6	450
35–39....	4767	54.8	261
40–44....	4719	18.3	86
45–49....	4646	1.5	7
Sum..	....	461.1	2222

is not because this population offers particularly interesting demographic conditions but because there exist long series of data on population and vital events. The data may be considered reliable and consistent. In addition, the author of this chapter is more familiar with their qualities than with data taken at random from the *Demographic Yearbook*. The practical calculation of gross and net reproduction rates may be illustrated by Table 36, for Sweden, 1950.

The second column, $L(x)$, gives the total number of years lived by an original group of 1,000 live-born girls when exposed to the mortality conditions during 1950. The age-specific fertility rates, $f(x)$, give the number of confinements during a specific age group per 1,000 of the average female population during the year.

Because the fertility rates are based on confinements rather than on live-born children, the sex proportion q here must be replaced by the quotient of the number of live-born girls and the number of confinements. For 1950 this is 0.479.

age distribution into married and non-married (unmarried, widows, and divorced) and can hence apply age-specific legitimate and illegitimate fertility (or confinement) rates. The total result can be reduced to number of live-born girls for each part separately or for the total. The calculations are indicated in Table 37.

If the percentage married is denoted

TABLE 37

CALCULATION OF NET REPRODUCTION RATE, STANDARDIZED FOR CIVIL STATUS

AGE x	PERCENT-AGE MARRIED $p(x)$	LEGITIMATE FERTILITY			ILLEGITIMATE FERTILITY		
		Stationary Age Distribution of Married $L_1(x)$	Age-specific Legitimate Confinement Rates $f_1(x)$	Calculated Number of Legitimate Confinements $L_1(x)f_1(x)$	Stationary Age Distribution of Non-married $L_2(x)$	Age-specific Illegitimate Confinement Rates $f_2(x)$	Calculated Number of Illegitimate Confinements $L_2(x)f_2(x)$
15–19........	3.6	175	556.3	97	4693	19.5	92
20–24........	39.7	1926	270.1	520	1925	31.1	60
25–29........	71.7	3463	169.9	588	1367	22.2	30
30–34........	81.0	3891	111.8	435	913	16.1	15
35–39........	81.2	3871	65.4	253	896	9.2	8
40–44........	78.5	3704	22.4	83	1015	3.4	3
45–49........	73.5	3415	2.0	7	1231	0.2	0
Sum.....		....	....	1983	....	....	208

Observing that the age is given in five-year groups, one obtains the gross reproduction rate by $R' = 0.479 \cdot 5 \cdot 461.1/1000 = 1.104$. The net reproduction rate becomes $R = 0.479 \cdot 2222/1000 = 1.064$.

From the age distribution of mothers, $L(x)f(x)$, the mean age is found to be slightly above twenty-eight years. From the life table for 1950 we find $l_{28} = 0.966$. The abridged calculation of the net reproduction (9) then gives $R = 1.066$, or almost the same as the value calculated above.

The use of separate legitimate and illegitimate fertility rates may be illustrated by dividing the stationary age distribution, given above, according to the distribution by civil status in the average population of 1950. In this way we obtain a division of the stationary

$p(x)$, the two parts of the stationary age distribution are given by

$$L_1(x) = L(x) p(x)$$

$$\text{and} \quad L_2(x) = L(x)[1 - p(x)].$$

The total number of calculated confinements is 2,191, which is a little lower than the figure previously derived (2,222). The net reproduction rate hence becomes 1.049. The difference can be attributed to the very crude age grouping used in this example and the way in which the division according to civil status is made. More detailed calculations would lead to close agreement.

The usefulness of introducing the civil status—or the nuptiality—as a separate factor in calculating reproduction rates becomes obvious when we compare populations with different marriage conditions. The above data for Sweden in 1950 may be used for an illustration.

Nuptiality in Sweden during the last two decades has been considerably higher than it was during the course of many generations previously. If we were to use proportions of married, $p(x)$, corresponding to previous "normal" marriage rates in Sweden, the net result of the fertility and mortality in 1950 would be much lower than the results given above. For simplicity, we will use here the percentages of married women according to the census of 1900 rather than calculate the proportions from any series of age-specific nuptiality rates. By the above-mentioned method, we find the net reproduction rate $R = 0.782$, as compared with $R = 1.049$ or 1.064. The difference may be interpreted as being the effect of changes in marriage conditions.

The use of male reproduction rates necessitates an estimation of the illegitimate part because usually only the legitimate children are classified according to the age of the father. Even if the ages of the fathers of illegitimate children are known, the fathers are sometimes found among the married men. The number of new fathers of legitimate confinements related to the average size of the male population (married and non-married) may be denoted $f^{(M)}(x)$, while the stationary male distribution is $L^{(M)}(x)$. The calculations are shown in Table 38.

The calculated number of legitimate confinements is 1,865. A reduction to number of live-born legitimate boys is made by the corresponding quotient from data observed in 1950: $q = 0.512$. The illegitimate fertility can be roughly estimated by the data previously given for legitimate and illegitimate female reproduction. We here obtain the factor $k = 2191/1983 = 1.105$. The male net reproduction rate thus becomes $R^{(M)} = 1.105 \cdot 0.512 \cdot 1865/1000 = 1.055$.

As shown in the following section, the male reproduction rate was once much higher than the female rate. However, the differences have disappeared, and the male rate is now even somewhat lower than the female rate.

The calculation of a replacement rate can be made for Sweden in 1950 by comparing the size of single one-year cohorts at the beginning and the end of the year.

TABLE 38

CALCULATION OF MALE NET REPRODUCTION RATE

Age x	Male Legitimate Fertility Rate (Confinements to Total Population) $f^{(M)}(x)$	Stationary Age Distribution $L^{(M)}(x)$	Calculated Number of Legitimate Confinements $L^{(M)}(x)f^{(M)}(x)$
15–19...	2.4	4823	12
20–24...	52.4	4793	251
25–29...	105.3	4756	501
30–34...	101.5	4721	479
35–39...	70.2	4675	328
40–44...	39.5	4621	183
45–49...	16.7	4535	76
50–54...	5.7	4402	25
55–59...	1.8	4198	8
60–64...	0.6	3896	2
Sum.	.....	....	1865

Letting the female population be

$$P^{(0)}_{x,\ x+1} \quad \text{and} \quad P^{(1)}_{x+1,\ x+2},$$

we calculate

$$k_x = P^{(1)}_{x+1,\ x+2}/P^{(0)}_{x,\ x+1}$$

and subsequently

$$K_x = \prod_0^{x+1} k_x.$$

Parts of the calculations are shown in Table 39.

We obtain the death rate $d = 1212/82308 = 14.7$ per thousand and the birth rate $b = 0.479 \cdot 2500/82308 = 14.5$ per thousand. The replacement rate is $S = 0.479 \cdot 2500/1000 = 1.198$. From this the annual replacement rate can be estimated as $s = 6.3$ per thousand. This value is not fully comparable with the annual net reproduction rate, which is 2.2 per thousand. Consistency can, however, be obtained by further calculations. Using the given value of s, we can calcuate the stable age distribution $K_x e^{-sx}$ and again apply f_x and m_x. In this way we obtain consistent values of the various vital rates.

COMPARISON OF CRUDE AND REFINED MEASURES OF POPULATION INCREASE

The main reason for constructing the various measures of population in-

tions given in the previous section, we will here give some time series of the population growth and its components for Sweden, confining ourselves to the hundred years 1851–1950. The figures and the diagrams are informative themselves about the differences between crude and refined measures, and only a few comments seem necessary.

Table 40 gives the female net reproduction rates, R_F, during single years 1851–1950. In Table 41, the corresponding male reproduction rates, R_M, are given for 1911–50. Table 42 presents the net reproduction rates for both sexes for five-year periods 1851–55

TABLE 39

CALCULATION OF REPLACEMENT RATE

	STABLE AGE DIS-	AGE-SPECIFIC RATES		CALCULATED NUMBERS	
AGE	TRIBUTION	Mortality	Fertility	Deaths	Confinements
x	K_x	m_x	f_x	$K_x m_x$	$k_x f_x$
0–4........	4916	4.2	.....	21	....
5–9........	4928	0.5	.....	2	....
10–14.......	4944	0.4	.....	2	....
15–19.......	5022	0.5	38.9	3	195
20–24.......	5295	0.8	126.0	4	667
.					
.					
.					
45–49.......	5526	3.8	1.5	21	8
.					
.					
75–79.......	2840	78.5	.....	223	....
80–ω........	2597	176.1	.....	457	....
Sum.....	82308	.....	.....	1212	2500

crease described in the previous sections is the need for indicators which can give information on what lies behind the crude measures and which allow certain conclusions concerning the general status of the population trends. In analogy with the improved measures of mortality and fertility, the reproduction rates are derived to serve analytical purposes. In some respects, however, the crude rates may give information of specific interest, and we are then faced with the desirability of using both crude and refined rates at the same time.

After the simple numerical illustra-

to 1946–50. In addition, the table also gives the replacement rates, S_F and S_M.

The amalgamation to five-year periods tends to eliminate minor fluctuations and to make the data more informative about the conditions of the specific periods. In order to allow a direct comparison between the reproduction and replacement rates and the crude vital rates, the former have been transformed from generation-long to annual rates. The result is presented in Table 43. The various (annual) rates given in this table, all per thousand, are:

Crude rates (for both sexes together):

$b =$ birth rate, $d =$ death rate, $n =$ $b - d =$ natural increase, $m =$ net migation, and $t = n + m =$ total increase.

Refined rates (for each sex separately): $r =$ annual reproduction rate (comparable with n), $s =$ annual replacement rate (comparable with t), and

Using first the female reproduction rate, this measure varied during the latter part of the eighteenth century between 0.84 and 1.37, with the exception of one single wartime value, 0.46, and with a mean 1.17. During the first half of the nineteenth century the

TABLE 40

NET REPRODUCTION RATES OF THE SWEDISH
FEMALE POPULATION, 1851–1950

YEAR END-ING WITH	1851–60	1861–70	1871–80	1881–90	1891–1900
1........	1.37	1.47	1.51	1.43	1.46
2........	1.27	1.37	1.50	1.43	1.40
3........	1.26	1.47	1.51	1.42	1.42
4........	1.44	1.48	1.42	1.48	1.43
5........	1.33	1.46	1.45	1.45	1.49
6........	1.28	1.49	1.41	1.50	1.46
7........	1.10	1.46	1.46	1.51	1.45
8........	1.39	1.22	1.40	1.51	1.49
9........	1.47	1.19	1.51	1.45	1.38
0........	1.59	1.34	1.43	1.43	1.43

	1901–10	1911–20	1921–30	1931–40	1941–50
1........	1.43	1.35	1.18	0.79	0.85
2........	1.49	1.33	1.08	0.77	0.98
3........	1.41	1.30	1.06	0.74	1.08
4........	1.43	1.26	0.99	0.73	1.16
5........	1.40	1.18	0.97	0.73	1.18
6........	1.44	1.15	0.92	0.76	1.17
7........	1.44	1.14	0.87	0.77	1.14
8........	1.43	0.95	0.86	0.80	1.11
9........	1.46	1.04	0.81	0.84	1.07
0........	1.39	1.26	0.82	0.83	1.06

TABLE 41

NET REPRODUCTION RATES OF SWEDISH
MALE POPULATION, 1911–50

YEAR END-ING WITH	1911–20	1921–30	1931–40	1941–50
1........	1.54	1.35	0.90	0.90
2........	1.52	1.24	0.88	1.03
3........	1.49	1.22	0.83	1.12
4........	1.45	1.15	0.82	1.19
5........	1.35	1.12	0.81	1.21
6........	1.33	1.07	0.83	1.19
7........	1.31	1.00	0.83	1.16
8........	1.03	1.00	0.86	1.13
9........	1.17	0.93	0.89	1.08
0........	1.42	0.94	0.87	1.06

$s - r =$ annual age-standardized net migration rate (comparable with m). The rounding of the annual reproduction and replacement rates to the nearest unit per thousand allows a rounding error in $s - r$ of the size one per thousand in each direction, corresponding to 3 per cent in the generation rate.

TABLE 42

NET REPRODUCTION RATES AND REPLACEMENT RATES OF SWEDISH FEMALE AND MALE POPULATIONS, 1851–55 TO 1946–50

PERIOD	FEMALES		MALES	
	R	S	R	S
1851–55.....	1.33	1.27	1.47	1.37
1856–60.....	1.36	1.35	1.50	1.43
1861–65.....	1.45	1.42	1.59	1.52
1866–70.....	1.34	1.07	1.45	0.98
1871–75.....	1.48	1.34	1.64	1.46
1876–80.....	1.44	1.25	1.63	1.26
1881–85.....	1.44	1.11	1.65	1.13
1886–90.....	1.48	1.06	1.73	1.06
1891–95.....	1.44	1.13	1.71	1.26
1896–1900...	1.44	1.29	1.67	1.47
1901–05.....	1.43	1.19	1.65	1.21
1906–10.....	1.43	1.30	1.65	1.39
1911–15.....	1.28	1.19	1.47	1.26
1916–20.....	1.11	1.10	1.25	1.26
1921–25.....	1.06	1.00	1.22	1.04
1926–30.....	0.86	0.84	0.98	0.90
1931–35.....	0.75	0.77	0.84	0.88
1936–40.....	0.80	0.81	0.85	0.87
1941–45.....	1.05	1.09	1.09	1.13
1946–50.....	1.10	1.17	1.12	1.19

range was from 0.76 (war year) to 1.62, with a mean 1.32. From 1851 to 1910 the range of single years was from 1.10 to 1.51, with a mean 1.42. From the beginning of the First World War there was a continuing decrease to a minimum of 0.73 in the year 1934–35.

quence of sex differences in mortality and in the heavy migration to America. These differences in the sex composition have since been leveled out, and during recent years the male reproduction measure has dropped below the female reproduction rates. The com-

TABLE 43

CRUDE AND REFINED RATES OF POPULATION CHANGES IN SWEDEN, 1851–55 TO 1946–50

(ANNUAL RATES PER 1,000)

[Lack of Correspondence between Birth Rates, Death Rates, and Natural Increase, etc., Is Due to Rounding]

PERIOD	CRUDE RATES BOTH SEXES					REFINED RATES					
						Males			Females		
	Birth Rate b	Death Rate d	Natural Increase $n = b - d$	Net Migration m	Total Increase $t = n + m$	Annual Reproduction r	Annual Replacement s	$s - r$	Annual Reproduction r	Annual Replacement s	$s - r$
1851–55...	32	22	10	−1	9	11	9	− 2	10	8	− 2
1856–60...	34	22	12	−0	12	12	11	− 1	10	10	− 0
1861–65...	33	20	13	−1	13	14	12	− 2	12	12	− 0
1866–70...	30	21	9	−7	3	11	− 1	−12	10	2	− 8
1871–75...	31	18	12	−2	10	15	11	− 4	13	10	− 3
1876–80...	30	18	12	−4	8	14	7	− 7	12	7	− 5
1881–85...	29	18	12	−7	5	15	4	−11	12	3	− 9
1886–90...	29	16	12	−8	4	16	2	−14	13	2	−11
1891–95...	27	17	11	−5	6	16	7	− 9	12	4	− 8
1896–1900.	27	16	11	−2	9	15	11	− 4	12	9	− 3
1901–05...	26	15	11	−5	6	14	6	− 8	12	6	− 6
1906–10...	25	14	11	−3	8	14	10	− 4	12	9	− 3
1911–15...	23	14	9	−2	7	11	7	− 4	8	6	− 2
1916–20...	21	15	7	−0	7	7	7	+ 0	3	3	− 0
1921–25...	19	12	7	−2	5	6	1	− 5	2	0	− 2
1926–30...	16	12	4	−1	3	− 1	− 3	− 2	− 5	− 6	− 1
1931–35...	14	12	2	+1	4	− 5	− 4	+ 1	−10	− 9	+ 1
1936–40...	15	12	3	+1	4	− 5	− 4	+ 1	− 7	− 7	+ 0
1941–45...	19	11	8	+1	9	3	4	+ 1	2	3	+ 1
1946–50...	18	10	8	+3	11	4	7	+ 3	4	8	+ 4

A new top was reached in 1945 with 1.18, followed by a new decrease.

Comparing this with the male reproduction rates, we observe that these were on a higher level until the last decades. Thus, during the period 1891–95, the rates were 1.44 and 1.71, respectively, owing to great discrepancies in the sex proportion as a conse-

parison of reproduction and replacement in Table 42 stresses the importance of the emigration during the five decades immediately before the First World War. It also indicates the differences between the two sexes with regard to the intensity of migration.

Tables 40–42 present summarizing generation-long age-standardized measures of population growth which have been derived for analytical purpose. It is obvious, however, that they fail to divulge the whole picture—just like the simple crude vital rates. In order to grasp at the same time both the size and changes of the demographic elements and of the age distribution, a comparison of the type given in Table 43 is desirable.

A few comments should be made in connection with Table 43. The observed crude rate of natural increase, *n*, and the female and male annual reproduction rates, *r*, coincide during the first few periods, but already during the 1860's the series begin to diverge. The reproduction rates indicate a higher natural increase than observed because of the progressive age distribution. These differences remained until the beginning of the twentieth century.

Up to the middle of the 1920's the reproduction rates were still above unity, and the annual rates thus positive, with the factual natural increase somewhat higher. During the three five-year periods 1926–30 to 1936–40 there was still a slight natural increase, but the reproduction rates for those periods were considerably below unity, and the annual rates negative. The subsequent changes to positive annual reproduction rates during the 1940's have appeared simultaneously with a relatively slight increase in the rate of natural increase.

The comparisons made here indicate a strong and increasing need for adequate measures. This is not less important in studying the effect of the net migration upon the total population growth. The observed crude net migration rate, *m*, may be compared with the calculated rates *s − r*. However, according to what has been mentioned previously, *s* and *r* are not fully consistent, being referred to different stable age distributions, and *s − r* therefore is not entirely satisfactory as

an age-standardized measure of the migration. The changes in age structure have also caused a diminution of the absolute value of the observed rates as compared with the refined rates.

The general remarks just made on the effects of the changing age distribution refer also to a comparison between the observed crude total population increase, *t*, and the annual replacement rate, *s*. The effect sometimes appears more pronounced here,

TABLE 44

REPRODUCTION RATES BY
GENERATIONS

Generation = Birth Period	Reproduction Rates by Generations	Moving Averages of Reproduction Rates by Periods
1826–30.........	1.34	1.38
1831–35.........	1.35	1.38
1836–40.........	1.36	1.42
1841–45.........	1.36	1.42
1846–50.........	1.32	1.45
1851–55.........	1.31	1.45
1856–60.........	1.25	1.45
1861–65.........	1.23	1.45
1866–70.........	1.20	1.44
1871–75.........	1.16	1.43
1876–80.........	1.11	1.38
1881–85.........	1.06	1.27
1886–90.........	0.95	1.15
1891–95.........	0.84	1.01
1896–1900......	0.75	0.89
1901–05.........	0.72	0.80
1906–10.........	0.75	0.87
1911–15.........	0.82	0.99
1916–20.........	0.91	1.08
1921–25.........	0.95	....

but in other periods the effects have been balanced.

Finally, some female generation reproduction rates are presented in Table 44, starting with the birth period 1826–30. This generation reached the age of fifteen years during 1841–45 and had the main part of its childbearing period in the beginning of the 1850's. In order to bring data as far up to date as possible, the mortality rates and the fertility rates have been estimated for 1951–55 on the basis of data up to June, 1955. Furthermore, the fertility above age thirty-five and the mortality have been extrapolated; the errors from this can be considered to be of very little importance.

In addition to the rates by generations, Table 44 also gives moving averages of the period rates. These are calculated on three five-year periods. The moving averages are placed opposite that birth period which lies thirty years before the middle of the three five-year period rates.

The generation rates were nearly constant at a level of 1.35 in the first few five-year generation groups. The decline in fertility which became evident during the 1870's affected the generation rates beginning with the generations born around 1850. A bottom was reached in generations born about fifty years later, in the very beginning of the twentieth century. Subsequently, the generation reproduction rates have increased, and for the generation born in 1921–25 the final rate has been calculated to a little below unity, 0.95.

The generation rates given here are subject to certain minor errors of various kinds, mainly owing to material and methods used, but certain conclusions can be drawn from the series of data. It has sometimes been felt that period rates are more influenced by short-time changes in fertility and hence that generation rates should be capable of giving a more precise picture of the general level and trend. A comparison between the generation reproduction rates in Table 44 and the period rates in Table 42 reveals, however, that even the generation rates are subject to considerable variation.

It is open for discussion to what extent the temporal changes in the generation rates express solely changes in the general level of reproductivity. If the changes are interpreted as mainly the result of changing reproductivity, the conclusion must be drawn that the rise in fertility (and nuptiality) during the two last decades not only means an end to the previous decrease during

several decades but also a new increase in the resulting reproduction to a more or less permanent higher level.

The generation reproduction rates, of course, cannot very well be compared with the period rates. In addition to the five-year period rates in Table 42, moving averages over three periods are given in Table 44. During the first periods of the table the differences are small, as could also be expected under conditions where the fertility still remains on a high level while the mortality is changing very slowly. During subsequent periods the differences become more pronounced. The first five-year generation which had a reproduction rate below unity was 1886–90, with 0.95.

The moving averages given for comparison are not in a fully comparable time position. They also have a strong tendency to eliminate the temporal changes. The low fertility during the 1930's thus becomes less important than indicated in either the original period rates or the generation rates. The general difference between the two series in Table 44 to some extent also depends on the continuing decrease in mortality, especially in younger ages. The comparison indicates that a simple use of period rates over some ten–fifteen–twenty years does not give a very good substitute for the generation rates. In order to get a more informative picture, it therefore seems necessary to analyze simultaneously a whole set of time series on fertility, nuptiality, mortality, and reproduction, each one giving its contribution to the analysis and each one meeting specific questions.

SELECTED BIBLIOGRAPHY

CLARK, C., and DYNE, R. E. 1946. "Applications and Extensions of the Karmel Formula for Reproductivity," *Economic Record*, XXII, 23–39.

HAJNAL, J. 1947. "The Analysis of Birth Statistics in the Light of the Recent International Recovery of the Birth-Rate," *Population Studies,* I, 137–64.

———. 1947. "Aspects of Recent Trends in Marriage in England and Wales," *ibid.,* pp. 72–98.

HYRENIUS, H. 1948. "La mesure de la reproduction et de l'accroissement naturel," *Population,* III, 271–92.

———. 1951. "Reproduction and Replacement," *Population Studies,* IV, 421–31.

———. 1954. "Reproduction and Replacement Rates," *REMP Bulletin,* II, 43–47; also in *Proceedings of the World Population Conference, 1954,* Vol. IV. New York: United Nations, 1955.

KARMEL, P. H. 1944. "Fertility and Marriages, Australia, 1933–42," *Economic Record.*

———. 1947. "The Relations between Male and Female Reproduction Rates," *Population Studies,* I, 249–74.

KUCZYNSKI, R. R. 1928–31. *The Balance of Births and Deaths.* Vol. I. New York: Macmillan Co. Vol. II. Washington, D.C.: Brookings Institution.

———. 1932. *Fertility and Reproduction.* New York: Falcon Press.

LOTKA, A. J. 1933. "Industrial Replacement," *Skandinavisk aktuarietidskrift,* pp. 51–63.

———. 1934–39. *Théorie analytique des associations biologiques.* Part I: *Principes.* Part II: *Analyse démographique avec application particulière à l'espèce humaine.* Paris: Hermann & Co.

———. 1936. "The Geographical Distribution of Intrinsic Natural Increase in the United States, and an Examination of the Relation between Several Measures of Net Reproductivity," *Journal of the American Statistical Association,* XXXI, 273–94.

———. 1938. "Some Recent Results in Population Analysis," *ibid.,* XXXIII, 164–78. Reprinted in *Population Theory and Policy,* ed. J. J. SPENGER and O. D. DUNCAN. Glencoe, Ill.: Free Press, 1956.

QUENSEL, C. -E. 1939. "Changes in Fertility Following Birth Restriction," *Skandinavisk aktuarietidskrift.*

THOMPSON, W. S. 1931. *Ratio of Children to Women: 1920.* (Census Monograph XI.) Washington, D.C., Government Printing Office.

VINCENT, P. 1946. "De la mesure du taux intrinsèque d'accroissement naturel dans les populations monogames," *Population,* I, 699–712.

WHELPTON, P. K. 1946. "Reproduction Rates Adjusted for Age, Parity, Fecundity, and Marriage," *Journal of the American Statistical Association,* XLI, 501–16.

WICKSELL, S. D. 1931. "Nuptiality, Fertility, and Reproductivity," *Skandinavisk aktuarietidskrift.*

WOLFENDEN, H. H. 1954. *Population Statistics and Their Compilation,* Sec. XIV. Rev. ed. Chicago: University of Chicago Press.

WOOFTER, T. J. 1947. "Completed Generation Reproduction Rates," *Human Biology,* XIX, 133–53.

21. Internal Migration[1]

DONALD J. BOGUE

WHY SHOULD DEMOGRAPHERS BE INTERESTED IN INTERNAL MIGRATION?

Migration often has been declared to be one of three major subjects that comprise the field of "formal demography." The other two subjects are mortality and fertility. These three phenomena are known as the "components of population change," for they are the mechanisms by which a population grows or declines in size. A community or nation can gain population only through the fertility of its inhabitants or by migration, and it can lose population only through deaths among its residents or by migration. As a component of population change, migration occupies a central place in demographic analysis.

By custom, the field of migration study is divided into two branches—international migration and internal migration. This division is purely one of convenience for classifying migrants, for specifying the cultural characteristics of migrants, and for describing the legal and other conditions under which migrants travel. Certainly internal and international migration are not independent of each other; they have a very strong reciprocal influence. International migration is discussed elsewhere in this volume, and the present statement should be regarded as a companion chapter. For a variety of reasons other than the fact that it is a component of population change, the movement of peoples in space is an important subject for scientific demographic analysis.

Migration frequently is a major symptom of basic social change. Every region and every nation that has undergone extensive industrial development has simultaneously undergone a redistribution of its population. The industrial revolution in Europe and North America has been paralleled by a great rural-to-urban migration of more than 150 years' duration. Other nations now experiencing technological change of this same type are being subjected to the same migration experience. The building of great metropolitan centers, the exploitation of new resources, and the opening-up of new regions have all involved large inflowing streams of migrants. These migrants have been drawn from areas of older settlement. The migration process has had a profound effect both upon the areas to which migrants have flowed and upon the areas from which they have come. During a period of rapid industrial development, the volume of migrants received in a community may greatly exceed the need. The streams may originate in communities different from those from which it is desired to draw migrants, or the streams may consist of persons with qualifications different from those needed at the given spot at a given time. Only a careful and detailed analysis of migration events can reveal the redistributive effects of rapid social change upon the people. If there is a desire to regulate or control these redistributive effects, this control must be based upon knowledge of internal migration.

[1] This chapter summarizes some methodological lessons of migration research acquired as a part of a long-range program of research in population distribution, the funds for which were provided by the Rockefeller Foundation.

Migration is a necessary element of normal population adjustment and equilibrium. Within most nations some areas have higher birth rates than others. Also, some communities are areas of expanding opportunities for employment, while other communities are areas of stationary or declining economic opportunities. Not infrequently the communities with declining economic opportunities have the highest birth rates. As a consequence, a large proportion of children are born and reared in places that offer them little promise of a satisfactory adjustment as adults. By siphoning off excess population into areas of greater opportunity, internal migration becomes a mechanism of personal adjustment for the citizen. For the nation it is a device for maintaining a social and economic balance among communities; if migration were suddenly to be stopped, only a very short time would be required for population to "pile up" in areas of rapid growth but of low opportunity for earning a livelihood. Thus, migration is a process for preserving an existing system.

Migration is an arrangement for making maximum use of persons with special qualifications. The special abilities of a particular person are useful to the nation only at certain sites, and persons who possess or acquire special abilities are not necessarily born or educated at the site where their talents are needed. Migration moves these specialized persons to the communities where their services can be used effectively. Youths who aspire to be physicians, engineers, scientists, artists, or other kinds of specialists frequently must move from their birthplace to a place where they can be trained and then to a place where they can be employed. This twofold migration is a normal aspect of the process of maturing and leaving the parental home. Even though a girl may not participate as directly in this adjustment as does a boy, girls tend to participate indirectly through the employment adjustments of their fiancés or husbands.

Migration frequently is a regional or national social problem. A prolonged drought or famine; the exhaustion of timber, minerals, or agricultural resources; a series of unfavorable growing seasons; or prolonged social or political oppression can lead to large-scale migration from an area to other parts of the nation. Since migration of this type usually has its stimulus in hardship and disaster, the migrants tend to be in need of assistance from the nation as a whole or from the communities through which they pass and at which they arrive. In accepting responsibility for caring for their needs, the nation should have accurate and detailed knowledge about the size, composition, and condition of the migration streams.

Migration is an instrument of cultural diffusion and social integration. The person who migrates from one community to another unites in himself two cultures. Temporarily, he tends to be a disruptive force in the community into which he enters. If members of one culture invade a community of another culture in large numbers, they tend to form a "community within a community" and to create cultural diversity and ethnic tension. Only by a slow process of assimilation, which sometimes requires a generation or more, the migrant group and the receiving community are finally adjusted to each other. In the process, the culture of the receiving community may be altered appreciably. Where internal migration distributes representatives from each region throughout all other regions, the resulting cultural diffusion can contribute to a reduction of intersectional and interregional differences, and to a building-up of a common nationwide culture within which regional variations persist but perhaps are less deviant from each other than otherwise they might be.

The migrant sometimes creates a

moral problem in the community at which he arrives. Migrants to cities from dissimilar cultures sometimes undergo personal disorganization—reputedly as a consequence of conflicts between two sets of folkways and systems of values. To the extent that migration weakens the traditional controls which neighborhoods, institutions, and communities exercise over the behavior of individuals it may lead to an increase of crime, delinquency, broken families, illegitimacy, and other problems indicative of social disorganization. The sudden arrival of large numbers of migrants in a community can lead to intergroup tensions and unrest. Inasmuch as a migrant tends to be a person with a problem which he is trying to solve through movement, not uncommonly he is poor, not well educated, unemployed or temporarily employed, in bad health, in need of public assistance or other community services. He may be a member of a minority group toward which there is strong economic and social discrimination in his home community. Even though the migrants may be arriving in large quantities—because job opportunities are plentiful and the migrants are the more resourceful citizens who perceive these opportunities and seize upon them to "do something about improving their lot"—members of the receiving community often feel they are being invaded by "cheap laborers," "parasites looking for charity," or people with inferior mental and social qualities. Experience has been that second-generation and third-generation descendants of migrants are well accommodated to the community to which their parents or grandparents moved.

There are several types of migration that are of interest as examples of unique social and economic adjustment. Foremost among them are the nomadic or seminomadic groups. Nomadic herdsmen; nomadic or seasonal agricultural laborers who help to plant, till, or harvest special crops; and itinerant workmen are examples of such groups. In nations with automobile cultures the "trailer nomad," or family with a home on wheels, is a special group worthy of intensive sociological study. The lone vagabond or "hobo" and the gypsy band are additional types of these nomads.

Migration is the major unknown component of population estimates and forecasts. Even where fertility and mortality can be projected with reasonable accuracy, estimates and forecasts for cities and regions cannot be made with any degree of reliability unless the demographer is able to forecast the probable future course of internal migration. Within a nation, migration is able to offset completely or to reinforce greatly the population change resulting from natural increase.

Because internal migration is involved in such a variety of social, economic, and political problems of a nation, there is widespread need for knowledge about it. A major source of this knowledge is population statistics, and the principal responsibility for furnishing this body of information rests upon the science of demography. However, the demographer who specializes in migration analysis must have interdisciplinary interests, for he finds many of his explanatory hypotheses in the fields of economics, sociology, geography, and technology. Moreover, he must not be a slave to census volumes but must be prepared to conduct his own sample surveys to obtain information that is essential but not available in official statistical reports.

THE PROBLEM OF DEFINING INTERNAL MIGRATION

Every member of a population resides at some point (or series of points) in space. A change in the location of his residence is termed "spatial mobility." Those who study spatial mobility are inclined to subdivide changes of residence into three major classes: local movement, or short-distance change of residence within the same community; internal migration, or change of residence from one community to another while remaining within the same national boundaries; and international migration, or change of residence from one nation to another.

For statistical purposes, there is no problem of identifying the population that is spatially mobile—it is necessary only to identify those who change dwelling places. Neither is it difficult to separate international migrants from the other mobile persons, in most cases. However, it is difficult to separate local movers from migrants in a way that is satisfactory for all purposes. The only practicable way yet devised for making such a separation, even approximately, is to set up boundaries which, if crossed in the act of changing residence, will constitute migration. Thus, rural-to-urban migration is the change of residence from a place outside the boundaries of an urban place to a residence inside. Interregional migration is the change of residence across a boundary separating two regions, etc. The amount of migration observed in a population is dependent, to no small degree, upon the number of kilometers of boundary that are established as migration-defining boundaries. If crossing the smallest minor civil division boundaries of a nation were to constitute migration, a much larger number of migrants would result than if migration were defined in terms of crossing major civil boundaries, such as the boundaries of provinces or states. This is necessarily true because major political boundaries also follow the lines of minor political boundaries so that the minor political boundaries include as many kilometers as do the major boundaries, plus many more kilometers.

At what point should the demographer try to make the distinction between local movers and migrants by erecting migration-defining boundaries? Theoretically, the term "migration" is re- served for those changes of residence that involve a complete change and readjustment of the community affiliations of the individual. In the process of changing his community of residence, the migrant tends simultaneously to change employers, friends, neighbors, parish membership, and many other social and economic ties. The local mover, by contrast, may simply move across the street or to a house a few blocks away. Very likely he retains his same job, breaks no community ties, and maintains most of his informal social relationships. Statistics of internal migration should purport to reflect major social adjustments and readjustments of the population, while statistics of local movement should purport to reflect less drastic individual adjustments and changes in local community structure. The boundaries that are established for separating migrants from non-migrants should make this subdivision, at least roughly.

When migration-defining boundaries are selected, there is little choice in most cases. The census or other statistics must necessarily follow civil boundaries of some kind. The choice usually must be between one of three levels of boundaries: the large provincial boundaries, the intermediate commune or county boundaries, and the minor civil boundaries—like those for cities, townships, or municipalities. The major boundaries are too gross for most purposes, and the minor boundaries usually are too detailed. This means that for most practical purposes the commune or county boundary is taken as the migration-defining boundary because it is the only choice between the two extremes. Statistics of internal migration are not fully comparable between nations because of differences in the average distance from a migration-defining boundary at which a member of the population may live. This distance may be greater in one nation than in another. However, once the migration boundaries are established, year-to-year comparisons or differentials among various socioeconomic or geographic groups can be made with less fear that changes in differences are due to boundary differences.

Any migration-defining boundary must be specified as a line upon the earth. There will always be a certain proportion of the population that can become migrants simply by moving across the street or other route that marks this boundary. For this reason, the boundary definition of migration can never completely separate the intercommunity migrants from local movers.

DEFINITIONS OF CONCEPTS AND TERMS USED IN MIGRATION ANALYSIS

Analysis of internal migration involves the use of certain concepts and terms that are more or less unique to it. Inasmuch as these terms must be used throughout the discussion to follow, they are defined in advance:

In-migrant—a migrant who crosses a migration-defining boundary in the process of changing residence and entering a given community from some other part of the same nation. The term "immigrant" refers to incoming international migrants.

Out-migrant—a migrant who crosses a migration-defining boundary while departing from a residence to reside in another area within the same nation. The term "emigrant" is the counterpart of this term in the study of international migration.

Net internal migration—the migration balance of a community or area. It consists of the number of in-migrants minus the number of out-migrants. The net balance may be either positive (representing a net gain to the community) or negative (representing a net loss to the community).

Area of origin—the area or community from which a migrant departs.

Area of destination—the area or community to which a migrant travels.

Migration interval—In order to analyze migration, it is necessary to break up time into intervals, with the data being assembled separately for each interval. Time intervals of one year, five years, or ten years have been used in migration analysis. In discussing migration statistics, it is always necessary to specify the interval of time, or migration interval, to which they relate.

Migration stream—a body of migrants that departs from a common area of origin and arrives at a common area of destination during a specified migration interval.

Differential migration—migration selectivity, or the tendency for some parts of the population to be more migratory than other parts. The incidence of migration is greater among some segments of the population than among others.

Migration rates—A rate is a measure of the comparative frequency of occurrence or prevalence of an event. In demography, it is usually expressed as a ratio of the number of events to the number of persons exposed to the likelihood of experiencing the event during a specified span of time. This same principle applies to the definition of migration rates; a migration rate is the ratio of migrants observed to the population exposed to the likelihood of migrating during a specified migration interval.

From the preceding, it follows directly that

$$m = \frac{M}{P} k , \qquad (1)$$

where $m =$ the rate of migration during a specified migration interval, $M =$ the number of persons defined as migrants during the interval, $P =$ the population exposed to the likelihood of migration during the interval, and $k =$ a constant, usually 1,000.

Theoretically, every person is exposed to the likelihood of migrating elsewhere during a migration interval. (It is true that some persons receive a more intensive "exposure" to migration, but this is also true in other areas of demographic research. For example, some groups are more exposed to the possibility of death, bearing a child, or getting married than others.) Hence, the denominator of a general migration rate should be the total population alive during the interval, and the numerator should be the total number of migrants observed among this population. But, as is well known, a population continuously changes in size. The population exposed to the likelihood of migration is the average population during the migration interval. Under the assumption that births, deaths, and migration are uniformly distributed throughout the migration interval, the best estimate of the population exposed to migration is the population at the midpoint of the migration interval.

Formula (1) may be used to establish three basic migration rates:

general in-migration rate

$$= m_i = \frac{I}{P} k \,, \quad (2)$$

general out-migration rate

$$= m_o = \frac{O}{P} k \,, \quad (3)$$

net migration rate $= m_n = \frac{I-O}{P} k \,, \quad (4)$

where $I =$ total number of in-migrants received by a community, $O =$ total number of out-migrants lost by a community, $P =$ total mid-interval population of the community, $k =$ a constant, usually 1,000.

These three rates should be thought of as the counterparts of crude birth rates, crude death rates, and crude rates of natural increase, respectively.

Just as refined fertility and mortality analysis depends upon using rates that are specific (cross-classified) for age, sex, and/or other characteristics, refined migration analysis makes use of rates that are specific for one or more characteristics. In general,

$$m_i = \frac{M_i}{P_i} k \,, \quad (5)$$

where $m_i =$ the rate of migration for a population all members of which are characterized by a particular category of trait i (for example, migration rate for an age group 20–24 years of age); M_i = the number of migrants characterized by a given category of trait i (for example, migrants aged 20–24 years); $P_i =$ the mid-interval population characterized by the same category of trait i as the migrants in the numerator (for example, population aged 20–24 at the midpoint of the migration interval); $k =$ a constant, usually 1,000.

If desired, migration rates may be made specific for two or more traits simultaneously. For example, age-sex-specific migration rates would provide a rate for each age group of males and a separate rate for each age group of females. These rates may be in-migration rates, out-migration rates, or net migration rates.

The incidence of migration, like that of mortality and fertility, varies with age, sex, and other population characteristics. In making comparisons aimed at measuring the effect of one trait upon migration rates, it will be necessary to hold constant the effect of age and other characteristics.

METHODS OF MEASURING MIGRATION: INDIRECT METHODS

A direct measurement of migration requires counting persons who change their residence across migration-defining boundaries. Such information is available only in nations where there is a system of residence registration or where a direct migration question has been asked at a census enumeration. Nations that lack statistics of this type need not be completely devoid of information about internal migration, however. If there is a reliable system of birth and death registration and/or if two or more reasonably good consecutive censuses with age tabulations are available, it is possible to estimate indirectly the amount of net migration that has taken place within the various communities of a nation. In order to estimate the net migration for a community, region, or province, it is necessary only that the data have been tabulated for the area for which the estimate is desired. The area boundaries then become the migration-defining boundaries for the purpose of the estimate.

Two procedures have been developed for estimating net migration from these data. They are termed "the vital statistics method" and "the survival ratio method." Each can accomplish results that the other cannot. The vital statistics method of measuring net intercensal migration estimates the total net gain or loss in population that a community experiences between two censuses as a result of migration. If measured directly, this net change would consist of the difference between the total number of persons that entered the community during the intercensal period and the total number of persons that departed from it during the same interval of time. The total population change that occurs in a community during the interval between two censuses consists of two major components—natural increase (total births minus total deaths) and net migration (total in-migration minus total out-migration). Net migration represents total population change minus total natural increase. Hence, where two consecutive, reliable censuses are available (from which total population change can be computed) and where a reliable count of births and deaths during the intercensal period is maintained (from which natural increase can be computed), a reliable estimate of net migration may be obtained simply by subtracting total natural increase for

the intercensal period from the total intercensal change in population.

Although this procedure is basically very simple, certain considerations should be taken into account that may require modification or adjustment of the results. Most of these problems arise from the fact that *the estimated net migration is a residual; it is what is "left over" after the other components of change have been removed.* All errors and discrepancies in the basic data enter directly into the determination of the residual and are defined, therefore, as in-migration or out-migration. Strictly speaking, the demographer should interpret migration estimates obtained by this method (and also estimated by the survival ratio method, which is a residual method) as a mixture of net migration and net balance of errors in the basic data. It is only where the net balance of error is near zero that the residual can be interpreted as a reliable measure of net migration.

The survival ratio method of measuring net migration rests on the following logic. If two censuses are taken exactly z years apart, the population that is age x at the first census will be age $x+z$ at the second. However, the number of people counted at the older age at the second census will be fewer in number, even in the absence of migration, because of mortality during the intercensal period. Each age group may be looked upon as a set of real cohorts, born in specified years, that pass through time together. If none of the initial group were to move to another community during the period and if a count could be maintained or estimated of the number of deaths that occurred to the cohort that was age x at the earlier census, it would be possible to know how many non-migratory persons should be expected to be alive and in the same community at the date of the final census. The difference between this "expected" number and the number actually counted at the second census may be accepted as a measure of net migration if other errors are not present.

In many cases, however, the number of deaths is unknown but can be estimated by applying a survival ratio, or a ratio that estimates what proportion of the population would be surviving at the date of the terminal census, assuming no migration during the intercensal interval. The difference between this surviving expected population and the actual population at the terminal census date is an estimate of net migration of the age group during the intercensal interval. If the "expected" population is smaller than the final census count, the community is assumed to have experienced net in-migration of the amount indicated by the difference. If the expected population is larger than the census count, the difference is taken as a measure of net out-migration.

If a survival ratio is established for each age group and used to make an estimate of net migration, a total count of net intercensal migration can be obtained simply by summing the results for all age groups. This total will not include the net migration of persons less than z years of age at the date of the terminal census, for these persons were born during the intercensal interval and have not survived for the full intercensal time. One virtue of this procedure, therefore, is that it yields an estimate of net migration by age groups; one weakness is that it fails to make such an estimate for the age group born during the intercensal period. There are special adaptations of the basic procedure that can be made to remove this latter deficiency.

This method of estimating net migration requires only two consecutive censuses, tabulated by age groups (usually five-year age groups), and a set of survival ratios that may be assumed to represent the force of mortality during the interval of time between the censuses. The method is highly useful in situations where there are no vital statistics for

deaths and births. For example, the survival ratio method can be used to estimate the net migration of the rural farm population, the migration of males and females, and the migration of white and non-white populations from small communities where births and deaths are not reported separately for these groups. It is also useful for estimating net migration between earlier censuses, at a time when vital statistics were not available.

Inasmuch as age data for two consecutive censuses are widely available in nations that lack other data for estimating net migration, this method holds considerable promise as a technique for estimating net migration in situations where other estimates could not be made.

In the past it has been customary to use either the vital statistics estimate or the survival ratio estimate, but not both, in the same research study. Where vital statistics data are available, some greatly improved and more detailed results can be obtained by using both methods simultaneously. The principles that would underlie this use would be as follows: Use vital statistics techniques wherever possible to establish the best available estimate of net migration for the province, state, or other area. In making these estimates, employ every refinement possible to make the estimates exact. Then use the survival-ratio estimation procedure for obtaining net migration by age and by any other characteristics or for any other subgroups for which vital statistics are not tabulated separately. Refine these estimates to the point that any errors in them are randomly distributed among the estimates (each estimate has an equal chance of being correct). In making these estimates, the net migration of population 0 to z years of age should be determined. Procedures for doing this are available. Make a survival ratio estimate for all parts into which the total population has been subdivided. When the work has reached this point, the demographer has estimated net migration two ways, once for over-all totals by the more accurate vital statistics method and once in much greater detail by the survival ratio estimate. The totals for these two estimates should be nearly alike. For a discussion of the reasons why they do not need to be identical, the reader is referred to Siegel and and Hamilton (1952).

The indirect measures of net migration described above cannot identify migration streams; i.e., they cannot determine where incoming migrants originate or where departing migrants end their journeys. A full analysis of the places of origin and destination of particular groups of migrants can be provided only by direct migration statistics. However, many nations that do not have such data do have place-of-birth statistics, from which certain indirect measures of migration streams can be made.

Place-of-birth statistics are derived from responses to a census question like, "In what place (nation, state, province) was he born?" The census records show the present residence (place at which enumerated) for each individual. By cross-tabulating place of birth by place of present residence, it is possible to identify separately all persons who are not residing in their place of birth at a given census. The persons who were born in each place may be subclassified according to their present place of residence. In this way it is possible to construct a place-of-origin by place-of-destination table. Tabulations of this type refer only to the native population, of course. The migration-defining boundaries are the boundaries used to specify place of birth. Most national censuses have used the province, state, or other major political unit for classifying places of birth. As a consequence, the streams of migration that can be separately identified and measured are only the major interprovincial, interstate, or interregional **streams.**

The net gain or loss through an interchange of migrants between any two areas may be obtained by subtracting the out-migrating stream from the in-migrating stream. This "birth-residence index" is the difference between the reported number of surviving native persons who have moved out of the specified area since they were born and the total number of native persons who have moved into the specified area since they were born.

The major drawback of the birth-residence index is that the time at which the migration occurred is unknown. Movement could have occurred at any time between birth and the time of enumeration. Some of the reported out-migrants and in-migrants are the survivors of groups who departed or arrived eighty or more years before the census date. It would be erroneous to interpret the birth-residence index as a statement of net migration during the decade immediately preceding the census.

This difficulty can be overcome partially by computing the birth-residence index for two consecutive decades and noting the intercensal change. Intercensal change in the birth-residence index does not estimate exactly the net flow of residents between two places during a decade, however, for it has several limitations. Among them are the following: (1) the number of moves and the specific place of origin of a migrant during an intercensal period are not known; (2) there are errors in reporting the place of birth for many people; (3) by far the most serious defect is the uncontrolled effect of mortality upon the estimates. After a group of persons has left a place of birth, each death that occurs to that group tends to lower the count of out-migrants that will be shown at the next census. A similar generalization holds for the count of in-migrants among incoming persons who were born in other places. Since migration tends to take place in waves, the age composition of in-migrants and out-migrants may be expected to be very unlike in different areas. As a consequence, the mortality among in-migrants and out-migrants will vary greatly from area to area. This can cause a change between two censuses in the number of in-migrants or out-migrants reported to be due entirely to differences in mortality.

THE DIRECT MEASUREMENT OF INTERNAL MIGRATION[2]

The techniques for measuring migration indirectly permit the demographer with no direct migration statistics to learn a great deal about the net effect of migration upon the various communities of a nation and the sources from which migrants are drawn. However, these indirect measures are incapable of furnishing the following information, which is of considerable importance for migration analysis: they cannot provide a full count of the numbers of persons in the streams flowing between individual communities or the characteristics of persons in these streams; they cannot provide detailed information about the social and economic characteristics of the migrants as compared with non-migrants; they cannot provide information with which to evaluate how rapidly and how well migrants adjust to the new community of their choice.

These aspects of migration can be explored efficiently only with statistics of migration obtained by direct methods, namely, by counts of boundary crossings. Statistics of this type are available for several European nations and for some nations of the Americas. One almost universal finding from these data is that the volume of gross migration (in-migration plus out-migration) for a community is much larger than the net migration. In fact, communities that may appear to be almost stationary from the point of

view of net migration (net migration near zero) frequently have extraordinarily high rates of gross migration, with a large in-migration being canceled by an equally large out-migration. Even though a situation of this type may not change the total size of the community, it is capable of effecting a drastic change in social, ethnic, and economic composition. In theory, the volume of migration from a place should be a response to a completely different set of factors from those that are related to the migration to the same place from outside areas. Net migration is not a single phenomenon related to a single set of factors but a complex resultant of two opposing phenomena, each represented by its own set of factors. The social and economic characteristics of net migration are a net balance between the social and economic characteristics of the in-migrating and out-migrating streams. The composition of the streams can be very unlike the composition of the net difference between the streams. Moreover, the volume of migration into or out of a community appears to fluctuate with the level of economic prosperity. Net migration does not fluctuate in exactly the same way as either in-migration or out-migration, for here also it is a compound of events rather than a unitary class of events. A full comprehension of net migration requires an untangling of the two sets of events (in-migration and out-migration) and a separate study of each. It is for reasons such as these that the establishment of direct measures of migration, accompanied by the detailed analysis of particular streams of movement, is a matter of importance in migration research.

A direct count of migration can be obtained either by establishing a system of continuous residential registration or by enumerating recent changes of residence as a part of a regular census enumeration. Some nations of Europe have systems of direct registration; each

[2] Much of this part has been abstracted from chapter i of Bogue, Shryock, and Hoermann (1957), and from Bogue and Hagood (1953).

change of residence requires official notification. When highly developed, these systems permit a summary of records at frequent intervals. Summaries of change-of-residence notifications provide direct information about intercommunity migration. Direct migration statistics can be made available on an annual basis for even very small communities. A limitation of registration statistics is that detailed and up-to-date information about the occupation, educational attainment, and other social and economic characteristics of migrants is not available from registration records.

A census count of migrations asks for a response to the question, "Where was he residing a year (or other time span) ago?" The place of residence as of the beginning of the migration interval is then compared with the place of residence at which the person is enumerated. A set of migration-defining boundaries (usually commune or county boundaries) are set up; a person enumerated in a different political unit than at the beginning of the migration interval is classified as a migrant. The migrants are then classified into streams according to their area of origin and their area of destination (residence as of the census date).

Statistics of migration streams obtained from census enumerations are subject to certain biases and errors. The census type of migration tabulation consists of a record of surviving migrants and misses those who move and then die before the census enumeration. Moreover, the census enumeration omits circulatory migrants—those who depart and return to the same area during the migration interval. Still another limitation of the census-type migration data is that the factor of memory is involved; faulty memory of time as well as faulty memory of place may lead to a rather wide margin of error. In recalling his place of residence at an earlier date, the informant may be vague about the exact location and may specify a large city when in reality it was a smaller community located near the large city. If the migration interval is long, such as five years, the informant may report a residence where he lived six years or four years ago rather than the residence as of the correct date.

Having taken direct observations of migration, classified the migrants according to streams between homogeneous areas of origin and destination, and computed appropriate rates of in-, out-, and net migration, one must ask a fundamental question: how can this information be used to determine what factors are conducive to mobility and migration? In a migration analysis of this type, migration rates (in-, out-, and net rates) should be taken as dependent variables, or variables whose behavior is to be explained or accounted for. The factors of "push" and "pull" are regarded as being independent variables, or variables whose correlations with migration rates tend to account for the behavior of the migration rates. The problem of identifying factors underlying migration becomes one of discovering (*a*) whether or not a significant statistical relationship exists between a dependent and one or more independent variables; (*b*) if so, what the direction and nature of the association is; and (*c*) whether or not there is a theoretical justification for the observed relationship.

Independent migration variables may be grouped into two classes: those dealing with attributes of persons and those dealing with attributes and conditions in the community of origin and destination. Techniques for identifying personal factors underlying migration will be discussed below. Techniques dealing with attributes and conditions in the environment and community of origin and of destination are discussed here.

If it were possible for the demographer to study migration under laboratory conditions, he could vary at will each of the various "push" and "pull" forces in the environment that, hypothetically, are related to migration. By manipulating the strength of each push and pull, holding other forces constant, he could observe the amount, direction, and composition of migration induced by each environmental factor. Lacking such ideal circumstances, the demographer can do only the next best thing. He can observe the migration that actually occurs in a variety of places under varying conditions of push and pull. By measuring the force of all variables simultaneously as they existed during a given migration interval, by means of statistical techniques he is able to estimate the influence of each independent variable, with other variables controlled. A variety of standard statistical techniques is available for this purpose. Among them are multiple-regression analysis, factor analysis, and analysis of simultaneously cross-classified variables.

Differential migration is selective migration. It notes the ways in which migrants are not a representative cross-section of the population, and especially in comparison with the populations in the communities of origin and destination. Selective migration in some form should be regarded as a necessary phenomenon of all modern, highly specialized societies. Persons with unique qualifications, training, or work histories need to be located where their activities can be used. A certain amount of reshuffling of the population is required to locate the various specialized categories of population where they are of most value and where they can best participate in the social and economic system. Moreover, as a result of depletion of resources, changes in technology, and changing patterns of consumption, the economic balance between various economic groups is constantly shifting in many parts of the country. A location that provided the maximum return for a given skill a few decades ago may provide much less than the maximum return now or a few years hence. Thus, in the life of a single person the need for movement may occur repeatedly. This view leads to the hypothesis that in modern industrialized societies most migration probably is selective in some respects; in such societies migration must be selective in order to be effective.

In order to transform counts of migrants having various characteristics and counts of the corresponding groups in the total population into a quantitative expression of migration selectivity, it is necessary to define differential migration explicitly and then to devise a statistical technique for measuring it. Although several different definitions might be adopted for this purpose, only two seem particularly worthy of intensive use with cross-classified data. These are: (*a*) definition by differential proportions and (*b*) definition by differential rates. These two definitions can be given statistical expressions which cause them to give identical results. This means that the major alternative techniques for detecting differential migration can be reduced to a single fundamental definition.

The definition of differential migration in terms of differential proportions is as follows: Evidence of differential migration exists with respect to a given category whenever a disproportionately greater or smaller percentage of migrants falls into that category than is found in the base population with which they are compared. A statistical technique for detecting differential migration which corresponds to this definition is simple to construct and may be easily interpreted. It is necessary only to compute a percentage distribution for migrants and a similar percentage distribution for the population with which the migrants are to be compared, and then to note the percentage point differences between the two distributions.

The definition of differential migration

in terms of differential rates is as follows: Evidence of differential migration exists with respect to a given category of the population whenever it is found that the rate of migration (number of migrants per 1,000 residents) for the particular category is significantly higher or lower than the rate for the general population of which the category is a part. A statistical measure of differential migration that corresponds to this definition may be devised by computing the amount by which the migration rate for the particular category differs from the rate for the general population. These differences may be expressed as a ratio of the average migration rate for the general population.

If each of the definitions stated above is given algebraic expression, both approaches can be made to yield a common result. Hence, the decision whether to use migration rates or percentage distributions in the study of differentials is a matter of secondary importance. The choice will depend upon considerations other than measuring the differentials themselves.

Throughout the preceding discussion the control population, with which migrants are to be compared in computing the indexes, has not been specified exactly. The population at the place of origin and the population at the place of destination are both logical candidates for this comparison. Some hypotheses about migration selectivity require for their testing a comparison of migrants with the population from which they were drawn, or the population at place of origin. Others require a comparison with the population at the place to which the migrants are attracted, or the population at place of destination. Each of the two sets of indexes is distinguished from the other by prefixing it with the name of the population used as a control group. Thus an "origin differential" is a set of indexes showing differential migration with re-

spect to the population at the place of origin. A "destination differential" is a set of indexes showing differential migration with respect to the population at the place of destination. Although the general patterns of origin differentials and of destination differentials are frequently found to be similar, they are far from identical.

The interpretation of origin differentials frequently is made difficult by the fact that the characteristics both of migrants and of the control population are those possessed at the time of enumeration and not at the date of migration or before. In many cases the migrant is able to change one or more of his characteristics during or after migrating. Thus one cannot interpret occupational, marital status, or other origin differentials derived from the characteristics of the migrants, when enumerated in the community of destination in terms of the migrants' relative positions in their home communities prior to their departure. Such differentials are only rough indicators of the migrants' social and economic status in comparison with the status of the population that stayed behind. If all such differences are interpreted as having resulted directly or indirectly from the act of migration, then it is valid to speak in very tentative terms of what benefits or changes in status, if any, have resulted from the departure from the place of origin.

A more direct interpretation may be made of destination differentials. From one point of view, the in-migrant may be regarded as an invader from outside the community. He enters an area with which he is unfamiliar and to which he must adjust if he is to survive and thrive. In making a controlled comparison of the characteristics of in-migrants with the population at the place of destination one asks and gets an answer to the questions, "How well did in-migrants fare in comparison with the receiving population?" Or, "Did the in-migrants have different characteristics from those of the receiving population?"

SUMMARY OF EXISTING KNOWLEDGE

One of the most important findings of empirical research on internal migration to date is that, like so many other events in the realm of human behavior, there are no "laws" of migration. The migration of human beings is not an instinctive action; nor is it generated by a simple or single impulse that may vary in intensity only from one person to another. Instead, as research studies accumulate it is becoming more and more evident that demographers are dealing with a highly complex class of events that can be triggered by a vast array of situations. When an individual person or family changes residence, the move is made for certain reasons, and the destination of the move is selected for the same or certain other reasons. These reasons may be looked upon as objective situations or as subjective responses to prejudices or values of which the persons involved may not be aware; reasons for migration are not necessarily known to the migrant, and his rationalization of his move may not be valid or logical. These reasons, or "causes," spring from many aspects of life—economic, social, political, medical, and psychological. Moreover, these "causes" can occur in a great many combinations, with each element of each combination being able to vary in intensity from one person to another or from one time to another. But this is only one-half of the complexity. The migration response that is made—the new residence that is selected—is also a product of many aspects of life—economic, social, political, medical, and psychological. And the factors that determine these responses can also occur in a great many combinations and with variable intensity.

If one were to compile a catalogue of the objective situations that stimulate a change of residence from one community to another, he would list the many events that may lead the person to review his whole economic, social, and personal position in his present residence, to re-evaluate the advantages and disadvantages of moving to certain other residences that he regards as possibly acceptable alternatives, and possibly to reach a decision to move.

Migration-stimulating situations for persons:

1. Graduation from grammar school, high school, or college
2. Marriage
3. Lack of an offer of marriage
4. Offers of good employment or better employment, or employment under conditions that satisfy some strong personal wish (to travel, to attain more prestige, to pursue particular hobbies)
5. News of bonanzas or good employment opportunities in other communities—gold rushes, distribution of free land, or construction of new factories and other establishments offering new jobs
6. Acceptance of employment that requires routine movement—migratory agricultural workers, construction workers, oil-well drillers, etc.
7. Development of proficiency in some specialty not marketable locally
8. Transfer by employer from one branch establishment to another within the firm
9. Sale of business or merger of businesses
10. Loss of a farm through consolidation, mechanization, or bankruptcy
11. Loss of non-farm employment through layoff or discharge
12. Prolonged receipt of low income or failure of income to increase, especially in comparison with known or believed situations elsewhere
13. Retirement from the labor force
14. Death of a spouse, parent, other relative
15. Military service
16. Onset of poor health under conditions requiring institutionalization or special medical care
17. Apprehension and conviction for a crime involving imprisonment
18. Oppression and discrimination—political, racial, religious

19. Disaster in the community—droughts, floods, pestilence
20. "Invasion" of the community by persons of a different occupational, income, ethnic, or other type
21. Personal bonanzas—receipt of gifts, inheritance of property
22. Acute personal maladjustment in present community due to incompatability with employer, spouse, or close associates
23. Restlessness and wanderlust urges, perhaps arising from the incipient onset of mental ill-health or from emotional immaturity and desire to escape the necessity of assuming the social responsibilities of adulthood
24. Social rejection by the community due to immoral or disapproved behavior—the ex-convict out of prison, the chronic alcoholic, the party to a public scandal
25. Forced movement resulting from legal enactment

This list could be supplemented by a second list of the situations that cause a migrant to choose to settle in a particular community.

Factors in choosing a destination:

1. Cost of moving
2. Presence of relatives or close friends
3. Possibility of living with relatives or close friends until "established"
4. Definite offer of desirable employment
5. Physical attractiveness of the community
6. The climate and topography of surrounding countryside
7. Recreational, educational, and other community facilities
8. The sex ratio, marital status, income level, occupational composition, other traits
9. Presence of special facilities or expanding employment opportunities in a migrant's field of competence
10. Familiarity and knowledge—through previous visits, vacations, military service, travel, reading
11. Possibility of special assistance in locating a job, attaining other advantages —relatives, friends, employment agencies

12. Special subsidies—train fare, extra pay to move, etc.
13. Hearsay information—reports of other migrants, newspaper advertisements, labor recruiters
14. General prestige or reputation of the community
15. Lack of alternative destinations

Finally, still a third list could be devised of "socioeconomic conditions" that can stimulate or retard mobility among a population. These conditions are, in many cases, simply the objective situation which the individual migrant experiences as a subjective migration-stimulating experience.

Socioeconomic conditions affecting migration:

1. Major capital investments in new plants, equipment, or other facilities for producing goods or services. This provides new jobs, both in the construction and in the operational phases.
2. Major business recessions or depressions and fluctuations in the business cycle which alter the volume of employment.
3. Technological change, which renders obsolete many existing enterprises and creates many new enterprises.
4. Changes in economic organization of enterprises which may destroy jobs at one place and create new jobs at other places.
5. Provisions among a population for retirement, medical care, insurance for dependents.
6. Provisions among a population for disseminating information about employment opportunities at distant places.
7. Regulations upon the movement of persons from one community to another.
8. Living conditions in the community. This would include quality of housing, quality of community facilities and services, and quality of commercially provided commodities and services—at prices residents can afford.
9. Degree of tolerance of ethnic, racial, religious, occupational, or other minority groups. This includes the presence

or absence of "colonies" of such groups in potential receiving communities.

10. Migration policy of the community. This may take the form of an active program to attract migrants or of unofficial sanctions against "outsiders." There may be an official policy prohibiting or regulating the number and types of persons that will be admitted.

The above three lists provide a useful starting point from which to evaluate present knowledge about migration. The individual migrant may experience a stimulus to migrate as a subjective impression of socioeconomic conditions in his community. He may also have subjective reactions to his objective social and personal position in his community or to events that happen in his private life (deaths, marriages, etc.). By comparing his position in the present community of residence with envisaged or possible positions in other communities, using information about socioeconomic conditions in those communities, he arrives at a decision to move or remain. When this process is viewed behavioristically, it can be noted that a certain measurable incidence (rate) of migration is associated with the occurrence of each of these situations or combinations of situations.

To date, there have been comparatively few opportunities to study migration in terms of a framework such as that described above. The statistics that have been available have been compiled from official population registers, from a census question on migration, or by one of the indirect methods described in the preceding section. These data are summaries of the operation of migration-stimulating forces. In the absence of explicit data concerning the migration-stimulating situations for individuals, it has been necessary to impute or infer these situations, using whatever information could be obtained.

Much valuable work has been done in this tradition. Demographers have grad-ually perfected techniques which enable them to break each population change into its basic components, reproductive change ("natural increase") and net migration. The types of communities and the parts of the nation that are growing rapidly can now be known for any place that has had two or more reliable censuses. Estimates of the numbers (or net numbers) of persons who have moved from rural to urban areas or from one region to another are known for almost all of western Europe and for the United States and Canada. In several of the larger metropolises of Europe the components of growth are known annually for each of several small subdivisions of the city and its environs (analogous to U.S. census tracts). This branch of migration analysis generates information that is much in demand by city planners, transportation experts, marketing analysts, housing officials, and many others who want to know where the population is growing fastest and at what rates and for what reasons. Such estimates can be made only if one has some objective basis upon which to forecast or project migration. An excellent example of this type of migration research is Gladys K. Bowles's recent set of estimates of the net migration of the rural farm population, by age, sex, and color for each state economic area in the United States during the decade 1940–50 (Bowles, 1956).

Demographers have been much less fortunate in obtaining data for migration streams. Although such information is potentially available from those nations having population registers, the task of tabulating the material in full detail has proved to be formidable and expensive. For this reason, such tabulations have been prepared only at infrequent intervals if at all, and under these circumstances comparatively little information has been obtained about the characteristics of migrants in each stream. Perhaps the most systematic research on this subject has been done with Swedish and United States data. (See Dorothy S. Thomas, 1941; Bogue, Shryock, and Hoermann, 1957.)

The standard research design has been to correlate rates of migration (in-, out-, and net) with known economic, social, or other conditions in the various communities of destination or origin. Although systematic work of this type is less plentiful than the more descriptive migration-measuring work, sufficient research has been accomplished to build up a fairly good interpretation of "what happened and why" during recent intercensal periods in at least a few nations. Full-scale demonstrations of what can be done in this area have only recently been made, and it is hoped that with the passage of time much more exploratory and analytical work of this type will be undertaken in nations throughout the world.

Following is a short summary of basic propositions about migration that have emerged from research thus far. It is not an exhaustive list but is intended to be illustrative. It is subdivided into two sections: knowledge about migration streams and knowledge about selective migration.

Knowledge about Migration Streams

Empirical research has supported the validity of each of the following generalizations:

1. The rate of in-migration to a central point from each of several other points lying at a distance tends to vary inversely with the distance (Zipf, 1949).

2. The rate of out-migration from a central point to each of several other central points lying at a distance tends to vary inversely with the distance (Zipf, 1949).

3. The amount of interchange between any two areas is directly proportional to the product of the population of the two areas and inversely proportional to the distance between them (Zipf, 1949).

4. Rates of net migration between two areas tend to be directly proportional to differences in level of living and inversely proportional to the distance between them (Mangus and McNamara, 1943; Folger, 1953).

5. If two areas are in different economic regions, the relationship between distance and number of migrants may be different from the relationship within an economically integrated area (Folger, 1953).

6. The number of persons going a given distance is directly proportional to the number of opportunities at that distance and inversely proportional to the number of intervening opportunities (Stouffer, 1940).

7. Areas of low level of living tend to be areas of net out-migration, while areas of high level of living tend to be areas of net in-migration (Goodrich, 1936).

8. The rate of migration between two communities varies with the type of community of origin and destination, the direction of migration, and the age and other characteristics of the migrant (Bogue and Hagood, 1953).

9. The rates of in-migration and out-migration in any community tend not to be independent of each other. A high rate of in-migration tends to be accompanied by a high rate of out-migration (Bogue, Shryock, and Hoermann, 1957).

10. A very high proportion of all migration streams is a flow between communities of the same type (urban to urban, farm to farm, etc.). In modern industrialized nations the urban-to-urban flow may be larger than all other flows combined (Bogue, Shryock, and Hoermann, 1957).

11. Migration streams tend to avoid areas of high unemployment and to flow with greatest velocity toward areas of low unemployment (Bogue, Shryock, and Hoermann, 1957).

12. The size, direction, and net effect of migration streams are not invariable, either in time or in place. Instead, they are highly sensitive to the social and economic changes that are occurring in the various communities of origin and destination (Bogue, Shryock, and Hoermann, 1957).

13. The regional pattern of net migration tends to remain constant for several decades, presumably reflecting the continued action of a given set of redistributive forces (Shryock and Eldridge, 1947).

The above generalizations suffer from four basic deficiencies:

a) None of them specifies what the level or rate of movement will be under any given set of conditions. They merely specify how a given batch of migrants (number unspecified) will be apportioned among possible destinations. Such formulas have analytical "hindsight" value in explaining the patterns of past migration but are completely incapable of estimating the amount of migration to be expected at any given place in the future—even if the economic and other conditions that are expected to prevail at that date are fully specified.

b) Some of them are inflexible in that they specify fixed relationships. In this sense, they are a throwback to the outmoded doctrine of migration "laws." In a recent paper, Anderson (1955) has pointed out appropriately that empirical study may show that the equations expressing these relationships are best expressed by writing some variables with a fractional or even a variable exponent.

c) These hypotheses are not mutually exclusive. Nor are the facts of migration expressed in such a way that the common element in the various alternative formulations is controlled, thereby permitting explicit comparative tests.

d) Each of these formulations is admittedly incomplete. Under test, they account for not more than 35 to 50 per cent of the observed variance in migration streams among areas. Yet each is not expressed in a context that facilitates the introduction of additional variables.

In a recent study, Bogue, Shyrock, and Hoermann (1957) suggest that marked improvements in the study of migration streams can be made if analysts cease using numbers of migrants, in-migration rates, out-migration rates, or net migration rates and employ instead a measure of relative stream velocity, defined as follows:

$$V = \frac{M}{P_o} \div \frac{P_d}{P_t} \, 100 , \quad \text{or} \quad V = \frac{M}{P_d} \div \frac{P_o}{P_t} \, 100 ,$$

where

$V =$ the rate of flow (velocity) of the migration stream,

$M =$ the number of migrants in the stream,

$P_o =$ the population in the area of origin,

$P_d =$ the population in the area of destination,

$P_t =$ the total population of all potential areas of destination, including the area of origin.

This is an abstract measure that takes the viewpoint neither of the place of origin nor of destination. The same result is obtained by using either the in-migration or the out-migration rate.

The important thing accomplished by this expression is control of the common elements in the above formulations, thereby permitting the expression to become a *dependent variable* rather than an *explanation*. The quantity V can then be subjected to a multiple-variable analysis in which distance, intervening opportunities, levels of living, regional location, and type of community are considered simultaneously. Furthermore (and what is more important), into this context it would be possible to insert several additional variables simultaneously that quantitatively express the socioeconomic conditions affecting migration. These additional items should express conditions in the community of origin, conditions in the community of destination, and differences between these communities and other possible destination communities. Moreover, this formulation permits the forecasting or projection of future volume of migration, given specified conditions and estimated future sizes of the communities involved. Another promising line of study would be to attempt to explain, by multiple-variable analysis, the quantity (V_a-V_b), where V_a and V_b are the velocities of the two streams flowing in opposite directions between pairs of communities.

Knowledge about Differential Migration

In this branch of study the focus of attention has been upon the problem of attempting to state in what respects and by how much migrants differ from the general population and (more specifically) how they differ from the community from which they depart and the community at which they arrive. Here, too, the earliest concern was to find inflexible laws or differentials that always held true—and here too the search was most disappointing. Only one migration differential seems to have systematically withstood the test—that for age. The following generalization has been found to be valid in many places and for a long period of time: (1) Persons in their late teens, twenties, and early thirties are much more mobile than younger or older persons. Migration is highly associated with the first commitments and acts of adjustment to adulthood that are made by adolescents as they mature. But even this is quite variable; in some streams of migration there is a much higher proportion of older people and children than in other streams. For example, the stream of migrants arriving in a great metropolis tends to be highly concentrated in the ages 20–29, whereas the movement from the central city

to the more distant suburbs tends to be a phenomenon that has a very high incidence among parents just getting their second or third child—ages 25–35.

Almost all of the migration differentials that one cares to state can be shown to have important exceptions. Following are five additional differentials that are valid at the present time in the United States population: (2) Men tend to be more migratory than women, especially over long distances and when the conditions at the destination are insecure or difficult. (3) The rate of migration from an area tends to vary inversely with the general level of educational attainment in that area. (4) Persons with professional occupations are among the most migratory segments of the population, while laborers and operatives are much below average in the degree of their mobility. (5) Unemployed persons are more migratory than employed persons. (6) Negroes are less migratory than white persons.

When we examine the characteristics of migrants in the streams between particular communities, we find frequent exceptions to all of these generalizations. If we were comparing the composition of the stream with the composition of the population of the whole nation, this would be expected because only persons with certain characteristics are available to move out of certain types of communities. For example, differential 3 would not apply to the very large volume of migration now pouring from the most rural areas of the state of Mississippi because Mississippi has comparatively fewer educated people to export than other states. During the depression years unemployed persons tended to be less migratory than employed persons. Immediately after World War II, Negroes were more migratory than whites. When the West was being opened up, the mass of migrants reportedly were not the professional and white-collar group, as now, but were common laborers seeking to become owners of farms. The recent removal of sharecroppers from plantation areas in the South has fed large numbers of older persons, semiliterate persons, and unskilled persons into the migration streams flowing toward the large metropolitan centers.

A little reflection convinces one that the search for universal migration differentials not only is doomed to failure but also fails to appreciate the reasons for migration selectivity. If migration arises from basic change and the need for adjustment and readjustment, then the streams of migration at any moment of history must be composed of persons who are actually executing the social changes that are taking place and who are, so to speak, "victims of circumstance." Migrants must be expected to reflect, in their characteristics, the social and economic changes that are taking place. Because these changes vary from place to place and from time to time, it is to be expected that the characteristics of migrants cannot remain fixed.

This does not mean that the study of differential migration is not a useful branch of demographic study; the reverse is true. It is only by studying selective migration that one can comprehend how particular changes in population composition have occurred. By studying the characteristics of migrants, one can gain deeper insights into the nature of changes that are occurring in the places of origin and of destination. By noting the relationships between the type of selectivity and the type of change that is occurring, one can gradually develop principles of selectivity that can be used to predict the future selective course of major types of migration.

NEXT STEPS IN RESEARCH

One of the most important next steps in migration research is to stop oversimplifying the migration situation and underestimating its variability from place to place and over time. Because

we have had access only to mass data, which yield only averages and rates for gross groupings, we have adopted models that are completely inadequate to lead to a body of profound and precise generalizations. For example, some of us have approached human migration as one would approach the study of the migration of birds or the dispersion of insects from a common source. Others have likened migration to the fundamental laws of descriptive mechanics, gravitation, or electrostatics. Still others have set up models that (implicitly or explicitly) assume that all migration is of only one of the types that have been listed. For example, the hypothesis of intervening opportunities implicitly takes as its model the semi-attentive shopper or half-informed job-seeker. In analyzing migration and distance, we do not know whether it is the cost of moving, the radius within which communication about job openings is effective, familiarity with the locality, or other variables that are responsible. To write the equation for a curve that fits the data without comprehending the underlying mechanisms is not scientific explanation but simply a form of curve-fitting. To use it as an explanation is simply extrapolation of past trends. The work that has been performed using these perspectives has served the very useful purpose of (*a*) demonstrating that migration is a non-random phenomenon and hence is subject to scientific explanation; (*b*) showing that human migration is not unique but shows several common elements with other types of migration, and (*c*) indicating the magnitude of the spatial and physical aspects of movement and some of their practical implications.

A recommended first step is to expand and refine the lists of factors affecting migration and then to measure the rate of migration associated with each of these items for several different subgroups in several different types of community. Variables from each of these lists should be cross-tabulated with each other and with those from the other lists. Little, if any, of this information is available from official sources. It could be obtained only by making special surveys. There has been a mistaken tendency to equate "objective" demographic research with the secondary analysis of official statistics in bound volumes and to equate "subjective" or "attitudinal" research with special sample surveys. This is a completely mistaken and prejudiced point of view. Registration records and census questions do not produce information about many of the objective situations that must receive central attention before a comprehensive theory of migration can be developed. Special surveys offer the only prospect of obtaining this information.[3] No attention need be given in these surveys to the social psychology of migration—the decision-making process—although this is itself an important unstudied aspect of the subject.

Another great need in migration research is a pooling of ideas among the several branches of mobility analysis. At the present time some provocative work is being done in the field of labor mobility (Kitagawa, 1953; Palmer, 1954; Rogoff, 1953). Much research energy is also going into the study of social mobility, the change of status from one social class to another (Glass, 1954). The study of migration shares common concepts and common methodological problems with these other fields. A systematic review of the concepts, methods, and research designs in these other fields should produce a common set of principles for the study of mobility and change of many types. This is especially important because the few exploratory studies that have been undertaken have shown that migration is intimately related both to labor mobility and to social mobility.

[3] A similar statement could be made for the other major branches of demography.

Several rather specific recommended lines of research have already been offered in the above review of previous research. Some additional ones can be enumerated:

a) There is need for a fuller exploitation of existing data relating to migration streams and selective migration. Much information has already been tabulated and remains underanalyzed. Arrangements for additional tabulations could be made not only in the United States but in several other nations.

b) Methodological studies in multiple-variable analysis need to be made. Migration, perhaps more than most topics in demography, demands research designs that take into account several variables simultaneously. The methodology now available for this kind of analysis is not fully satisfactory.

c) There is need for comparative international studies of internal migration. The rural-urban migration experience of several nations, when compared and generalized, could contribute much to demographic theory and would be of value in trying to predict the possible future course of events in other countries.

d) An unexplored and exciting opportunity for migration research lies in the study of the process of accommodation and adjustment of migrants to the new community. Strangely enough, demographers have focused upon migration only as a component of immediate population increase and have not studied its fuller implications. They implicitly assume, for example, that when high-fertility populations move into the urban environment their birth rates fall. But how long a period is required, the extent to which this happens, and which types of migrants are most and which are least affected are all topics about which there is little information. We have concentrated much on the migrant as a newcomer and as a social problem and have given too little attention to migration as a vehicle of long-run change in demographic processes. An application of the rapidly developing longitudinal analysis approach (the study of real cohorts) to the study of migration could make an outstanding contribution in this area.

SELECTED BIBLIOGRAPHY

ANDERSON, T. R. 1955. "Intermetropolitan Migration: A Comparison of the Hypotheses of Zipf and Stouffer," *American Sociological Review*, XX, 287–91.

———. 1956. "Intermetropolitan Migration: A Correlation Analysis," *American Journal of Sociology*, LXI, 459–62.

BOGUE, D. J. 1952. *A Methodological Study of Migration and Labor Mobility in Michigan and Ohio in 1947*. ("Scripps Foundation Studies in Population Distribution," No. 4.) Oxford, Ohio: Scripps Foundation, Miami University.

———, and HAGOOD, MARGARET J. 1953. *Subregional Migration in the United States, 1935–40*. Vol. II: *Differential Migration in the Corn and Cotton Belts*. ("Scripps Foundation Studies in Population Distribution," No. 6.) Oxford, Ohio: Scripps Foundation, Miami University.

———, SHRYOCK, H. S., JR., and HOERMANN, S. A. 1957. *Subregional Migration in the United States, 1935–40*. Vol. I: *Streams of Migration*. ("Scripps Foundation Studies in Population Distribution," No. 5.) Oxford, Ohio: Scripps Foundation, Miami University.

———, and THOMPSON, W. S. 1949. "Migration and Distance," *American Sociological Review*, XIV, 236–44.

BOWLES, GLADYS K. 1956. *Net Migration from the Rural-Farm Population, 1940–50*. (Agricultural Marketing Service, Statistical Bulletin No. 176.)

BRIGHT, MARGARET L., and THOMAS, DOROTHY S. 1941. "Interstate Migration and Intervening Opportunities," *American Sociological Review*, VI, 773–83.

CAIRNCROSS, A. K. 1949. "Internal Migration in Victorian England," *Manchester School of Economics and Social Studies*, XVIII, 67–87.

DAVIS, K. 1955. "Internal Migration and Urbanization in Relation to Economic Development," in *Proceedings of the World Population Conference, 1954*, Vol. II. New York: United Nations.

DORN, H. F., and LORIMER, F. 1936. "Migration, Reproduction, and Population Adjustment," *Annals of the American Academy of Political and Social Science*, CLXXXVIII, 280–89.

DUCOFF, L. J. 1951. "Migratory Farm Workers: A Problem in Migration Analysis," *Rural Sociology*, XVI, 217–24.

DUNCAN, O. D. 1940. Reprinted 1956. "The Theory and Consequences of Mobility of Farm Population," in *Population Theory and Policy*, ed. J. J. SPENGLER and O. D. DUNCAN. Glencoe, Ill.: Free Press.

FOLGER, J. 1953. "Some Aspects of Migration in the Tennessee Valley," *American Sociological Review*, XVIII, 253–60.

FREEDMAN, R. 1947. "Health Differentials for Rural-Urban Migration," *American Sociological Review*, XII, 536–41.

———. 1950. *Recent Migration to Chicago*. Chicago: University of Chicago Press.

GLASS, DAVID V. (ed.). 1954. *Social Mobility in Britain*. London: Routledge & Kegan Paul.

GOODRICH, C., *et al.* 1936. *Migration and Economic Opportunity*. Philadelphia: University of Pennsylvania Press.

HAGOOD, MARGARET J., and SHARP, E. F. 1951. *Rural-Urban Migration in Wisconsin, 1940–1950*. (Research Bulletin 176.) Madison: Agricultural Experiment Station, University of Wisconsin.

HAMILTON, C. H. 1951. Reprinted 1956. "Population Pressure and Other Factors Affecting Net Rural-Urban Migration," in *Demographic Analysis*, ed. J. J. SPENGLER and O. D. DUNCAN. Glencoe, Ill.: Free Press.

———, and HENDERSON, F. M. 1944. "Use of the Survival Rate Method in Measuring Net Migration," *Journal of the American Statistical Association*, XXXIX, 197–206.

HAWLEY, A. H. 1953. *Intrastate Migration in Michigan: 1935–1940*. ("Michigan Governmental Studies," No. 25.) Ann Arbor: University of Michigan Press.

HEBERLE, R. 1955. "Migratory Mobility: Theoretical Aspects and Problems of Measurement," in *Proceedings of the World Population Conference, 1954*, Vol. II. New York: United Nations.

HIRSCH, G. P. 1951. "Migration from the Land in England and Wales, 1871–

1950," *Farm Economics* (Oxford), VI, 270–80.

ISBELL, ELEANOR C. 1944. Reprinted 1956. "Internal Migration in Sweden and Intervening Opportunities," in *Demographic Analysis*, ed. J. J. SPENGLER and O. D. DUNCAN. Glencoe, Ill.: Free Press.

JAFFE, A. J., and WOLFBEIN, S. L. 1945. "Internal Migration and Full Employment in the United States," *Journal of the American Statistical Association*, XL, 351–53.

JEHLIK, P. J., and WAKELY, R. E. 1955. *Population Change and Net Migration in the North Central States, 1940–50*. (Research Bulletin 430.) Ames, Iowa: Iowa Agricultural Experiment Station, Iowa State College.

JOHNSON, D. G. 1948. Reprinted 1956. "Mobility as a Field of Economic Research," in *Population Theory and Policy*, ed. J. J. SPENGLER and O. D. DUNCAN. Glencoe, Ill.: Free Press.

KISER, C. V. 1932. *Sea Island to City: A Study of St. Helena Islanders in Harlem and Other Urban Centers*. ("Columbia University Studies in History, Economics, and Public Law," No. 368.) New York.

———. 1938. "Birth Rates among Rural Migrants in Cities," *Milbank Memorial Fund Quarterly*, XVI, 369–81.

KITAGAWA, EVELYN M. 1953. "Relative Importance—and Independence—of Selected Factors in Job Mobility, Six Cities, 1940–1949." Hectographed document, Chicago Community Inventory, University of Chicago.

KLINEBERG, O. 1935. *Negro Intelligence and Selective Migration*. New York: Columbia University Press.

KULLDORF, G. 1955. *Migration Probabilities*. ("Lund Studies in Geography," Ser. B, "Human Geography," No. 14.) Lund, Sweden: C. W. K. Gleerup for Royal University of Lund, Department of Geography and Statistics.

LEE, E. S. 1951. Reprinted 1956. "Negro Intelligence and Selective Migration: A Philadelphia Test of the Klineberg Hypothesis," in *Demographic Analysis*, ed. J. J. SPENGLER and O. D. DUNCAN. Glencoe, Ill.: Free Press.

———, et al. 1957. *Population Redistribution and Economic Growth: United States, 1870–1950*. Vol. I: *Methodological Considerations and Reference Tables*. Philadelphia: American Philosophical Society.

LIVELY, C. E., and TAEUBER, C. 1939. *Rural Migration in the United States*. (Research Monograph XIX, Division of Research, Works Progress Administration.) Washington, D.C.: Government Printing Office.

MAKOWER, H., MARSCHAK, J., and ROBINSON, H. W. 1938. "Studies in Mobility of Labour," *Oxford Economic Papers*, I, 83–123.

MALZBERG, B., and LEE, E. S. 1956. *Migration and Mental Disease: A Study of First Admissions to Hospitals for Mental Disease, New York, 1939–1941*. New York: Social Science Research Council.

MANGUS, A. R., and McNAMARA, R. L. 1943. *Levels of Living and Population Movements in Rural Areas in Ohio, 1930–40*. (Bulletin 639.) Wooster, Ohio: Ohio Agricultural Experiment Station.

MAULDIN, W. P. 1940. "Selective Migration from Small Towns," *American Sociological Review*, V, 748–58.

NEWTON, MARY P., and JEFFERY, J. R. 1951. *Internal Migration: Some Aspects of Population Movements within England and Wales*. (General Register Office, "Studies on Medical and Population Subjects," No. 5.) London: H. M. Stationery Office.

OGBURN, W. F. 1944. "Size of Community as a Factor in Migration," *Sociology and Social Research*, XXVIII, 255–61.

PALMER, GLADYS. 1954. *Labor Mobility in Six Cities*. New York: Social Science Research Council.

PRICE, D. O. 1948a. "Distance and Direction as Vectors of Internal Migration, 1935–1940," *Social Forces*, XXVII, 48–53.

———. 1948b. "Nonwhite Migrants to and from Selected Cities," *American Journal of Sociology*, LIV, 196–201.

———. 1951. "Some Socio-economic Factors in Internal Migration," *Social Forces*, XXIX, 409–15.

———. 1953. "Estimates of Net Migration in the United States, 1870–1940," *American Sociological Review*, XVIII, 35–39.

———. 1955. "Examination of Two Sources of Error in the Estimation of Net Internal Migration," *Journal of the American Statistical Association*, L, 689–700.

RAVENSTEIN, E. G. 1885–89. "The Laws of

Migration," *Journal of the Royal Statistical Society,* XLVIII, 167–235; and LII, 241–305.

ROGOFF, NATALIE. 1953. *Recent Trends in Occupational Mobility.* Glencoe, Ill.: Free Press.

SAUNDERS, H. W. 1943. Reprinted 1956. "Human Migration and Social Equilibrium," in *Population Theory and Policy,* ed. J. J. SPENGLER and O. D. DUNCAN. Glencoe, Ill.: Free Press.

SHRYOCK, H. S., JR., and ELDRIDGE, HOPE T. 1947. "Internal Migration in Peace and War," *American Sociological Review,* XII, 27–39.

SIEGEL, J. S., and HAMILTON, C. H. 1952. "Some Considerations in the Use of the Residual Method of Estimating Net Migration," *Journal of the American Statistical Association,* XLVII, 475–500.

STOUFFER, S. A. 1940. "Intervening Opportunities: A Theory Relating Mobility and Distance," *American Sociological Review,* V, 845–67.

———. 1957. "The Theory of Intervening Opportunities." Paper presented at fifty-second annual meeting of the American Sociological Society.

STRODTBECK, F. L. 1949. "Equal Opportunity Intervals: A Contribution to the Method of Intervening Opportunity Analysis," *American Sociological Review,* XIV, 490–97.

TAEUBER, C. 1940. "Migration and Rural Population Adjustment," *Rural Sociology,* V, 399–410.

———. 1947. "Recent Trends of Rural-Urban Migration in the United States," *Milbank Memorial Fund Quarterly,* XXV, 203–13.

THOMAS, B. 1955. "The Changing Pattern of Internal Migration in Great Britain, 1921–1951," in *Proceedings of the World Population Conference, 1954,* Vol. II. New York: United Nations.

THOMAS, DOROTHY S. 1936. "Internal Migrations in Sweden: A Note on Their Extensiveness As Compared with Net Migration Gain or Loss," *American Journal of Sociology,* XLII, 345–57.

———. 1938. *Research Memorandum on Migration Differentials.* (Bulletin 43.) New York: Social Science Research Council.

———. 1941. *Social and Economic Aspects of Swedish Population Movements, 1750–1933.* New York: Macmillan Co.

———. 1939. Reprinted 1956. "Selective Internal Migration: Some Implications for Mental Hygiene," in *Demographic Analysis,* ed. J. J. SPENGLER and O. D. DUNCAN. Glencoe, Ill.: Free Press.

THOMPSON, W. S. 1937. *Research Memorandum on Internal Migration in the Depression.* (Bulletin No. 30.) New York: Social Science Research Council.

THORNDIKE, E. L. 1942. "The Causes of Inter-state Migration," *Sociometry,* V, 321–35.

VANCE, R. B. 1938. *Research Memorandum on Population Redistribution within the United States.* (Bulletin 42.) New York: Social Science Research Council.

WENDEL, B. 1953. *A Migration Schema: Theories and Observations.* ("Lund Studies in Geography," Ser. B, "Human Geography," No. 9.) Lund, Sweden: University of Lund, Department of Geography.

ZIPF, G. K. 1949. *Human Behavior and the Principle of Least Effort.* Cambridge, Mass.: Addison-Wesley Press, Inc.

22. *International Migration*

BRINLEY THOMAS

In making a brief survey of the state of knowledge in any field, one must of necessity exercise restraint, but however careful the writer may be, there is always the danger that his own special interests will color his vision. This chapter is confined to modern migration movements, i.e., since the beginning of the nineteenth century. "Migration" is defined in this chapter as the movements (involving change of permanent residence) from one country to another which take place through the volition of the individuals or families concerned; forced population transfers, important though they have been, receive only the briefest mention. The sociological approach to the study of international migration, e.g., the contribution to the analysis of the problems of assimilation, is not covered in this chapter. It would be impossible to do justice to this important aspect within the compass here allowed. Finally, it would be idle to expect unanimity on the range of the generalizations that can be made in this branch of demography. In the section devoted to the existing state of knowledge, it has been thought desirable to survey the area where interesting work is being done rather than to limit the treatment to questions where reasonably satisfying answers have already been found.

DATA

Historical Development of Data

The evolution of records of international migration may be loosely divided into four phases corresponding to the changing preoccupations and policies of sovereign states. In the initial phase, covering roughly the first three-quarters of the nineteenth century, international movements of people were for the most part unrestricted, and the statistical records were by-products of legislation or administrative arrangements introduced for some other purpose, e.g., acts to regulate shipping (the United Kingdom and the United States), population registers kept by communal or ecclesiastical authorities (Belgium, Holland, and Sweden), or returns supplied by transport agencies and shipping companies concerning their contracts (Denmark and Switzerland).

As soon as states began to encourage or discourage the movement of certain categories of migrants, a demand arose for statistical information which would serve the purposes of policy. Each country tended to develop its statistics in the light of its own objectives; differences in concepts and in methods of collection and tabulation became more pronounced, and no attention was given to the need for defining an "international migrant." In the third phase, some governments established separate machinery for differentiating migrants in the strict sense of the term from other categories of international travelers. Finally, through the efforts of the International Labor Office and the Population Commission of the United Nations, the pathbreaking task of surveying the heterogeneous array of national statistics was carried out, and for the first time it became possible to present limited international tabulations. In the course of this work the difficulties of securing international comparability were found to be considerable.

Nature and Sources of Data

There are six main categories of migration data: statistics based on control at ports, control of land frontiers, passports, population registers, transport contracts, and coupons detached from certain documents. A significant difference may be noted between Europe and other continents. In the countries of North America, South America, Asia, and Africa there is a remarkable uniformity in method of collecting statistics; almost without exception it is done at frontiers and ports. The countries of Europe, however, have among them adopted every possible kind of system (United Nations, Population Division, 1949, Table 1, p. 8).

Port statistics.—This source has been in use in all parts of the world. In the United Kingdom it began with the Passengers' Act of 1803, which sought to alleviate the terrible hardships endured by emigrants sailing across the Atlantic. The act set a limit to the number of passengers which vessels were allowed to carry—one person for every two tons of unladen capacity. Masters of ships were required to present lists of their passengers to the customs authorities before they could receive clearance papers. Similarly, in the United States the Act of 1819 decreed that vessels arriving from foreign ports should furnish the collectors of customs with lists of passengers.

The chief advantage of port statistics is that they are collected at points where supervision is fairly easy, and they relate to specific times of departure and arrival. There are, however, a number of pitfalls. Some countries have simply included passengers traveling on emigrant ships or in the steerage class; this was the practice in the port of Hamburg up to 1924. It was not until 1912 that the British Board of Trade made a distinction between outward passengers who were

genuine emigrants and those who were not; a migrant was defined as a passenger who declared that he had lived for a year or more in one country and intended to settle down for a year or more in another country. In Hamburg after 1924, passengers of all classes going to America with immigration papers were classified as emigrants, and German-born residents of the United States returning to that country were excluded. As a result of this change, the German and American figures of emigrants from Germany to the United States showed hardly any difference.

In the second half of the nineteenth century the volume of international migration increased so much that some governments found it necessary to introduce controls, and this concern over the quantity and quality of the flow of migrants led to greater attention to the adequacy of port statistics. In the United States an act was passed in 1882 with the object of excluding undesirable classes of aliens, such as criminals and paupers. The contract labor laws of the eighties aimed at keeping out aliens arriving "under contract or agreement . . . express or implied, made previous to the importation of such aliens . . . to perform labor or service of any kind in the United States, its territories or the District of Columbia." In 1892 the Bureau of Immigration was set up with its own officials at the ports, and in that year the authorities began to define immigrants as aliens declaring their intention to live permanently in the Untied States. The increasing inflow from southern and eastern Europe prompted the introduction in 1899 of a classification of immigrants into racial groups by country of last residence. Interest was also aroused in the number of people leaving the United States. From 1868 to 1907 the information was based on returns made voluntarily by shipping companies showing the number of passengers departing for foreign countries outside North America; in 1907 the statistics of emigration were put on the same footing as those of immigration.

The refinement of port statistics in the United States lagged far behind the needs of the legislators. It is salutary to recall the conditions under which the records were actually collected at the busiest ports. The following statement was made to the Industrial Commission on October 12, 1899, by an official who had been Commissioner of Immigration at the port of New York, March, 1893—August, 1897.

I assumed charge of Ellis Island on the 1st of April 1893, just during the time when, in view of the new law about to take effect, there was an immense immigration into our country. . . . I had an opportunity during this time of acting under the old law . . . and I found, especially in looking up the old records which were all kept on Ellis Island, that while the few registry clerks in the office were supposed under the old law to take a statement from the immigrants about their nationality, destination and ages, as a matter of fact whole pages did not contain any reply to any of these points. They were nothing more than an index of names of people arriving at the port. It was, as a matter of fact, physically impossible for these people—the port officers—to do more. There were but a few of them who had to register sometimes 4000 or 5000 in a day. Now, under no circumstances could it be expected from them that they could examine the immigrants as to all these specific points, and put them down, and then expect that when through with the day's work they would make up the statistics [United States Senate, 1901, p. 179].

Port statistics can be very misleading unless the passenger lists distinguish clearly between passengers who are migrants or transmigrants and other international travelers.

Land frontier statistics.—Control at land frontiers is far less effective than at seaports. Where passports are compulsory only for emigrants, one can expect a great deal of clandestine move-

ment. Continental frontiers cannot possibly be watched at every point, particularly where there are no natural geographical barriers. It has become increasingly the practice to carry out inspection on the trains. A striking example of the unreliability of this source is the fact that in the years 1920–25 the statistics of Mexico recorded 489,748 Mexican immigrants re-entering the country from the United States, whereas American figures showed only 38,740 Mexicans crossing the frontier to their country of origin (International Labor Office, 1932, p. 67).

Passport statistics.—The utility of data based on passports varies widely according to the rules regarding their validity —whether passports are obligatory only for migrants and whether they are necessary only for certain countries or for certain voyages. Passports were one of the earliest sources of migration statistics, but this source can no longer be regarded as trustworthy. No country could have had a more efficient system of passport statistics than Hungary before World War I, and yet in the four years 1910–13 the number of Hungarian emigrants shown by this source (315,-498) was far below the number (433,-230) recorded by European port statistics (International Labor Office, 1932, p. 34).

Population register statistics.—Communal registers kept by local or ecclesiastical authorities enable an accurate count to be made of changes in residence as well as of births and deaths. The system was first established in Holland in 1849, and it was elaborated until by 1922 every commune was responsible for recording a wealth of detail relating to nationality, date of arrival, last residence, date of departure, and future residence. These registers can be made to yield important demographic facts about aliens as distinct from citizens and about external as distinct from internal migration. External migration can be divided into intracontinental and intercontinental movements. The figures are collected by officials who are in a position to insure accuracy. Unfortunately, much of this valuable information is buried out of sight in the published totals of outward and inward movements.

The Swedish registers, excellent as a source of data on births and deaths, were disappointing as a basis for external migration figures. The extent of their coverage varied from period to period; for example, after 1893, when emigration status ceased to carry exemption from military service, the totals seriously understated the real outflow. (See G. Sundbärg, 1910, pp. 250–52.)

One of the weaknesses of registers is that they often fail to distinguish between temporary migration and short-period tourist travel. This is part of an unavoidable difficulty whenever statistics are based on declarations of intention. Nevertheless, such are the advantages of population registers that this source has been proposed by the United Nations Population Commission (1949) as a possible substitute for frontier statistics in countries where such a change is feasible.

Transport contract statistics.—Figures obtained from copies of contracts furnished to the authorities by shipping companies are often deficient. Sometimes they fail to separate migrants from other travelers (transit migrants from residents of a country), and it is frequently impossible to trust the information about countries of last residence and future residence.

Statistics of detachable coupons from special documents.—When migrants are supplied with travel documents containing detachable coupons, the whole migratory history can be recorded in a manner combining the advantages of passport and frontier control statistics. The difficulty is that since the coupons must carry a host of necessary particulars, the system would be too cumbrous

to administer. The International Conference of Migration Statisticians in 1932 urged that the best way of measuring international migration would be to introduce a generally recognized identity document for migrants. This ambitious solution ignores the stubborn facts of state sovereignty which lie at the root of the problem of statistical comparability. The real task is to make heterogeneous systems yield reasonably comparable answers. In the words of a United Nations report (Population Division, 1949, p. 11) ". . . uniformity is not perhaps so desirable as equivalence of the information recorded on the documents, taking into account different connotations of the same words in the different countries, and different types of questions that may be required to elicit the same information under different conditions."

Problems of Definition, Classification, and Comparability

It is a melancholy fact that statistics of international migration are no better now than they were a quarter of a century ago, when they were reviewed by the International Labor Office in *Statistics of Migration: Definitions, Methods, Classifications* (1932). All that can be claimed is that there is a more widespread appreciation of what is desirable.

The basis on which everything else depends is a count of all departures and arrivals of civilian travelers, and these grand totals must be classified in such a way that the number of genuine migrants can be separated. The following scheme would command wide agreement among experts. (See United Nations, *Statistical Office*, 1953, p. 17.)

Arrivals from other countries

1. Permanent immigrants, i.e., non-residents (nationals and aliens) intending to remain for more than one year.
2. Temporary immigrants, i.e., non-residents intending to take up an occupation

remunerated within the country for a period of one year or less. Their dependents are placed in category 3.

3. Visitors, i.e., non-residents intending to remain for one year or less without engaging in an occupation remunerated within the country (including their dependents).
4. Residents (nationals and aliens) returning after being abroad for not more than one year.
5. Total arrivals (sum of categories 1–4).

Special groups.—Included in the above categories are groups which need to be shown separately, e.g., refugees, transferred populations, immigrants given special facilities such as government financial assistance, participation of intergovernmental organizations in cost of passage, facilities under bilateral or multilateral agreements.

Departures to other countries

1. Permanent emigrants, i.e., residents (nationals and aliens) intending to remain abroad for more than one year.
2. Temporary emigrants, departing dependents are placed in category 3.
3. Visitors departing, including their dependents.
4. Residents (nationals and aliens) intending to remain abroad for one year or less.
5. Total departures (sum of categories 1–4).

Special groups.—A classification similar to that under arrivals.

A general view of the actual performance of countries is given in Table 45. (See United Nations, Population Division, 1949, p. 25.)

The essential point about a permanent migrant is that he is changing his country of permanent residence; without this information it is impossible to distinguish migrants from other international travelers. Only sixteen out of forty-five countries publish a classification of emigrants by country of intended future residence or destination, and only seventeen give a classification of immigrants by country of last residence or origin. Only sixteen countries distinguish con-

tinental and intercontinental immigrants, and only ten distinguish continental and intercontinental emigrants. Although data on country of birth or nationality of migrants are more abundant, they cannot be regarded as a correct indication of country of last residence. Even greater difficulties are encountered in trying to compare national statistics which group persons according to "race" or ethnic origin. A detailed age classification of migrants by sex is available for twenty-two countries; but, owing to diversity of presentation, only eleven of these countries could yield a distribution such as: 0–14, 15–19, 20–24, 25–29, 30–39, 40–49, 50–59, 60 and over.

A major task of demographic analysis is to assess the impact of international migration on the population structure of sending and receiving countries. For this purpose it is necessary to have tabulations of migrants by marital status combined with distributions by sex and age. Sixteen countries give information on marital status, but in nine of them it is not combined with an age grouping, and in five there is no combination with sex. The omissions in these figures can sometimes be remedied by resorting to the distribution of migrants by occupation, where a distinction is drawn between economically active persons and their dependents. However, the only effective means of securing reliable primary data in this field is by sampling. (See, for example, the interesting analysis of the family structure of the emigrants from the United Kingdom, 1946–49, given by Dr. J. Isaac in *British Post-War Migration*, 1954, pp. 42–49.)

Data on the economic characteristics of migrants suffer from unavoidable weaknesses arising partly out of the unreliability of statements regarding "intended employment" and partly out of the fact that classifications which serve well in national statistics are often not applicable to migration statistics. Unfortunately, it is almost impossible in a number of countries to decide whether the grouping is occupational or industrial. (Details regarding the coverage and content of migration statistics in various countries are given in United Nations, Population Division, 1949, pp. 26–37.)

From the above summary it is clear

and the pace of improvement will necessarily be slow.

Adjustment of Data

The data discussed above are all direct records of migration movements. Some of their deficiencies can be remedied by applying appropriate methods to population census figures of foreign-

TABLE 45

TABULATIONS OF MIGRATION STATISTICS FOR DIFFERENT COUNTRIES

Emigration		Immigration	
Countries giving any data	41	Countries giving any data	42
Total numbers of emigrants		*Total numbers of immigrants*	
Countries giving data for		Countries giving data for:	
Nationals and aliens without distinction	29	Nationals and aliens without distinction	27
Nationals and aliens separately	1	Nationals and aliens separately	1
Nationals only	7	Nationals only	6
Aliens only	4	Aliens only	8
Countries giving data for:		Countries giving data for:	
Continental and intercontinental emigration without distinction	25	Continental and intercontinental immigration without distinction	22
Continental and intercontinental emigration separately	10	Continental and intercontinental immigration separately	16
Continental emigration only	2	Continental immigration only	2
Intercontinental emigration only	4	Intercontinental immigration only	2
Classifications by country of intended future residence, or destination		*Classifications by country of last residence or origin*	
Countries giving any data by this classification	16	Countries giving any data by this classification	17
Countries giving the classification for:		Countries giving the classification for:	
Nationals and aliens without distinction	11	Nationals and aliens without distinction	9
Nationals and aliens separately	0	Nationals and aliens separately	0
Nationals only	4	Nationals only	4
Aliens only	1	Aliens only	4
Classifications by sex and age		*Classifications by sex and age*	
Countries giving any data by this classification	12	Countries giving any data by this classification	13
Countries giving the classification for:		Countries giving the classification for:	
Nationals and aliens without distinction	9	Nationals and aliens without distinction	8
Nationals and aliens separately	0	Nationals and aliens separately	0
Nationals only	2	Nationals only	2
Aliens only	1	Aliens only	3

that serious problems of comparability are encountered in regard to total numbers of migrants in different countries and subdivisions according to various characteristics. This is particularly true of the countries of the Far East, where past records are so scanty that even the most elementary statistical analysis of migration has to be confined to recent decades. The problems to be surmounted are complex and deeply rooted,

born. The evolution of statistics of aliens in the censuses of various countries reflects phases similar to those noted in the history of migration sources. In the era of unrestricted migration and no discrimination (as between nationals and aliens), governments had no interest in collecting information about legal nationality; it is rare to find statistics on this subject in the censuses of the early nineteenth century. Even in the second half of the century the only countries which included such a question in the census forms were those where alien elements in the population were of some significance, e.g., France (1851), Norway (1855), and Germany (1871). The practice in the United Kingdom was to ask a question about place of birth. The modern census classifications by legal nationality, ethnic origin, country of birth, and race are fully reviewed and critically assessed in the admirable inquiry by the International Labor Office, *World Statistics of Aliens, A Compara-*

born, see Kuznets and Rubin, *Immigration and the Foreign Born*, 1954, Part III, "Statistical Methods and Problems," and the Appendixes, pp. 50–104. See also Brinley Thomas, *Migration and Economic Growth*, 1954, Appendix 1, "A Method of Estimating Net Migration from Population Census Data," pp. 242–52.)

Port statistics of the movement of passengers need to be subjected to certain tests if they are to be used as time series. It is necessary to discover how reliable they are as an index of *changes*

TABLE 46

UNITED KINGDOM: ADJUSTED BALANCE OF MIGRATION 1871–1911
(Nearest Thousand)

Census Decade	Net Loss by Migration (Census Figures) (1)	Outward Balance of Citizens (Board of Trade Passenger Figures) (2)	Estimated Inward Balance of Aliens (3)	Adjusted Outward Balance of Citizens and Aliens (Column 2 minus Column 3) (4)
1871–81............	918	1,030	62	968
1881–91............	1,557	1,650	95	1,555
1891–1901.........	586	680	177	513
1901–11............	1,083	1,500	116	1,384

tive Study of Census Returns 1910–1920–1930 (1936).

One of the first questions which a demographer in this field asks is how much of the population growth of a country has been due to immigration and how much has been due to the natural increase of the residents. The main part of the adjustment required in this operation is the use of life-table projections to calculate the number of survivors: the number of survivors through a decade is compared with the number of people enumerated at the end of a decade. An instructive example of this kind of work may be seen in Nathan Keyfitz' (1950) population balance sheet for Canada, 1851–1950, showing the number of births, deaths, immigration, and emigration in each decade. (For the reconciliation of the United States figures of immigration and emigration with population census data on resident foreign-

in the migratory stream over a long period. Possibilities of adjustment are illustrated in Table 46.

The most accurate estimate of external migration is obtained from the excess of births over deaths minus the decennial increase in the enumerated population. This is shown for the United Kingdom for the four decades 1871–1911 in Table 46, column 1. The recorded outward balance of passenger citizens, based on statistics collected at the ports, is shown in column 2, and the differences between these totals and those in column 1 call for explanation. First, British passenger figures do not cover movements to and from the continent of Europe. Second, the omission of aliens from these passenger statistics can be remedied by taking the number of foreign-born enumerated in the United Kingdom at each census and estimating the number of survivors from decade to decade; the decennial inward balance of aliens arrived at in this way is given in column 3. The adjusted outward balance of citizens and aliens in each decade (column 4) does not diverge much from column 1 except in the decade 1901–11, and that discrepancy is probably due to the incomplete coverage of cabin passengers and the inclusion of a certain number of alien transmigrants as British. (For an extended analysis see Brinley Thomas, 1954, pp. 50–52.)

British statistics of aggregate net passenger movement (i.e., for the period ending in 1912) are a good index of the course of total net emigration, but for individual countries of destination these figures are not to be trusted. Nor is it advisable to rely on land frontier statistics for a picture of international migration within a continent. The only way to arrive at a fairly reliable estimate of migration balances within Europe is to use the census classifications of persons by place of birth or political nationality. (See Kirk, 1946, chap. vi.) Valuable information may also be obtained from specific inquiries, such as the census of aliens taken in France in 1945 and the sampling experiments made in various countries, e.g., Ireland, Canada, and the United States.

METHODS

The methods which have been used in the study of international migration may be grouped under the usual three heads—historical, theoretical, and empirical. Historians of the subject have gathered together the basic facts about movements of population through the ages, and comparisons have been made between the experience of different countries and different periods. Theorists have applied a variety of methods, including comparative statics, cyclical analysis, process or period analysis, econometric models, and models of growth. Finally, there are the empirical studies embracing a wide range of sta-

tistical methods. The latter are of special interest, but they are not easy to classify. An enumeration of the main approaches in this category would include sampling, analysis of structure, time-series analysis, measurement of differentials, and sociological or socioeconomic analysis of processes of absorption.

Historical Methods

The fruits of the historical method are important in that they prevent the demographer from forming an unduly narrow conception of his problems. It is particularly useful for an investigator concerned with time-series analysis to be able to place his statistics against a full historical background. A vital question, for which the historical method is indispensable, is the extent to which political and institutional factors, legislative changes, technical innovations, or movements in public opinion have influenced the course of international migration. It is necessary to assess the causal significance of such factors as the disappearance of serfdom in Europe, the abolition of slavery, political or religious persecution, various systems of land tenure and inheritance, the evolution of transport, innovations in agriculture and industry, the policies of shipping companies, the development of savings banks, and the means of transmitting emigrants' remittances. Studies both of the determinants and of the consequences of migration must be firmly established on a bedrock of historical scholarship. Outstanding as pioneer in this field was the English historian, Archdeacon W. Cunningham (1897), and a notable contribution was also made by M. L. Hansen (1940).

Theoretical Methods

The formulation of questions to be addressed to the empirical data necessarily entails model-building. Lurking behind most inquiries into international migration is the shadowy and elusive concept of "optimum population." In the interests of precision, the investigator must first insure that, of the various kinds of optima, the appropriate one is selected for the problem at hand. (A thorough survey of the theory at different levels of abstraction is to be found in A. Sauvy, 1952.) The demographer here carries a heavy responsibility, for there is widespread popular interest in such questions as whether a particular country is "overpopulated" and, if so, whether emigration would be an effective remedy.

Economists employ several theoretical models. The method of comparative statics can be used, for example, to isolate a given flow of immigration, to elucidate the disturbance to the initial equilibrium of the economy, and to indicate how a new equilibrium is reached. The analysis would distinguish between aggregative or income effects and substitution effects (for example, J. J. Spengler, 1958). Second, models can be designed to establish the necessary and sufficient conditions for a cyclical fluctuation in the flow of population from one country to another. When the flow of capital is also taken into account, a two-country model can be constructed to demonstrate the conditions under which there will be an inverse relation between long swings in the rate of economic growth in the sending and receiving countries. Such models provide a theoretical interpretation of the nineteenth-century pattern of migration and foreign lending, particularly the movements from the Old World to the New; they also serve to bring out points of contrast between that pattern and the trends observed since World War II (see Brinley Thomas, 1958).

Third, an analysis of the process of monetary inflation, taking in the factor of large-scale immigration, is required to explain what happens during phases of rapid expansion in receiving countries. This approach is especially useful in interpreting recent experience in Australia and Israel. Fourth, the progress of econometrics has left its imprint on the study of migration. Interesting attempts have been made to use econometric models to calculate the most desirable rate of net external migration for countries such as the Netherlands, Australia, and Canada, assuming that the "target" is the attainment of the highest real income per head of the total population. (See J. Isaac assisted by C. A. van den Beld, 1953. See also the projection of extra-European emigration in Colin Clark, 1942.)

In recent years economists have given much attention to models of economic growth (e.g., R. F. Harrod, 1948; E. D. Domar, 1947; N. Kaldor, 1954; a useful review may be found in M. Abramovitz, 1952). In a dynamic analysis of advanced countries one is concerned with the rate of growth in investment which will insure a rate of increase in income equal to that of productive capacity. One of the key problems springs from the fact that population growth is not only a condition of economic growth but is also a consequence of it. Moreover, is it the trend rate of economic growth which governs the amplitude and span of fluctuations, or is it the amplitude and span of fluctuations which govern the trend rate of growth? Within these "hen or egg" problems may be found questions of immediate relevance to this chapter, i.e., when we are dealing with an open economy whose population growth is partly determined by international migration.

Empirical Methods

In view of the deficiencies of migration data in many countries, attention must be devoted to the problem of improving the basic material for quantitative analysis. By applying the method of sampling, we can establish new facts about the composition of migration streams, thereby opening up new avenues of inquiry. The possibilities of this approach may be seen in J. Isaac's *British Post-War Migration* (1954), the main source of which was a 10 per cent sample of all British emigrants shown in the shipping manifests for 1946–49. No attempt can be made here to do justice to the various statistical methods employed in the study of international migration; we shall merely select a few representative examples.

Projections.—A question of immediate interest to the demographer is the effect of migration on the size and structure of the population. By postulating alternative volumes of migration with varying sex and age composition, one can calculate projections of future population; such computations bring out the relative quantitative significance of the migration factor. As an example we may take England and Wales for the period 1950–90 and consider five possible projections as worked out in Carrier and Jeffery, *External Migration* (1953, Appendix 3). The five assumptions are selected in order to indicate the incidence of flows of net emigration varying according to size, sex-age structure and duration. They are as follows: (*a*) 100,-000 males aged 15–40, emigrating annually for forty years; (*b*) 100,000 males aged 15–40, emigrating annually for twenty years; (*c*) 100,000 persons of mixed sex and unrestricted ages emigrating annually for forty years; (*d*) 50,000 males aged 15–40, emigrating annually for forty years; and (*e*) 50,000 persons of mixed sex and unrestricted ages emigrating annually for forty years. The assumption of a net emigration of 100,00 persons per annum from England and Wales in 1950–90 implies an average annual rate of about 2.2 per cent of the population; this was the rate experienced in the decade 1881–91, the highest on record.

The standard case, where no migration is assumed, yields an increase in the population of England and Wales from 43.5 million to 46.5 million in 1950–90. Given assumption (*c*) (100,000 mixed emigration), the population would fall to 41.5 million by 1990; according to assumption (*a*) (100,000 male emigration), the population would decline to 43 million by 1990. Although in each case 4 million people are assumed to emigrate, the loss in the case of the mixed outflow includes about 1.5 million survivors of children whose parents would have left the country before they were born; no such adjustment was made in the computation for case (*a*). The results for case (*b*) show that, after the cessation of emigration in 1970, there is an appreciable increase in the number of males aged 15–44. Marked effects on the sex ratio are produced by the purely male outflows (*a*), (*b*), and (*d*): in case (*a*) the proportion of male to female in age group 15–44, which would have been 1.04, declines to 0.87. An authoritative analysis which includes migration projections may be found in "Population Projections for Great Britain 1947–2047" (United Kingdom, Royal Commission on Population, 1950*a*, pp. 213–301).

Correlation and lag analysis of fluctuations.—Each type of fluctuation, seasonal, cyclical, or minor secular, must be related to corresponding undulations in other economic or social variables. The following are some of the questions raised: To what extent do the timing and amplitude of seasonal, cyclical, and minor secular fluctuations in migration correspond with those of fluctuations in the level of economic activity in the receiving country? To what extent are fluctuations in migration determined by forces in the sending countries (the "push") and by forces in the receiving countries (the "pull")? What part does international migration play in the mechanism of the business cycle? Does it act as a stabilizer or a destabilizer? Is there any evidence of a regular recurrence of periods of extreme population pressure in Europe in the eighteenth and nineteenth centuries? Were such periods, during which the propensity to emigrate was high, governed by peaks of natural increase occurring about twenty years before? Did the relative strength of the "pull" and "push" change from one historical phase to the next? What was the relation between international migration and variations in the rate of growth in real income per head in the sending and receiving countries during the era of unrestricted movement? For examples of the use of correlation and lag analysis see H. Jerome (1926), Dorothy S. Thomas (1941, chaps. iii, ix), Brinley Thomas (1954, chaps. vii, x, xi), and H. Ravnholt, 1938, pp. 224–29).

Analysis of differentials.—Migration is a selective process, and it gives rise to various differentials. Detailed statistical analysis of the quality of migration movements can show the extent to which migrants differ from non-migrant populations in terms of age and sex composition, family status, income level, fertility, and intelligence, among other characteristics.

Effects of migration on demographic structure in sending and receiving countries.—Statistical investigation into the effects of migration on population structure contributes an important part of demographic research. What is the effect of migration on birth and death rates in sending and receiving countries? That these questions can assume considerable public importance is shown by the history of the famous "substitution theory" in the United States (F. A. Walker, 1891). In its original form this theory contended that immigration is neutral in its effect on the growth of population in the receiving country, any increase in numbers which it entails being offset by a diminution in the natural increase of the native-born people. Walker sought to prove that the fall in the rate of population growth in the United States which began in the 1830's was due

to the depressing influence of immigration on the living conditions of native stocks. The result of modern research (e.g., G. Mortara, 1942) has been to throw serious doubt on the validity of the Walker theory.

In view of the peculiarities of the age and sex composition of migrants, it is pertinent to inquire what will be the effect on the rate of growth of the immigrant section of the receiving country, assuming the inflow to be continuous. There is much scope here for mathematical analysis which would reveal the implications of alternative sets of assumptions. This kind of problem can have great political significance; for example, the Asian population of the Union of South Africa increased from 166,000 in 1921 to 285,000 in 1946. It is of interest to know under what conditions migrants carry their habits and attitudes regarding fertility with them into the new country; here the inquiry might become part of a general survey of the process of assimilation.

Effects of migration on the gainfully employed population and its occupational composition.—Under this heading the first problem is to devise a method of calculating the "money value of a worker." (See Dublin and Lotka, 1946; R. W. Goldsmith, 1950, pp. 23–114.) Attempts have been made to estimate the capital value which a receiving country obtains when it admits a certain volume of immigration. In a country such as Italy, which exports people, the view is widespread that the supply of "human capital" should command a price in exactly the same way as the supply of inanimate raw material. There can be no doubt that outlay on education, skills, health, and physical fitness is a form of capital investment, but there are serious methodological difficulties in thinking of a whole population as having a capital value which increases with immigration and diminishes with emigration.

A more practical exercise is to calculate the extent to which immigration adds to a country's labor force and alters the ratio of the number of young and old dependents to the total population. This has a direct bearing on the effect of migration on output per head. An instructive example of the kind of statistical technique which could be usefully applied to these problems can be seen in John D. Durand (1953, pp. 1–16).

Other questions which the foregoing method of analysis can be used to answer may be illustrated by taking the case of West Germany. The absorption of several million refugees from East Germany within a short period has had a marked effect on the demographic structure of West Germany. It is necessary to distinguish between the demographic and non-demographic elements in the growth of the labor force and to estimate the influence of the immigration on the technical coefficients of production. On the other hand, there are countries, such as Ireland, which have been heavy exporters of population, where the effects of prolonged emigration on the structure of the labor supply and the propensity to invest are of great interest.

Migration and the international monetary mechanism.—Insufficient attention has been given to the financial aspects of migration, especially the impact on the balance of payments of certain countries. Such research has no doubt been impeded by the imperfection of statistical data. One method of approach is indicated by J. Bourgeois-Pichat in his article, "Migrations et balance de comptes" (1949). We need to know the conditions under which an immigration country will experience unfavorable reactions through an adverse shift in the terms of trade or a decrease in foreign exchange reserves as a result of migrants' remittances. A poor country, suffering from disguised unemployment, can benefit considerably from an inflow of funds from its nationals abroad: to what extent does this benefit depend upon the manner in which this income is used?

The process of assimilation.—Various quantitative indexes have been devised to yield an approximate measure of the factors which facilitate or hinder the smooth assimilation of immigrants in their country of adoption. (See, e.g., W. D. Borrie, 1954.) It is often difficult to assess the psychosocial obstacles, and there are diverse views on the meaning of "assimilation." The following are some of the questions involved: Is economic growth a function of the social tension associated with immigration? To what extent does prejudice against foreigners exist apart from whether economic conditions are good or bad? Granted the permanent necessity to safeguard and promote a community core—the essence of nationhood—what is the "safe" rate of immigration? Illuminating comparisons could be made between different countries according to the size and character of the community core and the degree of cultural pluralism which is regarded as compatible with it.

SUMMARY OF EXISTING KNOWLEDGE

Facts

Volume and direction of migration flows.—Within the limits set by the imperfections of statistics, it is possible to present the main facts about the volume and direction of international migration in the nineteenth and twentieth centuries. The available figures for the period 1821–1932, given in Table 47, reflect trends during an era of relatively unrestricted movement. According to the data for countries of immigration, which are less defective than those for countries of emigration, 59 million people moved overseas during the period, but even this total is manifestly an underestimate. The vast majority of these migrants were Europeans, and over 90 per cent of them settled either in North or South America. In its heyday, international migration was largely an affair of the Atlantic community of nations.

This analysis is confined to normal migration movements, but in the twentieth century the volume of forced population transfers has been considerable. An outstanding example was the movement in-

400,000 Turks had to leave Greece. The separation of Pakistan from India led to an exchange of populations estimated in 1949 at 7 million in each country. The campaigns of World War II and the Nazi war machine resulted in vast movements of refugees and forced labor, and

TABLE 47

WORLD INTERCONTINENTAL MIGRATION*

(Thousands)

EMIGRATION: 1846–1932			IMMIGRATION: 1821–1932		
Country of Emigration	Period Covered†	Total	Country of Immigration	Period Covered‡	Total
Europe:			*America:*		
Austria-Hungary.....	....	5,196	Argentina..........	1856–1932	6,405
Belgium.............	....	193	Brazil...............	....	4,431
British Isles........	....	18,020	British West Indies..	1836–1932	1,587
Denmark............	....	387	Canada.............	....	5,206
Finland.............	1871–1932	371	Cuba..............	1901–32	857
France..............	....	519	Guadeloupe.........	1856–1924	42
Germany............	....	4,889	Dutch Guiana......	1856–1931	69
Italy................	....	10,092	Mexico.............	1911–31	226
Malta...............	1911–32	63	Newfoundland......	1841–1924	20
Holland.............	....	224	Paraguay...........	1881–1931	26
Norway.............	....	854	United States.......	....	32,244
Poland.............	1920–32	642	Uruguay...........	1836–1932	713
Portugal............	....	1,805			
Russia..............	....	2,253	Total (America)...	....	53,826
Spain...............	....	4,653			
Sweden.............	....	1,203	*Asia:*		
Switzerland........	....	332	Philippines........	1911–29	90
Total (Europe)....	....	51,696	*Oceania:*		
			Australia..........	1861–1932	2,913
Other countries:			Fiji.................	1881–1926	79
British India........	....	1,194	Hawaii.............	1911–31	216
Cape Verde........	1901–27	30	New Caledonia.....	1896–1932	32
Japan..............	....	518	New Zealand.......	1851–1932	594
St. Helena.........	1896–1924	12			
			Africa:		
			Mauritius..........	1836–1932	573
			Seychelles..........	1901–32	12
			South Africa........	1881–1932	852
Grand Total.....	....	53,450	Grand Total....	....	59,187

* Source: A. M. Carr-Saunders (1936, p. 49).
† 1846–1932, except where otherwise stated.
‡ 1821–1932, except where otherwise stated.

to Germany after World War I of Germans who had lived in Alsace-Lorraine and in areas ceded to Poland: it was estimated that over a million people were involved in this transfer. Then there was the exchange of populations between Greece and Turkey decreed by the Treaty of Lausanne of 1923. Over a million Greeks were moved out of Asia Minor and eastern Thrace, and about

the collapse of Germany set in motion a colossal chain of redistributions. (A detailed survey is given in E. M. Kulischer, 1948.) The permanent demographic consequences of these forced transfers are of the utmost significance, but an analysis of their determinants is outside our purview.

The situation since the end of World War II is sumarized in Table 48. The chief countries of emigration in the years 1945–52 were Great Britain (1,107,000), Italy (741,000), Netherlands (318,000), Spain (272,000), Portugal (152,000). The various categories of refugees taken together amounted to 1,200,000. At the beginning of the century—in the eight years 1900–1907—the outflow from Europe was equal to two years' natural increase; after World War II—in the eight years 1945–52—the outflow from Europe was equal to four-fifths of one year's natural increase. In the latter period the main receiving countries have been the United States, 1,104,000 (27 per cent); Argentina, Brazil, and Venezuela, 883,-000 (21 per cent); Canada, 726,000 (17 per cent); Australia, 697,000 (17 per cent); Israel, 526,000 (13 per cent); South Africa, 125,000 (3 per cent); New Zealand, 75,000 (2 per cent). It is interesting to note that North and South America still receive over two-thirds of the intercontinental migrants.

The Far East.—The first phase of emigration from the Far East to countries of America, Oceania, and Africa began as a result of the abolition of slavery in the British colonies in the 1830's. The demand for plantation labor was met by the recruitment of indentured laborers from India and later from China and Japan; this group migration was the dominating characteristic of Far Eastern population movements through the nineteenth century, but after the 1920's intercontinental migration from the Far East practically ceased. The decline in intercontinental migration has been accompanied by an increase in interregional migrations which has had important economic and demographic consequences. Immigrants have contributed greatly to the economic development of Malaya, Burma, Ceylon, Borneo, and Manchuria. International movements of migrants within the Far East continued on an appreciable scale during the 1920's and even during the world depression of the 1930's, in contrast to what happened in the West. The chief countries of emigration have been China, India, Pakistan, Japan, and Korea. There has also been a tremendous fillip to internal migration within certain Far Eastern countries; for example, it is estimated that the urban areas of Japan experienced a net gain between 1920 and 1940 of no less than 17.5 million persons, ten times the net emigration of civilians from Japan in that period.

The influence of emigration on the demographic evolution of the sending countries in the Far East has been negligible; it is estimated that between 1834 and 1937 about 30 million Indians settled abroad and about 24 million came back to India, the net outward balance being a mere 6 million. Since the end of

TABLE 48

INTERCONTINENTAL MIGRATION, 1945–52

Emigration from Europe........	4,452,000
Immigration into Europe.......	1,150,000
Non-European migration to non-European countries..........	460,000
Other intercontinental migration.	250,000
Total....................	6,312,000

World War II, while there has been a revival of international migration in the West, there has been a decline in the Far East. Political independence and economic and social reforms have resulted in a greater part being played by native labor in economic activities which formerly depended on immigrants. Internal migration is proving an effective substitute for immigration. (See "International Migrations in the Far East during Recent Times: The Countries of Emigration," United Nations, Population Division, 1951; "International Migrations in the Far East during Recent Times: The Countries of Immigration," United Nations, Population Division, 1952.)

Differentials. — Some generalizations can safely be put forward about the special characteristics of international migrants. The majority are comparatively young, between two-thirds and three-quarters of them falling in the age group 15–40. As a rule, the propensity to emigrate is highest in the age group 20–25. Sundbärg (1910), in his investigations of Swedish data for 1851–1900, found that if the rate of emigration for the population as a whole were expressed as 100, the specific rates for age groups were as follows: 15–20, 184; 20–25, 350; 25–30, 223; 30–35, 123. This was not an isolated phenomenon, for the same is true of British emigrants since World War II (see J. Isaac, 1954, p. 38). As a result of the age selectivity of immigration, a receiving country will have a high proportion of its foreign-born population in the adult age group. In the United States in 1930 over 40 per cent of the foreign-born whites were between 25 and 44 years of age, as compared with 27 per cent of the native whites. One of the effects of sudden restrictions is to diminish the proportion of young adult immigrants: as a result of the Restriction Act of 1924, the median age of immigrants into the United States went up from 24.9 years in 1925 to 33.0 years in 1940.

The sex composition of the main stream of transatlantic migrants in the period 1850–1920 showed a preponderance of males ranging between 58 per cent and 70 per cent. When a prolonged slump in migration occured, as in the 1920's and 1930's, the sex ratio changed in favor of females (this is partly due to the movement of women who are joining their husbands or relations who emigrated in an earlier period). In the case of mass emigration from a poor country, there may well be a preponderance of females among the youthful emigrants; in Ireland every year between 1860 and 1910 female emigrants outnumbered the male in the age group 15–20, and the reason must have been that the employment opportunities for girls in the United States, particularly in domestic service, remained fairly steady through boom and slump.

It is generally agreed that males are more mobile and migratory than females. A comparison between the number of foreign-born enumerated in a country at a particular date and the number of immigrants into that country in a period preceding that date gives a rough index of the degree of mobility. For example, the number of female immigrants into the United States in the thirty years 1890–1920 was about the same as the number of foreign-born females enumerated in the country in 1920, but in the case of males the number of immigrants in that period exceeded the number of foreign-born enumerated in 1920 by 4.5 million. W. F. Willcox (1931 *a*, p. 91 regarded this excess as ". . . a rough measure of the males who had left the United States during that period, temporarily or permanently either as repatriates or as birds of passage." Such reasoning led to the conclusion that about three out of four of the immigrants arriving in the United States in the decades before 1913 remained as permanent settlers.

The facts about occupational differentials are based on the experience of a minority of countries, since the data are notoriously defective. Clearly, it is impossible to generalize. The occupational composition of a migratory movement is relative to the phase of economic development of the countries concerned. Here we may anticipate one of the explanatory principles to be dealt with later, namely, that international migration has been a vast secular process of rural-urban transference, which is itself a necessary condition of economic growth. As the Malthusian Devil stalked across the Old World, from Ireland in the 1840's to the Balkans after 1900, surplus agricultural populations were uprooted and pitchforked into the New World. Early in the century the "old" migration from northwest Europe was largely rural in origin, but as time went on the industrial component increased in size. Even in Italy the proportion of migrants coming from agricultural districts fell from 57 per cent in 1886 to 34 per cent in 1906–10. On the receiving side, we find that as recently as 1926–30 over 50 per cent of the immigrants to Canada were grouped under "farming," while the corresponding proportion for the United States in those years was only 10 per cent.

It is necessary to sound a warning about false inferences that have been drawn from statistics concerning migrants' occupations. The Immigration Commission in the United States (1911–12) made use of statistical data purporting to demonstrate a considerable difference in quality between the "new" and the "old" immigration into the United States. Taking the immigrant flow (excluding Hebrews) from southeast Europe and from northwest Europe in the period 1899–1909, the commission declared that 60 per cent of the "new" immigrants were farm laborers and common laborers, i.e., unskilled, while the corresponding proportion for "old" immigrants was 24 per cent. This was used by commentators (e.g., Jenks and Lauck, 1912, p. 31) who contended that the "new" immigration was much inferior in quality to the "old" and much more difficult to assimilate. However, it was grossly misleading to compare the high tide from southeast Europe with the ebbing tide from northwest Europe. When Paul H. Douglas (1919, p. 401) compared the "new" immigration in 1899–1907 with the "old" immigration in 1871–82, he found that there was hardly any difference between the proportion of skilled workers in the two flows.

It follows from the special characteristics already indicated that migrants contain a relatively high proportion of economically active persons. In the United States from 1880 to 1910 immigration caused the economically active

population to increase at a rate which was one-third faster than the growth of total population. In the period 1870–1910 one-fifth of the net increase of 25 million in the American labor force was due to the increase in foreign-born (Kuznets and Rubin, 1954, p. 44). This differential is supported in Canada, where the proportion of gainfully occupied among foreign-born males in 1931 was 92 per cent, compared with 85.4 per cent among Canadian-born males. If immigration is to have this expansive effect on the labor force in the receiving country, it must of course be unaffected by selective restrictions. In the sending country the effect—though usually less perceptible—is to retard the growth of the economically active segment of the population more than it retards the growth of the population.

We turn now to qualitative differentials in which policy-makers have taken a keen interest—illiteracy and intelligence. These have been the subject of extensive investigation in the United States, but it cannot be said that any firm conclusions have emerged. At the zenith of the "new" immigration into the United States, 30 per cent of the immigrants were recorded as illiterate, i.e., unable to write any language, but all that this signified was that most of these aliens came from' countries where there was hardly any elementary education. That environment plays a decisive part is indicated by a study of the rate of illiteracy among the children of the foreign-born. The American census of 1900 revealed that the rate of illiteracy among native white children (10–14 years of age) of foreign-born or mixed parents was only one-fifth of the rate among native white children of native parents (9 per 1,000 as against 44 per 1,000). By 1920 the spread had been narrowed (5 per 1,000 as against 11 per 1,000). The explanation of this phenomenon is to be found in the geographical distribution of the children between rural and urban areas. Immigrants tended to concentrate in cities, and so their children benefited from the superior educational opportunities available there; in 1900, 60 per cent of the second-generation white Americans were living in towns and cities, as compared with only 30 per cent of the native white Americans of native parentage.

The evidence of intelligence tests is voluminous but inconclusive. No useful result could be expected by submitting, say, a Hungarian and a Scottish immigrant to the same test. The length of residence in the receiving country would certainly make a difference, and variations in social and cultural background complicate the issue. The whole problem of measuring the innate ability of different ethnic groups bristles with difficulties. (See Brigham, 1923; Kirkpatrick, 1926; Lorimer and Osborn, 1934.) In the field of internal migration one may note the interesting findings of Klineberg in his study of the northward migration of Negroes in the United States.

The intelligence tests showed no superiority of recent arrivals in the North over those of the same age and sex who were still in the southern cities. There is, on the other hand, very definite evidence that an improved environment, whether it be the southern city as contrasted with the neighboring rural districts, or the northern city as contrasted with the South as a whole, raises the test scores considerably; this rise in intelligence is roughly proportionate to length of residence in the more favorable environment [Klineberg, 1935, p. 59].

We are not in a position to say anything definite about the intelligence differential in international migration.

Secular phases.—Over the last century and a half the record of immigration countries reveals an interesting common pattern, the successive predominance of one ethnic group after another. France, the leading receiving country in Europe, is a good illustration; over the long period three ethnic phases may be identified —Germanic, Latin, and Slav. Up to the middle of the nineteenth century more than half the alien element in France comprised Germans, Swiss, and Belgians. By the middle of the 1920's this group had contracted to 20 per cent, for it had been overshadowed by the rapidly increasing Latin element; by 1913 three out of every four aliens were Italians or Spaniards. After the mid-twenties the Latin wave gave way to the Slav; the number of Polish, Czech, Yugoslav, Greek, and Armenian immigrants rose appreciably. There were signs of even a fourth ethnic element coming rapidly into the picture, i.e., Asians and Africans. Similar phases may be observed in the immigration into Brazil—the successive prominence of Latin, Slav, and Oriental inflows—and the history of the transition from the "old" to the "new" immigration in the United States is well known.

A strong propensity to emigrate showed itself first in the Anglo-Saxon peoples; it then affected other groups—Germanic, Scandinavian, Latin, Slav, and Oriental—in descending order of standard of living. The Anglo-Saxon nations overseas adopted a regime of selective restrictions at the very time when the urge to emigrate had begun to influence millions of people in the poorest countries of the world. A turning point had been reached: there was a profound conflict between the logic of dynamic industrialism and the sense of "self-preservation" in the new countries, their determination to prevent their societies from being swamped by unassimilable elements. If this fear of social fragmentation was less evident in France, it was because that country had long been haunted by the specter of depopulation.

Fluctuations.—Much research has been devoted to three types of fluctuation—seasonal, business cycle, and long swing. According to United States data for the pre-restriction period, the inflow of immigrants for gainful employment was usually at its peak in March, April, and May, while emigration was at its maximum in the later months of the year. The second quarter of the year thus registered a large net inward movement; there would be a less prominent peak early in the autumn and a considerable falling off in November and December; a net outward flow of alien males often took place in December. The extent to which seasonal fluctuations in immigration were in harmony with those in employment varied considerably from industry to industry. (See Jerome, 1926, chap. ix.)

The main facts about business cycle fluctuations in international migration were established by Jerome. Analyzing the inflow into the United States in the fifty years before the Restriction Act of 1924, he found that the migratory process in the short cycle was dominated by conditions in the receiving country: the "pull" was stronger than the "push." For the period beginning in 1889 the conclusion about the relationship between economic activity in the United States and the course of immigration was expressed as follows:

Frequently the turns in migration movement lag behind the corresponding change in employment, indicating that the passage of some time is required before the full effect of a change in employment is felt upon migration. The extent of this lag varies in different cycles, and is also frequently found to vary on the downturn and the upturn of the same cycle. In a few instances the effect of a change in employment conditions is not seen for almost a year afterward, but in other instances the fluctuations in employment and migration appear to be substantially concurrent. The more common lag in the migration fluctuations is from one to five months [Jerome, 1926, pp. 240–41].

Studies on emigration from Italy to the United States, France, and Argentina (Winsemius, 1939) and on the emigration from Scandinavia (A. Jensen, 1931) underline these findings.

An imporant amendment to Jerome's thesis was established by Dorothy Thomas in her examination of Swedish emigration. She observed that ". . . of the two factors, industrial pull to America and agricultural push from Sweden, the former played an overwhelmingly important role in respect to annual fluctuation from the seventies to the end of the emigration era just before the war." But she went on to demonstrate that

. . . cyclical upswings in Sweden were a far more powerful counter-stimulant than is generally recognized. In prosperous years, Swedish industry was able to compete successfully with the lure of America; and the latent agricultural push towards emigration became an active force only when a Swedish industrial depression occurred simultaneously with expanding or prosperous business conditions in the new world [1941, pp. 166–69].

Further knowledge of the dynamics of migration has been gained by concentrating not on the short cycle but on the long swings in international migration which have roughly the same span as the building cycle. Between 1845 and 1913 there were four major upswings and four major downswings in transatlantic migration, and there were corresponding fluctuations in the export of capital from Europe to the receiving countries. The proposition that the United Kingdom and the United States experienced simultaneous business fluctuations (which dominate the analysis of migration and business cycles) is not true when we look at the minor secular fluctuations. From the 1840's to the 1920's the construction cycles in the United Kingdom and the United States were inverse to one another. Transatlantic migration was positively correlated with American building activity. The mechanism of these long swings in migration and investment has been summarized by the present writer:

If we look at the process from the point of view of Great Britain we may describe it in terms of seasons of sowing and harvesting. When Britain was investing heavily in America and migrants from Europe were flocking there, the capital equipment of America grew rapidly and she received a surplus of imports financed by the London market; in this sowing season the British export sector was exceptionally busy, while the rate of capital construction at home tended to languish. In the following phase the inflow of capital and labour and the volume of investment in America slowed down, while her exports increased relatively to imports; this was the harvesting season in which British capital went into home construction, and foreign lending and exports slackened, while the volume of imports of raw materials and foodstuffs expanded. Part of these imports consisted of income on previous loans. When Britain was sowing her rate of economic development was low and that of America was high; when Britain was harvesting, her rate of economic development was high and that of America was low [B. Thomas, 1954, p. 233].

The inverse relation between British and American cycles of home construction ceased when the era of large-scale immigration into the United States came to an end.

Statistical analysis of long swings has brought out the fact that in the early phase of the development of America— up to the Civil War—railway construction (which was a major part of current investment) was preceded by an inflow of population. The driving forces in the Old World, causing the expulsion of millions of Irish and German migrants, were the operative factors: the "push" appears to have had a dominating influence. From the seventies on, however, the direction of lag is reversed, and railway construction precedes immigration. It is important to observe, nevertheless, that throughout the period 1845–1913, with the exception of the 1870's, immigration preceded American building activity. (For an extended account of this lag analysis see B. Thomas, 1954, chaps. vii, x, xi.) The conclusions about the operation of the "pull" factor reached in short-cycle analysis must be revised in the light of the analysis of long swings.

Determinants.–Numerous "facts" have been assembled by various writers purporting to explain the determinants of international migration, but no useful purpose would be served here by presenting a catalogue of them. A mere listing of factors under the heading of "push" and "pull" does not advance the frontiers of knowledge. In certain epochs forces other than economic have certainly had a dominant role in bringing about migrations, and this is true of the twentieth century. Leaving aside forced transfers, we can say that the economic motive has usually been stronger than religious or political motives in inciting people to move. The "facts" of migration as indicated by the statistical record show certain patterns which can best be explored in relation to the behavior of other relevant variables. We can interpret "determinants" in two ways: how the migration mechanism works and why the mechanism begins to work. In trying to answer the first of these questions, we cannot escape the most difficult problems of mutual interdependence; the second leads us into the mysteries of historical causation.

Demographic effects on sending countries.–The demographic significance of emigration arises mainly out of the fact that the incidence of emigration varies sharply from one age group to another. What a heavy outflow entails is vividly brought out in Table 49. In Eire in 1936, about 15 per 100 males aged 10–14, 21 per 100 aged 15–19, 19 per 100 aged 20–24, 10 per 100 aged 25–29, and 5 per 100 aged 30–35 emigrated in the following ten years. For earlier periods in the nineteenth century the rates of outflow were even heavier.

The loss through emigration is most severe in the age group 15–35, and this automatically lowers the number of births. Thus the age group 0–5 becomes smaller than its normal size in the absence of emigration. In view of the fact that school children are affected less by emigration than the population in general, the 0–5 infants, by the time they become aged 10–15, constitute a group which is relatively large. Thus we have the paradoxical result that a country experiencing a high and sustained volume of emigration always has a relatively large number of teen-agers. A self-generating mechanism is at work; fifteen years after the original thinning-out of the 15–35 age group, the number passing into the 15–20 group is abnormally large in relation to the population as a whole.

The change in the age structure of the population is shown by Table 50. The proportion of the population under 45 declined steadily from 1841 to 1951, and in 1951 persons aged 45 and over constituted 30 per cent of the population, compared with 16 per cent in 1941. The average age went up from 24.8 to 32.5 during the period. In Eire's population of 3 million in 1951 there were 117,000 more persons aged 65 and over than there were in the 1841 population of 6.5 million. It is significant, however, that even in this extreme case, the relative change in the economically active population was very small. The operating factors here were mortality and fertility rather than emigration.

In most countries emigration has re-

TABLE 49

EIRE: PERSONS AT EACH CENSUS PER HUNDRED OF THOSE TEN
YEARS YOUNGER AT PREVIOUS CENSUS*

PERIOD	MALES AGE AT BEGINNING OF PERIOD					FEMALES AGE AT BEGINNING OF PERIOD				
	10–14	15–19	20–24	25–29	30–34	10–14	15–19	20–24	25–29	30–34
1841–51.........	59	46	50	49	67	65	47	54	50	71
1851–61.........	65	49	53	57	80	68	48	52	58	82
1861–71.........	70	52	55	59	82	80	56	58	61	85
1871–81.........	73	61	65	66	85	77	62	67	66	87
1881–91.........	71	54	56	67	84	68	55	57	68	86
1891–1901.......	77	61	62	75	86	79	64	65	72	87
1901–11.........	82	67	68	83	87	78	68	66	76	82
1911–26†........	69	59	62	73	78	73	61	69	70	77
1926–36.........	89	78	76	91	91	83	74	77	88	87
1936–46.........	82	75	77	86	90	81	80	84	91	91
1936–46: Decrease due to deaths alone..	2.6	3.7	4.0	4.4	5.0	2.8	3.8	4.3	4.5	5.1
Decrease due to emigration....	15.4	21.3	19.0	9.6	5.0	16.2	16.2	11.7	4.5	3.9

* Source: Eire, Commission on Emigration and Other Population Problems, 1948–54, *Reports* (1955, p. 118).
† Fifteen years younger for the period 1911–26.

TABLE 50

EIRE: AGE DISTRIBUTION OF THE POPULATION, 1841 AND 1951*

PERCENTAGE DISTRIBUTION BY AGE GROUPS

CENSUS YEAR	0–14	15–44	45–64	65 and Over	All Ages	AVERAGE AGE IN YEARS
1841......	38.1	45.9	12.9	3.1	100	24.8
1951......	28.9	41.0	19.4	10.7	100	32.5

* Source: Eire, Commission on Emigration and Other Population Problems, 1948–54, *Reports* (1955, p. 14).

duced the marriage rate. One might expect the removal of so many from the 15–35 age group to make it easier for those left behind to earn a good living and, therefore, to marry. But this has not happened, except perhaps in Italy. The high marriage rate in England need not be considered, since her *net* emigration was not considerable. The experience of Ireland, Sweden, and Scotland, where net emigration was heavy, shows that the marriage rate was affected unfavorably. In Eire the number of married women under the age of 45 per 1,000 of the population in 1930 was 73, compared with 105 in Scotland, 123 in England and Wales, and 145 in the United States. One cannot be certain about the effect on fertility. In Sweden emigration, by taking away the poorest peasants, removed the most fertile; in Ireland, however, the low marriage rate was partly counterbalanced by a large number of children per marriage. With regard to the death rate, a heavy outflow of the best lives from the 15–35 age group may tend to make the mortality in that group higher than it would be otherwise. (On Sweden, see Sundbärg, 1910, pp. 63–67.)

Demographic effects on receiving countries.—Walker's "substitution theory," according to which the addition to numbers through immigration is offset by the depressing effect on the fertility of the native-born, can no longer be accepted. Thompson and Whelpton demonstrated that in any ten-, twenty-, or thirty-year period between 1830 and 1920 the direct increase in the population of the United States due to immigration was greater than the decline of fertility attributable to all causes (Thompson and Whelpton, 1933, pp. 304–7). Immigration may indirectly lower the natural increase of the native-born by promoting industrialization, but it need not do so. It is possible that heavy immigration into urban areas, by diminishing the volume of rural exodus in the receiving country, may cause the fer-

tility of the native population to be higher than it would otherwise be (C. Gini, 1946). Mortara's (1942) exhaustive analysis of the problem led to the conclusion that the migration movements of the last century had hardly any net effect on the course of natural increase of the native populations in the receiving countries. In the major countries of absorption, e.g., the United States and France, heavy immigration came after the natural increase of the native population had begun to fall.

When we consider the rate of growth of the immigrant section in the receiving country, the sex and age composition of the inflow normally promotes a high rate of natural increase. However, the increase depends upon the proportion of the immigration which is permanent. It is not possible to generalize on whether immigrants carry with them into the new country the habits and attitudes regarding fertility which exist in the country of origin. Arnold Rose (1942) found that the birth rate for Italian married couples not separating during migration was higher after they came to the United States than it would have been had they remained in Italy, and on the average 5 to 10 per cent more children survived to any given age in the United States than in Italy. On the other hand, Borrie (1948, p. 126) has shown that New Zealand women in Australia in 1933 had a gross reproduction rate lower than the rate for women in New Zealand. It has been said that there is no evidence that the non-marrying mores of the Irish persist in the second and third generations of Irish-Americans—where there *are* second and third generations! There is little doubt that whatever may be true of the foreign-born themselves, the second and third generations tend to adopt the family-building pattern of their country of adoption.

The empirical evidence on the long-period contribution of immigration to the growth of population may now be summarized. Net immigration into France in the period 1801–1936 has been estimated at 3,960,000, over a third of the increase of 14 million within the 1936 boundaries of France between 1801 and 1936 (Landry, 1945, pp. 513–14). The white population of the United States in 1790 was 3.2 million; allowing for a proportional contribution to persons of mixed parentage, its descendants living in the United States are estimated at 41.3 million in 1920. In the same year the survivors and descendants of immigrants since 1790 numbered about 53.5 million. The net immigration of white persons during this period is estimated at 26.5 million (United Nations, Population Division, 1953*b*, p. 139).

Explanatory Principles

A brief attempt will be made to sketch certain principles which offer an explanation of some of the phenomena of international migration viewed as a historical process over the last century and a half. Amid the maze of empirical data and the diversity of opinion as to the correct interpretation of them, this is not an easy task. We shall begin by drawing attention to an example of contradictory reasoning and by suggesting ways in which opposed points of view may be reconciled.

The interplay of migration and capital movements.—A contradiction is illustrated by the following quotations:

Continued development of non-agricultural industries on a large scale . . . may have the effect of removing the necessity of emigration from a country which was formerly unable, with a primarily agricultural economy, to provide suitable economic opportunities for all its people. . . .

Urbanization and industrialization of the major countries of immigration had the effect of increasing their attraction to immigrants, at least during the first decades of the twentieth century [United Nations, Population Division, 1953*b*, p. 114].

In sending countries industrialization inhibits emigration; in receiving countries industrialization stimulates immigration. This blurred picture can be made a little clearer if we look upon the countries concerned as if they constituted one economy, e.g., the Atlantic economy of the period 1830–1924. We then ask, other things being equal, what geographical redistribution of labor and capital was required in this economy if its rate of economic growth was to be maximized in that period? At the outset in the eastern sector of the economy—the Old World—labor and capital were plentiful, relative to land and natural resources; in the western sector—the New World—labor and capital were scarce, relative to land and natural resources. Given freedom to move and the means of transport, units of the plentiful factors would migrate from east to west. As long as the marginal social net product of labor in the New World was greater than in the Old World, east-west migration of workers would promote the economic efficiency of the Atlantic economy.

This transference did not proceed evenly through time. The highly industrialized creditor country was heavily dependent on the underdeveloped debtor countries for food and raw materials. When industrialization was advancing rapidly in the United States, with the aid of capital and immigrants from Europe, Great Britain was not able to have a big upsurge in her own capital formation at home. In one phase the debtor country pushed ahead with investment in capital equipment, and in the next phase it was the turn of the creditor country to do likewise, aided by a copious flow of imports from the debtor country. Transatlantic migration and the inverse cycles of home investment were necessary conditions for the economic growth of both lender and underdeveloped countries in the nineteenth century. We are now able to reconcile the apparent contradiction referred to above. In the upswing of the migration –foreign-lending cycle the rapid pace of industrialization overseas attracted immigration, and in the downswing of the migration–foreign-lending cycle the rapid pace of industrialization in Europe kept most would-be emigrants at home. There was a long-run community of interest between the sending and receiving countries. (See Brinley Thomas, 1958; 1954, chaps. vii, xi, and xiv.)

In the light of this explanatory principle, it is not possible to accept Jerome's (1926, p. 209) argument that ". . . the net effect of cyclical fluctuations in immigration is to aggravate on the whole the unemployment problem in the United States." Countries of emigration suffered more from unemployment than countries of immigration, and the United States got its severest dose of unemployment a few years after the drastic restrictions on immigration in 1924. In the fifty years ending in 1919–28 the average standard of living of the American people rose threefold; the most rapid rates of advance took place during the years when immigration was heaviest. In its upward phases immigration promoted the growth of investment, income, and employment, and in its downward phases it helped to relieve pressure in the labor market. (See Brinley Thomas, 1955, p. 171.)

We must now turn to a formally valid economic model which proves that in an international economy, under certain conditions, the prices of labor and capital will be equalized even if these factors cannot migrate from one country to another. The goal will be reached through commodity trade. The assumptions required for this result (free trade and free competition, a two-country, two-commodity, two-factor world, no specialization, identical production functions in both countries for the same products, small optimum units in comparison with markets) are extremely re-strictive. (See P. A. Samuelson, 1949; Tinbergen, 1949; I. F. Pearce, 1951–52; P. A. Samuelson, 1951–52.) When more realistic assumptions are made, it can be shown that if total production in the international economy is to be maximized, free trade must be accompanied by international migration of factors of production. Six possible reasons for this conclusion have been advanced by J. E. Meade (1953, pp. 72–73):

Differences in productive atmosphere in the different regions of our union; differences in the scale of production in the different regions; costs of transporting the products between the regions; the complete specializing of certain regions on certain lines of production; the existence of a large number of factors relatively to the number of standardized traded products made in many parts of the union; and marked differences in the technical possibility of substituting one factor for another in the different industries producing traded products.

These conditions were certainly true of the Atlantic economy of 1830–1924. Thus, both the comparative statics approach based on relative factor-proportions and the period analysis of fluctuations provide a logical explanation of the role of migration in the international economy.

Population pressure.—Many of the migrations of history can be explained by the theory of unavoidable population pressure. In the simplest Malthusian model a country is deprived of the fruits of technical improvement by the rapid growth of population. This eventually forces some of the people to seek subsistence in new territories. Given the notion of an optimum population, in the static sense of that size of population at any given time which maximizes real product per head, we may explain migration as transfers from countries above the optimum to countries below the optimum. This may be translated into dynamic terms by defining the optimum as that rate of growth of population which, other things being equal, maximizes the rate of growth of real product per head in a country over a given period of time. Sometimes a country is said to be over-populated if a tolerable level of subsistence cannot be secured without importing food. Finally, there is the notion of a population being so large that if some of it was removed total output would not diminish, the marginal product being negative. This condition, disguised unemployment, existed in several European agricultural countries in the nineteenth century and is today prevalent in China, India, Indonesia, Egypt, and eastern Europe.

It is illuminating to regard international migration as a vast secular process of rural-urban transference induced by the rise in agricultural productivity, which is the indispensable condition of economic growth. The demand for food does not keep pace with the rise in real income per head. If the productivity per person engaged in growing food in a closed community increases at a more rapid rate than food consumption per head of the population, then the proportion of the population engaged in agriculture must decline. It is the richest countries that have the smallest proportion of the population engaged in producing food.

Some of the movements of international migration in the nineteenth century were set off by intolerable pressure of disguised rural unemployment, brought to a head, e.g., in the case of Ireland, by the potato famine of 1846. The extent of the pressure varied from time to time: it might be that twenty years after a phase of an abnormally high birth rate the emigration age groups would be unduly swollen; or a wave of technical progress in agriculture, e.g., in Germany in the 1850's, might create a big pool of surplus labor; or the boomerang effect of agricultural and transport innovations in the New World might render obsolete whole tracts of

the agricultural economy of the Old World. In Schumpeter's (1939, p. 319) striking phrase, "The story of the way in which civilized humanity got and fought cheap bread is the story of American railroads and American machinery."

In the nineteenth century the rural-urban transference required by economic growth took place on a vast international scale because there were no serious racial conflicts between the migrants and the native populations of the countries of new settlement. Corresponding migrations in the twentieth century from the heavily overpopulated countries of Asia to Africa, Oceania, or the Americas are impossible for racial reasons. The elimination of disguised rural unemployment through a rise in agricultural productivity and a transfer of the surplus into manufacturing—the essence of economic growth—has to be enacted for the most part within the boundaries of the underdeveloped countries. This causes the rate of improvement to be much slower than if the process transcended national boundaries.

Theory of immigration.—In interpreting the effects of a flow of immigrants on the receiving country, it is essential to distinguish between the substitution effects and the income or aggregative effects. The arrival of a large number of unskilled workers means competition with native members of that grade of labor, and the relative incomes of the latter will tend to decline. Other grades, e.g., the skilled, professional, and executive, which stand in a complementary relationship to the unskilled, will benefit from the coming of the immigrants. This phenomenon contains an explanation of the change in the occupational character of British immigration to the United States after 1900; the proportion of unskilled fell sharply. Laborers from Britain were finding it very difficult to compete with laborers from southeast Europe. These "new" immigrants were complementary to the native-born skilled grades and bestowed prosperity on them.

The aggregative effects on the national income of the receiving country arise not only from the new inputs of labor but also from new ideas, methods, and techniques which individual immigrants bring with them. The aggregative effect can be very strong if the country is in the stage of increasing return. The experience of the United States up to 1923 shows that, given a high degree of vertical mobility and a potent aggregative effect, it is possible for huge inflows of immigrants to be absorbed without serious friction. (See J. J. Spengler, 1958, for a discussion of the aggregative and substitution approaches.)

To explain why immigration proceeds by fits and starts, we need to invoke the theory of the inflationary process in an open economy: the model could be either that of a demand inflation or of a cost inflation, or perhaps a mixture of both. Why does not a new country go on absorbing immigrants at an even rate? Let us take a simple example. Let the economy have an annual supply of output equal to 100, consumption comprising 90 and investment 10. Let the capital-output ratio be 3:1, and let immigration add 2 per cent per annum to the population. We assume full employment. Consumption goes up by 2 per cent, i.e., from 90 to 91.8; the capital stock of 300 would have to be increased by 2 per cent, i.e., by 6. Thus the aggregate real demand would rise from 100 to 107.8, whereas aggregate real supply would merely go up to 102. This inflaionary gap will be narrowed to the extent that the propensity to work hard, to save, and to abstain from demanding houses is relatively high among the migrants. The excess aggregate demand sucks into the home market products which would otherwise be exported and increases the flow of imported consumption and investment goods; this can be temporarily offset by an import of capi-

tal. But the situation is unstable, and eventually the government has to step in to curb the volume of imports by deflating incomes. At this point immigration falls. Australia ran into a crisis of this kind in 1951–52. (See P. H. Karmel, 1953. For a model of a cost inflation with special reference to Israel see A. P. Lerner, 1957.)

NEXT STEPS IN RESEARCH

Data

The prospects of empirical analysis will be much improved if the most glaring deficiencies of the primary data are eliminated in the developed countries and if the lessons of the past are borne in mind where new records are introduced in underdeveloped countries. The valuable work already done on migration statistics by the Population Commission of the United Nations needs to be extended; at the same time, much will depend on the initiative of those who seek to reform the statistics in each country. There is a powerful case for setting up an International Migration Institute which could concentrate the necessary expertise on the solution of the more urgent problems of data, methods, and analysis.

There are several tasks concerning countries with a long tradition of migration records. For example, what is the most effective way of recording the movements of international migrants by air? Since statistics of immigration are easier to collect and more accurate than statistics of emigration, the former should be the main object of reform. The activities of the United Nations Sub-Commission on Statistical Sampling should be expanded so that continuing sampling procedures can be organized in countries where conditions are favorable.

Second, the difficulties of making data consistent are so enormous that it would be a great mistake to be overambitious. Lack of comparability arises from heterogeneous methods of collecting national data, and it would be naïve to expect sovereign states suddenly to change their nature. It is discouraging but not surprising that migration statistics are no better today than they were twenty-five years ago. We shall not achieve an improvement in them by crying for the moon. It is necessary, first, to recognize that different types of questions must be asked in different countries if comparable information about a given datum is to be elicited, and it is the duty of scholars to show precisely what variety of questions is appropriate in each case. To try to force uniform questions on national authorities is not only fruitless but harmful. A uniform end-product can come only through a variety of means. Furthermore, it is the duty of scholars to draw up a *short* list of really important topics for which comparable data are indispensable. There is no limit to the curiosity of the academic mind, but there is a stern limit to what we can expect government departments to do for us. To present them with a vast shopping list (including a lot of luxuries which it would be very nice to have) is simply to invite the cold shoulder. We should bear in mind that statistics should be fruitful as well as illuminating. An organization such as the Intergovernmental Committee for European Migration faces operational problems which would be more easily solved if an adequate statistical service existed. A general reform of statistics would be achieved sooner if the usefulness of proposed changes as an aid in the execution of policy were first demonstrated. The academic battalions in Great Britain have waged a long campaign for better economic statistics without much success, but in April, 1956, the Chancellor of the Exchequer was stung into action by his discovery that, in his now famous words, "we are always, as it were, looking up a train in last year's Bradshaw."

Third, statisticians specializing in demography cannot escape some of the blame for the well-known inadequacies of migration time series. Every worker in this field has recognized the tremendous service performed by the International Labor Office and the National Bureau of Economic Research in carrying out the all-embracing survey, *International Migrations,* in 1929–31. Here was a unique inventory which should have inspired a rich advance in analysis. The historical series for many countries, so laboriously unearthed, needed to be critically appraised and subjected to various tests, particularly in the light of census information. But this vital task of adjustment was neglected or postponed. The United States possessed one of the oldest time series on immigration, but it was not until 1954 that the work of checking and reconciling immigration and emigration data with census data on resident foreign-born was carried out (it has been admirably done in Kuznets and Rubin, 1954). It would be easy to draw up a long list of needed jobs of adjustment, checking, and reconciliation in several departments of migration statistics in a host of countries. The aim should be to assemble, for those countries whose basic data warrant it, a comprehensive set of time series incorporating the best checks available. Few countries are as fortunate as Sweden in possessing a long series of unusually reliable population statistics. The recent compilation, *Historisk Statistik för Sverige, Befolkning, 1720–1850* ("Historical Statistics of Sweden, Population, 1720–1850"), published by the Central Statistical Office, Stockholm, is a model which could with variations be emulated in other countries.

Concepts and Methods

The words "overpopulated" and "underpopulated" are apt to mean a variety of things. When employed in a scientific argument they are usually part of the vocabulary of the optimum theory of population, a branch of comparative statics which flourished in the period between Wicksell and Keynes. In recent years there has been a remarkable revival of interest in the theory of economic growth, brought about partly by the Keynesian impetus and partly by the change in the type of problem which dominates the contemporary scene (cf. Harrod, 1948; Kuznets, 1956; W. Arthur Lewis, 1955; Joan Robinson, 1956).

The dynamic point of view which was implicit in the classical treatment of population is being recaptured. A valuable contribution to methodology has recently been made by Leibenstein in *A Theory of Economic-Demographic Development* (1954). He reaches the conclusion that

. . . optimum theory has nothing to say about the following: (1) the nature of the roles and the role distributions pertinent to the determination of population size; (2) the fields of action that can conceivably pertain to the process of demographic and economic changes; (3) the role of values in the determination of population size; (4) the choice distributions or behavior equations that lead to different population sizes. In short, existing optimum population theory says nothing about the determinants of population growth or decline, and hence the theory can say little that is of interest for policy purposes except when population happens to be the desired size [p. 188].

One of the most pressing tasks of the theorist is to rectify this state of affairs; intensive work on models of economic growth is required in order to attain concepts of "optima" in dynamic terms. Until this is done, much of the analysis of the economic implications of emigration and immigration will lack substance. At the World Population Conference in Rome in 1954 it was unfortunate that the four sessions devoted to international and internal migration showed hardly any connection with the theme of "population in relation to capital formation, investment, and employment" discussed

in later sessions. Migration was treated too much as a demographic phenomenon divorced from the process of economic growth; for example, hardly any attention was given to the interdependence of international capital and migration movements.

Current developments in analytical economics will have considerable effect on population study. The trend of thinking is well brought out in the following words of Kaldor (1954, p. 65):

. . . the very fact that different human societies experience such very different rates of growth—in fact, differences in rates of growth in different ages or in different parts of the world in the same age are one of the most striking facts of history—in itself provides powerful support for the view that technical invention and population growth, the two factors underlying the trend, are not like the weather or the movement of the seasons, that go on quite independently of human action, but are very much the outcome of social processes. The growth in population, in particular, is as much the consequence of economic growth as the condition of it.

There is abundant scope for the construction of models of growth in an *international* economy, with rates of change in population and in inflows or outflows of migrants as induced factors. It may be that as the economist reoccupies territory which has long been the preserve of sociologists and demographers, the gain in precision will be offset by a loss of realism. The economist is concerned only with his particular aspect of a many-sided situation; but, in view of past neglect, it is fair to say that we must now turn to economic dynamics if we are to fill the most important gap in our fundamental concepts.

Lines of Research

There are a number of fascinating problems arising out of the era of unrestricted movement which await analysis. Such research is far from being of mere academic interest, as Kuznets and Rubin (1954, p. vi) have said in relation to the United States:

An understanding of these past processes and of the implications of the decisions made about them is of great *practical* importance, today perhaps more than ever. Decisions about immigration, like those about the public domain, internal improvements, industrial organization, and protection, were among the basic secular decisions —basic in that they were far-reaching, and secular in that they were important for the long-term development of the economy. Although such decisions cannot be reversed easily, and often cannot be reversed at all, retrospective understanding of their consequences may forestall haste in future decisions and stimulate foresight where it is obscured by overconcern with the apparently pressing problems of the day. . . . Even a hasty survey of the data in this field and a glance at the implications of some of the findings reveal the vast need for a methodical quantitative analysis of this aspect of the country's past growth.

The following are some aspects of the migration process in the era of unrestricted movement which would well repay intensive analysis:

a) A re-examination of the long-period strength of the "push" factor in Europe, 1820–1920, with special reference to different phases of the period and different areas within the continent.

b) A re-examination of the long-period strength of the "pull" factor in America, 1820–1920, with special reference to different phases in the evolution of the American economy.

c) The mechanism of the long swings in transatlantic migration related to long swings in real investment in the United Kingdom and the United States. The bearing of migration on the determinants of the inverse relation between building cycles in the United States and the United Kingdom. A detailed lag analysis of the relation between migration and house construction in various countries.

d) The interaction between immigra-

tion and capital formation in the United States, using Kuznets' distinction between "population-sensitive" capital formation (e.g., residential construction and capital expenditure by railroads) and "other" capital formation. Testing the hypothesis of an inverse correlation between these two categories of capital formation.

e) Statistical verification of Kuznets' (1955, p. 17) speculation regarding a self-perpetuating long swing in population and product in the United States up to the 1920's.

Given the long swings in additions to per capita flow of goods to consumers, the result —with some lag—will be long swings first in the net migration balance and then in the natural increase, yielding swings in total population growth. The latter then induce, with some lag, similar swings in population-sensitive capital formation—residential housing and fixed capital expenditures by railroads. The latter cause inverted long swings in "other" capital formation, and in changes in additions to per capita flow of goods to consumers. The swings in the latter then start another long swing in the net migration balance and in natural increase, and so on.

f) Explanation of the factors responsible for the cessation of the mechanism outlined in (*e*).

g) A detailed sector analysis of the progress of mechanization, technical innovation, and capital-output ratios in the United States, 1890–1913, with special reference to the inflow of immigrant labor. To what extent, if any, did immigration exercise a causal influence on technical progess?

h) An analysis of the timing of building cycles and migration in European countries, e.g., Germany, Sweden, and France, and in overseas countries other than the United States. The results to be related to the conclusions under (*c*).

i) The interaction of emigration and internal migration in various countries at different times.

j) The interaction of immigration and internal migration in various countries at different times.

k) The effect of immigration on birth rates and death rates in different social and ethnic groups, e.g., an explanation of the fact that in the United States there was an *inverse* relation between the long swings in net increase of non-white population and in those in net increase of both native white and foreign-born. Test the hypothesis that the economic opportunities of Negroes varied inversely with the volume of alien immigration (Brinley Thomas, 1954, pp. 130–33).

l) The primary and secondary demographic consequences of emigration in sending countries.

A thorough analysis of the economic-demographic mechanism of mass emigration—the case of Ireland:

m) Migration and changes in social stratification.

n) The effect of declining rates of natural increase on the propensity to emigrate.

o) Historical inquiry into international flows of emigrants' remittances, and a consideration of the causal influence of these flows on the course of migration.

p) A re-examination of the existing body of generalizations on migration and business cycles. Did international migration act as a stabilizer or a destabilizer?

q) A thorough analysis of the economic and demographic consequences of the interwar restrictions on immigration.

The following are some of the leading problems of contemporary migration:

a) The determinants of the pace of immigration in Latin-American countries.

b) Private and public capital flows since 1945 in relation to migration movements.

c) Projections of the rate of increase of immigrant groups in multiracial societies.

d) Reactions of migration restrictions

on interregional migration in Asian countries.

e) Demographic consequences of forced population transfers in Europe and Asia.

f) Immigration as a factor in inflationary pressure.

g) What are the similarities and differences between waves of immigration at the present time in, say, Australia, Canada, or Brazil and nineteenth-century waves of immigration?

h) Migration and the dependency ratios of various countries.

i) Problems of capital requirements in relation to migration in various countries.

j) The implications of the population upsurge in rich countries, with particular reference to future migration trends.

k) Measurement of the beneficial effects in overpopulated countries of the homeward flow of emigrants' remittances, e.g., Italy and Greece.

l) Critical examination of migration projections and estimates of emigration potential in sending countries. Future effects of postwar increase in rates of natural increase.

m) Quantitative estimates of "multiplier" effects of various rates of immigration.

SELECTED BIBLIOGRAPHY

ABBOTT, E. (ed.). 1926. *Historical Aspects of the Immigration Problem: Select Documents.* Chicago: University of Chicago Press.

ABRAMOVITZ, M. 1952. "Economics of Growth," in *A Survey of Contemporary Economics,* ed. B. F. HALEY, Vol. II. Homewood, Ill.: Richard D. Irwin, Inc.

BERTHOFF, R. T. 1953. *British Immigrants in Industrial America 1790–1950.* Cambridge: Harvard University Press.

BORRIE, W. D. 1948. *Population Trends and Policies.* Sydney: Australian Publishing Co.

———. 1949. *Immigration: Australia's Problems and Prospects.* Sydney: Angus & Robertson.

——. 1954. *Italians and Germans in Australia: A Study in Assimilation.* Melbourne: F. W. Cheshire for the Australian National University.

——. 1955. "Australia," in *The Positive Contribution by Immigrants.* ("Population and Culture Series.") Paris: UNESCO.

BOURGEOIS-PICHAT, J. 1949. "Migrations et balance de comptes," *Population* (France), IV, 417–32.

BRIGHAM, C. C. 1923. *A Study of American Intelligence.* Princeton.

BUNLE, H. 1931. "Migratory Movements between France and Foreign Lands," in *International Migrations,* ed. W. F. WILLCOX, Vol. II. New York: National Bureau of Economic Research.

——. 1943. *Mouvements migratoires entre la France et l'étranger.* ("Études démographiques," No. 4, Service National de Statistique.) Paris: Imprimerie Nationale.

BURGDÖRFER, F. 1931. "Migration across the Frontiers of Germany," in *International Migrations,* ed. W. F. WILLCOX, Vol. II. New York: National Bureau of Economic Research.

BURTON, H. 1933. "Historical Survey of Immigration and Immigration Policy," in *The Peopling of Australia,* ed. F. W. EGGLESTON, Vol. II. ("Pacific Relations Series.") Melbourne.

CARPENTER, N. 1927. *Immigrants and Their Children, 1920.* (Census Monographs, No. VII.) Washington, D.C.: Government Printing Office.

CARR-SAUNDERS, A. M. 1936. *World Population.* Oxford: Clarendon Press.

CARRIER, N. H., and JEFFERY, J. R. 1953. *External Migration: A Study of the Available Statistics, 1815–1950.* (General Register Office, "Studies on Medical and Population Subjects," No. 6.) London: H.M. Stationery Office.

CARROTHERS, W. A. 1929. *Emigration from the British Isles.* London.

CHEN TA. 1940. *Emigrant Communities in South China.* New York: Institute of Pacific Relations.

CITROEN, H. A. 1948. *Les Migrations internationales: Un problème économique et sociale.* Paris: Librairie de Médicis.

CLARK, C. 1942. *The Economics of 1960.* New York: Macmillan.

COATS, R. H., and MACLEAN, M. C. 1943. *The American-Born in Canada.* Toronto: Ryerson Press.

COHN, S. S. 1934. *Die Theorie des Bevölkerungsoptimums.* Marburg.

CONNELL, K. H. 1950. *The Population of Ireland, 1750–1845.* Oxford: Clarendon Press.

CUNNINGHAM, W. 1897. *Alien Emigrants to England.* London.

DAVIE, M. R. 1936. *World Immigration.* New York: Macmillan.

DAVIS, K. 1947. "Future Migration into Latin America," *Milbank Memorial Fund Quarterly,* XXV, 44–62.

——. 1951. *The Population of India and Pakistan.* Princeton: Princeton University Press.

DAVIS, M. R. 1931. "Critique of Official United States Immigration Statistics," in *International Migrations,* ed. W. F. WILLCOX, Vol. II, Appendix 2. New York: National Bureau of Economic Research.

DOMAR, E. D. 1947. "Expansion and Employment," *American Economic Review,* Vol. XXXVII.

DOUGLAS, P. H. 1919. "Is the New Immigration More Unskilled Than the Old?" *Publications of the American Statistical Association,* N.S. XVI, No. 125, 393–403.

DUBLIN, L. I., and LOTKA, A. J. 1946. *The Money Value of a Man.* Rev. ed. New York: Ronald Press.

DURAND, J. D. 1953. "Population Structure as a Factor in Manpower and Dependency Problems of Under-developed Countries," *Population Bulletin of the United Nations,* No. 3.

ECKLER, A. R., and ZLOTNICK, J. 1949. "Immigration and the Labor Force," *Annals of the American Academy of Political and Social Science,* No. 262, pp. 92–101.

EIRE, COMMISSION ON EMIGRATION AND OTHER POPULATION PROBLEMS, 1948–54. 1955. *Majority and Minority Reports.* Dublin: Stationery Office.

ERICKSON, C. 1949. "The Encouragement of Emigration by British Trade Unions, 1850–1900," *Population Studies,* III, 248–73.

——. 1957. *American Industry and the European Immigrant, 1860–1885.* Cambridge: Harvard University Press.

FERENCZI, I. 1929. "A Historical Study of Migration Statistics," *International Labour Review*, XX, 356–84.

FOERSTER, R. F. 1919. *The Italian Emigration of Our Times*. Cambridge, Mass.: Harvard University Press.

FORSYTH, W. D. 1942. *The Myth of Open Spaces*. London: Oxford University Press.

GINI, C. 1940. "Europa und Amerika: Zwei Welten," *Weltwirtschaftliches Archiv*, LII, 1–37.

———. 1946. "Los efectos démográficos de las migraciones internacionales," *Revista internacional de sociologia*, IV, 351–88.

GOLDSMITH, R. W. 1950. "Measuring National Wealth in a System of Social Accounting," in *Studies in Income and Wealth*, Vol. XII. New York: National Bureau of Economic Research.

GOTTLIEB, M. 1945. "The Theory of Optimum Population for a Closed Economy," *Journal of Political Economy*, LIII, 289–316. Reprinted in *Population Theory and Policy*, ed. J. J. SPENGLER and O. D. DUNCAN. Glencoe, Ill.: Free Press, 1956.

HAMPEL, GUSTAV. 1957. *Einwanderungsgesetzgebung und innereuropäische Wanderung*. Kiel: Institut für Weltwirtschaft an der Universität Kiel.

HANSEN, M. L. 1940. *The Atlantic Migration 1607–1860*. Cambridge, Mass.: Harvard University Press.

HARROD, R. F. 1948. *Towards a Dynamic Economics*. London: Macmillan.

HOLBORN, LOUISE W. 1956. *The International Refugee Organization: A Specialized Agency of the United Nations: Its History and Work, 1946–52*. Oxford University Press.

HUTCHINSON, E. P. 1956. *Immigrants and their Children, 1850–1950*. New York: John Wiley & Sons.

ICHIHASHI, Y. 1931. "International Migration of the Japanese," in *International Migrations*, ed. W. F. WILLCOX, Vol. II. New York: National Bureau of Economic Research.

INTERNATIONAL LABOR OFFICE. 1922. *Methods of Compiling Emigration and Immigration Statistics*. Geneva.

———. 1932. *Statistics of Migration: Definitions, Methods, Classifications*. (Ser. N, No. 18.) Geneva.

———. 1936. *World Statistics of Aliens*. (Ser. O, No. 6.) Geneva.

———. 1954. *Analysis of the Immigration Laws and Regulations of Selected Countries*. Geneva.

ISAAC, J. 1947. *Economics of Migration*. New York: Oxford University Press.

———. 1954. *British Post-war Migration*. Cambridge: Cambridge University Press.

———, and BELD, C. A. VAN DEN. 1953. *The Effect of European Migration on the Economy of Sending and Receiving Countries: An Interim Report*. The Hague: Research Group for European Migration Problems.

JENKS, J. W., and LAUCK, W. J. 1912. *The Immigration Problem*. New York: Funk & Wagnalls.

JENSEN, A. 1931. "Migration Statistics of Denmark, Norway, and Sweden," in *International Migrations*, ed. W. F. WILLCOX, Vol. II. New York: National Bureau of Economic Research.

JEROME, H. 1926. *Migration and Business Cycles*. New York: National Bureau of Economic Research.

JOHNSON, S. C. 1913. *Emigration from the United Kingdom to North America*. London.

KALDOR, N. 1954. "The Relation of Economic Growth and Cyclical Fluctuations," *Economic Journal*, LXIV, 53–71.

KARMEL, P. H. 1953. "The Economic Effects of Immigration," in *Australia and the Migrant*, by H. E. HOLT et al. Sydney: Angus & Robertson.

KEYFITZ, N. 1950. "The Growth of the Canadian Population," *Population Studies*, IV, 47–63.

KIRK, D. 1946. *Europe's Population in the Inter-war Years*. Geneva: League of Nations.

———, and HUYCK, E. 1954. "Overseas Migration from Europe since World War II," *American Sociological Review*, XIX, 447–56.

KIRKPATRICK, C. 1926. *Intelligence and Immigration*. ("Mental Measurement Monographs," Ser. 2.) Baltimore: Williams & Wilkins.

KLINEBERG, O. 1935. *Negro Intelligence and Selective Migration*. New York: Columbia University Press.

KULISCHER, E. M. 1948. *Europe on the Move: War and Population Changes, 1917–47.* New York: Columbia University Press.

KUZNETS, S. 1955. "Long Swings in the Growth of Population and of Related Economic Variables." Unpublished manuscript.

———. 1956. *Toward a Theory of Economic Growth.* Baltimore: Johns Hopkins Press.

———, and RUBIN, E. 1954. *Immigration and the Foreign Born.* (Occasional Paper 46.) New York: National Bureau of Economic Research.

LANDRY, A. 1945. *Traité de démographie.* Paris: Payot.

LEIBENSTEIN, H. 1954. *A Theory of Economic-demographic Development.* Princeton: Princeton University Press.

LERNER, A. P. 1958. "Immigration, Capital Formation, and Inflationary Pressure," in *Economics of International Migration,* ed. B. Thomas. London: Macmillan.

LEWIS, W. A. 1955. *The Theory of Economic Growth.* London: Allen & Unwin.

LÖSCH, A. 1936. *Bevölkerungswellen und Wechsellagen.* Jena: Gustav Fischer.

LORIMER, F., and OSBORN, F. 1934. *Dynamics of Population.* New York: Macmillan.

MADGWICK, R. B. 1937. *Immigration into Eastern Australia 1788–1851.* London: Longmans.

MAUCO, G. 1932. *Les étrangers en France.* Paris: A. Colin.

MEADE, J. E. 1953. *Problems of Economic Union.* London.

MORTARA, G. 1942. "A Contribution to the Study of the Influence of Immigration on the Birth Rate," *Revista brasileira de estatística,* III, 575–84.

PAN CHIA-LIN. 1955. "Effects of Recent and Possible Future Migration on the Population of Argentina, Brazil, Italy, and India," *Proceedings of the World Population Conference, 1954,* Vol. II. New York: United Nations.

PEARCE, I. F. 1951–52. "The Factor-Price Equalization Myth," *Review of Economic Studies,* No. 49.

RAVNHOLT, H. 1938. "A Quantitative Concept of the International Mobility of Population and Its Application to Certain Countries in the Period 1851–1935," in *Les comptes-rendus du Congrès International de la Population,* Vol. I. Paris: Hermann & Co.

ROBINSON, JOAN. 1956. *The Accumulation of Capital.* London.

ROSE, A. M. 1942. "A Research Note on the Influence of Immigration on the Birth Rate," *American Journal of Sociology,* XLVII, 614–21.

RUBIN, E. 1947. "Immigration and Population Trends in the United States, 1900–1940," *American Journal of Economics and Sociology,* Vol. VI, No. 3.

SAMUELSON, P. A. 1949. "International Factor-Price Equalisation Once Again," *Economic Journal,* LVIII, 181–97.

———. 1951–52. "A Comment on Factor Price Equalization," *Review of Economic Studies,* No. 49.

SAUVY, A. 1952. *Théorie générale de la population,* Vol. I. Paris: Presses Universitaires de France.

SCHUMPETER, J. A. 1939. *Business Cycles: A Theoretical, Historical, and Statistical Analysis of the Capitalist Process,* Vol. I. New York: McGraw-Hill.

SKAUG, A. 1937. *Memorandum on Fluctuations in Migration from Norway since 1900, Compared with Other Countries, and Causes of These Fluctuations.* (Norwegian Memorandum No. 1.) Paris: International Institute of Intellectual Co-operation.

SPENGLER, J. J. 1949. "Theories of Socio-economic Growth," in *Problems in the Study of Economic Growth.* New York: National Bureau of Economic Research.

———. 1958. "On the Effects Produced in Immigration-receiving Countries by Pre-1939 Immigration," in *Economics of International Migration,* ed. B. THOMAS. London: Macmillan.

SUNDBÄRG, G. 1907. *Bevölkerungsstatistik Schwedens, 1750–1900.* Stockholm.

———. 1910. *Emigrationsutredningen.* Vol. IV: *Utvandringsstatistik.* ("Emigration Statistics.") Stockholm.

SWEDEN, ROYAL COMMISSION ON EMIGRATION. 1913. *Emigrationsutredningen: Betänkande.* ("Report of the Royal Commission on Emigration.") Stockholm.

———, CENTRAL STATISTICAL OFFICE. 1955. *Historisk Statistik för Sverige: Befolk-*

ning 1720–1950. ("Historical Statistics of Sweden: Population 1720–1950.") Stockholm.

TAEUBER, IRENE B. 1947. "Migration and the Population Potential of Monsoon Asia," *Milbank Memorial Fund Quarterly,* XXV, 21–43.

THOMAS, B. 1954. *Migration and Economic Growth.* Cambridge: Cambridge University Press.

———. 1955. "The Economic Aspect," in *The Positive Contribution by Immigrants.* ("Population and Culture Series.") Paris: UNESCO.

———. 1956. "International Movements of Capital and Labour Since 1945," *International Labour Review,* LXXIV, 225–38.

———. 1958. "Migration and International Investment," in *Economics of International Migration,* ed. B. THOMAS. London: Macmillan.

THOMAS, DOROTHY S. 1941. *Social and Economic Aspects of Swedish Population Movements, 1750–1933.* New York: Macmillan.

THOMPSON, W. S., and WHELPTON, P. K. 1933. *Population Trends in the United States.* New York: McGraw-Hill.

TINBERGEN, J. 1949. "The Equalization of Factor Prices between Free-trade Areas," *Metroeconomica.*

TRUESDELL, L. 1943. *The Canadian-born in the United States.* New Haven: Yale University Press.

UNITED KINGDOM. 1917. *Final Report of the Dominions Royal Commission.* (Cd. 8462.)

———. 1932. *Report of the Committee on Empire Migration.* (Cmd. 4075.)

———. 1949. *Report of the Royal Commission on Population.* (Cmd. 7695.) London: H. M. Stationery Office.

———. 1950a. *Papers of the Royal Commission on Population.* Vol. II: *Reports and Selected Papers of the Statistics Comitee.* London: H. M. Stationery Office.

———. 1950b. *Papers of the Royal Commission on Population.* Vol. III: *Report of the Economics Committee.* London: H. M. Stationery Office.

———. 1954–57. *Reports of Oversea Migration Board,* July, 1954 (Cmd. 9261);

August, 1956 (Cmd. 9835); December, 1957 (Cmd. 336).

UNITED NATIONS, DEPARTMENT OF SOCIAL AND ECONOMIC AFFAIRS. 1955a. "Summary Report." *Procedings of the World Population Conference, 1954.* New York: United Nations.

———. 1955b. *Proceedings of the World Population Conference, 1954,* Vol. II. New York: United Nations.

UNITED NATIONS, POPULATION DIVISION. 1949. *Problems of Migration Statistics.* ("Population Studies," No. 5.) Lake Success, N. Y.: United Nations.

———. 1951–53. *Population Bulletin,* Nos. 1–3. New York: United Nations.

———. 1953a. *International Research on Migration.* ("Miscellaneous Series," No. 18.) New York: United Nations.

———. 1953b. *The Determinants and Consequences of Population Trends.* ("Population Studies," No. 17.) New York: United Nations.

———. 1954. *Elements of Immigration Policy.* ("Miscellaneous Series," No. 19.) New York: United Nations.

UNITED NATIONS, STATISTICAL OFFICE. 1953. *International Migration Statistics.* ("Statistical Papers," Ser. M, No. 20.) New York: United Nations.

UNITED STATES, DEPARTMENT OF COMMERCE, BUREAU OF THE CENSUS. 1949. *Historical Statistics of the United States, 1789–1945.* Washington, D.C.: Government Printing Office.

———, DEPARTMENT OF JUSTICE. 1943 ff. "Annual Reports of the Immigration and Naturalization Service." Washington, D.C.: Department of Justice.

UNITED STATES SENATE. 1901. *Reports of the Industrial Commission,* Vol. XV. Washington.

———. 1902. *Final Report of the Industrial Commission,* Vol. XIX. Washington.

———, SIXTY-FIRST CONGRESS. 1911–12a. *Abstract of Reports of the Immigration Commission,* Vol. I, Document No. 747. Washington, D.C.: Government Printing Office.

———. 1911–12b. *Statistical Review of Immigration, 1820–1910: Report of the Immigration Commission,* Vol. III, Document No. 756. Washington, D.C.: Government Printing Office.

WALKER, F. A. 1891. "Immigration and Degradation," *Forum*, XI, 634–44.

WANDER, H. 1951. "Die Bedeutung der Auswanderung für die Lösung europäischer Fluchtlings- und Bevölkerungsprobleme," in *Kieler Studien*, No. 15.

WILLCOX, W. F. 1931*a*. "Immigration into the United States," *International Migrations*, ed. W. F. WILLCOX, Vol. II. New York: National Bureau of Economic Research.

———. (ed.). 1931*b*. *International Migrations*, Vol. II. New York: National Bureau of Economic Research.

WINSEMIUS, A. 1939. *Economische Aspecten der internationale Migratie*. (Netherlands Institute for Economic Research, Publication 29.) Haarlem: F. Bohn.

23. Population Estimates and Projections

JOHN V. GRAUMAN

THE FIELD OF POPULATION ESTIMATES

Definition and Importance of the Field

It might be said that knowledge of facts is the body of science and ability to predict its ultimate aim. Facts and their relationships are subject to definition, observation, and quantification. Assuming that the system of factual relationships is complete, prediction results from their synthesis; the validity of predictions is verifiable only by observation *post factum*.

The purpose of estimates is to provide quantification of facts not secured by accepted methods of measurement. A projection is a synthesis of factual relationships against some background; if the system of facts is sufficiently self-contained and if the background is the future, it is a prediction.

In demography, estimating and projection methods are so closely intertwined that together they form one field of scientific endeavor. In defining this field, we shall first regard estimates and projections separately. They will be considered jointly in the remainder of this report.

It is merely conventional to regard certain methods of quantification as scientific "measurement." In the physical sciences, the standards of acceptable mensuration are high in objectivity and precision; "estimates," i.e., other quantifications, are usually less objective or precise. Yet, even in physics, accurate measurement is subject to interferences; when these are taken into account, we arrive in an area in which measurement and estimation overlap.

Among interferences with rigorous measurement may be listed: (a) inadequacy of the observer's perception; (b) defects of the measuring instrument; (c) extraneous disturbing factors (e.g., humidity, temperature); (d) time, if observation does not coincide exactly with some occurrence; and (e) the disturbance introduced by the fact of observation itself. Usually slight, these interferences are sometimes appreciable, requiring some modification of the original "authentic" record. After adjustment, interpretation of the record may be more accurate and perhaps more objective than the record itself. But it is unclear whether a quantity so established is a measurement or an estimate.

This area of overlap is much wider in the social sciences. For example, economic index numbers are a measuring instrument of admitted structural weakness. In an opinion survey, the interview itself tends to disturb the facts. Often there is doubt whether the definition of facts to be measured is relevant. Finally, conventions as to what constitutes acceptable measurement are still in process of being formed.

Between such extremes, demography is in a middle position. Censuses and vital registers, despite recognized imperfections, are measuring devices of long standing. More recently, scientific sampling methods have gained prestige; when certain criteria (yet to be specified) are met, they may likewise come to attain the status of "measurements" rather than "estimates." But known imperfections of the measurements give rise to a large area of adjustment for errors. This area, where measured quantities are subject to reinterpretation, is already in the province of population estimates.

But the field of population estimates derives most of its scope from the fact that accepted measurement cannot be performed at every time and for every detail required by demographic analysis. Frequent, detailed, and accurate censuses are costly, and the collection of all facts pertinent to vital events meets with formidable administrative obstacles. Demographic information would have to remain very spotty indeed were it not possible to fill the gaps by means of estimates. In addition, useful estimates can often be made for places and times where conventional measurement is not yet possible.

Projections into the future can be predictions if the system of facts is sufficiently comprehensive. The ideal of a completely self-contained system of facts is attained in mathematics, where the assumption is implicit that no factors other than those defined enter the system. When a mathematical equation is solved, prediction is reduced to a logical identity.

A physical experiment is perfect if factors extraneous to some system are successfully excluded. Prediction can then be verified. If the predicted result does not appear, either the system of facts or the experimental conditions have been imperfect. Failure of an experiment, however, is no less instructive than its success. Failure can often lead to discovery of new facts or relationships previously left out of account.

In the social field, experimental conditions cannot be produced at will.

This circumstance precludes verification of a prediction in which only a limited number of factors are considered. But the number of possibly relevant factors is too great for human powers of conception. Prediction, then, is confined to systems in which only a manageable number of factors are included. It should, if possible, comprise a selection of those facts whose relevance is greatest. At the time when the prediction is made, the actual relevance of the selection of facts is in doubt; only the course of later events can prove whether a relevant choice has been made.

Useful demographic projections are often made for purposes other than prediction. "Conditional" projections reveal, like mathematical equations, the implications of a deliberately limited system of facts. Forward projections from a date in the past and reversed projections into the past are important aids in a variety of estimating procedures. But the usefulness of theoretical projections, however great, does not constitute an alibi where the public has been led to believe that a projection had been intended as a forecast.

According to popular understanding, scientific endeavors are warranted if they facilitate prediction. This applies also to demography where it is esteemed as a science. Disappointment with a population forecast which has "failed" is not decreased if the position is taken that social projections are "conditional" only. On the other hand, despite possible apparent "failure," the prediction will be appreciated where the divergence of events from prediction can be taken as positive evidence that new circumstances have arisen which give just cause for surprise.

Popular understanding of the business of weather forecasting seems to meet this condition. The public believes that forecasts seldom fail without "good" reason. Discovery of "good" reason for failure is believed to add to the stock of knowledge and to strengthen forecasting ability. The elements surrounding a population prospect cannot be yet as acceptably itemized as those which condition the weather.

Ramifications of the Field

In older textbooks, now "classic," the field of population estimates is subdivided into "intercensal" and "postcensal" estimates. This twofold division is still relevant today where censuses are taken periodically and provide the best possible measures of population size for the given dates. The division continues to be useful, since it facilitates clear distinction of estimates with varying degrees of definiteness.

Under the stated conditions, "intercensal" estimates are definite. Censuses, once taken, can no longer be improved upon. If estimates for the intercensal years are made with best available methods and made to agree with results of the preceding as well as the following census, no further improvement of the estimates appears possible.

"Postcensal" estimates vary in definiteness. When final results of noncensal information, if any (data on births, deaths, and migration), are utilized, the estimates will stand until a new census makes it possible, by one modification, to transform them into "intercensal" estimates. Estimates for very recent dates are "provisional" when extrapolation still has to be made pending the compilation of final data on births, deaths, and migration. The same type of estimate is "tentative" when the extrapolation is extended to a near date in the future. The definiteness of the latter resides in the possibility of unusual future events which, had they occurred in the recent past, would presumably have been taken into account even in a "provisional" current estimate.

The distinction between "intercensal" and "postcensal" estimates is standard administrative practice in many countries. The assumption that censuses, taken periodically, provide the most accurate bench marks of population size—though slightly incorrect—is of great administrative convenience. But there are many situations where the distinction is less relevant. More important than this, it has become inadequate as an outline of the entire field of population estimates in its present state of expansion.

The irrelevance of the "classic" twofold division of the field is obvious in countries where no censuses have been taken, where censuses are sporadic, where census results are reinterpreted after reappraisal of the census performance, and where population is measured by such diverse means as continuous population registers, annual lists of taxable households, sample enumerations, or the revenue of the salt tax.

The complexity of modern government and the modern approach to economic and social problems have heightened interest in a variety of population features other than mere size. It has become important to know a population's composition by sex, age, marital status, economic characteristics, urban and rural residence, and other features or cross-classifications, for various dates in the past, present, and presumable future. Births, deaths, and migration facts also require detailed examination with respect to various characteristics on which official statistics cannot inform us promptly, if at all.

New estimating tasks require constantly new techniques and, occasionally, new working models. So long as only intercensal and postcensal estimates of total population are needed, the task is met by a craftsman: both the theory and the application of the field can be easily handled by the same person.

Where new tasks arise constantly, the craftsman no longer suffices. He must be joined by an engineer who engages in the development and testing of methods. But even the specialty of the engineer might prove too narrow. Judicious use of techniques is not a mere matter of arithmetic but requires increasingly an insight into the total system of interrelations between demographic, social, and economic facts and tendencies. There is increasing scope for co-operation between computing experts, mathematicians, economists, and sociologists, as well as the practical experts in applied fields of endeavor.

Demographic estimates are not made exclusively for practical purposes but are also needed in the advancement of knowledge. The variety of estimates needed in support of detailed demographic and related studies, e.g., in studies of fertility or of genetic factors, is probably far greater than that required by a national administration.

These considerations lead to a multiple subdivision of the field of population estimates. At least the following criteria apply: (*a*) purpose (whether in support of practical action or the furtherance of knowledge); (*b*) level of work (applied, methodological, and critical); (*c*) demographic features (population, population characteristics, vital trends, etc.); (*d*) data used (censuses, registers, samples); and (*e*) time reference (past, current, future).

Objectives in Estimating

The question still to be considered is what constitutes a "good" estimate. Evidently, it is highly desirable that an estimate accord with the facts, i.e., that it be *accurate*. But accuracy as such is not always a practical criterion of the "goodness" of the estimate.

For practical purposes, accuracy is an elusive concept. How closely an estimate conforms to facts cannot be asserted unless the facts themselves are perfectly known. Such knowledge, if attained, would make an alternative estimate unnecessary and, in fact, impossible. An approximate idea of possible accuracy can sometimes be gained by comparison of estimates of the same quantity derived by alternative methods (including those of imperfect "measurement") with similar order of reliability.

This leads to a distinction between absolute accuracy and presumptive accuracy, i.e., *reliability*. A crude estimate can happen by mere chance to be accurate, while an elaborate estimate occasionally misses the facts by a wide margin. Accidental accuracy can be the result of compensating errors. Accidental failure can occur when, for the lack of past evidence to this effect, even an expert fails to recognize the possible relevance of some factor. Yet, so long as a clear idea of probable accuracy cannot be formed, greater reliance must be placed in an estimate whose chances of being accurate are deemed greatest.

Reliability cannot be quantitatively assessed. It is imputed to estimates made by methods of proven past success or by persons of demonstrated good judgment. As observable conditions change and new experience is made, methods once considered reliable may no longer be so. At best, frequency tests of approximate accuracy can lend support to estimates of one type instead of another type. Prior to such tests, reliability is the chief practical criterion of the "goodness" of an estimate.

Apart from acuracy, presumptive or otherwise, estimates should possess another virtue of sometimes greater importance. Especially when used in comparisons, estimates should be *consistent*. Valid comparison of consistent estimates is possible even if they are inaccurate, as appears from the following consideration. A population may have been enumerated in a census subject to an error of possibly 5 per cent. One year later, this population is estimated at a figure 1 per cent greater than the census result. If the two figures are consistent, the inference that population has increased by about 1 per cent is warranted. If the estimate is independent and more accurate than the census, no such conclusion is possible.

This observation throws more light on the merits of traditional series of "postcensal" and "intercensal" estimates. The known imperfections of censuses and vital registers would seem to taint this practice with hypocrisy, especially where new scientific appraisals of statistical performance permit the construction of estimates more accurate than the data themselves. As it turns out, the administrative routine of classifying some admittedly inaccurate estimates as "provisional" and others, hardly less accurate, as "definite," is a rather arbitrary device. Its justification is the consideration of expediency. The practice is certainly a poor one where errors in official demographic statistics are known to be large. Where they are minor, this small amount of hypocrisy is meritorious. Final census results require legal indorsement, as they form the basis for such political measures as the apportionment of voting districts or the allocation of educational grants. The results are part of a game whose rules cannot be changed while the game is in progress. It is doubtful whether estimates, even if more accurate than the official records, can be equally acceptable, since alternative estimates of possibly equal accuracy can always be made.

Legal sanction of official statistics leads to their wide acceptance. This makes it desirable to obtain estimates consistent with official data. Otherwise, frequent confusion could hardly be avoided. At the sacrifice of a small amount of accuracy, the unwarranted comparison of non-comparable figures

can be effectively prevented. Yet there are other purposes where absolute accuracy is more important than consistency, especially where inferences are to be made from observed differences. In an intercensal balancing equation, the difference between two successive census totals should, theoretically, equal the combined effects of births, deaths, and migration. A theoretical estimate of migration should then result from subtraction of natural increase from total increase as registered by the censuses. Yet this inference is in doubt while there is doubt as to the accuracy of censuses and vital registers.

Another case arises where the quality of official data is variable. Thus, according to official estimates, an improvement in birth registration would suggest, *ceteris paribus*, an acceleration of population growth, though actually growth has been constant.

The desire for estimates that are consistent is in partial conflict with the need for more accurate estimates. One way of resolving this conflict is to retain official estimates as they result from consistent practice and to qualify them with additional assessments of their probable errors. This practice appears most recommendable because accuracy is the higher of the two desiderata only in connection with comparatively specialized analytical problems. The virtue of consistency is supreme where theoretical estimates are derived from theoretical models. Accuracy is not relevant, since further modifications, to suit actual facts, can always be made.

Reconstruction of Unavailable Estimates

In recent years, various governments have "classified" certain types of information and withheld them from publication. Facts relating to population have come to constitute such "classified" information in certain areas, though population estimates exist at the government level. Yet international understanding is best aided if at least some essential facts of the social and demographic situation are internationally known. A new branch of specialized work has therefore come into existence.

Reconstruction of government estimates withheld from publication is like detective work. Occasional appearance of circumstantial information cannot be avoided. Painstaking search for published details which imply demographic estimates, however indirectly, can yield some clues. Whatever clues are obtained must be carefully related to each other to establish their probable relevance and consistency. Even if a quantity can be determined in this way, there remains the problem of its exact qualification, the definition of terms, the date to which an estimate refers, etc. This type of work differs a great deal from ordinary demographic estimating procedures. A high caliber of good judgment is necessary if useful and reasonably firm conclusions are to be drawn. A great deal of circumstantial reasoning is involved. The results may sometimes appear meager but are of great value because of their scarcity.

THE PRACTICAL ROLE OF POPULATION ESTIMATES

How Practical Requirements Are Met

Many scientifically established facts are tools in man's mastery of the environment. The most important part of that environment is man himself. Knowledge of human quantities and trends is a major prerequisite to rational social action. Such knowledge need not always be highly accurate but must be objective to the greatest possible degree. If estimates are to guide action, they must be made with the sincere intent to exclude any possible source of illusion or delusion.

Where governments are invested with diverse social functions, they require population estimates of varying degrees of detail and accuracy. But governments are managed by politicians and not by social scientists. The requirement of objectivity cannot be met unless politicians and scientific workers can reasonably coexist. This coexistence is facilitated in a democracy, and especially where public opinion is enlightened. Here, the politicians are under constraint to furnish detailed accounts of the affairs of the nation, while the public insists that the account rendered be objective. Within the limits of a desirable budget, the government will find it expedient to devote some funds to the provision of adequate population estimates.

Initiative in specifying the exact type of work to be undertaken is shared between those branches of the government which use the estimates and that particular unit—usually attached to the national census or statistical office—which produces them. The population specialists are in a good position to suggest what types of estimates can conveniently be made and which estimates will serve best in illustrating various issues of governmental concern. At the same time, other branches of the government must insist that priorities be met within stated limits of time and the budget. Disagreement as to what can and what should be done may arise frequently. Consistent work habits, standardized results, and general experience can best be cumulated under a civil service system where the specialists enjoy at least some minimum security of job tenure.

In other governments concerned with economic and social development the need for detailed population estimates is equally great, though publication is not always necessary. The conditions under which population statisticians cooperate with other organs of government probably vary with circumstances. The quality of demographic information secured can conceivably be high, but there may at times be some discouragement to the display of initiative and the exercise of independent judgment on the part of the experts.

Population-estimating work is still rudimentary where governments have only recently become agents of social policy and where public opinion is as yet rather innocent of a scientific spirit. These two circumstances impede progress no less than lack of trained personnel and financial resources. But the new concern with development of technologically retarded areas creates a great need for better demographic information. The Population Branch of the United Nations has assumed the task of developing demographic techniques suitable for countries in process of development.

Aside from governments, some academic institutions and other agencies are highly active in the development of population estimates and estimating methods. Relative independence from the political allocation of public funds enables such institutes to engage in work whose practical usefulness is not immediately apparent. Pioneer work in the improvement of techniques can be more readily undertaken at universities than in a public office. Especially in the United States, where some academic institutes are more richly endowed than elsewhere, private agencies have made great contributions to the public requirements for demographic information. The work done by semipublic institutes, such as the Institut National d'Études Démographiques in France, the Brazilian Institute of Geography and Statistics, and the Population Association of Japan, is likewise of great value. The vitality of such institutes is essential for progress in a field where the political and budgetary rigidities of government limit the possibilities of exploring new avenues of work.

Expectations and Disappointments

The astounding material applications of modern knowledge in physics are most conspicuous in the modern world. What would have previously been regarded a miracle is now solid achievement. This achievement is most dependable where preceding scientific analysis was most precise. There is an optimistic belief that, with precise scientific findings, almost any material achievement will be possible. Accordingly, precision of analysis has almost become the popular criterion of the "scientific." This criterion is very nearly met in many branches of physics but not within the social sciences. Among the latter, demography is relatively privileged, since its definitions, measurements, and estimates are more exact than those of most other social investigations. Social scientists rightly insist on the scientific nature of their endeavors, but popular expectation of precision endangers the prestige of social research.

It is important to consider the expectations and possible disappointments of the public to which population estimates can give rise. The demographer, after all, requires a measure of public confidence if his work is to continue. His hopes are very much those of the public he seeks to serve. High stakes were once set on the possibility of finding some universal "law" of population growth. Such a "law," if logically sound and empirically verified, would permit making reliable population estimates of the past and the future. But this hope has proven as chimeric as an earlier quest by physicists to build a *perpetuum mobile*.

Controlled experiments show that the multiplication of primitive organisms in a limited environment (e.g., fruit flies in a bottle) tends to conform to the formula of the logistic curve. Increment per unit of time accelerates as the colony increases in size; as the limitations of the environment assert themselves, increments diminish until saturation is reached.

These observations under controlled conditions do not support a universal biological "law" and, least of all, one for human populations. It is true that some human populations, for a limited time, have tended to grow logistically. But, as distinct from fruit flies, human beings act deliberately with respect to their fertility and mortality. And, as distinct from a bottle, their environment can be modified by migration and technical adaptations. It is the essence of all history that conditions of human existence change continuously, for "man, in his restless endeavors, forever undoes his own work."

The logistic "law" is not the only demographic model that had to be abandoned as new facts became known. An earlier model was that of exponential growth where resources are abundant and cyclical reversals where resources are in full use. (This model, used by T. R. Malthus for merely illustrative purposes, has been cited by Marxists as the "unscientific Malthusian law" which claims universality and forms the basis of a pseudo-science.) The model in vogue now is that of a transition from a near-balance of births and deaths under high fertility and mortality to a near-balance under low fertility and mortality. The logical foundations of the latter have, so far, not been seriously challenged, but confidence in generalizations of any kind is now much lower than it was on earlier occasions. Only Marxists, as recently as 1954, still upheld the claim that "specific population laws" are operative under each of several distinct forms of social organization. (Contributions by delegates from the U.S.S.R., Poland, Hungary, and Rumania to the World Population Conference in Rome, 1954, made this evident.)

Abandonment of the quest for solid ground upon which to base demographic models is perhaps unsatisfactory from the viewpoint of a public which expects scientific miracles. But the lessons of experience have made this necessary.

Four Facts in Need of Clear Exposition

Demographers have frankly relinquished the search for a universal demographic "law" of even remotely Newtonian force. Instead of this, "working models," aspiring to only limited and approximate validity, are now in use. It can no longer be denied that population estimates, in the absence of a discrete list of exactly quantifiable determinants, will always be subject to some measure of uncertainty. A second fact to be emphasized is that population estimates are scientific where an earnest attempt is made to survey all possibly relevant factors and to select at least those with presumably greatest relevance. This is the most rational thing to do, though the attempt may fail.

The third fact, that estimates though fallible are useful, is obvious enough. Some estimate is better than none, and a presumably good one is better than a presumably poor one. Anybody faced with the choice of taking or leaving his raincoat when departing from his house is intuitively aware of this. A fourth fact, yet to be fully appreciated, is that the theoretical value of a "wrong" estimate can be as great as that of a "correct" one. But a lesson can be drawn from a mistake only where the nature of the mistake can be adequately defined.

Good understanding of these simple facts is necessary if the expectations surrounding a population estimate are to be as realistic as those placed in a weather report. Disillusionment with particular estimates is bound to recur. But the general soundness of this business need not be questioned every time. It is well to consider further each of these four points. Formulated somewhat differently, they involve these principles: (*a*) limits to generalization, (*b*) the degree of objectivity attainable, (*c*) the role of estimates in decision-making, and (*d*) the scientific disposal of "errors."

In a sense, every estimate relies on the use of a model. The model is implicit and primitive where techniques are simple. Thus, interpolation or extrapolation of population figures from two measurements implies the model of a simple curve; the compounding of population figures from census and vital registers involves the assumption that these statistics are sufficient and adequate. Explicit and elaborate models occur in connection with more detailed or complicated estimates. The possible range of application of a model serving only theoretical purposes is irrelevant. If the system under study is the relationship of fertility trends and age structure, other factors can be deliberately excluded, and the theoretical conclusions will be accurate.

But where estimates are intended to conform as nearly as possible to facts, the relevance of the estimating model to the given situation must be seriously examined. No actual situation represents a perfect "closed system." Every situation is open to interference by at least several out of an infinity of possible factors. Not least among the hazards lurking in the background are possible inaccuracies of measurement. Others comprise the whole array of social and cultural variables, many of which are imponderable. A system encompassing all possible agents of mischief would be time-free and space-free but is beyond human powers of conception. Only limited models comprising a small group of relevant factors

can be practically used. They are valid to the extent, and for that period of time, that no serious disturbance by other factors arises. Fortunately, in a majority of situations this condition can be approximately met, especially if the period of time is reasonably short.

A practical model resembles a theoretical one, since both must of necessity be simple; the external resemblance is often so close that distinction is almost impossible. But this should never become a source of deception. The same model, used theoretically, yields findings which are eternally valid, while practical estimates derived from it are reliable only within the inherent limitations.

The question of objectivity is trivial with respect to estimates, such as the "intercensal" and "postcensal" ones, where large errors are unlikely to occur. It is fundamental in the case of future estimates and of estimates based on questionable statistics requiring careful interpretation.

Objectivity requires, in the first place, a perfectly unprejudiced approach to the facts. Numerous instances might be cited where, because of wishful or fearful thinking, census results have been manipulated, estimates inflated, or forecasts made on unreasonable assumptions. Such estimates might be useful in false propaganda but do not provide the most rational basis for action. Short-sighted discouragement of an objective approach, therefore, is likely to entail some real damage. Objectivity requires, in addition, a scrupulous search for factors which might affect the estimated quantity. This requirement can be relaxed where, at the risk of only small possible errors, routine procedures insure consistency and prevent possible confusion. Objectivity also requires accurate qualification of the estimated quantity, i.e., a statement on data used, adjustments, methods, and assumptions. Without adequate qualification any statistics are liable to misuse.

These and possibly other aspects of objectivity will be met if the person making the estimate is aware of his responsibility. Nevertheless, at some point or other, making an estimate involves a decision. And a decision, however cautious and dispassionate, stems from personal judgment.

The case may be likened to that of a businessman. In matters involving small contingencies he may very well proceed by rule of thumb; the routine of "intercensal" and "postcensal" estimates is of that nature. In an important venture he will have to weigh carefully all possible risks and gains. He will also be well advised to consult with experts and to review past experience. He will try to overcome, as best he can, every source of personal bias. But, on making his decision, his last word is still his own. In much the same way, an expert about to make a population forecast will draw on available experience and will exercise self-restraint to the best of his ability. But the judicious selection of assumptions remains his own business. At best, a population forecast will be an expert opinion. It may carry some weight in view of its author's expertise. But forecasts made independently by two experts are likely to differ, and, whether they differ or not, both might be in error.

Responsibility is partly evaded if a population projection, or forecast, is qualified as "conditional." This involves a prediction that a certain result will follow, *provided some specified set of conditions are met*. It does not imply that the conditions will be met. This attitude has been adopted all too frequently. Though understandable, it is not desired by the public. A farmer may be insured against crop failure, but this does not insure that he will deliver grain.

A "conditional" projection is a hybrid.

It is not fully practical, though it refers to practical conditions. It should never be made, except for reasons such as these: (*a*) to illustrate the effects of a contingency which deserves consideration, (*b*) to make abstraction from some secondary factor which is difficult to evaluate, or (*c*) to contrast a hypothetical consideration with reality. The first reason was met by some population projections made in the 1930's: they demonstrated that *if* fertility continued at its then current level, population decline was imminent in several countries. As an example of the second, we may regard a population projection in which the possible effects of migration, considered to be of secondary importance, are left out of account. A population projection of the third type was made by J. Bourgeois-Pichat (1952), showing the size and structure of the French population which would have resulted in 1946 *if* fertility had remained unchanged since 1776. To avoid misunderstanding, the reason for making a "conditional" projection should always be clearly stated.

In a recent discussion of population projections, the following sharp observation was made by Hajnal (1955*b*, p. 23):

Perhaps one should recognize that the demand for forecasts is generated in part by motives only weakly related to their accuracy; in other words that even very inaccurate forecasts fulfil a need. The point has been put in its sharpest form by Professor Devons when he compares the use of statistical forecasting as a guide for policy to the function of the magician in some primitive societies. For example, if you want to go out hunting and do not know whether the best hunting is to the north or to the south, you consult a magician; and that after all is a sensible thing to do because the important thing is to get on with the hunting. It would be disastrous to get bogged down in arguing. Much the same need lies behind the demand sometimes faced by demographers "Give me some figures, any figures are better than none." What such people want, perhaps, is someone to make up their mind.

If this observation contains a truth— and it certainly does—it reflects on the users of population estimates, but not necessarily on their authors. Some decisions can be made lightly, preferably by the flipping of a coin. But not so where large matters are involved. Not only must action be resolved, but it should also be wise. How can this be done if accuracy of an estimate cannot be guaranteed?

Only rarely can action be based on absolute certainty. Ordinarily, a wise course of action consists of successive approximations to the requirements of circumstances as they emerge. Action will be enlightened if circumstances are anticipated which then appear most likely. Enlightenment will be greater if other future possibilities, of smaller likelihood but greater possible impact, are also taken into account. The weight which each possible future contingency should bear on a decision may have to be proportional to the product of its likelihood and the gravity of its effect, or some similar function.

These requirements for wise action would be partly met by population estimates and forecasts if these could be presented not by single figures but by probability distributions of each figure. And they would be met almost entirely if, furthermore, every figure were instantly revised whenever one item of new information appeared. But these are exaggerated statements. The ideal can be approximated only to the extent that this is practical. Even so, there is room for improvement of current practices.

The relative probabilities of each of several possible future trends cannot be measured. The experienced student of population trends perceives, subjectively and intuitively, some shadings of likelihood in a set of several alternative future assumptions if they differ from each other significantly enough. This perception is not shared by persons less versed in the subject. Some of the demographer's talent is wasted if his perception of relative likelihood remains unconveyed. But how shall he convey it? It is a delicate matter, given the private nature of his personal judgment.

Only a slight hint can be derived from a consideration of the normal (bell-shaped) curve of error. Here, probabilities fall off most sharply where values deviate from the most likely one by plus or minus one standard error. The probability distribution relevant to a given case—if it can be conceived at all—is probably not normal and perhaps skew. But limiting values, governing the "high" and "low" assumptions, would probably be best selected at two points near which the likelihood of realization appears to diminish most sensibly.

This method of selecting limiting assumptions—if at all feasible—offers another important advantage. Population estimates and projections made on this basis, no matter by what techniques, are then perfectly comparable, both in respect of additivity and of the possibility of deriving inferences from their differences. The confidence interval between "high" and "low" estimates will naturally be wider in some cases then in others.[1]

The other desideratum, frequent and rapid revision of future estimates, is often difficult. In many cases, it would require repetition of the entire computing procedure. But the need for ready revision can hardly be overemphasized. The forecast should be furnished from the start with built-in provisions for ready revision when oppor-

[1] The author is indebted to Dr. H. Muhsam for development of some of these ideas.

tunity occurs. It might contain ready reference tables of correction factors or other devices for adjustment which enable the user of the forecast to apply simple revisions by himself when he possesses new figures. The simpler the forecast, the more easily it can be revised. Since an elaborate projection can hardly be more accurate, simplicity is of the essence. More ambitious schemes should be used occasionally to insure that the simpler and more practical models do not stray from judgments arrived at with weightier evidence. If such practice can be followed, the need to qualify population projections as "conditional" will no longer be felt.

Errors in estimates arise from two distinct sources: inaccuracy of basic data and the sum of economic, social, and cultural variables which can affect the estimating model. Estimates of the past and present are most sensitive to errors from the first source; the second type of error is most to be feared with respect to the future.

Errors of census enumeration and vital registration are best accounted for if field investigation permits some estimates of their direction and magnitude. But this is not often successfully done. A great deal can be learned from a balancing equation when a new census result permits the transformation of "postcensal" estimates into "intercensal" ones. The numerical facts of population size, births, deaths, and migration constitute a "closed system," and so do the corresponding statistics if the factor of their possible insufficiencies and inconsistencies is included. It is this factor, usually distributed *pro rata temporis*, by which postcensal estimates are adjusted. But the factor has several components of unknown magnitude, some of them possibly compensating.

In the equation $P_1 = P_0 + B - D + I - E + R$, where P_0 and P_1 are population size according to the two censuses, B and D the births and deaths registered in the interval, and I and E the recorded numbers of arrivals and departures of migrants, the composite factor of inaccuracies, R, is obtained as a residual. Hypothetically, it might be ascribed entirely to any one of the remaining factors. It would then have resulted from inaccurate enumeration at either one of the censuses or from inaccurate registration of births, deaths, arrivals, or departures. Some of these hypotheses will have to be rejected because they are quantitatively or qualitatively inconsistent with what is known about the recording of each of these facts. The remaining hypotheses can be examined for consistency by altering the form of the balancing equation and applying it to population segments by sex and age, populations of specified areas, or other categories. By the combination of strict arithmetic with qualitative judgment, useful conclusions are sometimes efficiently arrived at. The conclusion is useful not only because estimates can then be improved but also because it suggests at which points the collection of basic statistics is in need of overhauling.

Misjudgment of assumed trends can be subjected to similar analysis if component factors have been specified and are measurable. A population projection may be in "error" because mortality was misjudged. The assumption may have involved specific consideration of causes of death. Comparison with the pertinent statistics may show, however, that mortality from tuberculosis may have decreased, or mortality from cancer increased, more than anticipated. The conclusion is a lesson in the forecasting of mortality. More important than that, it points the way to a more rational allocation of health budgets between the prevention of tuberculosis and that of cancer.

The conclusion is less amenable to quantification if mortality from joint causes and mortality conditioned by social causes are involved. Alcoholism or suicide may be cases in point. If important, this observation should lead to the voting of funds for a more specialized investigation.

Errors of a forecast arising from misjudgment of unspecified or imponderable factors are most difficult to interpret. Why, in many countries, was the birth rate low in the 1930's but considerably higher in recent years? A complex of economic, social, and cultural factors contains but at the same time conceals the cause. Symptomatic relation of demographic with extra-demographic trends has been revealed in some socioeconomic factors, but strict causality has not been demonstrated. Even if strictly causal factors could some day be singled out, it remains doubtful whether the causal nexus could be measured quantitatively.

This baffling phenomenon has already stimulated much research yielding important by-products of learning. This is one useful result of forecasting errors. But an improvement in forecasting ability cannot be expected until the relevant factors become specifiable, preferably in accordance with a complete itemized list. Continued progress in the entire field of social research may gradually remedy our present ignorance. But many of the elements in the social situation have not yet been clearly conceptualized. The prospects of progress in this direction must still be viewed with modesty.

Dependence on Data

One might expect that good population estimates will result from judicious and efficient use of available techniques. But techniques only transform the raw material into a finished product. These raw materials are statistical data, in the widest possible sense. Techniques are, in fact, most easily distinguished by reference to the type of data they can use.

Demographic data form the subject of discussion in another chapter of this symposium. But formal measurements are not the only data used in estimating. Circumstantial information, appraisals of measurement, quantities consistent with "working models," and qualitative knowledge also form part of the stock-in-trade. It is no longer true that an estimate can be no more accurate than the data if censuses, vital registers, and migration records alone are considered. But it remains true if estimates must remain consistent with accepted results of conventional measurement.

The use of each technique is justified only where the data, formal or other, meet appropriate standards of accuracy or reliability. Gravel is sifted with a coarser sieve than sand. And there is a limit. When data are too few or too rough, estimating is reduced to guesswork. Of course, any quantity at any time can be vaguely conjectured or guessed at. Astronomers now believe that planetary systems like the solar one are very frequent. This makes it probable that physical conditions like those on earth exist also in many other places. It is not unlikely that organic life has evolved elsewhere. With this consideration, one might venture a guess of the number of beings resembling ourselves to be found in the universe, but this guess would hardly qualify as a population estimate.

As already indicated, "measurements" are distinguished from "estimates" by conventions. At the other extreme, a similar distinction of estimates from conjectures, and of these from fiction and fancy, would be helpful. It would enhance the status of "estimates" properly so called, while relegating "conjectures" to a lower plane of presumptive utility. The criteria, if they could be formulated, would have to be in terms of the quantity, quality, and relevance of the data employed.

The Classification of Methods

A comprehensive survey of demographic estimating and forecasting techniques is not possible at this time. The limits of the field are undefined, and there is no up-to-date textbook which covers the subject. This is regrettable. A classificatory scheme of estimating methods might provide a most useful frame of reference. In a given problem, the types of methods which seem possible could be inferred, and experience already made could be readily marshaled.

Literature on population estimating techniques is abundant but fragmentary. Here and there, articles in statistical journals delve into specific problems. Comparison of results of alternative methods in the estimation of some particular feature is sometimes made. Usually, it is taken for granted that a certain body of statistical data exists. The experience of one country or area is then not transferable to another area where statistical information is different. Nor is such experience of much avail where the demographic situations or trends are different in kind.

Estimating methods might be listed in accordance with any of three schemes. All methods serving in the estimation of a particular feature (e.g., population by sex and age, local populations, etc.) might be assembled, whatever the data and other circumstances which their use postulates. Again, methods relating to the estimation of any possible feature might be grouped in accordance with the amount and type of data which permit their use. Finally, methods might be classified by the logical principles on which their use depends; this type of classification would be most instructive. But this methodological exercise has scarcely made an appearance in demographic literature.

The logical principles of estimating involve the use of "data" and "assumptions," but this distinction, again, is a relative one. Is a quantification secured by a fairly representative sample a "datum"? Or are the sample results alone the data, while their supposed representativeness is an "assumption"? Are life-table functions "data" when official and "assumptions" when not? Where data are used uncritically, is not the "assumption" made that they are accurate? Evidently, "assumptions" are of varying degrees, depending on how well they suit given objectives. Customary distinctions are only made where required for convenience. Pragmatic tests of apparent success are, of course, decisive from the immediately practical point of view. But they do not lead us one step further in an analysis of the logical categories which make an estimate what it really is.

For the lack of a suitable classification, it is only possible here to select some estimating problems and to cite some methods by which they have been attacked. A group of methods has originated from actuarial practices. Another group traces its descent from "pure" demography. Some methods estimate theoretical concepts rather than facts of possible observation. Discussion must proceed along these, or similar, lines.

Totals and Components

Among the objectives of estimating are both total numbers and various subtotals, not only a country's whole population but also the numbers of inhabitants living in diverse localities or possessing various characteristics. It is useful to assess numbers of births or deaths, the migratory balance, and the resulting tempo of growth in these various categories.

Sometimes, only totals can be estimated, but as a rule, the aim is to estimate totals as well as various subtotals.

This can be done (*a*) by estimating totals first and then deriving subtotals by some device of redistribution of the total; (*b*) by estimating each subtotal separately, as if it were a total, and then obtaining the total as the sum of subtotals; and (*c*) by using both approaches and then reconciling the resulting estimates by adjustments for apparent discrepancies.

The third approach, if feasible, is best, especially if estimates made redistributively and additively are of comparable order of reliability. But bias can hardly be avoided unless each set of estimates is prepared by a different person or agency and some third party can be engaged in their reconciliation. Each of the first two approaches offers advantages and drawbacks, depending on the nature of the material in question. Generalization is difficult. Statistics for prior estimation of totals are usually more available and more reliable. Trends in totals sometimes exert a controlling influence on possible changes in component parts. If the redistributive formula can be reasonably well relied on, this is also the most efficient method. Sometimes, estimates for parts arrived at by uniform procedure are less open to questioning than estimates made separately by diverse means. Where, for reasons of convenience, due respect must be given to routine, consistency, and efficient procedure, it is sometimes wise to estimate first the whole and then its parts.

But separate estimates of parts can sometimes excel in accuracy. Information pertaining to each part, though not available for all parts, can be taken into account, and assumptions appropriate for each component, but not for the whole, can be judiciously selected. Furthermore, since errors tend to compensate, the relative error in the sum of subtotals is likely to be smaller than the relative error in each part. But in some instances the influences which diverse parts can exert on each other are difficult to take into account. Subject to this qualification, prior estimation of parts appears theoretically preferable, whereas prior estimation of totals is sometimes practically more expedient.

Estimates made by different approaches do not necessarily warrant the same conclusions. Where an assumption is made about some magnitude, trend, or relationship, inference of this same feature from the estimates would be a "foregone conclusion." Other inferences, however, are legitimate because they reflect the implications of data and assumptions. Some implications are more directly conditioned by assumptions than others. And some "assumptions" have considerable substance in observed fact, while others may have to be made more freely and arbitrarily. These considerations vary with the case. But, in a given case, there are conclusions which find better support in redistributive estimates, and others which can be more firmly based on additive estimates separately arrived at.

The proximity of an implication to a basic assumption depends on where exactly the assumption applies. A quantity can be determined as a one-time estimate, and also as a variable which changes in time according to a trend. But trends and their components are also quantities. The level of the rate of growth, the birth rate, death rate, or components thereof can also change in accordance with a trend. And where a trend is established, specific assumptions might require acceleration, deceleration, or reversal of the change. The higher the analytical level at which the assumption is made, the more conclusions are warranted from estimated quantities, provided, of course, that an assumption at that level of analysis can be reasonable.

These are some of the considerations

which recur in connection with almost every estimating problem. Other considerations depend on the exact nature of the problem. But one further generalization might be tentatively put forth. Demographic analysis, in many areas, has now progressed so far that it is no longer necessary, or desirable, to undertake exhaustive analytic research whenever an estimate is being prepared. Assumptions at a lower analytical level than attained by advanced investigation should now suffice in practical estimating work. These assumptions can be shaped to accord reasonably well with findings obtained in more searching specialized studies.

Total Population

Total population is the number of inhabitants, usually of a national territory, covered by a uniform statistical system. In some countries, different populations form separate totals mainly because different types of statistics are being secured (e.g., tribal Indians in South America, ethnic groups in South Africa, etc.). Estimates for parts of the same total population will be considered under a separate heading.

Total population can be assessed by a one-time estimate, by use of a trend in the total, or by use of component trends, i.e., births, deaths, and migration. In the last event, births, deaths, and migration may also have to be estimated first.

One-time estimates.—Where adequate direct enumeration of inhabitants has not been made, population is estimated by some parameter to which it is presumably related. Depending on the precision with which both the parameter and its presumable relation to population are known, these estimates can range from mere conjecture to fairly accurate measurement. The following is an example of a more conjectural type of estimate.

In 1885, travelling through the remote inner regions of China, the Russian explorer Potanin encountered a branch of sedentarized Mongols on the upper reaches of the Yellow River, near the present borders of Kansu and Chinghai Province, whom he called the Shirongol-Mongols. He estimated their numbers, by conjecture, as follows:

In San-chuan, i.e. in the area between Gyango-gol and Unchzhagol, there are 1,200 households; assuming five souls of either sex per household, we obtain 6,000 souls for San-chuan. If we allow for the population of Bouchzha-aral, Itel-gol, and Sombra with Badu-ol a figure of 2,000 souls, then the total population of this section amounts to 8,000. In Tun-syan one reports thirty-six imyks, i.e. villages; estimating that there are 100 households per village, one may put these at 18,000 inhabitants; however, assuming that the figure thirty-six is exaggerated, we may reduce the estimate for the population of Tun-syan to 10,000. The Shirongolian population of the lower part of Sinin-gol and of Day-tong-gol may also be accepted at 10,000. In the surroundings of U-yanbu and Mubayshintu there can hardly be more than 20,000 souls. Around Bou-nan there are, probably, no more than 2,000 souls. These estimates result in the folowing total:

	Persons
San-chuan	8,000
Day-tong-gol	10,000
Tun-syan	10,000
U-yan-bu	20,000
Bou-nan	2,000
Total	50,000

The author himself had travelled only through San-chuan and Bou-nan and had an opportunity to estimate these parts of the Shirongolian population from personal observations. Utilizing his personal knowledge regarding the average size of households, average numbers of households per village, and possible population densities, he proceeded to make an inference on possible numbers of population in neighboring areas which he had not visited but the approximate extent of which he knew from local reports.[2]

At the other extreme, we may consider a scientific sampling enumera-

[2] G. N. Potanin, *Tangutsko-tibetskaya okraina Kitaya i tsentralnaya Mongoliya* (Moscow, 1950), p. 377, as quoted in United Nations (1952), pp. 10–11.

tion. Multiplication of the sampling ratio by the sample result, provided pitfalls of sampling have been avoided, gives a figure of total population subject to a calculable percentage error. Sometimes this error may be less than those incurred in formal census enumerations, and it can be determined better than that of a census.

One-time estimates, by a variety of parameters and assumptions, have been characteristic of the assessment of population in colonial territories. The parameters have been land area, tax revenue, villages, households or persons from whom tax is collected, numbers of houses, numbers of workers—also incomplete demographic enumerations, such as agricultural or school censuses, voters' registers, and group enumerations where the group might be as large as a tribe or as small as the individual household. Ideally, these methods could attain the standards of accuracy of a scientific sample: efficient collection of taxes per hut and a representative sample to determine numbers of persons per hut might, conceivably, yield an accurate estimate of population. In practice, the procedures have resulted in estimates that fell far short of these standards. Especially the assumed relationship of the parameter to the number of inhabitants has rarely been well conceived. As shown by Kuczynski's exhaustive study, innumerable attempts to assess colonial populations, repeated year after year, have failed to provide satisfactory evidence even for a conclusion of whether population has increased or declined in the course of several decades.

Rough estimates are, of course, better than none. But repetition of one-time estimates of dubious quality does not permit an inference of a population trend. Some estimates are, however, made with a parameter that is very accurately known and whose correlation to population is presumably very close. The population estimates for the boroughs of New York City are derived from numbers of residential electrical service billings. Though not precise, these are probably accurate enough to suggest at what rates population is changing.

Estimates using a trend.—The trend in total population can be observed or assumed. It can also be arrived at by observation or assumption of trend components and subcomponents. The trend itself is a quantity of great interest, especially as it permits conjectures or estimates of the future. Estimates of population using a trend may or may not be more accurate than one-time estimates. They are certainly more consistent. But if the trend is merely assumed, users of the estimates must be cautioned lest they try to infer the trend from the estimates.

Often there is a failure to distinguish a trend from more accidental variations, as is generally done in the analysis of economic time series. In economics, the distinction of trend, cycles, periodic fluctuations, and accidental variations corresponds to a body of theory. There is no such theory in demography, and if there were, different categories of variation in time might be distinguished. But where a trend is based on the results of two or three censuses, taken perhaps at decennial intervals, it is conveniently assumed, without further justification, that the census results are values *on* the trend and not accidental deviations *from* it.

Also, the type of trend selected is often one of convenience. Two census results suggest, as the simplest device, an arithmetic or geometric progression. Three censuses can support a parabola; four or more, a logistic. Use of the most convenient type of trend sometimes finds support from general considerations of the demographic situation and its inherent tendencies. At other times, these considerations suggest a more or less arbitrary modification of the most convenient type of trend.

These general considerations prevail where the trend is merely assumed. Assumption is necessary for population estimates at different dates if there has been only one census or non-comparable one-time estimates. Where a census has been taken, the relevant considerations are strengthened by the qualitative knowledge of demographic conditions. If well substantiated, a freely assumed trend can be as reliable as one conveniently derived from successive population measurements. But in practice, free assumption is avoided where possible. It requires a choice whose possible wisdom cannot be clearly demonstrated. It is often preferred to support an even less plausible trend by given population measurements. Responsibility for failure is then shifted from the person making the estimate to the peculiarities in the data used. Routine and consistency are also better served by this course of procedure.

But free assumption of a trend can now be made more safely than previously. An estimate of the trend can be secured from a single census, like that of British East Africa in 1948, where sample data on births and deaths during the past year permit estimation of the birth rate, the death rate, and hence the rate of growth. Estimates can also be obtained from statistics on age composition; comparison with age structures of population models, such as a system of "stable" populations, permits an inference of the approximate level of fertility and sometimes also a conjecture of the possible level of mortality. The trend may then resemble that of a theoretical population whose structure is most nearly similar.

Births, Deaths, and Migration

The objective may be to estimate the current demographic events, the general population trend resulting from

these, or the population itself. The last, but not the first, objective is served if births, deaths, or migration are merely assumed. But these facts can also be estimated by using parameters or more detailed components.

Parameters are most pertinent where these facts can be conceived to arise not so much by their necessary relationship to population but under the influence of non-demographic phenomena. This applies especially to migration, most of which presumably occurs under the stimulus of changing economic opportunities. Demographic criteria are important insofar as migrants of various types cannot exceed the numbers of the population from which they originate. But migration research, so far, has developed few strictly demographic relationships. An attempt has been made to regard age-specific propensities to migrate jointly with age-specific risks of death, but it has not, so far, been widely applied in practical work.

The predominantly populational nature of deaths has been recognized since the beginnings of demographic analysis. Yet, at times, deaths can also be partly related to a non-demographic parameter, notably in times of war. The trend changes under the influence of social, cultural, and economic conditions but is conceived as a trend *in* the demographic measure. Deviations from a trend, such as mortality from famine or an epidemic, have sometimes been estimated separately, as "excess mortality"; but where disasters recur, distinction of "normal" from other deaths is a matter of academic debate.

The number of births depends on population size, in particular on the number of women of certain characteristics; but births are also responsive to other factors. The latter are essentially attitudinal, but attitudes are formed and modified by economic, social, and cultural conditions. Direct correlation with economic or social parameters can hardly be assumed, since their effects are further transformed through the psychological medium. Attempts were once made, not without success, to correlate marriages with economic indexes. But even if economic methods to estimate nuptiality could have been adopted, births within marriages would still have to be estimated demographically. Again, demographic trends are conceived as changing under the influence of non-demographic factors.

Difficulties of a formal nature arise in the use of demographic measures; their origin is the actuarial requirement of strict mathematical consistency. As births and deaths result from the population, while the population itself results from births and deaths, a mathematically precise birth rate or death rate can be only a differential, as of an infinitesimal moment of time. Symbols of integral summation alone can then represent accurately the relations between population and vital rates, assuming the latter to conform to an algebraic function for which integration is possible. But for most practical purposes this mathematical rigor must be relaxed. The births and deaths of a year are then related to a hypothetical "mean" population of that year. Even the latter concept can usually be abandoned for purposes of demography: unless conditions are exceptional, the population at the middle of a year, or even at the center of a period of a few years, differs from the "mean" population by a negligible quantity.

If there are statistics on births, deaths, and migration and if accuracy of the data is an "assumption," one might regard the statistics as an estimating parameter and the assumption as a one-to-one relationship. The assumption can be modified on the basis of evidence, and it usually is modified where postcensal estimates are being transformed into intercensal ones. But then a new assumption is substituted.

This is often a trivial matter; distribution of the estimating error *pro rata temporis* is then quite adequate. Sometimes there is reason to ascribe errors chiefly to one source, e.g., incomplete statistics of emigration; then the error can be prorated according to numbers in that set of statistics. Occasionally, some census result raises the greatest doubt; it can then be assumed that the series of estimates supersedes the result of that questionable census.

It would seem that an assumption made for the revision of intercensal estimates ought to apply also in subsequent years. But rarely is an assumption of possible inaccuracy of statistics applied in postcensal estimates. Here again, it is preferred to preserve the routine procedure rather than to apply an assumption that cannot be substantiated with absolute precision.

Component trend adjustments must be estimated in the absence of statistics. Birth and death statistics are not available for the future, nor for most recent dates. Very often, adequate migration statistics are unavailable. Demographically, the migratory balance might be inferred from the difference between intercensal total increase and recorded natural increase, but slight imperfections in those statistics can vitiate the estimated migratory residual. Parametrically, migration can be estimated from statistics on place of birth and citizenship or from the migration statistics of those countries whence migrants come and where they go. Nondemographic parameters can sometimes also be used. Fortunately, the effect of international migration on most national populations is relatively slight. This permits sometimes the "conditional" assumption that even if migration is left out of account, the resulting errors will not be appreciably greater than the estimating errors arising from other sources.

Extrapolation of births and deaths

requires the assumption of a trend in a relevant measure of fertility or mortality. Whatever the measure employed, the shape of the trend will be governed by non-demographic considerations. Demographic considerations, on the other hand, will determine which type of measure can relevantly portray the trend caused by external circumstances.

This point can be illustrated simply by considering a trend in the crude death rate. Everybody dies, once and no more often. The most relevant demographic condition under which deaths occur, however, is age. Non-demographic conditions will presumably bring about a general decline in "mortality" (however defined). At the same time, shifts in population age structure can be such that the general mortality decline is not reflected in a corresponding decline of the crude death rate. More detailed analysis, in some particular instance, might suggest that general mortality decline can be expected to result, e.g., in a constant crude rate. If it is intended to produce an extremely simple population projection, this finding of more detailed study can be employed as a "working assumption," and the crude death rate can be extrapolated accordingly. In some other instance, a very simple "working assumption" might be a certain percentage change in the crude rate, or perhaps a constant annual number of deaths.

The use of age-specific death rates in a projection is, of course, preferable. But the next most important consideration is the specificity of deaths by cause. This does not mean that causes of death must form part of the computations in the estimate. But the shape of trends assumed for age-specific rates should be in accordance with what appears plausible in the light of more specialized studies. And the shape should preferably be simple.

It is more difficult to decide which specific measure of fertility can portray a simple yet plausible trend. Demographically, a woman can remain childless but can also bear many offspring. Social factors influence fertility both positively and negatively, with a net effect that is incalculable. Mortality, however, invariably tends toward an attainable minimum.

Among the most relevant demographic criteria of fertility are age, duration of marriage, number of previous confinements, and interval since last previous birth. Statistics cross-classified by more than two categories are rare; with three categories they assume formidable proportions. But whatever the specificity of the fertility measure employed, detailed analysis has revealed that no stable trends and changes, in whatever terms, must be attributed to non-demographic circumstances. The use of analytic measures of fertility is, of course, desirable in a population projection. But the plausible shape in the trend of a comparatively simple measure should be inferred from the findings of more searching theoretical investigations. To this end, theoretical projections of high complexity may occasionally have to be carried out. But for practical estimates, the projections should be simple.

Local Populations and Population Distribution

Population estimates for territorial segments can be made by separate estimation of each segment but also by redistribution of the national total. As already indicated, both methods have their advantages and drawbacks. At the local level, more detailed information can be mustered, and methods can be adapted to the nature of local trends. At the national level, routine procedures can insure consistency and efficiency. But estimates prepared centrally can appear arbitrary from the local point of view and can give rise to misgivings. Reconciliation then becomes an act of diplomacy. Ideally, the services of a third party would be needed, but these can be secured in few practical situations.

The severe difficulty in estimates for territorial segments arises from internal migration. Its incidence among local or regional populations is of major, and sometimes decisive, importance. But statistics appropriate for its estimation are rare. Some countries have made it a practice to publish population estimates by territorial segments in which the factor of migration is deliberately disregarded. Though convenient, this practice is severely defective.

Methods of estimating local populations are diverse because of differences in available information, basic developmental factors, and research possibilities. This is obvious if we consider such different areas as agricultural districts, towns mainly dependent on one industry, cities with a great variety of economic activities, and residential suburban regions. The chief determining factors may be births and deaths, but migration is also related to the growth and decay of an industry, residential housing development, or general economic conditions.

Some methods try to seize the components of population trends. The use of birth and death data may suffice for areas of indifferent development. Migration statistics are usually not available, and migration can be estimated either by extrapolation of previous intercensal balances or with the use of a parameter. But, especially where migration is important and subject to fluctuation, the entire population trend can be so greatly affected that consideration of component trends is not encouraged. The trend in total population can then be extrapolated or estimated in relation to some parameter.

Diversity of methods is even greater with future estimates of local population. The usefulness of "component"

projections (by sex-and-age groups) is in doubt where migration can be a major factor. Sometimes, it may be conceived that migration generates further migration, but argument by analogy with different time periods can be as fallacious as analogy drawn from different areas. Migration, then, will have to depend on expectations of future economic activities, residential construction, transportation facilities, and the supply of energy. Expectations may be assessed in consultation with industrial management, public authorities, and practical experts in the various fields, but such expectations remain uncertain. Extrapolation of previous trends—which can be interpreted in a variety of ways—in migration or even in total population can sometimes be made with an equal amount of confidence.

Experience has shown that estimates and forecasts are generally more accurate the larger the population or the geographic extent of the area and the more varied its economic activities. Large industrial areas and cities have shown a remarkable capacity to generate new opportunities of activity even while major industries are depressed or declining. Such areas, therefore, show relative stability of population trends despite unpredictable variations of economic conditions.

The best estimates and forecasts are probably those which have been selected after trial of a great variety of methods, with greatest weight being given to those presumably most relevant to the situation. In this connection, a classification of situations might be helpful. Some situations permit adequate estimation by demographic methods only; in others, greatest reliance will have to be placed on the use of certain selected economic or related parameters, while in areas of relative stability some weight can be accorded to the inertia of mathematical trends.

Adequate and uniform national estimates of local populations can best be prepared if there is a good population parameter. The continuous population registers in Scandinavia and the issue of food ration cards in other countries have provided such an opportunity. Minor difficulties occur as, in the course of time, a residual of persons accumulates who have not been properly withdrawn from the records, and the definition of the rationed or "domiciled" population is at variance with the population definition for which estimates are sought. A migration parameter, such as changes in school enrolment in the United States, is sometimes used also.

But usually a suitable parameter cannot be secured for all of a country's geographic segments. The use of diverse parameters, besides being inefficient, would not lead to comparable estimates. Recourse must then be had to some mathematical redistribution method. With various modifications, two basic methods have been used: extrapolation of observed changes in the ratio of local to total populations and "apportionment," in accordance with ratios previously observed, of total national increase among the local populations. Each of these methods has an underlying rationale which is more relevant under some conditions and less so under others.

Though basically simple, these methods can be used in a variety of ways. Trends in ratios can be extrapolated from various base periods. The basis for apportionment of increase can be selected in several ways. Rules can be drawn up for adjustment in particular instances where, in accordance with some general criterion, unvaried use of the basic method would lead to a less plausible result. And the general formula can be modified so that particular results are avoided while yet the sum of local estimates equals the estimate for the total. Much ingenuity has been devoted to this latter problem, despite its mostly "formal" nature. Slight variations in the estimating formula, for the most part, produce only negligible differences in results. But the efforts have been prompted by the desire for one universal rule whose routine application can result in estimates which evoke a minimum of criticism. Yet the problem is unresolved. One method can avoid one type of inconsistency, and another method avoids other discrepancies with "normal" expectations. And what would seem abnormal under certain demographic conditions is not necessarily so under others. The search for a routine method that is also flexible is like the attempt to square the circle.

Local estimates prepared nationally can serve wider purposes than locally prepared estimates. With a consistent set of estimates, it is possible to assess population changes by groups of areas, e.g., economic regions or urban and rural areas. Also, with consistent estimates the local or regional gains and losses through internal migration are necessarily balanced. This control of local estimates by means of the estimate for the total is likely to eliminate some of the estimating biases which would be present in estimates locally prepared.

Population Structure (Unalterable Characteristics)

Some individual features are unalterably determined from the moment of birth, such as sex, parentage, and date and place of birth. To these features also belongs age, which is fixed at any one date relative to the date of birth. Other features, like marital status, economic activity, association with sociocultural groups, cultural attainments, change in the course of the lives of individuals. Unalterable population characteristics can be defined as "structural," whereas others are "compositional."

Population segments of equal structural characteristics can be treated by estimating methods analogous to those employed in estimating population totals. Age cohorts have the additional advantage that their numbers can change only by death and spatial migration. But, aside from this aspect, their distributional pattern also serves as an estimating aid.

Some well-known patterns of age distribution have been observed. But in demography the distributional pattern is not the result of an inherent mutual relationship of age segments—ages not being transferable—but a consequence of past trends in births and, to some extent, also in deaths and migration. To expect a distributional pattern, then, implies the assumption of a certain past trend in births. Depending on other extraneous information, this assumption can often be made, as a reasonable approximation.

The distributional pattern of ages then permits the detection of errors in age classification and, to a certain extent, also their correction. Though age is unalterable, age statements are notoriously transferable. Observed concentration of age statements at multiples of five might theoretically have been a result of sharp fluctuations in birth rates, but the precise recurrence of the fluctuation every five years is so unlikely that the periodicity of the concentration is conclusive evidence of age misstatement. This is not the only feature of age misstatement, but it is the one which is most evident in many statistics.

This effect of digit preference can be corrected by smoothing or graduation. Though the true composition by ages is probably not perfectly smooth, smoothed statistics are often a closer approximation to facts than the data originally recorded. This is sometimes done with highly elaborate methods. Their detailed discussion is not possible here, but the question is appropriate whether these methods, which originate from actuarial science, are well suited for demographic purposes.

Where high degrees of internal consistency are essential, actuarial graduation is, of course, excellent. It permits, for example, the derivation of a consistent set of age-specific death rates from the age distributions of deaths and of the population and the deduction of consistent survival ratios from the age statistics of successive censuses. On the other hand, if the chief purpose is that of estimating age structure at a given date as accurately as possible, the success of even the most refined actuarial techniques is questionable. Rougher methods of smoothing might secure an equally realistic result with much less labor. The degree of refinement in method ought really to be guided by the nature of the raw statistics, but suitable criteria for guidance still remain to be established.

None of these techniques attempts to deal with directional biases in age statements. Evidence of distortion of statistics by age owing to tendencies to understate age in some phases of the life span and to overstate it in others is plentiful and convincing. No amount of averaging, smoothing, and graduation can eliminate this type of bias. A free assumption that such bias is present, if judiciously applied to estimates, can result in a closer approximation to facts than the most elaborate actuarial graduation formula. Not the elaborateness of the procedure but its relevance determines how closely an estimate can approximate facts. This subject, for demographic purposes, still requires investigation.

Separate treatment of age groups in estimates and projections has become standard demographic procedure. This method of dealing with population phenomena is perhaps the strongest feature of modern demography. It is variously referred to as the "component" method, the "cohort-survival" method, or even simply the "demographic" method. It is highly convenient from several points of view: (*a*) age, as a reference to date of birth, is unalterable, so that age groups, i.e., birth cohorts, can be treated as separate populations; (*b*) age is by far the most relevant feature in the analysis of mortality and the synthesis of its effects; (*c*) age is also highly relevant in relation to nuptiality and fertility; (*d*) age is the most interesting population characteristic because of its very high correlation with economic, social, and cultural capacities; (*e*) statistics on various population characteristics as well as vital statistics are usually collected and tabulated with reference to age; and (*f*) as already stated, separate estimation of a population total by its constituent parts can reduce the relative error in the total. Since analysis by age has become almost the core of demographic techniques, various population models have been, and can be, elaborated in which age is the dominant feature.

Estimates of total population by sex and age components have not always been more accurate than estimates made by other methods. In particular, population projections have failed in respect of expected survivors from future births. It is now recognized that, though highly relevant, age is not as relevant to fertility as it is to mortality. Nevertheless, future survivors of age groups already living have been projected fairly accurately. Even if occasionally less accurate, estimates and projections of the population by age groups are more useful and instructive than mere estimated totals. It is justifiable and desirable to employ "cohort-survival" methods even where the basic "data" of age composition of the population or deaths must first be estimated

with reference to analogy or theoretical models.

Estimates of total population by prior estimation of age groups are additive. But the inverse procedure, the derivation of age distribution from populations initially estimated as totals, is also in use. Other procedures are based on the use of trends in ratios and apportionment of increments, which have already been mentioned in connection with estimates of geographic population distribution. From a modern demographic viewpoint such methods appear illogical; the same individuals advance in age as time passes, and there is no necessary relationship of numbers in the same age groups at different times. But the method is efficient and convenient, and it requires comparatively few data and computations. It is most justifiable under relatively stable conditions.

Redistributive estimates of age structure are made often for geographic segments where the use of other methods is hardly feasible. Numerous efforts have been made to find the perfect formula, which will yield results that are plausible and consistent at the same time. For practical purposes, such formality is hardly needed. The "square table" used by the English Registrar General does the trick equally well. In greatly simplified form, its operation is illustrated with fictitious data in Table 51.

In Table 51, let Panel A represent a census result, or earlier estimate, of population by three areas and age groups, and Panel B some current estimates of total population by areas and total population by age groups. These are the data. Fairly consistent and plausible estimates for the subcategories are then obtained as follows: First prorate the cells in A to the horizontal totals in B (Panel C); then prorate the results in C vertically to totals in B (Panel D); repeat alternating horizontal and vertical proration until discrepancies with predetermined totals are quite small (Panel E); the last can be readily eliminated by small direct adjustment of some of the larger figures (Panel F).

Population Composition (Changeable Features)

Various population characteristics are subject to change, and they can change in various ways. Some changes, like

separately a class of persons whose characteristic has changed once but cannot change again. A typical case is "ever-married women" (including married, widowed, divorced, and separated women), whose numbers can be determined more conveniently than those of "married women."

Some of the most interesting transfers of characteristics, notably marital status, economic activity, and educational attainment, are significantly re-

TABLE 51

FICTITIOUS DATA TO ILLUSTRATE ADJUSTMENT TO MARGINAL TOTALS

A

Area	AGE GROUPS			Total
	I	II	III	
A..........	80	80	40	200
B..........	100	180	20	300
C..........	120	340	40	500
Total...	300	600	100	1,000

B

Area	AGE GROUPS			Total
	I	II	III	
A..........	...	...	...	300
B..........	...	...	...	300
C..........	...	...	...	600
Total..	250	800	150	1,200

C

Area	I	II	III	Total
A..........	120	120	60	300
B..........	100	180	20	300
C..........	144	408	48	600
Total...	364	708	128	1,200

D

Area	I	II	III	Total
A..........	82	136	70	288
B..........	69	203	23	295
C..........	99	461	57	617
Total..	250	800	150	1,200

E

Area	I	II	III	Total
A..........	85	142	73	300
B..........	70	207	23	300
C..........	96	449	55	600
Total...	251	798	151	1,200

F

Area	I	II	III	Total
A..........	85	142	73	300
B..........	69	208	23	300
C..........	96	450	54	600
Total..	250	800	150	1,200

those in ethnic, linguistic, or religious affiliation, occur only infrequently during the lifetime of individuals; if mainly identified by parentage, as in the case of "racial origin," they are unalterable. But marital unions of men and women with originally different affiliations occur, and they pose an estimating problem where the presumable affiliation of the offspring remains to be determined. If affiliation is of a formal character, such as legal citizenship, changes can be determined from statistics of naturalization, etc.

For estimating and analytical purposes, it is often convenient to regard

lated to age. Hence, their estimation is best carried out with reference to each of the several age groups or sex-age groups involved. Age is not the only relevant factor; others such as economic conditions, social aspirations, and educational facilities may also have to be considered. But age is by far the most relevant of the measurable correlates of these changes in characteristics. Trends, therefore, can be most significantly expressed with specificity to age.

The relation of age to a changeable characteristic can be conceived in one of two ways. One may regard either age-specific propensities of *being in* a given class or age-specific propensities of *entering and leaving* the class. Which of the two techniques is appropriate will depend on the nature of available statistics, the frequency and repetitiveness with which changes can occur, and the number of changes possible from one class to another.

Changes in marital status generally occur with low frequency in an individual's lifetime. Single persons can terminate their condition, while living, only once and in only one way, i.e., by getting married. Age-specific propensities of getting married can then be treated like a life-table function. But marriages can be terminated by annulment, death of spouse, divorce, and separation, and persons whose marriages were terminated can marry again. The corresponding functions become more complicated than where only one type of change is possible. But the inflow-and-outflow model of marital condition is superior to one where only the age-specific propensities of being married are considered. The latter model, while easier to manipulate, can lead to inconsistent results, but it may suffice where relatively stable conditions can be assumed.

The two alternative models have also been used in the estimation of the economically active population, but here the more usual method is to consider age-specific propensities of *being in* the category of economically active persons, often referred to as "labor force participation ratios." Statistics of entry into, and departure from, the economically active group are generally not available in any comprehensive form, but estimates of inflow and outflow can be derived by life-table techniques, especially where there is a minimum of overlap in the ages of entry into, and those of cessation of, economic activity. Theoretically, the latter model appears superior, but its practical utility is still a matter of debate. Its relevance

may also depend on the manner in which "economic activity" is defined. If the definition approaches that of a status which endures in times of temporary inactivity, changes in this status are infrequent enough to make the inflow-and-outflow model appear pertinent. But changes under the concept of *de facto* activity as of a given moment of time can be very frequent and repetitive, as in the case of intermittent seasonal activities; from this point of view, the labor force participation ratios will appear better suited for practical application in estimates.

The inflow-and-outflow model is also pertinent where changes can occur successively, though each change occurs but once. The cases in point are numbers of women having had no live birth, one live birth, two live births, etc. The life-table technique is highly appropriate. But age, though relevant, is not necessarily as relevant as duration of marriage. A triple classification of number of children born by age as well as duration of marriage is theoretically desirable, but this imposes considerable difficulties both in computational work and in the interpretation of the detailed trends.

Theoretical Estimating Models

Various demographic quantities are more or less closely interrelated. For example, disregarding migration, age distribution is the result of births in various years of the past and deaths which intervened, prior to a given date, among each of the several birth cohorts. Given any two of the three data: births in each year, deaths to each cohort, or current age composition, the third can be inferred by computations, assuming that migration has been negligible.

Other demographic data show fairly stable relationships. For example, specific death rates among adjacent age groups are considerably correlated, whether death rates are high or low. The mean age of mothers at the birth of any child is usually in the area of twenty-seven to twenty-eight years. Under most conditions, between 102 and 107 boys are born per every 100 girls born.

Using some of these stable relationships, models can be constructed from which quantities can be inferred that are consistent with some given quantities *under average conditions*. In the absence of other specific information, it is reasonable to assume average conditions, especially if observed variability is small. With additional information, this assumption can be modified appropriately.

To give an example, it is possible, by using a variety of available statistics, to construct a model from which age-specific death rates likely to coexist under average conditions can be deduced. If expectation of life at birth, or any other age, can be assumed or estimated, plausible corresponding specific mortality conditions can be inferred. If there are some data on age composition, however summary, and on the total number of deaths (or the crude death rate), calculations carried out by means of the model can suggest those specific death rates which might be expected to obtain simultaneously with the given crude rate or total number of deaths.

For many populations, approximate stability of structure can be assumed. This is possible where fertility is presumably fairly constant, the effects of migration and changes in mortality on age structure being usually only of a minor nature. A model of theoretical "stable" populations, resulting from various levels of fertility and mortality, under average conditions, makes it possible to estimate, for approximately stable populations, a great variety of quantities, if only very few quantities are given.

Future estimates can also be derived from models in which average observations of relevant past trends are generalized. The assumption is then made that average trends of the past, or observed past changes in these trends, are relevant to future expectations. The use of a model, rather than specific *ad hoc* assumptions, has the advantage that estimates and projections so derived for a number of populations are systematic and comparable. Two examples of systematic population projections made with the use of estimating and forecasting models are those for European countries prepared under auspices of the League of Nations (Notestein *et al.*, 1944) and those for Latin-American countries put forth by the Population Branch of the United Nations (1954, 1955a).

The use of detailed working models permitting inference of interrelated quantities on the basis of observed regressions and correlations is a comparatively new approach to demographic estimating problems. Models cannot be expected to represent actual conditions with precision, though, within limits and for comparatively short periods of time, they may approximate them. Models promise to be particularly fruitful in countries with inadequate statistical services. Various demographic estimates can be made, especially in technologically retarded areas, with the use of only those few objective measurements which happen to be available.

Estimates of Theoretical Concepts

The need for demographic estimates is generated primarily by the practical objectives of social and economic policy in which the population factor must be taken into account. To a certain extent, this need can be met by convenient computational techniques. Judicious selection and use of techniques, however, must be derived from judgment regarding all possible interrelations between demographic, economic, social, and cultural factors. Comprehension of these is facilitated by development of explicit concepts in the entire field of social theory and, especially, in demography. At first, concepts often have to be formulated tentatively until logical experimentation can establish their utility. In that event, hypothesis leads to theory, and theory can become a powerful instrument in the marshaling and further advancement of objective knowledge.

Some specialized work is devoted to the formulation of new and possibly useful concepts. Quantification of concepts is then necessary to facilitate logical experiment. For example, modern eugenics makes extensive use of conceptual estimates. In demography, similar methods have characterized some of the outstanding work recently undertaken at the Institut National d'Études Démographiques in France. Among the concepts subject to estimation, the following might be cited: the incidence of "sterility" (however defined) in women; the extreme length of the human "life span"; mortality from "exogenous" and "endogenous" causes; average size of "genetic isolates." Abstract estimates like these are made with outstanding ingenuity. They are not common where emphasis in demographic research is given to the concrete facts of observation, with comparatively small reliance being given to deductive reasoning. But theory and knowledge advance by two avenues, of which empiricism is one and logical deduction the other.

CONDITIONS FOR FURTHER PROGRESS

The development of more refined and detailed estimates than hitherto made is recognized as pioneer work. But the pioneer character of endeavors designed to supply much simpler estimates, where statistical information is only rudimentary, does not yet meet equal recognition. The technicians experienced in advanced estimating work might, from their vantage point of statistical and academic accomplishments, tend to belittle the ingenuity needed where estimates must be developed with fewer statistics and in situations whose inherent tendencies have been little explored. The experience made in advanced areas can undoubtedly benefit areas of smaller experience, but many modifications and adaptations are necessary before techniques, transplanted from one climate to another, can be expected to thrive in new soil.

*General Reconsideration of
the Field*

The practical role of population estimates is in need of better appreciation. Its comprehension will be facilitated by means of the four considerations discussed in this chapter. These considerations, which could be expanded further, relate to (*a*) the limits to generalizations, (*b*) the degree of objectivity attainable, (*c*) the use of estimates in decision-making, and (*d*) the scientific disposal of "errors."

Different estimates of the same quantities can satisfy different practical objectives. The objectives, in a given instance, might be more clearly stated. It is desired that estimates be "reliable" (a somewhat vague but inevitable criterion), that they be "consistent" (with conventional measurements, with each other, or with general knowledge and expectations), that they be made "conveniently" (by simple, efficient, and yet plausible methods), and that their "accuracy" be submitted to verification.

But many estimates are also required for theoretical objectives. In that event, they may very well be "hypothetical" (i.e., independent of reality) or "conditional" (partly, but not entirely, related to reality), and they must be "consistent." Theoretical objectives should be kept distinct from practical ones, despite the similar external appearances of estimates made for either purpose.

There has been very little analysis of the inherent nature of estimates. Every estimate is made by means of data and assumptions, but even these two fundamental categories cannot yet be clearly distinguished. Progress is needed here because a classification of estimating methods by logical type, or of types of estimating problems, cannot be made in the absence of more fundamental definitions. The status of the field will be greatly enhanced once it can be surveyed.

Data and Methods

A quantity that is satisfactorily measured need no longer be estimated; in this respect, new data can displace the need for estimates. But data are also needed for estimating purposes. These data comprise not only conventional measurements (e.g., censuses, vital registers) but sample measurements, non-demographic parameters and observed relationships between those and demographic facts, observed interrelations between consistent demographic facts under average or "normal" conditions, observations on the shapes of trends, and various qualitative information and knowledge.

Some data, of only secondary immediate interest, can be crucial for estimating purposes. Objective information on underenumeration of infants at censuses, on tendentious misstatement of ages, on certain characteristics of migratory movements, etc., should be secured with these purposes in view. In the collection of data, specific needs for estimates which could be filled at the same time are often neglected.

Statistical measurements are not always highly satisfactory. Their reliability should always be checked. This can sometimes be done by estimating methods which permit tests of consistency, but the practice is not as frequent as it should be. The computational estimating techniques now in use are, on the whole, adequate and relevant. But because of their *ad hoc* development, their underlying nature and the prerequisites for their use are often insufficiently explored. The applicability of each technique remains conditional on available types of data and the general nature of the social and demographic situation.

The actuarial origin of certain techniques often places undue emphasis on internal consistency without achieving greater conformity to facts. Depending on criteria not yet formulated, simpler methods might often be substituted with advantage. The failure of actuarial graduations to take account of directional misstatement of ages can be serious for demographic purposes, but a suitable technique for dealing with this phenomenon still remains to be developed.

Demographic estimating techniques can be greatly expanded by the construction of estimating models where demographic quantities consistent with others under average conditions, or under certain typical conditions, can be directly inferred. This relatively new approach to estimating problems has already found some applications in systematic population projections. It promises to be most fruitful in the development of demographic estimates for countries where statistical information is only fragmentary or otherwise inadequate.

For many practical purposes, it is essential that techniques be simple, even if crude and, at first appearance, not entirely logical. Elaborate theoretical studies should suggest some of the simpler approximations which, within limitations, can suffice for estimating purposes. Modern fertility analysis will probably increase estimating ability. Estimates involving an assumption of migration are still in need of improvement. Research in the relationship of population movements and economic change may still prove helpful in the selection of economic or other parameters for estimates of population change.

Cumulation of Experience

Increased attention has recently been given to the relative success or failure of estimates made by different methods. The pragmatic tests are usually made in the form of frequency distributions of discrepancies of estimates from independent observations. They are highly pertinent because they make it possible to assess, somewhat intuitively, the likelihood of greater and lesser errors when an estimate is being made. But evaluation of experience should not stop here. The tests usually apply only to estimates made under similar conditions and with similar amounts and types of statistical data. The findings of such tests are most relevant to similar situations, but less so to others. Experience is not transferable without an appraisal of the types of situations in which the findings can be regarded as applicable.

The experience made in estimating can be marshaled only with difficulty. Some records of experience appear in the publications in which actual estimates are put forth. Others may be found by systematic perusal of some of the leading statistical journals. There is no suitable bibliographic compilation where systematic reference to experience in a variety of estimating techniques under diverse conditions can be found. The proper place for bibliographic reference might be a comprehensive textbook on population estimates. But a book with systematic coverage of this field still remains to be written.

The estimating experience in fields other than demography should also be considered. It is possible that useful hints for population estimating methods might be derived from economic time-series analysis. Even the experience in diverse fields, such as meteorology and astronomy, is possibly relevant. The Pareto curve, for example, is useful as a description of such diverse facts as the distribution of incomes, of stars of varying magnitude, and of population in localities of varying sizes.

Personnel and Training

Where estimating procedures are highly developed, three levels of work can now be distinguished: (*a*) the practical arrangement and execution of computational procedures, (*b*) the designing and testing of computing techniques, and (*c*) the critical evaluation of relevance in the light of a wider knowledge of social facts. But work at each level is not to be confined in watertight compartments. A computing clerk will work most intelligently if he participates in the design of methods. And the statistician who recommends the use of some methods will do well to consult with sociologists, economists, business managers, and public authorities. Furthermore, a higher level of work should preferably be assigned to persons with past experience in the lower echelon. Ideally, a computing clerk should be equipped to advance, as his experience widens, to posts involving larger responsibilities.

A specialized qualification is not to be desired. Of course, there must be some training and experience in persistent practical manipulation of routine procedures. But the capacity to develop and improve work methods derives its strength from knowledge in much wider fields than mere demographic-statistical computation. There has to be some understanding of the practical requirements for population estimates in government and business. And knowledge in one or several diverse fields, such as mathematics, statistics, economics, sociology, medicine, anthropology, and history, can be of great value. At least a fairly general education in a variety of fields should be combined with more specialized training.

One type of specialization, nevertheless, is essential. A person engaged in demographic estimating work must at least be endowed with the facility to deal imaginatively with quantitative terms. Whether this facility is a mere bent of mind or whether it has been acquired through work in another capacity, be it that of a bookkeeper, an engineer, or an astronomer, is immaterial, but it must be present. High intellectual accomplishment is sometimes achieved in entirely non-quantitative fields, such as law, literature, history, and philosophy. Though evidence of a good intellect, this accomplishment does not prove a person's ability to operate intelligently where quantities are concerned. One of the difficulties in recruiting demographic personnel in technologically less advanced areas lies in the fact that intellectual excellence is often confined to the non-quantitative disciplines.

International scholarships, seminars, and exchanges of experience can contribute greatly to an advancement of this field. But particularly in its present state of development, experience gained in one area is not directly transferable to another. Reference has been made to the failure of colonial administrations to produce adequate statistics of even the simplest quantities, despite the fact that a store of statistical competence has been at the disposal of the administering powers. The development and practical application of methods suitable to local conditions will depend to a large extent on a corresponding quickening of local genius in its familiar surroundings.

Taking a still broader view, one may assert that familiarity with general social conditions is necessary if estimating methods and assumptions are to be used judiciously. There have been many attempts to link some demographic phenomena to economic parameters. Quantified facts are found more abundantly in economics than in most other social studies, but this should not lead to exclusive preoccupation of demographers with the economic correlates of population trends. Cultural and sociological phenomena are at least as relevant. But many of the concepts in sociology are still in process of being formulated and not yet amenable to quantification. Much further progress in the entire field of social concepts is needed if ability to assess demographic situations within their wider setting is to be substantially improved.

SELECTED BIBLIOGRAPHY

Atsatt, Marjory. 1941. *Population Estimates for England and Wales from the Eleventh to the Nineteenth Century.* (Document 1459.) Washington, D.C.: American Documentation Institute, Offices of Social Service.

Bennett, M. K. 1954. *The World's Food,* chap. i. New York: Harper & Bros.

Bogue, D. J. 1950. "A Technique for Making Extensive Population Estimates," *Journal of the American Statistical Association,* XLV, 149–63.

Bourgeois-Pichat, J. 1952. *La mortalité en Europe: Chances et conséquences,* fasc. 1. Nancy: Centre Européen Universitaire, Departement des Sciences Sociales.

Cox, P. R. 1950. *Demography,* chap. xii–xiii. Cambridge: Cambridge University Press.

Dorn, H. 1950. "Pitfalls in Population Forecasts and Projections," *Journal of the American Statistical Association,* XLV, 311–34. Reprinted in *Demographic Analysis,* ed. J. J. Spengler and O. D. Duncan. Glencoe, Ill.: Free Press, 1956.

Glass, D. V. 1940. *Population Policies and Movements in Europe.* Oxford: Clarendon Press.

Hagood, Margaret J., and Siegel, J. S. 1951. "Projections of the Regional Distribution of the Population of the United States to 1975," *Agricultural Economics Research,* III, 41–52.

Hajnal, J. 1955a. "The Prospects for Population Forecasts," *Journal of the American Statistical Association,* L, 309–22.

———. 1955b. "Discussion on Current Population Problems with Particular Reference to the United Nations World Population Conference," *Journal of the Royal Statistical Society,* Ser. A, Vol. CXVIII, Part I.

HAUSER, P. M., and ELDRIDGE, HOPE T. 1947. "Projection of Urban Growth and Migration to Cities in the United States," *Milbank Memorial Fund Quarterly,* XXV, 293–307.

HAUSER, P. M., and TEPPING, B. J. 1944. "Evaluation of Census Wartime Population Estimates and of Predictions of Postwar Population Prospects for Metropolitan Areas," *American Sociological Review,* IX, 473–80.

KARPINOS, B. D. 1939. "Stabilized Method of Forecasting Population" ("United States Public Health Reports," LIV, 1807–22).

NOTESTEIN, F. W., et al. 1944. *The Future Population of Europe and the Soviet Union.* Geneva: League of Nations.

REED, L. J. 1936. "Population Growth and Forecasts," *Annals of the American Academy of Political and Social Science,* No. 188, pp. 159–66.

ROYAL COMMISSION ON POPULATION. 1950. *Reports and Selected Papers of the Statistics Committee.* London: H.M. Stationery Office.

SCHNEIDER, J. R. L. 1954. "Note on the Accuracy of Local Population Estimates," *Population Studies,* VIII, 148–50.

SIEGEL, J. S. 1953. "Forecasting the Population of Small Areas," *Land Economics,* XXIX, 72–88.

———, et al. 1954. "Accuracy of Postcensal Estimates of Population for States and Cities," *American Sociological Review,* XIX, 440–46.

SILCOCK, H. 1954. "Precision in Population Estimates," *Population Studies,* VIII, 140–47.

SPENGLER, J. J. 1936. "Population Prediction in Nineteenth-century America," *American Sociological Review,* I, 905–21.

SPIEGELMAN, M. 1955. *Introduction to Demography,* chap. xii. Chicago: Society of Actuaries.

TAEUBER, IRENE B. 1944. "The Development of Population Predictions in Europe and the Americas," *Estadística,* II, 323–46.

———. 1949. "Literature on Future Populations, 1943–1948," *Population Index,* XV, 2–30.

UNITED NATIONS, DEPARTMENT OF ECONOMIC AND SOCIAL AFFAIRS. 1949. *World Population Trends, 1920–1947.* ("Population Studies," No. 3.) New York: United Nations.

———. 1952. *Methods of Estimating Total Population for Current Dates.* ("Manuals on Methods of Estimating Population," Manual I, "Population Studies," No. 10.) New York: United Nations.

———. 1954. *The Population of Central America (Including Mexico), 1950–1980.* ("Population Studies," No. 16.) New York: United Nations.

———. 1955a. *The Population of South America, 1950–1980.* ("Population Studies," No. 21.) New York: United Nations.

———. 1955b. *Methods of Appraisal of Quality of Basic Data for Population Estimates.* ("Manuals on Methods of Estimating Population," Manual III, "Population Studies," No. 23.) New York: United Nations.

UNITED STATES, DEPARTMENT OF COMMERCE, BUREAU OF THE CENSUS. 1947. *Forecasts of the Population of the United States, 1945–1975,* by P. K. WHELPTON et al. Washington, D.C.: Government Printing Office.

UNITED STATES, NATIONAL RESOURCES COMMITTEE, COMMITTEE ON POPULATION PROBLEMS. 1938. *The Problems of a Changing Population.* Washington, D.C.: Government Printing Office.

WHELPTON, P. K. 1936. "An Empirical Method of Calculating Future Population," *Journal of the American Statistical Association,* XXXI, 457–73.

WHITE, HELEN R. 1954. "Empirical Study of the Accuracy of Selected Methods of Projecting State Populations," *Journal of the American Statistical Association,* XLIX, 480–98.

WORLD POPULATION CONFERENCE, 1954, MEETING 13. 1955. "Methods of Making Population Projections," in *Proceedings of the World Population Conference, 1954,* Vol. III. New York: United Nations.

24. Family Statistics

PAUL C. GLICK

Demographers in the field of family statistics are concerned chiefly with problems relating to family formation, family composition, social and economic characteristics of the family, and family dissolution. In many respects, family statistics deal with the same data as other fields of demography but with a different approach. Instead of treating individuals as units of observation, the family statistician more often considers as basic units the natural groups in which people live. Thus, the household, the family, the married couple, or the person living alone is generally the unit of analysis in studies of the family statistician, whereas the migrant or the income recipient or the labor force participant may be the unit of analysis for other demographic specialists. In family statistics, households and families are classified by age, sex, color, employment status, residence, and other characteristics of the head; in other population statistics, similar characteristics of people are generally treated without respect to family status. The family statistician is interested not only in how many persons are in the dependent ages or in how many people are married, widowed, or divorced but also in the living arrangements of these people. Vital statisticians in the field of the family specialize in data on such units as first marriages, divorces, and remarriages. They are concerned mainly with trends and differential patterns in marriage and divorce, but their interests also extend to such subjects as mortality data for persons classified by marital status.

The needs for statistics on families and households arise from the ways in which these natural groups of people act as units. The household is the unit of population which occupies one dwelling unit and which is therefore the most relevant population concept for use in housing analyses. The family, and not the person, is the primary unit of consumption used in various marketing and cost-of-living studies. The family is central to the study of dependency, migration, income maintenance, economic status, and social adjustment. In most instances, marriage marks the establishment of a family, and separation, divorce, or widowhood marks its dissolution. Students of marriage and the family are concerned with differential rates of family growth, patterns of family living arrangements, changes in economic welfare of families, and trends in the stability of families. In countries where family allowance systems are in effect or are being contemplated, there are obvious values in family statistics as a means of evaluating the scope and cost of such programs. Significantly, no mention is made here of the family as a unit of reproduction; this area is covered in another chapter, on "Fertility."

In this chapter, attention is focused on the development and evaluation of family statistics in the United States. Research in the field of the family was stimulated during the 1930's by many perplexing problems relating to poverty and unemployment. Out of the disturbed conditions of the depression years, a growing number of well-trained research workers developed an awareness of the deficiencies of available data on the family. These research workers saw the potential value of more adequate data in this field as a background for a rational appraisal of past trends and future prospects relating to family welfare. Many of the needs for family data were accordingly met through the consumer-purchases studies of the middle 1930's and through special tabulations of 1940 census data. The critical period of World War II brought new requests for information on marriage, divorce, the number of dependents of men of military age, and the wartime consumption needs of families. Later, the problems of postwar adjustment, especially in relation to housing, further stimulated interest in marriage and family data.

Currently, the demand for family statistics comes from many of the same sources as before, as well as from a rapidly growing number of research experts on the staffs of private industrial establishments. These experts are engaged in assessing the future potentials in production and marketing of their goods and services. Moreover, young people in the colleges and high schools have developed a keener interest in the factual study of marriage and family adjustments, and consumption patterns and textbooks on these subjects have drawn increasingly upon the available demographic data. Ministers, family counselors, and social workers have found the data on family statistics a useful standard against which to evaluate the circumstances of families needing moral and economic assistance.

DATA

Development of Family Statistics

Comprehensive statistics in the field of the family in this country, and in most other countries where such data are available, are of relatively recent origin. In the United States, a few characteristics of households in 1790 were compiled more than one century later for inclusion in an analysis of population changes up to 1900 (United States Bureau of the Census, 1909, chap. viii). Very limited data on households were compiled from the censuses of 1850 to 1880, but the coverage was not complete for certain censuses; and for other reasons the quality of these data was unsatisfactory. In 1890 and 1900, household data of a much wider range were compiled, partly for the light they threw on the subject of home ownership. More limited data in this field were compiled from the censuses of 1910 and 1920. Statistics on the marital status of persons have been published for each census date since 1890.

In the 1930 census the last of the six basic volumes on population was devoted to family statistics. Among the subjects covered were size of family, number of young members of different ages in the family, number of gainful workers in the family, number of lodgers living with the family, tenure and value or rent of home, and several characteristics of the head of the family, such as age, marital status, sex, race, and nativity. Data on these subjects were published for the United States, each state, and each large city, and selected data were shown for counties and smaller cities. Several tables for 1930 showing detailed cross-classifications of family items by marital status and sex of the head were compiled but not published except in summary tables included in some of the 1940 family reports.

The general design of the 1930 family tabulations was followed in the 1940 census, but in addition new types of data were compiled, notably on family income and housing characteristics in relation to family composition. Moreover, data on persons classified by relationship to the head of the household were compiled for the first time in 1940.

Many of the same types of family statistics were published from the 1950 censuses of population and housing, despite the fact that the family tabulation program was less extensive than that for 1940. New types of data from the 1950 census were published in the fields of marital status, family living arrangements, and duration of current marital status. Also, data on selected family items were published for the first time in 1950 for standard metropolitan areas and urbanized areas.

Since 1944, annual reports on marital status and family characteristics, based on the Current Population Survey, have provided current information on intercensal changes in patterns of family living in the United States as a whole. These publications are in the "P-20 Series" of the *Current Population Reports*. The sample data from these surveys have also been used to obtain certain types of family data not covered in decennial censuses, to test new family concepts, and to pretest the collection and processing of family data in advance of the decennial censuses. The Current Population Surveys are based on scientifically selected samples of households in many areas throughout the United States. In 1956 the size of the sample was increased by two-thirds, to about 35,000 households, and the number of local areas canvassed was similarly expanded.

Statistics on the numbers of marriages and divorces in the United States have been compiled for every year from 1867 to the present. Statistics in these fields are published by the National Office of Vital Statistics, which is an agency within the Public Health Service in the Department of Health, Education, and Welfare. During the 1920's and the early 1930's, reports showing marriages by age of the bride and groom and certain other subjects were published for those states with central files of marriage records. Since the late 1940's, annual reports containing more detailed figures of these types and other reports showing divorces by age of the husband and wife, number of children, legal grounds for the divorce, and related subjects have been tabulated by variable numbers of states and assembled and published by the National Office of Vital Statistics. In 1953 and 1954 data on several previously neglected characteristics of recently married persons were collected by the Bureau of the Census through its Current Population Survey. This project was sponsored jointly by the National Office of Vital Statistics and the Bureau of the Census. The results have been published in *Vital Statistics—Special Reports* by the National Office of Vital Statistics.

This brief outline of the development of census and vital-statistics data on marriage and the family shows that long-time trends can be traced for only a relatively small number of items but that recent data are available on a wide variety of subjects. These facts, in turn, are related to the recent development of active interest in demographic data in these areas.

Technical Problems Relating to the Data

An exhaustive treatment of the weaknesses in family data from past censuses and current surveys cannot be made within the scope of this chapter. Moreover, such a treatment would probably leave some readers with a much greater skepticism about the value of the published figures than the facts of the situation warrant. The majority of people give accurate and complete information to census enumerators and those in charge of vital records. As a rule, very few persons wilfully misreport or withhold information that is requested of them, even on the more personal items. Errors in the reporting do occur when exact answers are unknown and in occasional circumstances where a straightforward reply would be embarrassing to the respondent. In addition, errors may creep into the data at any stage from collection through processing and publication.

Some types of deficiencies in the data are more readily detectable than others. For instance, the reported duration of marriage for a young married person in a census or survey may be obviously too great to be consistent with his or her current age; such errors can be readily found and adjusted by substituting a more reasonable duration or age. In fact, systematic methods have been devised for estimating duration of marriage, when necessary. However, the reported duration of marriage for a person in his fifties may be in error by five or ten years without causing any apparent discrepancy with other particulars about him. Knowledge of the extent of such errors and of the randomness or directional bias among them can be obtained from re-enumeration of a sample of the population or from comparisons of census and vital statistics records. For many items covered in the 1950 census, but not for the one in question, rechecks of these types were made.

The quality of statistics on family life, as on other subjects, is generally related to the amount of attention devoted to the collection and processing of the data. Thus, the figures on the number of households for 1850 to 1870 are not very useful for several reasons, including the failure to count slave households in 1850 and 1860, the well-known shortage in the coverage of the census of 1870—which was taken during the disturbed conditions of the Reconstruction Period, the absence from the population schedule of the key item on relationship to the head of the household, and the slight attention given to household statistics during this period. When more (but not too many) questions are asked about households (or other subjects), it seems that more precision is developed in collecting and processing the data; that is, more attention is devoted to the reporting and editing of marginal cases, and more careful scrutiny is given to the inconsistencies in the basic data. For instance, if the enumerator is required to classify people according to their relationship to the head of the household, he is more likely to distinguish carefully where one household ends and another begins than he would be in the absence of such a question.

Data on number of households.— Family data from different sources for the same date may differ in quality for several reasons, such as differences in the training and experience of the enumerators, in the manner in which the enumerators are paid, and in the types of schedules and auxiliary forms used. These are believed to be some of the main factors underlying the differences between the counts of households obtained for 1950 from the decennial census and the Current Population Survey (CPS). The number of households in the United States according to the complete count of the 1950 census was 42,857,335, whereas the number from the CPS (as revised) was 43,554,000. The difference between these figures is too great to be readily accounted for by sampling variation in the CPS.

Where a complex grouping of persons in a given set of living quarters was encountered, the census enumerator was evidently more likely than the CPS enumerator to group the persons as members of a single household rather than two or more separate households, even though both enumerators had been given the same criteria for identifying a household. The census enumerators, unlike the enumerators in the

CPS, had relatively little training, were given no auxiliary forms covering previous enumerations of the people in question, and were paid on a piece-rate system rather than by the hour. In a doubtful case, the census enumerator evidently found it to his financial advantage to decide in favor of counting a group of persons as one household rather than two because that minimized the number of separate visits required. In support of this hypothesis, figures for identical persons enumerated in the 1950 census and in the CPS, classified

TABLE 52

Per Cent Distribution by Relationship to Head of Household According to 1950 Census and Current Population Survey, for Identical Persons*

Data for a Matched Group of about 69,000 Persons Enumerated in Both the 1950 Census and the Current Population Survey for April, 1950

Relationship to Head of Household	Census	Current Population Survey
Total..............	100.0	100.0
Head of household......	29.9	30.1
Wife of head............	23.6	23.6
Son or daughter of head .	36.7	36.6
Other relative of head...	6.9	7.2
Non-relative of head.....	2.7	2.4
Quasi-household member.	0.1	0.1

* Source: U.S. Bureau of the Census (1953–57, Part 2D, Marital Status, Table D).

by relationship to head of household, show a deficiency in the census of household heads and an excess of sons and daughters of the head and non-relatives of the head (Table 52).

Moreover, the Post-Enumeration Survey (PES) revealed a much larger proportional net deficit in the 1950 census count of households (2.5 per cent) than of persons (1.4 per cent). According to the PES, nearly three-fourths of the persons missed in the census were members of households which were entirely missed; this fact was contrary to a commonly accepted hypothesis that most people missed in censuses are infants or temporarily absent members of households that are enumerated. A special tabulation of PES data indicates that the average size of missed households was a little over 2.5 persons, whereas the average for enumerated households was considerably greater, about 3.4 persons.

Data on household relationship.—In classifying the population by family living arrangements, certain arbitrary decisions are sometimes made in one census and changed before the next census. These decisions affect, to some extent, the interpretation of data relating to family composition for a given date and comparisons over a period of time. To illustrate, the Bureau of the Census has consistently instructed the enumerators to list as the head of the household the person so reported by the respondent for the household. (In processing the returns, the wife is not counted as the head if her husband is present. This practice requires the editing of a small proportion—perhaps 0.5 per cent—of the schedules and is maintained in order to prevent the inclusion of a separate category for the few women involved.) Sometimes a different person would be listed as the head if, instead, the chief income recipient in the household were to be considered invariably as the head. However, using income as the criterion for determining who is the head would require the inclusion of questions on income in each census or survey and would often distort the pattern of dominant and subordinate relationships among the members. Probably the person classified as the head is generally the one in whose name the living quarters are owned or rented.

Technical problems arise also in enumerating college students. In 1940 and most of the previous censuses, unmarried college students were enumerated as members of their parents' households, but in the 1950 census they were counted where they lived while attending college. This was done as a means of improving the completeness of the count of such persons, on the assumption that persons away from home for several years at college might not be reported among the members of their parental households. However, the change in enumeration of college students affects the comparability of figures between 1940 and 1950 on population by geographic areas and on household and family members by age. This practice of counting college students where they live while attending school is not followed in the surveys based on the CPS because of difficulties in the changing rosters of household members during the summer months when students return home or go elsewhere for employment; the same households are covered for several months in the CPS. About two-thirds to three-fourths of a million students who were classified as residents of places where they were attending college in 1950 would have been classified as residents of places where their parents lived if the 1940 procedure had been followed.

Other types of persons involving problems of classification are lodgers, inmates of institutions, and members of the Armed Forces. In 1930 and 1940 if the number of lodgers exceeded ten, the occupants of the living quarters were regarded as residents in a lodging house rather than as a household. In 1950, the criterion was changed so that living quarters containing more than four lodgers were regarded as quasi-households. This change was intended to introduce a more realistic dividing line between commercial lodging houses and ordinary homes. A shift of roughly 100,000 households to the category of "quasi-households" was one of the results. The coverage of inmates of institutions was likewise increased in 1950 by the addition of tuberculosis hospitals and nursing and rest homes to the list of institutions, and by a systematic attempt in 1950 to identify, in

advance of the enumeration, the addresses of places that should be classified as institutions. Changes in the classification of lodgers, in the coverage of institutions, and in the size of the Armed Forces create difficulties in the interpretation of changes between 1940 and later dates in the population not in households. These difficulties are minimized, however, to the extent that data exist for the separate analysis of these groups.

Data on marital status.—Household relationship and marital status are almost always reported completely in censuses and surveys. In pretests of the 1950 census less than 1 per cent had no report on these items. In both 1940 and 1950, persons with no report on these subjects were assigned to one category or another on the basis of other data on the schedule. This procedure simplified table construction and made the data more usable. The scheme for assigning codes on marital status in 1950 was as follows: if the person had a spouse present, the code assigned was "married, spouse present"; if the person had no spouse present and was under twenty-five years old, the code assigned was "married, spouse absent," for those with children present and "single" (never married) for those with no children present; if the person had no spouse present, the code was "married, spouse absent," for those twenty-five to fifty-four years old and "widowed" for those fifty-five years old or older. Thus, in general, the person was assigned to the modal marital status class according to the presence of spouse or children and age. Special rules were established for selected groups of persons not reporting on marital status: for persons in convents and monasteries, the code assigned uniformly for those not reporting on marital status was "single"; for other persons in institutions a special scheme of random assignment was used, based on available data on marital status by age and sex for persons in institutions.

More serious deficiencies were found in the reporting on number of times married and duration of current marital status. The non-response rates on these items in 1950 were 7 per cent and 9 per cent, respectively. In processing the data for women, these non-responses were eliminated by the assignment of appropriate entries based on a complex, formalized, prorating process derived from data for a special national sample of 1950 census returns for approximately 60,000 women for whom information on these subjects was reported. The process of eliminating non-responses on number of times married for women made use of available data on current age, marital status, and color. The elimination of non-responses on duration of current marital status for women made use of data on current age, marital status, number of times married, color, and farm residence. Non-reports for men were not eliminated.

The number of persons reported in censuses and surveys as having been married for a relatively brief period tends to be considerably below the number expected on the basis of data from marriage records. This is attributable, in part, to differences in coverage; the CPS does not cover men in military barracks or overseas. Also, 5 per cent of the persons in the CPS in 1953 failed to report on duration of marriage. Aside from shortages due to these factors, the CPS showed about 9 per cent fewer marriages for the approximately three years prior to the survey of April, 1953, than the number indicated by data from marriage records. Among the possible reasons for this difference are errors in the survey in reporting a married person as single and errors in reporting year of marriage (usually reporting a year that is more remote than the actual year, presuma-

bly to hide premarital conceptions). To a lesser extent, the difference may be explained by overcounts of the marriage records arising from the inclusion for some areas of marriage licenses rather than marriages performed and from errors in estimates of marriages for areas from which data were not available.

Census and survey data provide information on the number of divorced persons who had not remarried by the census or survey date. These data may be compared with vital statistics data on the number of divorced persons for years previous to the census or survey date, adjusted downward to allow for deaths and remarriages of the divorced persons. Such comparisons have been made by Jacobson (1952, pp. 12–16). He has concluded that the numbers of divorced persons (who had not remarried) have been grossly understated in the census statistics but that the amount of the understatement has been declining. Thus, Jacobson has estimated that the number of divorced men as reported in the 1910 census was only one-fourth as large as it should have been and that in 1940 the number was about four-tenths as large as it should have been. For women, the shortage in 1940 may have been close to one-half, according to his estimates. Reasons for the undercount of divorced persons include the misreporting of marital status in order to avoid social disapproval and the relatively large proportion of divorced persons who live in lodging houses and other types of living quarters where information may be reported to enumerators by intermediate respondents; some of these intermediates do not know the person's marital status, and transient persons are often missed in the enumeration. Divorced women who have their children living with them and those without children who use the title "Mrs." probably find it less easy to avoid reporting themselves as divorced than divorced men—who seldom have custody of their children and who use the title "Mr." regardless of their marital status. Reporting of the correct marital status for divorced persons should continue to improve as attitudes toward divorce become more tolerant, and the enumeration of divorced persons should become more nearly complete as enumeration methods improve.

changes of classifications was between these two categories. The findings may have been affected by the inclusion of the response category "separated" in the census but not in the survey, as indicated by a footnote in the table. Interchanges between the categories "divorced," "widowed," and "married, spouse absent" were in general the most frequent, but numerous persons reported as "divorced" or "married,

TABLE 53

Per Cent Distribution by Marital Status According to 1950 Census, by Marital Status According to Current Population Survey, for Identical Persons Fourteen Years Old and Over*

Data for a Matched Group of about 51,000 Persons Enumerated in Both the 1950 Census and the Current Population Survey for April, 1950

Marital Status According to 1950 Census	Total	Single	Married			Widowed and Divorced		
			Total	Spouse Present	Spouse Absent	Total	Widowed	Divorced
Total..............	100.0	100.0	100.0	100.0	100.0	100.0	100.0	100.0
Single................	20.4	96.4	0.3	0.1	6.9	2.2	1.7	4.8
Married..............	69.9	1.7	99.3	99.7	80.1	6.2	4.3	15.3
Spouse present.......	67.7	0.3	97.4	99.6	2.8	0.6	0.5	1.1
Spouse absent†.......	2.2	1.5	1.9	0.2	77.3	5.6	3.7	14.2
Widowed and divorced..	9.7	1.9	0.5	0.2	13.0	91.6	94.1	79.8
Widowed...........	7.9	0.8	0.3	0.1	7.5	76.8	90.7	10.2
Divorced...........	1.8	1.1	0.2	0.1	5.5	14.8	3.3	69.6

* Source: U.S. Bureau of the Census, unpublished tabulation.

† In the 1950 census, included the response category "separated." In the Current Population Survey at that time, "separated" persons were to be reported as "married."

Further evidence of weaknesses in census and survey reporting of divorced persons is presented in Table 53. This table shows how a sample of persons enumerated in April, 1950, in both the 1950 census and the CPS were classified according to marital status in the two counts. The figures show the least agreement (70 per cent) in the category "divorced" and only slightly better agreement (77 per cent) in the category "married, spouse absent" (which includes "separated" persons). These facts are closely related, however, because a large proportion of the interchanges were between

spouse absent" in the CPS were reported as single in the 1950 census. All of these interchanges undoubtedly reflect the varied ways in which unwed mothers of illegitimate children misreport their marital status; very few such mothers are correctly reported as single.

If the marital status classification is limited to three broad categories, "single," "married," and "widowed or divorced," the results are likely to be reasonably stable, as Table 53 shows. About 96 per cent of those reported as single (never married) in the CPS were also reported as single in the 1950 census. The corresponding measure of agreement for married persons was 99 per cent and that for widowed or divorced persons was 92 per cent.

Data from marriage and divorce records.—The only nationwide data from marriage and divorce records are the total numbers of marriages and divorces. These data are limited in usefulness because they do not provide the fundamental distinction between persons in first marriages and those with remarriages. At present, thirty-six of the states have central files of marriage records, and thirty have central files of divorce records. Although the states with central files are not necessarily representative of all states, they are widely distributed throughout the nation. Efforts are being made to extend the coverage of these statistics and to make them more uniform.

For several states, figures are available on the residence status of persons who marry in the state, but until marriage statistics become available for all states, it will not be possible to allocate all marriages of non-residents to the usual state of residence of the bride and of the groom. Such allocation is needed in order to compute marriage rates in relation to the appropriate population bases by states.

Age at marriage tends to be overstated on marriage-reporting forms for persons below the legal age at marriage in the state. This undoubtedly accounts in part for the heaping of marriages with age eighteen reported for the bride. Twenty-one is by far the most often reported age at marriage for grooms. An opposite bias probably exists in the reported age at marriage in census enumerations because of a tendency to make the duration of the marriage consistent with the age of the oldest child. Recently, statistics from marriage records have become available on age at marriage in single years. These

are now published annually for those states which have such figures available; the list of states varies, however, from year to year.

Statistics from divorce records on number of children of the couple are reported in various ways by the several states, so that a precise understanding of the relationship between divorce and parenthood is obscured. The legal grounds for divorce are known to be at variance with the real causes of divorce in a large proportion of the cases. Entirely lacking from the statistics based on divorce and marriage records published by the National Office of Vital Statistics are any measures of the economic status of the persons concerned. However, under the stimulus of that agency, some states are beginning to assemble data on marriages by occupation and education of the bride and groom.

METHODS

Description of Methods Used in Family Statistics

The methods used in family statistics are essentially the same as those employed elsewhere in population research. These methods include survey methods, relating to the collection and processing of the data, and analytical methods, relating to the summarization and interpretation of the findings. Thus, information is collected from persons; the returns are reduced to tabular form; the tables are summarized in terms of distributions, averages, and rates; and the generalizations warranted by the summary results are prepared for circulation along with the detailed tables.

Survey methods.—One of the first steps in conducting a survey is the design of the reporting form. The items to be included are generally selected in the light of the known needs for information, the feasibility of obtaining accurate and complete responses, and the advice of budgetary and technical consultants. Advisory committees for the 1950 census and for the current program of the marriage and divorce branch of the National Office of Vital Statistics have had an important part in shaping the content of family statistics produced by these two agencies. Details involved in the editing, coding, and tabulating of the results have been largely the responsibilities of technicians on the staffs of the agencies.

One unique feature in the processing of census data on families is the preparation of data for family units from data collected for each person in the household. This process is referred to as "family transcription." After codes have been assigned to each person on marital status, education, occupation, and so on, one line of information is transcribed for each family to a special form with columns for items such as the size of family, number of children of specified ages, number of persons in the labor force, family income, and selected characteristics of the head and wife. Similar data, where relevant, are also recorded on separate lines for individuals who are not family members (such as heads of households living alone and lodgers and resident employees who have no relatives in the household). A punch card containing these items is then prepared for each family or individual. In 1950 most of the items on characteristics of family heads were transferred to the family card from another card containing these items.

The statistics on characteristics of persons obtaining a marriage or a divorce which are published by the National Office of Vital Statistics (NOVS) are obtained from tables prepared in the vital statistics offices of the states with central files of marriage and divorce records. An alternative procedure would be to have each state with central records submit to the NOVS a transcript or microfilm copy of the records or a punch card containing data for each marriage or divorce and to have the NOVS tabulate the results. This method is used for processing birth and death statistics, but for several reasons (including budgetary problems) the same method is not being used in processing marriage and divorce statistics.

Analytical methods.—Most of the summary measures used in family statistics, including percentage distributions, medians, arithmetic means, and crude rates, are prepared in a conventional manner. Attention is devoted here to selected instances in which special procedures have been developed for the treatment of family data.

In computing the median size of family, the interval containing the median is unconventional in the sense that the midpoint rather than the upper or lower limit of the interval is a whole number of persons. For example, the limits 2.50 and 3.49 are used instead of 2.00 and 2.99 or 3.00 and 3.99. This procedure can be defended on the grounds that persons are discrete rather than continuous variables. By this method, a population comprising families all of which contain three members would have a median size of family of 3.00 persons; if conventional limits of the median interval, 3.00 and 3.99, were used, the median size of family would be 3.50 persons. The median size of family, as computed, is nearer the mean size of family, as a rule, than it would be if conventional intervals were used. Following the same reasoning, the median number of children per family is computed also by the use of intervals with whole numbers as the midpoints.

In computing the median age at marriage from census data based on questions relating to age at census and duration of marriage, unconventional midpoints and intervals are used. The underlying reason can be best understood by presenting an example. In the published tables showing the distribution of ages at marriage derived from data on age at census and duration of marriage, the age at marriage shown is an approximation obtained by subtracting the number of (completed) years in the marriage from the age at census (in completed years). Thus, if a woman reported that she had been in her (most recent) marriage for three years and that she was twenty-three years old at the time of the census, she was tabulated as having been twenty years old at the time of marriage. This age at marriage is only approximate, however; there is a possible range of almost two years in the exact ages of such women at marriage. Furthermore, the single years of age at marriage shown in the tables represent midpoints rather than the lower limits of one-year intervals, as in conventional tables showing age distributions. This irregular procedure could have been avoided by adopting the equally irregular procedure of designating the intervals by half-years, such as 19.5 to 20.4 instead of 20, and 22.5 to 24.4 instead of 23 and 24. The following figures, using the ages cited above, illustrate this point:

1. If age in full years at census is "23" years, the range of exact ages is . . . . 23.00–23.99 years
2. If the duration of marriage is "3" years, the range of exact durations is . . . . 3.99– 3.00 years
3. The limits of the range of exact ages at marriage are, therefore . . . . 19.01–20.99 years
4. The midpoint of age at marriage is . . . . . . 20.00 years
5. The limits of the single year of age at marriage containing this midpoint are . . . 19.50–20.49 years
6. These limits are one-half year below the conventional limits used for age "20."

A method has been developed by the Bureau of the Census for the estimation of the median age at first marriage on the basis of census or survey data on marital status and age at the time of the enumeration. Because the description of this methodology is rather involved, it is omitted here.[1] The results obtained by this method agree closely with those obtained from questions relating to age at marriage or duration of marriage. This method is useful for the estimation of median age at marriage for remote and current dates when data are not collected directly on age at marriage or duration of marriage.

Various rates are used in relating marriage and other family data to meaningful bases in order to study underlying trends and differential patterns. For example, crude marriage and divorce rates may be computed by dividing the number of marriages (and divorces) by the total population as of the middle of the year in which these events occurred. If such rates are developed for a long period of time, they may be lacking in comparability because of changes in the proportion of the population in the ages when most marriages and divorces occur. Likewise, comparisons of crude rates for countries with unlike age compositions are open to similar criticism. To overcome this weakness, the rates may be related to population bases more narrowly restricted. Thus, a useful marriage rate, for analytical purposes, is one obtained by dividing the number of marriages by the number of single, widowed, and divorced females fifteen to fifty-four years old. (The males are omitted partly because of fluctuations over the years in the number of men in the Armed Forces.) This type of marriage rate can be computed in many countries only

[1] See U.S. Bureau of the Census, *Current Population Reports* (Series P-20, No. 62), "Marital Status and Family Status: April 1955," pp. 5–6.

for census years because of the absence of data for intercensal and postcensal years on the population by age, sex, and marital status.

Marriage and other rates for persons classified by social and economic groups require even more detailed basic data and may require further refinements in methods. Thus, for 1950 the National Office of Vital Statistics published first-marriage and remarriage rates by age and sex for those states with marriage data classified in the necessary detail; population figures by age, sex, and marital status by states were used as bases for the rates.[2]

Again, 1950 census data for persons who entered first marriages, remarriages, widowhood, divorce, or separation during the two years prior to April, 1950, and data for persons who were subject to entering these marital status categories[3] have been used to prepare rates of first marriage, remarriage, widowhood, divorce, and separation (Glick, 1957, chaps. vii, viii). Rates of these kinds were computed for women by age and color, classified further (separately) by education, labor force status, and (for remarriage) number of children ever born. Also, first-marriage and remarriage rates for men by income level were computed. In some of the detailed subdivisions of the persons for whom these rates were prepared, the rates were very high. In a few instances, the estimated number entering the marital status during the year before the census (half of those in the marital status less than two years) exceeded the number remaining in 1950

[2] National Office of Vital Statistics, *Vital Statistics of the United States, 1950,* Vol. I, Table 5.05. For similar rates based on data from the census bureau's Current Population Survey, see Carter, Glick, and Lewit (1955).

[3] Persons "subject to" entering first marriage are single persons; those subject to remarriage are widowed and divorced persons; and those subject to widowhood, divorce, or separation are married persons.

as subject to entering it. To illustrate, the estimated number of women in the upper education groups who remarried at younger ages during the year prior to the 1950 census exceeded the number of widowed and divorced women in comparable age and education groups at the time of the 1950 census. In view of this situation, the denominators for the rates were increased to include not only those subject to entering the specified marital status at the end of the period but also those who actually entered it during the preceding year; the latter group was also subject to entering the marital status at some time during the period in question.

Specialized methods for projecting the numbers of households, families, married couples, and other types of units have been developed to meet a growing demand from research workers, mainly in the fields of production and market research. These persons usually want to know approximately how many households there will be in future years—units which make use, as a rule, of only one product (one house, one furnace, one telephone, etc.). The projections in this field depend upon previously prepared projections of population by age and sex. To these population projections specially prepared projections of the proportions of persons in broad marital-status categories are applied; to the projected population by marital status derived in this manner, the proportions of persons in such categories as "head of household" and "wife of head" are applied in order to obtain projections of numbers of persons in these categories.[4] Different levels of projections are presented to illustrate the probable levels of the number of households or other units if

[4] See U.S. Bureau of the Census, *Current Population Reports* (Series P-20, No. 69), "Projections of the Number of Households and Families: 1960 to 1975." See also Glick, 1957, chaps. ix, x.

specified assumptions regarding the future trends in population growth and in the tendency to maintain units of the type in question eventually materialize. The research worker who makes use of the projections decides which one or more of the levels to rely upon.

The methods described above do not exhaust the list which might have been presented, but they do illustrate methodological developments in the demography of family life. Additional methods will be covered in the following section.

Technical Problems Relating to the Methods

Most of the problems discussed here relate to survey methods. These problems also have significance in relation to the quality of the results produced and hence to analytical methods.

In designing a schedule or other reporting form, several practices may be employed to minimize response variation on the items of information. One of these is to present the questions in the exact manner in which they are to be asked. For example, instead of having a column with the heading "age," the question "How old was he on his last birthday?" has obvious advantages. In asking for marital status in the 1950 census, the question used was: "Is he now married, widowed, divorced, separated, or never married?" This wording presented all of the response categories. Moreover, by using the expression "never married" instead of "single," as in earlier censuses, persons who were divorced or separated were discouraged fom replying that they were single (again). Another device which was probably in part responsible for the reduction in the number of non-reports in 1950, as compared with 1940, was the use of a box for "none" or "less than one" where applicable; this device tends to overcome the mistaken reaction on the part of many enumerators that entries of "0" are unimportant and may be skipped.

If data on family items are to be based on a sample of the census returns, as they were in 1940 and 1950, the use of a household sample is in most ways preferred to the use of a sample of persons. In those two censuses, certain questions were asked of every *n*th person listed on the large population schedule which had space for fifty persons (in 1940) or thirty persons (in 1950). Families for which data were transcribed were chosen from those with the head on a sample line. However, if the head was on a sample line, the wife was not; hence, there was no possibility of obtaining the same sample item for both the head and wife (such as education and income in 1950). If the sample items had been asked of all persons in a sample of households, this difficulty would have been avoided. This fact was recognized, but the person sample was nonetheless adopted because it was less expensive to administer. The use of a household sample in 1960 is under consideration. Sampling on a household basis is done regularly in the Current Population Survey.

In the United States, the population has always been enumerated on a *de jure* basis, that is, at their usual place of residence. Consideration has been given to the enumeration of the population in 1960 on a *de facto* basis, that is, where the people are found on the census date. This proposal is believed to be superior for the improvement of coverage in a census. It would have the disadvantage, however, of providing less realistic data on family composition, family income, and several other items, unless a costly procedure were followed to allocate persons enumerated away from home to their usual place of residence.

In actual practice, an area of judgment exists in the application of the usual residence concept for persons with living quarters in more than one place. Consider a son away from home serving in the Armed Forces and a husband staying in a distant city because his job is located there. According to census rules long in effect, both the son and the husband are enumerated at the place where they stay most of the time rather than with their relatives "back home." These men are counted as residents in the community where they work; however, their regular contributions to the mother or wife are counted as income for her.

In the editing operation, census or survey responses are sometimes changed in order to eliminate obvious inconsistencies, and non-reports on certain key items are assigned an entry on the basis of other information on the schedule. Although doing so makes the tabulated results more useful for most purposes, this practice conceals the irregularities in the original census returns and thus makes it impossible to evaluate the census returns in terms of the proportion of persons with no report on the item or of the proportion with inconsistent replies unless a supplemental operation is conducted to examine the original entries and the final entries after editing. A special punch card was prepared to serve this purpose for 1940, and the results on some but not all items were processed.

When figures on the same subject are included in two or more machine counts of the same card or in counts of two or more samples of different sizes, the results in a mass data operation are seldom identical. The punch cards may become damaged and lost after repeated use, sampling variability and sampling biases may cause the results from different samples to differ, and so on. In the 1950 census, distributions on different subjects within a given count of the cards were adjusted to the same totals, and distributions from different counts of the same cards on a given subject were sometimes reconciled; but the totals from two different samples (for example, the 20 per cent sample and the 3⅓ per cent sample) on the same subject were not made to agree because the cost of doing so was considered excessive. Although it is disturbing to find these inconsistencies when data from different samples are manipulated jointly, the position was adopted that funds necessary for reconciliation work could be better expended in producing statistics on a wider variety of cross-classifications of the data. It was believed that the samples would almost always lead to the same generalizations about distributions and averages based on the larger figures. Small figures are known to be subject to a large relative error because of sampling variability, response variation, and other reasons.

To illustrate the magnitude of the differences between figures based on different sizes of samples, the following numbers of households are cited. The total number of households in the United States in 1950 according to the complete census count was 42,857,335; that from the 20 per cent sample was 42,251,415; that from the 3⅓ per cent sample was 42,243,170; and that from the 1⅑ per cent sample was 42,286,230. The close similarity of the three sample figures is due to the fact that the last two are approximately random subsamples of the 20 per cent sample. All three sample figures for the total number of households are significantly lower than the complete count figure. This fact is probably the result of failure on the part of some enumerators to follow the instructions exactly in listing persons on the schedule. The 20 per cent sample had a shortage of about 1.45 per cent in the number of men twenty-five years old and over as compared with the complete count. Men of this age who were in the sample were the most likely to be asked questions on family income and war service; sometimes a great deal of time was required to obtain answers to such questions.

The sample from which 1950 census data on family composition were obtained (Sample F) was drawn from families with the head on the last (sixth) sample line on the population schedule. This line was chosen because only the persons on these lines were asked the questions on number of times

ulation side of the schedule in order to start the next household at the top of the next schedule; and so on.

The effects on the distribution by household relationship of the shortage of entries on the last sample line are given in Table 54. The figures show smaller proportions of persons on the last sample line than on all sample lines in the categories "head" and "wife of head of household," and larger proportions in nearly all of the other catego-

TABLE 54

Per Cent Distribution by Relationship to Head of Household, According to Data on All Six Sample Lines and on Last Sample Line of 1950 Census Population Schedule*

Data for a Subsample of about 0.1 Per Cent of the Persons Enumerated on Sample Lines

	MALE		FEMALE	
RELATIONSHIP TO HEAD OF HOUSEHOLD	All Six Sample Lines	Last Sample Line	All Six Sample Lines	Last Sample Line
Total†	100.0	100.0	100.0	100.0
In households	95.5	94.0	97.2	96.3
Head of household	48.5	45.6 ⎱	51.9	50.3
Wife of head	.....	..... ⎰		
Child of head	37.3	37.3	34.3	34.5
Son- or daughter-in-law	1.0	1.0	0.6	0.5
Grandchild of head	2.1	2.4	1.9	2.0
Parent of head	0.9	1.1	2.7	2.8
Other relative of head	2.8	3.4	3.3	3.6
Lodger	2.7	3.1	2.1	2.1
Resident employee	0.2	0.2	0.4	0.5
In quasi-households	4.5	6.0	2.8	3.7

* Source: U.S. Bureau of the Census, unpublished tabulation.

† The number actually enumerated on all six sample lines (in the subsample) was 74,698 for males and 75,994 for females; the number enumerated on the last sample line multiplied by six was 71,232 for males and 72,774 for females.

married and years in current marital status, and information on these items was desired for certain tables. On many of the sheets, however, the enumerator did not fill the last line for one of several reasons: the sheet was the last one for the enumeration district and was only partially filled; the area being covered was one in which households were small or many dwelling units were vacant, and the spaces for housing on the back of the schedule were filled before the spaces for population on the front were filled; the enumerator erroneously skipped the last few lines on the pop-

ries. Especially noteworthy are the excesses in the proportion of persons on the last sample line who were in categories characteristic of large families (such as "grandchild" and "other relative") and the excess in the proportion in quasi-households. All of the lines on the schedules are likely to be filled for residents in military installations, large institutions, and other large quasi-households.

In order to adjust for the shortage of heads of families on the last sample line, a procedure was adopted to supplement the sample by adding systematically selected family heads from the other sample lines. For these added family heads, information on the marriage items were, of course, not available.

FUND OF KNOWLEDGE

Frame of Reference and Basic Concepts

Family statistics, from the demographic viewpoint, consist mainly of summaries of recorded events, such as marriages and divorces, and summaries of cross-section studies covering items such as the marital and family status of the population and the composition and socioeconomic status of families. These statistics deal with measurable phenomena relating to family formation and dissolution and to the manner in which natural groupings of people live. These data provide information on pivotal points and dynamic aspects of family life.

Progress toward a scientific approach in the collection and treatment of family data has been manifested in numerous ways, including the development of concepts that are carefully defined and consciously designed to cover the wide range of family behavior in a systematic manner. In some instances, terms in common use elsewhere have been given specialized operational definitions; others have been created where no counterpart previously existed. Where feasible, the meanings in popular usage were preserved. Partly because of the recency of the development of family statistics and partly because of the lack of uniformity in the modes of family living in different parts of the world, much work remains before a universally consistent terminology will emerge.

The concepts relating to family formation and composition which are described here are those in use by demographers in the United States, but they could probably be used in most of the other countries with populations of European origin—and perhaps in much of the remainder of the world, with some modifications. These concepts are intended for use in the study of the family as a social and economic unit and not as a unit of reproduction, although they can be used for the latter purpose if a few concepts are added.

According to this system of concepts, persons may be divided into three broad groups: persons in families, inmates of institutions, and persons (other than inmates of institutions) who are not in families (called "unrelated individuals"). A family is defined as a group of two or more persons related by blood, marriage, or adoption who live together; the entire group of related persons living together is regarded as one family. A household is the entire group of persons (whether or not related) who are living together, or a person living alone, in one dwelling unit. A dwelling unit, in turn, is defined as a house, an apartment or other group of rooms, or a single room which is intended for occupancy as separate living quarters, that is, with separate cooking equipment or a separate entrance. Groups of persons living in hotels, rooming houses, labor camps, military barracks, and institutions are referred to as quasi-households. Usually there is one family in a household, but there may be two or more families or none. Thus, if the household head and his wife rent a room to a married couple unrelated to them, the household consists of two families. A widow living in a house alone does not constitute a family. A group of related persons in a quasi-household is considered as a family.

Families or unrelated individuals are referred to as primary families or primary individuals if they maintain a dwelling unit and as secondary families or secondary individuals if they do not maintain a dwelling unit. A married couple is defined, for census purposes, as a married man and his wife who are living together, that is, who are enumerated as members of the same household or quasi-household. If a married couple shares the living quarters of relatives, the couple is regarded as a subfamily. Likewise, one parent and his or her children who are sharing the home of relatives are counted as a subfamily. Although separate statistics are compiled for subfamilies, the total number of families does not include the number of subfamilies. Institutional inmates include persons confined for special care or treatment in such places as homes for delinquent or dependent children, homes and schools for the mentally or physically handicapped, places providing specialized medical care, homes for the aged, prisons, and jails.

The principal concepts relating to marriage and divorce have legal definitions and may vary according to differences in relevant state laws. For example, in a state where it is difficult to obtain a divorce, many persons with marital difficulties seek to have the marriage annulled (that is, have it voided on the grounds that it was illegally contracted) rather than seek a divorce. In census statistics, persons with annulled marriages are classified as single (never married) because, legally, the marriage has been cancelled. For statistical purposes, a procedure preferred by some research workers would be for census tables to show persons with annulled marriages among those who have been divorced, as do tables based on vital records. Persons in common-law marriages (living in consensual unions) are regarded as married according to census classifications even though the vital statistics may show no marriage for them. The number of persons with annulled marriages or in common-law marriages is probably quite small in the United States as a whole but is probably significant in a few states.

Trends, Differentials, and Prospects

Changes in marriage patterns in the 1940's and early 1950's contrasted sharply with those of earlier decades. During the half-century before 1940, the proportion married in the population fourteen years old and over showed a decline of only a couple of percentage points, according to data standardized on the 1940 age distribution. During the years from 1940 to 1950, however, the corresponding increase in the proportion married jumped up five or six percentage points. In the same recent period, the median age at first marriage fell more than a year, whereas for men it had evidently dropped about two years, and for women only half a year, from 1890 to 1940. These demographic developments have reverberated on the birth rate, on the demand for family consumption products, and on the movement of population to suburban communities.

For decades the number of households increased at a more rapid rate than the total population, as a corollary of the long-time decline in the average size of household, but there is some evidence that during the early 1950's the situation was reversed, largely because of the resurgence of the birth rate since 1940. The long-time decline in size of household probably resulted mainly from the falling birth rate, but it was a consequence, also, of several other factors: the decline in the number of persons living as lodgers and resident domestic helpers in households; the increasing percentage of couples and widowed persons surviving for a long time after their children had left home and continuing to maintain small households; the improvement in economic security in old age permitting more older persons to maintain separate homes; the increase in the marriage rate especially after World War II and the consequent increase in the number of small households of both the parental homes and the newlyweds' homes; and the sharp decline in the sharing of living quarters during the late 1940's and early 1950's as the housing shortage immediately after World War II abated.

The rate of marriage dissolution through widowhood has declined steadily for many decades, whereas the rate of marriage dissolution through divorce rose steadily until the early 1940's, rose sharply during and just after the war years, then fell steadily thereafter. The recent decline in divorce may be associated with such developments as the concurrent rise in the proportion of young married couples with children and in the proportion of households living in homes that they own. One hypothesis is that an increase in the time devoted to home life among couples below middle age is conducive to greater family stability. Consistent with these developments has been an increase in remarriage rates among persons (with broken marriages) who have not reached old age. The tendency for married men to be older than their wives and the higher death and remarriage rates among men have probably been largely responsible for the fact that widows outnumber widowers by a ratio of more than three to one.

The long-time decline in the birth rate until the middle 1930's brought a corresponding reduction in the average number of children ever born for women who had ever been married and who had reached the end of the childbearing period. In 1890 this figure was about 5.4 children. By 1950, when women who had been at the height of their childbearing in the 1930's had completed their family-building, the corre-

sponding figure was about 2.4 children. Even if the resurgence in the birth rate during the 1940's and early 1950's were to raise this average to, say, 2.8 children, the average woman will complete her childbearing by the time she is around twenty-six or twenty-seven years old, or about six years before the age when her grandmother bore her last child. The increased availability of time for women to devote to civic enterprises or to employment outside the home would be significant.

In 1940 there were more single women than married women in the labor force, but meantime this situation has been reversed. Close to 30 per cent of the married women in the middle 1950's were in the labor force. The high level of business activity, coupled with changes in the attitudes both of married women toward work outside the home and of employers toward hiring married women, have probably been responsible. Increases in marriage since 1940 have been most pronounced among women with a college education; these women, in turn, have perhaps always been the most likely to be labor force participants.

Illustrations of differential patterns of marriage and family life among different groups of the population are given in Tables 55 to 57. Table 55 shows that men have a median age at first marriage about three years above that for women. Although the data are for selected states only, the same type of differential has been noted in statistics for the entire country. In 1953 there was little difference between the median age at first marriage for white and non-white persons, but there is evidence that in the early 1940's non-whites tended to be younger at first marriage. The higher median age at the latest remarriage of non-white persons than of white persons is related to the tendency for non-whites to remarry more often. Less than a fourth of the white brides and grooms in 1953 were marrying for the second or subsequent time as compared with 30 per cent of the non-white brides and grooms.

The median age at remarriage for previously divorced persons was thirty-one years for brides and thirty-six years for grooms, whereas that for previously widowed persons was forty-six years for brides and fifty-six years for grooms. These differentials reflect differences in the age distributions of divorced and

and remarriage rates. Separation rates among non-white women were far above those for white women, but divorce rates did not differ much by color among those who had not completed high school; this includes a large majority of the non-whites. The fact that widowhood rates were significantly higher for persons in the lower education groups is evidence that mortality rates are negatively correlated with economic status. Additional findings support the conclusion that upper eco-

TABLE 55

MEDIAN AGE AT MARRIAGE BY SELECTED CHARACTERISTICS AND PER CENT ENTERING REMARRIAGE, FOR BRIDES AND GROOMS IN REPORTING STATES: 1953*

Subject	Bride	Groom	Subject	Bride	Groom
Median age at marriage:†			*Median age at marriage by previous marital status:*‡		
First marriage, total§	20.4	23.2	Total	21.6	24.6
White	20.3	23.2	Single	20.2	23.1
Non-white	20.6	23.6	Divorced	31.1	35.7
Negro	20.6	23.6	Widowed	46.2	55.7
Other races	21.2	24.4	*Median age at marriage by number of present marriage:*‖		
Remarriage, total§	34.9	39.7			
White	34.7	39.4			
Non-white	36.4	41.6	Total	21.6	24.5
Percentage entering remarriage:†			First	20.4	23.2
Total	25.3	24.1	Second	32.9	37.8
White	24.8	23.4	Third	40.4	46.1
Non-white	29.4	30.9	Fourth or more	44.2	51.5

* Source: National Office of Vital Statistics, *Vital Statistics—Special Reports*, Vol. XLII, No. 5, "Marriages: Detailed Statistics for Reporting Areas, 1953," Tables B, C, D.

† Based on data from eighteen states.

‡ Based on data from fifteen states.

§ Includes race not reported.

‖ Based on data from twelve states.

widowed persons and the tendency for the gap between the ages of brides and grooms to increase as age at marriage increases. The same tendency is revealed in the median ages at marriage by number of present marriage.

Evidence not shown here indicates that marriage rates for non-white women were formerly higher than those for white women, but the figures in Table 56 show that by the late 1940's the reverse was true. Women in 1950 who had attended college had lower marriage rates than other women, but the difference had undoubtedly diminished during the 1940's. Men with high incomes had the highest first marriage

nomic groups generally have greater permanence of marriage.

Men with the highest incomes soon after marriage are most likely to have been in their late twenties when they married. Those with earlier marriages are less likely to have had as much education, and those with later marriages may have more than the average amount of difficulty in making social adjustments. Women who drop out of high school have the youngest average age at marriage. Moreover, persons whose marriages have been broken were about two years younger at first marriage, on the average, than comparable persons with unbroken first marriages. Thus, persons who marry at a young age are less likely to have stable marriages.

The number of children per family is greater for poorly educated than for well-educated parents, but the gap was significantly reduced during the 1940's. Data collected in 1952 indicate that the number of young children per family was not significantly different for husbands in different income levels. These and other facts suggest that

sons and daughters in their homes (Table 57). Very few husband-wife families have children other than their own in the home. Likewise, there is only about one adult other than the head and wife in every fourth family; the largest proportion of couples with such adults occurs among those in which the husband is forty-five to sixty-four years old. Some of these adults are unmarried children who have not left home, and most of the others are

TABLE 56

First Marriage, Remarriage, Separation, Divorce, and Widowhood Rates per Thousand Women Subject to Entering Specified Marital Status, by Years of School Completed and Color, for the United States: 1948–50*

All Rates Standardized for Age

Type of Rate and Color	Total Women 15 to 54 Years Old	Years of School Completed				
		Elementary 0 to 8 Years	High School 1 to 3 Years	4 Years	College 1 to 3 Years	4 or More
First marriage rate:						
Total†	70	73	73	73	58	55
Non-white†	58	62	60	60	58	54
Remarriage rate:						
Total	75	71	81	79	78	81
Non-white	64	65	65	66	84	63
Separation rate:						
Total	5	7	5	3	2	2
Non-white	15	15	16	15	11	7
Divorce rate:						
Total	4	4	5	4	5	3
Non-white	4	3	5	6	9	6
Widowhood rate:						
Total	4	5	4	3	3	3
Non-white	6	7	6	5	6	6

* Source: Glick (1957, Tables 87, 90, 102).
† Women 14 to 59 years old.

childbearing is being increasingly shared more nearly equally by families in the several economic groups.

Families have changing composition and economic characteristics as they pass through the typical family life cycle. In 1953 the average married couple with the husband under twenty-five years old had one son or daughter under eighteen years old living in their home; couples with the husband thirty-five to forty-four years old had two dependent-age children, on the average, still living at home; older couples had diminishing numbers of young

married, widowed, or divorced sons and daughters or parents who share the couple's living quarters. Families are most likely to have preschool-age children in the home when the husband is under thirty-five years old and most likely to have school-age children at home when the husband is thirty-five to forty-four years old.

The economic well-being of the family, as measured by family income, increases until it reaches a peak when the head is forty-five to fifty-four years old, than declines. Some of the decline in economic status in older age, as inferred from cross-section data on families as of one point in time classified by age of the head, may be attributed to the fact that the older persons of today received less education and had fewer opportunities to acquire specialized skills in their work than those in succeeding generations. Families are less likely to move to other living quarters as the age of the head increases, and the quality of their housing tends

in the annual number of marriages are likely to occur during the 1960's and early 1970's. The future trend in the number of marriages seems likely to move upward in parallel with the rising numbers of women twenty to twenty-four years old. Growth in the number of households will probably depend mainly on the trend in the number of marriages during the next two decades. In contrast, the growth in number of

TABLE 57

SELECTED MEASURES OF FAMILY COMPOSITION, BY AGE OF HEAD, FOR HUSBAND-WIFE FAMILIES IN THE UNITED STATES: APRIL, 1953*

SUBJECT	ALL HUSBAND-WIFE FAMILIES	AGE OF HEAD (YEARS)					
		Under 25	25 to 34	35 to 44	45 to 54	55 to 64	65 and Over
Average number of members per family:							
All members.....	3.60	3.07	3.89	4.21	3.63	2.97	2.67
Members under 18 years..........	1.28	1.04	1.77	1.99	1.13	0.42	0.21
Own children of head	1.22	1.00	1.74	1.94	1.06	0.32	0.08
Other children......	0.06	0.04	0.03	0.05	0.07	0.10	0.13
Members 18 and over, other than head and wife..............	0.32	0.03	0.12	0.22	0.50	0.55	0.46
Percentage of families with one or more:							
Own children under 6..	32.5	61.5	69.8	40.6	11.9	1.7	0.6
Own children 6 to 17..	38.5	3.1	36.2	67.8	48.7	18.3	4.3
Members under 18....	58.6	62.8	81.4	81.3	54.3	24.0	12.1
Members 18 and over, other than head and wife..............	24.5	3.8	11.3	21.0	37.7	37.0	29.2

* Source: U.S. Bureau of the Census, *Current Population Reports* (Ser. P-20, No. 53), "Household and Family Characteristics: April 1953," Table 6 and unpublished tabulations.

to diminish after the head has passed middle age.

Little demographic research has been conducted on probable future trends in family life other than the preparation of projections of the numbers of households, families, and marriages. Marriage projections can be made by applying marriage rates to population projections by age and sex (Glick, 1957, chap. x).

The number of marriages is currently about 1.5 million per year. Persons now at the ages when most persons enter first marriage were born during the depression years of the 1930's, when birth rates were low. Marked increases

households during the first half of the 1950's depended greatly upon the subdivision of households containing two-generation families. This process of subdivision is evidently approaching its limit. Growth in the number of families in future years seems likely to follow closely the growth in number of households.

The average size of family (in terms of the number of family members living together) reached a low point about 1950 and rose slightly by 1955. This is the first time an upward movement in the average size of family has been recorded for this country, except for a short period after the end of World

War II. The family projections, considered in combination with the population projections, indicate a further increase in the average size of family by 1960, mainly because of an anticipated increase in the average number of young children living at home. Whether the average size of family stabilizes after 1960 or not will probably depend largely on the trend in the child population per family. The average number of children under eighteen per family in 1975 will be determined by the future course of the fertility rates. Figures on the average number of adults per family in future years reflect the assumptions made about the future rate of family formation. The higher the rate of family formation, the lower the average number of adults per family will be. Thus, the highest family projections show a further decline during the next two decades in adults per family, and the lowest family projections show a slight increase in adults per family.

Considerable interest is attached to future household growth patterns in farm and non-farm areas. Between 1940 and 1955, the number of farm households declined more than 1 per cent per year, whereas the number of non-farm households rose substantially. If farm households continue to decline in number during the next two decades because of farm–to–non-farm migration, as seems likely, the increase in the number of non-farm households will exceed that of the total number of households. This observation has importance to many types of research workers, including those concerned with the prospective demands for housing in farm and non-farm areas and those interested in the economy of agricultural areas.

NEXT STEPS IN RESEARCH

Demographers are seldom, if ever, satisfied with the quantity or quality of data obtained through population research. As a group, however, they are probably more critical of the available data than are the non-technical users of the data. That is as it should be. Demographic technicians are obliged to press steadily for more and better statistics to meet the increasing demand, which comes largely from persons less well equipped than they to evaluate the data. These observations are as relevant to family statisticians as they are to others in the field of demography.

Data

More information could be obtained about the current status and changing aspects of family composition in the United States as a whole by the introduction of some additional questions in the Current Population Survey or by the analysis of data collected on field "control cards" used in the CPS. Some of the information could be obtained for smaller areas through the decennial censuses or through local surveys. For example, types of changes in household composition over the course of a year might be studied for families in various phases of the life cycle. Annual gross changes in household composition, as well as net changes, could be estimated. Studies covering a longer period than a year might be made by use of a question on duration of marriage. Reasons for sharing the homes of others could be ascertained from groups living "doubled up." Studies of child-spacing could throw additional light on family composition and on patterns of family formation and dissolution.

The composition of households at the time of a change of residence, rather than at the time of enumeration, would sharpen the study of mobility on a family basis. The composition of families moving out of an area, such as the central city of a standard metropolitan area, could be compared with the composition of families remaining in the area and with that of families already living in the place of destination, such as suburban areas.

Little is known about the extent of orphanhood, child adoption, and informal shifting of children of living parents to the homes of relatives or non-relatives. Some information on orphans has been collected by the Bureau of the Census, but with only partial success (Fisher, 1950).

Data on reasons for the absence from home of persons ordinarily considered members of the family would be informative. Such data might be used to show the economic level and other characteristics of families with sons, daughters, or other members in college, in the Armed Forces, or in institutions, and of families with the chief breadwinner living in another part of the country. The degree of dependence of family members thus living apart could be investigated.

Questions could be asked to determine the extent of difference between the characteristics of parents and their grown children. Such characteristics might include education, farm residence, occupation, and marital status. Technical difficulties would be encountered in such a study, of course; these difficulties could be minimized if most of the data could be shown in terms of characteristics of members of the older generation at the time when they were about the same age as the current members of the younger generation.

Several aspects of the economic welfare of families need additional study. In a period of national emergency, it would be useful to know more about the availability of adult supervision for young children of mothers not in the labor force. The adult supervisor might be someone in the child's home or outside. Another subject about which little precise information exists is the labor-force participation of women in relation to family formation and family-building. This might be explored on a relatively small scale by inquiring about work done outside the home by women a few months immediately preceding marriage and also before the birth of each child. For a thorough study of this subject, the entire work history of the woman would probably be required. Additional aspects of family economics that might be studied are the extent to which women in different groups are self-supporting and the degree of dependence of family members on agriculture and on other types of industries.

Special note should be taken about next steps in the development of family data in the field of vital statistics. A marriage registration area, patterned after the birth and death registration areas, was established in 1957. This step should stimulate further interest in statistics from marriage records, encourage additional states to establish central files of marriages, insure more nearly uniform statistics on marriages, and expand the list of items for which most of the states will compile marriage statistics. One of the criteria for acceptance of a state in the marriage registration area is the completeness and accuracy of reporting. In 1958 the National Office of Vital Statistics announced the formation of a comparable divorce registration area. When comprehensive marriage and divorce statistics become available for all states, social research in the field of the family will advance more rapidly. In the meantime, data on these subjects can be used to study the effect of marriage and dissolution of marriage on the formation of households in states and other local areas where such data are available.

Methods

A new type of punch card, currently being developed by the Bureau of the Census, provides a basis for cross-classifying characteristics of the person with characteristics of his family. To illustrate, this type of card makes it possible to show, for teen-age workers, employed wives, and retired persons, the economic status of their family (family income, occupation of the family head, etc.). This device is also being used to obtain data on the dependence of persons on agriculture and on other industries, data on the chief earner in the family in relation to family income, and characteristics of persons in families of different sizes. A logical extension of this procedure would be to include on the same punch card characteristics of the person, his family, his home (housing items), and his neighborhood. Such a card could be used, for instance, to show the distribution (according to economic status of the family and type of neighborhood) of young persons with large enough homes to have separate rooms for each child.

Thus far unavailable on a nationwide basis are data on family histories. Such data might involve the collection of data on the ages of persons at each change of marital status and the ages of all their children. From these data, longitudinal studies of the life cycle of the family could be made. At present, such studies are made of cross-sections of the population as of one point in time. Improved data on child-spacing could also be obtained from this source. If economic items were included, changes in economic status (occupational mobility) could be correlated with changes in family composition. The probabilities of first marriage, separation, divorce, widowhood, and remarriage by economic status might also be developed from such data. This source might also be used to investigate the changes in social and economic characteristics from one generation to the next. A cohort approach to the study of family life might be developed from the family history questionnaires. Such questionnaires tend to be extensive and the tabulations complex unless the study is restricted to a well-defined group.

The method of setting up models of family composition and other characteristics might be more often adopted in family studies. Instead of making elaborate, general-purpose tabulations with many different cross-classifications of families, selected types or models of families (childless families, families with an only child, large families, families with one teen-age child and one younger child, families broken by divorce, etc.) might be established so as to focus the tabulations on specific problem areas in family life. Studies of consumer expenditures regularly employ such models in order to standardize the units of analysis from one month to the next. Many census tables are limited to husband-wife families or to women married once and husband present. However, census data on families serve as the source of information for many purposes rather than a single purpose, so that tabulations involving narrowly defined models are probably less appropriate than general-purpose tabulations.

Fund of Knowledge

A systematic inventory of demographic findings in the fields of marriage and the family might be undertaken by a committee of experts to determine the areas of knowledge that merit reinvestigation at specified periods of time. This committee could prepare recommendations on the information that should be provided on a national or local basis annually, decennially, or at other periods of time (including one-time studies) from marriage records, census returns, and other sources. The committee might use an inquiry of representative producers and users of family data to learn more about who needs various data, how frequently the figures should be brought up to date, and what the theoretical and practical applications of the data are. Such an inquiry might be used as a basis for discontinuing the publication of some types of data and the introduction of other types. In the absence of such an inquiry, the following suggestions are presented as the writer's appraisal of the existing needs and prospects.

A current study being made at the Bureau of the Census will indicate what type of person is reported as the head of the family. This study will show, among other things, the proportion of families in which the head, the wife, or some other relative of the head has the largest income (according to the age of the family head) and, in two-generation families, the frequency with which the head of the family or the head of the subfamily has the largest income.

The life cycle of the family for various social and economic groups could be analyzed on the basis of the most recent data available. Data on child-spacing among women in various strata are currently being developed by the National Office of Vital Statistics; these data should sharpen such an analysis. Other studies that would be informative might show the range of variation in family life cycles among couples marrying relatively early or relatively late, among large and small families, and among families with one or both spouses who had remarried after divorce or widowhood.

Generation first-marriage rates and generation median ages at first marriage are not available for this country. The lack of these measures is recognized as a gap in the current knowledge on marriage. The data required for the computation of these measures are annual series on single years of age at first marriage and annual numbers of births for long periods of time. Al-

though a nationwide annual series of births is available back to the beginning of this century, there is no nationwide series on age at first marriage. It may be possible, however, to estimate the age distributions of the single (never married) population for intercensal years back to 1890 and to derive from these distributions and from statistics on deaths some reasonable approximations of annual first marriages by age at marriage.

Much more could be learned about the stability of marriages contracted under different conditions. Existing nationwide data demonstrate that marriages entered at relatively young ages and by persons who leave high school before graduation are much less stable than other marriages. Other nationwide data might be assembled on the relationship between stability of marriage and many other factors, including differences between the age, education, income, and religion of the spouses and between the economic levels of their parents. The optimum combination of the husband's and wife's characteristics for stability of first marriages and remarriages could be studied. More information could be assembled on the living arrangements of persons prior to and following separation or divorce. Further study is needed on the characteristics of persons who remain in the status of divorce or widowhood for relatively short and relatively long periods. A similar analysis could be made of the characteristics of persons whose marriages have remained unbroken for varying lengths of time. The number of children whose parents have ever been widowed or divorced could be investigated. A study could be made to determine whether married couples have a greater probability of divorce as their youngest child approaches maturity.

The foregoing partial inventory of next steps in marriage and family research has been restricted to areas that are usually regarded as demographic and that seem to be feasible under favorable conditions. Obstacles in the path of further research include budgetary limitations, shortages of well-qualified research personnel, and encroachments on the good will of persons who are asked to give information for research purposes. It is probably true that research oriented toward the solution of practical, economic problems tends to be more readily supported than most other types of research. Thus the birth and death registration areas were extended to encompass the entire nation because of the many practical uses of birth and death records, and research workers have profited thereby. On the other hand, the development of marriage and divorce registration areas has lagged, perhaps because of the smaller number of practical uses of records in these fields. Steady progress is being made, nonetheless, in the accumulation of data from marriage and divorce records, from decennial censuses and current surveys, and from local studies. From these sources a growing fund of knowledge relating to theoretical problems as well as to action programs is being developed.

SELECTED BIBLIOGRAPHY

BEALE, C. L. 1950. "Increased Divorce Rates among Separated Persons as a Factor in Divorce since 1940," *Social Forces*, XXIX, 72–74.

BOSSARD, J. H. S. 1953. *Parent and Child: Studies in Family Behavior*. Philadelphia: University of Pennsylvania Press.

———, and BOLL, E. S. 1955. "Marital Unhappiness in the Life Cycle," *Marriage and Family Living*, Vol. XVII.

BOWERMAN, C. E. 1953. "Assortative Mating by Previous Marital Status," *American Sociological Review*, XVIII, 170–77.

CARTER, H. 1953. "Improving National Marriage and Divorce Statistics," *Journal of the American Statistical Association*, XLVIII, 453–61.

———, GLICK, P. C., and LEWIT, S. 1955.

"Some Demographic Characteristics of Recently Married Persons: Comparisons of Registration Data and Sample Survey Data," *American Sociological Review*, XX, 165–72.

CAVAN, R. S. 1953. *The American Family*. New York: Thomas Y. Crowell Co.

CHRISTENSEN, H. T., ANDREWS, R., and FREISER, S. 1953. "Falsification of Age at Marriage," *Marriage and Family Living*, XV, 301–4.

CHRISTENSEN, H. T., and MEISNER, H. H. 1953. "Studies in Child Spacing, III: Premarital Pregnancy as a Factor in Divorce," *American Sociological Review*, XVIII, 641–44.

COWLES, M. L. 1953. "Changes in Family Personnel, Occupational Status, and Housing Occurring over the Family's Life Cycle," *Rural Sociology*, XVIII, 35–44.

DAVIS, K. 1950. "Statistical Perspective on Marriage and Divorce," *Annals of the American Academy of Political and Social Science*, CCLXXII, 9–21.

EDWARDS, G. F. 1953. "Marital Status and General Family Characteristics of the Nonwhite Population in the United States," *Journal of Negro Education*, XXII, 280–96.

FISHER, J. 1950. "Orphans in the United States: Number and Living Arrangements," *Social Security Bulletin*, XIII, 13–18.

FOOTE, N. N. 1954. "Changes in American Marriage Patterns and the Role of Women," *Eugenics Quarterly*, Vol. I.

GLICK, P. C. 1955. "The Life Cycle of the Family," *Marriage and Family Living*, XVII, 3–9.

———. 1957. *American Families*. New York: John Wiley & Sons.

———, and LANDAU, E. 1950. "Age as a Factor in Marriage," *American Sociological Review*, XV, 517–29.

GOODE, W. J. 1949. "Problems in Postdivorce Adjustment," *American Sociological Review*, XIV, 394–401.

GRABILL, W. H. 1945. "Attrition Life Tables for the Single Population," *Journal of the American Statistical Association*, XL, 364–75.

GROVES, E. R., and OGBURN, W. F. 1928. *American Marriage and Family Relationships*. New York: Henry Holt & Co.

HAJNAL, J. 1954. "Analysis of Changes in the Marriage Pattern by Economic Groups," *American Sociological Review,* XIX, 295–302.

HAUSER, P. M., and JAFFE, A. J. 1947. "The Extent of the Housing Shortage," *Law and Contemporary Problems,* Vol. XII.

JACOBSON, P. H. 1949. "Total Marital Dissolutions in the United States: Relative Importance of Mortality and Divorce," in *Studies in Population,* ed. G. F. MAIR. Princeton: Princeton University Press.

———. 1950. "Differentials in Divorce by Duration of Marriage and Size of Family," *American Sociological Review,* XV, 235–44.

———. 1952. "Some Statistical Patterns of Marriage in the United States." Ph.D. thesis, Columbia University.

KISER, C. V. 1937. "Recent Analyses of Marriage Rates," *Milbank Memorial Fund Quarterly,* XV, 262–74.

———, and WHELPTON, P. K. 1949. "Social and Psychological Factors Affecting Fertility, IX: Fertility Planning and Fertility Rates by Socio-economic Status," *Milbank Memorial Fund Quarterly,* XXVII, 188–244.

KYRK, H. 1953. *The Family in the American Economy.* Chicago: University of Chicago Press.

LOCKE, H. J. 1941. "Tentative Knowledge about Marriage and Family Relations," *Marriage and Family Living,* Vol. III.

———, and MACKEPRANG, M. 1949. "Marital Adjustment and the Employed Wife," *American Journal of Sociology,* LIV, 536–38.

LORIMER, F., and ROBACK, H. 1940. "Economics of the Family Relative to Number of Children," *Milbank Memorial Fund Quarterly,* XVIII, 114–36.

METROPOLITAN LIFE INSURANCE COMPANY. 1955. "Cumulative Index to the *Statistical Bulletin,* Volumes 26 to 35, 1945–1954." Articles in this period of special relevance appear in issues for April, 1951; September and December, 1953; and March and May, 1954; for 1955, relevant articles appear in issues for January, February, May, October, and November.

MINER, H. 1938. "The French-Canadian Family Cycle," *American Sociological Review,* III, 700–708.

MONAHAN, T. P. 1951. *The Pattern of Age at Marriage in the United States.* Philadelphia: Stephenson Bros.

———. 1952. "How Stable Are Remarriages?" *American Journal of Sociology,* LVIII, 280–88.

———, and CHANCELLOR, L. E. 1955. "Statistical Aspects of Marriage and Divorce by Religious Denomination in Iowa," *Eugenics Quarterly,* II, 162–73.

NATIONAL CONFERENCE ON FAMILY LIFE. 1948. *The American Family: A Factual Background.* Washington, D.C.: Government Printing Office.

NEWMAN, S. C. 1950. "The Development and Status of Vital Statistics on Marriage and Divorce," *American Sociological Review,* XV, 426–29.

NIMKOFF, M. F. 1954. "The Family in the United States," *Marriage and Family Living,* Vol. XVI.

OGBURN, W. F., and NIMKOFF, M. F. 1955. *Technology and the Changing Family.* New York: Houghton Mifflin Co.

SPIEGELMAN, M. 1936. "The Broken Family: Widowhood and Orphanhood," *Annals of the American Academy of Political and Social Science,* CLXXXVIII, 117–30.

———. 1955. *Introduction to Demography.* Chicago: Society of Actuaries.

STOTT, A. L. 1955. "Population and Household Formation," from a study prepared in the statistical division, comptroller's department, American Telephone & Telegraph Co.

TIETZE, C., and LAURIAT, P. 1955. "Age at Marriage and Educational Attainment in the United States," *Population Studies,* IX, 159–66.

UNITED KINGDOM, REGISTRAR GENERAL. 1954. *The Registrar General's Statistical Review of England and Wales for the Five Years, 1946–1950.* London: H. M. Stationery Office.

UNITED NATIONS, POPULATION DIVISION. 1953. *The Determinants and Consequences of Population Trends.* New York: United Nations.

UNITED STATES, BUREAU OF THE CENSUS. 1909. *A Century of Population Growth.* Washington, D.C.: Government Printing Office.

———. "Current Population Reports" (periodic reports based on Current Population Survey):

1947 ff.*a*. Ser. P-20 (marital status, families, fertility, internal migration).

1947 ff.*b*. Ser. P-25 (population estimates and projections).

1947 ff.*c*. Ser. P-50 (labor force data on persons and families).

1948 ff. Ser. P-60 (income of persons and families).

———. *1950 Census of Population:*

1952–53. Vol. II: *Characteristics of the Population*. Part 1: "United States Summary." Parts 2–54: "Reports for States, Territories, and Possessions."

1953–57. Vol. IV: *Special Reports*. Part 2A: "General Characteristics of Families." Part 2C: "Institutional Population." Part 2D: "Marital Status." Part 2E: "Duration of Current Marital Status."

UNITED STATES, NATIONAL OFFICE OF VITAL STATISTICS. 1937 ff. "Vital Statistics of the United States" (annual volumes).

———. 1946 ff. "Vital Statistics: Special Reports."

(These are periodic publications, including analytical studies, of registration data on marriages, divorces, births, and deaths. Also included are other special studies, among which are reports on characteristics of recently married persons based on data compiled for the National Office of Vital Statistics by the Bureau of the Census; see Vols. XXXIX, XLV.)

———. 1952 ff. *Monthly Vital Statistics Report*.

WHELPTON, P. K. 1935. "Causes of the Decline in Birth Rates," *Milbank Memorial Fund Quarterly*, XIII, 237–51.

———. 1954. *Cohort Fertility: Native White Women in the United States*. Princeton: Princeton University Press.

———, and KISER, C. V. 1947. "Social and Psychological Factors Affecting Fertility, VI: The Planning of Fertility," *Milbank Memorial Fund Quarterly*, XXV, 63–111.

25. Working Force

A. J. JAFFE

RELATIONSHIP OF WORKING FORCE TO DEMOGRAPHY

Demography might be defined as study of the actions of people and the reasons therefor, with respect to fertility, mortality, and migration. Very many historical studies have been made describing past trends in birth and death rates, the movements of people, and population growth. These and other studies, furthermore, have attempted to explain why the historical patterns or events occurred. To the extent that demographers are able to explain why the birth rate (at some specified moment of time and in a specified place) is at the level observed or why it has changed over time or why people migrated as they did, then, of course, prediction becomes probable.

Other parts of this volume are concerned with the definition of demography and explore this subject at great length. For our purposes— namely, investigating the relationship of the working force to demography—the above very brief definition is sufficient. Let us now note how study of the working force relates to this definition.

The subject of the working force might be defined briefly as a study of the manner in which people earn their living, i.e., obtain the goods and purchasable services necessary to maintain the entire population—both those goods which are biologically necessary and those regarded as necessary in terms of the society's values. This very abbreviated definition immediately points to one of the crucial relationships between demography and the working force: the entire population consumes the goods and purchasable services, but these are produced by only a portion of the population. How, then, does one portion of the population become differentiated into the working force? What is the process, and why, whereby some people remain largely consumers, while others become both producers and consumers?

Implicit in these questions is the observation that all persons are born consumers and that some, ultimately, become producers. Undoubtedly this is true insofar as infants and very young children are concerned; under no imaginable definition can they be considered as producers. As these children grow up, some become producers and some can be said to continue as consumers. This differentiation raises another point, however—how should "consumer" be defined? In one sense almost everyone in a population produces something, whether it is money income or children or art objects. In another sense, however, most societies (with the possible exception of the economically most primitive; see International Labor Office, 1953) recognize that some parts of the population do not participate in the working force, however it may be defined. Our original question can then be revised to read as follows: What is the process, and why, within a given culture context, whereby some parts of the total population remain largely consumers, while others become producers as well as consumers? Furthermore, how might the answer vary in accordance with possible changes in the culture?

604

Once an attempt is made to separate the total population into producers and consumers—i.e., persons in the working force and those outside it—then a great many demographic elements become involved, both theoretical and empirical ones. Indeed, it might be said that most studies of fertility, mortality, migration, and closely related subjects—whether or not originally conceived for the purposes of studying the working force—also have relevance for studying this subject. Most findings which seem to be of a purely demographic nature also have considerable importance for an understanding of how and why the population becomes differentiated into producers and consumers—persons in the working force and those outside it.

Many examples of such studies with multiple implications are available. For example, many studies on fertility take into consideration the age and marital status of the woman and, in addition, whether or not she is in the working force (see, for example, Day, 1957). Participation in the working force is likely to be related to the birth rate; hence, this is one of the factors that must be taken into account in studying differential fertility or changing fertility. By the same token, however, if the focus of a study is the participation of married women in the working force, past and present childbearing behavior must be taken into account.

Having separated the total population into the two groups of those in and those out of the working force, we may inquire how those in the working force become differentiated into the occupational and industrial patterns observed at some given time and place and how such patterns may change. This process, which may be considered "division of labor," is also very closely related to many aspects of demography, both theoretical and practical, and cannot be studied independently of the demographic elements. For example, in the study of dif-ferential fertility, the status or class position of a family is an important factor; the criterion of status often employed is the occupation or industry of the husband.

However, we also recognize that the factors which make for occupational and industrial differentiation, i.e., which lead to social and class differentiation, also involve fertility patterns, both past and present. At the risk of oversimplification, this feedback relationship might be illustrated by an illiterate and poor farm laborer who has many children, only some of whom survive to adulthood. Since the family is poor, the children do not receive much education; since they remain relatively uneducated, they do not climb the occupational ladder to any appreciable extent; finally, the position of the now adult children on the occupational ladder helps determine how many children they, in turn, will have.

This example illustrates the interrelationships between demography and the working force. The birth rate and rate of population growth, the differentiation of the population into those in and those out of the working force, and the differentiation of the workers at various levels of the occupational ladder are all inextricably intertwined. The first point of relationship between working force and demography, then, involves the many theoretical and practical problems in one field which cannot be meaningfully studied without reference to the other. (See, for example, Durand, 1948; Garfinkle, 1955; Gordon, 1954; Hauser, 1951; Jaffe and Carleton, 1954; Palmer, 1954; United Nations, 1953; Wolfbein, 1949.) The second point of relationship derives from the first. Since many of the problems must be studied from both fields, or viewpoints, the same basic data are required. An age distribution, for example, is a datum with more than one function. The third point involves the fact that when the same data are analyzed, essentially the same methodologies must be employed, both in the collection of the original data and in their subsequent processing.

The Role of Historical "Accident"

Studies of the working force and demography are closely interrelated, both from the theoretical viewpoint and on the basis of much empirical research carried out to date. In addition, however, other events occurred which helped relate the two fields and which we believe have pertinence for an understanding of present-day developments; for want of a better name we will refer to these as historical "accidents."

The political economists of the nineteenth century and earlier generally failed to distinguish between total population (or its component age-sex groups) and the working population, and they considered the two as almost synonymous (i.e., highly interrelated). This lack of discrimination, in turn, may have reflected the earlier lord-serf culture in which the masses of the people, the serfs, existed primarily to work for the lord. It was unthinkable that a serf, capable of working, did not actually work; therefore, there was little reason for distinguishing between population and working force. Also, in societies of a century ago and earlier (and even today in grossly underdeveloped parts of the world) even in the absence of a lord-serf relationship, most people had to work because of the very low level of productivity per worker; hence, there was almost no reason for distinguishing between total and working population.

Another "accident" which may have helped relate demography to the working force involves the origin of life insurance. During the nineteenth century and earlier, life insurance companies as we know them today were largely nonexistent. If people wanted "assurance" they had to band together somehow for mutual insurance. This banding together was often accomplished via profession-al or other occupational organizations (Jack, 1912). Thus, in attempting to insure their individual lives, these labor unions and professional societies became involved in such working-force investigations as age composition by occupation (or industry), earnings by occupation, retirement patterns, rate of growth of occupation (or industries), etc.

A third historical "accident" which helped cement the relationship between the two fields involves "national egotism." Censuses of population had been taken in the eighteenth century and earlier. Whenever several such censuses, or inventories, had been taken in a country, efforts were made to use the findings for ascertaining the rate of economic growth, or the "increasing prosperity" of the country. Information on the occupational or industrial composition, and changes over time, were deemed of great importance in measuring such "progress." In part, they were considered so important because there were few other data available to measure "progress." Perhaps if good data on national income or gross national product had been available in the United States in 1800, for example, Thomas Jefferson would not have been so insistent that the census collect information on the occupations of the people, i.e., the United States working force.

These historical "accidents" were not pure chance affairs, of course. In large part they occurred because of underlying common interests between demography and the working force. In part, however, there is reason to think that they were accidental; if the early life insurance companies had been organized on a different basis or if Jefferson had not been so insistent that the United States census collect working-force information, perhaps the two fields would not have grown up so closely related. In any event, whether "pure chance" or not, the fact remains that in the mid-twentieth century there is a historical tradition at least two centuries old relating the two fields.

Interrelationships of Working Force to Other Disciplines

The subject matter of the working force has established close ties with a number of social science disciplines in addition to demography. These other subjects, in turn, have ties with demography; together the various disciplines form an interrelated matrix. Study of the entire matrix is clearly outside the scope of this chapter, which must be limited to discussion of the working force as related to the field of demography. Nevertheless, in order to obtain a fuller understanding of these two areas, we should view them against the background of the entire matrix of disciplines. Let us review very briefly the relationships between the working force and demography, on the one hand, and the various other disciplines, on the other.

Studies of motivation are becoming more prevalent. (See, for example, Bluestone, 1955; Hauser, 1951; Jaffe and Stewart, 1951, Part III; Parnes, 1954.) At one time, almost all research efforts were devoted to the problems of how to measure the working force and how to determine who was part of it and who was not. At present, questions are being asked about why people behave the way they do. Why do some women participate in the working force and others not? Do older men want to work or not? How does youth make occupational choices, if at all? These questions, which are so relevant for the supply of labor, are highly interrelated with certain fields of sociology. In particular, the entire area of attitude research has found considerable use in working-force and demographic studies; this is true both of the collection of the basic information and of its subsequent analysis. Psychology also has become involved in studying motivational problems of the working force.

Economics is also related to working-force analysis, particularly in respect to the demand for labor. Perhaps the single most important question being asked is, How, if at all, does the supply of labor adjust to the demand for it? Since there is a feedback relationship between supply and demand, one cannot be studied adequately without the other (Gordon, 1954; Wolfle, 1954). Hence, for questions of this type, the disciplines of economics and sociology become interrelated with that of the working force and, in turn, with the field of demography.

Working-force problems also become involved to some extent—perhaps to a lesser degree—with various other disciplines, including law, political science, health, and social welfare. Working-force interrelationships with law appear most clearly in the case of labor unions and labor law. Health also becomes involved with working force in certain questions. These include regulations governing the hours and working conditions of children and women and, to some extent, of all workers. Also, questions about the employment of physically handicapped or mentally retarded persons involve aspects of both disciplines. Unemployment is perhaps more closely related to social welfare than is any other aspect of the working force.

In short, the nature of the question determines the areas with which working-force analyses are interrelated. To date, both theoretical and practical questions and problems about the working force and about demography have been raised which involve all the social sciences.

DEFINITIONS, DATA, AND METHODS

Why Study the Working Force?

Basically we are asking why people act the way they do, specifically why they participate or do not participate in the working force, and if they do participate, why they are in one segment of the working force instead of another (defining segment as occupation, industry, class of worker, geographic area, or any other component of the working force). In attempting to discover answers to the basic question, however, we find immediately that we are also involved in problems of why people act the way they do with reference to demographic questions.

Some of the most important questions which can be asked about working behavior are:

(1) Just how is the fertility pattern of a woman related to her participation (or non-participation) in the working force? Does one "cause" the other, is there a feedback interrelationship, or are both phenomena manifestations of underlying factors? Under what conditions will more or fewer women be in the working force, and how will such behavior seem to affect the birth rate and, in turn, the rate of population growth? Over the lifetime of the family, how are childbearing and participation of the wives in the working force interrelated?

(2) For both men and women who enter the working force, how are choices of occupation or industry or patterns of working life made? Presumably such choices reflect past experiences of the persons involved; in addition, how, if at all, do they affect the social position of the family and its childbearing pattern?

(3) Just how are geographic mobility and population redistribution influenced by factors inherent in the job or occupation and by demographic factors? (Jaffe and Wolfbein, 1945.)

(4) How is the amount of a person's formal education related to fertility levels, on the one hand, and, on the other, to participation in the working force (among women) and position on the occupational ladder? Is the amount of formal education achieved a "cause" or an "effect"?

(5) In economically underdeveloped countries, perhaps the single most important question is how levels of fertility, population growth, occupational and industrial composition, population distribution within the country, and amount of capital investment are interrelated. Under what demographic and working-force conditions will maximum economic growth be achieved per unit of investment funds? And what are the underlying factors which will influence fertility and population growth rates?

These basic questions are some of the fundamental ones for research in the working force in relation to research on demography. The research which has actually been carried out in the United States since the 1930's, however, in large measure has centered about so-called "practical" or "administrative" problems. Funds and data became available for studying such problems, whereas little opportunity was granted to study the more basic questions. That answers to practical problems would be obtained more readily if fundamental research could be undertaken was largely ignored. The seeking of solutions to practical problems has been so instrumental in the growth of the working force as a field of study since the 1930's that this area must be mentioned briefly if the position of the working force in the 1950's as an area of scientific research is to be appreciated. (See, for example, President of the United States, annual; Stewart, 1955; U.S. Congress, 1955.)

In the United States impetus was given this topic during the depression of the 1930's; at this time the federal government undertook responsibility for alleviating unemployment either by finding jobs for the unemployed or by somehow removing them from the labor market. For accomplishing these aims, a great number of facts and their interrelationships were needed. How many unemployed were there? What skills did they have? Such questions led to the formation by the Works Progress Administration of what is now the monthly labor force survey conducted by the United States census bureau. It was hoped that these monthly surveys would provide the facts needed for formulating programs to combat unemployment.

By the time this monthly survey really got underway, World War II had drastically changed the economic scene. The important practical problems now centered about manpower shortages: Where and how could more workers be obtained? Following the end of World War II, questions involving both unemployment and labor shortages were asked at one time or another, although the need for action seemed not as necessary as during the depression and war periods. Simultaneously, a new set of problems arose in connection with presumed shortages of certain types of professional and skilled workers (Wolfle, 1954).

Whether these problems calling for action are genuine or not is often beside the point; the United States society believes them to be genuine and as a result makes available the kinds of data and research facilities which it believes will help lead to solutions. Data which are made available for "practical" purposes then become available for carrying on more basic research. Since the researcher has to "make do with what is available," so to speak, his own basic research may have to be adapted to and hitched onto the "practical" problems.

In economically underdeveloped societies, what emphasis has been given to study of the working force has centered on the problems of economic development (Hsieh, 1952; International Labor Office, 1950, 1954; Sierra Berdecia and Jaffe, 1955; United Nations, 1953). How many new jobs have to be created? How many native workers can be introduced into, or utilized by, modern manufacturing industry? How much underemployment is there? The practical questions seen by the administrators of an underdeveloped country appear to be quite different from the practical questions faced by the administrators of a developed country. Whether they are really different or whether both sets of questions revolve around a common basic core is not clear. This is a fundamental point on which working-force and demographic research ought to center.

Definition of the Working Force

For a country having a developed market economy, the following definition of the working force appears to be suitable:

That specialized portion of the market place in which the person is free to offer his services for hire may be called the labor market.

Those persons, then, who voluntarily offer their services for hire in the labor market (in exchange for which they receive wages or salaries) and who thereby participate (or attempt to participate) in the production of the gross national product, form the working force. Those persons in the population who fail or do not desire to offer their services in the labor market thereby automatically exclude themselves from the working force. [Jaffe and Stewart, 1951, p. 33. This definition includes self-employed persons even though they are not specifically mentioned in the quotation.]

This definition, as actually applied by the United States census bureau in its monthly population survey, becomes twofold. Those persons who had a job during the specified week are considered employed; those who report seeking a job during the same week are the unemployed. This application gets into trouble when one attempts to decide whether a person really had a job or not, or whether he really looked for work. The crucial breaking points thus are the person who did not actually work during the week but had (or may not have had) a claim on a job and the person who did not profess to have a claim on a job but whose job-seeking activities were so minimal as to make it difficult to decide whether he looked for work (Stephan, 1954).

In societies with poorly developed market economies there is no single precise definition of the working force which can be used successfully to encompass the entire population. On the one hand, in almost every such country at least some of the people live within a market economy; indeed, the very effort to achieve economic development means the growth of a market economy; indeed, the very effort to achieve economic development means the growth of a market economy. Hence, for at least some of the people the definition suitable for a developed market economy is applicable; it may be necessary to change some of the detailed collection procedures but not the basic definition.

In these same countries, on the other hand, there are also large segments of the adult population which have little contact with the market economy; these people live under subsistence or semi-subsistence conditions. For these people there is no precise definition which is very usable, if for no other reason than that the very intent of economic development is to take them out of these subsistence conditions. Hence, general demographic information (age, sex, etc.) serves to answer most, if not all, practical problems that are raised.

Many people within such societies, of course, are "half and half"—partly in and partly out of the market sphere. It is difficult to obtain statistics about those who are presumably in a transitional phase. Nevertheless, no new definition of the working force is needed in order to get information about such people that will be useful in a developmental program.

Types of Working-Force Data as Related to Demographic Data

Perhaps the most frequent statistics on the working force are those obtained in connection with population surveys, either complete censuses or sample surveys. Probably most countries of the world have collected such information. It is a very simple procedure to obtain information about the working force whenever demographic information is collected; after asking the person about his demographic characteristics (age, marital status, place of birth, etc.), one can ask him further questions about his employment, occupation, etc. Few countries have had many difficulties in obtaining some minimum information about the working force. This is true even for those countries in which much of the population lives outside the market sector and in which it is not very easy to distinguish, conceptually and otherwise, the working force from the general population. The reason for this close connection (as was noted previously) lies in the fact that the working-force data have to be interpreted in terms of the demographic characteristics of the population. The demographic factors of age, sex, marital status, etc., are all important elements for analyses of the working force. Hence, the two sets of information have to be collected and analyzed together.

In passing, we should note that there are a few items of information about the working force that are more or less unrelated to demographic considerations. For example, there may be good reason to know how many people are working (at any given moment) in the manufacture of paper as compared with the mining of copper. Questions of this nature generally involve the operation of the economy; information on the working force is used together with production data, financial data, etc., as indexes of the way the economy is operating.

Methods of Working-Force Analysis

Virtually all procedures devised for demographic analyses are suitable for working-force analyses, with but relatively slight modifications. The procedures described in *Handbook of Statistical Methods for Demographers* (Jaffe, 1951) or *Introduction to Demography* (Spiegelman, 1955) are all directly applicable to working-force analysis.

One set of procedures originally developed for demographic problems centers upon standardization procedures; Westergaard, for example, developed his procedures with population data. These standardization procedures are now used for working-force analyses. The conventional life table has been converted into the working-force life table. Procedures for calculating birth rates, with slight modifications, become procedures for calculating rates of new entries into the working force; at the other end of life, procedures for calculating death rates become procedures for calculating retirements from the working force. Even the well-known balancing equation, which is used so extensively and valuably in demographic analysis, is transferable almost without change to working-force analysis.

Another type of analysis sometimes employed involves the construction of mathematical models. Thus, for example, industrial mobility has been described in terms of a probability model (Blumen *et al.*, 1955). This procedure also has its counterpart in the various mathematical models which have been devised for the purpose of studying migration. In summary, if there are any procedures which have been used in demographic analysis and which cannot be adapted profitably to working-force analysis, this writer does not know of them.

The reason for this applicability of demographic procedures, of course, lies in the fact that demographic characteristics are used in combination with working-force characteristics. The demographic factors of age and sex are frequently used with working-force data; since many of the analytical procedures are built around the use of these two

variables, it is obvious that these same procedures can be used for analyses in both areas.

To the extent that the working-force data are used as economic indexes (as of the business cycle, for example), the analytical procedures described in most statistics textbooks can be used. These procedures—time-series analysis, correlation analysis, etc.—are also used in demographic analyses, however.

Another set of analytical procedures sometimes used in working-force analyses stems from attitude surveys. Thus, for example, procedures of analyzing the social importance of occupations or relating the social structure to the occupational structure (see, for example, Petersen, 1953) are identical with those used for analyzing the attitudes of the population to any other variable—sex, political parties and elections, housing, etc. It is impossible to draw lines and say that one set of procedures is used for demographic analyses, another for working-force analyses, still another for economic or sociological analyses.

WHAT WE THINK WE KNOW AND DO NOT KNOW ABOUT THE WORKING FORCE

The Conceptual Framework

The conceptual framework (see definition of the working force, above) has been developed largely in terms of the twentieth-century socioeconomic structure of the United States and other highly developed countries of the Western world. Some elements in this socioeconomic structure are relevant to this definition: the status of women is such that they are relatively free to participate in the working force if they so desire and to limit their fertility in accordance with their wishes; even those persons who must enter the working force, particularly adult men, are relatively free to choose occupation, industry, and type and location of job; the family structure is such that most people must depend on their own efforts or those of the immediate primary family (husband, wife with or without young children) for their support; education and literacy are widespread; considerable internal migration is possible; and, finally, work is considered a desirable value in itself and for its own sake, so that life tends to be divided into two parts—work first and play second.

Exactly how well this conceptual framework serves in socioeconomic structures which are quite different from that of the United States or western Europe is difficult to determine. For example, in some cultures (or subcultures) it is expected that everyone within certain age limits will work or be available for work at the behest of the community. The *kibbutzim* in Israel are of this nature. The adult individual has the right to choose whether or not he wants to be a member of such a co-operative agricultural community. Once he has decided to join, however, he no longer can decide to enter or remain outside of the working force, nor can he select his occupation or job. The community, through its administrative mechanism, makes all such decisions for the individual. As a result, it is difficult if not impossible to demarcate a working force separate from the total adult population.

Even in western Europe or the United States, in such special situations as during World War II, when the government could order people to enter the working force (as was the case with women in England) or could specify what jobs the workers must fill, it becomes difficult to apply the previously mentioned definition of the working force.

In parts of Latin-America, for example (and undoubtedly elsewhere in the world), work is not considered to be a particularly desirable activity. Work is necessary for some people, at least, but those who can, avoid it. "Enormous amounts of time, energy and money go into the celebration of particular festive events. In some rural villages, as much as a third of one's time, apart from Sundays, may be spent in *fiesta* activity. And much of the rest of one's time may well be spent in working for the next *fiesta*" (Whyte and Holmberg, 1956, p. 10). In a situation of this nature, how shall we distinguish between work and leisure activities? Indeed, is such a distinction possible?

Among the most primitive peoples, clearly the only ones to whom this definition can be applied are those who have left the tribal situation and have entered the labor market in some nearby area. In India, for example, those modern enterprises located in areas inhabited by aboriginal tribes draw large numbers of workers from among the aborigines (International Labor Office, 1953). Tribal members who have obtained such jobs or who have left the tribal territory to seek such employment can be encompassed within the definition of the working force. Those who have remained within the tribe and have continued to live and work as subsistence farmers or herdsmen or even as hunters and food gatherers cannot be encompassed within this definition.

In summary, the conceptual framework which we now have is one developed to fit the socioeconomic structure of twentieth-century United States and culturally similar nations. Insofar as the practical needs of these nations are concerned and insofar as we wish to measure the emergence of more or less similar types of working forces in other societies (originally quite different from our own), this conceptual framework appears to be useful. However, if we wish to have a more generalized framework which will encompass most of humanity, considerably more thought and research will have to be given to the subject (United Nations, 1956).

Classification Problems

Only in part do these problems stem from the nature of the conceptual framework used, i.e., the specific definition of the working force. Indeed, some of the most difficult problems posed in classifying people are largely operational; alternative forms of classification based on the same definition are possible, and the question is which set of procedures to adopt.

Why are classification problems important enough to be considered here? When conducting research on the working force—either of the United States or of some other country—in relation to demography, such research can be carried out only in terms of the available statistics. For example, in an underdeveloped country in which economic growth is occurring, we may ask how population growth, the growth of the working force, and occupational (or industrial) composition are interrelated. That there are interrelationships, both conceptual and empirical, is known to be the case. For purposes of scientific research, however, we wish to know as precisely as possible the size and direction of these relationships, and whether any bear a cause-and-effect relationship.

In trying to conduct such scientific research, we are faced with the fact that the answers (if any) which emerge may to a considerable extent be a product of the classification schemes adopted during the processes of data collection and tabulation (see, for example, Jaffe, 1957). Hence, the empirical investigations undertaken in an effort to test hypotheses may provide misleading results unless the researcher is fully aware of the possible effects upon his findings of the alternative classifications possible and the problems posed by each.

The classification problems most closely related to the concept of the working force are those which involve (*a*) separating out those persons deemed to be in the working force from those deemed to be outside of it, and (*b*) distinguishing among persons in the working force between those employed and those unemployed. It may seem, offhand, that such differentiations should be provided by the concept used in the collection of the statistics. The trouble is that the concept lays down the general principles but does not necessarily tell us exactly how they should be applied in specific cases.

This is because a concept attempts to distinguish among people and, in effect, draws boundary lines which separate the activities involved in earning a living from other activities. Actually, however, the activities of many people tend to differ one from another only by imperceptible degrees, so that there is no unique point where it is self-evident that a boundary line (or cutting point) should be drawn. This is seen most vividly in trying to distinguish "unemployed" from "not in the working force"; it also appears in trying to distinguish between "employed" and "unemployed." The conceptual basis on which the United States census bureau collects its monthly statistics about the working force is fairly clear about the distinction between these two groups. In actual practice, however, many persons who are not working (at a given moment) are on the borderline between seeking work and not seeking work. Elaborate instructions have been written for the supposed benefit of the enumerators, but these are *ad hoc* instructions which can be changed at any time *without* changing the basic concept (United States Congress, 1955, pp. 6 ff.).

Subclassification of the employed into at least two groups, fully employed and underemployed (sometimes referred to as "hidden unemployment"), is another area about which little is known (Hsieh, 1952; International Labor Office, 1957; Sierra Berdecia and Jaffe, 1955; United Nations, 1956). This classification problem seems to be most relevant for the underdeveloped countries, although it has relevancy for even the most developed.

There are several other classification problems which involve procedures rather than basic concepts and which have to do with demarcating the working force. One such is the time reference. The basic concept now being used begs the question entirely: "those persons who participate in the labor market" only implies a current activity without attempting to specify exactly when this activity was carried on, or for how long. When the United States census bureau applies it currently, it refers to "last week"; when the gainfully occupied procedures are used, the time reference is much more indefinite and encompasses some vague period probably not less than a year previous to the survey. We know empirically that by varying the time reference the number of persons who become classified as in the working force can be altered.

Another classification problem involves setting age limits on the working force. The basic concept itself sets no age limits. For various reasons, however, it is useful to set at least a minimum age limit. Here, also, further research is needed, both for developed and for underdeveloped countries. Once the problems of classifying persons as in or out of the working force and as employed or unemployed have been clarified, a whole host of other classification questions remain—questions which have nothing much to do with any basic concept. These involve classifying the members of the working force into groups which are meaningful for testing hypotheses or solving problems.

One such area, and perhaps the single most important, is concerned with occupations and industries. Within the United States (and other economically developed countries) studies leading to the improvement of occupational and industrial classification systems are con-

stantly being carried on. As a result of such improvements, the United States makes changes in its working-force statistics so often that it is difficult to reconstruct a historical series covering more than a couple of decades. These improvements, of course, are always directed toward making the data more useful for the purposes of solving current problems. More important from our viewpoint, however, such changes often make scientific research more difficult.

Thus there are at least three areas in which further investigation into problems of occupational and industrial classification are called for: (1) to make these classifications more suitable for analytical purposes in the developed countries; (2) to devise, if necessary, completely new classification schemes more suitable for the underdeveloped countries; (3) to determine whether there are any classification schemes which can be used for historical analyses extending over a half-century or longer, in both developed and underdeveloped countries.

What We Might Know about the United States Working Force

For the years since 1940, we have reasonably good descriptive information on the purely demographic aspects. (See, for example, Durand, 1948; Haber *et al.*, 1954; Industrial Relations Research Association, annual; Jaffe and Stewart, 1951; Jaffe and Carleton, 1954; Bakke *et al.*, 1954; Palmer, 1954; Parnes, 1954; United Nations, 1953.) We know the working-force participation rates by age, sex, and color; by marital and dependency status; as related to school attendance for the younger people; as related to internal migration and rural-to-urban movements; by education; among urban and rural areas; and by size of city. Furthermore, we know something about the dynamics of the relationships between job mobility and geographic mobility; family type and earnings as related to the working-force behavior of the various members; the role played by education in occupational mobility from one generation to another; demographic factors associated with the rates of entry into the working force by occupation and the rates of retirement by occupation; the number of years during the course of a lifetime spent by the average United States male in and out of the working force. We also have some descriptive information on the non-demographic aspects of the working force, for example: the working force and technological changes; the role of customs, habits, and attitudes as related to working-force behavior; economic demand for workers, secular, cyclical, and seasonal.

What We Do Not Know about the United States Working Force

There are at least two broad areas in which our knowledge is deficient. One has to do with the exact interrelationships between fertility rates and patterns and the participation of women in the working force (see Day, 1957, for example). On the purely descriptive side, we know that women who have "large numbers" of young children are seldom reported as in the working force. But beyond that we know very little.

The question which is highly important from an analytical viewpoint is this: Will women who take full-time jobs outside the home have smaller completed families than if they had not taken such jobs? Or does it work in reverse: Are women who will have smaller families (for whatever reason) the ones who take jobs outside the home? Or are both variables (size of completed family and working-force behavior of the woman) the resultants of other socioeconomic factors? Or is there a feedback relationship among a large number of variables so that a change introduced into any one will have repercussions on all other factors in the matrix?

Within the last twenty-five years the United States has experienced wide fluctuations in the birth rate and in the volume of employment of women. We know that these fluctuations have been related to the business cycle and to war conditions, but how are they related to each other? For example, in 1957, we know that a larger proportion of the women with no or few young children were in the working force than of the women with many young children; this implies a negative correlation. On the other hand, since the mid-1930's there has been an increase in fertility together with an increase in the proportion of women employed outside the home; this implies a positive correlation.

If the interrelationships between demographic and working-force factors can be ascertained with any reasonable degree of accuracy, then we shall have a valuable tool for estimating the answers to many practical problems. In particular, we should like to have good projections of the future size of the United States population and working force, say, for the year 2000 (U.S. Bureau of the Census, 1952). If such estimates could be made, they would help answer a multitude of subsidiary questions.

Our previous queries, in effect, have led us to a complex matrix of interrelated factors, a feedback switchboard, so to speak; this matrix may be described by the term "motivational factors." These are the factors—demographic, sociological, economic, technological, and other —which interact with each other and with the working force and which lead to the eventual shaping of the size and characteristics of the working force. Why are some women motivated to participate in the working force and others motivated to have more children? Why do boys choose one occupation instead of another (insofar as choice is permitted)? Why do some men change their jobs and others not?

How will automation fit into this matrix? Will it, perhaps, permit paying so much higher wages to a smaller number of workers that many married women will be motivated to remain out of the working force and have children instead of pay envelopes? Or will automation, via increased earnings, feed the consumer fires so that the more money people may have to spend on purchasable goods and services, the more money they will want? These are some of the questions which have to be answered if any realistic appraisal of future demographic and working-force trends is to be made. But the necessary studies have only begun.

Elsewhere in the World

The rest of the world comprises so many and such diverse countries that we cannot hope to review all of it in the same way as we reviewed the United States. Hence, we shall simply speak of the two extremes, the other developed countries and those which are largely underdeveloped, and mention briefly what we may know and do not know about each group.

Those which are well developed comprise the countries of northwestern Europe and the English-speaking areas outside of Europe, for the most part. All these countries have taken a number of population censuses, as part of which they have obtained considerable information about their working forces. By and large, as of the census dates, these countries have considerable descriptive materials about their people in their role as workers. With the exception of the periods of the two world wars, this information extends over a number of decades, in some instances back into the mid-nineteenth century.

Current working-force data on a monthly, quarterly, or annual basis are much scarcer; however, some information on employment and unemployment is available from various sources. Canada, for example, conducts a recurrent working-force sample survey quite similar to that of the United States. Other countries—England, for example—have well-developed social security systems (including unemployment compensation systems) whose by-product statistics provide much information on the working force.

There are two major hiatuses in these data and information about the well-developed countries (outside the United States). The first is the question of motivation; this is exactly the same question as was raised previously about the United States. In this connection, some very interesting and meaningful questions arise. For example, in England the proportion of women in the working force reached a level of around 35 per cent by the end of the nineteenth century and has remained at this level since then (with the exception of the period of World War II). This is about the same level of working-force participation for women as is found in the United States in the 1950's. Does this suggest that in our type of society 35 per cent to perhaps 40 per cent is the maximum participation of women which can be expected?

In attempting to answer such a question, we are confronted by the second major hiatus, the comparability of the data over time within any given country and among the various countries. Much talk has been devoted to this topic, but information is still scanty. In a number of these countries the national statisticians have attempted to adjust their historical information so as to achieve more or less comparable time series.[1] For comparing a number of

[1] Whether or not such statistically comparable time series are really comparable in terms of meaning which might be imputed to the data is another question. In some of these countries, as in the United States, the entire socioeconomic structure has changed so considerably over the last half-century that perhaps there never can be any data which mean the same for the various time periods. For the period since

countries, however, reasonably accurate information is lacking; the existing data are just not comparable enough for very meaningful analyses. For example, in the illustration given above in which the working-force participation of women in the United States and England were compared, we cannot be sure that our measurements are comparable. Do about the same proportion of women really participate in the working force in both countries, or does the apparent similarity accidentally result from the application of two quite different measuring devices? We know that the measuring devices are different, but we do not know how they affect the final statistics.

For the grossly underdeveloped countries the problems are simpler in some respects and more complicated in others. In the most underdeveloped countries the question of measuring and understanding the working force is simplified in that working-force and demographic analyses are virtually identical (International Labor Office, 1953; United Nations, 1951, p. 11). There is no clear demarcation of the working force from the total population, since virtually everyone has to work in order to live. Hence, knowledge of the demographic characteristics of the population tells us almost everything about the working force. Furthermore, since these people live under subsistence, or at best semi-subsistence, conditions, it is obvious that they are all occupied in agriculture; no question arises in trying to describe and explain their occupational and industrial composition. To the extent that non-agricultural activities are carried on, these are generally of secondary importance. For people living under such subsistence conditions, there is very little, if anything, that we need to know about their working force which cannot be determined from their population characteris-

tics. The major hiatus here is the lack of reliable and comprehensive demographic data. The international agencies are attempting to remedy this situation.

In most, if not all, of these underdeveloped countries, segments of the population live and work within the market sector and seem to constitute an embryonic modern working force. What do we know about them? The answer, unfortunately, is not much. We know little even about the proportions who work wholly within the original subsistence economy, the proportions who work within the market sector, and those who work in both sectors (United Nations, 1956). In short, we cannot even describe these working forces as well as we can describe that of the United States.

This lack of adequate descriptive materials stems, in part, from the fact that even when population censuses have been taken and data are available, little adequate differentiation has been made between those who live under the original subsistence conditions and those who live in the more modern market sector of the economy. The process whereby persons move from the subsistence into the market sectors, and factors associated with this process, are basic to our conceptualization of the working force; yet little is known about this process. The motivational side of the working-force behavior in an underdeveloped economy is as little understood as is that of our own society. Yet it is highly important to understand this process if socioeconomic development is to occur in these countries. In part, of course, the emergence of a modern type of working force from a primitive subsistence type is simply one part of the entire process of cultural change. In this sense, there may be little that is unique in any conceptual background for studying this problem.

From the practical viewpoint, however, as we pointed out previously, there are a large number of questions which

---

the beginning of World War II, however, this footnote probably has little relevance.

administrators want answered in order to carry on economic development in an orderly fashion. To answer these questions, better conceptual frameworks and more adequate measuring devices are the major needs. The procedures for measuring the working force devised in the United States and other developed countries are only partly useful in these underdeveloped countries. Thus, the major hiatuses for such underdeveloped countries may be summed up as: (1) lack of knowledge about how to obtain the needed data, (2) inadequate descriptive information about the people, (3) little understanding of the detailed nature of the process whereby subsistence farmers become modern workers, and (4) the manner in which demographic and working-force changes are interrelated.

FACILITIES FOR TRAINING AND RESEARCH

Working Force and Demography

Those aspects of working-force investigation which touch most closely upon demography have been largely neglected in American universities. In part, this stems from the fact that the study is relatively new, having come into prominence only about the time of World War II.[2] In part, however, its rejection by the universities lies in the fact that it is a subject which cuts across several officially demarcated academic lines. Exactly how many universities teach this subject is not known, but the total is small, indeed.

As for carrying on research, probably the majority of studies conducted in the United States in the past decade and in the 1950's are financed by the federal government. Probably most of this federally financed research is carried on by

employees within the various agencies of the federal government; the remainder is carried on in universities and other private organizations, with federal funds. State governments, private industry, and private foundations have financed only a small part of these investigations. If a student wishes to study this subject, he can take a course or two in the working force at some university, whatever courses are given in demography, and the full complement of courses in whatever official discipline he is taking his degree. After that, with some luck, he can become attached to an office which is conducting investigations. After serving an apprenticeship, he may then be qualified in this field.

Study of the Working Force of Foreign Countries

Few facilities are available in the United States for studying the working force of other countries. American universities have tended to avoid this subject matter. Sometimes United States students can obtain a smattering of such information as part of a course on economic development or social change, and sometimes as part of a course on world population. After that the student is on his own and can learn more only by reading, traveling, or obtaining an apprenticeship on a research study being carried on somewhere.

The foreign students, particularly those from underdeveloped countries who might want to learn something about this subject for scientific and administrative purposes in their own countries, also have few study facilities. The United States government provides some instruction for them on how the United States collects and analyzes working-force data, but little else.

The international agencies furnish no more facilities for training and research than does the United States government or American universities. An occasional "conference of experts" is held, but that

2 The first university course on this subject seems to have been given at the American University (Washington, D.C.) in the 1946 spring semester, by S. L. Wolfbein and A. J. Jaffe; this was entitled "The Labor Force of the United States."

is about all (United Nations, 1955, reports of meetings 15, 24, 26, 31). No international agency is functioning (as of 1958) to supply competent instruction and training on a world-wide basis; no agency is responsible for conducting research on methods for studying the working force under varying socioeconomic conditions. The net result is that the student who is interested in this subject—whether American or foreign—learns it as best he can.

SELECTED BIBLIOGRAPHY

BAKKE, E. W., *et al.* 1954. *Labor Mobility and Economic Opportunity.* New York: John Wiley & Sons.

BLUESTONE, ABRAHAM. 1955. "Major Studies of Workers' Reasons for Job Choice," *Monthly Labor Review,* LXXVIII, 301–6.

BLUMEN, ISIDORE, KOGAN, MARVIN, and McCARTHY, PHILIP J. 1955. *The Industrial Mobility of Labor as a Probability Process.* ("Cornell Studies in Industrial Relations," Vol. VI.) Ithaca, N.Y.

DAY, LINCOLN H. 1957. "Age at Completion of Childbearing and Its Relation to the Participation of Women in the Labor Force: United States, 1910–1955." Ph.D. dissertation, Columbia University.

DURAND, JOHN D. 1948. *The Labor Force in the U.S., 1890–1960.* New York: Social Science Research Council.

GARFINKLE, STUART. 1955. "Changes in Working Life of Men, 1900 to 2000," *Monthly Labor Review,* LXXVIII, 297–300.

GORDON, MARGARET S. 1954. *Employment Expansion and Population Growth.* Berkeley: University of California Press.

HABER, W., HARBISON, F. H., KLEIN, L. R., and PALMER, G. L. (eds.). 1954. *Manpower in the United States: Problems and Policies.* New York: Harper & Bros.

HAUSER, P. M. 1951. "The Labor Force as a Field of Interest for the Sociologist," *American Sociological Review,* XVI, 530–38.

HSIEH CHIANG. 1952. "Underemployment in Asia," *International Labour Review,* LXV, 703–25.

INDUSTRIAL RELATIONS RESEARCH ASSOCIATION. *Proceedings of the Annual Meetings.* (As of January, 1956, 7 volumes of proceedings were available.)

INTERNATIONAL LABOR OFFICE. "Yearbooks." Geneva.

———. 1950. *Action against Unemployment.* Geneva.

———. 1953. *Indigenous Peoples: Living and Working Conditions of Aboriginal Populations in Independent Countries.* Geneva.

———. 1954. *Employment and Unemployment Statistics.* (Report IV, prepared for the Eighth International Conference of Labor Statisticians.) Geneva.

———. 1957. *Measurement of Underemployment.* (Ninth International Conference of Labor Statisticians, Report IV.) Geneva.

JACK, A. FINGLAND. 1912. *An Introduction to the History of Life Assurance.* London.

JAFFE, A. J. 1951. *Handbook of Statistical Methods for Demographers.* Washington: Bureau of the Census.

———. 1957. "Suggestions for a Supplemental Grouping of the Occupational Classification System," *Estadística,* No. 54, pp. 13–23.

———, and CARLETON, R. O. 1954. *Occupational Mobility in the U.S., 1930–1960.* New York: King's Crown Press.

———, and STEWART, C. D. 1951. *Manpower Resources and Utilization.* New York: John Wiley & Sons.

———, and WOLFBEIN, SEYMOUR L. 1945. "Internal Migration and Full Employment in the United States," *Journal of the American Statistical Association,* XL, 351–63.

PALMER, GLADYS L. 1954. *Labor Mobility in Six Cities.* New York: Social Science Research Council.

PARNES, HERBERT S. 1954. *Research on Labor Mobility.* (Bulletin 65.) New York: Social Science Research Council.

PETERSEN, WILLIAM. 1953. "Is America Still the Land of Opportunity?" *Commentary,* XVI, 477–86.

PRESIDENT OF THE UNITED STATES (annual). "Economic Reports of the President." Washington, D.C.: Government Printing Office.

SIERRA BERDECIA, F., and JAFFE, A. J. 1955. "The Concept and Measurement of Underemployment," *Monthly Labor Review,* LXXVIII, 283–84.

SPIEGELMAN, MORTIMER. 1955. *Introduction to Demography.* Chicago: Society of Actuaries.

STEPHAN, F. F. (chairman, special advisory commitee on employment statistics). 1954. Report submitted to the Secretary of Commerce regarding the work of the census bureau's Current Population Survey.

STEWART, CHARLES D. 1955. "Uses of Unemployment Statistics in Economic Policy," *Monthly Labor Review,* LXXVIII, 279–82.

UNITED NATIONS. Various dates. *Population Studies.* (ST/SOA/Ser. A.) New York.

———. 1951. *Application of International Standards to Census Data on the Economically Active Population.* ("Population Studies." No. 9.) New York: United Nations.

———. 1953. "Population and Labor Supply," *The Determinants and Consequences of Population Trends,* chap. xi. New York: United Nations.

———. 1955. *Proceedings of the World Population Conference, 1954.* New York: United Nations.

———. 1956. *Manual on Statistics of Labor Force, Employment, and Unemployment.* Economic Commission for Asia and the Far East, Fourth Regional Conference of Statisticians. (STAT/Conf.4/20.)

UNITED STATES BUREAU OF THE CENSUS. 1952. "A Projected Growth of the Labor Force in the United States under Conditions of High Employment: 1950 to 1975," *Current Population Reports.* (Ser. P-53, No. 42.)

———. Various reports from the monthly population survey; see Ser. P-50, P-57, P-60.

UNITED STATES CONGRESS. 1955. "Interim Report of the Review of Concepts Subcommittee to the Committee on Labor Supply, Employment, and Unemployment Statistics," *Hearings before the Subcommittee on Economic Statistics of the Joint Committee on the Economic Report,* pp. 6 ff. (84th Cong., 1st sess., November 7–8, 1955.) Washington, D.C.: Government Printing Office.

UNITED STATES DEPARTMENT OF LABOR. 1954. *Techniques of Preparing Major BLS Statistical Series.* (Bulletin No. 1188.) Washington, D.C.

WHYTE, WILLIAM F., and HOLMBERG, ALLAN R. 1956. "Human Problems of U.S. Enterprise in Latin America," *Human Organization,* Vol. XV, No. 3.

WOLFBEIN, S. T. 1949. "The Length of Working Life," *Population Studies,* III, 286–94.

WOLFLE, DAEL. 1954. *America's Resources of Specialized Talent.* New York: Harper & Bros.

26. *Population and Natural Resources*

EDWARD A. ACKERMAN

The relation between population and resources may be one of the social equations first understood by man. From the earliest tribal life, the relation between the productivity of the hunting ground and the numbers and welfare of the tribe must have been very clear. It therefore is not surprising that we find mention of population-resource relations early in the recorded history of more complex societies. The administrators and intellectuals of early China, the Greek city-states, and Rome gave thought to population-resource problems. (See United Nations, Population Division, 1953, pp. 21 ff., for a résumé and useful list of references on the history of population study.)

Beginning with the records we have of the observations of Confucius, Plato, Aristotle, and lesser men among ancient civilizations, it is possible to trace remarkably continuous attention to this subject down to our time. Malthus was only one of a long series of analytical students of society who have found definite correlations between human groups and the attributes of those parts of the earth which support them. The dominant subject of interest has always been the relation of amount of resources to numbers of people, adequately sustained. This is still the point of departure for any general treatment of population-resource relations.

However, this simply described correlation, while most important, is only a beginning for the description of the relation of human social groups to the resources which support them. First, resources must be identified not only in

their amount but also in their quality (productivity) and stability and by their relation to other "conditioning" features of the natural environment. Second, resources become productive to men now mainly through the medium of culture. The technical attributes of the many cultures in the world differ widely and have vastly different meaning for the resources which are put to use through these cultures. In addition, cultures differ in the standard of living of the society, in the territorial extent of political jurisdiction, in institutional inheritances, in trading relations, in frugality, and in other respects. Finally, social groups differ not only in number and density of settlement on the earth's surface but also in health, age classes, mortality and natality, rates of natural increase, migration, and nature of employment. All these demographic features theoretically warrant examination for their correlation with the attributes of natural resources.

The relation of population and natural resources therefore concerns a relatively large number of variables. If all the attributes of culture, human demography, and resources are taken into account, a very large number of permutations occurs. Obviously, therefore, an understanding becomes possible only with some attempt to isolate or group the variables, analyzing the place of each major grouping in turn.

If one were to consider the relation of population and resources as species of equation, the equation might be described roughly in terms of a demand side and a supply side. On the demand

621

side are population numbers and standard of living; on the supply side, all the attributes of resources and all the attributes of culture except for standard of living. The equation might be written:

$$PS = RQ\,(TAS_t) + E_s + T_r \pm F - W\,,$$

or

$$P = \frac{RQ\,(TAS_t) + E_s + T_r \pm F - W}{S}\,,$$

where the symbols have these meanings:

P   numbers of people
S   standard of living
R   amount of resources
Q   factor for natural quality of resources
T   physical technology factor
A   administrative techniques factor
S_t resource stability factor
W   frugality element (wastage, or intensity of use)
F   institutional advantage and "friction" loss element consequent upon institutional characteristics of the society
E_s scale economies element (size of territory, etc.)
T_r resources added in trade

To most of the elements in this equation one cannot presently attach specific, accurate values in any population study. Nonetheless, the general composition of the relation involved in the resource-adequacy question would seem to be described in the equation.

In the succeeding discussion the component parts of this generalized equation will be analyzed briefly. Six steps will be taken in this analysis: (1) presentation of some observed general relations between numbers of people and the physical environment, including amount of resources; (2) mention of the effect of standard of living as it affects the demand side of the equation; (3) introduction of certain features of culture which affect the supply side of the

equation; (4) consideration of certain dynamic or "feedback" elements, wherein density of population in itself affects the productivity of resources—i.e., intensity of demand can and does affect the amount of supply; (5) consideration of all resource and pertinent culture attributes as they correlate with demographic attributes other than number; and (6) application of the above type of analysis to study of the world's population.

OBSERVED CORRELATION BETWEEN
NUMBERS OF PEOPLE AND THE
PHYSICAL ENVIRONMENT

The first step in understanding present-day resource-population relations is very easily taken with the aid of a few atlas maps of the world.[1] An examination of them readily reveals the following correlations:

(1) Concentration of the greater part of the world's population in a few regions (Far East, Indian peninsula, parts of southeast Asia, Mediterranean basin, western, central, and eastern Europe, and eastern United States). These densely populated regions generally are the sites of the past most productive agricultural lands. They usually have at least a one-hundred-day growing season, a favorable precipitation-evaporation ratio, and relatively extensive lands of low relief, suitable for unrestricted cultivation.

(2) Further concentration within the heavily settled regions in two types of environment, depending upon the prevalent culture: for the dominantly agrarian cultures of the Middle and Far East, concentration within the alluvial valleys of the great rivers, where irrigation agriculture has the best opportunity for de-

[1] Such as those in the *Encyclopaedia Britannica World Atlas* (Encyclopaedia Britannica, Chicago), *Goode's School Atlas* (Chicago: Rand McNally Co.), or the *Oxford Advanced Atlas* (New York: Oxford University Press).

velopment (the valleys of Ganges and the Yangtze are examples); for the industrialized Western cultures, concentration in those areas where access to mineral resources in combination encourages the growth of modern manufacturing and the cities which are based on manufacturing, directly or indirectly. Coal and iron have been the most important resource determinants of this type of population concentration in the past, but petroleum and natural gas also are now commencing to serve industrial concentrations which influence population growth. The belt of dense settlement which extends from French Flanders through the Low Countries and Germany into Bohemia and Polish Galicia is an example of the former; the Gulf Coast region of Texas and Louisiana in the United States is an example of the latter. Within the United States, California's growing concentration of population has been considered to depend mainly on the "amenities" afforded by an attractive physical environment (Ullman, 1954).

(3) Excepting some islands of development which have parallel environmental conditions with those of the large regions of heavy population concentration, the remainder of the world is made up of sparsely settled lands. These lands are of three main types: (a) The high latitude and high altitude environments, which have basic similarities. Agriculture in them generally must cope with infertile soils and short, undependable growing seasons; forest growth is slow or nonexistent; and natural livestock ranges are of very low capacity. Northern Canada, Iceland, and the larger part of the Scandinavian peninsula offer examples of this environment. (b) Arid and semiarid environments, generally characterized by evaporation potentials greater than the precipitation which they receive (deficit water budgets). The Great Basin of the United States, the Sahara, and Arabia, as examples, all contain fertile soils and other resources, but thus far they have been able to support only sparse populations because their water resources are so limited. (c) The tropical savannas and rain forests. Here a combination of infertile soils, insect annoyance and destruction, bacterial disease, stubbornly persistent and commercially unusable vegetation, and fungus decay have discouraged widespread dense settlement. The southern part of the Indian peninsula may be considered an exception in this environment, with central Africa and the Brazilian Amazon country more typical.

(4) The sparsely settled parts of the world are dotted with cases of denser settlement, depending almost entirely on local resources. Where water is available in arid regions, as in an exotic stream like the Nile or the Indus, a strip or a spot of dense settlement is certain. Where commercially exploitable industrial minerals exist, particularly petroleum (Arabia) or the metals (Great Basin of the United States), cases of denser settlement also may be found in all of these natural environments.

From these broad observations one can draw a few conclusions as to the correlation between resources and density of settlement: men are to be found in numbers only where there is a supply of fresh water usable through the techniques with which their culture has armed them; in mature agrarian civilizations numbers are a function of the amount of level land in combination with the amount of water available; for the industrial cultures numbers of people probably have a calculable direct relation to the amount and quality of industrially usable minerals available to an area, particularly iron and coal—however, this relationship is obscured and probably overshadowed by the technological attributes of the prevailing cultural differences among industrialized nations today. Taken the world over, the "conditioning" features of the natural environment, which include the thermal energy received in the atmosphere[2] and topography, share with resources the natural influences on density of settlement. A glance at any world map of temperature and surface configuration regions readily shows the direct correlation between present sparse populations and mountain lands and lands without a dependable growing season.

STANDARD OF LIVING AND RESOURCE-POPULATION RELATIONS

The simple relation of resources to numbers of people is altered by the quality of life which characterizes a social group. Most commonly this is referred to as the standard of living. It is the first of a series of cultural attributes which alter the basic relation of P (numbers of people) $= R$ (amount of resources). It is the only cultural attribute to be entered in the "demand" side of the balance. For purposes of resource-population relations, habits of material consumption are convenient measurements of the standard of living. A group which has a habitual 3,500-calorie daily diet composed of 40 per cent animal proteins obviously will have lesser numbers in relation to a given food-producing resource than a cereal-eating population with a 1,600-calorie diet dependent on the same resource. The disparity in consumption habits may be much greater in demands for fuel, clothing, shelter, and material consumption for aesthetic or recreational ends. Modern industrial nations show ranges in residential electricity consumption from 150 kilowatt hours to 8,000 kilowatt hours annually. Yearly paper consumption may range from 25 pounds for one group to 300 or more for another. The range is equally great for a long list of materials which enter daily life—high-strength textile fibers, metals, building materials of all kinds, and many other items. If a com-

[2] From insolation or through transfer by the air-mass movement system of the atmosphere.

parison is made between the underdeveloped non-industrial nations and the industrialized, the range of consumption averages is even greater.

While summary comparative measurements of the standard of living among different nations and different social groups are not easily compiled, data on average income do give some crude measure of the capacity of a social group to consume and of its habits of consumption. According to the Statistical Office of the United Nations (1950), the known range in average annual income among the nations of the world in 1949 was from $1,453 (United States) to $27 (China) and $25 (Indonesia). These figures, and the known differences in consumption rates of both food and materials, suggest that one inhabitant of the United States may equal twenty or more inhabitants of China or Indonesia when resource-population relations are considered. Standard of living thus adds another dimension to resource-population relations. It is not possible to consider population-support problems in terms of numbers of people alone; instead, numbers at a given or assumed standard of materials and food consumption must enter the calculation.

CULTURAL ALTERATIONS OF RESOURCE-POPULATION CORRELATIONS

There are four additional attributes of culture which may alter the simplified resource-population relation, $P = R$. They are technology (including transportation techniques), territorial extent of political jurisdiction, trading relations, and the "friction losses" caused by institutional inheritance. All of these must be entered on the "supply" side of the balance.

Technology

The history of most technological change has been a broadening of the supply base of resources, both geographically and in kind. Thus, little-known minerals of yesterday, like germanium, are vital to the technology of today. The petroleum resources of Arabia are essential to the economic health of Europe and Japan, while the United States draws uranium, copper, chrome, manganese, and other minerals from the corners of the earth. It is important to understand that nineteenth- and twentieth-century technological history does not constitute a story of liberation from dependence on resources; it is only a liberation from extreme dependence on *local* resources.

The centers of dense population today are dependent on resources, just as always before, but their resource base may be in hundreds of localities, separated by many thousands of miles. The technology of advanced industrial cultures like the United States has permitted them to command resources from wide areas, while less advanced groups are forced to continue dependence on a much more limited area of resource supply. A superior culture, like a vigorous vegetative growth, can obtain nourishment from a wide area which contributes to its size. We can say that a positive correlation of resources and size of population still obtains for technologically advanced cultures, even though some independence from adjacent resources becomes clear. Thus technology does not supplant resources but extends the geographical reach of the population group for resources and accordingly its capacity to grow.

Technology also gives value to local materials. The much-used example of Chinese peasant families burning grass for cooking fuel as they sat above great underground coal beds illustrates the meaning of technology-resource relations. Materials are given value as resources only insofar as technology can turn them to the use of people. In a sense, the true objective of technology is to make the most common materials serve as many of man's needs as possible.

The atmosphere was made a chemical resource when commercial nitrogen extraction became possible. Through technology, sea water has become a source of metal (magnesium); coal and silicon have become fiber resources; and granite may be a future source of energy. Thus technology can provide depth, as well as geographical breadth, to the resource base of a culture group. The ultimate in depth will be dependence on common materials for all major needs, no matter how complex the industrial structure of the social group. The more advanced the technical equipment of a social or political group, the larger the number of people which can be supported from a given set of resources.

Territorial Extent

Territorial extent of political jurisdiction also may alter simple population-resource relations. Its effects are noted mainly in economies of scale and in the diversity of resources employed. A group large enough in numbers to permit a very complex division of labor, and possessing a geographically extended territory, is likely to possess, employ, and exploit a greater diversity of natural resources than a geographically more restricted group. A diversity of resources, in fact, may lead to a variety of skills and encourage a complex division of labor. This is certainly true of the United States, and it is becoming true of the Soviet Union. The same population group can take advantage of economies of scale which a geographically more restricted group finds it difficult to organize. For instance, there appears to be an optimum size on the order of tens of thousands of square miles for an electric power generating and transmission system depending wholly or partly on hydroelectrical facilities. Efficient management of natural water supplies for irrigating land appears to require extended territory for the most productive combination. This is seen especially in arid, semiarid, and subhumid climates. The profitable exploitation of some low-grade ores also may have a scale attribute. Given a large enough domestic market, large-scale extraction facilities become possible, permitting the processing of low-grade materials. Other things being equal, a large territory like that of the United States or the Soviet Union can give added value to resources; one political jurisdiction permits economies of scale which are difficult to achieve under several political jurisdictions of lesser extent. A large group with geographically extended territory can produce more in relation to effort applied to natural resources than a smaller, geographically limited group.

Trading Relations

Trading relations, by extending the resource base of a group of people, afford a substitute for size of political jurisdiction. These relations usually have gone hand in hand with technological differences in the past, but they have favored the development of local specializations and therefore of certain scale economies. Trading relations explain the concentrations of people in Japan, Great Britain, Germany, Belgium, the Netherlands, Switzerland, and to a lesser extent France and Italy—concentrations far beyond the capacity of indigenous resources. Since they extend a population's geographical reach for resources, foreign-trading relations must always be considered an important alteration of domestic population-resource ratios.

A simple illustration of the effect of this cultural factor occurs in Iceland. Although that country depends mainly on one modest resource, a marine fishery, trade relations have permitted the development of a social group of number and economic quality unachievable under isolation. The situation of the Icelandic people today can be compared with that of Eskimo or other fishing-

hunting peoples under similar environmental conditions.

One can conclude that these cultural factors alter natural resource-population relations by creating resources from physical materials, by extending the geographical "reach" of the social group, and by permitting economies of scale. One must look to technology, territorial size of political jurisdiction, and trading relations, no less than to indigenous resources, for explanation of population concentrations.

Geographical Incidence of Three Major Culture Factors

The major areas in which resource-population relations thus far have been affected by the territorial extent of political jurisdiction have been the United States and the Soviet Union, although the full effects of this circumstance are only now coming into force in the Soviet Union. By the geographical extent of their territory alone, the peoples of both countries have opportunities for efficiency which smaller nations can acquire only through the more difficult route of trading relations. To a lesser extent, the same characteristic has operated in the British Commonwealth and in Brazil. In these countries, and in any other, this factor becomes influential only to the extent that a cohesive transportation system exists and operates. Because of transport deficiencies, economies of scale have never meant much to mainland China. Finally, the factor operates only in the presence of a moderate density of population. Transportation networks arise and economies of scale become possible only when there are numbers of people to be served. Thus Canada and Australia have large and diverse territories which predispose them to economies of scale in resource use, but they have profited little from their territories thus far because of sparsity of settlement.

Technology and trade relations have operated to a degree all over the earth, but their effects have been most pronounced on resource-population relations in the British Isles, in the European peninsula, and in Japan. The numbers of people in these parts of the earth are now far beyond the capacity of local resources to support without extensive trading relations, and therefore without extending the natural resource base. Particularly for the western European countries, technology has brought out the latent values of the indigenous resource base of the peninsula in a manner paralleled few other places in the world. The German chemical industry is a good case in point, in the way it has made use of coal, salt, potash, and a few other minerals. Perhaps more than for any other nation, the size of Germany during the twentieth century has been closely related to its technical proficiency.

Japan likewise is an interesting case of the effect of technology and trading relations on numbers. In a sense, its history offers very nearly a control situation to judge the broad effects of technology and trade relations. Until the Meiji Restoration in the late nineteenth century, Japan existed with very little trade and with a centuries-old technology which had changed very slowly. The story of the nation's overnight conversion to modern manufacturing and trading is well known. With this conversion the numbers of people in Japan also changed. From a nation which had remained at a relatively stable level somewhere between 25 and 30 millions for about 250 years, Japan commenced to grow at a striking rate. It now is three times the size of pre-Meiji Japan, and it is likely to grow to at least 100 million in the near future. The "inflationary" effect of technology and trade relations on numbers of people possessing a given domestic resource base is here clearly told.

Gains and Losses Associated with Institutional Inheritance

Institutional inheritance alone causes social groups throughout the world to function with varying effectiveness in transforming physical materials into resources and resources into consumers' goods. Economic institutions can favor or discourage savings and capital formation, the appearance of competent entrepreneurs, the provision of flexible and adequate training in skills, co-ordinated resource development planning, and other mechanisms which determine the progress of resource exploitation and the production of goods usable by men. (See Mason, 1955, for a concise description of the institutional factor in its association with energy resource development and use.) These institutions, which in part may be correlated with cultural advancement, are most effective within the advanced industrialized nations. Within countries like the United States, Canada, most western European nations, Australia, Japan, and the Soviet Union, the positive operation of these institutional factors is most clearly seen. To a lesser degree, their positive operation also characterizes countries like Mexico, Brazil, Venezuela, and India, which are in the process of industrialization and co-ordinating use of their resources. These factors are perhaps least favorable in some of the "underdeveloped" lands of low population density, like Madagascar, Angola, Borneo, and Paraguay.

These institutions are one of the most influential cultural attributes determining the effectiveness of resource exploitation. In a sense, the application of technology and the extension of trade depend on the vigor of these institutions, although the institutions themselves may differ greatly in form. Not all institutional inheritance represents gain in resource use. Nearly all, if not all, societies in the world have some institutional and ideological inheritances which cause losses in the supporting capacity of resources, as compared to the optimum obtainable under a given technological stage. The incidence of these losses has relatively little relation to cultural advancement. The industrially advanced nations suffer from them as well as the underdeveloped. Furthermore, there are collective losses from the point of view of the world as a whole, as well as from the point of view of the individual societies.

For the world as a whole, the most important of these inheritances are political boundaries and territorial restrictions, which in many instances prevent the achievement of scale economies which are known to be possible in large geographical units; prevent the movement of people from the densely settled, resource-deficient parts of the world to the lands which have low ratios of population to potential resources; permit artificial restrictions of production (like the United States "soil bank") which are of apparent national advantage; and deny to groups possessing both labor force and requisite techniques timely access to undeveloped resources.

In the same class we must place economic institutions which *in the balance* depress domestic economic benefits to social groups as a whole because they favor special interests within those groups. "Friction" of this kind may come in the form of pre-empting facilities, like storage sites for water, for use at levels below full productivity; maintenance of technically obsolete processes or procedures; needless "fashion" obsolescence of durable consumers' goods; depressing initiative toward efficient management (e.g., the tenant farmer problem); and in other ways.

In other words, there exists considerable "friction" in the process of matching people's needs against the resources upon which the world can draw. To the political inheritances should be added certain social inheritances which contribute to "friction"—like some customs following from religion or other social tradition. A good example is the Hindu attitude toward the existence of cattle, which in effect allows cattle to compete with human beings for the product of some land and water resources in India.

THE "FEEDBACK" ELEMENTS—EFFECTS OF DENSITY OF POPULATION UPON RESOURCES AND UPON CERTAIN RELATED CULTURAL ATTRIBUTES

Thus far we have considered a static correlation of resources and numbers of people. That is, density of settlement on the earth's surface varies according to observable attributes of the physical environment. Several facets of culture add different and larger dimensions to resources, but our interest still has centered on the numbers supportable at a specific standard of living by a given type and quantity of resource endowment. This is the effect of resources, in whatever dimensions several qualities of culture give them, upon numbers of people in specific geographical locations on the surface of the earth. At this point our "equation" is $PS = RT + E_s + T_r$, in which P equals number of people, S equals standard of living, R equals amount of resources, T equals physical technology factor, E_s equals scale economies element, and T_r equals resources added in trade.

The next step in understanding population-resource relations is the introduction of some dynamic elements or factors. Density of population in itself has some effect on resources and on some attributes of culture which in turn influence the productivity of resources. In other words, population density per se may alter both the physical resources and pertinent culture attributes in a manner which changes the resources' capacity to support people. While we have few statistical data to measure these features, historical information, methodical field observation, and cartographic analysis give us grounds for some qualitative comments.

The relation of density of settlement to resources may be examined in several particulars. The resource itself may be affected in its stability, productive life, and quality; the affected culture attributes are intensity or completeness of resource use (the wastage element) and administrative techniques, or the type of management. All of these appear to be correlatable with density or sparsity of settlement, and they all affect the "supply" side of the balance.

The density of settlement here considered is not that of numbers of people per unit of area. Instead, it is that of population as related to the *employed* resources upon which the social group depends. This relation may or may not coincide with geographical or areal density of settlement. A high population-resource ratio may be found in many regions with geographically sparse population, and employed and potential resources differ. (Potential resources are those natural resources which may be considered employable with the use of the most advanced, economically proven technology of the world, although not actually employed at the time in question.) China in the past has had a high ratio of population to employed resources. On the other hand, the ratio of population to potential resources was and presumably still is somewhat lower. Population-resource relations are here limited to those which concern resources employed under the culture existing in the area during the period treated.

Stability, Productive Life, and Quality of the Resource

Resource stability is a consideration particularly applicable to those resources which can endure near-permanent exploitation under proper management. Soil, water, forests, range lands, fisheries, and other animal life are the principal resources of this type, commonly referred to as the "renewable" resources. These also are the resources which have been used longest by men, and about which there is abundant historical evidence. The ideal management for these resources is "sustained-yield" production, whereby the resource is so maintained that it will continue in production at an optimum level indefinitely. Such management is particularly difficult for the renewable resources because their natural productivity varies, sometimes within a wide range. Most renewable resources respond to the vagaries of climate, particularly of precipitation, and to a certain degree also of temperature. At the same time, the human needs for production from the resources are at best a constant, and more likely an ascending, curve. Here we have the basis of one of the most frequently recurring resource-population problems: a capricious physical environment, but unchanging or increasing human needs. Most societies have attempted to meet the problem by coping with the environment rather than by adjusting human needs. In this process of adjustment, density of settlement has played an important role, although not always a consistent one.

Paradoxically, the most stable resources have been observed not under the conditions of dense or sparse settlement but where (and at times when) moderate to high densities prevail. The instability of the soil and forest resources of the United States during the last part of the nineteenth and the first part of the twentieth centuries exhibited the tendency of a social group with abundant resources to regard all of them as expendable. During this period the known abundance of unoccupied land containing a measure of naturally stored plant nutrients encouraged the "mining" of soils in many parts of the United States. While other factors certainly contributed, relatively sparse settlement made the development of new territory and farms on virgin land more tempting than the development of new management techniques for erosion-susceptible lands. The story of forest exploitation in the United States during the same period is even more striking. Because of the great abundance of forested land, the productivity of millions of acres was seriously impaired by poor cutting practices, burning, and other wasteful events. For a long period future needs seemed so distant to a relatively small population that sustained yield for the renewables had little attraction. In a land weighted with the problems of communication and transportation imposed by distance, the need for rapid development seemed much more important.

In different ways, parts of this story have been mirrored in Australia, Africa, South America, and the Soviet Union. Sparse settlement has been accompanied by exploitation which impaired the productivity of the renewable resources, in some cases making them locally barren.

We do not know at exactly what stage of settlement density resource management practices tend to favor the maintenance of more stable renewable resources. It is apparent that the United States entered into this stage in the 1930's and is still adjusting its management in the direction of more stable resources. Notable progress has been made since that time in both agriculture and forestry, although the transition is not yet complete, as shown in the unstable dry-farming of some semiarid lands.

This stage also is exhibited in western European countries and in Japan, where the adjustment toward stable renewable resources has become much more complete than in the United States. In this stage soil erosion is rare, dependence on fertilizers for agricultural production exceeds dependence on naturally provided plant nutrients, sustained yield is applied widely to biotic resources used in the economy, and waters are carefully controlled in settled areas. As long

as population density does not increase in relation to resources—because of migration, absence of natural increase, improved techniques of exploiting resources, extension of trading areas, or for other reasons—stable resources are the normal expectation for a social group having a moderately high density of population.[3] This appears to be illustrated in the histories of several western European countries, including Germany, France, the Netherlands, Belgium, the Scandinavian countries, Great Britain, and Switzerland. Japan also is a case in point.

However, if population densities move very high without the relief of demographic, technical, or trading outlets, the stability of renewable resources again appears to be affected adversely. Such undoubtedly was the case for mainland China for many decades. The same tendency has been shown in the past in India, Iran, Greece, Italy, and other Mediterranean lands. It is difficult to separate the effects of political instability upon the deterioration of resources from those of population pressure. An example may suggest the correlation between density and resource stability at this stage.

There can be little doubt that population pressure in China forced agriculture into topographic situations and climatic environments which were not suited to continued intensive cultivation. Eroding lands on a grand scale resulted during droughts. Population pressure also forced the collection of forest products in a manner which progressively shortened the wood-growing cycle, greatly reduced forest land productivity, and contributed further to erosion. These conditions contributed to the sediment loading of streams; in turn, aggrading lower channels increased the flood

[3] Statement of the numerical meaning of the generalized terms applied to population density here has been avoided because no satisfactory summary means exists to integrate varied resources into a total which can be compared with population numbers.

hazards and reduced the productivity of the normally stable alluvial lands of the lower valleys—the centuries-old heart of the Chinese economy. Permanent or lasting loss of productive sections of the renewable resources and sharply fluctuating production from the remaining resources characterized that very densely settled country. Excessively high population-resource ratios in this instance resulted in resource instability.

To a degree, productive life and quality of resources are implied in comment upon resource stability. However, a few additional comments are specifically appropriate to these characteristics of resource use.

For any "funded" resource (those not renewed by life or weathering processes), it is obvious that greater numbers of people decrease the life of an employed resource, other things being equal. It is also clear that as the intensity of use increases under population pressure, the actual service of the resource is greater, considering salvage, working of small mines or other small production units, etc. The conditions prevailing in Japanese coal mining are a good example. Thin, deep-lying, faulted, and otherwise broken seams, sometimes of low quality, are parts of working mines in Japan. Their counterparts in the United States are scarcely touched. Thus intensity of use does help to extend the useful life of the funded resources, but the employment of such marginal production is only a temporary alleviation to the accelerated use of a funded resource which accompanies increasing densities of population.

Water illustrates best the effect of numbers of people upon productive life and quality of a resource. Under given conditions of supply, the highest quality is generally that of the unused resource or the resource of the sparsely settled area. Because water is a convenient waste carrier, because micro-organisms survive and grow in it, and because it is a solvent for a number of minerals, water quality almost always has deteriorated as density of population increased in an area. While modern technology occasionally has effected a reversal of water conditions, the world as a whole shows a remarkably high positive correlation between density of settlement and decline of water quality, whether by bacterial pollution from residential waste, addition of organic or inorganic foreign materials by industry, mineralization through irrigation use, or sediment addition from eroding lands.

Under those conditions of population pressure (or sparsity) which have affected the stability of the land and biotic resources, the life of water resources at a given level of use has also been affected. This has been most commonly illustrated in the shortened life of storage sites where heavy sedimentation became part of the altered regimen of a stream. Conservation storage for consumptive use or energy production becomes ineffective as accumulated sediment leaves less space for water. While a certain amount of water continues to be available from runoff, the useful life of part of the water resource is shortened by population conditions which favor eroding land.

Intensity of Resource Use and Consumption Habits

Two attributes of culture which affect the capacity of resources show some correlation with density of population: the intensity of use and the type of administrative technique or management. Some statistical data (where they are available) give indications of the intensity of resource use. Per capita amounts of agricultural land, forest land, and data on unit area production in agriculture suggest the intensity of land use. The fact that Japan had about one-fifteenth as much cultivated land per capita as the United States in the 1950's (about 0.16 and 2.5 acres per capita) suggests that Japan uses its agricultural land more completely than the United States, which is the case. The same indication is given by data on the unit area productivity of Japanese farms (which hold world record yields for some crops, e.g., rice), by the ratio of irrigated area to total cultivated area, and by the percentage of multiple-cropped land. However, conclusions on the intensity of resource use may be safely derived only by supplementing the statistical data normally gathered with competent special field observation. The manner in which a social group uses the materials it has in everyday family life is a good indicator. Few statistics are to be found on such matters.

It is obvious that the denser the settlement, the more complete the use of resources, assuming a given stage of technology and a given standard of living. While the imprint of population will show on all resource use, the best illustrations come from the food-producing resources. These resources, and particularly the agricultural lands, have been significant in all societies of any size in nearly all ages. Differences in the use of cultivable lands which distinguish the lands of high-density settlement from the lands of lesser density are here used to illustrate the correlation between numbers of people and intensity of resource use.

The best illustrations occur in Japan and China, where aggressive and vital peoples have been faced with the problems of high population density for centuries. The cultivation of these lands, by comparison to that of the Western Hemisphere or even some European countries, has the following characteristics: (1) Wherever engineering knowledge has permitted and water supply was available, lands have been irrigated. Discovery of the vastly superior yields under irrigation, even in humid climates, was made long ago in the densely settled sections of the Far East. (2) Wherever

possible, cultivable land is multiple-cropped, making full use of the actual growing season. (3) To the full extent that materials are available, fertilizers are placed on the land. The Far Eastern habit of collecting night soil and applying it to crops is nothing more than a search for all the potential fertilizing materials. (4) Land is used sparingly for the support of livestock. Production of human food through livestock conversions (i.e., meat or dairy products) is avoided in favor of direct consumption of crops by human beings. (5) Crops with high calorie yields per unit area are favored. This is one reason for the popularity of rice in the Far East and for the production of maize, sweet potatoes, millets, and sorghums on sites not suited to rice. Production of sufficient calories is the usual problem of a people living close to the margin of its food resource productivity. The popularity of high-calorie crops therefore has been a natural evolution. (6) Cultivation generally extends onto lands considered poorly suited to agriculture under sparser settlement. Examples in Japan are the tilling of steep hillsides (usually through terrace preparation), planting of beach sands, and cropping of floodways. Few places naturally flat enough for cultivation (or suited to artificial leveling) are ignored. Land-use management is sparing in the use of cultivable lands for purposes other than agriculture. Roads and housing, wherever possible, are kept on the land of poorest agricultural quality in a locality, like the hill borders of a flood plain in Japan. Farm management also is efficient in use of the land. There are few idle field borders; even the dikes between irrigated fields customarily are planted during the growing season, and roadsides as well.

The impression given by these attributes of land use in the densely settled countries has been vividly summarized by Archibald MacLeish (1936):

In other countries a farm is meadows and a wood lot and a corner that the plow leaves: room to turn about and time to turn about in. In Japan a farm is as rigid and tight a thing as a city lot—a patch here and a triangle here and a square or so somewhere else; every road corner of land diked and leveled off even though the growing surface is less than a man's shirt; every field soaked with manure and worked and reworked as carefully and as continuously as a European farmer works a seedbed . . . nothing thrown away, nothing let go wild, nothing wasted.

All these characteristics of farming contrast with practices prevailing in lands of sparser population. For the United States in the past one might very well take the opposite of each of the land use attributes which were set down for Japan and China. There has been a tendency to depend on natural fertility of the soil; irrigation until recently was considered appropriate only to arid environments; animal conversion is favored by comparison to direct use of high-calorie crops; multiple-cropping generally is not economic; and so on. Parallels to United States practice could be found in Canada, Argentina, and Australia.

The description of how agricultural resources are used carries some implications about the characteristics of consumption under conditions of dense population. Minimal animal conversion of crops and concentration upon high-calorie crops could not be undertaken without corresponding adjustments, or willingness to adjust, by consumers. This is typical of the densely settled lands. Diets generally have been designed with a mineral protein, minimal animal protein, and low (but sometimes adequate) protective food content. The diets are relatively high in calorie-producing foods by comparison to the protein and protective food intake. At the same time, they are low-calorie diets by comparison to those of countries or societies with higher ratios of resources to people. The daily diets of the people of Japan, for

instance, have probably been within the 2,200–2,500-calorie range per person for many years. In the United States, on the other hand, a 3,300-calorie average prevails.[4]

Diet indicates one characteristic of consumption in the densely settled lands. Consumption of food and materials is adjusted (on the average) close to the minimal needs of the individual under the physical circumstances which prevail. For instance, both fuel consumption and housing space are low in the densely settled country. The average Japanese, for instance, has one-third the housing space of the average American.

There are other characteristics. Only low initial wastage is tolerated. When a tree is cut in a country like Japan, China, India, or Italy, the bark, limbs, and even the roots and needles are put to use as a matter of habit. Salvage is very carefully and consistently practiced by the people. Again Japan may serve as an example.

Most Japanese become conscious of conservation in their childhood. Even families in relatively comfortable circumstances teach their children at meals to clean every grain of rice from the bowls. No person with good manners would think of doing otherwise. Children from the more humble families, who constitute a large proportion of Japan's population are drilled in conservation even more unceasingly. It is they who are sent to glean animal dung from the streets for the home garden . . . to clean up the carpenter's shavings and sawdust, or to pick the unburned bits of coal out of the railroad or factory cinder piles. They gather the few papers and tins which may have been left at the roadside, and they are

[4] The 1951–52 daily average food supply per person entering the American home was estimated to be 3,225 calories, excepting alcoholic beverages. About 90 calories per person should be added from alcohol, making the total food available at the place of consumption 3,315 calories per day. Wastage is included in these totals and should be deducted if net actual consumption is sought (Dewhurst *et al.*, 1955, p. 156).

taught how carefully all inedible kitchen materials must be saved to be placed on the squash or eggplants of the back yard. Every child learns that nothing is wasted in a Japanese house or on the Japanese street (Ackerman, 1953, p. 490).

Population Density and Resource Management

Administrative techniques and concepts of management vary greatly with culture. Any attempt to suggest correlation between numbers of people and resource management therefore must isolate clearly the assumptions and specific situations under which it applies. Management in itself is a cultural reaction to the situation of the social group, since the group appraises the physical environment in which it lives and the technological assets at its command.

Management of resources may have a variety of objectives, including maximum short-term output, maximum long-term output, stablization of output, improvement of resource quality, territorial development, creation of employment opportunities, or still other objectives. Even from the point of view of groups, any one of these objectives may be present, or prevail.

The attributes of resource management which would seem to have some correlation with different densities of population are degree of public or private control over management, the application of planning or collective foresight, and the centralization or decentralization of administration over resource development and production.

Such correlations at present are imperfectly understood, but they obviously exist. Generally speaking, the land of sparse settlement has favored a high degree of control for private management and is apt to be concerned about short-term maximum output rather than long-term output; application of collective foresight has little stimulus, while territorial development and the creation of employment opportunities[5] are favored

objectives in resource management. Management in a situation of sparse settlement tends to be decentralized. This description certainly fitted the United States of almost the entire period from the time of first settlement to 1930. It fits Canada; it may be applied to Brazil and other South American countries, and to parts of Africa. The public-land policy of the United States and its prevailing forestry practices during the period mentioned were perfect illustrations of management within a society which had a high ratio of resources to population. The ideal was maximum short-term output and the most rapid possible territorial development with a minimum of public management responsibility.

On the other hand, dense settlement tends to be accompanied by the application of collective foresight, a higher degree of public (i.e., governmental) control over management, greater centralization of administration, and more concern for long-term maximum output. Almost every western European country illustrates this tendency, and the United States of the mid-twentieth century has been unable to escape it. Indeed, the United States of 1933–50 moved rapidly in the direction of this management pattern. Japan is an excellent example of the emergence of management characteristics of this kind.

An illustration of the meaning of these differences of management may be taken from forestry. Under the concepts of forest land use which prevailed in the United States for many decades, ownership of the forest land brought with it the right to use the land and trees in any way suited to the owner's taste or habit, including the destruction of the property if he so wished. In Japan, on the other hand, no forest landowner has had such control over his property, at least since 1907. Under national laws a Japanese

---

[5] Provision of land for farmers desiring property ownership is here considered one form of creating employment opportunities.

prefectural government administration may take over management of a private forest property considered to be managed poorly by the private owner.[6] While an owner does not lose title to net proceeds from his property, he does not have the choice of doing whatever he wishes with his land.

Correlations of population density and type of resource management must cover some apparent exceptions. China, for instance, has been a densely settled country for centuries. Yet within the twentieth century many of its resources were managed with little planning or foresight, and little public control over management appeared anywhere in the country. However, this could not be considered a contradiction of the tendencies here described, for China had few of the management characteristics of a sparsely settled land except the extreme decentralization of management. With a confused and somewhat anarchical governmental structure (in practice), the development of a strong public hand in resource management could hardly be expected nationally, even though the incentive for such action was very great. But there were within China some regional examples of careful public control, as on the famous Min River delta irrigation system in Szechwan. In a sense, these fitted the pattern of management for a densely settled country. Under a tightly organized national government, the national aspects of resource management are known to be changing already within China.

The case of the Soviet Union also may seem an exception, since it appears (at least popularly) to be a country with a relatively sparse settlement. Actually, the Soviet Union has had three lands, a densely settled west and sparsely settled Arctic and middle-latitude Asiatic sec-

[6] Forest Law No. 43 of Japan, amended in 1911, 1939, 1943, 1946, 1947, 1948, and 1950. Also the Afforestation Temporary Measures Law (No. 150), 1950.

tions. The resource-management pattern which has evolved for Soviet resources since 1918 is one which might be expected for the densely settled European and Caucasian parts of the Union in the presence of a well-organized national administration. The superposition of this type of management on relatively empty Soviet Asia is the same phenomenon as the reflection of United States resource-management trends in Alaska. Management, therefore, is not to be correlated with density of population within a given area but *with density of population within the dominant section of the political unit to which the area belongs.* With this in mind, the resource-management pattern of the Soviet Union does not appear to be an exception to the tendencies described above.

The management associated with population densities of the higher order generally tends to minimize or eliminate practices which tolerate wastage from a public point of view. This management tends also to institute the gains and economies which can be obtained from integrated planning and management of resources; it encourages long-term stability; and it tends to lengthen the productive life and long-term production. However, it may reduce the immediate, or short-term, productivity. Other things being equal, the dense settlement tends to introduce management directed toward a higher long-term productivity for the resources of a social group.

FURTHER DYNAMIC RELATIONS: CORRELATION OF RESOURCES AND PERTINENT CULTURE ATTRIBUTES WITH DEMOGRAPHIC ATTRIBUTES OTHER THAN NUMBER

In the foregoing discussion the only demographic attributes used in analyzing the relation among resources, culture, and population have been numbers of people and standard of living. As other demographic attributes are examined, further correlations may be observed. Where available resources and their productivity per capita differ, one may expect covariance to be shown between resources and health features, age classes, mortality and birth rates, rates of natural increase, migration, and employment, separately or severally.

Past analysis has not supported a direct correlation between employed resources and each of these demographic attributes, and it may be difficult and pointless at any time. There appears to be little doubt that per capita productivity of resources is a component in the variation of each of these attributes among different social groups in the world. However, covariance is most directly shown when the functioning economy of the group is examined as a whole, including the component of natural resource availability and productivity. In particular, the extension of the resource base through participation in the international trade community and the stage of technology characterizing a group must be considered in combination with resources for the supplement or multiplier which must be reckoned for the local resource base.

To illustrate such analysis and correlation, one may divide the major settled sections of the world into four types of area. The main distinctions are those of technology and population-resource ratios. Since the more important geographical expressions of culture correspond with political units rather than with features of the natural environment, the units of these four types are the countries of the world. On the one hand are the industrially organized technology-source areas, like western Europe and Anglo-America; on the other are the technology-deficient areas, like India, China, and most of Africa. (The technology-source areas are those where a general advance of technology is taking place under the stimulus of indigenous invention; the technology-deficient areas are those which are advancing—

if at all—by borrowing or adapting technology from the source areas.) Each of these may be divided into two subtypes, those having a low ratio of population to resources and those having a high ratio of population to resources. Thus there are technology-source areas with a relatively high ratio of population to employed and potential resources (western Europe, Japan), technology-source areas with a low ratio of population to resources (Canada, United States, Australia), technology-deficient areas with a high ratio of population to potential and employed resources (India, China, French North Africa), and technology-deficient areas with a low ratio of population to potential resources (central and east Africa, Latin-America, southeast Asia).

Where the employed-resource base is meager (and unrelieved by trade or technical advancement), the classical pattern in the past has been the one described for non-industrialized countries of dense population: high birth and mortality, low rates of natural increase, a predominance of the younger age classes, and lessened individual vigor because of the level of nutrition. There is strong incentive toward emigration, given an opportunity to emigrate, because underemployment is a chronic characteristic of the society. Actual mobility, considering the mass, however, is low. This is the pattern today for the technology-deficient areas having a high ratio of population to potential and employed resources.

The technology-deficient areas with a low ratio of population to potential local resources may exhibit some of the same characteristics as the dense population countries, reflecting their technical inability to make use of the resources which are at hand. This is well illustrated in Africa. On the other hand, the social groups within countries of this type would seem to have a somewhat different demographic pattern, considered over broad areas. They have shown high birth rates, moderate to high death rates, and moderate to high rates of natural increase. Health problems exist in major proportions, although health deficiences resulting from poor nutrition on the whole are less prominent than in the technology-deficient dense population areas. Incentives to migration still exist, in response to local conditions, and mobility on the whole would seem to be rather high. These areas have some attraction for emigrants from the dense population areas, but because of capital scarcity and technology deficiencies their capacity for absorbing numbers of immigrants is relatively low.

The more advanced industrial areas or countries, here labeled "technology-source areas," show a still different pattern of these demographic characteristics. Low death rates appear to be the outstanding characteristic of their demographic past, but they also exhibit low to middle-range birth rates, low to moderate rates of natural increase, high ratios of adults to children, and a relatively healthy population. The chief difference between the lands having abundant resources and those having a high ratio of population but advanced technology would appear to be in the recently higher birth rates of the former, with corresponding higher rates of natural increase. A difference in migration characteristics also appears. The resource-abundant areas have a high degree of internal mobility, while the high population areas (mainly western Europe and Japan) show more tendency to migration to other countries or continents. Even such general observations on the correlation of resources and natality, mortality, migration, natural increase, and health give some basis for later important conclusions. We are concerned here with the basic elements in the dynamics of population history. While the presentation of detailed statistical evidence is needed to give a full pattern, superficially it appears that the correlations between these demographic attributes and technology are closer than the correlation with resource conditions.

The ready correlation between population dynamics and technology, which obscures the correlation with resource conditions, may be more apparent than real. Technical advancement has given a social group not only the power to convert potential resources into employed resources but also the power to extend the group's reach to resources beyond the group's own immediate territory. Thus the technologically advanced but domestically resource-poor countries are not actually resource-poor when their ability to command food and materials in trade is considered. Technical proficiency has given a group the capacity to extend its resources both in depth within its own territory and extraterritorially, as previously observed. Considering the world trade community in peacetime operation, there has been no resource-poor but technically advanced country.

APPLICATION OF RESOURCE ANALYSIS TO POPULATION QUESTIONS

The attributes of resources and culture discussed above give at least a partial checklist for evaluating two important demographic questions: methods of making population projections and methods of estimating resource adequacy. The validity of Malthusianism or other deterministic concepts of resource-population relations is a specialized part of the latter question.

Resources, Culture, and Projections

Viewed both from a theoretical point of view and from the experience of history, the most direct response by numbers of people to resource conditions is under conditions of trade isolation, minimal standards of living (near the subsistence level), and little flexibility in technology. Under these conditions fluctuations in the natural productivity of resources have had immediate and sometimes violent effects on the numbers of people dependent on a given set of resources. These conditions and effects have been most pronounced among the agrarian societies of Asia (and Africa, to a lesser extent) as productivity of the land fluctuated from drought, flood, pests, permanent erosion or sedimentation injury, or other changes in the physical and biotic environment. In periods of low productivity the immediate effects on numbers of people come through starvation and migration, as classically illustrated in China and on the Indian peninsula many times.

The opposite situation is equally clear. As there are departures from these elemental conditions for social groups, there are intervening "cushions" which soften the impact of resource changes upon numbers of people dependent upon those resources. Where resources for a period have permitted high standards of consumption, where extensive trading connections have become normal, or where the society has an alert technical component, fluctuations in natural productivity have a lessened effect on numbers of people. Fluctuations (or a downward trend) in natural productivity of resources may be reflected in a lower standard of living; they may elicit technological efforts or increased efforts toward trade. Where one or all of these factors afford a cultural "cushion," resource changes may be reflected only in an upward trend of the population curve during productivity improvements. Declines in resource conditions tend to be absorbed by the cushions, with little visible effect on numbers.

A good illustration of the effect of a resource change under these conditions occurred in the 1933–38 "dust bowl" conditions on the Great Plains of the United States. Severe declines in the natural productivity of the cultivable and grazing lands of the plains were fol-

lowed by declines in standard of living for those most directly affected and by the application of technology to problems created by prevailing methods of occupancy. Severe as the dust bowl damages were physically, their net effect on numbers of people *in the United States* was probably very slight, both immediately and for the long term. Standard of living and technology effectively cushioned the impact of a natural event which would have had famine results in the China of the same day.

The meaning of these relations for population projections is easily outlined. As social and economic organization develops for any particular region or group of people, the isolation of resource-population ratios becomes increasingly difficult, and with it demographic projections which depend partly upon resource estimates. The uncertainty which attends estimates of resource effectiveness for modern nations is emphasized by (1) an imperfect understanding of the impact and even the direction of change which eventually will result from the overlap of many extraterritorial spheres of interest in resources; (2) our present inability to predict the exact temporal progress or the type of technical change in a society, even though we now can ascertain the direction of change and something of the general rate; and (3) our inability to appraise the meaning or limits of increasing appetites for material consumption on the part of social groups throughout the world. We can reasonably say that the culture variables at this time appear of dominant importance in the projection of relations between resources and numbers of people.

All three of the major culture attributes affecting resource supply show traits of rapid change. Trade relations may be subject to very rapid change, responding to intranational or international political events. Perhaps the most constant feature is the direction of change in technology, which during this century has been constantly in the direction of more efficient use of resources and materials. However, "breakthroughs" like those on nuclear fission and fusion may accelerate the rate of technical change unpredictably.

Standards of consumption also have a certain stability, considered on a group basis. While individual rates of consumption may vary considerably (as in wartime), the habits of group consumption, all products taken into account, generally have a consistent per capita trend in one direction or another. The sharpest fluctuations appear to be the temporary upward departures of wartime economies. Taken over a long period, the consumption rates for industrial nations in this century generally have had an upward trend. The non-industrial "Malthusian" populations have undoubtedly shown a downward tendency in per capita materials consumption.

In sum, resource data are of value in judging the accuracy of projections for non-industrialized societies; in them the relation of resources and numbers of people is at its simplest. For the more advanced cultures and social groups who participate in world trade, resource data are meaningful only in proportion to the accuracy of knowledge about the direction of change in technology, standards of living, trade relations, and other pertinent cultural features. Such knowledge is not accurate at the present time. For advanced cultures, therefore, the resource-adequacy check on population projections has very limited usefulness.

Analysis of World Resource Adequacy and Validity of Deterministic Theories

Consideration of resource-population relations inevitably ends in a summation of curves representing the dynamics of world population, the advance of technical skills, and the deteriorating earth. Since the days of Malthus the resultant of these curves has been interpreted in two principal ways: an open-ended view

of the future, which stresses the capacity of technical advance to overtake both population increase and deteriorating earth resources (Mather, 1944; Kellogg, 1949; Eldridge, 1952), and the Malthusian, or neo-Malthusian view (Osborn, 1948; Cook, 1951; Vogt, 1948; Huxley, 1956; Political and Economic Planning, 1955). These views necessarily become distilled into generally optimistic or pessimistic outlooks on the future of human society when they are translated into public consciousness.

Actually, the neo-Malthusian view or statements of the opposing position often are misleading in their simplification. It should be obvious from knowledge of biology that there are theoretical size limits to the total population which might be fed and settled on the face of the earth. (Deevey, 1956, offers an interesting fresh approach to the means of calculating the theoretical limits.) It should be equally obvious that the present-day population has not approached those theoretical limits, whatever they may be.[7]

On the other hand, there are very important existing regional population problems for which application of the neo-Malthusian view would appear to be fully justified. Examination of world data on diets (a good indicator of resource adequacy) gives convincing evidence of the influence which resource availability must have upon numbers of people and other demographic attributes in the technology-deficient areas with a high ratio of population to resources. All these areas have a diet close to the minimum needed for subsistence. (China, Korea, India, Egypt, Java, Pakistan, and a number of smaller countries all have a daily average per capita in-

[7] A number of estimates of the theoretical carrying capacity of the earth have been made in the past. They range from twice to about six times the earth's present population of 2.5 billion. See Boerman (1940), Penck (1941), Salter (1948), Mukerjee (1946).

take of less than 2,400 calories. See United Nations, Population Division, 1953, p. 402.) Where diets of 2,500 calories or less exist in technology-deficient countries with high population–potential resource ratios, it is probably safe to assume that some Malthusian "controls" exist or may become effective at any time. The most ominous thing about the world resource-population position is that about half the people of the world are to be found in countries which may be described in these terms. For them there is a present resource adequacy problem, and there is likely to be continued difficulty in matching resources to population.

Data on diets, furthermore, show that there is an additional large segment of the world's population which lives adjacent to potential resources of some size but which still exists close to the subsistence level of the technology-deficient densely settled lands. Most of the technology-deficient countries of low population–potential resource ratios fall into this group. They are exemplified by much of Africa and Latin-America. These people, who comprise about a sixth of the world's population, have a problem in the immediate adequacy of their employed resources, a position which they suffer because of technical deficiencies.

Third, an additional sixth of the world's people live in lands where industrial organization and technology have permitted them to extend their resource base through world trade, supplementing the low per capita productivity of their domestic resources. These are the western European countries and Japan. Their position is relatively secure, as far as resources are concerned, for the time being. Over the long run, however, these countries are vulnerable to competing demands from other lands for the resources which they now draw upon outside their own territory.

Finally, about a sixth of the world's

people live in technically advancing societies and possess territory affording relatively low ratios of population to potential resources. These are the people of the United States, the Soviet Union, Canada, Australia, and possibly Argentina and New Zealand. Presumably these peoples have room for future accommodation of increasing population.

In this general classification of the countries of the world there are the basic facts for considering the adequacy of world resources. Essentially, it is a question of the size of future population which the resources of the world can support. Considered ecologically, we know that the population of the world cannot go on increasing indefinitely, but is the day of final reckoning far off? How clear is our view of the limitations imposed by resources? How much can technical progress in the future inflate the present capacity of resources to support people?

Assuming a degree of international political stability and no catastrophic world conflicts, the emergence of a few changes in resource-population relations over the world appears likely within the next few decades.

a) Resource deterioration within the technology-deficient densely settled countries can be arrested and resources given substantial added carrying power by now feasible technical advances within their economies. Thus, either larger numbers of people in these countries at the present level of life or an improved standard of living for numbers equal to the present is possible. There is at least promise of some economic margin within which conditions may be more favorable to stabilization of population than at present.

b) Technical advances within the technology-deficient sparsely populated areas can add substantial carrying capacity to these lands. This capacity may be used for the support of a continuing natural increase within these countries, for the support of immigrants from densely settled lands, for an increased standard of living, or for all three. The economic margin for future population within lands like Brazil appears to be fairly large, although the practical obstacles to emigration may make it of relatively small importance to the densely settled lands. There must be reservations also about the *rate* of development because of serious biotic obstacles in the natural environment.

c) Nearly all the world's peoples have ambitions toward higher standards of living, to an extent never experienced before. Within at least some of the technology-source areas of low population-resource ratios like the United States and Canada, higher standards of living are being realized. Increased pressure for resource production is therefore generated even though the numbers of people remain the same. However, population is increasing in all these countries, thus hastening the time when the abundant potentials of these lands may be completely used by descendants of the present societies in them.

d) To a lesser but still significant extent, standards of living in other technology-source areas appear to have an upward tendency.

e) The dynamic technical centers of the world, like the United States, have recently had a rapidly increasing capacity to absorb materials and capital, not only from within their own boundaries, but from abroad as well. The development of Caribbean and Middle Eastern oil, South American copper and tin, African copper and uranium, and a variety of other minerals throughout the world illustrates the reach that even the nations with abundant resources can generate as technology moves ahead. The appetite of the technically advanced countries for the provision of materials from the world at large may very well increase.[8] This may be expected to continue at the same time that technically

retarded countries develop needs for foreign materials to support industrial economies.

f) Energy supplies are likely to be more mobile than at any time in previous world history. Energy is the key resource in technical advancement, not only in introducing industrial fabrication but also converting potential resources into employed ones. Furthermore, energy use enables the demand for materials to shift from scarce to abundant resources.[9] Many of the technology-deficient areas of the world have continued in that state because of the cost of obtaining adequate energy supplies within them. When the transportation of very small amounts of material can provide large supplies of energy, a distinctly new geographical relation of resources will prevail. (Moch, 1956, provides an interesting examination of this point.) This situation seems destined eventually to convert many of the now "potential" resources of the technology-deficient areas into employed resources.

g) International organization which gives new economies of scale in resource use will be experimented with and probably developed on a much more permanent basis than previously. The regional economic co-operation now being at-

[8] The appetite of the advanced industrial nations for raw materials from abroad may be illustrated by the minerals situation of the United States in recent years. It was almost wholly dependent on foreign countries for a supply of tin, nickel, asbestos, graphite, antimony, manganese, chromite, columbium, beryl, cobalt, diamonds, and quartz. More than half of the bauxite, lead, and mercury came from abroad, along with substantial quantities of tungsten, fluorspar, copper, zinc, iron ore, potash, and petroleum (Dewhurst *et al.*, 1955, p. 939).

[9] The manufacture of aluminum, which derives from an abundant natural resource, is a good example; aluminum has taken over many functions for which copper, a naturally more scarce material, formerly was essential. The substitution of plastics for many other metals also illustrates the place of energy in shifting economic demand away from scarce materials.

tempted in Europe may have other and later counterparts elsewhere in the world.[10]

h) Public health measures seem likely to influence death rates in an unprecedented manner in all the technology-deficient areas of the world. Assuming no corresponding immediate decrease in birth rates, demographic conditions in all the technology-deficient countries may present sharply increased demands for production within a relatively short period.

i) Taken the world over, there can be little doubt that substantial increases in food production are within technical reach. Furthermore, the capacity of applied biology to add still further to the potential food resources of the earth must be considered promising. Even if it is food at higher costs than those prevailing, it will be demographically significant food.

These new elements in judging the future balance of population and resources give both debits and credits. They all seem significant enough to warrant a summation of their meaning for the future capacity of resources to meet the needs of men. The practical objective of an analysis of resource adequacy is that of sensing the timing and location of social crisis before it occurs. What should be of interest is not the crude estimate of numbers of people possible on earth but the equilibrium between numbers of people as existing social groups and the resources they must draw upon for their life.[11]

Social crisis in this instance may be defined as deteriorating conditions of individual nutrition and material welfare, or the political crisis which arises in anticipation of such conditions. Crises of this kind have arisen countless times the world over during the period of recorded history. They have been met in four general ways: social disorder and reorganization, emigration (military conquest is one means of achieving emigration), technical advance, and the extension of resource base through trade.

The future of emigration, considering the friction of national boundaries, appears to be a very limited one, unlikely to make the world more of a unit in considering resource adequacy than it now is. Accordingly, world estimates of resource totals have only limited meaning in appraising this question. Total agricultural and food-production potentials certainly are far beyond the production of the present, and mineral exploration still has many opportunities facing it. However, these potentialities mean very different things to people of the four principal types of countries which have been described here.

The basic ingredients for judgment of impending population-resource crises for the type countries are the standard of living (or consumption) trend, the extent and condition of employed and potential resources, the technological advancement trend, trends in international economic organization, degree of group consciousness of impending crises, and the trend in numbers of people. Weighting one side of the balance at the present time are the general upward trend of both numbers and standard of living and the deteriorating productivity of employed resources. The three conspire to place increasing pressure upon resources. Other things remaining equal, the result would

[10] Generation and distribution of electric energy hitherto has been much cramped by national boundaries. This appears to be no longer necessary in western Europe (Bardon, Fleischer, and van Rhijn, 1956; Hoffman, 1956). Other experiments of importance to resource use include the European Coal and Steel Community and the Organization for European Economic Co-operation.

[11] This view is somewhat different from, although related to, a suggestion made by Sauvy (1949). He has maintained that the real population problem is not the earth's carrying capacity but how world and regional population trends may affect human welfare.

be certain and even sharp decline in per capita availability of resources, with eventual depressing effects first on standard of living and finally on numbers of people.

On the other side of the balance, tending to lift the level of resource availability or to lessen pressure upon resources, are technological advancement, group consciousness of crisis, and international economic organization. Technological advancement lifts the level of resource availability by exploring and discovering resources, by shifting demands from scarce to abundant resources, by adding production capacity to employed resources, and by converting potential to employed resources. Group consciousness of crisis can result in conscious stabilization of group numbers, as now appears to be the possibility in Japan. (This element is entering the national scene in India, in Indonesia, and possibly also in China. While its influence to date has been most profound in Japan, it would appear to be a factor which must be taken account of in the future of all the technology-deficient densely populated lands.) International economic organization, in turn, can raise the level of employed resource productivity through contributing scale economies, providing timely access to undeveloped resources, and removing artificial restrictions on production from employed resources.

A projected balance made up of these factors is not simply struck. In fact, it is doubtful that we have the data to arrive at an accurate understanding of the balance for any single social group, much less the balance for the world as a whole at any specific time in the future. To assess the effects of these forces, data on their present significance are needed. We also need the capacity to predict the rate and direction of the forces' change. We have little of such data or capacity at this time. Our view of technology especially may be thus characterized, and

that on international economic organization is similar, but to a lesser degree.

Recognizing the great need for additional data and the disturbing influence of technical "mutations" upon resource-use projections of any kind, identification of a few problem areas of future resource adequacy still seems possible. It seems reasonably clear that technical advance is likely to occur over almost the entire world. For all countries experiencing it, such advance certainly means a shift from land as a limiting resource in production to minerals as the limiting resources. Technological advances also generally have meant standard of living advances. Future population-resource crises therefore will be traceable as much to the standard-of-living pressure as to the number of people. In a sense, this means a double pressure on the limiting resources as compared to former times. Because the limiting resources for an industrial society are mainly mineral—and even the largest nation does not have mineral self-sufficiency—the resource pressures of the future are almost certain to be international as well as national. Until the present, limitations have been those of energy sources needed to commence industrial and technical advance. With the already forecast increased mobility and abundance of energy supplies, the pressure for production of metals and other industrial raw materials is likely to be increased greatly by the entry of new nations among the international buyers of industrial raw materials.

These likely events appear to have different meanings for five different types of country.[12] To the four types already described a fifth may be added to cover the sparsely populated lands of the world which have few potential land resources and probably little capacity to support a permanent population of

[12] Here used to mean a social group or groups and the territory recognized to be under the group's or groups' joint jurisdiction.

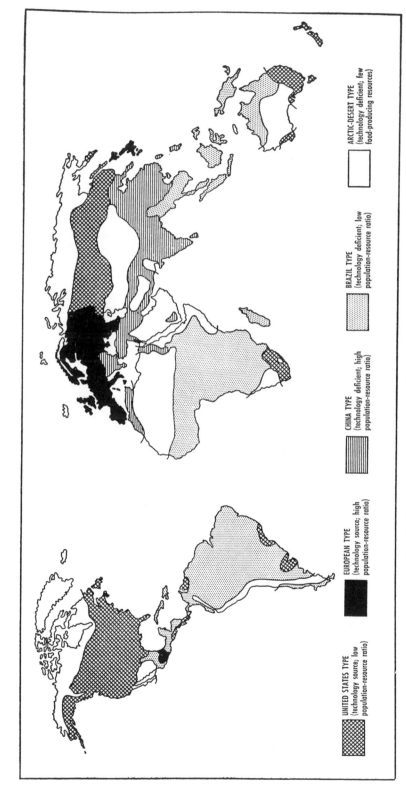

FIG. 5.—Type areas of resource-population correlation in the world

any large size. The five types of country then are: (1) the technology-source areas of low population–potential resource ratio, or the United States type; (2) the technology-source areas of high population-resource ratios, or the European type; (3) the technology-deficient areas of low population-resource ratio, or the Brazil type; (4) the technology-deficient areas of high population-resource ratio, or the China type; and (5) the arctic-desert type, technology-defi-

already revealed by these economies may continue to make them strong competitors for the product of some resources beyond their borders. Resource-population crises within these lands would seem unlikely for at least a century. These lands are likely to be disturbing in the world resource situation only as they draw minerals to support a high standard of living for their numbers, or the wartime equivalent, modern military machines.

TABLE 58

TRENDS AFFECTING RESOURCE ADEQUACY IN FIVE TYPE AREAS OF THE WORLD

Type	Application of Technology	Land Productivity	Mineral Productivity	Standard of Living	Numbers of People	Pressure for Use of Foreign Resources	Summary Characteristics
1. United States..	U+	U+	U	U+	U	U	Little resource limitation on numbers, some on standard of living; economically strong competition for product of foreign resources
2. European......	U+	U−	D	U−	U−	U+	Strong pressure for attachment to foreign resources; where frustrated, crisis possible
3. Brazil.........	U	U+	U+	U	U+	N	Little resource limitation on numbers; domestic orientation
4. China.........	U	U	U	U−	U	U	Continued consciousness of impending crisis; increasing pressure for attachment to foreign resources
5. Arctic-desert...	U	N	U+	U	N	N	Development by type 1, 2, 4 countries inevitable; strong competition for resources; however, few people

U+ strong upward trend
U ⎱
U− ⎰ upward trend

D downward trend
N very little or very few

cient and possessing few food-producing resources.

Considering substantial limitations of data, the forces which can affect the resource-population balance may be summarized for these five types of country about as follows (see also Table 58): The United States type has abundant resources and strong upward trends in the application of technology which are likely to encourage growth in numbers and rise in standard of living. The voracious capacity for mineral consumption

The European type, in spite of a certain strong technology, has limited domestic resources which place strong pressure for attachment of some sort to foreign resources. If their trade position does not permit them to continue and expand such attachments, crises are probable.

The China type, in spite of improving application of technology and the conversion of potential into employed resources, is likely to have continued consciousness of impending crisis; in this lies a principal hope for maintaining the population-resource balance in the face of ambitions for a rising standard of living. Increasing pressure for attachment to foreign mineral resources is certain as industrialization proceeds, a pressure likely to be felt internationally because of the great size of these social groups.

The Brazil type is characterized by limitations on numbers and standard of living likely to be in the rate of application of technology rather than potential resources. These countries are likely to have a domestic orientation and may continue to provide minerals for the three preceding types. They are more likely to contribute to an alleviation of crises elsewhere than to experience them. However, development is confronted with the unusual biotic obstacles of the tropical environments and may not be rapid for this reason.

The artic-desert type has water deficiencies, low energy receipt from the atmosphere, or other lacks which make these lands poor prospects for the support of many people. However, they are certain to provide mineral resources badly needed in other parts of the world. Countries of the United States, European, and China types are certain to support their development, as already has been the case with Middle Eastern petroleum. These lands, above all, are likely to contribute to the alleviation of crises elsewhere, while adding little to the world's total population. Should a technical "breakthrough" be reached in the economical conversion of salt water into fresh, the arid lands in this classification may be able to make substantial additions to the world's food-producing capacity, and they may be the site of some additional dense settlement.

Demographic Science and the Evaluation of Resource Adequacy

Considering these general observations and the paucity of firm data on forces which actually will determine resource adequacy in the several lands of the world, the immediate value of the neo-Malthusian and anti-Malthusian views must be qualified. A sense of impending *general* crisis is not factually supported; on the other hand, a sense of security in the future is no more firmly founded. Instead of analyzing the absolute supporting capacity of the entire earth, or parts of it, it may be most useful to identify conditions favoring crisis over a reasonably short future period. (A period on the order of fifty to seventy-five years is suggested.) This can be done if recognition of the diversity of the earth and its social groups is preserved. This approach will make the best use of the misty window from which we now view the forces in operation and will set up a framework within which a constant revision of view becomes essential. Because of the great uncertainty of the direction taken by social application of technical advances, this appears realistic.

Within these limitations, two important questions of resource adequacy appear for the next decades. The first concerns the countries of the China type. Will crisis in these countries be averted by the application of technology, by improved access to resources through trade, and by social action following consciousness of impending crisis? The second concerns countries of the European type. Will the continuing advance of technology and the needed further extension of trade for resources avert crisis in these countries? The certain increasing competition for the product of foreign mineral resources from almost all quarters of the earth makes the position of this type of country a particularly vulnerable one. It will be vulnerable until the time when technology has eliminated scarce mineral resources from the essential supplies of modern industrial plants. That is not yet in sight. A supplemental question changes the importance of these two questions only in degree. Will international economic organization be improved so as to lessen the risk of crisis arising in the above two areas, which contain two-thirds of the world's population?

Demography and the related sciences which treat resource adequacy have taken some important steps toward an understanding of these problems. Perfected systems for investigating and recording vital statistics are gradually being put into operation. Some knowledge of the feasibility of conscious population stabilization is being obtained. Better knowledge of the resource content of the earth's crust is being gained each year. It is now understood that the simple classification of the world's lands into industrialized and underdeveloped countries must give way to a more complex but also more meaningful classification when resource adequacy is analyzed.

The next steps will be the organization of more carefully co-ordinated population-resource-technology studies than have been possible in the past. Such studies might be applied to the problems of the two classes of countries within which the continuance of or first appearance of crises within the next few decades seems likely. Among other things, the studies might comprise (*a*) an appraisal of the limits of resource development in the problem lands, according to the existing technology available there or elsewhere in the world; (*b*) estimate of the demands of those populations for food and materials from other parts of the world community, assuming that adequate standards of consumption are to be established or preserved; (*c*) appraisal of the likelihood of competition for materials needed from the world community by these countries, and the intensity of that competition; (*d*) identification of fruitful subjects for the application of technical effort and social experiment; (*e*) identification of regional affinities among countries which have

resource deficiencies and potential complementary resource relations; (*f*) identification of the responsibility and capacity of international trade organization for reducing the risk of crisis within the problem classes of countries.

It is over this route that we are likely to arrive at some temporary understanding of what the limits of the earth amount to in the immediate future. It may be a long time before we understand the *permanent* limits of the earth—if, indeed, we ever discover them.

SELECTED BIBLIOGRAPHY

(Compiled with the assistance of Conrad Seipp, Resources for the Future, Inc., Washington, D.C.)

ACKERMAN, E. A. 1953. *Japan's Natural Resources and Their Relation to Japan's Economic Future.* Chicago: University of Chicago Press.

BARDON, FLEISCHER, and RHIJN, VAN. 1956. "La coordination de la production et du transport de l'électricité en Europe occidentale," *Proceedings, Fifth World Power Conference.* Section N.

BATES, M. 1955. *The Prevalence of People.* New York: Scribner.

BENNETT, M. K. 1954. *The World's Food: A Study of the Interrelations of World Populations, National Diets, and Food Potentials.* New York: Harper & Bros.

BLAKE, J., DAVIS, K., and STYCOS, J. M. "Economic Status and Fertility Control in Jamaica." Conservation Foundation.

BOERMAN, W. E. 1940. "De Voedelscapaciteit der Aarde en de toekomstige Wereldbevolking," *Tijdschrift voor economische Geographie,* XXXI, 121–32.

BONNÉ, A. 1953. "Land Resources and the Growth of World Population," in *Research Council of Israel, Special Publication No. 2,* pp. 464–77.

BROWN, H. 1954. *The Challenge of Man's Future.* New York: Viking.

———. 1956. "Raw Materials, Energy, Population, and the Spread of Industrialization," in *Resources of the World: A Speculative Projection.* California Institute of Technology.

CLARK, C. 1953. "Population Growth and

Living Standards," *International Labour Review*, LXVIII, 99–117.

COALE, A. J., and HOOVER, E. M. 1956. "Population Growth and Economic Development in India, 1956–1986." (Preliminary draft privately circulated for critical review.) Princeton: Office of Population Research, Princeton University.

COOK, R. C. 1951. *Human Fertility: The Modern Dilemma.* New York: William Sloane Associates.

DEEVEY, E. S., JR. 1956. "The Human Crop," *Scientific American*, CXCIV, 105–12.

DEWHURST, J. F., *et al.* 1955. *America's Needs and Resources: A New Survey.* New York: Twentieth Century Fund.

ELDRIDGE, H. T. 1952. "Population Growth and Economic Development," *Land Economics*, XXVIII, 1–9.

GREBENIK, E. 1955. "World Population and Resources," *Political Quarterly*, XXVI, 371–79.

HERTZLER, J. O. 1955. *The Crisis in World Population: A Sociological Examination, with Special Reference to the Underdeveloped Areas.* Lincoln: University of Nebraska Press.

HOFFMAN, G. W. 1956. "Toward Greater Integration in Europe: Transfer of Electric Power across International Boundaries," *Journal of Geography*, LV, 165–76.

HUXLEY, J. 1956. "World Population," *Scientific American*, CXCIV, 64–76.

KELLOGG, C. E. 1949. "The Earth Can Feed Her People," *Farm Policy Forum*, II, 1–5.

LEWIS, W. A. 1955. *The Theory of Economic Growth.* London: Allen & Unwin. (Esp. chap. vi, "Population and Resources," pp. 304–75.)

MacLEISH, A. 1936. "Of Many Men on Little Land," *Fortune.*

MATHER, K. F. 1944. *Enough and To Spare.* New York: Harper & Bros.

MASON, E. S. 1955. "Energy Requirements and Economic Growth." Washington, D.C.: National Planning Association.

MEIER, R. L. *Modern Society and the Human Fertility Problem* (in press).

MILBANK MEMORIAL FUND. 1954. *The In-terrelations of Demographic, Economic, and Social Problems in Selected Underdeveloped Areas.* New York.

MOCH, J. 1956. "Technology and the Future," *Bulletin of the Atomic Scientists*, XII, 112–18.

MUKERJEE, R. 1946. *Races, Lands, and Food.* New York.

OSBORN, F. 1948. *Our Plundered Planet.* Boston: Little, Brown & Co.

OSER, J. 1956. *Must Men Starve? The Malthusian Controversy.* New York: Abelard-Schuman.

PENCK, A. 1941. "Die Trägfahigkeit der Erde." in *Lebensraumfragen europäischer Völker*, ed. DIETZEL *et al.* Leipzig.

POLITICAL AND ECONOMIC PLANNING. 1955. *World Population and Resources.* London.

RUSSELL, SIR E. J. 1954. *World Population and World Food Supplies.* London: Allen & Unwin.

SALTER, R. M. 1948. "World Soil and Fertilizer Resources in Relation to Food Needs," in *Chronica Botanica*, XI (*Freedom from Want*), 226–35.

SAUVY, A. 1949. "Le 'faux problèm' de la population mondiale," *Population*, IV, 447–62.

SAX, K. 1955. *Standing Room Only: The Challenge of Overpopulation.* Boston: Beacon Press.

STAMP, L. D. 1955. *Natural Resources, Food, and Population in Intertropical Africa: A Report on a Geographical Symposium Held at Mekerere College.* Kampala, Uganda: University of East Africa.

ULLMAN, E. L. 1954. "A New Force in Regional Growth," in *Proceedings, Western Area Development Conference*, pp. 63–71.

UNITED NATIONS, POPULATION DIVISION. 1953. *Determinants and Consequences of Population Trends.* New York: United Nations.

UNITED NATIONS, STATISTICAL OFFICE. 1950. *National and Per Capita Income in 70 Countries, 1949.* New York: United Nations.

VOGT, W. 1948. *Road to Survival.* New York: William Sloane Associates.

Population Studies in Various Disciplines

Introduction to Part IV

This set of papers dealing with relationships of demography to other disciplines was placed last advisedly, for the authors of these chapters have assumed a reader well acquainted with the major problems of demography, its sources of data, and its techniques of analysis. In each case, the author's concern is to discuss these matters from the standpoint of the discipline which he represents. Collectively, the papers in Part IV suggest that while all population students share a more or less common body of data and the techniques of demographic analysis, the explanatory hypotheses they seek to test may stem from the theoretical concerns of one or another of the natural or social science disciplines. Indeed, the very manner in which they pose problems for investigation is to a large extent governed by the framework of the discipline whose concepts they employ.

The disciplines whose connections with demography are described include ecology, presented by Frank (chapter xxvii); human ecology, by Duncan (chapter xxviii); geography, by Ackerman (chapter xix); physical anthropology, by Spuhler (chapter xxx); genetics, by Kallmann and Rainer (chapter xxxi); economics, by Spengler (chapter xxxii); and sociology, by Moore (chapter xxxiii). These chapters are summarized individually, with certain editorial comments, in the last section of chapter ii.

27. Ecology and Demography

PETER W. FRANK

Several facets of ecology may be of interest to the demographer. Although man has to a great extent freed himself from the exigencies of his unmodified environment, he is, like other animals, bound by certain biological limitations. Such limits, defined by studies on human response and toleration physiology, may be significant demographic variables (for example, in an investigation of human populations at high altitudes). A second aspect that is of moment is the role of man in the community of other organisms with which he interacts and which he influences. It is perhaps a truism that the density of human populations has varied with man's cultural level. The latter, at the same time, may be considered in terms of his modification of the biota. It seems, however, that in the limited space allotted it will be profitable to neglect these phases and focus rather on a third, population ecology. In outlook as well as in methodology this rapidly developing field parallels demography rather closely—so closely that Hutchinson and Deevey (1949), in a review of the subject, coined for it the term "biodemography."

The premise that population ecology possesses attributes that make a closer rapport between demographers and ecologists desirable seemingly has found less than unanimous support. In large part this has resulted from premature and inaccurate broad generalizations to which biologists seem more prone than others. The consequent skepticism may have overcompensated. Although the specific mechanisms causing changes in human populations may and do differ from those found in other organisms, man is not basically different in any of the ultimate determinants of population change: reproduction, mortality, or movement.

Historically, population ecology as a distinct discipline is still in its infancy, going back perhaps to the second decade of this century. Properly, it has no history of its own. Early contributions were made almost exclusively by what might more properly be called demographers rather than biologists. In this connection, it is interesting to note that Graunt, in addition to his major work, published a short article on the multiplication of carp and the growth of salmon (Greenwood, 1942). Even though the essay of Malthus had wide influence in biology, ecology for some time was not prepared to follow a quantitative approach. This is clearly revealed by the almost complete neglect of the logistic curve, originally formulated by Verhulst (1838, 1844) but destined to have no influence until its rediscovery by Pearl and Reed (1920). Modern interests were foreshadowed by such events as the epidemiological studies of Brownlee (1906) and Ross (1916), but as late as 1930, of the three possibly most influential workers in the field of animal populations, neither Volterra nor Lotka but only Pearl was a biologist. Indirectly, it is apparent that the rapid development of statistics, in which biologists had recently been prominent, and the spectacular successes of quantitative methods in genetics now provided a favorable atmosphere not present heretofore. Pearl (1925) as well as others (Chapman, 1928; Gause, 1934) developed methods of investigating the behavior of animal populations in the laboratory and demonstrated the usefulness of this approach. Technical difficulties, however, largely prevented similar investigations on natural populations, and the complexities inherent in natural environments provide a sufficiently different set of circumstances from those of laboratory or mathematical models that a considerable gap arose within population ecology; it is only in recent years that this gap has begun to narrow.

Some insight into population ecology may be gained from the problems that have most engaged attention. In natural populations these have been primarily descriptive: attempts to describe changes in a population in time; or, singling out some pertinent part of population growth, such as natality or mortality, estimates of rates or changes in rates, sometimes both in time and space. Relatively little work has been done in measuring rates of migration or in attempting to refine gross birth and death rates. Often the objective of such descriptive studies is analytical, but specific rather than circumstantial evidence for analytical purposes is rare. In laboratory studies descriptive and analytical methods have often gone hand in hand, as in studies on population changes in a single species given a limited amount of requisites, usually replaced periodically. Such investigations usually attempt to describe the events occurring in a population in terms of numbers or volume of organisms and, more rarely, in terms of age structure, and to trace such changes to the proximate or ultimate factors responsible. In this analytical phase the role of density has been paramount and has led to a considerable literature on the physiological causes of effects accompanying changes in density. The

scope of inquiry has frequently been narrowed to an analysis of only mortality or fertility or broadened to include interactions between species. Predator-prey, host-parasite, and competitive relationships between two different organisms have been investigated, the last most thoroughly. Attempts to deal with a whole community of organisms, consisting of many species, along similar lines seem fruitless at present and have not been made. Instead, such studies have been concerned with the energy and material relations between the various species involved in a biological community, disregarding refined estimates within individual populations. Ultimately, in this area population and community ecology may meet.

When contrasted with demographic methods, those of the ecologist differ most markedly in the obtainable data. Furthermore, experimental and natural populations present a great contrast with each other. The regulation of conditions to which a population is exposed is, of course, the primary rationale underlying the experimental procedure. This means, ideally, that effects of single factors on a population may be assessed or may be combined with others in a systematic way. Populations with any arbitrary age structure may be assembled for analysis. This procedure becomes particularly useful, since experimental species are chosen with a sufficiently short life cycle to make the gathering of a cohort or generation life table, for example, reasonably simple. The experimental approach has arisen out of a need to systematize the often confusing multitude of effects impinging on natural populations and can effectively be defended on these grounds (Park, 1955). However it must be complemented both by theoretical and more immediately applicable attacks, by mathematical theory and field investigation.

At the outset it is essential to realize that natural populations of animals other than man present difficulties in methodology not experienced by the demographer. The problem of census, which, in principle at least, is not insurmountable in human populations, presents a major stumbling block to the student, say, of the mice in a corn field or the fish in a lake. Total census is rarely possible; when it is, it usually destroys the population. Some method of sampling is necessary. Such samplings often presuppose a knowledge of the way in which the organisms are distributed over the area under investigation, a problem which, in the case

TABLE 59

POPULATION ESTIMATES OF REDEAR
SUNFISH IN GORDY LAKE,
INDIANA, 1950*

SAMPLING METHOD	AGE GROUP		
	3	4	5
I.............	...	288	306
II..........	435	165	238
III.........	...	243	316
IV.........	566	288	263

* After Gerking (1952).

of animals at least, is subject to the same difficulty as that of census. The simplest assumption, that the animals are distributed at random, rarely holds. As a result, one often deals with an estimate of population whose variance cannot be ascertained with precision. Nevertheless, a number of sampling methods have been applied, with generally useful results. In recent years, the method of marking and recapture, which does not involve the assumption of random distribution, but only that marked animals distribute themselves like unmarked ones has become more and more popular and has undergone considerable theoretical refinement (Jackson, 1939; Chapman, D., 1951; Leslie, Chitty, and Chitty, 1953). In principle, the method consists of capturing and marking a group of animals that are then released. From their pro-

portion in a subsequent sampling, total population size may be estimated. If the procedure is repeated and if migration either is nonexistent or can be measured independently, it is possible to estimate birth and death rates and their variances, as well as population size. With further refinement, age-specific death rates may even be assessed. Some idea of the validity of sampling methods may be got from a fish population which was sampled by four independent methods (Gerking, 1952). Table 59 presents the pertinent estimates, which, considering the small size of the total population, are quite consistent.

A second difficulty that arises with natural populations as well as with those in the laboratory is that age often is impossible to determine. A number of organisms show discontinuous growth as individuals, which, as in tree rings, may be used to estimate age. Nevertheless, in nature, it may not be possible to establish the age distribution for a given species, since probability of capture may vary with age. To take an obvious example: fish populations are commonly sampled with some sort of net. Although the age of most fishes can be determined, nets of small mesh will not capture large fish, whereas those with large meshes allow the juveniles to escape. There is no simple way of using both methods and getting samples over a comparable area. Thus the limits of studies with field populations are set by limitations in techniques and methods to an extent that is difficult to appreciate. When one adds to this the complication arising from the tremendous environmental variation in space and time, the magnitude of the problem may be understood.

However, in some respects, particularly in application, the ecologist is not plagued with the same difficulties as the demographer. For instance, the problem of optimum population size for some population of an animal may be quite rigidly defined and has undergone considerable investigation. However, the reason this is possible is that what is desired is an estimate of population size and structure which will furnish the maximum continuous yield of certain age classes of that population without depleting the resources or the stock —clearly an entirely different problem from that faced by the student of human populations, unless he disregards

icance, the great majority of species in nature do not produce their young more or less continuously; they usually confine reproduction to a rather limited time span during the year. In the most extreme case, in semelparous species, this leads to completely discontinuous generations, a relative rarity; however, in the majority of instances, a combination of iteroparity and limited reproductive period produces discrete age classes. This may be contrasted to the situation in humans and

TABLE 60

RELATIVE DURATION OF ECOLOGICAL AGES IN SOME ANIMALS*

Animal	Development (Per Cent)	Reproduction (Per Cent)	Post-reproduction (Per Cent)	Average Longevity (in Days)
Homo sapiens (man), average	22.1	51.7	26.2	17,430
Homo sapiens (man), extreme	12.9	45.2	41.9	19,254
Rattus norvegicus (Norway rat), average	24.8	20.6	54.6	1,104
Rattus norvegicus (Norway rat), extreme	11.7	37.6	50.7	1,374
Drosophila melanogaster (fruit fly)	41.6	54.2	4.2	......
Pieris brassicae (cabbage butterfly)	95.9	4.1	....	......
Schistocerca gregaria (migratory locust)	50.5	17.5	32.0	......
Ephemeridae (May flies)	99.86	0.14	....	......
Panolis flammea (moth)	98.9	1.1	....	......
Periplaneta americana (cockroach)	69.9	27.2	2.8	......
Tenebrionides mauretanicus (beetle)	29.9	46.5	24.3	......
Trogoderma granarium (beetle)	83.0	11.9	5.1	......

* After Bodenheimer (1938).

with a cynicism not so far exhibited all aspects of individual welfare.

SURVEY OF TRENDS IN POPULATION ECOLOGY

Natality

Reproduction varies tremendously over the range of species. Cole (1954*a*) makes a useful distinction between iteroparous organisms (those which reproduce repeatedly) and semelparous species (in which reproduction is confined to a single effort). For a given individual, natality may vary anywhere from 2, in the case of organisms reproducing by binary fission, to 2×10^{13}, the figure given by Cole (1954*a*) for a giant puffball. In iteroparous species, moreover, the size of a clutch or litter may be either constant or variable with age. Of possibly even greater signif-

in the most commonly studied laboratory populations, where reproduction of the population is more or less constant in time, given a certain population composition. Finally, the actual as well as the relative age at first reproduction is extremely variable between species, as is the relative reproductive period in the organism's life span (Table 60). Certain effects of such differences have been investigated theoretically by Cole's study (1954*a*), which may serve as an excellent introduction to the use of mathematical models by biologists.

Precise measurements of age-specific fecundity (the maternity function m_x) have been made for relatively few populations, all of them under controlled laboratory conditions. While it is possible in some cases to form a crude estimate of this statistic from known life-history data, usually in natural populations it is not known what proportion of the organisms of breeding age are actually reproducing; such estimates must therefore be tentative and can give only the order of magnitude rather than any figure that can be trusted.

In many animals fecundity of individual females averages considerably below the physiological maximum. This phenomenon has been studied particularly in birds, notably by Lack (1947, 1948, 1954), and is strikingly illustrated by planktonic crustaceans

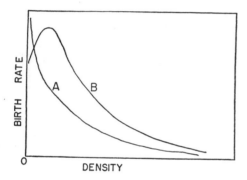

Fig. 6.—Relation between fertility and density (after Allee, 1951); explanation in text.

(Hutchinson, 1951). In many birds mean clutch size has been correlated with the maximum number in the clutch reaching reproductive age. Thus Lack interprets the basic phenomenon as the outcome of natural selection, the birds with the proper clutch size producing relatively the largest number of offspring. The problem has some interesting ramifications: clutch size in a number of bird species shows systematic increase from the equator poleward and, on the continent of Eurasia, in an east to west direction. The hypotheses that have been adduced to account for these facts are not entirely satisfactory; Lack believes the problem to be basically one of food supply, which may be correlated with time

available for feeding (day length) and perhaps with rainfall.

Density has a marked effect on reproduction in all species that have been studied in the laboratory. The general subject is reviewed in some detail by Allee *et al.* (1949, pp. 348–63, 399–408). Most animals may perhaps be expected to show characteristics within the range between the curves A and B of Figure 6 (Fujita, 1954). At increased density, in general, natality declines, perhaps exponentially. However, in a number of species studied—the flour beetle *Tribolium,* for example (MacLagen, 1932; Park, 1934, 1936) —the minimum density is not optimal, and the relation between density and fertility may be diagrammed as in curve B (Fig. 6). *Tribolium* has been chosen as an example, since here there has been considerable analytical work. In this species, copulation rate is directly correlated with fecundity, and chemical changes produced by the adults in the medium (conditioning) cause a decline in reproduction. The combined operation of these factors causes maximum fecundity to be achieved at a low, but not minimal, density. One other aspect may be of interest, since it points out the difficulties in measurement. The observed fecundity differs to some extent from the actual number of eggs produced, since some time elapses between the time an egg is laid and the time it is counted. A mortality factor—egg cannibalism, which is rather specific to *Tribolium*—thus enters into the observed fecundity. This aspect has been intensively studied by Rich (1956), who finds that cannibalism per animal decreases with density, although total cannibalism increases with increase in population. What the experimenter therefore observes when he notes that *Tribolium* shows an optimum density for natality is the interaction of these three factors, and probably of other lesser effects. Density here, as well as in other investigations, implies the collective measurement of specific ecologic factors, which may differ qualitatively as well as quantitatively from one case to the next.

Strangely, relatively little critical analysis of the enormous variation in fertility between different organisms has been undertaken. Cole has pointed out (1954a) that species such as parasites with complicated life histories, whose offspring have a low probability of survival, have high reproductive rates. Reasons for differences between similar species (Park and Frank, 1948) as well as for the low natality characterizing many organisms are much less readily understood. (It does not seem likely that the hypothesis advanced by Lack for birds can be generalized for all other organisms.) Perhaps the advantages involved may be reflected in increased stability of population growth form, but, lacking evidence, this is pure speculation.

Mortality

The ecological literature teems with statements on mortality rates; yet review reveals that many of these rates are such crude measures as to be valueless for our present purposes. However, in a number of instances life tables have been constructed, from natural as well as experimental populations. Such life tables are never so refined and precise as those obtainable for human populations for the simple reason that census of the magnitude undertaken for man is not feasible. Man provides the best data on survivorship even for the ecologist. In all other species for which data exist at all, these come from rather small numbers, usually less than a thousand, and do not merit the complex smoothing functions employed by the actuary.

Age-specific mortality has been estimated for a number of laboratory populations, including such diverse forms

as the rat (Wiesner and Sheard, 1935), the flour beetle *Tribolium* (Pearl, Park, and Miner, 1941), the water flea *Daphnia* (Pratt, 1943), the body louse (Evans and Smith, 1952), and a number of others (Pearl, 1922). The estimated life tables are of the fluent or generation type and are readily obtained by observing a cohort of newborn or newly emerged individuals. (For an analysis of the difference between fluent and static life tables, see Merrell, 1947.) Although the animals that have been investigated are quite different in a taxonomic sense, all these life tables exhibit a fundamental similarity: they are of a type in which the death rate increases more or less continuously with age. Perhaps the only conclusion that may be drawn is that experimenters find it too difficult to study animals with the extremely high early mortality that must obtain in some cases. Besides coming from a selected group of organisms, such life tables suffer from other defects. It is assumed that constant conditions exist throughout the course of observation of a cohort. In the laboratory it might seem that this would be readily achieved. However, as the cohort gradually dies off, the change in the density of animals may itself change the conditions of survivorship. Correction for this factor is technically difficult (Frank, 1952). Deevey (1947) emphasizes another difficulty: life tables of different species often do not start at equivalent biological ages and are therefore not comparable with each other.

In comparison with experimental data, similar information for natural populations is sparse. What statistics do exist have been recently reviewed (Deevey, 1947), and a number of life tables have been constructed. The essential data have been gathered by various methods: (1) marked animals of known age may be partly recovered at time of death, a procedure that has been much used by ornithologists; (2) a presumably random sample of a population may be collected, and, from the ages of these animals, a life table may be constructed—in a modified sense, this method is extensively used for gathering vital statistics in fisheries (Ricker, 1948); or (3) a cohort of animals, appropriately marked, may be observed repeatedly during its life span. The first two methods, although not as satisfactory as the third, provide most of the information that exists. Both assume a stationary population, a premise perhaps rarely satisfied

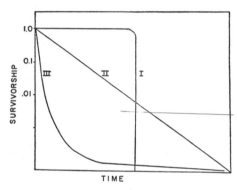

Fig. 7.—Types of survivorship curves (after Deevey, 1947); explanation in text.

even approximately. Recently, a number of attempts have been made to combine the last two methods, thus enabling the simultaneous estimation of a fluent and static life table (Jackson, 1948; Leslie and Chitty, 1951). As yet the method has not been sufficiently applied to assess its usefulness, although it seems to offer the best hope for relatively reliable vital statistics in natural populations.

Comparisons among different species as to the shape of the survivorship (l_x) function are dangerous, since different life tables start at varying biological ages. As Deevey (1947) has stated the problem: "Is it fair to com-

pare a bird life table, begining at early adult life with the Dall sheep life table, which begins at birth, or with the life table of a sessile invertebrate, beginning at attachment or metamorphosis? Evidently not; birth itself is not an age of universal biological equivalence outside the mammals, and for a broader view of comparative mortality the only safe point of reference would be the fertilized ovum." Unfortunately, such data are not available and, except in experimental populations, may be virtually impossible to gather. In most organisms, the young either are relatively inaccessible or, as in numerous insects, are exposed to an almost completely different set of ecological conditions from the adults. General theories of mortality that have been advanced must be viewed with this reservation in mind.

Pearl and Miner (1935) originally suggested that survivorship curves could be classified into three broad categories: (1) those which approached the negatively skew rectangular (Fig. 7, curve I) termed by Deevey (1947) conservative; (2) those in which mortality was essentially independent of age (curve II), the "indifferent" type of Deevey; and (3) (curve III) the positively skew rectangular or prodigal type, in which few animals attain the mean age. Bodenheimer (1938), in trying to make comparisons between different life tables of a single species under a variety of conditions, distinguished between two types of curves, an ideal physiological mortality function applying to animals under optimal conditions, and perhaps similar in form to the conservative type, and ecological mortality, the actual survival of the organisms under any set of conditions, presumably more similar to the indifferent or prodigal types. Ecologists seem to have formulated no mathematical functions applicable to the survivorship function, although such attempts have repeatedly been made for human populations (Elston, 1923). Behind this may lie the realization that, with the dearth of comparable data, discretion is the better part of valor. It does not seem unreasonable to suppose that many survivorship curves, particularly those of the higher insects, have a number of points of inflection when one considers the several shifts in ecological requisites that these organisms undergo. This is true in the spruce budworm, for example, for which Morris and Miller (1954) have prepared life tables from natural populations. It seems unlikely that such formulations could be simple and general at the same time; at best they would be descriptive without revealing underlying causes. Deevey concluded that it is premature to formulate a theory of mortality, a conclusion with which there must be almost universal agreement.

From the information available, it seems remarkable that very few organisms seem to possess survivorship curves of the prodigal type. This, as mentioned previously, is true for experimental populations and holds for the cases described by Deevey (1947) also. Many species, particularly birds and exploited fish populations, seem to be of the "indifferent" type. Again, this is more likely a matter of selection of species than a true view of the general picture. Sette (1943) estimates, for example, that larval mortality in the Atlantic mackerel varies at different ages between 10 and 45 per cent per day, so that in less than three months the original population of fertilized eggs is decimated to the extent of 99.9996 per cent. Similar relations must necessarily hold for those species in which reproductive rate is high.

Dissection of mortality by cause rather than by age suffers from even greater technical handicaps. More emphasis has probably been placed on study of the role of predation than on any other single factor, particularly from the point of view of the effect of various types of predation on population density, growth, and structure. The subject has been highly controversial, and most of it is not pertinent in the present context. It is clear, however, that in intensively managed fisheries human exploitation is a sufficient part of the total mortality above a certain age that other sources of mortality become negligible. Since after fish reach a certain size there may be little selection by the common fishing methods, from this size on a survivorship curve of the indifferent type must be expected. On the other hand, natural predation may have different effects. Errington (1946) particularly has asserted that predation in most vertebrates has no significant populational effect on mortality; the individuals falling victim to the predator are those that would otherwise have died in short order from other causes.

Paralleling those on natality have been efforts to determine relations between mortality and density. The ordinate of Fig. 6 may well represent survival rate rather than birth rate. Maximum survival at intermediate densities may have a number of interpretations. The phenomenon, which has been extensively reviewed by Allee (1931, 1951), may result from detoxification of some element of the surroundings or from some positive influence of sociality. This phenomenon is common though not universal in experimental populations and exists under uncontrolled conditions also, as in the barnacles studied by Hatton and analyzed by Deevey (1947). A remarkable case in a natural population of rotifers has been discovered by Edmondson (1945); *Floscularia,* a case-building rotifer, lives markedly longer if it settles on the case of another individual than if it is solitary. The populational significance of such optimum density effects is relatively obscure, although Odum and Allee (1954) have made an attempt to explain them as making possible population stability at higher density. It is easy to overemphasize the importance of these optima. Their absolute magnitude is commonly small; whether they occur or not, large-scale increase in density brings about increased mortality. The optimum density effects are little more than a ripple modifying this general relation. As might be expected, density may affect the shape of the survivorship curve as well as total mortality (Frank, 1952). In experimental populations of water fleas, increased density causes a gradual shift from a curve approaching the conservative to an indifferent type; this change seems to be largely independent of the total mortality, which initially declines with a moderate increase in density but later increases greatly.

Age Distribution and Growth Form

The combination of survivorship (l_x) and maternity-frequency (m_x) data supplies information that has recently received attention from population ecologists (Andrewartha and Birch, 1954, pp. 33 ff.). From these, the following relationships, called to the attention of biologists by Lotka (1925), may be established:

$$\int_0^\infty e^{-rx} l_x m_x\, dx = 1 , \qquad (1)$$

$$\int_0^\infty e^{-rx} l_x\, dx = \frac{1}{\beta} , \qquad (2)$$

$$\int_0^\infty \beta\, e^{-rx} l_x = c_x , \qquad (3)$$

where r is the true or intrinsic rate of natural increase, the rate at which a population with given survivorship and maternity frequency would grow were it to attain the stable age distribution; β is the instantaneous birth rate per head; and c_x is that fraction of the population with the stable age distribution with age between x and $x + dx$. Recent concern with these relations has been particularly with the intrinsic rate of natural increase. The history of this statistic in biology is revealing. Although ecologists must have been familiar with it, at least after publication of *The Elements of Physical Biology* (Lotka, 1925), fifteen years elapsed before this statistic was calculated for an animal population (Leslie and Ranson, 1940). Another eight years passed before r was calculated from empirical data for another species (Birch, 1948). Since that time, a number of other calculations for various groups of animals have appeared (Leslie and Park, 1949; Evans and Smith, 1952; Leslie, Venables, and Venables, 1952; Howe, 1953; Leslie et al., 1955), and more may be expected. One of the reasons for this interest is the realization that this statistic is a concise and unequivocal index of the ability of a population to increase at a given time. Simplification of calculation of the constant r (Birch, 1948) has undoubtedly also contributed to its use. Recently Leslie (1945, 1948) and Cole (1954a) have developed distinct derivations of the constant, both dealing with the discontinuous case rather than the continuous functions employed by Lotka.

Leslie (1945, 1948) has developed the analysis considerably by the use of matrix notation. The basic system he applies is as follows: an arbitrary age distribution may be operated on by a square matrix M, of which the first row represents essentially age-specific fertility, while the principal subdiagonal is a measure of survivorship. All other elements of the basic matrix are 0:

$$M = \begin{pmatrix} F_0 & F_1 & F_2 & F_3 & \cdots & & F_{m-1} & F_m \\ P_0 & 0 & 0 & 0 & \cdots & & \cdot & \cdot \\ 0 & P_1 & 0 & 0 & \cdots & & \cdot & \cdot \\ 0 & 0 & P_2 & 0 & \cdots & & \cdot & \cdot \\ 0 & 0 & 0 & P_3 & \cdots & & \cdot & \cdot \\ 0 & \cdot & & & & & & \cdot \\ \cdot & \cdot & & & & & & \cdot \\ \cdot & \cdot & & & & & & \cdot \\ \cdot & \cdot & & & & & & \cdot \\ \cdot & \cdot & & & & & & \cdot \\ \cdot & \cdot & \cdot & \cdot & \cdots & P_{m-2} & \cdot & \cdot \\ \cdot & \cdot & \cdot & \cdot & \cdots & & P_{m-1} & \cdot \end{pmatrix}$$

F_x may be defined as the number of daughters born in the interval t to $t+1$ who will be alive in the age group 0–1 at time $t+1$, per female aged x to $x+1$. P_x is the probability that a female aged x to $x+1$ at time t will be alive at time $t+1$.

The values for F_x and P_x may be calculated from maternity frequency and survivorship data by suitable interpolation, although there is no reason why they could not be empirically determined for experimental populations. (They are not, however, synonymous with m_x and l_x values.) By repeated pre- or post-multiplication by this matrix, one can, of course, calculate any population size and age distribution in the future or past from an existing one by a process that may be simplified by transformation; for the simplified matrix the characteristic roots can be more readily obtained, although the process, except for very small matrixes, is laborious. Leslie points out that the only real and positive root λ_1 corresponds to the finite rate of increase so that

$$r = ln\lambda_1;$$

the column vector representing the stable age distribution may also be calculated. In the later paper (Leslie, 1948), he applies this method to sev-

eral single and mixed species growth problems.

Another reason for the interest in the intrinsic rate of natural increase is its relation to some of the simple population growth equations that have been developed, in particular the logistic. Such curves usually consider population growth as a function of density alone:

$$dN/dt = f(N)$$

where t is time, and N a suitable measure of density. The logistic equation has had a controversial history among biologists as well as demographers. Its influence has been sufficiently great that it has been included in elementary college texts in biology (for example, in Hardin, 1949, p. 607, the legend to the proper graph is entitled "The curve of population increase for *any* population in a constant and finite environment"). The experiments of Gause (1934), in particular, seem to have fired the imagination of biologists. A reaction to the considerable confusion with which the curve has been made to serve as an inductive as well as a descriptive model has set in, and a number of recent critiques exist (Allee *et al.*, 1949, pp. 301–15; Smith, 1952).

In its differential form, the logistic may be derived as the simplest power series satisfying the following requirements:

when $N = 0$, $\qquad \dfrac{dN}{dt} = 0$;

when $N = K$, $\qquad \dfrac{dN}{dt} = 0$,

where K is a positive arbitrary constant. The resulting equation is

$$\frac{dN}{dt} = r_m N - \frac{r_m N^2}{K},$$

where r_m is a constant determining rate of increase. The formula can be interpreted as an arbitrary function describing population growth where some upper limit exists. This seems to be the sense in which Pearl originally employed the curve. Since, with a number of examples, he obtained a good fit, he was able to state (1924, p. 637): "We think that this evidence makes it probable that the curve is at least a first approximation to a descriptive law of population growth." Other workers, intrigued by the biological meaning that seemed to apply to the constants r_m and K, considered the curve in another sense, as an inductive model. Here r_m represents the intrinsic rate of natural increase in the absence of density effects, and K the population numbers when density has a sufficient influence just to cause the intrinsic rate of natural increase to become 0. The curve further implies that the intrinsic rate of natural increase decreases linearly with density. This meaning of the logistic seems clearly implied, for example, by the statement of Hardin cited above and seems the more common interpretation of the curve, despite the fact that it has never undergone critical tests to determine whether, in this sense, the curve provides even a first approximation. Besides these deterministic theories, there has been an increasing tendency to analyze biological populations by the probably more reasonable approach of stochastic processes (Feller, 1939; Reid, 1953).

Examination of numerous growth curves for a variety of populations (Allee *et al.*, 1949, p. 301–26) reveals that during the active growth phase the logistic provides, in nearly all cases, a fit that may be considered satisfactory. Growth form at this stage is usually sigmoid in character, and the logistic is sufficiently flexible that it can fit relatively well data which show a strong inflection as well as those in which even a straight line might provide a satisfactory approximation. Since human populations, from the

time that census has been practiced, fall into the steadily increasing category, it may not be surprising that they are, in general, so well fitted by the logistic. Moreover, Pearl's forecasts for human populations have on the whole proved surprisingly good, at least from the point of view of the biologist.

Lotka (1931, 1939) and Leslie (1948) have examined the relationship between logistic growth and age distribution. Both use the logistic not in the purely descriptive sense but as an inductive model. Lotka assumes that the population is growing logistically and investigates how the age distribution would change (1) with a constant life table, and (2) with a gradually improving one such as the fluent life table for man in the United States in the nineteenth and early twentieth centuries. The primary points with which we are concerned are that under either of these conditions, at any given stage in logistic growth, age distribution must be confined within rather narrow limits, and that the age structure shifts gradually from the stable to the stationary form. Leslie takes a somewhat different approach, asking how a population would, in theory, grow, given certain secular changes in fertility or mortality rates and some initial age distribution, but making no assumptions about the type of growth to be exhibited by the population. If mortality increases linearly with density regardless of age, logistic growth results, provided the initial age distribution is stable or Malthusian. If there are large-scale initial departures in age distribution, growth may be quite different from that specified by the corresponding logistic equation.

That age distribution has been a much neglected subject, particularly in the experimental study of populations, was pointed out by Bodenheimer (1938). His data for the bee and fruit fly *Drosophila* are in qualitative agreement, at least, with Lotka's theoretical development. Lotka (1931) similarly demonstrated that the actual human age distribution in the United States in 1920 corresponded well with what would be expected on the basis of logistic growth. Reasons for the lack of more extensive study of age structure are probably twofold: the technical difficulty of determining age and the lack of immediate applicability to the types of populations the ecologist commonly encounters in the field (see below).

For that portion of the logistic where the curve approaches the asymptote closely and where change in numbers is small, examples of populations that fit reasonably well are rare. Instead, highly irregular fluctuations are the rule. The amplitude and frequency of the fluctuations apparently depend both on the species and on the environment in which it lives (Park, 1948; Park and Frank, 1950) but are not contingent on environmental fluctuations. The usual explanation for such apparently intrinsic fluctuations is that there is a lag between the achievement of a certain density and its full physiological effect on birth and death rates. Wherever such a lag occurs, and biologically it would seem to be possibly universal, one may expect such fluctuations in population numbers as well as in age structure. The extent of the fluctuations must be related to the relation between the period occupied by the lag, its magnitude, the length of a generation, and the size of the system. During the growth phase of the logistic, although the lag effect presumably exists, it is not easily demonstrated, since it will merely alter the rate of increase somewhat, without thereby detracting much from the goodness of fit. An extreme though relatively well-analyzed example is provided by Pratt's laboratory study of the water flea *Daphnia magna* (1943).

Pratt determined birth rate and death rate as well as total numbers (Fig. 8). From Day 0 to Day 20, a logistic might, even here, provide a fair fit. During this period the death rate rises and then falls, the result of death of the original members of the population. The birth rate declines as a result of the increased numbers at a time when the death rate is low. It is only after Day 20 that the death rate is affected. During the period of high mortality, natality is almost nil. Not until the population has been at a low density for ten days or more does reproduction resume, causing another peak followed

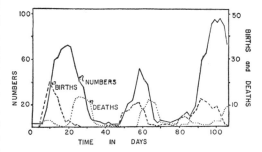

FIG. 8.—Population development in *Daphnia magna* at 25° C. (Redrawn from Pratt, 1943.)

by decline. Fluctuations may also arise as the result of discontinuous or partly discontinuous generations. As previously indicated, species which reproduce continuously or essentially so are a rarity, although experimental populations have been largely of this type. In natural populations, aside from such intrinsic fluctuations, the picture is further complicated by seasonal and other extrinsic ones. In many fishes, for instance, breeding success may show extreme variations from one year to the next. Figure 9, from a relatively lengthy study of the Pacific mackerel (Fitch, 1951), illustrates this point. The data have great imperfections. The first age class (0, representing fish in their first year of life) is not well represented in the catch, and it is doubtful that the next age class is. After this, however, the assumption that the percentage of fish of a given age in the catch is the same as that in the population is probably not far from the truth. It is clear, however, from the data on larval mortality cited earlier for the closely related Atlantic mackerel (Sette, 1943) that the 0 age class must encompass the great majority of the population. The Pacific mackerel is a good example of a heavily exploited population, and

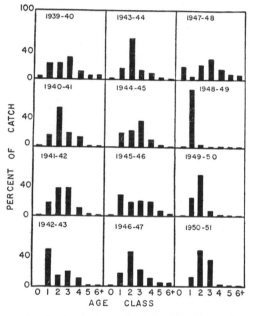

FIG. 9.—Percentage of catch of Pacific mackerel by season, in numbers of fish at each age. (Redrawn from Fitch, 1951.)

one should therefore expect an age distribution corresponding to the indifferent survivorship curve: succeeding age classes should be in a constant proportion to each other. This is far from the case, since recruitment into the population susceptible to catch is so highly variable. The years 1941–42 and 1947–48 were exceptionally good for the mackerel. The 1941–42 year class, although not captured to any great extent that year, makes up a higher than expected portion of the catch in 1942, 1943, 1944, and 1945, in age classes 1,

2, 3, and 4, respectively. The 1947–48 year class is even more spectacular, and was extensively caught even during its first year. Such phenomena are so common and so pronounced in many organisms that they may partially explain the dearth of analytical investigations of age distribution by biologists.

Any discussion of growth form would be incomplete without inclusion of the subject of cyclical fluctuations. Seemingly relatively regular periods of abundance followed by periods of scarcity characterize certain vertebrate populations, particularly in the arctic and subarctic. Similar fluctuations may occur in some insects. Many of the data are presented in a review by Elton (1942). Various intrinsic as well as extrinsic mechanisms have been suggested at one time or another to account for the apparent regularity, and active investigation of the problem continues. Despite this, not only is there no agreement on what mechanisms cause such fluctuations, but the regularity itself has recently been questioned (Cole, 1951, 1954b). Many of the data available can be interpreted as random series. Possibly the most prevalent interpretation of cycles involves interactions between several species and will be discussed in connection with interspecific relationships.

Not only does the logistic fail to describe fluctuations, but it is likely that any system based on density and the continuous calculus will be either too complex for manipulation or inadequate in representing the empirical data. The prospects for adequate theoretical development are not as good, perhaps, as those for an adequate theory for weather forecasts. (The analogy is chosen since the problems may be quite similar.) Besides treating population number as a function of density, it may be viewed in terms of a number of environmental variables, presumably different for each set of organisms. This approach, largely because of greater initial complexity, has not aroused nearly the same interest as has formulation in terms of density. Nevertheless, from two cases, its potential usefulness may be indicated. Davidson and Andrewartha (1948) have shown that most (78 per cent) of the variance of a thrips population studied by them could be explained by four components of weather. A difficulty with analyses of the type used by these authors, however, makes this particular investigation less meaningful than might at first appear. Multiple regressions, as fitted in this case, may coincidentally fit relatively well, without necessarily implying any causal relationship. An extremely ambitious investigation on oceanic plankton (Riley, Stommel, and Bumpus, 1949) suggests more clearly the possibilities of the use of physical and chemical factors (in this case, such things as radiation, temperature, current velocity) and biotic factors (nutrients and grazing rates). The plankton populations are considered as dependent on, and in turn influencing, certain of these factors, and by a series of simultaneous equations they may be predicted for any set of conditions. Such predictions, considering the heroic approximations involved, turn out to be surprisingly good, with an average departure from observed populations of about 25 per cent.

In an experimental population consisting of a single species given suitably renewed requisites there is no reason to expect extinction. Since organisms can exist only in a narrow environmental range, extinction at the level of the local population is certainly no rarity among those that live in highly variable natural environments. When, more rarely, some necessity for a species disappears throughout its range, the organism, if it fails to adapt, must disappear. Little sys-

tematized information exists on extinction, although there is no doubt that the influence of modern man is a potent accelerating cause. Extinction at the species level generally seems not to be catastrophic; a few members of the species persist for some time without, however, being able to increase effectively. About this phenomenon there has been considerable speculation, and it is often assumed that lack of genetic variability predestines the population to extinction once sufficiently low numbers are reached. This is possible, but remains pure conjecture. In face of the many successful accidental introductions of species into new areas, it is at most only a partial explanation.

Dispersal and Dispersion

The preceding section on growth form has been implicitly restricted to populations in a closed system, i.e., where emigration and immigration are absent. These systems are readily explored in the laboratory and may be approached by some natural populations. Such instances are, however, by no means the rule. We shall not be concerned here with directed, periodic mass migrations such as occur in many birds, as well as in some fishes and insects, but with the universal tendency of organisms to change or extend their spatial distribution. The whole subject has recently been reviewed in considerable detail (Andrewartha and Birch, 1954, pp. 86–125).

Dispersal certainly represents an adaptation to decrease the probability of extinction. Obversely, given suitable conditions, the ability to migrate permits a species to become more numerous by extensions of its range. Perhaps the most impressive example of this is the fulmar, which has apparently increased approximately geometrically since the seventeenth century. Fisher (1952) attributes the spread and increase of this bird to increased fishing, particularly for whales, which increases the fulmar's food supply.

The quantitative measurement of rates of dispersal, difficult enough in human populations, has been a piecemeal affair for other organisms. The information, mostly on birds, insects, and small mammals, is insufficient to determine whether it is subject to effective generalization. Distance is not the only determinant; organisms perceive and react to the patterning of the surroundings. Using distance alone as a measurement, there is evidence that dispersal is usually heterogeneous, so that a few individuals travel considerably farther than would be expected on the basis of random dispersal of the members of a population (Dobzhansky and Wright, 1943; Cragg and Hobart, 1955). That migration rates may be a function of density is illustrated by Kluyver's (1951) publication on the great tit, for which emigration from the study area was higher in the years of higher density than in others. Other more obvious although less well-documented examples, such as the well-known lemming migrations, are discussed by Elton (1942). The effect of such emigration for the part of the population that remains is to ameliorate the local environment, assuming that density was sufficiently high to have depressed natality or survivorship. The emigrating element usually has little chance of continued survival. Quantitative studies on rates of immigration and on rates of interchange between subpopulations of a single species—a subject that comes closer to the interests of the demographer—are lacking. Exchanges are particularly interesting biologically and have been most investigated in connection with problems of species formation, but so far only qualitatively.

Dispersal, jointly with natality and mortality, acts on the background of existing spatial differentiation ultimately determining dispersion. Diversity is imposed not only by the physical environment but by distribution of the major flora, giving rise to a complexity of pattern beautifully indicated in an essay by Elton (1949). Thus the basic physical irregularities set the stage for some degree of sociality, and it may not be surprising that random distribution of organisms, even in areas that seem homogeneous to the human observer, is rare (Cole, 1946; Hutchinson, 1953). Aggregating tendencies are common; superdispersion or spacing seems to be limited to relatively rare instances. Aggregations may be on a familial basis, as in many plants, social insects, and vertebrates, or may have no such conservative elements; the members of a particular aggregation may come together more or less randomly as a result of proximity of some limited favorable component of their environment. A more complete account of the various behavioral mechanisms resulting in sociality in different organisms would take us far afield (Allee, 1931; Allee *et al.*, 1949, chap. xxiii). Description and analysis of distribution by means of the Poisson and other theoretical distributions have reached a considerable level of complexity (Curtis and McIntosh, 1950; Bliss and Fisher, 1953) and still remain a fundamental problem of ecology.

Mixed Species Systems

Penetrating investigations have resulted from the theories of predator-prey and competitor relations advanced by Volterra (1926). The mathematical development is mainly an extension of logistic theory; additional assumptions that need to be made cause increased unreality of the models. Although it is obvious that they will not apply in detail, this by no means implies that they are useless. Certain qualitative predictions of the theory are not critically affected by changes in the mathematical functions, and the whole formulation provides a logical system subject to empirical evaluation.

The simplest models of Volterra concern the interaction of only two species. When these compete for the same resources, which are in limited supply, the major prediction is that two species occupying the same environments and with identical needs and behavior will not both persist. Which of the two survives depends on the characteristics of a given environment. The detailed exposition of this theory is not pertinent in the present context. The evidence has been reviewed by Crombie (1947). Although the main prediction has been abundantly demonstrated in the laboratory (Park, 1948, 1954), its significance in nature is difficult to evaluate. In a number of cases, closely related species that live together have consistently been found to differ in some critical characteristic, such as food requirement or period of feeding, so that competition is thought to be minimized. Andrewartha and Birch (1954) point out that this is what should be expected in different species whether competition is prevalent or not, and they do not consider the evidence to be crucial. Direct evidence of competition causing extinction is hard to come by in existing biological communities whose members have presumably been selected partly by the fact that competition did not cause their extinction. Although it might be possible to draw some fascinating parallels between the results of interspecies competition and competition between human groups, analogies of this sort are fraught with danger. Not only are the latter potentially capable of interbreeding, but the terms "needs and behavior" refer to more labile social patterns than is implied by their biological meaning.

The predator-prey model of Volterra differs from that of competition in that its main prediction is quantitative and more sensitive to small departures from the assumptions. Moreover, the latter in this case are quite far removed from biological reality. Nevertheless, the theory has been influential. Although it predicts coupled oscillations in the numbers of prey and predator, even in the laboratory only artifices have enabled the model to be approximated (Gause, 1935), and usually the species cannot coexist in simple two-species environments. In nature one would expect such oscillations to be masked by other factors; the primary problem becomes whether predators have any effect of this sort. As previously indicated, it may well be that in many vertebrate populations, predators do not function in this way (Errington, 1946) but that they merely destroy what may be termed a population excess. What is postulated is that above a certain critical density emigration from suitable habitats increases greatly, with the emigrants more subject to predation, as well as to other causes of mortality, than the resident portion of the population. The numerous instances of successful biological control of pest insects (Sweetman, 1936) attest that this is not the whole story of predation. The method of introducing insect predators to produce a decrease in the numbers of an economically undesirable species is far from universally effective, but the fact that it is ever practicable is sufficient to show that predation may cause significant populational effects. If this were not enough to make the point, one need merely consider the role of man as a predator. The dichotomy between effects of predation probably is more apparent than real, but the situation is so complex that no comprehensive theory has been achieved.

Of more immediate interest to demography are theories of interaction between parasite and host, or, more specifically, epidemic theory. Curiously, ecologists have not entered into this aspect to any extent; contributions come more from medical fields. Theories other than the original Martini-Ross equations (Lotka, 1923) have been developed (Costa Maia, 1952); fit of such a theory to single epidemic waves in human (boarding school) populations have been attempted with qualified success (Abbey, 1952). Interesting experimental epidemics in mice have been studied (Greenwood *et al.*, 1936). Aside from this, there are numerous statements in the ecological literature relating to epizoötics in natural populations, but in none has it been possible to separate disease from other causes of mortality. An interesting sidelight on the lack of evidence is provided by Park's studies on competition (Park, 1948; Park and Frank, 1950), which provide the only experimental data on the effects of an endemic parasite on animal population numbers. Some of the experimental populations in these studies were infected with a sporozoan parasite, while others were free of the disease. This sporozoan causes heavy mortality in the pre-reproductive stages of the flour beetle *Tribolium castaneum*. In populations this results in a reduction of average density for this species by more than half and an expected shift in the age distribution favoring a greater percentage of young stages.

The relations in systems containing more than two species have never been empirically evaluated in the ways discussed for the competitor and predator-prey situations. Confounding a difficult analytical problem by adding another major variable is not a choice method of attack. This has not kept investigators from speculations on more complex systems; such conjectures may be valuable in providing an impetus for gathering pertinent observational data. Since in the simple and spectac-

ular communities of organisms in the arctic the number of prevalent species is few and their populations seem to exhibit some regularity in time, these assemblages have proven particularly attractive. Attempts to explain the apparent cycles of many arctic mammals as coupled oscillations between predator and prey species have been common but have not been able to overcome the basic objection that the numbers of true predators are in no case sufficient to cause the major changes in the herbivore densities that exist. The main idea, however, has recently been revived by Lack (1954) in a slightly different sense. He considers the vertebrate herbivores, particularly the lemmings, as predators, and the vegetation as the prey species. It is conceivable that the vegetation under the unfavorable climatic conditions does not become restored at once, so that the conditions for the predator-prey fluctuations may be realized. Thus the lemming would undergo coupled fluctuations with its prey species. The true predators of the lemming—owls and other birds, weasels, and perhaps foxes—are thought by Lack to be limited by their food supply except in years of lemming abundance; they might be expected to show secondary cyclic fluctuations dependent on those of their prey, though without significant influence except when the prey is already on the decline. The idea is reasonable but, like other theories to account for population cycles, has virtually no supporting data.

On the whole, complex biological communities have not proven amenable to the approaches possible for simpler systems but have been studied in numerous other respects, of which one ultimately may be of paramount significance to the student of human populations: the relationship between the amounts of energy and matter received by components of the community. For this purpose one may think of organisms existing at a number of trophic levels (Lindeman, 1942). The first of these consists of all those organisms that obtain their energy not from other organisms but from sunlight and, to a small extent, from inorganic energy sources. Very little of the energy contained by these organisms is stored for long periods, and one can usually assume without great error that a steady state exists in a biotic community, so that the amount of energy entering equals that leaving it at any moment. This applies not only for the community as a whole but also for the individual trophic levels within it. The first or producer level is followed by that of the primary consumers, the herbivores, which in turn are followed by predators, which may form several more or less distinct trophic levels. However, the concept of discrete levels breaks down more and more the higher one goes in this food chain, since there is an increasing tendency for the organisms on top to invade food resources from several levels. The biological reasons for this are not particularly difficult to fathom: there is more food available at the lower stages as the result of the progressive wastage of energy in conversion, in respiration, and in the work required to procure food. This fact also limits the number of steps that a given food chain may have. The analysis of energy transfer by focusing on discrete trophic levels therefore involves some fairly gross approximation, but more critical dissection of a natural community would be a Herculean task.

Examination of the few studies of community productivity that exist reveals that the efficiency of conversion of incident light into chemical energy is very low, usually far below the 2 per cent which may be regarded as about maximal for cultivated crops. Theoretically, the efficiency of the process of photosynthesis is much better, about 25 per cent for the alga *Chlorella,* but such values are not approached even under laboratory conditions (Wassink, Kok, and Van Oorschot, 1953). Not all the energy absorbed is converted into a form usable by the next level, since there is some waste through respiration, and some may be tied up in an unavailable form. From the existing data one gets the impression that at successive trophic levels energy transfer becomes increasingly efficient, predators having an efficiency of perhaps 20–25 per cent. The efficiency of conversion increases as one moves up the energy pyramid because of the progressive wastage, but more and more of the energy absorbed is utilized not for growth but for maintenance. Thus very low amounts of energy are contained in the higher trophic levels. Clarke (1946) shows that the total efficiency of conversion of sunlight energy into fish protoplasm, a relatively high trophic level, was about 0.00015 per cent for the marine community he investigated. This is certainly a low value when compared with that of productivity of commercial livestock (Brody, 1952) but may be about the right order of magnitude for the top trophic level (except for man) of many natural communities. Clearly, the energy available as food for man ultimately is limited by such considerations. It is equally obvious that the amount of energy thus potentially available is subject to considerable increase, particularly by man's shortening of his food chain, but there are limits here also (Brody, 1952).

The discussion of trophic levels has dealt purely in terms of energy. One could equally well discuss it in terms of matter. In most respects the material relationships parallel the energetics. There is one basic distinction, however. Whereas the primary energy is a transient resource that is not stored if not used, the material out of which organisms are constructed usually persists in some form and may or may not be available for reconstruction. Thus we may speak of a cycle of matter, a situation that does not at all apply to the energy system. To the extent that vital materials such as phosphorus are not returned in some form usable by the community, their loss may cause an absolute shrinkage of the material available for maintenance of the community, so that its energy content may decline.

Comprehensive Theories of Population Regulation

There is no question about the fact that populations of organisms fluctuate within more or less definite limits, in space as well as in time. At first glance, it may seem strange that any phase of this subject should be controversial. However, for some time there has been a dichotomy between biologists who believe the causes for this limitation to lie in the reactions and interactions of the organisms themselves and those who think that the regulation is primarily imposed by climatic influences. Since the latter view negates the validity of studies on the relation of density to population growth, the controversy is by no means merely academic. In this extreme sense, this idea is not held by any vocal group. There is, however, a legitimate area of disagreement over the relative role played by the more or less chance fluctuations of the physical environment.

Instead of presenting any of the historical background, two modern positions will be briefly summarized. Both are the result of considerable thought on the subject and, I believe, have profited from critical appraisal of previous work. First to be presented will be the ideas of Nicholson (1954), who has elaborated his theory over a period of more than twenty years, so that it is now remarkably detailed. In order to understand his views, a number of Nicholson's definitions are needed. A requisite of the population is *responsive* when it is affected by change in population density; otherwise such a factor is termed *unresponsive*. A responsive factor is *reactive* if its response in turn modifies its influence on population growth. If it does not, the responsive factor may be grouped with unresponsive requisites and may be called *non-reactive*. A factor that causes a reaction on the part of the population opposing change in its numbers is termed *density-governing*. Nicholson thinks that, by definition, only reactive factors may be density-governing. Other effects may, however, profoundly influence population numbers, as is obviously the case in populations near the borders of their limits of distribution. Such factors, which Nicholson calls *legislative*, may consist of both unresponsive and responsive but non-reactive requisites. Both density-governing and density-legislative requisites are combined under the term *density-regulating*. These definitions, which may seem elaborations of the obvious, are useful, particularly since one of the main difficulties with the problem of population balance has been misunderstanding caused by confusion over the meaning of terms.

It is Nicholson's thesis that, although legislative factors may determine the level at which average density ("balance") is maintained in conjunction with governing factors, the latter alone serve to produce balance. Most of the governing factors Nicholson considers to be effects of competition, where competition is defined as a ". . . state of reciprocal interference which occurs when animals having similar needs live together, and which influences their success." Purely climatic factors cannot be governing, although indirectly spotty suitability of the physical environment may cause local competition, which in turn may lead to emigration. If the emigrating individuals are decimated by the unfavorable environment, it is clear that the latter is not the true governing factor. This raises the question of why food scarcity is not more noticeable, since one might expect from this theory that populations would usually be governed by their food. Certainly if animals in general were continuously limited by food, the amount of vegetation characteristic of the earth would not exist. Nicholson thinks that herbivore populations are governed primarily by their natural enemies, as well as by the availability of their food.

For populations in a constant environment, the type of balance achieved depends on a number of characteristics of the governing requisite, as well as on the way in which the population reacts to the requisite: (1) The population may not respond at all until the requisite has fallen below a certain threshold. (2) When the population does react to every change in the governing factor, the effect may be either immediate (prompt) or delayed (tardy). The governing requisites themselves may accumulate if not used; they may increase or reproduce; or they may be transient as is sunlight, and only immediately available. Depending on the combination of governing requisites and the nature of the reaction by the population, different types of growth form result, ranging from logistic growth to various types of oscillations. Nicholson thinks that the main effect of fluctuations in the environment on these formulations is to change the rate at which the governing factor operates. As it changes, it continually becomes appropriate to the environmental condition existing at the moment. It is possible for a population to be temporarily released from the regulation of a governing factor, as at times of stress when the population

may be extremely low and purely legislative factors may be limiting. If the population is to survive, however, these requisites must ease their effects, and some reactive requisite must sooner or later become limiting and governing.

Andrewartha and Birch (1954), the proponents of an alternative theory, seem to have only one fundamental quarrel with these views of Nicholson. They think that, in Nicholson's terminology, all requisites must be governing to an extent. They argue that simply because the individuals of a population of animals are themselves variable with regard to the needs for a given requisite, the probability of surviving a catastrophic event, whether caused by a responsive factor or not, increases with population size. This seems a valid objection to Nicholson's theory, although its importance is difficult to assess. There is also a difference between the part assigned to differences in space by the two theories, although this seems not to be so basic. Andrewartha and Birch consider that, given a certain amount of suitable space, this is so differentiated that the survival rate caused by a given catastrophe will be greater if there are few animals than if there are many. They attribute the governing effect to the decimating agency, whereas Nicholson would attribute it to competition of the members of the population for favorable space. Variability of space thus has an opposite effect from that of variability in the members of the population per se. The other difference between the two positions is one of relative emphasis placed on the role of density. While Nicholson believes that populations only rarely escape from the limitation by governing requisites, Andrewartha and Birch think this almost the rule. Catastrophe on a time-relative basis is viewed as a common method by which animal populations are kept in check. A relatively favorable environment is likely to permit the intrinsic rate of increase to be higher, to permit the periods between catastrophes to be longer, and to let the severity of a catastrophe be less than in an inferior environment. In each case the average numbers in the better environment will be higher. Since species are usually distributed in discontinuous, more or less favorable areas, extinction of populations in some of these areas is common rather than exceptional. After such local extinction, continued suitability of the locality will result in eventual reinvasion. Thus the most favorable areas for a species will be the ones where extinction is least probable, although even here not impossible. Only rarely would density under these conditions be sufficiently high for a requisite to act in a way that would effectively govern population numbers.

It is evident from the foregoing that neither of the theories proposed need be wrong in any major part. What is needed is a better knowledge of the relative role of density for various species, information that can be obtained only empirically. One handicap under which anyone contemplating a general theory of population balance works is that unless he is equally familiar with all sorts of animals, his views may be biased in a particular direction. Thus ornithologists, for example, are likely to reach different conclusions from entomologists, and laboratory ecologists are likely to differ in their views from those whose data are gathered in the field. It is this difficulty that has occasioned much of the controversy that still envelops the problem.

CONCLUSIONS

The foregoing summary has purposely steered clear of the applications the ecologist is inclined to make to human populations, since this would have injected an element with which the investigations discussed were not primarily concerned. Up to the present time, ecology has profited from demography much more than the reverse. Demography furnishes what constitutes the most extensive set of populational data, along with a methodology, much of which can be taken over bodily or adapted for non-human populations. Although it is possible, it does not seem likely that demographers will ever derive similar benefits from ecological methods of population measurement; this is one reason why these methods were not described in greater detail. If ecology has anything to offer the demographer, it must be looked for along theoretical lines.

It is eminently possible that the demographer or sociologist may be better able to evaluate what contributions general ecology can make to the field. Certainly ecologists are not agreed among themselves on what aspects of theory are applicable to human populations. At least some general population theory may provide a frame of reference: it should be able to define limits within which all organic populations must exist. A theory that is as broad as this may well be so general, however, that its usefulness is problematical. This raises once again the question of the similarities and differences between the populational behavior of man and that of other animals. Man's ultimate causes of population change are the same as those of other animals: natality, mortality, immigration, and emigration. Nor is man unique in having certain requisites which need to exist in specified amounts for these determinants to take on specific values. The requisites of man differ, however. Just as it is impossible to predict which factors are important in limiting a rat population from an analysis of population change in a forest insect, so it is useless to formulate such predictions for man from a study of other animals. The difference between most animals and man strikes a bit deeper, however. Human populations are unique in the rapidity with which they have been able to change their environments and thus their requisites. The recent shift to an industrial economy emphasizes, and perhaps overemphasizes, this fact. Compared with this basic distinction, other differences assume minor proportions. Nevertheless, it may be worth mentioning again that, from a purely pragmatic point of view, errors of a magnitude acceptable for non-human populations might prove extremely serious in the case of man.

The main aspect of human populations in which the ecologist tends not to be competent is, therefore, the effect of that part of man's social organization that is peculiar to him. Division of labor and a deliberate distribution of certain requisites occur in some social insects also, but neither on the same scale nor subject to so much modification as in man's case. Although suitable subjects for his interest, these effects seem often not to be fully appreciated by the ecologist. Granting that the effects of such organization in the immediately foreseeable future may overshadow any other factors, there remain a number of problems to which ecology should be able to contribute. There seems to be little doubt that the present is an unusual era for man in that there are no constant limits to population increase. Not at all times nor in all areas can it be expected that changes in social structure will occur and have this influence. If production and distribution facilities stabilize, some requisite or group of requisites must eventually become limiting again.

Judged by the relative volume of literature, which is not necessarily a good index, the majority of ecologists seem to be neo-Malthusians, and they evince great concern over the likelihood that food will again play this role. If this assumption is made, two distinct possibilities cause particular fear: (1) the likelihood that at the same time that the human population increases, the availability of the basic materials involved in food production may decrease, thus bringing about a possibly catastrophic decline, or (2) that, as in many other animals, there may be sufficient delay before the effects of density exert themselves in full force on human increase, likewise resulting in an abrupt and painful decrease in population. That food will ultimately be limiting is, of course, only one assumption; it is within the frame of general naturalistic theory, but other variants provide distinct alternatives.

It is once again at this point where ecologists, without detailed knowledge of cultural and institutional factors, suffer a handicap. If a naturalistic theory is to have validity, it must take into consideration, in the case of man, the various directed activities that form the base for institutional or economic theories of population. This might mean, for example, that population could be governed by the standard of living (in the broadest possible sense) to which its members become accustomed, an alternative also within the limits of general theory. Because of the indicated dangers of uncritical extrapolation, ecology as a delimited discipline must not be expected to provide specific theoretical statements about human populations. Even so, it is probable that ecology can function effectively, in combination with related disciplines, to produce a measure of integration for the ordering of human data.

SELECTED BIBLIOGRAPHY

ABBEY, HELEN. 1952. "An Examination of the Reed-Frost Theory of Epidemics," *Human Biology*, XXIV, 201–33.

ALLEE, W. C. 1931. *Animal Aggregations.* Chicago: University of Chicago Press.

———. 1951. *Cooperation among Animals, with Human Implications.* New York: Schuman.

———, EMERSON, A. E., PARK, O., PARK, T., and SCHMIDT, K. P. 1949. *Principles of Animal Ecology.* Philadelphia: W. B. Saunders Co.

ANDREWARTHA, H. G., and BIRCH, L. C. 1954. *The Distribution and Abundance of Animals.* Chicago: University of Chicago Press.

BIRCH, L. C. 1948. "The Intrinsic Rate of Natural Increase of an Insect Population," *Journal of Animal Ecology,* XXVII, 15–26.

BLISS, C. I., and FISHER, R. A. 1953. "Fitting the Negative Binomial Distribution to Biological Data," *Biometrics,* IX, 176–96.

BODENHEIMER, F. S. 1938. *Problems of Animal Ecology.* London: Oxford University Press.

BRODY, SAMUEL. 1952. "Facts, Fables, and Fallacies on Feeding the World Population," *Federation Proceedings,* XI, 681–93.

BROWNLEE, JOHN. 1906. "Statistical Studies in Immunity: The Theory of an Epidemic," *Proceedings of the Royal Society of Edinburgh,* XXVI, 484–521.

CHAPMAN, D. G. 1951. "Some Properties of the Hypergeometric Distribution with Applications to Zoölogical Censuses," *University of California Publications in Statistics,* I, 131–60.

CHAPMAN, R. N. 1928. "The Quantitative Analysis of Environmental Factors," *Ecology,* IX, 111–22.

CLARKE, G. L. 1946. "Dynamics of Production in a Marine Area," *Ecological Monographs,* XVI, 321–35.

COLE, L. C. 1946. "A Study of the Cryptozoa of an Illinois Woodland," *Ecological Monographs,* XVI, 49–86.

———. 1951. "Population Cycles and Random Oscillations," *Journal of Wildlife Management,* XV, 233–52.

———. 1954a. "The Population Consequences of Life History Phenomena," *Quarterly Review of Biology,* XXIX, 103–37.

———. 1954b. "Some Features of Random Population Cycles," *Journal of Wildlife Management,* XVIII, 2–24.

COSTA MAIA, JOAQUIM DE OLIVEIRA. 1952. "Some Mathematical Developments on the Epidemic Theory Formulated by Reed and Frost," *Human Biology,* XXIV, 167–200.

CRAGG, J. B., and HOBART, J. 1955. "A Study of a Field Population of the Blowflies *Lucilia caesar* (L.) and *L. sericata* (Mg.)," *Annals of Applied Biology,* XLIII, 645–63.

CURTIS, J. T., and McINTOSH, R. P. 1950. "The Interrelations of Certain Analytical and Synthetic Phytosociological Characters," *Ecology,* XXXI, 434–55.

DAVIDSON, J., and ANDREWARTHA, H. G. 1948. "The Influence of Rainfall, Evaporation, and Atmospheric Temperature on Fluctuations in the Size of a Natural Population of *Thrips imaginis* (Thysanoptera)," *Journal of Animal Ecology,* XVII, 200–222.

DEEVEY, EDWARD S., JR. 1947. "Life Tables for Natural Populations of Animals," *Quarterly Review of Biology,* XXII, 283–314.

DOBZHANSKY, T. and WRIGHT, S. 1943. "Genetics of Natural Populations, X: Dispersion Rates in *Drosophila pseudoobscura,*" *Genetics,* XXVIII, 304–40.

EDMONDSON, W. T. 1945. "Ecological Studies of Sessile Rotatoria, Part II: Dynamics of Populations and Social Structures," *Ecological Monographs,* XV, 141–72.

ELSTON, J. S. 1923. "Survey of Mathematical Formulas That Have Been Used To Express a Law of Mortality," *Records of the American Institute of Actuaries,* XII, 66–95.

ELTON, CHARLES. 1942. *Voles, Mice, and Lemmings.* Oxford: Clarendon Press.

———. 1949. "Population Interspersion: An Essay on Animal Community Patterns," *Journal of Ecology,* XXXVII, 1–23.

ERRINGTON, PAUL. 1946. "Predation and Vertebrate Populations," *Quarterly Review of Biology,* XXI, 144–77; 221–45.

EVANS, FRANCIS C., and SMITH, FREDERICK E. 1952. "The Intrinsic Rate of Natural Increase for the Human Louse, *Pediculus manus* L.," *American Naturalist,* LXXXVI, 299–316.

FELLER, W. 1939. "Die Grundlagen der

Volterraschen Theorie des Kampfes ums Daseins in wahrscheinlichkeitstheoretischer Behandlung," *Acta biotheoretica,* V, 11–40.

FISHER, JAMES. 1952. *The Fulmar.* London: Collins.

FITCH, JOHN E. 1951. "Age Composition of the Southern California Catch of Pacific Mackerel 1939–40 through 1950–51," *Bureau of Marine Fisheries, California Department of Fish and Game, Fish Bulletin,* LXXXIII, 3–73.

FRANK, P. W. 1952. "A Laboratory Study of Intraspecies and Interspecies Competition in *Daphnia pulicaria* (Forbes) and *Simocephalus vetulus* O. F. Müller," *Physiological Zoölogy,* XXV, 178–204.

FUJITA, HIROSHI. 1954. "An Interpretation of the Changes in Type of the Population Density Effect upon the Oviposition Rate," *Ecology,* XXXV, 253–57.

GAUSE, G. F. 1934. *The Struggle for Existence.* Baltimore: Williams & Wilkins.

———. 1935. "Vérifications expérimentales de la théorie mathématique de la lutte pour la vie," *Actualités scientifiques et industrielles,* CCLXXVII, 1–61.

GERKING, SHELBY D. 1952. "Statistics of the Fish Population of Gordy Lake, Indiana," *Transactions of the American Fisheries Society,* LXXXII, 48–67.

GREENWOOD, MAJOR. 1942. "Medical Statistics from Graunt to Farr," *Biometrika,* XXXII, 101–27, 203–25; XXXIII, 1–24.

———, HILL, A. B., TOPLEY, W. W. C., and WILSON, J. 1936. *Experimental Epidemiology.* ("Gt. Brit. M. R. C. Spec. Rep.," Ser. 209.) London: H.M. Stationery Office.

HARDIN, GARRETT. 1949. *Biology: Its Human Implications.* San Francisco: W. H. Freeman & Co.

HOWE, R. W. 1953. "The Rapid Determination of the Intrinsic Rate of Increase of an Insect Population," *Annals of Applied Biology,* XL, 134–51.

HUTCHINSON, G. E. 1951. "Copepodology for the Ornithologist," *Ecology,* XXXII, 571–77.

———. 1953. "The Concept of Pattern in Ecology," *Proceedings of the Academy of Natural Science of Philadelphia,* CV, 1–12.

———, and DEEVEY, E. S., JR. 1949. "Ecological Studies on Populations," *Surveys of Biological Progress,* I, 325–59.

JACKSON, C. H. N. 1939. "The Analysis of an Animal Population," *Journal of Animal Ecology,* VIII, 238–46.

———. 1948. "The Analysis of a Tsetse-Fly Population: III," *Annals of Eugenics,* XIV, 91–108.

KLUYVER, H. N. 1951. "The Population Ecology of the Great Tit *Parus m. major,*" *Ardea,* XIL, 1–135.

LACK, DAVID. 1947. "The Significance of Clutch Size," *Ibis,* XIC, 302–52.

———. 1948. "The Significance of Litter Size," *Journal of Animal Ecology,* XVII, 45–50.

———. 1954. *The Natural Regulation of Animal Numbers.* London: Oxford University Press.

LESLIE, P. H. 1945. "On the Use of Matrices in Certain Population Mathematics," *Biometrika,* XXXIII, 183–212.

———. 1948. "Some Further Notes on the Use of Matrices in Population Mathematics," *ibid.,* XXXV, 214–45.

———, and CHITTY, DENNIS. 1951. "The Estimation of Population Parameters from Data Obtained by Means of the Capture-recapture Method, I: The Maximum Likelihood Equations for Estimating the Death-Rate," *ibid.,* XXXVIII, 269–92.

———, CHITTY, DENNIS, and CHITTY, HELEN. 1953. "The Estimation of Population Parameters from Data Obtained by Means of the Capture-recapture Method, III: An Example of the Practical Applications of the Method," *ibid.,* XL, 137–69.

———, and PARK, T. 1949. "The Intrinsic Rate of Natural Increase of *Tribolium castaneum* Herbst," *Ecology,* XXX, 469–77.

———, and RANSON, R. M. 1940. "The Mortality, Fertility, and Rate of Natural Increase of the Vole (*Microtus agrestis*) As Observed in the Laboratory," *Journal of Animal Ecology,* IX, 27–52.

———, TEBNER, J. S., VIZOSO, M., and CHITTY, HELEN. 1955. "Longevity and Fertility of the Orkney Vole, *Microtus orcadensis,* As Observed in the Laboratory,"

Proceedings of the Zoölogical Society of London, CXXV, 115–25.

LESLIE, P. H., VENABLES, U. M., and VENABLES, L. S. V. 1952. "The Fertility and Population Structure of the Brown Rat (*Rattus norvegicus*) in Corn-Ricks and Some Other Habitats," *Proceedings of the Zoölogical Society of London*, CXXII, 187–238.

LINDEMAN, R. L. 1942. "The Trophic-dynamic Aspect of Ecology," *Ecology*, XXIII, 399–418.

LOTKA, A. J. 1923. "Contributions to the Analysis of Malaria Epidemiology," *American Journal of Hygiene*, III, Supplement I, 1–95.

———. 1925. *Elements of Physical Biology*. Baltimore: Williams & Wilkins Co.

———. 1931. "The Structure of a Growing Population," *Human Biology*, III, 459–93.

———. 1939. *Théorie analytique des associations biologiques*. Part II: *Analyse démographique avec application particulière à l'espèce humaine*. Paris: Hermann & Co.

MACLAGEN, D. S. 1932. "The Effect of Population Density upon the Rate of Reproduction with Special Reference to Insects," *Proceedings of the Royal Society of London*, Ser. B, CXI, 437–54.

MERRELL, MARGARET. 1947. "Time-specific Life Tables Contrasted with Observed Survivorship," *Biometrics*, III, 129–36.

MORRIS, R. F., and MILLER, C. A. 1954. "The Development of Life Tables for the Spruce Budworm," *Canadian Journal of Zoölogy*, XXXII, 283–301.

NICHOLSON, A. J. 1954. "An Outline of the Dynamics of Animal Populations," *Australian Journal of Zoölogy*, II, 9–65.

ODUM, H. T., and ALLEE, W. C. 1954. "A Note on the Stable Point of Populations Showing both Intraspecific Cooperation and Disoperation," *Ecology*, XXXV, 95–97.

PARK, T. 1934. "Studies in Population Physiology, III: The Effect of Conditioned Flour upon the Productivity and Population Decline of *Tribolium confusum* Duval and Its Populations," *Journal of Experimental Zoölogy*, LXVIII, 167–82.

———. 1936. "Studies in Population Physi-
ology, VI: The Effect of Differentially Conditioned Flour upon the Fecundity and Fertility of *Tribolium confusum* Duval," *ibid.*, LXXIII, 393–404.

———. 1948. "Experimental Studies of Interspecies Competition, I: Competition between Populations of the Flour Beetles, *Tribolium confusum* Duval and *Tribolium castaneum* Herbst," *Ecological Monographs*, XVIII, 265–308.

———. 1954. "Experimental Studies of Interspecies Competition, II: Temperature, Humidity, and Competition in Two Species of Tribolium," *Physiological Zoölogy*, XXVII, 177–238.

———. 1955. "Ecological Experimentation with Animal Populations," *Scientific Monthly*, LXXXI, 271–75.

———, and FRANK, M. B. 1948. "The Fecundity and Development of the Flour Beetles *Tribolium confusum* and *Tribolium castaneum* at Three Constant Temperatures," *Ecology*, XXIX, 368–74.

———. 1950. "The Population History of Tribolium Free of Sporozoan Infection," *Journal of Animal Ecology*, XIX, 95–105.

PEARL, RAYMOND. 1922. *The Biology of Death*. Philadelphia: Lippincott.

———. 1924. *Studies in Human Biology*. Baltimore: Williams & Wilkins Co.

———. 1925. *The Biology of Population Growth*. New York: Alfred A. Knopf.

———, and MINER, J. R. 1935. "Experimental Studies on the Duration of Life, XIV: The Comparative Mortality of Certain Lower Organisms," *Quarterly Review of Biology*, X, 60–75.

———, PARK, T., and MINER, J. R. 1941. "Experimental Studies on the Duration of Life, XVI: Life Tables for the Flour Beetle *Tribolium confusum* Duval," *American Naturalist*, LXXV, 5–19.

———, and REED, L. J. 1920. "On the Rate of Growth of the Population of the United States since 1790 and Its Mathematical Representation," *Proceedings of the National Academy of Sciences*, VI, 275–88.

PRATT, DAVID M. 1943. "Analysis of Population Development in Daphnia at Different Temperatures," *Biological Bulletin*, LXXXV, 116–40.

REID, A. T. 1953. "On Stochastic Processes in Biology," *Biometrics*, IX, 275–89.

RICH, EARL R. 1956. "Egg Cannibalism

and Fecundity in Tribolium," *Ecology*, XXXVII, 109–20.

RICKER, WILLIAM E. 1948. *Methods of Estimating Vital Statistics of Fish Populations.* ("Indiana University Publications, Science Series," Vol. XV.)

RILEY, GORDON A., STOMMEL, HENRY, and BUMPUS, DEAN F. 1949. "Quantitative Ecology of the Plankton of the Western North Atlantic," *Bulletin of Bingham Oceanography College*, XII, 1–169.

ROSS, RONALD. 1916. "An Application of the Theory of Probabilities to the Study of *a priori* Pathometry, Part I," *Proceedings of the Royal Society of London*, Ser. A, XCII, 204–30.

SETTE, O. E. 1943. "Biology of the Atlantic Mackerel (*Scomber scombrus*) of North America, Part I: Early Life History, Including the Growth, Drift, and Mortality of the Egg and Larval Populations," *United States Fish and Wildlife Service Fisheries Bulletin*, L, 147–237.

SMITH, F. E. 1952. "Experimental Methods in Population Dynamics: A Critique," *Ecology*, XXXIII, 441–50.

SWEETMAN, H. L. 1936. *The Biological Control of Insects.* Ithaca: Comstock Publishing Co.

VERHULST, P. F. 1838. "Notice sur la loi que la population suit dans son accroissement," *Correspondence mathématique et physique.* Paris: A. Quételet.

———. 1844. "Recherches mathématiques sur la loi d'accroissement de la population," *Nouveaux mémoires de l'Academie Royale des Sciences et Belles-Lettres de Bruxelles*, XVIII, 1–38.

VOLTERRA, VITO. 1926. "Variazioni e fluttuazioni del numero d'individui in specie animali conviventi," *Memorie della R. Accademia Nazionale dei Lincei*, II, 31–113.

WASSINK, E. C., KOK, B., and OORSCHOT, J. L. P. VAN. 1953. "The Efficiency of Light-energy Conversion in Chlorella Cultures As Compared with Higher Plants," in *Algal Culture from Laboratory to Pilot Plant*, ed. JOHN S. BURLEW. Washington, D.C.: Carnegie Institute.

WIESNER, B. P., and SHEARD, N. M. 1935. "The Duration of Life in an Albino Rat Population," *Proceedings of the Royal Society of Edinburgh*, LV, 1–22.

28. *Human Ecology and Population Studies*

OTIS DUDLEY DUNCAN

This chapter is concerned with problems of population insofar as they are both subject matter for what is usually called demographic research and of theoretical interest from the standpoint of human ecology. There are already available useful general statements of the differences between and interrelationships of demography and human ecology (McKenzie, 1934; Hawley, 1950, p. 70). Nonetheless, it seems desirable to proceed from a general consideration of the field of human ecology and its bearing upon population studies to a discussion of more specific substantive problems of population research. The thesis of the chapter is that human ecology provides a general perspective, heuristic principles and concepts, and specific hypotheses of first-rate significance to the demographer, while many problems in human ecology are most effectively attacked by research workers having at their disposal the techniques of modern demographic analysis.

THE FIELD OF HUMAN ECOLOGY

Preliminary Considerations

A major difficulty in framing the discussion is the uncertainty about its proper scope. One may adopt a broad or a narrow definition of the field of "demography," but either choice could be accepted by a general audience as a basis for discussion. On the other hand, even a provisional statement of the concerns of "human ecology" will doubtless encounter strong objections from one or another group of scientists

and thinkers who regard their studies of man as exemplifying the ecological viewpoint. Reasons for this divergency of intellectual positions would have to be sought in the circumstances attending the development of the ecological point of view in biology and its extension to discussion and research on human behavior. But without essaying such a historical digression it is well to suggest briefly the diversity of "ecological" orientations which a thorough survey would reveal. Several summaries of the variety of conceptions of human ecology—none of them comprehensive—may be referred to for additional details (Quinn, 1940; Shantz *et al.*, 1940; Hawley, 1944; Llewellyn and Hawthorn, 1945; Wirth, 1945; Deevey, 1951; Bates, 1953).

To indicate, first, something of the range of orientations, one may cite as the extreme of inclusiveness Adams' characterization of human ecology as "that general subject which deals with the relations and inter-relations between nature in general and human nature in particular . . . from the broadest possible point of view, and with all its ramifications" (Adams, 1951, p. 39). On the other hand, some writers seemingly have regarded human ecology as little more than a collection of techniques for the study of spatial distributions, or substantively as the discipline "concerned with explaining the territorial arrangements that social activities assume," whose task "is to discover and explain the regularities which appear in man's adaptations to space" (Firey, 1947, p.

3). The broad or "holistic" version of human ecology has sought an essentially philosophical underpinning (Bews, 1935), while the particularistic view of human ecology as the study of spatial distributions has some historical justification (Hawley, 1951): many studies labeled "ecological" have dealt primarily or solely with geographic distributions of social phenomena (Caldwell, 1938; Quinn, 1950, Part IV).

Leaving aside programmatic or propaedeutic statements of this kind, one can gain an impression of the ramifications of the ecological point of view by indicating some of the fields in which it has enlisted spokesmen and practitioners. First of all, the notion of including human ecology within the scope of bio-ecology, as developed by plant and animal ecologists (Clements and Shelford, 1939), continues to be debated by the biologists (Smith, 1951; Sears and Carter, 1952). However, few bio-ecologists have made a sustained effort to deal with a wide range of problems in human ecology, a significant exception being the treatise by Dice (1955).

Zoölogists and physical anthropologists are exploiting the ecological point of view in studies of human evolution and the differentiation of races (Bartholomew and Birdsell, 1953; Newman, 1953). Some geographers feel that human ecology provides a useful framework for presentation of findings in human geography (White and Renner, 1948) and urban geography (Dickinson, 1947); the terms "ecology" and "ecological" are probably appearing with increasing frequency in the geography literature, although from Hartshorne's review (1949) it would appear that only a minority of geographers accept the proposal of Barrows (1923) to make ecological relationships the primary focus of geographic research. Recent archeological writing has drawn upon materials of plant and animal ecology as aids to the interpretation of prehistoric economic development (Clark, 1952). Bennett (1944) points to a growing trend of attention to ecological problems in ethnography and ethnology; this is exemplified in studies by Steward (1938), Hallowell (1949), Thompson (1949), Birdsell (1953), Wedel (1953), and Meggers (1954). Some concepts of ecology are drawn on in recent statements of economic theory (Boulding, 1950; Bowen, 1954), the latter with special reference to population. Certain land economists (U.S. Federal Housing Administration, 1939) and location theorists (Hoover, 1948; Lösch, 1954; Isard, 1956) seemingly recognize an affinity between their work and human or general ecology.

A symposium on ecology and health (Corwin, 1949) and the continuing controversy over "ecological methods" for studying mental disorder (Dunham, 1947; Clausen and Kohn, 1954) attest to the impact of the ecological viewpoint on research in public health. A substantial literature has grown up in what one writer refers to as "political ecology" (Heberle, 1952), and ecological concepts have been used in a variety of studies in social organization, touching on such topics as organizational change (Boulding, 1953a) and social stratification (Duncan and Duncan, 1955a). There is also the large literature of "urban ecology," dealing with differentiation of residential areas (Schmid, 1950), segregation of population groups (Duncan and Duncan, 1955b), and such special problems as shopping habits (Jonassen, 1955), daytime population movements (Foley, 1954; Schnore, 1954), and other aspects of urban land use, structure, and functions. (See Hauser, 1956b, for a comprehensive review of these studies.) Some impact of this literature on approaches to city planning has been noted (Kligman, 1945; Demerath, 1947;

Dewey, 1950). Even psychologists have found it useful to conceptualize some of their research in language borrowed from ecology (Brunswik, 1947; Barker and Wright, 1955), and statisticians have coined the probably unfortunate terms "ecological correlation" (Robinson, 1950) and "ecological regression" (Goodman, 1953) to denote a particular problem of estimation that arises in connection with data tabulated by areal units. Lastly, "human ecology" or "social ecology" continues to serve as a platform for some social philosophers and reformers (Lindeman, 1940; Gutkind, 1953).

As one might suspect from the foregoing, the term "ecology" is sometimes applied rather casually—even irresponsibly. Many studies adopting the label bear only a tenuous relationship to any systematic, scientific conception of the field, while much research not labeled as "ecological" would have to be included in the purview of human ecology, however the problems of that discipline may be structured theoretically.

Additional documentation of the chaos engendered by subsuming so great a variety of undertakings under a single heading is unnecessary. Instead, three somewhat terse statements can be offered in summary evaluation of efforts to formulate the field of human ecology as a scientific discipline. (1) There is a "least common denominator" of nearly all attempts to delimit the field: "Human ecology studies relations between men and their natural environments" (Quinn, 1940, p. 192), whether the terms "man" and "environment" are given extensive or restricted (as in the limitation of "environment" to "space") connotations. (2) Many discussions of human ecology as a discipline are very inchoate, scarcely going beyond considerations of propaedeutic value. But there is available a careful theoretical treatise on human ecology, presenting a consistent, well-

elaborated version of the discipline (Hawley, 1950). While some of the views in this book are no doubt controversial (perhaps designedly so), it is hardly conceivable that any serious presentation of an alternative conception of human ecology can fail to reckon with Hawley's formulation. (3) Inasmuch as human ecology is undeniably immature as a discipline, little is to be gained by accepting any statement of its scope as final. On the contrary, extreme divergencies of viewpoint will persist and doubtless proliferate. However, one's impression (not a conclusion supported by careful scholarship) is that such divergencies now are being generated because workers dealing with an enormous variety of concrete problems have accepted an ecological point of view, whereas in the past these divergencies were largely produced by reasoning from different first principles or arguing about philosophic predispositions. If this impression is correct, then the confusing situation may actually be indicative of a healthy state of intellectual ferment and research exploration rather than a symptom of schizoid tendencies.

Actually, the intellectual disorganization may be less extreme or significant than it appears, for there is probably room for two conceptions of human ecology. For terminological clarity these may be distinguished as the "natural history of man" and "human ecology," using the latter term in a somewhat strict or limited sense. The "natural history of man" represents the extension of the ecological point of view to any study of the human species where it has promise of providing useful insights, however partial, and—largely as a task for the future—the synthesis of all such studies, however loose such synthesis must be in the light of the limitations of present knowledge. The "natural history of man" evidently is too broad a field to be dealt with by any single theorist or investigator or, indeed, by any presently established scientific discipline. Yet it seems desirable that scientists adopting the label of "ecology" and dealing with human problems recognize their affinity with others of the same kind; that they endeavor to share data, results, methods, and points of view; and that from time to time they consider the possibilities and problems of delineating a comprehensive picture of man in his environmental relations, including the ways in which these are mediated by relations between man and man and between man and his "cultural" equipment. Among other things, such a spirit might make possible the building of a badly needed bridge over the chasm the separates the natural and the social sciences.

There is no need to justify the limited conception of human ecology. In contrast with the "natural history of man," human ecology, *strictu senso,* is no mere prolegomenon but, with Hawley's (1950) achievement (based, of course, on the theoretical and research efforts of many workers), an accomplished fact. By whatever criteria one might accept any of the social sciences as sciences, human ecology must be acknowledged as one among their number, notwithstanding imperfections and incompleteness of its theoretical structure, crudeness of its methods, and limitations on the validity or generality of its empirical conclusions.

The remainder of this chapter will deal only with the limited conception of human ecology. Building primarily on Hawley's (1950) presentation of the discipline but departing from it in various ways, the chapter will outline the general frame of reference of human ecology, sketch some contact points between ecological theory and demographic research, and illustrate some of the more significant research developments and prospects in regard to these contact points.

Frame of Reference

The main problems of human ecology can be set forth in terms of four referential concepts: population, environment, technology, and organization. The unit of ecological analysis is a human population, more or less circumscribed territorially. Sociologists may recall that before the term "human ecology" was proposed, Cooley (1894) described part of its subject matter as "territorial demography." By referring observations to a concrete population of human organisms, human ecology (with demography) distinguishes itself from other social sciences whose data are referred to such units as the personality, the culture pattern, the market, or the state. That at least some spatially delimited population aggregates have unit character is one of the key assumptions of human ecology, as is the premise that there are significant properties of such an aggregate which differ from the properties of its component elements. It is reasonable to suppose that many of the fruitful consequences of these assumptions have yet to be worked out.

A concrete human population exists not in limbo but in an environment. Moreover, to continue to exist, it must cope with the problems posed by an environment which is indifferent to its survival but offering (in varying degree) resources potentially useful for the maintenance of life. By mere occupancy of an environment, as well as by the exploitation of its resources, a human population modifies its environment to a greater or lesser degree, introducing environmental changes additional to those produced by other organisms, geological processes, and the like. Thus, in the language of bioecology (Clements and Shelford, 1939), one may say that not only does the environment "act" upon the population but also the human population "reacts" upon its environment, either directly or through "coaction" with other species—notably those appropriated, cultivated, or husbanded for food, feed, fuel, and fiber. The "adjustment" of a population to its environment, therefore, is not a state of being or static equilibrium but a continuing, dynamic process.

For a human population—as distinguished from populations of other organisms—the problem of adjusting to an environment is both facilitated and complicated by man's possession of a culture. Contrary to the impression of some ill-informed critics, the modern human ecologist does not propose to construct a biologistic theory of human behavior that ignores or discounts the importance of culture. However, the human ecologist finds that the global or synthetic concept of culture developed in anthropology is ill-suited to an analysis of the system of interdependent factors with which ecology must deal. Moreover, as even some anthropologists are coming to recognize (Hallowell, 1949; Steward, 1955), the "culturological" viewpoint (save as a theory of culture per se) implies a determinism which is as logically objectionable and empirically fruitless as the "environmentalism" and "biological determinism" now rejected by all social scientists. In short, the functional and analytical approach of human ecology involves a concern not with culture as an undifferentiated totality but with aspects of culture as they play into the process of adaptation. The human ecologist is likely to regard some aspects of culture, especially "social organization," as dependent variables, i.e., phenomena to be explained within an ecological frame of reference. Other aspects of culture, notably "technology" in a broad sense, play an important role as explanatory factors. To be sure,

what is an "explanatory factor" in one context may more appropriately be treated as a "dependent variable" in another. The character of suitable analytical models cannot be prescribed in advance by a highly general frame of reference.

The concept of "technology" in human ecology refers not merely to a complex of art and artifact whose patterns are invented, diffused, and accumulated (the processes stressed by culturologists) but to a set of techniques employed by a population to gain sustenance from its environment and to facilitate the organization of sustenance-producing activity. Moreover, artifacts and apparatus are not only factors enabling a population to control—in a measure—its environment and leading to the transformation of the environment, but they are *part* of the environment insofar as they are incorporated into systems of activity. The environment in the contemporary city, for example, is so largely a product of human activity that for many purposes one can virtually ignore its "natural" features.

Patterns of social organization, like technology, are subsumed under the anthropologist's concept of culture. But ecology focuses attention on the functional aspect of organization rather than on the psychological mechanism of learning stressed by culturological interpretations of organization as an aspect of the social heritage. Functionally, human social organization bears many significant analogies to organization at all levels of life (Emerson, 1939, 1942; Allee, 1951) irrespective of the psychological mechanisms that may be involved in organized activity. For the ecologist, the significant assumptions about organization are that it arises from sustenance-producing activities, is a property of the population aggregate, is indispensable to the maintenance of collective life, and must be adapted to the conditions confronting a population—including the character of the environment, the size and composition of the population itself, and the repertory of techniques at its command.

Human ecology, then, is distinguished from other perspectives on man's nature and behavior neither by the phenomena it investigates (these are surveyed by many other disciplines) nor by the factors whose importance it recognizes. Rather, it lays claim to the status of a scientific discipline on the basis of its formulation of a problem and the heuristic principles employed in attacking that problem. Conceived as "a study of the morphology of collective life in both its static and dynamic aspects" (Hawley, 1950, p. 67), human ecology seeks one part of the answer to the persistent questions that have long inspired philosophic reflection and, recently, scientific research on the predicament of man. How is human social life possible? What is the nature of the bond that holds men together? How does it come about that societies of men differ from time to time and place to place—the problems of "cultural diversity" and "social change."

The general answers offered by human ecology provide a framework for its elaboration of theory and an outline of its research tasks. Society exists by virtue of the organization of a population of organisms, each of which is individually unequipped to survive in isolation. Organization represents an adaptation to the unavoidable circumstance that individuals are interdependent and that the collectivity of individuals must cope with concrete environmental conditions—including, perhaps, competition and resistance afforded by other collectivities—with whatever technological means may be at its disposal. The "social bond," in its most basic aspect, is precisely this

interdependence of units in a more or less elaborated division of labor, aptly described as a "functional integration." Societies differ because, among other things, each territorially delimited aggregate confronts a special set of environmental circumstances and differs from other such aggregates in size and composition. Even more important: since most environmental and demographic situations permit alternative solutions to the problems of adaptation and since such solutions have a tendency to persist as they are embodied in organizational forms and

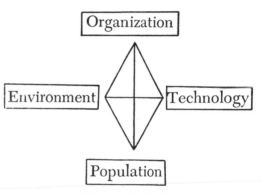

Fig. 10.—The ecological complex

technical apparatus, initial differences tend to produce continuing diversification. An ecological account of social change is attempted by referring to such instigating factors as environmental change (whether caused by man or by other agencies), changes in size and composition of population, introduction of new techniques, and shifts in the spatial disposition or organization of competing populations. The interdependence of factors in the adaptation of a population implies that change in any of them will set up ramifying changes in the others.

The diagram in Figure 10 suggests something of the scope of the ecological frame of reference. Each of the four vertexes of the diagram stands for a collection of analytically distinguishable elements, whose identification is part of the task of ecological theory. The lines are meant to suggest the idea of "functional interdependence," although in greatly oversimplified fashion. The diagram is entitled the "ecological complex" to avoid prejudgment of issues suggested by the term "system" or "ecosystem." Whether it is fruitful to regard this complex as a system with equilibrium-maintaining properties is a moot point of ecological theory. One thing is clear: a static equilibrium is seldom observable empirically. It may be possible, however, to derive significant hypotheses from the assumption that the "ecological complex" constitutes an equilibrium-seeking system whose path of change results from this tendency combined with dislocating forces impinging upon one or another point in the system.

Recent statements on ecological theory have moved toward the assumption that the *community* is the smallest ecological complex with properties approaching those of a system (Hawley, 1950; Dice, 1955). But it is only in a limiting case that the community approximates a closed or isolated system. The trend of social evolution is toward the elaboration of organization at the intercommunity or supralocal level to such an extent that it becomes necessary, for some purposes, to take account of a fabric of interdependence with planetary scope—the "world community," for want of a better term. Intermediate levels of organization must, of course, be recognized; the most prominent heuristic concept at present is the "region." To justify its continued preoccupation with analysis at the local community level, ecology resorts to two hypotheses: that territorially more inclusive forms of organization function primarily through the community nexus and that the community is the most accessible and manageable unit of observation and analysis among those

units exhibiting the full range of relationships postulated for the "ecological complex."

A final remark on the division of labor in ecological studies: The limited conception of human ecology implies a focus of interest upon the study of organization—in the context of the other factors of the ecological complex. Such a focus is a natural consequence of the fact that the limited conception of human ecology has been developed primarily by sociologists. Certainly there is little in the professional training of sociologists to equip them to study effectively all the problems implied in the notion of a "natural history of man." Moreover, other specialists are more likely to approach the analysis of the ecological complex via an interest in one of its other factors. The historical accident that training in demography (in the United States) has come to be concentrated in departments of sociology may help account for the fact that sociologists have gained the leadership in formulating problems of ecological theory even though they could hardly claim preeminence in many phases of ecological research. Recognition of the interrelations of organizational and demographic problems, while an incomplete basis for ecological theory, is one of the prerequisites to the development of such theory.

Interrelations of Demography and Human Ecology

A simple way to differentiate the disciplines of human ecology and demography is to characterize the former as, in part, the study of population as a factor in the "ecological complex" and the latter as the study of aggregates *qua* aggregates—i.e., in abstraction from their organization or structural properties. This, of course, implies a restricted scope for demography, embracing, first, the formal theory of aggregates—"population analysis," in Lotka's (1938) usage of the term—and, second, the descriptive study of the size, distribution, and composition of populations and the time changes in these characteristics. Clearly, most demographers *soi-disant* have not limited themselves to this narrow compass; they have investigated broader problems, notably the balance of population and resources and the impact of technology and organization on demographic processes, regarding the latter primarily as "dependent variables" (Ogburn, 1953). These broader interests of demographers have thrust them into a concern with ecological problems, whether or not the label of "ecology" has been accepted. This means, in practice, that it is difficult to distinguish a human ecologist from a demographer, save, perhaps, that some among the former group of specialists have not always had the command of demographic techniques that they should.

To state the relationship between demography and human ecology the other way around, the human ecologist concerns himself with a wide variety of demographic problems, uses freely (if not always effectively) demographic data, and relies heavily on demographic techniques. Oversimplifying the case, one might say that demographic variables come within the scope of ecological research (1) as "independent variables," determinants, or limiting conditions of ecological organization; (2) as "dependent variables," concomitants, or consequences of variations in ecological organization; and (3) as "indicators" of one or another aspect of ecological organization. Such relationships can be illustrated readily: (1) A small, dispersed population cannot, other things equal, have as elaborate social organization as a large, concentrated one. (2) The population of the suburbs of metropolitan centers in the United States, on the average, has a higher level of fertility than the central city population. (3) A spatial gradient in population composition may be interpreted as an indicator of the dominance of an urban agglomeration over its rural hinterland.

The following part of the paper indicates the relevance of ecological considerations to each of the conventional topics of demography; the penultimate part deals with some broader issues. The distribution of emphasis among the several topics reflects, of course, the writer's interests and limitations but also, to a degree, some lack of balance in the current preoccupations of human ecologists.

TREATMENT OF DEMOGRAPHIC PROBLEMS IN HUMAN ECOLOGY

Manifestly it is impossible to review here the whole corpus of demography in its relations with human ecology. The purpose of this section is, rather, to suggest that human ecology provides a distinctive and perhaps useful approach to or framework for the study of a wide variety of demographic matters.

Population Distribution

Abstracting two factors from the "ecological complex" (Figure 10), population and environment, and considering each of these factors in its simplest aspect—numbers and space—one is led directly into the study of population distribution. This subject, unfortunately, has been cultivated only sporadically, unsystematically, and impressionistically by the several specialties presumably most competent to deal with it: demography, human ecology, human geography, and location economics. A recent review of methodological problems of population distribution (Duncan, 1957) indicates that some of the most elementary questions of the measurement and description of population distribution patterns are in need of further clarification.

Investigators in this field have at their disposal a variety of techniques: measures of density, concentration, spacing, and potential of population; and frequency distributions of population by rural-urban or metropolitan-nonmetropolitan residence, by size of community, or by categories of a considerable number of classificatory schemes of areas. Unfortunately, the systematic use of each of these techniques has often been confined to single studies of particular countries or regions. Consequently, the growth of genuine comparative knowledge of population distribution has been slow. All too often, the discussion of distribution has been confined to the statement of impressionistic conclusions drawn from inspection of distribution maps. Maps, valuable as they are and highly esteemed as they may be by the geographer, are relatively unreliable tools. It is most difficult to tell by examining a series of maps, say, whether population is more "concentrated" in one region than in another, or at one time than at another. In fact, the very concept of "concentration" requires careful mathematical specification before a conclusion of this kind has any real meaning, let alone satisfactory reliability. This example of the measurement of concentration is aptly chosen, for this is one subject on which intensive methodological work has been done (Wright, 1937). Wright's analysis reveals unsuspected complexities in a problem which seems intuitively simple.

Methodological difficulties aside, it is obvious in a gross sense that the distribution of population is quite uneven over the earth's surface. This observation, of course, is what gives rise to the scientific problem of population distribution: to describe the pattern of unevenness, to measure variation in the degree of unevenness at different times and places, to explain the patterns and variations, and to discover their consequences for population dynamics and ecological organization. The human ecologist has been particularly concerned to note certain regularities in patterns of population distribution, to investigate functional correlates of distribution, and to develop the study of distribution in such a way as to provide indicators of ecological organization.

A striking empirical regularity which has captured considerable attention (largely from persons other than professional demographers) is the highly skewed frequency distribution of cities and towns by size. Practically all sizable countries with any appreciable degree of urbanization exhibit this pattern. For a number of such countries, as of recent dates, it is possible to make a rough, but for some purposes acceptable, approximation to the cumulative frequency distribution of communities by size with a simple logarithmic relationship, the so-called Pareto curve. Let $x =$ the size of city or town (number of inhabitants) and $y = y(x) =$ number of cities and towns of size x or greater; then the equation in question is $\log y = \log A - a \log x$, or $y = Ax^{-a}$, where A and a are constants estimated from the data. Some writers have emphasized the tendency of the parameter a to approximate unity, whereas others have emphasized temporal and national variations in a, interpreting it as a coefficient of concentration, urbanization, or metropolitanization. A recent review by Allen (1954) indicates that for a considerable number of countries this curve gives a moderately close fit to the size-of-place distribution. Several of the exceptions are "explained away" on the basis of the small size of the country or the lack of suitable data. There is some reason to think that an acceptable fit is more likely to be obtained if the data are tabulated on the basis of natural agglomerations or conurbations (cf. the U.S. census concept of "urbanized area") rather than by arbitrary political units.

Whereas writers with a background in economics have often expressed this regularity in the form given above, several others (notably Zipf, 1949) have tried to popularize the so-called "rank-size" rule, which in its generalized form merely reverses the axes of the graph and requires one to regard x as a function of y, a practice that has little justification in statistical theory. One unfortunate consequence of the "rank-size" formulation has been to focus attention on the fit of the curve at the very upper end of the size distribution. Thus critics of the "rank-size" rule are prone to point to countries where the largest city is either much too large or much too small for its size to be accurately estimated from the equation. Such discrepancies may have substantive significance; for example, they may furnish one criterion for the identification of "overgrown" or "primate" cities. But this is only one aspect of a size-of-place distribution, and an acceptable fit of the curve to a major portion of the distribution is surely not without interest, irrespective of the large deviation of a major city from the curve. Such a city may have unique, extraterritorial functions extending beyond the economy in which it is nominally located.

As a purely empirical proposition, the fact that many size-of-place distributions can be approximated by a Pareto curve is perhaps more of a curiosity than a scientific finding. However, what little theory there is on the relationship of community size to community function assigns some plausible significance to this form of distribution. Lösch (1954), Vining (1955), and Hoover (1955), among others, have discerned a connection between the size distribution and a theoretical hierarchy of functions ranging from the comparatively ubiquitous service functions of local trade and market centers up to the highly specialized functions of regional centers. It would be too much to say that this line of reasoning has produced a rigorous model that accounts for the Pareto distribution; for this reason the connection between size distribution and functional hierarchy was described as merely "plausible." Yet the recognition of this connection is probably one of the most promising leads to an empirically based theory of population distribution.

In pursuing research on this problem, we will have to give greater attention to the determination of the minimum size limit below which the Pareto relationship fails to hold. It is easy to show mathematically that there must be such a limit, but in many series of data it cannot be identified for lack of information on the number and size of smaller places or for lack of comparability between this information and that available for large places. It seems probable that, in some obscure way, this limit is related to the phenomenon of nucleation. One might hypothesize, for example, that the Pareto law will hold for all communities large enough to have a "complete" array of the relatively ubiquitous functions, but this is mere speculation at the present stage of research.

A remarkable extension of the work on community size distributions is Stewart's (1947) set of equations describing the "fundamental structure" of the United States population, 1790–1940. Stewart observed that the "rank-size" rule held approximately at each of the sixteen census dates during this period. He then fit an equation relating the proportion of the population classified as urban (i.e., living in places of 2,500 inhabitants or more) to the number of urban places. From these two relationships and the size of the total population at each census, it was possible to calculate the size of the largest city, the size of the urban population, and the size of the rural population. This system of equations may be written as follows:

$$M = 2,500C \tag{1}$$

$$U = 0.009782C^{1/2} \tag{2}$$

$$P_u = 2,500C \left(\log_e C + \frac{1}{2C} + 0.577\right) \tag{3}$$

$$P_t = P_u / U \tag{4}$$

$$P_r = P_t - P_u, \tag{5}$$

where M is a constant ($=$ size of largest city as calculated from the rank-size equation), C is the number of places of 2,500 inhabitants or more, U is the proportion of the population living in such places, and P_t, P_u, and P_r are the total, urban, and rural populations, respectively. Equations (1) and (2) are the two empirical relationships, the first the "rank-size" rule and the second the equation relating the urban proportion to the number of cities. The expression in parentheses in equation (3) is a mathematical approximation to the series $(1 + 1/2 + 1/3 + \ldots + 1/C)$. Equations (4) and (5) are identities that follow from the definition of the "rural" population as the total of inhabitants living outside places of 2,500 or more. It is clear that, given observed values of, say, C and P_t, it is possible to calculate the remaining parameters of the system. Comparisons of the computed with the observed values of the latter indicate a moderately good fit for most of the sixteen census years. Note that time does not enter explicitly into these equations although, of course, the several variables could vary only over time. It would be possible to introduce time into the system by, say, establishing a time trend for total population growth, such as the logistic curve.

Stewart presents this work as a strictly empirical result for which no theoretical justification is yet available. Yet his equations have value, if for no other reason, because they conform with the way in which the process of urbanization has been described conceptually. For example, Eldridge writes: "Urbanization is a process of population concentration. It proceeds in two ways: the multiplication of points of concentration and the increase in size of individual concentrations" (Eldridge, 1942). Urbanization also involves an increase in the proportion of population living in cities. All these changes are described in highly compressed form in Stewart's five equations, which make it clear that coupling these elements of change is not arbitrary but empirically necessary. Whether any significance is to be attached to the particular form of the equations is another matter. Equation (2), for example, when extrapolated, predicts U very poorly for 1950. This suggests, though it hardly demonstrates, that the parabola is not a suitable curve for expressing the relationship between U and C. On the other hand, the equations yield the gross prediction that the United States has entered a phase in which the rural population will undergo absolute as well as relative decline—a result in conformity with observations to date and consonant with our knowledge of technological trends. On balance, one concludes that Stewart's work merits closer examination, refinement, and extension by human ecologists.

Another aspect of population distribution, the spatial pattern of towns and cities, has been given more theoretical than empirical attention. As was mentioned earlier, long before the notion of "human ecology" was proposed, the sociologist Cooley (who was trained as an economist) proposed a discipline of "territorial demography." Its problem would be to investigate "the forces and laws that determine the territorial distribution of persons and wealth." As Cooley indicated, "Little is understood concerning the theory of settlement, the theory of the location of towns and cities, or the laws that determine their size, the density of their population and their internal structure" (Cooley, 1894). Cooley's own contribution to the problem of community location was summed up in his famous aphorism, "Population and wealth tend to collect wherever there is a break in transportation." To this description of locational forces, Harris and Ullman (1945) added the factors accounting for the location of cities whose primary function is to provide central services and the localizing effects of certain kinds of natural resources, resulting in various types of specialized-function cities. Their scheme posits a general correlation between three broad types of function and certain typical locational patterns: the location at ports and transportation junctions of commercial cities where break-of-bulk services are rendered, the more or less uniform spacing of central-place cities, and the response of specialized-function cities to geographic factors. Since most cities combine varying proportions of each of these three functions, it is too much to expect that a simple three-category scheme can be directly applied in empirical work with definitive results. Nonetheless, there is abundant unsystematic evidence illustrating the plausibility of this account of urban locational patterns. Careful empirical work perhaps could develop models of the spatial distribution of cities based on these factors which would have considerable explanatory value or predictive validity (in the statistical sense).

The notion of uniform spacing of central places has been developed in quite elaborate fashion by Christaller, whose work is summarized by Dickinson (1947) and Vining (1955). Lösch (1954) presents some fragmentary evidence of a tendency toward uniform spacing of towns and cities in regions where other locational factors are presumed to be minimal. His evidence suffers from the lack of a rigorous criterion of empirical conformity to the hypothesis. It is possible that further investigation of this kind will be stimulated by the plant ecologists' development (see Clark and Evans, 1954) of methods of measuring spacing and of determining the significance of observed departures from a random pattern of spacing. The writer, working informally with crude data, has found that in the state of Iowa and in the northern two-thirds of Indiana there is a statistically significant tendency for towns and cities to be more uniformly spaced than a random pattern would be. With the statistical tools provided by Clark and Evans, it is now practicable to compare regions in this respect, identifying those which exhibit a tendency toward uniform spacing of settlements and those in which towns and cities tend to be aggregated or clumped to a greater than chance extent. The theoretical background and methodological development appear to set the stage for intensive empirical work on this subject.

A third important topic in the analysis of distribution patterns is the study of density gradients with reference to central points. Clark (1951) suggested that in a number of large cities the relation of population density to mile distance from the city center could be summarized by the equation $y = Ae^{-bx}$, in which y is density of residential population in thousands per square mile, x is distance in miles from the center of the city, e is the base of natural logarithms, and A and b are empirical parameters, estimated from the data, which vary from city to city and over time. This relation would be valid, of course, only outside the central business district, which is predominantly non-residential; presumably the fit of the data to the curve is improved if in computing densities for the remaining zones large tracts of non-residential land (parks, vacant areas, industrial areas, and the like) are eliminated. Clark also gives evidence that the time changes in the parameters A and b are in the direction anticipated on the basis of a knowledge of developments in the technology of local transportation. For example, he gives as values for A and b, respectively, in Chicago, 110 and 0.45 in 1900 and 120 and 0.30 in 1940. Thus the density gradient was less steep in the latter year.

Density gradients in the zone immediately surrounding metropolitan centers, extending to some forty-five miles from their centers, are presented by Hawley (1956). These show a more or less regular decline with increasing distance by five-mile intervals, although the gradients do not seem to follow closely a curve of the form proposed by Clark for intra-urban densities. The density gradient is much steeper for large metropolitan centers than for small ones.

Finally, the density pattern of the entire United States has been shown by Bogue (1949) to be clearly related to distance from principal metropolitan centers. Each county in the country was classified by its distance to the nearest of sixty-seven major centers, and densities were computed from the aggregate population and aggregate land area falling in successive class intervals of distance. Over the range of approximately 15 to 500 miles of distance from a metropolis, Bogue's data suggest an approximately linear relationship between the logarithms of density and of distance. However, it is well not to exaggerate the importance of the seeming linearity of the relationship, first, because of the crude distance measurement and, second, because of the use of open-end intervals at both ends of the distance scale. Perhaps of equal importance is Bogue's demonstration that the height and slope of the density gradient, at any given distance, are modified by the proximity of minor urban centers, intermetropolitan highways, and variations in size of the nearest metropolis.

The three studies just cited are by no means the only ones that investigate density patterns, but they are outstanding in the breadth of the comparisons presented. Even so, they furnish only a starting point for systematic study, which needs to deal exhaustively with temporal and spatial variations in density patterns and to develop more decisive results on factors apparently determining variations in density. It is unfortunate that this aspect, at least, of the study of Cooley's "territorial demography" had to wait for half a century before reliable comparative studies began to accumulate.

The human ecologist is interested in population distribution not only for its own sake, or solely as a dependent variable. He wishes also to discover the consequences of variations in patterns of distribution for ecological organization. The typical pattern of inquiry here, then, is to take one or another aspect of ecological organization as a dependent variable and examine its relationship to various measures of population distribution as independent variables. This kind of study reinforces the need for powerful techniques of describing or measuring distribution, since it requires that data on population distribution be expressed in summary form to be manipulated analytically. The identification of certain variables in a set as "dependent" and others as "independent" for purposes of analysis does not guarantee that a "causal" connection will be established; usually the functional relationship is much more complex than is suggested by this simple analytical model.

Perhaps the topic of greatest interest under this heading is the study of the causes and consequences of urbanization. Much of the discussion in this field is worthless because "urbanization" is accepted as a slogan rather than being carefully defined in operational terms. A capital example is the catch phrase "urbanism as a way of life," coined by Louis Wirth (1938). Many writers have seized upon the notion of a "way of life" without noting that Wirth's principal contribution was to dissect "urbanism" into its elements —which he identified as size, density, and heterogeneity of population—and to investigate how these elementary variables are related to other aspects of community life. Consistent with this effort to reduce the notions of urbanism and urbanization to their most general and indispensable elements is Eldridge's definition quoted earlier, "a process of population concentration. . . ." Eldridge (1942) ably defends the "strictness and simplicity" of her definition, notes the confusion that results if certain apparent correlates of urbanization are incorporated in its definition, and sketches a broad framework within which one can investigate the demographic and technological determinants of urbanization as well as its social consequences. The worst fault of theories of urbanization employing definitions that violate the criterion of "strictness and simplicity" is that they conceal empirical hypotheses within the definitions. Thus one is led to expect certain universal concomitants of urbanization, and these expectations may be quite unrealistic, as is evident from the preliminary results of studies of urbanization in non-Western countries. The indicated strategy for the comparative study of urbanization, then, is to define the phenomenon closely and to test hypotheses about its concomitants in systematic studies of longitudinal and cross-sectional data.

Current investigations under the direction of Davis illustrate the comparative approach to the study of urbanization on a world basis. Besides compiling basic information on the growth and distribution of cities and urban population in the world—thus, in a sense, bringing up to date A. F. Weber's (1899) classic study—this project is studying interrelations among certain basic correlates of urbanization. For example, Davis and Golden (1954) report a correlation of $-.86$ between the percentage of the male labor force engaged in agriculture (X) and the percentage of the population living in cities of 100,000 or more (Y), taking the countries and territories of the world as units. Their figures indicate that the regression equation relating these two variables on a country-by-country basis is approximately $Y = 38.7 - 0.44 X$. This relationship, incidentally, is remarkably close to the one that would be obtained by correlating Y and X for successive census dates for the United States, 1820–1950, although the United States was probably less urbanized (on this particular criterion) over most of this period than would be anticipated from Davis and Golden's relationship. Here, then, is a problem for which illuminating results should be obtained from comparing cross-sectional and longitudinal relationships. Moreover, with such relationships established, one has a norm for identifying regions that are "over-urbanized" or "under-urbanized"; Davis and Golden present some interesting speculations on the consequences of these conditions for economic development. There are grounds for hope that the methodology sketched in this illustration may put to crucial test a number of the current plausible hypotheses concerning determinants and consequences of urbanization.

Another promising approach to the study of correlates of population distribution arises from the concept of population potential, set forth by Stewart (1947). Taking any specified point in a given universe of territory, population potential at that point is defined as the sum of the reciprocals of the distances of each inhabitant of the territory from that point. In practice, of course, the computations are made for areal units rather than for individuals; consequently, potential at a point may be defined as $\Sigma(P_i/D_i)$, where D_i is the distance of the center of the *i*th areal unit from the designated point, P_i is the population of that unit, and the summation is over all units. Having computed potential at a suitable number of selected points, one can interpolate values for other points. It is usual to present the results of such computations in the form of a map showing isopotential lines; the configuration of these lines suggests the location of areas of maximum demographic "influence," on the supposition that "influence" is directly proportional to numbers of people and inversely proportional to distance. Stewart (1948) presents evidence of a number of relationships between potential and other demographic and economic variables. To illustrate some of the results that may be obtained employing potential as an independent variable in studies of ecological organization: for a sample of 100 non-metropolitan state economic areas in the United States in 1950, population potential correlated .35 with per cent of farm land in crop land, .39 with value of farm products sold per acre of farm land, and .54 with density of rural farm population per 1,000 acres of land in farms (from a current study by Beverly Duncan, under the writer's direction). These results suggest that the total pattern of population distribution is one deter-

minant of the intensity of agricultural activity; thus they support a hypothesis held by land economists since the time of Von Thünen but also suggest a means of releasing this hypothesis from the prison of pure theory and permitting it to be verified. Inasmuch as the pattern of potential values over a territory is primarily determined by the configuration of major centers of population, the potential measure also suggests itself as an alternative approach to the study of metropolitan dominance or concomitants of urbanization.

This affords an opportunity to bring out a methodological point of some significance. A substantial positive relationship is observed between potential of population and agricultural density within the United States. However, Davis and Golden (1954) report an inverse relationship between urbanization and agricultural density on a country-by-country basis; they found that in countries with less than 10 per cent of the inhabitants residing in cities of 100,000 or more, the average number of agricultural males per square mile of agricultural land was 136, as compared with 13 in countries with 30 per cent or more of the population in these large cities. There is, of course, no logical contradiction between the two findings. Rather, they pose what might be termed a "fruitful paradox," for it becomes a matter of some interest to work out a reconciliation of the apparently discrepant results. Without entering into a discussion of the matter here, one can simply say that the illustration points out the necessity of regarding "urbanization" and "population distribution" as complex notions requiring careful analysis and operational specification. Their study has already advanced to the point where loose hypotheses about global relationships are rapidly ceasing to have much heuristic value and must be replaced by sophisticated research designs employing multivariate analysis.

As was suggested earlier, human ecologists employ data on population distribution in a variety of studies where the data serve as indicators of aspects of ecological organization. For example, Bogue (1949) interpreted density gradients as indexes of metropolitan dominance, in effect providing an indirect measurement of a concept hitherto prominent primarily in the theoretical and speculative ecological literature. Students recently have been concerned with comparing spatial distributions of two or more population groups; a summary of this literature on measurement of "ecological segregation" is given by Duncan and Duncan (1955b), who indicate the dangers in *ad hoc* construction of index numbers without careful consideration of the rationale for such indexes. Among the substantive results obtained from this approach to population distribution is the demonstration that the pattern of spatial separation of occupation groups closely parallels the socioeconomic differentiation of these groups (Duncan and Duncan, 1955a; Wilkins, 1956), confirming Park's insight that "physical distances so frequently are, or seem to be, the indexes of social distance" (in Burgess, 1926, p. 18).

Distribution data are used in yet another way in studies employing what is sometimes inappropriately called the "ecological method." A demographic example is the study of differential fertility among socioeconomic groups, where these groups are established by aggregating data for inhabitants of small areas having similar average socioeconomic levels (e.g., Kitagawa, 1953). In effect, an individual or a family is classified by, say, the average income of the neighborhood in which he lives; and, since neighborhoods are by no means perfectly homogeneous in income, considerable numbers of individuals may be classified differently from the way they would be on the basis of their own incomes. Viewed in one way, areal classification may be regarded simply as a crude approximation to the presumably preferable individual basis. It would then be justified primarily on the grounds that individual data are unavailable in many instances where useful indications of differentials may be obtained from the areal data. Investigators must be cautious, however, in making inferences about individual characteristics from areal data (Robinson, 1950), although limited inferences of this kind can sometimes be justified mathematically (Goodman, 1953; Duncan and Davis, 1953). Looked at in another way, areal differentials are significant in their own right. There is even some sociological basis for supposing that such differentials may reflect factors influencing demographic phenomena that would not come to light in studying individual characteristics solely. This supposition should be tested by investigators in this field in order to resolve some of the issues concerning so-called "ecological correlations" (Robinson, 1950).

The example just given is but one of an indefinitely large class of problems in which areal variation in demographic phenomena is the object of study, either by itself or in conjunction with other analyses. The areal approach, in fact, is applicable to almost any aspect of population composition and dynamics. Here, then, the study of population distribution begins to merge with general demography, as is brought out by Bogue (chap. xvii) in this symposium.

Population Composition

The principal interests of the human ecologist in the study of population composition are the exploitation of data on composition as indicators of ecological organization and the study of the impact of variations in composition on ecological organization. Several illustrations of these interests are given in Hawley's chapter (xvi) on population composition in this volume.

Of primary concern to the human ecologist are data describing the division of labor and allocation of population among the various sustenance activities. It is probably true, as Hauser (1951) states, that human ecologists have given insufficient attention to the ecological analysis of the labor force. However, one important problem that calls for the use of these data—the functional classification of communities—has been the subject of considerable study. Beginning with Ogburn (1937) and Harris (1943), there has been a succession of studies proposing operational criteria for distinguishing among major functional types of cities. Although these classifications vary in details, they exhibit certain convergences in broad outline. It is generally conceded that fairly clear distinctions can be made among manufacturing cities, trade cities, and centers highly specialized in such functions as transportation services, higher education, recreational services, and government. Subcategories of these classes may also be recognized, as well as additional classes of specialization occurring less frequently. Recent studies in this field have recognized that the problem of functional classification is closely related to that of measuring the "economic base" of the urban community; for most significant results the two problems should be handled together. Of interest to the demographer is the demonstration that several aspects of population composition tend to vary systematically with type of functional specialization (Duncan and Reiss, 1956).

Population composition data also indicate degrees and rates of assimilation of groups of in-migrants to cities. The general assumption of such studies is that similarity and convergence in demographic characteristics as between new and old residents of a community indicate, respectively, a high level of or substantial progress in assimilation. Aside from such an obvious indicator as mother tongue, characteristics like occupation, family size and composition, age and sex distribution, home ownership, and educational attainment are relevant. When combined with evidence of decreasing spatial segregation or diminishing differentiation between residential patterns of old and new residents (Cressey, 1938), "favorable" changes in such characteristics are strong presumptive evidence that assimilation would be revealed by measures of social interaction or social participation.

Spatial gradients in indexes of population composition, as well as in population density, are used by the ecologist to test hypotheses about the territorial organization of communities and regions. For example, comparisons of the nominally rural population living in the vicinity of large urban centers with those of the more remote rural population indicate the extent to which "suburbanization" or "fringe development" extends beyond the recognized limits of urban settlement (Duncan and Reiss, 1956). Usually studies of this phenomenon analyze changes in average levels of selected indexes of composition, but an ingenious study by Kish (1954) indicates that the variability of composition indexes is inversely related to distance. Thus suburbs close to the central city differ from each other to a greater degree than do satellite towns farther away.

Many other illustrations of the human ecologist's attention to population composition could be given. Like other social scientists, he uses composition data to study social differentiation and social stratification (Duncan and Duncan, 1955a). He may investigate the impact of certain aspects of composition on the functioning of certain units of community structure (Hawley, 1941). There is a long-standing interest in studying the differentiation of residential areas within the metropolitan community. In a recent study, for example, Sheldon (1954) demonstrated a neat correlation between the age of suburbs and the age composition of their populations. Striking variations in the population pyramid among various parts of the city were noted by Booth in the 1890's (see Pfautz, 1947), and were re-examined in this country when census-tract data became available (Park, 1929; McKenzie, 1933). Perhaps the distinctive thing about the ecologist's treatment of such variations in population composition is his effort to relate them to processes shaping the structure of the community. Therefore, ecological thinking is a rich source of hypotheses for the demographic study of population composition.

Population Growth

Given a strong interest in the structure of the community, the human ecologist has a distinctive slant on the problem of population growth. He is interested not merely in the increase (or decrease) in the size of a specified aggregate but also in the concomitant processes of community expansion and reorganization. Growth data undoubtedly provide the most accessible indication of expansion over extended periods of time and under careful scrutiny can be used to develop important inferences about the nature of changes in community structure. Consequently, human ecologists have produced a considerable literature analyzing changes in size of communities and their correlates (e.g., Bogue, 1953; Hawley, 1956). Some of the older literature (cf. Hollingshead, 1939) recognized "ag-

gregation" as one of the basic ecological processes, but this concept has not been emphasized in much empirical work. One of the most influential schemes in ecological research, the system of urban "zones" developed by Burgess (1925), derived from a consideration of urban growth and expansion. Despite the title of Burgess' paper, "The Growth of the City," many writers have treated this conception as a static typology rather than as an attempt to specify the concomitants and consequences of a growth process.

The supposition that growth and expansion entail structural changes in the community is made plausible by a consideration of the principle of non-proportional change (Boulding, 1953b). For example, if a circular city expands uniformly, its radius will increase as the square root of its area. The fact that accessibility is essentially a function of linear distance, therefore, makes it possible for cities to increase to large population sizes and still maintain the accessibility of various parts to the center (Weber, 1899, p. 471). However, at an early stage of expansion the community can no longer function efficiently with but a single nucleus, and subcenters tend to arise, usurping certain of the functions of the original nucleus.

By another line of argument one arrives at a conception of the relationships among growth, expansion, and structural change. There is systematic evidence of structural differentiation of communities according to size (e.g., Duncan, 1951). Since variations in size are produced by variations in timing and/or rate of growth, present structural differentiation may be regarded as a product of past growth. However, there is need for research to examine the connection of growth and structure longitudinally; cross-sectional relationships between size and structure permit only rather tenuous inferences about the order in which structural changes occur.

Population growth and community expansion are readily observed to produce a "succession" of land uses in the community area. The best documented descriptions of the process of succession pertain to cities that grew rapidly from small towns during the nineteenth and twentieth centuries in the context of of major developments in the technology of transportation and production. Under these conditions it is believed that the major impulse to succession is the radial expansion of the city from its center outward; functions localized at the community center then tend to encroach upon those in adjacent areas; these, in turn, must move in upon those at some distance from the center (Burgess, 1925). While the pressure to expand occasioned by population growth may be more or less steady and continuous, adjustments to this pressure tend to be sporadic and discontinuous, owing to the inertia of established land uses. The complex distribution of time lags in adjustments to expansion is commonly supposed to be the source of many community problems, notably the formation of slums and blighted areas. The picture is complicated when—as was the case with most American cities—population growth and expansion are accompanied by changes in ethnic composition. Two forces then come into opposition, the tendency of the area occupied by a given ethnic group to expand to accommodate increasing numbers and the resistance to that expansion by other groups. Where the latter force is strong enough, there may even occur a distortion of the typical pattern of radial expansion of the community as a whole. Associated with recent rapid increases in Negro population in certain cities are reversals in the trend of growth rates in the central portions of those cities (Redick, 1956;

Duncan and Duncan, 1956). One of the more obvious aspects of urban expansion and consequent succession, the change of land from agricultural to urban use, has, curiously enough, received little direct study (see, however, Bogue, 1956). However, problems of land use and residential adjustment in "fringe" areas undergoing this transition have attracted a good deal of attention in the last two decades (Firey, 1946; Blizzard and Anderson, 1952).

The foregoing paragraphs no more than sketch the basis of the ecologist's interest in growth, but they make it evident that his preoccupation with problems of community structure leads him to state a number of hypotheses about growth that would not emerge from a narrowly demographic concern with the subject. To conclude the discussion, a few examples of concrete research may be cited.

One of the most active fields of current interest is the study of population redistribution within and among metropolitan areas (see summaries and discussion by Reiss, 1956; Shryock, 1956). On the one hand, the question of why some cities grow more rapidly at a given time than others is being investigated with rigorous methods (Bogue and Harris, 1954). As Reiss (1956) indicates, there is no clear-cut relationship between degree of industrialization and current rate of growth; many of the more rapidly growing communities are those specialized in so-called tertiary industries. The well-known association of industrial and urban growth in the past contrasts with the comparatively static sizes of present-day manufacturing centers; this suggests a secular change in the bases of urban growth which needs intensive study. Comparative study of correlates of growth designed to elucidate "causes" of differential growth rates has thus far neglected one theoretically important aspect of the problem. Modern communities are not independent entities but are implicated in widely ramifying networks of intercommunity relationships. Hence, growth at one point in a system of cities cannot be without consequences for growth and reorganization at other points. There is, then, a need for research designs that attack the problem of differential growth, taking account of evidence like that of Madden (1956) that a system of cities exhibits significant stabilities in its pattern of growth rates.

The other focus of current interest in metropolitan population redistribution is what is popularly known as the "suburban trend." Extensive attempts to measure the trend and efforts to isolate its determinants are prominent in the literature (Bogue, 1950c; Gross, 1954; Hawley, 1956). This is a field of research with more than ordinary difficulties of conceptualization and measurement. All too often researchers (not particularly the ones just cited) have naïvely accepted findings of differential growth rates between central and peripheral portions of urban communities as evidence of a specific process of "suburbanization" or "decentralization," without attempting an operational distinction between these alleged processes and the normal tendency for expansion to occur on the periphery of the community area (Duncan, 1956; Schmitt, 1956; Shryock, 1956). One may hazard a guess as to the approach needed to clarify this problem. Comparative studies in considerable longitudinal depth should match a city of a given size at a recent date with one of the same size at a remote date and note whether the recent pattern of growth is a more dispersed or "suburban" one than that occurring at the earlier period. An adequate comparison would require detailed examination of patterns and changes of population

density; Clark's approach (1951) is suggestive in this respect.

Another group of studies on community growth concerns concomitants and consequences of growth. There is a tendency to regard community growth as a normal and desirable state of affairs and to view a decline in growth rates with some alarm. Of course, any theory of growth or superficial observation of growth suggests that high rates cannot be maintained indefinitely (see National Industrial Conference Board, 1953). Comparisons between growing and static communities, therefore, might well be conceptualized as comparisons between different phases of the growth cycle (if such a term may be used without suggesting any specific norm of growth). However, most of the literature to date (e.g., Ogburn, 1937; Hauser, 1940; Roterus, 1946; Duncan and Reiss, 1956) has presented more or less uncontrolled comparisons between attributes of cities which have grown rapidly in a recent period and those of cities growing slowly in the same period. Among the concomitants and effects of growth that can be demonstrated in this fashion, the economic are perhaps most evident. Rapidly growing places in the United States have a considerably larger volume of residential construction than those growing slowly, and there must be other stimuli to economic activity occasioned by growth. An important problem in the comparative study of urbanization is analyzing the contrast in causes and correlates of city growth in highly modernized countries with those in certain of the less-developed regions where rapid growth is likewise taking place (Hauser, 1956a).

The Vital Processes

Like all students of demographic phenomena, the human ecologist deals with the vital processes as components of population growth. But there is little to distinguish the ecologist's interest in this topic from that of other demographers except, perhaps, for a somewhat specialized need for data and estimates on a small-area basis. Symptomatic are the contributions of ecologists to methods of estimating changes in population distribution in postcensal periods (Bogue, 1950a) and the intensive application of residual methods of estimating net migration based on vital statistics or survival rates, even down to the intracommunity level (Duncan and Duncan, 1957). Use of small-area data in studying variation in fertility rates has been mentioned; the same approach is, of course, available for mortality studies (e.g., Mayer and Hauser, 1950; DeWolff and Meerdink, 1952). As was indicated, there is not much that is specifically "ecological" about this method, unless one confuses ecology with any use of areal data.

The distinctively ecological contributions to the study of the vital processes may be grouped under two headings: (1) studies of vital rates as indexes of the adjustment of a population to its environment and investigations of the impact of variations in community structure and function on the vital processes; (2) investigations employing vital rates as indexes of community structure or ecological processes.

A substantial body of literature under the first heading concerns the topic of rural-urban differences in fertility and mortality. The study of "urbanization and fertility" (Jaffe, 1942), for example, has been developed from gross rural-urban comparisons, comparisons by community-size groups, comparisons of highly-urbanized with less-urbanized regions, and examination of spatial gradients in fertility by distance from urban centers. Two widely accepted generalizations emerge from these studies. First, lowered fertility is a typical adaptation to conditions of urban life in a variety of historical and cultural settings. Second, declining regional and national levels of fertility often are led by the population of cities, and cities function as foci for the diffusion of patterns of controlled fertility. These propositions imply, of course, that the magnitude of the rural-urban differential in fertility is not constant, but varies over time and from region to region. Studies of this variation are no doubt of equal or greater importance for future research than further documentation of the occurrence of a differential. Moreover, situations in which the expected fertility concomitants of urbanization fail to appear merit intensive investigation as a basis for refining the foregoing propositions. For example, the suggestion that the maintenance of unexpectedly high levels of urban fertility during the last decade in the United States is associated with the "suburban trend" needs more careful examination than it has yet received.

The ecological study of mortality has been cultivated along somewhat the same lines as that of fertility. Demographers long ago took note of the high death rates in cities and have related improvements in urban mortality to progress in sanitation and public health. The modern city is no longer unequivocally a less salubrious environment than rural territory; meaningful comparisons must take account of variations in the pattern of rural-urban differences by age and cause of death. There is evidence that in some respects the advantages in regard to medical care facilities of large cities outweigh the hazards to health incident upon population concentration. Nonetheless, it probably remains true that the long-run environmental impact of the city is adverse to survival, apart from the hazards of specific occupations that may be peculiar to the city (Duncan, 1951). Unfortunately, it is hard to make meticulous longitudinal studies of mortality in relation to urbanization because of changes in classifications of urban and rural population and difficulties in allocating deaths to the area of residence of the decedent. To an even greater extent than is the case for fertility, statements of relationship between mortality and community structure require strict qualification as to the time and place for which they have been established, and the progress of knowledge depends on the accretion of extensive comparative studies with a maximum of refinement in research design.

Levels of the vital rates, like indexes of population composition, are studied by ecologists for clues to the operation of the processes of assimilation, selection, segregation, and the like. For example, Hauser's (1938) demonstration of a spatial gradient in fertility rates in Chicago conforms with other information on socioeconomic levels and family characteristics. An intriguing aspect of such relationships awaits exploration—the connection of intracommunity residential mobility and the cycle of family formation and dissolution. It is quite likely that increments and decrements to family size engender typical streams of movement within the community which have not yet been measured for lack of the requisite detailed information.

Movement

Along with an interest in "migration," as the term is usually understood in demography, the human ecologist has reason to study movements of population which differ from migration in two characteristics, i.e., in being confined to change of place within a local community area and/or in being routine and repetitive rather than disruptive of a rhythm of activity. Although it is difficult to suggest a terminology without misleading connotations, the rele-

vant distinctions may be conveyed by the following fourfold classification:

	Recurrent	Non-recurrent
Local	(a)	(b)
Extra-local	(c)	(d)

In this scheme what is ordinarily regarded as "migration," whether internal or international, falls in cell (d). Movements of type (c) have been described for some nomadic populations, but, except for studies of traffic volume, they have not been studied much for relatively sedentary populations. Non-recurrent local movements—cell (b)—comprise the frequent and significant changes of residence within the local community. These may be studied from the standpoint of the adjustment of the population to such processes as household formation, social mobility, job changes, and changes in household composition associated with the family cycle; or they may be examined in the context of such processes of community change as residential succession (Duncan and Duncan, 1957). Finally, movements of type (a) have recently been emphasized as an area for demographic-ecological research needed to supplement the traditional interest of demographers in internal and international migration (see Breese, 1949; Foley, 1954; Schnore, 1954).

The special interest of the human ecologist in recurrent and local movements means that conventional sources of demographic data often are of limited usefulness. For example, whereas the United States census gives some information on the volume of "residential mobility," or changes of residence not classifiable as "migration," it gives no information on the direction of such movement. Studies of residential succession, while they involve certain problems formally quite similar to those of selective migration (Cressey, 1938; Gibbard, 1941), usually must depend on rather uncertain inferences from net changes in population composition and distribution instead of data on movements as such. It is significant that one of the most influential contemporary models of internal migration—Stouffer's (1940) theory of intervening opportunities—was worked out with non-census data on intracity changes of residence. Most of the research on commuting and other forms of recurrent local movement has been carried out with little aid from censuses, although certain foreign censuses compile statistics on the journey to work, and there has been considerable interest in introducing their procedures into the United States census.

Migration proper is studied in human ecology as a component of population growth and redistribution, although it is unfortunately not often that gross or even net changes due to migration can be distinguished satisfactorily from the reproductive component of change in population size or distribution. Most of the studies of "suburbanization," for example, have proceeded in the absence of direct measurements or even reliable estimates of the streams of movement between central and outlying portions of metropolitan areas.

Like other students of migration, ecologists have been concerned with two major problems: the "causes" of migration and the spatial patterns of movement. On the first point, Hawley has developed the thesis that an ecological explanation of migration should be based on aspects of the environmental and community context of migration, rather than the analysis of the expressed motives of individual migrants. In simplified summary, his theory is that

. . . migration presupposes a condition of disequilibrium in the form of an excess number of people in one locality, and either incompletely used resources or disequilibrium in the form of too few people in an alternative place of settlement. The effect of migration is to permit a restoration of equilibrium at both the point of origin and the point of destination [Hawley, 1950, p. 332].

A similar statement on migration as an equilibrating process has been presented by Saunders (1943). This theory, though made plausible by a considerable amount of fragmentary evidence, has yet to be specified in operational detail for research purposes, and its systematic verification is an important task for future investigation.

Following Stouffer's (1940) restatement of Ravenstein's (1885 and 1889) hypothesis of intervening opportunities, human ecologists have emphasized the search for simple empirical regularities in patterns of migration capable of summary expression in mathematical form. This search has been attended by moderate success (Anderson, 1955), but other studies have made it clear that more complicated models than those so far developed will be required for a high order of descriptive accuracy (Bogue and Thompson, 1949; Price, 1948).

There seems to have been little effort to bring ecological theory to bear on the problem of selective migration. However, Dorothy Thomas (1938, p. 62) points out the probable relevance of the "socio-economic structure of the sending and receiving communities" for the pattern and intensity of migration selectivity as well as for the volume and direction of migration. Recent work on functional classification of communities should therefore be of interest to students of differential migration.

The problem of the assimilation of in-migrants into the social structure of the receiving community has been of considerable interest to human ecologists as well as to other students of, particularly, urban communities. The theoretical importance of the recruitment of urban populations by migration was indicated by Wirth's (1938) inclusion of "heterogeneity" as a criterion of urbanism. Wirth referred, of course, to functional differentiation of the population by roles in the division of labor, as well as to ethnic heterogeneity produced by the diversified sources of the city's population, but the latter aspect of heterogeneity is the one that has received most attention in discussions of Wirth's formulation.

SELECTED PROBLEMS AND ISSUES

The preceding section sketched some demographic problems that are of theoretical interest from an ecological standpoint and indicated some contributions to their study by ecologists, as well as a number of fruitful problems for further research emerging from an ecological perspective on population. In following the conventional topical outline of demography, certain subjects, especially population distribution, have been emphasized at the expense of others. This differential emphasis reflects, in part, the writer's judgment that both disciplines would profit from a greater allocation of research effort to the topic of distribution. At the same time, it should be clear that the ecologist's interest in population is not confined to spatial analysis in any narrow sense. In this section of the paper attention will be given to two major ecological problems that exhibit some further ramifications of the relationships between human ecology and demography.

The Environment and Regional Analysis

In their authoritative résumé of the field of animal ecology, Allee *et al.* (1949) recognize "analysis of the environment" as one of four major subdivisions of the field and devote no less than fourteen chapters to discussions of specific environmental factors in animal life. One would not find this performance duplicated in a systematic treatise on human ecology. Various reasons for this gap in the literature of human ecology—if it is such—can be suggested. For one thing, the emergence of human ecology as a subfield of sociology occurred at a time when sociologists were busy discovering empirical errors and speculative excesses in the literature of "environmental determinism." They were—perhaps had to be—primarily concerned with establishing the legitimacy of the study of society per se rather than as a mere reflex of organisms in their environmental relations. Thus they were all too willing to "explain away" various correlations discerned between social forms and environmental conditions, finding this task simplified by the relatively crude methods that had been used in establishing such correlations. Moreover, a direct concern with characteristics of the environment appeared to early writers on human ecology as an unwarranted invasion of the field of geography, and it seemed necessary in presenting working formulations of the scope of human ecology to differentiate it clearly from human geography (McKenzie, 1934).

One might suppose, therefore, that the task of providing an ecological "analysis of the environment" would have been accepted by geography, or at any rate by those geographers sympathetic to an ecological approach. Such, indeed, was implied by the program of Barrows (1923) to develop "geography as human ecology" focusing on "relationships existing between natural environments and the distribution and activities of man." Under such an approach, presumably, geographic classifications and descriptions of the environment would be developed in terms of their relevance for the adaptation of human populations to the environment, rather than, say, reflecting only geological or physiographic considerations. It appears, however, that Barrows' suggestion was not accepted by the majority even of human geographers, who, like other students of the discipline, seem to be in reasonable consensus that geography is or should be "the study of the areal differentiation of the earth's surface" (Hartshorne, 1949, p. 130 and *passim*). Human occupancy is generally recognized as a major factor in areal differentiation, but this does not mean, of course, that it is necessarily studied as an ecological problem.

The net situation, then, is that students identifying themselves as human ecologists have failed to study the environment in the systematic, intensive fashion that seems to be required by the very notion of ecology, while specialists in the study of the human environment have not ordered their investigations in terms of ecological considerations. But this is not to say that the chapter on "analysis of the environment" could not be written for lack of knowledge. There are, indeed, both abundant empirical data and pertinent theoretical formulations. The information amassed by human geographers is, of course, raw material for the ecological analysis of the environment. Many particular studies would be found, on inspection, to represent an ecological point of view, if only implicitly. For example, the "functional theory of resources" is formulated by Zimmerman (1951) in a fashion very similar to the outline of the "ecological complex" sketched earlier in this chapter. It is perhaps significant, by the way, that this theory was developed by an economist working in a field usually cultivated by economic geographers and physical scientists. It appears that interdisciplinary approaches to the study of the environment naturally come up with something approximating an ecological statement of the problem; further evidence on this point is

the symposium, *Man's Role in Changing the Face of the Earth* (Thomas, W., 1956), in which many discussions are explicitly referred to as involving "ecological" considerations. Moreover, the recent investigations of "ecological" problems by anthropologists are motivated by a reawakening interest in the environment and its influence on forms of social organization.

Realizing that a systematic treatment of the environment is one of the neglected chapters of the discipline, human ecologists with a sociological background have begun to approach the problem somewhat obliquely, working with the concept of "region." Sociology, of course, has entertained an active school of "regionalism" for a long time. Until recently, however, there seemed to be little interest in bringing about a rapprochement between the "regionalists" and the "ecologists." What distinguishes the current ecological interest in regions from the "regionalism" of a decade or two ago is the attempt to fashion regions as a tool for investigating ecological relationships. Increasing interest in problems of ecological organization at the supracommunity level also has been congenial to the attempt to refurbish regional methodology. Whereas the older "regionalism" was as likely as not to be motivated by a concern with "folk culture" and to lead to mere appreciation of regional distinctiveness rather than to systematic research, the contemporary tendency is to approach regional analysis primarily as a methodological problem. The reification of the "region" and the somewhat unproductive empiricism of many regional studies are dangers that now are clearly recognized.

The leading spokesman for the incorporation of regional analysis into human ecology, Bogue (1950*b*, 1955), has indicated that the study of the environment comprises two major steps: first, the subdivision of the total environment into a set of internally homogeneous subareas for each of which observations of environmental conditions, demographic phenomena, and organizational traits are available; second, the formal test of hypotheses concerning environmental relationships employing procedures of multivariate analysis, analysis of variance and co-variance, and the like (Hagood and Eaton, 1939). The details of this ap-proach, expounded with special ref-erence to demographic problems, are set forth in Bogue's contribution to this symposium and need not be elaborated here. However, it is well to call atten-tion to some issues and problems aris-ing from this approach which are in need of further study.

The "internally homogeneous sub-areas" developed for this approach to environmental analysis are the State Economic Areas (SEA's) adopted by the United States Bureau of the Cen-sus for the 1950 census (Bogue, 1950*b;* U.S. Bureau of the Census, 1951). These units are combinations of counties de-vised after examination of a variety of socioeconomic indexes, comparison of tentative areas with other similar de-limitations, and consultation with ex-perts in the several states. An inspec-tion of the list of statistical indexes em-ployed in the SEA delimitation makes it clear that environmental criteria were included only in an indirect manner. If the SEA's were designed specifically for use in testing hypotheses about en-vironmental relationships, one might expect that factors like climate, topog-raphy, proximity to navigable waters, mineral deposits, and soil fertility would be the bases of delimiting the areas. Instead, attention was given to industrial composition of the labor force, land use, levels of living, rates of population growth, and economic char-acteristics of agriculture, with the heaviest emphasis falling on the last. No doubt each of these items in one

way or another reflects environmental conditions, but only as the latter are mediated and modified by technology and organization. Consequently, there is a circular element in the proposal to use SEA's to test environmental in-fluences when it is the indexes of the influences rather than measures of the environment itself which have been used to identify areas of homogeneity. This point should perhaps not be over-emphasized, since the description of procedures for delimiting SEA's indi-cates that informal attention was given to climate and physiography. How-ever, it is quite explicit in this descrip-tion that the SEA's were delimited pri-marily on the basis of the "economy" of the areas rather than strictly in terms of environmental features.

It is, of course, recognized that the "homogeneity" of units like SEA's is only a relative homogeneity. Inevitably, there is variation within them as well as differentiation among them. It is well, however, to gain some quantita-tive feeling for the relative importance of these two sources of areal variation. Table 61 presents some illustrative in-formation. A systematic sample of some 200 counties was drawn. For each county in the sample a list was made of all counties contiguous to it, and one of these contiguous counties was selected at random, using a scheme of random numbers. Each pair of counties selected in this manner was classified as to whether the two counties fell in the same or in different SEA's. Indexes of five characteristics of the counties were taken from census reports, and the intraclass correlation was computed as a measure of the similarity of ad-joining counties in respect to these characteristics, as compared with coun-ties paired wholly at random.

The salient feature of the results summarized in Table 61 is that con-tiguous counties manifest a considera-ble degree of homogeneity, irrespective of whether they fall in the same or in different SEA's. For the four indexes pertaining to cross-sectional characteristics, the intraclass correlations run around .8 for the entire sample. In each case the homogeneity is somewhat greater for counties in the same SEA than for counties in different SEA's; correlations for the first group are .8–.9, as compared with .6–.7 for

implications. First, any grouping of contiguous areal units (like counties) is likely to produce "regions" with a comparatively high degree of homogeneity in certain characteristics. This is true because variation from place to place is relatively continuous and gradual for many characteristics; such gradation produces a general "space correlation" which will be reflected in the

TABLE 61

INTRACLASS CORRELATIONS BETWEEN PAIRS OF COUNTIES IN SAME AND DIFFERENT STATE ECONOMIC AREAS, FOR SELECTED VARIABLES: 1950

VARIABLE AND AREA	COUNTIES IN SAME SEA		COUNTIES IN DIFFERENT SEA		ALL COUNTIES	
	Number of Pairs*	Correlation	Number of Pairs*	Correlation	Number of Pairs*	Correlation
Per cent of land in farms:						
United States†	117	.79	88	.68	205	.75
North central	42	.88	28	.66	70	.80
South	53	.75	41	.57	94	.68
Per cent of farms tenant-operated:						
United States†	117	.85	88	.71	205	.80
North central	42	.88	28	.76	70	.84
South	53	.82	41	.65	94	.74
Median gross monthly rent, non-farm dwelling units:						
United States†	111	.78	84	.62	195	.71
North central	39	.60	28	.28	67	.50
South	51	.66	38	.48	89	.57
Per cent of families with 1949 incomes under $2,000:						
United States†	112	.83	85	.71	197	.78
North central	41	.73	28	.56	69	.64
South	50	.77	39	.49	89	.67
Per cent increase in population, 1940–50:						
United States†	117	.32	88	.44	205	.36
North central	42	.51	28	.59	70	.54
South	53	.34	41	.43	94	.38

* Number varies because census data are not shown for certain counties with small frequencies.
† Includes counties in northeast and west, not numerous enough to show separately.

the second. This difference holds up if counties in the North Central States or in the South are examined separately. The fifth characteristic in the table pertains to change over time, i.e., the per cent increase in population between 1940 and 1950. Here the findings are somewhat different. These intraclass correlations are much lower than those for the static characteristics. Moreover, the higher correlations are observed for counties in different SEA's.

These results—which are, of course, only suggestive—have some important

relative homogeneity of composite areal units, whether these are created by arbitrary grouping or by careful study of the spatial pattern of statistical indexes. Second, the degree of homogeneity will vary from characteristic to characteristic and, in particular, may differ as between static characteristics and measures of change. The finding that counties in different SEA's were more homogeneous in terms of a measure of growth than counties in the same SEA is somewhat disconcerting if one accepts a viewpoint like that of

Hoover and Fisher (1948, p. 4): "The use of any concept of an economic region is justified by the hypothesis that a region grows or decays as an entity, rather than having its changes in income represent merely the random sum of independent experience in individual types of economic activity which happen to be located there." Third, the fact that there is considerable similarity between counties in different SEA's means that adjacent SEA's tend to be similar. Or, in other words, indexes of SEA characteristics are not statistically independent. This circumstance seriously compromises the use of techniques, such as multiple regression or analysis of covariance, that assume independence. In general, the number of degrees of freedom involved in these statistics is much smaller than the number of areal units employed in their computation. However, to the writer's knowledge, there is no statistical theory available to indicate the extent of the loss of degrees of freedom. The problem is analogous to that of serial correlation in time series.

The proposed method of establishing environmental relationships raises the issue of "ecological correlation," albeit in a somewhat different form from that already discussed in the literature (Robinson, 1950; Goodman, 1953). Suppose that an investigator is concerned with an environmental variable, X, and a demographic index or ecological attribute, Y. If data are available for two orders of areal unit, say counties and SEA's, he has the choice of computing a measure of relationship such as the correlation r_{XY} for either unit. It can be shown from certain identities underlying the analysis of covariance (see Robinson, 1950) that

$$r_t = r_w \sqrt{1 - \eta_{XA}^2} \sqrt{1 - \eta_{YA}^2}$$
$$+ r_b \eta_{XA} \eta_{YA},$$

where r_t is the correlation for counties (or "total" correlation); r_w is the average within-SEA correlation for counties (computed from the pooled sums of squares and products within SEA's); r_b is the (weighted) between-SEA correlation, which usually differs only slightly from the correlation obtained from SEA data; η_{XA}^2 is the squared correlation ratio of variable X on SEA, i.e., the ratio of the between-SEA variation in X by counties to the total variation in X by counties; and η_{YA}^2 is the the squared correlation ratio of Y on SEA.

Now, if the counties composing each SEA had identical values of the environmental variable, X, i.e., if SEA's were perfectly homogeneous with respect to X, the measure of regional differentiation, η_{XA}, would be unity, and the foregoing equation would reduce to $r_t = r_b \eta_{YA}$. Unless SEA's were perfectly homogeneous in Y as well as in X, the measure of relationship based on SEA's, r_b, would have to be larger than that based on counties, r_t. To the extent that the size of "regional" units is a matter of somewhat arbitrary determination, there can be no unique measure of the degree of relationship between an environmental variable and a demographic or ecological variable. Moreover, the comparison of the relative importance of two environmental variables, X_1 and X_2, in producing variation in Y must be somewhat ambiguous or indeterminate. Because the correlation ratios of the two variables on SEA need not be equal, in general, it is quite possible for their correlations with Y to undergo a reversal in order of magnitude in shifting from a county to an SEA basis of calculation.

Whereas the type of research design under discussion raises problems of statistical inference for which there is as yet no solution, it also brings out the complexity of environmental relationships and therefore guards against the oversimplified deterministic hypotheses that characterized the old "environmentalism" and, to a degree, the early versions of "regionalism." It is clearly recognized that mere variation in a demographic or ecological variable by region does not demonstrate an environmental influence. One observes, to begin with, what may be called a "regional effect" in the dependent variable Y, as measured by η_{YA}. Then the measure of relationship, r_t, affords a preliminary test of the hypothesis that this regional effect represents the "influence" of a particular environmental variable, X. As a further test, one might calculate $\eta_{Y'A}$ and subject it to a test of significance, where Y' is the standardized value of Y from which the statistical influence of X has been removed. If the relationship between Y and X is taken to be linear, then $Y' = Y - b_{YX}(X - \overline{X})$. It can be shown that

$$\eta^2_{Y'A} = (\eta^2_{YA} + r^2_t \eta^2_{XA} - 2 r_t r_w \eta_{XA} \eta_{YA}) / (1 - r^2_t),$$

in the notation of the preceding paragraphs. Note that it is possible for $\eta_{Y'A}$ not to differ significantly from zero while r_t is substantially below unity. If this were true, one might entertain the hypothesis that X accounts for *regional variation* in Y without having to conclude that X completely determines Y, since there might be considerable within-region variation in Y not statistically accounted for by X. On the other hand, if $\eta_{Y'A}$ is significant, then one must seek explanatory variables other than X, and, of course, one may have to consider variables other than environmental characteristics. A significant "residual regional effect," as measured by $\eta_{Y'A}$ may have heuristic importance insofar as a general knowledge of regional differences may suggest to the investigator the importance of variables other than X producing variation in Y.

The regional approach contributes to the ecological analysis of the environment by bringing into the open some difficult methodological questions obscured by a less rigorous approach. These difficulties, of course, are not peculiar to this particular scheme of regional delimitation. Moreover, the merits of a system of statistical tabulation units like SEA's are not to be judged solely on the basis of their contribution to the solution of this kind of ecological problem. If the present tentative developments in regional analysis appear to involve grave difficulties, it is equally true that a scientifically adequate alternative approach to the ecological analysis of the environment has yet to be suggested.

Population Balance

The traditional problem of "population and resources" is not only the leading theme of a great deal of demographic research; it is also a topic which exhibits clearly the close reciprocal relationship between demography and human ecology. In fact, the problem cannot be stated within a strictly demographic frame of reference, i.e., solely in terms of size, composition, and changes in the human aggregate. In essence, it concerns the relationship of these variables to other elements in the "ecological complex" (Fig. 10, *supra*).

Hawley has indicated that the concept of balance "concerns the ratio of numbers to the opportunities for living" (Hawley, 1950, p. 149). No doubt the selection of a somewhat vague and global expression, "opportunities for living," was deliberate. This formulation forces the recognition that any particular index of "opportunities for living" is, in fact, only an index; determinants of the variation of any plausible index may or may not be the same as those of another, equally plausible one. It is notorious that social scientists have been unable to reach consensus on the "best" single indicator of the level of living, to use the more conventional term (United Nations, 1954). There are reasons for supposing that the diversity of viewpoints reflects the inherent nature of the problem: to "measure" the level of living, one has the alternatives of selecting a more or less accessible single index and neglecting other aspects of the concept, aggregating by an inevitably arbitrary formula several indicators which are likely to be highly but not perfectly intercorrelated, or investigating separately the determinants of each of a number of aspects of level of living. This is the "index number problem" par excellence; methodological nuances of it have been thoroughly explored by economists, but other social scientists have scarcely learned to grapple with the problem.

For purposes of argument or abstract exposition, it is customary to suppose that a suitable index number, L, of the level of living can be defined and quantified. Then determinants of L are identified and perhaps combined in some kind of formal or empirical model. This convention will be followed in the present discussion, whose only purpose is to bring out some of the ecological ramifications of the problem of population balance.

The major heuristic hypothesis to be entertained is that L is a measure or aspect of ecological adaptation and that it is consequently a function of all the principal elements of the "ecological complex." One might therefore be tempted to write the equation, $L = f(P, E, T, O)$, where the letters on the right stand for the four factors in the "ecological complex" identified earlier. However, we are not prepared to sim-

plify the discussion to the point of assuming that each of these four factors is expressible by a single index number, as we are assuming for L. For example, not only size of population but also composition, rate of growth, and levels of fertility and mortality are related to variation in L. For E, instead of a single number, it is necessary to consider a lengthy list of "resources," as well as several categories of "resistances" (Zimmerman, 1951). Although useful indexes of technological development are available—for example, per capita use of inanimate energy—still there are various qualitative considerations that must be acknowledged. The form of available "energy converters" is, no doubt, one of the prime considerations (Cottrell, 1955). Finally, O is perhaps the most complex "variable" of all. If one chose to symbolize the several aspects of each of the four factors, the above equation might be rewritten giving each of them a variable subscript. However, this elaboration of the notation would serve no useful purpose here, provided one keeps in mind that each symbol, P, E, T, and O, stands for a whole set of variables and not for any single index number.

One might well classify the major theories of population balance by the simplifications they introduce into the basic equation. Malthus, of course, emphasized P, or rather the ratio, P/E, attributing only secondary importance to T and O. Marx's theory was notable for its emphasis on O. The theoretical and empirical case for the importance of T has been presented by Ogburn (1951). The first major contribution, then, of the ecological formulation is to suggest that a partial theory of population balance—i.e., one neglecting any of the four factors on the right side of the equation—is likely to be unsatisfactory.

The second contribution is the emphasis on the interrelations of the four "independent variables" as relevant to the problem of population balance. It is, of course, well known that one cannot identify or "measure" E apart from T. An aspect of the environment (e.g., a body of water) classifiable as a "resistance" at one level of technology becomes a "resource" at another stage. Fossil fuels are "resources" only for those populations equipped with energy converters that make relatively efficient use of such fuels. Even the amount of "land" is not a fixed quantity if one has in mind productive land and the possibilities of irrigation, drainage, and soil improvement.

One relationship emphasized by ecologists is the connection between P and O. On the one hand, size and distribution of population are major limiting factors in the evolution of organization. Any elaborate form of organization is virtually precluded if population is small and dispersed. On the other hand, growth and concentration of population appear to be major forces behind the emergence of functional specialization, territorial and occupational, and the elaboration of the division of labor (Durkheim, 1947; Halbwachs, 1946). When, in turn, attention is focused on the territorial division of labor, it becomes clear that growth of population may be accompanied by an expansion of the areal extent of the "ecological complex," e.g., by the establishment of trade relations. Consequently, the determinants of L become progressively less localized, and the relevant observations of E cease to be solely those taken within a circumscribed area (Halbwachs, 1946; Hawley, 1950).

The equation presented above is generalized to the point of being able to accommodate any substantive hypothesis on the interrelationships of the "dependent" and "independent" variables. In devising more specific models, one has a number of alternatives: to "hold constant" certain factors in the equation, to assume that one or more of them can be adequately represented by a single variable, or to introduce assumptions as to the form of relationship among variables, perhaps introducing time as an additional variable. Several such possibilities are illustrated by Boulding (1955). One constraint which usually enters into such models is the assumption that there is a value of L, say, L_s, such that the growth rate of population, $dP/dt \to 0$ as $L \to L_s$. The "subsistence level," L_s, is then the level of living which establishes a maximum size of population. It is usual to point out that L_s need not be construed as some kind of physiological minimum for survival and that the "standard of living," or level of living to which a population aspires (Saunders, 1943), in effect determines the "subsistence level" below which a population will inhibit further growth.

The problem of empirically ascertaining L_s is one that has scarcely been tackled on account of its evident difficulty. Without trying to set forth a satisfactory empirical approach, one may suggest that the ecological framework puts the question differently from the conventional statement. Ecologically, the "subsistence level" is not a mere psychological "level of aspiration" or "cultural standard" experienced as a norm by individuals. It may be conceived, rather, as a minimal adaptation of a population, failing which organization would be disrupted, technology would cease to function, or environmental problems would become overwhelming. It is, of course, in a somewhat complicated society where population is not solely dependent on local resources and where L has advanced well beyond any physiological minimum that the conception of a conventional "standard of living" becomes most pertinent. In such a society there has already evolved a fabric of interdependence which, though representing an extraordinary adaptation, is nevertheless vulnerable. A decrease in L (which is, of course, an average over the whole population of a quantity that varies among its segments) means that relationships among certain units of organization will be adversely modified, and these disruptions will be transmitted to still other units. Should this process continue, the entire network of inter-unit relationships would be imperiled. It is not far-fetched to suppose that this condition was approximated during the Great Depression, when, significantly, the net reproduction rate fell below unity for the first time in the United States. It is significant too that this threat was met not only by reduction in the fertility rate (not by an increase in mortality) but by modifications of organization as well. While in comparison with most countries and historical periods L remained high, the subsistence level, L_s, had likewise increased to a high level, so that even a relatively small decline in L set in motion sizable demographic and organizational changes.

Recognizing the speculative character of the preceding paragraph, one is still at liberty to suggest that the possibility of operationalizing the "subsistence theory" depends on gaining a firmer understanding of the interrelations of the factors in the ecological complex rather than on acquiring data on psychological processes. The latter, no doubt, are relevant to the understanding of individual behavior, but whether their study can produce a cogent theory of population balance is questionable.

RECAPITULATION AND EVALUATION

One would not set out to write a treatise on human ecology without including a rather full exposition of matters ordinarily regarded as "demographic." This is because ecology, like demography, is concerned with the population as its unit of study. If one followed the model of animal ecology (cf. Allee *et al.*, 1949), an important section of the treatise would be headed "population ecology" and would treat such topics as size, growth, distribution, and composition of population in relation to the vital processes and migration. In the human field, however, demography is a recognized specialty, and it hardly enlightens practitioners of that specialty to tell them that their work is theoretically classifiable as an aspect of human ecology. Consequently, this chapter has emphasized the connections between demography and ecology that arise from ecology's concern with the ways in which populations are or become organized to cope with problems afforded by their environments. Without suggesting that the problem of organization can be studied only at the local community level, most illustrations have been drawn from community ecology, reflecting the present run of attention in the discipline.

Demographic variables appear in ecological investigations as "dependent variables" influenced by one or another aspect of organization, as "independent variables" affecting the character of organization, and as "indicators" of one or another aspect of organization. Such a formulation reflects the limitations of the present methodological resources of human ecology as much as it aids in the formulation of problems. Variables are designated as "dependent" or "independent" only as a convenience to the analyst, who generally proceeds on the assumption that functional interrelationship rather than unilateral "causation" would be revealed by a sufficiently flexible method. The validity of assumptions about demographic "indicators" depends, in the last analysis, on the existence of such relationships.

Human ecology is in part an evolutionary study. The study of the evolution of the human species falls to the physical anthropologist and human biologist, both of whom are evincing interest in ecological formulations of their problem. But the human ecologist must recognize that not only the species and the genetic structure of human populations undergo evolution. The same is true of patterns of organization, systems of technology, and even the environment. One of the most prominent evolutionary hypotheses in current ecological thinking is that the metropolitan community has emerged from earlier stages of village and town economy (McKenzie, 1933; Bogue, 1949). Explicit attention has been given to the process of technological accumulation (Ogburn, 1922), more specifically, to the successive emergence of major forms of energy converters (White, 1943; Cottrell, 1955) and modes of local and long-distance transportation (McKenzie, 1927; Ogburn, 1946; Gilmore, 1953). That the environment evolves as technology and organization change is virtually a truism, but one whose implications are not always appreciated. Not only do these changes in other factors of the ecological complex entail modifications of the habitat, but the environmental significance of the physical and biotic world shifts with such changes. These observations imply that demographic phenomena appear historically in a shifting context and suggest that there is small likelihood of discovering empirical laws of demographic change that can be stated in complete abstraction from that context.

Whether human ecology offers a "theory" of population hinges on the meaning of "theory." What is clear is that the ecological framework provides one means of ordering demographic data intelligibly; it suggests a number of researchable hypotheses; when it is applied in various specialized fields of investigation, it almost invariably leads to a recognition of the importance of demographic data and to an appreciation of the ramifications of population problems.

Human ecology has its own conceptual difficulties and controversial issues, of course. With many of these, population specialists need not be greatly concerned. The issue of "dualism" arising from certain early statements of the scope and character of human ecology is resolved when one recognizes that any science involves a typical pattern of abstraction from the concrete world. But there remains the task of developing operational counterparts to a number of ecological concepts that have thus far figured mainly in general discussions or served as plausible interpretations of casual observations. In this task the methodological skills of the demographer should prove invaluable. Presumably, the road to progress lies in the co-operation of demographers and human ecologists in the study of a number of their common problems, the variety and importance of which it has been the aim of this paper to show.

SELECTED BIBLIOGRAPHY

(Items marked with asterisk constitute a brief selected bibliography.)

ADAMS, CHARLES C. 1951. "The Application of Biologic Research Methods to Urban Areal Problems," *Scientific Monthly*, LXXIII, 39–40.

ALLEE, W. C. 1951. *Cooperation among Animals with Human Implications*. New York: Schuman.

———, EMERSON, A. E., PARK, O., PARK, T., and SCHMIDT, K. P. 1949. *Principles of Animal Ecology*. Philadelphia: W. B. Saunders Co.

ALLEN, G. R. 1954. "The 'Courbe des Populations': A Further Analysis," *Bulletin of the Oxford University Institute of Statistics*, XVI, 179–89.

ANDERSON, THEODORE R. 1955. "Intermetropolitan Migration: A Comparison of the Hypotheses of Zipf and Stouffer," *American Sociological Review*, XX, 287–91.

BARKER, ROGER G., and WRIGHT, HERBERT F. 1955. *Midwest and Its Children: The Psychological Ecology of an American Town*. Evanston, Ill.: Row, Peterson & Co.

BARROWS, H. H. 1923. "Geography as Human Ecology," *Annals of the Association of American Geographers*, XIII, 1–14.

BARTHOLOMEW, GEORGE A., JR., and BIRDSELL, JOSEPH B. 1953. "Ecology and the Protohominids," *American Anthropologist*, LV, 481–98.

*BATES, MARSTON. 1953. "Human Ecology," in *Anthropology Today*, ed. A. L. KROEBER. Chicago: University of Chicago Press.

BENNETT, JOHN W. 1944. "The Interaction of Culture and Environment in the Smaller Societies," *American Anthropologist*, XLVI, 461–78.

BEWS, J. W. 1935. *Human Ecology*. New York: Oxford University Press.

BIRDSELL, JOSEPH B. 1953. "Some Environmental and Cultural Factors Influencing the Structuring of Australian Aboriginal Populations," *American Naturalist*, LXXXVII, 171–207.

BLIZZARD, SAMUEL W., and ANDERSON, WILLIAM F., II. 1952. *Problems in Rural-urban Fringe Research: Conceptualization and Delineation*. (Progress Report No. 89.) State College, Pa.: Pennsylvania Agricultural Experiment Station.

*BOGUE, DONALD J. 1949. *The Structure of the Metropolitan Community*. Ann Arbor: University of Michigan Press.

———. 1950a. "A Technique for Making Extensive Population Estimates," *Journal of the American Statistical Association*, XLV, 149–63.

———. 1950b. "Economic Areas as a Tool for Research and Planning," *American Sociological Review*, XV, 409–16.

———. 1950c. *Metropolitan Decentralization: A Study of Differential Growth*. ("Studies in Population Distribution," No. 2.) Oxford, Ohio: Scripps Foundation.

———. 1953. *Population Growth in Standard Metropolitan Areas, 1900–1950*. Washington, D.C.: Housing & Home Finance Agency.

———. 1955. "Nodal versus Homogeneous Regions, and Statistical Techniques for Measuring the Influence of Each," preprint, *Proceedings of the Conference of the International Statistical Institute*. Rio de Janeiro.

———. 1956. *Metropolitan Growth and the Conversion of Land to Nonagricultural Uses*. ("Studies in Population Distribution," No. 11.) Oxford, Ohio: Scripps Foundation.

———, and HARRIS, DOROTHY L. 1954. *Comparative Population and Urban Research via Multiple Regression and Covariance Analysis*. ("Studies in Population Distribution," No. 8.) Oxford, Ohio: Scripps Foundation.

———, and THOMPSON, WARREN S. 1949. "Migration and Distance," *American Sociological Review*, XIV, 236–44.

BOULDING, KENNETH E. 1950. *A Reconstruction of Economics*. New York: John Wiley & Sons.

———. 1953a. *The Organizational Revolution*. New York: Harper & Bros.

———. 1953b. "Toward a General Theory of Growth," *Canadian Journal of Economics and Political Science*, XIX, 326–40.

*———. 1955. "The Malthusian Model as a General System," *Social and Economic Studies*, IV, 195–205.

BOWEN, IAN. 1954. *Population*. London: James Nisbet & Co.

BREESE, GERALD. 1949. *The Daytime Population of the Central Business District in Chicago*. Chicago: University of Chicago Press.

BRUNSWIK, E. 1947. *Systematic and Representative Design of Psychological Experiments*. Berkeley: University of California Press.

*BURGESS, ERNEST W. 1925. "The Growth of the City," in *The City*, by R. E. PARK, E. W. BURGESS, and R. D. MCKENZIE. Chicago: University of Chicago Press.

——— (ed.). 1926. *The Urban Community*. Chicago: University of Chicago Press.

CALDWELL, MORRIS G. 1938. "The Sociological Tract: The Spatial Distribution of Social Data," *Psychiatry*, I, 379–85.

CLARK, COLIN. 1951. "Urban Population

Densities," *Journal of the Royal Statistical Society*, Ser. A, CXIV, 490–96.

CLARK, J. G. D. 1952. *Prehistoric Europe: The Economic Basis.* New York: Philosophical Library.

CLARK, PHILIP J., and EVANS, FRANCIS C. 1954. "Distance to Nearest Neighbor as a Measure of Spatial Relationships in Populations," *Ecology*, XXXV, 445–53.

CLAUSEN, JOHN A., and KOHN, MELVIN L. 1954. "The Ecological Approach in Social Psychiatry," *American Journal of Sociology*, LX, 140–49.

CLEMENTS, FREDERIC E., and SHELFORD, VICTOR E. 1939. *Bio-ecology.* New York: John Wiley & Sons.

COOLEY, C. H. 1894. Reprinted 1930. "The Theory of Transportation," in *Sociological Theory and Social Research.* New York: Henry Holt & Co.

CORWIN, E. H. L. (ed.). 1949. *Ecology of Health.* New York: Commonwealth Fund.

*COTTRELL, FRED. 1955. *Energy and Society.* New York: McGraw-Hill.

CRESSEY, PAUL F. 1938. "Population Succession in Chicago: 1898–1930," *American Journal of Sociology*, XLIV, 59–69.

DAVIS, KINGSLEY, and GOLDEN, HILDA HERTZ. 1954. "Urbanization and the Development of Pre-industrial Areas," *Economic Development and Cultural Change*, III, 6–26.

DEEVEY, EDWARD S., JR. 1951. "Recent Textbooks of Human Ecology," *Ecology*, XXXII, 347–51.

DEMERATH, N. J. 1947. "Ecology, Framework for City Planning," *Social Forces*, XXVI, 62–67.

DEWEY, RICHARD. 1950. "The Neighborhood, Urban Ecology, and City Planners," *American Sociological Review*, XV, 502–7.

DICE, LEE R. 1955. *Man's Nature and Nature's Man: The Ecology of Human Communities.* Ann Arbor: University of Michigan Press.

*DICKINSON, ROBERT E. 1947. *City, Region, and Regionalism: A Geographical Contribution to Human Ecology.* London: Kegan Paul.

DUNCAN, OTIS DUDLEY. 1951. "Optimum Size of Cities," in *A Reader in Urban Sociology,* ed. PAUL K. HATT and ALBERT J. REISS, JR. Glencoe, Ill.: Free Press.

———. 1956. "Research on Metropolitan Population: Evaluation of Data," *Journal of the American Statistical Association*, LI, 591–96.

———. 1957. "The Measurement of Population Distribution," *Population Studies*, XI, 27–45.

———, and DAVIS, BEVERLY. 1953. "An Alternative to Ecological Correlation," *American Sociological Review*, XVIII, 665–66.

———, and DUNCAN, BEVERLY. 1955a. "Residential Distribution and Occupational Stratification," *American Journal of Sociology*, LX, 493–503.

———. 1955b. "A Methodological Analysis of Segregation Indexes," *American Sociological Review*, XX, 210–17.

———. 1956. *Chicago's Negro Population: Characteristics and Trends.* Chicago: Office of the Housing and Redevelopment Coordinator & Chicago Plan Commission.

———. 1957. *The Negro Population of Chicago: A Study of Residential Succession.* Chicago: University of Chicago Press.

*———, and REISS, ALBERT J., JR. 1956. *Social Characteristics of Urban and Rural Communities, 1950.* New York: John Wiley & Sons.

DUNHAM, H. WARREN. 1947. "Current Status of Ecological Research in Mental Disorder," *Social Forces*, XXV, 321–26.

*DURKHEIM, ÉMILE. 1947. *The Division of Labor in Society.* Glencoe, Ill.: Free Press.

ELDRIDGE, HOPE TISDALE. 1942. Reprinted 1956. "The Process of Urbanization," in *Demographic Analysis*, ed. JOSEPH J. SPENGLER and OTIS DUDLEY DUNCAN. Glencoe, Ill.: Free Press.

EMERSON, ALFRED E. 1939. "Social Coordination and the Superorganism," in *Plant and Animal Communities*, ed. T. JUST. South Bend: University of Notre Dame Press.

———. 1942. "Basic Comparisons of Human and Insect Societies," in *Levels of Integration in Biological and Social Systems*, ed. ROBERT REDFIELD. Lancaster, Pa.: Jaques Cattell Press.

FIREY, WALTER. 1946. "Ecological Considerations in Planning for Urban Fringes,"

American Sociological Review, XI, 411–23.

———. 1947. *Land Use in Central Boston.* Cambridge: Harvard University Press.

FOLEY, DONALD L. 1954. "Urban Daytime Population: A Field for Demographic-ecological Analysis," *Social Forces*, XXXII, 323–30.

GIBBARD, HAROLD A. 1941. "The Status Factor in Residential Successions," *American Journal of Sociology*, XLVI, 835–42.

*GILMORE, HARLAN W. 1953. *Transportation and the Growth of Cities.* Glencoe, Ill.: Free Press.

GOODMAN, LEO A. 1953. "Ecological Regressions and Behavior of Individuals," *American Sociological Review*, XVIII, 663–64.

GROSS, EDWARD. 1954. "The Role of Density as a Factor in Metropolitan Growth in the United States of America," *Population Studies*, VIII, 113–20.

GUTKIND, E. A. 1953. *Community and Environment: A Discourse on Social Ecology.* London: Watts & Co.

HAGOOD, MARGARET JARMAN, and EATON, MARY ALICE. 1939. "An Examination of Regional Differentials in Fertility by Analysis of Variance and Covariance," *Social Forces*, XVII, 495–502.

*HALBWACHS, MAURICE. 1946. *Morphologie sociale.* 2d ed. Paris: Librairie Armand Colin.

HALLOWELL, A. IRVING. 1949. "The Size of Algonkian Hunting Territories: A Function of Ecological Adjustment," *American Anthropologist*, LI, 35–45.

HARRIS, CHAUNCY D. 1943. "A Functional Classification of Cities in the United States," *Geographical Review*, XXXIII, 86–99.

———, and ULLMAN, EDWARD L. 1945. "The Nature of Cities," *Annals of the American Academy of Political and Social Science*, No. 242, pp. 7–17.

HARTSHORNE, RICHARD. 1949. *The Nature of Geography.* Lancaster, Pa.: Association of American Geographers.

HAUSER, PHILIP M. 1938. "Differential Fertility, Mortality, and Net Reproduction in Chicago, 1930." Unpublished Ph.D. dissertation, Department of Sociology, University of Chicago.

———. 1940. "How Declining Urban Growth Affects City Activities," *Public Management*, XXII, 355–58.

———. 1951. "The Labor Force as a Field of Interest for the Sociologist," *American Sociological Review*, XVI, 530–38.

*———. 1956a. "World and Asian Urbanization in Relation to Economic Development and Social Change." Mimeographed paper, United Nations Economic and Social Council.

*———. 1956b. "Ecological Aspects of Urban Research," in *The State of the Social Sciences*, ed. LEONARD D. WHITE. Chicago: University of Chicago Press.

HAWLEY, AMOS H. 1941. "An Ecological Study of Urban Service Institutions," *American Sociological Review*, VI, 629–39.

———. 1944. "Ecology and Human Ecology," *Social Forces*, XXII, 398–405.

*———. 1950. *Human Ecology.* New York: Ronald Press.

———. 1951. "The Approach of Human Ecology to Urban Areal Research," *Scientific Monthly*, LXXIII, 48–49.

———. 1956. *The Changing Shape of Metropolitan America: Deconcentration Since 1920.* Glencoe, Ill.: Free Press.

HEBERLE, RUDOLF. 1952. "On Political Ecology," *Social Forces*, XXXI, 1–9.

*HOLLINGSHEAD, A. B. 1939. "Human Ecology," in *An Outline of the Principles of Sociology*, ed. ROBERT E. PARK. New York: Barnes & Noble.

HOOVER, EDGAR M. 1948. *The Location of Economic Activity.* New York: McGraw-Hill.

———. 1955. "The Concept of a System of Cities: A Comment on Rutledge Vining's Paper," *Economic Development and Cultural Change*, III, 196–98.

———, and FISHER, JOSEPH L. 1948. "Regional Aspects of Economic Growth and Decay." Mimeographed paper, National Bureau of Economic Research.

ISARD, WALTER. 1956. *Location and Space-Economy.* New York: John Wiley & Sons.

JAFFE, A. J. 1942. "Urbanization and Fertility," *American Journal of Sociology*, XLVIII, 48–60.

JONASSEN, C. T. 1955. *The Shopping Center versus Downtown.* Columbus: Bureau of Business Research, Ohio State University.

KISH, LESLIE. 1954. "Differentiation in Metropolitan Areas," *American Sociological Review*, XIX, 388–98.

KITAGAWA, EVELYN M. 1953. "Differential Fertility in Chicago, 1920–40," *American Journal of Sociology*, LVIII, 481–92.

KLIGMAN, MIRIAM. 1945. "Human Ecology and the City Planning Movement," *Social Forces*, XXIV, 89–95.

LINDEMAN, EDUARD C. 1940. "Ecology: An Instrument for the Integration of Science and Philosophy," *Ecological Monographs*, X, 367–72.

LLEWELLYN, EMMA C., and HAWTHORN, AUDREY. 1945. "Human Ecology," in *Twentieth Century Sociology*, ed. GEORGES GURVITCH and WILBERT E. MOORE. New York: Philosophical Library.

LÖSCH, AUGUST. 1954. *The Economics of Location*. New Haven: Yale University Press.

LOTKA, ALFRED J. 1938. Reprinted 1956. "Some Recent Results in Population Analysis," in *Population Theory and Policy*, ed. JOSEPH J. SPENGLER and OTIS DUDLEY DUNCAN. Glencoe, Ill.: Free Press.

McKENZIE, R. D. 1927. "Spatial Distance and Community Organization Pattern," *Social Forces*, V, 623–27.

*——. 1933. *The Metropolitan Community*. New York: McGraw-Hill.

*——. 1934. "The Field and Problems of Demography, Human Geography, and Human Ecology," in *The Fields and Methods of Sociology*, ed. L. L. BERNARD. New York: Ray Long & Richard R. Smith, Inc.

MADDEN, CARL H. 1956. "On Some Indications of Stability in the Growth of Cities in the United States," *Economic Development and Cultural Change*, IV, 236–52.

MAYER, ALBERT J., and HAUSER, PHILIP M. 1950. "Class Differentials in Expectation of Life at Birth," *Revue de l'Institut International de Statistique*, XVIII, 197–200.

MEGGERS, BETTY J. 1954. "Environmental Limitation on the Development of Culture," *American Anthropologist*, LVI, 801–24.

NATIONAL INDUSTRIAL CONFERENCE BOARD. 1953. *Growth Patterns of Cities*. ("Studies in Business Economics," No. 39.) New York: The Board.

NEWMAN, MARSHALL T. 1953. "The Application of Ecological Rules to the Racial Anthropology of the Aboriginal New World," *American Anthropologist*, LV, 311–27.

OGBURN, WILLIAM FIELDING. 1922. *Social Change*. New York: B. W. Huebsch, Inc.

——. 1937. *Social Characteristics of Cities*. Chicago: International City Managers' Association.

——. 1946. "Inventions of Local Transportation and the Patterns of Cities," *Social Forces*, XXV, 313–19.

*——. 1951. Reprinted 1956. "Population, Private Ownership, Technology, and the Standard of Living," in *Population Theory and Policy*, ed. JOSEPH J. SPENGLER and OTIS DUDLEY DUNCAN. Glencoe, Ill.: Free Press.

——. 1953. Reprinted 1956. "On the Social Aspects of Population Changes," in *Population Theory and Policy*, ed. JOSEPH J. SPENGLER and OTIS DUDLEY DUNCAN. Glencoe, Ill.: Free Press.

PARK, ROBERT E. 1929. "Sociology," in *Research in the Social Sciences*, ed. WILSON GEE. New York: Macmillan.

PFAUTZ, HAROLD W. 1947. "Charles Booth's Contribution to the Theory and Methods of Human Ecology and Social Organization." Unpublished M.A. thesis, Department of Sociology, University of Chicago.

PRICE, DANIEL O. 1948. "Distance and Direction as Vectors of Internal Migration, 1935–1940," *Social Forces*, XXVII, 48–53.

*QUINN, JAMES A. 1940. "Topical Summary of Current Literature on Human Ecology," *American Journal of Sociology*, XLVI, 191–226.

——. 1950. *Human Ecology*. New York: Prentice-Hall, Inc.

RAVENSTEIN, E. G. 1885–89. "The Laws of Migration," *Journal of the Royal Statistical Society*, XLVIII, 167–235; LII, 241–305.

REDICK, RICHARD W. 1956. "Population Growth and Redistribution in Central Cities, 1940–1950," *American Sociological Review*, XXI, 38–43.

REISS, ALBERT J., JR. 1956. "Research Problems in Metropolitan Population Redistribution," *American Sociological Review*, XXI, 571–77.

ROBINSON, W. S. 1950. "Ecological Correlations and the Behavior of Individuals," *American Sociological Review*, XV, 351–57.

ROTERUS, VICTOR. 1946. "Effects of Population Growth and Non-growth on the Well-being of Cities," *American Sociological Review*, XI, 90–97.

SAUNDERS, HAROLD W. 1943. Reprinted 1956. "Human Migration and Social Equilibrium," in *Population Theory and Policy*, ed. JOSEPH J. SPENGLER and OTIS DUDLEY DUNCAN. Glencoe, Ill.: Free Press.

*SCHMID, CALVIN F. 1950. "Generalizations Concerning the Ecology of the American City," *American Sociological Review*, XV, 264–81.

SCHMITT, ROBERT C. 1956. "Suburbanization: Statistical Fallacy?" *Land Economics*, pp. 85–87.

*SCHNORE, LEO F. 1954. "The Separation of Home and Work: A Problem for Human Ecology," *Social Forces*, XXXII, 336–43.

SEARS, PAUL B., and CARTER, GEORGE F. 1952. "Ecology and the Social Sciences: A Reply," *Ecology*, XXXIII, 299–300.

SHANTZ, H. L., *et al.* 1940. "Relation of Ecology to Human Welfare: The Human Situation," *Ecological Monographs*, X, 308–72.

SHELDON, HENRY D. 1954. "Suburban Growth and Age Structure." Unpublished paper presented to the annual meeting of the American Sociological Society.

SHRYOCK, HENRY S., JR. 1956. "Population Redistribution within Metropolitan Areas: Evaluation of Research," *Social Forces*, XXXV, 154–59.

SMITH, FREDERICK E. 1951. "Ecology and the Social Sciences," *Ecology*, XXXII, 763–64.

STEWARD, JULIAN H. 1938. *Basin-Plateau Aboriginal Sociopolitical Groups*. (U.S. Bureau of American Ethnology Bulletin 120.) Washington, D.C.: Government Printing Office.

———. 1955. *Theory of Culture Change*. Urbana: University of Illinois Press.

*STEWART, JOHN Q. 1947. "Empirical Mathematical Rules Concerning the Distribution and Equilibrium of Population," *Geographical Review*, XXXVII, 461–85.

———. 1948. "Demographic Gravitation: Evidence and Applications," *Sociometry*, XI, 31–58.

STOUFFER, SAMUEL A. 1940. "Intervening Opportunities: A Theory Relating Mobility and Distance," *American Sociological Review*, V, 845–67.

THOMAS, DOROTHY SWAINE. 1938. *Research Memorandum on Migration Differentials*. (Bulletin 43.) New York: Social Science Research Council.

*THOMAS, WILLIAM L., JR. (ed.). 1956. *Man's Role in Changing the Face of the Earth*. Chicago: University of Chicago Press.

THOMPSON, LAURA. 1949. "The Relations of Men, Animals, and Plants in an Island Community (Fiji)," *American Anthropologist*, LI, 253–76.

UNITED NATIONS. 1954. *Report on International Definition and Measurement of Standards and Levels of Living*. New York.

UNITED STATES BUREAU OF THE CENSUS. 1951. *State Economic Areas*. By DONALD J. BOGUE. Washington, D.C.: Government Printing Office.

UNITED STATES FEDERAL HOUSING ADMINISTRATION. 1939. *The Structure and Growth of Residential Neighborhoods in American Cities*. By HOMER HOYT. Washington, D.C.: Government Printing Office.

VINING, RUTLEDGE. 1955. "A Description of Certain Spatial Aspects of an Economic System," *Economic Development and Cultural Change*, III, 147–95.

WEBER, A. F. 1899. *The Growth of Cities in the Nineteenth Century*. New York: Columbia University Press.

WEDEL, WALDO R. 1953. "Some Aspects of Human Ecology in the Central Plains," *American Anthropologist*, LV, 499–514.

WHITE, C. LANGDON, and RENNER, GEORGE T. 1948. *Human Geography: An Ecological Study of Society*. New York: Appleton-Century Crofts.

*WHITE, LESLIE A. 1943. "Energy and the Evolution of Culture," *American Anthropologist*, XLV, 335–56.

WILKINS, ARTHUR H. 1956. "The Residential Distribution of Occupation Groups in Eight Middle-sized Cities of the United States in 1950." Unpublished Ph.D. dissertation, Department of Sociology, University of Chicago.

*WIRTH, LOUIS. 1938. "Urbanism as a Way of Life," *American Journal of Sociology*, XLIV, 1–24.

*———. 1945. "Human Ecology," *ibid.*, L, 483–88.

WOLFF, P. DE, and MEERDINK, J. 1952. "La mortalité à Amsterdam selon les quartiers," *Population*, VII, 639–59.

WRIGHT, JOHN K. 1937. "Some Measures of Distributions," *Annals of the Association of American Geographers*, XXVII, 177–211.

*ZIMMERMAN, ERICH W. 1951. *World Resources and Industries*. Rev. ed. New York: Harper.

ZIPF, G. K. 1949. *Human Behavior and the Principle of Least Effort*. Cambridge, Mass.: Addison-Wesley Press.

29. Geography and Demography[1]

EDWARD A. ACKERMAN

Professional geographers have long interested themselves in the study of population, and those scholars concerned with human geography inevitably have studied attributes of human populations and their settlement characteristics. In this they have touched common ground with demographers. This chapter discusses the areas of common interest through the distinctive approach of the geographer in his research, the aspects of population study covered by geographers in the past, and the outlook for research in geography which bears upon the study of population.

THE CHARACTER OF GEOGRAPHIC RESEARCH

Geography is one of the oldest of the sciences. Like astronomy, geography is concerned with the content of space, and it treats the distributive relations of objects in space. The "universe" of geography[2] is mainly two dimensional, limited to the zone of contact between land surface, water surface, and atmosphere. It is particularly a science of spatial distribution, and the matrix for its distributional analysis is the earth's surface. (This presentation follows the methodological discussion of Ackerman, 1958.) Geography undoubtedly began with isolated students' attempts to establish the space relation of particular localities to other localities within the range of the

individual's experience. We can only guess when this first took place, but embryonic geography certainly began in remote prehistory. It was present at the time when the written record of human cultures began.

Men in early Egypt and Babylon began to measure the relation of localities or points on earth to the movements of the sun and stars; with this they began a science which has continued through each passing generation. Throughout much of its long history, geography has been concerned with identifying the pattern of simple space relations among the physical and biotic features of the earth's surface—the pattern compounded from distance and extent, direction and orientation. Inevitably there has been included in this work the identification of the space relations of cultural features. Thus even the earliest maps included the location of the most readily recognized cultural features—routes, towns, or settlements—along with the location of physical features.

Modern geographical research has been carried on in several specific steps. It starts with the description of the earth as a site,[3] that is, with accurate determination of the shape and extent of the physical matrix. Explorers, geographers, and others took centuries to produce an accurate determination, but it was finally accomplished by navigational reckoning, surveying, geodesy, and cartography. The objective was to determine the exact position which points on the earth's surface have in relation to each other. While

---

[1] The author was assisted by Donald Patton of the University of Maryland. Dr. Patton's bibliographic research and recommendations are represented in many of the references cited.

[2] "Universe" here is used in the sense of the total field for investigation within which a science actually or potentially may be a valid instrument of inquiry and synthesis.

[3] The term "site" here denotes that attribute which gives a specific position in space to any phenomenon.

the major works in this step have been completed, refinement of detail and new geodetic data on poorly known regions like the Antarctic are still necessary.

A second step in modern research is identification of the specific phenomenal content of earth space: quantity, qualities, degree. This has been carried on for centuries, but generally in an unsystematic manner. The tools were field observation and the written word. As cartographic techniques have been developed, this work has become more precise. Aerial photography in particular has improved the geographer's capacity to observe and record accurately, but other devices, like the use of fractional symbols in mapping, also have contributed.

The third step is the identification of generic relations: categorization, classification, differentiation. The objective of this is to reduce to comprehensible limits the myriad possible observations which may be made about the distribution of earth phenomena. This step may be illustrated by the classification of weather phenomena into climatic types, and further into climatic regions. Climatic regions and other special-purpose regions show space relations generically considered.

A fourth step is the identification of genetic relations; this seeks determination of the dynamic aspects of space content. For example, a land-forms region is not static but changing. The processes[4] at work, their speed of action, and the conditions under which they arrive at stable equilibrium are all significant to genetic relations. This is a phase of study which geography shares with other disciplines and in which it often carries a secondary role, but geography's view and its objectives are uniquely centered on distributional problems.

The fifth step is the determination of

covariant relations among earth features. Settlement types may covary with transportation routes, transportation routes with land forms, land forms with climatic types, and so on. Study of covariant features is important in ascertaining space relations.

The integration of data on site, phenomenon, and process so as to reveal the full pattern of space relations is the final step. Geography is an "integrative" discipline, with some resemblance to history in this respect (Hartshorne, 1939, pp. 243–45). In this sense it culminates in an understanding of, and capacity to describe, those aspects of a region which are significant in areal differentiation. In this step the science is concerned with the analysis and synthesis of earth-space content in such a way that reality may be comprehended.

In its first modern flowering in the nineteenth century, geography concentrated on the physical and biotic world. This strong physical interest was continued until a relatively few years ago, but geography now has changed to a different form. Within the twentieth century, geographers have turned to a dominant interest in those phases of the discipline which collectively are known as human geography: study of the space relations of cultural attributes in the setting of the natural environment. While the cultural phases of geography were known as far back as the time of Strabo (63 B.C.?–A.D. 24?), methodical study appeared only on the eve of the twentieth century. Recording of population numbers within settlements and political groupings seems to have been among the most continued efforts toward cultural study in premodern geography.

Recent geographers have studied the features of culture in the same general manner as their immediate predecessors analyzed the physical environment. They have taken the cultural features of the earth, analyzed them generically and genetically in their space relations,

---

[4] "Process" here and hereafter denotes a succession of physical, biotic, or cultural events dependent on characteristic energizing agents.

and established covariant relations of cultural features with each other and with those of the physical and biotic environment. Much of this study has concerned economic features, but distributional features of concern to demography also have been studied.

GEOGRAPHIC STUDIES OF POPULATION

During the period in which professional geographic activity has centered on human geography, there has been consistent attention to the description and analysis of the distributional aspects of population. Like population studies in other disciplines, such study has included a number of separate subjects. The following are considered significant from the point of view of demography: (1) design of the collection of demographic data; (2) an analysis and comprehensible synthesis of data on areal differentiation of population as shown by census enumeration; (3) study of the several population attributes in their distributional aspects; (4) study of settlement patterns and settlement interrelation; and (5) study of the geographic pattern of population sustenance. Of these, the first four will be discussed in this chapter. The fifth is treated in chapter xxvi of this volume, under the title "Population and Natural Resources." The present chapter refers primarily to American studies and to the subjects considered distinctively suited to geographical research methods. (The European geographical literature in the fields is extensive, as illustrated in the bibliography by Dörries, 1940.) References, furthermore, will be illustrative rather than exhaustive.

DESIGN OF THE COLLECTION OF DEMOGRAPHIC DATA

Every census enumeration must be conducted within a geographic framework, and few other research works or data collections are so closely tied to units of area on the earth's surface. It follows that perceptive understanding of the areal characteristics of the enumeration unit can facilitate a census considerably and make its results more meaningful. It is not surprising, therefore, that some of the earliest and most consistent geographic work related to demography has been applied to census design. Henry Gannett, as Geographer of the Census, in 1881 drafted a plan of territorial division to facilitate enumeration in the following census (James, 1954; Von Struve, 1940). Geographers have assisted in the design of each decennial United States census since Gannett's time. The Division of Geography of the United States Bureau of the Census in 1958 was staffed with fifteen professional geographers assisting in preparation for the 1960 enumeration.[5] Other countries—Japan, the Soviet Union, Great Britain, and some Latin-American countries—have used geographical assistance in census design.

Census design improvements have been at least partly dependent upon and related to other aspects of geographic population research, notably the study of settlement patterns. Problems attending census design have become increasingly complex as single urban areas have spread within the last thirty years over many adjacent units of political jurisdiction, but census design is an important research function because understanding of the regional economic structures which affect population dynamics depends in large part on the manner in which census data are organized.

AREAL DIFFERENTIATION OF POPULATION: ANALYSIS AND COMPREHENSIBLE SYNTHESIS

Once an enumeration has been made, problems of meaningful interpretation of the returns arise. Geographers have made analyses of the static areal differ-

[5] Information supplied by the Division of Geography, United States Bureau of the Census, January, 1958.

entiation shown in a single enumeration; they have compared a succession of returns so as to reveal the trends in areal distribution patterns; they have evaluated the returns according to how they reflect the actual situation; they have interpolated data to show actual geographical patterns; and they have studied the relation of the different units in population distribution (e.g., the rural-urban relations and the hierarchy of central places).

The earliest such studies of note are still relatively recent, dating mainly from the years following the First World War. In this period the work of the Inquiry, a research group directed by Isaiah Bowman, studied areal differentiation of Central European populations in unprecedented detail. While an important objective of the Inquiry was the study of cultural differentiation, other results rested on a thorough description of the details of numerical distribution (partly reported in Bowman, 1921). In the same period Sten de Geer (1922) undertook a classic study of the distribution of population in Sweden, in which a very helpful technique for urban-rural cartographic comparison was used for the first time. Aurousseau (1921, 1923) in France and Jefferson in the United States were other geographical scholars examining the problems of describing population distributions during the same years. Among other things, Aurousseau devoted attention to developing a usable method of distinguishing rural and urban population. Jefferson (1909, 1911) was among the first to study the shortcomings of enumerations within arbitrary census areas, and he noted the important difference between geographical concentrations and political cities (see James, 1954).

Since the time of Jefferson and Aurousseau, there has been a succession of geographical studies which try to analyze census and other statistical data and to present these data so as to show areal differentiation. Some have sought refinements of method, giving more realistic presentation of distributional patterns (Wright, 1936, 1937). Others have worked with the problem of meaningful distributional descriptions in the presence of fragmentary or unreliable data (Louis, 1952), and still others with the extension of distributional knowledge into areas of underdeveloped economies, poorly developed governmental structure, or other characteristics conducive to retarded or previously fragmentary information (e.g., Trewartha and Zelinsky, 1954*a, b*). Perhaps most numerous have been the straightforward interpretations of national or regional enumerations, which attempt to provide a description of the most recently known static pattern (e.g., Fawcett, 1932; James, 1938; Melón, 1952; Ahmad, 1953; Cumberland, 1953; Stevens, 1946).

Some of the most careful and interesting studies have concerned the dynamics of population distribution as they could be interpreted from a series of census returns. Even before 1900, one study based on the returns of 1870, 1880, and 1890 had appeared in the United States (Whitney, 1894). Stanley Dodge's work (1946) on the relation of population dynamics to the frontier in the United States is a good example of geographical methods applied to an illumination of trends. Dodge's study covers two and one-half centuries, and the entire country. More typically, geographical studies of this kind treat limited periods (Neuvy, 1956; Willatts and Newson, 1953; Friis, 1940) or limited areas (Kollmorgen and Jenks, 1951–52; Schwind, 1954).

Some prominent geographers consider these and other geographic studies of population of basic importance to the entire field of human geography (James, 1954). Trewartha (1953) especially has presented the case for geographic population study as "pivotal" to the entire field of human geography, and he urges greater attention to it. This would suggest that population distribution studies are likely to be undertaken by geographers as a necessity in their own field, whatever the relation of geographic study to demography. It would also suggest that the refinement and extension of demographic data are of great importance to the human geographer and will be a stimulus to his further application in this field.

STUDY OF THE SEVERAL POPULATION ATTRIBUTES IN THEIR DISTRIBUTIONAL ASPECTS

Geographers generally have devoted less of their effort to distributional studies of specific demographic attributes beyond straight enumeration. Nonetheless, they have paid some attention to these subjects. Specific studies of natality and mortality are not common in geographical literature, but examples can be found—Dodge's (1946) study of population trends, for example, describes trends in United States fertility rates specifically. For this reason, only a few original studies of population projection problems have been undertaken. (One example is Steigenga, 1954. Studies on natural resources or other economic phenomena—of indirect significance to projections—have been numerous.) Where needed, the projections used by the geographer generally have been drawn from the work of the demographer (for example, the projections used in the post-World War II sustenance study of Japan; see Ackerman, 1953, p. 7).

Distributional studies of other specific demographic attributes also have been undertaken. Migrations and their distributional consequences have been attractive subjects for geographers, as might be expected. Proudfoot's (1956) study of European refugee movements during and after the Second World War is the most detailed research undertaken by a geographer on this subject. While its content goes beyond the distinctively geographic, it illustrates well the geographer's affinity to problems of areal change in population. Geographers also have treated migration in terms of its mechanism (Porter, 1956) and its correlation with environmental features (Ullman, 1954) or settlement (Gottmann, 1957). A number of specific regional or national studies also might be cited, for example, Nelson (1953), Mather (1956), Dyer (1952), and Hart (1957).

Geographic studies describing ethnic distributions (Calef and Nelson, 1956; Price, 1953; Schroeder, 1956), health conditions, and age and sex ratios (Franklin, 1958) also have been undertaken. The extensive studies of disease distribution supported by the American Geographical Society have been noteworthy among these special distributional studies (e.g., May, 1952). They illustrate the results to be obtained from competent collaborative effort between geographers and workers in other disciplines in studying specialized aspects of demographic geography.

SETTLEMENT PATTERNS AND SETTLEMENT INTERRELATION

The relation between population dynamics and economic and other societal phenomena has long been appreciated; in fact, investigation of this relation can be traced to the beginnings of demography. Prominent among the phenomena investigated have been settlement forms and the several determinants of economic productivity. In part because of the world's demographic history since 1940, we now know that the interrelations of these elements and population growth are extremely complex and intricate, subject to no simple interpretation (see United Nations, 1953). We perhaps are still closer to the beginning than to the completion of conclusive analysis of these elements and their interrelation.

One obvious entry into this complex field is through the study of settlement forms, their distribution, and the evolution of their distribution. This is one important point of contact between people and the earth to which they are bound. Geographers perhaps have pursued these studies more assiduously than any others related to demography. The field of urban geography has been particularly well cultivated, but studies of the general nature of settlement and of rural farm and non-farm settlement also have been pursued. German geographers have devoted much attention to analyzing settlement types and distinctions among them (e.g., Christaller, 1938; Gradmann, 1937).[6] This was a natural consequence of German geographic methodology's emphasis on *Länderkunde* and *Landschaftskunde*. (See Hartshorne, 1939, pp. 207–10, 224–27, for explanation of these terms.) While the German view has notably influenced the practice of American geography, United States studies have turned much more in the direction of urban geography. The pioneering studies of Jefferson (1921, 1931) indicated a choice of direction which since has become popular among American geographers, and a copious American, British, and European professional literature has accumulated on urban geography. (See Mayer, 1954*a*, pp. 162–66, for a recent illustrative bibliography of urban geographic studies, especially of the United States.) Many studies have treated the morphology and functions of towns or sections of cities, and there is a notable series undertaken under the direction of Charles C. Colby and others of the University of Chicago faculty (e.g., Klove, 1942; Harris, 1940). Treatment of mapping techniques (e.g., Jones, 1931; Applebaum, 1952) and a variety of specialized studies of the internal structure of cities also were undertaken (e.g., Proudfoot, 1937).

From a study of cities' morphology and functions a natural step is to investigate the over-all structural pattern of urban settlement and the relation of cities, towns, and villages to each other. While geographers recently have shared this subject increasingly with economists, sociologists, and planning analysts, provocative analysis was undertaken early by geographers (Christaller, 1933; Jefferson, 1939; Ullman, 1941). Their attention to it has been continued (e.g., Dickinson, 1947; Smailes, 1946; Mayer, 1954*b*). Further study has been devoted to articulating parts of the settlement pattern, especially the function of transportation (e.g., Brush, 1953). Although not specifically directed toward the problem of articulation, the very extensive set of regional studies which twentieth-century geography has produced could serve as background material for research in this field. (For a descriptive summary of the methods of regional geography, see Whittlesey, 1954.)

While less cultivated in recent years than urban geography, study of rural settlement also has been conducted by geographers in a number of countries. Much investigation has centered on forms related to agricultural pursuits (e.g., Demangeon, 1920; Barrows, 1910; Hall, 1931; Stevens, 1946; Thorpe, 1952),[7] but the treatment of rural non-farm settlement also has appeared recently (e.g., Kant, 1957).

Studies of settlement often, and sometimes inevitably, have included attention to functions represented in the settlement forms. This interest has been extended into study of functional relations of different types of population distribution (e.g., McCarty, 1942) and of the relation of population dynamics to functions of settlements (e.g., Roterus, 1946). Geographers have undertaken

---

[6] Christaller generally has been considered an economist; however, works like the *Siedlungsgeographie* have become part of geography's professional literature. While Christaller was an economist first, he was a geographer too.

[7] These are taken only to illustrate the time span and type of hundreds of studies in this subfield.

studies which localize functional relations of interest to demographers and which investigate the meaning of local demographic events of concern to students of areal phenomena. At one stage in the field's progress, geographers' attraction to studies of the relation (or covariation) of population distribution, settlement forms, and functions prompted one leading geographer (Barrows, 1923) to propose human geography as human ecology. However, geography has not followed the trend proposed by Professor Barrows, although it has continued to have a preoccupation with covariants in the composite pattern of physical and cultural features on the earth.

COMMON INTERESTS OF OTHER DISCIPLINES IN FIELDS TREATED BY GEOGRAPHY

Within recent years students from other disciplines also have become concerned with the manifold problems of distribution and distributional relations. This is illustrated in the discussion of human ecology and population distribution presented elsewhere in this volume (chap. xxviii). Although the Barrows proposal did not anticipate a trend in geography, it did anticipate the growth of another field of study. The common ground of human ecology and human geography is suggested by Duncan's reference to the works of ten different geographers in the presentation of his chapter. Distributional studies are of obvious concern to the human ecologist.

Sociologists, economists, physicists, and others have profitably turned their attention to distributional problems associated with depicting the reticulated structure of settlement, population agglomeration, and social function. The works of Bogue (1955) in sociology, Isard (1956) in economics, and of the physicist Stewart (1947) have been considered helpful contributions to the subjects which have preoccupied geographers for decades. These and similar

works have been well received among geographers because they afforded fresh insights, although not necessarily conclusive approaches, to the increasingly complex problems of understanding the distributional structure of man's relation to the earth.

LOGICAL FUTURE RESEARCH INTEREST IN GEOGRAPHY

At least two prominent American geographers in recent years have stressed the importance of population studies to their field. James (1954, p. 107) has summarized the situation: "The irregularity of the distribution of mankind over the earth and the differences from place to place in the racial and societal character of the population are facts which underlie all studies in social science, including those of human geography." Trewartha (1953, p. 83), in the most thoughtful American analysis of the meaning of geographic population studies, states that "numbers, densities, and qualities of the population provide the essential background for all geography. *Population is the point of reference from which all other elements are observed, and from which they all, singly and collectively, derive significance and meaning.*" While partisans of the landscape school of geography might dispute Trewartha's emphasis, the significance of population study was indorsed by one of the most influential methodologists in the field, Alfred Hettner (Trewartha, 1953, p. 75). Furthermore, even geographers of the landscape school have contributed studies of indirect importance to demography through studies of settlement. While relatively few geographers have undertaken comprehensive studies of geography of population per se (one exception is Pierre George, 1951), it is safe to say that a majority of them today would recognize a significant relation between geographic and demographic research. This seems especially true since the end of the Second World War, when the demographer began to broaden his vision in seeking an answer to population dynamics.

A further point of interest in this relation is the connection between geographic research, resource-use planning, and settlement planning. It is patent that the technology of the future will contain an increasing element of these techniques and that they must eventually be taken into account in any evaluation of population dynamics. The techniques of geographic research and its results are basic to efficient planning (see Mayer, 1954a, p. 162). Accordingly, any evaluation of the technological element in settlement influences and sustenance patterns as they affect population characteristics may be illuminated by appropriate geographic study.

If the above assumptions are accepted, a further view of the possible character of forthcoming geographical research may form a helpful conclusion. One view of this prospect has been presented as follows (see Ackerman, 1958, for an elaboration of the statement given here): Geography treats areal differentiations, and all significant areal differentiation has a time dimension. A near universal characteristic of space-relation patterns on the earth is constant change. Study of the *evolution* of space content on the earth's surface is geography's research frontier. Geographers can seek understanding of the evolution of earth distributions in the operation of at least eight different physical, biotic, and cultural processes: movement of the soil mantle; movement of water over land; climate; biotic processes, particularly the vegetative; demographic movement; organizational evolution; development of the resource-converting techniques; and development of the space-adjusting techniques.[8] Demographic movement is at the heart of these forces which influence the change in space content.

Within this framework the following general research problems are recognized: study of distributions in the abstract and development of the general theory of area distribution, perfection of techniques of observation, study of the action of the processes on a given class of phenomena, study of the covariance of the processes as reflected in space relations, and integration of data on the several processes with those of site. Quantification is considered a major problem in describing the space-relations effect of the significant processes causing change (see, for example, Robinson and Bryson, 1957), and observational techniques need much further development if they are to match the need for quantification. Finally, study of the covariance of the significant processes is only at its beginning.

In the future, geographic research is likely to proceed on the assumption that the cultural, physical, and biotic worlds are something of a continuum for the understanding of space relations. However, disaggregative research stressing quantification may be most influential in determining the future direction taken by the discipline. In this the data and interpretations of demography will be very important to geography. Geography, on the other hand, will aspire to illuminate the scene on which population growth and decline runs its course.

SELECTED BIBLIOGRAPHY

Ackerman, E. A. 1953. *Japan's Natural Resources.* Chicago: University of Chicago Press.

———. 1958. *Geography as a Fundamental*

---

[8] Resource-converting techniques are those which turn the materials of the physical world and the life products of the biotic world to satisfaction of the needs of men (i.e., land-use techniques, techniques of mineral exploitation, etc.).

Space-adjusting techniques are those which shorten the effective distance of travel and transportation or those which permit intensification of space employment beyond that possible on the natural land surface (e.g., civil engineering, architecture, city and regional planning).

Research Discipline. ("Department of Geography Research Series.") Chicago: University of Chicago.

AHMAD, Q. S. 1953. "Distribution of Population in Pakistan," *Pakistan Geographical Review*, VIII, 94–112, maps.

APPLEBAUM, W. 1952. "A Technique for Constructing a Population and Urban Land Use Map," *Economic Geography*, XXVIII, 240–43.

AUROUSSEAU, M. 1921. "The Distribution of Population: A Constructive Problem," *Geographical Review*, XI, 563–92.

———. 1923. "The Geographic Study of Population Groups," *ibid.*, XIII, 266–82.

BARROWS, H. H. 1910. *Geography of the Middle Illinois Valley.* (Illinois State Geological Survey Bulletin No. 15.) Urbana, Ill.

———. 1923. "Geography as Human Ecology," *Annals of the Association of American Geographers*, XIII, 1–14.

BOGUE, D. J. 1955. "Nodal versus Homogeneous Regions, and Statistical Techniques for Measuring the Influence of Each," preprint, *Proceedings of the Conference of the International Statistical Institute.* Rio de Janeiro.

BOWMAN, I. 1921. *The New World: Problems in Political Geography.* New York and Chicago. 4th ed.; 1928.

BRUSH, J. E. 1953. "The Hierarchy of Central Places in Southwestern Wisconsin," *Geographical Review*, XLIII, 380–402, map.

CALEF, W. C., and NELSON, H. J. 1956. "Distribution of Negro Population in the United States," *Geographical Review*, XLVI, 82–97.

CHRISTALLER, W. 1933. *Die zentralen Orte in Süddeutschland.* Jena: Fischer.

———. 1938. "Siedlungsgeographie und Kommunalwissenschaft," *Petermanns geographische Mitteilungen*, LXXXIV, 49–53.

CUMBERLAND, KENNETH. 1953. "Population Growth in New Zealand: A Review of Recent Census Returns," *The Scottish Geographical Magazine*, LXIX, 97–105, map.

DEMANGEON, A. 1920. "L'habitation rurale en France: Essai de classification des principaux types," *Annales de géographie*, XXIV, 352–75.

DICKINSON, R. E. 1947. *City, Region and Regionalism.* London: Kegan Paul, Trench, Trubner & Co.

DODGE, S. D. 1946. "Periods in the Population History of the United States," *Papers of the Michigan Academy of Science, Arts, and Letters*, XXXII, 253–60.

DÖRRIES, H. 1940. "Siedlungs und Bevölkerungsgeographie (1908–38)," *Geographisches Jahrbuch*, LV, 3–380.

DYER, D. 1952. "The Place of Origin of Florida's Population," *Annals of the Association of American Geographers*, XLII, 283–94, maps.

FAWCETT, C. B. 1932. "Distribution of the Urban Population in Britain in 1931," *Geographical Journal*, LXXIX, 100–116.

FRANKLIN, S. H. 1958. "The Age Structure of New Zealand's North Island Communities," *Economic Geography*, XXXIV, 64–79.

FRIIS, H. R. 1940. "A Series of Population Maps of the Colonies and the United States, 1625–1790," *Geographical Review*, XXX, 463–70.

GEER, S. DE. 1922. "A Map of the Distribution of Population in Sweden: Method of Preparation and General Results," *Geographical Review*, XII, 72–83.

GEORGE, PIERRE. 1951. *Introduction à l'étude géographique de la population du monde.* Paris: Institut National d'Études Démographiques.

GOTTMANN, J. 1957. "Expansion urbaine et mouvements de population," *Research Group for European Migration Problems Bulletin*, No. 5, pp. 53–61.

GRADMANN, R. 1937. "Zur siedlungsgeographischen Methodik," *Geographische Zeitschrift*, XLIII, 353–61.

HALL, R. B. 1931. "Some Rural Settlement Forms in Japan," *Geographical Review*, XXI, 93–123.

HARRIS, C. D. 1940. *Salt Lake City: A Regional Capital.* Chicago: University of Chicago.

HART, J. F. 1957. "Migration and Population Change in Indiana," *Indiana Academy of Science*, LXVI, 195–203.

HARTSHORNE, RICHARD. 1939. *The Nature of Geography: A Critical Survey of Current Thought in the Light of the Past.* Lancaster, Pa.: Association of American Geographers.

ISARD, WALTER. 1956. *Location and Space Economy.* New York: Wiley.

JAMES, P. E. 1938. "The Distribution of People in South America," in *Geographic Aspects of International Relations*. Chicago: University of Chicago Press.

———. 1954. "The Geographic Study of Population," in *American Geography: Inventory and Prospect*, ed. P. E. JAMES and C. F. JONES. Syracuse, N.Y.: Association of American Geographers.

JEFFERSON, MARK. 1909. "The Anthropogeography of Some Great Cities," *Bulletin of the American Geographical Society*, XLI, 537–66.

———. 1911. "The Real New York," *ibid.*, XLIII, 737–40.

———. 1921. "Great Cities of the United States, 1920," *Geographical Review*, XI, 437–41.

———. 1931. "Distribution of the World's City Folks," *ibid.*, XXI, 446–65.

———. 1939. "The Law of the Primate City," *ibid.*, XXIX, 226–32.

JONES, W. D. 1931. "Field Mapping of Residential Areas in Metropolitan Chicago," *Annals of the Association of American Geographers*, XXI, 207–14.

KANT, E. 1957. "Suburbanization, Urban Sprawl, and Commutation: Examples from Sweden," in *Migration in Sweden: A Symposium*, ed. D. HANNERBERG *et al.* ("Lund Studies in Geography," Ser. B, "Human Geography," No. 13.) Lund: C. W. K. Gleerup.

KLOVE, R. C. 1942. *The Park Ridge–Barrington Area*. Chicago: University of Chicago Press.

KOLLMORGEN, W. M., and JENKS, G. F. 1951–52. "A Geographic Study of Population and Settlement Changes in Sherman County, Kansas," *Transactions, Kansas Academy of Sciences*, LIV, 449–94; LV, 1–37, map.

LOUIS, H. 1952. "Über Aufgabe und Möglichkeiten einer Bevölkerungsdichtekarte der Erde: Begleitworte zur beigegebenen Karte 1:80 Mill.," *Petermanns geographische Mitteilungen*, XCVI, 284–88.

McCARTY, H. H. 1942. "A Functional Analysis of Population Distribution," *Geographical Review*, XXXII, 282–93.

MATHER, D. B. 1956. "Migration in the Sudan," in *Geographical Essays on British Tropical Lands*, ed. R. W. STEEL and C. A. FISHER. London: G. Philip & Son.

MAY, J. M. 1952. "Map of the World Distribution of Dengue and Yellow Fever," *Geographical Review*, XLII, 283–86.

MAYER, H. M. 1954a. "Urban Geography," in *American Geography: Inventory and Prospect*, ed. P. E. JAMES and C. F. JONES. Syracuse, N.Y.: Association of American Geographers.

———. 1954b. "Urban Nodality and the Economic Base," *Journal of the American Institute of Planners*, XX, 117–21.

MELÓN, AMANDO. 1952. "La población de España en 1950 (datos y comentarios)," *Estudios geográficos*, XIII, 441–54.

NELSON, H. J. 1953. "Die Binnenwanderung in den USA, am beispiel Kaliforniens," *Die Erde*, II, 109–21.

NEUVY, PIERRE. 1956. "L'évolution de la population japonaise," *Annales de géographie*, LXV, 40–53.

PORTER, R. 1956. "Approach to Migration through Its Mechanism," *Geografiska Annaler*, XXXVIII, 317–43.

PRICE, E. T. 1953. "A Geographic Analysis of White-Negro-Indian Racial Mixtures in Eastern United States," *Annals of the Association of American Geographers*, XLIII, 138–55, maps.

PROUDFOOT, M. J. 1937. "City Retail Structure," *Economic Geography*, XIII, 425–28.

———. 1956. *European Refugees, 1939–52: A Study in Forced Population Movement*. Evanston, Ill.: Northwestern University Press.

ROBINSON, A. H., and BRYSON, R. A. 1957. "A Method for Describing Quantitatively the Correspondence of Geographical Distributions," *Annals of the Association of American Geographers*, XLVII, 379–91.

ROTERUS, V. 1946. "Effects of Population Growth and Non-Growth on the Wellbeing of Cities," *American Sociological Review*, XI, 90–97.

SCHROEDER, K. 1956. "Bevölkerungsgeographische Probleme in Grenzraum der USA gegenüber Mexico," *Die Erde*, VIII, 229–63, map.

SCHWIND, M. 1954. "Bevölkerungsdichte und Bevölkerungsverteilung in Schleswig, 1800–1950," *Berichte zur deutschen Landeskunde*, XIII, 32–43, maps.

SMAILES, A. 1946. "The Urban Mesh of England and Wales," *Transactions of the Institute of British Geographers*, No. 11, pp. 87–101, maps.

STEIGENGA, W. 1954. "Het Vraagstuk der regionale Bevolkingsprognose," *Tijdschrift voor economische en sociale Geographie*, XLV, 80–88.

STEVENS, A. 1946. "The Distribution of Rural Population in Great Britain," *Transactions of the Institute of British Geographers*, No. 11, pp. 23–53.

STEWART, J. Q. 1947. "Empirical Mathematical Rules Concerning the Distribution and Equilibrium of Population," *Geographical Review*, XXXVII, 461–85.

STRUVE, A. W. VON. 1940. "Geography in the Census Bureau," *Economic Geography*, XVI, 275–80.

THORPE, H. 1952. "The Influence of Inclosure on the Form and Pattern of Rural Settlement in Denmark," *Transactions of the Institute of British Geographers*, No. 17, 111–29, maps.

TREWARTHA, G. T. 1953. "The Case for Population Geography," *Annals of the Association of American Geographers*, XLIII, 71–97.

———, and ZELINSKY, W. 1954*a*. "Population Patterns in Tropical Africa," *Annals of the Association of American Geographers*, XLIV, 135–62, map.

———. 1954*b*. "The Population Geography of Belgian Africa," *ibid.*, pp. 163–93, map.

ULLMAN, E. L. 1941. "A Theory of Location for Cities," *American Journal of Sociology*, XLVI, 853–64.

———. 1954. "Amenities as a Factor in Regional Growth," *Geographical Review*, XLIV, 119–32.

UNITED NATIONS, POPULATION DIVISION. 1953. *The Determinants and Consequences of Population Trends*. New York: United Nations.

WHITNEY, J. D. 1894. *The United States: Facts and Figures Illustrating the Physical Geography of the Country and Its Material Resources. Supplement 1, Population: Immigration: Irrigation*. Boston: Little, Brown & Co.

WHITTLESEY, D. 1954. "The Regional Concept and the Regional Method," in *American Geography: Inventory and Prospect*, ed. P. E. JAMES and C. F. JONES. Syracuse, N.Y.: Association of American Geographers.

WILLATTS, E. C., and NEWSON, MARION C. C. 1953. "The Geographical Pattern of Population Changes in England and Wales, 1921–1951," *Geographical Journal*, CXIX, 431–54, maps.

WRIGHT, J. K. 1936. "A Method of Mapping Densities of Population: With Cape Cod as an Example," *Geographical Review*, XXVI, 103–10.

———. 1937. "Some Measures of Distributions," *Annals of the Association of American Geographers*, XXVII, 177–211.

30. Physical Anthropology and Demography

J. N. SPUHLER

"Demography" is defined in the *Oxford Universal Dictionary* (1955) as "that branch of anthropology which treats of the statistics of births, deaths, diseases, etc." In current American practice, both in the professions and in the universities, demography is not a branch of anthropology. Until recent times the two sciences have had little connection. Demography is characterized by the quantitative treatment of four principal topics: fertility, mortality, marriage, and migration. Other qualitative and quantitative population characteristics, such as biological attributes, gene frequencies, or culture traits, have indeed received attention by demographers, but such material has in general been treated as borderline subject matter associated with demography only insofar as such topics have an important effect upon the four principal constitutents (Cox, 1950).

During the last two decades demography and anthropology have come to overlap in some points of view and items of subject matter because of quite independent developments in the two fields. Traditional demographic theory with its search for species-wide population regularities has required substantial modification or supplementation to understand satisfactorily such new phenomena as the combination of rapid population growth with widespread poverty in the "anthropological" (i.e., non-Western) areas of the world or the unexpected, "unlawful" (i.e., non-logistic), recent population growth in the United States. Demographers no longer speak of *the* world population problem, but, as anthropologists would do initially, of the *different* population problems in Egypt, India, Jamaica, Japan, and Taiwan—to mention some of the areas which have received serious demographic analysis from the newer relative-comparative point of view.

Traditionally, physical anthropology has been concerned with three major problems: the evolution of man and the primates, especially the higher primates; the ontogenetic development of man, especially after birth; and the classification of the living varieties of man. Current theoretical views on the first and third problems have been substantially modified by the rise of population genetics, the synthesis of certain aspects of genetics, paleontology and evolution, and especially the view that evolution is a population phenomenon and not an individual one (see, for example, Washburn, 1951, 1953; Spuhler, 1954). Most physical anthropologists today interpret both long-term human evolution and ongoing biological differentiation of local populations in terms of changes in gene frequency. They have borrowed from population genetics what appears to be an exhaustive list of the determinate modes of change in gene frequency (see Wright, 1949, 1950): mutation, selection, gene flow, random genetic drift, and selective mating. Contemporary physical anthropology has fresh interest in the "demographic" topics—fertility, mortality, mating, migration, population number, and composition—because these variables are of fundamental importance in the study of changes in gene frequency.

The purpose of this chapter is to show

728

some of the ways in which information on the "demographic variables" is utilized in physical anthropology. In addition, two further topics will be reviewed to show how morphological techniques of physical anthropology can provide unique background information with time-depth on certain demographically interesting aspects of extinct populations.

The many important recent connections between cultural anthropology and demography will not be discussed in this chapter. The study by Lorimer and his associates on *Culture and Human Fertility* (1954) and some of the papers listed by Kluckhohn (1956) in his review of Lorimer give an excellent general view of this area.

DIFFERENCES IN GENE FREQUENCIES BETWEEN TWO POPULATIONS

Throughout this chapter an elementary knowledge of the terminology and theory of genetics will be assumed; some parts of elementary population genetics will be outlined as needed. (See Snyder and David, *Principles of Heredity*, 5th ed., 1957, for an introduction to general genetics; Neel and Schull, *Human Heredity*, 1954, for a more advanced treatment of human genetics; and Li, *Population Genetics*, 1955, for details of that subject.)

The population frequency of single, autosomal alleles will be symbolized pA and qa where A, a are the alleles and $p = 1 - q$ are their frequencies. The frequencies in a second population may be designated rA and sa where $r = 1 - s$. Genotype or zygotic frequencies will be designated p^2AA, etc. Note that pA means that gene "A" has a population frequency of "p", and that p^2AA means genotype "AA" has a frequency of "p^2" and not some product of p and A. About 5 per cent of the gene material in man is carried in the sex chromosomes—these non-autosomal genes will not be considered here.

We may represent the possible difference between any two populations in autosomal gene frequencies in this way:

Pop. 1: $(pA + qa)(p'B + q'b) \ldots$

$$(p''N + q''n) = 1 ,$$

Pop. 2: $(rA + sa)(r'B + s'b) \ldots$

$$(r''N + s''n) = 1 .$$

If all the p's are equal to corresponding r's throughout, the two populations are identical in gene frequencies. If none of the p's and r's are equal to zero or unity, the gene frequencies may differ between the two populations in degree but not in kind. This last is the general type of difference observed between local populations and geographical races of man both for normal genetic variations (see Mourant, 1954, and Spuhler, 1951, for examples) and for most of the identified deleterious genes (Komai, 1947). However, a number of populations are known where alleles common in other populations at one or more loci are absent from a given population—for instance, the gene associated with blood group A of the ABO series is absent in some American Indian populations, and the gene for B is absent in many American Indian groups.

A basic problem in genetically-oriented physical anthropology is to study the conditions for stability and the modes of change of population gene frequencies. Before outlining the major modes of change in gene frequencies, we will consider some conditions for their stability over two or more generations.

Hardy-Weinberg Steady State

Hardy in England and Weinberg in Germany independently showed in 1908 that population gene frequencies remain constant from generation to generation under a system of random mating (random union of gametes in fertilization) when the frequencies of the heterozygous genotype are equal to twice the product of the square roots of the two homozygous genotype frequencies: $p^2AA + 2pqAa + q^2aa = 1$, where p and q are the relative proportions of alleles A and a in the population. This steady state holds in theory for a breeding population which is ideally large, with non-overlapping generations, where there are no changes in gene frequency due to mutation, selection, gene flow, or genetic drift. (These four modes of change will be discussed below.)

Where multiple alleles are present, the genotypic frequencies are given by the square of the multinomial representing the gene frequencies: for example, if triple alleles occur with frequencies p, q, r summing to unity, their stable genotypic frequencies are given by the expansion of $(p + q + r)^2$. For traits controlled by multiple genes, the equilibrium frequencies of the various genotypes are given by expansion of the products of the squares of the allelic frequencies for each locus involved; for example, for two pairs of alleles, the frequencies of the nine genotypes are given by expansion of $(p + q)^2(p' + q')^2 = 1$.

In the case of single alleles, equilibrium is reached in the first generation after random mating regardless of the initial genotypic composition of the population. In the case of multiple genes, there is a constant approach toward equilibrium which in theory is never reached and which is slower for linked genes than for those at independent loci.

Random Mating

Strictly speaking, no human population has a system of random mating. The assumption of random mating implies that if a breeding population is composed of N_0 females and N_1 males and if a given female is the mother of a child by a given father the probability that her next child will have the same father is $1/N_1$. In all known human populations the empirical value of this probability is closer to unity than to $1/N_1$ because most fertile matings tend to endure long enough to produce two or more offspring. This brings about a higher correlation between uniting gametes than that expected under a strictly random system of mating and will account for small departures for the expected proportions of the various genotypes given by the Hardy-Weinberg rule. All known human populations tend to avoid close inbreeding, which tends to decrease the proportion of heterozygous genotypes over that expected under random mating. However, for many cases where the theory of population genetics is used to interpret empirical gene frequency data for human populations, the departures from randomness in mating are sufficiently slight to be negligible. This is especially the case for the genes associated with the red-blood cellular antigens, which provide the largest and most useful body of gene frequency data for anthropological use (Boyd, 1939; Mourant, 1954; Kelus *et al.*, 1953). For example, in the vast majority of known human populations where the ABO blood groups have been specified with reliable testing reagents and technique, the observed phenotype-genotype frequencies do not depart significantly from those expected under random mating (Mourant, 1954).

For the purposes of comparison, in the following sections we will consider an ideal breeding population where the distribution of genes into genotypes is in equilibrium under random mating. We will consider changes in gene distribution brought about by two general types of departures from random mating: inbreeding and assortative mating.

Inbreeding

A first general class of departures from random mating is inbreeding, or the mating of individuals who have one or more biological ancestors in common. Inbreeding should be distinguished from endogamy, the selection of mates within some social group. If sufficiently large, endogamous groups need not be highly inbred. For example, Sanghvi and his associates (1956) estimate that the Desasth Rigveda Brahman, an endogamous caste in India numbering over 300,000 members, has a negligible amount of inbreeding.

Inbred individuals can be joined with their common ancestor(s) by inbreeding loops composed of parent-child steps. The degree of inbreeding is measured by the coefficient of inbreeding, f, which gives the probability that an inbred individual who received some particular gene from a common ancestor over one side of an inbreeding loop will receive the same (in the sense of derivation) gene over the other side of the inbreeding loop and thus be homozygous for the gene in question. The inbreeding coefficient may be defined

$$f = \Sigma \left(\tfrac{1}{2}\right)^{n-1}$$

where n is the number of parent-child steps in an inbreeding loop and the summation is over all loops connecting the inbred individual and his common ancestors. The calculation of f is illustrated in Figure 11, where the parents of the inbred child are related as first cousins, first cousins once removed, and third cousins.

The Hardy-Weinberg steady state modified to represent the population effects of inbreeding on the distribution of genotypes may be written:

$$(p^2 + pqf)\,AA + 2pq\,(1 - f)\,Aa$$
$$+ (q^2 + pqf)\,aa = 1 .$$

The population consequences of certain regular systems of inbreeding are illustrated in Table 62, which starts with a random-bred population where single autosomal alleles have the frequencies of $p = q = 1/2$. Inbreeding reduces the proportion of heterozygotes expected under random mating ($= 2pq$) by a fraction $(1-f)$. Inbreeding as such does

not change gene frequencies but only the distribution of genes into genotypes. When inbreeding is associated with selection, gene frequencies may be altered at comparatively fast rates (Wright, 1921).

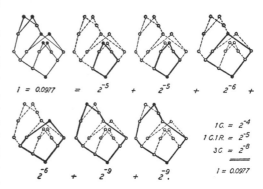

$$l = 0.0977 \;=\; 2^{-5} \;+\; 2^{-5} \;+\; 2^{-6} \;+$$

$$2^{-6} \;+\; 2^{-9} \;+\; 2^{-9}.$$

$$1C. = 2^{-4}$$
$$1C.1R. = 2^{-5}$$
$$3C = 2^{-8}$$
$$\overline{\overline{}}$$
$$l = 0.0977$$

Fig. 11.—Diagrams to illustrate the calculation of the inbreeding coefficient. The parents of the inbred child are related as first cousins, first cousins once removed, and third cousins. The six inbreeding loops connecting the inbred child and his six common ancestors are shown (Spuhler and Kluckhohn, 1953).

TABLE 62

Changes in Percentage of Heterozygotes under Various Regular Systems of Inbreeding[*]

Generation	Brother-Sister	Double First Cousins	Single First Cousins	Single Second Cousins
0....	0.500	0.500	0.500	0.500
1....	.375	.438	.469	.491
2....	.312	.406	.453	.491
3....	.250	.375	.439	.491
4....	.203	.344	.427	.491
5....	.164	.316	.416	.491
10....	.057	.208	.374	.491
15....	.020	.137	.344	.491
∞....	0.000	0.000	0.000	0.491

[*] Source: Wright (1921).

Since a considerable proportion of all rare deleterious genes carried in a human population are recessives in single dose, inbreeding increases the incidence of deleterious homozygous recessive genotypes. This is the explanation for the well-known observation that the degree of consanguinity is greater among the parents of offspring with rare recessive abnormalities than in the general population.

Probably no natural and lasting human populations have experienced the degree of inbreeding common for some farm animals and laboratory organisms, that is, population levels of $f > 0.4$. No known human society, for example, has practiced a regular system of brother-sister mating, although this has been a preferred mating in the upper classes of a few societies, of which the Ptolemies of Egypt are perhaps the best known. Actually, it would be impossible

tion estimates of f values. Even in the few cases where a large number of marriages have been classified according to kinship of the spouses (two African examples with relatively extensive data are Ashton, 1952, for the Sotho of Basutoland and Schapera, 1953, for the Tswana of Bechuanaland), it is not possible to make accurate estimates of population values of f because the relationship of the published sample to the total population is unknown or unreported. Cultural anthropologists have been slow to adopt proper sampling procedures: the neces-

TABLE 63

ESTIMATES OF INBREEDING LEVELS IN VARIOUS POPULATIONS*

Population	Period	Number	f
L'Yonne, France	1926–45	. . . . . .	.0002
Nagasaki, Japan	1945–49	842	.0004
Germany (rural Catholics)	1848–72	5,283	.0005
Argentina	1954	23,000	.0005
Austria (urban Catholics)	1901–2	40,498	.0006
Uruguay	1952	5,370	.0006
Rio de Janeiro, Brazil	1954	1,272	.0008
Puerto Rico	1954	6,013	.0013
Corse, France	1926–45	. . . . . .	.0024
Hiroshima, Japan	1948–49	10,547	.0029
Kure, Japan	1948–49	5,510	.0033
Waifu, Japan	1949	2,908	.0046
Midori, Japan (Eta village)	1949	147	.0045
Rhineland (Protestants)	1840–89	376	.0050
Alagoas, Brazil	1954	3,566	.0055
Ramah Navaho Indians, New Mexico	1948	1,118	.0066

* Data from Freire-Maia (1957); Neel *et al.* (1949); Schull (1953); Spuhler and Kluckhohn (1953); Sutter and Tabah (1948).

to practice a regular system of brother-sister mating in a human population if all adults reproduced because a considerable proportion of all sibships are composed of sibs of the same sex. Representative samples of the inbreeding level in various populations are given in Table 63.

As might be inferred from Table 63, considerably more data are available on inbreeding levels in national populations or in local groups within national populations than on primitive tribes. Although anthropologists have long been interested in systems of kinship and marriage (Murdock, 1949), they have published very little quantitative information of the kind needed to make popula-

sities of intensive field work using ethnographical techniques make representative sampling for population data difficult but not impossible or impractical.

France is the only country where inbreeding levels have been extensively studied on a national scale. In a series of excellent studies, Sutter and Tabah (1948) give inbreeding levels for all the departments of France for the period 1926–45 (their $\alpha = f$). In this connection, the less extensive but nonetheless large studies of Friere-Maia (1957) for Brazil and several investigations for Japan (see Schull, 1953) should be mentioned.

Many human breeding populations of anthropological interest are small in size and prohibit marriage of relatives as close as first cousins. A necessary consequence is that distant relationships will contribute greatly to the mean f of the population. For example, Spuhler and Kluckhohn (1953) estimate that about 57 per cent of the known inbreeding of the Ramah Navaho Indians (population 619 in 1948) would have been neglected had the study been restricted to degrees of relationship equal to or greater than third cousins and to specification of a single (closest) type of relationship for each inbred mating. Thus, accurate estimation of inbreeding levels in small populations with restricted immigration requires ascertainment of all

becomes increasingly small according to the general formula $(1/2)^{2i+2}$ where i is the degree of full cousinship.

There is considerable experimental evidence to suggest an optimum proportion of heterozygosity in bisexual populations of fruit flies, chickens, and the larger farm animals (Lerner, 1954), where survival to reproduction or some other given age is taken as the standard of reference. Inbreeding reduces the proportion of all loci which are heterozygous. Thus if heterozygosity in itself is beneficial to the population as judged by survival, then inbreeding, from the viewpoint of population survival, is harmful. This is particularly the case in

TABLE 64

DISTRIBUTION OF DEATHS DURING THE FIRST EIGHT YEARS AFTER BIRTH BY
PARENTAL RELATIONSHIP, ATOMIC BOMB CASUALTY COMMISSION
SAMPLE, HIROSHIMA, JAPAN, 1948–56*

Parental Relationship	f	Number of Infants Born Alive	Number of Deaths	Per Cent Deaths
First cousins....................	.0625	352	41	11.65
First cousins once removed.......	.0312	106	9	8.49
Second cousins................	.0156	144	8	5.56
Unrelated.....................	0	567	31	5.47
Totals	......	1169	89	7.61

* Source: Schull (1957).

degrees of relationship between spouses; a complete genealogy of the population over several generations is needed rather than an enumeration of, say, first- and second-cousin marriages alone. However, in human breeding populations which are fairly large and where cousin marriage is neither prohibited nor preferred, as in certain Japanese communities, estimates of mean f based on counts up to third cousin alone may be quite accurate. In populations where kinship marriages are not disapproved, rough estimates of the degree of inbreeding can be derived from the rate of full first-cousin marriage—a rough approximation is that f is equal to one-tenth of the percentage of first-cousin marriages among all marriages. The contribution of the more remote cousin relationships to f

large animals like man with usually single births and relatively low fertility.

Schull (1957) found that the regression of percentage mortality in the first eight years of life on degree of inbreeding based on four f values had a coefficient of $b = 0.99$ for a sample of 1179 live births in Hiroshima, Japan, of which 567 were from unrelated parents (Table 64). The regression of percentage mortality on inbreeding is even more striking for the Ramah Navaho population (where $b = 33.91$), although the available data are not fully satisfactory for regression analysis due to the small size of the population. Sutter (1957) feels that inbreeding leads to higher pre-reproductive mortality only in economically distressed populations. The carefully controlled results obtained by

Schull in Japan as well as evidence from experimental organisms make it difficult to accept this conclusion as having general validity. Morton *et al.* (1956), using information on increased mortality in children of inbred marriages in two French departments (1919–25) and in the United States (nineteenth century), estimate that the average person carries heterozygously the equivalent of three to five recessive lethals which act between late fetal and early adult stages.

If the total number of gene loci in man is of the order 20,000 (Spuhler, 1948),

TABLE 65

OBSERVED FREQUENCIES OF THE ABO BLOOD GROUPS AND MN BLOOD TYPES IN 458 RAMAH NAVAHO INDIANS WITH MEAN POPULATION $f = 0.007$ COMPARED TO VALUES EXPECTED UNDER RANDOM MATING*

System	Phenotypes	Genotypes	Inbred $f = .007$	Random $f = 0$
ABO	A	AA	0.017	0.016
		Aa	.218	.220
	O	aa	.765	.764
MN	M	MM	.829	.830
	MN	Mm	.163	.162
	N	mm	0.008	0.008

* Source: Spuhler and Kluckhohn (1953).

even low levels of inbreeding (of the order $0.001 < f < 0.01$ or, say, an average for inbred individuals corresponding to the level for second cousins where $f = 0.0156$) would make the average inbred individual homozygous for 78 more loci than the average non-inbred individual, assuming that one-half of all loci are heterozygous in the random-bred portion of the population.

With regard to some specified single locus, the degree of inbreeding experienced in most human populations including those with the higher f levels does not lead to marked changes in the distribution of genotypes from those expected under random mating. This conclusion may be illustrated by comparing the genotype frequencies (Table 65) ex-

pected under random mating with those actually observed in the Ramah Navaho population, where the degree of inbreeding is toward the higher end of the known distribution for human populations ($f = 0.007$) for the ABO blood group genes A and a (the gene for group B is absent from this population) and for the MN blood type genes.

Haldane (1938) has shown that departures in the amount of heterozygosity from that expected under random mating can be used to estimate the degree of inbreeding in natural populations (if similar effects on gene distribution due to assortative mating can be excluded). The population mean f for the Ramah Navaho population was found to be 0.007 from a genealogical study of the population over seven generations since its founding. We can obtain an indirect estimate of f for this population using data on the distribution of the MN blood types where the three genotypes can be determined directly by serological tests.

The expected ratios of the genotypes in an inbred population with inbreeding coefficient f may be written:

$$(u^2 + fu) \text{ MM} : 2(1 - f) u \text{ Mm} :$$
$$(fu + 1) \text{ mm} .$$

If we let the observed phenotype-genotype frequencies be

$$a \text{ M} + b \text{ MN} + c \text{ N} = n ,$$

then

$$u = (2a + b) / (b + 2c) ,$$

and

$$f = (4ac - b^2) / (2a + b)(b + 2c) .$$

Although the observed frequencies of the MN blood types ($380 \text{ M} + 74 \text{ MN} + 4 \text{ N} = 458$) do not depart significantly from the proportions expected under random mating ($\chi^2 = 0.0358$, $0.8 < P < 0.9$), the directly observed value of f is sufficiently small that larger deviations from the theoretical proportions appropriate under random mating are not to be expected. With this in mind, and noting that the N gene is rare in this population and that estimates of its frequency are subject to considerable error in such small samples, it is of interest that the observed departure from random expectation is in the direction expected with inbreeding and that the indirect estimate gives a value of $f = 0.009$, which is remarkably close to the directly observed value of $f = 0.007$ for the mean inbreeding coefficient of all members of sibships belonging to generations five through eight (the latest) of the population.

Assortative Mating

A second general class of departures from random mating is assortative mating. When mates in a breeding population have more attributes in common than would be expected by chance, the system is called positive assortative mating; when they have less attributes in common than would be expected by chance, the system is called negative assortative mating. The degree of assortment is usually measured by some association statistic ranging from $+1$ for perfect positive assortative mating to -1 for perfect negative assortative mating. The population consequences of positive assortative mating are similar to those for inbreeding in that the proportion of heterozygous genotypes is reduced, and that of homozygous genotypes increased, in comparison to the proportions expected under random mating. The consequences for multiple gene modes of inheritance differ from those with inbreeding in that fewer of the homozygous genotypes are preserved. For example, if five phenotypes $(1, 2, \ldots 5)$ are controlled by two pairs of genes at different loci $(A, a; B, b)$ as follows: 1—*AABB*, 2—*AaBB, AABb*, 3—*AAbb, AaBb, aaBB*, 4—*Aabb, aaBb*, 5—*aabb*, a system of close inbreeding will result in a genotype distribution with all homozygous classes (*AABB, AAbb, aaBB, aabb*) preserved, while one of perfect positive assortative mating will preserve only two homozygous classes (*AABB, aabb*). The population consequences of negative assortative mating are in the opposite direction, with an increase in the proportion of heterozygous genotypes, although long continued negative assortment does not lead to a population with all members heterozygous. The results to be expected from assortative mating for different modes of inheritance are given in Table 66.

Assortative mating alone is not of evolutionary consequence; it changes the distribution of genes into genotypes but not the frequency of genes. However, assortative mating in association with selection can rapidly change gene frequencies.

We have poorer information on assortative mating in human populations than on inbreeding. Some data are available, however, for physical, psychological, and social characteristics. Only about one-tenth of the published information is summarized in Table 67.

A study of assortative mating for body size has been carried out by Spuhler and Clark (1957) on the adult population of Ann Arbor, Michigan. A random sample of 205 married pairs, 111 single males, and 109 single females together with 205 of their relatives (parent, child, or sibling) was observed for forty-three traits including age, weight, and measurements of body lengths, breadths, and circumferences. Twenty-nine of the measurements (67.4 per cent) show between-mate correlations significant at the 5 per cent level. Until a multivariate analysis is carried out, stress should not be placed on the exact number of significant correlations obtained because some of the traits are themselves intercorrelated.

Like-sex parent-child and sib-sib correlations computed for the related members of the Ann Arbor sample suggest that a considerable portion of the variance in the twenty-nine measurements of body size is due to genetic factors. This conclusion is given additional support by a study of the heritability of these anthropometric characters in eighty-one pairs of twins of the same sex observed from the same general southeastern Michigan population (Clark, 1956).

In order to determine if the married pairs of our sample who were similar in body size differed in fertility from those who were dissimilar in body size, we calculated within-pair indexes of fertility and similarity. A square-root transformaton of years of exposure to pregnancy plotted against the number of live-born children showed a strong, approximately linear relationship between exposure and fertility. From this relationship a score was obtained giving the difference between observed and expected fertility for each couple. The range in this fer-

TABLE 66

PERCENTAGE OF HETEROZYGOSIS IN VARIOUS GENE SYSTEMS UNDER VARIOUS DEGREES (r) OF ASSORTATIVE MATING

n = Number of Pairs of Genes. A Condition of No Dominance Is Assumed*

GENERA-TION	PERFECT ASSORTATIVE MATING			IMPERFECT ASSORTATIVE MATING						PERFECT NEGATIVE ASSORTATIVE MATING	
	$r = +1.00$			$r = +.80$		$r = +.50$		$r = +.25$		$r = -1.00$	
	$n=1$	$n=2$	$n=10$	$n=1$	$n=10$	$n=1$	$n=10$	$n=1$	$n=10$	$n=1$	$n=4$
0......	.500	.500	.500	.500	.500	.500	.500	.500	.500	.500	.500
1......	.250	.375	.475	.300	.480	.375	.488	.438	.494	.750	.563
2......	.125	.312	.462	.220	.472	.344	.484	.430	.493	.625	.531
3......	.063	.266	.451	.188	.465	.336	.482	.429	.493	.687	.535
4......	.031	.227	.439	.175	.459	.334	.481	.429	.492	.656	.533
5......	.016	.193	.428	.170	.454	.333	.479	.429	.492	.672	.533
10......	.001	.088	.376	.167	.436	.333	.477	.429	.492	.667	.533
15......	.000	.040	.330	.167	.427	.333	.476	.429	.492	.667	.533
∞......	0	0	0	.167	.417	.333	.476	.429	.492	.667	.533

* From Wright (1921) with additions.

TABLE 67

ASSORTATIVE MATING FOR PHYSICAL, PSYCHOLOGICAL, AND SOCIOLOGICAL CHARACTERISTICS

(Tetrachoric Correlations Are Marked with an Asterisk)

Characteristic	Population	Number of Pairs	Authors	
Age......................	U.S.	2500	Lutz '05	.76 ± .01
Stature....................	English	1000	Pearson and Lee '03	.28 ± .02
Eye color.................	English	774	Pearson '06	.26 ± .03
Weight....................	U.S.	989	Burgess and Wallin '44	.21 ± .03
Cephalic index	U.S.	319	Harris and Govaerts '22	.02 ± .04
Memory....................	U.S.	80	Schooley '36	.57 ± .05
Intelligence (Stanford)	U.S.	174	Burks '28	.47 ± .04
Association (Kent-Rosanoff)....	U.S.	80	Schooley '36	.47 ± .08
Neurotic tendency (Thurstone).	U.S.	80	Schooley '36	.30 ± .07
Dominance (Benreuter)........	U.S.	100	Hoeffeditz '34	.15 ± .07
Religious affiliation...........	U.S.	941	Burgess and Wallin '44	.75*
Drinking habits...............	U.S.	989	Burgess and Wallin '44	.55*
Number of children desired	U.S.	951	Burgess and Wallin '44	.51*
Years of education...........	U.S.	1000	Burgess and Wallin '44	.40*
Number of siblings...........	U.S.	988	Burgess and Wallin '44	.10*

tility score was from — 2.57 to + 3.49, with a mean of + 0.0003 and a standard deviation of 1.06. The distribution of the fertility scores was found to be satisfactorily close to a normal distribution. An index of similarity made up of the ratio of the husband's measurement to the sum of the husband's and wife's measurements had an approximately normal distribution for both stature (not significantly skewed in our sample) and middle finger length (the most highly skewed in our sample).

A study of the correlation (for each of the twenty-nine traits with significant correlations between mates) between the indexes of similarity and of fertility for the married couples found only one correlation (minimum wrist circumference, with $r = + 0.175$) significantly different from zero at the 5 per cent level, whereas more than one would be expected by chance alone. A similar negative result was obtained with an analysis of variance, which does not require the assumption of a linear relationship between similarity and fertility.

Assortative mating is acting to change the distribution of genotypes concerned with size inheritance in Ann Arbor, but it is not an important mode of evolutionary change in this population because there is little or no differential association between assortative mating for body size and fertility.

Very little empirical information is available regarding the effect of assortative mating on the distribution of known human genes. Hart (1944) has shown that assortative mating for religious affiliation has important consequences for the distribution of the ABO blood group genes in the population of Northern Ireland.

The Elementary Factors of Evolution

Change in gene frequency (q) may be considered the elementary evolutionary process. Wright (1949) distinguished three primary modes of change according to the degree of determinacy in the variations they bring about:

(1) Systematic change: Since Δq is determinate in principle, the following three modes of change are capable of precise mathematical formulation which would make possible prediction of the magnitude of evolutionary change over specified times if there were no processes of an indeterminate nature: (a) recurrent mutation, (b) gene flow, and (c) intragroup selection.

(2) Random fluctuations: In the following two modes of change, δq is indeterminate in direction but determinate in variance: (d) random genetic drift, (e) fluctuations in mutation, gene flow, and intragroup selection.

(3) Non-recurrent change: The following four modes of change in gene frequency are indeterminate for each locus. Although the distinction between (3), and (1) and (2), above, is somewhat arbitrary, it is convenient to consider separately events that are unique or nearly so in the history of the human species: (f) non-recurrent mutation, (g) non-recurrent gene flow, (h) non-recurrent selective incidents, and (i) non-recurrent extreme reduction in numbers.

Mutation

Mutation is the source of all new gene variation. In the course of normal human growth and reproduction each gene must, in general, repeatedly duplicate exactly its own fine structure. On occasion, however, a gene is not an exact duplicate of its parent gene—a mutant gene comes into being. Mutant genes have a different effect on the development of the organism from that of their parent alleles and they are capable of reproducing their own modified fine structure. The combined properties of stability (exact self-reduplication) and mutability (self-reduplication after the new type) of genes make possible the existence of hereditary variability.

A number of mutagenic agents are

known: ionizing radiation which reaches the gonads, temperature shocks, and chemical shocks. Multiple alleles are formed when a set of alleles of one type mutates in a number of different ways. Beneficial mutation should occur much more rarely than deleterious mutation. Man's present set of genes have been selected from a long series of diverse mutations in the species set of genes. In a highly complex entity like a gene, most

reverse rate, and t is the time in generations.

Data on some spontaneous mutation rates per gene per generation are given in Table 68. The list would be nearly twice as long had all published rates been included. These rates tend to cluster about 1 in 50,000 in the more reliable estimates, although higher rates of the order 1 in 10,000 are as securely established as any of the better estimates.

TABLE 68

SPONTANEOUS MUTATION RATES (PER GENE PER GENERATION) IN MAN*

Character	Population	Mutant Genes per Million Gametes	Authors
Epiloia	England	8–12	Penrose, '36
Chondrodystrophy	Denmark	42	Mørch, '41
Chondrodystrophy	Sweden	70	Böök, '52
Chondrodystrophy	Denmark (mothers over 40 years)	200	Krooth, '53
Pelger's nuclear anomaly	Germany, *inter alia*	27	Nachtsheim, '53
Aniridia	Denmark	12	Møllenbach, '47
Retinoblastoma	England	14	Philip and Sorsby
Retinoblastoma	Michigan	23	Neel and Falls, '51
Retinoblastoma	Germany	4	Vogel, '54
Neurofibromatosis	Michigan	100	Crowe, Schull, and Neel, '55
Multiple polyposis colon	Michigan	10–30	Reed and Neel, '55
Microphthalmos+anopthalmos	Sweden	10–20	Sjögren and Larson, '49
Albinism	Japan	28	Neel *et al.*, '49
Total colorblindness	Japan	28	Neel *et al.*, '49
Infantile amaurotic idiocy	Japan	11	Neel *et al.*, '49
Ichthyosis congenita	Japan	11	Neel *et al.*, '49
Cystic fibrosis pancreas	Minnesota	700–1000	Goodman and Reed, '52
Epidermolysis bullosa	Sweden	50	Böök, '52
Amyotonia congenita	Sweden	20	Böök, '52
Microcephaly	Japan	22–76	Komai, '54
Hemophilia	England	20	Haldane, '48
Hemophilia	Denmark	32	Andreassen, '43

* See Spuhler (1956) for references.

random changes in fine structure would be expected to have low survival value. Beneficial results of mutation would have been selected in the past. A large proportion of new gene mutations do not survive to the next generation. Some recent reviews on mutation in man are by Glass (1954), Neel and Schull (1954), Nachtsheim (1954), and Spuhler (1956).

The net mutation rate per generation for single alleles is given by

$$\Delta q = dq/dt = v(1-q) - uq$$

where u is the mutation rate from a gene with frequency q to its allele, v is the

Estimates of reverse mutation rates are not available for man. Probably most of the values given for spontaneous mutation in man are overestimates. Statistical estimates of the error of mutation rates have not been devised for the non-experimental procedures used in human genetics, but in some cases maximum estimates can be made. The rough agreement in the several results for different characters gives some hope that they are of the right order of magnitude.

On theoretical grounds we should expect differences in mutation rates in populations with diverse mutagenic environments. Muller (1954) speculates that people living on the high plateaus of Bolivia and Tibet receive from cosmic sources about 5 roentgens per generation more radiation than those living at sea level—an extra dosage which would increase a mutation rate of 10^{-5} by about 6 per cent. There is considerable geographical variation in amount of background irradiation due to differing amounts of radioactive minerals in the earth's crust. Inhabitants of stone or brick houses receive more radiation than those living in structures made of plant or animal materials. If mutation rates are constant, population number is important for total mutation. Krooth (1953) has suggested that mutation rates for chondrodystrophy go up with age of mothers, and a similar finding is supported by Penrose (1955) for fathers.

Morton *et al.* (1956) used data on the increased mortality in children of related parents and a guess as to the number of loci per gamete to estimate the total mutation rate to lethal and detrimental genes in man as $6–15 \times 10^{-6}$ per locus per generation. In fruit flies (*Drosophila*) lethal, semilethal, and deleterious mutations are fifteen to twenty times more common than visible ones. Lacking evidence to the contrary, a similar relationship may be assumed to hold for man.

Probably the mutation rate for common human genes, like those for the blood groups, is sufficiently low and the average effective size of breeding groups sufficiently small that mutation pressure is not a major determinant of observable local and regional differences in gene frequencies.

Gene Flow

Gene flow refers to recurrent introduction of genes into a population by outbreeding. It is not strictly parallel with migration in the full sense of the latter. Genes may regularly enter a human breeding population from the outside without the individuals who introduced the genes (usually males) becoming integrated into the population. Wife-lending, "hereditary" friendships, and perhaps general promiscuity are examples of social customs which allow gene flow without immigration. However, in general, this more or less casual outbreeding is of only secondary importance in changing gene frequencies. A more important type of gene flow involves a regular introduction of individuals from neighboring groups which are partially isolated reproductively.

The effects of gene flow on local frequencies is similar to those of mutation (Li, 1955). Their joint systematic effect may be written:

$$\Delta q = (u + m\bar{q})\, p - (v + m\bar{p})\, q$$

where m is the rate of gene flow per generation, u and v are forward and reverse mutation rates, and

$$\bar{p} + \bar{q} = 1$$

are the gene frequencies in the migrants.

Some of the more spectacular cases of race mixture should be viewed as unique events rather than as examples of gene flow. The Dunns of Zululand are an interesting case in point. This mixed group was founded by John Dunn, who was born in Port Elizabeth in 1833 of white parents. In 1857 Dunn became military advisor to the Zulu King Cetshwayo on the promise of a grant of land and wives. His one Malay-white and forty-eight Zulu wives bore him more than 100 children. His descendants did not become assimilated into the native tribes but became an independent community ranging in physical type from Negro to white. In 1936 the Dunn Reserve in Zululand had about 235 members (Burrows *et al.*, 1953). For a general summary of physical anthropological studies on race mixture, see Trevor (1953).

Unfortunately, much of the vast literature by demographers on international and internal migration, while of great background interest, cannot be applied directly to the study of gene flow in population genetics and physical anthropology. Much of the published information on internal migration cannot be used to provide close estimates of the amount of gene flow because dispersal is *classified* into "migration" and "not migration" according to movement or lack of movement across the boundary of a political unit which may be larger than average dispersal distances between generations.

Seemingly, an appropriate mathematical model is not available for estimating the size of a breeding neighborhood centering about some point within a quasi-continuous population of variable density. Wright (1946, 1950) developed a model which, given certain simplifying assumptions, gave an estimate of the effective size of a local breeding neighborhood within an indefinitely large population with uniform density and areal continuity. A basic assumption in Wright's model is that the locations of parents at a given point in their life cycle are distributed according to a bivariate normal distribution with standard deviation σ for both X and Y co-ordinates of the parental locations relative to the progeny's locations at the same point in the life cycle. This model does not require the assumption of random mating. But the assumption of uniform density is a major difficulty in application of Wright's model to human data. While the assumption may be appropriate for certain known human societies which have a relatively small amount of discontinuous aggregation and low dispersal rates (e.g., the Navaho Indians of the American Southwest or the Cree and other hunting tribes of Canada), clearly it is not appropriate for contemporary populations of the United States which have variable density and high internal migration rates.

In an unpublished study, Spuhler and Clark used birth certificate data to find the distance in miles between the birth-places of parents living in Ann Arbor, Michigan, in 1947 and their 1059 children born alive during that year. The co-ordinates of the birthplaces were ascertained to the nearest minute, and the longitudinal (X) and latitudinal (Y) distances from Ann Arbor were obtained by differencing. Great circle distances were obtained by solution of the required spherical triangle using an IBM electronic calculator. In a few cases, especially in rural areas, measurements were made to the geographical center of the smallest known political unit, usually townships or counties, more rarely states or countries.

Great circle distances, r, from Ann Arbor to each parent's birthplace were used to estimate the proportion, p, of parents whose birthplace is less than r from Ann Arbor. The frequency distribution of $x = \log (r + 1)$, although usually non-normal, is much less skewed than that of r. The data were analyzed separately for the two sexes and two occupational categories. Occupation of the fathers was classified into professional and non-professional according to Edwards (1940), and mothers were classified according to the occupation of their husbands.

The distribution of x was found adequately to approximate the Pearson Type III probability function. Estimates of the mean, median, standard deviation, and skewness of x were made. From these values, estimates of p corresponding to any desired r, or the reverse, could be obtained from tabulations of the Type III function (see Table 69).

In choosing a boundary to define a local breeding neighborhood within a continuous population, two opposite sorts of error can be made. If the area is too small, an appreciable proportion of the parents of children who are actually born in the local breeding population will be excluded. If the area is too large, an appreciable proportion of individuals who may be parents but who are not parents of children born in the local breeding population would be included within the area and number. An ideal definition requires a model in which these two opposite errors exactly compensate for one another. Wright's model for areal continuity (1946) achieves this result at the expense of making the assumption of uniform density of population distribution. But the known distribution of the population in the area surrounding Ann Arbor is far from uniform density.

Although we lack a model which will compensate satisfactorily the two types of errors, we can define the breeding population size to be the number of reproductive individuals within a radius about Ann Arbor equal to the median distance between the birthplace of children born to residents of Ann Arbor and the birthplaces of their parents. This definition does not incorporate the desired compensation of the two types of errors. Nonetheless, the definition is of some interest in providing a basis for comparison among different communities and time periods.

The total population included within a radius of 126 miles from Ann Arbor was about 8.9 million in 1950 and about 3.2 million in 1920, the latter year approximating the median year of birth of the parents in question. If we reduce these numbers to include only married females of reproductive age with one or more children, we obtain 1.1 million for 1950 and 0.4 million for 1920 as a rough approximation of the number of mates available (considering only isolation by distance) for a male resident in Ann Arbor.

A breeding population of 400,000 to one million is, from one point of view, large. Such a size, however, is small compared to the world population or the population of the United States and Canada, and this segment of the population has, of course, a highly complex structure. An interplay of geographical,

biological, social, cultural, and psychological factors operates to reduce greatly the number of potential mates for a specific member of the larger areal population. Factors including race, age, "accidents" of dispersal, residential propinquity, national background, social status, economic status, religion, personality, and individual physical traits combine to restrict greatly the potential number of mates for any specific individual.

No empirical information is available on the effects of gene flow in a local population where frequencies in both the migrants and the sedentes are known. Glass and Li (1953) estimated the rate

TABLE 69

DISTANCE BETWEEN BIRTHPLACES
OF PARENTS

PARENTAL CATEGORY	NUMBER	DISTANCE IN MILES	
		Mean	Median
Professional males...	247	245	190
Non-professional males............	812	142	106
Professional females.	247	262	205
Non-professional females............	812	135	102
Males.............	1059	166	125
Females............	1059	165	126
Total parents.......	2118	165	126

of gene flow from the United States white into the American Negro population from the equation

$$(1 - m)^k = (q_k - Q) / (q_o - Q) ,$$

where k is the number of generations of hybridization, q_k is the gene frequency in the hybrid population, q_o the frequency of the same gene in the African populations, Q that in the white population, and m the percentage of genes per generation in the mixed population which derive from the white population.

For a relatively short period of intermixture ($k < 8$) the change in the estimate of m per unit change in k is considerable; when k is over ten generations the change in m per unit change in k is small. Thus it is important to make a minimum estimate of k. Glass and Li assume that intermixture was well under way by 1675 and, letting an average generation equal 27.5 years, obtain a minimum estimate of $k = 10$.

Gene frequency estimates for the mixed and parental populations were derived from samples of Baltimore Negroes, west African Negroes, and whites from New York City, North Carolina, and Ohio. m was assumed to be constant over time. Seven sets of allele frequencies (R^0 R^1, R^2, and r of the Rhesus blood types; I^A and I^B of the ABO blood groups; and T/t of the taste response to phenylthiocarbamide) were used to obtain independent estimates of m. The values of m (in order of the genes listed above) were: .036, .029, .041, and .028 for the Rhesus factors; .033 and .056 for the ABO blood groups; and .033 for the taste reaction. The estimate based on R^0, which is rare in European and common in African Negro populations, was considered the most reliable. From this value of $m - .036$, the accumulated amount of white admixture in the American Negro of the United States is estimated to be 30.6 per cent.

Some caution is needed in interpreting as evidence for gene flow any single-locus frequency found to be distributed in clines. Differences in selection intensity may also account for smooth geographical gradients in gene frequencies. When clines are actually reflections of gene flow, the gene frequencies of several loci should show similar cline distribution when the migrating and the receiving populations differ with regard to those frequencies. Additional information on gene flow is to be found in Birdsell (1950, 1953) and Glass (1954).

Selection

Selection can be defined to include in an exhaustive way all systematic modes of change in gene frequency which do not involve mutation or gene flow. Although gene flow could be regarded as a form of intergroup selection, we will here restrict selection to its within-popu-

lation action. Selection occurs when individuals of one generation are differentially represented by offspring in later generations. In demographic terms, family size is the ultimate measure of selection. Differences in rates of reaching maturity, mating, fecundity, mortality, and emigration control differences in selection.

The general formula for systematic selection pressure is

$$\Delta q_c = \partial q_c / \partial t = q_c (W_c - \bar{W}) / \bar{W}$$

where W_c is the selective value of the gene in question (weighted for the frequencies and selective values for all genotypes) and $\bar{W} = \Sigma W_i q_i$ is the mean selective value for the population as a whole (Wright, 1949).

Selection can change gene frequencies only when different genotypes contribute different numbers of progeny to future generations. Much ongoing selection in human populations maintains genetic equilibrium by eliminating deleterious mutants or by keeping up systems of balanced polymorphism (see the section on hemoglobin varieties below). Unlike mutation or gene flow, selection is inoperative for gene frequencies of zero or unity. Selection is the most important condition for cumulative change in gene frequencies, i.e., for evolution, but it works only on variation provided by mutation and gene flow.

An illustration of the effects of differential fertility and survival on total selection intensity in a small human population can be obtained by counting the number of descendants of some initial generation. Table 70 presents data on the number of descendants of the twenty-nine "Founders" of the Ramah Navaho population. The count was made over paternal and maternal lines of descent through four generations. The number of descendants is greater than twice the number of offspring in the four generations because lines of descent include parts of inbreeding loops. Not all of the sibships of the fourth descendant generation are completed.

The "Founder" with the largest number of descendants accounts for 14.18 per cent of the total. Six "Founders" (20.69 per cent) account for more than half (52.68 per cent), and fifteen (51.72 per cent) account for 86.45 per cent; the fourteen least prolific lines of descent (48.28 per cent) account for only 13.56 per cent of the descendants over four generations. These general results differ very little when the incomplete fourth

the total selection intensity, I, can be separated into components associated with mortality, I_m, and differential fertility, I_f:

$$I = I_m + 1/p_s (I_f),$$

where

$$I_m = V_m / \bar{x}^2 = p_d / p_s, \text{ and } I_f = V_f / \bar{x}_s^2,$$

where V_m is the variance in mortality, V_f that in fertility, and $\bar{x}_s$ is the mean number of births per fertile individual. The index of total selection gives the

TABLE 70

NUMBER OF DESCENDANTS OF RAMAH NAVAHO "FOUNDERS" BY
DESCENDING ORDER OF NUMBER OF DESCENDANTS

RANK	DESCENDANT'S GENERATION				TOTAL DESCENDANTS	PERCENTAGE OF TOTAL	CUMULATIVE PERCENTAGE
	1	2	3	4			
1	9	66	230	106	411	14.18	14.18
2	23	107	123	57	310	10.69	24.87
3	12	71	162	46	291	10.04	34.91
4	4	30	83	86	203	7.00	41.91
5	8	40	60	58	166	5.73	47.64
6	8	67	66	5	146	5.04	52.68
7	21	53	57	11	142	4.90	57.58
8	12	35	79	5	131	4.52	62.10
9	2	21	42	65	130	4.48	66.58
10	8	63	53	5	129	4.45	71.03
11	6	17	50	37	110	3.79	74.82
12	6	32	68	...	106	3.66	78.48
13	8	32	57	...	97	3.34	81.82
14	12	35	30	...	77	2.66	84.48
15	7	16	34	...	57	1.97	86.45
16–29	37	108	182	66	393	13.56	100.01
Totals	183	793	1376	547	2899	100.01	100.01

generation is excluded from the summations.

Despite man's low fertility, selection can be fairly intense, if only to maintain the genetic status quo. All populations experience considerable mortality before and during the reproductive period. Crow (1958) suggests that total selection intensity in man is best measured by the ratio of the variance in number of progeny (V) to the square of the mean number of progeny ($\bar{x}^2$), where parents and offspring are counted at the same point in the life cycle, e.g., at birth. Assuming p_d individuals counted at birth die prematurely, and $p_s = (1 - p_d)$ survive until maturity and have i births ($i = 0, 1, 2, \ldots$), Crow has shown that

maximum change by selection; the actual change in a character would depend also on its heritability and correlation with fitness.

Crow gives some numerical examples of the total intensity of selection based on United States census data for 1910 and 1950 (Table 71). The birth distributions are based on children ever born to women who were of age forty-five to forty-nine in the census year. Corrections were not made for pooling of offspring in the higher parities or for women who died after having one or more children. The hypothetical mortality values were chosen to approximate the total mortality of women from birth to the end of the child-bearing period for 1957 (10 per cent), during the lifetime of women who were forty-five to forty-nine in 1950 (30 per cent) and during that of women who were forty-five to forty-nine in 1910 (50 per cent).

Comparison of rows 2 and 6 shows a drop in total intensity of selection from 2.6 to 2.1 (about 20 per cent) in a forty-year period. The component of selection due to differential fertility increased during this period. Despite a drop in fertility rates from 3.9 to 2.3 children per woman (including unmarried), the pattern of marriages and births was such as to enlarge the component due to differential fertility. Comparison of the total intensity of selection compares favorably with that of United States whites.

Although no area of human population genetics has a surplus of empirical data, the available knowledge for systems of mating and population size, mutation, gene flow, and genetic drift is well advanced when viewed in the light of the virtual absence of good data on selection (Neel, 1958). A number of cases are known where the selective advantage of a particular genotype is zero or near zero (infantile amaurotic idiocy, retinoblastoma without surgical intervention) or comparatively low (hemo-

TABLE 71

SELECTION INTENSITIES IN THE UNITED STATES AND
RAMAH NAVAHO POPULATIONS*

POPULATION	HYPOTHETICAL MORTALITY, PERCENTAGE	SELECTION INTENSITY			
		Mortality	Fertility	I_f/p_s	Total
(1) U.S., 1950 births.....	10	0.111	1.143	1.270	1.381
(2)	30	0.429	1.143	1.633	2.062
(3)	50	1.000	1.143	2.286	3.286
(4) U.S., 1910 births.....	10	0.111	0.784	0.871	0.982
(5)	30	0.429	0.784	1.120	1.549
(6)	50	1.000	0.784	1.568	2.568
(7) Ramah Navaho......	27	0.374	1.572	2.159	2.533

* See text for explanation; United States values from Crow (1957).

columns for the total and that for premature mortality alone indicates that with relatively low death rates differential postnatal mortality contributes only a small part to total intensity of selection.

The bottom of Table 71 gives data for the Ramah Navaho population. The mean (2.10) and variance (11.18) in number of progeny were determined for the last 100 women in the population who were born before 1910 and who survived into the reproductive period. The actual pre-reproductive mortality in this population was probably higher than 27 per cent. Although the economic status of the Navaho is depressed in comparison to that of the whites, their reproductive pattern is such that the philia, sickle cell anemia, or chondrodystrophy)—each of these lists could be increased by about two dozen—but these abnormalities are rare in all populations. We have practically no reliable information on selective values for the more common genotypes in man. Unless some mechanism like balanced polymorphism is involved, we must suppose that the selective differentials for such characters will be relatively low, probably less than 1 per cent, and thus extremely difficult to demonstrate statistically. The difficulty is further compounded because the selective act of reproduction involves the "whole child" and not single alleles alone. This is one reason why many physical anthropologists and human geneticists are skeptical about the empirical bases of some of the demographic literature on population quality. Probably investigations now under way will produce secure knowledge on selective differentials in the three-allele system involving hemoglobins A, C, and S (see Neel, 1956, and the section on hemoglobin varieties below).

Levine (1958) has presented the first information on selection in man where two independent loci are involved. He established that ABO incompatibility between the Rh negative mother and the Rh positive child diminishes the probability of isoimmunization and thus reduces the incidence of Rh hemolytic disease of the newborn. Among the ABO incompatible matings, the greatest protection is found in matings in which the husband is AB, while in compatible matings the least protection is observed in matings with AB mothers. The essential requirement for isoimmunization and hemolytic disease is that the Rh positive fetal red blood cells survive long enough in the maternal circulation to provide the antigenic stimulus. Only ABO compatible blood is capable of surviving; group incompatible fetal red cells are destroyed by the maternal anti-A or anti-B substances before there is an opportunity for the Rh positive red cells to be antigenic.

Random Drift in Gene Frequencies

The two genes which occupy each autosomal locus are a sample of the four genes in that locus in the two parents. In small populations gene frequencies may fluctuate from generation to generation due to this sampling process. The action of random drift in gene frequencies, usually called "genetic drift," may be illustrated by considering a human breeding population of two maintained by brother-sister mating. If we start with two heterozygous individuals, Aa and Aa, the frequency of A is 0.5 and that of a is 0.5. The next generation could have

any of the six following compositions with the probabilities indicated:

GENOTYPES	PROBABILITY	GENE FREQUENCIES A	a
AA, AA ...	1/16	1.00	0
AA, Aa ...	1/4	0.75	0.25
AA, aa ...	1/8	0.50	0.50
Aa, Aa ...	1/4	0.50	0.50
Aa, aa ...	1/4	0.25	0.75
aa, aa ...	1/16	0	1.00

In a large number of such populations, random genetic drift would be expected to bring about loss of one allele and fixation of the other in one-eighth of the cases, change in allelic frequencies in one-half, and no change in three-eighths.

When the number of males and females in the breeding population is equal, the ultimate rate of decrease in the proportion of heterozygotes (H) is approximately $1/(2N) - 1/(4N^2)$ for small N, and $1/(2N+1)$ or $1/(2N)$ for moderately large N. After a number of generations, heterozygosis will decrease at the constant proportion $1/(2N)$ per generation. If we put

$$dH/dt = - (1/2N) H$$

where t is the number of generations, we obtain

$$H_t = H_o e^{-t/2N}$$

where H_o is the initial proportion of heterozygotes and H_t is the proportion after t generations (Li, 1955). An indication of the time trend toward loss of one allele and fixation of the other due to random drift, in closed populations of various sizes where other modes of change are neglected, is given in Table 72. Random drift in theory should not be neglected as a possible mode of change in gene frequencies in small, isolated breeding populations. And human breeding populations have been "large" only during a small fraction of the time that (anatomically) modern man has existed. Before the urban revolution with its reliance on trade and manufactures, the upper size limit for local, largely endogamous agricultural groups seems to have been about 350 to 400. The world average for local population number for agricultural peoples was probably between 100 and 150. The bands of hunters and food gatherers were usually much smaller, probably 50 to 100 (Linton, 1936). Throughout most of man's history the average size of Mendelian populations has been much closer to 100 than to 1,000.

Since random genetic drift is essentially an error term for the determinate evolutionary processes, it is difficult to

erations" (age groups 1–27, 28–55, and 56 + years) of the Dunker community in Franklin County, Pennsylvania, whose estimated effective population size was ninety. He found no evidence of random gene drift in the ABO and Rh blood groups nor in the phenotype frequencies of mid-digital hair, ear lobe, hyperextensibility of the thumb, and diastema between the upper central incisors. He interprets observed changes between generations to indicate the operation of drift in the case of the MN blood types, relative length of the little finger, and possibly handedness.

TABLE 72

GENETIC DRIFT IN A CLOSED, RANDOM-BRED POPULATION OF SIZE N

NUMBER OF GENERATIONS	NUMBER OF YEARS	GENE FREQUENCY				
		$N=50$	$N=100$	$N=500$	$N=1000$	$N=50000$
0......	0	.500	.500	.500	.500	.500
10......	200	.343	.393	.450	.468	.495
20......	400	.281	.343	.429	.450	.493
30......	600	.245	.313	.413	.441	.491
40......	800	.213	.281	.400	.429	.490
50......	1000	.186	.264	.390	.423	.489
100......	2000	.103	.186	.343	.390	.484
200......	4000	.035	.103	.281	.343	.478
300......	6000	.013	.060	.245	.313	.473
400......	8000	.005	.035	.213	.281	.468
500......	10000	.002	.021	.186	.269	.465
1250......	25000	.000001	.0005	.078	.159	.444

produce empirical demonstration of its operation in human populations. A number of anthropologists have suggested that drift might account for local variations in ABO and MN blood group gene frequencies (Boyd, 1950). Laughlin (1950) has shown that the ABO gene frequencies vary considerably among local Eskimo groups, whereas the cephalic index shows a gradient increasing from east to west. Since a trait controlled by multiple genes should be more stable under drift than one controlled by genes at a single locus, it is plausible to use drift as an explanatory factor for the observed distribution of the blood groups and selection for the distribution of head shape.

Glass (1956) made an age-group analysis of gene and phenotype frequencies for nine inherited traits in three "gen-

Hulse (1955) reports marked fluctuations in ABO frequencies over four generations in the Tulalip, a small tribe of northwest coast Indians. Such changes have not been found in successive generations of large populations, for example, in a study of 2,000 consecutive London mothers and their infants (Boorman, 1950).

The relative importance of gene flow and genetic drift needs to be established separately for each particular population and generation. Yet, in general, the rates of gene flow are very often high enough to prevent development of wide local variations by random drift (Lasker, 1954). Man is now in a period of genetic amalgamation. Table 73 gives some basic data for gene flow and drift in several populations.

Wright (1950) has shown that the distribution, $\phi\,(q)$, of gene frequencies [q + $(1-q)$ for a local breeding population and $q_t + (1-q_t)$ for the total population supplying migrants to the local population] is

$$\phi\,(q) = C q^{4Nmq_t-1} (1-q)^{4Nm(1-q_t)-1},$$

where N is the effective size of the local breeding unit, m is the rate of gene flow, and the constant C is such that

$$\int_0^1 \phi\,(q)\,d\,q = 1,$$

and mutation and selection are neglected. If mutation and selection are not negligible,

$$\phi\,(q) = C e^{4Nsq} q^{4N(mq_t+v)-1}$$
$$\times (1-q)^{4N[m(1-q_t)+u]-1},$$

where s is the difference between selec-

frequencies would drift to zero or unity —that local populations would become homozygous for one allele to the exclusion of the other. If Nm is of the order 0.05, genetic drift is an important agent making for differences in gene frequencies; if Nm is much larger than 5, random genetic drift is relatively unimportant.

Distribution and Frequency of Hemoglobin Varieties in West Africa

It is a commonly accepted general principle that cultural variables may be important codeterminants of geographical distribution and frequency of biological variables in human populations. Demographers in particular have stressed this principle in recent publications, and they have presented consider-

TABLE 73

DEMOGRAPHIC DATA ON POPULATION SIZE, RANDOM GENETIC DRIFT, AND
ADMIXTURE IN SOME SMALL POPULATIONS*

(Rough Estimates Are Marked with a Dagger)

Population	Community Size	Effective Size of Breeding Population	Rate of Random Genetic Drift per Generation for a Gene with Frequency of 0.5 Per Cent	Percentage of Individuals Born Elsewhere	Rate of Mixture
Paracho, Michoacán.......	4593	967	±1.1	34.9	20.2
Quiroga, Michoacán.......	3161	665†	1.4	22.6	22.6†
Mitla, Oaxaca............	2951	621†	1.4	19.0†	3.5†
Tzintzuntzan, Michoacán..	1231	259†	2.2	11.8	11.8†
Tajin....................	1102	232†	2.3	29.4	29.4†
Aguacate................	777	163†	2.8	22.9	22.9†
Panajachel, Guatemala....	688–780	145–64†	2.8–2.9	16.4	5.2†
Ramah Navaho..........	614–34	129–33†	3.1	4.9	5.6
Havasupai..............	177	39	5.7	....	7.5–16.2
Australian aborigines......	100–1500	20.7–316†	2.0–7.8	....	3.5–10.5
Ranchos of Quiroga......	133	28†	6.7	10.3	10.3†
Camayura, Brazil........	110	23†	7.4	11.8–13.6	11.8–13.6†

* Source: Lasker (1954).

tion in the local group and that of the species population as a whole.

Assuming a value for the gene frequencies, the distribution for various values of Nm may be found. In general, if m is small relative to $1/4N$, the distribution of gene frequencies in a local breeding population is U-shaped, and the probability is relatively high that

able concrete data to illustrate interplay of social-cultural-psychological and biological factors as determinants of various demographic rates, especially those non-biological factors having to do with fertility (Lorimer *et al.*, 1954, and the papers reprinted in Spengler and Duncan, 1956, chap. iii). These demonstrations suffer from the fact that the demographic variables, such as rates of birth or death, are themselves highly complex in the biological sense. Recent information on the distribution and frequency of hemoglobin varieties in native populations of West Africa allows us to make some plausible inferences on the effect of cultural variables on a simply inherited biological entity.

Our example will have to do with normal adult (A) and fetal (F) hemoglobin and with two varieties of abnormal hemoglobin called C and S (sickle cell hemoglobin). There is not space here to outline even briefly the multifold ways in which the varieties of human hemoglobin are studied. The subject is an excellent example of the unity of science in the sense that variation in hemoglobins is now being investigated in an integrated way from the molecular to the species and even biotic levels (see the reviews of Neel, 1956; Zuelzer *et al.*, 1956).

About a dozen varieties of hemoglobin, each under simple genetic control, are known. Most of these, including A, C, and S, can be distinguished physically by differences in motility in an electrophoretic field, indicating differences in molecular structure. Biochemical investigation shows that S differs from A by the substitution of a single amino acid in the globin part of the molecule. Genetical study finds that this biochemical difference is controlled by a single autosomal gene which is an allele of the genes for hemoglobins A and C. Morphological observation shows that red blood cells containing S take on an elongated and sickle shape under reduced oxygen tension. Clinical genetical analysis demonstrated that individuals homozygous for S develop a severe anemia, whereas those heterozygous for the gene do not develop anemia but are more susceptible to blackout in high-altitude flight than those homozygous for A. Field studies by hematologists and physical anthropologists establish that

hemoglobin S is virtually absent from many human populations and fairly common in peoples indigenous to the area bounded by Italy on the northwest, India on the northeast, and Africa on the south. Malariologists find that hemoglobin S affords some protection against the killing forms of *Plasmodium falciparum*. Ecological studies indicate that the mosquito which is the vector of this form of malaria does not live in the unbroken tropical forest, but rather in areas where man is the dominant large mammal and where agriculture is practiced. Finally, the cultural anthropologist can trace the genesis of this complex interrelationship between man, mosquito, and protozoan as a sequel to the introduction of iron tools for clearing the forest, the cultivation of plants suitable for the tropical soils, and the formation of settled agricultural communities with high local population density compared to the low density of hunters and gatherers.

The metabolic difference recognized as hemoglobin S is controlled by a single autosomal gene which we will symbolize as hgb^S. This gene together with its normal allele hgb^A provides three genotypes, all of which can be recognized phenotypically:

Genotypes	Phenotypes
$hgb^A\,hgb^A$	Normal hemoglobin A
$hgb^A\,hgb^S$	Sickle cell trait; about 22–45 per cent of the hemoglobin is S and the rest is A.
$hgb^S\,hgb^S$	Sickle cell anemia; 80 per cent plus is of type S, the rest of type F.

Hemoglobin C is controlled by a third allele, hgb^C, at the same locus. These three alleles can occur two at a time, making a total of six different genotypes:

$hgb^A\,hgb^C$	Hemoglobin C trait; 25–39 per cent C, the rest A.
$hgb^C\,hgb^C$	Hemoglobin C disease; a mild anemia with splenomegaly and increased target cells.

$hgb^C hgb^S$ Hemoglobin C–Sickle Cell disease; 50–67 per cent of type C, the remainder of type S; a milder anemia than sickle cell disease.

In the following discussion, the genotypic designations will be abbreviated to their superscripts: *AA, AC, AS, CC, CS,* and *SS.*

Since the fertility of the homozygous sicklers (SS) in West Africa is essentially zero, in the absence of counterbalancing forces we would expect the population supply of S genes to be reduced by a proportion q^2 in each generation where $q =$ the frequency of S and $p = (1 - q)$ is the frequency of its normal allele. Yet more than 100 African populations are observed to have frequencies from 20 to 30 per cent of sicklers (Mourant, 1954). This observation suggests that some force is acting to maintain the population supply of genes for hemoglobin S even though these genes are definitely deleterious in the homozygous condition.

At least three genetic mechanisms are known which in theory could account for the observed situation: recurrent mutation, meiotic drive, and balanced polymorphism due to a selective advantage of the heterozygotes. In theory, mutation could supply new sickle cell genes to the population at a rate sufficiently high to hold the gene frequencies in equilibrium and to maintain the heterozygote frequencies at the observed level. Three kinds of information argue against high recurrent mutation as an explanation: (*a*) the mutation rate required (about 10^{-2} per gene per generation) is much higher than estimated rates for known human genes (Spuhler, 1956); (*b*) unless one postulates highly different mutation rates for this locus in different populations, the absence of the sickle cell gene from hundreds of breeding populations, including some of African Negroes, would be difficult to explain on the postulate of a high mutation

rate for normal to sickle cell; (*c*) Vandepitte *et al.* (1955) found a maximum mutation rate of 1.7×10^{-3} in a study of 233 families in the Belgian Congo, which is only one-tenth the rate required to maintain the observed frequency of 25 per cent sickle cell trait in this population.

Meiotic drive refers to a segregation ratio departing from 1:1 in the formation or survival of gametes by heterozygous individuals (Sandler and Novitski, 1957). Although the phenomenon is well established in *Drosophila* and the house mouse, there is no evidence to support such an explanation in the case of hemoglobin S, and there is some evidence to the contrary.

Balanced polymorphism could explain the incidence of sickle cell trait in African populations if the heterozygotes had a selective advantage (compared to the homozygous normals) sufficiently high to balance the loss of sickle genes through low reproductive fitness of the homozygous sicklers.

Two mechanisms are known to account for the selective advantage of the heterozygotes for the sickle cell trait in areas where falciparum malaria is holoendemic: (*a*) Allison (1954) has shown that sicklers have a relative immunity to falciparum malaria compared to nonsicklers. Raper (1956) and others have shown that infant sicklers do not suffer from cerebral malaria and blackwater fever despite high parasite densities, while non-sickler infants do develop these killing forms of malaria and thus have higher mortality rates than the sicklers in the same environment. (*b*) A number of investigators (Bruce-Chwatt, 1952) find that falciparum infections of the placenta are associated with higher abortion, stillbirth, and neonatal death rates. Livingstone (1957) has suggested that if falciparum infections of the placenta did not develop to the same extent in sickling mothers as in non-sickling mothers, the former should have a proportionally higher number of live-born offspring, and these a higher survival rate.

Probably the two mechanisms of increased fertility and higher survival value of AS can account for the postulated increased fitness of the AS relative to AA. A small supply of gene S could become available in a population originally through mutation or gene flow.

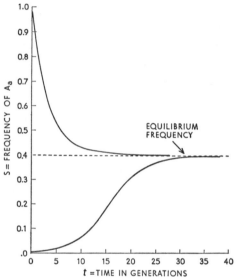

FIG. 12.—Changes in the frequency of the sickle cell heterozygote (AS) in the adult population, with time. Fitness of the homozygote (SS) = 0, and that of the heterozygote (AS) = 1.26 compared to unity for (AA). (From Smith, 1954.)

Probably the latter mechanism would be the more common source for most local populations, since known rates of gene flow are higher per generation than the most plausible estimates of the mutation rate $A \rightarrow S$, which is 10^{-4} to 10^{-6} per gene per generation. Given such a supply, if we assume a selective advantage of 1.26 for AS relative to AA, and a fitness of zero for SS, the gene frequencies would approach an equilibrium value of about 40 per cent AS, as illustrated in Figure 12, in about thirty-five generations, or about 700–900 years (Smith, 1954).

As Livingstone has emphasized, the estimated selective advantage of AS can account for the observed *frequencies* of the sickle cell trait in West Africa where they are found in areas with holoendemic falciparum malaria, but this phenomenon cannot account for the observed *geographical distribution* of S genes because areas with holoendemic falciparum malaria and low or zero frequencies of S are known. It turns out that the pockets of low frequency are in the right places in that we can make sense of the situation by reference to the anthropological history of the populations that occupy the pockets. Before turning to these anthropological factors we need to outline the distribution of S in West Africa and to report a few details about the vector of falciparum malaria in this region.

From the latitude of the Gambia River to the south, West Africa is characterized by hyper- or holoendemic malaria. In much of this area, the frequency of the gene for hemoglobin S is 0.15 or more (Fig. 13). Of course, this figure does not show the details of local variation in gene frequencies. There are some significant variations within tribes; the Fulani have frequencies from 0.08 to 0.25, and the Mandingo from 0.06 to 0.28. There is some indication of a north-south gradient in frequencies with the higher values of S in the south. The distribution of falciparum malaria shows a similar gradient, and, in general, areas with hyper- or holoendemic malaria have 0.15 + of S.

Yet in three small pockets, populations with rather low S frequencies (0–.02) are known: coastal Portuguese Guinea, eastern Liberia, and northern Ghana. Since the situation is complicated in northern Ghana by considerable frequencies of hemoglobin C, which like S seems to give some protection against malaria in heterozygous individuals, and since the relative fitness of the three additional genotypes involving C are not known in detail, we will consider only coastal Portuguese Guinea and eastern Liberia.

Anopheles gambiae is the most common vector of malaria in West Africa. This mosquito does not live in the shady floors of the unbroken tropical forest; rather, it likes sunlight, breeds in exposed pools of water in areas cleared for agricultural purposes, and is attracted to the permanent habitations of the agriculturists, where it rests in the grass-thatched roofs. The ecology of *A. gambiae* suggests that there is a relation between the incidence of hemoglobin S and the cultural practice of slash-and-burn agriculture in West Africa. The low human population density and the lack of suitable breeding places for this particular mosquito prevent malaria from reaching holoendemic status in virgin tropical forests inhabited by peoples with a hunting and gathering economy.

The frequency of S is not closely correlated with linguistic affiliation—suggesting that linguistic diversification occurred before the introduction of the S gene. However, the pockets of low frequency in Portuguese Guinea and eastern Liberia are occupied by peoples considered on linguistic grounds to be the earlier inhabitants of the area. This and other anthropological data suggest that S was introduced into the western part of West Africa by migrants from the vicinity of the middle Niger valley and then spread along the Guinea coast. Livingstone (1958) has shown that the cultural factors responsible for the spread of S have only recently reached the isolated groups of these two pockets of low frequency and that there has not yet been time for the frequencies of S to reach equilibrium through the action of selection in the malarial environment

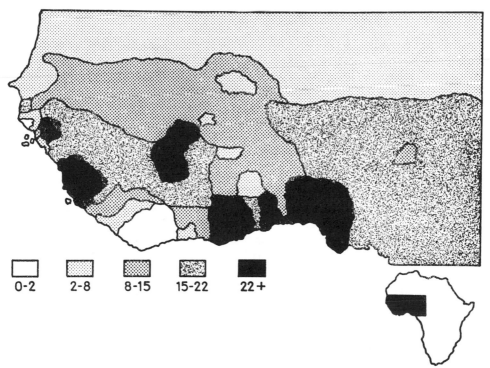

0-2   2-8   8-15   15-22   22+

Fig. 13.—Distribution of sickle cell trait (AS) in West African populations. (From Livingstone, 1958.)

made possible by the introduction of agriculture.

Both iron-working and agriculture were introduced into West Africa from Asia Minor via Egypt over several routes of diffusion. The first evidence of agriculture in Africa is from the Fayum of Egypt at about 4000 B.C. Wheat and barley were the earliest principal crops in Egypt. Later, the cultivation of millet and sorghum spread through the Sudan but did not penetrate into the tropical rain forest, which was not exploited agriculturally until after the spread of iron tools and the cultivation of tropical plants like rice, yams, and cassava. In the tropics the yield in calories per unit area of cultivation is about twice as great for yams as for millet and sorghum, and that of cassava is over three times as great.

The archeological evidence indicates that, at the time of introduction of agriculture into Africa, Negro peoples with microlithic tools and a hunting-gathering economy were living around the fringes and, at places, in the middle of the Sahara, while most of South and East Africa was inhabited by Bushmen-like peoples. The great spread of the Bantu peoples into these latter regions was postagricultural and well within the last two millenia. Rice culture, based on a native species, did not reach the pocket in Portuguese Guinea until about 600 years ago. Intensive agriculture of the slash-and-burn type is considerably later in this area, and the clearing of the forest for farming is still in progress.

There is a general correspondence in the clines for hemoglobin S and for yam agriculture in West Africa. Some peoples have low frequencies except where they come in contact with yam cultivators; the areas with established yam culture in the eastern Ivory Coast, southern Ghana, and Nigeria all have high frequencies of S.

The food-producing revolution was an important event in man's cultural and somatic evolution. Agriculture results in vast changes in man's non-human environment as well as in the increase in population numbers due to a larger supply of calories. Haldane (1949) has suggested that disease becomes an important evolutionary factor only in organisms with dense populations. Many human populations with agriculture and high density possess considerable immunity to measles, while hunting and gathering peoples with low densities do not.

When agriculture spread in West Africa, the forests were cut and the fauna disrupted, with extinction or great reduction in numbers of especially the larger mammals. Elsewhere, there are a number of examples of the parasites of the larger animals adapting to man as a new host in the absence of the old ones, e.g., bubonic plague (Heisch, 1956). Most probably holoendemic malaria did not develop in West Africa until after the spread of agriculture. The anopheline mosquito then became adapted to the environment modified by man, who became the most available blood meal for the mosquito and the host for *P. falciparum*.

Now if the complex relationship between parasite, host, and vector that characterizes holoendemic malaria could not develop in human populations living by hunting and gathering in unbroken tropical forests, the selective advantage of the individuals heterozygous for S would not hold, and the selective disadvantage of the homozygote for S would tend to keep the population frequencies of S at a low level. And if, as Livingstone has postulated, the "pocket people" in Portuguese Guinea, eastern Liberia, and the western Ivory Coast are descendants of the aboriginal hunters and gatherers of the tropical forests, we have an explanation of their low frequencies of S in the relatively late spread of agriculture to these areas and in a lack of the conditions that give a selective advantage to the heterozygotes for S.

Up to this point I have stressed the part of physical anthropology which emphasizes a genetical point of view because that part of physical anthropology has considerably more interest in the central subject matter of demography than does morphological anthropology. However, genetical anthropology is only one side of the larger subject. The concluding sections will outline two contributions of morphology to demography: the study of populations known only from skeletal remains and the comparative study of the duration of the stages of the ontogenetic cycle in primates.

Demography of Skeletal Populations

Some historical depth to our knowledge of the age and sex distributions of ancient populations, as well as something about their morbidity, can be gotten through the study of skeletal remains. Often archeological investigation can recover useful information on the cultural and ecological situation of such populations from the past. Of course, the probability of survival and archeological recovery vary greatly with locality and type of interment. But when skeletal remains are interpreted with caution, useful information on the ancient history of demographic variables can be obtained. Sex can be determined with considerable accuracy on the adult skeleton. The older morphological methods may have an error as high as 15 per cent, but modern methods of discriminant analysis using multiple characters give a high degree of accuracy. Thieme and Schull (1957) have constructed a discriminant function using seven skeletal measurements which correctly classified sex in known material in 98.5 per cent of 198 skeletons. Age can be determined on the skeleton with an error of about one year

up to age twelve, about two or three years up to age forty, and about five years up to age sixty (Stewart and Trotter, 1954). Age determinations on skeletal material are thus of approximately the same accuracy as those obtained through interviews with living members of non-literate societies.

There is space here to report only results on life span (see Goldstein, 1953, for some other vital statistics based on skeletal material). All estimates of mean life span based on skeletons recovered by excavation are likely to be much too high because of lack of salvage of infant skeletons. Probably infant mortality was 50 per cent or more in many primitive groups. Angel (quoted in Goldstein, 1953) found that only 22 per cent of infant graves had skeletal fragments, as contrasted to about 90 per cent for adult graves, in Macedonian burials at Olynthus.

Weidenreich (1939) identified some thirty-eight individuals among the fossil skeletal remains of Peking Man from the Lower Cave at Choukoutien, a site occupied during the Middle Pleistocene about 200,000 years ago. Fifteen of the thirty-eight were classified as children up to fourteen years of age. The age at death could be determined with some accuracy only on seven of the twenty-three adults. Of these, three died before age thirty, three between forty and fifty, and one between fifty and sixty. Estimates of age in Pleistocene hominids are apt to be too high because the various stages of physiological age probably occur chronologically earlier than in modern man.

Skeletal remains of seven individuals were recovered from the Upper Cave at Choukoutien, a site occupied during the Upper Pleistocene perhaps 25,000 years ago. Three of the seven individuals died before adulthood—one as a fetus or newborn, one about five years, and one between fifteen and twenty years of age. Two of the adults, probably females, were slightly over twenty, one was of middle age, and one male was at least sixty years at death (Weidenreich, 1939). The fragmentary evidence suggests that an advanced age was seldom reached in either the *Sinanthropus* or the Upper Pleistocene Homo sapiens of northern China.

In a study with more extensive material, Vallois (1937) determined the approximate age at death in Neanderthal, Upper Paleolithic, and Mesolithic societies of Europe (Table 74). Of 187 indi-

A.D. 850–1700 was estimated by Goldstein (1953) as 30.5 years on the basis of a study of 767 of their skeletons. When corrected for non-recovery of infants, the mean age at death is reduced to about 24 years. About 25 per cent of males and 48 per cent of females died in the age period 20–34 years. Only 14 per cent survived middle age, males seemingly living longer than females. The Pueblo agriculturalists of New Mexico enjoyed a longer life span than these Texas food gatherers. The average Pecos

TABLE 74

APPROXIMATE AGE AT DEATH IN VARIOUS EARLY POPULATIONS*

POPULATION	PERIOD	NUMBER	PER CENT DYING IN AGE PERIODS				
			0–14	15–20	21–40	41–60	61–x
Neanderthal............	c. 100000 B.C.	20	40.0	15.0	40.0	5.0	....
Upper Paleolithic, Europe.	c. 30000 B.C.	102	24.5	9.8	53.9	11.8	....
Mesolithic, Europe	c. 8000 B.C.	65	30.8	6.2	58.5	3.0	1.5
Bronze Age, lower Austria.	c. 2500 B.C.	273	7.0†	17.2	39.9	28.6	7.3†
Egyptians, Roman Period.	c. 30 B.C.	141	19.9†	14.2†	39.7	16.3	9.9†

* After Vallois (1937) with time periods added. Values marked with a dagger are corrected from misprints by reference to the original data in Pearson (1902) and Franz and Winkler (1936).

viduals whose ages are determinable, 55 per cent of the Neanderthal, 34 per cent of the Upper Paleolithic, and 37 per cent of the Mesolithic people died before reaching twenty years of age.

Angel (1954) gives the following estimates of mean age at death in ancient Greeks dying at fifteen years or older over a time span of 5,000 years:

Period	Number	Mean Age
Pre-Greek (3500 B.C.) ..	59	31.3
Middle Bronze (2000 B.C.)	94	34.9
Mycenaean (1450 B.C.) .	167	35.9
Early Iron Age (1150 B.C.)	110	35.8
Classical (680 B.C.)	127	40.8
Hellenistic (300 B.C.) ...	118	40.4
Imperial Roman (120 B.C.)	81	38.1
Medieval (A.D. 600)	78	34.7
Turkish (A.D. 1400)	52	31.3
Romantic (A.D. 1750) ..	233	39.8

Mean age at death of Indians living in present-day Texas during the period

Indian lived to an age of 42.9 during the period A.D. 800–1700.

Duration of Periods in the Primate Life Cycle

The total human population today is something like 2700 million. According to Schultz (1948), it is doubtful that this figure is equaled by the total numbers of all living non-human primates. The single species, Homo sapiens, exists in numbers in excess of the sum of all members of more than 500 other extant primate species. This fact is all the more spectacular if we consider the reproductive potential of the non-human primates and the indications that most tropical regions could support much larger numbers of these animals than now exist. Man has the longest period of fecundity of all primates, but he also has the longest period between successive generations because menarche is delayed to a much more advanced age in man than in other primates. The fertile period lasts about twenty-eight years in man, not more than sixteen in the chimpanzee, and about seven years in the marmoset, a South American monkey. The average onset of fertility is in the seventeenth year in man, the ninth year in the chimpanzee, about the third year in the marmoset. The age of onset of female fertility added to the gestation period together equal the minimum interval between generations. This interval is about three years in marmosets, nine to ten years in chimpanzees, and about eighteen years in man. If we take as unity the maximum number of offspring where the sexes are born in equal numbers to an initial human couple over a period of

living animals, there exists among primates a general evolutionary trend to increase the duration of the main periods of the life cycle. The evidence is presented in Table 75, where the more primitive primates are placed early and the more advanced forms late in the list. In the great apes the gestation period is lengthened to at least thirty-four weeks, full growth is attained by the end of the eleventh year, and animals in their third decade are senile. In man the duration of the prenatal period has changed little, if any, from that characteristic of the great apes, but the duration of period of postnatal growth has almost

TABLE 75

AVERAGE DURATION OF PRENATAL AND POSTNATAL GROWTH PERIODS
AND OF LIFE SPAN IN DIFFERENT PRIMATES*

Primate Species	Gestation (Weeks)	Menarche (Years)	Eruption of First and Last Permanent Teeth (Years)	Completion of General Growth (Years)	Life Span (Years)
Lemur.........	18	?	?	3	14
Macaque.......	24	2	1.8– 6.4	7	24
Gibbon........	30	8.5	? – 8.5	9	30
Orangutan.....	39	?	3.5– 9.8	11	30
Chimpanzee....	34	8.8	2.9–10.2	11	35
Gorilla........	?	9	3 –10.5	11	?
Man..........	38	13.7	6.2–20.5	20	75

* Source: Schultz (1956).

forty-five years (the average age when female fertility ceases in man), the reproductive potential in the chimpanzee is about six times, and in the marmoset millions of times, greater than in man.

Despite man's relatively low reproductive potential, he represents the only primate species that has persistently increased in total numbers. Growth in numbers of a species is influenced by a complex interplay of ecological, physiological, pathological, psychological, and sociological factors. During the course of human evolution some of these factors have changed in a way which allowed a continual increase in human numbers despite the phylogenetic decrease in the human reproductive potential.

Insofar as phylogenetic information can be deduced from observations on

doubled, and the total life span has more than doubled. Man is not unique with regard to the gestation period, but he is specialized in the marked elongation of the period of postnatal growth and the long postponement of the onset of senility. These human specializations are extremes of trends found to lesser degrees in the evolutionary history of other primates (Schultz, 1956).

Man, then, is not much different from the other primates, especially the anthropoid apes, in the general sequence of events from conception to birth. After birth, the ontogenetic pattern in man differs markedly from the situation in all non-human primates, but differs in a direction forecast by the general trend of primate evolution. I would guess that this elongation of the life periods after birth in man is a consequence of somatic adaptation to the acquisition of culture. Culture is a biological adaptation with a non-genetic mode of inheritance depending on symbolic contact rather than fusion of gametes. It has greatly supplemented somatic evolution. In all known human societies individuals participate in social systems whose members represent more than single nuclear families. No human family is a self-sufficient system of social action. All known non-human families are self-sufficient systems of action. It may be assumed that the genetic factors controlling the ontogenetic cycle in man have modified through selection to man's *human* environment.

SELECTED BIBLIOGRAPHY

ALLISON, A. C. 1954. "Notes on Sickle-cell Polymorphism," *Annals of Human Genetics,* XIX, 39–57.

ANGEL, J. L. 1954. "Human Biology, Health, and History in Greece from First Settlement until Now," *Year Book of the American Philosophical Society,* pp. 168–72.

ASHTON, H. 1952. *The Basuto.* London: Oxford University Press.

BIRDSELL, J. B. 1950. "Some Implications of the Genetical Concept of Race in Terms of Spatial Analysis," *Cold Spring Harbor Symposia on Quantitative Biology,* XV, 259–314.

———. 1953. "Some Environmental and Cultural Factors Influencing the Structuring of Australian Aboriginal Populations," *American Naturalist,* LXXXVII, 169–207.

BOORMAN, K. E. 1950. "An Analysis of the Blood Types and Clinical Condition of 2000 Consecutive Mothers and Their Infants," *Annals of Eugenics,* XV, 120–34.

BOYD, W. C. 1939. "Blood Groups," *Tabulae biologica,* XVII, 113–240.

———. 1950. *Genetics and the Races of Man.* Boston: Little, Brown & Co.

BRUCE-CHWATT, L. J. 1952. "Malaria in African Infants and Children in Southern Nigeria," *Annals of Tropical Medicine and Parasitology,* XLVI, 173–200.

BURROWS, H. R., *et al.* 1953. *The Dunn Reserve, Zululand.* (*Natal Regional Survey,* Additional Report No. 4.) Pietermaritzburg: University of Natal Press.

CLARK, P. C. 1956. "The Heritability of Certain Anthropometric Characters As Ascertained from Measurements of Twins," *American Journal of Human Genetics,* VIII, 49–54.

COX, P. R. 1950. *Demography.* Cambridge: Cambridge University Press.

CROW, J. F. 1958. "Some Possibilities for Measuring Selection Intensities in Man," *Human Biology,* XXX, 1–13.

EDWARDS, A. M. 1940. *Alphabetical Index of Occupations and Industries.* Washington, D.C.: Government Printing Office.

FREIRE-MAIA, N. 1957. "Inbreeding Levels in Different Countries," *Eugenics Quarterly,* IV, 127–38.

GLASS, B. 1954. "Genetic Changes in Human Populations, Especially Those Due to Gene Flow and Genetic Drift," *Advances in Genetics,* VI, 95–139.

———. 1956. "On the Evidence of Random Genetic Drift in Human Populations," *American Journal of Physical Anthropology,* XIV, 541–55.

GLASS, B., and LI, C. C. 1953. "The Dynamics of Racial Intermixture: An Analysis Based on the American Negro," *American Journal of Human Genetics,* V, 1–20.

GOLDSTEIN, M. S. 1953. "Some Vital Statistics Based on Skeletal Material," *Human Biology,* XXV, 3–12.

HALDANE, J. B. S. 1938. "Indirect Evidence for the Mating System in Natural Populations," *Journal of Genetics,* XXXVI, 213–20.

———. 1949. "Disease and Evolution," *La ricerca scientifica,* Supplement, pp. 3–10.

HART, E. W. 1944. "An Analysis of the Blood Group Composition of a Population in Northern Ireland," *Annals of Eugenics,* XII, 89–101.

HEISCH, R. B. 1956. "Zoonoses as a Study in Ecology," *British Medical Journal,* I, 669–73.

HULSE, F. S. 1955. "Blood-Types and Mating Patterns among Northwest Coast Indians," *Southwestern Journal of Anthropology,* XI, 93–104.

KELUS, A., *et al.* 1953. "Badania nad częstością grup krwi ze szczególnym uwzględnieniem Polski," *Materiały I Prace Antropologiczne* (Wrocław), No. 2.

KLUCKHOHN, C. 1956. "Review of Lorimer, *et al.*, *Culture and Human Fertility*," *American Journal of Physical Anthropology*, XIV, 527–32.

KOMAI, T. 1947. *Pedigrees of Hereditary Diseases and Abnormalities Found in the Japanese Race.* (Japan Society for the Promotion of Scientific Research, fourth special committee, Report No. 2. Japanese with English summary.)

KROOTH, R. S. 1953. "Comments on the Estimation of the Mutation Rate for Achondroplasia," *American Journal of Human Genetics*, V, 373–76.

LASKER, G. W. 1954. "Human Evolution in Contemporary Communities," *Southwestern Journal of Anthropology*, X, 353–65.

LAUGHLIN, W. S. 1950. "Blood Groups, Morphology, and Population Size of the Eskimos," *Cold Spring Harbor Symposia on Quantitative Biology*, XV, 165–73.

LERNER, I. M. 1954. *Genetic Homeostasis.* Edinburgh: Oliver & Boyd.

LEVINE, P. 1958. "The Influence of the ABO System on Rh Hemolytic Disease," *Human Biology*, XXX, 14–28.

LI, C. C. 1955. *Population Genetics.* Chicago: University of Chicago Press.

LINTON, R. 1936. *The Study of Man.* New York: D. Appleton-Century Co.

LIVINGSTONE, F. B. 1957. "Sickling and Malaria," *British Medical Journal*, I, 762–63.

———. 1958. "Anthropological Implications of Sickle Cell Gene Distribution in West Africa," *American Anthropologist*, LX, 533–62.

LORIMER, F., *et al.* 1954. *Culture and Human Fertility.* Paris: UNESCO.

MORTON, N. E., CROW, J. F., and MULLER, H. J. 1956. "An Estimate of the Mutational Damage in Man from Data on Consanguineous Marriages," *Proceedings of the National Academy of Sciences*, XLII, 855–63.

MOURANT, A. E. 1954. *The Distribution of the Human Blood Groups.* Oxford: Blackwell Scientific Publications.

MULLER, H. J. 1954. "The Manner of Dependence of the 'Permissible Dose' of Radiation on the Amount of Genetic Damage," *Acta radiologica*, XLI, 5–20.

MURDOCK, G. P. 1951. *Social Structure.* New York: Macmillan Co.

NACHTSHEIM, H. 1954. "Die Mutationsrate menschlicher Gene," *Die Naturwissenschaften*, XLI, 385–92.

NEEL, J. V. 1956. "The Genetics of Human Haemoglobin Differences: Problems and Perspectives," *Annals of Human Genetics*, XXI, 1–30.

———. 1958. "The Study of Natural Selection in Primitive and Contemporary Human Populations," *Human Biology*, XXX, 43–72.

———, *et al.* 1949. "The Incidence of Consanguineous Matings in Japan," *American Journal of Human Genetics*, I, 156–78.

———, and SCHULL, W. J. 1954. *Human Heredity.* Chicago: University of Chicago Press.

PENROSE, L. S. 1955. "Parental Age and Mutation," *Lancet*, pp. 312–13.

RAPER, A. B. 1956. "Sickling in Relation to Morbidity from Malaria and Other Diseases," *British Medical Journal*, I, 965–69.

SANDLER, L., and NOVITSKI, E. 1957. "Meiotic Drive as an Evolutionary Force," *American Naturalist*, XCI, 105–10.

SANGHVI, L. D., *et al.* 1956. "Frequency of Consanguineous Marriages in Twelve Endogamous Groups in Bombay," *Acta genetica*, VI, 41–49.

SCHAPERA, I. 1953. *The Tswana.* London: International African Institute.

SCHULL, W. J. 1953. "The Effect of Christianity on Consanguinity in Nagasaki," *American Anthropologist*, LV, 74–88.

———. 1957. Personal communication.

SCHULTZ, A. H. 1948. "The Number of Young at Birth and the Number of Nipples in Primates," *American Journal of Physical Anthropology*, VI, 1–24.

———. 1956. "Postembryonic Age Changes," *Primatologia*, I, 887–964.

SMITH, S. M. 1954. "Appendix to Notes of Sickle-Cell Polymorphism," *Annals of Human Genetics*, XIX, 51–57.

SNYDER, L. H., and DAVID, P. R. 1957. *The Principles of Heredity.* 5th ed. Boston: D. C. Heath & Co.

SPENGLER, J. J., and DUNCAN, O. D. (eds.). 1956. *Demographic Analysis: Selected Readings*. Glencoe, Ill.: Free Press.

SPUHLER, J. N. 1948. "On the Number of Genes in Man," *Science*, CVIII, 279–80.

———. 1951. "Some Genetic Variations in American Indians," in *Physical Anthropology of the American Indian*, ed. W. S. LAUGHLIN. New York: The Viking Fund, Inc.

———. 1954. "Some Problems in the Physical Anthropology of the American Southwest," *American Anthropologist*, LVI, 604–25.

———. 1956. "Estimation of Mutation Rates in Man," *Clinical Orthopaedics*, VIII, 34–43.

———, and CLARK, P. C. 1957. "Assortative Mating for Body Size." Manuscript.

———, and KLUCKHOHN, C. 1953. "Inbreeding Coefficients of the Ramah Navaho Population," *Human Biology*, XXV, 295–317.

STEWART, T. D., and TROTTER, M. (eds.). 1954. *Basic Readings on the Identification of Human Skeletons: Estimation of Age*. New York: Wenner-Gren Foundation for Anthropological Research, Inc.

SUTTER, J. 1957. "Recherches sur les effets de la consanguinité chez l'homme." Manuscript.

———, and TABAH, L. 1948. "Frequence et répartition des mariages consanguins en France," *Population* (France), III, 607–30.

THIEME, F. P., and SCHULL, W. J. 1957. "Sex Determination from the Skeleton," *Human Biology* (in press).

TREVOR, J. C. 1953. *Race Crossing in Man: The Analysis of Metrical Characters.* ("Eugenics Laboratory Memoirs," No. 36.) London: Cambridge University Press.

VALLOIS, H. V. 1937. "La durée de la vie chez l'homme fossile," *Anthropologie*, XLVII, 499–532.

VANDEPITTE, J. M., *et al.* 1955. "Evidence Concerning the Inadequacy of Mutation As an Explanation of the Frequency of the Sickle Cell Gene in the Belgian Congo," *Blood*, X, 341–50.

WASHBURN, S. L. 1951. "The New Physical Anthropology," *Transactions of the New York Academy of Sciences*, Ser. 2, XIII, 298–304.

———. 1953. "The Strategy of Physical Anthropology," in *Anthropology Today: An Encyclopedic Inventory*, ed. A. L. KROEBER. Chicago: University of Chicago Press.

WEIDENREICH, F. 1939. "The Duration of Life of Fossil Man in China and the Pathological Lesions Found in His Skeleton," *Chinese Medical Journal*, LV, 34–44.

WRIGHT, S. 1921. "Systems of Mating," *Genetics*, VI, 111–78.

———. 1946. "Isolation by Distance under Diverse Systems of Mating," *ibid.*, XXXI, 33–59.

———. 1949. "Adaptation and Selection," in *Genetics, Paleontology, and Evolution*, ed. G. L. JEPSEN *et al.* Princeton: Princeton University Press, pp. 365–89.

———. 1950. "The Genetical Structure of Populations," *Annals of Eugenics*, XV, 323–54.

ZUELZER, W. W., NEEL, J. V., and ROBINSON, A. R. 1956. "Abnormal Hemoglobins," *Progress in Hematology*, pp. 91–137.

31. Genetics and Demography[1]

FRANZ J. KALLMANN, M.D., AND JOHN D. RAINER, M.D.

Linked by a concern with the dynamics and variable stratifications of human populations, the descriptive science of demography and the biological discipline of human genetics meet on common ground. Their mutual interests lie in the physical and mental characteristics that cause men to strive and create, to maintain health or succumb to adversity, to choose a proper mate, to work, to reproduce and grow old, to die in harness or in the feeble shadows of retirement. There are biological foundations for each of these functions, and all of them are genetically controlled.

While the primary objective of demographic research is to furnish an inventory of quantitative and qualitative population changes, the aim of genetic studies is to search for the basic causes. The changing composition of populations and the various modes of interaction with physical and social surroundings depend on determining basic factors which, in turn, follow certain laws. Some of these underlying principles are elementary; others are highly complex. A few are still the subject of much hypothetical controversy. With the science of human genetics less than sixty years old and its offshoot of population genetics barely twoscore, a wealth of data has nevertheless been produced for man's study of himself and his origins.

[1] The assistance of Dr. Arnold Kaplan in preparing the bibliographical material of this chapter and the most helpful advice of our statistical consultant, Professor W. Edwards Deming, are gratefully acknowledged.

An attempt will be made here to review the results of statistical and experimental studies, their clinical and biological correlates, and the theoretical and practical principles of genetics as reflected in the demography of the present and of the future.

GENERAL GENETIC PRINCIPLES

The modern theory of genetics, which is basic for a biological approach to human populations, began with Gregor Mendel's report on his garden pea experiments before the Brünn Natural Science Society in February, 1865. His observations of the "unblended" separation and subsequent recombination of stable genetic units, confirmed in 1900, led to the first description of populations in mathematical terms—frequency and distribution of types on a genetic basis. Stimulated by advances in cellular biology, biophysics, and clinical medicine, and reinforced by painstaking experiments with lower organisms, the development of genetics merged with that of the theory of evolution. Since then, genetic progress has been steadily directed toward presenting ever more precise explanations of early experimental data, in terms of the biochemically-oriented chromosome theory.

As originally formulated, Mendel's conclusions were strictly statistical in nature. Variations observed in the offspring of certain matings were counted in relation to such individual characteristics as shape and color. Deriving a number of general principles from these statistics, the Austrian biologist inferred that single characters behaved as if determined by paired particles (later called *genes*) in the germ plasm. Of the two members of a pair that join to form the zygote (one-celled stage of the new individual), one is derived from the father (male germ cell) and the other from the mother (female germ cell). When new germ cells are formed by the matured individual, the paired members separate again, without having had a chance to influence each other or to enter the same germ cell. This basic phenomenon is known as the law of segregation. The members of a pair of genes—assumed to be specific nucleoprotein molecules located on ribbon-like chromosomes in the nucleus of a cell—are called *alleles*.

A person is a *homozygote* for a particular gene, and certain to show its characteristics under proper environmental conditions, if he receives that gene from both parents. A *heterozygote* (hybrid) originates when the given gene is received from only one parent, and a different one at the corresponding *locus* from the other parent.

In some cases, the Mendelian trait displayed by the heterozygous individual will be *intermediate* between the traits represented by homozygotes. In others, the possession of only one member of a gene pair suffices to produce the trait (*dominant*), while its partner remains unexpressed (*recessive*). Homozygousness is necessary for the expression of a recessive trait in the individual's appearance (*phenotype*), as heterozygousness merely allows the gene to remain part of the individual's genic formula (*genotype*), which will be transmitted to the offspring.

Discovery of the chromosomes in the cell nucleus (Waldeyer, 1888) took place in the thirty-four-year interval during which Mendel's findings remained unnoticed. These thread-like bodies with a peculiar staining reaction were seen to divide in the process of ordinary cell division and be redistributed as exact duplicates, with each germ cell receiving half the parental chromosome structure. This mode of behavior was consistent with Mendel's experimental data, making it possible to combine knowledge derived from breeding experiments with the microscopic study of cells and chromosomes (*cytogenetics*).

In this context, the construct of *genes* emerged as a set of microscopically invisible particles strung like beads along the chromosome. More precisely, genes may be thought of as clearly differentiated regions (*loci*) that preserve their identity, produce specific effects, and are capable of duplicating themselves. In chemical terms, they seem to consist of nucleoproteins with the property of self-duplication (Beadle, 1955; McElroy and Glass, 1957, p. 6).

Combined chromosome and gene analyses yielded an enormous body of data, including Morgan's early chromosome maps in the fruit fly (1919). Before long, the new science of genetics was expected to explain a variety of phenomena in human populations. Ideally, its major goals may be described as follows: (1) prediction of the potentialities of the offspring in any given marriage; (2) prediction of future population trends on the basis of more or less detailed information about the present composition of a population and the matings contracted within it; (3) exploration of the phenomena of variation, species formation, and evolution, as well as the specific mechanisms whereby those genes producing pathological changes are brought into play and may be accessible to therapeutic influence.

In the crucial area of genetic changes, both evolutional and pathological, the phenomenon of *mutation* holds one of the key positions. The ensuing change in the germ plasm may occur either spontaneously and with predictable frequency or reactively in response to ionizing radiation (Muller, 1927) or other mutagenic agents. Either way, the change is transmitted to the next generation via the germ cells.

Depending on whether the affected chromosomal portion or point is altered to a greater or lesser extent—chemically or structurally in the form of a deletion, duplication, inversion, or translocation—the effect may be extremely deleterious (lethal) or moderately severe or slight and only detectable statistically in large populations by a change in certain health and survival values. Other types of variation may result from the reassortment of parental genes in the process of fertilization (*recombination*) or may be environmentally produced and so *modify* only the phenotype, in the sense of Goldschmidt's non-hereditary *phenocopies* (1938, p. 7).

Where a single mutant gene is potent enough to express itself distinctly against a vast number of other genetic background factors, its phenotypical effect will tend to be pathological. In this *single-factor* type of inheritance, the distribution between the sexes of a dominant or recessive gene is usually equal (*autosomal*). Exceptions are due to the effect of genes transmitted on the *sex chromosomes* (XX in females, XY in males). In recessive X-borne conditions males are more frequently affected than females, while Y-borne traits such as webbed toes can occur only in males.

Characterized by transmission in the direct line of descent and by inheritance from one parent, *simple dominant* traits tend to be rare (self-eliminating) and incompletely expressed. They require only one member of a gene pair (heterozygousness) and are easily studied in pedigrees (Fig. 14, *a*). Since most affected persons are heterozygotes, the distinguishing feature of the dominant mode of inheritance is "once free, free forever," a fact which has both clinical and social significance (selection pressure). Unions between two afflicted persons are most unlikely, and, for the same reason, a negligible role is played by consanguineous marriages.

Simple recessive traits, expressed only by homozygotes, require inheritance from both parents, who are frequently phenotypically unaffected (heterozygotes), as assumed in Figure 14, *b*. No parent, whether heterozygous or homozygous for such a trait (Fig. 14, *c*), can possibly have an affected child (homozygote) unless he marries another carrier of the given gene (Fig. 14, *d*). Consanguineous marriages are apt to increase the chances of this type of mating, especially in the case of a relatively rare and severe disorder. Transmission along collateral, rather than direct, lines of descent is the rule.

Since many human traits are known to be recessive, it is a mistake to accept the verdict of an "inherited" disorder only where the symptoms are clinically traceable to one of the direct ancestors of the patient. Conversely, the family background of a child that has a healthy father with normal family history but a mother afflicted with a severe recessive condition should not be regarded as "alarmingly poor" merely because of an unusual accumulation of affected persons among the mother's relatives. Whether she has one, two, or twenty-seven disordered uncles and aunts, the mother cannot be more than a homozygote. Genetically, it would be worse for the child if both parents were heterozygous carriers due to the presence of one affected uncle on each side. The prospects for a child's health cannot be statistically determined by counting the number of identifiable carriers of a trait in a particular family, although such timeworn misconceptions still appear all too often in the medical and demographic literature.

For statistical purposes it is important to understand that many mutant genes in man do not conform to simple schemes of single-factor inheritance. A gene does not directly produce a given trait. It merely sets in motion

press itself mildly in a heterozygote whose corresponding factor for health is only incompletely dominant. Such modifications are of practical significance, since they may lead to new techniques for the detection of carriers.

Subsidiary genes, which cause quantitative changes in the expression of a major mutant gene, are referred to as

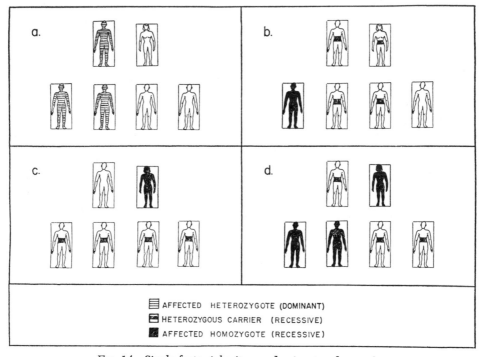

FIG. 14.—Single-factor inheritance, dominant and recessive

a chain reaction which may be modified by environmental factors (prenatal or postnatal), as well as by the action of other genes, before culminating in the production of the trait. Hence a certain gene effect may vary from complete expression to no apparent expression, and there may be some genes that are neither strictly dominant nor strictly recessive but somewhere in between (*incomplete* dominance or recessiveness). While a dominant trait may not be manifested by every heterozygote, a recessive gene tends to ex-

modifier genes if they contribute to the *variable expressivity* of a trait. Although generally difficult to identify, they are called *suppressor genes* if they are responsible for *incomplete penetrance* of the main gene. The failure of a major mutant gene to be expressed at all (lack of penetrance) can be determined by studying populations known to be homozygous for the given trait, i.e., children of two affected parents or one-egg cotwins of affected persons. The extent to which either group falls short of an expected manifestation rate of 100 per cent represents the degree of incompleteness of the gene's penetrance.

When it comes to personality variations showing numerous small gradations in a population within the range of normalcy, a genetic analysis is further complicated by the fact that certain traits are determined by the interaction of several or many genes. In this *multi-factor type* of inheritance, cumulative contributions are made by an assortment of genes which individually produce only minor effects. These *"polygenes"* (Mather, 1949, p. 7) are neither dominant nor recessive but "intermediate" in their additive effect. Figure 15 illustrates the expected distribution of polygenically controlled height variations in a population in which normal stature differences vary from 152 to 192 centimeters (Kallmann, 1953, p. 49).

Within this range, persons between 152 and 162 centimeters have been classified as short, those between 162 and 182 centimeters as medium-height, and those between 182 and 192 centimeters as tall. The range of environmentally produced variations is marked by two broken lines, while the genetically determined height potentials are indicated by a straight line. Sex-specific height differences are disregarded in the diagram, which shows only the growth potentials of the children of two medium-height parents.

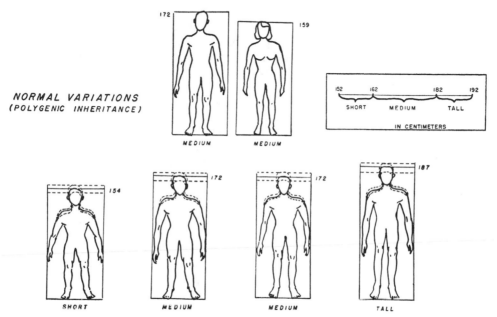

Fig. 15.—Multifactor type of inheritance (stature)

Medium-height results from matings between tall and short persons, since the height of the offspring tends to be intermediate between the height of the two parents. Similarly, the children of short parents will be short, and the children of tall parents will be tall. In matings between two medium-height parents, however, the children are expected to be short, medium, and tall (1:2:1), since they receive in varying combinations the multiple genes producing shortness, medium height, and tallness.

In an intermarrying population, with

random mating and all varieties of multiple genes for body size, the distribution of the resultant crosses can be plotted in a bell-shaped curve showing variations from the lowest to the highest grades, with a majority of medium-height persons and with the tallest and smallest persons the least numerous. Some extremely short persons may approach a pathological degree of dwarfism, usually produced by a major mutant gene or a non-hereditary hormonal disturbance, but genetically they would be as much a part of the general population as those who are in the upper section of the general distribution curve for height. Other polygenically determined traits are intelligence, the capacity for longevity, and variable resistance to selective types of infectious disease (Kallmann, 1953, p. 156).

As to the genes contributing to the production of any of these traits, it is axiomatic that their total effect is not expected to be in the pathological range unless one of them is altered either in chemical composition or chromosomal position (*mutation*). According to classical genetic theory, a gene may produce different effects depending upon its location on the chromosome (*position effect*) or it may exert different effects upon various organs from one and the same location (*pleiotropic effect*). Positional changes may subject the gene to different cytoplasmic influences or make it necessary for the gene to express itself in different linkage groups. The effect of a major mutant gene may also be simulated by a chromosomal aberration (*supergene*).

The action of single genes with a distinguishable normal or pathological effect is not an independent entity but rather "a unified action of a field type which results in a hierarchical order of not strictly delimited fields" (Goldschmidt, 1955, p. 192). In addition, every gene may undergo a number of mutational changes, although only two of these mutants (present in a population) can form a pair occupying a certain position on a particular chromosome in any one individual. A good example of such a series of *multiple alleles* is represented by the blood groups.

The occurrence of a rearranged pairing of four allelic genes in the offspring of two heterozygous parents (*position pseudo-allelism*) is still a disputed topic (Lewis, 1955). The phenomenon may be regarded as a transitional stage in the evolution of new genes or as evidence for the theory of chromosomal hierarchy.

Taken as a whole, this array of genetic mechanisms, consonant with the basic theory of organic inheritance, constitutes a body of knowledge which is one of the landmarks of those modern sciences concerned with variations of health in populations. While insufficient to explain the total range of demographic variants without the complex concepts of adaptation and selection (discussed elsewhere), the given phenomena are indispensable for an understanding of a multitude of population data.

The gene-specific foundation of human health has so many and such far-reaching ramifications that no essential biological or demographic parameter can be considered independent of this vital influence, "although mutants which affect general features like growth, fertility, sterility and viability frequently cannot be isolated and localized like the standard mutants of elementary Mendelism" (Goldschmidt, 1955, p. 132).

Ultimately, it is reasonable to expect that genetic theory will be sufficiently broadened to include within its scope those balanced interactions of normal human functions so closely related to demographic variables. When that time comes, it will be possible for the discipline of genetics to make its contribution not only to the analysis of relatively rare pathological traits but to all aspects of human existence.

To be effective, an approach to the genetics of populations requires not only an understanding of general genetic principles but also a definition of "population" that is sufficiently precise for use in both demographic and genetic investigations.

The main criterion for this purpose is the "intrabreeding" modality of a sexually reproducing species—a group of individuals tending to mate among each other (Strandskov, 1950). Hence the most inclusive Mendelian (intrabreeding) population is the *species*. Defined as "a reproductive community of individuals who share a common gene pool" (Dobzhansky, 1955), it serves as the investigative unit in population genetics. In line with this description, subspecies or races are "subordinate Mendelian populations differing in relative frequencies of genes or chromosomal structures, and usually also in external appearance and . . . physiological properties."

A particular gene pool consists of the sex cells contributed by all persons forming the population and can be described in terms of the percentage frequencies of the possible alleles at each of an estimated 10,000 loci. This gene frequency formula is known as the *allelotype* of the population.

In the human species, other distinguishing features of a population may be geographic, cultural, socioeconomic, ethnic, or psychological in nature. They tend to function as isolating factors and may serve to define subpopulations, but from a biological standpoint they are secondary to the intrabreeding characteristic. Since subpopulations undergo continuous boundary changes and are apt to overlap, their stratification exercises a definite effect on the genetic composition of the given population groups.

The cornerstone of a methodical approach to population genetics is a formula called the *Hardy-Weinberg law* (Hardy, 1908; Weinberg, 1908). It describes the state of equilibrium that exists in an ideal population, or, statistically speaking, the "expected values" of the various genotypes, under the following conditions: random mating (panmixia), with every male having the same chance to mate with any female; no selective advantage of one allele over the others at any locus; and absence of mutations. Failure to fulfil any of these conditions is bound to interfere in various ways with the equilibrium of a population.

In a simplified version of an ideal state of equilibrium, we may consider a single locus with only two possible alleles, A and A'. If p is the frequency of A in the population's gene pool, and q that of A', the sum of p and q equals 1. After one generation of random mating, the offspring will be represented by the following expected values:

		Spermatozoa	
		pA	qA'
Ova	pA	p^2AA	$pqA'A$
	qA'	$pqAA'$	$q^2A'A'$

In this filial population, the expected proportion of individuals homozygous for A will be p^2, that of A' homozygotes q^2, and that of heterozygotes for the two alleles $2pq$, according to the formula $(pA + qA')^2 = p^2A^2 + 2pqAA' + q^2A'^2$. Confirming that the given genotypic proportions are in equilibrium and will be so redistributed in all future generations, the gene frequencies in this generation may be calculated as follows:

Apt to appear in all sex cells of p^2 homozygotes as well as in half the sex cells of $2pq$ heterozygotes, the allele A will recur in the poportions p^2 and pq. Since $p + q$ equals 1, the total frequency of A will be $p^2 + pq = p(p + q) = p$. Similarly, the frequency of A' will be $q^2 + pq = q(q + p) = q$. With the gene frequencies in the first filial generation remaining unchanged, each succeeding generation will have the same gene frequencies and a distribution of genotypes according to the binomial expansion explained before.

The importance of the Hardy-Weinberg law lies in the fact that the continuation of intrapopulation variations from generation to generation is demonstrated as a corollary of the simplest Mendelian principles. A trend toward increasing uniformity, as would be observed either in a "blending" type of inheritance with a consequent reduction of individual differences or in a non-sexually reproducing species, is thus precluded. Lacking such a trend, the major causes of modifications in the expected generation-to-generation equilibrium are limited to assortative mating, undersized populations, and the phenomena of mutation and selection.

One type of modification takes place as a change in the relative proportions of homozygotes and heterozygotes and does not affect the actual gene frequencies. Modifying the phenotypic composition of successive generations through *interference with random mating*, such a change may be brought about by consanguineous marriage, assortative mating, and the development of isolates.

Since each of these phenomena may move toward two opposite poles, the following trends are to be considered: (*a*) an increase above the expected number of marriages among relatives (*endogamy*); (*b*) a decrease below the expected number of such marriages (*exogamy*); (*c*) an increase of marriages among people with the same traits (*positive assortative mating*); (*d*) resistance to marriage on the part of people with the same traits (*negative assortative mating*); and (*e*) the formation of *isolates;* or (*f*) their gradual breakup.

A tendency to increase the proportion of homozygotes and decrease that of heterozygotes results from *inmarriage* and, to a lesser extent, from *positive assortative mating*, the consequences of which may be either desirable (intelligence, musical talent) or undesirable (deafness). As a rule, the increase in recessive phenotypes due to inmarriage will be noticeable only in the case of relatively rare conditions, thus limiting the untoward effect upon the total population of any single trait. Commonly found conditions are as likely to be encountered in unrelated persons as in related ones. It has been well established, however, that many deleterious traits are both recessive in inheritance and rare in appearance. Cousin marriages are therefore important from the standpoint of individual mating prospects and are usually discouraged by genetically-oriented marriage counselors.

The demographic significance of *isolates* has been carefully studied by geneticists, particularly by Wahlund (1928), Wright (1943), and Dahlberg (1948). Defined as a randomly mating population group wherein an individual can find his mate, an isolate may be formed for one or more of the following reasons: (*a*) isolating geographic factors; (*b*) social, religious, or ethnic qualities; and (*c*) similar severe afflictions such as total deafness from birth or early childhood. Accordingly, the make-up of such a population group may be altered in one of the following three directions:

1. In a small isolate, there will be an increased chance of two heterozygous carriers of recessive genes marrying and producing homozygous offspring. An extreme example is that of an isolate constituted by persons with a common gene-specific defect. In the group of the deaf, the disorder in at least 50 per cent of the persons is of genetic origin.

2. Even with random mating in a small population, the relative frequency of alleles will show chance variations of a stochastic nature (*genetic drift*) from generation to generation. Instead of complete equilibrium as specified by the Hardy-Weinberg formula, there will be a tendency to fluctuations in gene frequencies despite the absence of mutative, selective, or assortative mating influences.

3. New patterns in industrialization, transportation, and migration are responsible for the *breakup* of isolates. As a result, deleterious genes will be more widely dispersed, since the proportion of heterozygous carriers will increase and that of homozygotes will decrease. Hence the immediate effect is likely to be advantageous for the population. With a decline in homozygotes, however, vigorous selective factors will cease to operate, thus creating a possible disadvantage for future generations.

A simple method of estimating the size of an isolate (Dahlberg, 1948) is based on the assumption that within such a population group, whose members practice random mating, consanguineous marriages will also take place at random. Thus the frequency of cousin marriages is expressed by the proportion of the average number of opposite-sex cousins per individual (a constant depending on the mean family size) to the number of opposite-sex persons in the isolate. It follows, then, that the size of the isolate varies inversely with the frequency of cousin marriages.

In the absence of ecological factors favoring or restricting matings between relatives in an isolate, a trend toward its breakup is indicated by a decrease in cousin marriages. This trend may be partly offset by the operation of assortative mating, which leads to increased homozygosis. On the whole, the effect of an isolate's breakup on the population's state of health is supposed to be beneficial, as was confirmed by the results of a recent French study (Sutter and Tabah, 1954). Expected to reduce the frequency of rare traits as well as the contingencies of homozygosis and selective emigration, the breakup in two French districts was shown to have resulted in lower infant mortality rates among the offspring of non-consanguineous matings than of consanguineous ones.

While the phenomena of isolates, assortative mating, and endogamy tend to change the proportions of homozygotes and heterozygotes in the ideal Hardy-Weinberg equilibrium and not the gene frequencies themselves, theoretically the original proportions can be re-established by a return to random mating in an infinitely large population. Social factors, however, may prevent this reversion. Moreover, whenever selection operates, it has a close relation to the homozygote-heterozygote balance of the population and is apt to lead to gene frequency changes—the distinguishing feature of the second type of modification in an ideal random-mating equilibrium. In addition to selection, the mechanisms to be considered in this group include mutation, genetic drift, and migration (gene flow).

Mutation rates in man have been less intensively studied than those in lower organisms. They can be estimated in two different ways, yielding figures which are of the order of 1 in 10^5

(Neel, 1952). The first procedure, known as the direct method, is primarily applied to dominant mutations. It simply consists in counting the number of affected children born to normal parents in a given population. Among 94,075 children born in Copenhagen, for instance, ten were found to be chondrodystrophic dwarfs, eight of whom had no affected parents (Mørch, 1941). Thus there was one dwarf in 12,000 births, yielding a mutation rate of one mutant allele per 24,000 loci, or about 4 in 10^5, provided the condition is dominant and fully penetrant and involves only one locus.

The indirect method rests on an important hypothesis. As the reproductive rate is lowered in individuals affected by abnormal traits and as the frequency of the particular alleles decreases from one generation to another, this trend may be counterbalanced by constantly occurring mutations—with a hypothetical equilibrium as the result. In dominant traits, this equilibrium is expressed by the following equation where u is the mutation rate, f is the reproductive fitness (frequency of abnormal offspring born to affected persons compared to that of normal offspring born to normal siblings), and x represents the frequency of the abnormality: $u = \frac{1}{2}(1-f)x$.

For estimating the mutation rate of recessive genes, a modification of this formula is used. However, the results are questionable for two reasons: while the method assumes complete recessiveness, the heterozygote may either be mildly affected or possess some selective advantage, and while equilibrium is assumed in all other respects, demographic factors may be at work in modern populations, tending to increase the proportion of heterozygotes through the breakup of isolates.

In any case, mutations occur in man with calculable frequency and with definite effects upon the gene pool for future generations. Whether they change a chromosomal pattern or the chemical composition of a gene, their frequency has been shown in animal experiments to be increased by such agents as radiation, ultraviolet light, and certain chemicals. The implications of a possible similar increase in human populations form the basis for much current concern and investigative work. According to Neel (1952), mutation rates are known at present for a total of seventeen human traits, with an approximate average frequency of $3:10^5$.

In an otherwise randomly mating population, it would take thousands of generations for the products of mutation alone to become noticeable. With m representing the mutation frequency per generation, the frequency of mutated genes at the end of n generations may be expressed as $1 - e^{-mn}$. This quantity increases with n and shows that in an infinite number of generations, and in the absence of specific adaptive effects, all genes will have mutated.

In reality, of course, mutations tend to cause changes in adaptedness as well as in gene frequencies. In this process of adaptive change, individuals become subject to the action of *selection,* a phenomenon defined as "a differential contribution of alleles by one generation to the succeeding one" (Strandskov, 1950). According to Wright (1949), selection may be mediated by differences in mating, fertility, and emigration as well as in mortality, but its result will always consist in a predictable change in gene frequency (other variables being equal).

Since the ensuing genetic advantage or disadvantage is usually measured in terms of mean family size, the production of an increased number of offspring by individuals of a certain genetic constitution is called *positive selection.* By contrast, extreme *negative* selection is the elimination of a dominant trait in one generation, with all affected persons dying without offspring. A similar result may be produced by a single recessive trait in the homozygotes. The frequency of such a gene in the nth generation will be $r/[1 + (n-1)r]$ (r being the initial gene frequency). At first, therefore, elimination of affected homozygotes will be rapid, but it will gradually slacken. The corresponding decrease in heterozygous carriers will be much slower.

The attenuation of selection also retards its speed of action. As the disadvantage of a mutated gene becomes less and less selective, other factors affecting gene frequency gain in importance.

Further complications, especially from the standpoint of population dynamics and demography, arise when general genetic aspects of fitness and adaptedness to the environment are considered, rather than the effect of one allele determining a unit character. A major problem is that of *heterosis* (heterozygous advantage) where a heterozygous carrier of a gene possesses a selective advantage over either type of homozygote.

Other factors to be scrutinized as basic to demographic genetics are changing environmental features and the truism that the individual's state of adaptedness is determined not by one gene-specific trait but by a balanced organization of many genes or chromosomal structures. Finally, the action of selection may be affected by inbreeding, assortative mating, and isolate formation, since they alter the proportions of heterozygotes and homozygotes, and the pressure of new mutations may be exerted in the same or opposite direction.

As to the flow of genes between two intermingling populations (migration), what it accomplishes in terms of the frequency of any gene is to yield a final frequency that is the weighted mean of the two original frequencies. Since the frequency of homozygotes varies inversely with the square of population size, the effect of such intermingling upon the population's phenotypic composition duplicates that which results from the breakup of isolates. Demographic data on gene flow in relation to space and time were recently reviewed by Glass (1954), while the distinction between inter-isolate differences due to gene flow and those caused by genetic drift was extensively studied by Birdsell (1950), mainly in Australian tribes.

The remaining mechanism which is a potential source of gene frequency changes is that of genetic drift, a measure of random deviations from ideal Mendelian frequencies. Whether operating independently of or in interaction with mutative and selective phenomena, it essentially reflects the fact that Mendelian ratios are approximated rather than ideally achieved in populations of finite size. A chance deviation in favor of one allele may either lead to the total loss of another allele within a few generations, or perpetuate itself in the same direction, thus resulting in a new gene frequency. That this occurrence would be more probable in a small rather than a large population was first shown by the geneticist who described the phenomenon, Sewall Wright (1931, 1932, 1940, 1943, 1948).

In a population of effective size N, if N is greater than $1/2m$, $1/2s$, or $1/2f$ (where m is the mutation pressure, s the coefficient of selection, and f the flow of genes into the population), the most pronounced changes in the frequency of any particular allele will be produced by mutation, selection, or gene flow. On the other hand, in smaller populations genetic drift may occur, consisting of oscillations in gene frequencies from generation to generation, due to random variations of expected ratios, and possibly resulting in complete fixation or elimination.

Since inbred populations are apt to be limited in size, they are subject to both increased homozygosis and genetic drift. How such a random departure from original gene frequencies may occur within two or three generations was observed by Glass *et al.* (1952) and Glass (1954, 1956) in a small religious isolate of less than 350 people. Significant differences from the surrounding population were estab-

TABLE 76

MODES OF IMMEDIATE CHANGE
OF GENE FREQUENCY*

1. *Directed processes:*
   a. Recurrent mutation
   b. Recurrent immigration and cross-breeding
   c. Mass selection

2. *Random processes:*
   a. Fluctuations in the rate of mutation
   b. Fluctuations in the effect of immigration
   c. Fluctuations in selection
   d. Stochastic movement (genetic drift) from the "expected" proportions

3. *Unique events:*
   a. Novel favorable mutation
   b. Unique hybridization
   c. Mass immigration
   d. Unique selective incident
   e. Unique reduction in numbers

* Adapted from a table published by Sewall Wright, 1955. "Classification of the factors of evolution" (*Cold Spring Harbor Symposia on Quantitative Biology*, XX, 16–24).

lished for MN blood groups, ABO groups, mid-digital hair types, and ear lobes.

Using a steadily growing body of population data on gene frequency changes due to the separate and interacting effects of mutation, selection, gene flow, and genetic drift, Wright (1955) proposed an over-all system of classification according to the *degree of determinacy* in these changes (Table 76).

In this frame of reference, the following types of *genic equilibrium* are distinguishable in an analysis of genetic population changes:

1. Neutral equilibrium:
   (a) with random mating (Hardy-Weinberg formula)
   (b) with deviations from random mating
2. Stable equilibrium with selection:
   (a) with recurrent mutation
   (b) with heterozygote advantage
   (c) with more than one environmental niche
3. Unstable equilibrium with heterozygote disadvantage

As previously noted, neutral equilibrium is found in an ideal randomly mating population in the absence of both mutation and selection. Deviations from random mating, in the form of inbreeding or assortative mating, affect the ratio of homozygotes to heterozygotes but do not change the gene frequency. A similar effect is produced by the breakup of isolates or migration, while chance effects due to sampling error are perpetuated.

Following an alteration in gene frequency under the conditions of a stable equilibrium, the original frequency is gradually re-established. This type of equilibrium is found where selection against a certain gene is balanced either by recurrent mutations or by an advantage conferred upon the heterozygote. Even if slight, this advantage may suffice to maintain an equilibrium at which the gene frequencies are entirely determined by the selection coefficients against the homozygotes (Li, 1955, p. 259). The stability of this equilibrium can be disturbed by increasing homozygosis due to inbreeding and assortative mating, unless the selective advantage of the heterozygote increases proportionally.

Another variety of stable equilibrium is encountered when the environment is not uniform but consists of a number of different local environments (niches), each favoring a different allele (Levene, 1953). Stability may be attained with both alleles present. The result will be a form of balanced polymorphism, an important phenomenon in both demography and ecology.

An unstable equilibrium ensues if the heterozygote is less fit than either type of homozygote and the two alleles about equal in frequency. With an increased proportion of one allele at the expense of the other, the rarer allele will eventually be reduced to a very low frequency. In the case of the Rh blood factor, for instance, heterozygotes born to homozygous (recessive) mothers are subject to hemolytic disease which lowers their survival rate (Race and Sanger, 1954). Since this gene is known to have a frequency of about 0.38 in the United States, it should be well on the way to extinction. Its failure to follow the expected pattern has given rise to a number of hypothetical explanations (Glass, 1950; Lewontin, 1953; Li, 1955). As one theory has it, mothers may continue to produce children beyond the average family size (*reproductive overcompensation*). If the father is a heterozygote, the living children will be homozygotes and will actually serve to increase the frequency of the recessive gene.

A discussion of population genetics would be incomplete without reference to the most inclusive current theory of genetic adaptedness in human populations, Dobzhansky's *balance hypothesis* (1955, p. 3). In terms of classical Mendelian principles heterozygosity would be (*a*) a transient state, (*b*) the result of adaptively neutral mutants, or (*c*) the product of environmental diversity, while populations would tend by selection to become homozygous for each of the more advantageous variants of a large number of genes.

In the balance hypothesis two well-established phenomena are taken into consideration: (*a*) the increased fitness of heterozygotes (selective advantage) and (*b*) the concept of gene interaction (equivalent to chromosomal hierarchy in Goldschmidt's framework), with a selective advantage of particular combinations of genes. If it is a genic combination or chromosomal organization resulting in phenotypes best adapted to the environment in which they arise, this combination or organization (sometimes called a supergene) will have the real selective advantage. Accordingly, a heterozygote possessing this coadapted genic complex will, as an individual, be more fit, vigorous, and better adapted to the environment than a homozygote.

Called *euheterosis* or *overdominance*, this concept implies that in the process of evolution a number of gene complexes or a set of alleles somehow acquired a combined advantage over the single advantages of any one of them. It is a moot point whether heterozygosis may also act as a kind of physiological stimulus to growth and vigor (luxuriance). Even on the individual level, however, a geneticist's willingness to think in terms of broadened qualities of fitness and adaptedness leads to extending the classical concepts of dominance, recessivity, and independence of action to those of overdominance, heterosis, and balanced organization.

On the level of populations, it is safe to assume that heterozygous advantage produces a stable equilibrium. In this balanced state many well-adapted heterozygotes will coexist with a limited number of homozygotes, who may be regarded as a necessary by-product distinguished by a lesser degree of adaptedness. As a trait qualifying the gene pool of a population, however, such a "balanced polymorphism" tends to confer the capacities both for adaptedness to the present environment and for adaptability to future environmental changes. It is this balanced state, called *homeostasis* by Lerner (1954), that endows the population with its best chance of survival in the widest variety of potential environments.

METHODS OF GENETIC INVESTIGATION

The methods used in genetic studies differ according to whether an analysis deals with the health problems of certain groups of families or of entire populations. In either case, it is necessary to bear in mind that gene-specific variations follow the theory of probabilities.

Mendelian ratios express no more than the average expectancy of a gene-controlled trait in a representative population sample. Diversified statistical procedures are needed to determine the validity of inferences drawn from individual observations (Schulz, 1936). This principle applies to all genetic mechanisms and attributes, physical or mental, normal or pathological, frequent or infrequent. Here, however, only those statistical methods will be discussed which are peculiar to family and population studies in man.

Since statistically representative samples of certain groups of people or populations are a principal requirement, genetic data obtained from individual families (pedigrees) or sets of relatives (one pair of concordant or discordant twins) usually prove of doubtful value. Family histories are seldom published because of familial concentration of exceptionally fine health in one generation after another or because of the rare occurrence of an important pathological trait in a particular family. Also, it is obvious that an affected person must be fertile in order to have a similarly afflicted child and that unless his parents had at least seven children, he cannot have six affected sibs.

At best, therefore, the usefulness of the ordinary family history method is restricted to rare pathological conditions that are easily traced genealogi-cally and known to be fairly constant in penetrance and clinical expression. While single pedigree studies may serve to demonstrate how often similar varieties of a familial trait tend to occur in the members of an affected family, they are not likely to furnish conclusive proof of the operation of heredity as such or of the mode of inheritance involved.

At the present stage of incomplete knowledge regarding the biology of man, systems of *constitutional typology* are largely the equivalent of pedigree studies in the area of population genetics. They have been used either in compiling correlations between main types of body build and personality (by means of anthropometric indexes taken directly or from standardized photographs) or in classifying somato-typal measurements according to the technique of factor analysis. In the opinion of Rees and Eysenck (1945), the major part of the measurable variation in any human group is accounted for by two factors alone—growth in length and growth in breadth. However that may be, there are no adequate data to substantiate the premise that a particular body type, the relative distribution of constitutional components, or a certain dysplastic variation tends to remain constant throughout a person's life or during a major part of it. What is more, the genetic phenomena responsible for the differentiation of the main constitutional variations are largely unidentified.

For the purpose of a comprehensive genetic analysis, the applications of total population surveys (census method) are also limited. Exceptions are surveys concerned with small and sufficiently co-operative populations (isolates) as well as those dealing with relatively uncomplicated traits that can be ascertained by enumerative procedures, that is, without close personal contact with the members of the communities to be surveyed (questionnaires, vital statistics, registries of reportable diseases and defects). In this way, adequate population data may be obtained on the distribution of freckles, pellagra, or blood groups (if blood samples are available), but not on possible linkage phenomena, the selectivity of dietary deficiencies among the members of certain families, or the genetics of a special form of blood incompatibility between mother and child.

Similarly, a dividing line is to be drawn between the relative frequencies of tasters and non-tasters, on the one hand, and inquiries into possible psychological deviations of non-tasters, on the other, or between the number of married couples and their fertility, and qualitative variations in marital adjustment as related to intelligence, economic prosperity, or philoprogenitiveness. In other words, the census method is neither economical nor fruitful when it comes to genetic problems presenting difficulties of diagnosis or ascertainment (reluctance of families to disclose embarrassing private affairs to nonspecialized research personnel), or requiring data on differential fertility rather than general marital fertility rates. The application of usual census procedures is equally unsuited to those areas where differential morbidity-risk estimates, rather than actual prevalence statistics, are needed.

With respect to the genetically important aspects of differential fertility, disease expectancy, and the etiology of pathological conditions, special population surveys will have to be conducted so long as public health authorities are chiefly concerned with the actual frequency on a given date of all persons affected by, hospitalized for, or dying of a certain disease. From a genetic standpoint, these general population statistics are particularly insufficient when it is known that many persons affected by a given trait are not hospitalized or that, following hospitalization, their chances of mate selection and reproductivity are reduced.

Since differential mating and fertility patterns in genetically homogeneous groups may have a profound effect on gene frequencies in the general population, they have been studied in many special surveys, especially in relation to different educational levels (Cook, 1951; Whelpton and Kiser, 1943–54; Muckermann, 1932; Tietze and Grabill, 1957) and the matings of physically handicapped, mentally defective, or psychotic persons (Dahlberg, 1933; Essen-Möller, 1935; Juda, 1934; Kallmann, 1938; Weinberg, 1913). The demographic results of differential fertility are discussed elsewhere, but it may be mentioned here that under conditions of negative selection, reproductive quotas (marital and extramarital) are to be obtained in terms of absolute and net fertility, per year of reproductivity with and without the years of institutionalization falling into the reproductive period, and relative to the crucial dates of the type of ill health investigated (onset of disease, first admission, and so forth). As to the effects of migration and differences in socioeconomic status, it has been established that social mobility tends to result in the transfer of gene complexes from more fertile to less fertile subpopulations.

For ascertaining normal control data, comparable to selected sets of differential fertility and morbidity risk figures, the Munich school (Luxenburger, 1928) devised a simple yet most satisfactory method. It is based on the premise that families forming a representative general population tend to be easily located and relatively co-operative while they have a relative in the general or special hospital where the study is conducted. To facilitate procuring identifying data on a sample of control families at the time of admission (when routine family histories are obtained), the old master-statisticians of human genetics recommended the use of the siblings of the mates of any group of hospital patients (afflicted with a disease other than the one under study) as "general population." Of course, the same diagnostic criteria and statistical corrections (expectancy rates related to the manifestation period of the condition studied, differences in age distribution) are to be used in both sets of data.

Regarding the need for statistically corrected expectancy rates in all areas of clinical genetics, the main interest here is on the probable or empirically observed morbidity risk (expectancy) of members of certain families with respect to specific traits and their variations in different periods of time or life and in various ethnic or socioeconomic settings (Kallmann, 1953, p. 60). According to Strömgren's definition (1950), the disease expectancy of a person is "the risk of becoming ill during one's lifetime, if one lives long enough to pass the period of risk"— that is, the time during which the disease may develop. Of course, some expectancy rates have only a theoretical value, since it is expected that the majority of persons will die before they have passed all possible risks. In any event, the two principal methods for obtaining expectancy rates are Weinberg's system (*proband-sibship and abridged methods*) and certain extensions of the twin-study method (*twin-family method*).

In Weinberg's system, the chief objective of a comparative analysis is to determine whether a particular trait occurs more frequently in blood relatives of a representative number of probands or index cases (persons disclosing clinical evidence of the trait in question) than in the general population or, more precisely, in a group of

persons not ascertained through known consanguinity to the given type of proband. The observed number of affected persons among the siblings of the probands (full sibs, half-sibs, stepsibs) is analyzed in terms of varying parental matings (affected or unaffected, but in the case of full sibs always distinguished by the fact of having produced at least one affected child, the proband). This statistical bias in the ascertainment of index sibships (parental matings with no affected child cannot be reached in this manner) is corrected by omitting from the statistical analysis all patients obtained as probands (according to the most consistent method of ascertaining patients who show clinical evidence of the given trait within the boundaries of the area covered by the study).

In addition, inequalities in age distribution are to be corrected by the use of the abridged method (Weinberg, 1927, 1930) or such similar procedures as morbidity tables or Ilse's and Strömgren's methods (Kallmann, 1938, pp. 135–42). In Weinberg's method, the actually observed (absolute) morbidity figures are related to the total number of persons who have survived the given period of manifestation, increased by half the number of persons who at the time of the study are still within the age limits of this period. Persons who did not reach (because of death), or are too young to have reached, the beginning of the manifestation period are not counted. The resulting morbidity rates are average expectancy figures, valid for persons who are old enough to have developed the usual clinical symptomatology of a certain disease. The range of the given manifestation period is to be chosen in accordance with clinical experience. Obviously, statistical accuracy in employing the abridged method depends as much on a fairly uniform distribution of the persons observed within the accepted period of manifestation as on the representative size and diagnostic uniformity of the total group studied.

Methods for testing the biological uniformity of clinical subgroups (Kallmann, 1938, pp. 146–47) have been devised by Weinberg (*double proband method*) and Schulz (*double case method* based on Bernstein's *a priori method*). In both procedures only sibships with at least two probands are included in the analysis. While the other members of these sibships are counted singly (according to the principles of the ordinary proband method), the two probands are statistically treated as a "double proband entity." In the absence of statistically significant differences between the expectancy rates yielded by the ordinary and the double proband methods, the clinical subgroups compared may be considered biologically homogeneous.

The corrective procedures of Weinberg's system are also used in the twin-family method (Kallmann and Reisner, 1943; Kallmann, in press), which combines the principles of the proband-sibship and abridged methods with those of the *twin-study method*, the most effective procedure for exploring the genetics of human behavior, both normal and abnormal. Introduced as a genetic research tool by Galton (1876), the method is based on the regular occurrence of two genetically different types of twins—those derived from one fertilized ovum, and those derived from two fertilized ova. While one-egg twins are always of the same sex, two-egg twins may be of the same or opposite sex.

In the original version of the twin-study method, the comparison of observable similarities and dissimilarities in the histories of genetically similar or dissimilar genotypes is limited to twin subjects. This procedure requires access to a representative series of one-

egg and two-egg twins, of either or different sex, presenting evidence of a diagnostically well-defined trait to which the principles of the proband method can be applied.

In another version called the *co-twin-control method* (Gesell and Thompson, 1941), observational or experimental data are obtained from a few selected pairs of one-egg twins whose aptitudes, physiological reactions, or adjustive patterns can be compared under different life conditions, or in response to planned differences in management.

In the third version (*twin-family method*) the collection of comparative data is extended to complete sibships of twin index cases and their parents. The six dissimilar sibship groups compared in this manner are one-egg twins, two-egg twins of the same sex, two-egg twins of opposite sex, full sibs, half-sibs, and step-sibs. This procedure provides a unique opportunity of investigating intrafamily variations with a minimum of uncontrolled variables, especially with respect to traits that present complex sampling problems and that require comparisons in both cross-sectional and longitudinal directions.

So broad is the scope of this combined procedure that it fulfils nearly all the requirements specified by Cattell (1953) for the use of the *multiple variance method* in investigating functionally, but not necessarily genetically, unitary traits in the normal range of personality development. In his scheme, measurable test data are obtained from five different subgroups in pairs: (*a*) a sample group of one-egg twins in their own families, (*b*) siblings in their own families, (*c*) siblings with each member of the pair in a different family, (*d*) unrelated persons in pairs in the same families, and (*e*) unrelated persons in different families.

For determining the zygosity of

same-sex twins, the method of choice at present is a refined version of the *similarity method,* originally developed by Siemens (1924) and Von Verschuer (1928). The fetal-membrane method is no longer in use, since it is now known that not all one-egg pairs are born with only one placenta. The most reliable criteria of the modern similarity method are dermatoglyphic and blood group data. Where these criteria prove indecisive in a scientifically important case, reciprocal skin grafts may be performed. Full-thickness homografts are not successful in two-egg twins, although initial takes may last three to four weeks (Rogers, 1957). By the same token, a given pair of twins cannot be monozygotic if the blood groups are different. The dermatoglyphic analysis should be extended, whenever possible, to both qualitative and quantitative aspects (Kallmann, 1953, p. 63).

Since generalized conclusions cannot be drawn from observations made on single pairs or an unrepresentative series of pairs, the importance of adequate sampling procedures with complete ascertainment of twin index cases (rather than pairs) in a certain district or group of institutions is axiomatic. The most useful evidence of unbiased sampling in a twin study is provided by an approximate agreement between a twin sample and the parent population, with respect to the proportion of either opposite-sex pairs or, when known, one-egg pairs (Allen, 1955). Roughly speaking, the population twin rate is 2 per cent, with the proportion of twins from opposite-sex pairs about one-third of all twins. Any series of twins differing significantly from the parent population in either of these two characteristics may be regarded as non-representative. Of course, the given statistics are to be related to twin individuals rather than pairs, since even random samples may deviate considerably from the parent

population in statistical estimates based on pairs.

In the United States, the precise twin rate is 2.19 per cent of all babies born since 1928. This rate is reduced to about 1.9 per cent by excess twin mortality within the first year of life, while the 2:1 ratio of same-sex to opposite-sex pairs observed at birth remains virtually unchanged in all age groups (Allen, 1955). After the first year of life, there is no significant difference between the mortality rates of twins and non-twins, so that the proportion of twin individuals in the population remains nearly the same at all ages. However, as pairs are broken by mortality and migration, the number of intact pairs is reduced at successive ages, thus making it necessary to analyze twin data in terms of individuals rather than twin pairs. Among people who survive to an advanced age, the relative frequency of pairs represented by at least one twin may be nearly twice as great as at birth.

When analyzing twin family samples in terms of expectancy rates, it is essential to compute all statistics from twin index cases rather than twin pairs if some or many pairs are represented by a single index case and if morbidity risk figures for various groups of sibs and cotwins are to be compared within the sample. The same means of computation is required for estimating penetrance and concordance rates. In the latter instance, however, the number of index cases from concordant pairs must be halved in order to correct for the twofold representation of concordant pairs in the sample. With this stipulation, it is apparent that differences beween one-egg and two-egg groups of twins will have the same statistical significance whether evaluated in terms of concordance or morbidity expectancy.

In the study of normal personality variations in twin samples (Newman *et al.*, 1937), the best-known statistical technique employed in estimates of genetic components is Holzinger's h^2: the variance of the two-egg twins minus the variance of the one-egg twins, divided by the variance of the two-egg twins. In order to establish the significance of the h^2 values, an F test may be used for the ratio of the two-egg over the one-egg variance.

As a general rule for analyzing normal traits, it would be well to express twin data in terms of varying degrees of intrapair similarity or dissimilarity rather than in terms of concordance or discordance. Twins may be concordant or discordant as to rheumatic heart disease but not as to the normal shape of their hearts or the possession of a cardiovascular system.

GENETIC ASPECTS OF PUBLIC HEALTH (EUGENICS)

It is in the public health area of demography that the effects of changes in the frequency and distribution of genes in a given population find their broadest application. Variations in the genotypic composition of a population are associated in one way or another with changing demographic trends, which may be *eugenic* or *dysgenic* in nature.

The term "eugenic," as used here, connotes no moral value judgments. It describes changes toward desirable public health goals, either from the standpoint of over-all population fitness or in relation to specific genetic aspects of a deviation from usual health patterns.

The genetically oriented demographer, concerned with gene-specific population trends that may be capable of promoting health for the sake of human betterment (eugenics), is in the same position with respect to dysgenic phenomena as are experts in mental hygiene when it comes to mental defect and disorder. In short, the student of human genetics and eugenics is against dysgenic principles in much the same way as the prudent politician is against sin.

Eugenic ideas, as an instrument of public health planning, have long been linked to the need for further evolutionary progress of the human species, biologically and socially (Huxley, 1953; Riddle, 1954; Kallmann and Sank, in press). It is assumed that this need exists because modern man has been forced by a multitude of technical and scientific advances to adjust to radical changes in his mode of living. With educability his most outstanding quality, it is inevitable that man should find himself in a position where he will have to recognize that he can plan the future of both the world around him and, more important, himself.

In genetic terms, the *modern eugenic thesis* is based on the supposition that man's evolution to his present station of leadership over all other forms of organic life on earth and his gradual conquest of nature have resulted in a uniquely unstable state of affairs. Up to the time modern man made his appearance, all living organisms were subject to natural selection in the same manner and to the same extent. More recently, a second potent force has been in operation—that of *artificial selection*. This man-made type of selection may be either voluntary (directed), as in the domestication of plants and animals, or involuntary (undirected), as in haphazard use of birth-control information and marked inconsistencies in the lowering of the overall death rate with the progress of medicine.

Some experts in human genetics are quite pessimistic about the effect of an unchecked relaxation of natural selection. Others are less gloomy or even deny the need for any such fears at this time. Actually, few specific eugenic programs have been announced, as it is widely recognized that the eugenic objectives of public health planning must necessarily vary from nation to nation, from culture to culture, and from generation to generation. Since a specimen of the standard man would be impossible to find, it is apparent that demographic problems connected with measures of population control extend far beyond the borders of those scientific disciplines that are concerned with the study of man's genetically determined capacities and frailties. It is quite undisputed, however, that man can and perhaps should learn to exert some degree of control over his future in regard to population size and composition.

In line with this premise, it is logical to suppose that procedural effectiveness would be considerably increased if any eugenic program were thought of as a means to promote general welfare and public health. Even then, it would be well to bear in mind that public opinion would not respond to efforts to arouse an interest in the activation of eugenic population policies that had not previously existed, at least latently. People have an inscrutable talent for knowing what it is they want and do not want to accomplish through their children.

In a bipolar scheme of eugenically meaningful population trends, the following man-made (artificially selective) factors are regarded as dysgenic, although potentially controllable by man:

1. Wars, because they reduce the proportions of the most physically and mentally fit, in either camp.

2. Differential reproductive patterns with a negative effect on the genotypic composition of a subpopulation: (a) cousin marriage, (b) assortative mating trends, (c) differential fertility lowering the reproductivity of genetically well-endowed groups of families, (d) migration trends likely to have a differentiating effect on previously stabilized fertility rates, and (e) overcompensatory mechanisms.

3. Other circumstances favoring an uncontrolled spread of deleterious genes and traits, especially in the presence of a condition which might confer an immediate adaptive advantage (apparent or real) in a particular environment.

4. Improvement in the efficacy of therapeutic procedures, unaccompanied by directed guidance as to reproduction, designed to counteract the relaxation of natural selection.

5. Procedures tending to increase the mutation rate of genes with a deleterious effect: (a) irradiating methods of medical treatment and (b) exposure to atomic radiation.

While there is no disagreement on the first point, the dysgenic effect of warfare between nations, the same cannot be said of differential reproductive patterns, if only because pertinent population data are still at a premium in this area. Little is known about selective factors of this kind in primitive populations, and in modern societies selective conditions have become increasingly complex.

The frequency of marriages between first cousins has been investigated in the United States (Herndon and Kerley, 1952; Woolf *et al.*, 1956) as well as in other countries, including France (Sutter and Tabah, 1948), Germany (Rüdin, 1956), Italy (Fraccaro, 1957), Japan (Neel *et al.*, 1949) and Sweden (Dahlberg, 1938; Böök, 1956*a*). The general trend seems to be toward a decline in such matings, although cultural attitudes differ from one country to another, and the given data have been obtained for various purposes (mutation rate calculations, estimates of the size of isolates, and the like). Apparently, the need for cousin marriages decreases as isolates are broken up by advancing civilization and as isolated rural or frontier conditions of life yield to modern communication, transportation, and social mobility.

That the general population effect of a continually high cousin-marriage rate is largely dysgenic, and its gradual decline eugenic, is not disputed. To be sure, the union of two favorable recessive genes may be prevented by such a decline, but most single-factor traits are pathological in their effect. Moreover, heterozygosis confers adaptive advantages (general fitness) as measured by such indexes as fertility (Böök, 1956b) and mortality at an early age (Sutter and Tabah, 1954). It has also been shown that induced mutations, including those caused by radiation, tend to manifest themselves more quickly with a higher prevalence of inbreeding (Neel *et al.*, 1949). By the same token, they will be eliminated by selection in fewer generations where inbreeding is prevalent.

Compared to the dysgenic implications of an unusually high rate of consanguineous marriages, those of assortative mating call for definitive demographic criteria and corroborative data even more urgently. While the differentiating significance of "mating based on phenotypic resemblance" is rather obvious, its precise effect upon the genotypic composition of a population has been demonstrated mainly on a theoretical basis (Dahlberg, 1948; Li, 1955).

As previously noted (Hardy-Weinberg law), an increase in marriages among people with the same traits (positive assortative mating) changes only the proportions of homozygotes and heterozygotes and not the gene frequencies themselves. Positive assortative mating trends may be incomplete or complete. If they are incomplete, an equilibrium condition of heterozygosis will be reached. In the event of completeness, however, a slow but progressive decrease in heterozygotes will be observed in accordance with the following formula: $H_n = 2pH_0/(2p + nH_0)$. Here H_0 is the initial proportion of heterozygotes, H_n the proportion after n generations of continued assortative mating, and p the frequency of the dominant gene.

In applying these principles to human populations, two major difficulties are encountered: (1) No quantitative assortative-mating data (frequencies) are available for individual traits, not even for comparatively obvious ones. In fact, it is frequently unknown whether there is a positive or negative assortment. Possible exceptions are height, skin color, total deafness, and such a nebulous quality as musical talent. (2) Although many human traits (physical, intellectual, and emotional) are of demographic interest as a probable source of assortative mating trends, very few have been defined clearly enough or are measurable in their genetic components. The learning process, for instance, "supposed to be the key to the intellectual gift, is itself a highly complex, and by no means well-understood phenomenon; . . . and even the simplest cognitive functions, such as perception, and recall, lend themselves very badly indeed to conceptualization in terms of the units with which the student of heredity deals" (Murphy, 1954, p. 210). In order to clarify "possible relationships between traits, factors and genes," highly specialized and comprehensive investigations will be required, using such procedures as factor analysis (Cattell, 1953), animal experiments (Thompson, 1957), criterion analysis (Eysenck, 1950), and comparative twin studies (Kallmann, in press).

With continuing progress in the genetic analysis of human behavior patterns, extensive studies of the population dynamics of assortative mating will become imperative and will probably be most productive. It is reasonable to assume that current population trends are toward an increasing size of isolates, a wider choice of mates, and a greater frequency of assortative mating. As a consequence, the expected decrease in homozygosis due to diminished inbreeding will be counteracted, at least partly, by increases commensurate with positive assortment. Obviously, the genetic aspects of assortative mating will become increasingly important both demographically and eugenically, and particularly in a democratic and mobile society, but they will require much systematic research.

In this investigative program, careful attention should be given to special subpopulations, such as the deaf, who are forced by a severe form of sensory deprivation into a state of semi-isolation, with concomitant effects on both mate selection and reproductivity (Rainer and Kallmann, in press). Reduced in their potentialities for culture-specific speech development, learning, and socializing, the deaf—more specifically, persons with total deafness from birth or early childhood—are shut off from the hearing world to a variable extent, forming a society within a society. Out of either necessity or choice they merge into groups that cut across many boundaries, including those conventionally drawn for geographic, ethnic, cultural, or socioeconomic reasons.

Demographically as well as eugenically, it is particularly important that the deaf are distinguished by the tendency to cluster within families. It has been estimated that nearly one-half of total deafness cases are genetically determined, that about 47 per cent of the deaf population in America marry, and that the majority of the mates come from the same group. The dysgenic consequences of this assortative-mating trend are somewhat mitigated by the fact that marriages in which one or both partners are deaf tend to be only half as productive of children as those

contracted by a comparable group of hearing couples. It is apparent, however, that the genetic factors operating in such semi-isolate-forming conditions as early deafness (known to accumulate in certain families) represent an important set of variables which call for a thorough analysis of differential reproductive patterns.

As to the reproductivity of the population as a whole, differential fertility is another potentially dysgenic phenomenon where much additional information is needed on intragroup variations. Although there is considerable evidence for a decreased reproductivity rate being associated with a higher socioeconomic level, some investigators assume that this association operates without disrupting the homeostatic (self-regulating) forces necessary to maintain genetically balanced, well-adapted individuals and populations. According to Osborn (1951a, b, 1952a, b), such differentials are not likely to have a dangerous effect on the genetic potential of the population, though the possibility of some negative influence on cultural and technological advances is acknowledged. In the opinion of Cook (1955), however, there is an urgent need for a broad educational program that would provide the public with essential facts and stimulate the desire of future parents to have perfect children.

Osborn's belief that if there is a decrease in average reproduction with increasing educational and socioeconomic status, it may be a reflection of a transitional period marked by uneven use of birth control is based on the results of the much-discussed Indianapolis study (Whelpton and Kiser, 1943–54). With the universal practice of effective contraception, individual psychological factors are expected by Osborn's group to become a major determinant of who will have children. According to this hypothesis, persons with desirable physical, mental, and moral qualities would then tend to distinguish themselves by a high degree of philoprogenitiveness. In this manner, it may come about that the best-endowed individuals would be habitually selected as the parents to contribute the largest number of children to the next generation.

Whether or not this goal can be achieved only through a well-organized program of "positive eugenics" (education), there is little doubt that attempts to enforce such a program at this time would be premature, mainly because of incomplete genetic data on the complex population problems involved. Nevertheless, consideration of a minimum population program for the relief of pressures (genetic and social) arising from interference with the operation of natural selection is very much in order.

Planning of eugenic population policies in this area requires essentially the same additional genetic data as were discussed in relation to assortative mating. For purposes of positive selection (best-endowed parents), accurate trait descriptions, particularly in the intellectual and emotional range, are needed in a form that meets the standards of a genetic analysis. The prerequisites for any recommended program of negative selection are improved methods of detecting heterozygous carriers.

Although complete selection against a dominant gene will eliminate it in one generation, selection against a recessive genotype, even if complete, tends to lower the gene frequency only slowly. Where q_0 is the initial frequency of the recessive gene before the operation of selection, the expression for q_n, the frequency of a recessive gene after n generations of complete elimination of homozygous recessives, is $q_n = q_0/(1 + nq_0)$. For instance, if the initial gene frequency is 1/50, the frequency expected after the passing of fifty generations (in approximately 1500 years) will still be ½ of its original value, with the number of affected persons (homozygotes) amounting to $(\frac{1}{2})^2$ or ¼. Under conditions of partial selection, of course, the process of elimination will take even longer, while the operational mechanism of selection itself will be slowed down by an intensified trend toward heterozygosis due to the breakup of isolates. It is obvious, therefore, that no eugenic program aimed at a quantitative reduction of undesirable offspring could possibly be effective without being extended to the heterozygous carriers as well.

While the difficulties encountered in the detection of these carriers by means of clinical or biochemical criteria are pronounced, they are probably not insurmountable (Neel, 1949). Equally valuable would be reliable methods for the early identification of persons destined to succumb to the severe symptoms of a late-developing dominant trait such as Huntington's chorea, which rarely begins in the early part of the reproductive period. If the given persons (50 per cent of the children of an affected parent) could receive some expert advice as to their health prospects (Kallmann, 1956), they would be certain to benefit in one way or another (relief from anxiety, prophylactic measures, and the chance to weigh the question of parenthood).

The need for intelligent deliberation of this kind requires no particular emphasis in view of the possibility of overcompensatory influences. The mechanism of overcompensation may induce parents, following the loss of some children affected by a gene-specific trait, to replace them abundantly. That such couples may eventually have more living children than is true for normal controls has been reported by Fisher (in Race, 1944), Spencer (1947), and Glass (1950) in regard to erythroblastosis fetalis, by Race (1942) in regard to acholuric jaundice, and by Silvestroni *et al.* (1950) with respect to thalassemia. A similar overcompensatory force may operate in the members of families so severely afflicted as those with Huntington's chorea, manifesting itself relatively late in life. Apparently, some of these persons tend to overcompensate for their own anticipated loss (Reed and Palm, 1951).

An allied population phenomenon, which may also be followed by a potentially dysgenic differentiation of reproductive patterns, is that of selective migration. When motivated by drastic social changes and flowing toward genotypically different populations, migratory movements alter the gene distribution in the emigration as well as the immigration area—a factor which is often overlooked in epidemiologic studies of physical or mental illness. Regardless of whether the given migration trends are on a national or international scale, between rural and urban groups, or from one socioeconomic level to another, the ensuing gene frequency changes should always be taken into consideration when environmental influences are evaluated in terms of differential fertility or disease prevalence.

Migration, a factor that is likely to modify the genetic fitness of a population, serves to spread certain genes on an enlarged scale. By favoring heterozygosis (increase in the number of carriers at the expense of affected homozygotes), its immediate effect is probably beneficial. However, what happens in the long run will depend on trends which are reversible only in theory. One would have to balance the possibly deleterious consequences of broken gene combinations, which proved to be adaptive from an evolutionary standpoint, against the selective advantage of heterozygosis. It is possible, of course, that future genera-

tions may succeed in forming new adaptive combinations.

Apart from changes in the patterning of reproduction and adaptedness, there are other demographic variables which may be dysgenic in their effect. Their common denominator may be seen in an active or passive form of partiality for an uncontrolled spread of deleterious genes and traits, especially in the presence of a condition associated with an immediate adaptive advantage (imaginary or real) in a particular environment. Circumstances conducive to this spreading include (*a*) a tolerant attitude toward dissemination of misinformation regarding human heredity; (*b*) failure of public health authorities to provide adequate facilities for the education and guidance of morally responsible people who seek advice on problems of marriage, parenthood, and human genetics; and (*c*) establishment of legalized population policies fostering dysgenic or potentially genocidal practices.

As to the propriety of medicogenetic guidance activities, it may be stressed that most intelligent persons would rather have the truth about possible genetic implications of their family problems than a well-intentioned denial, however comforting, of the operation of heredity in man (Kallmann, 1953, p. 263). Many people ask for and are grateful for frank information regarding expectancy rates of a known familial disorder or the advisability of marrying and having children under certain circumstances. Countless physicians and other health-guidance workers would no doubt exert greater care in advising prospective parents or marriage partners as to predictable genetic contingencies, could they foresee the misery brought on some of these families, often many years later, by the recurrence of a severe gene-controlled trait.

To be sure, the family physician of a

young woman who happened to be born with a cleft palate, subsequently well repaired, is not obliged to volunteer information on the expected recurrence of the defect in her offspring. Indeed, if such an unsolicited disclosure were made under potentially traumatic conditions, it would be inconsistent with accepted standards of medical ethics. On the other hand, if the young woman requests the information and is capable of making intelligent use of available predictive data, she is entitled to the benefit of a truthful discussion of her chances of having a similarly malformed child.

The need for competent eugenic (medicogenetic) advice will be most apparent in those instances where a realistic appraisal of the health prospects of a family group might be helpful in early recognition of insidious pathologic symptoms or where careful guidance as to reproduction might safeguard an unstable state of health in affected family members who benefited from improved therapeutic procedures to the extent that they survived until the beginning of their reproductive period.

From the standpoint of the contemporary disciplines of demography and population genetics, an ostrich-like insistence on avoiding speculation about problems of fitness and survival in the distant future is a poor excuse for complete indifference toward the extrapolation of current medical activities in terms of future public health values. It is true that there are still many technical and procedural uncertainties regarding the determination and nature of selection pressures bearing upon the phenotypic expressions of mutant genes, especially in relation to traits that are neither lethal nor near-lethal. However, no one questions the necessity of continual vigilance as to apparently dysgenic practices which may increase either the distribution or the mutation rate of genes with a deleterious effect.

The theory that an increasing load of mutations in future generations will be the penalty for relaxing natural selection by medical advances has been supported by many genetic experts, especially by Muller (1950), Neel (1952), and Morton *et al.* (1956). It is based on Muller's estimate that the average person is heterozygous for at least eight genes of the following variety: (*a*) having a marked detrimental effect in the homozygous state and (*b*) exerting a lesser detrimental effect even in the heterozygous state (effective dominance). Under the conditions of equilibrium prevailing for the present gene frequencies, there would be an effective genetic loss in the population of 20 per cent, resulting from the total of these "more or less familial patterns of weaknesses."

Since a large proportion of this segment will be saved for reproduction by modern medical procedures, the frequency of mutant genes will inevitably rise to a new level. When that happens, even if medical techniques continue to improve, inordinate demands will be made on national resources to counteract the accumulation of gene-specific disabilities. Obviously, only the voluntary decision of persons with the greatest number of mutant genes to refrain from reproduction could prevent this occurrence altogether. By the same token, a further increase in the mutation rate, such as may arise from the use of ionizing radiation, would proportionally overburden the genetic load, possibly beyond a critical value for the population's survival.

The total mutation rate in man, per generation, is assumed by Muller to be as high as 0.1 to 0.5 and to represent the maximum compatible with the successful survival of the species. Neel's estimate is even higher, 1.0, but slightly more optimistic regarding its adverse consequences for future generations. In his opinion, selection at the cellular level "may act upon combinations of genes having to do with a particular reaction rather than single genes."

As to Muller's theory, it will be noted that it presupposes a certain degree of dominance for most mutant genes, that is, a diminished but significant effect even in heterozygotes. Under such conditions, it may be assumed that "selection, both negative and positive, is more effective and rapid in its action than had been thought," with the amount of inbreeding practiced becoming "a matter of lesser consequence."

By contrast, Lerner's theory of overdominance (1954) is based on the assumption that recessive genes, although deleterious in the homozygous state, may actually be selectively advantageous in the heterozygote. Hence, the ideal genotype would be the *balanced polymorph*, wherein the optimum combination of recessive genes produces the maximum adaptedness to present environmental conditions and a high degree of adaptability to future environmental changes.

Apart from observations in lower organisms which have been cited as evidence for either theory, one recently discovered example in human populations of the overdominance effect is sickle cell anemia (Allison, 1955). While fatal in the homozygote, this condition seems to confer resistance to malaria in the heterozygous state. Whereas the postulated selective advantage of heterozygotes is interpreted by Lerner as "a phenomenon extending beyond isolated cases of polymorphism," it is considered by Muller as an isolated event occurring only occasionally in transitional periods.

In line with Muller's conviction that "the great majority of mutant genes, even in man of today, have a detrimental effect not only homozygously but also heterozygously," the genetic (dysgenic) hazards of ionizing radiation have become a matter of serious concern to everyone in recent years. Despite some unresolved disagreement on various theoretical points, scientific groups are united in urging precautions against exposure to mutagenic energy sources. The prevailing views were jointly studied by the Committee on Genetic Effects of Atomic Radiation of the National Academy of Sciences and the National Research Council (1956) and summarized as follows:

1. Radiations cause mutations, and practically all radiation-induced mutations which have effects large enough to be detected are harmful.

2. The most common mutations are those with the smallest direct effect on any one generation—the slight detrimentals, rather than those resulting in monstrosities or freaks.

3. Since the genetic damage caused by radiation is cumulative, what counts is not the rate of radiation received by an individual with reasonable safety to his own person but the total accumulated dose to the reproductive cells of the individual from the beginning of his own life up to the time the child is conceived.

4. As the average age of fathers at the births of all children is 30.5 years (according to 1950 data for the United States), the average person ought not receive more than 10 roentgens of man-made radiation up to age 30, and preferably less. No individual should receive more than 50 roentgens during his first 30 years of life.

5. The fall-out from weapons testing, so far, has led to considerably less irradiation of the population than have the medical uses. However, there remains a proper concern to see to it that the fall-out does not increase to more serious levels.

6. The present state of advancement

in atomic and nuclear physics on the one hand, and in genetics on the other hand, are seriously out of balance.

Very similar conclusions were reached in Great Britain in a simultaneous statement made by the Medical Research Council, *The Hazards to Man of Nuclear and Allied Radiation* (1956), wherein it was strongly emphasized that "as an essential basis for future studies of the genetic effects of radiation, further data are required on the genetic structure of human populations." To this end, "the collection of more detailed information, when births, marriages and deaths are registered" was urgently recommended.

As brought out in the American report, "we badly need to know much more about genetics—about all kinds and all levels of genetics, from the most fundamental research on various lower forms of life to human radiation genetics." The current consensus, therefore, is that "our society should take prompt steps to see to it that the support of research in genetics is substantially expanded and that it is stabilized."

EUGENIC POPULATION TRENDS

In formulating a set of prophylactic population measures that are potentially eugenic from the standpoint of public health, a simple rule can be followed, namely, to obvert the order of dysgenic trends previously noted. Accordingly, the following factors are expected to have a eugenic effect upon the composition of future generations:

1. Enlightened public health policies in a flourishing nation which is at peace.

2. Differential reproductive patterns with a positive effect on the genetic structure of a subpopulation:

a) assortative-mating trends that favor genetically desirable characteristics;

b) differential fertility that raises the reproductivity of genetically well-endowed groups of families.

3. Measures forestalling any preventable spread of deleterious genes and traits.

4. Public health programs designed to guard progress in the efficacy of therapeutic procedures by providing directive guidance for marriage and parenthood.

5. Procedures tending to decrease the mutation rate of genes with a deleterious effect:

a) limiting medical irradiation to safe lifetime amounts and to the lowest doses consistent with medical necessity, with proper safeguards for minimizing radiation to the reproductive cells and a national system for recording individual exposure to X-rays and all other gamma radiation (as recommended by the Committee on Genetic Effects of Atomic Radiation);

b) adequately protecting workers in atomic energy plants and similar laboratories, preferably restricting employment to persons who expect no additional offspring, and eliminating further significant increase in the quantity of fall-out from weapons testing;

c) promoting comprehensive research on the chromosomal effects of radiation and the genetic structure of human populations.

The methodological aspects of eugenic procedures for future public health protection belong in the province of demographic policy rather than basic genetic theory and will therefore be discussed only briefly here. Generally speaking, the aims of eugenic population policies are related to either quantitative or qualitative modes of population control.

On the quantitative level, eugenic measures deal with the general growth pattern of the population. In overpopulated areas, education in birth-control methods is an essential part of the program, while underpopulation may call for systematic encouragement of increased reproductivity through preferential housing and taxation for families with many children. Application of these measures can be safeguarded sufficiently to meet the requirements of a non-discriminatory population policy.

Qualitative measures are aimed at changes in the actual composition of the population. When applied with a view to inducing favorable biological responses to contemporary standards of civilization (*affirmative* or *positive* eugenics), such measures are largely educational in their objectives and focused on the planning of a well-spaced family. For this reason, they can be effective only in a favorable environment that lends itself to eugenic selection. Intelligence, a sense of duty to the community, and the desire to perpetuate worthy family traditions and to utilize emotional capacities for making a success of marriage are all prerequisites for the application of affirmative eugenic ideas.

Negative or *preventive* eugenic measures serve the purpose of determining and possibly forestalling obvious biological failure to respond even to a good environment. Accordingly, such measures may be applied either for reasons of public health protection or in the management of individual adjustive problems of unknowing or emotionally unstable persons. In the former application, these measures range from prevention of child marriages to establishment of laws regulating divorce on biological principles or enforcing the segregation of hopelessly asocial and grossly defective individuals in special institutions. Further, obligatory health certificates for couples applying for a marriage license, contraceptive birth-control methods, medically induced abortion, and surgical sterilization are procedures which have been used for

eugenic purposes. Of course, in a democracy, recommendation of these procedures is based on the voluntary cooperation of the patient and his family.

Preventive measures, when motivated by medicogenetic considerations of individual adjustment and family welfare, lie strictly in the province of medical indication and require adequate supervision by public health authorities. Moreover, complex health problems of this kind should be handled only by genetically trained and psychotherapeutically experienced specialists.

This requirement holds for premarital as well as marital and pre-parenthood guidance work wherever obvious maladjustment exists or is clearly predictable. More specifically, it extends to all legalized approaches to medicogenetic questions calling for advice on the prospects of a marriage, deliberate childlessness in marriage, or the predictable biological qualities of additional offspring.

The diversity and complexity of the counseling problems encountered in this important public health area have created the need for a sufficient number of regional genetics departments to conduct the work. Needless to say, these departments should be adequately motivated and equipped. First and foremost, they require a staff of experienced and emotionally mature counselors with a sense of social responsibility based on an attitude of empathetic understanding of human needs. No counselor should be employed who is not aware of his part in raising the physical and mental health level of the population.

The paramount consideration in these counseling centers should always be to make it possible for families or professional agencies requesting eugenic guidance to receive the best advice that can be rendered at the current stage of scientific knowledge. No one will dispute the magnitude of this task or the need for a far better understanding of genetic phenomena and eugenic measures. Demographically, however, it is also certain that "society should begin to modify its procedures to meet inevitable new conditions" (Committee on Genetic Effects of Atomic Radiation, 1956).

What is most needed at this time, in addition to increased genetic knowledge, is the foresight implicit in a concern with the health prospects of future generations, a general willingness to exercise voluntary restraints recommended by public health authorities, and a promise of concerted action on the part of all the sciences dealing with current and future health problems of families and populations.

SELECTED BIBLIOGRAPHY

ALLEN, G. 1955. "Comments on the Analysis of Twin Samples," *Acta geneticae medicae et gemellogiae*, IV, 143–60.

ALLISON, A. C. 1955. "Aspects of Polymorphism in Man," *Cold Spring Harbor Symposia on Quantitative Biology*, XX, 239–55.

BEADLE, G. W. 1955. "What Is a Gene?" *Bulletin of the American Institute of Biological Sciences*, V, 15.

BIRDSELL, J. B. 1950. "Some Implications of the Genetical Concept of Race in Terms of Spatial Analysis," *Cold Spring Harbor Symposia on Quantitative Biology*, XV, 123–28.

BÖÖK, J. A. 1956a. "Genetical Investigations in a North-Swedish Population: Population Structure, Spastic Oligophrenia, Deaf Mutism," *Annals of Human Genetics* (Cambridge), XX, 239–50.

———. 1956b. "Genetical Morbidity of Children from First Cousin Marriages." Paper read at meeting of First International Congress of Human Genetics, Copenhagen.

CATTELL, R. B. 1953. "Research Designs in Psychological Genetics with Special Reference to the Multiple Variance Method," *American Journal of Human Genetics*, V, 76–93.

COMMITTEE ON GENETIC EFFECTS OF ATOMIC RADIATION. 1956. *The Biological Effects of Atomic Radiation*. Washington, D.C.: National Academy of Sciences, National Research Council.

COOK, R. C. *Human Fertility: The Modern Dilemma*. New York: William Sloane Associates.

———. 1955. "Eugenic Hypothesis B," *Eugenics Quarterly*, II, 129–32.

DAHLBERG, G. 1933. "Die Fruchtbarkeit der Geisteskranken," *Zeitschrift für die gesamte Neurologie und Psychiatrie*, CXLIV, 427–54.

———. 1938. "On Rare Defects in Human Populations with Particular Regard to Inbreeding and Isolate Effects," *Proceedings of the Royal Society of Edinburgh*, LVIII, 213–32.

———. 1948. *Mathematical Methods for Population Genetics*. New York: Interscience Publishers.

DOBZHANSKY, T. 1955. "A Review of Some Fundamental Concepts and Problems of Population Genetics," *Cold Spring Harbor Symposia on Quantitative Biology*, XX, 1–15.

ESSEN-MÖLLER, E. 1935. "Untersuchungen über die Fruchtbarkeit gewisser Gruppen von Geisteskranken," *Acta psychiatrica et neurologica*, Supplement VIII. Copenhagen: Levin & Munksgaard.

EYSENCK, H. J. 1950. "Criterion Analysis: An Application of the Hypothetico-deductive Method to Factor Analysis," *Psychological Review*, LVII, 38–53.

FRACCARO, M. 1957. "Consanguineous Marriages in Italy," *Eugenics Quarterly*, IV, 36–39.

GALTON, F. 1876. "The History of Twins as a Criterion of the Relative Powers of Nature and Nurture," *Journal of the Anthropological Institute of Great Britain and Ireland*.

GESELL, A., and THOMPSON, H. 1941. "Twins T and C from Infancy to Adolescence: A Biogenetic Study of Individual Differences by the Method of Co-twin Control," *Genetic Psychology Monographs*, XXIV, 3–121.

GLASS, B. 1950. "The Action of Selection on the Principal Rh Alleles," *American Journal of Human Genetics*, II, 269–78.

———. 1954. "Genetic Changes in Human

Populations, Especially Those Due to Gene Flow and Genetic Drift," *Advances in Genetics*, VI, 95–139.

GLASS, B. 1956. "On the Evidence of Random Genetic Drift in Human Populations," *American Journal of Physical Anthropology*, XIV, 541–55.

——, SACKS, M. S., JAHN, E. F., and HESS, C. 1952. "Genetic Drift in a Religious Isolate: An Analysis of the Causes of Variation in Blood Group and Other Gene Frequencies in a Small Population," *American Naturalist*, LXXXVI, 145–59.

GOLDSCHMIDT, R. B. 1938. *Physiological Genetics*. New York: McGraw-Hill.

——. 1955. *Theoretical Genetics*. Berkeley: University of California Press.

HARDY, G. H. 1908. "Mendelian Proportions in a Mixed Population," *Science*, XXVIII, 49–50.

HERNDON, C. N., and KERLEY, E. R. 1952. "Cousin Marriage Rates in Western North Carolina." Paper read at meeting of the American Society of Human Genetics.

HUXLEY, J. 1953. *Evolution in Action*. New York City: Harper & Bros.

JUDA, A. 1934. "Über Anzahl und psychische Beschaffenheit der Nachkommen von schwachsinnigen und normalen Schülern," *Zeitschrift für die gesamte Neurologie und Psychiatrie*, CLI, 244–313.

KALLMANN, F. J. 1938. *The Genetics of Schizophrenia*. New York: J. J. Augustin.

——. 1953. *Heredity in Health and Mental Disorder*. New York: W. W. Norton & Co.

——. 1956. "Psychiatric Aspects of Genetic Counseling," *American Journal of Human Genetics*, VIII, 97–101.

——. (in press). "Psychogenetic Studies of Twins," in *Study of the Status and Development of Psychology in the United States*, ed. S. KOCH. New York: McGraw-Hill Book Co.

——, and REISNER, D. 1943. "Twin Studies on the Significance of Genetic Factors in Tuberculosis," *Annual Review of Tuberculosis*, XLVII, 549–74.

——, and SANK, D. (in press). "Genetik, Eugenik, und geistige Hygiene," in *Lehrbuch der Psycholhygiene*, ed. H. MENG. Vol. I. Basel: B. Schwabe.

LERNER, I. M. 1954. *Genetic Homeostasis*. New York: John Wiley & Sons.

LEVENE, H. 1953. "Genetic Equilibrium When More Than One Ecological Niche Is Available," *American Naturalist*, LXXXVII, 331–33.

LEWIS, E. B. 1955. "Some Aspects of Position Pseudoallelism," *American Naturalist*, LXXXIX, 73–89.

LEWONTIN, R. C. 1953. "The Effect of Compensation on Populations Subject to Natural Selection," *American Naturalist*, LXXXVII, 375–81.

LI, C. C. 1955. *Population Genetics*. Chicago: University of Chicago Press.

LUXENBURGER, H. 1928. "Demographische und psychiatrische Untersuchungen in der engeren biologischen Familie von Paralytikergehalten," *Zeitschrift für die gesamte Neurologie und Psychiatrie*, CXII, 331–491.

McELROY, W. D., and GLASS, B. (eds.). 1957. *The Chemical Basis of Heredity*. Baltimore: Johns Hopkins Press.

MATHER, K. 1949. *Biometrical Genetics*. New York: Dover Publications.

MEDICAL RESEARCH COUNCIL. 1956. *The Hazards to Man of Nuclear and Allied Radiations*. London: H.M. Stationery Office.

MØRCH, E. T. 1941. "Chondrodystrophic Dwarfs in Denmark," *Opera ex domo biologiae hereditariae humanae universitatis hafniensis* (Copenhagen), Vol. III.

MORGAN, T. H. 1919. *The Physical Basis of Heredity*. Philadelphia: J. B. Lippincott Co.

MORTON, N. E., CROW, J. F., and MULLER, H. J. 1956. "An Estimate of the Mutational Damage in Man from Data on Consanguineous Marriages," *Proceedings of the National Academy of Sciences*, XLII, 855–63.

MUCKERMANN, H. 1932. "Vergleichende Untersuchungen über differenzierte Fortpflanzung in einer Stadt- und Landbevölkerung," *Zeitschrift für induktive Abstammungs und Vererbungslehre*, LXII, 188–203.

MULLER, H. J. 1927. "The Problem of Genic Modification," *Verhandlungen V. Internationaler Kongress für Vererbungswissenschaften* (Berlin).

——. 1950. "Our Load of Mutations," *The*

American Journal of Human Genetics, II, 111–76.

MURPHY, G. 1954. "Editorial Comment (a Research Program for Qualitative Eugenics)," *Eugenics Quarterly*, I, 209–12.

NEEL, J. V. 1949. "The Detection of the Genetic Carriers of Hereditary Disease," *American Journal of Human Genetics*, I, 19–36.

———. 1952. "The Study of Human Mutation Rates," *American Naturalist*, LXXXVI, 129–44.

———, KODANI, M., BREWER, R., and ANDERSON, R. C. 1949. "The Incidence of Consanguineous Matings in Japan, with Remarks on the Estimation of Comparative Gene Frequencies and the Expected Rate of Appearance of Induced Recessive Mutations," *American Journal of Human Genetics*, I, 156–78.

NEWMAN, H. H., FREEMAN, F. N., and HOLZINGER, K. J. 1937. *Twins: A Study of Heredity and Environment*. Chicago: University of Chicago Press.

OSBORN, F. 1951*a*. *Preface to Eugenics*. New York: Harper & Bros.

———. 1951*b*. "The Eugenic Hypothesis," *Eugenical News*, XXXVI, 19–21.

———. 1952*a*. "The Eugenic Hypothesis," ibid., XXXVII, 6–9.

———. 1952*b*. "Possible Effects of Differential Fertility on Genetic Endowment," ibid., pp. 47–54.

RACE, R. R. 1942. "On the Inheritance and Linkage Relations of Acholuric Jaundice," *Annals of Eugenics*, XI, 365–84.

———. 1944. "Some Recent Observations on the Inheritance of Blood Groups," *British Medical Bulletin*, II, 160–65.

———, and SANGER, R. 1954. *Blood Groups in Man*. 2d ed. chap. xx. Springfield, Ill.: Charles C Thomas.

RAINER, J., and KALLMANN, F. J. (in press). "Genetic and Demographic Aspects of Disordered Behavior Patterns in a Deaf Population," *Symposium on Epidemiology of Mental Disorder*. Washington, D.C.: American Association for the Advancement of Science.

REED, S. C., and PALM, J. D. 1951. "Social Fitness versus Reproduction Fitness," *Science*, CXIII, 294–96.

REES, W. L., and EYSENCK, H. J. 1945. "A Factorial Study of Some Morphological and Psychological Aspects of Human Constitution," *Journal of Mental Science*, XCI, 8–21.

RIDDLE, O. 1954. *The Unleashing of Evolutionary Thought*. New York: Vantage Press.

ROGERS, B. O. 1957. "The Genetics of Skin Homotransplantation in the Human," *Annals of the New York Academy of Science*, LXIV, 741–66.

RÜDIN, E. 1956. "Nachkommen aus Ehen Zwischen nahen Blutsverwandten." Paper read at meeting of First International Congress of Human Genetics, Copenhagen.

SCHULZ, B. 1936. *Methodik der medizinischen Erbforschung*. Leipzig: Georg Thieme.

SIEMENS, H. W. 1924. *Zwillingspathologie*. Berlin: Springer.

SILVESTRONI, E., BIANCO, I., MONTALENTI, G., and SINISCALCO, M. 1950. "Frequency of Microcythaemia in Some Italian Districts," *Nature*, CLXV, 682–83.

SPENCER, W. P. 1947. "On Rh Gene Frequencies," *American Naturalist*, LXXXI, 237–40.

SPUHLER, J. N. 1956. "Estimation of Mutation Rates in Man," *Clinical Orthopaedics*, VIII, 34–43.

STRANDSKOV, H. H. 1950. "The Genetics of Human Populations," *Cold Spring Harbor Symposia on Quantitative Biology*, XV, 1–11.

STRÖMGREN, E. 1950. *Psychiatrie sociale*. (*Comptes-Rendus du Premier Congrès International de Psychiatrie, de Neurologie, de Psychologie, et de l'Assistance des Aliénés*, VI, 156–92.)

SUTTER, J., and TABAH, L. 1948. "Fréquence et répartition des marriages consanguins en France," *Population*, IV, 607–30.

———. 1954. "The Breakup of Isolates: Its Genetic Consequences in Two French Départements," *Eugenics Quarterly*, I, 148–54.

THOMPSON, W. R. 1957. "Traits, Factors, and Genes," *Eugenics Quarterly*, IV, 8–16.

TIETZE, C., and GRABILL, W. H. 1957. "Differential Fertility by Duration of Marriage," *Eugenics Quarterly*, IV, 3–7.

VERSCHUER, O. VON. 1928. "Die Ähnlichkeitsdiagnose der Eineiigkeit von Zwillingen," *Anthropologischer Anzeiger*, V, 244–48.

WAHLUND, S. 1928. "Zusammensetzung von Populationen und Korrelationserscheinungen vom Standpunkt der Vererbungslehre aus betrachtet," *Hereditas*, XI, 65–106.

WALDEYER, W. 1888. *Über Karyokinese und ihre Beziehungen zu den Befruchtungsvorgängen*. Bonn: Max Cohen & Son.

WEINBERG, W. 1908. "Über den Nachweis der Vererbung bein Menschen," *Verein für vaterländische Naturkunde in Württemberg*, LXIV, 368–82.

——. 1913. *Die Kinder der Tuberkulösen*. Leipzig: S. Hirzel.

——. 1927. "Mathematische Grundlagen der Probandenmethode," *Zeitschrift für induktive Abstammungs und Vererbungslehre*, XLVIII, 179–228.

——. 1930. "Zur Probandenmethode und zu ihrem Ersatz," *Zeitschrift für de gesamte Neurologie und Psychiatrie*, CXXIII, 809–12.

WHELPTON, P. K., and KISER, C. (eds.). 1943–54. *Social and Psychological Factors Affecting Fertility*. 4 vols. New York: Milbank Memorial Fund.

WOOLF, C. M., STEPHENS, F. E., MULAIK, D. D., and GILBERT, R. E. 1956. "An Investigation of the Frequency of Consanguineous Marriages among the Mormons and Their Relatives in the United States," *American Journal of Human Genetics*, VIII, 236–52.

WRIGHT, S. 1931. "Size of Population and Breeding Structure in Relation to Evolution," *Science*, LXXXVII, 430–31.

——. 1932. "The Roles of Mutation, Inbreeding, Crossbreeding, and Selection in Evolution," *Proceedings of the Sixth International Congress of Genetics*, I, 356–65.

——. 1940. "Breeding Structure of Populations in Relation to Speciation," *American Naturalist*, LXXIV, 232–48.

——. 1943. "Isolation by Distance," *Genetics*, XXVIII, 114–38.

——. 1948. "On the Roles of Directed and Random Changes in Gene Frequency in the Genetics of Populations," *Evolution*, II, 279–94.

——. 1949. "Population Structure in Evolution," *Proceedings of the American Philosophical Society*, XCVIII, 471–78.

——. 1955. "Classification of the Factors of Evolution," *Cold Spring Harbor Symposia on Quantitative Biology*, XX, 16–24.

32. Economics and Demography

JOSEPH J. SPENGLER

This chapter is divided into five main parts. In the first part, concerned with the major connections between economics and demography, the principal points at which the two sciences presently converge are indicated and the history of the development of these points of convergence is briefly summarized. The second part has to do with relevant data; it is quite short because the sources, the nature, and the deficiencies of available data are dealt with in other chapters of this volume. The third part is given to a brief description of the economist's methods of analysis and of their significance for economic and demographic subject matter. The fourth part, much the longest section, is devoted to what we know and what we do not know respecting problems and issues in areas in which economics and demography converge. In the fifth part some next steps in research are noted.

ECONOMICS AND DEMOGRAPHY: INTERCONNECTIONS

Economics and Demography: Points of Convergence

The points at which the subject matter of economics and demography converge may be indicated in terms of economic variables, changes in which may affect demographic variables, and in terms of demographic variables, changes in which may affect economic variables. For the present these variables will merely be identified. A number of matters, some of which will be considered in the fourth part, are

passed over in the present section: that economic (demographic) variables may be complexly interrelated; that between economic and demographic variables a relation of mutual interdependence rather than one of unilateral "causation" may obtain; that the relation between given economic and demographic variables may be conditioned by the presence or absence of intervening but non-identified variables; that effects of changes in demographic (economic) variables may be mediated through the system of prices; that the short-run effects of demographic (economic) changes may differ from their long-run effects; that varying time intervals may separate a demographic (economic) change from its economic (demographic) effect.

What appear to be the main demographic and economic variables of significance for an analysis of economic-demographic convergence are listed below. For purposes of brevity of exposition, they have been symbolized.

Demographic Variables:

M Mortality (general or age-specific)
F Fertility (general or age-specific)
r Natural increase
M_d Differential mortality (intergroup differences in fertility)
F_d Differential fertility (intergroup differences in fertility)
e Emigration
i Immigration
n Net international migration
m Internal migration
m_d Differential internal migration
T Population total or population density

791

T_d Internal distribution of population total

R Rate of growth of total population

C_a Age composition of population

C_s Sex composition of population

C_q Qualitative composition of population (e.g., genetic, educational)

C_{qs} Qualitative composition of a component of the total population (e.g., occupational group, population of a region)

Economic Variables:

Y Net national product or national income

y Per capita net national product or national income

K Total stock of capital or income-producing wealth

k Per capita amount of capital or income-producing wealth

l Land or other resources per capita

t International terms of trade

D Functional distribution of income into wages, interest, etc.

D_y Distribution of income among persons composing population

E Index of fulness of employment

S Annual volume of savings

I Annual volume of investment

c Consumption

c_c Qualitative composition of consumption

I_c Qualitative composition of investment

O_c Occupational composition of population

The demographic variables may be divided into those, changes in which are capable of affecting immediately some of the economic variables, and those, changes in which are not capable of affecting the economic variables immediately *and* significantly. In the first category are R, T, T_d, C_a, C_s, C_q, and possibly C_{qs}, all of which may also be looked upon as secondary demographic variables. In the second category are M, F, M_d, F_d, e, i, m, and m_d, all of which may be looked upon as primary variables. The variables r and n are also secondary in character but are embraced in R. The values assumed by the secondary variables depend upon those assumed by the primary variables. This dependence may be summarized as follows:

Secondary demographic variable	Its determining primary demographic variables
$R; r, n$	M, F, e, i
T	Past values for M, F, e, i
C_a	M, F, e, i
C_q	F_d, M_d, e, i
C_s	e, i
T_d	e, i, F_d, M_d, m
C_{qs}	m_d, F_d, M_d

Similarly, the economic variables may be divided into those, changes in which are capable of immediately affecting some of the demographic variables, and those, changes in which are not capable of affecting the demographic variables immediately *and* significantly. In the first category are Y, y, D_y, E, c, O_c, and possibly c_c. While these variables might be described as *secondary* for the purposes of this section, it does not appear advisable so to describe them, since the values of each may be affected by the values of other variables included in the same category. In the second category fall the variables K, k, l, t, D, S, I, I_c, O_c, and upon these variables Y, y, D_y, E, c, and c_c depend as follows:

Economic variable	Economic variables whereupon dependent
Y	$K, l, t, S, I, I_c, O_c, D_y$
y	$k, l, t, S, I, I_c, O_c, D_y$
D_y	D, t, k, l, I, S, O_c
E	I, S, c, O_c
c, c_c	D, O_c, D_y
O_c	y, k, l, t, I, D_y

Abstracting from the fact that economic variables both affect and are affected by demographic variables, convergence may be illustrated by listing, together with each economic variable, those demographic variables by changes in which this economic variable is most likely to be directly affected.

Economic variable	Demographic variables by which affected
Y and y	$R, T, T_d, C_a, C_q, C_s,$ and possibly C_{qs}
K and k	R, T, C_a, C_q, C_s
l	T, R, T_d
D	R, T, C_q, T_d
D_y	R, T, C_q, T_d, C_a, C_s
t	R, T, C_q
S	R, T, C_q, C_a, C_s, T_d
I	R, C_q, C_a, C_s, T_d
E	R, T, C_a, C_q, C_s, T_d
c and c_c	R, T, C_a, T_d
I_c	R, C_a, T_d
O_c	C_q, C_s, T_d

Abstracting from the fact that demographic variables both affect and are affected by demographic variables, convergence may be illustrated by listing, together with each primary demographic variable and with T_d, C_q, and C_{qs}, those economic variables by changes in which this demographic variable is most likely to be directly and significantly affected. C_s is disregarded on the ground that usually it is unimportant; it depends principally upon i.

Demographic variable	Economic variables by which affected
$M, F, e, i; (r, R)$	$Y, y, D_y, E, c, O_c, c_c$
F_d, M_d	O_c, D_y, E
m, m_d, T_d	O_c, E, D_y
C_q, C_{qs}	O_c, D_y, E

It is quite possible that the set of variables on the left—i.e., the "demographic variables"—needs to be subdivided somewhat, since these variables appear to be differentially sensitive to changes in economic variables. Of these demographic variables, e, i, m, and m_d appear to be most sensitive to economic change, for each of these movements usually is dominated by decisions and activities designed to

improve the economic situation of the moving individual or family. If this be the case, the direction and possibly the relative volume of the movements in question should be comparatively predictable in the light of the underlying economic situation. The variables M, F, F_d, M_d, and (probably) C_q appear to be considerably less sensitive to economic change than are e, i, m, and m_d; for their movement is not so dominated by activities designed to better the economic situation of the individual, and the course of their movement is not so predictable in the light of the underlying economic situation.

The main points of convergence between economic and demographic subject matter having been identified, the historical development of this convergence will be summarized. The interrelations between economic and demographic variables will be examined in some detail in the fourth part.

Economics and Demography: History of Interconnections

In this section attention will be given primarily to the relations which post-sixteenth-century students of economics have supposed to exist between demographic and economic growth. Although students of economics, together with students of statistical and actuarial methods, were perhaps the first to give considerable attention to questions of population, they did not explore effectively the data available for the analysis of interrelations between economic and demographic movements. Accordingly, opportunity remains for correlating nineteenth-century economic data (e.g., data pertaining to the movement of wages, interest, rent, profits, income, wealth, prices) and demographic data (mortality, fertility, migration, etc.), and some opportunity remains for extending this type of analysis into the eighteenth and earlier centuries. But these data, though they contribute to our knowledge of economic history and growth, are imperfectly suited to yield precise answers respecting many questions of population. The data are incomplete, and other relevant information is inadequate. Only rough answers to some questions of interest to the student of economics *and* demography are to be had for periods antedating World War I (cf. Bennett, 1954; Kuznets, 1956; Russell, 1948).

As has been shown in many studies (e.g., Stangeland, 1904; United Nations, 1953; Spengler, 1936, 1938, 1942; Stassart, 1947; Johnson, 1937), men have for many centuries manifested interest in population movements. This interest seems to have been intensified, so far as European peoples are concerned, by the discovery of the New World, by changes in the political structure of Europe, by the growth of international political and commercial rivalry, by improvements in the arts and methods of war, and by modifications of the manner in which goods and services were produced. Greater importance came to be attached to numbers on military, political, and economic grounds. These grounds, of course, were considered to be interrelated. Men took for granted that (presumably within limits) an increment in any one of these three sources of power was associated with an increment in the other sources of power.

Before the eighteenth century and to some extent in that century, land and labor were looked upon as the principal factors of production or sources of productive power, and labor was considered much the more important. The significance of the roles of capital and of enterprise seems to have been greatly underestimated. The importance of technological and related improvements (a steadily expansible source of productive power even

though not definable as a factor of production) likewise was greatly underestimated, in part because the rate of both technological change and its diffusion long remained low. In sum, therefore, in and after the sixteenth century great importance came to be attached to population and its growth because it was believed that such growth entailed a corresponding growth of the labor force, then considered the principal source of productive power, given that the labor force was effectively employed.

If a country's labor force was the major source of its productive power, and if it was desirable that this power be increased, it followed that population growth should be stimulated. Such at least was the conclusion of many who wrote about public policy or were charged with its formulation. It was often urged, therefore, especially before the mid-eighteenth century, that numbers be increased. It was supposed that this objective could be realized through direct measures designed to increase nuptiality and fertility, to decrease mortality, to augment immigration, and to diminish emigration (except in those instances when it was deemed essential for colonial development or for the operation of highly profitable centers of trade situated in foreign parts). Measures of this sort were advocated frequently, and in a number of countries some measures were enacted into law or decree, although few if any were effectively implemented.

This direct approach to the stimulation of population growth came to be questioned in the eighteenth century. After 1750 it was accepted increasingly that population would tend to grow only so long as means of subsistence (or existence) were available and to be had through income-yielding employment. It was concluded therefore that measures designed to stimulate population growth directly were not only unnecessary but harmful in that they tended to make fertility higher than the flow of subsistence warranted and in that they diverted resources from productive to unproductive uses. It was necessary only that an economy function efficiently and effectively, and it would tend to do this so long as conditions of what Adam Smith called "natural liberty" prevailed. Then there would certainly be adequate population growth; in fact, there would probably be too many births unless prevailing institutions and habits underwent suitable modification and made for sufficient prudential restraint. This new view, given classic formulation by Malthus and Ricardo, remained dominant in the literature of economics at least until World War I; but it was subjected to a variety of criticism, especially in the late nineteenth century when the climate of opinion was again becoming somewhat more favorable to the intervention of the state in economic and related affairs. This view was, of course, rejected by Karl Marx and most of his disciples, by various other critics of orthodox political economy, and by many essentially orthodox economists.

Economists opposed measures to stimulate population growth on value grounds as well as upon the ground that such measures were both ineffective and resource-wasting. Economists generally accepted the view that the objective of economic activity was a relatively high and rising scale or standard of living. Or, in income terms, they favored a relatively high and rising per capita income. This objective could not be realized if, as often tended to be the case, population grew unduly. For as numbers grew, they pressed ever harder upon the limited supply of land and other resources, and this increasing pressure made more difficult the elevation of per capita income even

when technological change was augmenting men's skill. Increasing numbers, moreover, absorbed capital which might otherwise have been used to increase capital per head and therewith output per head. It followed that measures designed to increase a state's political and military power by increasing its numbers tended to slow down if not to prevent advances in the average level of living.

The population policies of states conformed rather closely to the precepts of economists in the nineteenth century and even until after World War I. Not much legislation designed specifically to stimulate population growth was kept in effect; moreover, in the first half of the century some legislation intended to check population growth was introduced. At the same time, a number of circumstances made for increases in per capita income in Europe even though the rate of natural increase and that of population growth continued to be relatively high. Technology steadily improved and income-producing wealth per head rose. Migration being free, many millions moved to the Americas and Oceania, contributing to (among other things) the agricultural development of those parts whence, after the middle of the nineteenth century, much cereal and other agricultural produce flowed to Europe and served to hold down food costs there. Even so, economists remained concerned lest the continuing growth of numbers eventually swamp the forces then conducing to the increase of food and output generally. This concern was virtually transformed into alarm during and after World War I, when Malthus' so-called geometrical ratio of increase was rediscovered, and it was inferred that numbers inside and outside of Europe might grow faster than the output of goods and services (cf. Glass, 1940; O'Brien, 1948; Wolfe, 1928–29).

This concern must have played a part in the development and eventual enactment of measures for the restriction of immigration into major countries of immigration. Apparently it was but one among many factors, for in the United States immigration restriction was advocated on non-economic as well as on economic grounds. Even so, much of the support of restrictionism based upon economic grounds came from particular groups who believed that their economic interests would be adversely affected by continuation of large-scale immigration. The history of legislation for the restriction of immigration suggests, however, that the opinions of economists respecting the economic effects of population growth affected a legislation pertaining thereto in only a limited way (Thomas, B., 1956).

Economists' concern lest population growth unduly slow down the rate at which the average scale of living rises was translated into terms of what is now called income-optimum population theory (Leibenstein, 1954). This theory, anticipated at least as early as 1848, had two purposes: to show how per capita income varies with population density and to shift the burden of proof to those who favored continuing population growth. The income-optimum theory allowed for the fact that, within limits, as population grew and became more dense in relatively new and unsettled regions or countries, division of labor would increase and thus make for increases in per capita productive power and income (Young, 1928; Jones, G., 1933). There was a limit to this process, however, and when that limit was reached, increases in over-all population density within a country would no longer make for increases in per capita income. Accordingly, when this limit had been reached in a state, its population would be of optimum size, and further increase in population would make per capita income lower than it otherwise would have been. While some economists believed that this limit might shift, given certain changes (e.g., improvements in technology and industrial structure, increased imports and exports), and make the magnitude of the optimum larger or smaller, others did not consider it likely that, under conditions such as obtained at the close of the nineteenth century, the optimum magnitude would increase. It may be said, therefore, that exponents of the income-optimum theory favored the view that increases in population density beyond the level obtaining in most countries in the early twentieth century would tend to make the average level of living lower than it otherwise would have been. They believed, in other words, that the capacity of technological improvements, capital formation, etc., to elevate the level of living would be diminished by further increases in population density in most countries (cf. Buquet, 1956; Cohn, 1934; Fua, 1940; Gottlieb, 1945, 1949).

With the accumulation in some countries of statistics reflecting changes in the age composition of the population that were attributable largely to the decline in fertility, it was observed that some age structures are more favorable to output per capita than are others. This was found to be the case, for example, in France, where natality had long been falling and where a relatively large fraction of the population was of working age. It came to be true also of other countries.

Although considerable attention was given to the impact of the trade cycle upon marriage and birth rates, very little attention was given to possible economic effects of variations in the rate of natural increase or in the rate of growth of the population of working age. Not until some time after World War I did attention begin to be given to the response of cyclical, structural, and general unemployment to population movements (Beveridge, 1930; Royal Commission, 1950).

In the second quarter of the present century economists made some changes in their approach to population questions. Interest in the impact of economic change upon fertility persisted; it was, in fact, intensified by the discovery that the birth rate had fallen markedly in many countries and that the net reproduction rate was approaching a level close to replacement if not below. These discoveries, together with the onset of depression, directed attention to possible economic effects of changes in the rate of natural increase and helped give currency to the view that the slowing-down of population growth might be accompanied by a reduction in the rate of investment and hence by an increase in involuntary unemployment. The causes and the consequences of internal migration also came to command far more attention than formerly. A number of circumstances operated in combination to intensify interest in natality-stimulating measures (e.g., family wage) of the sort that theretofore had been seriously considered only in France: fear that net reproduction would fall below the replacement level, belief that increases in consumption might be essential to the maintenance of full employment, increasing acceptance of a distributivist philosophy favoring greater equality in income distribution, and so on (Glass, 1940; Myrdal, G., 1940; Reddaway, 1939).

It may be said, in sum, that while some of the points of convergence listed in the preceding section were noted already in the early nineteenth century, it is only in more recent decades that careful consideration began to be given to these points. This more careful analysis, furthermore, has revealed the frequent dependence of functional relationships between economic and demographic variables upon the degree of presence of variables that are not essentially economic or demographic in character.

THE DATA AVAILABLE

If research on interrelations between economic and demographic variables is conditioned by the availability of data, it is also essential that data be available in such form as to permit their correlation, association, etc.; only then can functional relationships, with appropriate time lags, be established between changes in specific economic (demographic) variables and changes in specific demographic (economic) variables.

Available demographic data are of four sorts: (*a*) those assembled in census and similar enumerations; (*b*) those to be found, usually on a national basis, in such compilations as the *Demographic Yearbook* issued by the United Nations; (*c*) those to be found, usually on a subnational class or regional basis, in such compilations as national statistical yearbooks; and (*d*) those gathered in the course of specific-purpose investigations, such as those undertaken in conjunction with the Indianapolis Study (referred to elsewhere in this volume).

Available economic data may be similarly classified into four categories: (i) those assembled in census and similar enumerations; (ii) those to be found, usually on a national basis, in such collections as are brought together by the United Nations; (iii) those to be found, usually on a subnational class or regional basis, in such compilations as national statistical yearbooks; and (iv) those gathered in the course of specific-purpose investigations, such as those undertaken by sampling organizations (e.g., Survey Research Center).

Data falling within the (*a*) and (i)

and the (*d*) and (iv) categories differ significantly in their usefulness from data falling in the remaining categories. The methods employed to obtain information of the (*a*) or (i) sort bring together data on the demographic, economic, social, and perhaps other characteristics of specific units (individuals, etc.) which permit the investigator to determine statistically the extent to which specific interindividual demographic (economic) differences are associated with specific individual economic (demographic) differences. The methods employed to obtain information of the (*d*) or (iv) sort bring together somewhat similar data and hence permit somewhat similar inquiries into the sources of interindividual differences. These methods are superior, moreover, to those used for the assembly of (*a*) or (i) data, in that (*d*) and (iv) data usually are gathered to test the validity of specific hypotheses or to serve other particular purposes, whereas (*a*) and (i) data usually are collected to serve non-specific purposes. In contrast with data of the (*a*), (i), (*d*), and (iv) sorts, data of the (*b*), (ii), (*c*), and (iii) sorts are no longer available in forms that disclose, for each unit (e.g., individual, family), information relating to specific demographic, economic, social, and other characteristics of that unit.

Because of the superiority of data gathered by (*d*) and (iv) methods to data gathered by (*a*) and (i) methods, it is likely that the relative importance of (*d*) and (iv) methods will increase. This tendency will be strengthened by improvements in sampling procedures and by diminutions in the comparative cost and flexibility of such procedures. It will be strengthened also by the tendency of explanatory hypotheses to increase in number; it usually is possible to test new hypotheses by recourse to (*d*) and (iv) methods, whereas it is difficult to adapt (*a*) and (i) methods to the task of assembling new and hitherto unassembled data.

Information concerning the availability of data pertaining to the impact of economic change upon fertility and mortality is provided in the chapters dealing with fertility, mortality, and the family. Information about available data on the impact of economic change upon migration is supplied in the chapters dealing with that subject. It is evident, of course, that since relatively few available data are of the (*d*) and (iv) types, explanations of the behavior of fertility, mortality, and migration—and of the motivation processes underlying this behavior—are incomplete. Moreover, because the response of fertility and migration to economic change is not so much an immediate response as one of varying time lag (cf. Katona, 1951, chaps. iii–iv), eliciting the necessary information is more difficult than it would be were there no time lag. Some information about migration comes also from the literature on labor mobility (e.g., Parnes, 1954), though this literature may at times underestimate the importance of motivation describable as "economic."

Information concerning the impact of demographic change upon economic change is not plentiful. There is, of course, considerable information (most of it assembled under governmental auspices) on wage and income movements and structures, employment levels, variations in savings and investment, and so on; but it does not run back many decades, and it does not lend itself readily to analysis of the impact of demographic change upon economic change. The economic behavior which we can infer from these data usually reflects many causes other than demographic movements, but not in a manner that permits careful measurement, directly or residually, of the incidence of demographic change upon the behavior of economic variables.

So far, we have noted only information relating to the supposed functional relationships between economic and demographic variables. Of importance, however, from a policy and a welfare point of view, are data on the extent and the international distribution of land and natural resources and on the contribution these agencies make to the incomes of nations. Unfortunately, data of this sort are limited in quantity, often of uncertain value, and frequently inaccessible; some such data are to be found in the report of the President's Materials Policy Commission (1952), in Woytinsky (1953), in publications of the United Nations, and in governmental reports. These data are especially important in that they indicate the boundaries within which solutions to problems of population pressure are to be found (Spengler, 1956*b*; Zimmerman, 1951).

THE ECONOMIST'S METHODS OF ANALYSIS

The economist usually looks upon the economy which is the subject of his analysis as a system of mutually interdependent variables, the values assumed by which are conditioned by data external to the economy. Among these data, as a rule, is population. The approach and methods of the economist may be suggested by selections drawn from representative works. His handling of lagged effects and of the impact of autonomous and non-recurrent changes is best illustrated in models adapted to this purpose (Allen, 1956). George J. Stigler (1952, p. 1) states:

Economics is the study of the operation of economic organizations, and economic organizations are social (and rarely, individual) arrangements to deal with the production of economic goods and services. . . . The central element of the "economic problem" is scarcity: the inability of the society to provide all the bread, television sets, and

bombers its members desire. The problem of scarcity is of long standing: it has survived enormous advances of science and, what is perhaps more fundamental, enormous advances in social organization.

Milton Friedman (1953, pp. 39–40) writes:

Economics as a positive science is a body of tentatively accepted generalizations about economic phenomena that can be used to predict the consequences of changes in circumstances. Progress in expanding this body of generalizations, strengthening our confidence in their validity, and improving the accuracy of the predictions they yield is hindered not only by the limitations of human ability that impede all search for knowledge but also by obstacles that are especially important for the social sciences in general and economics in particular, though by no means peculiar to them. Familiarity with the subject matter of economics breeds contempt for special knowledge about it. The importance of its subject matter to everyday life and to major issues of public policy impedes objectivity and promotes confusion between scientific analysis and normative judgment. The necessity of relying on uncontrolled experience rather than on controlled experiment makes it difficult to produce dramatic and clear-cut evidence to justify the acceptance of tentative hypotheses. Reliance on uncontrolled experience does not affect the fundamental methodological principle that a hypothesis can be tested only by the conformity of its implications or predictions with observable phenomena; but it does render the task of testing hypotheses more difficult and gives greater scope for confusion about the methodological principles involved. More than other scientists, social scientists need to be self-conscious about their methodology.

According to Paul A. Samuelson (1947, pp. 4, 5, 19–20), operationally meaningful theorems, i.e., hypotheses

about empirical data which could conceivably be refuted, if only under ideal conditions . . . proceed almost wholly from two types of very general hypotheses. The first is that the conditions of equilibrium are equivalent to the maximization (minimization) of some magnitude. . . . However, when we leave single economic units, the determination of unknowns is found to be unrelated to an extremum position . . . there is lacking symmetry in the conditions of equilibrium so that there is no possibility of directly reducing the problem to that of a maximum or minimum. Instead the dynamical properties of the system are specified, and the hypothesis is made that the system is in "stable" equilibrium or motion.

Samuelson goes on to say:

a. For theoretical purposes an economic system consists of a designated set of unknowns which are constrained as a condition of equilibrium to satisfy an equal number of consistent and independent equations. . . . These are implicitly assumed to hold within a certain environment and as of certain data. Some parts of these data are introduced as explicit parameters; and, as a result of our equilibrium conditions, our unknown variables may be expressed in function of these parameters. . . .

b. The method of *comparative statics* consists of the study of the responses of our equilibrium unknowns to designated changes in parameters; i.e., we wish to know the properties of the functions. . . . In the absence of complete quantitative information concerning our equilibrium equations, it is hoped to be able to formulate qualitative restrictions on slopes, curvatures, etc., of our equilibrium equations so as to be able to derive definite qualitative restrictions upon the responses of our system to changes in certain parameters.

Having shown that "the usefulness of any theoretical structure lies in the light which it throws upon the way economic variables will change when there is a change in some datum or parameter" and that this statement holds in "the realm of dynamics as in statics," Samuelson (1947, pp. 351–52) proceeds to formulate a theory of comparative dynamics:

The central notion of *comparative dynamics* is simple enough. We change something (just *what* need not concern us at the moment), and we investigate the effect of this change on the whole motion or behavior over time of the economic system under investigation. It will be seen that comparative statics involves the special case where a "permanent" change is made, and only the effects upon final levels of stationary equilibrium are in question.

In *comparative dynamics* we consider a much broader class of changes. (*a*) We may make a change in *initial conditions*. By definition this alters the immediate behavior of the system in a known way. By the assumption of continuity we may infer that the position of the system for some region adjacent to the initial conditions is also altered in the same direction. For intermediate lapses of time a separate investigation is necessary to determine what happens to the system. However, for a *stable* system it is clear by virtue of the definition of stability that for sufficiently long time periods there will be no final alteration in the behavior of the system.

(*b*) We may make a change in some *force* acting on the system. Thus, we may cause autonomous investment to vary. Actually, there are a variety of cases which must be considered. The change in force may be permanent; it may be intermittent; it may be transient or instantaneous. In this very last case the analysis may be subsumed under the heading of a shift in initial conditions. In the case of stable systems the response to a permanent alteration gives us a description of the actual path followed by a system in going from one "comparative static level" to another.

. . . .

(*c*) Finally, there may be a change in some internal parameter of the system. We may ask, for example, what the effect of a change in the marginal propensity to consume or in the "relation" may have on the behavior of a system. Again, the change in question may be permanent, varying, transient, etc.

Because the economy is made up of mutually interdependent variables, one must employ the concept of causation with care; Samuelson (1947, pp. 9–10, 315 n.) notes:

> The only sense in which the use of the term causation is admissible is in respect to changes in external data or parameters. As a figure of speech, it may be said that changes in these *cause* changes in the variables of our system. . . . Even here, when several parameters change simultaneously, it is impossible to speak of causation attributable to each except in respect to limiting rates of change (partial derivatives).

. . . .

The notion of causation in a closed interdependent system is exceedingly slippery and ambiguous. As used here, a system is said to be causal if from an initial configuration it determines its own behavior over time. While it is not appropriate to say that one subset of variables causes another to move, it is permissible to speak of change in a given parameter or datum as causing changes in the system or in its behavior over time.

As was indicated at the outset of this section, a population change is usually looked upon as a change in a datum, in response to which the magnitudes of the variables composing an economic system undergo change. However, inasmuch as population data may change in consequence of changes in economic variables, it may become necessary to take into account such mutual interdependence as obtains between economic variables and demographic data. It is always necessary, of course, to take into account the channels through which changes in the behavior of individuals at the economic (population or demographic) level may affect the behavior of individuals at the population or demographic (economic) level (Simon, 1957).

The difficulties which attend efforts to determine empirically the effects changes in data or parameters may have upon an economic system have frequently been stressed. Thus, as Leontief writes (1951, pp. 33–34), it is hard to trace the diffusion of the impact of a change through the system of economic variables:

> The principal merit of the general equilibrium theory is that it enables us to take account of the highly complex network of interrelationships which transmits the impulses of any local primary change into the remotest corners of the economic system. While in the case of partial analysis, which operates simultaneously with only two or three variables, the interrelation among these few elements can often be perceived directly, such intuitive inference becomes practically impossible as soon as the number of variables increases up to four or five, not to say ten or twenty. A doubtful reader of these lines can ascertain the limitation of his own common-sense intuition by trying to hazard at least an approximate solution of a system of three simple linear equations with three variables; or, after having found the right answer mathematically, by trying to guess out intuitively what effect a change in one of the constants would have on the values of all three unknowns.

The problem becomes greater, given mutability of the elements composing the matrix of conditions within which the functional relationships connecting economic variables are supposed to hold. In fact, considerable support could be marshaled for the view that economic dynamics in the sense that it has been defined above is too constrained and non-dynamic, too neglectful of the role of changes in the matrix of conditions that are taken as given. Presumably Kuznets has this shortcoming in mind when he writes (1953, pp. 294–95):

> In the social sciences we have need of a new group of workers who combine the mastery of detail and careful procedures essential to the specialized research scientist with the wider horizon of the historian and social philosopher; and we have need on the part of our specialist groups of greater awareness of the variety of historical experience and the mutability of the social framework within which lie the more narrowly

defined phenomena that they study. With specific reference to the statistical tools and techniques for dealing with social data, one might suggest that the statistician needs to be receptive to the results of the analytical theorist, to the suggestion of the student of the historical scene, and even to the claims and clamor of the reformers. And he must beware especially of the danger of identifying mechanically derived lines with trends; calculated ratios with immutable and natural laws of constitution, and correlation coefficients with inviolable laws of causation and association.

It is even contended that the methods of economics are unsuited to prediction. Schoeffler (1955, pp. 40–41) has observed:

As a result, the structure of economic analysis is not isomorphic with the structure of economic reality. In attempting to bridge the gap, economists have become accustomed to committing a considerable variety of artificialities in their collection, treatment, and interpretation of data. They artificially mechanize, artificially simplify, artificially generalize, artificially systematize, artificially fixate, artificially factorize, artificially close, artificially semiclose and artificially isolate. They employ an artificial indirectness. They assume the heterogeneous to be homogeneous, the complex to be simple, the complexly related to be simply related, the unknown to be known, the variable to be fixed, the open to be closed, the connected to be isolated, and the indeterminate to be determinate. Unavoidably, therefore, predictions about economic reality which are produced with the aid of these techniques are quite undependable.

Population changes frequently work themselves out through one or the other or both of two "modes" or formal channels, which may be identified, in Keirstead's terminology (1948, pp. 109–10):

Any process of change which we may select can best be observed as it works itself out through two forms or modes. These we shall call the "aggregative mode" and the "real mode." By the "aggregative mode"

we mean the form or mode through which any change works its effect on the economy via its effect on aggregate income. By the "real mode" we mean the form or mode through which the change affects the economy via the alteration in the margin of substitution of one good, or group of goods, or one factor, for another good, group of goods, or factor, the structure of the market, the level of real income and welfare, and the real rates of reward. Thus an increase in population may increase aggregate demand and in so doing work certain changes in the economy. This would be the "income mode." The same population change would affect the labour-capital combination, under certain conditions increasing the proportion of labour to capital, and this would work further changes, not necessarily in the same direction, in the economy. This would be the "real mode." It is important, we shall show, to sort out these two modes through which effects from causes of change work themselves out, and as far as possible, estimate the probable predominance of the one or the other when they appear to operate in opposite directions. This can only be done, if at all, by careful selection of the processes to be analysed and definition of the level of abstraction.

These two modes are similar to (though more general than) what economists, following Hicks (1946, pp. 27–33), call "income" and "substitution" effects. Since these effects may work in opposite directions, it is not always easy to determine the net effect of a population change accompanied by both effects.

While it may be easy to determine the direction of an economic effect accompanying a change in some dimension of population, it frequently is not easy to determine the magnitude of such an effect. The population change may be accompanied by some other change in the matrix of conditions within which economic effects work themselves out; for example, an influx of immigrants of superior technological culture entails an increase in the size of the labor force and possibly also an alteration of the methods of production in use. Furthermore, when population changes are studied historically and when the period is one marked by various changes in the matrix of conditions, it may not be possible to describe all these changes with quantitative precision. In this event it is impossible to determine precisely the effects imputable to the recorded population change.

It is only in the economic effects of population change that the economist's analytical methods are particularly relevant. These methods have not been contrived to deal with the impact of economic change upon the dimensions of a population. Accordingly, when one tries to analyze this impact, it is necessary to employ methods not peculiar to economics. Furthermore, when longer-run interrelations of economic and demographic behavior are analyzed, both the methods of economics and the methods of other relevant sciences must be employed, since not all the changes taking place can be dealt with solely by the methods of economics or by those of other relevant sciences.

THE PRESENT STATE OF ECONOMIC-DEMOGRAPHIC KNOWLEDGE

In this section discussion is focused upon the nature of functional relationships rather than upon the specific empirical content of these relationships, for the manner in which economic (demographic) variables respond to demographic (economic) change may depend significantly, in concrete situations, upon the state of other conditions present (even though not being analyzed) which may vary greatly in time and space. It is, in fact, because economic (demographic) response to demographic (economic) change may be significantly conditioned by these extraneous factors that the instruments of economic analysis do not always yield adequate explanations.

Demographic Change and Economic Response

Demographic changes may be subdivided, for purposes of analyzing their economic effects, in at least two ways. First, these changes may be subdivided somewhat after the fashion in which they were subdivided in the first section, and the economic changes associated with given demographic changes may then be indicated. This arrangement is used here. Second, economic effects of demographic change may be viewed in terms of "comparative statics," or in terms of the process of economic change associated with the process of demographic change, and demographic changes may be classified accordingly. When the method of comparative statics is employed, investigation is confined to "changes in a system from one position of equilibrium to another without regard to the transitional process involved in the adjustment" (Samuelson, 1947, pp. 7–8). Such an approach would be employed, for example, if equilibrium values were determined before and after a specified change in the magnitude of a population and its labor-force component. If, however, the demographic events involved in a change in the size of a population and its labor-force component were ordered in time and the economic effects associated with these demographic events were ordered in time accordingly, the approach employed would be that of economic dynamics or process analysis. This approach is superior to the former approach in that the final equilibrium position is conditioned by the process of adjustment eventuating in stable equilibrium (Baumol, 1951, chaps. i, vii–viii). This approach, furthermore, compels the analyst to take more explicitly into account the impact of changes in data that tend to be ignored on the ground that they lie outside the province of economists.

Demographic changes are classified in terms of what were called *secondary*, or derivative, demographic variables, and the nature of the economic changes associated therewith are briefly described. What were called *primary* demographic variables are disregarded, not because they are unimportant but because they make their influence felt through the medium of the secondary variables. An over-all view of the influence exercised by these secondary demographic variables may be had from the following:

Secondary demographic variable	Economic variables sensitive thereto
$R;\ (r, n)$	$Y, y, K, k, l, D, D_y, t, S, I, E, c, c_c$
T	$Y, y, K, k, l, D, D_y, t, S, E, c, c_c$
C_a	$Y, y, K, k, D_y, t, S, I, E, c, c_c$
C_q	$Y, y, K, k, D, D_y, S, I, E$
C_s	Y, y, K, k, D_y, S, I, E
T_d	$Y, y, l, D, D_y, S, I, E, c, c_c$

The relationships indicated can now be examined in more detail.

T. Population total; population density.—With increases in a country's total population (and hence in its density), T, are normally associated increases in the magnitude of national income (Y), if only because the labor force is larger, and increases in savings (S) and the national stock of capital (K), if only because of the increase in Y, the rise in the marginal productivity of capital, and the disposition of societies to provide capital for the equipment of increments in their numbers (Matthews, 1954–55). The effect of increases in T upon y are considered below. While the magnitudes of S and k are affected by various circumstances, increases in y are more likely to induce increases in S/Y and k than is invariance of y.

Increases in T are associated with a tendency for the ratio of export to import prices (i.e., t) to fall, other conditions being given, since an increase in T usually entails an increase in both imports and exports (Royal Commission, 1950, pars. 41 ff.; Rybczynski, 1955; Corden, 1955; Robinson, 1951, pp. 188–89). A decrease in t, other conditions given, operates to make Y lower than it otherwise would have been. In the event, however, that the increase in T gives rise to increasing return and/or improvements in technology, the resulting increase in output per capita will probably more than offset the effect of the accompanying decrease in t. Although it has been suggested that the behavior of t may be used as an index of changes in a country's population maladjustment, this suggestion is not considered practicable, since changes in t are affected by many circumstances not connected with changes in the magnitude of T or R (Dalton, 1928; Cohn, 1934; Fua, 1940; Rostow, 1952). In general, analysis of the impact of increases in T upon t must take into account whether essentially static conditions obtain or whether there is associated with the increase in T so great a transformation of the economy and so great a change in the composition of imports and exports that a new price structure and a new set of initial conditions is coming into being; this distinction is pertinent, in fact, in analyses of most sequels to increases in T.

Increases in T, by modifying the relative prices at which factors of production are to be had in a country, modify the comparative prices at which finished goods are supplied and therewith alter the composition and the volume of both exports and imports. Because of this potential sequence of events, increases in T may be accompanied either by emigration from the country in question or by adjustment through international trade

(Ohlin, 1933; Lewis, 1950, 1955; Hansson, 1952). Emigration tends to develop when increases in T press wages significantly below the level which potential emigrants believe themselves capable of earning in countries of immigration. If, however, emigration does not take place under these circumstances, the internal economy and the price structure of the affected country may undergo modification until new increments in the labor force have become employed under as favorable circumstances as are realizable, given the country's resource equipment and technology. Inquiry concerning the extent to which international trade is a substitute for international migration and is capable of preventing wage declines (as sequels to increases in T) indicates trade to be a substitute, but one that is imperfect and only partly capable of offsetting increases in T (cf. Samuelson, 1953–54, Bibliography; Laursen, 1952; McKenzie, 1955; Robinson, 1956; Haberler, 1955, pp. 18 ff.). Account is not taken of the fact that efforts to absorb population growth through industrialization are much more likely than emigration to eventuate in a decline in age-specific fertility.

Within limits, increases in T may operate to increase y (given as constant all conditions except those affected by increases in T) and thereafter serve to reduce y. For up to a point increases in T give rise to improvements in organization and other sources of increasing return (Jones, 1933; Clark, 1940; Young, 1928), and these improvements more than offset such adverse effects as eventually accompany decreases in the amount of land and other resources available per head (i.e., decreases in l). Eventually the decline in l constitutes a drag on the upward movement of y. When increases in T no longer give rise to improvements sufficient to offset these adverse effects and those accompanying declines in t, further increases in T operate to make y lower than it otherwise would have been, and this tendency is accentuated when population growth serves to slow down the rate at which capital per head is formed or to affect adversely the terms of trade. In concrete situations, of course, when a society is dynamic and progressive, there usually are circumstances which make for the growth of y even though T is already too great (Tinbergen, 1942; Tinbergen and Polak, 1950). Even in these situations, however, the increase of T may be depriving the population of advantages whose loss is not compensated by the increase of y (Leibenstein, 1954; Meade, 1955, chap. vi; Stone, 1955; Spengler, 1954). It has also been suggested that increase in T, by directing attention to obstacles to income growth and compelling their removal, may itself be a source of technological and organizational progress, but not much evidence on this score has as yet been convincingly presented. There exists an extensive body of literature whose value is necessarily impaired by the fact that it has not yet been possible to assess with quantitative precision the various sources of increases in income (cf. Kuznets, 1956–57; Gottlieb, 1945, 1949; Clark, 1940, pp. 291 ff.; Dijkmans, 1938; Villard, 1955; Whelpton, 1939; Robinson, 1952, pp. 104–11; Royal Commission, 1950; Spengler, 1947–48).

Increases in T may affect the distribution of income (i.e., D, D_y). If increases in T slow down the rate at which capital per head (k) is formed and reduce the value of resources per head (l), the human agent, labor, becomes more plentiful, compared with capital and land, and the rate at which the human agent is productive and remunerated, compared with the rates at which capital and land are productive and remunerated, becomes lower than it otherwise would have been. Under these circumstances the relative share of the national income going to labor may or may not change; it will not change if the elasticity of substitution of labor for other factors of production approximates unity, and it may not change if institutional conditions are modified sufficiently to offset the decrease in labor's comparative scarcity. Should D change in consequence of changes in T, D_y would change in the same direction in the absence of compensatory institutional changes. While we cannot predict with certainty what will be the net effect on distribution (i.e., D and D_y) of an increase in T, the presumption is that the share of the human agent will be affected adversely unless the economy remains in the stage of increasing returns or unless the increase in T is counterbalanced by an increase in K. Of course, if K continues to increase faster than T and if there is sufficient technical progress, wages will continue to increase (cf. Dickinson, 1954–55; Marty, 1953; Mitra, 1955; Peacock, 1952, 1954).

Sauvy (1954) has suggested that if the territory on which a population is multiplying is relatively small, a hierarchy of social status tends to develop, in turn accompanied by notably great inequality of income. Presumably, however, such a development can ensue only if there are present social variables which make for a positive association between the relative magnitude of incomes and their relative rates of growth (cf. Simon, 1957, chap. ix).

Increases in T may affect the level of employment, E, if K does not increase sufficiently. If labor is combinable with capital in sufficiently variable proportions, only a decline in the capital-labor ratio tends to result. If, however, the proportions in which capital and labor are combined are not sufficiently variable, it may not prove im-

mediately possible to redistribute labor among industries rapidly enough to provide employment for all; hence, some unemployment and underemployment may result. This situation appears to obtain in overpopulated countries where there is an insufficiency of agents of production to combine with labor and where technological change and the redistribution of workers among employments does not proceed rapidly enough to permit all increments in the labor force to be combined promptly, if at all, with other agents of production (cf. Dorfman *et al.*, 1954; Eckhaus, 1955; Fukuoka, 1955).

It is possible that increases in T may occasion increase in c at the expense of S, with the result that the ratio of S to Y (i.e., the average propensity to save) may fall. This result need not follow, of course, but it would become likely if the increase in T were accompanied by a decline in y. The composition of consumption (c_c) would change as a result of an increase in T either if y fell and caused a shift in consumption toward cheaper commodities or if the price structure of consumer goods underwent changes resulting in a considerable substitution of now relatively cheaper for now relatively more expensive goods.

Those interested in measuring or projecting consumption in general, or consumption of particular commodities, must take into account the movement of population (i.e., T), since, the price structure and consumer tastes being given, consumption is governed both by the movement of population and by that of per capita income (Belshaw, 1956). Here it is needful merely to indicate that the movement of consumption may be associated either with that of the total population or with that of some component of the population (e.g., young people, old people, families, households) and that special studies of consumption usually deal with this subject (e.g., Blank, 1954; Fisher, 1952; Zwick, 1957; Mack, 1954; Klein, 1950, pp. 44–45, 81, 91). Ferber's (1953) evaluation of various types of aggregate consumption functions indicates that the predictive accuracy of such functions is always improved when they are deflated by population and expressed in per capita terms.

R. Rate of population growth.—Abstracting from the changes in age composition that accompany a change in R until a population's age composition has become stable, the economic variables apparently most sensitive to changes in R are y, k, S, I, and E. Because a change in R entails a change in the rate of change of T, the variables I, t, D, D_y, c, and c_c may be affected somewhat after the manner described above when the effects of increases in T were under consideration; there is no need, therefore, to consider these changes further.

An increase in R, other conditions being given, tends to slow down the rate of increase in k and hence eventually to slow down the rate of increase in y (Koo, 1955; Spengler, 1951), which is conditioned by the rate of increase in k. Population growth absorbs resources which might otherwise be used partly to increase k, for resources are invested in increments to the population (Bowen, 1937; Ghosh, 1946), and resources must be used to provide equipment for these increments. Accordingly, so long as there is not considerable unemployment and a plethora of potential savings, an increase in the rate of population growth tends to slow down the progress of k and y. The capital-absorbing power of population growth may be suggested in several ways. On the assumption that national wealth approximates four to five times national income, a saving rate of 4 to 5 per cent of national income is required to keep the wealth-population ratio constant if population is growing 1 per cent per year. The cost of a 1 per cent rate of population growth, expressed in terms of per capita income, appears to be in the neighborhood of 0.5 per cent. Studies of the response of family expenditure patterns to increase in the number of children indicate that, family income being given, family savings per annum diminish (Henderson, 1949–50; Brady and Froeder, 1955; Goldsmith *et al.*, 1956).

The past two decades have witnessed the appearance of a voluminous literature purporting to show that a decline in R, or the advent of a low-level R, tends to be accompanied by a condition of underemployment and possibly by circumstances comparatively unfavorable to the expansion of per capita income (cf. Barber, 1953; Daly, 1940; Davis, J., 1953; Hansen, 1939, 1940, 1941, 1951; Hicks, 1946; Reddaway, 1937, 1939; Higgins, 1950; Goldenberg, 1946; Ardant, 1950; Arndt, 1948; Adler, 1945; Keynes, 1937; Timlin, 1951; Royal Commission, 1950; Tsiang, 1942; Gordon, 1956; Corbett, 1951; Matthews, 1954–55; also Achinstein, 1950; Kurihara, 1954; Hamberg, 1956, and Jones, M., 1944). Some of the arguments may be indicated. Since a decline in R tends to be accompanied by a decline in the rate of investment and an increase in the rate of savings, investment will no longer suffice to offset savings under conditions of full employment (as it did in the nineteenth century when supposedly around one-half of all investment was population-oriented, being undertaken to equip new increments to the population and the labor force and to finance the extension of settlement). Population growth, furthermore, is a dynamic and catalytic agent that makes for economic growth in general. Since a continually growing population insures a continually expanding market, enterpreneurs are not hesitant about investing in improved, resource-saving equipment. They expect to sell at a profit whatever they produce. Consequently, new and improved methods are introduced at a relatively high rate. Given that population growth had been so important a force of economic expansion and so significant a source of demand for investment goods, it seemed to follow that a marked decline in the rate of population growth would result in a decline in technological progress, investment, and employment, with the multiplier effect and probably also the accelerator principle serving to intensify greatly the diminution in employment (Stolper, 1941). The role which variations in the rate of population growth may play in trade-cycle models involving intermittent shocks, or the presence of moving floors and ceilings, remains to be fully developed (Hicks, 1950; Hansen, 1951; Goodwin, 1951).

Critics of this view have indicated that although in the past population growth has absorbed a considerable volume of savings, population growth is not necessarily essential to the absorption of such savings as are forthcoming under conditions of full employment. The composition (I_c) of investment may change but not its quantity I. Population-oriented investment, relatively heavy in periods of great population growth, tends to be replaced in part by other forms of investment when population growth slackens and savings can be devoted to other purposes. In the past, savings have usually fallen within a range of 5 to 15 per cent of national income (Kuznets, 1956). Investment has been of the same order of magnitude, with consumption and net government expenditures providing the remainder of the demand for net national product. Apparently a quite small increase in

consumption and government expenditure would offset a significant decrease in investment expenditure and thus insure continuation of something like full employment. Such action, moreover, is considered quite feasible under modern conditions. It has been observed, of course, that in the United States the rate of investment remained high long after the rate of population growth began to decline (cf. Terborgh, 1945; Neisser, 1944; Fellner, 1947; Schiff, 1946; Hoover, C. B., 1948; Royal Commission, 1950; Robinson, 1951, pp. 115–32; Spengler, 1956a).

It has been noted that just as a low rate of population growth may conduce to unemployment, so a high rate may conduce to inflation. If, with a relatively high rate of population growth, a nation endeavors both to equip new increments to its population and also to augment the equipment of its existing population, the aggregate volume of investment resulting may exceed the aggregate volume of voluntary savings. If the gap between savings and investment is made up through privately sponsored or governmentally supported inflationary borrowing, prices will tend to rise until the gap is removed through forced savings and other adjustments (cf. Lewis, 1955).

It has been remarked also that variation in the rate at which population and the labor force are growing may affect the course of the trade cycle. During expansion phases of the trade cycle both unemployed and new members of the labor force become gainfully employed. While those without employment during the upswing of the cycle do not constitute a homogeneous group, it is still true that a growing shortage of labor may check a cyclical upswing and that, insofar as this is the case, variation in the rate of growth of the labor force (resulting from past variation in R) may occasion some variation in cyclical behavior. Furthermore, insofar as variation in the rate of growth of population and the labor force is the source of variation in investment, it may somewhat affect behavior of the cycle through the medium of investment. Variation in the rate of population growth may also affect the cycle through the medium of saving (Matthews, 1954–55). Literature on the cyclical effects of variations in population growth is much smaller than that on the secular influences of population growth (cf. Lösch, 1936; Haberler, 1941, chap. xi; Neisser, 1944; Pederson, 1948; Robinson, 1952, pp. 107–10; Duesenberry, 1950).

Structural unemployment might tend to become more common when the rate of population growth is low than when it is high, though for a somewhat different reason than cyclical and general unemployment, for which relief may flow out of a sufficiency of investment. When a population is growing, this growth partly offsets declines in the per capita demand for the products of particular industries, with the result that fewer workers need to transfer out of such declining industries. It has been indicated, however, that in the absence of new recruits to an occupation, the number attached to it will shrink at an increasing rate, after starting in the neighborhood of as little as 2 per cent per year (cf. Wolfbein, 1949; Royal Commission, 1950, pars. 148–72).

T_d. Distribution of population in space.—While the distribution of population in space is largely the consequence of what has taken place in the past, together with current socio-economic population-conglomerating forces that give rise to internal migration (Lösch, 1954; Isard, 1956; Hoover, E. M., 1948), distribution is affected also by intercommunity differences in the rate of natural increase. Population redistribution serves to increase

per capita output when, as is frequently but not always the case, it accompanies or makes possible a more nearly optimal distribution of economic activities in space. When this is the case, Y and y rise in consequence, and this rise may be intensified slightly if population redistribution entails a use of land and resources that might otherwise lie outside the orbit of use because of location rather than because of inferior quality. Redistribution may, as international migration sometimes does (Clark, 1951, pp. 206–7), produce changes in habits and attitudes and thereby conduce to the use of improved methods of production. Redistribution tends to increase wages somewhat and thereby to modify D and D_y slightly. Redistribution also tends to increase the rate of investment and may thereby affect the character and progress of the trade cycle (Isard, 1942; Myrdal, G., 1933). Redistribution operates to reduce the supply of savings in the long run if, as appears to be the case, it transfers people from situations in which the propensity to consume is relatively low to situations in which it is relatively high and if the effects of this transfer are not offset by accompanying increases in per capita income. Since consumption and value and other behavior patterns vary somewhat with community, population redistribution may somewhat modify national consumption (c_c) as well as related patterns. Selective redistribution of population in space, at either the national or the international level, may serve to improve the occupational structure (or other structures) of the populations of immigrant-receiving countries (Sauvy, 1952, pp. 100 ff.).

Composition of Population.—Three kinds of population composition have been identified: sex, age, and qualitative. It suffices to indicate that income levels, savings, capital formation, income distribution, labor-force participation, and possibly the level of employment tend to be affected by a population's sex composition (C_s); but since major divergences from normality of sex composition tend to be transitory, they are not of long-run economic importance. (cf. Durand, 1948; Frumkin, 1950). Of the two forms of qualitative composition (C_q), genetical and environmental, the former is neglected in this discussion, not because it is unimportant but because the economic effects of variations in genetical composition have not been effectively related to economic processes. In general, while a population's potential capacity to perform is limited by its genetical composition, the ratio of its actual level of performance to its potential level is governed by non-genetical conditions. Environmental composition is important because values, aspiration levels, attitudes, educational and occupational and related opportunities, and other behavior-affecting conditions vary with social environment. In consequence, the aggregate behavior patterns of a population will be affected by variations in the proportions of children who are born or moved into some social environments as distinguished from other such environments. The resultant changes in behavior patterns may affect such economic tendencies as the disposition to save or to invest or to work.

Occupational composition may be affected by differential fertility when fertility is relatively high in occupational groups, the price and income elasticity of demand for whose services is relatively low, and labor mobility also is relatively low. Agriculture often is a case in point. Movement from agricultural occupations often is indicated because, given the relatively high fertility usually found there and the fact that the demand for agricultural services does not keep pace with the rate

of supply of these services, more agricultural labor tends to be available than can be employed at rates of remuneration at all commensurate with others in the economy (cf. Simon, 1957, chap. xii). If movement out of agriculture does not occur, therefore, agricultural income levels tend to fall relative to those obtaining elsewhere in the economy.

Most important of the forms of population composition is age composition (C_a), in part because it is uniquely determined by the movement of age-specific fertility and mortality, subject on occasion to a small amount of modification through international migration (Coale, 1956; United Nations, 1951, 1953, 1954). Most important of the effects of changes in age composition is that emerging from its influence upon the ratio of persons of economically productive age to the total population, since the magnitude of the fraction of the population that can be absorbed into the labor force depends upon this ratio (New York Legislative Committee, 1948; Durand, 1948, 1953). The ratio tends to be higher when the rate of natural increase is low than when it is high, at least in a stable population, since the increase in the relative number of older persons associated with a low rate of natural increase is more than offset by the decrease in the relative number of persons below productive age (Lorimer, 1950; United Nations, 1954, 1956).

Changes in age composition, other conditions being given, are usually associated with changes in y, k, S, and probably t, each of which tends to be positively correlated with output per head, which in turn tends to vary with the ratio of the labor force to the population (Dorfman *et al.*, 1954). Changes in age composition are also associated with changes in the composition of consumption, since the members of different age groups differ in their habits of consumption and in their purchasing power. Moreover, age composition is partly reflected in the relative number and composition of households, by which consumption is affected (Henderson, 1949–50a, b; Glass and Davidson, 1951; Brown, 1954).

It has been suggested that savings will vary with age composition because per capita income is affected thereby. Savings also vary with age, in part because income varies with age and in part because needs vary with age (Fisher, 1952; Duesenberry, 1949; Lydall, 1955; Miller, 1955; Friedman, 1956; Brady and Froeder, 1955; Zwick, 1957).

What the impact of changes in age composition upon investment and employment will be is not self-evident. Capital per head (k) tends to increase as the ratio of persons of productive age to total population rises. But whether the rate of investment then tends to be high enough to maintain full employment cannot be empirically determined with precision. Those who believe that labor mobility will diminish as the average age of the labor force rises, and as the ratio of persons entering the labor force to persons departing falls, suggest that employment will not be full (Myrdal, G., 1940; Reddaway, 1939). The predominating tendency remains to be determined, however, as does the variation of this tendency with other circumstances.

The impact of an increase in the relative number of older persons, consequent upon a decline in age-specific fertility, is conditioned, of course, by the manner in which this increase is met. In general, an increase of this sort is less likely to produce adverse effects when there are no institutional obstacles to employing older workers and when inflation is not permitted to nibble away the accumulated financial security of retired persons. Whether because of a possible tendency for pub-

lic debt to increase in comparison with national income or because of other reasons, inflationary tendencies are greater in a slowly growing than in a rapidly growing population remains to be determined, however. In this instance, as in so many others, what takes place is not intimately connected with the growth of a population or with its age structure (cf. Derber, 1950; New York Legislative Committee, 1948; Bourgeois-Pichat, 1950; Webber, 1956).

Some writers have sought to explore the relation between the distribution of ability and the functional distribution of income, and some of these same writers have found the distribution of abilities to be based in part upon the genetical composition of the population (Staehle, 1943; Spengler, 1953, Bibliography). If the distribution of income is closely related to that of ability, as it must in a significant degree be, and if the distribution of ability appears susceptible to significant change through genetical selection and resulting changes in the genetical composition of population, further inquiry into these relationships is indicated.

Economic Change and Demographic Response

Demographic variables have been divided into two categories, the primary (i.e., M, F, M_d, F_d, e, i, m, m_d) and the secondary (i.e., R, T, T_d, C_a, C_s, C_q, and possibly C_{qs}). The secondary variables were described as derivative variables, since changes in their values are compounded of changes in the values of the primary variables. Economic change, therefore, produces demographic change by producing changes in the primary demographic variables, changes in which, in turn, give rise to change in the secondary demographic variables. As has been indicated, changes in the secondary demographic variables are of most significance for students of economic change.

The discussion presented in this section is organized in terms of the primary demographic variables upon which changes in economic circumstances operate. While T is a secondary demographic variable, its value at any time having been determined by the preceding behavior of primary variables, T may be grouped with these primary variables when attention is being given to the direction of change in T produced by economic changes.

M, F. Mortality; fertility.—Age-specific mortality is somewhat negatively correlated with level of per capita income, other conditions being given, as is indicated in the chapter on mortality. The degree of this dependence varies with other conditions; it appears to be significant only within a certain income range. Insofar as such dependence obtains, mortality shows some tendency to diminish in population aggregates and in subgroups of population aggregates when over-all per capita income rises and also when forces making for greater equality in income distribution occasion income increases in subgroups. The relationship between the movement of y and that of mortality is complex, however, depending on what intervening variables are present, on the uses to which increments in income are put, and so on. In many underdeveloped countries this relationship has come to differ from what it was in the early nineteenth century; for the present, at least, crude mortality is quite low and life expectancy relatively high in many countries in which per capita real income remains very low (Davis, 1956).

Age-specific fertility tends to be correlated positively with increments in per capita income arising from increases in employment (Kirk, 1942), improvements in technology, etc., when other conditions, especially the living pattern, stay put (cf. Leibenstein and Galenson, 1955). Other conditions rarely stay put, however, so decreasing age-specific fertility often is associated with increasing per capita income among those of reproductive age. In fact, until recently, the long-run tendency has been for per capita income to rise and for age-specific fertility, or at least gross reproduction, to fall. It is possible, furthermore, that large increments in income may modify the recipients' living patterns in ways that serve to reduce fertility or that the changes giving rise to income increases may also render living patterns less favorable to fertility. Again, it is possible for fertility to be affected by the degree to which the income recipient believes his income to be secure at various stages in life, whether because he owns property or because he participates in collective arrangements designed to protect him against unfavorable events. (Collective arrangements designed to insure a given number of participants against such events, of course, furnish security at less cost, in terms of resources set aside for this purpose, than would be necessary were each participant to establish his own insurance reserve fund; the relative magnitude of deviation from normal expectancy, against which protection is sought, diminishes as the number of participants increases. Such arrangements thus increase the uncommitted fraction of an individual's income, but they may also increase somewhat his average propensity to consume.) It has been suggested that a population, finding itself in a situation wherein growth of numbers continually depresses income near to the subsistence level, is most likely to escape from this Malthusian trap through policies that increase income significantly, thus serving as destabilizers (Leibenstein, 1957).

The population policies in effect in many countries are based in part upon the supposition that age-specific fertility tends to be stimulated by family allowances and various other grants-in-aid geared to the number of dependent children in a family (e.g., Watson, 1954*a*, *b*; Susswein, 1948; Doublet, 1948; Gille, 1948*a*, *b*, 1952, 1954). While these policies presumably tend to elevate fertility in the short run (Spengler, 1950), their long-run effect is not so clear. This effect turns in part upon the incidence of the costs of the policies in question. Under the family wage system, the cost is incident in part at least upon wage and salary earners, with this incidence varying according to type of system. Under some arrangements, however, the cost may be largely incident upon those who provide the bulk of the savings out of which capital formation is financed; in this event, therefore, capital formation will be retarded, with the result that income growth also will be retarded (Boulding, 1953*b*). What the ultimate net effect upon population growth will be is not so clear.

The circumstances which underlie the connections between income and fertility are not well known. In fact, the information available about the social-psychological processes which connect change in income with the responses of the individual experiencing this income change is very slight. Most studies of consumption have dealt with relatively large numbers of subjects in given periods of time and have established only gross functional relationships. The nature of the underlying processes has not been adequately studied, perhaps because the economist is not very interested in the sociopsychological nexus between change in income and change in its use. Presumably, not until we make a detailed study of these processes will we be able to explain fully why income change produces now one type of response and now another, and why such change

often is not reversible. The information obtained through such studies would throw light also on why the average propensity to save of aggregate populations, or of subgroups of such aggregates, behaves as it does (cf. Kuznets, 1956; Burns, 1952).

M_d, F_d. *Differential mortality; differential fertility.*—Among the circumstances responsible for intergroup differences in mortality are intergroup differences in total economic situations, above all, perhaps, differences in per capita real consumption. The impact of these differences varies with the character of societies, however, and with the absolute level of real income enjoyed, as is indicated in the chapter on mortality. Apparently, when minimum real incomes move above some critical level, intergroup income differences no longer greatly affect intergroup differences in mortality.

Among the circumstances responsible for intergroup differences in age-specific and total fertility appear to be differences in per capita income and differences in the level and composition of aspirations or wants. Inasmuch as both income and aspirations tend to increase together, but not necessarily in the same proportion, fertility differentials may increase even though income differentials do not, and fertility differentials may remain unchanged or decline even though income differentials increase. Intergroup differences in fertility are probably greater in open or less stratified than in closed or rigidly stratified societies, both because social capillarity or social promotion leads to family limitation and because social promotion may favor the ascent of the less fecund and thereby reduce fecundity in the upper social classes (Burks, 1941). Insofar as these two propositions hold, economic changes which reduce the impermeability of interclass barriers may increase intergroup differences in fertility. We will not know precisely the extent to which differences in fertility, by group, are attributable to economic, as distinguished from non-economic, circumstances in different types of societies until we know much more about other determinants of age-specific and total fertility.

e, i. Emigration, immigration.—While the movement of migrants from one country to another is affected by non-economic conditions, it appears to be dominated by economic conditions when legal barriers do not prevent movement. The demand for labor (or for population) in a country, together with the range of prices at which labor is demanded, depends on that country's resources, its stock of equipment and rate of capital formation, the state of its technology, the fluidity of its occupational composition, and the stage of its industrial development. If the ruling circumstances make the demand for labor relatively inelastic and non-expandable, much of the increase in population that takes place, especially in rural sectors, will move abroad if the monetary and distance and psychic costs of movement are not too great; this tendency will be especially strong if the income and other economic advantages anticipated abroad are decidedly superior to what appears to be in store for the potential migrant if he remains at home. If, on the contrary, the non-rural branches of the domestic economy are expanding, the disposition to emigrate is likely to be much weaker, even if the level of wages in prospect at home is significantly inferior to those that might be had abroad (cf. Thomas, D., 1941). In sum, abstracting from the existence of legal barriers and from the transient influence of the trade cycle (Thomas, B., 1954; Jerome, 1926), the international movement of migrants tends to be dominated by real and anticipated international wage and salary differences, and the weight of this dominance is greater when inter-national trade is not free and when the demand for labor in countries of potential emigration is not sufficiently augmented by foreign demand for its exports (Ohlin, 1933; Hansson, 1952; Samuelson, 1949, 1953–54).

For purposes of exposition and analysis, the attraction of one country for another country's potential migrants may be said to vary more or less directly with the spread between the set of opportunities available in the country of potential emigration and that available in the country of immigration, and it may be said to vary more or less inversely with the costs of movement from the one country to the other, with these costs depending principally upon expenses of transport and differences in culture, and perhaps above all on the distance intervening between the two countries, since both transport costs and the disposition to discount the attractiveness of opportunities available in countries of immigration are much affected by the distance they are removed from the country of potential emigration. Thus migration, like trade (cf. Isard, 1949, 1951, 1954, 1956; Isard and Peck, 1954; Stewart, 1947, 1948; Lösch, 1954; Spengler, 1952, pp. 117–26; Bogue, 1949), is much affected by distance. While some writers continue to look upon emigration as a means of easing population pressure, others believe that it is more effective to invest in a country suffering population pressure the productive agents required to move its emigrants abroad and equip them; for such investment may accomplish what emigration is unlikely to do, namely, transform the country's economy and thereby bring down its rate of natural increase.

m, m_d. Internal migration; differential internal migration.—While the volume of internal migration may be affected by interregional differences in fertility, it is dominated by the forces which make for the conglomeration and agglomeration of economic activities and hence of population. These forces are predominantly economic in character (Hoover, E. M., 1948; Lösch, 1954; Isard, 1952, 1956; Hoyt, 1941, 1951; Isard and Whitney, 1949, 1955; Isard and Kavesh, 1954) and subject to the incidence of the cost of distance, just as international movements of men and goods are. The selective and differential impact of these agglomerative forces also partly accounts for the fact that the migrant stream usually differs in composition from both that of the community of origin and that of the community of destination, though the bulk of this difference appears to be of non-economic origin (cf. the chapter on internal migration). Fluidity of occupational structure is favorable to migration, since it widens the range of opportunities accessible to the migrant.

It is impossible to deal in brief compass with these forces of agglomeration, both because the literature is extensive and because the corpus of location theory being developed to explain the distribution of activities and individuals in space is by no means fully developed. Important contributions of Isard and his co-workers, of Vining, of Stewart, of Lösch, of Bogue, of Zipf, of Simon, and of others are indicated, however, in the Bibliography. There also are listed several works (Piddington, Sears) which testify to increasing concern at the non-expansibility of space in countries wherein space enters importantly into the standard of living.

Interrelations of Economic and Demographic Response

The response of economic variables to demographic change has been examined in isolation, as has that of demographic variables to economic change. This approach is justifiable in that it facilitates analysis; yet it is misleading. It is misleading because both economic response and demographic response are parts of an all-inclusive growth process (cf. Boulding, 1953a; Svennilson, 1954). It is not possible to describe adequately the process of population growth in the past or to project convincingly the process of population growth into the future unless population growth is treated as a component of a larger growth process whose participants are mutually interrelated. At the same time, it is not easy to generalize empirically this growth process, since so many of the relationships are behavioral rather than technological and since, therefore, the growth process appears to vary considerably in time and from country to country (Kuznets, 1956, 1956–57), with high rates of increase in per capita income associated with both high and low rates of increase in population and vice versa.

The nature of the interrelation between income growth and population growth may be suggested. Let e represent population elasticity, the ratio of a small proportionate increase in population to the small proportionate increase in community income upon which the population increase is consequent. Presumably a time lag would separate the initiating change in income and the response of population. Let E represent the elasticity of productivity of population, the ratio of a small proportionate increase in community income to the small proportionate increase in population upon which the indicated income increase is consequent. Now suppose that the community's income, Y, increases two units per year because of changes unconnected with population growth. In consequence (assuming that time lags may be disregarded) population would increase, and as a result of the increase in population (labor force), income would increase, and so on. Under the conditions stated, Y would eventually increase by the following amount (ΔY) per year: $k(1 + Ee + E^2 \, e^2 + E^3 \, e^3 + \ldots)$, and population ($T$) would increase by $e\Delta Y$. In reality, of course, this sequence would not be realized. An increase in population cannot increase income until the increment to population enters the labor force, and the time from birth to such entry might be as much as sixteen to twenty-five years. T might also respond to increases in Y only after a time lag.

The problem is that of stating in satisfactory terms the nature of the interdependent changes. Some attention has been given to the formulation of statements that are realistic and satisfactory (Vianelli, 1936; Haavelmo, 1954; Leibenstein, 1954), but not much real progress has been made; nor is the prospect of progress very promising. Presumably, because of the time lags involved, difference-equation models are indicated; and because different components of population (income) respond differently to changes in different components of income (population), both population and income must be appropriately subdivided.

Reference has been made above only to the nature of the interrelation between changes in income and changes in population, together with the cumulative effect of such changes. One might proceed similarly with other pairs of interconnected variables, one from the economic realm and the other from the demographic realm. Unfortunately, little such inquiry has been attempted. Instead, it has been customary to postulate a rate of change, say, in the size of the labor force, and then to build upon it estimates of the rate of growth of net national product. Or it has been explicitly assumed only that population would grow at a certain rate, on the implicit assumption that net national product would grow at a rate sufficient to sustain the postu-lated increase in population (Pearl, 1939).

NEXT STEPS IN RESEARCH

Two steps may be indicated: improvements in methods and approaches in analysis and identification of substantive areas in special need of study. Most studies of population problems deal with the behavior of groups and subgroups of individuals through time. The kind of analysis called for, therefore, can be labeled dynamic process analysis, for it entails determining the changing demographic situation of a population as it progresses through a sequence of time periods, in each of which the situation then resulting flows out of the situation that, having evolved from situations existing in earlier time periods, came to obtain in the time period immediately preceding that under consideration. The situation of a population in any given time period is what it is in virtue of the situation obtaining in the immediately preceding time period, together with the functional relations that interrelate the major demograpic, economic, and social dimensions of the population whose sequence of situations is under analysis. The progress of a population from one situation to the next is always conditioned, of course, by exogenous circumstances that operate either as restraints or as facilitating agencies, but the importance of these exogenous circumstances is likely to become relatively great only if an analysis relates to a considerable number of time periods in the course of which the cumulative influence of these exogenous circumstances can become significant.

It appears to be essential, if dynamic process analysis is resorted to, that social-psychological considerations be taken into account as well as those which are of an essentially economic or demographic order. For, as an examination of points of convergence shows, most of the relevant relations are behavioral rather than technological or purely mechanical; and when relations are behavioral, it is always possible, and frequently probable, that social-psychological as well as economic and demographic circumstances condition their concrete form. When this is the case, therefore, the study of the progress of a population through time, if it is to be optimally effective, presupposes consideration of social-psychological circumstances also. Hence an interdisciplinary rather than a purely economic or a purely demographic approach is indicated.

The movement of a population through time entails change in many interrelated variables. Two technical problems therefore confront the analyst. On the one hand, the techniques of multivariate analysis are called for whenever one anticipates significant changes in a number of these interrelated variables. On the other hand, because analysis of variables becomes increasingly difficult with a greater number of variables, factor analysis or an analogous set of techniques to reduce the number of variables may be called for. Of course, given electronic computers and given sufficient specificity respecting variables and their possible interrelations, complicated models, stochastic and non-stochastic, may be utilized.

At present, two sorts of models are commonly employed, economic and demographic. In economic models most or all dimensions of population usually are treated as data or exogenous elements. In demographic models relevant economic variables are disregarded or considered only implicitly. Such procedures are justifiable for some purposes and under some conditions, and they would be justifiable under all conditions if both the economic and the demographic worlds were self-contained, autonomous, and hence in-

dependent of all other worlds. But a very high degree of independence is seldom approximated. It is desirable, therefore, when both economic and demographic variables are significantly involved, to deal with these variables explicitly in the models prepared for analysis—in short, to employ economic-demographic models when their use is indicated. It would be possible, for example, after having specified the conditions of demographic stability, to specify sets of economic and non-economic conditions suited to maintain these conditions of demographic stability and then to utilize the resulting stable economic-demographic systems to facilitate further analysis.

The role of time lags in dynamic demographic process analysis also calls for careful statement and assessment. Here concern is just with what have been called economic and demographic variables. Change in one variable is not followed promptly by change in other variables, nor is the time interval between initiatory and consequential change of uniform length. In some instances the time interval is short (e.g., between the addition of a child to a family and modification of the family's expenditure pattern). In other instances the time interval is very long (e.g., between a change in age-specific fertility and natural increase and the consequent change in the rate of increase of the working-age population). Until we can determine precisely the quantitative dimensions of the time lags involved in dynamic demographic process analysis, together with the degree of stability characteristic of such time lags, the empirical content that can be given to dynamic demographic process analysis will be limited. Inquiry into these time lags presupposes inquiry into mechanical, institutional, and social-psychological relationships, since some time lags are essentially mechanical (e.g., those between earlier and later changes in age structure), some are institutional (e.g., those between birth and entry into labor force), and some are predominantly social-psychological (e.g., those between family-income change and change in family fertility pattern).

A major shortcoming of much of the analysis touched upon in this chapter is that it tends to be shaped too much by the kinds of information supposedly available and too little by the kinds of questions that are of great significance even though not effectively answerable through analysis of data presently available. An assembly of questions or problems, together with an indication of their comparative priority appears necessary; the object then in view would be specifying the data needed to provide both answers to these questions and the resolution of associated problems.

The scope for illuminating empirical research, with information presently available, is very limited and is likely to remain so. It has already been noted that many, though not all (e.g., age composition), of the economic and demographic variables discussed earlier may undergo modification because of changes taking place in other variables, some of which were not included in the lists assembled earlier. In a sense, therefore, the changes in question may have multiple causes, some of which may be interrelated, and the methods of analysis indicated are of the multivariate sort. However, models designed to guide such analysis cannot be translated into empirical terms until the variables entering into such models are precisely defined, given precise and unambiguous and quantitative expression, and made adequate in number to make the system represented by the model essentially a closed (though perhaps an evolving) system. Data gathered in censuses and other enumerations of the usual not clearly defined multiple-purpose sort do not, as a rule, meet the requirements laid down. This being the situation, it is not likely that many questions can be nicely formulated and resolved until data are gathered, presumably by sampling methods, in response to carefully stated questions, answers to which are obtained through carefully executed surveys.

Parenthetically, when the data at hand are quite limited in quantity and quality, recourse must be had to the use of theory and models into which enter functional relations, the general character and direction of which, but not their specific and concrete content, are known. For many purposes of policy, recourse to the use of such models is quite adequate. For example, the average propensity to save and the elasticity of productivity of labor and capital may not be very well known, and information concerning the prospective course of technological change may be even less adequate. Even so, one can easily demonstrate that, in many situations, a lower rather than a higher rate of population growth is preferable, if only because the lower rate absorbs less capital and hence is less unfavorable to the progress of per capita income than is the higher rate. In sum, the direction of the economic effects of demographic change frequently is known and their magnitude is roughly determinable, even in the absence of much information. Within limits also, the direction of demographic effects on economic change may also be known, but the range of uncertainty is much greater than that of the economic effects of demographic change.

It may be relevant, in this connection, to inquire into the nature and causes of the apparent appeal made by Marxian views on population to public spokesmen and policy-makers in some countries, and particularly to those in countries in which population pressure, by most standards, is great. In essence, Marxian views appear to find little if any functional connection between population movements and the movement of per capita income, and this despite the fact that much emphasis is placed upon technological progress and capital formation; at least the second is adversely affected by population growth. The kind of inquiry here indicated lies within the area of the sociology of knowledge, but its significance lies in the field of international relations.

Effective inquiry into the determinants of age-specific fertility in a dynamic world presupposes fairly complete knowledge of the acquisition of patterns of consumption. Yet, on this score, there is a decided shortage of relevant information. The information available is essentially cross-sectional rather than longitudinal in character and hence falls short of what is required in much the same manner that the information underlying the synthetic net reproduction rate falls short of what is required. It would appear that the type of inquiry indicated is the longitudinal sort that underlies cohort analysis. Conceivably, small but truly representative cohorts of consumers could be selected at some stage in life, perhaps at entry into some level of education or into the labor force, and their behavior as consumers observed and studied throughout life. A series of such cohorts would have to be selected, of course, to represent a sequential series of years. The response of the consumption patterns of specific members of representative cohorts to income and other changes could be recorded and studied longitudinally and the results could be contrasted with those presently obtained through cross-sectional inquiry and analysis. Such study could be financed by foundation funds and carried on by an institution somewhat after the manner of the Terman

studies of gifted children. In time, a great deal of information concerning the social-psychological processes involved in the modification of living patterns would be assembled and this in turn could be used to improve greatly the results obtained from cross-sectional analysis of consumption. An inquiry of this sort would automatically provide fertility information of the sort obtained by cohort analysis, and this information could be carefully correlated with the economic and related information obtained for the same cohort.

Assessment of the possibilities of making population forecasts is indicated, since if these cannot be made with a high degree of precision as to time and magnitude of increase, it follows that effective economic adjustment to population change is best achieved, as in the past, through keeping the economy highly flexible and capable of being accommodated to considerable variation in the rate of population growth. Whelpton (1954, p. 276) has suggested that the demographer's task of forecasting births would be much simplified "if economists and other social scientists could provide reliable forecasts of changes in business and social conditions during the next decade or more." It is doubtful, however, whether economists could provide such forecasts, since the conditions prerequisite to satisfactory economic forecasts are not present and are not likely to be present (cf. Schoeffler, 1955). This doubt needs to be resolved, nonetheless, and it needs also to be determined, insofar as possible, whether major fluctuations in per capita income remain likely.

Much more work needs to be done on the interrelations of the trade cycle and age-specific fertility (Thomas and Galbraith, 1941; Hogben, 1938; Hyrenius, 1946), a subject that has not received a great deal of attention in recent years, though it ties in nicely with cohort analysis. Information from such research would have various uses and would contribute to assessing the predictability of population movements. We would have to take account of a new factor in the situation—the state's disposition to provide unemployment compensation and to furnish family allowances and related grants-in-aid.

As has been indicated, economic changes may be translated into terms of substitution and aggregative or income effects. The former set of effects is represented principally by changes in the structure of prices; the latter is represented principally by changes in aggregate and/or per capita income. When prices change, costs attendant upon the reproduction and rearing of children may become relatively greater or less than the costs of goods and services which compete with those entering into the reproduction and rearing of children, and fertility may be affected accordingly. Probably the progress of age-specific fertility through time has been notably affected by changes in the price structure (e.g., the decline in the relative prices of what once were called luxury goods). We might therefore inquire into the effect of changes in the price structure upon the course of fertility. Similarly, we might inquire into the effect of changes in the wage and/or salary structure of nations upon the course of differential fertility and into the various sources (e.g., immigration, differential migration, technological change) of these changes in wage and salary structure. Since the impact of aggregate or income effects upon demographic variables has received far more attention than that of substitution effects, the importance of aggregate effects need not again be stressed; but we should make a clearer distinction between aggregate and substitution ef-

fects, if for no other reason than that the distinction is of considerable significance to policy (Spengler, 1950).

It is possible to prepare either a brief or an extended list of substantive areas in need of further study. In fact, the United Nations (1954, pp. 1 ff.) has recently prepared such a list and many defects in the information available were reported earlier in a United Nations (1953) study. Here only a few such needed studies will be indicated.

Perhaps the most important of possible economic studies is a report on the land and natural resources of the world, on their distribution and use, on their entry into international and interregional trade, and on the degree to which they enter into national incomes and into the composition of specific commodity groups. At present there exists considerable though scattered information on these questions. But it is incomplete; it is not in accessible form; it has not been carefully assessed in the light of technological prospects; and it has not been put in a form sufficiently suitable for policy considerations.

Information concerning land and other natural resources is important because it is by the stock of these that the course of aggregate and per capita income is ultimately determined, given the course of population growth and the state of technology. It is the stock of these resources (among which is space itself, that is, space for economic activity, habitation, and recreation) that ultimately is fixed in quantity. Yet, at present, the long-run significance of the availability of land and resources receives little attention, concern being restricted to what will be available in one, two, or three decades.

We also need more information on age-structural change, together with the implications of this kind of change for the relative magnitude of the labor force, for the recruitment of occupations, for the interoccupational mobility of labor, for retirement policies, and for the economic aspects of social security (which could be weakened by inflationary policies or by obsolete investment policies). There is much scattered information on these questions, and a number of special studies have been undertaken; but there has not yet been a definitive inquiry of really authoritative significance for public and private policy.

A third subject in need of careful inquiry is the possible economic effect of differential fertility. We noted earlier that economic effects might arise from economically significant changes in the genetical composition of populations or from significant changes in the cultural or value composition of populations consequent upon the course of differential fertility. On these matters scattered papers have appeared, but no one has yet brought together a sufficiently inclusive body of well-assembled and assessed information to permit answers of salient importance in this field and to provide a satisfactory basis for policy which, at present, may unduly neglect effects of differential fertility.

A fourth subject greatly in need of inquiry is the range of response of which so-called underdeveloped countries, whether already densely populated or not so heavily populated, are capable. We presume that in many of these countries much of the fruits of development programs will be consumed by increments in population brought into being by these programs, and the progress of per capita income will be retarded or checked. Much of what is significant in this connection is treated in the chapters dealing with fertility and mortality. It remains true, nonetheless, that fertility levels may be affected by the composition of investment (Leibenstein and Galenson, 1955; Leibenstein, 1957; Spengler, 1956c), by the character of the price structure,

by the impact of the economic policies pursued when the population gains access to effective means of population control, and by the population's disposition to regulate its numbers. It is essential, therefore, that the information available on these questions be gotten together, assessed for gaps, and oriented to policy considerations. It is desirable also that studies be undertaken of the probable cost of population growth in terms of per capita income (e.g., Coale and Hoover, 1958).

A fifth subject is the impact of population and income growth upon the availability in the near and the more distant future of recreational facilities and perhaps also upon the significance of this availability for the population's general health. This availability has been disregarded, though it is shrinking in per capita terms, because it is camouflaged by the methods used in calculating gross and net national product.

A sixth and related subject is the impact of population growth upon goods and services that at one time were free. Real income is being affected adversely by the decline in that component of living which is free in the sense that its use costs no one resources that bear a price because scarce. As population grows, the role of free goods and services diminishes, but the effect of this diminution is ignored in income studies, since they disregard the role of goods and services other than those which command a price because scarce. How has the availability of free goods been affected by population growth? This question is of importance from a policy point of view, since we must consider it when we give attention to the comparative attractiveness of different rates of population growth.

Seventh, although a considerable amount of theoretical work is being published on interregional economic relations and the determinants of industrial location, we should carefully assess the long-run trends in industrial location in the United States. Much remains to be done on the factors that play a major part in determining the location of industry. The locational alternatives open need to be specified and assessed. The impact of prospective technological change needs to be estimated and evaluated. Finally, alternative sets of locational objectives need to be isolated and contrasted.

SELECTED BIBLIOGRAPHY

ACHINSTEIN, ASHER. 1950. *Introduction to Business Cycles.* New York: Thomas Y. Crowell Co.

ADLER, H. A. 1945. "Absolute or Relative Rate of Decline in Population Growth," *Quarterly Journal of Economics,* LIX, 626–34.

ALLEN, R. G. D. 1956. *Mathematical Economics.* London: Macmillan & Co.

ANGELL, R. C. 1951. "The Moral Integration of American Cities," *American Journal of Sociology,* LVII, Part 2, 1–140.

ARDANT, G. 1950. "Les diables de Malthus," *Population,* V, 229–50.

ARNDT, H. W. 1948. "Savings in a State with a Stationary Population: Comment," *Quarterly Journal of Economics,* LXII, 623–29.

——. 1955. "External Economies in Economic Growth," *Economic Record,* XXXI, 192–214.

AYRES, EUGENE, and SCARLOTT, C. A. 1952. *Energy Sources: The Wealth of the World.* New York: McGraw-Hill.

BAKER, O. E. 1948. *The Population Prospect in Relation to the World's Agricultural Resources.* College Park: University of Maryland Press.

BARBER, C. L. 1953. "Population Growth and the Demand for Capital," *American Economic Review,* XLIII, 133–39.

BAUMOL, W. J. 1951. *Economic Dynamics: An Introduction.* New York: Macmillan Co.

BELSHAW, H. 1956. *Population Growth and Levels of Consumption.* New York: Institute of Pacific Relations.

BENNETT, M. K. 1954. *The World's Food.* New York: Harper & Bros.

BEVERIDGE, SIR WILLIAM H. 1930. *Unemployment.* London: Longmans, Green & Co.

BILLING, G. C. 1935. "Some Economic Effects of a Stationary Population," *Economic Record,* XI, 167–75.

BLANK, DAVID M. 1954. *The Volume of Residential Construction, 1889–1950.* (Technical Paper 9.) New York: National Bureau of Economic Research, Inc.

BOERMAN, W. E. 1940. "De Voedselcapaciteit der Aarde en de toekomstige Wereldbevolking," *Tijdschrift voor economische Geographie,* XXXI, 121–32.

BOGUE, D. J. 1949. *Structure of the Metropolitan Community.* Ann Arbor: University of Michigan Press.

——. 1950. *Metropolitan Decentralization: A Study of Differential Growth.* Oxford, Ohio: Scripps Foundation.

——, and THOMPSON, W. S. 1949. "Migration and Distance," *American Sociological Review,* XIV, 236–44.

BOULDING, K. E. 1950. *A Reconstruction of Economics.* New York: Wiley & Sons.

——. 1953a. "Toward a General Theory of Growth," *Canadian Journal of Economics and Political Science,* XIX, 326–40.

——. 1953b. "The Fruits of Progress and the Dynamics of Distribution," *American Economic Review,* XLVIII, No. 2, 473–83.

BOURGEOIS-PICHAT, J. 1949. "Migrations et balance des comptes," *Population,* IV, 417–32.

——. 1950. "La structure de la population et la sécurité sociale," *ibid.,* V, 435–92.

BOWEN, H. 1937. "Capital in Relation to Optimum Population," *Social Forces,* XV, 346–50.

BRADY, DOROTHY S., and FROEDER, MARTHA M. 1955. "Influence of Age on Saving and Spending Patterns," *Monthly Labor Review,* LXXVIII, 1240–44.

BRESARD, MARCEL, and GIRARD, ALAIN. 1950–51. "Mobilité sociale et dimension de la famille," *Population,* V, 533–66; VI, 103–24.

BROCKIE, M. D. 1950. "Population Growth and the Rate of Investment," *Southern Economic Journal,* XVII, 1–15.

BROWN, J. A. C. 1954. "The Consumption of Food in Relation to Household Composition and Income," *Econometrica*, XXII, 444–60.

BUQUET, L. 1956. *L'optimum de population*. Paris: Presses Universitaires de France.

BURKS, BARBARA. 1941. "Social Promotion In Relation to Differential Fecundity," *Human Biology*, XIII, 103–13.

BURNS, ARTHUR F. 1952. *The Instability of Consumer Spending*. New York: National Bureau of Economic Research, Inc.

CANNAN, E. 1894. *A History of the Theories of Production and Distribution in English Political Economy from 1776–1848*. London: P. S. King & Sons.

CARTER, HUGH (ed.). 1949. "Reappraising Our Immigration Policy," *Population and Population Studies, Annals of the American Academy of Political and Social Science*, CCLXII, 1–192.

CHANDRASEKHAR, S. 1954. "Population Growth, Socio-economic Development, and Living Standards," *International Labour Review*, LXIX, 527–46.

CLARK, C. 1940. *The Conditions of Economic Progress*. 1st ed., London: Macmillan & Co. 2d ed., 1951.

——. 1945. "The Economic Functions of a City," *Econometrica*, XIII, 97–113.

——. 1953. "Population Growth and Living Standards," *International Labour Review*, LXVIII, 99–117.

——. 1954. "World Supply and Requirements of Farm Products," *Journal of the Royal Statistical Society*, CXVII, 263–96.

COALE, A. J. 1956. "The Effects of Changes in Mortality and Fertility on Age Composition," *Milbank Memorial Fund Quarterly*, XXXIV, 79–114.

——, and HOOVER, E. M. 1958. *Population Growth and Economic Development in Low Income Countries*. Princeton: Princeton University Press.

COHN, S. S. 1934. *Die Theorie des Bevölkerungsoptimums: Ein Beitrag zur dogmengeschichtlichen und dogmenkritischen Behandlung des Bevölkerungsproblems*. Marburg: Buchdruckerei Hans Michel.

COLLINS, S. D. 1927. *Economic Status and Health*. (United States Public Health Bulletin No. 165.) Washington, D.C.

CORBETT, D. C. 1951. "Immigration and Economic Development," *Canadian Journal of Economics and Political Science*, XVII, 360–68.

CORDEN, W. M. 1955. "The Economic Limits to Population Increase," *Economic Record*, XXXI, 242–60.

COWGILL, D. O. 1949. "The Theory of Population Growth Cycles," *American Journal of Sociology*, LV, 163–70.

CRESSEY, GEORGE B. 1953. "Land for 2.4 Billion Neighbors," *Economic Geography*, XXIX, 1–9.

DALTON, H. 1928. "The Theory of Population," *Economica*, VIII, 28–50.

DALY, M. C. 1940. "An Approximation to a Geographical Multiplier," *Economic Journal*, L, 248–58.

DANIEL, G. H. 1939. "Labour Migration and Age Composition," *Sociological Review*, XXXI, 281–308.

DARIC, JEAN. 1948. *Vieillissement de la population et prolongation de la vie active*. Paris: Presses Universitaires de France.

——. 1949. "Mortalité, profession, et situation sociale," *Population*, IV, 671–94.

DAVIS, JOSEPH. S. 1953. "The Population Upsurge and the American Economy, 1945–80," *Journal of Political Economy*, LXI, 369–88.

——. 1954. "Adam Smith and the Human Stomach," *Quarterly Journal of Economics*, LXVIII, 275–86.

DAVIS, KINGSLEY. 1951. *The Population of India and Pakistan*. Princeton: Princeton University Press.

——. 1956. "The Amazing Decline of Mortality in Underdeveloped Areas," *American Economic Review*, XLVI, No. 2, 305–18.

DEAN, W. H. 1938. *The Theory of the Geographic Location of Economic Activities*. Ann Arbor: Edwards Brothers.

DERBER, MILTON (ed.). 1950. *The Aged and Society*. Champaign, Ill.: Industrial Relations Research Association.

DICKINSON, H. D. 1954–55. "A Note on Dynamic Economics," *Review of Economic Studies*, XXII, 169–79.

DIJKMANS, G. 1938. "Déterminisme démographique et sociologie économique pure," *Annales de la Société Scientifique de Bruxelles*, Ser. 3, fasc. 3, LVIII, 197–221.

DODD, S. C. 1950. "The Interactance Hypothesis," *American Sociological Review,* XV, 245–56.

DORFMAN, ROBERT. 1953. "Mathematical, or 'Linear,' Programming: A Nonmathematical Exposition," *American Economic Review,* XLIII, 797–825.

———, et al. 1954. "Economic Implications of an Aging Population: Review of the University of California Research Project," *American Economic Review,* XLIV, No. 2, 634–79.

DOUBLET, J. 1948. "Family Allowances in France," *Population Studies,* II, 219–39.

DUESENBERRY, JAMES S. 1949. *Income, Saving, and the Theory of Consumer Behavior.* Cambridge: Harvard University Press.

———. 1950. "Some Aspects of the Theory of Economic Development," *Explorations in Entrepreneurial History,* III, 63–102.

DURAND, JOHN. 1948. *The Labor Force in the United States, 1890–1960.* New York: Social Science Research Council.

———. 1953. "Population Structure as a Factor in Manpower and Dependency Problems of Underdeveloped Countries," *Population Bulletin of the United Nations,* III, 1–16.

ECKHAUS, R. S. 1955. "The Factor Proportions Problem in Underdeveloped Areas," *American Economic Review,* XLV, 539–65.

FAWCETT, C. B. 1947. "The Numbers and Distribution of Mankind," *Scientific Monthly,* LXIV, 389–96.

FELLNER, W. 1940–41. "The Technological Argument of the Stagnation Thesis," *Quarterly Journal of Economics,* LV, 638–51.

———. 1946. *Monetary Policies and Full Employment.* Berkeley: University of California Press.

———, et al. 1951. *Money, Trade, and Economic Growth: In Honor of Henry Williams.* New York: Macmillan Co.

FERBER, ROBERT. 1953. *A Study of Aggregate Consumption Functions.* (Technical Paper 8.) New York: National Bureau of Economic Research, Inc.

FISHER, JANET A. 1952a. "Postwar Changes in Income and Savings among Consumers in Different Age Groups," *Econometrica,* XX, 47–70.

———. 1952b. "Income, Spending, and Saving Patterns of Consumer Units in Different Age Groups," in *Studies in Income and Wealth.* New York: National Bureau of Economic Research.

FORSYTH, W. D. 1942. *The Myth of Open Spaces.* Melbourne and London: Melbourne University Press.

FRANZSEN, D. G. 1942. "The Secular Stagnation Thesis and the Problem of Economic Stability," *South African Journal of Economics,* X, 282–94.

FRIEDMAN, MILTON. 1953. *Essays in Positive Economics.* Chicago: University of Chicago Press.

———. 1957. *A Theory of the Consumption Function.* Princeton: Princeton University Press.

FRUMKIN, G. 1950. "Pre-war and Post-war Trends in Manpower of European Countries," *Population Studies,* IV, 209–40.

FUA, G. 1940. *La conception économique de l'optimum du peuplement; population et bien-être.* Lausanne: Concorde.

FUKUOKA, MASAO. 1955. "Full Employment and Constant Coefficients of Production," *Quarterly Journal of Economics,* LXIX, 23–44.

GHOSH, D. 1946. *Pressure of Population and Economic Efficiency in India.* New Delhi: Indian Council of World Affairs.

GILLE, H. 1948a. "Recent Developments in Swedish Population Policy, Part I," *Population Studies,* II, 3–70.

———. 1948b. "Recent Developments in Swedish Population Policy, Part II," *ibid.,* 129–84.

———. 1952. "Family Welfare Measures in Denmark," *ibid.,* VI, 172–210.

———. 1954. "Scandinavian Family Allowances: Demographic Aspects," *Eugenics Quarterly,* I, 182–90.

GINI, CORRADO. 1946. "Los efectos demográficos de las migraciones internacionales," *Revista internacional de sociología,* IV, 351–88.

GLASS, D. V. 1940. *Population Policies and Movements in Europe.* Oxford: Oxford University Press.

GLASS, R., and DAVIDSON, F. G. 1951. "Household Structure and Housing Needs," *Population Studies,* IV, 395–420.

GOLDENBERG, LEON. 1946. "Saving in a State with a Stationary Population,"

Quarterly Journal of Economics, LXI, 40–65.

GOLDSMITH, RAYMOND, *et al.* 1956. *A Study of Saving in the United States.* Princeton: Princeton University Press.

GOODWIN, R. W. 1951. "The Nonlinear Accelerator and the Persistence of Business Cycles," *Econometrica,* XIX, 1–17.

GORDON, R. A. 1956. "Population Growth and the Capital Coefficient," *American Economic Review,* XLVI, 307–22.

GOTTLIEB, M. 1945. "The Theory of Optimum Population for a Closed Economy," *Journal of Political Economy,* LIII, 289–316.

———. 1949. "Optimum Population, Foreign Trade, and World Economy," *Population Studies,* III, 151–69.

HAAVELMO, T. 1954. *A Study in the Theory of Economic Evolution.* Amsterdam: North Holland Publishing Co.

HABERLER, GOTTFRIED. 1941. *Prosperity and Depression.* 3d ed. Geneva: League of Nations.

———. 1955. *A Survey of International Trade Theory.* Princeton: Princeton University Press.

HAJNAL, J., and HENDERSON, A. 1950. "The Economic Position of the Family," *Papers of the Royal Commission on Population,* V, 1–23.

HALEY, B. F. (ed.). 1952. *Survey of Contemporary Economics.* Homewood, Ill.: Richard D. Irwin, Inc.

HAMBERG, D. 1956. *Economic Growth and Instability.* New York: W. W. Norton & Co., Inc.

HANSEN, A. H. 1939. "Economic Progress and Declining Population Growth," *American Economic Review,* XXIX, 1–15.

———. 1940. "Extensive Expansion and Population Growth," *Journal of Political Economy,* XLVIII, 583–85.

———. 1941. *Fiscal Policy and Business Cycles.* New York: W. W. Norton & Co.

———. 1947. *Economic Policy and Full Employment.* New York: McGraw-Hill.

———. 1951. *Business Cycles and National Income.* New York: W. W. Norton & Co.

HANSSON, K. E. 1952. "A Theory of the System of Multilateral Trade," *American Economic Review,* XLII, 59–69.

HARROD, R. F. 1939. "Modern Population Trends," *Manchester School of Economic and Social Studies,* X, 1–20.

———. 1940. "The Population Problem: A Rejoinder," *Manchester School of Economic and Social Studies,* XI, 47–58.

———. 1948. *Towards a Dynamic Economics.* London: Macmillan & Co.

HEALEY, DEREK T., and NILSON, STEN S. 1954. "Population Growth and Living Standards: Replies to Mr. Clark's Article," *International Labour Review,* LXIX, 68–76.

HENDERSON, A. M. 1949–50a. "The Cost of a Family," *Review of Economic Studies,* XVII, 127–48.

———. 1949–50b. "The Cost of Children," *Population Studies,* III, 130–50; IV, 267–98.

HICKS, J. R. 1946. *Value and Capital.* Oxford: Oxford University Press.

———. 1950. *A Contribution to the Theory of the Trade Cycle.* Oxford: Oxford University Press.

HIGGINS, B. H. 1950. "The Theory of Increasing Underemployment," *Economic Journal,* LX, 255–74.

HILDEBRAND, G. H., and MACE, A. 1950. "The Employment Multiplier in an Expanding Industrial Market: Los Angeles County, 1940–47," *Review of Economics and Statistics,* XXXII, 241–49.

HOFSTEE, E. W. 1950. "Population Pressure and the Future of Western Civilization in Europe," *American Journal of Sociology,* LV, 523–24.

HOGBEN, LANCELOT (ed.). 1938. *Political Arithmetic.* New York: George Allen & Unwin.

HOOVER, C. B. 1948. "Keynes and the Economic System," *Journal of Political Economy,* LVI, 392–402.

HOOVER, E. M. 1948. *The Location of Economic Activity.* New York: McGraw-Hill.

HOPKIN, W. A. B. 1953. "The Economics of an Aging Population," *Lloyds Bank Review,* 25–36.

HOSELITZ, BERT F. 1953. "The Role of Cities in the Economic Growth of Underdeveloped Countries," *Journal of Political Economy,* LXI, 195.

HOYT, HOMER. 1941. "Forces of Urban Centralization and Decentralization,"

American Journal of Sociology, XLVI, 843 ff.

HOYT, HOMER. 1951. "Is City Growth Controlled by Mathematics or Physical Laws?" *Land Economics*, XXVII, 259–62.

HYRENIUS, HANNES. 1946. "The Relation between Birth-Rates and Economic Activity in Sweden, 1920–1940," *Bulletin of the Oxford University Institute of Statistics*, VIII, 15 ff.

———. 1949. "Summary Indices of the Age Distribution of a Population," *Population Studies*, II, 454–60.

ISAAC, J. 1947. *Economics of Migration*. New York: Oxford University Press.

ISARD, WALTER. 1942. "Transport Development and Building Cycles," *Quarterly Journal of Economics*, LVII, 90–112.

———. 1949. "The General Theory of Location and Space Economy," *ibid.*, LXIII, 476–506.

———. 1951. "Interregional and Regional Input-Output Analysis: A Model of a Space Economy," *Review of Economic Statistics*, XXXIII, 318–28.

———. 1952. "A General Location Principle of an Optimum Space-economy," *Econometrica*, XX, 406–30.

———. 1954. "Location Theory and Trade Theory: Short-run Analysis," *Quarterly Journal of Economics*, LXVIII, 305–20.

———. 1956. *Location and Space-economy*. New York: John Wiley & Sons.

———, and KAVESH, ROBERT. 1954. "Economic Structural Interrelations of Metropolitan Regions," *American Journal of Sociology*, LX, 152–62.

———, and PECK, MERTON. 1954. "Location Theory and International and Interregional Trade Theory," *Quarterly Journal of Economics*, LXVIII, 97–114.

———, and WHITNEY, VINCENT. 1949. "Metropolitan Site Selection," *Social Forces*, XXVII, 263–69.

———. 1951. "Distance Inputs and the Space Economy," *Quarterly Journal of Economics*, LXV, 181–298, 373–99.

———. 1955. *Atomic Power: An Economic and Social Analysis*. Philadelphia: Blakiston Co.

JEROME, H. 1926. *Migration and Business Cycles*. New York: National Bureau of Economic Research.

JEWKES, J. 1939. "The Population Scare," *Manchester School of Economic and Social Studies*, X, 101–21.

JOHNSON, E. A. J. 1937. *Predecessors of Adam Smith*. New York: Prentice-Hall.

JONES, G. T. 1933. *Increasing Return*. Cambridge: Cambridge University Press.

JONES, MARTIN V. 1944. "Secular Trends and Idle Resources," *Journal of Business of the University of Chicago*, XVII, Part 2, 1–72.

KATONA, GEORGE. 1951. *Psychological Analyses of Economic Behavior*. New York: McGraw-Hill.

KEIRSTEAD, B. S. 1948. *The Theory of Economic Change*. Toronto: Macmillan Co. of Canada.

KEYNES, J. M. 1937. "Some Economic Consequences of a Declining Population," *Eugenics Review*, Vol. XXIX.

KIRK, DUDLEY. 1942. "The Relation of Employment to the Level of Births in Germany," *Milbank Memorial Fund Quarterly*, XX, 126–38.

———. 1946. *Europe's Population in the Interwar Years*. Geneva: League of Nations.

KLEIN, LAWRENCE R. 1950. *Economic Fluctuations in the United States, 1921–41*. New York: John Wiley & Sons.

KOO, A. Y. C. 1955. "Per Capita Rate of Economic Growth," *Weltwirtschaftliches Archiv*, LXXIV, 47–61.

KURIHARA, K. K. (ed.). 1954. *Post-Keynesian Economics*. New Brunswick: Rutgers University Press.

KUZNETS, SIMON. 1949. *Problems in the Study of Economic Growth*. New York: National Bureau of Economic Research.

———. 1953. *Economic Change*. New York: W. W. Norton & Co.

———. 1956. *Toward a Theory of Economic Growth*. Baltimore: Johns Hopkins University.

———. 1956–57. "Quantitative Aspects of the Economic Growth of Nations" (in two parts), *Economic Development and Cultural Change*, Vol. V, Supplements.

LAFITTE, F. 1941. "The Economic Effects of a Declining Population," *Eugenics Review*, XXXII, 121–34.

LANGE, O. 1939. "Is the American Economy Contracting?" *American Economic Review*, XXIX, 503–13.

LAURSEN, SVEND. 1952. "Production Functions and the Theory of International Trade," *American Economic Review,* XLII, 540–57.

LEIBENSTEIN, H. 1954. *A Theory of Economic-demographic Development.* Princeton: Princeton University Press.

———. 1957. *Economic Backwardness and Economic Growth.* New York: John Wiley & Sons.

———, and GALENSON, W. 1955. "Investment Criteria, Productivity, and Economic Development," *Quarterly Journal of Economics,* LXIX, 343–70.

LEONTIEF, W. 1951. *The Structure of American Economy.* 2d ed. London: Oxford University Press.

LÉTINIER, GEORGES. 1946. "Progrés technique, destructions de guerre, et optimum de population," *Population,* I, 35 ff.

LEWIS, W. A. 1950. *Industrial Development in the Caribbean.* Port of Spain: Caribbean Commission.

———. 1951. "Food and Raw Materials," *District Bank Review,* No. 99, pp. 1–11.

———. 1955. *The Theory of Economic Growth.* London: George Allen & Unwin.

LINDBERG, J. 1945. "Food Supply under a Program of Freedom from Want," *Social Research,* XII, 181–204.

LÖSCH, AUGUST. 1936. *Bevölkerungswellen und Wechsellagen.* Jena: Gustav Fischer.

———. 1936–37. "Population Cycles as a Cause of Business Cycles," *Quarterly Journal of Economics,* LI, 649–62.

———. 1954. *The Economics of Location.* New Haven: Yale University Press.

LORIMER, F. 1951. "Dynamics of Age Structure in a Population with Initially High Fertility and Mortality," *Population Bulletin of the United Nations,* I, 31–41.

———, and ROBACK, H. 1940. "Economics of the Family Relative to the Number of Children," *Milbank Memorial Fund Quarterly,* XVIII, 114–36.

LYDALL, HAROLD. 1955. "The Life Cycles in Income, Saving, and Asset Ownership," *Econometrica,* XXIII, 113–50.

MACK, RUTH P. 1954. *Factors Influencing Consumption: An Experimental Analysis of Shoe Buying.* Technical Paper 10. New York: National Bureau of Economic Research, Inc.

McKENZIE, LIONEL W. 1955. "Equality of Factor Prices in World Trade," *Econometrica,* XXIII, 239–57.

MAKOWER, HELEN, et al. 1940. "Studies in Mobility of Labour," *Oxford Economic Papers,* IV, 39–62.

MARTY, A. L. 1953. "Diminishing Returns and the Relative Share of Labor," *Quarterly Journal of Economics,* LXVII, 614–18.

MATTHEWS, R. C. O. 1954–55. "The Saving Function and the Problem of Trend and Cycle," *Review of Economic Studies,* XXII, 75–95.

MEADE, J. E. 1955. *Trade and Welfare.* London: Oxford University Press.

MILLER, HERMAN P. 1955. *Income of the American People.* New York: John Wiley & Sons.

MITRA, ASHOK. 1955. *The Share of Wages in National Income.* The Hague: Nijhoff.

MOORE, W. E. 1944. *Economic Demography of Southern and Eastern Europe.* Geneva: League of Nations.

MUKERJEE, RADAHAKAMAL. 1943. *The Political Economy of Population.* Bombay: Longmans, Green.

MYRDAL, ALVA. 1941. *Nation and Family.* New York: Harper & Bros.

MYRDAL, G. 1933. "Industrialization and Population," in *Economic Essays in Honour of Gustav Cassel.* London: George Allen & Unwin.

———. 1940. *Population: A Problem for Democracy.* Cambridge: Harvard University Press.

NEISSER, H. 1944. "The Economics of a Stationary Population," *Social Research,* XI, 470–90.

NEW YORK STATE LEGISLATIVE COMMITTEE ON PROBLEMS OF AGING. 1948. *Birthdays Don't Count.* Albany: Newburgh.

O'BRIEN, G. O. 1948. *The Phantom of Plenty.* Dublin: Clonmore & Reynolds.

OHLIN, B. 1933. *Inter-regional and International Trade.* Cambridge: Harvard University Press.

PAISH, F. W., and PEACOCK, A. T. 1954. "Economics of Dependence (1952–82)," *Economica,* XXI, 279–99.

PARNES, H. S. 1954. *Research on Labor Mobility.* New York: Social Science Research Council.

PEACOCK, ALAN T. 1952. "Theory of Population and Modern Economic Analysis," *Population Studies*, VI, 114–22.

PEACOCK, ALAN T. 1954. "Theory of Population and Modern Economic Analysis," *Population Studies*, VII, 227–34.

PEARL, R. 1939. *The Natural History of Population*. New York: Oxford University Press.

PEARSON, F. A., and HARPER, F. A. 1945. *The World's Hunger*. Ithaca: Cornell University Press.

PEDERSEN, JORGEN. 1948. "Interest Rates, Employment, and Changes in Population," *Kyklos*, II, 1–15.

PENROSE, E. F. 1934. *Population Theories and Their Application, with Special Reference to Japan*. Stanford, Calif.: Food Research Institute.

PIDDINGTON, R. A. 1956. *The Limits of Mankind*. Bristol: John Wright & Sons.

PRESIDENT'S MATERIALS POLICY COMMISSION. 1952. *Resources for Freedom*. Washington, D.C.: Government Printing Office.

PRICE, D. O. 1948. "Distance and Direction as Vectors of Internal Migration, 1935 to 1940," *Social Forces*, XXVII, 48–53.

———. 1951. "Some Socio-economic Factors in Internal Migration," *ibid.*, XXIX, 410–15.

PROKOPOVICH, S. N. 1946. *L'industrialisation des pays agricoles et la structure de l'économie mondiale après la guerre*. Paris: Neuchâtel, Éditions de la Baconniére.

RAUBER, EARL L. 1956. "The Realm of the Red Queen," *Monthly Review of the Federal Reserve Bank of Atlanta*, January, 1956, pp. 3–4.

REDDAWAY, W. B. 1937. "Special Obstacles to Full Employment in a Wealthy Community," *Economic Journal*, XLVII, 297–307.

———. 1939. *The Economics of a Declining Population*. New York: Macmillan Co.

ROBINSON, JOAN. 1951. *Collected Economic Papers*. New York: Augustus M. Kelley, Inc.

———. 1952. *The Rate of Interest and Other Essays*. London: Macmillan & Co.

ROBINSON, ROMNEY. 1956. "Factor Proportions and Comparative Advantage," *Quarterly Journal of Economics*, LXX, 169–92, 346–63.

ROSEN, M. M. 1942. "Population Growth, Investment, and Economic Recovery," *American Economic Review*, XXXII, 122–25.

ROSTOW, W. W. 1952. *The Process of Economic Growth*. New York: W. W. Norton & Co.

ROTERUS, VICTOR. 1946. "Effects of Population Growth and Non-growth on the Well-being of Cities," *American Sociological Review*, XI, 90–97.

ROYAL COMMISSION ON POPULATION. 1950. "Report of the Economics Committee," *Papers of the Royal Commission on Population*, Vol. III. London: H.M. Stationery Office.

RUSSELL, J. C. 1948. *British Medieval Population*. Albuquerque: University of New Mexico Press.

RYBCZYNSKI, T. M. 1955. "Factor Endowment and Relative Commodity Prices," *Economica*, XXII, 336–41.

SALTER, R. M. 1948. "World Soil and Fertilizer Resources in Relation to Food Needs," *Chronica botanica*, XI, 226–35.

SAMUELSON, P. A. 1947. *Foundations of Economic Analysis*. Cambridge: Harvard University Press.

———. 1948. "International Trade and the Equilisation of Factor Prices," *Economic Journal*, LVIII, 163–84.

———. 1949. "International Factor-Price Equalisation Once Again," *ibid.*, 181–97.

———. 1953–54. "Prices of Factors and Goods in General Equilibrium," *Review of Economic Studies*, XXI, 1–20.

SAUVY, ALFRED. 1948. "Social and Economic Consequences of the Aging of Western European Populations," *Population Studies*, II, 115–24.

———. 1952. *Théorie générale de la population*. Paris: Presses Universitaires de France.

———. 1954. "Sociétés verticales et classes moyennes," *Cahiers internationaux de sociologie*, I, 568–86.

SCHIFF, ERIC. 1946. "Family Size and Residential Construction," *American Economic Review*, XXXVI, 97–112.

SCHMID, C. F. 1950. "The Ecology of the American City," *American Sociological Review*, XV, 264–81.

SCHOEFFLER, S. 1955. *The Failures of Eco-*

nomics: A Diagnostic Study. Cambridge: Harvard University Press.

SEARS, PAUL B. 1958. "The Inexorable Problem of Space," *Science,* CXXVII, 9–16.

SIMON, H. A. 1957. *Models of Man.* New York: John Wiley & Sons.

SINGER, H. W. 1936. "The 'courbe des populations,' a Parallel to Pareto's Law," *Economic Journal,* XLVI, 254–63.

SMITH, KENNETH. 1952. "Some Observations on Modern Malthusianism," *Population Studies,* VI, 92–105.

SOLOMON, MORTON. 1948. "The Structure of the Market in Underdeveloped Economies," *Quarterly Journal of Economics,* LXII, 519–41.

SPENGLER, J. J. 1936. "French Population Theory since 1800," *Journal of Political Economy,* XLIV, 577–611, 743–66.

———. 1938. *France Faces Depopulation.* Durham: Duke University Press.

———. 1942. *French Predecessors of Malthus.* Durham: Duke University Press.

———. 1947–48. "Aspects of the Economics of Population Growth," *Southern Economic Journal,* XIV, 124–47, 233–65.

———. 1950. "Some Economic Aspects of the Subsidization by the State of the Formation of 'Human Capital,'" *Kyklos,* IV, 316–43.

———. 1951. "The Population Obstacle to Human Betterment," *American Economic Review,* XLI, 343–54.

———. 1952. "Population Theory," in *A Survey of Contemporary Economics,* ed. B. F. HALEY. Homewood, Ill.: Richard D. Irwin, Inc.

———. 1953. "Changes in Income Distribution and Social Stratification: A Note," *American Journal of Sociology,* LIX, 247–59.

———. 1954. "Welfare Economics and the Problem of Overpopulation," *Scientia,* LXXXIX, 128–38, 166–75.

———. 1956a. "Population Threatens Prosperity," *Harvard Business Review,* XXXIV, 85–94.

———. 1956b. "The Population Problem: Dimensions, Potentialities, Limitations," *American Economic Review,* Vol. XLVI.

———. 1956c. "Capital Requirements and Population Growth in Underdeveloped Countries: Their Interrelations," *Econom-*

ic Development and Cultural Change, Vol. IV.

STAEHLE, HANS. 1943. "Ability, Wages, and Income," *Review of Economic Statistics,* XXV, 77–87.

STANGELAND, C. E. 1904. *Pre-Malthusian Doctrines of Population.* New York: Columbia University Press.

STASSART, J. 1957. *Malthus et la population.* Liège: Faculté de Droit de l'Université de Liège.

STAUDINGER, H. 1939. "Stationary Population: Stagnant Economy?" *Social Research,* VI, 141–53.

STEWART, J. Q. 1947. "Empirical Mathematical Rules Concerning the Distribution and Equilibrium of Population," *Geographical Review,* XXXVII, 461–85.

———. 1948. "Demographic Gravitation: Evidence and Applications," *Sociometry,* XI, 31–58.

———. 1950. "Potential of Population and Its Relationship to Marketing," in *Theory in Marketing,* ed. REAVIS COX and WROE ALDERSON. Chicago: R. D. Irwin.

STIGLER, GEORGE J. 1952. *The Theory of Price.* Rev. ed. New York: Macmillan Co.

STOLPER, W. F. 1941. "The Demand for Houses: The Population Factor," *Quarterly Journal of Economics,* XLV, 79–107.

STONE, RICHARD. 1955. "Misery and Bliss," *Proceedings of the World Population Conference,* V, 779–816. New York: United Nations.

SUSSWEIN, E. 1948. "Family Allowances in Belgium," *Population Studies,* II, 278–91.

SVENNILSON, I. 1954. *Growth and Stagnation in the European Economy.* Geneva: United Nations.

SWEEZY, A. R. 1940–41. "Population Growth and Investment Opportunity," *Quarterly Journal of Economics,* LV, 64–79.

———. 1942. "Wages and Investment," *Journal of Political Economy,* L, 117–29.

TERBORGH, GEORGE. 1945. *The Bogey of Economic Maturity.* Chicago: Machinery & Allied Products Institute.

THOMAS, BRINLEY. 1954. *Migration and Economic Growth.* Cambridge: Cambridge University Press.

———. 1958. *Economics of International Migration.* London: Macmillan & Co.

THOMAS, D. S. 1941. *Social and Economic Aspects of Swedish Population Movements, 1750–1933.* New York: Macmillan Co.

——, and GALBRAITH, V. L. 1941. "Birth Rates and Interwar Business Cycles," *Journal of the American Statistical Association,* XXXVI, 465–76.

THOMPSON, W. S. 1947. *The Growth of Metropolitan Districts in the United States, 1900–40.* Washington, D.C.: Bureau of the Census.

THORNDIKE, E. L. 1939. *Your City.* New York: Harcourt Brace & Co.

——. 1940. *144 Smaller Cities.* New York: Harcourt Brace & Co.

TIETZE, CHRISTOPHER. 1943. "Life Tables for Social Classes in England," *Milbank Memorial Fund Quarterly,* XXI, 182 ff.

TIMLIN, M. F. 1951. *Does Canada Need More People?* Toronto: Oxford University Press.

TINBERGEN, JAN. 1942. "Zur Theorie der langfristigen Wirtschaftsentwicklung," *Weltwirtschaftliches Archiv,* LV, 511–47.

——. 1949. "The Equalization of Factor Prices between Free-trade Areas," *Metroeconomica,* I, 39–47.

——, and POLAK, J. J. 1950. *The Dynamics of Business Cycles.* Chicago: University of Chicago Press.

TSIANG, S. C. 1942. "The Effect of Population Growth on the General Level of Employment and Activity," *Economica,* IX, 325–32.

ULLMAN, E. 1941. "A Theory of Location for Cities," *American Journal of Sociology,* XLVI, 853–64.

UNITED NATIONS. 1951. "Some Quantitative Aspects of the Aging of Western Populations," *Population Bulletin of the United Nations,* I, 42-57.

——. 1953. *The Determinants and Consequences of Population Trends.* New York: United Nations.

——. 1954. "The Cause of the Aging of Populations: Declining Mortality or Declining Fertility?" *Population Bulletin of the United Nations,* IV, 30–38.

——. 1956. *The Aging of Populations and Its Economic and Social Implications.* ("Population Studies," No. 26.) New York: United Nations.

USHER, A. P. 1947. "The Resource Requirements of an Industrial Economy," *Journal of Economic History,* VII, Supplement, 35–46.

USHER, THOMAS H. 1951. "An Appraisal of the Canadian Family Allowance System," *Review of Social Economy,* IX, 124–36.

VIANELLI, S. 1936. "A General Dynamic Demographic Scheme and Its Application to Italy and the United States," *Econometrica,* IV, 269–83.

VILLARD, HENRY H. 1955. "Some Notes on Population and Living Levels," *Review of Economics and Statistics,* XXXVII, 189–95.

VINCENT, P., and HENRY, L. 1947. "Rythme maximum d'accroissement d'une population stable," *Population,* II, 663–80.

VINING, RUTLEDGE. 1949. "The Region as an Entity and Certain Variations To Be Observed in the Study of Systems of Regions," *American Economic Review,* XXXIX, 89–104.

——. 1955. "A Description of Certain Spatial Aspects of an Economic System," *Economic Development and Cultural Change,* III, 147–95.

WATSON, C. 1952*a.* "Birth Control and Abortion in France since 1939," *Population Studies,* V, 261–86.

——. 1952*b.* "Recent Developments in French Immigration Policy," *ibid.,* VI, 3–38.

——. 1953. "Housing Policy and Population Problems in France," *ibid.,* VII, 14–45.

——. 1954*a.* "A Survey of Recent Belgian Population Policy," *ibid.,* VIII, 152–87.

——. 1954*b.* "Population Policy in France: Allowances and Other Benefits," *ibid.,* VII, 263–86; VIII, 46–93.

WEBBER, I. L. 1956. *Aging: A Current Appraisal.* Gainesville: University of Florida Press.

WHELPTON, P. K. 1939. "Population Policy for the United States," *Journal of Heredity,* XXX, 401–6.

——. 1954. *Cohort Fertility.* Princeton: Princeton University Press.

WOLFBEIN, S. L. 1949. "The Length of Working Life," *Population Studies,* III, 286–94.

WOLFE, A. B. 1928–29. "The Population

Problem since the World War: A Survey of Literature and Research," *Journal of Political Economy*, XXXVI, 662–85, 529–59.

WOOL, HAROLD. 1950. *Tables of Working Life*. (United States Department of Labor Bulletin No. 1001.) Washington, D.C.: Government Printing Office.

WOYTINSKY, W. S., and WOYTINSKY, E. S. 1953. *World Population and Production*. New York: Twentieth Century Fund.

YOUNG, A. A. 1928. "Increasing Returns and Economic Progress," *Economic Journal*, XXXVIII, 527–40.

ZIMMERMAN, E. W. 1951. *World Resources and Industries*. 2d ed. New York: Harper & Bros.

ZIPF, G. K. 1949. *Human Behavior and the Principle of Least Effort*. Cambridge, Mass.: Addison-Wesley Press.

ZWICK, CHARLES. 1957. "Demographic Variation: Its Impact on Consumer Behavior," *Review of Economics and Statistics*, XXXIX, 451–56.

33. Sociology and Demography

WILBERT E. MOORE

The development of all knowledge proceeds both by specialization and by the bridging of specialties. At any time the modes of specialization are likely to be conventional, arbitrary, and perhaps even accidental. And since ordered scientific knowledge is always abstracted from the raw materials of reality, there develop marked tendencies for specialties to intersect and overlap and for questions to arise that can be answered only by transcending conventional boundaries, by adopting points of view and postures typical of other disciplines. If these circumstances justify an examination of the relations between scientific fields, they do not warrant attempts to set precise boundaries, adjudicate jurisdictional disputes, or allocate a specialty that intersects a number of disciplines to the exclusive control of one of them.

Demography is first discussed below as a subfield of sociology, with full recognition that the jurisdiction of sociology is not exclusive. Attention is then turned to sociological theory in relation to demography and finally to demographic theory in relation to sociology.

DEMOGRAPHY AS A SUBFIELD OF SOCIOLOGY

Although demography deals with a somewhat distinctive body of data, has specialized techniques for analyzing those data, and has some unifying theory or general perspective, it is generally regarded as a "branch" of other fields (commonly sociology, economics, or geography). The simple test of

this assertion is the absence of college and university "departments" of demography or population studies and the rarity even of "chairs" of demography in other departments. Whether this represents historical accident rather than a "correct" administration of education is not likely to be settled by dispassionate discussion. It is perhaps noteworthy that the last two decades or so have witnessed an increasing number of university-sponsored research institutes in population studies which normally conduct advanced training either through formal seminars or through supervised research.

At least in American college organization, demography is allocated to sociology more frequently than to other disciplines. The majority of courses are offered in sociology departments, and sociology is consequently the formal field in which at least a plurality of practicing demographers have received advanced degrees. Since the field of advanced training is likely to have some bearing on the direction of research interests, some of the intimate connections between sociology and demography may be traced to this source rather than to the interpenetration of "independent" disciplines.

Whether the American student of sociology specializes in demography or not, he is at least likely to get some elementary introduction to the study of population in general sociology courses. Most of the standard "introductory" or "principles" texts in sociology have larger or smaller sections explicitly devoted to population size and composition, fertility, mortality, and migration. The level of theoretical and methodological sophistication in the treatment of demographic subjects is of course highly variable among the widely-used texts. The primary point of present interest is not the adequacy of their introduction to a technical field, but rather the fact that the attempt is made to treat demography as a subfield of sociology.

As a final, and admittedly incidental, indication of American practice in classification of specialties, it may be noted that in the *Dictionary of Occupational Titles*, "Demographer" is listed and briefly described under the general heading "Sociologist" (U.S. Department of Labor, 1949, p. 1241).

Since demography is related to a number of standard scientific disciplines, it might be argued that the predominant American practice of treating the field as a part of sociology is merely arbitrary and conventional. This again is a question not likely to be easily settled on strictly logical grounds. Nor is it necessary to make the attempt for present purposes; it seems more appropriate to accept current practice and identify some of its major consequences before turning to the relations between the fields as somewhat independent but interdependent ways of organizing and analyzing social phenomena.

If demography be accepted, for the moment, as a subfield of sociology, what are its special characteristics in the more general field? Three points of emphasis in demography are distinct from other sociological thought and research.

(1) Demography entails a persistent emphasis on quantitative variables and measurement. Much of sociology comprises non-quantitative description and generalizations about social patterns and structures that are not expressed in terms readily amenable to quantifi-

cation. Demography is accordingly recognized by sociologists as one of the more "advanced" specialties in the field and one of the few that uses precise mathematical models as well as statistical techniques. It may be added, without attempting to discount this position of some "prestige" in sociology, that the sheer existence of statistics collected at public expense has greatly aided the development of demography in the direction of measurement. Other sociological specialties must rely on less comprehensive and less adequate statistical sources or, very commonly, "manufacture" their own statistics in experiments or expensive field surveys. Moreover, the primary demographic elements (persons and vital events—births and deaths), although involving some problems of definition, are easier to identify than are many elements in other sociological fields (e.g., role, pattern, norm, and even community).

(2) In general, demography deals with the "distributive" characteristics of a society, as compared with unifying concepts like "culture" or "social structure." Population size and growth and such characteristics as age and sex provide some of the basic dimensions of social phenomena that may then be analyzed with reference to other variables. This distinction should not be exaggerated, however. Demographers deal also with various population "characteristics" which are primarily social and which vary among societies and cultures. Perhaps because of the close professional ties with sociology, demographers even seem occasionally to neglect current "distributive" aspects of population in favor of analyses more closely linked to aspects of social structure as commonly studied by sociologists. For example, current research on fertility appears to be more concerned with completed size of family—a subsystem of society—than with variations

in current fertility rates applicable to the society as a whole. The latter may vary through time somewhat independently of the former and yet retain social and even sociological significance: for example, variations in school populations, entrants to the labor force, proportions of new voters, dependency ratios, and consumption patterns. It will be suggested later that sociological theory and analysis is especially weak with reference to social change. It appears that to the extent that current demographic research attempts to derive benefit from sociology, demography is likely to rely more on static and segmental analysis than on an explanation of temporal variations, particularly over a short period.

(3) It is, then, precisely in its explicit concern with time and change that demography offers another special characteristic as a subfield of sociology. Much demographic measurement involves rates and trends in rates. It is true that these may be, and often are, used essentially for static cross-sectional comparison (as in fertility and mortality differentials, or in the classification of populations into growth types). However, it is also true that persistent emphasis on historic changes in population size and composition and on population projections provides the non-demographically oriented sociologist with examples and models for the analysis of other trends. For example, a demographic growth model may be applied, with minor modifications, to any segment of a social system. Analysis of trends in formally organized associations may be concerned solely with total size or with internal composition also. For the latter, especially, "component rate" projections are indicated, just as they are with standard demographic forecasts. Organizational accessions may be treated as births or inmigrants, separations as deaths or outmigrants. Rates of accessions and sep-

arations may be applied to various parts or sections or to other social categories within an association. So much is fairly obvious, although not thereby standard practice in sociological research. There are also somewhat subtler applications of demographic analysis. Again a single example may suffice. It is well known that a population may be growing by natural increase and still not be *effectively* reproducing itself for the long run if the growth is in considerable measure a result of an age composition temporarily favorable to fertility, but the actual size of families is too small to insure continuous replacement in subsequent generations, given intervening mortality. A similar view of "underlying trend" applies to the replacement of persons in skilled and professional occupations; their numbers may be currently growing owing to past occupational choices, but subject to subsequent decline in view of the failure of similar choices and/or training facilities at the appropriate younger ages.

In the remainder of this chapter demography is treated as a largely independent discipline, which intersects sociology in various ways and at numerous points. The organization of the discussion is essentially fourfold: (1) functional theory in sociology and its relation to demography, (2) the relation of special fields and topics in sociology to demography, (3) "the" population problem and its relation to sociology, and (4) the relation of special fields and topics in demography to sociology. This organization represents an attempt to focus, initially, on a central feature of the theory of each field, and then, since in neither field is it readily feasible to speak of integrated theory, to attend to additional points of interrelation. An inevitable result of this organization will be some overlapping of points discussed, but this seems to reflect the actual situation.

SOCIOLOGICAL THEORY AND DEMOGRAPHY

To refer to sociological theory in the singular is still somewhat hazardous in a rapidly developing and highly variegated scholarly field. Yet recent years have seen some convergences on central concepts and frames of reference and substantial agreement on at least some theoretical orientations despite the multiple terminologies and research specialties.

Requisite Functions as a Key to Universal Structures

One major concern of sociological theory at the highest level of generalization is the identification of universals in social systems. This development has many intellectual sources, which will not be traced here. Recent formulations of issues and propositions, however, derive fairly directly from the so-called structural-functional approach. In general this "approach" or frame of reference studies repeated patterns of action (structures) and their consequences (functions). Although such questions are very old in sociological analysis, under these or other names, and can be highly particular in their applications, they also prompt further questions at a more general level. Prime among these questions is: What functions (structural consequences) are essential to the continuity or survival of any society?

There are several available lists of such "requisite functions." Those presented by Davis (1949, p. 30) and Levy (1952, pp. 149–97) are among the clearest and most comprehensive. As they stand, the lists constitute the basis for propositions of the order: "Any society (as suitably defined), if it is to survive, must provide for. . . ." Such propositions are as a matter of fact implicit in many standard general texts in sociology, but often in chapter titles rather than in explicit formulation.

The points of present interest in functional theory are several. (1) Since human societies comprise human populations, their survival depends in part upon provision for what Levy (1952, p. 151) calls "an adequate physiological relationship to the setting and . . . sexual recruitment." In other words, human societies require reproduction and some minimum control of mortality. This point is scarcely startling, and gains significance only in combination with others. (2) Human societies also depend for survival upon such essential functions as socialization (the transformation of ignorant and amoral children into knowledgeable and conforming adults), language and communication, economic production, preservation of order, maintenance of motivation, and integrative values. (3) Thus human fertility and mortality are not simply biological phenomena which in their balance determine growth, decline, and at the extremes sheer biological survival, but are also sociological phenomena that are interrelated with other essential features of human societies.

The theoretical importance of this approach is fundamental. Not only does it avoid a disturbingly common fallacy of treating population as an essentially exogenous variable in the analysis of social systems, but it leads to the question, How? That is, requisite functions provide the steppingstone to a consideration of the *structural* characteristics of human societies. Since clear-cut structural or organizational specialization is highly unequal among societies, and in any event could not precisely match the identified functions, the conceptualization and analysis are necessarily complex. Nevertheless, starting from universal functions and their interrelations alerts the analyst to look for common patterns that are related to those functions, that is, have consequences for, say, fertility and mortality. Moreover, proceeding at this level of generalization avoids, or at least postpones, reliance upon explanations in terms of the *differences* among societies.

To recapitulate, analysis of demographic as well as other social phenomena in terms of requisite functions invites consideration at the highest level of generalization that the empirical data will bear, and at the same time places population and vital events solidly within the patterns of human relations. Those patterns, we have suggested, are not simply random. More explicitly, they are limited in several ways. First, there is the principle of *structural suitability.* Thus, to take an obvious but not completely frivolous example, male monastic orders are unsuited to the bearing and probably the rearing of children. Second, this suitability is limited not only at the most general level (any society) but also by other structural characteristics of given societies and types of societies. Thus current sociological theory of fertility argues that extended family systems and high fertility are structurally inconsistent with urban-industrial societies. Third, since we are dealing with social *systems* and thus with patterns of action that are intricately interrelated, we may expect significant consequences for such phenomena as fertility and longevity from sectors of the system that seem superficially to be primarily related to such functions as the maintenance of a system of stratification (division of labor and orderly inequality) or the performance of various passage rituals.

Certain generalizations can be derived from this theoretical approach. Nothing like a complete set of derivations will be attempted here, but some illustrative propositions of considerable significance for demographic analysis may be noted.

Fertility is always under institutional controls, even if not under calculated individual control. (On this and many of the subsequent points see Davis, 1949, pp. 551–86; Davis and Blake, 1956.) Although extramarital sexual relations and even conception are treated with various degrees of tolerance among societies, the general principle prevails that children will be born within a normatively prescribed family system. Such universal structures combine legitimate reproduction with initial social placement and socialization of children. Moreover, the rules relating to marriage and remarriage and to sexual relations within marriage do not uniformly lead to "maximum" fertility even where fertility is given a high positive value. Indeed, as Davis points out (1949, p. 557), no society does or could reproduce at its biological maximum, for to do so would entail sacrifice of other essential social functions in the interest of sheer biological maintenance. Exclusive attention to the latter would destroy the continuing effectiveness of the social system and, paradoxically, prejudice even its biological survival.

Conversely, human fertility cannot be assumed to be simply an outcome of natural biological urges. Since deliberate controls (contraception, abortion, infanticide) are always potentially available and since sexual relations can be separated from effective fertility with some degree of success, fertility behavior is socially motivated behavior. The motivational patterns relating to fertility are in principle as problematical as is any other aspect of approved, but controlled, social behavior.

"Natural selection" in the human species is always social selection. The notion held by some demographers concerned with the biological (including intellectual) quality of populations, that populations "formerly" were subject to natural selection but are now prone to deterioration by the protection of the unfit, rest at best upon a misunderstanding of the elementary facts of social systems. The biological fitness of human populations is always somewhat relative to the particular demands of differing social structures.

Mortality is subject to both deliberate controls and the often unintended consequences of other features of social systems. Health and longevity being very nearly universal values, it is not surprising that all societies exhibit types of action deliberately (even if often inefficiently or inconsequentially) directed at restoring and maintaining health and preventing death. At the same time, short of modern scientific medicine and public health measures, mortality control has probably derived more from effective economic production and distribution and the maintenance of political order and protection than from explicit health practices.

Migration, which has been neglected to this point, also is clearly determined by the characteristics of social systems. (See, for example, Davis, 1949, pp. 586–92; Isaac, 1947.) Whether we are concerned with movement of people within social systems or among them, the type of migration, its magnitude, selectivity, and direction are socially determined but with consequences that are both social and demographic (in the narrow sense of the latter term— that is, affecting fertility and mortality patterns in sending and receiving areas).

It remains true of course that generalization at the level illustrated in the preceding paragraphs "loses information" available in particular observations or lesser generalizations. The sociologist and demographer are often more interested in accounting for differences within and among social systems than they are in the circumstance

that fertility is commonly encompassed by familial organization or that some form of health practice is universal. Yet the emphasis on general characteristics of human societies has the additional merit of placing bounds on the escape into "cultural relativism" or highly particular and descriptive approaches to social phenomena.

A recent controversy concerning the sociological approach to demographic problems may serve to illustrate the role of sociological theory in this area. The dispute, if it may be called such, involves two sociologist-demographers, Lorimer (1954) and Davis (see Davis and Blake, 1956; Davis, 1949). Both accept the importance of sociological theory in demographic analysis, and both are, explicitly, "functionalists." However, Davis employs functionalism to reach levels of generalization applicable to all societies or to differentiate among a limited number of types of societies for which in turn generalizations are attempted. Lorimer, on the other hand, starts from the somewhat older view of functionalism, namely, the interrelation of the segments or characteristics of *particular* societies. He then proceeds to types of societies, or at least to types of cultural-fertility relations, without, however, any systematic derivation from general structural principles. Thus Lorimer, after stating a generally relativistic position, suggests certain type-relations. For example, he finds an association between high fertility and "corporate unilateral kinship groups" (1954, pp. 58–90) and between controlled fertility and "marginal and isolated areas" (1954, pp. 101–9), and limited means of subsistence (1954, pp. 151–83). Lorimer also discusses the influence of acute social disorganization, religious values, and the introduction of Western influences on health and economic production (1954, pp. 115–33, 183–98, 204–17, respectively). His general summary

(1954, pp. 198–203, 247–51) reasserts the variable features of distinct cultures.

Davis is explicitly critical of this approach for its failure to deal systematically with the "intermediate variables" that must implement any relation between social structure and fertility. He is also, if less explicitly, critical of Lorimer's emphasis on cultural differences among non-industrial societies. However, Davis, at least in the cited article, is primarily concerned with a theoretical analysis. Lorimer's orientation is more strongly in the direction of deliberate policy for effecting demographic change in areas undergoing modernization. For these purposes, whether the analysis is good or bad, it can be expected to be more concerned with local variations.

Lest the thread of the discussion be lost, it may be well to restate the position taken here. It is, essentially, that a view of human societies in terms of requisite functions explicitly brings demographic variables into the scheme of sociological theory. This position has substantive implications at high levels of generalization, briefly illustrated above. It also has methodological implications in the sense that it warns the sociologist or demographer that treating demographic variables as exogenous to social systems involves a mode of abstraction that runs grave risks of errors of fact and interpretation.

It may also be repeated, however, that the "functional approach" is not limited to the search for universal structural features of human societies. Functions are consequences of patterns of action, whether explicit and deliberate or not. Thus the typological relationship illustrated by Lorimer's work also involves establishing connections among elements of social systems. At the extreme, this represents a "relativistic" position that emphasizes "cultural" differences and that attempts to establish detailed connections between

structural elements in particular social systems and the demographic characteristics of those systems. (See also Landis and Hatt, 1954.) This leads, of course, to predictive propositions of a very low order of generality, presumably applicable only to the given society and only under the assumption of constant relevant conditions.

Two closely related further qualifications are in order here. First, a social system is "looser" than a biological organism, and it is unlikely therefore that even a fairly comprehensive and detailed specification of structural characteristics will yield a precisely determined single possibility for fertility and mortality behavior. Rather, such an analysis should typically yield a limited range of alternatives. Thus to the principle of structural suitability we must add the corollary principle of *structural substitutability*. Within the specified range, the precise demographic structure may have to be regarded as a consequence of "historical accident," at least in view of available information and analytical techniques.

Second, structural-functional analysis is commonly, and usually correctly, charged with being "static." That is, relations among elements in a social system are traced, but not changes in those relationships or in the system as a whole. Here then is a situation in which the dynamic elements inherent in the relation between fertility and mortality—changes in size and composition of populations—can be used to modify the original theoretical approach. Since, particularly in view of the looseness of social systems, it is extremely improbable that the fertility, mortality, or migration consequences of social structures will result in their precise duplication from generation to generation, we find one key to the freeing of functional analysis from some of its static assumptions and predilections. This represents in part the view taken by Halbwachs in his discussion of "social morphology," which emphasizes demography and demographic elements in the analysis of social organizations (Halbwachs, 1946).

This dynamic perspective becomes even more pointed with the recognition that especially mortality but also fertility may in some circumstances be substantially altered without prior changes in the fabric of social relations. Thus, natural disasters, spraying with insecticide, or the sterilizing effects of radiation constitute examples of essentially external influences on demographic changes that will have consequences in turn for social structures. The insistance that demographic variables operate in a social matrix need not blind us to some independent variability. If the analysis is thereby complicated, this seems regrettable but appropriate.

Special Fields and Topics

In the most general sense, all sociological theory may be said to be structural-functional. The "special topics" discussed here represent concern either for specific, organized subsystems of societies (e.g., the family or the urban community) or for particular aspects of patterned social behavior, whether or not represented by concrete organizations (e.g., political sociology or social stratification). In either case the sociologists' interest is in patterns and consequences. The latter, in turn, may be viewed in terms of establishing essentially "static" interrelations (e.g., the connection between occupational status and residential location in a city) or "dynamic" relations (e.g., the sequential connections between technical innovations in production and the development of leisure activities).

The approach in this particular section is to start with an area of sociological concern and indicate how demographic data and procedures are relevant and, to a lesser extent, the way general sociological principles have specific applications of primary interest to demographers. For example, propositions concerning the ecological differentiation internal to cities will rely in part on such specifically demographic variables as fertility differentials and such additional distributive "characteristics" of populations as occupation and income. But propositions concerning the functioning of cities as centers of communication and agencies of diffusion of new values and techniques may have specific demographic applications in the analysis of *trends* in vital rates and their rural-urban differentials.

Demography thus is considered not only as a subfield of sociology, with somewhat specialized variables and analytical techniques, but as an aspect of other special fields. A recent general textbook (Broom and Selznick, 1955) may be taken not as representative, since it gives exceptional attention to population, but as indicating some of the range of interpenetration of social and demographic variables.

Broom and Selznick treat population as one of some nine principal "elements of sociological analysis." (The others are social organization, culture, socialization, primary groups, social stratification, associations, collective behavior, and ecology.) Each of these nine "elements," including population, is then used in the discussion of six special topics—family, city, minorities, industrial sociology, political sociology, and criminal behavior. Note that it is not demographic *theory* that is used in these special fields, but questions of size, distributive characteristics, and numerical changes are introduced as important elements for the description of social systems and derivation of propositions about the relation among elements.

For example, not only is the family

in a general and distributive sense responsible for reproduction and, to a lesser degree, for biological sustenance and for prevention and treatment of accidents and illness, but the family structure itself is molded or conditioned by its fertility and mortality and by its age and sex composition. Size of family, that is, the number of children, affects individual consumption levels at given income levels, probably affects adult economic opportunities of both parents and children and also the pattern of socialization of the young, since in large families a large share of the care of younger siblings is likely to be the responsibility of the older ones. Age compositions and sex ratios in the community and society affect marriage rates and perhaps even age at marriage.

An even more specific illustration of the combination of demographic and sociological facts relates to household composition. Several component generalizations must be combined to derive a further generalization and put it in perspective: (1) The "norm" in the American family system is for neolocal residence, that is, the residential separation of generations upon marriage of children. (2) The principal exceptions are (*a*) "temporary" doubling-up during the initial years of marriage, where the "head" of the household is still of the older generation, and (*b*) residence of an aged parent (rarely both) with a married offspring, where the "head" of the household is of the younger generation. It is this latter situation in which we are here interested. One can predict that this aged parent is more likely to be female than male. This prediction stems from two further facts: the demographic fact of the greater average longevity of females and the sociological fact that widowers remarry in considerably higher proportion than do widows. (This prediction is borne out by census data, which unfortunately do not permit de-

termination of whether the widow is more likely to live with a son or a daughter.)

Brief illustrations of the way sociological queries require in part demographic answers will be presented with reference to several other special fields dealt with by Broom and Selznick. A few should suffice, for the methodological principles involved are fairly uniform.

The city not only is typically characterized by distinctive fertility and mortality patterns but also typically grows in part by migratory accretions as well as by natural increase. These demographic variables are the result of, and result in, distinctive age and sex compositions. Sociological analysis of the city, including the theory and methods of human ecology, thus relies in part upon the use of demographic data and procedures. But these data are significant not only for static or cross-sectional analysis, as causes, conditions, or correlates of other social phenomena. In sociological theory the principle of "metropolitan dominance" and the role of the city as a center of diffusion of new values and practices ascribe to urbanization a major link in the causal chain resulting in reduced fertility and the small-family system.

With respect to minority groups, the sociologists' prime concern relates to the social sources of prejudice and discrimination, the internal as well as external factors tending to preserve the solidarity of the groups, the operation of residential segregation, and the types of relations with the broader society. However, even here, the sociologist may be concerned with the demographic consequences of various "subcultures," both as a correlate of other characteristics and as a clue to future changes in size and composition or the extent to which the group loses its identity through assimilation of majority norms and practices. Again, we may use an illustration of combining sociological and demographic facts. Some religious and ethnic minorities in American society are dwindling rapidly by the joint effect of defection and low fertility. Thus in some sectarian religious communities subject to the impact of the public school and other secular influences, young men tend to leave both the community and their religious affiliation. Even though the girls remain, the strict norm of religious endogamy presents them with the choice either of violating that norm, whereby they and their children are also lost to the sect, or of remaining unmarried and failing to produce a new generation of sectarians.

Incidentally, the foregoing example brings us full circle to our previous discussion of "requisite functions." Given the circumstances just sketched plus the additional circumstance that recruitment to sectarian communities is almost entirely by birth (and these communities may thus be viewed, and indeed explicitly attempt to be, small self-subsistent societies), we have a situation in which survival of the system is threatened by failure of reproduction. Moreover, this situation illustrates that the specification of biological reproduction as essential for societal survival is not as banal as at first glance it appears. Since human reproductive behavior is motivated and normatively sanctioned behavior, it cannot be taken for granted or assumed to be sociologically unproblematical.

"Political sociology" is a rather loosely distinguishable special field which includes the relation of political organization to other aspects of society, the analysis of political ideologies and structures, and such topics as the social origins and careers of political and administrative officials, the formation and implementation of political opinion, and voting behavior. Here there are both substantive and methodological

grounds for considering demographic data. Substantively, political structures and voting behavior, for example, will be substantially affected by age and sex characteristics of a population, and even by the trends in vital rates. A rapidly growing population has political implications, especially for economic planning, educational budgets, or policy on encouraging emigration. Methodologically, any attempt by survey techniques or other sampling techniques to appraise political trends, to determine opinion on public issues, or to analyze the effectiveness of political communications will have to take into account various population characteristics. Social science sampling techniques generally rely on various demographic characteristics of the population.

Social stratification, one of Broom and Selznick's "principal elements" of social systems, also has demographic aspects. As will be noted in the following section, various indexes of class or socioeconomic status are standard bases for the analysis of fertility differentials. Here our focus is different. Starting from questions about social stratification, what demographic data are needed, and how do these demographic phenomena, in turn, affect the operation of systems of status differentiation? Social status on the one hand and fertility and mortality on the other clearly stand in a reciprocal relation (Sibley, 1942). "Class" position affects fertility patterns and also life expectancy. On the other hand, fertility and mortality differentials generally result in a situation in which various strata do not precisely, or even proportionally, reproduce themselves. This means a changing "class structure" through time and/or class mobility between generations.

The Broom and Selznick text in sociology was used as a partial checklist of special fields and topics in sociological theory of particular significance for demography because of the unusually extensive attention given to population in that book. However, there are at least two additional aspects of sociological theory which are not primarily emphasized in that text but which deserve attention in the present context. These topics are motivation and social change. Both of them are commonly recognized as "messy" subjects in the current state of theory but, perhaps for that reason, of considerable importance.

Sociology may seem to bypass questions of motivation by using such concepts as "values" and "social control." Clearly, however, these are only a short step removed from motivational counterparts. Values have behavioral consequences only as they are matched by attitudes toward them. Social control depends upon some combination of internalized social norms (moral conformity through socialization) and a balance of positive and negative sanctions that will effectively motivate individuals to prescribed and expected actions. Motivational categories, or their combination in character or personality types, seem especially important under the dual conditions that the relevant behavior in attempting to predict behavior is in its nature intimate or even furtive (c.g., sexual behavior and violation of criminal codes) and that in complex societies standard social categories (various status indicators, rural or urban birth and residence, religious affiliation, ethnic origin, etc.) are multiple and partially contradictory in their impact on any individual or aggregate of individuals. The fact is that under these conditions the predictability of behavior from knowledge of group memberships and norms is, from the scientific standpoint, distressingly feeble. Given large enough samples and refinements of statistical analysis, correlations may be improved by a process which may be called typo-

logical prediction, or its equivalent, refinement of stipulated conditions bearing on the relations among variables. The point of present concern is that the development of personality types *may* elevate motivational categories to full-fledged analytical status, rather than their usual present position as intervening variables, adduced in a rather *ad hoc* fashion. (An interesting experiment, related in this instance to the theory of the demographic transition, is presented in Riesman, 1955, pp. 21–38.)

To recapitulate, what is being suggested here is that current knowledge and techniques for the analysis of the relation of, say, fertility to various differentiating social categories leaves considerable variance unaccounted for. It seems probable that greater precision can be achieved at a "strictly sociological" level by finer analysis of the interrelations among such variables as residence, current occupation, mobility history, and formal education. It also seems possible that a correlative development of "psychological" variables may not only increase detailed predictability but also lead eventually to a closer integration of social and psychological theory.

The theory of social change is a generally neglected aspect of sociological analysis, partly under the pervasive influence of structural-functional theory in sociology, partly as a consequence of dissatisfaction with attempts at such sweeping theoretical doctrines as various "social evolution" formulas a half-century ago. Yet it seems evident that this is an aspect of social theory in which the connections between sociological theory and demography are potentially very important.

The analysis of social change may be divided, with some degree of arbitrariness, into (*a*) changes of primarily internal origin in human societies, and (*b*) change from external sources ("culture contact" and diffusion). Although these two, and their interrelations, logically exhaust the relevant phenomena, it is also convenient to distinguish (*c*) theories attempting laws of long-term changes applicable to human societies generally.

Although explicit or implicit "equilibrium" models have pervaded most sociological theory over recent decades, all social structures change through time, and not simply on haphazard or accidental bases. Thus every social system, no matter how small and how seemingly bound by the power of tradition, has internal flexibilities and inherent strains. Societies may, although this is apparently not universal, also organize and institutionalize deliberate change. Each of these principles may have demographic consequences.

With reference to "flexibilities," no society is so constituted, or probably could be, as to achieve precise, perfect, and continuing control over the details of socializing the young—always partially "decentralized" to nuclear family units—or over exact demographic reproduction of appropriate structural categories. Various "demographic imbalances" are at the very least elements of change in social systems. Two general hypotheses, not adequately supported by available evidence, may be noted. The one is that because of the combination of reproduction and early socialization in the same agency, the family, initial differentials may be perpetuated through successive generations. Thus children of large families would tend to have large families not primarily because of differences in hereditary fecundity but because of more specific social-psychological differences in attitudes and values as they relate to fertility behavior. The other is that, even outside the modern experience of industrial societies, fertility differentials tend to lead to higher reproductivity in lower status categories than

in elites, a principle which would lead in turn to support of theories of "circulation of the elite."

With reference to "strains" inherent in social systems, these include various standard "scarcity situations"—time, treasure, and affective energy or loyalty—and consequent role and value conflicts. These, in turn, may be related to various normative alternatives which seem to stand in dialectical relations in every society. Thus no society has norms that lead exclusively to high or low fertility, and slight changes in the relevant norms and in their relative weights may lead to substantial changes in effective fertility (Davis and Blake, 1956). The same is true in principle with reference to mortality and migration (Davis, 1949, pp. 562–93). These considerations suggest the hypothesis—which available evidence does not permit testing—that in nonindustrial societies the population balance of high fertility checked by high mortality (the usual generalization) is more nearly a cyclical pattern of both fertility and mortality.

Societies may also change deliberately. This is an especially marked characteristic of industrial societies, where both mortality and, more rarely, fertility may be a matter of official, governmental concern. Contemporary "underdeveloped" countries are now showing some concern over the demographic consequences of deliberate mortality-reducing innovations and are moving toward changes that would encourage or facilitate reduced fertility. There is much room here for both theory and research, since deliberate changes will almost certainly have unintended consequences, and there is no assurance that the latter will be entirely "positive," whether judged in terms of explicit values or in terms of the more neutral "functional" standpoint.

A great deal of social change in the

modern world, and particularly in the so-called underdeveloped areas, is primarily "external" in origin as viewed from a particular social system. Clearly, the situation is always one of complex interplay, and it includes the amenability to change of particular societies. However, "Western" culture in one or another of its forms (including the Communist version) now is a persuasive influence throughout the world. Sociologists and anthropologists have attempted to work out general principles of "acculturation" (e.g., Herskovits, 1938; Sorokin, 1947, chaps. xxxvii–xxxviii). The various propositions will not be repeated here, but two applications to demographic analysis will be indicated. The first relates to the general theory of the demographic transition. Briefly, it may be predicted that new techniques of mortality control will be readily accepted in most societies because of consistency with pre-existing values (although still with possible "negative," unintended consequences). It may also be predicted that new techniques of fertility control will be less readily accepted, or positively rejected, because of inconsistency with pre-existing values (Davis, 1944).

The second application of acculturation theory to demographic analysis derives from the first. Given the "gap" between mortality decline and fertility decline, it may be said that, "In a sense, Western enterprise helps provide its own labor supply in new areas. . ." (Moore, 1951*b*, p. 305). Failing a rapid expansion of commercial and industrial employment opportunities, modernization in one aspect of life—public health—may thus actually increase the number and proportion of the population dependent on archaic modes of agricultural production but potentially available for new employment opportunities.

Various unifying theories of long-term change in social systems have been put forth in the historical development of social thought. These range from various "cyclical" theories to "evolutionary" theories that seek to account for the evident complexity of modern Western societies. Since most of these simplifying formulations have failed to withstand theoretical and empirical criticism and since they also generally have only tenuous implications for demographic analysis, they will not long detain us.

One particular type of evolutionary theory is, however, of special interest. This links complexity, or specialization, to size—a well-established "static" relationship—but views the latter as generally increasing on partially demographic grounds. In Durkheim's famous work on "division of labor," organic solidarity, based on specialization, is related to "moral" density, which in turn is linked to demographic density and growth (Durkheim, 1933, especially pp. 256–82). In a simplified way, therefore, this may be viewed as a *demographic* theory of social change. However, Durkheim, a notable "functionalist" in his theoretical orientations, uses demographic growth as but one link in a chain of interrelations, whether static or sequential, with the main emphasis on the characterization of the components of the normative order.

Recent developments toward a more limited, but still rather general, theory of long-term change have focused on economic development or, in a loose sense, industrialization. Here the sociologists (and also the economists and other social scientists) deal with gross historical facts of sweeping generality in terms of societies or other social units affected. Modern forms of economic production and distribution are remarkably and increasingly pervasive in their impact on the world's cultures. The historical record in the West is beginning to be compared with near-contemporary experience in currently "underdeveloped" areas, and attempts have begun not only to formulate empirical generalizations but also to account for the relationships among component elements. (See Kuznets, 1956; Moore, 1955*a, b.*) Demographic data are relevant to these theoretical and research developments in two principal ways: growth trends and population compositions affect both consumer demand and manpower potential, and the industrial system has a complex but definitely negative impact on extended kinship systems and, in an even more complex way, on high fertility.

These relationships lead directly to a primary focus on demographic theory, for that theory is centrally concerned with the relationship between population and the means for its subsistence or, more generally, the links between demographic variables, taken as criteria, and social systems.

DEMOGRAPHIC THEORY AND SOCIOLOGY

If a standard complaint about sociology is that it has "too much" theory, a standard complaint about demography is that it has "too little." Such judgments tend to be pointless without further specification. What is generally meant in the case of sociology is that competing conceptual systems and theories have not been adjudicated and that empirical generalizations are often not related in any systematic way. What is generally meant in the case of demography is that a pervasive preoccupation with refinement of measurement and with *ad hoc* explanations for observations leads to an avoidance of the fundamental question, What do we want to know?

"The" Population Problem: Relation of Population to the Means for Its Support

Despite the charge that demography has "too little" theory, there is a matter of central concern to much demographic research that serves as a partial integration. That is "the" population problem, meaning by that the relation of population to the means for its support, or, in still more general terms, the interrelation between demographic phenomena and their social settings.

This focus of theoretical concern antedates the work of Malthus but conventionally and conveniently may be discussed on the basis of the Malthusian position. Malthus' formulation is sufficiently well known not to require elaborate restatement at this point (see Malthus, n.d.). Indeed, the formulation may be too well known, for modifications through successive editions of the *Essay* plus ambiguities throughout argue against a completely simplified summary. (For a short, critical summary see Wrong, 1956, pp. 97–118; also, Glass, 1953.) The essence of this position is that population will tend to grow more rapidly than the "means of subsistence" and that the growth will be held to those means of subsistence only by positive checks (raising the death rate) or preventive checks (lowering the birth rate). From this basic relationship Malthus draws various gloomy conclusions about the possibilities of substantial increases in material well-being and particularly comes to conclusions of a "conservative" character about the distribution of consumption through various social strata.

We are not here concerned with an empirical refutation of Malthus, which is easy and obvious enough in the modern history of the Western world. Our concern is with the central problem as posed by Malthus and as modified and amended in subsequent theoretical development. This may be done in summary fashion for a number of central issues.

(1) A population is clearly limited

by the means of subsistence, but not only by that. No human population is controlled solely by the means for its biological survival, as noted earlier (see Davis, 1949, pp. 553–55). Those means of survival are themselves variable, as Malthus recognized, and human reproductivity is subject to both unintended and intended controls.

(2) Any population is related to the means for its support in complex ways. Although simplified formulas like

$$\frac{\text{resources}}{\text{population}} = \text{level of consumption,}$$

or even the somewhat more sophisticated

$$\frac{\text{product}}{\text{population}} = \text{level of consumption,}$$

are inviting, they court theoretical disaster. The numerator of the fraction needs to take into account technology and its counterpart in occupational and skill distributions, and product specialization and trade. The denominator of the fraction must take into account the circumstance that each individual does not count as one, not only because of different consumption "needs" by age and sex but also because of distribution differentials related to systems of social stratification, which, in some form or other, are universal (Davis and Moore, 1945).

(3) Biological survival in relation to non-human resources, accordingly, affects, but does not determine, the relation of a population to its setting. Here we face once more the basic fallacy of treating population as a primarily biological variable, exogenous to social systems, rather than as inherently imbedded in social structures that always must perform functions (or offer "services") beyond those required for sheer biological survival. The progress of this aspect of demographic theory, therefore, has been away from the crude Malthusian formulation, through various conceptions that take into account what we may call economic variables, to full recognition of the sociological character of "the" population problem. (On various treatments of "optimum" population theory, principally representing the incorporation of economic variables, see Penrose, 1934; Sauvy, 1952–54; United Nations, 1953. On more specifically sociological analyses, see Davis, 1949, pp. 551–93; Moore, 1951a, pp. 455–62, 1955c.)

(4) The relation between a population and its setting is dynamic and reciprocal. Although much of the treatment of "the" population problem has been cast in static, distributive models, the original Malthusian formulation involved a dynamic tension, and some subsequent developments have taken into account rates of change and the complex interrelations in social systems through time. Thus, if particular rates of population growth "challenge" the productive and distributive system, the latter in turn will affect fertility and mortality rates. Changing age compositions—the consequence of past trends in fertility, mortality, and migration—affect the population as consumers and also as producers. Whether a particular problem of meager levels of consumption is phrased as "too many people" or "too little product" may involve questions of social strategy, moral and political ideologies, or genuine differences in theoretical interpretations (United Nations, 1953, especially pp. 21–44). No theory claiming to be scientific, however, can well avoid the interplay between demographic and social phenomena.

The theory of "the" population problem has thus proceeded from a simple kind of relation between biology and geography to a complex analysis involving the essential and crucial middle terms that lie between a biological group and its non-human setting. This line of development leads to a consideration of the theory of the "demographic transition," although the latter is not commonly placed in this context.

It is perhaps idle to speculate whether the Malthusian theory was amended and rejected because of scientific development or by the crude course of events. The events were, in order, an extremely rapid expansion of economic production, yielding rising per capita levels of consumption despite the rapid population growth from sharply reduced mortality, and reductions in family size and fertility to a point at some times and places below long-run population replacement levels.

These historic phenomena led to a group of related empirical generalizations: (1) Prior to what may be called tentatively "social modernization," population balances have been maintained by high fertility eroded by high mortality. (2) Subsequent to such modernization, low mortality is matched by low fertility. (3) In the transition, death rates fall before, and more rapidly than, birth rates, with a consequent rapid expansion of total population. These three generalizations have been converted into a typology for classifying particular populations—"high growth potential," "incipient decline," and "transitional growth," or equivalent terms (Davis, 1949, pp. 603–8; Thompson, 1944, chap. vi).

A first set of questions revolves around the generalizations and classification. Do the classes adequately comprise the empirical range, and is classification of a particular population unambiguous? What are the temporal dimensions of the transition? What are the growth dimensions in the process? These queries do not necessarily challenge the basic propositions, but seek to refine them or put limits on their range of validity.

A second set of questions concerns the predictive validity of the general-ization of a dynamic process rather than a simple historical summary or convenient typology. Will the sequence and dimensions remain essentially the same in other areas if they go through a process of social, including economic, modernization? What if "expansion room," locally or by emigration, for absorption of large population increases, is missing? Are the unspecified intervening variables severable from the particular historic context of urban industrialization so that, for example, fertility may be reduced in densely settled agrarian societies? (See Davis, 1951, 1954; Milbank Memorial Fund, 1944, 1950, 1954; Notestein, 1944, 1950, 1952; Vance, 1952a, b.) These queries seek to determine the range of applicability but thereby raise the kind of question that always marks the progress from empirical generalization to theory, how and why?

A third set of questions, then, concerns the precise links between "modernization" and the "demographic transition." Why are death rates more amenable to reduction than birth rates? Since deliberate fertility control is at least an incipient possibility in any society, what, precisely, is the connection between urban life or industrial employment and the voluntary limitation of size of families? If these links can be established, is the functional relation so close as to require the entire matrix for effective restoration of population balance or so loose as to permit direct and deliberate fostering of the "intervening" changes either to speed the transition, to reduce total growth, or possibly to make the full Western social pattern unnecessary for the predictable future?

This line of development once more illustrates the process of starting from overly simple formulations and moving to more elaborate analyses. In this process sociological variables are brought squarely into the picture. On structural grounds we know that extended kinship ties and large families are inconsistent with geographical and occupational mobility, between generations and within careers. Children in an urban setting become relatively more expensive as "items of consumption" and practically useless as "factors of production." New, and moving, aspiration levels are inconsistent with concentration on child-rearing.

These and other factors have been noted as explanatory principles to account for the "demographic transition." The analytical problem becomes one of separating various nexuses in a system of multiple causation (Feldman, 1956) and determining the relevance of contemporary conditions in underdeveloped areas that differ from the historical experience. Moreover, since neither deaths nor births declined simultaneously throughout all sectors of the population, it becomes relevant to ask about mortality and fertility "differentials," and to raise the issue of whether current fertility differentials and their correlates (differences in space) provide clues to historic trends (differences in time).

Starting, then, as a rough empirical generalization based on limited historical experience, the theory of demographic transition provides avenues for wider empirical generalization, integration with sociological theory, and incorporation of other areas of demographic research into a "main body" of principles of social, including demographic, change applicable to the modern world.

Special Fields and Topics

Births, deaths, and migrations are the essential components of population size and changes in size. Since the time that fertility was regarded as an essentially unproblematical, "natural" phenomenon, changes in fertility rates and cross-sectional fertility differentials have raised the whole problem of fertility as a *social* phenomenon. The "standard" inverse correlation between various indexes of socioeconomic status and size of family belied any simple economic interpretation, and other equally rationalistic social or psychological models failed to account for observed differentials. Much current demographic research, therefore, is designed to explore social and psychological correlates of differential fertility in greater detail and with more specific hypotheses drawn from general theory in those fields. At the present time it is probably safe to say that the relation of fertility to the social and psychological aspects of mobility is the most promising lead to part of the "intervening links" between "structural" characteristics and fertility behavior (Westoff, 1953; see also Milbank Memorial Fund, 1955; Whelpton and Kiser, 1946–54; Wrong, 1956, pp. 69–83). A more general basis for examining these connections needs to be established before the demographic and sociological propositions are firmly wedded (Davis and Blake, 1956).

Like fertility, mortality and migration may be treated by the demographer as essentially unproblematical, with primary attention focused on their consequences for age-sex composition of populations, fertility, growth, and relation to economic product. They may, in other words, be treated as independent variables. But they may also be treated as dependent variables, with attention then shifting to the social context of mortality and migration phenomena. The consequence of this shift is to make it clear that biological or even economic explanations will not suffice to account for observed trends and differentials. The search for social correlates tends to be piecemeal and *ad hoc,* but it may lead in these areas also to more systematic integration with the theory of social systems.

If demography be defined as what self-identified or professionally recognized demographers do, it is clear that the field is broader than most of the foregoing discussion implies. The study of populations also commonly includes attention to various "characteristics." Some of these—age, sex, and various indexes of biological "quality"—are closely related to population as a partially biological system. Thus age and sex compositions are the product of past fertility, mortality, and migration and are relevant for the same phenomena in the future. No society does or could ignore these characteristics. Also, however, no society does or could limit their significance to the "purely" demographic, since they are made directly or indirectly relevant to the whole interlocking system of social positions and normative expectations.

The question of population "quality" is a moot one, with one extreme position maintaining that the inverse relation between social status and fertility tends to deterioration of intelligence and physical vigor. Such a position, of course, implies a theory of social stratification—that the rich are biologically superior—for which there is no substantial evidence. Any system of social selection, as noted earlier, is not a system of "natural" selection in the usual sense, and to confuse the two is a basic sociological fallacy. This is a special field, then, in which the major impact of sociological theory has been to rectify, or at least to place serious limits on, an older aspect of demographic theory. (On the alleged dysgenic effects of fertility differentials, see Lorimer and Osborn, 1934; for a critique of "natural selection" fallacy, see MacIver and Page, 1949, pp. 538–51.)

Other population "characteristics" are in principle virtually infinite. In practice, they include attributes which can be readily enumerated and which the determiners of enumeration policy think useful and important. Some of the characteristics are fairly standard in demographic analysis of fertility, mortality, and migration, where they are usually approached in terms of "differentials." Some characteristics useful for demographic analysis, on the other hand, are not enumerated in censuses—for example, attitudes and personality traits. Indeed, the preoccupation of many demographers with the analysis of census data gives partial foundation to the exaggerated charge that demography has "no" or "too little" theory. The circumstance that fertility differentials have been more often related to current residence and occupation than to residential changes and occupational histories probably stems from *both* the greater availability of some types of data and the absence of any clear-cut theory of fertility differentials.

Population characteristics, to repeat, figure in demographic theory only as they relate to size and the components of demographic change. Residence, economic position, religion, national or regional origin, education, marital status, and many other distributive attributes of populations may all provide bases for the analysis of the relation between populations and their social settings. These enumerated characteristics may also provide data relevant for quite different analytical purposes. Both demographic and sociological theory, the interrelations between which have concerned us here, will benefit by making the questions explicit and systematic, so that the answers will gain in precision, predictability, and power of generalization.

SELECTED BIBLIOGRAPHY

Broom, Leonard, and Selznick, Philip. 1955. *Sociology.* Evanston, Ill.: Row, Peterson & Co.

Davis, Kingsley. 1944. "Demographic Fact and Policy in India," in *Demographic*

Studies of Selected Areas of Rapid Growth. New York: Milbank Memorial Fund.

DAVIS, KINGSLEY. 1949. *Human Society.* New York: Macmillan.

——. 1951. "Population and the Further Spread of Industrial Society," *Proceedings of the American Philosophical Society,* XCV, 8–19.

——. 1954. "Fertility Control and the Demographic Transition in India," in *The Interrelations of Demographic, Economic, and Social Problems in Selected Underdeveloped Areas,* pp. 66–89. New York: Milbank Memorial Fund.

——, and BLAKE, JUDITH. 1956. "Social Structure and Fertility," *Economic Development and Cultural Change,* IV, 211–35.

——, and MOORE, WILBERT E. 1945. "Some Principles of Stratification," *American Sociological Review,* X, 242–49.

DUBLIN, LOUIS I., LOTKA, ALFRED J., and SPIEGELMAN, MORTIMER. 1949. *Length of Life.* New York: Ronald Press Co.

DURKHEIM, ÉMILE. 1933. *On the Division of Labor in Society.* Translated by GEORGE SIMPSON. New York: Macmillan Co. 1st French edition; 1893.

FELDMAN, ARNOLD S. 1956. "Social Structure and Fertility in Puerto Rico." Unpublished doctoral dissertation. Evanston, Ill.: Northwestern University Library.

GLASS, D. V. (ed.). 1953. *Introduction to Malthus.* New York: John Wiley & Sons.

HALBWACHS, MAURICE. 1946. *Morphologie sociale.* 2d ed. Paris: Librairie Armand Colin.

HANKINS, FRANK H. 1940. "Demographic and Biological Contributions to Sociological Principles," in *Contemporary Social Theory,* ed. HARRY ELMER BARNES, HOWARD BECKER, and FRANCES BENNETT BECKER. New York: D. Appleton-Century Co.

HERSKOVITS, MELVILLE. 1938. *Acculturation: A Study of Culture Contact.* New York: J. J. Augustin.

ISAAC, JULIUS. 1947. *Economics of Migration.* New York: Oxford University Press.

KUZNETS, SIMON. 1956. "Toward a Theory of Economic Growth." Expanded mimeographed reproduction of a paper published in *National Policy for Economic Welfare at Home and Abroad,* ed. ROBERT LECACHMAN. Garden City, N.Y.: Doubleday & Co., 1955.

LANDIS, PAUL H., and HATT, PAUL K. 1954. *Population Problems: A Cultural Interpretation.* 2d ed. New York: American Book Co.

LEVY, MARION J., JR. 1952. *The Structure of Society.* Princeton: Princeton University Press.

LORIMER, FRANK. 1954. *Culture and Human Fertility.* Paris: UNESCO.

——, and OSBORN, FREDERICK. 1934. *Dynamics of Population.* New York: Macmillan Co.

MACIVER, R. M., and PAGE, CHARLES H. 1949. *Society: An Introductory Analysis.* New York: Rinehart & Co.

MALTHUS, T. R. n.d. *An Essay on Population.* Everyman's Library Edition. New York: E. P. Dutton & Co. 1st ed.; 1798.

MILBANK MEMORIAL FUND. 1944. *Demographic Studies of Selected Areas of Rapid Growth.* New York.

——. 1950. *Modernization Programs in Relation to Human Resources and Population Problems.* New York.

——. 1954. *The Interrelations of Demographic, Economic, and Social Problems in Selected Underdeveloped Areas.* New York.

——. 1955. *Current Research in Human Fertility.* New York.

MOORE, WILBERT E. 1951a. *Industrial Relations and the Social Order.* Rev. ed. New York: Macmillan Co.

——. 1951b. *Industrialization and Labor.* Ithaca: Cornell University Press.

——. 1955a. "Creation of Common Culture," *Confluence,* IV, 229–38.

——. 1955b. *Economy and Society.* New York: Doubleday & Co.

——. 1955c. "Population and Labor Force in Relation to Economic Growth," in *Economic Growth: Brazil, India, Japan,* ed. SIMON KUZNETS, WILBERT E. MOORE, and JOSEPH J. SPENGLER. Durham, N.C.: Duke University Press.

NOTESTEIN, FRANK W. 1944. "Problems of Policy in Relation to Areas of Heavy Population Pressure," in *Demographic Studies of Selected Areas of Rapid*

Growth. New York: Milbank Memorial Fund.

———. 1950. "The Reduction of Human Fertility as an Aid to Programs of Economic Development in Densely Settled Agrarian Regions," in *Modernization Programs in Relation to Human Resources and Population Problems*. New York: Milbank Memorial Fund.

———. 1952. "Economic Problems of Population Change," *Eighth International Conference of Agricultural Economists*. Michigan State College.

PENROSE, E. F. 1934. *Population Theories and Their Application*. Stanford, Calif.: Food Research Institute.

RIESMAN, DAVID. 1955. *The Lonely Crowd*. Rev. ed. Garden City, N.Y.: Doubleday Anchor Books.

SAUVY, ALFRED. 1952–54. *Théorie générale de la population*. Vol. I: *Économie et population*. Vol. II: *Biologie sociale*. Paris: Presses Universitaires de France.

SIBLEY, ELBRIDGE. 1942. "Some Demographic Clues to Stratification," *American Sociological Review*, VII, 322–30.

SOROKIN, PITIRIM A. 1947. *Society, Culture, and Personality*. New York: American Book Co.

THOMPSON, WARREN S. 1944. *Plenty of People*. Lancaster, Pa.: Jaques Cattell Press.

UNITED NATIONS, DEPARTMENT OF SOCIAL AFFAIRS, POPULATION DIVISION. 1953. *The Determinants and Consequences of Population Trends*. New York: United Nations.

UNITED STATES DEPARTMENT OF LABOR, BUREAU OF EMPLOYMENT SECURITY, UNITED STATES EMPLOYMENT SERVICE. 1949. *Dictionary of Occupational Titles*, Vol. I. Washington, D.C.: Government Printing Office.

VANCE, RUPERT B. 1952a. "The Demographic Gap: Dilemma of Modernization Programs," in *Approaches to Problems of High Fertility in Agrarian Societies*. New York: Milbank Memorial Fund.

———. 1952b. "Is Theory for Demographers?" *Social Forces*, XXXI, 9–13.

WESTOFF, CHARLES F. 1953. "The Changing Focus of Differential Fertility Research: The Social Mobility Hypothesis," *Milbank Memorial Fund Quarterly*, XXXI, 24–35.

WHELPTON, P. K., and KISER, CLYDE V. 1946–54. *Social and Psychological Factors Affecting Fertility*. 4 vols. New York: Milbank Memorial Fund.

WRONG, DENNIS H. 1956. *Population*. New York: Random House.

List of Contributors

List of Contributors

EDWARD A. ACKERMAN, director of the Water Resources Program, Resources for the Future, Inc., was formerly professor of geography at the University of Chicago and assistant general manager (program analysis), Tennessee Valley Authority. Among his publications are *American Resources* (with J. Russell Whitaker, 1951) and *Japan's Natural Resources and Their Relation to Japan's Economic Future* (1953).

DONALD J. BOGUE, professor of sociology and associate director of the Population Research and Training Center, University of Chicago, is the editor of the series, "Scripps Foundation Studies in Population Distribution," and author of *The Structure of the Metropolitan Community* (1949) and numerous monographs on internal migration and population distribution.

C. CHANDRASEKARAN, professor of statistics at the All-India Institute of Hygiene and Public Health, is the author of numerous studies on the interrelationship of social, economic, and population changes and on reproductive patterns in India, including "Some Aspects of Parsi Demography" (1948) and "Fertility in Mysore State, India" (1955). He has served as social affairs officer, United Nations Population Branch.

ALESSANDRO COSTANZO, professor of statistics at the University of Parma, is author of *Costituzione e mortalità* (1936) and other studies in demography and biometry.

HAROLD F. DORN, chief of the Biometrics Branch, Division of Research Services, National Institutes of Health, is author of "Prospects of Further Decline in Mortality" (1952), "Pitfalls in Population Forecasts and Projections" (1950), and other studies on mortality trends and population growth. He has served as president of the Population Association of America.

OTIS DUDLEY DUNCAN, research associate in human ecology and associate director, Population Research and Training Center, University of Chicago, is co-author of *The Negro Population of Chicago* (1957) and other studies in human ecology and population distribution.

PETER W. FRANK, associate professor of biology, University of Oregon, is author of several studies on experimental population ecology, including "Interspecific Competition and Related Phenomena in Two Species of Daphnia" (1957) and (with others) "Vital Statistics of Laboratory Cultures of *Daphnia pulex DeGeer* as Related to Density" (1957).

PAUL C. GLICK, chief of the Social Statistics Branch, Population Division, United States Bureau of the Census, is the author of *American Families* (1957) and numerous studies on the demography and sociology of families.

JOHN V. GRAUMAN, of the Population Branch, Bureau of Social Affairs, United Nations Secretariat, is the officer in charge of the United Nations program and publications in the field of population estimates and projections.

E. GREBENIK, professor of social studies, University of Leeds, is co-author of *The Trend and Pattern of Fertility in Great Britain* (1954) and author of monographs on population and demographic methods.

PHILIP M. HAUSER, professor and chairman of the department of sociology and director of the Population Research and Training Center, University of Chicago, is editor of *Population and World Politics* (1958) and *Urbanization in Asia and the Far East* (1957). He has served as president of the Population Association of America and as United States representative on the United Nations Population Commission.

855

Amos H. Hawley, professor of sociology at the University of Michigan, is the author of *Human Ecology* (1950), *The Changing Shape of Metropolitan America* (1956), and numerous studies in population distribution.

Hannes Hyrenius, professor of statistics at the University of Gothenburg, is author of *Population and Society* (1951) and of a number of monographs and studies in mathematical statistics, agricultural statistics, and methods of forecasting and measuring reproduction.

A. J. Jaffe, director of the Manpower and Population Program, Bureau of Applied Social Research, Columbia University, is co-author of *Manpower Resources and Utilization* (1951) and author of *Handbook of Statistical Methods for Demographers* (1951) and numerous research studies in demography and labor-force analysis.

Franz J. Kallmann, M.D., professor of psychiatry, Columbia University, and principal research scientist, New York State Psychiatric Institute, is author of *Heredity in Health and Mental Disorder* (1953), *The Genetics of Schizophrenia* (1938), and numerous publications in medical genetics.

Forrest E. Linder, director of the National Health Survey Program, United States Public Health Service, was formerly chief of the Demographic and Social Statistics Branch, Statistical Office, United Nations. He is co-author of *Vital Statistics Rates in the United States, 1900–1940* (1943).

Frank Lorimer, professor of sociology at American University, is the author of *Culture and Human Fertility* (1954), *The Population of the Soviet Union* (1946), and other studies in population dynamics and policy. He has served as president of the Population Association of America and is president (1957——) of the International Union for the Scientific Study of Population.

Wilbert E. Moore, professor of sociology and research associate at the Office of Population Research, Princeton University, is the author of *Industrialization*

and Labor (1951), *Economic Demography of Eastern and Southern Europe* (1945), and numerous sociological treatises and research studies.

Giorgio Mortara, professor and director of the Institute of Demography at the Università degli Studi, Rome, and formerly technical advisor to the Conselho Nacional de Estatística of Brazil, is the author of *Methods of Using Census Statistics* (1949), "The Development and Structure of Brazil's Population" (1954), and other studies on demographic methods and population problems. He has served as president of the International Union for the Scientific Study of Population.

John D. Rainer, M.D., research associate, Columbia University, and associate research scientist, New York State Psychiatric Institute, is author of "Genetic and Demographic Aspects of Disordered Behavior Patterns in a Deaf Population" (1956) and other studies in medical genetics.

N. B. Ryder, assistant professor of sociology and anthropology at the University of Wisconsin, is author of "Problems of Trend Determination During a Transition in Fertility" (1956), "The Influence of Declining Mortality on Swedish Reproductivity" (1955), and other studies in cohort analysis.

Alfred Sauvy, director of the Institut National d'Études Démographiques, Paris, is the author of *Théorie générale de la population* (1952 and 1954), *La nature sociale* (1957), and numerous monographs on population movements and the economics of population. He is a member and former chairman of the United Nations Population Commission.

Hermann Schubnell, chief of the branch of population censuses and cultural statistics, Statistisches Bundesamt, Wiesbaden, and lecturer in demography, University of Freiburg (Breisgau), is the co-author of *Grundriss der Bevölkerungswissenschaft (Demographie)* (1950) and other studies on population and economic statistics.

Joseph J. Spengler, professor of economics at Duke University, is the author of *French Predecessors of Malthus* (1942), *France Faces Depopulation* (1938), and numerous studies on the history of population theories and the economics of population. He has served as president of the Population Association of America.

J. N. SPUHLER, associate professor of anthropology and of human genetics, University of Michigan, is author of numerous studies on human population genetics, including "Inbreeding Coefficients of the Ramah Navaho Population" (with Clyde Kluckhohn, 1953) and "Estimation of Mutation Rates in Man" (1956).

IRENE B. TAEUBER, research associate at the Office of Population Research, Princeton University, is the author of *The Population of Japan* (1958), *General Censuses and Vital Statistics in the Americas* (1943), and numerous research studies and biblio-graphic essays in international demography. She has served as president of the Population Association of America.

BRINLEY THOMAS, professor of economics and social science at University College of South Wales and Monmouthshire, Cardiff, is author of *Migration and Economic Growth* (1954) and other studies on migration, and editor of *Economics of International Migration* (1958).

RUPERT B. VANCE, professor of sociology at the University of North Carolina, is the author of *All These People* (1945), *Research Memorandum on Population Redistribution within the United States* (1938), and other studies of population movements and regionalism. He has served as president of the Population Association of America.

Index

[Names of individuals and organizations are indexed only if their work is discussed at considerable length in the text.]

859